The United States Government Manual 1991/92

Office of the Federal Register
National Archives and Records Administration

BERNAN PRESS
Lanham, Maryland

Revised July 1, 1991

Martha L. Girard,
Director of the Federal Register.

Don W. Wilson,
Archivist of the United States.

Bernan Press
An Imprint of Bernan Associates
4611-F Assembly Drive
Lanham, MD 20706

ISBN 0-89059-001-X

Printed in the United States of America

Preface

As the official handbook of the Federal Government, *The United States Government Manual* provides comprehensive information on the agencies of the legislative, judicial, and executive branches. The *Manual* also includes information on quasi-official agencies; international organizations in which the United States participates; and boards, commissions, and committees.

A typical agency description includes a list of principal officials, a summary statement of the agency's purpose and role in the Federal Government, a brief history of the agency, including its legislative or executive authority, a description of its programs and activities, and a "Sources of Information" section. This last section provides information on consumer activities, contracts and grants, employment, publications, and many other areas of public interest.

The 1991/92 *Manual* was prepared by the Legislative Unit, Office of the Federal Register. Gwendolyn J. Henderson was Managing Editor; Gregory R. Walton, Rochelle A. Cohen, and Alfred W. Jones were Assistant Editors.

This year's *Manual* cover depicts a view of the Washington Monument facing east from Constitution Gardens.

The Federal Register and Its Special Editions

The *Manual* is published as a special edition of the *Federal Register* (*see* 1 CFR 9.1). Its focus is on programs and activities. Persons interested in detailed organizational structure, the regulatory documents of an agency, or Presidential documents should refer to the *Federal Register* or one of its other special editions, described below.

Issued each Federal working day, the *Federal Register* provides a uniform system for publishing Presidential documents, regulatory documents with general applicability and legal effect, proposed rules, notices, and documents required to be published by statute.

The *Code of Federal Regulations* is an annual codification of the general and permanent rules published in the *Federal Register*. The *Code* is divided into 50 titles that represent broad areas subject to Federal regulation. The *Code* is kept up to date by the individual issues of the *Federal Register.*

The *Weekly Compilation of Presidential Documents* serves as a timely, up-to-date reference source for the public policies and activities of the President. It contains the remarks, news conferences, messages, statements, and other Presidential material of a public nature issued by the White House during the week reported.

A companion publication to the *Weekly Compilation* is the *Public Papers of the Presidents,* which contains public Presidential documents and speeches in convenient book form. Volumes of the *Public Papers* have been published for every President since Herbert Hoover, with the exception of Franklin D. Roosevelt, whose papers were published privately.

Other Office of the Federal Register Publications

The Office of the Federal Register publishes slip laws, which are pamphlet prints of each public and private law enacted by Congress. Slip laws are compiled annually as the *United States Statutes at Large*. The *Statutes* volumes contain all public and private laws and concurrent resolutions enacted during a session of Congress; recommendations for executive, legislative, and judicial salaries; reorganization plans; proposed and ratified amendments to the Constitution; and Presidential proclamations. Included with many of these documents are sidenotes, U.S. Code and statutes citations, and a summary of their legislative histories.

The *Codification of Presidential Proclamations and Executive Orders* provides in one reference source proclamations and Executive orders issued from the Truman through the Reagan administrations that have general applicability and continuing legal effect. The *Codification* is divided into 50 chapters representing broad subject areas. Incorporated into each codified document are all amendments that were in effect on the most recent revision date.

Publication Availability

The publications of the Office of the Federal Register are available for sale by writing:

Superintendent of Documents
Government Printing Office
Washington, DC 20402–9325

and are also sold at Government Printing Office bookstores located in several major cities. Telephone inquiries should be directed to 202–783–3238.

The *Federal Register* and *Code of Federal Regulations* are available in microfiche form as well as bound paper copies. In addition, these publications are available to the public at designated Government depository libraries and many other libraries. For more information, see the "Sources of Information" section of the Government Printing Office's statement in this book.

Further Information

Information on the contents of *The United States Government Manual* and other publications of the Office of the Federal Register may be obtained by writing:

Office of the Federal Register
National Archives and Records Administration
Washington, DC 20408

Telephone inquiries concerning the editorial content of the *Manual* should be directed to 202–523–5230.

Contents

The Declaration of Independence

IN CONGRESS, JULY 4, 1776

THE UNANIMOUS DECLARATION of the thirteen united STATES OF AMERICA

WHEN in the Course of human events, it becomes necessary for one people to dissolve the political bands which have connected them with another, and to assume among the powers of the earth, the separate and equal station to which the Laws of Nature and of Nature's God entitle them, a decent respect to the opinions of mankind requires that they should declare the causes which impel them to the separation.— We hold these truths to be self-evident, that all men are created equal, that they are endowed by their Creator with certain unalienable Rights, that among these are Life, Liberty and the pursuit of Happiness.—That to secure these rights, Governments are instituted among Men, deriving their just powers from the consent of the governed,— That whenever any Form of Government becomes destructive of these ends, it is the Right of the People to alter or to abolish it, and to institute new Government, laying its foundation on such principles and organizing its powers in such form, as to them shall seem most likely to effect their Safety and Happiness. Prudence, indeed, will dictate that Governments long established should not be changed for light and transient causes; and accordingly all experience hath shown, that mankind are more disposed to suffer, while evils are sufferable, than to right themselves by abolishing the forms to which they are accustomed. But when a long train of abuses and usurpations, pursuing invariably the same Object evinces a design to reduce them under absolute Despotism, it is their right, it is their duty, to throw off such Government, and to provide new Guards for their future security.—Such has been the patient sufferance of these Colonies; and such is now the necessity which constrains them to alter their former Systems of Government. The history of the present King of Great Britain is a history of repeated injuries and usurpations, all having in direct object the establishment of an absolute Tyranny over these States. To prove this, let Facts be submitted to a candid world.—He has refused his Assent to Laws, the most wholesome and necessary for the public good.—He has forbidden his Governors to pass Laws of immediate and pressing importance, unless suspended in their operation till his Assent should be obtained; and when so suspended, he has utterly neglected to attend to them.—He has refused to pass other Laws for the accommodation of large districts of people, unless those people would relinquish the right of Representation in the Legislature, a right inestimable to them and formidable to tyrants only.—He has called together legislative bodies at places unusual, uncomfortable, and distant from the depository of their public Records, for the sole purpose of fatiguing them into compliance with his measures.—He has dissolved Representative Houses repeatedly, for opposing with manly firmness his invasions on the rights of the people.—He has refused for a long time, after such dissolutions, to cause others to be elected; whereby the Legislative powers, incapable of Annihilation, have returned to the People at large for their exercise; the State remaining in the mean time exposed to all the dangers of invasion from without, and convulsions within.—He has endeavored to prevent the population of these States; for that purpose obstructing the Laws for Naturalization of Foreigners; refusing to pass others to encourage their migration hither, and raising the conditions of new Appropriations of Lands.—He has obstructed the Administration of Justice, by refusing his Assent to Laws for establishing Judiciary powers.—He has made Judges dependent on his Will alone, for the tenure of their offices, and the amount and payment of their salaries.—He has erected a multitude of New Offices, and sent hither swarms of Officers to harrass our people, and eat out their substance.—He has kept among us, in times of peace, Standing Armies, without the Consent of our legislatures.—He has affected to render the Military independent of and superior to the Civil power.—He has combined with others to subject us to a jurisdiction foreign to our constitution, and unacknowledged by our laws; giving his Assent to their Acts of pretended Legislation:—For quartering large bodies of armed troops among us:—For protecting them, by a mock Trial, from punishment for any Murders which they should commit on the Inhabitants of these States:—For cutting off our Trade with all parts of the world:—For imposing Taxes on us without our Consent:—For depriving us in many cases, of the benefits of Trial by Jury:—For transporting us beyond Seas to be tried for pretended offences:—For abolishing the free System of English Laws in a neighbouring Province, establishing therein an Arbitrary government, and enlarging its Boundaries so as to render it at once an example and fit instrument for introducing the same absolute rule into these Colonies:—For taking away our Charters, abolishing our most valuable Laws, and altering fundamentally the Forms of our Governments:—For suspending our own Legislatures, and declaring themselves invested with power to legislate for us in all cases whatsoever.—He has abdicated Government here, by declaring us out of his Protection and waging War against us.—He has plundered our seas, ravaged our Coasts, burnt our towns, and destroyed the lives of our people.—He is at this time transporting large Armies of foreign Mercenaries to compleat the works of death, desolation and tyranny, already begun with circumstances of Cruelty & perfidy scarcely paralleled in the most barbarous ages, and totally unworthy the Head of a civilized nation.—He has constrained our fellow Citizens taken Captive on the high Seas to bear Arms against their Country, to become the executioners of their friends and Brethren, or to fall themselves by their Hands.—He has excited domestic insurrections amongst us, and has endeavoured to bring on the inhabitants of our frontiers, the merciless Indian Savages, whose known rule of warfare, is an undistinguished destruction of all ages, sexes and conditions. In every stage of these Oppressions We have Petitioned for Redress in the most humble terms: Our repeated Petitions have been answered only by repeated injury. A Prince, whose character is thus marked by every act which may define a Tyrant, is unfit to be the ruler of a free people. Nor have We been wanting in attentions to our Brittish brethren. We have warned them from time to time of attempts by their legislature to extend an unwarrantable jurisdiction over us. We have reminded them of the circumstances of our emigration and settlement here. We have appealed to their native justice and magnanimity, and we have conjured them by the ties of our common kindred to disavow these usurpations, which, would inevitably interrupt our connections and correspondence. They too have been deaf to the voice of justice and of consanguinity. We must, therefore, acquiesce in the necessity, which denounces our Separation, and hold them, as we hold the rest of mankind, Enemies in War, in Peace Friends.—

WE, THEREFORE, the REPRESENTATIVES of the UNITED STATES OF AMERICA, in General Congress, Assembled, appealing to the Supreme Judge of the world for the rectitude of our intentions, do, in the Name, and by Authority of the good People of these Colonies, solemnly publish and declare, That these United Colonies are, and of Right ought to be FREE AND INDEPENDENT STATES; that they are Absolved from all Allegiance to the British Crown, and that all political connection between them and the State of

Great Britain, is and ought to be totally disolved; and that as Free and Independent States, they have full Power to levy War, conclude Peace, contract Alliances, establish Commerce, and to do all other Acts and Things which Independent States may of right do.—And for the support of this Declaration, with a firm reliance on the protection of Divine Providence, we mutually pledge to each other our Lives, our Fortunes and our sacred Honor.

John Hancock
Button Gwinnett
Lyman Hall
Geo. Walton
Wm. Hooper
Joseph Hewes
John Penn
Edward Rutledge
Thos. Heyward, Jr.
Thomas Lynch, Jr.
Arthur Middleton
Samuel Chase
Wm. Paca
Thos. Stone
Charles Carroll of Carrollton
George Wythe
Richard Henry Lee
Th. Jefferson

Benj. Harrison
Thos. Nelson, Jr.
Francis Lightfoot Lee
Carter Braxton
Robt. Morris
Benjamin Rush
Benj. Franklin
John Morton
Geo. Clymer
Jas. Smith
Geo. Taylor
James Wilson
Geo. Ross
Caesar Rodney
Geo. Read
Tho. M: Kean
Wm. Floyd
Phil. Livingston
Frans. Lewis

Lewis Morris
Richd. Stockton
Jno. Witherspoon
Fras. Hopkinson
John Hart
Abra. Clark
Josiah Bartlett
Wm. Whipple
Saml. Adams
John Adams
Robt. Treat Paine
Elbridge Gerry
Step. Hopkins
William Ellery
Roger Sherman
Sam. Huntington
Wm. Williams
Oliver Wolcott
Matthew Thornton

The Constitution of the United States

We the People of the United States, in Order to form a more perfect Union, establish Justice, insure domestic Tranquility, provide for the common defence, promote the general Welfare, and secure the Blessings of Liberty to ourselves and our Posterity, do ordain and establish this Constitution for the United States of America.

Article I

Section 1. All legislative Powers herein granted shall be vested in a Congress of the United States, which shall consist of a Senate and House of Representatives.

Section 2. The House of Representatives shall be composed of Members chosen every second Year by the People of the several States, and the Electors in each State shall have the Qualifications requisite for Electors of the most numerous Branch of the State Legislature.

No Person shall be a Representative who shall not have attained to the Age of twenty five Years, and been seven Years a Citizen of the United States, and who shall not, when elected, be an Inhabitant of that State in which he shall be chosen.

Representatives and direct Taxes shall be apportioned among the several States which may be included within this Union, according to their respective Numbers, which shall be determined by adding to the whole Number of free Persons, including those bound to Service for a Term of Years, and excluding Indians not taxed, three fifths of all other Persons. The actual Enumeration shall be made within three Years after the first Meeting of the Congress of the United States, and within every subsequent Term of ten Years, in such Manner as they shall by Law direct. The Number of Representatives shall not exceed one for every thirty Thousand, but each State shall have at Least one Representative; and until such enumerations shall be made, the State of New Hampshire shall be entitled to chuse three, Massachusetts eight, Rhode-Island and Providence Plantations one, Connecticut five, New-York six, New Jersey four, Pennsylvania eight, Delaware one, Maryland six, Virginia ten, North Carolina five, South Carolina five, and Georgia three.

When vacancies happen in the Representation from any State, the Executive Authority thereof shall issue Writs of Election to fill such Vacancies.

The House of Representatives shall chuse their speaker and other Officers; and shall have the sole Power of Impeachment.

Section 3. The Senate of the United States shall be composed of two Senators from each State, chosen by the Legislature thereof, for six Years; and each Senator shall have one Vote.

Immediately after they shall be assembled in Consequence of the first Election, they shall be divided as equally as may be into three Classes. The Seats of the Senators of the first Class shall be vacated at the Expiration of the second Year, of the second Class at the Expiration of the fourth Year, and of the third Class at the Expiration of the sixth Year, so that one third may be chosen every second Year; and if Vacancies happen by Resignation, or otherwise, during the Recess of the Legislature of any State, the Executive thereof may make temporary Appointments until the next Meeting of the Legislature, which shall then fill such Vacancies.

No Person shall be a Senator who shall not have attained to the Age of thirty Years, and been nine Years a Citizen of the United States, and who shall not, when elected, be an Inhabitant of that State for which he shall be chosen.

The Vice President of the United States shall be President of the Senate, but shall have no Vote, unless they be equally divided.

The Senate shall chuse their other Officers, and also a President pro tempore, in the Absence of the Vice President, or when he shall exercise the Office of President of the United States.

The Senate shall have the sole Power to try all Impeachments. When sitting for that Purpose, they shall be on Oath or Affirmation. When the President of the United States is tried, the Chief Justice shall preside: And no Person shall be convicted without the concurrence of two thirds of the Members present. Judgment in Cases of Impeachment shall not extend further than to removal from Office, and disqualification to hold and enjoy any Office of honor, Trust or Profit under the United States: but the Party convicted shall nevertheless be liable and subject to Indictment, Trial, Judgment and Punishment, according to law.

Section 4. The Times, Places and Manner of holding Elections for Senators and Representatives, shall be prescribed in each State by the Legislature thereof; but the Congress may at any time by Law make or alter such Regulations, except as to the Places of chusing Senators.

The Congress shall assemble at least once in every Year, and such Meeting shall be on the first Monday in December, unless they shall by Law appoint a different Day.

Section 5. Each House shall be the Judge of the Elections, Returns and Qualifications of its own Members, and a Majority of each shall constitute a Quorum to do business; but a smaller Number may adjourn from day to day, and may be authorized to compel the Attendance of absent Members, in such Manner, and under such Penalties as each House may provide.

Each House may determine the Rules of its Proceedings, punish its Members for disorderly Behaviour, and, with the Concurrence of two thirds, expel a Member.

Each House shall keep a Journal of its Proceedings, and from time to time publish the same, excepting such Parts as may in their Judgment require Secrecy; and the yeas and Nays of the Members of either House on any question shall, at the Desire of one fifth of those Present, be entered on the Journal.

Neither House, during the Session of Congress, shall, without the Consent of the other, adjourn for more than three days, nor to any other place than that in which the two Houses shall be sitting.

Section 6. The Senators and Representatives shall receive a Compensation for their Services, to be ascertained by Law, and paid out of the Treasury of the United States. They shall in all Cases, except Treason, Felony and Breach of the Peace, be privileged from Arrest during their Attendance at the Session of their respective Houses, and in going to and returning from the same; and for any Speech or Debate in either House, they shall not be questioned in any other Place.

No Senator or Representative shall, during the Time for which he was elected, be appointed to any civil Office under the Authority of the United States, which shall have been created, or the Emoluments whereof shall have been encreased during such time; and no Person holding any Office under the United States, shall be a Member of either House during his Continuance in Office.

Section 7. All Bills for raising Revenue shall originate in the House of Representatives; but the Senate may propose or concur with Amendments as on other Bills.

Every Bill which shall have passed the House of Representatives and the Senate, shall, before it become a Law, be presented to the President of the United States; If he approve he shall sign it, but if not he shall return it, with his Objections to that House in which it shall have originated, who shall enter the Objections at large on their Journal, and proceed to reconsider it. If after such Reconsideration two thirds of that House shall agree to pass the Bill, it shall be sent, together with the Objections, to the other House, by which it shall likewise be reconsidered, and if approved by two thirds of that House, it shall become a Law. But in all such Cases the Votes of both Houses shall be determined by yeas and Nays, and the Names of the Persons voting for and against the Bill shall be entered on the Journal of each House respectively. If any Bill shall not be returned by the President within ten Days (Sundays excepted) after it shall have been presented to him, the Same shall be a Law, in like Manner as if he had signed it, unless the Congress by their Adjournment prevent its Return, in which Case it shall not be a Law.

Every Order, Resolution, or Vote to which the Concurrence of the Senate and House of Representatives may be necessary (except on a question of Adjournment) shall be presented to the President of the United States; and before the Same shall take Effect, shall be approved by him, or being disapproved by him, shall be repassed by two thirds of the Senate and House of Representatives, according to the Rules and Limitations prescribed in the Case of a Bill.

Section 8. The Congress shall have Power To lay and collect Taxes, Duties, Imposts and Excises, to pay the Debts and provide for the common Defence and general Welfare of the United States; but all duties, Imposts and Excises shall be uniform throughout the United States;

To borrow Money on the Credit of the United States;

To regulate Commerce with foreign Nations, and among the several States, and with the Indian Tribes;

To establish an uniform Rule of Naturalization, and uniform Laws on the subject of Bankruptcies throughout the United States;

To coin Money, regulate the Value thereof, and of foreign Coin, and fix the Standard of Weights and Measures;

To provide for the Punishment of counterfeiting the Securities and current Coin of the United States;

To establish Post Offices and post Roads;

To promote the Progress of Science and useful Arts, by securing for limited Times to Authors and Inventors exclusive Right to their respective Writings and Discoveries;

To constitute Tribunals inferior to the supreme Court;

To define and punish Piracies and Felonies committed on the high Seas, and Offences against the Law of Nations;

To declare War, grant Letters of Marque and Reprisal, and make rules concerning Captures on Land and Water;

To raise and support Armies, but no Appropriation of Money to that Use shall be for a longer Term than two Years;

To provide and maintain a Navy;

To make rules for the Government and Regulation of the land and naval Forces;

To provide for calling forth the Militia to execute the Laws of the Union, suppress Insurrections and repel Invasions;

To provide for organizing, arming, and disciplining, the Militia, and for governing such Part of them as may be employed in the Service of the United States, reserving to the States respectively, the Appointment of the Officers, and the Authority of training the Militia according to the discipline prescribed by Congress;

To exercise exclusive Legislation in all Cases whatsoever, over such District (not exceeding ten Miles square), as may, by Cession of particular States, and the Acceptance of Congress, become the Seat of the Government of the United States, and to exercise like Authority over all Places purchased by the Consent of the Legislature of the State in which the Same shall be for the Erection of Forts, Magazines, Arsenals, dock-Yards, and other needful Buildings;—And

To make all Laws which shall be necessary and proper for carrying into Execution the foregoing Powers, and all other Powers vested by this Constitution in the Government of the United States, or in any Department or Officer thereof.

Section 9. The Migration or Importation of such Persons as any of the States now existing shall think proper to admit, shall not be prohibited by the Congress prior to the Year one thousand eight hundred and eight, but a Tax or duty may be imposed on such Importation, not exceeding ten dollars for each Person.

The Privilege of the Writ of Habeas Corpus shall not be suspended, unless when in Cases of Rebellion or Invasion the public Safety may require it.

No Bill of Attainder or ex post facto Law shall be passed.

No Capitation, or other direct, Tax shall be laid, unless in Proportion to the Census or Enumeration herein before directed to be taken.

No Tax or Duty shall be laid on Articles exported from any State.

No Preference shall be given by any Regulation of Commerce or Revenue to the Ports of one State over those of another: nor shall Vessels bound to, or from, one State, be obliged to enter, clear, or pay Duties in another.

No money shall be drawn from the Treasury, but in Consequence of Appropriations made by Law; and a regular Statement and Account of the Receipts and Expenditures of all public Money shall be published from time to time.

No Title of Nobility shall be granted by the United States: And no Person holding any Office of Profit or Trust under them, shall, without the Consent of the Congress, accept of any present, Emolument, Office, or Title, of any kind whatever, from any King, Prince, or foreign State.

Section 10. No State shall enter into any Treaty, Alliance, or Confederation; grant Letters of Marque and Reprisal; coin Money; emit Bills of Credit; make any Thing but gold and silver Coin a Tender in Payment of Debts; pass any Bill of Attainder, ex post facto Law, or Law impairing the Obligation of Contracts, or grant any Title of Nobility.

No State shall, without the Consent of the Congress, lay any Imposts or Duties on Imports or Exports, except what may be absolutely necessary for executing it's inspection Laws: and the net Produce of all Duties and Imposts, laid by any State on Imports or Exports, shall be for the Use of the Treasury of the United States; and all such Laws shall be subject to the Revision and Controul of the Congress.

No State shall, without the Consent of Congress, lay any Duty of Tonnage, keep Troops, or Ships of War in time of Peace, enter into any Agreement or Compact with another State, or with a foreign Power, or engage in War, unless actually invaded, or in such imminent Danger as will not admit of delay.

Article II

Section 1. The executive Power shall be vested in a President of the United States of America. He shall hold his Office during the Term of four Years, and, together with the Vice President, chosen for the same term, be elected, as follows

Each State shall appoint, in such Manner as the Legislature thereof may direct, a Number of Electors, equal to the whole Number of Senators and Representatives to which the State may be entitled in the Congress: but no Senator or Representative, or Person holding an Office of Trust or Profit under the United States, shall be appointed an Elector.

The Electors shall meet in their respective States, and vote by Ballot for two Persons, of whom one at least shall not be an Inhabitant of the same State with themselves. And they shall make a List of all the Persons voted for, and of the Number of Votes for each; which List they shall sign and certify, and transmit sealed to the Seat of the Government of the United States, directed to the President of the Senate. The President of the Senate shall, in the Presence of the Senate and House of Representatives, open all the Certificates, and the Votes shall then be counted. The Person having the greatest Number of Votes shall be the President, if such Number be a Majority of the whole Number of Electors appointed; and if there be more than one who have such Majority, and have an equal Number of Votes, then the House of Representatives shall immediately chuse by Ballot one of them for President: and if no Person have a Majority, then from the five highest on the List the said House shall in like Manner chuse the President. But in chusing the President, the Votes shall be taken by States, the Representation from each State having one Vote; A quorum for this Purpose shall consist of a Member or Members from two thirds of the States, and a Majority of all the States shall be necessary to a Choice. In every Case, after the Choice of the President, the Person having the greatest Number of Votes of the Electors shall be the Vice President. But if there should remain two or more who have equal Votes, the Senate shall chuse from them by Ballot the Vice President.

The Congress may determine the Time of chusing the Electors, and the Day on which they shall give their Votes; which Day shall be the same throughout the United States.

No Person except a natural born Citizen, or a Citizen of the United States, at the time of the Adoption of this Constitution, shall be eligible to the Office of President; neither shall any Person be eligible to that Office who shall not have attained to the Age of thirty five Years, and been fourteen Years a Resident within the United States.

In Case of the Removal of the President from Office, or of his Death, Resignation, or Inability to discharge the Powers and Duties of the said Office, the Same shall devolve on the Vice President, and the Congress may by Law provide for the Case of Removal, Death, Resignation or Inability, both of the President and Vice President, declaring what Officer shall then act as President, and such Officer shall act accordingly, until the Disability be removed, or a President shall be elected.

The President shall, at stated Times, receive for his Services, a Compensation, which shall neither be encreased nor diminished during the Period for which he shall have been elected, and he shall not receive within that Period any other Emolument from the United States, or any of them.

Before he enter on the Execution of his Office, he shall take the following Oath or Affirmation:—"I do solemnly swear (or affirm) that I will faithfully execute the Office of President of the United States, and will to the best of my Ability, preserve, protect and defend the Constitution of the United States."

Section 2. The President shall be Commander in Chief of the Army and Navy of the United States, and of the Militia of the several States, when called into the actual Service of the United States; he may require the Opinion, in writing, of the principal

Officer in each of the executive Departments, upon any Subject relating to the Duties of their respective Offices, and he shall have Power to grant Reprieves and Pardons for Offences against the United States, except in Cases of Impeachment.

He shall have Power, by and with the Advice and Consent of the Senate, to make Treaties, provided two thirds of the Senators present concur; and he shall nominate, and by and with the Advice and Consent of the Senate, shall appoint Ambassadors, other public Ministers and Consuls, Judges of the supreme Court, and all other Officers of the United States, whose Appointments are not herein otherwise provided for, and which shall be established by Law: but the Congress may by Law vest the Appointment of such inferior Officers, as they think proper, in the President alone, in the Courts of Law, or in the Heads of Departments.

The President shall have Power to fill up all Vacancies that may happen during the Recess of the Senate, by granting Commissions which shall expire at the End of their next Session.

Section 3. He shall from time to time give to the Congress Information of the State of the Union, and recommend to their Consideration such Measures as he shall judge necessary and expedient; he may, on extraordinary Occasions, convene both Houses, or either of them, and in Case of Disagreement between them, with Respect to the Time of Adjournment, he may adjourn them to such Time as he shall think proper; he shall receive Ambassadors and other public Ministers; he shall take Care that the Laws be faithfully executed, and shall Commission all the Officers of the United States.

Section 4. The President, Vice President and all civil Officers of the United States, shall be removed from Office on Impeachment for, and Conviction of, Treason, Bribery, or other High Crimes and Misdemeanors.

Article III

Section 1. The judicial Power of the United States, shall be vested in one supreme Court, and in such inferior Courts as the Congress may from time to time ordain and establish. The Judges, both of the supreme and inferior Courts, shall hold their Offices during good Behaviour, and shall, at stated Times, receive for their Services, a Compensation, which shall not be diminished during their Continuance in Office.

Section 2. The judicial Power shall extend to all Cases, in Law and Equity, arising under this Constitution, the Laws of the United States, and Treaties made, or which shall be made, under their Authority;—to all Cases affecting Ambassadors, other public Ministers and Consuls;—to all Cases of admiralty and maritime Jurisdiction;—to Controversies to which the United States shall be a Party;—to Controversies between two or more States; between a State and Citizens of another State;—between Citizens of different States;—between Citizens of the same State claiming Lands under Grants of different States, and between a State, or the Citizens thereof, and foreign States, Citizens or Subjects.

In all Cases affecting Ambassadors, other public Ministers and Consuls, and those in which a State shall be Party, the supreme Court shall have original Jurisdiction. In all the other Cases before mentioned, the supreme Court shall have appellate Jurisdiction, both as to Law and Fact, with such Exceptions, and under such Regulations as the Congress shall make.

The Trial of all Crimes, except in Cases of Impeachment, shall be by Jury; and such Trial shall be held in the State where the said Crimes shall have been committed; but when not committed within any State, the Trial shall be at such Place or Places as the Congress may by Law have directed.

Section 3. Treason against the United States, shall consist only in levying War against them, or in adhering to their Enemies, giving them Aid and Comfort. No Person shall be convicted of Treason unless on the Testimony of two Witnesses to the same overt Act, or on Confession in open Court.

The Congress shall have Power to declare the Punishment of Treason, but no Attainder of Treason shall work Corruption of Blood, or Forfeiture except during the Life of the Person attainted.

Article IV

Section 1. Full Faith and Credit shall be given in each State to the public Acts, Records, and judicial Proceedings of every other State. And the Congress may by general Laws prescribe the Manner in which such Acts, Records and Proceedings shall be proved, and the Effect thereof.

Section 2. The Citizens of each State shall be entitled to all Privileges and Immunities of Citizens in the several States.

A Person charged in any State with Treason, Felony, or other Crime, who shall flee from Justice, and be found in another State, shall on Demand of the executive Authority of the State from which he fled, be delivered up, to be removed to the State having Jurisdiction of the Crime.

No person held to Service or Labour in one State, under the Laws thereof, escaping into another, shall, in Consequence of any Law or Regulation therein, be discharged from such Service or Labour, but shall be delivered up on Claim of the Party to whom such Service or Labour may be due.

Section 3. New States may be admitted by the Congress into this Union; but no new State shall be formed or erected within the Jurisdiction of any other State; nor any State be formed by the Junction of two or more States, or Parts of States, without the Consent of the Legislatures of the States concerned as well as of the Congress.

The Congress shall have Power to dispose of and make all needful Rules and Regulations respecting the Territory or other Property belonging to the United States; and nothing in this Constitution shall be so construed as to Prejudice any Claims of the United States, or of any particular State.

Section 4. The United States shall guarantee to every State in this Union a Republican Form of Government, and shall protect each of them against Invasion; and on Application of the Legislature, or of the Executive (when the Legislature cannot be convened) against domestic Violence.

Article V

The Congress, whenever two thirds of both Houses shall deem it necessary, shall propose Amendments to this Constitution, or, on the Application of the Legislatures of two thirds of the several States, shall call a Convention for proposing Amendments, which, in either Case, shall be valid to all Intents and Purposes, as Part of this Constitution, when ratified by the Legislatures of three fourths of the several States, or by Conventions in three fourths thereof, as the one or the other Mode of Ratification may be proposed by the Congress; Provided that no Amendment which may be made prior to the Year One thousand eight hundred and eight shall in any Manner affect the first and fourth Clauses in the Ninth Section of the first Article; and that no State,without its Consent, shall be deprived of its equal Suffrage in the Senate.

Article VI

All Debts contracted and Engagements entered into, before the Adoption of this Constitution, shall be as valid against the United States under this Constitution, as under the Confederation.

This Constitution, and the Laws of the United States which shall be made in Pursuance thereof; and all Treaties made, or which shall be made, under the Authority of the United States, shall be the supreme Law of the Land; and the Judges in every State shall be bound thereby, any Thing in the Constitution or Laws of any State to the Contrary notwithstanding.

The Senators and Representatives before mentioned, and the Members of the several State Legislatures, and all executive and judicial Officers, both of the United States and of the several States, shall be bound by Oath or Affirmation, to support this Constitution; but no religious Test shall ever be required as a Qualification to any Office or public Trust under the United States.

Article VII

The Ratification of the Conventions of nine States, shall be sufficient for the Establishment of this Constitution between the States so ratifying the Same.

done in Convention by the Unanimous Consent of the States present the Seventeenth Day of September in the Year of our Lord one thousand seven hundred and Eighty seven and of the Independence of the United States of America the Twelfth *In witness whereof We have hereunto subscribed our Names,*

G^{o} Washington—Presid^{t}
and deputy from Virginia

New Hampshire	John Langdon Nicholas Gilman
Massachusetts	Nathaniel Gorham Rufus King
Connecticut	Wm Sam:^{l} Johnson Roger Sherman
New York	Alexander Hamilton
New Jersey	Wil: Livingston David Brearley. Wm Paterson. Jona: Dayton
Pennsylvania	B Franklin Thomas Mifflin Robt Morris Geo. Clymer Thos FitzSimons Jared Ingersoll James Wilson Gouv Morris

Delaware	Geo: Read Gunning Bedford jun John Dickinson Richard Bassett Jaco: Broom
Maryland	James McHenry Dan of St Thos Jenifer Danl Carroll
Virginia	John Blair— James Madison Jr.
North Carolina	Wm Blount Richd Dobbs Spaight. Hu Williamson
South Carolina	J. Rutledge Charles Cotesworth Pinckney Charles Pinckney Pierce Butler.
Georgia	William Few Abr Baldwin

Amendments

(*The first 10 Amendments were ratified December 15, 1791, and form what is known as the Bill of Rights*)

Amendment 1

Congress shall make no law respecting an establishment of religion, or prohibiting the free exercise thereof; or abridging the freedom of speech, or of the press; or the right of the people peaceably to assemble, and to petition the Government for a redress of grievances.

Amendment 2

A well regulated Militia, being necessary to the security of a free State, the right of the people to keep and bear Arms, shall not be infringed.

Amendment 3

No Soldier shall, in time of peace be quartered in any house, without the consent of the Owner, nor in time of war, but in a manner to be prescribed by law.

Amendment 4

The right of the people to be secure in their persons, houses, papers, and effects, against unreasonable searches and seizures, shall not be violated, and no Warrants shall issue, but upon probable cause, supported by Oath or affirmation, and particularly describing the place to be searched, and the persons or things to be seized.

Amendment 5

No person shall be held to answer for a capital, or otherwise infamous crime, unless on a presentment or indictment of a Grand Jury, except in cases arising in the land or naval forces, or in the Militia, when in actual service in time of War or public danger; nor shall any person be subject for the same offence to be twice put in jeopardy of life or limb; nor shall be compelled in any criminal case to be a witness against himself, nor be deprived of life, liberty, or property, without due process of law; nor shall private property be taken for public use, without just compensation.

Amendment 6

In all criminal prosecutions, the accused shall enjoy the right to a speedy and public trial, by an impartial jury of the State and district wherein the crime shall have been committed, which district shall have been previously ascertained by law, and to be informed of the nature and cause of the accusation; to be confronted with the witnesses against him; to have compulsory process for obtaining witnesses in his favor, and to have the Assistance of Counsel for his defence.

Amendment 7

In Suits at common law, where the value in controversy shall exceed twenty dollars, the right of trial by jury shall be preserved, and no fact tried by a jury, shall be otherwise re-examined in any Court of the United States, than according to the rules of the common law.

Amendment 8

Excessive bail shall not be required, nor excessive fines imposed, nor cruel and unusual punishments inflicted.

Amendment 9

The enumeration in the Constitution, of certain rights, shall not be construed to deny or disparage others retained by the people.

Amendment 10

The powers not delegated to the United States by the Constitution, nor prohibited by it to the States, are reserved to the States respectively, or to the people.

Amendment 11

(*Ratified February 7, 1795*)

The Judicial power of the United States shall not be construed to extend to any suit in law or equity, commenced or prosecuted against one of the United States by Citizens of another State, or by Citizens or Subjects of any Foreign State.

Amendment 12

(*Ratified July 27, 1804*)

The Electors shall meet in their respective states, and vote by ballot for President and Vice-President, one of whom, at least, shall not be an inhabitant of the same state with themselves; they shall name in their ballots the person voted for as President, and in distinct ballots the person voted for as Vice-President, and they shall make distinct lists of all persons voted for as President, and of all persons voted for as Vice-President, and of the number of votes for each, which lists they shall sign and certify, and transmit sealed to the seat of the government of the United States, directed to the President of the Senate;—The President of the Senate shall, in the presence of the Senate and House of Representatives, open all the certificates and the votes shall then be counted;—The person having the greatest number of votes for President, shall be the President, if such number be a majority of the whole number of Electors appointed; and if no person have such majority, then from the persons having the highest numbers not exceeding three on the list of those voted for as President, the House of Representatives shall choose immediately, by ballot, the President. But in choosing the President, the votes shall be taken by states, the representation from each state having one vote; a quorum for this purpose shall consist of a member or members from two-thirds of the states, and a majority of all the states shall be necessary to a choice. And if the House of Representatives shall not choose a President whenever the right of choice shall devolve upon them, before the fourth day of March next following, then the Vice-President shall act as President, as in the case of the death or other constitutional disability of the President.—The person having the greatest number of votes as Vice-President, shall be the Vice-President, if such number be a majority of the whole number of Electors appointed, and if no person have a majority, then from the two highest numbers on the list, the Senate shall choose the Vice-President; a quorum for the purpose shall consist of two-thirds of the whole number of Senators, and a majority of the whole number shall be necessary to a choice. But no person constitutionally ineligible to the office of President shall be eligible to that of Vice-President of the United States.

Amendment 13

(*Ratified December 6, 1865*)

Section 1. Neither slavery nor involuntary servitude, except as a punishment for crime whereof the party shall have been duly convicted, shall exist within the United States, or any place subject to their jurisdiction.

Section 2. Congress shall have power to enforce this article by appropriate legislation.

Amendment 14

(*Ratified July 9, 1868*)

Section 1. All persons born or naturalized in the United States, and subject to the jurisdiction thereof, are citizens of the United States and of the State wherein they reside. No State shall make or enforce any law which shall abridge the privileges or immunities of citizens of the United States; nor shall any State deprive any person of life, liberty, or property, without due process of law; nor deny to any person within its jurisdiction the equal protection of the laws.

Section 2. Representatives shall be apportioned among the several States according to their respective numbers, counting the whole number of persons in each State, excluding Indians not taxed. But when the right to vote at any election for the choice of electors for President and Vice President of the United States, Representatives in Congress, the Executive and Judicial officers of a State, or the members of the Legislature thereof, is denied to any of the male inhabitants of such State, being twenty-one years of age, and citizens of the United States, or in any way abridged, except for participation in rebellion, or other crime, the basis of representation therein shall be reduced in the proportion which the number of such male citizens shall bear to the whole number of male citizens twenty-one years of age in such State.

Section 3. No person shall be a Senator or Representative in Congress, or elector of President and Vice President, or hold any office, civil or military, under the United States, or under any State, who, having previously taken an oath, as a member of Congress, or as an officer of the United States, or as a member of any State legislature, or as an executive or judicial officer of any State, to support the Constitution of the United States, shall have engaged in insurrection or rebellion against the same, or given aid or comfort to the enemies thereof. But Congress may by a vote of two-thirds of each House, remove such disability.

Section 4. The validity of the public debt of the United States, authorized by law, including debts incurred for payment of pensions and bounties for services in suppressing insurrection or rebellion, shall not be questioned. But neither the United States nor any State shall assume or pay any debt or obligation incurred in aid of insurrection or rebellion against the United States, or any claim for the loss or emancipation of any slave; but all such debts, obligations and claims shall be held illegal and void.

Section 5. The Congress shall have power to enforce, by appropriate legislation, the provisions of this article.

Amendment 15

(*Ratified February 3, 1870*)

Section 1. The right of citizens of the United States to vote shall not be denied or abridged by the United States or by any State on account of race, color, or previous condition of servitude.

Section 2. The Congress shall have power to enforce this article by appropriate legislation.

Amendment 16

(*Ratified February 3, 1913*)

The Congress shall have power to lay and collect taxes on incomes, from whatever source derived, without apportionment among the several States, and without regard to any census or enumeration.

Amendment 17

(*Ratified April 8, 1913*)

The Senate of the United States shall be composed of two Senators from each State, elected by the people thereof for six years; and each Senator shall have one vote. The electors in each State shall have the qualifications requisite for electors of the most numerous branch of the State legislatures.

When vacancies happen in the representation of any State in the Senate, the executive authority of such State shall issue writs of election to fill such vacancies: *Provided,* That the legislature of any State may empower the executive thereof to make temporary appointments until the people fill the vacancies by election as the legislature may direct.

This amendment shall not be so construed as to affect the election or term of any Senator chosen before it becomes valid as part of the Constitution.

Amendment 18

(*Ratified January 16, 1919. Repealed December 5, 1933 by Amendment 21*)

Section 1. After one year from the ratification of this article the manufacture, sale, or transportation of intoxicating liquors within, the importation thereof into, or the exportation thereof from the United States and all territory subject to the jurisdiction thereof for beverage purposes is hereby prohibited.

Section 2. The Congress and the several States shall have concurrent power to enforce this article by appropriate legislation.

Section 3. This article shall be inoperative unless it shall have been ratified as an amendment to the Constitution by the legislatures of the several States as provided in the Constitution, within seven years from the date of the submission hereof to the States by the Congress.

Amendment 19

(*Ratified August 18, 1920*)

The right of citizens of the United States to vote shall not be denied or abridged by the United States or by any State on account of sex.

Congress shall have power to enforce this article by appropriate legislation.

Amendment 20

(*Ratified January 23, 1933*)

Section 1. The terms of the President and Vice President shall end at noon on the 20th day of January, and the terms of Senators and Representatives at noon on the 3d day of January, of the years in which such terms would have ended if this article had not been ratified; and the terms of their successors shall then begin.

Section 2. The Congress shall assemble at least once in every year, and such meeting shall begin at noon on the 3d day of January, unless they shall by law appoint a different day.

Section 3. If, at the time fixed for the beginning of the term of the President, the President elect shall have died, the Vice President elect shall become President. If a President shall not have been chosen before the time fixed for the beginning of his term, or if the President elect shall have failed to qualify, then the Vice President elect shall act as President until a President shall have qualified; and the Congress may by law provide for the case wherein neither a President elect nor a Vice President elect shall have qualified, declaring who shall then act as President, or the manner in which one who is to act shall be selected, and such person shall act accordingly until a President or Vice President shall have qualified.

Section 4. The Congress may by law provide for the case of the death of any of the persons from whom the House of Representatives may choose a President whenever the right of choice shall have devolved upon them, and for the case of the death of any of the persons from whom the Senate may choose a Vice President whenever the right of choice shall have devolved upon them.

Section 5. Sections 1 and 2 shall take effect on the 15th day of October following the ratification of this article.

Section 6. This article shall be inoperative unless it shall have been ratified as an amendment to the Constitution by the legislatures of three-fourths of the several States within seven years from the date of its submission.

Amendment 21

(*Ratified December 5, 1933*)

Section 1. The eighteenth article of amendment to the Constitution of the United States is hereby repealed.

Section 2. The transportation or importation into any State, Territory, or possession of the United States for delivery or use therein of intoxicating liquors, in violation of the laws thereof, is hereby prohibited.

Section 3. This article shall be inoperative unless it shall have been ratified as an amendment to the Constitution by conventions in the several States, as provided in the Constitution, within seven years from the date of the submission hereof to the States by the Congress.

Amendment 22

(*Ratified February 27, 1951*)

Section 1. No person shall be elected to the office of the President more than twice, and no person who has held the office of President, or acted as President, for more than two years of a term to which some other person was elected President shall be elected to the office of the President more than once. But this Article shall not apply to any person holding the office of President when this Article was proposed by the Congress, and shall not prevent any person who may be holding the office of President, or acting as President, during the term within which this Article becomes operative from holding the office of President or acting as President during the remainder of such term.

Section 2. This article shall be inoperative unless it shall have been ratified as an amendment to the Constitution by the legislatures of three-fourths of the several States within seven years from the date of its submission to the States by the Congress.

Amendment 23

(*Ratified March 29, 1961*)

Section 1. The District constituting the seat of Government of the United States shall appoint in such manner as the Congress may direct:

A number of electors of President and Vice President equal to the whole number of Senators and Representatives in Congress to which the District would be entitled if it were a State, but in no event more than the least populous State; they shall be in addition to those appointed by the States, but they shall be considered, for the purposes of the election of President and Vice President, to be electors appointed by a State; and they shall meet in the District and perform such duties as provided by the twelfth article of amendment.

Section 2. The Congress shall have power to enforce this article by appropriate legislation.

Amendment 24

(*Ratified January 23, 1964*)

Section 1. The right of citizens of the United States to vote in any primary or other election for President or Vice President, for electors for President or Vice President, or for Senator or Representative in Congress, shall not be denied or abridged by the United States or any State by reason of failure to pay any poll tax or other tax.

Section 2. The Congress shall have power to enforce this article by appropriate legislation.

Amendment 25

(*Ratified February 10, 1967*)

Section 1. In case of the removal of the President from office or of his death or resignation, the Vice President shall become President.

Section 2. Whenever there is a vacancy in the office of the Vice President, the President shall nominate a Vice President who shall take office upon confirmation by a majority vote of both Houses of Congress.

Section 3. Whenever the President transmits to the President pro tempore of the Senate and the Speaker of the House of Representatives his written declaration that he is unable to discharge the powers and duties of his office, and until he transmits to them a written declaration to the contrary, such powers and duties shall be discharged by the Vice President as Acting President.

Section 4. Whenever the Vice President and a majority of either the principal officers of the executive departments or of such other body as Congress may by law provide, transmit to the President pro tempore of the Senate and the Speaker of the House of Representatives their written declaration that the President is unable to discharge the powers and duties of his office, the Vice President shall immediately assume the powers and duties of the office as Acting President.

Thereafter, when the President transmits to the President pro tempore of the Senate and the Speaker of the House of Representatives his written declaration that no inability exists, he shall resume the powers and duties of his office unless the Vice President and a majority of either the principal officers of the executive department or of such other body as Congress may by law provide, transmit within four days to the President pro tempore of the Senate and the Speaker of the House of Representatives their written declaration that the President is unable to discharge the powers and duties of his office. Thereupon Congress shall decide the issue, assembling within forty-eight hours for that purpose if not in session. If the Congress, within twenty-one days after receipt of the latter written declaration, or, if Congress is not in session, within twenty-one days after Congress is required to assemble, determines by two-thirds vote of both Houses that the President is unable to discharge the powers and duties of his office, the Vice President shall continue to discharge the same as Acting President; otherwise, the President shall resume the powers and duties of his office.

Amendment 26

(*Ratified July 1, 1971*)

Section 1. The right of citizens of the United States, who are eighteen years of age or older, to vote shall not be denied or abridged by the United States or by any State on account of age.

Section 2. The Congress shall have the power to enforce this article by appropriate legislation.

THE GOVERNMENT OF THE UNITED STATES

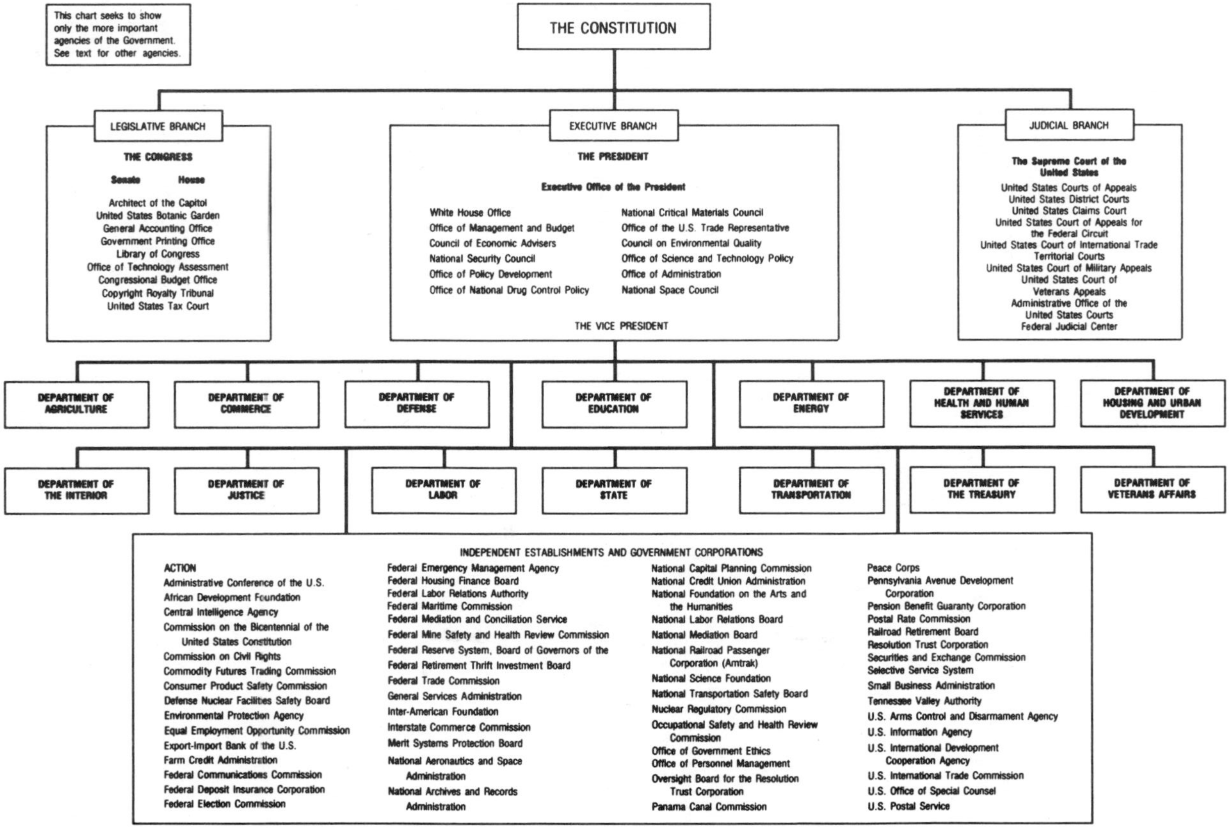

Legislative Branch

LEGISLATIVE BRANCH

CONGRESS

One Hundred and Second Congress, First Session

The Senate

The Capitol, Washington, DC 20510
Phone, 202–224–3121

President of the Senate (Vice President of the United States)	Dan Quayle
President pro tempore	Robert C. Byrd
Majority Leader	George J. Mitchell
Minority Leader	Bob Dole
Secretary	Walter J. Stewart
Sergeant at Arms	Martha S. Pope
Secretary for the Majority	C. Abbott Saffold
Secretary for the Minority	Howard O. Greene, Jr.
Chaplain	Richard C. Halverson

The House of Representatives

The Capitol, Washington, DC 20515
Phone, 202–224–3121

The Speaker	Thomas S. Foley
Clerk	Donnald K. Anderson
Sergeant at Arms	Jack Russ
Doorkeeper	James T. Molloy
Postmaster	Robert V. Rota
Chaplain	Rev. James David Ford

The Congress of the United States was created by Article I, section 1, of the Constitution, adopted by the Constitutional Convention on September 17, 1787, providing that "All legislative Powers herein granted shall be vested in a Congress of the United States, which shall consist of a Senate and House of Representatives."

290-950 o 91 = 2

UNITED STATES SENATE

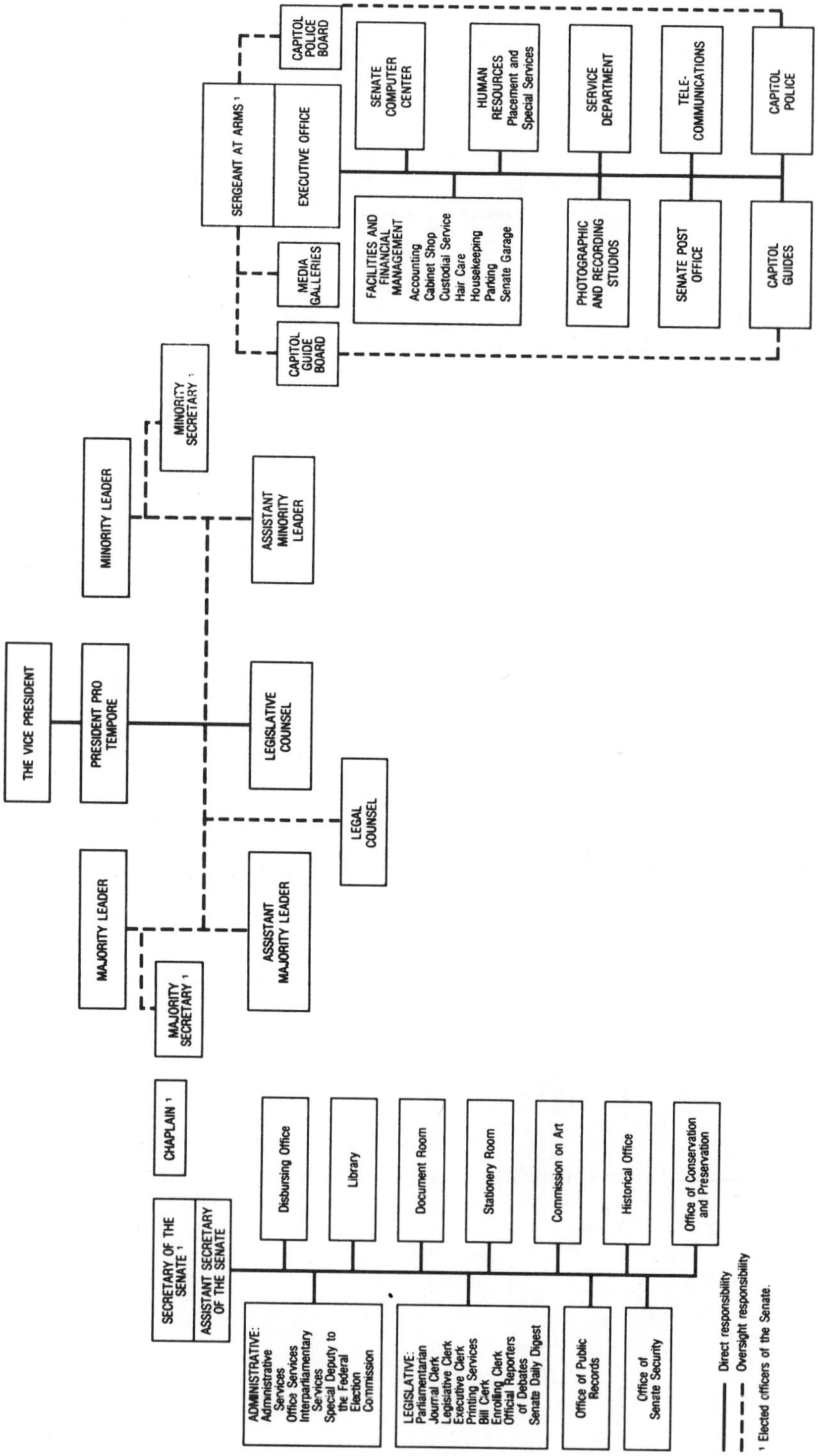

¹ Elected officers of the Senate.

HOUSE OF REPRESENTATIVES

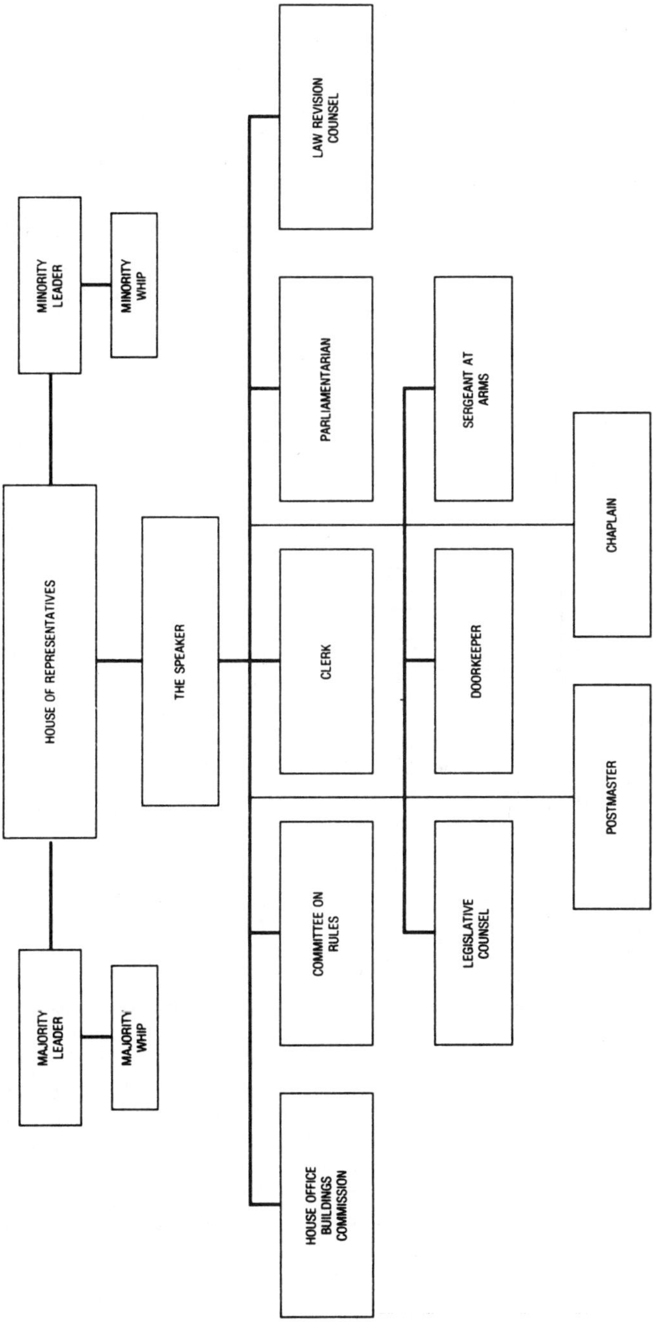

The first Congress under the Constitution met on March 4, 1789, in the Federal Hall in New York City. The membership then consisted of 20 [1] Senators and 59 Representatives.

The Senate is composed of 100 Members, 2 from each State, who are elected to serve for a term of 6 years. Senators were originally chosen by the State legislatures. This procedure was changed by the seventeenth amendment to the Constitution, adopted in 1913, which made the election of Senators a function of the people. There are three classes of Senators, and a new class is elected every 2 years.

The House of Representatives comprises 435 Representatives. The number representing each State is determined by population, but every State is entitled to at least one Representative. Members are elected by the people for 2-year terms, all terms running for the same period.

Both the Senators and the Representatives must be residents of the State from which they are chosen. In addition, a Senator must be at least 30 years of age and must have been a citizen of the United States for at least 9 years; a Representative must be at least 25 years of age and must have been a citizen for at least 7 years.

A Resident Commissioner from Puerto Rico (elected for a 4-year term) and Delegates from American Samoa, the District of Columbia, Guam, and the Virgin Islands complete the composition of the Congress of the United States. Delegates are elected for a term of 2 years. The Resident Commissioner and Delegates may take part in the floor discussions, but have no vote. They do vote in the committees to which they are assigned.

Officers The Vice President of the United States is the Presiding Officer of the Senate; in his absence the duties are taken over by a President pro tempore, elected by that body, or someone designated by him. The Presiding Officer of the House of Representatives, the Speaker, is elected by the House; he may designate any Member of the House to act in his absence.

The positions of Senate majority and minority leader have been in existence only since the early years of the 20th century. Leaders are elected at the beginning of each new Congress by a majority vote of the Senators in their political party. In cooperation with their party organizations, leaders are responsible for the design and achievement of a legislative program. This involves managing the flow of legislation, expediting noncontroversial measures, and keeping Members informed regarding proposed action on pending business. Each leader serves as an *ex officio* member of his party's policymaking and organizational bodies and is aided by an assistant floor leader (whip) and a party secretary.

The Secretary of the Senate, elected by vote of the Senate, performs the duties of the Presiding Officer of the Senate in the absence of the Vice President and pending the election of a President pro tempore. The Secretary is the custodian of the seal of the Senate, draws requisitions on the Secretary of the Treasury for moneys appropriated for the compensation of Senators, officers, and employees, and for the contingent expenses of the Senate, and is empowered to administer oaths to any officer of the Senate and to any witness produced before it. The Secretary's executive duties include certification of extracts from the Journal of the Senate; the attestation of bills and joint, concurrent, and Senate resolutions; in impeachment trials, issuance, under the authority of the Presiding Officer, of all orders, mandates, writs, and precepts authorized by the Senate; and certification to the President of the United States of the advice and consent of the Senate to ratification of treaties and the names of persons confirmed or rejected upon the nomination of the President.

[1] New York ratified the Constitution on July 26, 1788, but did not elect its Senators until July 15 and 16, 1789. North Carolina did not ratify the Constitution until November 21, 1789; Rhode Island on May 29, 1790.

The Sergeant at Arms of the Senate is elected by and serves as the Executive Officer of that body. She directs and supervises the various departments and facilities under her jurisdiction. She is also the Law Enforcement and Protocol Officer. As Law Enforcement Officer, she has statutory power to make arrests; to locate absentee Senators for a quorum; to enforce Senate rules and regulations as they pertain to the Senate Chamber, the Senate wing of the Capitol, and the Senate Office Buildings. She serves as a member of the Capitol Police Board and as its chairman each odd year; and, subject to the Presiding Officer, maintains order in the Senate Chamber. As Protocol Officer, she is responsible for many aspects of ceremonial functions, including the inauguration of the President of the United States; arranging funerals of Senators who die in office; escorting the President when he addresses a Joint Session of Congress or attends any function in the Senate; and escorting heads of state when they visit the Senate.

The Clerk of the House is the chief legislative, administrative, and budgetary officer of the U.S. House of Representatives. The Clerk is responsible for directing legislative activities of the House such as keeping the Journal, taking all votes, certifying passage of bills, and processing all legislation. The Clerk also prepares the budget for the House, disburses funds, and serves as the contracting officer of the House. In addition, the Clerk is the purchaser and provider of all furnishings, office equipment, and office supplies.

Committees The work of preparing and considering legislation is done largely by committees of both Houses of Congress. There are 16 standing committees in the Senate and 22 in the House of Representatives. The standing committees of the Senate and the House of Representatives are shown in the list below. In addition, there are special committees in each House, and various congressional commissions and joint committees composed of members of both Houses. Each House may also appoint special investigating committees.

The membership of the standing committees of each House is chosen by a vote of the entire body; members of other committees are appointed under the provisions of the measure establishing them.

Each bill and resolution is usually referred to the appropriate committee, which may report a bill out in its original form, favorably or unfavorably, recommend amendments, or allow the proposed legislation to die in committee without action.

Standing Committees of the Congress

House Committee	Room [1]	Senate Committee	Room [2]
Agriculture	1301	Agriculture, Nutrition, and Forestry	SR-328A
Appropriations	H-218	Appropriations	S-128
Armed Services	2120	Armed Services	SR-228
Banking, Finance and Urban Affairs	2129	Banking, Housing, and Urban Affairs	SD-534
Budget	214 [3]	Budget	SD-621
District of Columbia	1310	Commerce, Science, and Transportation	SD-508
Education and Labor	2181	Energy and Natural Resources	SD-364
Energy and Commerce	2125	Environment and Public Works	SD-458
Foreign Affairs	2170	Finance	SD-205
Government Operations	2157	Foreign Relations	SD-446
House Administration	H-326	Governmental Affairs	SD-340
Interior and Insular Affairs	1324	Judiciary	SD-224
Judiciary	2138	Labor and Human Resources	SD-428
Merchant Marine and Fisheries	1334	Rules and Administration	SR-305
Post Office and Civil Service	309	Small Business	SR-428A
Public Works and Transportation	2165	Veterans' Affairs	SR-414
Rules	H-312		
Science, Space, and Technology	2321		
Small Business	2361		
Standards of Official Conduct	HT-2		
Veterans' Affairs	335		
Ways and Means	1102		

[1] Room numbers with three digits are in the Cannon House Office Building, four digits beginning with 1 are in the Longworth House Office Building, and four digits beginning with 2 are in the Rayburn House Office Building.
[2] Room numbers preceded by S are in the main Capitol building; those preceded by SD are in the Dirksen Office Building; and those preceded by SR are in the Russell Office Building.
[3] O'Neill House Office Building.

Congressional Record Proceedings of Congress are published in the *Congressional Record,* which is issued when Congress is in session. Publication of the *Record* began March 4, 1873; it was the first record of debate officially reported, printed, and published directly by the Federal Government. The Daily Digest of the *Congressional Record,* printed in the back of each issue of the *Record,* summarizes the proceedings of that day in each House, and before each of their committees and subcommittees, respectively. The Digest also presents the legislative program for each day and, at the end of the week, gives the program for the following week. Its publication was begun March 17, 1947.

Sessions Section 4 of Article I of the Constitution makes it mandatory that "The Congress shall assemble at least once in every Year. . . ." Under this provision, also, the date for convening Congress was designated originally as the first Monday in December, "unless they shall by Law appoint a different Day." Eighteen acts were passed, up to 1820, providing for the meeting of Congress on other days of the year. From 1820 to 1934, however, Congress met regularly on the first Monday in December. In 1934 the Twentieth Amendment changed the convening of Congress to January 3, unless Congress "shall by law appoint a different day." In addition, the President, according to Article II, section 3, of the Constitution "may, on extraordinary Occasions, convene both Houses, or either of them, and in Case of Disagreement between them, with Respect to the Time of Adjournment, he may adjourn them to such Time as he shall think proper. . . ."

Powers of Congress Article I, section 8, of the Constitution defines the powers of Congress. Included are the powers to assess and collect taxes—called the chief power; to regulate commerce, both interstate and foreign; to coin money; to establish post offices and post roads; to establish courts inferior to the Supreme Court; to declare war; and to raise and maintain an army and navy. Congress is further empowered "To provide for calling forth the Militia to execute the Laws of the Union, suppress Insurrections and repel Invasions;" and "To make all Laws which shall be necessary and proper for carrying into Execution the foregoing Powers, and all other Powers vested by this Constitution in the Government of the United States, or in any Department or Officer thereof."

Amendments to the Constitution Another power vested in the Congress is the right to propose amendments to the Constitution, whenever two-thirds of both Houses shall deem it necessary. Should two-thirds of the State legislatures demand changes in the Constitution, it is the duty of Congress to call a constitutional convention. Proposed amendments shall be valid as part of the Constitution when ratified by the legislatures or by conventions of three-fourths of the States, as one or the other mode of ratification may be proposed by Congress.

Special Powers of the Senate Under the Constitution, the Senate is granted certain powers not accorded to the House of Representatives. The Senate approves or disapproves certain Presidential appointments by majority vote, and treaties must be concurred in by a two-thirds vote.

Special Powers of the House of Representatives The House of Representatives is granted the power of originating all bills for the raising of revenue.

Both Houses of Congress act in impeachment proceedings, which, according to the Constitution, may be instituted against the President, Vice President, and all civil officers of the United States. The House of Representatives has the sole power of impeachment, and the Senate has the sole power to try impeachments.

Prohibitions upon Congress Section 9 of Article I of the Constitution also imposes prohibitions upon Congress. "The Privilege of the Writ of Habeas Corpus shall not be suspended, unless when in Cases of Rebellion or Invasion the public Safety may require it." A bill of attainder or an ex post facto law cannot be passed. No export duty can be imposed. Ports of one State cannot be given preference over those of another State. "No money shall be drawn from the Treasury, but in Consequence of Appropriations made by Law. . . ." No title of nobility may be granted.

Rights of Members According to section 6 of Article I, Members of Congress are granted certain privileges. In no case, except in treason, felony, and breach of the peace, can Members be arrested while attending sessions of Congress "and in going to and returning from the same. . . ." Furthermore, the Members cannot be questioned in any other place for remarks made in Congress. Each House may expel a Member of its body by a two-thirds vote.

Enactment of Laws All bills and joint resolutions must pass both the House of Representatives and the Senate and must be signed by the President, except those proposing a constitutional amendment, in order to become law, or be passed over the President's veto by a two-thirds vote of both Houses of Congress. Section 7 of Article I states: "If any Bill shall not be returned by the President within ten Days (Sundays excepted) after it shall have been presented to him, the Same shall be a Law, in like Manner as if he had signed it, unless the Congress by their Adjournment prevent its Return, in which Case it shall not be a Law."

When a bill or joint resolution is introduced in the House, the usual procedure for its enactment into law is as follows:

Assignment to House committee having jurisdiction;

If favorably considered, it is reported to the House either in its original form or with recommended amendments;

If the bill or resolution is passed by the House, it is messaged to the Senate and referred to the committee having jurisdiction;

In the Senate committee the bill, if favorably considered, may be reported in the form as received from the House, or with recommended amendments;

The approved bill or resolution is reported to the Senate, and if passed by that body, is returned to the House;

If one body does not accept the amendments to a bill by the other body, a conference committee comprised of Members of both bodies is usually appointed to effect a compromise;

When the bill or joint resolution is finally approved by both Houses, it is signed by the Speaker (or Speaker pro tempore) and the Vice President (or President pro tempore or acting President pro tempore) and is presented to the President;

Once the President's signature is affixed, the measure becomes a law. If the President vetoes the bill, it cannot become a law unless it is repassed by a two-thirds vote of both Houses.

Publications The *Congressional Directory,* the *Senate Manual,* and the *House Rules* and *Manual* may be obtained from the Superintendent of Documents, Government Printing Office, Washington, DC 20402.

Senators

[Democrats in roman (56); Republicans in italic (44); total, 100]

Room numbers preceded by SR are in the Russell Office Building (Delaware and Constitution Avenues); those preceded by SD are in the Dirksen Office Building (First Street and Constitution Avenue); and those preceded by SH are in the Hart Office Building (Second and C Streets). Members offices may be reached by phone at 202–224–3121.

Name	State	Room
Adams, Brock	Washington	SH–513
Akaka, Daniel K	Hawaii	SH–720
Baucus, Max	Montana	SH–706
Bentsen, Lloyd	Texas	SH–703
Biden, Joseph R., Jr	Delaware	SR–221
Bingaman, Jeff	New Mexico	SH–524
Bond, Christopher S	Missouri	SR–293
Boren, David L	Oklahoma	SR–453
Bradley, Bill	New Jersey	SH–731
Breaux, John B	Louisiana	SH–516
Brown, Hank	Colorado	SH–717
Bryan, Richard H	Nevada	SR–364
Bumpers, Dale	Arkansas	SD–229
Burdick, Quentin N	North Dakota	SH–511
Burns, Conrad	Montana	SD–183
Byrd, Robert C	West Virginia	SH–311
Chafee, John H	Rhode Island	SD–567
Coats, Dan	Indiana	SR–411
Cochran, Thad	Mississippi	SR–326
Cohen, William S	Maine	SH–322
Conrad, Kent	North Dakota	SH–724
Craig, Larry	Idaho	SH–302
Cranston, Alan	California	SH–112
D'Amato, Alfonse M	New York	SH–520
Danforth, John C	Missouri	SR–249
Daschle, Thomas A	South Dakota	SH–317
DeConcini, Dennis	Arizona	SH–328
Dixon, Alan J	Illinois	SH–331
Dodd, Christopher J	Connecticut	SR–444
Dole, Bob	Kansas	SH–141
Domenici, Pete V	New Mexico	SD–434
Durenberger, Dave	Minnesota	SR–154
Exon, J. James	Nebraska	SH–528
Ford, Wendell H	Kentucky	SR–173A
Fowler, Wyche, Jr	Georgia	SR–204
Garn, Jake	Utah	SD–505
Glenn, John	Ohio	SH–503
Gore, Albert, Jr	Tennessee	SR–393
Gorton, Slade	Washington	SH–730
Graham, Bob	Florida	SD–241
Gramm, Phil	Texas	SR–370
Grassley, Charles E	Iowa	SH–135
Harkin, Tom	Iowa	SH–531
Hatch, Orrin G	Utah	SR–135
Hatfield, Mark O	Oregon	SH–711
Heflin, Howell	Alabama	SH–728
Helms, Jesse	North Carolina	SD–403
Hollings, Ernest F	South Carolina	SR–125
Inouye, Daniel K	Hawaii	SH–722

Senators—Continued

Room numbers preceded by SR are in the Russell Office Building (Delaware and Constitution Avenues); those preceded by SD are in the Dirksen Office Building (First Street and Constitution Avenue); and those preceded by SH are in the Hart Office Building (Second and C Streets). Members offices may be reached by phone at 202-224-3121.

Name	State	Room
Jeffords, James M	Vermont	SD-530
Johnston, J. Bennett	Louisiana	SH-136
Kassebaum, Nancy Landon	Kansas	SR-302
Kasten, Robert W., Jr	Wisconsin	SH-110
Kennedy, Edward M	Massachusetts	SR-315
Kerrey, J. Robert	Nebraska	SH-316
Kerry, John F	Massachusetts	SR-421
Kohl, Herb	Wisconsin	SH-330
Lautenberg, Frank R	New Jersey	SH-506
Leahy, Patrick J	Vermont	SR-433
Levin, Carl M	Michigan	SR-459
Lieberman, Joseph I	Connecticut	SH-502
Lott, Trent	Mississippi	SR-487
Lugar, Richard G	Indiana	SH-306
Mack, Connie	Florida	SH-517
McCain, John	Arizona	SR-111
McConnell, Mitch	Kentucky	SR-120
Metzenbaum, Howard M	Ohio	SR-140
Mikulski, Barbara A	Maryland	SH-320
Mitchell, George J	Maine	SR-176
Moynihan, Daniel Patrick	New York	SR-464
Murkowski, Frank H	Alaska	SH-709
Nickles, Don	Oklahoma	SH-713
Nunn, Sam	Georgia	SD-303
Packwood, Bob	Oregon	SR-259
Pell, Claiborne	Rhode Island	SR-335
Pressler, Larry	South Dakota	SH-133
Pryor, David	Arkansas	SR-267
Reid, Harry	Nevada	SH-324
Riegle, Donald W., Jr	Michigan	SD-105
Robb, Charles S	Virginia	SR-493
Rockefeller, John D., IV	West Virginia	SH-109
Roth, William V., Jr	Delaware	SH-104
Rudman, Warren B	New Hampshire	SH-530
Sanford, Terry	North Carolina	SH-716
Sarbanes, Paul S	Maryland	SD-309
Sasser, Jim	Tennessee	SR-363
Seymour, John	California	SD-361
Shelby, Richard C	Alabama	SH-313
Simon, Paul	Illinois	SD-462
Simpson, Alan K	Wyoming	SD-261
Smith, Robert	New Hampshire	SD-332
Specter, Arlen	Pennsylvania	SH-303
Stevens, Ted	Alaska	SH-522
Symms, Steve	Idaho	SH-509
Thurmond, Strom	South Carolina	SR-217
Wallop, Malcolm	Wyoming	SR-237
Warner, John W	Virginia	SR-225
Wellstone, Paul	Minnesota	SH-702

Senators—Continued

Room numbers preceded by SR are in the Russell Office Building (Delaware and Constitution Avenues); those preceded by SD are in the Dirksen Office Building (First Street and Constitution Avenue); and those preceded by SH are in the Hart Office Building (Second and C Streets). Members offices may be reached by phone at 202-224-3121.

Name	State	Room
Wirth, Timothy E	Colorado	SR-380
Wofford, Harris	Pennsylvania	SR-277

Representatives

[Democrats in roman (267); Republicans in italic (164); Independents in bold (1); vacancies (3); [1] total, 435]

Room numbers with three digits are in the Cannon House Office Building (New Jersey and Independence Avenues), four digits beginning with 1 are in the Longworth House Office Building (between South Capitol Street and New Jersey Avenue on Independence Avenue), and four digits beginning with 2 are in the Rayburn House Office Building (between First and South Capitol Streets on Independence Avenue). Members offices may be reached by phone at 202-224-3121.

Name	State (District)	Room
Abercrombie, Neil	Hawaii (1)	1440
Ackerman, Gary L	New York (7)	238
Alexander, Bill	Arkansas (1)	233
Allard, Wayne	Colorado (4)	513
Anderson, Glenn M	California (32)	2329
Andrews, Michael A	Texas (25)	303
Andrews, Robert E	New Jersey (1)	1005
Andrews, Thomas H	Maine (1)	1724
Annunzio, Frank	Illinois (11)	2303
Anthony, Beryl, Jr	Arkansas (4)	1212
Applegate, Douglas	Ohio (18)	2183
Archer, Bill	Texas (7)	1236
Armey, Richard K	Texas (26)	130
Aspin, Les	Wisconsin (1)	2336
Atkins, Chester G	Massachusetts (5)	123
AuCoin, Les	Oregon (1)	2159
Bacchus, Jim	Florida (11)	431
Baker, Richard H	Louisiana (6)	404
Ballenger, Cass	North Carolina (10)	328
Barnard, Doug, Jr	Georgia (10)	2227
Barrett, Bill	Nebraska (3)	1607
Barton, Joe	Texas (6)	1225
Bateman, Herbert H	Virginia (1)	1030
Beilenson, Anthony C	California (23)	1025
Bennett, Charles E	Florida (3)	2107
Bentley, Helen Delich	Maryland (2)	1610
Bereuter, Doug	Nebraska (1)	2348
Berman, Howard L	California (26)	137
Bevill, Tom	Alabama (4)	2302
Bilbray, James H	Nevada (1)	319

[1] 15th District, Illinois; 1st District, Massachusetts; 3d District, Texas.

Representatives—Continued

Room numbers with three digits are in the Cannon House Office Building (New Jersey and Independence Avenues), four digits beginning with 1 are in the Longworth House Office Building (between South Capitol Street and New Jersey Avenue on Independence Avenue), and four digits beginning with 2 are in the Rayburn House Office Building (between First and South Capitol Streets on Independence Avenue). Members offices may be reached by phone at 202-224-3121.

Name	State (District)	Room
Bilirakis, Michael	Florida (9)	2432
Bliley, Thomas J., Jr	Virginia (3)	2241
Boehlert, Sherwood L	New York (25)	1127
Boehner, John A	Ohio (8)	1020
Bonior, David E	Michigan (12)	2242
Borski, Robert A	Pennsylvania (3)	407
Boucher, Rick	Virginia (9)	405
Boxer, Barbara	California (6)	307
Brewster, Bill K	Oklahoma (3)	1407
Brooks, Jack	Texas (9)	2449
Broomfield, Wm. S	Michigan (18)	2306
Browder, Glen	Alabama (3)	1221
Brown, George E., Jr	California (36)	2300
Bruce, Terry L	Illinois (19)	419
Bryant, John	Texas (5)	208
Bunning, Jim	Kentucky (4)	116
Burton, Dan	Indiana (6)	120
Bustamante, Albert G	Texas (23)	1113
Byron, Beverly B	Maryland (6)	2430
Callahan, Sonny	Alabama (1)	1330
Camp, Dave	Michigan (10)	511
Campbell, Ben Nighthorse	Colorado (3)	1530
Campbell, Tom	California (12)	313
Cardin, Benjamin L	Maryland (3)	117
Carper, Thomas R	Delaware (At Large)	131
Carr, Bob	Michigan (6)	2439
Chandler, Rod	Washington (8)	223
Chapman, Jim	Texas (1)	236
Clay, William (Bill)	Missouri (1)	2470
Clement, Bob	Tennessee (5)	325
Clinger, William F., Jr	Pennsylvania (23)	2160
Coble, Howard	North Carolina (6)	430
Coleman, E. Thomas	Missouri (6)	2468
Coleman, Ronald D	Texas (16)	440
Collins, Barbara-Rose	Michigan (13)	1541
Collins, Cardiss	Illinois (7)	2264
Combest, Larry	Texas (19)	1527
Condit, Gary	California (15)	1529
Conyers, John, Jr	Michigan (1)	2426
Cooper, Jim	Tennessee (4)	125
Costello, Jerry F	Illinois (21)	119
Coughlin, Lawrence	Pennsylvania (13)	2309
Cox, C. Christopher	California (40)	412
Cox, John W., Jr	Illinois (16)	501
Coyne, William J	Pennsylvania (14)	2455

Representatives—Continued

Room numbers with three digits are in the Cannon House Office Building (New Jersey and Independence Avenues), four digits beginning with 1 are in the Longworth House Office Building (between South Capitol Street and New Jersey Avenue on Independence Avenue), and four digits beginning with 2 are in the Rayburn House Office Building (between First and South Capitol Streets on Independence Avenue). Members offices may be reached by phone at 202-224-3121.

Name	State (District)	Room
Cramer, Robert E. (Bud), Jr	Alabama (5)	1431
Crane, Philip M	Illinois (12)	1035
Cunningham, Randy (Duke)	California (44)	1017
Dannemeyer, William E	California (39)	2234
Darden, George (Buddy)	Georgia (7)	228
Davis, Robert W	Michigan (11)	2417
DeFazio, Peter A	Oregon (4)	1233
de la Garza, E	Texas (15)	1401
DeLauro, Rosa L	Connecticut (3)	327
DeLay, Tom	Texas (22)	308
Dellums, Ronald V	California (8)	2136
Derrick, Butler	South Carolina (3)	201
Dickinson, William L	Alabama (2)	2406
Dicks, Norman D	Washington (6)	2429
Dingell, John D	Michigan (16)	2328
Dixon, Julian C	California (28)	2400
Donnelly, Brian J	Massachusetts (11)	2229
Dooley, Calvin M	California (17)	1022
Doolittle, John T	California (14)	1223
Dorgan, Byron L	North Dakota (At Large)	203
Dornan, Robert K	California (38)	301
Downey, Thomas J	New York (2)	2232
Dreier, David	California (33)	411
Duncan, John J., Jr	Tennessee (2)	115
Durbin, Richard J	Illinois (20)	129
Dwyer, Bernard J	New Jersey (6)	2428
Dymally, Mervyn M	California (31)	1717
Early, Joseph D	Massachusetts (3)	2349
Eckart, Dennis E	Ohio (11)	1111
Edwards, Chet	Texas (11)	425
Edwards, Don	California (10)	2307
Edwards, Mickey	Oklahoma (5)	2330
Emerson, Bill	Missouri (8)	438
Engel, Eliot	New York (19)	1213
English, Glenn	Oklahoma (6)	2206
Erdreich, Ben	Alabama (6)	439
Espy, Mike	Mississippi (2)	216
Evans, Lane	Illinois (17)	1121
Fascell, Dante B	Florida (19)	2354
Fawell, Harris W	Illinois (13)	435
Fazio, Vic	California (4)	2113
Feighan, Edward F	Ohio (19)	1124
Fields, Jack	Texas (8)	108
Fish, Hamilton, Jr	New York (21)	2269
Flake, Floyd H	New York (6)	1034

Representatives—Continued

Room numbers with three digits are in the Cannon House Office Building (New Jersey and Independence Avenues), four digits beginning with 1 are in the Longworth House Office Building (between South Capitol Street and New Jersey Avenue on Independence Avenue), and four digits beginning with 2 are in the Rayburn House Office Building (between First and South Capitol Streets on Independence Avenue). Members offices may be reached by phone at 202-224-3121.

Name	State (District)	Room
Foglietta, Thomas M	Pennsylvania (1)	231
Foley, Thomas S	Washington (5)	1201
Ford, Harold E	Tennessee (9)	2305
Ford, William D	Michigan (15)	2371
Frank, Barney	Massachusetts (4)	2404
Franks, Gary A	Connecticut (5)	1609
Frost, Martin	Texas (24)	2459
Gallegly, Elton	California (21)	107
Gallo, Dean A	New Jersey (11)	1318
Gaydos, Joseph M	Pennsylvania (20)	2186
Gejdenson, Sam	Connecticut (2)	2416
Gekas, George W	Pennsylvania (17)	1519
Gephardt, Richard A	Missouri (3)	1432
Geren, Pete	Texas (12)	1730
Gibbons, Sam	Florida (7)	2204
Gilchrest, Wayne T	Maryland (1)	502
Gillmor, Paul E	Ohio (5)	1203
Gilman, Benjamin A	New York (22)	2185
Gingrich, Newt	Georgia (6)	2438
Glickman, Dan	Kansas (4)	2311
Gonzalez, Henry B	Texas (20)	2413
Goodling, William F	Pennsylvania (19)	2263
Gordon, Bart	Tennessee (6)	103
Goss, Porter J	Florida (13)	224
Gradison, Willis D., Jr	Ohio (2)	1125
Grandy, Fred	Iowa (6)	418
Gray, William H., III	Pennsylvania (2)	2454
Green, Bill	New York (15)	2301
Guarini, Frank J	New Jersey (14)	2458
Gunderson, Steve	Wisconsin (3)	2235
Hall, Ralph M	Texas (4)	2236
Hall, Tony P	Ohio (3)	2162
Hamilton, Lee H	Indiana (9)	2187
Hammerschmidt, John Paul	Arkansas (3)	2110
Hancock, Mel	Missouri (7)	318
Hansen, James V	Utah (1)	2421
Harris, Claude	Alabama (7)	1009
Hastert, J. Dennis	Illinois (14)	515
Hatcher, Charles	Georgia (2)	2434
Hayes, Charles A	Illinois (1)	1131
Hayes, James A	Louisiana (7)	503
Hefley, Joel	Colorado (5)	222
Hefner, W.G. (Bill)	North Carolina (8)	2161
Henry, Paul B	Michigan (5)	215
Herger, Wally	California (2)	1108

Representatives—Continued

Room numbers with three digits are in the Cannon House Office Building (New Jersey and Independence Avenues), four digits beginning with 1 are in the Longworth House Office Building (between South Capitol Street and New Jersey Avenue on Independence Avenue), and four digits beginning with 2 are in the Rayburn House Office Building (between First and South Capitol Streets on Independence Avenue). Members offices may be reached by phone at 202-224-3121.

Name	State (District)	Room
Hertel, Dennis M	Michigan (14)	2442
Hoagland, Peter	Nebraska (2)	1710
Hobson, David L	Ohio (7)	1338
Hochbrueckner, George J	New York (1)	124
Holloway, Clyde C	Louisiana (8)	1206
Hopkins, Larry J	Kentucky (6)	2437
Horn, Joan Kelly	Missouri (2)	1008
Horton, Frank	New York (29)	2108
Houghton, Amo	New York (34)	1217
Hoyer, Steny H	Maryland (5)	1705
Hubbard, Carroll, Jr	Kentucky (1)	2268
Huckaby, Jerry	Louisiana (5)	2182
Hughes, William J	New Jersey (2)	341
Hunter, Duncan	California (45)	133
Hutto, Earl	Florida (1)	2435
Hyde, Henry J	Illinois (6)	2262
Inhofe, James M	Oklahoma (1)	408
Ireland, Andy	Florida (10)	2466
Jacobs, Andrew, Jr	Indiana (10)	2313
James, Craig T	Florida (4)	1408
Jefferson, William J	Louisiana (2)	506
Jenkins, Ed	Georgia (9)	2427
Johnson, Nancy L	Connecticut (6)	227
Johnson, Tim	South Dakota (At Large)	428
Johnston, Harry	Florida (14)	1028
Jones, Ben	Georgia (4)	514
Jones, Walter B	North Carolina (1)	241
Jontz, Jim	Indiana (5)	1317
Kanjorski, Paul E	Pennsylvania (11)	424
Kaptur, Marcy	Ohio (9)	1228
Kasich, John R	Ohio (12)	1133
Kennedy, Joseph P., II	Massachusetts (8)	1208
Kennelly, Barbara B	Connecticut (1)	204
Kildee, Dale E	Michigan (7)	2239
Kleczka, Gerald D	Wisconsin (4)	226
Klug, Scott L	Wisconsin (2)	1224
Kolbe, Jim	Arizona (5)	410
Kolter, Joe	Pennsylvania (4)	212
Kopetski, Michael J	Oregon (5)	1520
Kostmayer, Peter H	Pennsylvania (8)	2436
Kyl, Jon	Arizona (4)	336
LaFalce, John J	New York (32)	2367
Lagomarsino, Robert J	California (19)	2332
Lancaster, H. Martin	North Carolina (3)	1417
Lantos, Tom	California (11)	1526

Representatives—Continued

Room numbers with three digits are in the Cannon House Office Building (New Jersey and Independence Avenues), four digits beginning with 1 are in the Longworth House Office Building (between South Capitol Street and New Jersey Avenue on Independence Avenue), and four digits beginning with 2 are in the Rayburn House Office Building (between First and South Capitol Streets on Independence Avenue). Members offices may be reached by phone at 202-224-3121.

Name	State (District)	Room
LaRocco, Larry	Idaho (1)	1117
Laughlin, Greg	Texas (14)	218
Leach, Jim	Iowa (1)	1514
Lehman, Richard H	California (18)	1319
Lehman, William	Florida (17)	2347
Lent, Norman F.	New York (4)	2408
Levin, Sander M	Michigan (17)	323
Levine, Mel	California (27)	2443
Lewis, Jerry	California (35)	2312
Lewis, John	Georgia (5)	329
Lewis, Tom	Florida (12)	1216
Lightfoot, Jim	Iowa (5)	1222
Lipinski, William O	Illinois (5)	1501
Livingston, Bob	Louisiana (1)	2368
Lloyd, Marilyn	Tennessee (3)	2266
Long, Jill L	Indiana (4)	1513
Lowery, Bill	California (41)	2433
Lowey, Nita M	New York (20)	1313
Luken, Charles J	Ohio (1)	1632
McCandless, Alfred A. (Al)	California (37)	2422
McCloskey, Frank	Indiana (8)	127
McCollum, Bill	Florida (5)	2453
McCrery, Jim	Louisiana (4)	429
McCurdy, Dave	Oklahoma (4)	2344
McDade, Joseph M	Pennsylvania (10)	2370
McDermott, Jim	Washington (7)	1707
McEwen, Bob	Ohio (6)	2431
McGrath, Raymond J	New York (5)	205
McHugh, Matthew F	New York (28)	2335
McMillan, J. Alex	North Carolina (9)	401
McMillen, C. Thomas	Maryland (4)	420
McNulty, Michael R	New York (23)	414
Machtley, Ronald K	Rhode Island (1)	132
Manton, Thomas J	New York (9)	331
Markey, Edward J	Massachusetts (7)	2133
Marlenee, Ron	Montana (2)	2465
Martin, David O'B	New York (26)	442
Martinez, Matthew G	California (30)	2446
Matsui, Robert T	California (3)	2353
Mavroules, Nicholas	Massachusetts (6)	2334
Mazzoli, Romano L	Kentucky (3)	2246
Meyers, Jan	Kansas (3)	1230
Mfume, Kweisi	Maryland (7)	217
Michel, Robert H	Illinois (18)	2112
Miller, Clarence E	Ohio (10)	2308

Representatives—Continued

Room numbers with three digits are in the Cannon House Office Building (New Jersey and Independence Avenues), four digits beginning with 1 are in the Longworth House Office Building (between South Capitol Street and New Jersey Avenue on Independence Avenue), and four digits beginning with 2 are in the Rayburn House Office Building (between First and South Capitol Streets on Independence Avenue). Members offices may be reached by phone at 202-224-3121.

Name	State (District)	Room
Miller, George	California (7)	2228
Miller, John	Washington (1)	322
Mineta, Norman Y	California (13)	2350
Mink, Patsy T	Hawaii (2)	2135
Moakley, John Joseph	Massachusetts (9)	221
Molinari, Susan	New York (14)	315
Mollohan, Alan B	West Virginia (1)	229
Montgomery, G.V. (Sonny)	Mississippi (3)	2184
Moody, Jim	Wisconsin (5)	1019
Moorhead, Carlos J	California (22)	2346
Moran, James P	Virginia (8)	1523
Morella, Constance A	Maryland (8)	1024
Morrison, Sid	Washington (4)	1434
Mrazek, Robert J	New York (3)	306
Murphy, Austin J	Pennsylvania (22)	2210
Murtha, John P	Pennsylvania (12)	2423
Myers, John T	Indiana (7)	2372
Nagle, David R	Iowa (3)	214
Natcher, William H	Kentucky (2)	2333
Neal, Richard E	Massachusetts (2)	437
Neal, Stephen L	North Carolina (5)	2463
Nichols, Dick	Kansas (5)	1605
Nowak, Henry J	New York (33)	2240
Nussle, Jim	Iowa (2)	507
Oakar, Mary Rose	Ohio (20)	2231
Oberstar, James L	Minnesota (8)	2209
Obey, David R	Wisconsin (7)	2462
Olin, Jim	Virginia (6)	1410
Ortiz, Solomon P	Texas (27)	1524
Orton, Bill	Utah (3)	1723
Owens, Major R	New York (12)	114
Owens, Wayne	Utah (2)	1728
Oxley, Michael G	Ohio (4)	2448
Packard, Ron	California (43)	434
Pallone, Frank, Jr	New Jersey (3)	213
Panetta, Leon E	California (16)	339
Parker, Mike	Mississippi (4)	1504
Patterson, Elizabeth J	South Carolina (4)	1641
Paxon, Bill	New York (31)	1314
Payne, Donald M	New Jersey (10)	417
Payne, Lewis F., Jr	Virginia (5)	1118
Pease, Donald J	Ohio (13)	2410
Pelosi, Nancy	California (5)	109
Penny, Timothy J	Minnesota (1)	436
Perkins, Carl C	Kentucky (7)	1004

Representatives—Continued

Room numbers with three digits are in the Cannon House Office Building (New Jersey and Independence Avenues), four digits beginning with 1 are in the Longworth House Office Building (between South Capitol Street and New Jersey Avenue on Independence Avenue), and four digits beginning with 2 are in the Rayburn House Office Building (between First and South Capitol Streets on Independence Avenue). Members offices may be reached by phone at 202-224-3121.

Name	State (District)	Room
Peterson, Collin C	Minnesota (7)	1725
Peterson, Douglas (Pete)	Florida (2)	1415
Petri, Thomas E	Wisconsin (6)	2245
Pickett, Owen B	Virginia (2)	1204
Pickle, J.J	Texas (10)	242
Porter, John Edward	Illinois (10)	1026
Poshard, Glenn	Illinois (22)	314
Price, David E	North Carolina (4)	1406
Pursell, Carl D	Michigan (2)	1414
Quillen, James H. (Jimmy)	Tennessee (1)	102
Rahall, Nick Joe, II	West Virginia (4)	2104
Ramstad, Jim	Minnesota (3)	504
Rangel, Charles B	New York (16)	2252
Ravenel, Arthur, Jr	South Carolina (1)	508
Ray, Richard	Georgia (3)	225
Reed, John F	Rhode Island (2)	1229
Regula, Ralph	Ohio (16)	2207
Rhodes, John J., III	Arizona (1)	326
Richardson, Bill	New Mexico (3)	332
Ridge, Thomas J	Pennsylvania (21)	1714
Riggs, Frank D	California (1)	1517
Rinaldo, Matthew J	New Jersey (7)	2469
Ritter, Don	Pennsylvania (15)	2202
Roberts, Pat	Kansas (1)	1110
Roe, Robert A	New Jersey (8)	2243
Roemer, Tim	Indiana (3)	415
Rogers, Harold	Kentucky (5)	343
Rohrabacher, Dana	California (42)	1039
Ros-Lehtinen, Ileana	Florida (18)	416
Rose, Charles	North Carolina (7)	2230
Rostenkowski, Dan	Illinois (8)	2111
Roth, Toby	Wisconsin (8)	2352
Roukema, Marge	New Jersey (5)	2244
Rowland, J. Roy	Georgia (8)	423
Roybal, Edward R	California (25)	2211
Russo, Marty	Illinois (3)	2233
Sabo, Martin Olav	Minnesota (5)	2201
Sanders, Bernard	Vermont (At Large)	509
Sangmeister, George E	Illinois (4)	1032
Santorum, Richard John	Pennsylvania (18)	1708
Sarpalius, Bill	Texas (13)	126
Savage, Gus	Illinois (2)	2419
Sawyer, Thomas C	Ohio (14)	1518
Saxton, Jim	New Jersey (13)	324
Schaefer, Dan	Colorado (6)	1007

Representatives—Continued

Room numbers with three digits are in the Cannon House Office Building (New Jersey and Independence Avenues), four digits beginning with 1 are in the Longworth House Office Building (between South Capitol Street and New Jersey Avenue on Independence Avenue), and four digits beginning with 2 are in the Rayburn House Office Building (between First and South Capitol Streets on Independence Avenue). Members offices may be reached by phone at 202-224-3121.

Name	State (District)	Room
Scheuer, James H	New York (8)	2221
Schiff, Steven	New Mexico (1)	1427
Schroeder, Patricia	Colorado (1)	2208
Schulze, Richard T	Pennsylvania (5)	2267
Schumer, Charles E	New York (10)	2412
Sensenbrenner, F. James, Jr	Wisconsin (9)	2444
Serrano, José E	New York (18)	1107
Sharp, Philip R	Indiana (2)	2217
Shaw, E. Clay, Jr	Florida (15)	2338
Shays, Christopher	Connecticut (4)	1531
Shuster, Bud	Pennsylvania (9)	2188
Sikorski, Gerry	Minnesota (6)	403
Sisisky, Norman	Virginia (4)	426
Skaggs, David E	Colorado (2)	1507
Skeen, Joe	New Mexico (2)	2447
Skelton, Ike	Missouri (4)	2134
Slattery, Jim	Kansas (2)	1512
Slaughter, D. French, Jr	Virginia (7)	1404
Slaughter, Louise McIntosh	New York (30)	1424
Smith, Christopher H	New Jersey (4)	2440
Smith, Lamar S	Texas (21)	422
Smith, Lawrence J	Florida (16)	113
Smith, Neal	Iowa (4)	2373
Smith, Robert F. (Bob)	Oregon (2)	118
Snowe, Olympia J	Maine (2)	2464
Solarz, Stephen J	New York (13)	1536
Solomon, Gerald B.H	New York (24)	2265
Spence, Floyd	South Carolina (2)	2405
Spratt, John M., Jr	South Carolina (5)	1533
Staggers, Harley O., Jr	West Virginia (2)	1323
Stallings, Richard H	Idaho (2)	1122
Stark, Fortney Pete	California (9)	239
Stearns, Cliff	Florida (6)	1123
Stenholm, Charles W	Texas (17)	1226
Stokes, Louis	Ohio (21)	2365
Studds, Gerry E	Massachusetts (10)	237
Stump, Bob	Arizona (3)	211
Sundquist, Don	Tennessee (7)	230
Swett, Dick	New Hampshire (2)	128
Swift, Al	Washington (2)	1502
Synar, Mike	Oklahoma (2)	2441
Tallon, Robin	South Carolina (6)	432
Tanner, John S	Tennessee (8)	1232
Tauzin, W.J. (Billy)	Louisiana (3)	2342
Taylor, Charles H	North Carolina (11)	516

Representatives—Continued

Room numbers with three digits are in the Cannon House Office Building (New Jersey and Independence Avenues), four digits beginning with 1 are in the Longworth House Office Building (between South Capitol Street and New Jersey Avenue on Independence Avenue), and four digits beginning with 2 are in the Rayburn House Office Building (between First and South Capitol Streets on Independence Avenue). Members offices may be reached by phone at 202-224-3121.

Name	State (District)	Room
Taylor, Gene	Mississippi (5)	1429
Thomas, Craig	Wyoming (At Large)	1721
Thomas, Lindsay	Georgia (1)	240
Thomas, William M	California (20)	2402
Thornton, Ray	Arkansas (2)	1214
Torres, Esteban Edward	California (34)	1740
Torricelli, Robert G	New Jersey (9)	317
Towns, Edolphus	New York (11)	1726
Traficant, James A., Jr	Ohio (17)	312
Traxler, Bob	Michigan (8)	2366
Udall, Morris K	Arizona (2)	235
Unsoeld, Jolene	Washington (3)	1508
Upton, Frederick S	Michigan (4)	1713
Valentine, Tim	North Carolina (2)	1510
Vander Jagt, Guy	Michigan (9)	2409
Vento, Bruce F	Minnesota (4)	2304
Visclosky, Peter J	Indiana (1)	330
Volkmer, Harold L	Missouri (9)	2411
Vucanovich, Barbara F	Nevada (2)	206
Walker, Robert S	Pennsylvania (16)	2369
Walsh, James T	New York (27)	1238
Washington, Craig A	Texas (18)	1711
Waters, Maxine	California (29)	1207
Waxman, Henry A	California (24)	2418
Weber, Vin	Minnesota (2)	106
Weiss, Ted	New York (17)	2467
Weldon, Curt	Pennsylvania (7)	316
Wheat, Alan	Missouri (5)	1210
Whitten, Jamie L	Mississippi (1)	2314
Williams, Pat	Montana (1)	2457
Wilson, Charles	Texas (2)	2256
Wise, Robert E., Jr	West Virginia (3)	1421
Wolf, Frank R	Virginia (10)	104
Wolpe, Howard	Michigan (3)	1535
Wyden, Ron	Oregon (3)	2452
Wylie, Chalmers P	Ohio (15)	2310
Yates, Sidney R	Illinois (9)	2109
Yatron, Gus	Pennsylvania (6)	2205
Young, C.W. Bill	Florida (8)	2407
Young, Don	Alaska (At Large)	2331
Zeliff, William H., Jr	New Hampshire (1)	512
Zimmer, Dick	New Jersey (12)	510

Representatives—Continued

Room numbers with three digits are in the Cannon House Office Building (New Jersey and Independence Avenues), four digits beginning with 1 are in the Longworth House Office Building (between South Capitol Street and New Jersey Avenue on Independence Avenue), and four digits beginning with 2 are in the Rayburn House Office Building (between First and South Capitol Streets on Independence Avenue). Members offices may be reached by phone at 202-224-3121.

Delegates

Blaz, Ben Garrido	Guam	1130
de Lugo, Ron	Virgin Islands	2238
Faleomavaega, Eni F.H	American Samoa	413
Norton, Eleanor Holmes	District of Columbia	1631

Resident Commissioner

Fuster, Jaime B.	Puerto Rico	427

For further information concerning the United States Senate, contact the Secretary of the Senate, The Capitol, Washington, DC 20510. Phone, 202-224-2115. For further information concerning the House of Representatives, contact the Clerk, The Capitol, Washington, DC 20515. Phone, 202-225-7000.

Telephone directories for the United States Senate and the House of Representatives are available for sale by the Superintendent of Documents, Government Printing Office, Washington, DC 20402.

ARCHITECT OF THE CAPITOL

U.S. Capitol Building, Washington, DC 20515
Phone, 202-225-1200

Architect of the Capitol	George M. White

The Architect of the Capitol is responsible for the care and maintenance of the Capitol Building and nearby buildings and grounds while implementing reconstruction and landscape improvement projects according to the original intent of the Capitol's designers.

The first Architect of the Capitol was appointed in 1793 by the President of the United States. During the period of the construction of the Capitol (1793-1865), appointments were made to the position of Architect at such times and for such periods as the various stages of the construction work required. The office of Architect has been continuous, however, from 1851 to the present.

Originally, the duties of the Architect of the Capitol were to plan and construct the Capitol Building and, later, to supervise its care and maintenance. The functions of the office have changed materially through the years in accordance with the increased activities imposed upon it by Congress, due principally to the addition of new buildings and grounds.

Permanent authority for the care and maintenance of the Capitol Building is provided by act of August 15, 1876 (40 U.S.C. 162, 163). This act has been amended from time to time to provide for the care and maintenance of the additional buildings and grounds placed under the jurisdiction of the Architect of the Capitol by Congress in subsequent years.

The Architect of the Capitol, acting as an agent of Congress, is in charge of the structural and mechanical care of the United States Capitol Building and making arrangements with the proper authorities for ceremonies held in the building and on the grounds; is responsible for the care, maintenance, and improvement of the Capitol Grounds, comprising approximately 221 acres of landscaping, parks, streets, and parking; is responsible for the structural and mechanical care of the Library of Congress Buildings and the United States Supreme Court Building; and under the direction of the Senate Committee on Rules and Administration and the Committee on House Administration, respectively, is charged with the operation of the United States Senate and House restaurants.

In addition to these activities, the Architect has the following duties and responsibilities:

—under the direction and approval of the House Office Building Commission, the structural, mechanical, and domestic care and maintenance of the House Office Buildings, including the maintenance and operation of the mechanical, electrical, and electronic equipment and the care, maintenance, and operation of the Capitol Power Plant, which supplies heat and air-conditioning refrigeration for the Capitol, Senate and House Office Buildings, Library of Congress Buildings, and the United States Supreme Court Building; heat for the United States Botanic Garden and the Senate and House garages; steam heat for the Government Printing Office, Washington City Post Office, and Union Station; and steam heat and chilled water for the Folger Shakespeare Library;

—subject to the approval of the Senate Committee on Rules and Administration as to matters of general policy, the structural, mechanical, and domestic care and maintenance of the Senate Office Buildings, including the maintenance and operation of the mechanical, electrical, and electronic equipment;

—the jurisdiction and control, including care and maintenance of the Senate garage, subject to such regulations respecting the use thereof as may be promulgated by the Senate Committee on Rules and Administration; and

—under the direction of the Joint Committee on the Library, serving as Acting Director of the United States Botanic Garden.

The Architect of the Capitol also is charged with the planning and construction of such buildings as may be committed to his care by Congress from time to time. Current projects include extension, reconstruction, alteration, and improvement of the United States Capitol; procurement and installation of permanent television broadcasting facilities for the Senate Chamber; procurement and installation of hydraulic security barriers and bollards at the vehicular entrances to the Capitol square; development of design and cost estimates associated with the construction aspects of the congressional joint leadership proposal to improve security of the Capitol and House and Senate Office Buildings; interior restoration and renovation of the Thomas Jefferson and John Adams Buildings of the Library of Congress; and direction of the Master Plan for Future Development of the U.S. Capitol Grounds and related areas.

Pursuant to the provisions of the Judiciary Office Building Development Act (40 U.S.C. 1201 *et seq.*), the Architect, under the direction of the Commission for the Judiciary Office Building, is responsible for supervising the design, development, and maintenance of a building east of Union Station to meet the current and future needs of the Administrative Office of the U.S. Courts, the Federal Judicial Center, and other judicial functions and to accommodate such other governmental activities as may be appropriate.

The Architect of the Capitol serves as a member of the District of Columbia Zoning Commission, the Capitol Police Board, the Capitol Guide Board, the Board of Directors of the Pennsylvania Avenue Development Corporation, the Advisory Council on Historic Preservation, the Art Advisory Committee to the Washington Metropolitan Area Transit Authority, the House of Representatives Page Board, the National Capital Memorial Advisory Committee to the Secretary of the Interior, the International Centre Committee (Rome Centre), the National Conservation Advisory Council, and as the Civil Defense Coordinator for the Capitol buildings.

For further information, contact the Office of the Architect of the Capitol, U.S. Capitol Building, Washington, DC 20515. Phone, 202–225–1200.

UNITED STATES BOTANIC GARDEN

Office of Director, 245 First Street SW., Washington, DC 20024
Phone, 202–225–8333

Conservatory, Maryland Avenue, First to Second Streets SW., Washington, DC 20024
Phone, 202–225–6646

Nursery, Poplar Point, 700 Howard Road SE., Anacostia, DC 20020
Phone, 202–225–6420

Director (Architect of the Capitol)	George M. White, *Acting*
Executive Director	David Scheid

The United States Botanic Garden collects, cultivates, and grows various vegetable productions of this and other countries for exhibition and display to the public and for study material for students, scientists, and garden clubs.

The Botanic Garden contains a large variety of palms, cycads, ferns, cacti, orchids, and other miscellaneous tropical and subtropical plants, many of which are rare species. There are special displays during most of the months of the year, and in their proper seasons banana, papaya, orange, lemon, tangerine, kumquat, averrhoa, coffee, and surinam cherry are to be seen in luxuriant fruiting. The entire collection of the Garden includes over 10,000 species and varieties of plant growth. The collection attracts many visitors annually, including botanists, horticulturists, students, and garden club members.

The Garden, though not operated as a scientific institution, offers educational facilities in that it makes available for study to students, botanists, and floriculturists many rare and interesting botanical specimens. Every year botanical specimens are received from all over the world with requests for identification, and one of the services rendered by the Garden to the public is the identification of such specimens and the furnishing of information relating to the proper methods of growing them.

The United States Botanic Garden was founded in 1820 under the auspices of the Columbia Institute for the Promotion of Arts and Sciences, an organization that was the outgrowth of an association known as the Metropolitan Society and that received its charter from Congress on April 20, 1818. The Garden continued under the direction of this Institute until 1837, when the Institute ceased to exist as an active organization.

It remained abandoned until 1842, when it became necessary for the Government to provide accommodations for the botanical collections brought to Washington, DC, from the South Seas by the United States Exploring Expedition of 1838–42, under the leadership of Capt. Charles Wilkes. The collections were placed temporarily on exhibition at the Patent Office upon return of the expedition in June 1842. The first greenhouse for this purpose was constructed in 1842 on a lot behind the Patent Office Building under the direction and control of the Joint Committee of Congress on the Library, from funds appropriated by Congress.

The act of May 15, 1850 (9 Stat. 427), provided for the relocation of the Botanic Garden under the direction of the Joint Committee on the Library. The site selected was on the Mall at the west end of the Capitol Grounds, practically the same site the Botanic Garden occupied during the period it functioned under the Columbia Institute. This site was later enlarged, and the main area continued to serve as the principal Botanic Garden site from 1850 to 1933, when the Garden was relocated to its present site.

Although the Botanic Garden began functioning as a Government-owned institution in 1842, the records indicate that it was not until 1856 that the maintenance of the Garden was specifically placed under the direction of the Joint Committee on the Library and a regular, annual appropriation was provided by Congress (11 Stat. 104).

At the present time the Joint Committee exercises its supervision through the Architect of the Capitol, who has been serving as Acting Director since 1934.

The Botanic Garden is open to the public from 9 a.m. to 9 p.m. daily, June through August, and from 9 a.m. to 5 p.m. the rest of the year.

For further information concerning the United States Botanic Garden, contact the Office of the Architect of the Capitol, U.S. Capitol Building, Washington, DC 20515. Phone, 202–225–1200.

GENERAL ACCOUNTING OFFICE

441 G Street NW., Washington, DC 20548
Phone, 202–275–5067

Comptroller General of the United States	Charles A. Bowsher
Deputy Comptroller General of the United States	(vacancy)
Special Assistant to the Comptroller General	Milton J. Socolar
Assistant Comptroller General	Harry S. Havens
Assistant Comptroller General for Planning and Reporting	Donald J. Horan
Assistant Comptroller General for Operations	James L. Howard
Assistant Comptroller General for Policy	Werner Grosshans
Assistant Comptroller General, General Government Division	Richard L. Fogel
Assistant Comptroller General, Human Resources Division	Lawrence H. Thompson
Assistant Comptroller General, National Security and International Affairs Division	Frank C. Conahan
Assistant Comptroller General, Resources, Community, and Economic Development Division	J. Dexter Peach
Assistant Comptroller General, Accounting and Financial Management Division	Donald H. Chapin
Assistant Comptroller General, Information Management and Technology Division	Ralph V. Carlone
Assistant Comptroller General, Program Evaluation and Methodology Division	Eleanor Chelimsky
General Counsel	James F. Hinchman
Director, Office of Affirmative Action Plans	Arnold P. Jones
Director, Office of the Chief Economist	Sidney G. Winter
Director, Civil Rights Office	Nilda Aponte
Director, Office of Congressional Relations	M. Thomas Hagenstad
Director, Office of Counseling and Career Development	Howard N. Johnson
Director, General Services and Controller	Richard L. Brown
Director, Office of Information Management and Communications	F. Kevin Boland
Director, Office of Internal Evaluation	Joe E. Totten

Director, Office of International Audit Organization Liaison	PETER V. ALIFERIS
Director, Personnel	FELIX R. BRANDON II
Director, Office of Program Planning	WILLIAM J. GAINER
Director, Office of Public Affairs	CLEVE E. CORLETT
Director, Office of Recruitment	FRANCES GARCIA
Director, Office of Special Investigations	RICHARD STIENER
Director, Training Institute	TERRY HEDRICK
Chair, Personnel Appeals Board	ROGER P. KAPLAN

The General Accounting Office is the investigative arm of Congress and is charged with examining all matters relating to the receipt and disbursement of public funds.

The General Accounting Office (GAO) was established by the Budget and Accounting Act of 1921 (31 U.S.C. 702), to independently audit Government agencies. Over the years, the Congress has expanded GAO's audit authority, added new responsibilities and duties, and strengthened GAO's ability to perform independently.

The General Accounting Office is under the control and direction of the Comptroller General of the United States, who is appointed by the President with the advice and consent of the Senate for a term of 15 years.

Activities

Audits and Evaluations Supporting the Congress is GAO's fundamental responsibility. In meeting this objective, GAO performs a variety of services, the most prominent of which are audits and evaluations of Government programs and activities. The majority of these reviews are made in response to specific congressional requests. The Office is required to do work requested by committee chairmen and, as a matter of policy, assigns equal status to requests from ranking minority Members. To the extent possible, GAO also responds to individual Member requests. Other assignments are initiated pursuant to standing commitments to congressional committees, and some reviews are specifically required by law. Finally, some assignments are independently undertaken in accordance with GAO's basic legislative responsibilities.

The ability to review practically any Government function requires a multidisciplined staff able to conduct assignments wherever needed. GAO's staff has expertise in a variety of disciplines—accounting, law, public and business administration, economics, the social and physical sciences, and others.

The Office is organized so that staff members concentrate on specific subject areas, enabling them to develop a detailed level of knowledge. When an assignment requires specialized experience not available within GAO, outside experts are called in to assist the permanent staff. GAO's staff goes wherever necessary on assignments, working onsite to gather data, test transactions, and observe firsthand how Government programs and activities are carried out.

Questions GAO considers include:

—Are Government programs being operated in compliance with applicable laws and regulations, and is data furnished to the Congress on these programs accurate?

—Do opportunities exist to eliminate waste and inefficient use of public funds?

—Are funds being spent legally and is accounting for them accurate?

—Are programs achieving desired results, or are changes needed in Government policies or management?

—Are there better ways of accomplishing each program's objectives at lower costs?

—What emerging or key issues should the Congress consider?

GENERAL ACCOUNTING OFFICE

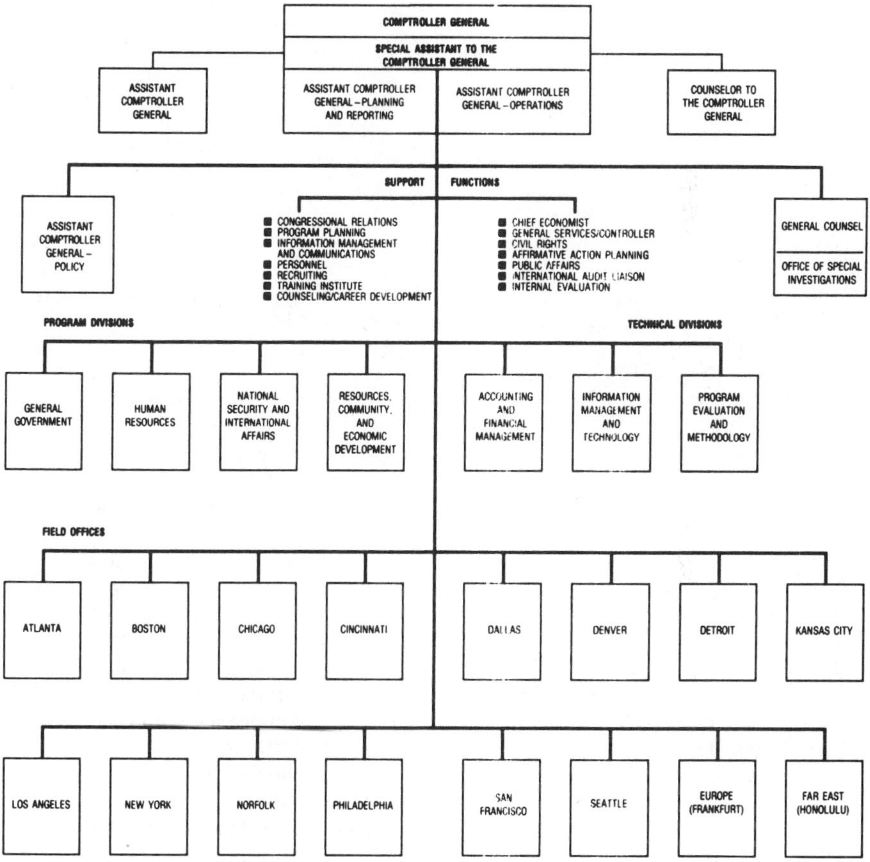

Accounting and Financial Management Policy The Office helps ensure that the Congress has available for its use current, accurate, and complete financial management data. To do this, GAO:

—prescribes accounting principles and standards for the executive branch;

—advises other Federal agencies on fiscal and related policies and procedures; and

—prescribes standards for auditing and evaluating Government programs.

In addition, the Comptroller General, the Secretary of the Treasury, and the Director of the Office of Management and Budget develop standardized information and data processing systems. This includes standard terminology, definitions, classifications, and codes for fiscal, budgetary, and program-related data and information.

Legal Services The Office provides various legal services to the Congress. In response to inquiries from committees and Members, the Comptroller General provides advice on legal issues involving Government programs and activities. GAO is also available to assist in drafting legislation and reviewing legislative proposals before the Congress. In addition, GAO reviews and reports to the Congress on proposed rescissions and deferrals of Government funds.

Other legal services include resolving bid protests that challenge Government contract awards, assisting Government agencies in interpreting the laws governing the expenditure of public funds, and adjudicating claims for and against the Government.

In addition, GAO has a staff of trained investigators who conduct special investigations and assist auditors and evaluators when they encounter possible criminal and civil misconduct. When warranted, GAO refers the results of its investigations to the Department of Justice and other law enforcement authorities.

Reporting Authorities The Office offers a range of products to communicate the results of its work. The type of product depends on the assignment's objectives and the needs of the intended user. Product types include testimony, oral briefings, and written reports. All of GAO's unclassified reports are available to the public; however, GAO will honor a requester's desire to postpone release of a report for up to 30 days. The report will be made public automatically following the requester's release or public disclosure of the report's contents.

A list of GAO reports issued or released during the previous month is furnished monthly to Congress, committees, and Members. Copies of GAO reports are furnished to interested congressional parties; Federal, State, local, and foreign governments; members of the press; college faculty, students, and libraries; and nonprofit organizations.

Copies of unclassified reports are available from the U.S. General Accounting Office, P.O. Box 6015, Gaithersburg, MD 20877. Phone, 202-275-6241. The first five copies of each report are free; additional copies are $2 each. There is a 25-percent discount on orders of 100 or more copies mailed to a single address. Orders must be prepaid by cash or by check or money order made out to the Superintendent of Documents.

For further information, contact the Office of Public Affairs, General Accounting Office, 441 G Street NW., Washington, DC 20548. Phone, 202-275-2812.

GOVERNMENT PRINTING OFFICE

North Capitol and H Streets NW., Washington, DC 20401
Phone, 202–275–2051

Public Printer	ROBERT W. HOUK
Deputy Public Printer	WILLIAM A. HOHNS
Chief of Staff	RICHARD C. BARNETT
General Counsel	ANTHONY J. ZAGAMI
Inspector General	LEWIS L. SMALL
Director, Office of Congressional, Legislative, and Public Affairs	NANCY A. GUIDEN
Director, Office of Information Dissemination Policy	JUDITH C. RUSSELL
Director, Office of Workforce Planning and Training	LOIS SCHUTTE
Administrative Law Judge	STUART M. FOSS
Assistant Public Printer (Administration and Resources Management)	JAMES N. JOYNER
Director, Security and Support Services	MANUEL M. BRITO
Director, Equal Employment Opportunity Service	CLAUDETTE BOULDIN
Director, Labor and Employee Relations Service	NEAL H. FINE
Director, Occupational Health and Environmental Services	WILLIAM T. HARRIS
Director, Personnel Service	LAWRENCE W. GARDNER
Assistant Public Printer (Chief Financial Officer)	VINCENT F. ARENDES
Comptroller/Office of Financial Management	ROBERT B. HOLSTEIN
Director, Office of Information Resources Management	RAYMOND J. PLUTO
Director, Office of Planning	THOMAS J. MULDOON
Assistant Public Printer (Operations and Procurement)	MICHAEL F. DiMARIO
Director, Analysis and Review Staff	JOHN D. CHAPMAN
Manager, Customer Service Department	BURKEY W. BOGGS
Director, Engineering Service	JOSEPH A. PALANK
Director, Materials Management Service	THOMAS M. HUGHES
Manager, Printing Procurement Department	JAMES T. SMITH
Production Manager	GLENN H. ROTTMANN
Manager, Quality Control and Technical Department	GEORGE J. COLLINS
Assistant Public Printer (Superintendent of Documents)	(VACANCY)
Director, Documents Sales Service	JAMES D. YOUNG
Director, Library Programs Service	BONNIE TRIVIZAS
Director, Marketing	CHARLES B. McKEOWN

The Government Printing Office prints, binds, and distributes the publications of the Congress as well as the executive departments and establishments of the Federal Government.

GOVERNMENT PRINTING OFFICE

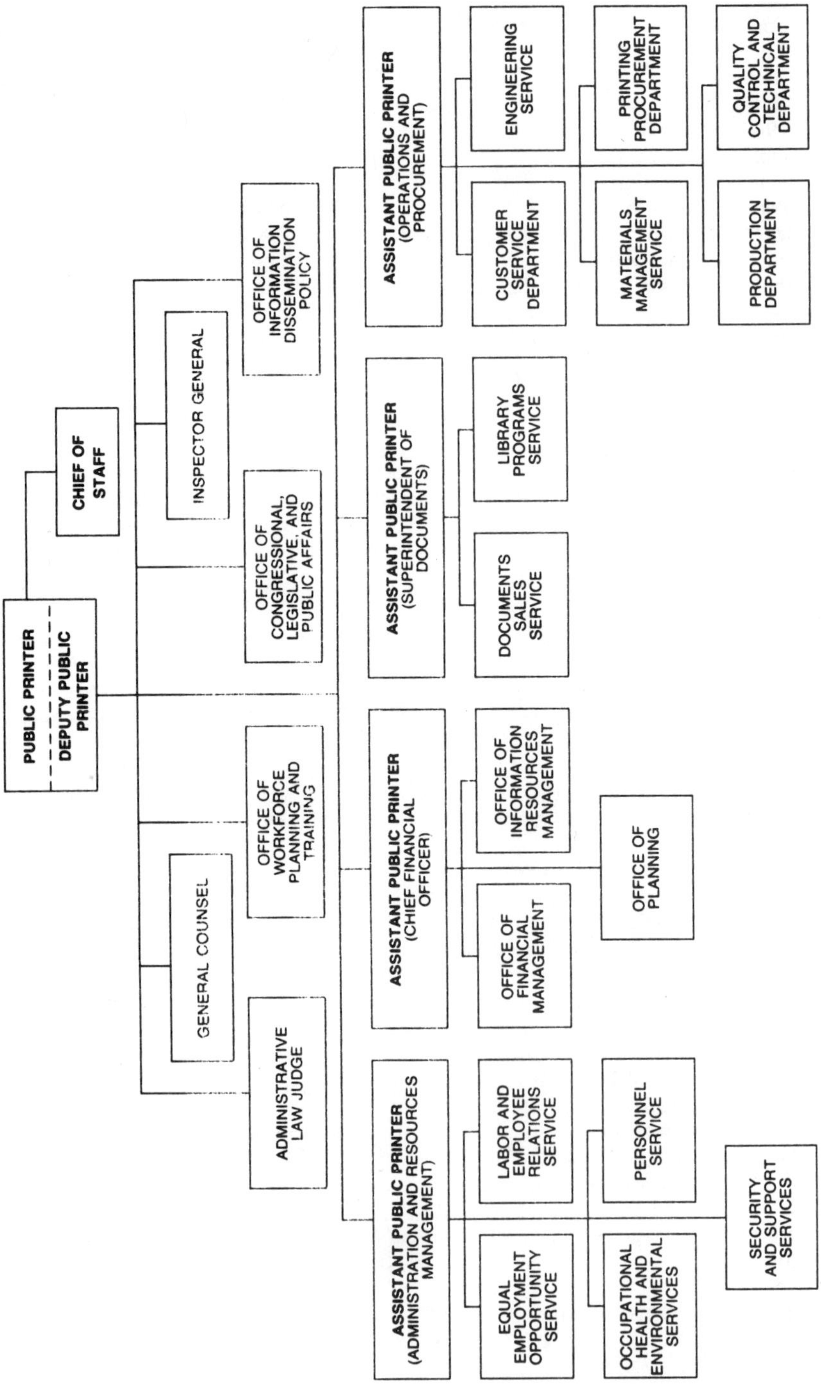

The Government Printing Office (GPO) began operations in accordance with Congressional Joint Resolution 25 of June 23, 1860. The activities of the Government Printing Office are outlined and defined in the act of October 22, 1968, as amended (44 U.S.C. 101 *et seq.*).

The congressional Joint Committee on Printing serves in an oversight capacity for the Government Printing Office. The Public Printer, who serves as the head of the agency, is required by law to be a practical printer versed in the art of bookbinding and is appointed by the President with the advice and consent of the Senate.

Activities

The Government Printing Office executes orders for printing and binding placed by Congress and the departments and establishments of the Federal Government. It furnishes blank paper, inks, and similar supplies to all governmental activities on order. It prepares catalogs and distributes and sells Government publications.

The Office invites bids from commercial suppliers on a wide variety of printing and binding services, awards and administers contracts, and maintains liaison between ordering agencies and contractors.

Printing and binding processes used are electronic photocomposition; linotype and hand composition; letterpress printing and photopolymer platemaking; offset photography, stripping, platemaking, and press; and manual and machine bookbinding.

The Office sells through mail orders and Government bookstores approximately 20,000 different publications that originate in various Government agencies, and administers the depository library program through which selected Government publications are made available in libraries throughout the country.

Sources of Information

Contracts Printing and binding enterprises should direct inquiries to the Manager, Printing Procurement Department, Government Printing Office, Washington, DC 20401 (phone, 202-275-2265), or contact the GPO Regional Printing Procurement Office in the following cities: Atlanta, GA; Boston, MA; Chicago, IL; Columbus, OH; Dallas, TX; Denver, CO; Hampton, VA; Los Angeles, CA; New York, NY; Philadelphia, PA; St. Louis, MO; San Francisco, CA; or Seattle, WA.

Suppliers of paper and kindred products; printing and binding equipment, related parts, and supplies; purchasers of scrap or surplus printing and binding equipment, waste, and salvage materials; and freight carriers should contact the Director of Materials Management, Government Printing Office, Washington, DC 20401. Phone, 202-275-2701.

The booklet *How To Do Business with the Government Printing Office, A Guide for Contractors* is available on request from any regional procurement office mentioned.

Employment Office of Personnel Management registers are used in filling administrative, technical, and clerical positions. Inquiries should be directed to the Chief, Employment Branch, Government Printing Office, Washington, DC 20401. Phone, 202-275-2951.

Publications Orders and inquiries concerning publications and subscriptions for sale by the Government Printing Office should be directed to the Superintendent of Documents, Government Printing Office, Washington, DC 20402. Phone, 202-783-3238.

To keep abreast of Government publications, the public is offered listings of varying scope.

The *GPO Sales Publications Reference File (PRF)* provides author, title, and subject access to Government publications available for sale through the Superintendent of Documents. Issued in biweekly magnetic tape and bimonthly microfiche editions, it is available for purchase from the Superintendent of Documents.

The *Monthly Catalog of U.S. Government Publications* is the most comprehensive listing of Government publications issued by Federal departments and agencies. It is available for purchase from the Superintendent of Documents.

There also are two free catalogs of new or popular publications available: *U.S. Government Books,* which lists hundreds of best selling titles, and *New Books,* a bimonthly list of all Government publications placed on sale in the preceding 2 months. These publications can be obtained by writing to the Superintendent of Documents, Government Printing Office, Washington, DC 20402.

Remittance for all publications ordered from the Superintendent of Documents must be received in advance of shipment by check or money order payable to the Superintendent of Documents. Orders also may be charged to MasterCard or VISA accounts or a GPO deposit account.

A list of depository libraries is available from the Superintendent of Documents.

Popular Government publications may be purchased at the GPO Bookstores listed below:

Bookstores—Government Printing Office

City	Address	Telephone
Washington, DC, area:		
Main Bookstore	710 N. Capitol St. NW.	202-275-2091
Farragut West	1510 H St. NW.	202-653-5075
Retail Sales Outlet	8660 Cherry Lane, Laurel, MD	301-953-7974
Atlanta, GA	Rm. 100, 275 Peachtree St. NE.	404-331-6947
Birmingham, AL	2021 3d Ave. N.	205-731-1056
Boston, M,	Rm. 179, 10 Causeway St.	617-720-4180
Chicago, IL	Rm. 1365, 219 S. Dearborn St.	312-353-5133
Cleveland, OH	Rm. 1653, 1240 E. 9th St.	216-522-4922
Columbus, OH	Rm. 207, 200 N. High St.	614-469-6956
Dallas, TX	Rm. 1C50, 1100 Commerce St.	214-767-0076
Denver, CO	Rm. 117, 1961 Stout St.	303-844-3964
Detroit, MI	Suite 160, 477 Michigan Ave.	313-226-7816
Houston, TX	801 Travis St.	713-228-1187
Jacksonville, FL	Rm. 158, 400 W. Bay St.	904-353-0472
Kansas City, MO	120 Bannister Mall, 5600 E. Bannister Rd.	816-767-8225
Los Angeles, CA	C-Level, ARCO Plaza, 505 S. Flower St.	213-239-9844
Milwaukee, WI	Rm. 190, 517 E. Wisconsin Ave.	414-297-1304
New York, NY	Rm. 110, 26 Federal Plz.	212-264-3825
Philadelphia, PA	100 N. 17th St.	215-597-0677
Pittsburgh, PA	Rm. 118, 1000 Liberty Ave.	412-644-2721
Portland, OR	1305 SW. 1st Ave.	503-221-6217
Pueblo, CO	720 N. Main St.	719-544-3142
San Francisco, CA	Rm. 1023, 450 Golden Gate Ave.	415-252-5334
Seattle, WA	Rm. 194, 915 2d Ave.	206-553-4271

For further information, contact the Director, Office of Public Affairs, Government Printing Office, North Capitol and H Streets NW., Washington, DC 20401. Phone, 202-275-3204.

LIBRARY OF CONGRESS

101 Independence Avenue SE., Washington, DC 20540
Phone, 202-707-5000

Librarian of Congress	JAMES H. BILLINGTON
Deputy Librarian of Congress	WINSTON TABB, *Acting*
Associate Librarian for Management	RHODA W. CANTER
Associate Librarian for Collections Services	HENRIETTE D. AVRAM
Associate Librarian for Constituent Services	DONALD C. CURRAN
Associate Librarian for Cultural Services	JOHN Y. COLE, *Acting*

Associate Librarian for Special Projects	RHODA W. CANTER, *Acting*
Director, Congressional Research Service	JOSEPH E. ROSS
Associate Librarian of Congress (Register of Copyrights)	RALPH OMAN
Law Librarian	M. KATHLEEN PRICE
General Counsel	JOHN J. KOMINSKI
Legislative Liaison	ADOREEN M. MCCORMICK
Inspector General	JOHN W. RENSBARGER
Director, Human Resources	BEN BENITEZ
Chief, Loan Division	CHRISTOPHER WRIGHT

Library of Congress Trust Fund Board

Ex Officio Members:	
Chairman (Librarian of Congress)	JAMES H. BILLINGTON
(Secretary of the Treasury)	NICHOLAS F. BRADY
(U.S. Representative from Illinois and Chairman, Joint Committee on the Library)	FRANK ANNUNZIO
Appointive Members	MILDRED LOIS NICHOLS TEAS
	(VACANCY)

The Library of Congress is the national library of the United States, offering diverse materials for research including the world's most extensive collections in many areas such as American history, music, and law.

The Library of Congress was established under the law approved April 24, 1800 (2 Stat. 56), appropriating $5,000 "for the purchase of such books as may be necessary for the use of Congress...." The Library's scope of responsibility has been widened by subsequent legislation (2 U.S.C. 131–168d). The Librarian, appointed by the President with the advice and consent of the Senate, directs the Library.

Supported mainly by the appropriations of Congress, the Library also has the use of the income from funds received from foundations and other private sources and administered by the Library of Congress Trust Fund Board; it has the use also of gifts of money presented for direct application (2 U.S.C. 154–163).

Under the organic law, the Library's first responsibility is service to Congress. As the Library has developed, its range of service has come to include the entire governmental establishment in all its branches and the public at large, so that it has become a national library for the United States.

Activities

Collections The Library's extensive collections are universal in scope. They include books and pamphlets on every subject and in a multitude of languages. Among them are the most comprehensive collections of Chinese, Japanese, and Russian language books outside Asia and the Soviet Union; volumes relating to science and legal materials outstanding for American and foreign law; the world's largest collection of published aeronautical literature; and the most extensive collection in the Western Hemisphere of books printed before 1501 A.D.

The manuscript collections relate to manifold aspects of American history and civilization and include the personal papers of most of the Presidents from George Washington through Calvin Coolidge. The music collections contain volumes and pieces—manuscript and published—from classic works to the newest popular compositions. Other materials available for research include maps and views; photographic records from the daguerreotype to the latest news photo; recordings, including folksongs and other music, speeches, and poetry readings; prints, drawings, and posters; government documents, newspapers, and periodicals from all over the world; and motion pictures, microforms, and audio and video tapes.

Reference Resources Admission to the various research facilities of the Library is free. No introduction or credentials are required for persons over high school age. Readers must submit appropriate personal identification and, certain collections, like those of the Manuscript, Rare Book and Special Collections, and Motion Picture, Broadcasting and Recorded Sound Divisions, can be used only by those with a serious purpose for doing so. As demands for service to Congress and Federal Government agencies permit, limited reference service is available through correspondence. The Library must, however, decline some requests with the suggestion that a library within the correspondent's area can provide satisfactory assistance. While priority is given to inquiries pertaining to its holdings of special materials or to subjects in which its resources are unique, the Library does attempt to provide helpful responses to all inquirers.

Copyrights Since 1870 the Library has been responsible for copyrights, which are now registered by the Copyright Office (acts of July 8, 1870 (16 Stat. 212–217), February 19, 1897 (29 Stat. 545), March 4, 1909, as codified and amended, and October 19, 1976 (90 Stat. 2541)). All copyrightable works, whether published or unpublished, are subject to a system of statutory protection that gives the copyright owner certain exclusive rights, including the right to reproduce the copyrighted work and distribute it to the public by sale, rental, lease, or lending. Works of authorship include books, periodicals, and other literary works, musical compositions, song lyrics, dramas and dramatico-musical compositions, pictorial, graphic, and sculptural works, pantomimes and choreographic works, motion pictures and other audiovisual works, and sound recordings.

Extension of Service The Library extends its service through:

—an interlibrary loan system;

—the photoduplication, at reasonable cost, of books, manuscripts, maps, newspapers, and prints in its collections;

—the sale of sound recordings, which are released by its Recording Laboratory;

—the exchange of duplicates with other institutions;

—the sale of printed catalog cards and magnetic tapes and the publication in book format or microform of cumulative catalogs, which make available the results of the expert bibliographical and cataloging work of its technical personnel;

—a centralized cataloging program whereby the Library of Congress acquires material published all over the world, catalogs it promptly, and distributes cataloging information in machine-readable form as well as by printed cards and other means to the Nation's libraries;

—a cooperative cataloging program whereby the cataloging of data, by name authority and bibliographic records, prepared by other libraries becomes part of the Library of Congress data base and is distributed through the MARC Distribution Service;

—a cataloging-in-publication program in cooperation with American publishers for printing cataloging information in current books;

—the National Serials Data Program, a national center that maintains a record of serial titles to which International Standard Serial Numbers have been assigned and serves, with this file, as the United States Register; and

—the development of general schemes of classification (Library of Congress and Dewey Decimal), subject headings, and cataloging, embracing the entire field of printed matter.

Furthermore, the Library provides for:

—the preparation of bibliographical lists responsive to the needs of Government and research;

—the maintenance and the publication of *The National Union Catalogs* and other cooperative publications;

—the publication of catalogs, bibliographical guides, and lists, and of texts of original manuscripts and rare books in the Library of Congress;

—the circulation in traveling exhibits of items from the Library's collections; and

—the provision of books in raised type and "talking book" records, as well as books on tape, for the blind and the physically handicapped through 150 cooperating libraries throughout the United States.

Congressional Research Service The Congressional Research Service (CRS) serves the public through its elected representatives in the Congress. The Service provides objective, nonpartisan research, analysis, and informational support of the highest quality to assist Congress' legislative, oversight, and representative functions. It also helps to ensure an informed national legislature.

CRS evolved from the Legislative Reference Bureau, whose statutory authority dates back to the Legislative Reorganization Act of 1946, as amended (2 U.S.C. 72a note, 166), authorizing increased emphasis on in-depth research and analysis. Its mandate has grown over the years in response to the increasing scope and complexity of public policy issues to encompass nonpartisan technical, reference, and research assistance to Congress. The Service's staff anticipates and responds to congressional technical informational and policy analysis needs in an interdisciplinary, integrated manner.

CRS is organized to respond in a timely and objective manner to congressional inquiries for information and analysis at every stage of the legislative process and in subject areas relevant to policy issues before Congress. The CRS director, assisted by a deputy director and a management team, oversees and coordinates the work of seven research divisions, which span an encyclopedic range of subjects and disciplines. These research divisions contain scholars and experts in the following subject areas: American law, economics, education and public welfare, environment and natural resources policy, foreign affairs and national defense, government, and science policy. CRS also contains two reference divisions: Congressional Reference Division and Library Services Division. These divisions provide reference, bibliographic, and other informational services, employing sophisticated computerized systems to identify and locate appropriate material for requestors. CRS also creates and maintains a number of specialized reading lists for Members of Congress and their staffs, and disseminates other materials found to be of interest.

The Service also maintains those parts of the Library of Congress' automated information system that cover legislative matters, including digests of all public bills and briefing papers on major legislative issues. Other CRS offices include Special Programs, Operations, Policy, Research Coordination, and the Director's office.

In addition to responding to individual requests for information and analysis, CRS anticipates congressional needs, and develops and presents timely seminars that provide a forum for discussion among Members of Congress and their staffs, CRS specialists, and nationally recognized experts on important legislative issues. Audio and visual materials on a variety of topics of congressional interest are also produced and aired on the congressional cable television system. A language service section provides a variety of services including translations, interpreting, and research.

For further information, call 202–707–7904.

American Folklife Center The Center, which was established in the Library of Congress by act of January 2, 1976 (20 U.S.C. 2102 *et seq.*), has a coordinative function both in and outside the Federal Establishment to carry out appropriate programs to support, preserve, and present American folklife through such activities as receiving and maintaining folklife collections, scholarly research, field projects, performances, exhibitions, festivals, workshops, publications, and audiovisual presentations. The Center is directed by a Board of Trustees consisting of four members appointed by the President from Federal agencies, four each appointed by the President pro tempore of the Senate and the Speaker of the House from private life, and five

290-950 O 91 - 3

ex officio members: the Librarian of Congress, the Secretary of the Smithsonian Institution, the Chairmen of the National Endowment for the Arts and the National Endowment for the Humanities, and the Director of the Center.

The Center has conducted projects in many locations across the country, such as the ethnic communities of Chicago, IL; southern Georgia; a ranching community in northern Nevada; the Blue Ridge Parkway in southern Virginia and northern North Carolina; and the States of New Jersey, Rhode Island, and Montana. The projects have provided large collections of recordings and photographs, which are being incorporated into the Library's collections. The Center administers the Federal Cylinder Project, which is charged with preserving and disseminating music and oral traditions recorded on wax cylinders dating from the late 1800's to the early 1940's. A cultural conservation study was developed at the Center, in cooperation with the Department of the Interior, pursuant to a congressional mandate. Various conferences, workshops, and symposia are given throughout the year. A series of outdoor concerts of traditional music are scheduled monthly at the Library, April through September.

The *Folklife Center News,* a quarterly newsletter, and other informational publications are available upon request. The Government Printing Office sells additional Center publications, including the *Folklife Annual* and catalogs produced by the Federal Cylinder Project.

The American Folklife Center maintains and administers the Archive of Folk Culture, an extensive collection of folk music and lore in published and unpublished forms. It is a national repository for folk-related recordings, manuscripts, and other materials. The Center's reading room contains over 3,500 books and periodicals; a sizable collection of magazines, newsletters, unpublished theses, and dissertations; field notes; and many textual and some musical transcriptions and recordings.

For further information, call 202-707-6590.

Center for the Book The Center was established in the Library of Congress by act of October 17, 1977 (2 U.S.C. 171 *et seq.*), to stimulate public interest in books, reading, and libraries, and to encourage the study of books and print culture. The Center is a catalyst for promoting and exploring the vital role of books, reading, and libraries—nationally and internationally. As a partnership between the Government and the private sector, the Center for the Book depends on tax-deductible contributions from individuals and corporations to support its programs.

The Center's activities are directed toward the general public and scholars. The overall program includes reading and promotion projects with four television networks, symposia, lectures, exhibitions, special events, and publications. First Lady Barbara Bush was Honorary Chair of the Center's "1991—The Year of the Lifetime Reader" campaign.

Since 1984, 24 States have established statewide book centers that are affiliated with the Center for the Book in the Library of Congress. State centers plan and fund their own projects, involving members of the State's "community of the book," including authors, readers, prominent citizens, and public officials who serve as honorary advisors.

For further information, call 202-707-5221.

National Preservation Program The Library provides technical information related to the preservation and restoration of library and archival material. A series of leaflets on various preservation and conservation topics has been prepared by the Preservation Office. Information and publications are available from the National Preservation Program Office, Library of Congress, Washington, DC 20540. Phone, 202-707-1840.

Sources of Information

Books for the Blind and Physically Handicapped Talking and braille books and magazines are distributed through 150 regional and subregional libraries to blind and physically handicapped residents of the United States and its territories. Information is available at public libraries throughout the United States and from the headquarters office, National Library Service for the Blind and Physically Handicapped, Library of Congress, 1291 Taylor Street NW., Washington, DC 20542. Phone, 202-707-5100.

Cataloging Data Distribution Cataloging and bibliographic information in the form of printed catalog cards, microfiche catalogs, book catalogs, magnetic tapes, bibliographies, and other technical publications is distributed to libraries and other institutions. Kits describing the procedure for ordering materials are available from the Cataloging Distribution Service, Library of Congress, Washington, DC 20541. Phone, 202-707-6171.

Library of Congress card numbers for new publications are now assigned by the Cataloging in Publication Division. Direct inquiries to CIP Division, Library of Congress, Washington, DC 20540. Phone, 202-707-6372.

Contracts Persons seeking to do business with the Library of Congress should contact the Contracts and Logistics Services, Library of Congress, Landover Center Annex, 1701 Brightseat Road, Landover, MD 20785. Phone, 202-707-8717.

Copyright Service Information about the copyright law (title 17 of the United States Code), the method of securing copyright, and registration procedures may be obtained by writing to the Copyright Office, Library of Congress, Washington, DC 20559. Phone, 202-479-0700. Registration application forms may be ordered by calling the forms hotline at 202-707-9100. Reports on copyright facts found in the records of the Copyright Office may be obtained for a fee of $20 an hour; any member of the public, however, may use without charge the Copyright Card Catalog in the Copyright Office. The Copyright Information Office is located in Room LM-401, James Madison Memorial Building, 101 Independence Avenue SE., Washington, DC 20559.

Employment Employment inquiries and applications (on Standard Form 171, Application for Federal Employment) should be directed to the Human Resources Operations Office, Library of Congress, Washington, DC 20540. Potential applicants are encouraged to visit the Employment Office, Room LM-107, 101 Independence Avenue SE., where current vacancy announcements and application forms are available. A recorded announcement on 202-707-5295 provides general information on the employment process.

National Translations Center Copies of existing unpublished translations of scientific papers gathered from private and public sources are supplied for a fee. Information on other related products, order procedures, and prices are available from the National Translations Center, Library of Congress, Washington, DC 20541. Phone, 202-707-0100. Fax, 202-707-6147.

Photoduplication Service Copies of manuscripts, prints, photographs, maps, and book material not subject to copyright and other restrictions are available for a fee. Order forms for photoreproduction and price schedules are available from the Photoduplication Service, Library of Congress, Washington, DC 20540. Phone, 202-707-5640.

Publications A list of *Library of Congress Publications in Print,* many of which are of interest to the general public, is available free upon application to Office Systems Services, Library of Congress, Washington, DC 20540. A monthly *Calendar of Events,* listing programs and exhibits at the Library of Congress, can be mailed regularly to persons requesting it from the same office.

Reference and Bibliographic Services Guidance is offered to readers in the identification and use of the material in the Library's collections, and reference service in answer to inquiries is offered to those who have exhausted local, State, and regional resources. Persons requiring services that cannot be performed by the Library staff can be supplied with names of private researchers who work on a fee basis.

Requests for information should be directed to the General Reading Rooms Division, Library of Congress, Washington, DC 20540. Phone, 202-707-5522.

Research and Reference Services in Science and Technology Reference specialists in the Science and Technology Division answer without charge brief technical inquiries entailing a bibliographic response. Of special interest is a technical report collection exceeding 3 million titles. Most of these are in microform and are readily accessible for viewing in the Science Reading Room. Requests for reference service should be directed to the Science and Technology Division, Library of Congress, Washington, DC 20540. Phone, 202-707-5639.

An informal series of reference guides is issued by the Science and Technology Division under the general title *LC Science Tracer Bullet*. These guides are designed to help a reader locate published material on a subject about which he or she has only general knowledge. For a list of available titles, write to the Reference Section, Science and Technology Division, Library of Congress, Washington, DC 20540. Phone, 202-707-5580.

For further information, contact the Public Affairs Office, Library of Congress, 101 Independence Avenue SE., Washington, DC 20540. Phone, 202-707-2905.

OFFICE OF TECHNOLOGY ASSESSMENT, U.S. CONGRESS

600 Pennsylvania Avenue SE., Washington, DC 20510-8025
Phones: Personnel locator, 202-224-8713; Congressional and Public Affairs, 202-224-9241; Press, 202-228-6204; Publications, 202-224-8996; FAX, 202-228-6098

Director	JOHN H. GIBBONS
Executive Assistant to the Director	SUE BACHTEL
Director, Congressional Affairs	JAMES JENSEN
Director, Press Affairs	JEAN K. MCDONALD
General Counsel	HOLLY GWIN
Assistant Director, Energy, Materials and International Security Division	LIONEL S. JOHNS
Energy and Materials Program Manager	PETER BLAIR
International Security and Commerce Program Manager	ALAN SHAW
Industry, Technology and Employment Program Manager	AUDREY B. BUYRN
Assistant Director, Health and Life Sciences Division	ROGER C. HERDMAN
Food and Renewable Resources Program Manager	WALTER E. PARHAM
Health Program Manager	CLYDE BEHNEY
Biological Applications Program Manager	MICHAEL GOUGH
Assistant Director, Science, Information and Natural Resources Division	JOHN P. ANDELIN
Telecommunication and Computing Technologies Program Manager	JAMES CURLIN
Oceans and Environment Program Manager	ROBERT W. NIBLOCK
Science, Education and Transportation Program Manager	NANCY C. CARSON

Operations Manager	BART J. MCGARRY
Congressional Board	
Chairman	REPR. GEORGE E. BROWN, JR.
Vice Chairman	SEN. TED STEVENS
Senate Members	TED STEVENS, ORRIN G. HATCH, ERNEST F. HOLLINGS, CLAIBORNE PELL, CHARLES E. GRASSLEY
House of Representatives Members	MORRIS K. UDALL, GEORGE E. BROWN, JR., JOHN D. DINGELL, DON SUNDQUIST, AMO HOUGHTON
OTA Member (nonvoting)	JOHN H. GIBBONS
Advisory Council	
Chairman	CHASE N. PETERSON
Vice Chairman	JOSHUA LEDERBERG
Members	CHARLES A. BOWSHER, LEWIS M. BRANSCOMB, MICHEL T. HALBOUTY, NEIL E. HARL, JAMES C. HUNT, HENRY KOFFLER, SALLY RIDE, JOSEPH E. ROSS, MARINA VON NEUMANN WHITMAN

The Office of Technology Assessment reports to the Congress on the scientific and technical impact of government policies and proposed legislative initiatives.

The Office of Technology Assessment (OTA) was created by the Technology Assessment Act of 1972 (2 U.S.C. 472) to serve the United States Congress by providing objective analyses of major public policy issues related to scientific and technological change. The Office began operations in January 1974.

The bipartisan 13-member Board includes 6 Senators appointed by the President pro tempore, 6 Members of the House of Representatives appointed by the Speaker, and the Director of OTA, who is a nonvoting member.

The Technology Assessment Advisory Council comprises 10 public members eminent in science and technology. The Council is appointed by the Board and advises the Board and OTA on assessments and other matters.

The Office's assessments explore complex issues involving science and technology, helping Congress resolve uncertainties and conflicting claims, identifying alternative policy options, and providing foresight or early alert to new developments that could have important implications for future Federal policy. Requests for assessments may be made by the chairman of any congressional committee acting for himself or on behalf of a ranking minority member, or a majority of committee members; by the OTA Board; or by the OTA Director, in consultation with the Board.

The Office's work centers on comprehensive assessments that may take 1 to 2 years to complete. It also draws upon its past and current work to provide a variety of responses to meet immediate congressional needs, such as briefings, testimony, and special reports.

Office assessment teams work closely with congressional staff and support agencies to ensure that major committee concerns are addressed and to stay in touch with the published work and current activities of analysts and researchers in the Executive branch and throughout the public and private interest sectors. Each project is guided by an advisory panel of experts on a particular

OFFICE OF TECHNOLOGY ASSESSMENT

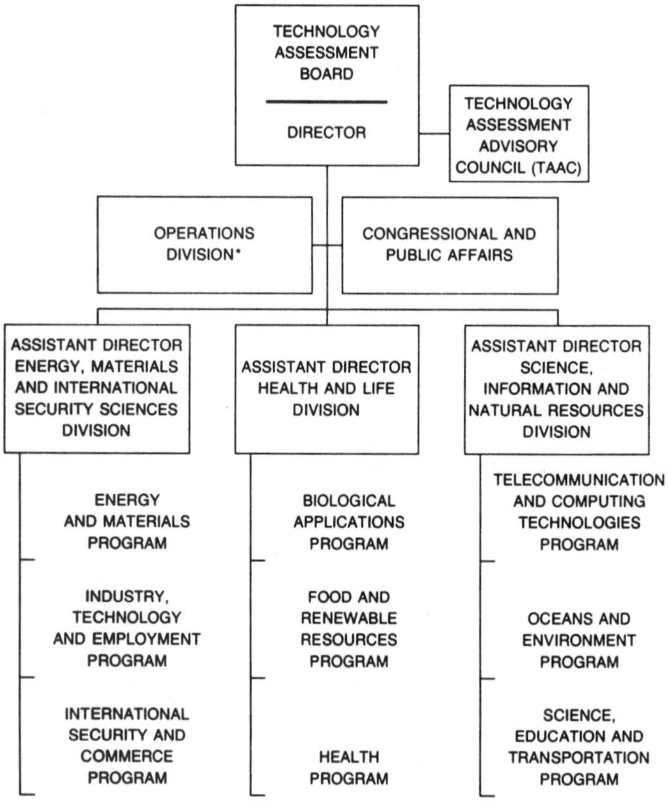

*Operations Division consists of the following units: Finance and Administrative Services; Information Management and Publishing Services; and Personnel.

subject as a way of ensuring that reports are objective, fair, and authoritative.

After approval for release by the Board, OTA assessment reports are distributed to the requesting committees, with summaries provided to all Members of Congress. The reports are available to the public through the Government Printing Office.

Sources of Information

Information may be obtained from the following sources:

Congressional and Public Affairs Office (documents for congressional use and general information about OTA). Phone, 202-224-9241.

Publications Request Department (OTA documents for general public use). Phone, 202-224-8996.

Personnel locator. Phone, 202-224-8713.

CONGRESSIONAL BUDGET OFFICE

Second and D Streets SW., Washington, DC 20515
Phone, 202-226-2621

Director	ROBERT D. REISCHAUER
Deputy Director	ROBERT W. HARTMAN, *Acting*
General Counsel	ALFRED B. FITT
Director, Office of Intergovernmental Relations	STANLEY L. GREIGG
Assistant Director for Budget Analysis	JAMES L. BLUM
Assistant Director for Fiscal Analysis	FREDERICK RIBE
Assistant Director for Tax Analysis	ROSEMARY MARCUSS
Assistant Director for Natural Resources and Commerce	ELLIOT SCHWARTZ, *Acting*
Assistant Director for Human Resources and Community Development	NANCY M. GORDON
Assistant Director for National Security	ROBERT F. HALE

The Congressional Budget Office provides the Congress with assessments of the economic impact of the Federal budget.

The Congressional Budget Office (CBO) was established by the Congressional Budget Act of 1974 (2 U.S.C. 601), which also created a procedure by which the United States Congress considers and acts upon the annual Federal budget. This process enables the Congress to have an overview of the Federal budget and to make overall decisions regarding spending and taxing levels and the deficit or surplus these levels incur.

The Congressional Budget Office provides Congress with basic budget data and with analyses of alternative fiscal, budgetary, and programmatic policy issues.

Activities

Economic Forecasting and Fiscal Policy Analysis The Federal budget affects and is affected by the national economy. The Congressional Budget Office provides Congress with biannual forecasts of the economy and analyses of economic trends and alternative fiscal policies.

Scorekeeping Under the budget process the Congress establishes, by concurrent resolution, targets (or ceilings) for overall expenditures, budget authority and budget outlays, and for broad functional categories. The Congress also establishes targets (or ceilings) for the levels of revenues, the deficit, and the public debt. CBO "keeps score" for the Congress by monitoring the results of congressional action on individual authorization, appropriation, and revenue bills against the targets (or ceilings) specified in the concurrent resolution.

Cost Projections The Congressional Budget Office prepares 5-year cost estimates for carrying out any public bill or resolution reported by congressional committees. As soon as practicable after the beginning of each fiscal year, CBO also provides 5-year projections on the costs of continuing current Federal spending and taxation policies.

Annual Report on the Budget The Congressional Budget Office is responsible for furnishing the House and Senate Budget Committees by February 15 of each year with a report that includes a discussion of alternative spending and revenue levels and alternative allocations among major programs and functional categories, all in the light of major national needs and the effect on the balanced growth and development of the United States.

Special Studies The Congressional Budget Office undertakes studies requested by the Congress on budget-related areas. As required by the establishing act, such service is provided in the following order of priority to: the House and Senate Budget Committees, the House and Senate Appropriations Committees, the Senate Finance and the House Ways and Means Committees, and all other congressional committees.

Sequestration Report This advisory report is mandated by the Balanced Budget and Emergency Deficit Control Act of 1985, as amended (2 U.S.C. 901). The report estimates whether proposed spending levels breach categorical spending limits or cause a deficit in excess of the target and, if so, it estimates the amount and percentage of budget resources that should be sequestered to eliminate any excesses.

Pay-As-You-Go The Balanced Budget and Emergency Deficit Control Act of 1985, as amended (2 U.S.C. 901), requires CBO to provide the Office of Management and Budget with an estimate of the amount of change in outlays or receipts for each fiscal year through 1995 for any direct spending or receipts legislation as soon as practicable after Congress completes action on that legislation.

For further information, contact the Office of Intergovernmental Relations, Congressional Budget Office, Second and D Streets SW., Washington, DC 20515. Phone, 202–226–2600.

COPYRIGHT ROYALTY TRIBUNAL

1825 Connecticut Avenue NW., Washington, DC 20009
Phone, 202–673–5400

Chairman	MARIO F. AGUERO
Commissioners	J.C. ARGETSINGER
	CINDY S. DAUB
General Counsel	ROBERT L. CASSLER

[For the Copyright Royalty Tribunal statement of organization, see the *Code of Federal Regulations,* Title 37, Part 301]

The Copyright Royalty Tribunal adjusts copyright royalty rates and distributes copyright royalties for certain uses of copyrighted works.

The Copyright Royalty Tribunal was established by the act of October 19, 1976 (17 U.S.C. 801). The Tribunal is composed of three Commissioners appointed by the President with the advice and consent of the Senate.

The Tribunal adjusts copyright royalty rates for cable retransmission of broadcast signals, for recording new versions of previously recorded songs, and for noncommercial educational stations that broadcast musical, pictorial, graphic, and sculptural works.

The Tribunal also has stand-by authority to adjust the rates for jukeboxes and satellite retransmission of broadcast signals to satellite home dish owners if the parties are unable to reach voluntary agreements among themselves. In addition, the Tribunal distributes the royalty fees deposited with the Copyright Office by cable operators and satellite carriers to the proper copyright owners.

In making its distribution determinations, the Tribunal considers primarily the harm incurred by the copyright owners, the benefit to the user, and the marketplace value of the work.

For further information, contact the Copyright Royalty Tribunal, Suite 918, 1825 Connecticut Avenue NW., Washington, DC 20009. Phone, 202-673-5400.

Judicial Branch

JUDICIAL BRANCH

THE SUPREME COURT OF THE UNITED STATES

United States Supreme Court Building
1 First Street NE., Washington, DC 20543
Phone, 202–479–3000

Members:

Chief Justice of the United States	WILLIAM H. REHNQUIST
Associate Justices	BYRON R. WHITE
	THURGOOD MARSHALL
	HARRY A. BLACKMUN
	JOHN PAUL STEVENS
	SANDRA DAY O'CONNOR
	ANTONIN SCALIA
	ANTHONY M. KENNEDY
	DAVID H. SOUTER

Officers:

Clerk	WILLIAM K. SUTER
Reporter of Decisions	FRANK D. WAGNER
Librarian	SHELLEY L. DOWLING
Marshal	ALFRED WONG

Article III, section 1, of the Constitution of the United States provides that "[t]he judicial Power of the United States, shall be vested in one supreme Court, and in such inferior Courts as the Congress may from time to time ordain and establish." The Supreme Court of the United States was created in accordance with this provision and by authority of the Judiciary Act of September 24, 1789 (1 Stat. 73). It was organized on February 2, 1790.

The Supreme Court comprises the Chief Justice of the United States and such number of Associate Justices as may be fixed by Congress. Under that authority, and by virtue of act of June 25, 1948 (28 U.S.C. 1), the number of Associate Justices is eight. Power to nominate the Justices is vested in the President of the United States, and appointments are made with the advice and consent of the Senate. Article III, section 1, of the Constitution further provides that "[t]he Judges, both of the supreme and inferior Courts, shall hold their Offices during good Behaviour, and shall, at stated Times, receive for their Services, a Compensation, which shall not be diminished during their Continuance in Office." A Justice may, if so desired, retire at the age of 70 after serving for 10 years as a Federal judge or at age 65 after 15 years of service.

The Clerk, the Reporter of Decisions, the Librarian, and the Marshal are appointed by the Court to assist in the performance of its functions. Other Court officers, including the Administrative Assistant, the Court Counsel, the Curator, the Director of

Data Systems, and the Public Information Officer, are appointed by the Chief Justice to assist him with the administrative aspects of his position.

The library is open to members of the bar of the Court, attorneys for the various Federal departments and agencies, and Members of Congress. Only members of the bar of the Court may practice before the Supreme Court.

The term of the Court begins, by law, the first Monday in October of each year and continues as long as the business before the Court requires, usually until about the end of June. Six members constitute a quorum. Approximately 5,000 cases are passed upon in the course of a term. In addition, some 1,200 applications of various kinds are filed each year that can be acted upon by a single Justice.

Jurisdiction According to the Constitution (art. III, sec. 2), "[t]he judicial Power shall extend to all Cases, in Law and Equity, arising under this Constitution, the Laws of the United States, and Treaties made, or which shall be made, under their Authority;—to all Cases affecting Ambassadors, other public Ministers and Consuls;—to all Cases of admiralty and maritime Jurisdiction;—to Controversies to which the United States shall be a Party;—to Controversies between two or more States;—between a State and Citizens of another State;—between Citizens of different States;—between Citizens of the same State claiming Lands under Grants of different States, and between a State, or the Citizens thereof, and foreign States, Citizens or Subjects.

"In all Cases affecting Ambassadors, other public Ministers and Consuls, and those in which a State shall be Party, the supreme Court shall have original Jurisdiction. In all the other Cases before mentioned, the supreme Court shall have appellate Jurisdiction, both as to Law and Fact, with such Exceptions, and under such Regulations as the Congress shall make."

Appellate jurisdiction has been conferred upon the Supreme Court by various statutes, under the authority given Congress by the Constitution. The basic statute effective at this time in conferring and controlling jurisdiction of the Supreme Court may be found in 28 U.S.C. 1251, 1253, 1254, 1257–1259, and various special statutes. Congress has no authority to change the original jurisdiction of this Court.

Rulemaking Power Congress has from time to time conferred upon the Supreme Court power to prescribe rules of procedure to be followed by the lower courts of the United States. Pursuant to these statutes there are now in force rules promulgated by the Court to govern civil and criminal cases in the district courts, bankruptcy proceedings, admiralty cases, appellate proceedings, and the trial of misdemeanors before U.S. magistrates.

For further information concerning the Supreme Court, contact the Public Information Office, United States Supreme Court Building, 1 First Street NE., Washington, DC 20543. Phone, 202–479–3211.

Lower Courts

Article III of the Constitution declares, in section 1, that the judicial power of the United States shall be invested in one Supreme Court and in "such inferior Courts as the Congress may from time to time ordain and establish." The Supreme Court has held that these constitutional courts ". . . share in the exercise of the judicial power defined in that section, can be invested with no other jurisdiction, and have judges who hold office during good behavior, with no power in Congress to provide otherwise."

United States Courts of Appeals The courts of appeals are intermediate appellate courts created by act of March 3, 1891 (28 U.S.C. ch. 3), to relieve the

Supreme Court of considering all appeals in cases originally decided by the Federal trial courts. They are empowered to review all final decisions and certain interlocutory decisions (18 U.S.C. 3731,3734; 28 U.S.C. 1291, 1292) of district courts. They also are empowered to review and enforce orders of many Federal administrative bodies. The decisions of the courts of appeals are final except as they are subject to discretionary review or appeal in the Supreme Court.

The United States is divided geographically into 12 judicial circuits, including the District of Columbia. Each circuit has a court of appeals (28 U.S.C. 41, 1294). Each of the 50 States is assigned to one of the circuits, and the Territories are assigned variously to the first, third, and ninth circuits. There is also a Court of Appeals for the Federal Circuit, which has nationwide jurisdiction defined by subject matter. At present each court of appeals has from 6 to 28 permanent circuit judgeships (179 in all), depending upon the amount of judicial work in the circuit. Circuit judges hold their offices during good behavior as provided by Article III, section 1, of the Constitution. The judge senior in commission who is under 65 years of age, has been in office at least 1 year, and has not previously been chief judge serves as the chief judge of the circuit for a 7-year term. One of the justices of the Supreme Court is assigned as circuit justice for each of the 13 judicial circuits. Each court of appeals normally hears cases in panels consisting of three judges but may sit *en banc* with all judges present.

The judges of each circuit by vote determine the size of the judicial council for the circuit, which consists of the chief judge and an equal number of circuit and district judges. The council considers the state of Federal judicial business in the circuit and may "make all necessary and appropriate orders for [its] effective and expeditious administration . . ." (28 U.S.C. 332). The chief judge of each circuit summons annually a judicial conference of all circuit and district judges in the circuit, and sometimes members of the bar, to discuss the business of the Federal courts of the circuit (28 U.S.C. 333). The chief judge of each circuit and a district judge elected from each of the 12 geographical circuits, together with the chief judge of the Court of International Trade, serve as members of the Judicial Conference of the United States, of which the Chief Justice of the United States is chairman. This is the governing body for the administration of the Federal judicial system as a whole (28 U.S.C. 331).

Judicial Circuits—United States Courts of Appeals

Circuit	Judges	Official Station
	District of Columbia Circuit	
(*Clerk:* Constance L. Dupre; *Circuit Executive:* Linda Finkelstein; Washington, DC)	*Circuit Justice*	
	Chief Justice William H. Rehnquist	
	Circuit Judges	
	Abner J. Mikva, *Chief Judge*	Washington, DC
	Patricia M. Wald	Do.
	Harry T. Edwards	Do.
	Ruth B. Ginsburg	Do.
	Laurence H. Silberman	Do.
	James L. Buckley	Do.
	Stephen F. Williams	Do.
	Douglas Ginsburg	Do.
	David Bryan Sentelle	Do.
	Clarence Thomas	Do.
	A. Raymond Randolph	Do.
	Karen LeCraft Henderson	Do.
	First Circuit	
Districts of Maine, New Hampshire, Massachusetts, Rhode Island, and Puerto Rico	*Circuit Justice*	
	Justice David H. Souter	

Judicial Circuits—United States Courts of Appeals—Continued

Circuit	Judges	Official Station
(*Clerk:* Francis P. Scigliano; *Circuit Executive:* Vincent F. Flanagan; Boston, MA)	*Circuit Judges*	
	Stephen G. Breyer, *Chief Judge*	Boston, MA
	Levin H. Campbell	Boston, MA
	Juan R. Torruella	San Juan, PR
	Bruce M. Selya	Providence, RI
	Conrad K. Cyr	Bangor, ME
	(Vacancy)	
	Second Circuit	
Districts of Vermont, Connecticut, northern New York, southern New York, eastern New York, and western New York (*Clerk:* Elaine B. Goldsmith; *Circuit Executive:* Steven Flanders; New York, NY)	*Circuit Justice*	
	Justice Thurgood Marshall	
	Circuit Judges	
	James L. Oakes, *Chief Judge*	Brattleboro, VT
	Thomas J. Meskill	New Britain, CT
	Jon O. Newman	Hartford, CT
	Amalya Lyle Kearse	New York, NY
	Richard J. Cardamone	Utica, NY
	Ralph K. Winter, Jr.	New Haven, CT
	George C. Pratt	Uniondale, NY
	Roger J. Miner	Albany, NY
	Frank X. Altimari	Uniondale, NY
	J. Daniel Mahoney	Milford, CT
	John J. Walker, Jr.	New York, NY
	Joseph M. McLaughlin	Brooklyn, NY
	(Vacancy)	
	Third Circuit	
Districts of New Jersey, eastern Pennsylvania, middle Pennsylvania, western Pennsylvania, Delaware, and the Virgin Islands (*Clerk:* Sally Mrvos; *Circuit Executive:* John P. Hehman; Philadelphia, PA)	*Circuit Justice*	
	Justice David H. Souter	
	Circuit Judges	
	Dolores Korman Sloviter, *Chief Judge*	Philadelphia, PA
	Edward R. Becker	Philadelphia, PA
	Walter K. Stapleton	Wilmington, DE
	Carol Los Mansmann	Pittsburgh, PA
	William D. Hutchinson	Pottsville, PA
	Robert E. Cowen	Trenton, NJ
	Morton I. Greenberg	Trenton, NJ
	Anthony J. Scirica	Philadelphia, PA
	Richard Lowell Nygaard	Erie, PA
	Samuel A. Alito, Jr.	Newark, NJ
	(2 vacancies)	
	Fourth Circuit	
Districts of Maryland, northern West Virginia, southern West Virginia, eastern Virginia, western Virginia, eastern North Carolina, middle North Carolina, western North Carolina, and South Carolina (*Clerk:* John Greacen; *Circuit Executive:* Samuel W. Phillips; Richmond, VA)	*Circuit Justice*	
	Chief Justice William H. Rehnquist	
	Circuit Judges	
	Sam J. Ervin III, *Chief Judge*	Morganton, NC
	Donald S. Russell	Spartanburg, SC
	H. Emory Widener, Jr.	Abingdon,VA
	Kenneth K. Hall	Charleston, WV
	James Dickson Phillips, Jr.	Durham, NC
	Francis D. Murnaghan, Jr.	Baltimore, MD
	James M. Sprouse	Lewisburg, WV
	James Harvie Wilkinson III	Charlottesville, VA
	William W. Wilkins, Jr.	Greenville, SC
	Paul V. Niemeyer	Baltimore, MD
	(Vacancy)	
	Fifth Circuit	
Districts of northern Mississippi, southern Mississippi, eastern Louisiana, middle Louisiana, western Louisiana, northern Texas, southern	*Circuit Justice*	
	Justice Antonin Scalia	
	Circuit Judges	
	Charles Clark, *Chief Judge*	Jackson, MS

Judicial Circuits—United States Courts of Appeals—Continued

Circuit	Judges	Official Station
Texas, eastern Texas, and western Texas (*Clerk:* Gilbert F. Ganucheau; *Circuit Executive:* Lydia Comberrel; New Orleans, LA)	Henry A. Politz	Shreveport, LA
	Carolyn Dineen King	Houston, TX
	William L. Garwood	Austin, TX
	E. Grady Jolly	Jackson, MS
	Patrick E. Higginbotham	Dallas, TX
	W. Eugene Davis	Lafayette, LA
	Edith H. Jones	Houston, TX
	Jerry Edwin Smith	Houston, TX
	John M. Duhe, Jr.	Lafayette, LA
	Rhesa H. Barksdale	Jackson, MS
	Jacques L. Wiener, Jr.	Shreveport, LA
	Emilio M. Garza	San Antonio, TX
	(3 vacancies)	
	Sixth Circuit	
Districts of northern Ohio, southern Ohio, eastern Michigan, western Michigan, eastern Kentucky, western Kentucky, eastern Tennessee, middle Tennessee, and western Tennessee (*Clerk:* Leonard Green; *Circuit Executive:* James A. Higgins; Cincinnati, OH)	*Circuit Justice*	
	Justice John Paul Stevens	
	Circuit Judges	
	Gilbert S. Merritt, *Chief Judge*	Nashville, TN
	Damon J. Keith	Detroit, MI
	Cornelia G. Kennedy	Detroit, MI
	Boyce F. Martin, Jr.	Louisville, KY
	Nathaniel R. Jones	Cincinnati, OH
	Robert B. Krupansky	Cleveland, OH
	H. Ted Milburn	Chattanooga, TN
	Ralph B. Guy, Jr.	Ann Arbor, MI
	James L. Ryan	Detroit, MI
	David A. Nelson	Cincinnati, OH
	Danny J. Boggs	Louisville, KY
	Alan E. Norris	Columbus, OH
	Richard F. Suhrheinrich	Detroit, MI
	(2 vacancies)	
	Seventh Circuit	
Districts of northern Indiana, southern Indiana, northern Illinois, central Illinois, southern Illinois, eastern Wisconsin, and western Wisconsin (*Clerk:* Thomas F. Strubbe; *Circuit Executive:* Collins T. Fitzpatrick; Chicago, IL)	*Circuit Justice*	
	Justice John Paul Stevens	
	Circuit Judges	
	William J. Bauer, *Chief Judge*	Chicago, IL
	Walter J. Cummings	Chicago, IL
	Harlington Wood, Jr.	Springfield, IL
	Richard D. Cudahy	Chicago, IL
	Richard A. Posner	Chicago, IL
	John L. Coffey	Milwaukee, WI
	Joel M. Flaum	Chicago, IL
	Kenneth F. Ripple	South Bend, IN
	Frank H. Easterbrook	Chicago, IL
	Daniel A. Manion	South Bend, IN
	Michael S. Kanne	Lafayette, IN
	Eighth Circuit	
Districts of Minnesota, northern Iowa, southern Iowa, eastern Missouri, western Missouri, eastern Arkansas, western Arkansas, Nebraska, North Dakota, and South Dakota (*Clerk:* (Vacancy); *Circuit Executive:* June L. Boadwine; St. Louis, MO, and St. Paul, MN)	*Circuit Justice*	
	Justice Harry A. Blackmun	
	Circuit Judges	
	Donald P. Lay, *Chief Judge*	St. Paul, MN
	Theodore McMillian	St. Louis, MO
	Richard S. Arnold	Little Rock, AR
	John R. Gibson	Kansas City, MO
	George G. Fagg	Des Moines, IA
	Pasco M. Bowman II	Kansas City, MO
	Roger L. Wollman	Pierre, SD
	Frank J. Magill	Fargo, ND
	Clarence Arlen Beam	Lincoln, NE
	James B. Loken	St. Paul, MN
	Ninth Circuit	
Districts of northern California, eastern	*Circuit Justice*	
	Justice Sandra Day O'Connor	

Judicial Circuits—United States Courts of Appeals—Continued

Circuit	Judges	Official Station
California, central California, southern California, Oregon, Nevada, Montana, eastern Washington, western Washington, Idaho, Arizona, Alaska, Hawaii, Territory of Guam, and District Court for the Northern Mariana Islands (*Clerk:* Cathy Catterson Hansen; *Circuit Executive:* Gregory B. Walters; San Francisco, CA)	*Circuit Judges*	
	J. Clifford Wallace, *Chief Judge*	San Diego, CA
	James R. Browning	San Francisco, CA
	Proctor Hug, Jr.	Reno, NV
	Thomas Tang	Phoenix, AZ
	Mary M. Schroeder	Phoenix, AZ
	Betty B. Fletcher	Seattle, WA
	Jerome Farris	Seattle, WA
	Harry Pregerson	Woodland Hills, CA
	Arthur L. Alarcon	Los Angeles, CA
	Cecil F. Poole	San Francisco, CA
	Dorothy W. Nelson	Pasadena, CA
	William C. Canby, Jr.	Phoenix, AZ
	William A. Norris	Los Angeles, CA
	Stephen Reinhardt	Los Angeles, CA
	Robert R. Beezer	Seattle, WA
	Cynthia Holcomb Hall	Pasadena, CA
	Charles E. Wiggins	Reno, NV
	Melvin Brunetti	Reno, NV
	Alex Kozinski	Pasadena, CA
	David R. Thompson	San Diego, CA
	John T. Noonan, Jr.	San Francisco, CA
	Diarmuid F. O'Scannlain	Pasadena, CA
	Edward Leavy	Portland, OR
	Stephen S. Trott	Boise, ID
	Ferdinand F. Fernandez	Los Angeles, CA
	Pamela A. Rymer	Los Angeles, CA
	Thomas G. Nelson	Boise, ID
	(Vacancy)	
	Tenth Circuit	
Districts of Colorado, Wyoming, Utah, Kansas, eastern Oklahoma, western Oklahoma, northern Oklahoma, and New Mexico (*Clerk:* Robert L. Hoecker; *Circuit Executive:* Eugene J. Murret; Denver, CO)	*Circuit Justice*	
	Justice Byron R. White	
	Circuit Judges	
	William J. Holloway, Jr., *Chief Judge*	Oklahoma City, OK
	Monroe G. McKay	Salt Lake City, UT
	James K. Logan	Olathe, KS
	Stephanie K. Seymour	Tulsa, OK
	John P. Moore	Denver, CO
	Stephen H. Anderson	Salt Lake City, UT
	Deanell Reece Tacha	Lawrence, KS
	Bobby R. Baldock	Roswell, NM
	Wade Brorby	Cheyenne, WY
	David M. Ebel	Denver, CO
	Eleventh Circuit	
Districts of northern Georgia, middle Georgia, southern Georgia, northern Florida, middle Florida, southern Florida, northern Alabama, middle Alabama, southern Alabama (*Clerk:* Miguel J. Cortez, Jr.; *Circuit Executive:* Norman E. Zoller; Atlanta, GA)	*Circuit Justice*	
	Justice Anthony M. Kennedy	
	Circuit Judges	
	Gerald B. Tjoflat, *Chief Judge*	Jacksonville, FL
	Peter T. Fay	Miami, FL
	Phyllis A. Kravitch	Savannah, GA
	Frank M. Johnson, Jr.	Montgomery, AL
	Joseph Woodrow Hatchett	Tallahassee, FL
	R. Lanier Anderson III	Macon, GA
	Thomas A. Clark	Atlanta, GA
	J.L. Edmondson	Atlanta, GA
	Emmett Ripley Cox	Mobile, AL
	Joel F. Dubina	Montgomery, AL
	Stanley F. Birch, Jr.	Atlanta, GA
	(Vacancy)	

United States Court of Appeals for the Federal Circuit This court was established under Article III of the Constitution pursuant to the Federal

Courts Improvement Act of 1982 (28 U.S.C. 41) as the successor to the United States Court of Customs and Patent Appeals and the Court of Claims. The jurisdiction of the court is nationwide (as provided by 28 U.S.C. 1295) and includes appeals from the district courts in patent cases; appeals from the district courts in contract, and certain other civil actions in which the United States is a defendant; and appeals from final decisions of the U.S. Claims Court and the U.S. Court of International Trade. The jurisdiction of the court also includes the review of administrative rulings by the Patent and Trademark Office, U.S. International Trade Commission, Secretary of Commerce, agency boards of contract appeals, and the Merit Systems Protection Board.

The court consists of 12 circuit judges. It sits in panels of three or more on each case and may also hear or rehear a case *en banc.* The court sits principally in Washington, DC, and may hold court wherever a court of appeals sits (28 U.S.C. 48). Like the other courts of appeals, the U.S. Court of Appeals for the Federal Circuit has a clerk, staff attorneys, technical assistants, librarian, and supporting staff.

Federal Circuit—United States Court of Appeals

Official Station: Washington, DC

Circuit Justice
Chief Justice William H. Rehnquist

Chief Judge
Helen W. Nies

Judges
Giles S. Rich
Glenn L. Archer, Jr.
Pauline Newman
Haldane Robert Mayer
Paul R. Michel
S. Jay Plager
Alan D. Lourie
Randall R. Rader
(2 vacancies)

Clerk: Francis X. Gindhart

For further information, contact the Clerk, United States Court of Appeals for the Federal Circuit, 717 Madison Place NW., Washington, DC 20439. Phone, 202–633–6550.

United States District Courts The district courts are the trial courts of general Federal jurisdiction. Each State has at least one district court, while some of the larger States have as many as four. Altogether there are 89 district courts in the 50 States, plus the one in the District of Columbia. In addition, the Commonwealth of Puerto Rico has a district court with jurisdiction corresponding to that of district courts in the various States.

At present, each district court has from 2 to 27 Federal district judgeships, depending upon the amount of judicial work within its territory. Only one judge is usually required to hear and decide a case in a district court, but in some limited cases it is required that three judges be called together to comprise the court (28 U.S.C. 2284). The judge senior in commission who is under 65 years of age, has been in office for at least 1 year, and has not previously been chief judge serves as chief judge for a 7-year term. There are altogether 610 permanent district judgeships in the 50 States and 15 in the District of Columbia. There are 7 district judgeships in Puerto Rico. District judges hold their offices during good behavior as provided by Article III, section 1, of the Constitution. However, Congress may create temporary judgeships for a court with the provision that when a vacancy occurs in that district, such vacancy shall not be filled. Each district court has a clerk, a United States attorney, a United States marshal, one or more United States magistrates and bankruptcy judges, probation officers, court reporters, and their staffs. The jurisdiction of the district courts is set forth in title 28, chapter 85, of the United States Code and at 18 U.S.C. 3231.

Cases from the district courts are reviewable on appeal by the applicable court of appeals.

Territorial Courts Pursuant to its authority to govern the Territories (art. IV, sec. 3, clause 2, of the Constitution), Congress has established district courts in the territories of Guam and the Virgin Islands. The District Court of the Canal Zone was abolished on April 1, 1982, pursuant to the Panama Canal Act of 1979 (22 U.S.C. 3601 note). Congress has also established a district court in the Northern Mariana Islands, which presently are administered by the United States under a trusteeship agreement with the United Nations. These Territorial courts have jurisdiction not only over the subjects described in the judicial article of the Constitution but also of many local matters that, within the States, are decided in State courts. The district court of Puerto Rico, by contrast, is established under Article III, is classified like other "district courts," and is called a "court of the United States" (28 U.S.C. 451). There is one judge each in Guam and the Northern Mariana Islands, and two in the Virgin Islands. The judges in these courts are appointed for terms of 10 years.

For further information concerning the lower courts, contact the Administrative Office of the United States Courts, Washington, DC 20544.

Judicial Panel on Multidistrict Litigation The Panel, created by act of April 29, 1968 (28 U.S.C. 1407), and consisting of seven Federal judges designated by the Chief Justice from the courts of appeals and district courts, is authorized to temporarily transfer to a single district, for coordinated or consolidated pretrial proceedings, civil actions pending in different districts that involve one or more common questions of fact.

For further information, contact the Clerk, Judicial Panel on Multidistrict Litigation, Suite 1002, 1120 Vermont Avenue NW., Washington, DC 20005. Phone, 202–653–6090.

Special Courts

The Supreme Court has held that ". . . Article III [of the Constitution] does not express the full authority of Congress to create courts, and that other Articles invest Congress with powers in the exertion of which it may create inferior courts and clothe them with functions deemed essential or helpful in carrying those powers into execution." Such courts, known as legislative courts, have functions which ". . . are directed to the execution of one or more of such powers and are prescribed by Congress independently of section 2 of Article III; and their judges hold office for such term as Congress prescribes, whether it be a fixed period of years or during good behavior." Appeals from the decisions of these courts, with the exception of the U.S. Tax Court and the U.S. Court of Military Appeals, may be taken to the U.S. Court of Appeals for the Federal Circuit. Appeals from the decisions of the Tax Court may be taken to the court of appeals in which judicial circuit the case was initially heard. Certain decisions of the U.S. Court of Military Appeals are reviewable by writ of certiorari in the Supreme Court.

United States Claims Court The Court was established on October 1, 1982, as an Article I court (28 U.S.C. 171, Article I, U.S. Constitution). The Claims Court succeeds to the original jurisdiction of the Court of Claims, as provided for in 28 U.S.C. 1491 *et seq.* The Court is composed of a chief judge, designated by the President, and 15 associate judges. All judges are appointed for 15-year terms by the President with the advice and consent of the Senate.

The court has jurisdiction over claims to render money judgments against the United States. A claim must be founded either upon: the United States Constitution; an act of Congress; the regulation of an executive department; an express or implied-in-fact contract with the United States; or damages, liquidated or unliquidated, in cases not sounding in tort.

If a bidder files a claim with the Court before the award of a Government contract, it has jurisdiction to grant declaratory judgments and equitable relief. Under the Contract Disputes Act (41 U.S.C. 601 *et seq.*), the Court may render judgments upon a claim by or against, or any dispute between a contractor and the United States Government arising under the act.

The Congress, from time to time, also grants the Court jurisdiction over specific types of claims against the United States. The National Vaccine Injury Compensation Program, established by 42 U.S.C. 300aa–10 (the Vaccine Act), is an example of such special jurisdiction.

The Court also furnishes reports to Congress on bills referred by either the House of Representatives or the Senate.

Judgments of the Court are final and conclusive on both the claimant and the United States. All judgments are subject to appeal to the United States Court of Appeals for the Federal Circuit. Collateral to any judgment, the Court may issue orders directing the restoration to office or status of any claimant or the correction of applicable records.

The Court's jurisdiction is nationwide. Trials are conducted before individual judges at locations most convenient for the claimants and their witnesses.

For further information, contact the Clerk of Court, United States Claims Court, 717 Madison Place NW., Washington, DC 20005. Phone, 202–633–7257.

United States Court of International Trade This court was originally established as the Board of United States General Appraisers by act of June 10, 1890, which conferred upon it jurisdiction theretofore held by the district and circuit courts in actions arising under the tariff acts (19 U.S.C. ch. 4). The act of May 28, 1926 (19 U.S.C. 405a), created the United States Customs Court to supersede the Board; by acts of August 7, 1939, and June 25, 1948 (28 U.S.C. 1582, 1583), the court was integrated into the United States court structure, organization, and procedure. The act of July 14, 1956 (28 U.S.C. 251), established the court as a court of record of the United States under Article III of the Constitution.

The Customs Courts Act of 1980 (28 U.S.C. 251) constituted the court as the United States Court of International Trade and revised provisions relating to its jurisdiction. The Court of International Trade has all the powers in law and equity of a district court.

The Court of International Trade has jurisdiction over any civil action against the United States arising from Federal laws governing import transactions. This includes classification and valuation cases, as well as authority to review certain agency determinations under the Trade Agreements Act of 1979 (19 U.S.C. 2501) involving antidumping and countervailing duty matters. In addition, it has exclusive jurisdiction of civil actions to review determinations as to the eligibility of workers, firms, and communities for adjustment assistance under the Trade Act of 1974 (19 U.S.C. 2101). Civil actions commenced by the United States to recover customs duties, to recover on a customs bond, or for certain civil penalties alleging fraud or negligence are also within the exclusive jurisdiction of the court.

The court is composed of a chief judge and eight judges, not more than five of whom may belong to any one political party. Any of its judges may be temporarily designated and assigned by the Chief Justice of the United States to sit as a court of appeals or district court judge in any circuit or district. The court has a clerk and deputy clerks, a librarian, court reporters, and other supporting personnel. Cases before the court may be tried before a jury. Under the Federal Courts Improvement Act of 1982 (28 U.S.C. 1295), appeals are taken to the U.S. Court of Appeals for the Federal Circuit, and ultimately review may be sought in appropriate cases in the Supreme Court of the United States.

The principal offices are located in New York, NY, but the court is empowered to hear and determine cases arising at any port or place within the jurisdiction of the United States.

For further information, contact the Clerk, United States Court of International Trade, 1 Federal Plaza, New York, NY 10007. Phone, 212–264–2814.

United States Court of Military Appeals This court was established under Article I of the Constitution of the United States pursuant to act of May 5, 1950, as amended (10 U.S.C. 867). Subject only to certiorari review by the Supreme Court of the United States in a limited number of cases, the court serves as the final appellate tribunal to review court-martial convictions of all the armed services. It is exclusively an appellate criminal court, consisting of five civilian judges who are appointed for 15-year terms by the President with the advice and consent of the Senate. The court is called upon to exercise jurisdiction to review the record in all cases:

—extending to death;

—certified to the court by a Judge Advocate General of an armed service or by the General Counsel of the Department of Transportation, acting for the Coast Guard; or

—petitioned by accused who have received a sentence of confinement for 1 year or more, and/or a punitive discharge.

The court also exercises authority under the All Writs Act (28 U.S.C. 1651 (a)).

In addition, the judges of the court are required by law to work jointly with the senior uniformed lawyer from each Armed Force, the Chief Counsel of the Coast Guard, and two members of the public appointed by the Secretary of Defense, to make an annual comprehensive survey and to report annually to the Congress on the operation and progress of the military justice system under the Uniform Code of Military Justice, and to recommend improvements wherever necessary.

For further information, contact the Clerk, United States Court of Military Appeals, 450 E Street NW., Washington, DC 20442–0001. Phone, 202–272–1448.

United States Tax Court This is a court of record under Article I of the Constitution of the United States (26 U.S.C. 7441). Currently an independent judicial body in the legislative branch, the court was originally created as the United States Board of Tax Appeals, an independent agency in the executive branch, by the Revenue Act of 1924 (43 Stat. 336) and continued by the Revenue Act of 1926 (44 Stat. 105), the Internal Revenue Codes of 1939, 1954, and 1986. The name was changed to the Tax Court of the United States by the Revenue Act of 1942 (56 Stat. 957), and the Article I status and change in name to United States Tax Court were effected by the Tax Reform Act of 1969 (83 Stat. 730).

The court is composed of 19 judges. Its strength is augmented by senior judges who may be recalled by the chief judge to perform further judicial duties and by 17 special trial judges who are appointed by the chief judge and serve at the pleasure of the court. The chief judge is elected biennially from among the 19 judges of the court.

The Tax Court tries and adjudicates controversies involving the existence of deficiencies or overpayments in income, estate, gift, and generation-skipping transfer taxes in cases where deficiencies have been determined by the Commissioner of Internal Revenue. It also hears cases commenced by transferees and fiduciaries who have been issued notices of liability by the Commissioner.

The Tax Court has jurisdiction to redetermine excise taxes and penalties imposed on private foundations. Similar jurisdiction over excise taxes has been conferred with regard to public charities, qualified pension plans, and real estate investment trusts.

At the option of the individual taxpayer, simplified procedures may be utilized for the trials of small tax cases, provided that in a case conducted under these procedures the decision of the court would be final and not subject to review by any court. The jurisdictional maximum for such cases is $10,000 for any disputed year.

In disputes relating to public inspection of written determinations by the Internal Revenue Service, the Tax Court has jurisdiction to restrain disclosure or to obtain additional disclosure of written determinations or background file documents and, at the request of any person, to order disclosure of the identity of any person to whom the written determination pertains, if there has been a third party contact noted on the determination made public.

The Tax Court has jurisdiction to render declaratory judgments relating to the qualification of retirement plans, including pension, profit-sharing, stock bonus, annuity, and bond purchase plans; the tax-exempt status of a charitable organization, qualified charitable donee, private foundation, or private operating foundation; and the status of interest on certain governmental obligations. Additional jurisdiction was conferred on the Tax Court by the Technical and Miscellaneous Revenue Act of 1988 (102 Stat. 3342). Such jurisdiction includes injunctive authority over certain procedure assessments, authority to review certain jeopardy assessments and jeopardy levies, and authority to hear and decide appeals by taxpayers from the denial of administrative costs by the Internal Revenue Service.

All decisions other than small tax cases are subject to review by the courts of appeals and thereafter by the Supreme Court of the United States upon the granting of a writ of certiorari.

The office of the court and all of its judges are located in Washington, DC, with the exception of a field office located in Los Angeles, CA. The court conducts trial sessions at various locations within the United States as reasonably convenient to taxpayers as practicable. Each trial session is conducted by a single judge or a special trial judge. All proceedings are public and are conducted judicially in accordance with the court's Rules of Practice and the rules of evidence applicable in trials without a jury in the U.S. District Court for the District of Columbia. A fee of $60 is prescribed for the filing of a petition. Practice before the court is limited to practitioners admitted under the court's Rules.

For further information, contact the Administrative Office, United States Tax Court, 400 Second Street NW., Washington, DC 20217. Phone, 202-376-2751.

Temporary Emergency Court of Appeals The Economic Stabilization Act Amendments of 1971 (85 Stat. 743) created a special court known as the Temporary Emergency Court of Appeals of the United States. The court has exclusive jurisdiction over all appeals from the district courts of the United States in cases and controversies arising under the economic stabilization and energy conservation laws, and consists of eight circuit and district judges designated by the Chief Justice. The court has been in operation since February 1972, and its principal location is at the United States Courthouse in the District of Columbia.

The court operates under its own rules (28 U.S.C. app.) and the Federal Rules of Appellate Procedure. Under the rules, the hearing divisions sit when necessary at Washington, DC; St. Paul, MN; Atlanta, GA; Houston, TX; and San Francisco, CA; and at such other places and times as the Chief Judge may designate.

For further information, contact the Clerk, Temporary Emergency Court of Appeals, United States Courthouse, Washington, DC 20001. Phone, 202-535-3390.

United States Court of Veterans Appeals The United States Court of Veterans Appeals was established on November 18, 1988 (102 Stat. 4105, 38 U.S.C. 4051) pursuant to Article I of the Constitution, and given exclusive jurisdiction to review decisions of the Board of Veterans Appeals. However, the Court may not review the schedule of ratings for disabilities or actions of the Administrator in adopting or revising that schedule. Decisions of the Court of Veterans Appeals may be appealed to the United States Court of Appeals for the Federal Circuit.

The Court consists of a chief judge and at least two, but not more than six, associate judges. All judges are appointed by the President with the advice and consent of the Senate for terms of 15 years.

The court's principal office is in the District of Columbia, but the Court can also act at any place within the United States.

Other Courts There have also been created two courts of local jurisdiction for the District of Columbia: the District of Columbia Court of Appeals and the Superior Court.

Business of the Federal Courts

The business of all the Federal courts described here, except the Court of Military Appeals, the Tax Court, and the Court of Veterans Appeals is discussed in detail in the text and tables of the *Annual Report of the Director of the Administrative Office of the United States Courts (1940–90).*

ADMINISTRATIVE OFFICE OF THE UNITED STATES COURTS

Washington, DC 20544
Phone: See "Sources of Information" section at end of statement

Director	L. Ralph Mecham
Deputy Director	James E. Macklin, Jr.
General Counsel	William R. Burchill, Jr.
Legislative and Public Affairs Officer	Robert E. Feidler
Chief, Judicial Conference and Management Coordination	Karen K. Siegel
Assistant Director for Administration and Human Resources	Clarence A. Lee, Jr.
Deputy Assistant Director for Special Projects	R. Townsend Robinson
Assistant Director for Automation and Technology	Edwin L. Stoorza, Jr.
Deputy Assistant Director for Automation and Technology	Charles F. McBride
Assistant Director for Court Programs	(vacancy)
Court Security Officer	William A. Cohan, Jr.
Assistant Director for Finance, Budget, and Program Analysis	Raymond A. Karam
Assistant Director for Judges Programs	Peter G. McCabe
Chief, Long Range Planning OFfice	Charles W. Nihan
Chief, Accounting Division	Alexander L. Lloyd, *Acting*
Chief, Article III Judges Division	John E. Howell
Chief, Audit Division	David L. Gellman
Chief, Automation Resources Division	Albert E. Ball
Chief, Bankruptcy Division	Francis F. Szczebak
Chief, Budget Division	Dewey R. Heising
Chief, Court Administration Division	Duane R. Lee
Chief, Court Systems Division	Dennis E. Morey
Chief, Contracts and Services Division	Ralph J. Simmons
Chief, Defender Services Division	Theodore J. Lidz
Chief, Evaluation and Assessment Division	Robert M. Crowder
Chief, Human Resources Division	Charlotte G. Peddicord
Chief, Financial Applications and Analysis Division	Penny G. Jacobs, *Acting*
Chief, Integrated Technology Division	Pamela B. White
Chief, Magistrate Judges Division	John T. Jones
Chief, Policy and Management Coordination Division	Cathy A. McCarthy
Chief, Probation and Pretrial Services Division	Donald L. Chamlee
Chief, Space and Facilities Division	P. Gerald Thacker

Chief, Statistics Division	DAVID L. COOK
Chief, Systems Technology Division	FRANK S. DOZIER

The Administrative Office of the United States Courts is charged with the nonjudicial, administrative business of the United States Courts, including the maintenance of workload statistics, and the disbursement of funds appropriated for the maintenance of the U.S. judicial system.

The Administrative Office of the United States Courts was created by act of August 7, 1939 (28 U.S.C. 601). The Office was established November 6, 1939. Its Director and Deputy Director are appointed by the Chief Justice of the United States after consultation with the Judicial Conference.

Administering the Courts The Director is the administrative officer of the courts of the United States (except the Supreme Court). Under the supervision and direction of the Judicial Conference of the United States he is required, among other things, to:

—supervise all administrative matters relating to the offices of clerks and other clerical and administrative personnel of the courts;

—examine the state of the dockets of the courts, secure information as to the courts' need of assistance, and prepare and transmit quarterly to the chief judges of the circuits statistical data and reports as to the business of the courts;

—submit to the annual meeting of the Judicial Conference of the United States, at least 2 weeks prior thereto, a report of the activities of the Administrative Office and the state of the business of the courts;

—fix the compensation of employees of the courts whose compensation is not otherwise fixed by law;

—regulate and pay annuities to widows and surviving dependent children of judges;

—disburse moneys appropriated for the maintenance and operation of the courts;

—examine accounts of court officers;

—regulate travel of judicial personnel;

—provide accommodations and supplies for the courts and their clerical and administrative personnel;

—establish and maintain programs for the certification and utilization of court interpreters and the provision of special interpretation services in the courts; and

—perform such other duties as may be assigned to him by the Supreme Court or the Judicial Conference of the United States.

The Director is also responsible for the preparation and submission of the budget of the courts, except the budget of the Supreme Court.

Probation Officers The Administrative Office exercises general supervision of the accounts and practices of the Federal probation offices, subject to primary control by the respective district courts that they serve. The Office publishes quarterly, in cooperation with the Bureau of Prisons of the Department of Justice, a magazine entitled *Federal Probation,* which is a journal "of correctional philosophy and practice."

The Director also has responsibility with respect to the establishment of pretrial services in the district courts under the Pretrial Services Act of 1982 (18 U.S.C. 3152). These offices report to their respective courts information concerning pretrial release of persons charged with Federal offenses and supervise such persons who are released to their custody.

Bankruptcy The Bankruptcy Amendments and Federal Judgeship Act of 1984 (28 U.S.C. 151) provided that the bankruptcy judges for each judicial district shall constitute a unit of the district court to be known as the bankruptcy court. Bankruptcy judges shall be appointed by the courts of appeals in such numbers as authorized by Congress and shall serve for a term of

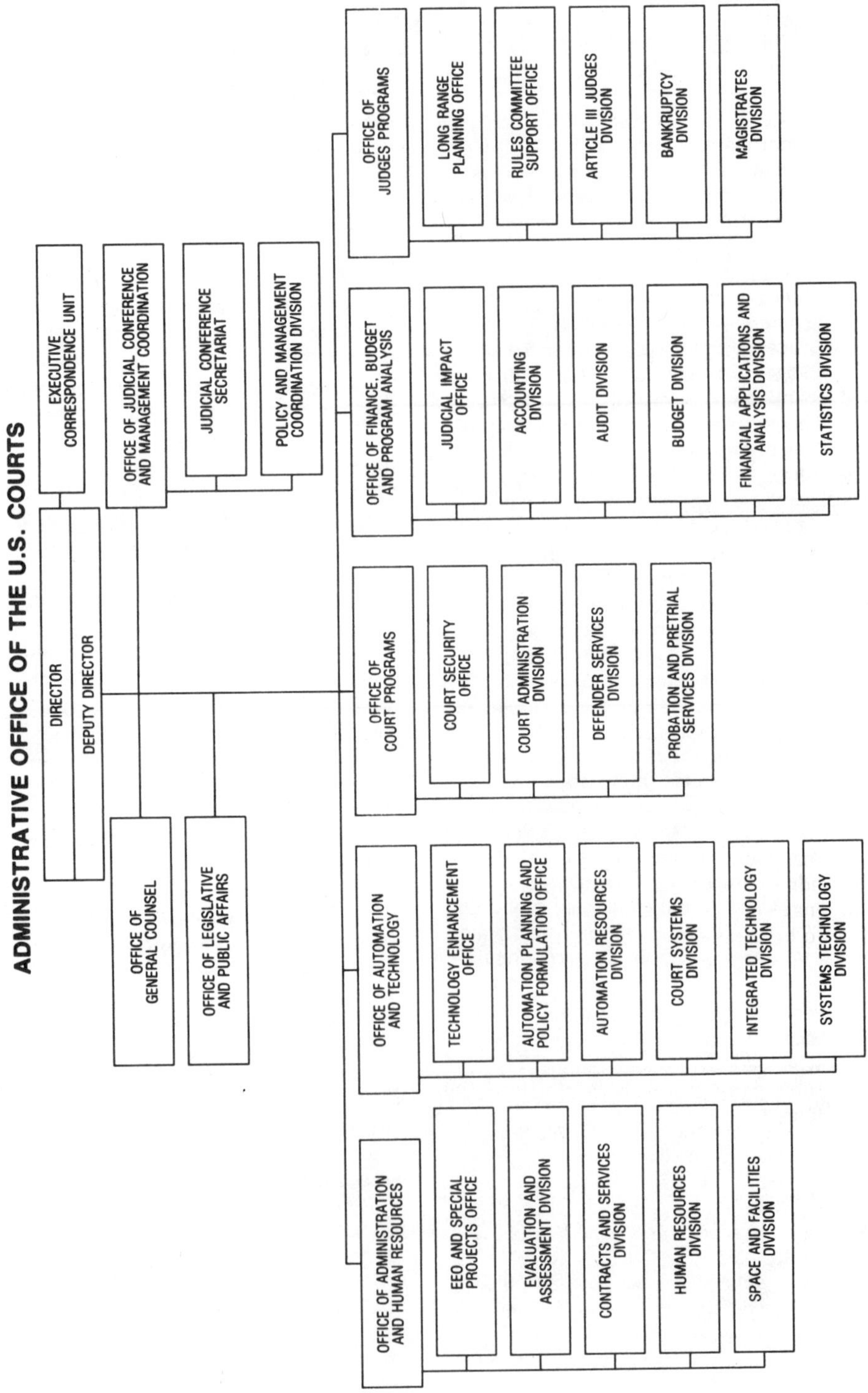
ADMINISTRATIVE OFFICE OF THE U.S. COURTS
DIRECTOR
DEPUTY DIRECTOR
EXECUTIVE CORRESPONDENCE UNIT
OFFICE OF JUDICIAL CONFERENCE AND MANAGEMENT COORDINATION
JUDICIAL CONFERENCE SECRETARIAT
POLICY AND MANAGEMENT COORDINATION DIVISION
OFFICE OF GENERAL COUNSEL
OFFICE OF LEGISLATIVE AND PUBLIC AFFAIRS
OFFICE OF JUDGES PROGRAMS
LONG RANGE PLANNING OFFICE
RULES COMMITTEE SUPPORT OFFICE
ARTICLE III JUDGES DIVISION
BANKRUPTCY DIVISION
MAGISTRATES DIVISION
OFFICE OF FINANCE, BUDGET AND PROGRAM ANALYSIS
JUDICIAL IMPACT OFFICE
ACCOUNTING DIVISION
AUDIT DIVISION
BUDGET DIVISION
FINANCIAL APPLICATIONS AND ANALYSIS DIVISION
STATISTICS DIVISION
OFFICE OF COURT PROGRAMS
COURT SECURITY OFFICE
COURT ADMINISTRATION DIVISION
DEFENDER SERVICES DIVISION
PROBATION AND PRETRIAL SERVICES DIVISION
OFFICE OF AUTOMATION AND TECHNOLOGY
TECHNOLOGY ENHANCEMENT OFFICE
AUTOMATION PLANNING AND POLICY FORMULATION OFFICE
AUTOMATION RESOURCES DIVISION
COURT SYSTEMS DIVISION
INTEGRATED TECHNOLOGY DIVISION
SYSTEMS TECHNOLOGY DIVISION
OFFICE OF ADMINISTRATION AND HUMAN RESOURCES
EEO AND SPECIAL PROJECTS OFFICE
EVALUATION AND ASSESSMENT DIVISION
CONTRACTS AND SERVICES DIVISION
HUMAN RESOURCES DIVISION
SPACE AND FACILITIES DIVISION

14 years as judicial officers of the district courts.

This act placed jurisdiction in the district courts over all cases under title 11, United States Code, and all proceedings arising in or related to cases under that title (28 U.S.C. 1334). The district court may provide for such cases and proceedings to be referred to its bankruptcy judges (as authorized by 28 U.S.C. 157).

The Director of the Administrative Office recommends to the Judicial Conference the official duty stations and places of holding court of bankruptcy judges, surveys the need for additional bankruptcy judgeships to be recommended to Congress, and determines the staff needs of bankruptcy judges and the clerks of the bankruptcy courts.

Federal Magistrates Under the Federal Magistrates Act, as amended (28 U.S.C. 631), the Director of the Administrative Office, under the supervision and direction of the Judicial Conference, exercises general supervision over administrative matters in offices of United States magistrates, compiles and evaluates statistical data relating to such offices, and submits reports thereon to the Conference. The Director reports annually to Congress on the business that has come before United States magistrates and also prepares legal and administrative manuals for the use of the magistrates. The act provides for surveys to be conducted by the Administrative Office of the conditions in the judicial districts in order to make recommendations as to the number, location, and salaries of magistrates, which are determined by the Conference subject to the availability of appropriated funds.

Federal Defenders The Criminal Justice Act (18 U.S.C. 3006A) establishes the procedure for the appointment of counsel in Federal criminal cases for individuals who are unable to afford adequate representation under plans adopted by each district court. The act also permits the establishment of Federal public defender or Federal community defender organizations by the district courts in districts where at least 200 persons annually require the appointment of counsel. Two adjacent districts may be combined to reach this total.

Each defender organization submits to the Director of the Administrative Office an annual report of its activities along with a proposed budget or, in the case of community defender organizations, a proposed grant for the coming year. The Director is responsible for the submission of the proposed budgets and grants to the Judicial Conference for approval. The Director also makes payments to the defender organizations out of appropriations in accordance with the approved budgets and grants, as well as compensating private counsel appointed to defend criminal cases in the U.S. courts.

Sources of Information

Information may be obtained from the following offices:

Bankruptcy Division. Phone, 202-633-6231.

Budget Division. Phone, 202-633-6122.

Court Administration Division. Phone, 202-633-6236.

Defender Services Division. Phone, 202-633-6051.

General Counsel. Phone, 202-633-6127.

Human Resources Division. Phone, 202-633-6112.

Magistrates Division. Phone, 202-633-6251.

Probation Division. Phone, 202-633-6226.

Statistics Division. Phone, 202-633-6094.

For further information, contact one of the offices listed above, Administrative Office of the United States Courts, Washington, DC 20544.

FEDERAL JUDICIAL CENTER

Dolley Madison House,
1520 H Street NW., Washington, DC 20005
Phone, 202–633–6011

Director	WILLIAM W SCHWARZER
Deputy Director	CHARLES W. NIHAN
Director of Research	WILLIAM B. ELDRIDGE
Director of Innovations and Systems Development	(VACANCY)
Director of Continuing Education and Training	DANIEL L. SKOLER
Director of Special Educational Services	RUSSELL R. WHEELER
Director of Publications	SYLVAN A. SOBEL
Information Specialist	LEONARD E. KLEIN

The Federal Judicial Center is the judicial branch's agency for policy research, systems development, and continuing education.

The Federal Judicial Center was created by act of December 20, 1967 (28 U.S.C. 620), to further the development and adoption of improved judicial administration in the courts of the United States.

The Center's basic policies and activities are determined by its Board, which is composed of the Chief Justice of the United States, who is, by statute, permanent Chairman of the Board, and two judges of the United States courts of appeals, three judges of the United States district courts, and one bankruptcy judge, all of whom are elected for 4-year terms by the Judicial Conference of the United States. The Director of the Administrative Office of the United States Courts is also a permanent member of the Board.

Congress assigned the Center the following basic functions:

—to conduct research on the operation of the United States courts and to stimulate and coordinate such research on the part of other public and private persons and agencies;

—to stimulate, create, develop, and conduct programs of continuing education and training for judges and support personnel of the judicial branch;

—to study and determine ways in which automatic data processing and systems procedures may be applied to the administration of the courts;

—to provide staff, research, and planning assistance to the Judicial Conference and its committees, consistent with the performance of the other functions set forth above;

—to develop recommendations for improvement in the administration and management of the courts and to submit recommendations to the Judicial Conference of the United States;

—to submit to government agencies recommendations for improvement of their programs or activities that relate to the administration of justice; and

—to conduct, coordinate, and encourage programs relating to the history of the judicial branch.

For further information, contact the Information Specialist, Federal Judicial Center, Dolley Madison House, 1520 H Street NW., Washington, DC 20005. Phone, 202–633–6011.

Executive Branch

EXECUTIVE BRANCH

THE PRESIDENT OF THE UNITED STATES

THE PRESIDENT OF THE UNITED STATES	GEORGE BUSH

Article II, section 1, of the Constitution provides that "the executive Power shall be vested in a President of the United States of America. He shall hold his Office during the Term of four Years, * * * together with the Vice President, chosen for the same Term * * *." In addition to the powers set forth in the Constitution, the statutes have conferred upon the President specific authority and responsibility covering a wide range of matters (United States Code Index).

The President is the administrative head of the executive branch of the Government, which includes numerous agencies, both temporary and permanent, as well as the 14 executive departments.

The Cabinet

The Cabinet, a creation of custom and tradition dating back to George Washington's administration, functions at the pleasure of the President. Its purpose is to advise the President upon any subject on which he requests information (pursuant to Article II, section 2, of the Constitution).

The Cabinet is composed of the heads of the 14 executive departments—the Secretaries of Agriculture, Commerce, Defense, Education, Energy, Health and Human Services, Housing and Urban Development, Interior, Labor, State, Transportation, Treasury, and Veterans Affairs, and the Attorney General—and certain other executive branch officials to whom the President accords Cabinet rank. Additionally, the Office of Management and Budget and the Office of the U.S. Trade Representative have Cabinet rank in the Bush administration. The Vice President also participates in Cabinet meetings, and from time to time, other individuals are invited to participate in discussions of particular subjects. A Secretary to the Cabinet is designated to provide for the orderly handling and followup of matters brought before the Cabinet.

EXECUTIVE OFFICE OF THE PRESIDENT

Under authority of the Reorganization Act of 1939 (5 U.S.C. 133–133r, 133t note), various agencies were transferred to the Executive Office of the President by the President's Reorganization Plans I and II of 1939 (5 U.S.C. app.), effective July 1, 1939. Executive Order 8248 of September 8, 1939, established the divisions of the Executive Office and defined their functions. Subsequently, Presidents have used Executive orders, reorganization plans, and legislative initiatives to reorganize the Executive Office to make its composition compatible with the goals of their administrations.

EXECUTIVE OFFICE OF THE PRESIDENT

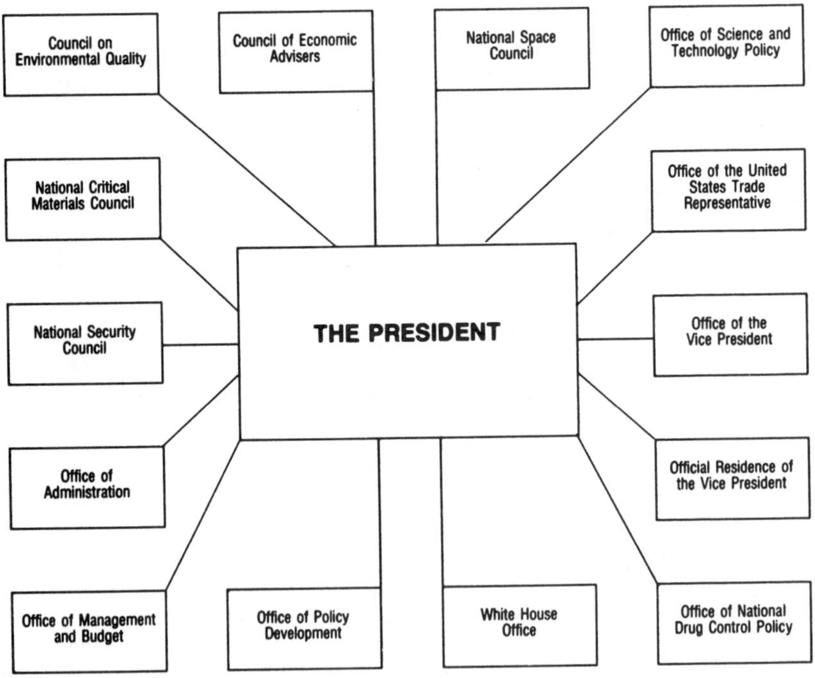

The White House Office

1600 Pennsylvania Avenue NW., Washington, DC 20500
Phone, 202–456–1414

Chief of Staff to the President	John H. Sununu
Assistant to the President and Deputy Chief of Staff	Andrew H. Card, Jr.
Assistant to the President and Staff Secretary	Phillip D. Brady
Assistant to the President for Science and Technology	D. Allan Bromley
Assistant to the President for Communications	David F. Demarest, Jr.
Assistant to the President and Press Secretary	Max Marlin Fitzwater
Assistant to the President and Deputy for National Security Affairs	Robert M. Gates
Counsel to the President	C. Boyden Gray
Assistant to the President and Secretary of the Cabinet	Edith E. Holiday
Physician to the President	Burton J. Lee III, M.D.
Assistant to the President for Legislative Affairs	Frederick D. McClure
Assistant to the President and Director, Office of National Service	C. Gregg Petersmeyer
Assistant to the President for Economic and Domestic Policy	Roger B. Porter
Assistant to the President for Public Events and Initiatives	Sigmund A. Rogich
Assistant to the President for National Security Affairs	Gen. Brent Scowcroft, USAF (Ret.)
Assistant to the President for Media Affairs	J. Dorrance Smith
Assistant to the President for Presidential Personnel	Charles G. Untermeyer
Deputy Assistant to the President and Director, Office of Intergovernmental Affairs	Debra Anderson
Deputy Assistant to the President for Management and Director, Office of Administration	Paul W. Bateman
Deputy Assistant to the President for Legislative Affairs (House)	Gary J. Andres
Deputy Assistant to the President and Director, Office of Cabinet Affairs	Stephen I. Danzansky
Deputy Assistant to the President for Legislative Affairs (Senate)	James W. Dyer
Deputy Assistant to the President for Political Affairs	Ronald C. Kaufman
Deputy Assistant to the President for Public Liaison	Bobbie G. Kilberg
Deputy Assistant to the President for Domestic Policy	Charles E.M. Kolb

290-950 0 91 - 4

Deputy Assistant to the President and Deputy Director of Presidential Personnel	JEANNETTE L. NAYLOR
Deputy Assistant to the President for Policy Planning	JAMES P. PINKERTON
Deputy Assistant to the President and Deputy Press Secretary	ROMAN POPADIUK
Deputy Assistant to the President	PATRICIA PRESOCK
Deputy Assistant to the President and Executive Assistant to the Chief of Staff	EDWARD M. ROGERS, JR.
Deputy Assistant to the President and Chief of Staff to the First Lady	SUSAN PORTER ROSE
Deputy Counsel to the President	JOHN P. SCHMITZ
Deputy Assistant to the President for Public Liaison	SICHAN SIV
Deputy Assistant to the President for Cabinet Liaison	GARY R. BLUMENTHAL
Deputy Assistant to the President for Communications and Director of Speechwriting	ROBERT ANTHONY SNOW
Deputy Assistant to the President for Appointments and Scheduling	KATHERINE SUPER
Deputy Assistant to the President and Director of White House Operations	ROSE M. ZAMARIA
Special Assistant to the President for Communications	DEBORAH A. AMEND
Special Assistant to the President for Legislative Affairs (House)	ARNOLD I. HAVENS
Special Assistant to the President for Intergovernmental Affairs	WILLIAM J. CANARY
Special Assistant to the President and Director, Office of Political Affairs	DAVID M. CARNEY
Special Assistant to the President for Political Affairs	PAUL J. COLLINS, JR.
Special Assistant to the President for National Security Affairs	TIMOTHY E. DEAL
Special Assistant to the President for Policy Development	STEPHEN FARRAR
Special Assistant to the President and Assistant Staff Secretary	JOHN S. GARDNER
Special Assistant to the President for Presidential Press Advance	SPENCER E. GEISSINGER
Special Assistant to the President and Senior Director for European and Soviet Affairs	DAVID C. GOMPERT
Special Assistant to the President and Associate Director of Presidential Personnel	MARTHA H. GOODWIN
Special Assistant to the President for Policy Development	TERESA A. GORMAN
Special Assistant to the President for Presidential Messages and Correspondence	SHIRLEY M. GREEN
Special Assistant to the President for Intergovernmental Affairs	GEORGE O. GRIFFITH, JR.
Special Assistant to the President and Associate Director of Presidential Personnel	ANNE B. GWALTNEY
Special Assistant to the President for National Security Affairs	RICHARD N. HAASS

Special Assistant to the President and Deputy Press Secretary	STEPHEN T. HART
Special Assistant to the President for National Security Affairs	EDWARD A. HEWETT
Associate Counsel to the President	JEFFREY R. HOLMSTEAD
Special Assistant to the President for Legislative Affairs (House)	JOHN W. HOWARD
Special Assistant to the President and Deputy Director, Office of Administration	HECTOR F. IRASTORZA, JR.
Special Assistant to the President and Executive Secretary for Cabinet Liaison	MICHAEL P. JACKSON
Special Assistant to the President for National Security Affairs	ARNOLD KANTER
Special Assistant to the President for National Security Affairs	VIRGINIA A. LAMPLEY
Associate Counsel to the President	LEE S. LIBERMAN
Special Assistant to the President for Policy Development	LAWRENCE LINDSEY
Associate Counsel to the President	NELSON LUND
Special Assistant to the President and Associate Director of Presidential Personnel	JOSÉ E. MARTINEZ
Special Assistant to the President for Intergovernmental Affairs	MARY A. MCCLURE
Special Assistant to the President for Policy Development	MARIANNE MCGETTIGAN
Special Assistant to the President for Public Liaison	LEIGH ANN METZGER
Special Assistant to the President and Associate Director of Presidential Personnel	NANCY F. MILLER
Special Assistant to the President for Legislative Affairs	FRANCES MCMURTRAY NORRIS
Special Assistant to the President for National Security Affairs	DOUGLAS PAAL
Special Assistant to the President and Director of Presidential Advance	JAKE L. PARMER
Special Assistant to the President for Legislative Affairs	NELL PAYNE
Special Assistant to the President and Executive Secretary, Domestic Policy Council	RICHARD W. PORTER
Special Assistant to the President for National Security Affairs	WILLIAM T. PRYCE
Special Assistant to the President for National Security Affairs	C. NICHOLAS ROSTOW
Associate Counsel to the President	GENE C. SCHAERR
Executive Secretary, National Security Council	WILLIAM F. SITTMANN
Special Assistant to the President for Legislative Affairs (Senate)	SHAWN H. SMEALLIE
Special Assistant to the President and Deputy Press Secretary	JUDY A. SMITH
Military Assistant to the President and Director, White House Military Office	LT. GEN. RICHARD G. TREFRY, USA (RET.)
Special Assistant to the President for Legislative Affairs	BRIAN K. WAIDMANN
Associate Counsel to the President	GREGORY S. WALDEN

Special Assistant to the President and Executive Secretary, Economic Policy Council	OLIN LEWIS WETHINGTON
Special Assistant to the President for National Security Affairs	WILLIAM W. WORKING

The White House Office serves the President in the performance of the many detailed activities incident to his immediate office.

The staff of the President facilitates and maintains communication with the Congress, the individual Members of the Congress, the heads of executive agencies, the press and other information media, and the general public.

The various Assistants to the President assist the President in such matters as he may direct.

Office of Management and Budget

Executive Office Building, Washington, DC 20503
Phone, 202–395–3080

Director	RICHARD G. DARMAN
Deputy Director	(VACANCY)
Executive Associate Director	FRANK HODSOLL
General Counsel	ROBERT DAMUS, *Acting*
Deputy Director for External Affairs and Spokeswoman	KIM TIMMONS-GIBSON
Associate Director for Economic Policy	AHMAD AL-SAMARRIE
Associate Director for Legislative Affairs	(VACANCY)
Assistant Director for Budget	BARRY ANDERSON
Deputy Assistant Director for Budget Analysis and Systems	PHIL DAME
Deputy Assistant Director for Budget Review and Concepts	DICK EMERY
Associate Director for Legislative Reference and Administration	JAMES C. MURR
Assistant Director for Legislative Reference	BERNARD H. MARTIN
Assistant Director for Administration	DARRELL A. JOHNSON
Associate Director for National Security and International Affairs	ROBERT HOWARD
Deputy Associate Director, National Security Division	DONALD E. GESSAMAN
Deputy Associate Director, International Affairs Division	PHILIP DUSAULT
Deputy Associate Director, Special Studies Division for National Security and International Affairs	DANIEL H. TAFT
Associate Director for Human Resources, Veterans and Labor	THOMAS A. SCULLY
Deputy Associate Director, Health and Income Maintenance Division	DAVID KLEINBERG
Deputy Associate Director, Labor, Veterans and Education Division	BARBARA S. SELFRIDGE
Associate Director for Economics and Government	JANET HALE

Deputy Associate Director, Transportation, Commerce and Justice Division	KENNETH L. SCHWARTZ
Deputy Associate Director, Housing, Treasury and Postal Division	KENNETH F. RYDER
Deputy Associate Director, Special Studies Division for Economics and Government	HARRY MEYERS
Associate Director for Natural Resources, Energy and Science	ROBERT GRADY
Deputy Associate Director, Natural Resources Division	DAVID GIBBONS
Deputy Associate Director, Energy and Science Division	JOSEPH HEZIR
Deputy Associate Director, Special Studies Division for Natural Resources, Energy and Science	KENNETH G. GLOZER
Administrator, Office of Information and Regulatory Affairs	(VACANCY)
Deputy Administrator for Information and Regulatory Management	JAMES MACRAE
Assistant Director, General Management	STEVE LIEBERMANN
Deputy Assistant Director, General Management	FRANKLIN S. REEDER
Assistant Director, Financial Management	SUSAN GAFFNEY, *Acting*
Administrator, Office of Federal Procurement Policy	ALLAN V. BURMAN

The Office of Management and Budget evaluates, formulates, and coordinates management procedures and program objectives within and among Federal departments and agencies. It also controls the administration of the Federal budget, while routinely providing the President with recommendations regarding budget proposals and relevant legislative enactments.

The Office of Management and Budget (OMB), formerly the Bureau of the Budget, was established in the Executive Office of the President pursuant to Reorganization Plan No. 1 of 1939 (5 U.S.C. app.), effective July 1, 1939.

By Executive Order 11541 of July 1, 1970, all functions transferred to the President of the United States by part I of Reorganization Plan No. 2 of 1970 (5 U.S.C. app.) were delegated to the Director of the Office of Management and Budget. Such functions are to be carried out by the Director under the direction of the President. Reorganization Plan No. 1 of 1977 (5 U.S.C. app.) and Executive orders issued pursuant to that plan amended further the functions of OMB. The Office's functions include the following:

—to assist the President in his program to develop and maintain effective government by reviewing the organizational structure and management procedures of the executive branch to ensure that they produce the intended results;

—to assist in developing efficient coordinating mechanisms to implement Government activities and to expand interagency cooperation;

—to assist the President in the preparation of the budget and the formulation of the fiscal program of the Government;

—to supervise and control the administration of the budget;

—to assist the President by clearing and coordinating departmental advice on proposed legislation and by making recommendations as to Presidential action on legislative enactments, in accordance with past practice;

—to assist in the development of regulatory reform proposals and in programs for paperwork reduction, especially reporting burdens of the public;

—to assist in the consideration and clearance and, where necessary, in the preparation of proposed Executive orders and proclamations;

—to plan and develop information systems to provide the President with program performance data;

—to plan, conduct, and promote evaluation efforts to assist the President in the assessment of program objectives, performance, and efficiency; and

—to keep the President informed of the progress of activities by Government agencies with respect to work proposed, initiated, and completed, together with the relative timing of work between the several agencies of the Government, all to the end that the work programs of the several agencies of the executive branch of the Government may be coordinated and that the moneys appropriated by the Congress may be expended in the most economical manner with the least possible overlapping and duplication of effort.

Office of Federal Procurement Policy

The Office of Federal Procurement Policy Act (41 U.S.C. 404) established the Office of Federal Procurement Policy (OFPP) within the Office of Management and Budget to improve the economy, efficiency, and effectiveness of the procurement processes by providing overall direction of procurement policies, regulations, procedures, and forms. The establishment of OFPP implemented the first recommendation made by the Commission on Government Procurement in its report to Congress in December 1972. Its authority applies to procurement by executive agencies and recipients of Federal grants or assistance of property, other than real property in being; services, including research and development; and construction, alteration, repair, or maintenance of real property.

For further information, contact the Office of the Administrator, Office of Federal Procurement Policy, Room 350, Old Executive Office Building, Washington, DC 20503. Phone, 202-395-5802.

Sources of Information

Employment Various civil service examinations and registers are used for filling positions, such as economist, budget examiner, and management analyst. Inquiries on employment should be directed to the Personnel Division, Office of Administration, Washington, DC 20500. Phone, 202-395-3765.

Inquiries Contact the Associate Director for External Affairs, Office of Management and Budget, Executive Office Building, Washington, DC 20503. Phone, 202-395-3080.

Publications *The Budget of the U.S. Government; Historical Tables, Budget of the U.S. Government; The Budget System and Concepts;* and *Catalog of Federal Domestic Assistance* are for sale by the Superintendent of Documents, Government Printing Office, Washington, DC 20402.

Council of Economic Advisers

Old Executive Office Building, Washington, DC 20500
Phone, 202-395-5084

Chairman	Michael J. Boskin
Members	Richard L. Schmalensee
	John B. Taylor
Special Assistant to the Chairman and Senior Economist	Harry G. Broadman

The Council of Economic Advisers primarily engages in the analysis and appraisal of the national economy for the purpose of providing policy recommendations to the President.

The Council of Economic Advisers was established in the Executive Office of the President by the Employment Act of 1946 (15 U.S.C. 1023). It now functions under that statute and Reorganization Plan No. 9 of 1953 (5 U.S.C. app.), effective August 1, 1953.

The Council consists of three members appointed by the President with the advice and consent of the Senate, and one of the members is designated by the President as Chairman.

The Council analyzes the national economy and its various segments; advises the President on economic developments; appraises the economic programs and policies of the Federal Government; recommends to the President policies for economic growth and stability; assists in the preparation of the economic reports of the President to the Congress; and prepares the Annual Report of the Council of Economic Advisers.

For further information, contact the Council of Economic Advisers, Old Executive Office Building, Washington, DC 20500. Phone, 202–395–5084.

National Security Council

Old Executive Office Building, Washington, DC 20506
Phone, 202–395–4974

Members:	
The President	GEORGE BUSH
The Vice President	DAN QUAYLE
The Secretary of State	JAMES A. BAKER III
The Secretary of Defense	DICK CHENEY
Statutory Advisers:	
Director of Central Intelligence	WILLIAM H. WEBSTER
Chairman, Joint Chiefs of Staff	GEN. COLIN L. POWELL, USA
Officials:	
Assistant to the President for National Security Affairs	GEN. BRENT SCOWCROFT, USAF (RET.)
Assistant to the President and Deputy for National Security Affairs	ROBERT M. GATES
Executive Secretary	WILLIAM F. SITTMANN

The National Security Council was established by the National Security Act of 1947 (50 U.S.C. 402), as amended by the National Security Act Amendments of 1949 (50 U.S.C. 401 *et seq.*). By Reorganization Plan No. 4 of 1949 (5 U.S.C. app.), the Council was placed in the Executive Office of the President.

The National Security Council is chaired by the President. Its statutory members, in addition to the President, are the Vice President and the Secretaries of State and Defense. The Chairman of the Joint Chiefs of Staff is the statutory military adviser to the Council, and the Director of Central Intelligence is its intelligence adviser.

The statutory function of the Council is to advise the President with respect to the integration of domestic, foreign, and military policies relating to national security.

Office of Policy Development

1600 Pennsylvania Avenue NW., Washington, DC 20500
Phone, 202–456–1414

Deputy Assistant to the President for Domestic Policy	CHARLES E.M. KOLB
Special Assistant to the President for Policy Development and Associate Director for Domestic Economic Policy	LAWRENCE LINDSEY
Special Assistant to the President for Policy Development and Associate Director for International Economic Policy	STEPHEN FARRAR
Special Assistant to the President for Policy Development and Associate Director for Legal Policy	MARIANNE MCGETTIGAN
Special Assistant to the President for Policy Development and Associate Director for Energy, Environment, and Natural Resources Policy	TERESA A. GORMAN
Associate Director for Health and Social Services Policy	JOHANNES KUTTNER
Deputy Associate Director for Education Policy	RAE NELSON
Director of Administration	DAVID R. ALEXANDER

The Office of Policy Development, formerly the Domestic Policy Staff, was redesignated as such in 1981 to replace the Domestic Policy Staff, which was established in the Executive Office of the President by Reorganization Plan No. 1 of 1977 (5 U.S.C. app.), effective March 26, 1978, pursuant to Executive Order 12045 of March 27, 1978.

The Office of Policy Development advises and assists the President in the formulation, evaluation, and coordination of long-range domestic and economic policy. In addition, the Office supports the operations of the Domestic Policy Council, the Economic Policy Council, and the President's Education Policy Advisory Committee.

Office of the United States Trade Representative

600 Seventeenth Street NW., Washington, DC 20506
Phone, 202–395–3230

United States Trade Representative	CARLA A. HILLS
Chief of Staff and Counselor	GARY EDSON
Deputy U.S. Trade Representatives	JULIUS L. KATZ
	S. LINN WILLIAMS

Deputy U.S. Trade Representative—Geneva	RUFUS YERXA
General Counsel	JOSHUA BOLTEN
Principal Deputy General Counsel and Assistant U.S. Trade Representative for Dispute Resolution	A. JANE BRADLEY
Deputy General Counsel	DANIEL M. PRICE
Chief Textile Negotiator	RON SORINI
Assistant U.S. Trade Representative for Public Affairs	TORIE CLARKE
Assistant U.S. Trade Representative for Congressional Affairs	MARY TINSLEY
Assistant U.S. Trade Representative for Canada and Mexico	CHARLES E. ROH, JR.
Executive Director Trade Policy Coordination	DAVID WEISS
Assistant U.S. Trade Representative for Europe and the Mediterranean	PETER F. ALLGEIER
Assistant U.S. Trade Representative for Latin America, Caribbean and Africa	JAMES M. MURPHY, JR.
Assistant U.S. Trade Representative for Japan and China	JOSEPH A. MASSEY
Assistant U.S. Trade Representative for Asia and the Pacific	SANDY KRISTOFF
Assistant U.S. Trade Representative for Multilateral Trade Negotiations	WARREN LAVOREL
Assistant U.S. Trade Representative for GATT Affairs	W. DOUGLAS NEWKIRK
Assistant U.S. Trade Representative for Industry	DONALD PHILLIPS
Assistant U.S. Trade Representative for Services, Investment, Intellectual Property, and Science and Technology	S. BRUCE WILSON
Assistant U.S. Trade Representative for Agriculture	SUZANNE EARLY
Assistant U.S. Trade Representative for Administration	DAVID BURNS

The United States Trade Representative is responsible for the direction of all trade negotiations of the United States and for the formulation of trade policy for the United States.

The Office of the United States Trade Representative was created as the Office of the Special Representative for Trade Negotiations by Executive Order 11075 of January 15, 1963. The Trade Act of 1974 (19 U.S.C. 2171) established the office as an agency of the Executive Office of the President charged with administering the trade agreements program under the Tariff Act of 1930 (19 U.S.C. 1654), the Trade Expansion Act of 1962 (19 U.S.C. 1801), and the Trade Act of 1974 (19 U.S.C. 2101). Other powers and responsibilities for coordinating trade policy were assigned to the Office by the Trade Act of 1974 and by the President in Executive Order 11846 of March 27, 1975, as amended.

Reorganization Plan No. 3 of 1979 (5 U.S.C. app.), implemented by Executive Order 12188 of January 4, 1980, charged the Office with responsibility for setting and administering overall trade policy. It also provides that the United States Trade Representative shall be chief representative of the United States for:

—all activities concerning the General Agreement on Tariffs and Trade;

—discussions, meetings, and negotiations in the Organization for Economic Cooperation and Development when such activities deal primarily with trade and commodity issues;

—negotiations in the United Nations Conference on Trade and Development and other multilateral institutions when such negotiations deal primarily with trade and commodity issues;

—other bilateral and multilateral negotiations when trade, including East-West trade, or commodities is the primary issue;

—negotiations under sections 704 and 734 of the Tariff Act of 1930 (19 U.S.C. 1671c and 1673c); and

—negotiations concerning direct investment incentives and disincentives and bilateral investment issues concerning barriers to investment.

The Omnibus Trade and Competitiveness Act of 1988 codified these prior authorities and added additional authority, including the implementation of section 301 actions (regarding enforcement of U.S. rights under international trade agreements).

The Office is headed by the United States Trade Representative, a Cabinet-level official with the rank of Ambassador, who is directly responsible to the President. There are three Deputy United States Trade Representatives, who also hold the rank of Ambassador, two located in Washington and one in Geneva. The Chief Textile Negotiator and the Uruguay round coordinator also hold the rank of Ambassador.

The United States Trade Representative serves as an *ex officio* member of the Boards of Directors of the Export-Import Bank and the Overseas Private Investment Corporation and serves on the National Advisory Council for International Monetary and Financial Policy.

For further information, contact the Office of Public Affairs, Office of the United States Trade Representative, 600 Seventeenth Street NW., Washington, DC 20506. Phone, 202-395-3230.

Council on Environmental Quality

722 Jackson Place NW., Washington, DC 20503
Phone, 202-395-5750

Chairman	MICHAEL R. DELAND
Special Assistant	DALE CURTIS
Members	(2 VACANCIES)
Chief of Staff	DAVID B. STRUHS
General Counsel	DINAH BEAR
Director, President's Commission on Environmental Quality	PATRICIA KEARNEY
Associate Director, International Law and Policy	PATRICIA BLISS-GUEST
Associate Director, Pollution Control and Prevention	SCOTT FARROW
Associate Director, Legislative Affairs	LARRY FLICK
Assocaite Director, Natural Resources	ROBIN O'MALLEY
Associate Director, Statistical Analysis and Reporting	FRANK SKIDMORE

The Council on Environmental Quality was established within the Executive Office of the President by the National Environmental Policy Act of 1969 (42 U.S.C. 4341 *et seq.*) to formulate and recommend national policies to promote the improvement of the quality of the environment. Additional responsibilities were provided by the Environmental Quality Improvement Act of 1970 (42 U.S.C. 4371 *et seq.*).

The Council consists of three members appointed by the President with the advice and consent of the Senate, and one of the members is designated by the President as Chairman.

The Council develops and recommends to the President national policies that further environmental quality; performs a continuing analysis of changes or trends in the national environment; reviews and appraises programs of the Federal Government to determine their contributions to sound environmental policy; conducts studies, research, and analyses relating to ecological systems and environmental quality; assists the President in the preparation of the annual environmental quality report to the Congress; and oversees implementation of the National Environmental Policy Act. The Chairman of the Council also serves as Chair of the President's Commission on Environmental Quality.

For further information, contact the Information Office, Council on Environmental Quality, 722 Jackson Place NW., Washington, DC 20503. Phone, 202–395–5750.

Office of Science and Technology Policy

Old Executive Office Building, Washington, DC 20506
Phone, 202–395–7347

Assistant to the President for Science and Technology and Director	D. ALLAN BROMLEY
Chief of Staff	KENNETH P. YALE
Executive Assistant	DAMAR HAWKINS
Associate Director for Life Sciences	D.A. HENDERSON
Associate Director for Industrial Technology	WILLIAM D. PHILLIPS
Associate Director for Policy and International Affairs	J. THOMAS RATCHFORD
Associate Director for Physical Sciences and Engineering	EUGENE WONG
Assistant Director for the Federal Coordinating Council for Science, Engineering and Technology	MARYANNE BACH
Assistant Director for Physical Sciences and Engineering	KARL ERB
Assistant Director for Health and Life Sciences	RACHEL LEVINSON
Assistant Director for the Environment	NANCY MAYNARD
Assistant Director for the Social Sciences	PIERRE PERROLLE
Assistant Director for National Security	MICHELLE VAN CLEAVE
Assistant Director for the President's Council of Advisors on Science and Technology	THOMAS J. WELCH
Assistant Director for Industrial Technology	(VACANCY)

The Office of Science and Technology Policy was established within the Executive Office of the President by the National Science and Technology Policy, Organization, and Priorities Act of 1976 (42 U.S.C. 6611).

The Office serves as a source of scientific, engineering, and technological analysis and judgment for the President with respect to major policies, plans, and programs of the Federal Government. In carrying out this mission, the act provides that the Office shall advise the President of scientific and technological considerations involved in areas of national concern, including the economy, national security, health, foreign relations, and the environment; evaluate the scale, quality, and effectiveness of the Federal effort in science and technology; provide advice and assistance to the President, the Office of Management and Budget, and Federal agencies throughout the Federal budget development process; and assist the President in providing leadership and coordination for the research and development programs of the Federal Government.

For further information, contact the Office of Science and Technology Policy, Old Executive Office Building, Washington, DC 20506. Phone, 202-395-7347.

Office of National Drug Control Policy

Executive Office of the President, Washington, DC 20500
Phone, 202-673-2520

Director	BOB MARTINEZ
Special Assistant to the Director	GRAHAM GILLETTE
Chief of Staff	JOHN P. WALTERS
National Security Affairs Liaison	THEODORE GRABOWSKY
Director, Office of Research	HENRY MARSDEN
Deputy Chief of Staff	(VACANCY)
General Counsel	TERENCE J. PELL
Director of Public Affairs	(VACANCY)
Executive Secretariat/White House Liaison	LISA GRIFFIN
Director of Congressional Affairs	JOSEPH MCHUGH
Director of Planning, Budget and Administration	BRUCE M. CARNES
Director, Planning Staff	GABRIELLE LUPO
Director, Budget and Legislative Review Staff	FRANK KALDER
Director, Administrative Staff	SARA T. BASS
Deputy Director for Supply Reduction	STANLEY E. MORRIS
Deputy Director for Demand Reduction	HERBERT D. KLEBER
Associate Director for State and Local Affairs	REGGIE B. WALTON

The Office of National Drug Control Policy coordinates Federal, State, and local efforts to control illegal drug abuse and devises national strategies to effectively carry out antidrug activities.

The Office of National Drug Control Policy was established by the National Narcotics Leadership Act of 1988 (21 U.S.C. 1501 *et seq.*), effective January 29, 1989.

The Office is headed by the Director of National Drug Control Policy, who is appointed by the President with the advice and consent of the Senate. The Director is assisted by the Deputy Director for Demand Reduction and the Deputy Director for Supply Reduction. The Bureau of State and Local Affairs is a separate division of the Office, headed by an Associate Director for National Drug Control Policy.

The Director of National Drug Control Policy is responsible for establishing policies, objectives, and priorities for the National Drug Control Program, and for annually promulgating a National Drug Control Strategy to be submitted to the Congress by the President. The Director advises the President regarding necessary changes in the organization, management, budgeting, and personnel allocation of Federal agencies involved in drug enforcement activities, and is also responsible for notifying Federal agencies if their policies are not in compliance with their responsibilities under the National Drug Control Strategy.

For further information, contact the Office of National Drug Control Policy, Executive Office of the President, Washington, DC 20500. Phone, 202-673-2520.

National Critical Materials Council

725 Seventeenth Street NW., Washington, DC 20506
Phone, 202-395-7200

Chairman	D. ALLAN BROMLEY
Executive Director	DAVID L. HUBER, *Acting*

The National Critical Materials Council ensures that sufficient supplies of strategic minerals and materials are maintained for national security, economic well-being, and industrial productivity.

The National Critical Materials Council was established by the National Critical Materials Act of 1984 (30 U.S.C. 1801 *et seq.*).

The Council is composed of three members, each of whom is designated by the President. Designees who are not already Senate-confirmed Government officials must be appointed with the advice and consent of the Senate. The length of each member's term is determined by the President.

The Council advises the President on policies related to strategic and critical materials and reviews Federal programs, activities, and budget priorities with respect to these policies. The Council also monitors domestic and foreign industry trends and requirements in order to ensure that national materials policies reflect the latest developments in technology and resource availability.

For further information, contact the National Critical Materials Council, 725 Seventeenth Street NW., Washington, DC 20506. Phone, 202-395-7200.

Office of Administration

725 Seventeenth Street NW., Washington, DC 20503
Phone, 202-395-6963

Deputy Assistant to the President for Management and Director	PAUL W. BATEMAN
Special Assistant to the President and Deputy Director	HECTOR F. IRASTORZA, JR.
Director, Administrative Operations Division	(VACANCY)
Director, Facilities Management Division	LEWIS M. PEARSON
Director, Financial Management Division	RON RASMUSSEN

Director, Information Resources Management Division	(VACANCY)
Director, Library and Information Services Division	MARY HESTER ANTON
Director, Personnel Management Division	PHILLIP D. LARSEN
Executive Secretary	JONATHAN H. MERTZ
General Counsel	BRUCE L. OVERTON

The Office of Administration was established within the Executive Office of the President by Reorganization Plan No. 1 of 1977 (5 U.S.C. app.). The Office was activated, effective December 4, 1977, by Executive Order 12028 of December 12, 1977.

The Office of Administration, headed by the Director, provides administrative support services to all units within the Executive Office of the President. The services provided include information, personnel, and financial management; data processing; library services; records maintenance; and general office operations, such as mail, messenger, printing, procurement, and supply services.

For further information, contact the Executive Secretary, Office of Administration, Washington, DC 20503. Phone, 202–395–6963.

OFFICE OF THE VICE PRESIDENT OF THE UNITED STATES

Old Executive Office Building, Washington, DC 20501
Phone, 202–456–2326

THE VICE PRESIDENT	DAN QUAYLE
Chief of Staff to the Vice President	WILLIAM KRISTOL
Assistant to the Vice President and Deputy Chief of Staff and Executive Director of the Council on Competitiveness	AL HUBBARD
Assistant to the Vice President for National Security Affairs	KARL JACKSON
Assistant to the Vice President and Deputy Assistant for National Security Affairs	JON D. GLASSMAN
Assistant to the Vice President and Press Secretary	DAVID C. BECKWITH
Counsel to the Vice President	JOHN L. HOWARD
Assistant to the Vice President and Chief of Staff for Mrs. Quayle	MARGUERITE SULLIVAN
Assistant to the Vice President for Legislative Affairs	WILLIAM J. GRIBBIN
Assistant to the Vice President for Domestic Policy and Deputy Director of the Council on Competitiveness	DAVID MCINTOSH
Assistant to the Vice President for Scheduling and Public Liaison	CECILE KREMER
Assistant to the Vice President for Advance and Special Projects	TOM PERNICE

Deputy Assistant to the Vice President for Political Affairs	JIM PITTS
Deputy Assistant to the Vice President and Director of Administration	LES J. NOVITSKY
Personal Aide to the Vice President	DAN MURPHY
Director of Constituent Affairs	LORETTA COUPLAND
Special Assistant to the Vice President and Staff Secretary	MYRNA DUGAN

Article II, section I, of the Constitution provides that the President "shall hold his Office during the Term of four Years * * * together with the Vice President * * *." In addition to his role as President of the Senate, the Vice President is empowered to succeed to the Presidency, pursuant to Article II and the 20th and 25th amendments to the Constitution.

The executive functions of the Vice President include participation in Cabinet meetings and, by statute, membership on the National Security Council and the Board of Regents of the Smithsonian Institution.

Departments

DEPARTMENT OF AGRICULTURE

Fourteenth Street and Independence Avenue SW., Washington, DC 20250
Phone, 202–447–2791

SECRETARY OF AGRICULTURE	EDWARD R. MADIGAN
Deputy Secretary	ANN M. VENEMAN
Associate Deputy Secretary	CHARLES R. HILTY
Chief of Staff	WILLIAM O'CONNER
Executive Assistants to the Secretary	SALLY I. BUIKEMA
	DIANE R. LIESMAN
	WILLIAM O'CONNER
	JACQUELINE A. PARKE
General Counsel	ALAN C. RAUL
Deputy General Counsel	J. ROBERT FRANKS
Inspector General	LEON SNEAD
Deputy Inspector General	CHARLES R. GILLUM
Assistant Inspector General, Policy Development and Resource Management	PAULA F. HAYES
Assistant Inspector General, Audit	JAMES R. EBBITT
Assistant Inspector General, Investigations	CRAIG L. BEAUCHAMP
Director, Office of Budget and Program Analysis	STEPHEN B. DEWHURST
Associate Director for Budget, Legislation, and Program Review	LAWRENCE WACHS
Associate Director for Resource Programs and Special Studies	JOHN FEDKIW
Director, Office of Public Affairs and Press Secretary	KELLY M. SHIPP
Deputy Directors	CAMERON D. WOODS
	ALBERT MARUGGI
Director, Intergovernmental Affairs	LARRY WERRIES
Director, Press and Media Relations	ERIC RUFF
Director, Public Liaison	CHRIS GUNDERSON
Director, Publishing and Visual Communication	SUSAN FERTIG-DYKS
Under Secretary, International Affairs and Commodity Programs	RICHARD T. CROWDER
Deputy Under Secretaries	JOHN B. CAMPBELL
	ANN M. VENEMAN
Administrator, Agricultural Stabilization and Conservation Service	KEITH D. BJERKE
Associate Administrator	JOHN A. STEVENSON

Deputy Administrator for Management	SARITA G. SCHOTTA
President, Commodity Credit Corporation	RICHARD T. CROWDER
Executive Vice President	KEITH D. BJERKE
Secretary	JAMES V. HANSEN
Deputy Secretary	ALBERT REAGAN
Assistant Secretary	BRENDA B. KING
Controller	ANGELENA V. BRACHT
Treasurer	JAMES R. LITTLE
Chief Accountant	DWIGHT T. TAYMAN
Administrator, Foreign Agricultural Service	DUANE ACKER
Associate Administrator	STEPHEN CENSKY
Associate Administrator and General Sales Manager	F. PAUL DICKERSON, JR.
Assistant Administrator, Management	EARL C. HADLOCK
Administrator, Office of International Cooperation and Development	(VACANCY)
Associate Administrator	STEPHEN N. ABRAMS
Under Secretary, Small Community and Rural Development	ROLAND R. VAUTOUR
Deputy Under Secretary	JONATHAN I. KISLAK
Assistant Under Secretary	WALTER E. HILL
Administrator, Farmers Home Administration	LAVERNE G. AUSMAN
Associate Administrator	DAVID T. CHEN
Deputy Administrator, Management	(VACANCY)
Manager, Federal Crop Insurance Corporation	JAMES E. CASON
Deputy Manager	JANE A. WITTMEYER
Administrator, Rural Electrification Administration	GARY C. BYRNE
Deputy Administrator for Program Operations	GEORGE E. PRATT
Assistant Administrator for Management	BLAINE D. STOCKTON
Assistant Secretary for Administration	ADIS M. VILA
Deputy Assistant Secretary	ELIZABETH BOARD
Chairperson, Board of Contract Appeals	EDWARD HOURY
Judicial Officer	DONALD A. CAMPBELL
Chief Judge, Office of Administrative Law Judges	VICTOR W. PALMER
Director, Office of Advocacy and Enterprise	JO ANN C. JENKINS
Director, Office of Finance and Management	LARRY WILSON
Director, Office of Information Resources Management	JOHN L. OKAY, *Acting*
Director, Office of Operations	MARILYN WAGNER, *Acting*
Director, Office of Personnel	LARRY B. SLAGLE
Assistant Secretary for Congressional Relations	FRANKLIN E. BAILEY
Deputy Assistant Secretary	GARY K. MADSON
Assistant Secretary for Economics	BRUCE L. GARDNER
Deputy Assistant Secretary	DANIEL A. SUMNER
Director, Economic Analysis Staff	KEITH J. COLLINS
Director, Economic Management Staff	ALLAN S. JOHNSON
Administrator, Economic Research Service	JOHN E. LEE, JR.
Associate Administrator	(VACANCY)
Administrator, National Agricultural Statistics Service	CHARLES E. CAUDILL
Deputy Administrator	DONALD M. BAY

Director, Office of Energy	Roger Conway
Chairperson, World Agricultural Outlook Board	James R. Donald
Deputy Chairperson	Gerald A. Bange
Assistant Secretary for Food and Consumer Services	Catherine A. Bertini
Deputy Assistant Secretary	(vacancy)
Administrator, Food and Nutrition Service	Betty Jo Nelsen
Associate Administrator	George A. Braley
Deputy Administrator, Management	Joseph J. Leo
Administrator, Human Nutrition Information Service	Sue Ann Ritchko
Director, Office of the Consumer Advisor	Ann C. Chadwick
Assistant Secretary for Marketing and Inspection Services	Jo Ann D. Smith
Deputy Assistant Secretary	John E. Frydenlund
Administrator, Agricultural Cooperative Service	Randall E. Torgerson
Deputy Administrator	James E. Haskell
Administrator, Agricultural Marketing Service	Daniel D. Haley
Deputy Administrator for Management	Linda P. Massaro
Administrator, Animal and Plant Health Inspection Service	James W. Glosser
Associate Administrator	Robert Melland
Deputy Administrator for Management	Robert L. Buchanan
Administrator, Federal Grain Inspection Service	John C. Foltz
Deputy Administrator	David R. Galliart
Administrator, Food Safety and Inspection Service	Lester M. Crawford
Associate Administrator	Ronald J. Prucha
Deputy Administrator for Administrative Management	William J. Hudnall
Administrator, Packers and Stockyards Administration	Virgil M. Rosendale
Deputy Administrator	Calvin W. Watkins
Assistant Secretary for Natural Resources and Environment	James R. Moseley
Deputy Assistant Secretary	John H. Beuter
Chief, Forest Service	F. Dale Robertson
Associate Chief	George M. Leonard
Deputy Chief for Administration	(vacancy)
Chief, Soil Conservation Service	William T. Richards
Associate Chief	R. Mack Gray
Deputy Chief for Administration	William L. Rice
Assistant Secretary for Science and Education	Charles E. Hess
Deputy Assistant Secretary	Harry C. Mussman
Administrator, Agricultural Research Service	Ronald D. Plowman
Associate Administrator	Mary E. Carter
Administrator, Cooperative State Research Service	John P. Jordan
Associate Administrator	Claire I. Harris
Administrator, Extension Service	Myron D. Johnsrud
Associate Administrator	Mitchell Geasler

Director, National Agricultural Library	JOSEPH D. HOWARD
Associate Director	MARIA PISA

[For the Department of Agriculture statement of organization, see the *Code of Federal Regulations,* Title 7, Part 2]

The Department of Agriculture benefits all Americans daily. It works to improve and maintain farm income and to develop and expand markets abroad for agricultural products. The Department helps to curb and to cure poverty, hunger, and malnutrition. It works to enhance the environment and to maintain our production capacity by helping landowners protect the soil, water, forests, and other natural resources. Rural development, credit, and conservation programs are key resources for carrying out national growth policies. Department research findings directly or indirectly benefit all Americans. The Department, through inspection and grading services, safeguards and ensures standards of quality in the daily food supply.

The Department of Agriculture (USDA) was created by act of May 15, 1862 (7 U.S.C. 2201), and was administered by a Commissioner of Agriculture until 1889 (5 U.S.C. 511, 514, 516). By act of February 9, 1889 (7 U.S.C. 2202, 2208, 2212), the powers and duties of the Department were enlarged. The Department was made the eighth executive department in the Federal Government, and the Commissioner became the Secretary of Agriculture.

Staff Offices

Administration The Assistant Secretary for Administration serves as the principal adviser to the Secretary on all administrative management and related matters. Five departmental staff offices report to the Assistant Secretary and assist in providing staff support to top policy officials and program agencies to ensure the efficient and effective management and operation of the Department. These are the Office of Personnel, the Office of Finance and Management, the Office of Information Resources Management, the Office of Advocacy and Enterprise, and the Office of Operations. These offices coordinate the Department's personnel management program; equal opportunity and civil rights activities; safety and health activities; management improvement programs; accounting, fiscal, and financial activities; automated data processing administration; procurement and contracts; and management of real and personal property.

In addition, two quasi-judicial agencies, the Office of Administrative Law Judges and the Board of Contract Appeals, report to the Assistant Secretary. Both organizations operate autonomously when adjudicating cases and deciding contract disputes.

The Assistant Secretary for Administration serves as the Department's Director of Equal Employment Opportunity and oversees all equal opportunity and civil rights programs within USDA.

General Counsel The General Counsel is the chief law officer of the Department and is responsible for providing legal services for all programs, operations, and activities of the Department. The functions of the General Counsel's Office are performed in the Washington Headquarters, and in 5 regional and 17 branch offices. The headquarters legal staff is divided into four sections; each directed by an Associate General Counsel, and include: Regulatory and Marketing; International Affairs, Commodity and Food Assistance Programs; Community Development and Natural Resources; and Legislation, Litigation, Research and Operations. In general, the regional and branch offices provide legal services relating to the activities of the Agricultural Stabilization and Conservation Service, the Commodity Credit Corporation, the

DEPARTMENT OF AGRICULTURE

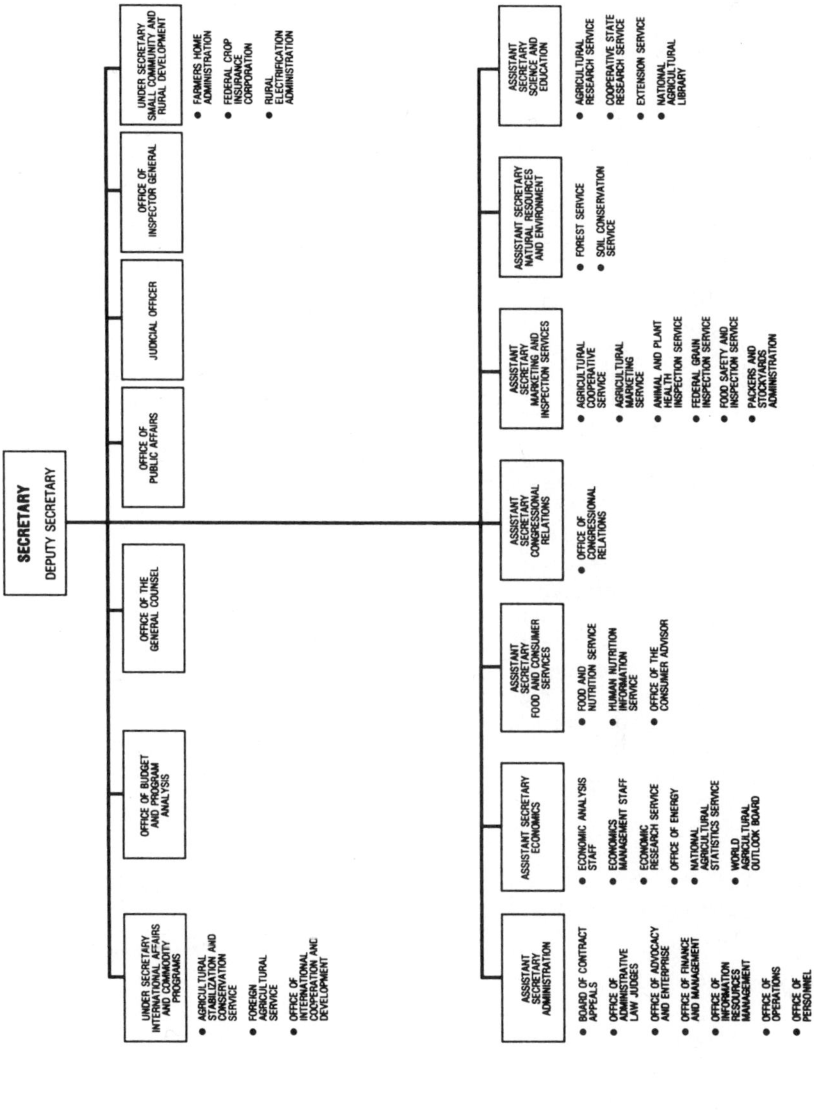

Farmers Home Administration, the Federal Crop Insurance Corporation, the Forest Service, the Soil Conservation Service, and the Food and Nutrition Service.

The Office also provides a full range of legal services to the Department's agencies, offices, and corporations. These legal services include: rendering opinions on legal questions; preparing or reviewing rules and regulations; preparing or interpreting contracts, mortgages, leases, deeds, and other documents; representing departmental agencies in litigation debt collection programs; processing applications for patents or inventions by the Department's employees; representing departmental agencies in State water rights adjudication; considering and determining claims by and against the United States arising out of the Department's activities; assisting the Department of Justice in the preparation and trial of cases involving the Department; and representing the Secretary of Agriculture and the Commodity Credit Corporation before the Interstate Commerce Commission, the Federal Maritime Commission, and the International Trade Commission.

Inspector General The Office of the Inspector General was established administratively by the Secretary of Agriculture in 1962. The Inspector General Act of 1978 (5 U.S.C. app.) created statutory inspectors general in the Department of Agriculture and a number of other Federal executive departments and independent agencies. The Inspector General conducts and supervises all audits and investigations relating to the programs and operations of the Department. The Office also is responsible for coordinating, conducting, or supervising all other activities carried out by the Department for the purpose of promoting program economy and efficiency and preventing and detecting fraud. The investigation of employee complaints, physical security of the Secretary, review of legislation and regulations for their impact on program efficiency and susceptibility to abuse, and relations with governmental and nongovernmental units concerning program efficiency and prevention of fraud also are responsibilities of the Office. The Office is headed by an Inspector General who is appointed by the President and confirmed by the Senate.

For further information, call 202–447–8001.

Budget and Program Analysis The Office of Budget and Program Analysis coordinates the preparation of departmental budget estimates and legislative reports; administers systems for the management and control of funds; provides policy, program, and budgetary analysis of USDA proposals; and provides staff assistance to USDA agencies in meeting their responsibilities for the development and review of regulations.

Office of Public Affairs The Office of Public Affairs is the communication pulse of USDA, providing services to all of the Department's 43 agencies to ensure that the communications objectives of the entire Department are achieved. The Director of Public Affairs orchestrates the activities of four offices: Public Liaison, Intergovernmental Affairs, Resources Management, and Information Technology Management; and oversees seven divisions. The Director also coordinates major events for the Secretary and the Department, and communicates USDA's policy to the media, America's farmers, commodity organizations, agribusiness, and consumers. In addition, the Office acts as a liaison with State departments of agriculture, local governmental agencies, and Indian tribes.

Judicial Officer The Judicial Officer serves as the final deciding officer, in the place of the Secretary, in regulatory proceedings and appeals of a quasi-judicial nature where a hearing is statutorily required.

Office of the Assistant Secretary for Congressional Relations The Office establishes policy and procedures for the conduct of relations with Congress. It serves as the principal point of departmental contact with the Congress and provides guidance to the Secretary and all departmental staff on congressional issues.

Small Community and Rural Development

Farmers Home Administration

[For the Farmers Home Administration statement of organization, see the *Code of Federal Regulations,* Title 7, Part 2003]

The Farmers Home Administration, an agency within the Department of Agriculture, provides credit for those in rural America who are unable to get credit from other sources at reasonable rates and terms.

The Administration operates principally under the Consolidated Farm and Rural Development Act (7 U.S.C. 1921) and title V of the Housing Act of 1949 (42 U.S.C. 1471).

Applications for loans are made at the agency's 2,200 local county and district offices, generally located in county seats. A county or area committee of three individuals, at least two of whom are farmers, certifies or recommends as to eligibility of individual farm loan applicants and reviews borrowers' progress. The Administration makes loans from three revolving funds: the Agricultural Credit Insurance Fund, the Rural Housing Insurance Fund, and the Rural Development Insurance Fund.

The Administration provides financial and management assistance through the following types of loans:

Operating Loans Loans are made to farmers who operate family-size farms and who cannot get the credit they need from conventional sources. They may be farming as individuals, joint operators, cooperatives, or corporations. Operating loan funds may be used to acquire needed resources, to make improved use of their land and labor resources, and to make adjustments necessary for successful farming and nonfarm enterprises. Funds may be advanced to pay for equipment, livestock, feed, seed, fertilizer, other farm and home operating needs; refinance chattel debts; provide operating credit to fish farmers; carry out forestry purposes; and develop income-producing, nonfarm enterprises.

For loans made directly by the Administration, the interest rate is set periodically, based on the Federal Government's cost of borrowing. For loans made by other lenders and guaranteed by the Administration, the interest rate is negotiated between the lender and the borrower. The limit on farm operating loans made by the Administration is $200,000, and on guaranteed loans the limit is $400,000. Loans may be repaid over 1 to 7 years. Other reliable agricultural credit sources are encouraged to support as much of the essential needs of loan applicants as possible with the balance supplied from operating loan funds of the agency. Operating loan borrowers are expected to refinance their operating loans and return to conventional credit when able to do so.

Youth Project Loans The Administration makes loans to individual rural residents between the ages of 10 and 21 to establish and operate income-producing enterprises of modest size, either on the farm or in other locations. The interest rate is determined by formula periodically. Repayment terms depend upon the type of project for which the loan is made. This program is designed to help 4–H Clubs, Future Farmers of America, and other youth group members finance their agricultural or nonagricultural projects.

Emergency Loans Emergency loans are made to eligible farmers, ranchers, and aquaculture operators for losses arising from natural disasters. In order to be eligible to apply for an emergency loan, farmers must carry multiperil crop insurance if it is available. Only family-size farms qualify for these loans.

Each loan is scheduled for repayment as rapidly as feasible, in annual installments, consistent with the borrower's reasonable ability to pay. The schedule varies according to the purpose of the loan.

The interest rate for emergency loans offsetting actual losses is 4.5 percent. Loans are limited to $500,000 or 80 percent of actual losses, less any insurance protection.

Farm Ownership Loans These loans enable farmers and ranchers to buy farms and owners of inadequate or underimproved farms to enlarge or develop farms. Loans are limited to farms that are not larger than family-size farms. Loans may include funds to construct or repair farm homes and service buildings and facilities; improve land; develop water, forestry, and fish farming resources; establish nonfarm enterprises to supplement farm income; and refinance debts.

Repayment is scheduled according to the borrower's ability to repay, but the maximum term is 40 years. The interest rate is set periodically, based on the cost of Government borrowing. The maximum for insured loans is $200,000 and for guaranteed loans is $300,000. The loan may not exceed the market value of the farm or other security.

Loans to Limited-Resource Farmers The Administration makes loans to help low-income farmers and ranchers improve their farming and earn a better living. These loans are made on easier terms than ordinary farm loans and are intended to give the limited-resource farmer a chance to become more successful in farming.

Limited-resource farmers are owners or tenants of small farms yielding low production and low income due to factors such as lack of land, equipment, or opportunity to get necessary financing, or limited education in farming or management.

Loans to limited-resource farmers may be made for farm purchases or operating expenses. Loans for the purchase of farm real estate are made at lower interest rates. Production loans also are made at lower interest rates and evaluated every 2 years. Repayment terms vary according to the purposes of the loan. While the needs of limited-resource farmers are usually well below its limits, the agency can make a real estate loan and a production loan of up to $200,000 under this program. Farm Ownership and Operating Loan Funds are targeted to members of socially disadvantaged groups.

Soil and Water Conservation Loans Loans are made to owners or operators of farms and ranches, including farming partnerships and domestic corporations to assist them in developing, conserving, and making proper use of their land and other resources. Loans are repayable within 40 years. The interest rate for insured loans is determined by the Secretary of Agriculture and does not exceed the cost of money to the Government, plus up to 1 percent additional. Loans may be made by the Administration or by other lenders with an agency guarantee. Guaranteed loans bear an interest rate negotiated by the lender and the borrower.

Loans to Indian Tribes Loans to Indian tribes and tribal corporations are made for the acquisition of lands, including those within the reservation or community. Loans are made for up to 40 years. The interest rate is set periodically, based on the cost of Government borrowing.

Rural Housing Loans Section 502 loans are made to low-income families for housing in rural areas. Loans can be made to build, purchase, repair, and refinance homes. The maximum term can be 38 years, and the loan may be for 100 percent of the appraised value. The basic interest rate is determined periodically, based on the cost of money. Borrowers may qualify for annual subsidy on the loan, which can reduce the interest rate to as low as 1 percent. Cosigners on promissory notes may be permitted for applicants who are deficient in repayment ability.

Builders may obtain from the Administration "conditional commitments" that are assurances to a builder or seller that if their houses meet agency lending requirements, then the agency may make loans to qualified applicants to buy the houses.

An owner-occupant may obtain a section 504 loan of up to $15,000, or, in the case of senior citizens, a grant of up to $5,000 to remove hazards to the health and safety of the family. These loans, available to very low-income families, are made at 1 percent interest.

Loans are made to private, nonprofit corporations, consumer cooperatives, State or local public agencies, and individuals or organizations operating on a profit or limited profit basis to provide rental or cooperative housing in rural areas for persons of low and moderate income. Maximum term is 50 years. Rental assistance may be available to help defray rent paid by low-income families.

Loans and grants are authorized for housing for farm laborers.

Loans repayable in 2 years are authorized to nonprofit organizations to purchase and develop land for resale as homesites for persons of low-to-moderate income.

Watershed Protection and Flood Prevention Loans These loans enable local organizations approved by the Soil Conservation Service to finance projects that protect and develop land and water resources in small watersheds.

Loans may be repaid over 50 years at an interest rate based on the average rate paid by the U.S. Treasury on obligations of similar maturity. Total loans outstanding on any one watershed project may not exceed $10 million. Authority for these loans is contained in section 8 of the Watershed Protection and Flood Prevention Act of 1964 (16 U.S.C. 1006a).

Resource Conservation and Development Loans These loans enable sponsors of projects approved for operation by the Soil Conservation Service to finance projects for natural resource conservation and development in designated areas. Such loans may be made for periods up to 30 years with repayment of principal and interest deferred up to 5 years, if necessary. Authority for these loans is contained in section 32(e) of the Bankhead-Jones Farm Tenant Act (7 U.S.C. 1011(e)) and subtitle A of the Consolidated Farm and Rural Development Act (7 U.S.C. 1921).

Community Programs Loans Direct and guarantee loans are authorized to public and quasi-public bodies, nonprofit associations, and certain Indian tribes for essential community facilities, such as water and waste disposal systems, fire and rescue, and health care. Necessary related equipment may also be purchased.

The interest rate is set periodically for direct loans and is based on yields of municipal bonds. Guarantee loans bear an interest rate negotiated by the lender and the borrower.

Water and waste disposal projects may serve residents of open country and rural towns of not more than 10,000 population. Community facility loans may be made in towns of up to 20,000.

Grants may be made for up to 75 percent of the cost for water and waste disposal projects when necessary to bring user costs to a reasonable level.

Business and Industry Loans The Administration is authorized to make or guarantee loans to public, private, or cooperative associations organized for profit or nonprofit; to certain Indian tribes or tribal groups; or to individuals for the purpose of improving, developing, or financing business, industry, and employment and improving the economic and environmental climate in rural communities.

The purpose is to develop business enterprises in rural areas and cities of less than 50,000 population, with priority to applications for projects in open country, rural communities and towns of 25,000 and smaller.

Private lenders initiate, process, close, service, and supervise guaranteed loans; the Farmers Home Administration guarantees a lender against loss on up to 90 percent of principal and interest. Interest rates are determined between borrower and lender.

Intermediary Relending Program Loans Loans are made to nonprofit corporations, public agencies, Indian tribes, or cooperatives to establish revolving loan funds from which the borrower, in turn, makes loans to finance businesses or community development projects. Entities that receive loans from FmHA are referred to as "intermediaries" and entities that receive loans from intermediaries are referred to as "ultimate recipients." Loans to intermediaries may be for up to $3,000,000, to be repaid over up to 30 years, at 1 percent interest. Loans to ultimate recipients must not exceed $150,000. The term and interest rate to ultimate recipients are set by the intermediary. Ultimate recipients must not be located in a city with a population of 25,000 or more.

For further information, contact the Information Staff, Farmers Home Administration, Department of Agriculture, Washington, DC 20250. Phone, 202-447-4323.

Rural Electrification Administration

[For the Rural Electrification Administration statement of organization, see the *Code of Federal Regulations,* Title 7, Part 1700]

The Rural Electrification Administration (REA) is a credit agency of the U.S. Department of Agriculture that assists rural electric and telephone utilities in obtaining financing. This assistance may include insured loans, agency guarantees of loans made by others, and agency approval of security arrangements that permit agency borrowers to obtain financing from other lenders without a guarantee.

Approximately 1,000 rural electric and approximately 1,000 rural telephone utilities in 47 States, Puerto Rico, the Virgin Islands, Guam, the Republic of the Marshall Islands, the Northern Mariana Islands, and the Federated States of Micronesia have received REA loans, loan guarantees, or other assistance to construct, expand, and improve rural electric and telephone systems.

The Administration was established by Executive Order 7037 of May 11, 1935, as part of a general program of unemployment relief. It was given statutory authority by the Rural Electrification Act of 1936, as amended (7 U.S.C. 901–950b). Its Administrator is appointed by the President with the advice and consent of the Senate.

Electric Program The Rural Electrification Act of 1936, as amended (7 U.S.C. 901–950b), established REA as a lending agency with responsibility for developing a program for rural electrification.

The act requires that preference be given to nonprofit and cooperative associations and to public bodies. With the agency's assistance, rural electric utilities have obtained financing to construct electric generating plants and transmission and distribution lines to provide initial and continued adequate electric service to persons in rural areas.

Telephone Program In 1949 REA was authorized to make loans to provide telephone service in rural areas. Congress directed that the rural telephone program be conducted to "assure the availability of adequate telephone service to the widest practicable number of rural users of such service." About 75 percent of the telephone systems financed by the agency are commercial companies, and about 25 percent are subscriber-owned cooperatives.

Loans Loans are made from the Rural Electrification and Telephone Revolving Fund, which was established in 1973 in the U.S. Treasury. By law, REA loans are made at a 5-percent interest rate. The Administrator may approve loans at interest rates as low as 2 percent in cases of extreme hardship.

Since 1973 the Administration has advanced more loan funds to its borrowers than it has received in payments on loans. The Fund obtains the additional funds necessary to meet its interest expenses and loan advances from the U.S. Treasury by direct borrowing and sale of Certificates of Beneficial Ownership to the Federal Financing Bank (FFB), which is located in the Treasury. Interest paid by the agency on funds obtained from the Treasury is several points higher than the agency is permitted to charge borrowers.

Loan Guarantees The Administration also guarantees loans made by other lenders, mainly for large-scale electric and telephone facilities. Guarantees are considered if such loans could have been made by the agency under the Rural Electrification Act, and may be obtained from any legally organized lending agency qualified to make, hold, and service the loan. All policies and procedures of the agency are applicable to a guaranteed loan.

In 1974 the Agency entered into an agreement with FFB, whereby the Bank agreed to purchase obligations guaranteed by the Administrator. The Administration acts as the agent for the Bank and all borrower dealings are with the agency. In 1981 the Rural Electrification Act was amended to require the Bank to make loans under an agency guarantee if requested to do so by a borrower with such a guarantee. Most guaranteed loans received by agency borrowers are made by the Bank.

Supplemental Financing A 1973 amendment of the Rural Electrification Act states that it is the policy of Congress "...that rural electric and telephone systems should be encouraged and assisted in developing their resources and ability to achieve the financial strength needed to enable them to satisfy their credit needs from their own financial organizations and other sources at reasonable rates and terms consistent with the loan applicant's ability to pay and achievement of the act's objectives."

When REA approves electric loans, it requires most borrowers to obtain 30 percent of their loan needs from nonagency sources without an agency guarantee. These nonagency sources include the National Rural Utilities Cooperative Finance Corporation, which is owned by electric cooperatives and the Bank for Cooperatives.

Telephone borrowers obtain supplemental financing from the Rural Telephone Bank (RTB), an agency of the United States that was established in 1971. Loans are made to telephone systems able to meet RTB's requirements. Bank loans are made for the same purposes as loans made by REA but bear interest at a rate consistent with the Bank's cost of money. Effective in fiscal year 1988, the budget act changed the method of determining Bank interest rates.

The Rural Telephone Bank is managed by a 13-member board of directors. The Administrator serves as Governor of the Bank until conversion to private ownership, control, and operation. This will take place when 51 percent of the Class A stock issued to the United States and outstanding at any time after September 30, 1995, has been fully redeemed and retired. The Bank board holds at least four regularly scheduled meetings a year. Activities of RTB are carried out by REA employees and the Office of the General Counsel of the U.S. Department of Agriculture.

Rural Development Effective in fiscal year 1988, the Omnibus Budget Reconciliation Act gave rural electric distribution systems an option to invest their general funds, in an amount up to 15 percent of their total plant value, in rural development and other non-utility projects, without obtaining approval of the Administrator. In addition, it established a Rural Development Program to provide interest-free loans and grants to electric and telephone borrowers for the promotion of rural economic development and job creation projects.

For further information, contact the Public Information Office, Rural Electrification Administration, Department of Agriculture, Washington, DC 20250. Phone, 202-382-1255.

Federal Crop Insurance Corporation

[For the Federal Crop Insurance Corporation statement of organization, see the *Federal Register* of June 10, 1976, 41 FR 23443]

The Federal Crop Insurance Corporation (FCIC) was created within the Department of Agriculture under the Federal Crop Insurance Act, as amended (7 U.S.C. 1501). The primary goal of FCIC is to improve the economic stability of agriculture through a sound system of crop insurance. The Federal Crop Insurance Act of 1980 lifted many limitations of the crop insurance program, which expanded the availability of crop insurance and the number of insurable crops.

The Food, Agriculture, Conservation, and Trade Act of 1990 (7 U.S.C. 1421 note) strengthened the actuarial foundation of the program. An insurance program is considered actuarially sound when total premiums equal or exceed anticipated losses. Further revisions allowed field offices of the Agricultural Stabilization and Conservation Service (ASCS) to distribute material and lists of qualified agencies offering crop insurance.

All capital stock of FCIC is owned by the United States. Administrative and other costs are financed by annual appropriations. The Corporation's management is vested in a Board of Directors, subject to the general supervision of the Secretary of Agriculture. A Manager and Deputy Manager, appointed by the Secretary, are responsible for coordinating the day-to-day operations of FCIC and for providing policy leadership.

The Federal Crop Insurance Act of 1980 requires FCIC to contract, as much as possible, with private companies and encourage insurance sales through licensed agents and brokers. As a result, FCIC's delivery system has been shifted largely to the private sector, which offers insurance through two sales mechanisms. In the first, sales and service agencies provide insurance of Federal papers. Loss adjustment, claims functions, and training are carried out by FCIC, which also supervises marketing services and quality control. The second mechanism uses reinsured companies that offer crop insurance under private brand names and provide marketing, distribution, servicing, training, quality control, premium collection, and adjustment functions. The Corporation reinsures these companies against extraordinary operational and actuarial losses.

Federal crop insurance covers unavoidable production losses due to adverse weather conditions, including drought, excessive rain, hail, wind, hurricanes, tornadoes, and lightning. It also covers unavoidable losses due to insect infestation, plant disease, floods, fires, and earthquakes. It is available in 3,026 counties on 51 crops; however, not every crop is insurable in every county. Federal crop insurance does not cover losses due to neglect, poor farming practices, or theft; nor does it cover financial losses resulting from low farm product prices.

Participation in the program is voluntary, and the producer must pay a premium for the coverage. Producers select from three coverage levels (50, 65, or 75 percent) and from three price elections on each commodity. Premium rates vary on the basis of productivity and risk of loss. The premium is generally not collected until harvest, can be deducted from the indemnity, and is fully tax deductible.

Field Service Offices—Federal Crop Insurance Corporation

Office	Address	Director	Telephone
BILLINGS, MT—Montana, Wyoming	Suite 108, 2110 Overland Ave., Billings, MT 59102	E. Burdette Lortz	406-657-6196
BISMARCK, ND—North Dakota, South Dakota	309 N. Mandan St., Bismarck, ND 58501	Donald Welken	701-250-4271
COLLEGE STATION, TX—New Mexico, Oklahoma, Texas	Suite 240, 7607 E. Mark Dr., College Station, TX 77840	F.W. Crouch, Jr.	409-260-9391
COLUMBIA, SC—Florida, Georgia, South Carolina	Rm. 1222, 1835 Assembly St., Columbia, SC 29201	J. Porter Bull	803-765-5766
DES MOINES, IA—Iowa, Missouri	Rm. 509, 210 Walnut St., Des Moines, IA 50309	Roberta E. Waggoner	515-284-4316
HARRISBURG, PA—Connecticut, Delaware, Maine, Maryland, Massachusetts, New Hampshire, New Jersey, New York, Pennsylvania, Rhode Island, Vermont	1 Credit Union Pl., Harrisburg, PA 17110	John J. Gartside	717-782-4803
INDIANAPOLIS, IN—Indiana, Michigan, Ohio	Suite B, 5969 Lakeside Blvd., Indianapolis, IN 46278	Joan Sutter, *Acting*	317-290-3050
JACKSON, MS—Alabama, Arkansas, Louisiana, Mississippi	Suite 1201, 100 W. Capitol, Jackson, MS 39269	Mitchell T. Crouther	601-965-4328
LINCOLN, NE—Nebraska	Rm. 259, 100 Centennial Mall, Lincoln, NE 68508	Richard E. Moore	402-471-5531
MANHATTAN, KS—Colorado, Kansas	2601 Anderson Ave., Manhattan, KS 66502	Thomas V. Link	913-537-4980
NASHVILLE, TN—Kentucky, Tennessee	Rm. 301, U.S. Courthouse, Nashville, TN 37203	Larry Whitford	615-736-5591

Field Service Offices—Federal Crop Insurance Corporation—Continued

Office	Address	Director	Telephone
RALEIGH, NC—North Carolina, Virginia, West Virginia	Rm. 608, 310 New Bern Ave., Raleigh, NC 27601	Robert Fenton	919-551-1717
SACRAMENTO, CA—Arizona, California, Nevada	Suite 470, 1303 J. St., Sacramento, CA 95814	Max Cain	916-551-1717
SPOKANE, WA—Idaho, Oregon, Utah, Washington	Suite 507, W. 601 1st Ave., Spokane, WA 99204	O.D. Christiansen	509-353-2319
SPRINGFIELD, IL—Illinois	Suite 2, 2305 W. Monroe St., Springfield, IL 62704	Joan Sutter	217-492-4280
ST. PAUL, MN—Minnesota, Wisconsin	Rm. 300, 375 Jackson St., St. Paul, MN 55101-1810	Kenneth F. Krefting	612-290-3871

Field Underwriting Offices—Federal Crop Insurance Corporation

Office	Address	Director	Telephone
BILLINGS, MT—Montana, North Dakota, half of Wyoming	Suite 106, 2110 Overland Ave., Billings, MT 59102-6440	Robert Pechal	406-657-6447
HARRISBURG, PA—Delaware, Maryland, New Jersey, New York, West Virginia, Pennsylvania	Suite 310, 1 Credit Union Pl., Harrisburg, PA 17110	John J. Gartside	717-782-4807
JACKSON, MS—half of Alabama, Arkansas, Kentucky, Louisiana, Mississippi, Tennessee	Suite 318, 100 W. Capitol St., Jackson, MS 39269	Thomas J. Smith	601-965-4771
OKLAHOMA CITY, OK—New Mexico, Oklahoma, Texas	Suite 210, 205 63d St. NW., Oklahoma City, OK 73118	John B. Blankenship	405-231-5057
RALEIGH, NC—North Carolina, Virginia	Suite 150, 4407 Bland Rd., Raleigh, NC 27609	C. Dewey Botts	919-790-2990
SACRAMENTO, CA—Arizona, California, Nevada	Suite 450, 1303 J. St., Sacramento, CA 95814	Larry Dell	916-551-2153
SPOKANE, WA—Idaho, Oregon, Utah, Washington	Suite 204, N. 112 University Rd., Spokane, WA 99206	Leroy F. Knox	509-456-2147
SPRINGFIELD, IL—Illinois, Indiana, Michigan, Missouri, Ohio	Suite 3, 2305 W. Monroe St., Springfield, IL 62704	Thomas L. McKean	217-492-4186
ST. PAUL, MN—Iowa, Minnesota, Wisconsin	Rm. 624, 7th and Roberts Sts., St. Paul, MN 55101	William R. Archer	612-290-3304
TOPEKA, KS—Colorado, Kansas, Nebraska, South Dakota, half of Wyoming	Rm. 135, 444 SE. Quincy, Topeka, KS 66683	Richard Moore	913-295-2570
VALDOSTA, GA—half of Alabama, Florida, Georgia, South Carolina	Rm. M-113, 401 N. Patterson St., Valdosta, GA 31601	Jerry D. Scheuerman	912-242-3044

Compliance Offices—Federal Crop Insurance Corporation

Office	Address	Director	Telephone
DALLAS, TX—Alabama, Arkansas, Louisiana, Mississippi, New Mexico, Texas	Suite 280, 1111 W. Mockingbird Lane, Dallas, TX 75247	Billy Pryor	214-767-7700
KANSAS CITY, MO—Colorado, Illinois, Iowa, Kansas, Missouri, Nebraska	9435 Holmes St., Kansas City, MO 64131	Timothy Hoffman	816-926-7963
RALEIGH, NC—Connecticut, Delaware, Florida, Georgia, Indiana, Kentucky, Maine, Maryland, Massachusetts, Michigan, New Hampshire, New Jersey, New York, North Carolina, Ohio, Pennsylvania, Puerto Rico, Tennessee, Virginia, West Virginia	Suite 201, 1 Copley Pkwy., Morrisville, NC 27560	Johnnie Perdue	919-856-4479
SACRAMENTO, CA—Alaska, Arizona, California, Hawaii, Idaho, Nevada, Oregon, Utah, Washington	Suite 460, 1303 J St., Sacramento, CA 95814	William J. Murphy	916-551-1024
ST. PAUL, MN—Minnesota, Montana, North Dakota, South Dakota, Wisconsin, Wyoming	Suite 145, 3440 Federal Dr., Eagan, MN 55122	Patrick Morris	612-725-3730

For further information, contact the Manager, Federal Crop Insurance Corporation, Department of Agriculture, Washington, DC 20250. Phone, 202-447-6795.

Marketing and Inspection Services

Agricultural Cooperative Service

The Agricultural Cooperative Service helps farmers to help themselves through the use of cooperative organizations. Studies are conducted to support cooperatives that market farm products, purchase production supplies, and perform related business services. These studies concentrate on the financial, organizational, legal, social, and economic aspects of cooperative activity in U.S. agriculture. The Service provides technical assistance and research to improve cooperative performance in organizing new cooperatives, the merits of merging cooperatives, the changing business structure, and developing strategies for growth. Applied research is conducted to give farmers relevant and expert assistance pertaining to their cooperatives.

The Service also collects and publishes basic statistics regarding the role and scope of cooperative activity in U.S. agriculture. Its monthly magazine, *Farmer Cooperatives,* reports current developments and research for cooperative management.

For further information, contact the Agricultural Cooperative Service, Department of Agriculture, P.O. Box 96576, Washington, DC 20090–6576. Phone, 202–245–5358.

Agricultural Marketing Service

The Agricultural Marketing Service was established by the Secretary of Agriculture on April 2, 1972, under the authority of Reorganization Plan No. 2 of 1953 (5 U.S.C. app.) and other authorities. The Service administers standardization, grading, inspection, market news, marketing orders, and research, promotion, and regulatory programs.

Market News The Service provides current, unbiased information to producers, processors, distributors, and others to assist them in the orderly marketing and distribution of farm commodities. Information is collected on supplies, demand, prices, movement, location, quality, condition, and other market data on farm products in specific markets and marketing areas. The data is disseminated nationally via a modern satellite system.

Standardization, Grading, and Classing Grade standards have been established for nearly 200 agricultural commodities to help buyers and sellers trade on agreed-upon quality levels. Standards are developed with the benefit of views from those in the industries directly affected and others interested.

Grading and classing services also are provided to certify the grade and quality of products. These services are provided to buyers and sellers of live cattle, swine, sheep, meat, poultry, eggs, rabbits, fruits, vegetables, tree nuts, peanuts, dairy products, tobacco, wool, and mohair. Classing services are provided to buyers and sellers of cotton and cotton products. These services are mainly voluntary and are provided upon request and for a fee. The Service also is responsible for the certification of turpentine and other naval stores products, and the standardization and testing of seed.

Laboratory Testing The Service provides scientific and laboratory support to its commodity programs relating to testing of microbiological and chemical factors in food products through grading, certification, acceptance, and regulatory programs; processing and finishing tests for cotton fiber and yarn; testing of peanuts for aflatoxin, and testing of imported flue-cured and burley tobacco for pesticide residues. The agency also carries out quality assurance and safety oversight activities with respect to the Service's commodity division laboratory and testing activities relating to milk market administrators, resident grading programs, and State and private laboratory programs.

The Service also administers the new Pesticide Data Program which, in cooperation with States, samples and analyzes fresh fruits and vegetables for pesticide residues. It shares residue test results with the Environmental Protection Agency and other public agencies.

Food Quality Assurance Under a Governmentwide quality assurance program, AMS is responsible for the development and revision of specifications used by Federal agencies in food procuring for military and civilian uses. The Service coordinates and approves certification programs designed to ensure that purchased products conform to the specification requirements.

Section 32 Programs Under section 32 of the act of August 24, 1935, as amended (7 U.S.C. 612c), 30 percent of customs receipts collected during each calendar year are automatically appropriated for expanding outlets for various commodities. Portions of these funds are transferred to the Food and Nutrition Service of USDA and to the Department of Commerce. Remaining funds are used to purchase commodities for the National School Lunch Program and other feeding programs, for diversion to other outlets, and for administering agreement and order programs.

Regulatory Programs The Service administers several regulatory programs designed collectively to protect producers, handlers, and consumers of agricultural commodities from financial loss or personal injury resulting from careless, deceptive, or fraudulent marketing practices. Such regulatory programs encourage fair trading practices in the marketing of fruits and vegetables, require truth in seed labeling and advertising, and protect farmers' rights to organize cooperatives.

Under the Egg Products Inspection Act (21 U.S.C. 1031–1056), the Service provides mandatory inspection for wholesomeness in all plants processing liquid, dried, or frozen egg products, and controls the disposition of restricted shell eggs—eggs that are a potential health hazard.

Marketing Agreements and Orders These programs, under authority of the Agricultural Marketing Agreement Act of 1937 (7 U.S.C. 601 *et seq.*), help to establish and maintain orderly marketing conditions for certain commodities. Milk marketing orders establish minimum prices that handlers or distributors are required to pay producers. Programs for fruits, vegetables, and related specialty crops like nuts and spearmint oil help stabilize supplies and market prices. In some cases, they also authorize research and market development activities, including advertising supported by assessments that handlers pay. Through orderly marketing, adjusting the supply to demand, and avoiding unreasonable fluctuations during the marketing season, the income of producers is increased by normal market forces, and consumer interests are protected through quality and quantity control.

Federal marketing orders originate with a request from a producer group to the Secretary of Agriculture. The Secretary can conduct hearings and referenda based on the producer group's proposal for a marketing order. Producer and handler assessments would finance their operations.

In carrying out the Government role, the Service ensures that persons interested in the development and operation of the programs have a fair hearing and that each marketing order works according to Federal law and established rules and guidelines.

Plant Variety Protection Program Under authority of the Plant Variety Protection Act (7 U.S.C. 2321 *et seq.*), the Service administers a program that provides for the issuance of "certificates of plant variety protection." These certificates afford developers of novel varieties of sexually reproduced plants exclusive rights to sell, reproduce, import, or export such varieties, or use them in the production of hybrids or different varieties for a period of 18 years.

Research and Promotion Programs The Service monitors certain industry-sponsored research, promotion, and information programs authorized by Federal laws. These programs provide farmers with a means to finance and operate various research, promotion, and information activities for cotton, potatoes, eggs, milk and dairy products, beef, pork, honey, wool, lamb, mohair, limes, mushrooms, pecans, and soybeans.

Transportation Programs The Service is also responsible for the development of an efficient transportation system for rural America that begins at the farm gate, moves agricultural and other rural products through the Nation's highways, railroads, airports, and waterways, and into the domestic and international marketplace. To accomplish this, AMS conducts economic studies and analyses of these systems, and represents agricultural and rural transportation interests in policy and regulatory forums. To provide direct assistance to the transportation community, AMS supplies research and technical information to producers, producer groups, shippers, exporters, rural communities, carriers, government agencies, and universities.

The Service carries out responsibilities of USDA's former Office of Transportation under the Agricultural Adjustment Act of 1938 (7 U.S.C. 1281), the Agricultural Marketing Act of 1946 (7 U.S.C. 1621), the Agricultural Trade Development and Assistance Act of 1954 (7 U.S.C. 1691), the Rural Development Act of 1972 (7 U.S.C. 1921 note), the International Carriage of Perishable Foodstuffs Act (7 U.S.C. 4401), and the Cooperative Marketing Act of 1926 (7 U.S.C. 451–457).

Other Programs Other marketing service activities include financial grants to States for marketing improvement projects. The agency also has responsibility for the conduct of studies of the facilities and methods used in the physical distribution of food and other farm products; for research designed to improve the handling of all agricultural products as they move from farm to consumers; and for increasing marketing efficiency by developing improved operating methods, facilities, and equipment for processing, handling, and distributing dairy, poultry, and meat products.

Field Organization Programs and activities in the field are carried out through a variety of different types of organizations reporting to their respective Washington components.

For further information, contact the Information Staff, Agricultural Marketing Service, Department of Agriculture, P.O. Box 96456, Washington, DC 20250. Phone, 202–447–8999.

Animal and Plant Health Inspection Service

[For the Animal and Plant Health Inspection Service statement of organization, see the *Code of Federal Regulations,* Title 7, Part 371]

The Animal and Plant Health Inspection Service was reestablished by the Secretary of Agriculture on March 14, 1977, pursuant to authority contained in 5 U.S.C. 301 and Reorganization Plan No. 2 of 1953 (5 U.S.C. app.).

The Service was established to conduct regulatory and control programs to protect and improve animal and plant health for the benefit of man and the environment. In cooperation with State governments, the agency administers Federal laws and regulations pertaining to animal and plant health and quarantine, humane treatment of animals, and the control and eradication of pests and diseases. Regulations to prevent the introduction or interstate spread of certain animal or plant pests or diseases are also enforced by the Service. It also carries out research and operational activities to reduce crop and livestock depredations caused by birds, rodents, and predators.

Plant Protection and Quarantine Programs Plant protection officials are responsible for programs to control or eradicate plant pests and diseases. These programs are carried out in cooperation with the States involved, other Federal agencies, farmers, and private organizations. Pest control programs use a single tool or a combination of pest control techniques, both chemical and nonchemical, which are both effective and safe.

Agricultural quarantine inspection officials administer Federal regulations that prohibit or restrict the entry of foreign pests and plants, plant products, animal products and byproducts, and other materials that may harbor pests or diseases. Inspection service is maintained at all major ocean, air, border, and interior ports of entry in the continental

United States and in Hawaii, Alaska, Puerto Rico, U.S. Virgin Islands, Bahamas, and Bermuda. Services also are provided on a regular or on-call basis at some 500 outlying ports and military installations throughout the country.

Other responsibilities include the inspection and certification of domestic commodities for export, regulation of the import and export of endangered plant species, and ensuring that imported seed is free of noxious weeds.

Veterinary Services Animal health officials are responsible for determining the existence and extent of outbreaks of communicable diseases and pests affecting livestock and poultry. They organize and conduct control and eradication programs in cooperation with State officials.

Service officials maintain inspection and quarantine service at designated ports of entry for imported animals and birds. They are responsible for the health certification of livestock and poultry exported to other countries.

Regulatory Enforcement and Animal Care The Service administers Federal laws concerned with the humane handling of livestock and poultry in interstate commerce and governing the transportation, sale, and handling of dogs, cats, circus and zoo animals, and other animals intended to be sold at the wholesale level or to be used in laboratory research or for exhibition. The agency also is responsible for enforcing the Horse Protection Act of 1970 (15 U.S.C. 1821 note), a Federal law that prohibits soring of horses shipped interstate to be shown or sold.

International Services Service officials carry out cooperative plant pest programs with Canada, Mexico, and other nations when the pest is a joint problem or presents a threat to this country. They also cooperate with animal health officials in other countries in planning and conducting disease control efforts in those countries. In addition, inspectors work in several foreign countries to supervise preclearance of agricultural materials for entry into the United States.

Biotechnology, Biologics, and Environmental Protection Service officials are responsible for the regulation of genetically engineered organisms and products that present a plant pest risk. Regulation is carried out through a permit system. The Service also administers a Federal law intended to ensure that all veterinary biological products, whether developed by conventional or new biotechnological procedures, used in the diagnosis, prevention, and treatment of animal disease are safe, pure, potent, and effective. This responsibility is met by regulating firms that manufacture veterinary biological products subject to the act. This includes licensing the manufacturing establishment and its products; inspecting production facilities and production methods; and testing products under a surveillance program.

Animal Damage Control Animal damage control officials cooperate with States, counties, local communities, and agricultural producer groups to reduce crop and livestock depredations caused by birds, rodents, and predators. The officials conduct research into predator-prey relationships, new control methods, and more efficient and safe uses of present methods such as toxicants, repellants and attractants, biological controls, scare devices, and habitat alteration. Using methods and techniques that are biologically sound, environmentally acceptable, and economically feasible, they participate in efforts to educate and advise farmers and ranchers on proper uses of control methods and techniques; they suppress serious nuisances and threats to public health and safety caused by birds, rodents, and other wildlife in urban and rural communities; and they work with airport managers to reduce risks of bird strikes.

For further information, contact Legislative and Public Affairs, Animal and Plant Health Inspection Service, Department of Agriculture, Washington, DC 20250. Phone, 202–447–2511.

Federal Grain Inspection Service

The Federal Grain Inspection Service was established in the U.S. Department of

290-950 O 91 - 5

Agriculture on November 20, 1976. The primary task of the Service is to carry out the provisions of the United States Grain Standards Act (7 U.S.C. 71 *et seq.*) and to ensure integrity in the inspection, weighing, and handling of domestic grain. An Administrator, appointed by the President with the advice and consent of the Senate, heads the agency.

The Service is responsible for establishing official U.S. standards for grain and other assigned commodities and for administrating a nationwide official inspection and weighing system. The Service may, in response to formal application, authorize private and State agencies to perform official services under the authority contained in the act.

Three of the Service's four divisions are located in Washington, DC; the fourth is located in Kansas City, MO. Most employees work in field offices around the Nation.

Inspection The United States Grain Standards Act requires, with some exceptions, all domestic export grain be officially inspected. At export port locations, inspection is performed by the Service or by State agencies that have been delegated export inspection authority by the Administrator. For domestic grain, marketed at inland locations, the Administrator designates private and State agencies to provide official inspection services upon request. Both export and domestic services are provided on a fee basis.

To ensure that the official U.S. grain standards are applied uniformly nationwide, Service field offices provide oversight, guidance, and assistance to non-Federal agencies performing inspection activities, both at export and inland inspection points.

Buyers and sellers may request appeal inspections of original inspection results, first from a field office and then, if desired, from the Service's Board of Appeals and Review. The Service maintains a quality control program to monitor the national inspection system and to ensure that all field locations accurately and uniformly apply the U.S. grain standards.

Weighing Official weighing of domestic export grain is performed at port locations by the Service or by State agencies that have been delegated export weighing authority by the Administrator. For domestic grain marketed at inland locations, the weighing services may be provided by the Service or by designated private or State agencies. Weighing services are provided on a fee basis upon request.

As with inspection activities, Service field offices provide oversight, guidance, and assistance to non-Federal agencies performing official weighing services. With the support of the Association of American Railroads and user fees, the Service conducts a railroad track scale-testing program which includes an annual testing service for all State and railroad company-owned master scales. The Service is the only entity, public or private, which connects all railroad track scales to the national standards.

Standardization The Service is responsible for establishing, maintaining, and, as needed, revising official U.S. standards. Such standards exist for corn, wheat, rye, oats, barley, flaxseed, sorghum, soybeans, triticale, sunflowerseed, and mixed grain. The Service has been authorized to perform applied research for the purpose of developing methods to improve accuracy and uniformity in grading grain.

The Service is also responsible for the standardization and inspection activities for rice, dry beans, peas, lentils, hay, straw, hops, and related processed grain commodities under the Agricultural Marketing Act of 1946, as amended (7 U.S.C. 1621). Although standards no longer exist for hay, straw, and hops, the Service maintains inspection procedures for and retains authority to inspect these commodities.

Compliance The Service's compliance activities ensure accurate and uniform implementation of the act, applicable provisions of the Agricultural Marketing Act of 1946, and related regulations—including designating States and private agencies to carry out official inspection and weighing functions and monitoring, overseeing, and reviewing the operations of such agencies to ensure adequate performance.

The Service administers a registration program for all grain firms that export grain from the United States. In conjunction with the Office of the Inspector General, the Service carries out a program for investigating reported violations, and initiates followup and corrective actions when appropriate. The total compliance program ensures the integrity of the national inspection and weighing system.

For further information, contact the Federal Grain Inspection Service, Department of Agriculture, Washington, DC 20250. Phone, 202–382–0219.

Food Safety and Inspection Service

The Food Safety and Inspection Service (FSIS) was established by the Secretary of Agriculture on June 17, 1981, pursuant to authority contained in 5 U.S.C. 301 and Reorganization Plan No. 2 of 1953 (5 U.S.C. app.). The Service is responsible for regulating the meat and poultry industry to ensure that meat and poultry products moving in interstate and foreign commerce are safe, wholesome, and accurately labeled.

Meat and Poultry Inspection Federal inspection is mandatory for the following animals and birds used for human food: cattle, calves, swine, goats, sheep and lambs, horses and other equines, chickens, turkeys, ducks, geese, and guineas. The work includes inspection of each animal or bird at slaughter, and inspection of processed products during various stages of production. The Service tests product samples for microbial or chemical contaminants to monitor trends or for enforcement purposes. Facilities and equipment are approved by FSIS before inspection is granted, and each product label must be approved by the agency before products can be sold. It monitors products in storage, distribution, and retail channels; and takes necessary compliance actions to protect the public, including detention of products, voluntary product recalls, court-ordered seizures of products, administrative withdrawal of inspection, and referral for criminal prosecution. The Service also conducts surveillance of foreign inspection systems exporting meat or poultry products to the United States, and oversight of and cooperation with State programs for the inspection of meat and poultry products sold only within the State in which produced, by authority of sections 450 through 470 and sections 601 through 691 of title 21, United States Code.

The Service also monitors livestock upon arrival at federally inspected facilities to ensure compliance with the Humane Slaughter Act (7 U.S.C. 1901–1906); conducts voluntary reimbursed inspection for rabbits and other domestic food animals not covered by the inspection law (7 U.S.C. 1622); and ensures that inedible products from meat or poultry, such as offal rendered for animal feed, are properly identified and isolated from edible products (7 U.S.C. 1624).

The Service conducts a toll-free Meat and Poultry Hotline (800–535–4555) to answer questions about labeling and safe handling of meat and poultry products. The hotline is also accessible by TDD.

For further information, contact the Director of Information and Legislative Affairs, Food Safety and Inspection Service, Department of Agriculture, Washington, DC 20250. Phone, 202–447–7943.

Packers and Stockyards Administration

[For the Packers and Stockyards Administration statement of organization, see the *Code of Federal Regulations,* Title 9, Part 204]

The Packers and Stockyards Administration administers the provisions of the Packers and Stockyards Act of 1921, as amended (7 U.S.C. 181–229), the Truth in Lending and Fair Credit Billing Acts (15 U.S.C. 1601 *et seq.*), and the Equal Credit Opportunity Act (15 U.S.C. 1691 *et seq.*) with respect to firms subject to the Packers and Stockyards Act. The Administration also administers the provisions of section 1324 of the Food Security Act of 1985 (7 U.S.C. 1631), certifying State central filing systems for notification of liens against farm products.

The Packers and Stockyards Act is an antitrust, trade practice, and financial protection law. Its principal purpose is to maintain effective competition and fair trade practices in the marketing of livestock, meat, and poultry for the protection of livestock and poultry producers. Members of the livestock, poultry, and meat industries are also protected against unfair or monopolistic practices of competitors. The act also protects consumers against unfair business practices in marketing of meats and poultry and against restrictions of competition that could unduly affect meat and poultry prices.

The provisions of the Packers and Stockyards Act are enforced by investigations of violations of the act with emphasis on payment protection; detecting instances of commercial bribery, fraud in livestock marketing, and false weighing; requiring adequate bond coverage for commission firms, dealers, and packers; and the surveillance of marketing methods at public markets and in geographical market areas of the country.

For further information, contact the Office of the Administrator, Packers and Stockyards Administration, Department of Agriculture, Washington, DC 20250. Phone, 202-447-7051.

Food and Consumer Services

Food and Nutrition Service

[For the Food and Nutrition Service statement of organization, see the *Federal Register* of June 6, 1970, 35 FR 8835]

The Food and Nutrition Service is the agency of the Department that administers the programs to make food assistance available to people who need it. These programs are operated in cooperation with States and local governments.

The Service was established on August 8, 1969, by the Secretary of Agriculture, under authority of 5 U.S.C. 301 and Reorganization Plan No. 2 of 1953 (5 U.S.C. app.).

Food Stamps The Food Stamp Program provides food coupons through State and local welfare agencies to needy persons to increase their food purchasing power. The coupons are used by program participants to buy food in any retail store that has been approved by FNS to accept and redeem the food coupons.

Special Nutrition Programs The Service administers several programs designed to improve the nutrition of children, and particularly those who come from low-income families. Principal among these is the National School Lunch Program, which provides financial assistance to public and nonprofit private schools of high school grade and under, in operating nonprofit school lunch programs.

The School Breakfast Program provides cash assistance to State educational agencies to help schools in operating nonprofit breakfast programs meeting established nutritional standards. It is especially important in improving the diets of needy children who may receive breakfast free or at reduced prices.

The Summer Food Service Program for Children helps to get nutritious meals to needy preschool and school-aged children in schools, residential summer camps, or during vacations in areas operating under a continuous school calendar.

The Child Care Food Program is a companion activity that helps to get nutritious meals to preschool and school-aged children in child care facilities.

The Special Milk Program for Children, which is administered in schools, institutions, and split-session kindergartens that do not participate in any other Federal food program, is designed to help child nutrition by paying a share of the cost of increased servings of fluid milk made to children.

Food Distribution The Food Distribution Program makes foods available, in kind, to eligible recipients. Foods purchased by the Department are made available principally to children in school lunch and breakfast programs, in summer camps and child care centers, and to the nutrition program for the elderly. Also, surplus commodities are distributed to needy families through food banks, charitable institutions, and local government agencies.

The program on Indian reservations provides Indians on or near reservations with access to a wide range of donated foods, including meat, fruit, vegetables, and dairy and grain products.

Supplemental Food Programs The Special Supplemental Food Program for Women, Infants and Children—the WIC Program—provides specified nutritious food supplements to and nutrition education for pregnant women, nursing women up to 12 months postpartum, non-nursing women up to 6 months postpartum, and children up to 5 years of age. Participants are determined by competent professionals (physicians, nutritionists, nurses, and other health officials) to be health risks because of nutritionally related medical conditions or inadequate nutrition.

Cash grants are made available to participating State health departments or comparable State agencies, or recognized Indian tribes, bands, or groups. The State agencies distribute funds to the local agencies, and the funds are used to provide foods for WIC recipients and to pay specified administrative and clinical costs.

Commodity Supplemental Food Program This program provides supplemental foods and nutrition education to infants and children and to pregnant, postpartum, and breastfeeding women, and elderly persons with low incomes who are vulnerable to malnutrition and reside in approved project areas. The Department purchases the foods for distribution through State agencies.

Nutrition Education and Training Under this program funds are granted to the States for the dissemination of nutrition information to children and for in-service training of food service and teaching personnel.

No person may be discriminated against—in the operation of any of the programs administered by the Food and Nutrition Service—because of race, color, sex, creed, national origin, or handicap.

For further information, contact the Public Information Officer, Food and Nutrition Service, Department of Agriculture, Alexandria, VA 22302. Phone, 703–756–3276.

Human Nutrition Information Service

The Human Nutrition Information Service conducts research in human nutrition to improve professional and public understanding of the nutritional adequacy of diets and food supplies as well as the nutritive value of food. It helps develop knowledge needed to improve the nutritional quality of diets, thereby improving the general health of the American public.

Service activities fall into two broad categories: research, analysis, and technical assistance; and information collection and dissemination. The nationwide food consumption surveys and annual continuing surveys of food intake by individuals monitor food and nutrient consumption of households and individuals in the United States. The Nutrient Data Bank compiles information on the nutritive value of foods and publishes representative values in Agriculture Handbook No. 8.

Composition of Foods Additional activities include nutrition education research, dissemination of information through technical and nontechnical publications, machine-readable forms, professional journals, and responses to individual requests.

For further information, contact the Human Nutrition Information Service, Department of Agriculture, Hyattsville, MD 20782. Phone, 301–436–7725.

Office of the Consumer Advisor

The Office of the Consumer Advisor serves as the focal point for coordinating USDA actions on problems and issues of importance to consumers. The Office:

—consults and advises USDA policymakers on issues and questions of importance to consumers;

—represents the Department in policy discussions related to consumer-oriented issues before Congress, in meetings with other departments and agencies, and in various public forums;

—monitors the policies, practices, and procedures of USDA programs in the area of consumer affairs;

—assists in informing consumers of USDA's functions, policies, and procedures so that consumers may know where services are to be found, what regulations consist of, and how to participate in these activities;

—develops and monitors procedures for handling consumer complaints and followup actions; and

—analyzes consumer complaints for policy and program evaluation purposes.

For further information, contact the Office of the Consumer Advisor, Department of Agriculture, Washington, DC 20250. Phone, 202-382-9681.

International Affairs and Commodity Programs

Agricultural Stabilization and Conservation Service

The Agricultural Stabilization and Conservation Service was established June 5, 1961, by the Secretary of Agriculture under authority of revised statutes (5 U.S.C. 301), and Reorganization Plan No. 2 of 1953 (5 U.S.C. app.), as well as all other statutes and prior reorganization plans vesting authority in the Secretary of Agriculture.

The Service administers commodity and related land use programs designed for voluntary production adjustment, resource protection, and price, market, and farm income stabilization.

In each State, operations are supervised by a State committee of three to five members appointed by the Secretary. A State Executive Director, appointed by the Secretary, and staff carry on day-to-day operations of the State office. The State Director of the Agricultural Extension Service is an *ex officio* member of the State committee.

In each of approximately 3,080 agricultural counties, a county committee of three farmer members is responsible for local administration. While two are held over, one is elected yearly, either directly by farmers or by farmer-elected delegates, to a county convention. The county agricultural Extension agent is a nonvoting *ex officio* member or secretary of the county committee. A county executive director, with other necessary staff, is employed to carry on day-to-day operations of the county office, usually located in the county seat.

Commodity Programs The Service administers the Commodity Credit Corporation's commodity stabilization programs for wheat, corn, cotton (upland and extra long staple), seed cotton, soybeans, peanuts, rice, tobacco, milk, wool, mohair, barley, oats, sugarbeets, sugarcane, grain sorghum, rye, and honey. Commodity stabilization is achieved through commodity loans, purchases, and payments to eligible producers.

For most commodities, loans are made directly to producers on the unprocessed commodity through the Service's county offices. Some commodities are also purchased from producers. Price support loans and purchases also can be made available through cooperative marketing associations. The price of milk is stabilized through purchases of processed dairy products. Price stabilization programs for tobacco and peanuts are carried out through loans to producer associations that, in turn, make program benefits available to producers. Stabilization of sugarbeet and sugarcane prices is carried out through loans to sugar processors, who in turn make program benefits available to producers.

Loans to producers, except for seed cotton, are "nonrecourse." If market prices rise above loan levels, producers or their agents can pay off their loans and market their commodity. If market prices fail to rise above loan levels, producers or their agents can forfeit or deliver the commodity to the Commodity Credit Corporation, thereby discharging their obligations in full.

Commodity stabilization for wool and mohair is accomplished through the National Wool Act of 1954 (7 U.S.C. 1781 note) by making payments to producers to bring the national average price received by all producers up to a support level required by the act.

Eligibility for commodity loans, purchases, and payments is, in most cases, conditional upon participation in acreage reduction, paid-land diversion, payment-in-kind, allotment, or quota programs in effect for the particular crop.

Under the Food, Agriculture, Conservation, and Trade Act of 1990, payments are limited to an annual ceiling of $50,000 per person on the total payments of upland cotton, extra long staple cotton, wheat, rice, and feed grain programs for the 1991 through 1995 crops.

The act greatly expanded flexibility for participating farmers to shift program crop plantings, as well as options for oilseeds and industrial and experimental crops. The acreage reduction program requirement for the 1991 crop year is 15 percent for wheat; 7.5 percent for corn, barley, and sorghum; 5 percent for upland and extra-long staple cotton; and 0 percent for oats.

Emergency Assistance Such programs offered to farmers in emergency-designated areas may include any or all of the following:

—furnishing assistance for feed purchases or making available Corporation-owned feed grains at reduced prices to eligible producers, and, in some instances, donation of feed grains;

—cost-sharing with farmers who carry out emergency conservation practices to rehabilitate farmland damaged by natural disaster; and

—allowing haying and grazing on acreage diverted to conserving uses under the commodity programs or long-term land retirement program on a county-by-county basis, as needed, in the event of drought or excess moisture.

Farm Facility Loan Program This program helps qualifying farmers obtain on-site storage for their crops. Applications for these loans are accepted by county ASCS offices only during periods announced by the Secretary of Agriculture.

Grain Reserve Program The Food, Agriculture, Conservation, and Trade Act of 1990 reauthorized the Grain Reserve Program for farmer-owned wheat, corn, grain sorghum, oats, and barley. When entry into the Reserve is authorized by the Secretary of Agriculture, producers may enter into a contract extending their 9-month loan for an additional 27 months and receive quarterly storage payments.

Loans may be repaid at any time. Interest may be charged when prices exceed 105 percent of the target; however, storage payments cease when prices exceed 95 percent of the target price.

Indemnity Program The Dairy Indemnity Payment Program provides indemnity payments to dairy farmers whose milk has been removed from the commercial market because it contained residues of chemicals or toxic substances, including nuclear radiation or fallout.

The Service is responsible for defense preparedness plans and programs relating to food production, conservation, and stabilization; food processing, storage, and wholesale distribution; controlled distribution of farm machinery, equipment and repair parts, distribution of fertilizer, feed, and seed; and the handling, storage, and distribution of all grains before export or processing.

The Service also provides services relating to expansion of productive capacity, materials, and facilities under the Defense Production Act of 1950, as amended (50 U.S.C. 2061); plans for management, control, and allocation of water to be used for agricultural production and food processing; consolidates all claims for material, labor, equipment, supplies, and services needed to support the defense responsibilities of USDA; and guarantees payments or makes loans, as needed, for the continuation of food and agriculture activities in a national defense emergency.

Accounting and budget support is provided by the Service for the General

Sales Manager of the Foreign Agricultural Service in administering Commodity Credit Corporation export credit sales and guarantee programs and Food for Peace programs.

To carry out the Agricultural Foreign Investment Disclosure Act of 1978 (7 U.S.C. 3501), the Department assigned the Service the primary responsibility of collecting information through a reporting system involving all States and most counties. The agency assesses penalties on late filed information and refusals to file. The Administrator rules on appeals resulting from penalties assessed for violations of the act.

Resource Conservation Programs Under the Food, Agriculture, Conservation, and Trade Act of 1990, new incentives for preserving and protecting agricultural resources have been implemented.

The major component of a new Environmental Conservation Acreage Reserve Program (ECARP) is the revised Conservation Reserve Program which will, beginning in 1991, put greater emphasis on preserving and upgrading water quality, identifying environmentally sensitive areas for special conservation treatment, and planting trees. Also included under ECARP is a new Wetlands Reserve Program which features easements to implement approved plans for wetland restoration and protection of farms.

Another new program is the Agricultural Water Quality Protection Program, a voluntary program with a goal of enrolling 10 million acres of farmland under agricultural water protection plans by the end of 1995.

The Integrated Farm Management Program Option is a voluntary program to encourage participants to plant resource conserving crops on commodity base acres.

In addition, producers who farm highly erodible land without an approved conservation plan will be considered ineligible for USDA program benefits. Other provisions of the new law are designed to discourage farming practices that may have adverse environmental impacts.

Other previously authorized conservation programs provide assistance to install a variety of soil-saving practices and other measures to control erosion, to plant trees and improve timberstands, to prevent the loss of wetlands for migratory waterfowl, and to control nonpoint source water pollution in rural America.

For further information, contact the Information Division, Agricultural Stabilization and Conservation Service, Department of Agriculture, P.O. Box 2415, Washington, DC 20013. Phone, 202–447–5237.

Commodity Credit Corporation

The Commodity Credit Corporation was organized October 17, 1933, pursuant to Executive Order 6340 of October 16, 1933, under the laws of the State of Delaware, as an agency of the United States. From October 17, 1933, to July 1, 1939, the Corporation was managed and operated in close affiliation with the Reconstruction Finance Corporation. On July 1, 1939, the agency was transferred to the Department of Agriculture by the President's Reorganization Plan No. I of 1939 (5 U.S.C. app.). Approval of the Commodity Credit Corporation Charter Act on June 29, 1948 (15 U.S.C. 714), subsequently amended, established the Corporation, effective July 1, 1948, as an agency and instrumentality of the United States under a permanent Federal charter.

The Corporation stabilizes, supports, and protects farm income and prices, assists in maintaining balanced and adequate supplies of agricultural commodities and their products, and facilitates the orderly distribution of commodities.

The Corporation is managed by a Board of Directors, subject to the general supervision and direction of the Secretary of Agriculture, who is an *ex officio* Director and Chairman of the Board. The Board consists of seven members (in addition to the Secretary of Agriculture), who are appointed by the President of the United States.

The Corporation is capitalized at $100 million and has statutory authority to borrow up to $30 billion from the U.S.

Treasury. It utilizes the personnel and facilities of the Agricultural Stabilization and Conservation Service and, in certain foreign assistance operations, the Foreign Agricultural Service to carry out its activities.

A commodity office in Kansas City, MO, has specific responsibilities for the acquisition, handling, storage, and disposal of commodities and products held by the Corporation.

Commodity Stabilization Loan, purchase, and/or payment programs of the Corporation are administered by the Service for wheat, corn, upland and extra-long staple cotton, peanuts, rice, tobacco, milk, wool, mohair, honey, barley, oats, grain sorghum, rye, soybeans, sugarbeets, and sugarcane.

Commodities acquired under the stabilization program are disposed of through domestic and export sales, transfers to other Government agencies, and donations for domestic and foreign welfare use. The Corporation also is authorized to exchange surplus agricultural commodities it has acquired by the Corporation for strategic and other materials and services produced abroad.

Foreign Assistance Under Public Law 480, the Agricultural Trade Development and Assistance Act of 1954, as amended (7 U.S.C. 1691), the Corporation carries out assigned foreign assistance activities, such as guaranteeing the credit sale of U.S. agricultural commodities abroad. Major emphasis is also being directed toward meeting the needs of developing nations under the Food for Peace Act of 1966 (7 U.S.C. 1691) that further amends the Agricultural Trade Development and Assistance Act of 1954. Under these authorities, agricultural commodities are procured and exported to combat hunger and malnutrition and to encourage economic development in the developing countries.

The Corporation encourages U.S. financial institutions to provide financing to developing countries under the Export Credit Guarantee Programs. The Foreign Agricultural Service Administers the programs under titles I and II of Public Law 480 (7 U.S.C. 1701, 1721) and the Export Credit and Guarantee Programs.

For further information, contact the Information Division, Commodity Credit Corporation, Department of Agriculture, P.O. Box 2415, Washington, DC 20013. Phone, 202–447–5237. For information about Commodity Credit Corporation export programs, contact the Information Division, Foreign Agricultural Service, Department of Agriculture. Phone, 202–447–3448.

Foreign Agricultural Service

The Foreign Agricultural Service (FAS) has primary responsibility for USDA's overseas market information, access, and development programs. It also administers USDA's export assistance and foreign food assistance programs. The Service carries out its tasks through its network of agricultural counselors, attachés, and trade officers stationed overseas and its U.S.-based team of analysts, marketing specialists, negotiators, and other professionals.

The Foreign Agricultural Service maintains a worldwide agricultural intelligence and reporting system through its attaché service. This service consists of a team of more than 100 U.S. professional agriculturalists posted at more than 60 American embassies around the world. Their areas of responsibility encompass approximately 110 countries. They represent the Department of Agriculture and provide information and data on foreign government agricultural policies, analyses of supply and demand conditions, commercial trade relationships, and market opportunities. They report on more than 100 farm commodities, weather, economic factors, and related subjects that affect agriculture and agricultural trade.

At FAS in Washington, DC, agricultural economists and marketing specialists analyze these and other reports. These analyses are supplemented by accumulated background information and by the Crop Condition Assessment system, which analyzes Landsat satellite, weather, and other data.

To improve access for U.S. farm products abroad, FAS' international trade policy specialists coordinate and direct USDA's responsibilities in international trade agreement programs and negotiations. They maintain an ongoing effort to reduce foreign trade barriers and practices that discourage the export of U.S. farm products.

To follow foreign governmental actions that affect the market for U.S. agricultural commodities, FAS relies on its agricultural counselors and attachés. In Washington, a staff of international trade specialists analyzes the trade policies and practices of foreign governments to ensure conduct in conformance with international treaty obligations. During international negotiations, FAS provides staff and support for U.S. agricultural representation.

The FAS Trade Assistance and Planning Office, established in November 1988, serves agricultural exporters who need foreign market information, as well as those believed to have been injured by unfair trade practices. In addition, the Office coordinates reports on long-term trade strategy, foreign agricultural export assistance, and market opportunities for U.S. agricultural exports.

The Service has a continuing market development program to create, service, and expand commercial export markets for U.S. agricultural products. It carries out programs with nonprofit commodity groups called Cooperators, trade associations, and State agriculture departments and their regional associations. It manages market opportunity referral services and organizes trade fairs and sales teams.

The Service's Office of the General Sales Manager also oversees agricultural functions under the Public Law 480 Food for Peace Program, title I (7 U.S.C. 1701); section 416(b) of the Agricultural Act of 1949 (7 U.S.C. 1431); the Commodity Credit Corporation's (CCC) Export Credit Guarantee Programs; several other export assistance programs; and direct sales of Corporation-owned surplus commodities.

The Service also participates in the Public Law 480 donations program, title II, which is administered by the Agency for International Development (AID). Public Law 480 is aimed at long-range improvement in the economies of developing countries. As a result of the Food, Agriculture, Conservation, and Trade Act of 1990, USDA has the entire responsibility for title I; AID has total responsibility for title III; and the two agencies share responsibility for title II.

Title I, the concessional sales section of Public Law 480, provides for low-interest, long-term credit to recipients of U.S. farm commodities. Payment is generally made in dollars, and proceeds from sales into commercial channels are used by the recipient country for agricultural self-help measures and general economic development.

Title II of Public Law 480 authorizes the donation of agricultural commodities to foreign governments, voluntary relief agencies, or intergovernmental organizations. The commodities are donated for use abroad in meeting famine or other urgent or extraordinary relief requirements, economic development, and school lunch programs in developing areas.

Section 416(b) authorizes CCC to donate its commodities overseas. Certain sales and barter of the commodities are also authorized. The program functions are shared between USDA and AID. The Commodity Credit Corporation has the responsibility for determining the types and quantities of products for programming and for making funds available in any fiscal year for programming and related specific expenditures. Program proposals must be approved by the appropriate interagency groups. In addition, section 416(b) also is a source of funding for multiyear Food for Progress Development Programs. These programs are focused on agricultural policy changes and private-sector promotions.

The Commodity Credit Corporation Export Credit Guarantee (GSM-102) and the Intermediate Export Credit Guarantee (GSM-103) Programs encourage the development or expansion of overseas markets for U.S. agricultural commodities by providing guarantees on private financing of U.S. exports to foreign buyers purchasing on credit terms.

The foreign buyer contracts for the purchase of U.S. commodities on a deferred-payment basis of 3 years or less under GSM–102, or between 3 and 10 years under GSM–103. The foreign buyer's bank issues a letter of credit to guarantee payment to the U.S. exporter or an assignee U.S. lending institution. To receive the payment guarantee, the exporter registers the sale with CCC prior to export and pays a guarantee fee. The payment guarantee is implemented only if the foreign bank fails to pay the exporter or the assignee U.S. lending institution.

The Corporation considers coverage on sales of any U.S. agricultural commodity that has the potential of expanding U.S. export markets. A U.S. exporter, private foreign buyer, or foreign government may submit requests that may result in authorized guarantee coverage.

Several export assistance programs are designed to counter or offset the adverse effects from competitors' unfair trade practices on U.S. agriculture. These programs include the Export Enhancement Program (EEP), the Dairy Export Incentive Program (DEIP), the Sunflowerseed Oil Assistance Program (SOAP), and the Cottonseed Oil Assistance Program (COAP).

Under EEP, USDA provides Corporation-owned commodities or cash as export bonuses to make U.S. commodities more competitive in the world marketplace. The DEIP and EEP programs are similar, but EEP is restricted to dairy products. The SOAP and COAP programs are also like EEP, except bonuses provided to U.S. exporters are crude sunflowerseed oil and cottonseed oil rather than CCC certificates.

The Foreign Agriculture Service is also responsible for sales of Corporation-owned surplus commodities to private trade, foreign government, and nonprofit organizations. Direct sales may be negotiated on a case-by-case basis and on a cash or credit basis. The only criteria for financing direct sales are a 3-year maximum credit plan and the arrangement of suitable payment terms.

Another program authorized by the Food, Agriculture, Conservation, and Trade Act of 1990 is the Market Promotion Program, formerly known as Targeted Export Assistance (TEA). The Market Promotion Program provides assistance in the form of cash or commodities to trade promotion organizations to help fund their market development activities overseas, particularly in those markets where the United States encounters unfair trade practices by foreign competitors or importers.

For further information, contact the Information Staff, Foreign Agricultural Service, Deparment of Agriculture, Washington, DC 20250. Phone, 202–447–3448.

Office of International Cooperation and Development

The mission of the Office of International Cooperation and Development (OICD) is helping other USDA agencies, U.S. universities, and others enhance America's agricultural competitiveness globally; and increasing income and food availability in developing nations by mobilizing expertise for agriculturally led economic growth.

OICD programs enhance U.S. agriculture's competitiveness by providing U.S. agriculturalists and scientists with linkages to world resources. These linkages often produce new germplasm and technologies that can be vital to improving our current agricultural base and producing new and alternative products. They also foster relationships and understandings that result in trade opportunities and strengthened strategic and political ties.

The Office also serves as a link between the technical expertise of the U.S. agricultural community and Third World nations. By sharing agricultural knowledge with less-developed nations, the United States provides tools to help build stable economies and a more prosperous world. In the process, less-developed nations overcome the barriers of hunger and poverty and gain the economic means to buy needed goods and services in the world marketplace.

To accomplish its dual mission, OICD manages programs to exchange visits, germplasm, and technologies between U.S. and international scientists; supports collaborative research projects of mutual interest to the United States and other nations; taps the U.S. agricultural community to provide technical assistance and professional development and training programs to assist economic development in lower income nations; serves as U.S. liaison with international organizations; and organizes overseas trade and investment missions.

These activities serve the needs of other USDA agencies, the Agency for International Development, other public and private institutions, foreign nations, development banks, and the U.S. university and agricultural communities.

For further information, contact the External Affairs Staff, Office of International Cooperation and Development, U.S. Department of Agriculture, Washington, DC 20250–4300. Phone, 202–245–5800.

Science and Education

Agricultural Research Service

The Agricultural Research Service administers fundamental and applied research to solve problems in animal and plant protection and production; the conservation and improvement of soil, water, and air; the processing, storage, and distribution of farm products; and human nutrition. The research applies to a wide range of goals, commodities, natural resources, fields of science, and geographic, climatic, and environmental conditions.

Research activities are carried out at 122 domestic locations, including Puerto Rico and 8 overseas laboratories. Much of this research is conducted in cooperation with State partners in the universities and experiment stations, other Federal agencies, and private organizations. A national program staff, headquartered at Beltsville, MD, is the focal point in the overall planning and coordination of the Service's national research programs. Day-to-day management of the various national research programs for specific field locations is assigned to 8 area offices.

Area Offices—Agricultural Research Service

Office	Address
BELTSVILLE AREA—Beltsville Agricultural Research Center, National Arboretum, Washington, DC	Bldg. 003, Beltsville Agricultural Research Center, W. Beltsville, MD 20705
MIDSOUTH AREA—Alabama, Kentucky, Louisiana, Mississippi, Tennessee	P.O. Box 225, Stoneville, MS 38776
MIDWEST AREA—Illinois, Indiana, Iowa, Michigan, Minnesota, Missouri, Ohio, Wisconsin	1815 N. University St., Peoria, IL 61604
NORTHERN PLAINS AREA—Colorado, Kansas, Montana, Nebraska, North Dakota, South Dakota, Utah, Wyoming	Suite 350, 2625 Redwing Rd., Ft. Collins, CO 80526
NORTH ATLANTIC AREA—Connecticut, Delaware, Maine, Maryland, Massachusetts, New Hampshire, New Jersey, New York, Pennsylvania, Rhode Island, Vermont, West Virginia	600 E. Mermaid Ln., Philadelphia, PA 19118
PACIFIC WEST AREA—Alaska, Arizona, California, Hawaii, Idaho, Nevada, Oregon, Washington	800 Buchanan St., Albany, CA 94710
SOUTH ATLANTIC AREA—Florida, Georgia, North Carolina, Puerto Rico, South Carolina, Virginia, Virgin Islands	P.O. Box 5677, Athens, GA 30613
SOUTHERN PLAINS AREA—Arkansas, New Mexico, Oklahoma, Texas	Suite 230, 7607 Eastmark Dr., College Station, TX 77840

For further information, contact the Information Staff, Agricultural Research Service, Department of Agriculture, Beltsville, MD 20705. Phone, 301–344–2264.

Cooperative State Research Service

The Cooperative State Research Service facilitates the advancement of science and technology in the nationwide agricultural research system by providing Federal resources, participating in cooperative program planning and evaluation, and developing a forum for coordination between the State Agricultural Experiment Stations, the Department of Agriculture, and Federal research scientists.

The Service's primary function is to administer the acts of Congress that authorize Federal appropriations for agricultural research carried on by the State Agricultural Experiment Stations of the 50 States, Puerto Rico, Guam, the Virgin Islands, American Samoa, Micronesia, the Northern Marianas, the District of Columbia, approved schools of forestry, the 1890 land-grant institutions and Tuskegee University, colleges of veterinary medicine, and other eligible institutions.

Research programs administered by the Service include the agricultural research act (Hatch Act revised) that provides for State/Federal cooperative funding for agricultural research programs at State agricultural experiment stations (including the Regional Research Program that facilitates collaboration on problems of national and regional significance); the cooperative forestry research program; the 1890 land-grant colleges and Tuskegee University research program; the animal health and disease research program; a special research grants program on specific problems in agriculture; the critical materials research program (including domestic rubber); a rangeland research program; aquacultural research centers; an international trade centers research program; an agricultural productivity research program; a groundwater research program; a supplemental and alternative crops research program; a small business innovative research program; a low-input agriculture research program; a small farms research program; a research facilities improvement program; a program of competitive and extramural grants to State agricultural experiment stations, colleges, universities, research organizations, and individuals to promote basic research; and a competitive support program in higher education.

In fulfilling its mission of advancing science and technology in support of agriculture, forestry, people, and communities, the scientific staff allocates Federal resources for the acquisition of new knowledge, promotes excellence in research, encourages the emergence of creativity in science, develops improved awareness and analysis of national problems, supports the efficient management of research institutions and programs, enhances effective leadership in science, promotes the facilitation of new scientific approaches, and strives for improved cooperation between individuals and institutions in the agricultural scientific community.

The Service also provides support and assistance for the Joint Council on Food and Agricultural Science, the National Agricultural Research and Extension Users Advisory Board, and the Committee of Nine (for regional programs).

For further information, contact the Office of the Administrator, Cooperative State Research Service, U.S. Department of Agriculture, Washington, DC 20250–2200. Phone, 202–447–4423.

Extension Service

The Extension Service was created by the Smith-Lever Act of 1914, as amended (7 U.S.C. 341 *et seq.*). The Service is the educational agency of the Department of Agriculture and the Federal partner in the Cooperative Extension System. The System consists of the Extension Service; Extension professionals at the 1862 land-grant universities in the 50 States, American Samoa, the District of Columbia, Guam, Micronesia, the Northern Marianas, Puerto Rico, and the Virgin Islands—plus sixteen 1890 land-grant universities with Tuskegee University as the State partner; and staff in nearly all of the Nation's 3,150 counties as the local partners. All three partners share in financing, planning, and conducting the Cooperative Extension System's educational programs.

As a nationwide educational network, the Cooperative Extension System helps people improve their lives through an educational process that uses scientific knowledge focused on issues and needs. Key functions include:

—providing nationwide leadership in adapting and transferring science and technology;

—anticipating and responding educationally to critical national issues affecting the food and agricultural system;

—mobilizing resources to respond to natural disasters and catastrophes;

—initiating educational programs to help implement Federal regulations and policies; and

—developing more than 3 million volunteers to serve the Nation, the States, and local communities with educational program support.

Through an interactive, strategic planning process, Extension educational programs target critical issues. Current national issues being addressed are food safety and quality, international marketing, revitalizing rural America, sustainable agriculture, waste management, water quality, and youth at risk.

The Extension Service has a small professional staff that formulates national policy and provides leadership, coordination, and evaluation to support State and county educational programs.

The Cooperative Extension at the land-grant universities has State, county, and area staff who work with clientele to determine their needs and develop educational programs to assist farmers, families, individuals, and communities. All Extension programs are designed to apply new communication technologies—including computers, videos, satellites, and teleconferences to develop and deliver educational programs. The national Cooperative Extension System also assures citizens access to research-finding and information from anywhere in the Nation.

For further information, contact the Director, Communication, Information, and Technology, Extension Service, Department of Agriculture, Washington, DC 20250. Phone, 202–447–3029.

National Agricultural Library

The National Agricultural Library provides information services over a broad range of agricultural interests to a wide cross-section of users, from research scientists to the general public. The Library assists its users through a variety of specialized information centers. Its staff utilizes advanced information technologies to generate new information products, creating an electronic library as it improves access to the knowledge stored in its multi-media collection of over 2 million items. At the same time, the Library is sharing resources, cooperating with land-grant university and other libraries in many projects, and using telecommunications to share information among all the libraries and their users.

Information on agriculture is made available through loans, photocopies, reference services, and literature searches. A subject profiling system for selective searches of agricultural data bases is available for USDA scientists. Citations to the agricultural literature are stored in the AGRICultural OnLine Access (AGRICOLA) data base, available through online computer systems and on compact disc. The Library also distributes in the United States the AGRIS data base of citations to the agricultural literature prepared by centers in various parts of the world and coordinated by the Food and Agriculture Organization of the United Nations.

Access to information is strengthened by the use of innovative technology, including compact disc, as noted above; digital videodisc, containing fully searchable full text of publications; laser videodisc, containing photo collections; interactive videodisc for instruction in the use of the online AGRICOLA data base; and expert systems serving as reference advisors. Instructor-led workshops are also conducted for training at the basic and advanced levels in use of the AGRICOLA data base.

Specialized information centers on subjects of current concern—agricultural trade and marketing, alternative farming systems, animal welfare, aquaculture, biotechnology, food and nutrition, plant genome, rural development, technology transfer, water quality, and youth development—provide enhanced information services to the Library's current clientele as well as develop new service relationships with the public and private sectors. Information center staff concentrate their efforts on strengthening the Library collection, developing information products, coordinating outreach activities, and establishing dissemination networks.

The products and services of the Library are available to Department of Agriculture personnel, other Federal agencies, land-grant universities, the agricultural community in the U.S. and worldwide, and others with an interest in the Library's resources.

The main Library is located at 10301 Baltimore Boulevard, Beltsville, MD 20705-2351. The DC Reference Center of the National Agricultural Library, located in Room 1052, South Building, U.S. Department of Agriculture, 14th and Independence Avenue SW., Washington, DC 20250, offers reference resources, periodicals, newspapers, and services including data base searching, end-user training, demonstrations of new technology, and document delivery from Beltsville.

For further information, contact the Office of the Director, National Agricultural Library, Beltsville, MD 20705-2351. Phone, 301-344-4248.

Natural Resources and Environment

Forest Service

[For the Forest Service statement of organization, see the *Code of Federal Regulations,* Title 36, Part 200.1]

The Forest Service was created by the Transfer Act of February 1, 1905 (16 U.S.C. 472), which transferred the Federal forest reserves and the responsibility for their management from the Department of the Interior to the Department of Agriculture. The forest reserves were established by the President from the public domain under authority of the Creative Act of March 3, 1891 (26 Stat. 1103). The protection and development of the reserves (which became the national forests in 1907) are governed by the Organic Act of June 4, 1897, as amended (16 U.S.C. 473–478); the Multiple Use-Sustained Yield Act of June 12, 1960 (16 U.S.C. 528–531); the Forest and Rangeland Renewable Resources Planning Act of 1974 (16 U.S.C. 1601–1610); and the National Forest Management Act of 1976 (90 Stat. 2947). The Weeks Law of March 1, 1911, as amended (16 U.S.C. 480), allowed the Government to purchase and exchange land for national forests.

Objectives The Forest Service has the Federal responsibility for national leadership in forestry. Its mission is to provide a continuing flow of natural resource goods and services to help meet the needs of the Nation and to contribute to the needs of the international community. To accomplish this, it has adopted the following objectives:

—to provide a sustained flow of renewable resources—outdoor recreation, forage, wood, water, wilderness, wildlife, and fish—in a combination that best meets the needs of society now and in the future;

—to administer the nonrenewable resources of the National Forest System to help meet the Nation's needs for energy and mineral resources;

—to promote a healthy and productive environment for the Nation's forests and rangelands;

—to develop and make available scientific and technological capabilities to advance renewable natural resource management, use, and protection; and

—to further natural resource conservation through cooperation with other Federal agencies and State and local governments.

National Forest System The Service manages 156 national forests, 19 national grasslands, and 15 land utilization projects on 191 million acres in 44 States, the Virgin Islands, and Puerto Rico under the principles of multiple-use and sustained yield. The Nation's tremendous need for wood and paper products is balanced with the other vital, renewable resources or benefits that the national forests and grasslands provide: recreation and natural beauty, wildlife habitat, livestock forage, and water supplies. The guiding principle is the greatest good to the greatest number in the long run.

These lands are protected as much as possible from wildfire, epidemics of disease and insect pests, erosion, floods, and water and air pollution. Burned areas get emergency seeding treatment to prevent massive erosion and stream siltation. Roads and trails are built where needed to allow for closely regulated timber harvesting and to give the public access to outdoor recreation areas and provide scenic drives and hikes. Picnic, camping, water-sport, skiing, and other areas are provided with facilities for public convenience and enjoyment. Timber harvesting methods are used that will protect the land and streams, assure rapid renewal of the forest, provide food and cover for wildlife and fish, and have minimum impact on scenic and recreation values. Local communities benefit from the logging and milling activities. These lands also provide needed oil, gas, and minerals. Rangelands are improved for millions of livestock and game animals. The national forests provide a refuge for many species of endangered birds, animals, and fish. Some 32 million acres are set aside as wilderness and 175,000 acres as primitive areas where timber will not be harvested.

Cooperation With the States The Service provides national leadership and financial and technical assistance to non-Federal forest landowners, operators, processors of forest products, and urban forestry interests. Through its cooperative State and private forestry programs, the Service protects and improves the quality of air, water, soil, and open space and encourages uses of natural resources on non-Federal lands that best meet the needs of the Nation, while protecting the environment.

Cooperative programs are carried out through the State foresters or equivalent State officials, who receive grant funding under the Cooperative Forestry Assistance Act of 1978 (16 U.S.C. 2101). Cooperators at the State and local level provide the delivery system for most State and private forestry programs.

Grant funds and technical assistance are available for rural forestry assistance, forestry incentives, insect and disease control, urban forestry assistance, rural fire prevention and control, organization management assistance, State forest resource planning, and technology implementation.

The Service also cooperates with the Soil Conservation Service, the Agricultural Stabilization and Conservation Service, and other USDA agencies in providing leadership and technical assistance for the forestry aspects of conservation programs.

State and private forestry also is responsible for ensuring that the Service and its cooperators keep abreast of the best knowledge and technology in carrying out its programs, and helping to develop technology transfer plans for implementing research results for a broad range of potential users.

Forest Research The Service carries on basic research throughout the country, often in cooperation with State agricultural colleges, under the authority of the McSweeney-McNary act of May 22, 1928, as amended and supplemented (45 Stat. 699). Research is carried on in all the fields previously mentioned in addition to many others including genetics, nutrition, improved methods of harvesting, prevention, detection, and mapping of lightning fires, better processing methods for forest products, and environmental improvement.

Human Resource Programs The Service operates the Youth Conservation Corps and the Volunteers in the National Forests programs and participates with the Department of Labor on several human resource programs that involve the Nation's citizens, both young and old, in forestry-related activities. Included in these programs are the Job Corps and the Senior Community Service Employment Program. These programs annually accomplish millions of dollars worth of conservation work, while providing participants with such benefits as training, paid employment, and meaningful outdoor experience.

Field Offices—Forest Service

	Address
National Forest System Regions [1]—Regional Forester	
1. Northern	Federal Bldg. (P.O. Box 7669), Missoula, MT 59807
2. Rocky Mountain	11177 W. 8th Ave. (P.O. Box 25127), Lakewood, CO 80225
3. Southwestern	517 Gold Ave. SW., Albuquerque, NM 87102
4. Intermountain	324 25th St., Ogden, UT 84401
5. Pacific Southwest	630 Sansome St., San Francisco, CA 94111
6. Pacific Northwest	319 SW. Pine St. (P.O. Box 3623), Portland, OR 97208
8. Southern	1720 Peachtree Rd. NW., Atlanta, GA 30367
9. Eastern	310 W. Wisconsin Ave., Milwaukee, WI 53203
10. Alaska	Federal Office Bldg. (P.O. Box 21628), Juneau, AK 99802
Forest and Range Experiment Stations—Director	
Intermountain	324 25th St., Ogden, UT 84401
North Central	1992 Folwell Ave., St. Paul, MN 55108
Northeastern	370 Reed Rd., Broomall, PA 19008
Pacific Northwest	P.O. Box 3890, Portland, OR 97208
Pacific Southwest	1960 Addison St. (P.O. Box 245), Berkeley, CA 94701
Rocky Mountain	240 W. Prospect Ave., Fort Collins, CO 80526
Southeastern	200 Weaver Blvd. (P.O. Box 2860), Asheville, NC 28804
Southern	701 Loyola Ave., U.S. Postal Service Bldg., New Orleans, LA 70113
Forest Products Laboratory	1 Gifford Pinchot Dr., Madison, WI 53705
State and Private Forestry Areas [2]—Director	
Northeastern	370 Reed Rd., Broomall, PA 19008

[1] There is no Region 7.
[2] In Regions 1 through 6, 8, and 10, State and private forestry activities are directed from regional headquarters.

For further information, contact the Public Affairs Office, Forest Service, Department of Agriculture, P.O. Box 96090, Washington, DC 20090–6090. Phone, 202–447–3760.

Soil Conservation Service

[For the Soil Conservation Service statement of organization, see the *Code of Federal Regulations,* Title 7, Parts 600 and 601]

The Soil Conservation Service (SCS) was established under authority of the Soil Conservation Act of 1935 (16 U.S.C. 590a-f). It has responsibility for developing and carrying out a national soil and water conservation program in cooperation with landowners and operators and other land users and developers, with community planning agencies and regional resource groups, and with other Federal, State, and local government agencies. The Service also assists in agricultural pollution control, environmental improvement, and rural community development.

The soil and water conservation program is carried on through technical help to locally organized and operated conservation districts; local sponsors of watershed protection projects and resource conservation and development projects; and consultative assistance to other individuals and groups. About 3,000 conservation districts cover more than 2 billion acres in the 50 States, Guam, Puerto Rico, and the Virgin Islands.

Conservation Operations The Service provides technical assistance through conservation districts to landowners and operators in carrying out locally adapted soil and water conservation programs.

Technical assistance is given to district cooperators and other landowners in the development of conservation plans and application of conservation treatment. Assistance to district cooperators (individuals and communities) includes: providing a soil map and other resource data; providing information about practical alternatives for treating and using the land; developing a plan for installing the treatment measures and making the land use changes needed; and helping to apply parts of the plan that require special skills or knowledge.

In response to the President's Water Quality Initiative, the Service is carrying out, in cooperation with other Federal and State agencies, a 5-year plan to direct its activities relative to water quality and quantity. Elements addressed in this plan include program application, technology development, information and education, and evaluation and assessment. The implementation of the plan will focus on the expansion and improvement of technical assistance utilizing the agency's extensive field delivery system through local soil and water conservation districts. A major part of the assistance required by SCS to implement the USDA's Water Quality Initiative is provided through conservation operations.

Soil surveys are made to determine soil use potentials and conservation treatment needs, and publication of soil surveys with interpretations useful to cooperators, other Federal agencies, and State and local organizations. One important basis for conservation planning is the National Cooperative Soil Survey for which SCS has the Federal part of the responsibility. The work is carried out in cooperation with State agricultural experiment stations and other State and Federal agencies.

Plant materials centers are operated to assemble, test, and encourage increased use of promising plant species in conservation programs; and snow surveys in the Western States are made to develop water supply forecasts.

Under the Soil and Water Resources Conservation Act of 1977 (16 U.S.C. 2001), the Service is responsible for appraising the status and condition of soil, water, and related resources and trends in their use; designing long-range conservation programs with the aid of local soil conservation districts and the public; and evaluating progress in meeting conservation needs. The Service's inventory and monitoring data are used at all governmental levels for conservation, use and development of land, and for protecting environmental quality. The Service also helps prepare maps showing the location of important farmlands, usually on a county basis.

Under the Food Security Act of 1985 and the Food, Agriculture, Conservation, and Trade Act of 1990, the Service helps producers determine if their cropland or potential cropland is highly erodible, wetland, wetland on which the conversion would result in minimal effect, or converted wetland. Service field staffs assist producers in preparing conservation compliance plans and installing appropriate conservation systems so that eligibility for USDA program benefits is maintained.

River Basin Surveys and Investigations The Service, along with the Economic Research Service and Forest Service, cooperates with other Federal, State, and local agencies in studying the watersheds of rivers and other waterways. These studies include:

—cooperative river basin surveys, which serve as a basis for developing coordinated water resource programs;

—flood plain management studies, which furnish technical data, assistance, and information for State and local governments to use in flood plain management programs;

—joint investigations and reports with the Department of the Army in accordance with Pub. L. 87–639 (16 U.S.C. 1009); and

—interagency coordination.

Watershed Planning The Service has general responsibility for administration of activities consisting of investigations and surveys of proposed small watershed projects in response to requests made by sponsoring local organizations, and for assisting sponsors in the development of watershed plans.

Watershed and Flood Prevention Operations The Service has general responsibility for administration of activities that include cooperation with local sponsors, State, and other public agencies in the installation of planned works of improvement to reduce erosion, floodwater, and sediment damage; conserve, develop, utilize, and dispose of water; plan and install works of improvement for flood prevention including the development of recreational facilities and the improvement of fish and wildlife habitat; and loans to local organizations to help finance the local share of the cost of carrying out planned watershed and flood prevention works of improvement. The Farmers Home Administration administers the loan program.

The Service also has responsibility for carrying out emergency watershed protection under section 403 of the Agricultural Credit Act of 1978 (16 U.S.C. 2203).

Great Plains Conservation Program The Service has general responsibility for administration of the program designed to promote conservation and greater agricultural stability in the Great Plains area. Activities include cost-sharing of conservation practices under 3- to 10-year contracts with farmers and ranchers in designated counties of the 10 Great Plains States, and technical services to help make needed land use adjustments and install conservation measures specified in conservation plans in accordance with contract schedules.

Resource Conservation and Development Program The Service has general responsibility for administering the program designed to assist local government units in accelerating planning and development of land and water resources in multiple county areas. Projects include work for such things as erosion control, flood prevention, farm irrigation, fish and wildlife facilities, agriculture-related pollutant control, and water quality. Plans also are directed toward improving recreation facilities, including historic and scenic attractions; encouraging new industries to locate in the area and to process products of the area; improving markets for crop and livestock products; upgrading and protecting the quality of the environment; and long-range planning to coordinate public efforts in the area.

Activities include investigations and surveys to help develop programs and plans of land conservation and utilization, technical services and financial assistance to sponsors, local groups, and individuals, and making loans for resource improvements and developments in approved projects. The Farmers Home Administration administers the loans.

Rural Abandoned Mine Program The Service has USDA leadership for administration of the program to assist land users in reclaiming abandoned or inadequately reclaimed coal-mined lands and water, provided there is no continuing reclamation responsibility on the part of the mine operator, permit holder, or agent. The program provides cost-sharing aid ranging from 25 to 100 percent, as well as technical assistance to land users, under contracts of 5 to 10 years. The goal is to reclaim, conserve, and develop unreclaimed coal lands that adversely affect people or their environment.

Other Programs The Service gives technical help to the Farmers Home Administration in making soil and water conservation loans to landowners and operators and assists landowners and operators in developing recreation areas and facilities on private land.

Participants in the Agricultural Conservation Program, Rural Clean Water Program, Conservation Reserve Program, Colorado River Salinity Control Program, and the Water Bank Program are provided with technical assistance by the Service. Under these programs, it provides technical assistance in developing conservation plans that are the basis of long-term agreements between the Department and landowners and operators. The Service assists in the design, layout, and certification of some conservation practices installed under these programs.

For further information, contact the Public Information Division, Soil Conservation Service, Department of Agriculture, P.O. Box 2890, Washington, DC 20013. Phone, 202–447–4543.

Economics

Economic Research Service

The mission of the Economic Research Service (ERS) is to provide economic and other social science information and analysis for improving the performance of agriculture and rural America. The Service produces such information as a benefit to the general public and to help Congress and the administration develop, administer, and evaluate agricultural and rural policies and programs. The wide range of topics covered by ERS include:

—U.S. and world agricultural production and demand for production resources, agricultural commodities, and food and fiber products;

—costs of and returns to agricultural production and marketing;

—economic performance of U.S. agricultural production and marketing;

—effects of Governmental policies and programs on farmers, rural residents and communities, natural resources, and the public; and

—organization and institutions of the U.S. and world agricultural production and marketing systems, natural resources, and rural communities.

ERS-produced information is made available to the public through research monographs, situation and outlook reports, standardized data products in electronic media, professional and trade journals (including *The Journal of Agricultural Economics Research*), magazines (including *Agricultural Outlook, Farmline, National Food Review,* and *Rural Development Perspectives*), radio, television, newspapers, and frequent participation of ERS staff at various public forums.

For further information, contact the Information Division, Economics Management Staff, Department of Agriculture, Washington, DC 20005–4789. Phone, 202–786–1504.

National Agricultural Statistics Service

The National Agricultural Statistics Service prepares estimates and reports on production, supply, price, and other items necessary for the orderly operation of the U.S. agricultural economy.

The reports include statistics on field crops, fruits and vegetables, cattle, hogs, sheep, poultry, and related commodities or processed products. Other estimates concern farm numbers, prices received by farmers for products sold, prices paid for commodities and services, indexes of prices received and paid, parity prices, farm employment, and farm wage rates.

The Service prepares these estimates through a complex system of sample surveys of producers, processors, buyers, and others associated with agriculture. Information is gathered by mail, telephone, personal interviews, and field visits.

The 45 State-Federal offices, serving all 50 States, and the national office prepare weekly, monthly, annual, and other periodic reports for free distribution to the news media, Congress, and survey respondents. The reports are available to others on a subscription basis. Data on crop and livestock products appears in over 300 reports issued annually. Cooperative agreements with State agencies also permit preparation and publication of estimates of individual crops and livestock by counties in most States.

The Service performs reimbursable survey work and statistical consulting services for other Federal and State agencies and provides technical assistance for developing agricultural data systems in other countries.

For further information, contact the Information Division, Economics Management Staff, Department of Agriculture, Washington, DC 20005–4789. Phone, 202–786–1504.

Economic Analysis Staff

The Economic Analysis Staff assists in developing, organizing, coordinating, and synthesizing economic and statistical analyses to be used as a basis for planning and evaluating short- and intermediate-range agricultural policy. The Staff also develops economic and statistical analyses to evaluate complex interagency domestic and foreign agricultural problems and issues. The staff also is responsible for departmental regulations on agricultural labor under the Immigration and Nationality Act (8 U.S.C. 1101 note).

The Staff reviews and evaluates recommendations submitted by USDA agencies, task forces, and study groups for their impact upon the agricultural economy. It analyzes the economic policy implications of legislative proposals of the Department and of Congress. The Staff also represents the Department in meetings with agriculture, industry, and consumer groups to discuss the economic impact of existing and proposed Department policies.

For further information, contact the Information Division, Economics Management Staff, Department of Agriculture, Washington, DC 20005–4789. Phone, 202–786–1504.

Office of Energy

The Office of Energy serves as the focal point for all energy-related matters within the Department. The Office is responsible for developing and coordinating all USDA energy policies, reviewing and evaluating all USDA energy and energy-related programs, and providing liaison with the Department of Energy and other Federal agencies and departments on energy activities that may affect agriculture and rural America. The Office also represents the Department in meetings with agriculture, industry, and consumer groups to discuss impacts of departmental energy policies, programs, and proposals.

For further information, contact the Information Division, Economics Management Staff, Department of Agriculture, Washington, DC 20005–4789. Phone, 202–786–1504.

World Agricultural Outlook Board

The World Agricultural Outlook Board coordinates the development of and reviews all commodity and aggregate agricultural forecasts issued by the Department. The Board's objective is to improve the consistency, objectivity, and reliability of the outlook information provided to the public.

The Board serves as a focal point for the Department's economic intelligence effort of gathering, interpreting, and summarizing developments affecting domestic and world agriculture. The Board brings together interagency experts to develop official forecasts of supply, utilization, and prices for commodities.

The Board participates in planning and developing research programs related to improving departmental analyses and forecasts, including departmentwide activities involving remote sensing, weather, and climate. The Board jointly operates a Joint Agricultural Weather Facility with the National Oceanic and Atmospheric Administration which continually monitors world weather and assesses its effects on agriculture.

The Board also plans and participates in departmental, interdepartmental, regional, and international outlook conferences and briefings.

For further information, contact the Information Office, World Agricultural Outlook Board, Department of Agriculture, Washington, DC 20250–3800. Phone, 202–447–5447.

Economics Management Staff

The Economics Management Staff provides management services to the National Agricultural Statistics Service, the Economic Research Service, the World Agricultural Outlook Board, the Economic Analysis Staff, and the Office of Energy. These services include budget, financial management, personnel and related programs, administrative services, information, equal opportunity and civil rights, and general management assistance.

For further information, contact the Information Division, Economics Management Staff, Department of Agriculture, Washington, DC 20005–4789. Phone, 202–786–1504.

Graduate School, U.S. Department of Agriculture

Fourteenth Street and Independence Avenue SW., Washington, DC 20250
Phone, 202–447–4419

Director	PHILIP H. HUDSON
Deputy Director	LYNN EDWARDS
Program Director, Correspondence Study	NORMA HARWOOD
Director of Information and Public Affairs	BRIAN GRAY
Program Director, Evening and Saturday	RONALD MACNAB
Program Director, Government Audit Training Institute	DONALD SMULAND

Program Director, International Training	ROBERT MASHBURN
Program Director, International Visitor and Exchange	LILY PARSONS
Director of Administration	LANSING WILLIAMS
Registrar	CAROLYN NELSON

The Graduate School, U.S. Department of Agriculture, is a continuing education school offering career-related training to adults. It is self-supporting and does not receive direct appropriated funds from Congress or the Department of Agriculture. Fees charged individuals and Government agencies are nominal. Courses are planned with the help of Government professionals and specialists. The faculty is mostly part-time and is drawn from throughout Government and the community at large. They are selected because of their professional and specialized knowledge and experience and thus bring a practicality and experience to their classrooms. Faculty holding regular Government positions take annual leave or leave without pay when teaching during their normal work hours. The school does not grant degrees but does provide planned sequences of courses leading to certificates of accomplishment in a number of occupational and career fields important to government. Training areas include management, auditing, computer science, communications, foreign language, procurement, financial management, and others.

The Graduate School's objective is to improve Government services by providing needed continuing education and training opportunities for Government employees and agencies. The Graduate School, administered by a Director and governed by a General Administration Board appointed by the Secretary of Agriculture, was established by the Secretary of Agriculture on September 2, 1921, pursuant to act of May 15, 1862 (7 U.S.C. 2201); joint resolution of April 12, 1892 (27 Stat. 395); and the Deficiencies Appropriation Act of March 3, 1901 (20 U.S.C. 91).

For further information, contact the Information Office, Graduate School, U.S. Department of Agriculture, Room 129, 600 Maryland Avenue SW., Washington, DC 20024. Phone, 202–447–4419.

Sources of Information

Consumer Activities Educational, organizational, and financial assistance is offered to consumers and their families in such fields as rural housing and farm operating programs, improved nutrition, family living and recreation, food stamp, school lunch, donated foods, and other food programs. Phone, 202–447–2791.

Contracts and Small Business Activities Contact the Office of Advocacy and Enterprise, Department of Agriculture, Washington, DC 20250. Phone, 202–447–7117.

Employment Most jobs in the Department are in the competitive service and are filled by applicants who have established eligibility under an appropriate examination administered by the Office of Personnel Management or Department Special Examining Units.

General employment inquiries may be sent to the Staffing and Personnel Information Systems Staff, Office of Personnel, Department of Agriculture, Washington, DC 20250. Phone, 202–426–3964.

Persons interested in employment in the Food and Nutrition Service should contact the Regional Offices located in Atlanta, Chicago, Dallas, San Francisco, Denver, Boston, and Robbinsville, NJ, or the national headquarters in Washington, DC. Phone, 703–756–3326.

Persons interested in employment in the Office of the Inspector General should contact the USDA Office of

Personnel, Room 6-W, Administration Building, Washington, DC 20250. Phone, 202-447-5781.

In addition, all Forest Service field units listed on page 137 will accept employment applications.

Environment Educational, organizational, technical, and financial assistance is offered to local citizens, their organizations and communities in such fields as watershed protection, flood prevention, soil and water conservation practices to reduce erosion and sedimentation, community water and waste disposal systems, safe use of pesticides, and the development of pesticide alternatives.

Contact the nearest county Extension agent or USDA office, or write to the Office of Public Affairs, Department of Agriculture, Washington, DC 20250, for information on consumer activities and the environment, as described above. Phone, 202-447-2791.

Films Motion pictures on a variety of agricultural subjects are available for loan through various State Extension Service film libraries. Contact the Video and Teleconference Division, Office of Public Affairs, Department of Agriculture, Washington, DC 20250, for a listing of cooperating film libraries. Phone, 202-447-6072.

Color filmstrips and slide sets on a variety of subjects are available for purchase. For a listing of titles and prices, contact the Photography Division, Office of Public Affairs, Department of Agriculture, Washington, DC 20250. Phone, 202-447-6633.

Whistleblower Hotline Persons wishing to register complaints of alleged improprieties concerning the Department should contact one of the Regional Offices or the Inspector General's "Whistleblower Hotline"—outside Washington, DC, phone toll-free, 800-424-9121; within the Washington, DC, metropolitan area. Phone, 202-475-5022.

Reading Rooms Located at each USDA agency; addresses indicated in text.

Speakers Contact the nearest Department of Agriculture office or county Extension agent. In the District of Columbia, contact the Office of Public Liaison, Office of Public Affairs, Department of Agriculture, Washington, DC 20250. Phone, 202-447-2798.

For further information concerning the Department of Agriculture, contact the Office of Public Affairs, Department of Agriculture, Washington, DC 20250. Phone, 202-447-2791.

DEPARTMENT OF COMMERCE

Fourteenth Street between Constitution Avenue and E Street NW., Washington, DC 20230
Phone, 202–377–2000

SECRETARY OF COMMERCE	ROBERT A. MOSBACHER
Chief of Staff and Assistant Secretary of Commerce	THOMAS J. COLLAMORE
Counselor to the Secretary	BRUCE A. SOLL
Deputy Counselor	TIMOTHY P. HECHT
Director, Office of White House Liaison	MARY ANN FISH
Director, Executive Secretariat	BARBARA J. GOLDKAMP
Deputy Secretary of Commerce	ROCKWELL A. SCHNABEL
Associate Deputy Secretaries	MARC G. STANLEY
	MARK S. LIEBERMAN
Special Assistant to the Deputy Secretary	KARLTON C. ADAM
Director, Office of Commercial Space Programs	JAMES J. FRELK
Director, Office of Small and Disadvantaged Business Utilization	JAMES MARUCA
General Counsel	WENDELL L. WILLKIE II
Deputy General Counsel	DAN HAENDEL
Counselor to the General Counsel	ALDEN F. ABBOTT
Assistant General Counsel for Administration	BARBARA S. FREDERICKS
Assistant General Counsel for Legislation and Regulation	MICHAEL A. LEVITT
Assistant General Counsel for Finance and Litigation	JAMES K. WHITE
Chief Counsel for Economic Affairs	PHILIP FREIJE, *Acting*
Chief Counsel for Export Administration	THOMAS H. STILLMAN
Chief Counsel for Import Administration	STEPHEN J. POWELL
Chief Counsel for International Commerce	ELEANOR ROBERTS LEWIS
Chief Counsel for Minority Business Development	ERIC MOLL
Chief Counsel for Technology Administration	JAMES V. LACY
Assistant Secretary for Legislative and Intergovernmental Affairs	CRAIG R. HELSING
Deputy Assistant Secretary for Legislative Affairs	MICHAEL R. GALE
Director for Intergovernmental Affairs	ALISON KAUFMAN
Inspector General	FRANK D. DEGEORGE
Deputy Inspector General	MICHAEL ZIMMERMAN
Counsel to the Inspector General	K. WAYNE WEAVER
Assistant Inspector General for Auditing	JOHN D. NEWELL
Assistant Inspector General for Investigations	FREDERICK J. PINCIARO
Assistant Inspector General for Inspections and Resource Management	CHARLES M. HALL
Assistant Inspector General for Compliance and Audit Resolution	GEORGE R. ROSS

Director, Office of Public Affairs	(VACANCY)
Deputy Director	(VACANCY)
Director, Office of Business Liaison	DIANE G. TERPELUK
Director, Office of Consumer Affairs	(VACANCY)
Assistant Secretary for Administration and Chief Financial Officer	PRESTON MOORE
Deputy Assistant Secretary for Administration	OTTO J. WOLFF
Director for Budget, Planning and Organization	ALAN P. BALUTIS
Director, Office of Budget	MARK E. BROWN
Director, Office of Program Planning and Evaluation	CHARLES F. TREAT
Director, Office of Management and Organization	STEPHEN C. BROWNING
Director, Office of Civil Rights	GERALD R. LUCAS
Director for Federal Assistance and Management Support	SONYA G. STEWART
Director, Office of Budget Operations	URIEL GOTTESMAN
Director, Office of Federal Assistance	BARBARA LAMBIS
Director, Office of Management Support	(VACANCY)
Director for Financial Management	GARY T. MAUPIN
Deputy and Director, Office of Financial Planning and Analysis	DOUGLAS K. DAY
Director, Office of Financial Systems	JOSEPH SCLAFANI
Director, Office of Financial Policies and Procedures	ROGER J. MALLET
Director, Office of Financial Operations and Reports	JOAN BOZZONETTI
Director, Office of Financial Compliance and Review	(VACANCY)
Director for Information Resources Management	REED PHILLIPS, JR.
Director, Office of Information Policy and Technology	JAMES E. MCNAMEE
Director, Office of Systems and Telecommunications	RONALD P. HACK
Director, Office of Information Planning and Review	THOMAS H. SCOTT
Director, Office of Computer Services	RALPH J. HURD
Director of Personnel	ELIZABETH W. STROUD
Deputy Director	(VACANCY)
Director, Office of Personnel Operations	(VACANCY)
Director for Procurement and Administrative Services	HUGH L. BRENNAN
Deputy Director	DAVID FARBER
Director, Office of Procurement	ROBERT A. WELCH
Director, Office of Administrative Services Management	MARY T. DIGIULIAN
Director, Office of Administrative Operations	ROBERT A. GALPIN
Director, Office of Federal Property Programs	HARRY E. BRADLEY, JR.
Director, Office of Security	STEPHEN E. GARMON
Director, Office of Library and Information Services	ANTHONY J. STEINHAUSER

Under Secretary for Economic Affairs and Administrator	MICHAEL R. DARBY
Deputy Under Secretary	MARK W. PLANT
Deputy Assistant Secretary for Statistical Affairs	HARRY SCARR
Director, Office of Policy Analysis	JEFFREY L. MAYER
Director, Office of Business Analysis	JOHN E. CREMEANS
Associate Under Secretary (External Relations)	SUSANNE H. HOWARD
Executive Director	F.T. KNICKERBOCKER
Director of Administration	B. JEROME JACKSON
Chief Economist	J. ANTONIO VILLAMIL
Director, Office of Macroeconomic Analysis	SUMIYE O. MCGUIRE
Director, Office of Economic Conditions	CARL E. COX
Director, Bureau of the Census	BARBARA E. BRYANT
Deputy Director	C.L. KINCANNON
Associate Director for Management Services	BRYANT BENTON
Associate Director for Field Operations	ROLAND H. MOORE
Associate Director for Demographic Programs	WILLIAM P. BUTZ
Associate Director for Economic Programs	CHARLES A. WAITE
Associate Director for Statistical Design, Methodology and Standards	ROBERT M. GROVES
Associate Director for Decennial Census	CHARLES D. JONES
Director, Bureau of Economic Analysis	ALLAN H. YOUNG
Deputy Director	CAROL S. CARSON
Associate Director for National Economic Accounts	ROBERT P. PARKER
Associate Director for Regional Economics	HUGH W. KNOX
Associate Director for International Economics	J. STEVEN LANDEFELD
Under Secretary for Export Administration	(VACANCY)
Deputy Under Secretary	JOAN M. MCENTEE
Associate Deputy Under Secretary	STANLEY SIENKIEWICZ
Director of Administration	ROBERT F. KUGELMAN
Assistant Secretary for Export Administration	MICHAEL P. GALVIN
Deputy Assistant Secretary	JAMES M. LEMUNYON
Director, Office of Export Licensing	IAIN S. BAIRD
Director, Office of Technology and Policy Analysis	WILLIAM CLEMENTS
Director, Office of Foreign Availability	STEVE GOLDMAN
Assistant Secretary for Export Enforcement	QUINCY M. KROSBY
Deputy Assistant Secretary	KENNETH A. CUTSHAW
Director, Office of Export Enforcement	FRANK DELIBERTI
Director, Office of Antiboycott Compliance	WILLIAM SKIDMORE
Director, Office of Enforcement Support	THOMAS ANDRUKONIS
Assistant Secretary for Economic Development	L. JOYCE HAMPERS
Deputy Assistant Secretary	DOUGLAS J. ALLER
Deputy Assistant Secretary for Program Operations	HUGH M. FARMER
Deputy Assistant Secretary for Program Support	RUTH L. KLEINFELD
Chief Counsel	JOSEPH M. LEVINE
Under Secretary for International Trade	J. MICHAEL FARREN

Deputy Under Secretary	ROGER W. WALLACE
Deputy Assistant Secretary for Planning	TIMOTHY J. HAUSER
Director of Administration	ALAN NEUSCHATZ
Assistant Secretary for International Economic Policy	THOMAS J. DUESTERBERG
Deputy Assistant Secretary for International Economic Policy	RICHARD L. JOHNSTON, JR.
Deputy Assistant Secretary for the Western Hemisphere	ANN HUGHES
Deputy Assistant Secretary for Europe	FRANKLIN J. VARGO
Deputy Assistant Secretary for Africa, the Near East and South Asia	DAVID A. JENSEN
Deputy Assistant Secretary for East Asia and the Pacific	JON HUNTSMAN
Deputy Assistant Secretary for Japan	MARJORY SEARING
Assistant Secretary for Import Administration	ERIC I. GARFINKEL
Deputy Assistant Secretary for Import Administration	MARJORIE A. CHORLINS
Deputy Assistant Secretary for Compliance	JOSEPH SPETRINI
Deputy Assistant Secretary for Investigations	FRANCIS J. SAILER
Assistant Secretary for Trade Development	TIMOTHY J. MCBRIDE
Deputy Assistant Secretary for Trade Development	JAMES C. LAKE
Deputy Assistant Secretary for Capital Goods and International Construction	CHRISTINA M. BOLTON
Deputy Assistant Secretary for Basic Industries	FREDERICK W. VOLCANSEK
Deputy Assistant Secretary for Science and Electronics	ALAN M. DUNN
Deputy Assistant Secretary for Automotive Affairs and Consumer Goods	MARY A. TOMAN
Deputy Assistant Secretary for Aerospace	SALLY H. BATH, *Acting*
Deputy Assistant Secretary for Services	LINDA POWERS
Deputy Assistant Secretary for Trade Information and Analysis	BARBARA N. MCLENNAN
Deputy Assistant Secretary for Textiles and Apparel	AUGUSTINE D. TANTILLO
Assistant Secretary and Director General of the U.S. and Foreign Commercial Service	SUSAN C. SCHWAB
Deputy Assistant Secretary for the U.S. and Foreign Commercial Service	JOSEPH A. VASQUEZ
Deputy Assistant Secretary for Domestic Operations	DANIEL E. SULLIVAN
Deputy Assistant Secretary for International Operations	THEODORE A. ROSEN
Manager, Export Promotion Services	(VACANCY)
Director, Minority Business Development Agency	JOE A. LIRA
Deputy Director	WILLIAM H. BAILEY
Assistant Director for External Affairs	JOHN R. WINSTON
Executive Officer for Administration	GEORGE S. PARISH
Associate Director for Operations	(VACANCY)
Assistant Director for Program Development	BHARAT BHARGAVA

Under Secretary for Oceans and Atmosphere and Administrator	John A. Knauss
Assistant Secretary for Oceans and Atmosphere and Deputy Administrator	Jennifer Joy Wilson
Deputy Under Secretary for Oceans and Atmosphere	Gray Castle
Chief Scientist	Sylvia Earle
Deputy Assistant Secretary for International Interests	Carmen J. Blondin
Assistant Administrator for Fisheries	William W. Fox, Jr.
Assistant Administrator for Ocean Services and Coastal Zone Management	Virginia K. Tippie
Assistant Administrator for Oceanic and Atmospheric Research	Ned A. Ostenso
Assistant Administrator for Weather Service	Elbert W. Friday, Jr.
Assistant Administrator for Environmental Satellites, Data, and Information Services	Thomas N. Pyke, Jr.
General Counsel	Thomas A. Campbell
Comptroller	Andrew Moxam
Director of Administration	(vacancy)
Director, National Oceanic and Atmospheric Administration Corps Operations	Sigmund R. Petersen
Assistant Secretary for Communications and Information	Janice I. Obuchowski
Deputy Assistant Secretary	Thomas J. Sugrue
Chief Counsel	Jean M. Prewitt
Director, Policy Coordination and Management	Dennis R. Connors
Associate Administrator for Spectrum Management	Richard D. Parlow
Associate Administrator for Policy Analysis and Development	William F. Maher
Associate Administrator for Telecommunication Sciences	William F. Utlaut
Associate Administrator for International Affairs	Charles M. Rush
Assistant Secretary and Commissioner of Patents and Trademarks	Harry F. Manbeck, Jr.
Deputy Assistant Secretary and Deputy Commissioner	Douglas B. Comer
Assistant Commissioner for Patents	James E. Denny
Assistant Commissioner for Trademarks	Jeffrey M. Samuels
Assistant Commissioner for Administration	Theresa A. Brelsford
Assistant Commissioner for Finance and Planning	Bradford R. Huther
Assistant Commissioner for External Affairs	Michael K. Kirk
Assistant Commissioner for Information Systems	Thomas P. Giammo
Under Secretary for Technology	Robert M. White
Deputy Under Secretary	Nancy H. Mason
Chief Counsel	James V. Lacy
Executive Director, Office of Management Services	Nancy L. Darr
Director, Public Affairs	John F. Sargent
Director, Congressional Affairs	Mark O. Hatfield

Director, Technology Analysis Group	CARY GRAVATT
Assistant Secretary for Technology Policy	DEBORAH L. WINCE-SMITH
Deputy Assistant Secretary for Technology Policy	(VACANCY)
Director, Office of Technology Policy	JACK WILLIAMS
Director, Office of Technology Commercialization	JOSEPH P. ALLEN
Director, Office of International Technology Policy and Programs	CHARLES WESSNER
Director, Office of Metric Programs	ALAN WHELIHAN
Director, National Institute of Standards and Technology	JOHN W. LYONS
Deputy Director	RAYMOND G. KAMMER
Associate Director	SAMUEL KRAMER
Director of Administration	GUY W. CHAMBERLIN, JR.
Director, Technology Services	DONALD R. JOHNSON
Director, Electronics and Electrical Engineering Laboratory	JUDSON C. FRENCH
Director, Manufacturing Engineering Laboratory	JOHN A. SIMPSON
Director, Chemical Science and Technology Laboratory	HARRY S. HERTZ
Director, Physics Laboratory	KATHERINE A. GEBBIE
Director, Materials Science and Engineering Laboratory	LYLE H. SCHWARTZ
Director, Building and Fire Research Laboratory	RICHARD N. WRIGHT
Director, Computer Systems Laboratory	JAMES H. BURROWS
Director, Computing and Applied Mathematics Laboratory	FRANCIS E. SULLIVAN
Director, Advanced Technology Program	GEORGE A. URIANO
Director, Manufacturing Technology Centers Program	PHILIP NANZETTA, *Acting*
Director, Office of Quality Programs	CURT W. REIMANN
Director, National Technical Information Service	JOSEPH F. CAPONIO
Deputy Director	JOSEPH E. CLARK
Under Secretary for Travel and Tourism	JOHN KELLER
Deputy Under Secretary	WYLIE H. WHISONANT, JR.
Assistant Secretary for Tourism Marketing	LINDA M. MYSLIWY
Director, Office of Policy and Planning	DAVID L. EDGELL
Director, Office of Research	HARVEY SHIELDS
Director, Office of Strategic Planning and Administration	LEE J. WELLS

The Department of Commerce encourages, serves, and promotes the Nation's international trade, economic growth, and technological advancement. Within this framework and together with a policy of promoting the national interest through the encouragement of the competitive free enterprise system, the Department provides a wide variety of programs. It offers assistance and information to increase America's competitiveness in the world economy; administers programs to prevent unfair foreign trade competition; provides social and economic statistics and

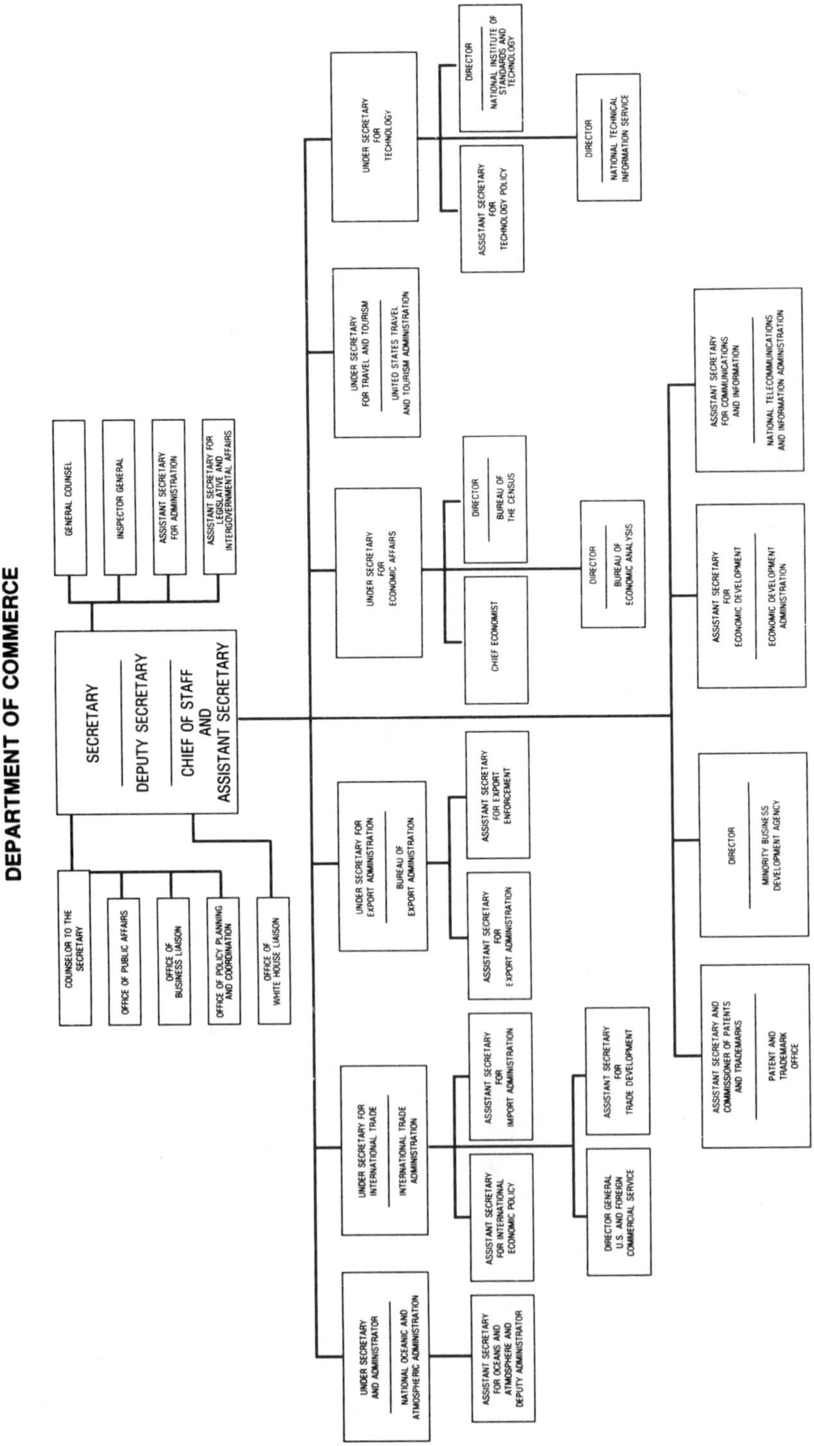
DEPARTMENT OF COMMERCE
SECRETARY
DEPUTY SECRETARY
CHIEF OF STAFF AND ASSISTANT SECRETARY
GENERAL COUNSEL
INSPECTOR GENERAL
ASSISTANT SECRETARY FOR ADMINISTRATION
ASSISTANT SECRETARY FOR LEGISLATIVE AND INTERGOVERNMENTAL AFFAIRS
COUNSELOR TO THE SECRETARY
OFFICE OF PUBLIC AFFAIRS
OFFICE OF BUSINESS LIAISON
OFFICE OF POLICY PLANNING AND COORDINATION
OFFICE OF WHITE HOUSE LIAISON
UNDER SECRETARY FOR TECHNOLOGY
DIRECTOR NATIONAL INSTITUTE OF STANDARDS AND TECHNOLOGY
ASSISTANT SECRETARY FOR TECHNOLOGY POLICY
DIRECTOR NATIONAL TECHNICAL INFORMATION SERVICE
UNDER SECRETARY FOR TRAVEL AND TOURISM
UNITED STATES TRAVEL AND TOURISM ADMINISTRATION
UNDER SECRETARY FOR ECONOMIC AFFAIRS
DIRECTOR BUREAU OF THE CENSUS
CHIEF ECONOMIST
DIRECTOR BUREAU OF ECONOMIC ANALYSIS
UNDER SECRETARY FOR EXPORT ADMINISTRATION
BUREAU OF EXPORT ADMINISTRATION
ASSISTANT SECRETARY FOR EXPORT ENFORCEMENT
ASSISTANT SECRETARY FOR EXPORT ADMINISTRATION
UNDER SECRETARY FOR INTERNATIONAL TRADE
INTERNATIONAL TRADE ADMINISTRATION
ASSISTANT SECRETARY FOR IMPORT ADMINISTRATION
ASSISTANT SECRETARY FOR INTERNATIONAL ECONOMIC POLICY
ASSISTANT SECRETARY FOR TRADE DEVELOPMENT
DIRECTOR GENERAL U.S. AND FOREIGN COMMERCIAL SERVICE
UNDER SECRETARY AND ADMINISTRATOR
NATIONAL OCEANIC AND ATMOSPHERIC ADMINISTRATION
ASSISTANT SECRETARY FOR OCEANS AND ATMOSPHERE AND DEPUTY ADMINISTRATOR
ASSISTANT SECRETARY FOR COMMUNICATIONS AND INFORMATION
NATIONAL TELECOMMUNICATIONS AND INFORMATION ADMINISTRATION
ASSISTANT SECRETARY FOR ECONOMIC DEVELOPMENT
ECONOMIC DEVELOPMENT ADMINISTRATION
DIRECTOR
MINORITY BUSINESS DEVELOPMENT AGENCY
ASSISTANT SECRETARY AND COMMISSIONER OF PATENTS AND TRADEMARKS
PATENT AND TRADEMARK OFFICE

analyses for business and government planners; provides research and support for the increased use of scientific, engineering, and technological development; works to improve our understanding and benefits of the Earth's physical environment and oceanic resources; grants patents and registers trademarks; develops policies and conducts research on telecommunications; provides assistance to promote domestic economic development; promotes travel to the United States by residents of foreign countries; and assists in the growth of minority businesses.

The Department was designated as such by act of March 4, 1913 (15 U.S.C. 1501), which reorganized the Department of Commerce and Labor, created by act of February 14, 1903 (15 U.S.C. 1501), by transferring all labor activities into a new, separate Department of Labor. The Department of Commerce (DOC) is composed of the Office of the Secretary and the operating units.

Office of the Secretary

Secretary The Secretary is responsible for the administration of all functions and authorities assigned to the Department of Commerce and for advising the President on Federal policy and programs affecting the industrial and commercial segments of the national economy.

Deputy Secretary The Deputy Secretary of Commerce serves as the principal deputy of the Secretary, performing continuing and special duties as the Secretary may assign. The Deputy Secretary serves as acting Secretary in the Secretary's absence.

Inspector General The Office of the Inspector General is responsible for conducting and supervising audits, inspections, and investigations relating to the programs and operations of the Department. The Office provides leadership and coordination for, and recommends policies and corrective actions concerning activities designed to promote economy and efficiency and prevent and detect fraud, waste, abuse, and mismanagement in departmental programs and operations. The Office provides a means for keeping the Secretary and Congress fully and currently informed about problems and deficiencies in the administration of such programs and operations and the necessity for corrective action.

General Counsel The Office of the General Counsel supervises all legal activities and is responsible for developing the legislative program of the Department.

Administration The Assistant Secretary for Administration is responsible for the administrative management functions of the Department, including program planning, budget, management analysis and controls, productivity improvement, personnel, finance, automated data processing management, contracting and procurement, and administrative services, as well as for equal employment activities.

Legislative and Intergovernmental Affairs The Assistant Secretary for Legislative and Intergovernmental Affairs directs both the Office of Legislative Affairs and the Office of Intergovernmental Affairs, advising the Secretary on matters of concern to the Department relating to Congress and State and local officials. The Assistant Secretary is also responsible for advising Congress and State and local officials on the Department's programs and policies and for communicating to the Secretary the concerns that are most significant to these officials.

For further information, call 202-377-5485.

Public Affairs The Director of Public Affairs is the principal adviser on public affairs matters and is responsible for the overall public information program of the Department, supervising the information activities of the 12 bureaus within the Department. The Director serves as the primary departmental public affairs liaison with other Federal departments and the White House.

For further information, call 202-377-3263.

Business Liaison The Office of Business Liaison develops and promotes a cooperative working relationship and ensures effective communication between the Department of Commerce and the business community. The Office's objectives are to keep the business community aware of Department and administration resources, policies, and programs, and to keep Department and administration officials aware of issues of concern to business. The Office also promotes business involvement in departmental policymaking and program development, provides technical assistance to businesses that desire help in dealing with the Government, and serves as the focal point for all Department of Commerce agencies' contacts with the business community.

For further information, call 202–377–3942.

Consumer Affairs The Office of Consumer Affairs works with the business community on behalf of consumers and assists consumers with marketplace problems. To help businesses improve their customer relations, the Office develops cooperative projects with companies, trade and professional associations, consumer organizations, and Federal, State, and local agencies. The Director is the Department's representative to the White House Consumer Affairs Council.

For further information, call 202–377–5001.

Economics and Statistics Administration The Under Secretary for Economic Affairs advises the Secretary and other Government officials on matters relating to economic developments and forecasts and on the development of macroeconomic and microeconomic policy. The Under Secretary, as Administrator of the Economics and Statistics Administration, exercises general supervision over the Bureau of the Census and the Bureau of Economic Analysis.

Current economic data is available to the public through the National Trade Data Bank and the Economic Bulletin Board.

For further information, call 202–377–1986.

Small and Disadvantaged Business Utilization The Office of Small and Disadvantaged Business Utilization (OSDBU) serves as an advocate for small business to ensure that minority, women-owned, and 8(a) concerns receive a fair share of Commerce contracts and subcontracts. The Office was established by act of October 24, 1978 (92 Stat. 1757) and serves as a focal point in the Department's efforts to set aside procurements for the socioeconomic programs. It provides procurement assistance, publishes a yearly forecast of Commerce contracting opportunities, and screens procurements for possible small business set-asides. The Office oversees administration of the Small Business Innovation Research and Research and Development Goaling Programs; develops policies and procedures to assist small firms; maintains a computer listing of small businesses; and monitors small business legislation. In conjunction with the Small Business Administration, OSDBU establishes procurement goals for all small business programs, including subcontracting, and provides an outreach network to assist small businesses in becoming Federal contractors.

For further information, call 202–377–3387.

Bureau of the Census

[For the Bureau of the Census statement of organization, see the *Federal Register* of Sept. 16, 1975, 40 FR 42765]

The Bureau of the Census was established as a permanent office by act of March 6, 1902 (32 Stat. 51). The major functions of the Bureau are authorized by the Constitution, which provides that a census of population shall be taken every 10 years, and by laws codified as title 13 of the United States Code. The law also provides that the information collected by the Bureau from individual persons, households, or establishments be kept strictly confidential and be used only for statistical purposes.

The Bureau is a general purpose, statistical agency that collects, tabulates, and publishes a wide variety of statistical data about the people and the economy of the Nation. These data are utilized by the Congress, by the executive branch, and by the public generally in the development and evaluation of economic and social programs.

In addition to its headquarters at Suitland, MD, the Bureau includes a Data Preparation Division at Jeffersonville, IN, a Personal Census Service Branch at Pittsburg, KS, and 12 regional offices.

The principal functions of the Bureau include:

—decennial censuses of population and housing;

—quinquennial censuses of agriculture, State and local governments, manufacturers, mineral industries, distributive trades, construction industries, and transportation;

—current surveys that provide information on many of the subjects covered in the censuses at monthly, quarterly, annual, or other intervals;

—compilation of current statistics on U.S. foreign trade, including data on imports, exports, and shipping;

—special censuses at the request and expense of States and local government units;

—publication of estimates and projections of the population;

—current data on population and housing characteristics; and

—current reports on manufacturing, retail and wholesale trade, services, construction, imports and exports, State and local government finances and employment, and other subjects.

The Bureau makes available statistical results of its censuses, surveys, and other programs to the public through printed reports, computer tape, CD-ROM's, microfiche, and other media and prepares special tabulations sponsored and paid for by data users. It also produces statistical compendia, catalogs, guides, and directories that are useful in locating information on specific subjects. Upon request, the Bureau makes searches of decennial census records and furnishes certificates to individuals for use as evidence of age, relationship, or place of birth. A fee is charged for such searches.

Field Organization—Bureau of the Census

Office	Address
REGIONAL OFFICES:	
ATLANTA—Alabama, Florida, Georgia (all counties except Columbia, McDuffie, and Richmond), Tennessee (all counties except Shelby and Tipton), Virginia (counties of Bristol City, Scott, and Washington)	Rm. 625, 1365 Peachtree St. NE., Atlanta, GA 30309-3147
BOSTON—Connecticut, Maine, Massachusetts, New Hampshire, New York (counties of Albany, Allegany, Broome, Cattaraugus, Cayuga, Chautauqua, Chemung, Chenango, Clinton, Cortland, Erie, Essex, Franklin, Fulton, Genesee, Greene, Hamilton, Herkimer, Jefferson, Lewis, Livingston, Madison, Monroe, Montgomery, Niagara, Oneida, Onondaga, Ontario, Orleans, Oswego, Otsego, Rensselaer, St. Lawrence, Saratoga, Schenectady, Schoharie, Schuyler, Seneca, Steuben, Tioga, Tompkins, Warren, Washington, Wayne, Wyoming, and Yates), Pennsylvania (Susquehanna County), Rhode Island, Vermont	Rm. 553, 10 Causeway St., Boston, MA 02222-1084
CHARLOTTE—District of Columbia, Georgia (counties of Columbia, McDuffie, and Richmond), Indiana (counties of Clark, Floyd, and Harrison), Kentucky (all counties except Boone, Campbell, Henderson, and Kenton), Maryland (counties of Calvert, Charles, Frederick, Montgomery, Prince Georges, and St. Mary's), North Carolina, Ohio (Lawrence County), South Carolina, Virginia (all counties except Bristol City, Scott, and Washington), West Virginia (counties of Boone, Cabell, Lincoln, Logan, McDowell, Mercer, Mingo, Wayne, and Wyoming)	Suite 505, 222 S. Church St., Charlotte, NC 28202-3220
CHICAGO—Illinois (all counties except Clinton, Jersey, Madison, Monroe, and St. Clair), Indiana (all counties except Clark, Dearborn, De Kalb, Floyd, and Harrison), Iowa (Scott County), Kentucky (Henderson County)	Rm. 557, 175 W. Jackson Blvd., Chicago, IL 60604-2689

Field Organization—Bureau of the Census—Continued

Office	Address
DALLAS—Arkansas, Louisiana, Mississippi, New Mexico, Oklahoma (counties of Le Flore, McCurtain, and Sequoyah), Tennessee (counties of Shelby and Tipton), Texas	Rm. 3C-54, 1100 Commerce St., Dallas, TX 75242-0399
DENVER—Arizona, Colorado, Iowa (Pottawattamie County), Kansas (all counties except Atchison, Bourbon, Crawford, Douglas, Franklin, Jackson, Jefferson, Johnson, Leavenworth, Linn, Miami, Neosho, Osage, Shawnee, and Wyandotte), Montana (all counties except Lincoln), Nebraska, North Dakota (all counties except Cass), Oklahoma (all counties except Le Flore, McCurtain, and Sequoyah), South Dakota, Utah, Wyoming	P.O. Box 26750, 7655 W. Mississippi Ave., Denver, CO 80226-0750
DETROIT—Indiana (counties of Dearborn, De Kalb, and Steuben), Kentucky (counties of Boone, Campbell, and Kenton), Michigan, Ohio (all counties except Lawrence), Pennsylvania (Mercer County), West Virginia (counties of Brooke, Hancock, Marshall, and Ohio)	Rm. 565, 231 W. Lafayette, Detroit, MI 48226-2769
KANSAS CITY—Illinois (counties of Clinton, Jersey, Madison, Monroe, and St. Clair), Iowa (all counties except Pottawattamie and Scott), Kansas (counties of Atchison, Bourbon, Crawford, Douglas, Franklin, Jackson, Jefferson, Johnson, Leavenworth, Linn, Miami, Neosho, Osage, Shawnee, Wyandotte), Minnesota, Missouri, North Dakota (Cass County), Wisconsin	Suite 500, 1 Gateway Ctr., 4th and State Sts., Kansas City, KS 66101
LOS ANGELES—California (counties of Fresno, Imperial, Inyo, Kern, Kings, Los Angeles, Madera, Mariposa, Merced, Monterey, Orange, Riverside, San Benito, San Bernardino, San Diego, San Luis Obispo, Santa Barbara, Santa Cruz, Tulare, Ventura), Hawaii, Nevada (Clark County)	Suite 300, 15350 Sherman Way, Van Nuys, CA 91406-4224
NEW YORK—New Jersey (counties of Bergen, Essex, Hudson, Middlesex, Morris, Passaic, Somerset, Union), New York (counties of Bronx, Columbia, Delaware, Dutchess, Kings, Nassau, New York, Orange, Putnam, Queens, Richmond, Rockland, Suffolk, Sullivan, Ulster, Westchester)	Rm. 37-130, 26 Federal Plz., New York, NY 10278-0044
PHILADELPHIA—Delaware, Maryland (counties of Allegany, Anne Arundel, Baltimore, Baltimore City, Caroline, Carroll, Cecil, Dorchester, Garrett, Harford, Howard, Kent, Queen Annes, Somerset, Talbot, Washington, Wicomico, Worcester), New Jersey (counties of Atlantic, Burlington, Camden, Cape May, Cumberland, Gloucester, Hunterdon, Mercer, Monmouth, Ocean, Salem, Sussex, Warren), Pennsylvania (all counties except Mercer and Susquehanna), West Virginia (all counties except Boone, Brooke, Cabell, Hancock, Lincoln, Logan, Marshall, McDowell, Mercer, Mingo, Ohio, Wayne, Wyoming)	105 S. 7th St., Philadelphia, PA 19106-3395
SEATTLE—Alaska, California (counties of Alameda, Alpine, Amador, Butte, Caleveras, Colusa, Contra Costa, Del Norte, El Dorado, Glenn, Humboldt, Lake, Lassen, Marin, Mendocino, Modoc, Mono, Napa, Nevada, Placer, Plumas, Sacramento, San Francisco, San Joaquin, San Mateo, Santa Clara, Shasta, Sierra, Siskiyou, Solano, Sonoma, Stanislaus, Sutter, Tehama, Trinity, Tuolumne, Yolo, Yuba), Idaho, Montana (Lincoln County), Nevada (all counties except Clark), Oregon, Washington	Suite 500, 101 Stewart St., Seattle, WA 98101-1098
DATA PREPARATION DIVISION	1201 E. 10th St., Jeffersonville, IN 47132
PERSONAL CENSUS SERVICE BRANCH	1600 N. Walnut St., Pittsburg, KS 66762

For further information, contact the Public Information Office, Bureau of the Census, Department of Commerce, Washington, DC 20233. Phone, 301-763-4040.

Bureau of Economic Analysis

[For the Bureau of Economic Analysis statement of organization, see the *Federal Register* of Dec. 29, 1980, 45 FR 85496]

The Bureau of Economic Analysis, formerly the Office of Business Economics, was established by the Secretary of Commerce on December 1, 1953, and operates under authorities contained in Department Organization Order No. 35-1A.

The goal of the Bureau is to provide a clear picture of the U.S. economy through the preparation, development, and interpretation of the national income and product accounts, summarized by the gross national product; the wealth accounts, which show the business and other components of the national wealth; the input-output accounts, which trace the interrelationships among industrial markets; other national economic accounts within the framework of the system of national accounts; personal income and related economic series by geographic area; the balance-of-payments accounts and associated foreign investment accounts; and measures relating to environmental change within the framework of the national economic accounts.

The work on the national economic accounts is supplemented by the preparation and analysis of other measures of economic activity, including various tools for forecasting economic developments such as surveys of investment outlays and a system of leading, coincident, and lagging economic indicators. The data and analyses prepared by the Bureau are disseminated primarily through its monthly *Survey of Current Business* and other publications and associated computed media.

For further information, contact the Public Information Office, Bureau of Economic Analysis, Department of Commerce, Washington, DC 20230. Phone, 202–523–0777.

Bureau of Export Administration

[For the Bureau of Export Administration statement of organization, see the *Federal Register* of June 7, 1988, 53 FR 20881]

The Bureau of Export Administration was established as a separate agency within the Department of Commerce on October 1, 1987, to separate the functions of export promotion and export control as mandated by the Export Administration Act, as amended (50 U.S.C. app. 2401 *et seq.*).

The Bureau is headed by the Under Secretary for Export Administration. The Under Secretary coordinates all matters related to the mission of BXA, which is to direct the Nation's export control policy. Major functions include processing license applications, conducting foreign availability studies to determine when products should be decontrolled, and enforcing U.S. export control laws.

Export Administration The Assistant Secretary for Export Administration oversees export licensing, technology and policy analysis, and foreign availability determinations. These responsibilities are linked to the Administration's objectives of reducing processing times for granting export licenses, decontrolling those technologies that offer no real threat to U.S. security, and eliminating unilateral controls in areas where widespread foreign availability exists. This office also works with our allies in pushing for stronger, more uniform ways of controlling strategic exports.

Export Enforcement The Assistant Secretary for Export Enforcement investigates breaches of U.S. export control laws and analyzes export intelligence to assess diversion risks. In addition, this office administers and enforces the antiboycott provisions of the Export Administration Act.

Field Offices—Bureau of Export Administration

City	Address
Boston, MA	Rm. 350, 10 Causeway St., 02222
Dallas, TX	Rm. 622, 525 Griffin St., 75202
Des Plaines, IL	Suite 300, 2400 E. Devon St., 60018
Fort Lauderdale, FL	Suite 500, 200 S. Andrews Ave., 33301
Irvine, CA	Suite 301, 2601 Main St., 92714
Nashua, NH	547 Amherst St., 03063
New York, NY	Rm. 3704, 26 Federal Plz., 10278
Newport Beach, CA	Suite 345, 3300 Irvine Ave., 92660
Portland, OR	Rm. 241, 121 SW. Salmon St., 97204
San Jose, CA	Suite 350, 96 N. 3d St., 95112-5519

Field Offices—Bureau of Export Administration—Continued

City	Address
Santa Clara, CA	Suite 226, 5201 Great America Pkwy., 95054
Springfield, VA	Rm. 201, 8001 Forbes Pl., 22161

For further information, contact the Bureau of Export Administration, Office of Public Affairs, Room 3895, Fourteenth Street and Constitution Avenue NW., Washington, DC 20230. Phone, 202–377–2721.

Economic Development Administration

[For the Economic Development Administration statement of organization, see the *Code of Federal Regulations,* Title 13, Part 301, Subpart C]

The Economic Development Administration was established under the Public Works and Economic Development Act of 1965 (42 U.S.C. 3121), to generate new jobs, to help protect existing jobs, and to stimulate commercial and industrial growth in economically distressed areas of the United States. Assistance is available in rural and urban areas of the Nation experiencing high unemployment, low income levels, or sudden and severe economic distress. The basic programs include:

—public works grants to public and private nonprofit organizations and Indian tribes to help build or expand public facilities essential to industrial and commercial growth. Typical projects are industrial parks, access roads, water and sewer lines, and port and airport terminal developments;

—loan guarantees to industrial and commercial firms. Proceeds from the loans may be used for working capital to maintain and expand operations or for fixed assets such as purchase of land, construction of plants, and the purchase of machinery and equipment;

—technical assistance and grants to enable communities and firms to find solutions to problems that stifle economic growth. Under the technical assistance program, funds are used for studies to determine the economic feasibility of resource development to establish jobs and to provide on-the-scene assistance to help businesses overcome a wide range of management and technical problems through university centers;

—planning grants to States, cities, districts, and Indian reservations to help pay for the expertise needed to plan, implement, and coordinate comprehensive economic development programs; and

—special economic adjustment assistance to help State and local governments in solving recent and anticipated severe adjustment problems, resulting in abrupt and serious job losses, and to help areas implement strategies to reverse and halt long-term economic deterioration.

Regional Offices—Economic Development Administration

Region	Address
ATLANTA, GA	401 W. Peachtree St. NW., 30308–3510
Alabama	Rm. 134, 474 S. Court St., Montgomery, AL 36104
Florida	Rm. 423, 80 N. Hughey Ave., Orlando, FL 32801
Georgia	401 W. Peachtree St. NW., 30308–3510
Kentucky	Rm. 209, 333 Waller Ave., Lexington, KY 40504
Mississippi	100 W. Capitol St., Jackson, MS 39269
North Carolina	Rm. 128, 300 Fayetteville St. Mall, P.O. Box 2522, Raleigh, NC 27601

Regional Offices—Economic Development Administration—Continued

Region	Address
South Carolina	Rm. 840, Strom Thurmond Federal Bldg., Columbia, SC 29201
Tennessee	261 Cumberland Bend Dr., Nashville, TN 37228
AUSTIN, TX	Suite 201, 611 E. 6th St., 78701
Arkansas	Rm. 2509, 700 W. Capitol St., Little Rock, AR 72201
Louisiana	2027 One American Pl., 500 N. 4th St., Baton Rouge, LA 70825
New Mexico	P.O. Box 2662, 120 S. Federal Pl., Santa Fe, NM 87501
Oklahoma	Rm. 202, 215 Dean McGee St., Oklahoma City, OK 73102
Texas	Suite 201, 611 E. 6th St., Austin, TX 78701
CHICAGO, IL	Suite A-1630, 175 W. Jackson Blvd., 60604
Illinois	Suite 204, 509 W. Capitol St., Springfield, IL 62701
Indiana	Rm. 114, 46 E. Ohio St., Indianapolis, IN 46204
Michigan	Rm. 221, 315 W. Allegan St., Lansing, MI 48933
Minnesota	515 W. 1st St., Duluth, MN 55802
Ohio	Rm. 405, 8 N. Court St., Athens, OH 45701
Wisconsin	Rm. 202, 505 S. Dewey St., Eau Claire, WI 54701
DENVER, CO	Suite 670, 1244 Speer Blvd., 80204
Colorado	Rm. 632, 1244 Speer Blvd., Denver, CO 80204
Iowa	Rm. 593A, 210 Walnut St., Des Moines, IA 50309
Missouri	Rm. S-305H, 1222 Spruce St., St. Louis, MO 63101
Montana	196 Federal Bldg., Helena, MT 59626
North Dakota	P.O. Box 1911, Bismarck, ND 58501
South Dakota	346 Federal Bldg., Pierre, SD 57501
Utah	125 S. State St., Salt Lake City, UT 84138
PHILADELPHIA, PA	105 S. 7th St., 19106
Connecticut	450 Main St., Hartford, CT 06103
Maine	Rm. 410-D, 40 Western Ave., Augusta, ME 04330
Maryland	2d Fl., 2568 Riva Rd., Annapolis, MD 21401
Massachusetts	Rm. 420, 10 Causeway St., Boston, MA 02222-1036
New Hampshire	Rm. 332, 55 Pleasant St., Concord, NH 03301
New Jersey	Rm. 703, 44 S. Clinton St., Trenton, NJ 08608
New York	Rm. 1225, 100 S. Clinton St., Syracuse, NY 13260
Pennsylvania	Rm. 406B, 301 Market St., Lewisburg, PA 17837
Puerto Rico	Rm. 620, Federal Office Bldg., 150 Carlos Chardon, Hato Rey, PR 00918-1738
Virginia	400 N. 8th St., Richmond, VA 23240
West Virginia	Rm. 305, 550 Eagan St., Charleston, WV 25301
SEATTLE, WA	Rm. 1856, 915 2d Ave., 98174
Alaska	Rm. G-80, 605 W. 4th Ave., Anchorage, AK 99501-7594
Arizona	Rm. 3406, 230 N. 1st Ave., Phoenix, AZ 85025
California	Rm. 11105, 11000 Wilshire Blvd., Los Angeles, CA 90024
	Rm. B-10, 1351 2d St., Napa, CA 94559
	Suite 150, 1510 J St., Sacramento, CA 95814
Hawaii	P.O. Box 50264, Honolulu, HI 96850
Idaho	Rm. 441, 304 N. 8th St., Boise, ID 83702
Oregon	Suite 244, 121 SW. Salmon St., Portland, OR 97204
Washington	915 2d Ave., Seattle, WA 98174

For further information, contact the Economic Development Administration, Department of Commerce, Washington, DC 20230. Phone, 202-377-5113.

International Trade Administration

[For the International Trade Administration statement of organization, see the *Federal Register* of Jan. 25, 1980, 45 FR 6148]

The International Trade Administration was established on January 2, 1980, by the Secretary of Commerce to promote world trade and to strengthen the international trade and investment position of the United States.

The Administration is headed by the Under Secretary for International Trade, who coordinates all issues concerning import administration, international economic policy and programs, and trade development. It is responsible for nonagricultural trade operations of the U.S. Government and supports the trade policy negotiation efforts of the U.S. Trade Representative. The Office of the

Under Secretary includes a Deputy Under Secretary and the Director of Administration, who is responsible for providing administrative management and support services for the Administration. The Office also includes the Deputy Assistant Secretary for Planning who is responsible for international trade policy planning and interdepartmental coordination. The Under Secretary is assisted by three Assistant Secretaries and the Director General of the U.S. and Foreign Commercial Service.

International Economic Policy The Assistant Secretary for International Economic Policy advises on the analysis, formulation, and implementation of international economic policies of a bilateral, multilateral, or regional nature. Reporting to the Assistant Secretary are five Deputy Assistant Secretaries (for Europe; the Western Hemisphere; East Asia and the Pacific; Africa, the Near East and South Asia; and Japan) who have responsibility for trade and investment issues with particular countries and regions of the world. These officials maintain in-depth commercial and economic information on the countries and regions for which they are responsible. In addition, there is a Deputy Assistant Secretary for International Economic Policy who has responsibility for multilateral affairs and for overall policy coordination.

Import Administration The Assistant Secretary for Import Administration defends American industry against injurious and unfair trade practices by administering efficiently, fairly, and in a manner consistent with U.S. international trade obligations the antidumping and countervailing duty laws of the United States; the U.S.-European Economic Community Arrangement and 19 other steel trade arrangements under the President's policy for the steel industry; the machine tool arrangements with Japan and Taiwan under the President's Machine Tool Program; the U.S.-Japan Semiconductor Agreement; and the U.S.-Canada Memorandum of Understanding on Softwood Lumber. The Administration plays a leading role in Federal efforts to improve functioning of the GATT antidumping code. The Assistant Secretary also ensures the proper administration of foreign trade zones and advises the Secretary on establishment of new zones; and administers programs governing the importation of strategic industrial resources, watch assemblies, and other statutory import programs.

Trade Development The Assistant Secretary for Trade Development advises on international trade and investment policies pertaining to U.S. industrial sectors, carries out programs to strengthen domestic export competitiveness, and promotes U.S. industry's increased participation in international markets. The Assistant Secretary manages an integrated Trade Development Program that includes policy development, industry analysis, and promotion organized by the following U.S. industry sectors: aerospace, automotive affairs and consumer goods, basic industries, capital goods and international construction, science and electronics, services, and textiles and apparel.

The Assistant Secretary:

—provides support for sectoral aspects of the Multilateral Trade Negotiations and obtains industry's views of trade policy issues through 17 industry-sector advisory committees;

—gathers, analyzes, and disseminates trade information;

—reports on foreign investment in the United States;

—serves as the Department's primary source of information and analysis on U.S. industrial sectors; and

—promotes the formation of export trading companies and issues certificates of review providing them with limited exemption from liability under the antitrust laws.

U.S. and Foreign Commercial Service The Assistant Secretary and Director General of the U.S. and Foreign Commercial Service develops, produces, markets, and manages an effective line of high-quality products and services geared to the marketing information needs of the U.S. exporting and international business community and manages the delivery of

Administration programs through 47 district offices and 21 branch offices located in the United States and 129 posts located in 67 countries throughout the world. The Assistant Secretary and Director General manages trade fairs and exhibitions, trade missions, overseas trade seminars, and other promotional events; promotes U.S. products and services throughout the world market; conducts conferences and seminars in the United States; assists State and private-sector organizations on export financing; and promotes the export of U.S. fish by working with the domestic fishing industry and the National Oceanic and Atmospheric Administration.

District Offices—International Trade Administration

District/Address	Director	Telephone
Anchorage, AK (319 World Trade Ctr. Alaska, 4201 Tudor Ctr. Dr., 99508)	Charles Becker	907-261-4237
Atlanta, GA (4360 Chamblee-Dunwoody Rd., 30341)	George T. Norton, Jr.	404-452-9101
Baltimore, MD (413 U.S. Customhouse, 40 S. Gay St., 21202)	David Earle	301-962-3560
Birmingham, AL (Rm. 302, 2015 2d Ave. N., 35203)	Gayle C. Shelton, Jr.	205-731-1331
Boston, MA (Suite 307, World Trade Ctr., Commonwealth Pier Area, 02210)	Francis J. O'Connor	617-565-8563
Buffalo, NY (Rm. 1312, 111 W. Huron St., 14202)	George Buchanan	716-846-4191
Charleston, WV (Suite 809, 405 Capitol St., 25301)	Roger L. Fortner	304-347-5123
Chicago, IL (1406 Mid-Continental Plaza Bldg., 55 E. Monroe St., 60603)	LoRee P. Silloway	312-353-4450
Cincinnati, OH (9504 Federal Office Bldg., 550 Main St., 45202)	Gordon B. Thomas	513-684-2944
Cleveland, OH (Rm. 600, 668 Euclid St., 44114)	Toby Zettler	216-522-4750
Columbia, SC (Suite 172, 1835 Assembly St., 29201)	Edgar L. Rojas	803-765-5345
Dallas, TX (Rm. 7A5, 1100 Commerce St., 75242)	(Vacancy)	214-767-0542
Denver, CO (Suite 680, 1625 Broadway, 80202)	James Manis	303-844-3246
Des Moines, IA (Rm. 817, 210 Walnut St., 50309)	John H. Steuber	515-284-4222
Detroit, MI (1140 McNamara Bldg., 477 Michigan Ave., 48226)	Donald L. Schilke	313-226-3650
Greensboro, NC (P.O. Box 1950, Rm. 203, 324 W. Market St., 27402)	Samuel P. Troy	919-333-5345
Hartford, CT (Rm. 610-B, 450 Main St., 06103)	Eric B. Outwater	203-240-3530
Honolulu, HI (P.O. Box 50026, 400 Ala Moana Blvd., 96850)	George Dolan	808-541-1782
Houston, TX (Rm. 2625, 515 Rusk St., 77002)	James Cook	713-229-2578
Indianapolis, IN (Suite 520, 1 N. Capitol St., 46204)	Andrew W. Thress	317-226-6214
Jackson, MS (328 Jackson Mall Office Ctr., 300 Woodrow Wilson Blvd., 39213).	Mark E. Spinney	601-965-4388
Kansas City, MO (Rm. 635, 601 E. 12th St., 64106)	John Kupfer	816-426-3141
Little Rock, AR (Suite 811, 320 W. Capitol Ave., 72201)	Lon J. Hardin	501-378-5794
Los Angeles, CA (Rm. 9200, 11000 Wilshire Blvd., 90024)	Sherwin Chen, *Acting*	213-575-7104
Louisville, KY (Rm. 636B, 601 W. Broadway, 40202)	Patrick T. Wall, *Acting*	502-582-5066
Miami, FL (Suite 224, 51 SW. 1st Ave., 33130)	Ivan A. Cosimi	305-536-5267
Milwaukee, WI (Rm. 606, 517 E. Wisconsin Ave., 53202)	Johnny Brown	414-297-3473
Minneapolis, MN (Rm. 108, 110 S. 4th St., 55401)	Ronald E. Kramer	612-348-1638
Nashville, TN (Suite 1114, Parkway Towers, 404 James Robertson Pkwy., 37219).	James Charlet	615-736-5161
New Orleans, LA (432 World Trade Ctr., 2 Canal St., 70130)	Paul L. Guidry	504-589-6546
New York, NY (Rm. 3718, 26 Federal Plz., 10278)	Joel Barkan	212-264-0600
Oklahoma City, OK (6601 Broadway Extension, 73116)	Ronald L. Wilson	405-231-5302
Omaha, NE (11133 O St., 68137)	George H. Payne	402-221-3664
Philadelphia, PA (Suite 202, 475 Allendale Rd., King of Prussia, 19406)	Robert E. Kistler	215-962-4980
Phoenix, AZ (Rm. 3412, 230 N. 1st Ave., 85025)	Donald W. Fry	602-379-3285
Pittsburgh, PA (Rm. 2002, 1000 Liberty Ave., 15222)	John McCartney	412-644-2850
Portland, OR (Suite 242, 1 World Trade Ctr., 121 SW. Salmon St., 97204)	Richard Lenahan	503-326-3001
Reno, NV (1755 E. Plumb Lane, No. 152, 89502)	Joseph J. Jeremy	702-784-5203
Richmond, VA (Rm. 8010, 400 N. 8th St., 23240)	Philip A. Ouzts	804-771-2246
Salt Lake City, UT (Suite 105, 324 S. State St., 84111)	Stephen P. Smoot	801-524-5116
San Diego, CA (Suite 145, 6363 Greenwich Dr., 92122)	Richard Powell	619-557-5395
San Francisco, CA (Box 36013, 450 Golden Gate Ave., 94102)	Betty D. Neuhart	415-556-5860
San Juan, PR (Hato Rey) (Rm. G-55, Federal Bldg., 00918)	J. Enrique Vilella	809-766-5555
Savannah, GA (Rm. A-107, 120 Barnard St., 31401)	Barbara Prieto	912-944-4204
Seattle, WA (Suite 290, 3131 Elliott Ave., 98121)	Charles Buck	206-553-5615
St. Louis, MO (Suite 610, 7911 Forsyth Blvd., 63105)	Donald R. Loso	314-425-3302
Trenton, NJ (Suite 100, Bldg. 6, 3131 Princeton Pike, 08648)	Thomas J. Murray	609-989-2100

For further information, contact the International Trade Administration, Department of Commerce, Washington, DC 20230. Phone, 202-377-3808.

Minority Business Development Agency

[For the Minority Business Development Agency statement of organization, see the *Federal Register* of Mar. 17, 1972, 37 FR 5650, as amended]

The Minority Business Development Agency, formerly the Office of Minority Business Enterprise, was established by the Secretary of Commerce on November 1, 1979, and operates under the authority of Executive Order 11625 of October 13, 1971. The Agency develops and coordinates a national program for minority business enterprise.

The Agency was created to assist minority business in achieving effective and equitable participation in the American free enterprise system and in overcoming social and economic disadvantages that have limited their participation in the past. The Agency provides national policies and leadership in forming and strengthening a partnership of business, industry, and government with the Nation's minority businesses.

Management and technical assistance is provided to minority firms on request, primarily through a network of minority business development centers funded by the Agency. Specialized business assistance is available to minority firms or potential entrepreneurs.

The Agency promotes and coordinates the efforts of other Federal agencies in assisting or providing market opportunities for minority business, primarily through its affiliate network of Minority Business Development Centers. It coordinates opportunities for minority firms in the private sector. Through such public and private cooperative activities, the Agency promotes the participation of Federal, State, and local governments, and business and industry in directing resources for the development of strong minority businesses. The Agency also operates an Information Clearinghouse for catalogs, publications, and other information for and about the Nation's minority businesses.

The Minority Business Development Agency conducts most of its activities through its six Regional Offices (Atlanta, Chicago, Dallas, New York, San Francisco, Washington) and four District Offices.

Regional Offices—Minority Business Development Agency

Region/Address	Director	Telephone
Atlanta, GA (Suite 1930, 401 W. Peachtree St. NW., 30309)	Carlton Eccles	404-730-3300
Chicago, IL (Suite 1440, 55 E. Monroe St., 60603)	David Vega	312-353-0182
Dallas, TX (Suite 7823, 1100 Commerce St., 75242)	Melda Cabrea	214-767-8001
New York, NY (Suite 37-20, 26 Federal Plz., 10278)	John Iglehart	212-264-3262
San Francisco, CA (Rm. 1280, 221 Main St., 94105)	Xavier Mena	415-974-9597
Washington, DC (Rm. 6723, 14th St. and Constitution Ave. NW., 20230)	Georgina Sanchez	202-377-8275

District Offices—Minority Business Development Agency

District/Address	Officer	Telephone
Boston, MA (Rm. 418, 10 Causeway St., 02222-1041)	Rochelle K. Schwartz	617-565-6850
Los Angeles, CA (Suite 201, 977 N. Broadway, 90012)	Joseph Galindo	213-894-7157
Miami, FL (Rm. 928, 51 SW. 1st Ave., 33130)	Rodolfo Suarez	305-536-5054
Philadelphia, PA (Rm. 10128, 600 Arch St., 19106)	Alfonso C. Jackson	215-629-9841

For further information, contact the Office of Public Affairs, Minority Business Development Agency, Department of Commerce, Washington, DC 20230. Phone, 202-377-1936.

National Oceanic and Atmospheric Administration

U.S. Department of Commerce, Washington, DC 20230
Phone, 202–377–2985

[For the National Oceanic and Atmospheric Administration statement of organization, see the *Federal Register* of Feb. 13, 1978, 43 FR 6128]

The National Oceanic and Atmospheric Administration was formed on October 3, 1970, by Reorganization Plan No. 4 of 1970 (5 U.S.C. app.). Its principal functions are authorized by title 15, chapter 9, United States Code (National Weather Service); title 33, chapter 17, United States Code (National Ocean Survey); and title 16, chapter 9, United States Code (National Marine Fisheries Service). The Administration's mission was further defined by the Coastal Zone Management Act of 1972; the Marine Mammal Protection Act of 1972; the Marine Protection, Research, and Sanctuaries Act of 1972, as amended; the Weather Modification Reporting Act of 1972; the Endangered Species Act of 1973; the Offshore Shrimp Fisheries Act of 1973; the Fishery Conservation and Management Act of 1976; and the Land Remote Sensing Act of 1984.

The Administration's mission is to explore, map, and chart the global ocean and its living resources and to manage, use, and conserve those resources; to describe, monitor, and predict conditions in the atmosphere, ocean, Sun, and space environment; to issue warnings against impending destructive natural events; to assess the consequences of inadvertent environmental modification over several scales of time; and to manage and disseminate long-term environmental information.

Among its principal activities, the Administration reports the weather of the United States and its possessions and provides weather forecasts to the general public; issues warnings against such destructive natural events as hurricanes, tornadoes, floods, and tsunamis; and provides services in support of aviation, marine activities, agriculture, forestry, urban air-quality control, and other weather-sensitive activities. The Administration also monitors and reports all non-Federal weather modification activities conducted in the United States.

The Administration conducts an integrated program of management, research, and services related to the protection and rational use of living marine resources and their habitats, and protects marine mammals and endangered marine species. It prepares and issues nautical and aeronautical charts, provides the Nation's precise geodetic surveys, and conducts broad research programs in marine and atmospheric sciences, solar-terrestrial physics, and experimental meteorology, including weather modification. The Administration also predicts tides, currents, and the state of the oceans; conducts research and development aimed at providing alternatives to ocean dumping; and develops sound national policies in the areas of ocean mining and energy. It provides Federal leadership in promoting wise and balanced management of the Nation's coastal zone.

In addition, the Administration provides satellite observations of the environment by operating a national environmental satellite system; and conducts an integrated program of research and services relating to the oceans and inland waters, the lower and upper atmosphere, space environment, and the Earth to increase understanding of the geophysical environment. It acquires, stores, and disseminates worldwide environmental data through a system of meteorological, oceanographic, geodetic, and seismological data centers.

The Administration also administers and directs the oceanic research programs by providing grants to institutions for marine research, education, and advisory services; develops a system of data buoys for automatically obtaining and disseminating marine environmental data; and promotes the development of technology to meet future needs of the marine community.

Field Organization—National Oceanic and Atmospheric Administration

Organization	Address	Director	Telephone
NATIONAL WEATHER SERVICE			
Alaska region	Rm. 507, No. 23, 222 W. 7th Ave., Anchorage, AK 99513-7575.	Richard J. Hutchcon	907 271 5136
Central region	Rm. 1836, 601 E. 12th St., Kansas City, MO 64106-2897.	Richard P. Augulis	816-426-5400
Eastern region	Airport Corporate Ctr., 630 Johnson Ave., Bohemia, NY 11716.	Susan F. Zevin	516-244-0100
National Meteorological Center.	5200 Auth Rd., Camp Springs, MD 20746.	Ronald D. McPherson	301-763-8016
Pacific region	P.O. Box 50027, Honolulu, HI 96850	Richard Hagermeyer	808-541-1641
Southern region	Rm. 10A26, 819 Taylor St., Fort Worth, TX 76102.	Harry S. Hassel	817-334-2668
Western region	P.O. Box 11188, Federal Bldg., Salt Lake City, UT 84147-0188.	Thomas D. Potter	801-524-5122
NATIONAL MARINE FISHERIES SERVICE			
Alaska region	P.O. Box 21668, Juneau, AK 99802-1668.	Steven Pennoyer	907-586-7221
Northwest region	7600 Sand Point Way NE., BIN C15700, Bldg. 1, Seattle, WA 98115-0070.	Rolland Schmitten	206-526-6150
Northeast region	1 Blackburn Dr., Gloucester, MA 01930.	Richard B. Roe	617-281-9210
Southeast region	9450 Koger Blvd., St. Petersburg, FL 33702.	Andrew J. Kemmerer	813-893-6208
Southwest region	300 S. Ferry St., Terminal Island, CA 90731.	Ellsworth Fullerton	213-514-6208
NATIONAL ENVIRONMENTAL SATELLITE, DATA, AND INFORMATION SERVICE			
National Climatic Data Center.	Federal Bldg., Asheville, NC 28801-2696.	Kenneth D. Hadeen	704-259-0476
National Geophysical Data Center.	RL-3, 325 Broadway, Boulder, CO 80303-3328.	Michael Chinnery	303-497-6215
National Oceanographic Data Center.	1825 Connecticut Ave. NW., Washington, DC 20235.	Gregory W. Withee	202-673-5594
NATIONAL OCEAN SERVICE			
Alaska office	Rm. A13, No. 56, 222 W. 8th Ave., Anchorage, AK 99513-7543.	Jawed Hameedi	907-271-3033
Pacific office	7600 Sandy Point Way NE., Seattle, WA 98115-0070.	John H. Robinson	206-526-6317
Key Largo National Marine Sanctuary.	P.O. Box 020197, Miami, FL 33102-0197.	Michael W. White	305-526-7152
All other sanctuaries and reserves.	1825 Connecticut Ave. NW., Washington, DC 20235.	Joseph A. Uravitch	202-673-5122
OFFICE OF OCEANIC AND ATMOSPHERIC RESEARCH			
Atlantic Oceanographic and Meteorological Laboratory.	4301 Rickenbacker Causeway, Miami, FL 33149.	Hugo F. Bezdek	305-361-4450
Environmental Research Laboratories.	325 Broadway, Boulder, CO 80303-3328.	Joseph O. Fletcher	303-497-6000
Geophysical Fluid Dynamics Laboratory.	P.O. Box 308, Princeton, NJ 08542	J.D. Mahlman	609-452-6502
Great Lakes Environmental Research Laboratory.	2205 Commonwealth Blvd., Ann Arbor, MI 48105-1593.	Alfred M. Beeton	313-668-2244
National Severe Storms Laboratory.	1313 Halley Circle, Norman, OK 73069.	Robert A. Maddox	405-366-0427
Pacific Marine Environmental Research Laboratory.	BIN C 15700, 7600 Sand Point Way NE., Seattle, WA 98115-0070.	Eddie N. Bernard	206-526-6239
ADMINISTRATIVE SUPPORT CENTERS			
Central Administrative Support Center.	601 E. 12th St., Kansas City, MO 64106-2897.	Martha R. Lumpkin	816-426-2050
Eastern Administrative Support Center.	253 Monticello Ave., Norfolk, VA 23510-2314.	Robert S. Smith	804-441-6864
Mountain Administrative Support Center.	325 Broadway, Boulder, CO 80303-3328.	Curtis T. Hill	303-497-6431
Western Administrative Support Center.	7600 Sand Point Way NE., Seattle, WA 98115-0070.	Kelly C. Sandy	206-526-6026

Field Organization—National Oceanic and Atmospheric Administration—Continued

Organization	Address	Director	Telephone
NOAA CORPS OPERATIONS CENTERS			
Atlantic Marine Center	439 W. York St., Norfolk, VA 23510-1114.	Rear Adm. Freddie Jefferies	804-441-6776
Commissioned Personnel Center.	11400 Rockville Pike, Rockville, MD 20852.	Capt. Theodore Wyzewski	301-443-8950
Pacific Marine Center	1801 Fairview Ave. E., Seattle, WA 98102-3767.	Rear Adm. Raymond L. Speer	206-442-7656

For further information, contact the Office of Public Affairs, National Oceanic and Atmospheric Administration, Department of Commerce, Washington, DC 20230. Phone, 202-377-4190.

National Telecommunications and Information Administration

[For the National Telecommunications and Information Administration statement of organization, see the *Federal Register* of June 5, 1978, 43 FR 24348]

The National Telecommunications and Information Administration (NTIA) was established in 1978 in response to Executive Order 12046 of March 27, 1978.

The reorganization that accompanied this Executive order combined within NTIA the resources of the Office of Telecommunications of the Commerce Department and the Office of Telecommunications Policy from the Executive Office of the President. It thus provided a broad national role in telecommunication and information issues for the Department of Commerce.

The broad goals of NTIA include formulating policies to support the development and growth of telecommunications, information, and related industries; furthering the efficient development and use of telecommunications and information services; providing policy and management for Federal use of the electromagnetic spectrum; and providing telecommunications facilities grants to public service users.

For further information, contact the National Telecommunications and Information Administration, Department of Commerce, Washington, DC 20230. Phone, 202-377-1832.

Patent and Trademark Office

[For the Patent and Trademark Office statement of organization, see the *Federal Register* of Apr. 14, 1975, 40 FR 16707]

The patent system was established by Congress ". . . to promote the progress of . . . the useful arts. . ." under Article I, section 8, U.S. Constitution (*see also* title 35 United States Code, Patents; and title 15 United States Code, chapter 22, Trademarks). Patents are granted and trademarks are registered by the Patent and Trademark Office.

The Office examines applications for three kinds of patents: design patents (issued for 14 years), plant patents, and utility patents (issued for 17 years). Also, the Office issues Statutory Invention Registrations, which have the defensive but not the enforceable attributes of a patent. It also processes international applications for patents under the provisions of the Patent Cooperation Treaty, including, as of July 1, 1986, the examination provisions of chapter II of the Treaty.

About 97,000 patents were issued for fiscal year 1990 that provide inventors with exclusive rights to the results of their creative efforts. Patents may be reviewed and searched in the Office and in over 69 public libraries around the country. The patent system is intended to promote incentives to invent, to invest in research and development, to commercialize new technology, and to make public inventions that would otherwise go unnoticed.

About 64,000 trademarks were registered for fiscal year 1990, and 7,100 trademark registrations were renewed. A trademark includes any distinctive word, name, symbol, device, or any combination thereof adopted and used, or intended to be used, by a manufacturer or merchant to identify his goods or services and distinguish them from those manufactured or sold by others. Trademarks, registered for 10 years, with renewal rights of equal term, are examined by the Office for compliance with various statutory requirements to prevent unfair competition and consumer deception.

In addition to the examination of patent and trademark applications, issuance of patents, and registration of trademarks, the Patent and Trademark Office:

—sells printed copies of issued patents and trademark registrations;

—records and indexes documents transferring ownership;

—maintains a scientific library and search files containing over 30 million documents, including U.S. and foreign patents and U.S. trademarks;

—provides search rooms for the public to research their applications;

—hears and decides appeals from prospective inventors and trademark applicants;

—participates in legal proceedings involving the issue of patents or registration of trademarks;

—helps represent the United States in international efforts to cooperate on patent and trademark policy;

—compiles the Official Gazettes—a weekly notice of patents issued and trademarks registered by the Office, including other information; and

—maintains a roster of patent agents and attorneys qualified and recognized to practice before the Office.

For further information, contact the Office of Public Affairs, Patent and Trademark Office, Washington, DC 20231. Phone, 703–557–3341. The Office's operations are located at 2011 Crystal Drive, Arlington, VA 22202.

Technology Administration The Under Secretary for Technology identifies opportunities or barriers affecting U.S. commercial innovation, quality, productivity, and manufacturing; advocates Federal policies and programs to eliminate governmentwide statutory, regulatory, or other barriers to the rapid commercialization of U.S. science and technology; consults and collaborates with the U.S. industrial and nonprofit sectors to identify priority technologies, analyze foreign competitors' progress in technology, and provide a forum for U.S. industry to discuss issues of mutual interest; advises the Secretary of Commerce and the President's science adviser regarding the needs and commercial relevance of federally funded research and development; fosters and promotes Federal investment in research and development, technical standards, and intellectual property protection necessary for optimal U.S. commercial development of new products and processes; represents U.S. commercial interests in international science and technology agreements and forums; and promotes joint efforts involving business, industry, educational institutions, and State and local organizations to encourage technology commercialization.

The Office of the Assistant Secretary for Technology Policy has the primary responsibility to maximize the role and contribution of technology to U.S.

competitiveness and economic security. This Office is also the central point for developing and coordinating technology policies, programs, and issues; reviewing programs for consistency with Department science and technology policies and objectives; and promoting commercialization of technology. The Office is also the focal point in DOC for developing and advocating international science and technology policies that promote U.S. competitiveness and coordinates review of federally supported international science and technology negotiations and related activities. Additionally, the Office advises other components in the Department on how their programs and activities affect the climate for technological advancement in the United States.

The Office also manages the National Medal of Technology, the Nation's highest honor awarded by the President to American technologists, as well as the Clearinghouse for State and Local Initiatives, which maintains an active data base of hundreds of State and local programs created to foster technology, innovation, and productivity.

The Under Secretary for Technology exercises general supervision over the National Institute of Standards and Technology and the National Technical Information Service.

For further information, call 202–377–1091.

National Institute of Standards and Technology

Headquarters: Gaithersburg, MD (Route I–270 and Quince Orchard Road)
Mailing address: Gaithersburg, MD 20899
Phone, 301–975–2000

[For the National Institute of Standards and Technology statement of organization, see the *Federal Register* of Apr. 13, 1978, 43 FR 15473]

The National Institute of Standards and Technology (NIST), founded in 1901 as the National Bureau of Standards, was renamed in 1988 by the Omnibus Trade and Competitiveness Act and directed specifically to assist industry in developing technology to improve product quality; to modernize manufacturing processes; to ensure product reliability; and to facilitate rapid commercialization of products based on new scientific discoveries.

This explicit mission builds on a long-standing agency responsibility to both assist industry and to develop, maintain, and retain custody of the national standards of measurement. As a nonregulatory agency of the Department's Technology Administration, NIST aids U.S. industry through research and services; carries out selected programs in public health and safety and environmental improvement; and supports the U.S. scientific and engineering research communities through fundamental research.

As a world-class center for physical science and engineering research, NIST develops generic technology and measurement techniques and standards. NIST researchers work at the frontiers of science and technology in such areas as chemical science and technology, physics, materials science and engineering, electronics and electrical engineering, manufacturing engineering, computer systems, building technology and fire safety, and computing and applied mathematics.

The Institute has been a valuable behind-the-scenes partner to industry, providing many of the tools U.S. businesses need to compete in the marketplace. Several new NIST programs have been set up to spur innovation and accelerate the adoption of new ideas and technology by U.S. companies. For example, the Advanced Technology Program provides seed money to help U.S. businesses conduct research on precompetitive, generic technologies with high commercial potential. Through its regional Manufacturing Technology Centers, NIST provides technical and financial support to nonprofit centers that assist small- and medium-sized companies in gaining expertise with new manufacturing technologies.

The Malcolm Baldrige National Quality Award, managed by NIST in cooperation with the private sector, encourages industry to improve quality. Established by Congress in 1987, the award recognizes U.S. companies that excel in quality achievement and total quality management. The award promotes awareness of quality as an increasingly important element in competitiveness, understanding requirements for quality excellence, and sharing information on successful quality strategies.

To further aid businesses in building a competitive advantage, NIST makes available at its headquarters in Gaithersburg, MD, and its site in Boulder, CO, research and testing facilities for cooperative and proprietary work. A 20-megawatt research reactor with a cold neutron facility, a metals processing laboratory, an automated manufacturing research facility, and a computer network and security facility are some of the facilities made available by NIST.

Major Field Organizational Units and Stations—National Institute of Standards and Technology

Units and Stations	Address
Office of the Director, NIST/Boulder Laboratories	National Institute of Standards and Technology, Boulder, CO 80303
Quantum Physics Division	Joint Institute of Laboratory Astrophysics, University of Colorado, 80302
Standard Frequency Stations, WWV and WWVB	200 E. County Rd. 58, Fort Collins, CO 80524
Standard Frequency Station WWVH	Box 417, Kekaha, Kauai, HI 96752

For further information, contact the Office of Information Services, National Institute of Standards and Technology, Department of Commerce, Gaithersburg, MD 20899. Phone, 301–975–3058.

National Technical Information Service

[For the National Technical Information Service statement of organization, see the *Federal Register* of May 5, 1976, 41 FR 18538]

As a cornerstone of the technology information publishing structure in the United States, the National Technical Information Service (NTIS) is a key participant in the development, production, and dissemination of advanced information products and services for the achievement of U.S. productivity and international competitiveness goals for the 1990's. The Service provides access to U.S.- and foreign government-sponsored research and development and applied engineering studies. As the source for Government scientific and technical information, NTIS each year announces 150,000 summaries of ongoing, as well as completed, Government-sponsored research projects. These summaries detail the knowledge and technology generated through those projects funded by the U.S. Government's annual multibillion-dollar research and development effort, as well as those funded by the governments of leading developed countries.

In addition, NTIS provides the full text of the technical reports resulting from most research activities; manages the Federal Computer Products Center which provides access to software, data files, and databases produced by Federal agencies; manages the Federal Software Exchange Program for intragovernmental distribution; gives U.S. firms access to more than 15,000 foreign government research and engineering programs each year; and manages the Center for the

Utilization of Federal Technology (CUFT), which operates one of the most active patent licensing programs in the Government and, with its directories and catalogs, links U.S. firms to Federal laboratory contacts and technologies. The Service is also the lead Government agency in international research and development and technical information exchange through agreements with dozens of organizations in such leading industrialized nations as Japan, Great Britain, France, and the Federal Republic of Germany, among others.

The NTIS information collection presently contains some 2 million items, all of which are available for sale in print, microform, audiovisual, and/or electronic format. The Service ships some 12,000 information products every day as technical reports and Government-sponsored journals in paper and microfiche, as datafiles or software on tape, diskette, or CD-ROM, and a wide range of audiovisual materials. All of these items are acquired, indexed, cataloged, and announced by NTIS in a broad range of alerting journals, newsletters, specialized bibliographies, annual indexes, and online databases.

Anyone seeking the latest Government research reports may search the NTIS Bibliographic Database online using the services of organizations that offer the database for public use. NTIS also has contractual arrangements with several vendors to provide the database in CD-ROM format. Updated twice monthly, the NTIS database is also available to organizations and agencies having substantial internal research and development information needs by means of a direct lease from NTIS. Another NTIS database, FEDRIP (Federal Research in Progress), also available online through the private sector, provides status reports and investigative information on current research funded by the Government. The full text of all progress reports in FEDRIP is searchable and printable only online, since there are no printed counterpart publications.

Customers with well-defined, continuing interests subscribe to a current awareness microfiche service, which enables them to receive automatically the full text of reports relating to their unique, custom-profiled information requirements.

The Service sells its information products and services under the provisions of title 15, United States Code, which establishes NTIS as a clearinghouse for scientific, technical, and engineering information and directs it to be self-supporting. The cost of NTIS salaries, marketing, printing, product distribution, and all associated operating costs is recovered solely through sales income. An information center and bookstore is located at the NTIS operations center, 5285 Port Royal Road, Springfield, VA 22161. Phone, 703-487-4604; or Fax, 703-321-8547.

For further information, contact the National Technical Information Service at the address immediately above. Phone, 703-487-4650.

United States Travel and Tourism Administration

[For the United States Travel and Tourism Administration statement of organization, see the *Federal Register* of June 25, 1982, 47 FR 27594]

The United States Travel and Tourism Administration was established by the National Tourism Policy Act of 1981 (22 U.S.C. 2121 note).

The Administration is headed by the Under Secretary of Commerce for Travel and Tourism who advises the Secretary of Commerce on the formulation and execution of policy affecting the American tourism industry and its contribution to the Nation's economic development and international trade objectives. The Administration also maintains trade development, trade policy, and statistical research programs designed to increase the American travel industry's awareness of the export market, facilitate the entry of medium- and small-sized American travel companies into the market, and eliminate barriers to market entry for those companies.

The Administration maintains nine regional offices located in Amsterdam, Frankfurt, London, Mexico City, Milan, Paris, Sydney, Tokyo, and Toronto; an International Congress Office located in Paris; and an office servicing five South American markets located in Miami.

For further information, contact the United States Travel and Tourism Administration, Department of Commerce, Washington, DC 20230. Phone, 202-377-3811.

Sources of Information

Age and Citizenship Age search and citizenship information is available from the Personal Census Service Branch, Walnut and Pine Streets, Pittsburg, KS 66762. Phone, 316-231-7100.
Environment The National Oceanic and Atmospheric Administration monitors the conditions in the ocean, atmosphere, and Earth-Sun environment; prepares and issues weather warnings and forecasts; provides Federal leadership in managing the living resources of the sea and the Nation's coastal zone; ensures that marine mammals and endangered marine species are protected under the law; and provides worldwide environmental data and information products and services in the atmospheric, marine, solid earth, and solar terrestrial sciences. It also conducts research aimed at remote sensing of the physical environment and provides a variety of environmental quality control services, including those for urban airborne pollution control, estuarine water movement, and water resources management. Write to the Office of Public Affairs, National Oceanic and Atmospheric Administration, Washington, DC 20230. Phone, 202-377-8090.

The Patent and Trademark Office has priority programs for the processing of applications for patents that could aid in materially enhancing the environment. Write to the Assistant Secretary and Commissioner of Patents and Trademarks, Washington, DC 20231. Phone, 703-557-3811.

Field Employment

National Oceanic and Atmospheric Administration The Department of Commerce has field employment offices at the Western Administrative Support Center, Bin C15700, 7600 Sand Point Way NE., Seattle, WA 98115 (phone, 206-526-6053); the Mountain Administrative Support Center, 325 Broadway, Boulder, CO 80303 (phone, 303-497-6305); the Central Administrative Support Center, 601 East Twelfth Street, Kansas City, MO 64106 (phone, 816-426-2056); and the Eastern Administrative Support Center, 253 Monticello Avenue, Norfolk, VA 23510 (phone, 804-441-6516).

Publications

The titles of selected publications are listed below with the operating units responsible for their issuance. These and other publications dealing with a wide range of business, economic, environmental, scientific, and technical matters are announced in the weekly *Business Service Checklist,* which may be purchased from the Superintendent of Documents, Government Printing Office, Washington, DC 20402. Phone, 202-783-3238.

Further information on Commerce publications is available at any of the Department's International Trade Administration district offices.
National Technical Information Service *Products and Services Catalog* (PR-827), *Government Reports Announcements and Index* (PR-195), *Abstract Newsletters* (PR-797), *Annual Index* (PR-273), and *Published Searches Catalog* (PR-186). Available from NTIS,

5285 Port Royal Road, Springfield, VA 22161. Phone, 703-487-4650.

Also available are approximately 2 million technical reports on completed Government research—all available in microform, paper, or electronic media. All the report titles and abstracts may be searched by computer, addressing the NTIS Bibliographic Database online or via CD-ROM, available through private vendors.

Bureau of the Census *Census Catalog and Guide; Statistical Abstract of the U.S.; Historical Statistics of the United States, Colonial Times to 1970; County and City Data Book, 1988;* and *State and Metropolitan Area Data Book, 1991.* Available from the Government Printing Office.

Bureau of Economic Analysis *The Survey of Current Business; Business Statistics: 26th Biennial Edition; Local Area Personal Income, 1983–1988; Foreign Direct Investment in the United States: Operations of U.S. Affiliates of Foreign Companies;* and *U.S. Direct Investment Abroad: Operations of U.S. Parent Companies and Their Foreign Affiliates.* Available from the Government Printing Office.

International Trade Administration *Business America* (published biweekly). Available from the Government Printing Office and at ITA District Offices.

Minority Business Development Agency *Minority Business Today, Guide to Federal Minority Enterprise and Related Assistance Programs, Director of MBDA Regional and District Offices and Funded Organizations, MBDA Performance Highlights Report for FY '85,* and *Federal Agency Performance for Minority Business Development for FY '85.* Available from MBDA, Information Clearinghouse, Department of Commerce, Washington, DC 20230. Phone, 202-377-2414.

National Institute of Standards and Technology *Journal of Research; Publications of the National Institute of Standards and Technology; Handbook of Mathematical Functions; Experimental Statistics; and Accuracy, Integrity and Security in Computerized Vote Tallying.* Available from the Government Printing Office.

National Oceanic and Atmospheric Administration *Floods, Flash Floods and Warnings* and *Tornado Safety.* Available from the Government Printing Office. Also available from NOAA's Office of Public Affairs are technical memoranda, technical reports, and monographs, nautical and aeronautical charts, coastal zone maps, magnetic tape, and a wide variety of raw and processed environmental data. Phone, 202-377-8090. Schools should contact the Educational Affairs Division, Office of Legislation, Education, Outreach and Intergovernmental Affairs, 1825 Connecticut Avenue NW., Washington, DC 20235. Phone, 202-673-5381.

National Telecommunications and Information Administration Several hundred Technical Reports, Technical Memoranda, Special Publications, Contractor Reports, and other information products have been published by NTIA or its predecessor agency since 1970. The publications are available from the National Telecommunications and Information Administration, Department of Commerce, Washington, DC 20230 (phone, 202-377-1832); or the National Telecommunications and Information Administration, Institute for Telecommunication Sciences, Department of Commerce, Boulder, CO 80302 (phone, 303-497-3572).

Patent and Trademark Office *General Information Concerning Patents, Basic Facts About Trademarks, Official Gazette of the United States Patent and Trademark Office,* and *Attorneys and Agents Registered to Practice Before the U.S. Patent and Trademark Office.* Available from the Government Printing Office.

Reading Rooms See address of specific operating unit.

Small Business and Minority Business Activities See statement on page 152.

Telephone Directory The Department of Commerce telephone directory is available for sale by the Superintendent of Documents, Government Printing Office, Washington, DC 20402. Phone, 202-783-3238.

For further information concerning the Department of Commerce, contact the Office of Public Affairs, Department of Commerce, Fourteenth Street between Constitution Avenue and E Street NW., Washington, DC 20230. Phone, 202-377-4901.

DEPARTMENT OF DEFENSE

Office of the Secretary, The Pentagon, Washington, DC 20301–1155
Phone, 703–545–6700

SECRETARY OF DEFENSE	DICK CHENEY
Executive Assistant to the Secretary of Defense	KATHLEEN EMBODY
Senior Military Assistant	REAR ADM. T. JOSEPH LOPEZ, USN
Military Assistant	LT. COL. JOHN L. BERRY, USAF
Director of Protocol for the Secretary of Defense	DONNA M. LARSEN
Deputy Secretary of Defense	DONALD J. ATWOOD, JR.
Senior Military Assistant	COL. GARRY R. TREXLER, USAF
Executive Assistant	KIM F. MCKERNAN
Special Assistant to the Secretary and Deputy Secretary of Defense	DAVID S. ADDINGTON
Assistant to the Secretary of Defense	(VACANCY)
Assistant to the Secretary of Defense for Special Projects and White House Fellow	ROBERT R. GRUSKY
Executive Secretary of the Department of Defense	COL. JOHN A. DUBIA, USA
Deputy Executive Secretary	LT. COL. MICHAEL G. LEE, USAF
Military Assistants	LT. COL. B.E. BOEVERS, USA
	LT. COL. ROBERT E. LEE, JR., USMC
	LT. COMDR. D.G. COOPER, USN
Military Assistant for Special Projects	LT. COL. MICHAEL C. RYAN, USA
Military Assistant for Special Projects	LT. COL. BETTY J. PRICE, USAF
Under Secretary of Defense for Acquisition	DONALD J. YOCKEY
Principal Deputy Under Secretary of Defense for Acquisition	(VACANCY)
Assistant to the Under Secretary of Defense for Acquisition (Quality Management)	LAURA BROEDLING
Deputy Under Secretary of Defense (International Programs)	ALBERT J. KELLEY
Director, Acquisition Education Training and Career Development Policy	JAMES D. MCMICHAEL
Director, Defense Procurement	ELEANOR R. SPECTOR
Director, Office of Administration	B.A. REESE
Chairman, Defense Science Board	JOHN S. FOSTER, JR.
Director, Defense Research and Engineering	CHARLES M. HERZFELD
Deputy Director, Defense Research and Engineering (Research Advanced Technology)	RAYMOND F. SIEWART, *Acting*
Deputy Director, Defense Research and Engineering (Strategic and Theater Nuclear Forces)	GEORGE R. SCHNEITER, *Acting*

Deputy Director, Defense Research and Engineering (Tactical Warfare Programs)	FRANK KENDALL III, *Acting*
Deputy Director, Defense Research and Engineering (Test Evaluation)	CHARLES E. ADOLPH
Assistant to the Secretary of Defense for Atomic Energy	ROBERT B. BARKER
Chairman, Nuclear Weapons Council	CHARLES M. HERZFELD
Chairman, Nuclear Weapons Council Standing Committee	ROBERT B. BARKER
Assistant Secretary of Defense (Production and Logistics)	COLIN MCMILLAN
Principal Deputy Assistant Secretary of Defense (Production and Logistics)	DAVID J. BERTEAU
Deputy Assistant Secretary (Production Resources)	NICHOLAS M. TORELLI, JR.
Deputy Assistant Secretary (Logistics)	DIANE K. MORALES
Deputy Assistant Secretary (Installations)	ROBERT A. STONE
Deputy Assistant Secretary (Environment)	THOMAS E. BACA
Director, Acquisition Policy and Program Integration	JOHN CHRISTIE
Director, Small and Disadvantaged Business Utilization	HORACE J. CROUCH
Director, Special Programs	REAR ADM. DENNIS A. JONES, USN
Under Secretary of Defense for Policy	PAUL B. WOLFOWITZ
Assistant Secretary of Defense (International Security Affairs)	HENRY S. ROWEN
Principal Deputy Assistant Secretary	CARL W. FORD, JR.
Director, Foreign Military Rights Affairs	PHILIP E. BARRINGER
Deputy Assistant Secretary (African Affairs)	JAMES L. WOODS
Deputy Assistant Secretary (East Asian and Pacific Affairs)	CARL W. FORD, JR.
Deputy Assistant Secretary (Inter-American Affairs)	NANCY P. DORN
Deputy Assistant Secretary (Near East and South Asian Affairs)	ARTHUR H. HUGHES
Deputy Assistant Secretary (Global Affairs)	ROBERT K. WOLTHUIS
Assistant Secretary of Defense (International Security Policy)	STEPHEN J. HADLEY
Principal Deputy Assistant Secretary	J.D. CROUCH II
Deputy Assistant Secretary (European and NATO Policy)	W. BRUCE WEINROD
Deputy Assistant Secretary (Nuclear Forces and Arms Control Policy)	FRANKLIN C. MILLER
Deputy Assistant Secretary (Strategic Defense Space and Verification Policy)	DOUGLAS R. GRAHAM
Deputy Assistant Secretary (Conventional Forces and Arms Control Policy)	WILLIAM B. INGLEE
Assistant Secretary of Defense (Special Operations and Low Intensity Conflict)	JAMES R. LOCHER III
Principal Deputy Assistant Secretary	(VACANCY)
Deputy Assistant Secretary (Missions and Applications)	BRIG. GEN. CHARLES E. WILHELM, USMC

Deputy Assistant Secretary (Forces and Resources)	RAYMOND DOMINQUEZ
Deputy Assistant Secretary (Policy and Requirements)	ALBERTO COLL
Principal Deputy Under Secretary (Strategy and Resources)	I. LEWIS LIBBY
Assistant Deputy Under Secretary (Policy Planning)	ZALMAY M. KHALILZAD
Assistant Deputy Under Secretary (Plans)	DALE A. VESSER
Assistant Deputy Under Secretary (Soviet and East European Affairs)	ERIC S. EDELMAN
Director, Competitive Strategies	DANIEL I. GOURE
Deputy Under Secretary (Security Policy)	CRAIG ALDERMAN, JR.
Director, Defense Investigative Service	JOHN F. DONNELLY
Director, Emergency Planning	JOSEPH E. MUCKERMAN II
Director, Crisis Coordination Center	SHIRLEY AXTELL
Director, Psychologial Operations	COL. LOUIS H. ANDERSON, USA
Assistant Deputy Under Secretary (Counterintelligence and Security)	MAYNARD C. ANDERSON
Director, Counterintelligence and Investigative Program	RAY W. POLLARI
Deputy Under Secretary (Trade Security Policy) and Director, Defense Technology Security Administration	WILLIAM N. RUDMAN
Assistant Deputy Under Secretary	PETER M. SULLIVAN
Director, Net Assessment	ANDREW W. MARSHALL
Chairman, Defense Policy Board	ADM. SEYMOUR WEISS
Comptroller of the Department of Defense	SEAN C. O'KEEFE
Principal Deputy Comptroller	DONALD B. SHYCOFF
Deputy Comptroller (Program/Budget)	L. PAUL DUBE
Deputy Comptroller (Management Systems)	ALVIN TUCKER
Assistant Secretary of Defense (Command, Control, Communications and Intelligence)	DUANE P. ANDREWS
Principal Deputy Assistant Secretary/Deputy Assistant Secretary (Strategic and Tactical C^3)	THOMAS P. QUINN
Deputy Assistant Secretary (Defense-wide C^3)	JOHN G. GRIMES
Deputy Assistant Secretary (Intelligence)	C.A. HAWKINS, JR.
Deputy Assistant Secretary (Plans and Resources)	NATHANIEL M. CAVALLINI
Deputy Assistant Secretary (Information Systems)	CYNTHIA KENDALL
Assistant Secretary of Defense (Force Management and Personnel)	CHRISTOPHER JEHN
Principal Deputy Assistant Secretary	R.S. SILBERMAN
Chairperson, Armed Forces Chaplains Board	REAR ADM. A.B. KOENEMAN, USN
Deputy Assistant Secretary (Civilian Personnel Policy/Equal Opportunity)	SARA B. RATCLIFF
Deputy Assistant Secretary (Personnel Support, Families and Education)	MILLICENT W. WOODS
Deputy Assistant Secretary (Military Manpower and Personnel Policy)	LT. GEN. DONALD W. JONES, USA

Deputy Assistant Secretary (Requirements and Resources)	Carl J. Dahlman
Director, Office of Economic Adjustment	Robert M. Rauner
Assistant Secretary of Defense (Health Affairs)	Enrique Mendez, Jr., M.D.
Principal Deputy Assistant Secretary	Jack O. Lanier
Deputy Assistant Secretary (Health Budget and Programs)	Katherine D. Ladd
Deputy Assistant Secretary (Health Services Financing)	Martin L. Kappart
Deputy Assistant Secretary (Health Services Operations)	Rear Adm. Harold M. Koenig, MC, USN
Deputy Assistant Secretary (Medical Readiness)	Peter B. Collis, M.D.
Deputy Assistant Secretary (Professional Affairs and Quality Assurance)	Edward O. Martin, M.D.
Assistant Secretary of Defense (Legislative Affairs)	Dave Gribbin
Principal Deputy Assistant Secretary (Legislative Affairs)	Patty Howe
Deputy Assistant Secretary (Senate Affairs)	Jim Dykstra
Executive Director (House Affairs)	Terry Nyhous
Director, Research and Administration	Susan Lockard
Assistant Secretary of Defense (Program Analysis and Evaluation)	David S.C. Chu
Principal Deputy Assistant Secretary	Michael Leonard
Deputy Assistant Secretary (General Purpose Programs)	Herbert C. Puscheck
Deputy Assistant Secretary (Resource Analysis)	David L. McNicol
Deputy Assistant Secretary (Theater Assessments and Planning)	Deborah P. Christie
Deputy Assistant Secretary (Strategic Programs)	Michael L. Ioffredo
Assistant Secretary of Defense (Public Affairs)	Pete Williams
Principal Deputy Assistant Secretary of Defense (Public Affairs)	Robert Taylor
Deputy Assistant Secretary (Information)	Robert Hall
Deputy Assistant Secretary (Communication)	Daniel J. Kalinger
Director for Management	Ted L. Daniel
Director for Defense Information	Col. Miguel E. Monteverde, USA
Director for Plans	Col. Peter Alexandrakos, USAF
Director for Community Relations	Lt. Col. Alan Defend, USAF
Director for Public Communication	Harold Heilsnis
Director for Freedom of Information and Security Review	William M. McDonald
Director for Editorial Services	Jeffrey Salmon
Director for Programs	Janice Barbier
Assistant Secretary of Defense (Reserve Affairs)	Stephen M. Duncan
Principal Deputy Assistant Secretary	George G. Kundahl
Deputy Assistant Secretary (Manpower and Personnel)	Roger P. Scheer
Deputy Assistant Secretary (Readiness and Training)	Maj. Gen. Thomas P. McHugh, USA

Deputy Assistant Secretary (Materiel and Facilities)	JOHN B. ROSAMOND
Deputy Assistant Secretary (Program and Budget)	JOHN L. LAUGHLIN
Director, Analysis	J. ANTHONY ENGLISH
Director, Mobilization Policy and Plans	COL. REX WILLIAMS, USMCR
Chairman, Reserve Forces Policy Board	JOHN O. MARSH, JR.
National Chairman, National Committee for Employer Support of the Guard and Reserve	JOHN G. MCELWEE
Executive Director	G. ANDREW LAWRENCE
General Counsel and Director, Defense Legal Services Agency	TERRENCE O'DONNELL
Deputy General Counsel and Deputy Director	LEONARD NIEDERLEHNER
Assistant General Counsel (International and Intelligence)	JOHN H. MCNEILL
Assistant General Counsel (Fiscal and Inspector General)	MANUEL BRISKIN
Assistant General Counsel (Legal Counsel)	MICHAEL A. STERLACCI
Assistant General Counsel (Personnel and Health Policy)	ROBERT L. GILLIAT
Assistant General Counsel (Logistics)	DENNIS H. TROSCH
Director, Operational Test and Evaluation	ROBERT C. DUNCAN
Deputy Director (Resources and Administration)	NICHOLAS A. TOOMER
Deputy Director (Strategic Systems)	GEORGE G. WAUER
Deputy Director (Conventional Systems)	LEE S. FRAME, JR.
Deputy Director (C^3I Systems)	DONALD FRASER
Department of Defense Coordinator for Drug Enforcement Policy and Support	STEPHEN M. DUNCAN
Deputy Assistant Secretary (Drug Enforcement Plans and Support)	MAJ. GEN. ARNOLD SCHLOSSBERG, JR., USA
Deputy Assistant Secretary (Drug Enforcement Policy)	MICHAEL A. WERMUTH
Inspector General, Department of Defense	SUSAN J. CRAWFORD
Deputy Inspector General	DEREK J. VANDER SCHAAF
Assistant Inspector General for Administration and Information Management	NICHOLAS T. LUTSCH
Assistant Inspector General for Analysis and Followup	DAVID A. BRINKMAN
Assistant Inspector General for Auditing	(VACANCY)
Assistant Inspector General for Audit Policy and Oversight	MICHAEL R. HILL
Assistant Inspector General for Criminal Investigation Policy and Oversight	MORRIS B. SILVERSTEIN
Assistant Inspector General for Inspections	KATHERINE A. BRITTIN
Assistant Inspector General for Investigations/Director, Defense Criminal Investigative Service	DONALD MANCUSO
Assistant Inspector General for Departmental Inquiries	MICHAEL B. SUESSMAN
Assistant to the Secretary (Intelligence Oversight)	WERNER E. MICHEL

Deputy Assistant to the Secretary (Intelligence Oversight)	FRANK J. AURELIO
Assistant to the Secretary (Intelligence Policy)	RICHARD L. HAVER
Deputy Assistant to the Secretary (Intelligence Policy)	JEREMY C. CLARK
Director of Administration and Management and Director, Washington Headquarters Services	D.O. COOKE

Joint Chiefs of Staff

Chairman	GEN. COLIN L. POWELL, USA
Vice Chairman	ADM. D.E. JEREMIAH, USN
Chief of Staff, Army	GEN. CARL E. VUONO, USA
Chief of Naval Operations	ADM. FRANK B. KELSO II, USN
Chief of Staff, Air Force	GEN. MERRILL A. MCPEAK, USAF
Commandant, Marine Corps	GEN. ALFRED M. GRAY, JR., USMC

Joint Staff

Director	LT. GEN. MICHAEL P.C. CARNS, USAF
Vice Director	MAJ. GEN. GENE A. DEEGAN, USMC
Director for Manpower and Personnel—J–1	BRIG. GEN. MICHAEL G. VERGAMINI, USAF
Director for Operations—J–3	LT. GEN. M.L. ARANDTNER, USMC
Director for Logistics—J–4	VICE ADM. JIMMY PAPPAS, USN
Director for Strategic Plans and Policy—J–5	LT. GEN. E.S. LELAND, JR., USA
Director for Command, Control, and Communications Systems—J–6	MAJ. GEN. JAMES S. CASSITY, USAF
Director for Operational Plans and Interoperability—J–7	MAJ. GEN. MALCOLM B. ARMSTRONG, USAF
Director for Force Structure, Resource and Assessment—J–8	MAJ. GEN. JOHN D. ROBINSON, USA
Director for Information and Resource Management	COL. WILLIAM O. NATIONS, USAF

[For the Department of Defense statement of organization, see the *Code of Federal Regulations,* Title 32, Chapter I, Subchapter R]

The Department of Defense is responsible for providing the military forces needed to deter war and protect the security of our country.

The major elements of these forces are the Army, Navy, Marine Corps, and Air Force, consisting of about 2.1 million men and women on active duty. Of these, some 518,000—including about 67,000 on ships at sea—are serving outside the United States. They are backed, in case of emergency, by the 1.7 million members of the reserve components. In addition, there are about 1.1 million civilian employees in the Defense Department.

Under the President, who is also Commander in Chief, the Secretary of Defense exercises direction, authority, and control over the Department, which includes the separately organized military departments of Army, Navy, and Air Force, the Joint Chiefs of Staff providing military advice, the unified and specified combatant commands, and various defense agencies established for specific purposes.

Every State in the Union has some defense activities. Central headquarters of the Department is at the Pentagon, the "world's largest office building."

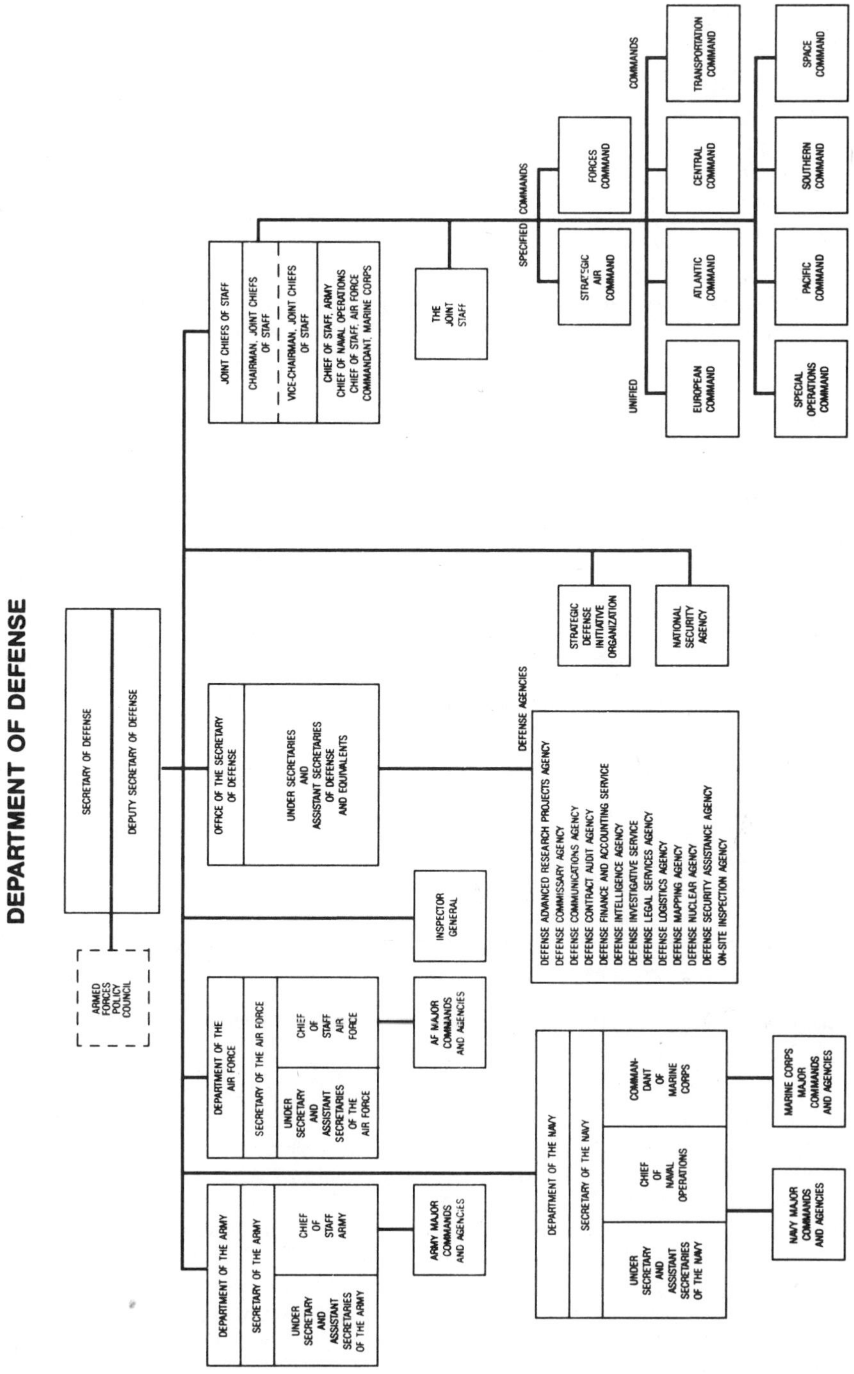
DEPARTMENT OF DEFENSE
SECRETARY OF DEFENSE
DEPUTY SECRETARY OF DEFENSE
ARMED FORCES POLICY COUNCIL
JOINT CHIEFS OF STAFF
CHAIRMAN, JOINT CHIEFS OF STAFF
VICE-CHAIRMAN, JOINT CHIEFS OF STAFF
CHIEF OF STAFF, ARMY
CHIEF OF NAVAL OPERATIONS
CHIEF OF STAFF, AIR FORCE
COMMANDANT, MARINE CORPS
THE JOINT STAFF
SPECIFIED COMMANDS
STRATEGIC AIR COMMAND
FORCES COMMAND
UNIFIED COMMANDS
EUROPEAN COMMAND
ATLANTIC COMMAND
CENTRAL COMMAND
TRANSPORTATION COMMAND
SPECIAL OPERATIONS COMMAND
PACIFIC COMMAND
SOUTHERN COMMAND
SPACE COMMAND
STRATEGIC DEFENSE INITIATIVE ORGANIZATION
NATIONAL SECURITY AGENCY
OFFICE OF THE SECRETARY OF DEFENSE
UNDER SECRETARIES AND ASSISTANT SECRETARIES OF DEFENSE AND EQUIVALENTS
DEFENSE AGENCIES
DEFENSE ADVANCED RESEARCH PROJECTS AGENCY
DEFENSE COMMISSARY AGENCY
DEFENSE COMMUNICATIONS AGENCY
DEFENSE CONTRACT AUDIT AGENCY
DEFENSE FINANCE AND ACCOUNTING SERVICE
DEFENSE INTELLIGENCE AGENCY
DEFENSE INVESTIGATIVE SERVICE
DEFENSE LEGAL SERVICES AGENCY
DEFENSE LOGISTICS AGENCY
DEFENSE MAPPING AGENCY
DEFENSE NUCLEAR AGENCY
DEFENSE SECURITY ASSISTANCE AGENCY
ON-SITE INSPECTION AGENCY
INSPECTOR GENERAL
DEPARTMENT OF THE AIR FORCE
SECRETARY OF THE AIR FORCE
UNDER SECRETARY AND ASSISTANT SECRETARIES OF THE AIR FORCE
CHIEF OF STAFF AIR FORCE
AF MAJOR COMMANDS AND AGENCIES
DEPARTMENT OF THE ARMY
SECRETARY OF THE ARMY
UNDER SECRETARY AND ASSISTANT SECRETARIES OF THE ARMY
CHIEF OF STAFF ARMY
ARMY MAJOR COMMANDS AND AGENCIES
DEPARTMENT OF THE NAVY
SECRETARY OF THE NAVY
UNDER SECRETARY AND ASSISTANT SECRETARIES OF THE NAVY
CHIEF OF NAVAL OPERATIONS
COMMANDANT OF MARINE CORPS
NAVY MAJOR COMMANDS AND AGENCIES
MARINE CORPS MAJOR COMMANDS AND AGENCIES

The Department of Defense (DOD) is the successor agency to the National Military Establishment created by the National Security Act of 1947 (50 U.S.C. 401). It was established as an executive department of the Government by the National Security Act Amendments of 1949 with the Secretary of Defense as its head (5 U.S.C. 101). Since that time, many legislative and administrative changes have occurred, evolving the Department into the structure under which it currently operates.

Structure

The Department of Defense is composed of the Office of the Secretary of Defense; the military departments and the military services within those departments; the Chairman of the Joint Chiefs of Staff and the Joint Staff; the unified and specified combatant commands; the Defense agencies; DOD field activities; and such other offices, agencies, activities, and commands as may be established or designated by law, or by the President or the Secretary of Defense.

In providing immediate staff assistance and advice to the Secretary of Defense, the Office of the Secretary of Defense and the Chairman of the Joint Chiefs of Staff, and the Joint Staff, though separately identified and organized, function in full coordination and cooperation.

The Office of the Secretary of Defense includes the offices of the Deputy Secretary of Defense; the Special Assistant to the Secretary and the Deputy Secretary of Defense; the Executive Secretary of the Department of Defense; the Assistant to the Secretary of Defense; the Assistant to the Secretary of Defense for Special Projects and White House Fellow; the Under Secretary of Defense for Acquisition; the Under Secretary of Defense for Policy; the Comptroller of the Department of Defense; Assistant Secretaries of Defense; the General Counsel; the Director of Defense Research and Engineering; the Director of Operational Test and Evaluation; the Inspector General; and such other staff offices as the Secretary of Defense establishes to assist him in carrying out his duties and responsibilities. The heads of these offices are staff advisers to the Secretary and perform such functions as he assigns to them.

The Joint Chiefs of Staff consist of the Chairman; the Chief of Staff, U.S. Army; the Chief of Naval Operations; the Chief of Staff, U.S. Air Force; and the Commandant of the Marine Corps. Supported, subject to the authority of the Chairman, by the Joint Staff, they constitute the immediate military staff of the Secretary of Defense. The Chairman is the principal military adviser to the President, the National Security Council, and the Secretary of Defense. The other members of the Joint Chiefs of Staff are the senior military officers of their respective services and are military advisers to the President, the National Security Council, and the Secretary of Defense. The Vice Chairman of the Joint Chiefs acts as Chairman when there is a vacancy in the Office of the Chairman or in the absence or disability of the Chairman.

Each military department (the Department of the Navy includes naval aviation and the United States Marine Corps) is separately organized under its own Secretary and functions under the direction, authority, and control of the Secretary of Defense. The Secretary of a military department is responsible to the Secretary of Defense for the operation and efficiency of his department. Orders to the military departments are issued through the Secretaries of these departments, or their designees, by the Secretary of Defense or under authority specifically delegated in writing by the Secretary of Defense or provided by law.

The commanders of unified and specified combatant commands are responsible to the President and the Secretary of Defense for accomplishing the military missions assigned to them and exercising command authority over forces assigned to them. The operational chain of command runs from the President to the Secretary of Defense to the commanders of the unified and specified combatant commands. The Chairman of the Joint Chiefs of Staff functions within the chain of command by transmitting the orders of the President or the Secretary of Defense to the commanders of the unified and specified combatant commands.

Office of the Secretary of Defense

Secretary of Defense The Secretary of Defense is the principal defense policy adviser to the President and is responsible for the formulation of general defense policy and policy related to all matters of direct and primary concern to DOD, and for the execution of approved policy. Under the direction of the President, the Secretary exercises direction, authority, and control over the Department of Defense.

Deputy Secretary of Defense The Deputy Secretary of Defense is delegated full power and authority to act for the Secretary of Defense and to exercise the powers of the Secretary on any and all matters for which the Secretary is authorized to act pursuant to law.

Special Assistant to the Secretary and Deputy Secretary of Defense The Special Assistant is the principal immediate office adviser to the Secretary and Deputy Secretary.

Assistant to the Secretary of Defense The Assistant to the Secretary of Defense represents the Secretary with the White House offices of Intergovernmental Affairs, Political Affairs, and Presidential Personnel; manages the selection of noncareer appointees throughout the Department; handles appointments to boards, committees, and consultancies; and carries out special projects.

Assistant to the Secretary of Defense for Special Projects and White House Fellow The Assistant for Special Projects performs tasks and initiates actions relating to projects of special interest to the Secretary and Deputy Secretary.

Executive Secretary of the Department of Defense The Executive Secretary supports the Secretary and Deputy Secretary by executing the following responsibilities:

—managing and controlling all action and information documents for the Secretary and Deputy Secretary;

—performing liaison functions with the White House military office, including Presidential support activities;

—processing requests for DOD support from other departments or agencies;

—coordinating assignments of executive agents, and assignments of DOD personnel to non-DOD agencies;

—validating military airlift transportation requests for the Office of the Secretary and non-DOD agencies;

—coordinating and editing the Secretary's *Annual Report to the Congress* and the annual production of *Soviet Military Power;* and

—performing other special projects as directed by the Secretary or Deputy Secretary.

Acquisition The Under Secretary of Defense for Acquisition is the principal staff assistant and adviser to the Secretary of Defense for all matters relating to the acquisition system; research and development; production; logistics; military construction; and procurement. The Under Secretary serves as the Defense Acquisition Executive with responsibility for supervising the performance of the entire DOD acquisition system and chairing the Defense Acquisition Board.

Research and Engineering The Director of Defense Research and Engineering is the Principal Staff Assistant to the Under Secretary of Defense (Acquisition) for DOD scientific and technical matters, basic and applied research, and the development of weapon systems. The Director:

—conducts analyses, develops policies, provides advice, makes recommendations, and issues guidance for DOD programs;

—develops systems and standards for the administration and management of approved plans and programs;

—initiates programs, actions, and taskings to ensure adherence to DOD policies and national security objectives, and ensures that programs are designed to accommodate operational requirements;

—reviews and evaluates programs for carrying out approved policies and standards;

—informs appropriate organizations and personnel of new and significant trends or initiatives;

—reviews proposed resources programs, formulates budget estimates, recommends resource allocations, and monitors the implementation of approved programs;

—participates in planning, programming, and budgeting activities that relate to the office's responsibilities; and

—reviews and evaluates recommendations on requirements and priorities.

Production and Logistics The Assistant Secretary of Defense for Production and Logistics is the principal staff assistant and adviser to the Under Secretary of Defense for Acquisition for management of DOD production procurement, development of procurement regulations, career management of the procurement workforce, logistics, installations, associated support functions, and related matters.

Small and Disadvantaged Business Utilization This office, which is under the direction of the Under Secretary of Defense for Acquisition, administers Department responsibilities under the Small Business Act, as amended (15 U.S.C. 631). The Director:

—ensures that a fair share of Department procurements are placed with small businesses, small disadvantaged businesses, and women-owned small businesses;

—conducts surveillance reviews of selected Department contracting activities' small business programs as well as those of major Department prime contractors;

—establishes and reviews policies, procedures, and initiatives for inclusion in the Defense supplement to the Federal Acquisition Regulation for the improvement of Department small business and small disadvantaged business programs;

—manages the Department's labor surplus program;

—develops and reviews legislative initiatives for increased small business participation in Department procurements; and

—manages the small business research and development program.

Policy The Under Secretary of Defense for Policy is the principal staff assistant to the Secretary of Defense for policy matters relating to overall international security policy and political-military affairs. Functional areas include NATO affairs; net assessments; foreign military sales; arms limitation agreements; international trade and technology; regional security affairs; intelligence analysis and collection requirements; integration of departmental plans and policies with overall national security objectives; and issuance of policy guidance affecting departmental programs.

International Security Affairs The Assistant Secretary of Defense for International Security Affairs is the principal staff assistant to the Under Secretary of Defense (Policy) for policy planning regarding political-military activities related to international affairs, excluding the North Atlantic Treaty Organization, other European countries, and the U.S.S.R. Oversight is provided for DOD activities relating to law of the sea. The Assistant Secretary oversees bilateral defense relationships and provides supervision in the areas of security assistance (i.e., foreign military sales and military assistance programs), Military Assistance Advisory Groups and Missions, and the negotiation and monitoring of agreements with foreign governments, excluding NATO, other European countries, and the U.S.S.R. In the area of international economic and energy affairs, the Assistant Secretary provides advice and recommends policies, formulates programs, develops plans, and issues guidance to DOD components. The Assistant Secretary formulates plans and policy related to general purpose forces, non-European regional security requirements, and related budget considerations. The Assistant Secretary provides defense policy oversight on matters pertaining to prisoner of war and missing in action affairs and acts as principal adviser to the Secretary of Defense on such matters.

International Security Policy The Assistant Secretary of Defense for International Security Policy is the principal staff assistant to the Under Secretary of Defense (Policy) for policy planning regarding strategic international security matters concerning European and North Atlantic Treaty Organization affairs, strategic and theater nuclear force planning, and all matters concerning nuclear and conventional, bilateral and multilateral negotiations on arms reductions, defense and space, and East-West security negotiations. The Assistant Secretary formulates policy related to strategic offensive and defensive forces, theater nuclear matters and capabilities, European conventional defense, and the relationship between strategic and theater force planning and budgets. Responsibilities also include implementing policy on nuclear nonproliferation matters and other treaties and agreements, as well as oversight of DOD activities related to NATO and bilateral issues with European countries.

Special Operations and Low Intensity Conflict The Assistant Secretary of Defense for Special Operations and Low Intensity Conflict is the principal staff assistant and adviser to the Under Secretary of Defense (Policy) concerning DOD policy for special operations and low-intensity conflict and exercises overall supervision (including oversight of policy and resources) of special operations and low-intensity conflict activities of the Department of Defense.

Oversight is provided for special operations policy, plans, and programs in the areas of direct action, strategic reconnaissance, unconventional warfare, foreign internal defense, civil affairs, psychological operations, counterterrorism, humanitarian assistance, theater search and rescue, and such other activities as may be specified by the Secretary of Defense. Also provided is DOD oversight and policy guidance for DOD activities in low-intensity conflict.

With the advice and assistance of the Commander-in-Chief of the Special Operations Command, the Assistant Secretary provides overall supervision of the preparation and justification of program recommendations and budget proposals to be included in FYDP Program 11. In conjunction with the Commander-in-Chief, the Assistant Secretary provides oversight of the development and acquisition of special operations-peculiar equipment and acquisition of other material, supplies, or services that are peculiar to special operations activities.

The Assistant Secretary provides representatives, staffing, and interface with national level or interagency boards or committees relating to special operations or low-intensity conflict activities.

Net Assessment The Director of Net Assessment is under the direction, authority, and control of the Under Secretary of Defense for Policy, but maintains a direct channel to the Secretary of Defense while keeping the Under Secretary informed. The Director formulates, plans, conducts, and prepares net assessments for the Secretary of Defense.

Comptroller The Comptroller of the Department of Defense is the principal adviser and assistant to the Secretary of Defense for budgetary and fiscal matters, including financial management, accounting policy and systems, budget formulation and execution, contract audit administration and organization, and general management improvement programs. In addition, the Comptroller is the Chief Financial Officer of DOD. Through the Comptroller, resource management information is collected, analyzed, and reported for the Office of Management and Budget, the Congress, the General Accounting Office, and other agencies outside the Department of Defense. Supervision, direction, and review of the preparation and execution of the Defense budget is provided.

Command, Control, Communications and Intelligence The Assistant Secretary of Defense (Command, Control, Communications and Intelligence (C^3I)) is the principal adviser and assistant to the Secretary of Defense for C^3I policy, requirements, priorities, systems, resources, and programs, including related warning and reconnaissance activities, and those national programs and intelligence-related activities for which the Secretary of Defense has execution authority. Additionally, the Assistant Secretary is responsible for developing counterintelligence policies and coordinating their implementation, and for implementing information management principles throughout DOD, including ensuring the proper integration of DOD computing, systems security, telecommunications, and information management activities.

Health Affairs The Assistant Secretary of Defense (Health Affairs) is the principal staff assistant and adviser to the Secretary of Defense for all DOD health policies, programs, and activities, which include the following functional areas: medical readiness; disease prevention; health promotion; health benefits programs; alcohol and drug abuse treatment; cost containment; quality assurance; medical information systems; DOD HIV Program and Research on Acquired Immunodeficiency Syndrome; procurement, professional development, retention of medical and dental personnel and related health care specialists and technicians; and military medical construction.

Force Management and Personnel The Assistant Secretary of Defense (Force Management and Personnel) is responsible for the following functional areas:

—civilian and military personnel policy, management programs and systems, (including attraction and retention of personnel); personnel utilization; compensation; retired pay; per diem travel and transportation allowances; career development, training, and education; labor-management relations; morale, discipline, and welfare; community services; nonappropriated fund activities; commercial affairs, credit unions and post exchanges;

—development of programs and procedures for detecting both drug and alcohol dependency within the DOD Dependent Schools system and during pre-accession and new-entrant screenings for military personnel;

—civilian and military equal opportunity programs, including employment and utilization of personnel, education in race and human relations, and compliance with nondiscrimination requirements of federally assisted programs;

—family policy and support, including dependents' education, health affairs liaison, and child and spouse abuse;

—resource management and support, including force structure analysis as related to quantitative and qualitative manpower requirements, manpower utilization, manpower programs development, and control of military and civilian manpower strengths; provision of Department resources to other agencies; Federal-State relations; force readiness and sustainability; goal-setting and management supervision for the force management and personnel research program; and

—mobilization planning and requirements, including coordination of Department efforts for mobilization of conventional forces.

Legislative Affairs The Assistant Secretary of Defense (Legislative Affairs) is responsible for the following functional areas:

—maintenance of direct liaison with the Congress, the Executive Office of the President, and other Government agencies with regard to legislative investigations and other pertinent matters affecting the relations of the Department of Defense with the Congress;

—advice and assistance to the Secretary of Defense and other officials of the Department of Defense on congressional aspects of departmental policies, plans, and programs;

—coordination of departmental actions relating to congressional consideration of the legislative program of the Department;

—coordination of the development, clearance, and furnishing of information in response to requests received in the Office of the Secretary of Defense from Members of the Congress and the committees of the Congress and their staffs; and

—arrangements for witnesses from the Office of the Secretary of Defense, Defense agencies, and the military departments at congressional hearings on Defense matters.

Program Analysis and Evaluation The Assistant Secretary of Defense (Program Analysis and Evaluation) assists the Secretary in development of the force planning, fiscal, programming, and policy guidance upon which DOD force structure, system acquisition, and other resource allocation actions are to be based. The staff analyzes and evaluates military forces, weapons systems, and equipment in relation to projected threats, U.S. objectives, resource constraints, and priorities established by the Secretary of Defense. Based upon these analyses, the staff develops alternative program proposals for consideration by the Secretary of Defense. In carrying out these responsibilities, the staff proposes, guides, monitors, and evaluates studies and analyses by other DOD components and conducts or participates in special studies as directed by the Secretary of Defense. Finally, the staff leads the Department in developing and promoting improved analytic tools and methods for analyzing national security planning and resource allocation decisionmaking.

Public Affairs The Assistant Secretary of Defense (Public Affairs) is responsible for the functional areas which include Defense public and internal information; audiovisual activities; community relations; review of information intended for public release to ensure compliance with security policies; implementation of the Freedom of Information Act and the access portion of Federal Privacy Act programs within the Department of Defense; long-range coordination and planning of public schedules of senior Defense officials; and providing editorial services to the Secretary of Defense and the Deputy Secretary of Defense. Liaison is maintained with and assistance is provided to information media and national and civic organizations with respect to matters relating to activities of the Department of Defense. Approvals are required for military participation in public exhibitions, demonstrations, and ceremonies of national or international significance. The Assistant Secretary of Defense (Public Affairs), limited only by national security constraints and statutory considerations, ensures a free flow of news and information to the media, appropriate forums, and the American people.

Reserve Affairs The Assistant Secretary of Defense (Reserve Affairs) is responsible for exercising overall supervision of Reserve component matters in the Department of Defense: manpower, personnel, and compensation; research, studies, and evaluation; operations, training, and force structure; mobilization, demobilization, and reconstitution; force mix; weapons systems, equipment, and materiel; construction, installations, and facilities; and readiness and sustainability.

General Counsel The General Counsel is the chief legal officer of the Department of Defense with responsibility for all legal services performed within or involving the Department of Defense. The General Counsel is responsible for the preparation and processing of legislation, executive orders and proclamations, and reports and comments thereon. In addition, the General Counsel serves as Director of the Defense Legal Services Agency, providing legal advice and service for the Office of the Secretary of Defense, its field activities, and the Defense agencies. Additional responsibilities include the administration of the Defense Industrial Security Clearance Review program and the Standards of Conduct Ethics program, which provides services to the Office of the Secretary of Defense, its field activities, and Defense agencies, and establishes departmental ethics policies.

Operational Test and Evaluation The Director of Operational Test and Evaluation serves as the principal staff assistant and adviser to the Secretary of Defense on operational test and evaluation in the Department of Defense and the principal test and evaluation official within the senior management of the Department. The Director prescribes policies and procedures for the conduct of operational test and evaluation within the Department; provides advice and makes recommendations to the Secretary of Defense and issues guidance to and consults with the heads of Defense components with respect to such activities in the Department in general, and to specific programs to be conducted in connection with a major defense acquisition program; monitors and reviews all test and evaluation programs in the Department to ensure adherence to approved policies and standards; and reviews and makes recommendations to the Secretary of Defense on all budgetary and financial matters relating to such activities, including operational test facilities and equipment. The Director approves the adequacy of service operational test plans for major programs prior to execution and provides to the Secretary of Defense, the Under Secretary of Defense for Acquisition, and Congress an assessment of the operational effectiveness and suitability of each system before it proceeds beyond a low rate of production.

Intelligence Oversight The Assistant to the Secretary of Defense (Intelligence Oversight):

—conducts independent oversight inspections of DOD intelligence and counterintelligence activities to ensure compliance with legal requirements and standards of propriety;

—reviews all allegations that raise questions of legality or propriety involving intelligence, intelligence-related, or counterintelligence activities in DOD to ensure that investigations are rigorously and thoroughly accomplished and that appropriate corrective measures are implemented;

—reviews results of inspections conducted by the Inspectors General of the National Security Agency, Defense Intelligence Agency, and military service intelligence and counterintelligence organizations; and

—serves as the focal point for all DOD contacts with the President's Intelligence Oversight Board (established under Executive Order 12334 of December 4, 1981) and, at least quarterly, reports jointly with the DOD General Counsel to the Board on any DOD intelligence activities of questionable legality or propriety, as well as on significant oversight activities undertaken by the DOD to ensure compliance with Executive Order 12333 of December 4, 1981, and DOD policies.

Intelligence Policy The Assistant to the Secretary of Defense (Intelligence Policy):

—provides advice, makes recommendations, and monitors the implementation of DOD intelligence policies and programs;

—reviews all intelligence programs and resource management activities, including resource allocation, and recommends changes to the Secretary of Defense and OSD officials responsible for staff supervision of these activities;

—reviews requirements and priorities to determine if DOD user requirements are fully considered in the development of intelligence plans and programs; and

—conducts a continuing assessment of the effectiveness of DOD intelligence activities, including the production of finished intelligence.

DOD Coordinator for Drug Enforcement Policy and Support The DOD Coordinator for Drug Enforcement Policy and Support, as the principal staff assistant and adviser to the Secretary of Defense for drug control policy, requirements, priorities, systems, resources, and programs:

—develops policies, conducts analysis, provides advice, makes recommendations, and issues guidance on DOD drug control plans and programs;

—develops systems and standards for the administration and management of approved DOD drug control plans and programs;

—promulgates plans, programs, actions, and tasks pertaining to the DOD drug control program, consistent with the National Drug Control Strategy and DOD drug control policies and objectives;

—serves as the DOD contact for the Office of the Director of National Drug Control Policy and other Federal and State agencies;

—coordinates and monitors DOD support of civilian drug-law enforcement;

—coordinates and monitors interagency detection of maritime and aerial transit of illegal drugs into the United States;

—coordinates and monitors, in conjunction with the Assistant Secretary of Defense (Reserve Affairs), National Guard support to State drug-law enforcement operations, and to DOD, as required;

—coordinates and monitors, in conjunction with the Assistant Secretary of Defense (Command, Control, Communications, and Intelligence), DOD intelligence and communications support of drug-law enforcement operations; and

—proposes policy guidelines for the DOD counterdrug role and recommends the distribution of DOD resources for counterdrug support, based upon advice and assistance from OSD officials, the Chairman of the Joint Chiefs of Staff, and appropriate DOD components.

Inspector General The Inspector General serves as an independent and objective official in the Department of Defense who is responsible for conducting, supervising, monitoring, and initiating audits, investigations, and inspections relating to programs and operations of the Department of Defense. The Inspector General provides leadership and coordination and recommends policies for activities designed to promote economy, efficiency, and effectiveness in the administration of, and to prevent and detect fraud and abuse in, such programs and operations. The Inspector General is also responsible for keeping the Secretary of Defense and the Congress fully and currently informed about problems and deficiencies relating to the administration of such programs and operations and the necessity for, and progress of, corrective action.

Administration and Management The Director of Administration and Management serves as the principal staff assistant and advisor to the Secretary and Deputy Secretary of Defense on departmentwide organizational and administrative management matters, and also serves as the Director, Washington Headquarters Service.

Joint Chiefs of Staff

Joint Chiefs of Staff

The Joint Chiefs of Staff consists of the Chairman of the Joint Chiefs of Staff; the Chief of Staff, United States Army; the Chief of Naval Operations; the Chief of Staff, United States Air Force; and the Commandant of the Marine Corps.

The Chairman of the Joint Chiefs of Staff is the principal military adviser to the President, the National Security Council, and the Secretary of Defense. The other members of the Joint Chiefs of Staff are military advisers who may provide additional information upon request from the President, the National Security Council, or the Secretary of Defense. They may also submit their advice when it does not agree with that of the Chairman.

Subject to the authority of the President and the Secretary of Defense, the Chairman of the Joint Chiefs of Staff is responsible for:

—assisting the President and the Secretary of Defense in providing for the strategic direction and planning of the Armed Forces;

—allocating resources to fulfill strategic plans;

290-950 O 91 - 7

—making recommendations for the assignment of responsibilities within the Armed Forces in accordance with and in support of those logistic and mobility plans;

—comparing the capabilities of American and allied Armed Forces with those of potential adversaries;

—preparing and reviewing contingency plans that conform to policy guidance from the President and the Secretary of Defense;

—preparing joint logistic and mobility plans to support contingency plans; and

—recommending assignment of logistic and mobility responsibilities to the Armed Forces to fulfill logistic and mobility plans.

The Chairman also advises the Secretary of Defense on critical deficiencies and strengths in force capabilities (including manpower, logistic, and mobility support) and assesses the effect of such deficiencies and strengths on meeting national security objectives and policy and on strategic plans. He establishes and maintains a uniform system for evaluating the preparedness of each unified and specified combatant command to carry out assigned missions.

The Chairman advises the Secretary of Defense on the priorities of the requirements identified by the commanders of the unified and specified combatant commands and on the extent to which program recommendations and budget proposals of the military departments and other DOD components for a fiscal year conform with priorities established in requirements of the unified and specified combatant commands. He is responsible for submitting to the Secretary alternative program recommendations and budget proposals with, guidance provided by the Secretary, in order to achieve greater conformance with priorities established by the unified and specified combatant commands. The Chairman advises the Secretary on the extent to which major programs and policies of the Armed Forces in the area of manpower conform with strategic plans and assesses military requirements for defense acquisition programs.

Additionally, the Chairman:

—formulates doctrine and training policies and coordinates military education and training;

—represents the United States on the Military Staff Committee of the United Nations;

—performs such other duties as may be prescribed by law or by the President and the Secretary of Defense;

—convenes and presides over regular meetings of the Joint Chiefs of Staff;

—assists the Joint Chiefs in carrying on their business as promptly as practicable; and

—schedules issues for consideration by the Joint Chiefs.

The Chairman, while so serving, holds the grade of general or admiral and outranks all other officers of the Armed Forces.

The Vice Chairman of the Joint Chiefs performs duties assigned by the Chairman, with the approval of the Secretary of Defense. The Vice Chairman acts as Chairman when there is a vacancy in the office of the Chairman, or in the absence or disability of the Chairman. He participates in all meetings of the Joint Chiefs of Staff, but may not vote except when acting as Chairman. The Vice Chairman, while so serving, holds the grade of general or admiral and outranks all other officers of the Armed Forces except the Chairman of the Joint Chiefs of Staff.

Joint Staff

The Joint Staff under the Chairman of the Joint Chiefs of Staff assists the Chairman and, subject to the authority of the Chairman, the other members of the Joint Chiefs of Staff, including the Vice Chairman, in carrying out their responsibilities.

The Joint Staff is headed by a Director who is selected by the Chairman in consultation with the other members of the Joint Chiefs of Staff, and with the approval of the Secretary of Defense. Officers assigned to serve on the Joint Staff are selected by the Chairman in approximate equal numbers from the Army, Navy, Marine Corps, and Air Force. The Joint Staff is composed of all members of the Armed Forces and civilian employees assigned or detailed to permanent duty to perform the functions assigned to the Chairman of the Joint Chiefs of Staff.

Sources of Information

Contracts and Small Business Activities Contact the Director, Small and Disadvantaged Business Utilization, Office of the Secretary of Defense, Room 2A340, The Pentagon, Washington, DC 20301-3061. Phone, 703-697-9383.

DOD Directives and Instructions Correspondence and Directives Directorate, Washington Headquarters Services, Room 2A286, The Pentagon, Washington, DC 20301-1155. Phone, 703-697-4111.

Employment Almost all positions are in the competitive service and are filled from civil service registers. College recruiting requirements are limited primarily to management intern positions at the B.S. and M.S. levels. For additional information, inquiries should be addressed to the Chief, Staffing Division, Directorate for Personnel and Security, Washington Headquarters Services, Room 3B347, The Pentagon, Washington, DC 20301-1155. Phone, 703-697-4211.

Films The Department of Defense has certain motion pictures and videotapes available for public, nonprofit exhibition. These are productions required to support training and internal information objectives. There is a catalog of productions available to the public for sale from the National Technical Information Service, 5285 Port Royal Road, Springfield, VA 22161. Each Service has its own catalog for internal use. Interested persons should contact the nearest installation of each Service to obtain the appropriate address of the film/videotape distribution center serving that area. Additionally, the Public Affairs Office of each Service at its Headquarters, Washington, DC, should be contacted. There is no charge for listings of films. No admission or any other fees may be charged for viewing of films and each film must be shown in its entirety, including all titles at beginning and end; no portion of the film may be reproduced, edited, or cut in any manner; and qualified operators must be provided by the borrower. Interested purchasers of Department of Defense films may also contact the Sales Branch, National Audio-Visual Center, 8750 Edgeworth Drive, Capitol Heights, MD 20743-3701. Phone, 301-763-1896.

Pentagon Tours Guided tours of the Pentagon are available Monday through Friday, excluding Federal holidays. The 1-hour tours start at the Concourse. For further information or reservations, call 703-695-1776 or write: Pentagon Tour Director, Room 3C1054, Washington, DC 20301-1400.

Speakers Scheduling of speaking engagements for civilian and military representatives of the Department of Defense is a responsibility of the Director for Programs, Office of the Assistant Secretary of Defense (Public Affairs). Speakers on a variety of defense subjects are available in response to invitations at no cost to the local sponsor. However, any speaker can accept transportation, meals, and lodging, if offered by the sponsor of the public event in which he is to participate.

Written requests for speakers should be forwarded to the Director for Community Relations, Office of the Assistant Secretary of Defense (Public Affairs), The Pentagon, Washington, DC 20301-1400 (phone, 703-695-6108) or to the Public Affairs Officer of the nearest military installation.

Telephone Directory The Department of Defense telephone directory is available for sale by the Superintendent of Documents, Government Printing Office, Washington, DC 20402. Phone, 703-783-3238.

For further information concerning the Department of Defense, contact the Director, Directorate for Public Communication, Office of the Assistant Secretary of Defense (Public Affairs), The Pentagon, Washington, DC 20301–1400. Phone, 703–697–5737.

DOD FIELD ACTIVITIES

American Forces Information Service The American Forces Information Service, established in 1977 under the supervision of the Assistant Secretary of Defense (Public Affairs), is responsible for the Department's internal information program and visual information policy. The Armed Forces Radio and Television Service, the American Forces Press and Publications Service (which includes among its many products the *Current News* Early Bird), and the Armed Forces Radio and Television Service Broadcast Center function under the Director of American Forces Information Service. In addition, the Service provides policy guidance and oversight for departmental periodicals and pamphlets, *Stars and Stripes* newspapers, military command newspapers, the broadcast elements of the military departments, departmental audiovisual matters, and the Defense Information School.

(American Forces Information Service, Department of Defense, Suite 311, 601 North Fairfax Street, Alexandria, VA 22314–2007. Phone, 703–274–4839.)

DOD Dependents Schools The office of Department of Defense Dependents Schools was established in 1974. Under the policy guidance of the Assistant Secretary of Defense (Force Management and Personnel), the office is charged with providing quality education, from kindergarten through grade twelve, to eligible minor dependents of military and civilian personnel of the Department of Defense stationed overseas. The office, in turn, advises the Assistant Secretary of Defense (Force Management and Personnel) on all matters pertaining to Dependents Schools.

(Department of Defense Dependents Schools, Room 164, Hoffman Building, Alexandria, VA 22331. Phone, 703–325–0885.)

Office of Civilian Health and Medical Program of the Uniformed Services The Office of Civilian Health and Medical Program of the Uniformed Services (OCHAMPUS) was established as a field activity in 1974 under the policy guidance and operational direction of the Assistant Secretary of Defense (Health Affairs). The Office is responsible for administering a civilian health and medical care program for retirees and the spouses and dependent children of active duty, retired, and deceased service members. Also included are spouses and dependent children of totally disabled veterans. The Office also administers, for the Uniformed Services, a program for payment of emergency medical/dental services provided to active duty service members by civilian medical personnel.

(Office of Civilian Health and Medical Program of the Uniformed Services, Department of Defense, Denver, CO 80045. Phone, 303–361–8606.)

Defense Medical Systems Support Activity The Activity, under the policy guidance and operational direction of the Assistant Secretary of Defense (Health Affairs), is comprised of two principal elements: the Defense Medical Systems Support Center and the Defense Medical Facilities Office.

The Defense Medical Systems Support Center ensures that information systems and related communications function efficiently, are supportive of the Department's functional requirements for both peacetime and contingency operations, and are integrated to support a planned systems architecture. The four principal subdivisions are the Tri-Service Medical Information System, the Defense Enrollment Eligibility Reporting System, the Office of Mobilization Support and Communications, and the Management Information Support Directorate.

(Defense Medical Systems Support Center, Department of Defense, Suite 502, Skyline 6, 5109 Leesburg Pike, Falls Church, VA 22041–3201. Phone, 703–756–2530.)

The Defense Medical Facilities Office develops and maintains an integrated system for planning, programming, and budgeting for medical facility construction projects (which include construction, replacement, modification, modernization, and supporting facilities) throughout the Department of Defense and for managing the allocation of the financial resources approved for such projects.

(Defense Medical Facilities Office, Suite 817, Skyline 6, 5109 Leesburg Pike, Falls Church, VA 22041–3201. Phone, 703–756–0900.)

Defense Technology Security Administration The Defense Technology Security Administration was established by the Deputy Secretary of Defense on May 10, 1985, under the policy and overall management of the Under Secretary of Defense (Policy). The Administration is responsible for reviewing the international transfer of defense-related technology, goods, services, and munitions consistent with U.S. foreign policy and national security objectives.

(Defense Technology Security Administration, Department of Defense, Suite 300, 400 Army Navy Drive, Arlington, VA 22202. Phone, 703–693–1158.)

Office of Economic Adjustment The Office of Economic Adjustment, under the policy guidance and operational direction of the Assistant Secretary of Defense (Force Management and Personnel), is responsible for planning and managing the Department's economic adjustment programs and for assisting Federal, State, and local officials in cooperative efforts to alleviate any serious social and economic side effects resulting from major departmental realignments or other actions. The Office also supports the Secretary of Defense in his capacity as Chairperson of the Economic Adjustment Committee, an interagency group established by Executive Order 12049 of March 27, 1978, to coordinate Federal economic adjustment activities. In addition, the Director of the Office of Economic Adjustment also serves as the economic adjustment policy adviser on the staff of the Assistant Secretary of Defense (Force Management and Personnel).

(Office of Economic Adjustment, Department of Defense, Room 4C767, The Pentagon, Washington, DC 20301–4000. Phone, 703–697–9155.)

Washington Headquarters Services The Director of Administration and Management serves in a dual capacity as the Director, Washington Headquarters Services. The agency's mission is to provide administrative and operational support to certain Department of Defense activities in the National Capital region. Such support includes budget and accounting, personnel management, office services, security, correspondence, directives and records management, travel, building administration, information and data systems, voting assistance program, and other administrative support as required.

(Washington Headquarters Services, Department of Defense, Room 3D972, The Pentagon, Washington, DC 20301-1155. Phone, 703–695–4436.)

DEPARTMENT OF THE AIR FORCE

The Pentagon, Washington, DC 20330–1000
Phone, 703–545–6700

SECRETARY OF THE AIR FORCE	DONALD B. RICE
Military Assistant	BRIG. GEN. DAVID W. MCILVOY
Deputy Military Assistant	LT. COL. THOMAS D. DICKSON
Executive Assistant	MAJ. DON ALSTON
Chief, Secretary's Staff Group	COL. JOHN W. BROOKS
Under Secretary of the Air Force	ANNE N. FOREMAN
Military Assistant	COL. DON W. RAKESTRAW
Executive Officer	JOHN S. GRAHAM
Deputy Under Secretary (International Affairs)	ELIZABETH J. KEEFER
Director of Small and Disadvantaged Business Utilization	ANTHONY J. DELUCA
Assistant Secretary (Manpower, Reserve Affairs, Installations, and Environment)	JEROME G. COOPER
Principal Deputy Assistant Secretary (Manpower, Reserve Affairs, Installations, and Environment)	JUDY ANN F. MILLER
Deputy Assistant Secretary (Manpower and Personnel)	WILLIAM G. NORTON
Deputy Assistant Secretary (Reserve Affairs)	MICHAEL P. REARDON
Deputy Assistant Secretary (Installations)	JAMES F. BOATRIGHT
Deputy Assistant Secretary (Readiness Support)	JACK B. DAVIS
Deputy Assistant Secretary (Environment, Safety, and Occupational Health)	GARY D. VEST
Deputy, Air Force Review Boards	JOE G. LINEBERGER
Executive Director, Air Force Board, Correction of Military Records	C. BRUCE BRASWELL
Director, Air Force Personnel Council	BRIG. GEN. ELLWOOD P. HINMAN III
Director, Civilian Appellate Review Agency	MICHAEL I. MCGUIRE
Deputy (Equal Opportunity)	DORA G. ALCALA
Assistant Secretary (Financial Management and Comptroller of the Air Force)	MICHAEL B. DONLEY
Principal Deputy Assistant Secretary (Financial Management)	C. RONALD HOVELL
Deputy Assistant Secretary (Budget)	MAJ. GEN. GEORGE W. LARSON, JR.
Director, Budget Management and Execution	ROBERT W. ZOOK
Director, Budget Investment	ROBERT D. STUART
Director, Budget Operations	BRIG. GEN. JOHN L. FINAN
Deputy Assistant Secretary (Cost and Economics)	LEROY T. BASEMAN
Deputy (Management Systems)	A. ERNEST FITZGERALD
Deputy Assistant Secretary (Plans, Systems and Analysis)	JOHN J. NETHERY
Assistant Secretary (Acquisition)	JOHN J. WELCH, JR.

Principal Deputy Assistant Secretary (Acquisition)	LT. GEN. JOHN E. JAQUISH
Deputy Assistant Secretary (Acquisition)	DANIEL S. RAK
Deputy Assistant Secretary (Support and Analysis)	(VACANCY)
Competition Advocate and Director of Contracted Advisory Assistant Services	BENEDICT A. KAUSAL
Deputy Assistant Secretary (Communications, Computers, and Logistics)	LLOYD K. MOSEMANN II
Deputy Assistant Secretary (Contracting)	MAJ. GEN. JOHN D. SLINKARD
Deputy Assistant Secretary (Management Policy and Program Integration)	BRIG. GEN. STEPHEN P. CONDON
Director of Strategic/Special Operations Forces/Airlift Programs	MAJ. GEN. STEPHEN B. CROKER
Director of Electronics and Special Programs	COL. JESSE T. MCMAHAN
Director of Tactical Programs	MAJ. GEN. JOSEPH W. RALSTON
Director of Space and Strategic Initiative Programs	MAJ. GEN. DONALD G. HARD
Director of Test and Evaluation	CARROLL G. JONES
Deputy, Resources	LT. COL. JAMES KOTORA
Director of Science and Technology	BRIG. GEN. STEPHEN P. CONDON, *Acting*
Director, Air Force Program Executive Office (AFPEO)	JOHN J. WELCH, JR.
Assistant Secretary (Space)	MARTIN C. FAGA
Principal Deputy Assistant Secretary (Space)	JIMMIE D. HILL
Deputy Assistant Secretary (Space Plans and Policy)	RICHARD M. MCCORMICK
Director of Space Systems	BRIG. GEN. DONALD R. WALKER
General Counsel	ANN C. PETERSEN
Deputy General Counsel	MYRON H. NORDQUIST
The Inspector General	(VACANCY)
Deputy Inspector General	BRIG. GEN. HAROLD H. RHODEN
Deputy Inspector General for Inspection and Safety	MAJ. GEN. ALEXANDER K. DAVIDSON
Administrative Assistant to the Secretary	ROBERT J. MCCORMICK
Deputy Administrative Assistant	WILLIAM A. DAVIDSON
Chief (Civilian Personnel)	KATHLEEN L. PEYTON
Director (Information Management)	COL. EDWARD A. PARDINI
Chief, Plans, Programs and Budget Division	LT. COL. PIERRE JOUBERT
Chief, Personnel Division	LT. COL. ROBERT G. LINN, JR.
Chief (Supply Support Services)	HECTOR T. DITTAMO
Deputy (Security and Investigative Programs)	COL. MARV T. FURUSHO
The Auditor General of the Air Force	JOHN W. BODDIE
Deputy Auditor General	(VACANCY)
Director of Legislative Liaison	BRIG. GEN. BUSTER C. GLOSSON
Deputy Director of Legislative Liaison	BRIG. GEN. JOHN O. MCFALLS III
Chief, Congressional Inquiry Division	COL. THOMAS ALISON
Deputy Chief, Congressional Inquiry Division	LT. COL. DAVID L. HAYES
Director of Public Affairs	BRIG. GEN. HALLIE E. ROBERTSON
Deputy Director of Public Affairs	COL. JAMES L. GREER
Chief, Community Relations Division	BARBARA HOLKUM
Chief, National Affairs Division	COL. HAROLD L. ROTHGEB, JR.
Chief, Media Relations	COL. DOUGLAS J. KENNETT

Chief, Management Division	Col. Samuel T. Martin, Jr.
Chief of Security Review	Col. Neil J. Buttimer
Deputy Chief of Security Review	June Forte
Director, Air Force News Command Liaison Office	Lt. Col. Robert A. Gibson

Air Staff

Chief of Staff	Gen. Merrill A. McPeak
Vice Chief of Staff	Gen. Michael P.C. Carnes
Assistant Vice Chief of Staff	Lt. Gen. Charles A. May, Jr.
Chief Master Sergeant of the Air Force	CMSgt. Gary R. Pfingston
Director of Safety	Brig. Gen. James L. Cole, Jr.
Chief of Security Police	Brig. Gen. Frank K. Martin
Chairman, Scientific Advisory Board	Edwin B. Stear
Director, Morale, Welfare and Recreation	Col. Normand G. Lezy
Director, Programs and Evaluation	Brig. Gen. Ralph E. Eberhart
Director, Manpower and Organization	Maj. Gen. Eugene H. Fischer
The Civil Engineer	Maj. Gen. Joseph A. Ahearn
Deputy Civil Engineer	Brig. Gen. James E. McCarthy
Air Force Historian	(vacancy)
Chief Scientist of the Air Force	Robert W. Selden
Chief, Air Force Reserve	Maj. Gen. John J. Closner III
Deputy Chief, Air Force Reserve	Brig. Gen. Wallace W. Whaley
Chief, National Guard Bureau	Lt. Gen. John B. Conaway
Director, Air National Guard	Maj. Gen. Philip G. Killey
Surgeon General of the Air Force	Lt. Gen. Alexander M. Sloan
Deputy Surgeon General	Maj. Gen. James G. Sanders
Chief, Chaplains	Maj. Gen. John P. McDonough
Deputy Chief, Chaplains	Brig. Gen. Donald J. Harlin
The Judge Advocate General	Maj. Gen. David C. Morehouse
Deputy Judge Advocate General	Brig. Gen. Nolan Sklute
Deputy Chief of Staff (Personnel)	Lt. Gen. Billy J. Boles
Deputy Chief of Staff (Plans and Operations)	Lt. Gen. Michael A. Nelson
Deputy Chief of Staff (Logistics)	(vacancy)
Deputy Chief of Staff (Command, Control, Communications, and Computers)	Lt. Gen. Robert H. Ludwig
Assistant Chief of Staff (Intelligence)	Maj. Gen. James R. Clapper, Jr.

Major Commands:

Air Force Logistics Command (Wright-Patterson Air Force Base, OH 45433–5001)	Gen. Charles C. McDonald
Air Force Space Command (Peterson Air Force Base, CO 80914–5001)	Lt. Gen. Thomas S. Moorman, Jr.
Air Force Special Operations Command (Hurlburt Field, FL 32544–5000)	Maj. Gen. Thomas E. Eggers
Air Force Systems Command (Andrews Air Force Base, DC 20334–5000)	Gen. Ronald W. Yates
Air Training Command (Randolph Air Force Base, TX 78150–5001)	Lt. Gen. Joseph W. Ashy
Air University (Maxwell Air Force Base, AL 36112–5001)	Lt. Gen. Charles G. Boyd
Electronic Security Command (San Antonio, TX 78243–5000)	Maj. Gen. Gary W. O'Shaughnessy
Military Airlift Command (Scott Air Force Base, IL 62225–5001)	Gen. Hansford T. Johnson

Strategic Air Command (Offutt Air Force Base, NE 68113-5001)	GEN. GEORGE L. BUTLER
Tactical Air Command (Langley Air Force Base, VA 23665-5001)	GEN. JOHN M. LOH
Overseas Commands:	
Pacific Air Forces (Hickam Air Force Base, HI 96853-5001)	GEN. JIMMIE V. ADAMS
United States Air Forces in Europe (Ramstein Air Base, Federal Republic of Germany, APO New York 09094-5001)	GEN. ROBERT C. OAKS
Field Operating Agencies:	
Air Force Audit Agency (Norton Air Force Base, CA 92409-6001)	JOHN W. BODDIE
Air Force Center for Studies and Analyses (Washington, DC 20330-5420)	COL. THOMAS A. CARDWELL III
Air Force Civilian Personnel Management Center (Randolph Air Force Base, TX 78150-6421)	PAT L. SCHITTULLI
Air Force Combat Operations Staff (Washington, DC 20330-5050)	LT. GEN. MICHAEL A. NELSON
Air Force Commissary Service (Kelly Air Force Base, TX 78241-6290)	MAJ. GEN. ROBERT F. SWARTS
Air Force Communications Agency (Scott Air Force Base, IL 62225-6001)	MAJ. GEN. JOHN S. FAIRFIELD
Air Force Cost Center (Falls Church, VA 22041-5101)	COL. RONALD S. BOWEN
Air Force Engineering and Services Center (Tyndall Air Base, FL 32403-6001)	COL. MARSHALL W. NAY, JR.
Air Force Inspection and Safety Center (Norton Air Force Base, CA 92409-7001)	MAJ. GEN. ALEXANDER K. DAVIDSON
Air Force Intelligence Agency (Ft. Belvoir, VA 22060-5788)	BRIG. GEN. BILLY J. BINGHAM
Air Force Legal Services Center (Bolling Air Force Base, Washington, DC 20332-6128)	COL. THOMAS L. HEMINGWAY
Air Force Management Engineering Agency (Randolph Air Force Base, TX 78150-6431)	COL. RONALD W. BLAKE
Air Force Military Personnel Center (Randolph Air Force Base, TX 78150-6001)	MAJ. GEN. JOHN E. JACKSON, JR.
Air Force Morale, Welfare and Recreation Center (Arlington, VA 20330-5000)	COL. ROY D. SHEETZ
Air Force News Center (Kelly Air Force Base, TX 78241-5000)	COL. PAUL F. HEYE
Air Force Office of Medical Support (Brooks Air Force Base, TX 78235-5000)	COL. CHARLES W.B. MORRISON
Air Force Office of Security Police (Kirtland Air Force Base, NM 87117-5000)	COL. FREDERIC L. MILLER
Air Force Office of Special Investigations (Bolling Air Force Base, Washington, DC 20332-6001)	BRIG. GEN. FRANCIS R. DILLON
Air Force Program Executive Office (Washington, DC 20330-1000)	JOHN J. WELCH, JR.
Air Force Reserve (Washington, DC 20330-5440)	MAJ. GEN. JOHN J. CLOSNER III

Air Force Review Boards Office (Washington, DC 20330–5000)	JOE G. LINEBERGER
Air Force Technical Applications Center (Patrick Air Force Base, FL 32925–6001)	COL. JOHN P. CASCIANO
Air Reserve Personnel Center (Denver, CO 80280–5000)	COL. JOSEPH C. RAMSEY, JR.
Air Weather Service (Scott Air Force Base, IL 62225–5001)	COL. GEORGE L. FREDERICK
USAF Historical Research Center (Maxwell Air Force Base, AL 36112–5000)	COL. ELLIOTT V. CONVERSE III
7 Communications Group (Washington, DC 20330–6345)	COL. WILLIAM B. RANKIN
Direct Reporting Units:	
Air Force District of Washington (Washington, DC 20332–6001)	BRIG. GEN. JAMES L. VICK
Air Force Operational Test and Evaluation Center (Kirtland Air Force Base, NM 87117–7001)	MAJ. GEN. PETER D. ROBINSON
U.S. Air Force Academy (Colorado Springs, CO 80840–5001)	LT. GEN. BRADLEY C. HOSMER

The Department of the Air Force is responsible for providing an Air Force that is capable, in conjunction with the other Armed Forces, of preserving the peace and security of the United States.

The Department of the Air Force was established as part of the National Military Establishment by the National Security Act of 1947 and came into being on September 18, 1947. The National Security Act Amendments of 1949 redesignated the National Military Establishment as the Department of Defense, established it as an executive department, and made the Department of the Air Force a military department within the Department of Defense (63 Stat. 578). The Department of the Air Force is separately organized under the Secretary of the Air Force. It operates under the authority, direction, and control of the Secretary of Defense (10 U.S.C. 8010). The Department consists of the Office of the Secretary of the Air Force, the Air Staff, and field organizations.

Office of the Secretary

The Office of the Secretary consists of the offices of the Under Secretary, four Assistant Secretaries, the General Counsel, the Administrative Assistant, Legislative Liaison, Public Affairs, International Affairs, Small and Disadvantaged Business Utilization, Auditor General, and the Inspector General. The heads of these offices are staff advisers to the Secretary for functions he assigns to them.

The Department of the Air Force is administered by the Secretary of the Air Force, who is responsible for and has the authority to conduct all affairs of the Department. The principal assistant to the Secretary is the Under Secretary, who acts with full authority of the Secretary on all affairs of the Department.

Assistant Secretaries and the General Counsel The Assistant Secretary (Manpower, Reserve Affairs, Installations, and Environment) is responsible for providing guidance, direction, and oversight for the Department of the Air Force on all matters pertaining to the formulation, review, and execution of plans, policies, programs, and budgets relative to manpower; military and civilian personnel; reserve component affairs; counternarcotics support; installations; environment, safety, and occupational health; and readiness support.

The Assistant Secretary (Financial Management and Comptroller) directs and manages the financial management activities and operations of the Department of the Air Force and ensures that financial management systems comply with Comptroller General standards. The Assistant Secretary is authorized to supervise and direct Air Force budget estimate preparations; project to design, approve, and supervise or enhance a financial management system (to include accounting, internal control, and financial reporting); and establish and supervise Air Force asset management systems.

The Assistant Secretary (Acquisition) is responsible for the formulation and execution of Department of the Air Force research, development, and acquisition policies and programs. As the Air Force acquisition executive, the Assistant Secretary is responsible to the Secretary for all decisions relating to the acquisition of weapons systems and the command and control systems that support them. Additionally, the Assistant Secretary is the senior Air Force Information Resource Management official. Also, the Assistant Secretary is responsible for the Air Force Program Executive Offices (AFPEO's). The Assistant Secretary manages the planning and execution of the major and other selected United States Air Force acquisition programs. An outgrowth of the Defense Management Review, AFPEO's ensure clear acquisition command channels from the Air Force Service Acquisition Executive through the mission area Program Executive Officers to the Program Directors.

The Assistant Secretary (Space) is responsible for the formulation, review, and execution of Air Force plans, policies, and programs relating to space.

The General Counsel is the chief legal officer of the Air Force. The General Counsel is responsible for furnishing legal advice and assistance to the Office of the Secretary of the Air Force. The General Counsel also provides legal counsel to the Air Staff in selected areas such as procurement, real property, civil aviation, authorization and appropriation legislation, and environmental matters. Finally, the General Counsel represents the Secretary when dealing with other agencies of the Government regarding negotiation of international agreements.

Supporting Offices The Inspector General is responsible to the Secretary of the Air Force for optimum effectiveness of Air Force inspection; safety; investigation; security; counterintelligence; complaint; law enforcement; fraud, waste, and abuse; and antiterrorism programs. The Inspector General assures resources are used effectively to accomplish the mission of the Air Force.

The Administrative Assistant to the Secretary of the Air Force serves as principal advisor to the Secretary and other statutory appointees on all phases of internal administration and management policies. The Administrative Assistant assures administrative continuity in the Office of the Secretary during changes of top officials. Additionally, the Administrative Assistant provides worldwide administrative oversight and policy formulation as the senior information management official for the Air Force, and is the senior Air Force official for the personnel security and information security programs. The Administrative Assistant manages Air Force contingency funds, including official representational funds. The Administrative Assistant makes medical designee determinations and final determinations on claims against the Air Force. The Administrative Assistant is also the appellate authority for appeals under the Freedom of Information Act and the Privacy Act.

The Air Force Audit Agency (AFAA) is headed by the Auditor General, who reports directly to the Secretary of the Air Force. It is responsible for the internal audit function of the Air Force and for liaison on audit and audit-related matters with the General Accounting Office, the

Department of Defense Inspector General, and other Government audit agencies. The mission of AFAA is to provide all levels of Air Force management with independent, objective, and constructive evaluations of the economy, efficiency, and effectiveness with which management carries out financial, operational, and support responsibilities. All Air Force functions, organizations, and activities are subject to audit.

The Director of Small and Disadvantaged Business Utilization is responsible for the implementation and execution of the Air Force program to counsel and help small and disadvantaged firms obtain a fair proportion of prime Air Force contracts and subcontracts. The Office also provides assistance and counseling for women-owned business firms.

The Director of Legislative Liaison advises and assists the Secretary and other principal civilian and military officials of the Department concerning Air Force legislative affairs and congressional relations.

The Deputy Under Secretary of the Air Force (International Affairs) is responsible for overall direction, guidance, and supervision of international programs affiliated with the United States Air Force.

The Director of Public Affairs advises the Secretary of the Air Force and Chief of Staff on aspects of the Air Force mission affecting the public, and establishes programs for communicating with Air Force personnel and the public, including news media worldwide, to gain informed public support.

Air Staff

Mission The mission of the Air Staff is to furnish professional assistance to the Secretary, the Under Secretary, the Assistant Secretaries, and the Chief of Staff.

Structure The Air Staff is a management headquarters functional organization under the Chief of Staff, United States Air Force. Titles throughout all organizational levels reflect the functions involved.

Functions and Activities Air Staff functions are specialized into well-defined areas to effect the management principles of functionality, integration, flexibility, simplicity, and decentralization. The Air Staff retains those management functions that legally cannot be delegated or decentralized, are needed by the Secretary and Chief of Staff, are essential to respond promptly to the Secretary of Defense, or are required to determine the design and structure of the Air Force in the future.

Chief of Staff The Chief of Staff is directly responsible to the Secretary of the Air Force for the efficiency and operational readiness of the United States Air Force. He is a member of the Joint Chiefs of Staff (JCS) of the Department of Defense. The Chief of Staff is assisted by the Vice Chief of Staff in all areas of responsibility except JCS. The Assistant Vice Chief of Staff assists the Chief and Vice Chief in the discharge of their duties.

Special Staff The Special Staff is an adjunct to the Chief of Staff, independent of the basic staff structure, and provides advisory and support services to both the Chief of Staff and the Air Staff. The Special Staff consists of: Director, Safety; Chief of Security Police; Director, Morale, Welfare and Recreation; Chief, Air Force History; Air Force Scientific Advisory Board; The Surgeon General; Chief, Chaplains; The Judge Advocate General; Chief, Air Force Reserve; Director, Programs and Evaluation; Director, Manpower and Organization; Assistant Chief of Staff, Intelligence; the Civil Engineer; and the Chief Scientist.

Deputy Chiefs of Staff The Deputy Chiefs of Staff (DCS) function primarily as a coordinating level on policy matters and represent the corporate structure.

Substantive functions are organized under DCS in homogeneous groups called directorates. Under the directorates, functions are further broken down into descriptive groups, divisions, and branches.

Field Organizations [1]

The major commands, field operating agencies, and direct reporting units together represent the field organizations of the United States Air Force. These commands are organized primarily on a functional basis in the United States and on an area basis overseas. These commands are responsible for accomplishing certain phases of the worldwide activities of the United States Air Force. They also are responsible for organizing, administering, equipping, and training their subordinate elements for the accomplishment of assigned missions.

Major Commands

The Continental Commands

Air Force Logistics Command The Air Force Logistics Command provides worldwide logistical support to the United States Air Force. This support includes procurement, storage, and distribution of supplies, and the performance or arrangement of depot-level maintenance on material.

Air Force Space Command The Air Force Space Command provides resource management and operation of assigned assets for space control, space force application, force enhancement, space support, and strategic aerospace defense. The Command provides a close link between its space activities and, through the United States Space Command, the unified command structure.

Air Force Special Operations Command The responsibility of the Air Force Special Operations Command is to organize, train, and equip Air Force special operations forces. It is the USAF component of the United States Special Operations Command (USSOCOM).

Air Force Systems Command The responsibility of the Air Force Systems Command is to advance aerospace technology, adapt it into operational aerospace systems, and acquire qualitatively superior aerospace systems and materials needed to accomplish the United States Air Force mission.

Air Training Command The Air Training Command is responsible for Air Force recruiting and individual training of the officers and airmen of the United States Air Force. Training includes basic training and indoctrination for recruits; Air Force Reserve Officer Training Corps (ROTC); flight training; and technical, field, and special training.

Air University The Air University is responsible for the higher education of officers of the United States Air Force. Educational activities include: the Air War College, Air Command and Staff College, Air Force Institute of Technology, Civil Air Patrol, Extension Course Institute, and the Ira C. Eaker Center for Professional Development.

Electronic Security Command The Electronic Security Command monitors Air Force communications in all parts of the world to ensure compliance with established communication security practices and procedures. In addition, Electronic Security Command units occasionally conduct research in

---

[1] Writeups on Defense Agencies and Defense Joint Service Schools begin on pages 237 and 257, respectively.

communication phenomena in support of various elements of the Government.

Military Airlift Command The Military Airlift Command (MAC) is a major command of the United States Air Force and the Air Force Component of the U.S. Transportation Command. Its primary mission is to provide air transportation for personnel and cargo for all the military services on a worldwide basis. In addition, it furnishes rescue and audiovisual services for the Air Force.

Strategic Air Command The Strategic Air Command is a major command of the United States Air Force and a Joint Chiefs of Staff specified command. Its primary mission is to organize, train, equip, administer, and prepare strategic air forces for combat, including bombardment, missile, special mission, and strategic reconnaissance units, and to conduct strategic air and air refueling operations.

Tactical Air Command The Tactical Air Command is a major command of the United States Air Force. Its primary mission is to organize, train, and equip forces to participate in tactical air operations. This includes tactical fighter, tactical air reconnaissance, air defense, close combat air support, and joint amphibious and airborne operations. It is the Air Force component of the U.S. Atlantic Command and provides the Air Force components of the U.S. Central Command, U.S. Southern Command, and forces for North American Aerospace Defense Command. It participates with other services in developing doctrine, procedures, tactics, techniques, training, and equipment for joint operations.

Overseas Commands

Pacific Air Forces The Pacific Air Forces is a major command of the United States Air Force and is the Air Force component of the U.S. Pacific Command. Its primary mission is to organize, train, equip, administer, and prepare assigned forces for combat, including tactical fighter, tactical air reconnaissance, tactical air control, close air support, and defense suppression units to conduct defensive and offensive air operations. It provides combat-ready air elements to the U.S. Pacific Command and participates in joint and combined air operations.

United States Air Forces in Europe The United States Air Forces in Europe is a major command of the United States Air Force and is the Air Force component of the U.S. European Command. Its primary mission is to organize, train, equip, administer, and prepare assigned forces for combat, including tactical fighter, tactical air reconnaissance, tactical air control, close air support, and defense suppression units to conduct defensive and offensive air operations. It provides combat-ready air elements to the U.S. European Command and participates in joint and combined air operations.

Field Operating Agencies

Air Force Audit Agency The Air Force Audit Agency provides independent internal audit and appraisal of financial, operational, management, and support activities as a service to all levels of management.

Air Force Center for Studies and Analyses The Air Force Center for Studies and Analyses performs studies to assist and support the decision-making process of the Air Force. The Center performs independent studies and evaluations of Air Force requirements, proposals, plans, and programs, while providing comparisons and trade-off analyses. The Center also evaluates critical technical and operational issues, and monitors applicable tests and evaluations that address such issues.

Air Force Civilian Personnel Management Center The Air Force Civilian Personnel Management Center directs, develops, manages, and evaluates the wide range of Federal and internal policies and programs affecting Air Force civilians, including foreign nationals, worldwide.

Air Force Combat Operations Staff The Air Force Combat Operations Staff provides readiness-oriented, combat-related support to the Chief of Staff, United States Air Force. The Staff serves as the permanent nucleus of a centralized, highly responsive and integrated combat support structure. It includes the combat-related activities of functions such as operations, operations plans, intelligence, logistics, and personnel.

Air Force Commissary Service The Air Force Commissary Service provides subsistence support to appropriated and nonappropriated fund food activities and to authorized individual patrons. It also operates a resale store system to provide service and facilities for the sale of Department of Defense authorized merchandise at the lowest practical price to authorized patrons.

Air Force Communications Agency The Air Force Communications Agency provides base and point-to-point communications, computer facilities, air traffic control, and automated data processing services, primarily to the United States Air Force, but also to other agencies—governmental and civil, national and foreign.

Air Force Cost Center The Air Force Cost Center is responsible for developing the cost analysis tools, methods, data bases, models, and automated systems used in resource allocation and cost management decisions departmentwide.

Air Force Engineering and Services Center The Air Force Engineering and Services Center provides specialized engineering and services, technical assistance, and operating support to Air Force bases and organizations. This includes food, laundry, dry-cleaning, and linen exchange services; regional civil engineering; and the highly specialized, interdisciplinary civil engineering functions.

Air Force Inspection and Safety Center The Air Force Inspection and Safety Center directs the Air Force inspection and safety programs, evaluating operational readiness, accident prevention, and management systems.

Air Force Intelligence Agency The Air Force Intelligence Agency provides specialized intelligence service in support of United States Air Force operations through the conduct of comprehensive research, direction of collection activities, processing and dissemination of intelligence information, and the exercise of management and control of intelligence systems and special security systems.

Air Force Legal Services Center The Air Force Legal Services Center provides Air Force-wide legal services in the functional areas of military justice, patents, claims and tort litigation, general litigation, labor law, preventive law, and legal aid. It also administers the Federal Legal Information Through Electronics Program for the Air Force as Executive Agent for the Department of Defense.

Air Force Management Engineering Agency The Air Force Management Engineering Agency develops and maintains Air Force manpower standards to improve manpower utilization, implements the Air Force Management Engineering Program, and exercises direct supervision over Management Engineering Teams responsible for developing specialized and functional manpower standards and related data.

Air Force Military Personnel Center The Air Force Military Personnel Center executes personnel plans and programs and supervises procedures applicable to the worldwide management and administration of Air Force military personnel.

Air Force Morale, Welfare and Recreation Center The Air Force Morale, Welfare and Recreation Center (MWR) manages worldwide Air Force MWR operations for Air Force members and their families to improve United States Air Force readiness.

Air Force Office of Medical Support The Air Force Office of Medical Support assists and supports the Air Force Surgeon General in developing and implementing practices for health care in peacetime and wartime environments. It also performs studies and research on how Air Force medical policies and programs are executed and recommends appropriate modifications to the Air Force Surgeon General.

Air Force News Center The Air Force News Center plans and executes the United States Air Force internal information program for all military and civilian personnel. It develops, produces, and distributes materials in support of information, orientation, motivation, and unit morale goals and provides information about Air Force people and missions to hometown news media and national commercial magazines.

Air Force Office of Security Police The Air Force Office of Security Police develops operational policies and practices in peacetime and wartime environments to carry out programs for the security of Air Force resources and information and the delivery of law enforcement services. The Office implements plans, policies, and programs for base defense; management of security police personnel, training, systems and equipment programs, and the physical security of Air Force resources; information, personnel and industrial security programs, and the wartime information security program; maintenance of law and order; prisoner rehabilitation and corrections programs; vehicle traffic management; and the military working dog program.

Air Force Office of Special Investigations The Air Force Office of Special Investigations provides criminal, counterintelligence, personnel security, and special investigative services to Air Force activities. It collects, analyzes, and reports significant information about these matters.

Air Force Program Executive Office The Air Force Program Executive Office oversees major United States Air Force acquisition programs in selected weapons systems and other categories. An outgrowth of the Defense Management Review, it is headed by the USAF Service Acquisition Executive and includes the Program Executive Officers who oversee Program Managers in the major commands.

Air Force Reserve The Air Force Reserve performs the United States Air Force Chief of Staff field responsibilities of command of the Air Force Reserve and is responsible for participating in the formulation of plans for the management, administration, and execution of programs affecting Air Force Reserve units and mobilization of these reserves when needed.

Air Force Review Boards Office The Air Force Review Boards Office consists of the Air Force Board for Corrections of Military Records (AFBCMR), the Air Force Civilian Appellate Review Agency (AFCARA), and the Air Force Personnel Council. AFBCMR and AFCARA ensure compliance with appropriate legal and policy guidelines in the correction of military records and in resolving civilian employee complaints. The Personnel Council advises the Air Force Secretariat on matters relating to various personnel policies and the effective management of active and reserve components of the Air Force. Boards under the Council examine such matters as discharges, physical disability cases, and decorations.

Air Force Technical Applications Center The Air Force Technical Applications Center operates and maintains the United States Atomic Energy Detection System (AEDS). Specific responsibilities include: monitoring compliance with various nuclear test ban treaties; installing and operating equipment for detection and identification of foreign nuclear weapon tests; and identifying whether events are produced by humans or by nature. In addition, the Air Force Technical Applications Center conducts research to improve atomic energy detection systems.

Air Reserve Personnel Center The Air Reserve Personnel Center develops personnel management policies, plans, and programs pertaining to Air Force Reserve personnel when they are not on extended active duty. The Center also provides personnel management for reserve forces of the Air Force and personnel support for mobilization of these forces.

Air Weather Service The Air Weather Service provides or arranges for staff and operational weather services to active and reserve Air Force and Army units, designated unified or specified commands, and other agencies as directed by the Chief of Staff.

United States Air Force Historical Research Center The United States Air Force Historical Research Center provides Air Force commanders historical assistance in carrying out their assigned missions and responsibilities and implements the United States Air Force history program (AFR 210–3). It serves as a repository for Air Force historical records; determines lineage and honors of Air Force units; and prepares books and other historical works on United States Air Force and military aviation.

7 Communications Group The 7 Communications Group (CG) provides the Secretary of Defense, the Joint Chiefs of Staff, the Secretary of the Air Force, and the Chief of Staff of the Air Force with command, control, communication and computer systems (C^4) to satisfy critical national defense requirements, automated systems for preparing and submitting the President's budget, and decision-making aides for top DOD officials. The 7 CG also secures C^4 for the National Command Authority to evaluate global events and respond to crises.

Direct Reporting Units

Air Force District of Washington The Air Force District of Washington (AFDW) provides logistical and administrative support to Air Force activities in the Washington, DC, area that do not have their own internal support, including Headquarters United States Air Force and the Air Force Secretariat. In addition, AFDW represents the Air Force in matters pertaining to the National Capital Region.

Air Force Operational Test and Evaluation Center The Air Force Operational Test and Evaluation Center manages the Air Force Operational Test and Evaluation (OTE) Program; assesses the operational utility of all major and selected nonmajor Air Force systems using and implementing supporting commands, as required; and recommends policy and planning, directing, evaluating, and reporting on the Air Force OTE Program.

United States Air Force Academy The United States Air Force Academy provides instruction and experience to each cadet in preparation for graduating with the knowledge and character essential to leadership, and the motivation to become a career officer in the United States Air Force.

Sources of Information

Speakers The Air Force will make speakers available for private organizations or community groups. Requests for speakers should be addressed to the Public Communications Branch, HQ USAF (SAF/PAGP), Washington, DC 20330. Phone, 703–697–2769.

DEPARTMENT OF THE ARMY

The Pentagon, Washington, DC 20310
Phone, 202–545–6700; Information during nonoffice hours, 202–695–0441

SECRETARY OF THE ARMY	MICHAEL P.W. STONE
Executive	COL. JOSEPH E. DEFRANCISCO
Military Assistant	MAJ. MARY L. TORGERSEN
Under Secretary of the Army	JOHN W. SHANNON
Executive	COL. MONTE L. PICKENS
Military Assistants	LT. COL. JIMMY O. JACOBS
	MAJ. MARY A.B. TYSON
Deputy Under Secretary of the Army	(VACANCY)
Assistant to the Under Secretary	WILLIAM K. TAKAKOSHI
Deputy Under Secretary of the Army (Operations Research)	WALTER W. HOLLIS
Executive for the National Board for the Promotion of Rifle Practice	COL. M.S. GILCHRIST
Assistant Secretary of the Army (Civil Works)	(VACANCY)
Principal Deputy	G. EDWARD DICKEY, *Acting*
Executive	COL. DENNIS C. COCHRANE
Deputy for Planning Policy and Legislation	MORGAN R. REES
Deputy for Policy and Evaluation	G. EDWARD DICKEY
Deputy for Management and Budget	STEVE DOLA
Deputy for Project Management	ROBERT STEARNS
Assistant for Water Resources Management	ROBERT KAIGHN
Assistant for Regulatory Affairs	MICHAEL DAVIS
Fiscal Program Management Officer	CLAUDIA L. TORNBLOM
Assistant for Interagency and International Affairs	KEVIN COOK
Water Resources Specialist	JAMES SMYTH
Military Assistant	LT. COL. GEORGE CAJIGAL
Civil Works Planning Specialist	JUANITA WHEELER
Assistant Secretary of the Army (Financial Management)	DOUGLAS A. BROOK
Comptroller of the Army	LT. GEN. MERLE FREITAG
Principal Deputy Assistant Secretary of the Army	NEIL R. GINNETTI
Executive	COL. WILLIAM J. CONNOLLY
Assistant Executive	LT. COL. WILLIAM F. CONNOLLY
Deputy Assistant Secretary of the Army for Financial Operations	CHARLES A. CHASE
Deputy Assistant Secretary of the Army for Resource Analysis and Business Practice	CYNTHIA BAKER
Deputy for Cost Analysis	ROBERT W. YOUNG
Deputy Assistant Secretary of the Army for Army Budget	BRIG. GEN. JOSUE ROBLES, JR.
Assistant Secretary of the Army (Installations, Logistics and Environment)	SUSAN LIVINGSTONE
Principal Deputy	MICHAEL W. OWEN
Executive Officer	WILLIAM S. PAVLICK
Deputy Assistant Secretary for Environment, Safety and Occupational Health	LEWIS D. WALKER
Deputy Assistant Secretary for Installations and Housing	PAUL W. JOHNSON

Deputy Assistant Secretary for Logistics	ERIC A. ORSINI
Deputy for Programs and Installation Assistance	COL. ROBERT W. WHITTON, *Acting*
Assistant Deputy for Chemical Demilitarization	COL. ERIC K. AZUMA
Assistant Secretary of the Army (Manpower and Reserve Affairs)	G. KIM WINCUP
Principal Deputy Assistant Secretary (Manpower and Reserve Affairs)	WILLIAM D. CLARK
Deputy Assistant Secretary (Review Boards and Equal Employment Opportunity Compliance and Complaint Review Agency)	JOHN W. MATTHEWS
Deputy Assistant Secretary (Readiness, Force Management and Manpower)	(VACANCY)
Deputy Assistant Secretary (Training and Education)	PATRICIA M. HINES
Deputy Assistant Secretary (Military Personnel Management and Equal Opportunity Policy)	ROBERT M. EMMERICHS
Executive	COL. ROBERT B. MAGRUDER
Assistant Deputy for Military Personnel and Equal Opportunity Policy	WILLIAM K. MERRILL
Assistant Deputy for Military Personnel Procurement and Manpower Systems	LT. COL. JEANNE G. HAMILTON
Assistant Deputy for Reserve Forces and Mobilization	(VACANCY)
Assistant Deputy for Force Management, Manpower and Budget	ROBERT BARTHOLOMEW III
Assistant Deputy for Training, Education and Simulation	COL. JOHN SCHNEEBERGER, JR.
Assistant Deputy for Civilian Personnel Policy	CAROL D. SMITH
Assistant Deputy for Security Policy	THOMAS D. HOWARD, JR.
Assistant Deputy for Force Modernization and Readiness	JOHN J. MCGINN

Army Military Review Boards Agency:

Director	JOHN W. MATTHEWS
Director, Army Council of Review Boards	COL. JOSEPH E. NICKENS
Executive Secretary, Army Board for Correction of Military Records	DAVID R. KINEER
Chairman, Army Clemency Boards Application Status	J. EDWARD VICK
Director, Management Information Support Directorate	GEORGE G. DONOVAN
Director, Equal Employment Opportunity Complaint and Compliance Review Agency	DOLORES SYMONS

Equal Employment Opportunity Agency:

Director	LUTHER L. SANTIFUL
Director, Federal Women's Program	JUNE HAJJAR
Director, Hispanic Employment Program	FELIX ROSARIO
Director, Program for Individuals with Disabilities	KATHRYN F. VITEK
Director, Black Employment Program	ISIAH GATLING

Assistant Secretary of the Army (Research, Development and Acquisition)	STEPHEN K. CONVER
Military Deputy to Assistant Secretary	LT. GEN. AUGUST M. CIANCIOLO
Executive	LT. COL. ROBERT C. ATWELL
Military Assistant	LT. COL. WALLACE B. OLSON III
Deputy Director Army Acquisition Corps	COL. AL GREENHOUSE
Deputy Assistant Secretary for Procurement	GEORGE E. DAUSMAN
Deputy for Systems Management	MAJ. GEN. RICHARD D. BELTSON
Deputy Assistant Secretary for Plans and Programs	KEITH CHARLES
Deputy Assistant Secretary for Research and Technology	GEORGE T. SINGLEY III
Deputy for Program Assessment and International Cooperation	BRIG. GEN. JOSEPH RAFFIANI, JR.
Director for Contracting	BRIG. GEN. NICHOLAS R. HURST
Assistant Deputy for Plans and Programs	MAURICE R. DONNELLY
Assistant Deputy for Systems Management	COL. JOHN E. LONGHAUSER
General Counsel	WILLIAM J. HAYNES II
Principal Deputy	(VACANCY)
Deputy General Counsel (Acquisition)	ANTHONY H. GAMBOA
Deputy General Counsel (Military and Civil Affairs)	DARRELL L. PECK
Deputy General Counsel (Installation and Operations)	THOMAS W. TAYLOR
Deputy General Counsel (Fiscal Law and Policy)	MATT RERES
Administrative Assistant to the Secretary of the Army	MILTON H. HAMILTON
Deputy Administrative Assistant	PETER STEIN
Director, Plans and Projects	JOEL B. HUDSON
Director, Executive Communications and Control	COL. B.T. BROOKS
Director, Resource Management Office	ROBERT L. JAWORSKI
Director, Internal Review	AL D. COMBS
Director, Management Systems and Support	ROBERT LAYCHAK
OSA/OCSA Correspondence and Records	D.P. GRAF
Director, Personnel	PETER B. HORN
EEO Officer	SHAWN D. LAND, *Acting*
Headquarters Services—Washington:	
Coordinator for Headquarters Services	PETER STEIN
Director, Defense Supply Service	CHARLES C. O'DONNELL
Director, Defense Telephone Service	MICHAEL A. NEWTON
Director, Personnel and Employment Service	PETER B. HORN
Director, Military Personnel Service Center	CWO2 MICHAEL J. MOLNAR
Director, HQDA Recreation Services	QUINTIN B. CARY
Director, Safety, Security and Support Services	JOEL B. HUDSON
Commander, USA Service Center for the Armed Forces	COL. DENNIS P. VASEY
Director, Administrative Services and Crafts	W. DENNIS MCGHEE
Director, Environmental Suppport Group	DONALD C. HAKENSON
Director, Headquarters Services, Safety and Occupational Health	GEORGE A. PETRELLO

Director, HQDA Security	Ronald E. Adams
Director, Space and Building Management Service	Edward E. Pavlick
Chief of Public Affairs	Brig. Gen. C.W. McClain
Deputy Chief	Col. David Fabian
Executive Officer	Lt. Col. Michael V. Sullivan
Chief, Security Review Office	James W. Hill
Chief, Policy and Plans Division	Lt. Col. George W. Stinnett
Chief, Media Relations Division	Col. David K. Kiernan
Chief, Community Relations Division	Tansill Johnson
Chief, Command Information Division	Lt. Col. Donald P. Maple
Chief, Army Broadcasting Service	Col. Bruce R. Eaton
Chief of Legislative Liaison	Maj. Gen. Charles E. Dominy
Special Assistant for Legislative Affairs	Robert J. Winchester
Executive	Col. William P. Dickens, Jr.
Assistant Executive	Lt. Col. William B. Loper
Chief, Investigation and Legislative Division	Col. John McLaurin III
Chief, House Liaison Division	Col. M. James Littig
Chief, Senate Liaison Division	Col. Frank Norton
Chief, Programs Division	Col. Cordis B. Colburn
Chief, Congressional Inquiry Division	Col. John J. McNulty III
Chief, Congressional Operations Division	Andrea Buel
Director of Small and Disadvantaged Business Utilization	D.R. Gill

Office of the Chief of Staff:

Chief of Staff, United States Army	Gen. Gordon R. Sullivan
Vice Chief of Staff	(vacancy)
Director of the Army Staff	Lt. Gen. Ellis D. Parker
Director, Program Analysis and Evaluation	Maj. Gen. Thomas P. Carney
Director of Management	Maj. Gen. William A. Stoft
Commanding General, Operational Test and Evaluation Agency	Maj. Gen. Richard E. Stephenson
Commanding General, Strategic Defense Command	Lt. Gen. Robert D. Hammond

Army General Staff:

Deputy Chief of Staff for Operations and Plans	Lt. Gen. Dennis J. Reimer
Deputy Chief of Staff for Personnel	Lt. Gen. William H. Reno
Deputy Chief of Staff for Logistics	Lt. Gen. Jimmy D. Ross
Deputy Chief of Staff for Intelligence	Lt. Gen. Charles B. Eichelberger

Special Staff:

Chief of Engineers	Lt. Gen. Henry J. Hatch
The Surgeon General	Lt. Gen. Frank F. Ledford
Chief of Chaplains	Maj. Gen. Norris L. Einertson
The Judge Advocate General	Maj. Gen. John L. Fugh, *Acting*
Chief, National Guard Bureau	Lt. Gen. John B. Conaway
Chief, Army Reserve	Maj. Gen. William F. Ward

Functional Commands:

Superintendent, U.S. Military Academy	Lt. Gen. Dave R. Palmer
Commanding General, U.S. Army Health Services Command	Maj. Gen. Alcide M. Lanoue
Commanding General, U.S. Army Military District of Washington	Maj. Gen. William F. Streeter
Commanding General, U.S. Army Criminal Investigation Command	Brig. Gen. Peter T. Berry

Commanding General, Military Traffic Management Command	Maj. Gen. John R. Piatak
Commanding General, Intelligence Security Command	Maj. Gen. Charles F. Scanlon
Commanding General, Information Systems Command	Lt. Gen. Alonzo E. Short, Jr.
Commanding General, U.S. Army Recruiting Command	Maj. Gen. Jack C. Wheeler
Army Materiel Command:	
Commanding General, Army Materiel Command	Gen. William G.T. Tuttle, Jr.
Deputy Commanding General, Research Development and Acquisition	Lt. Gen. Billy M. Thomas
Deputy Commanding General, Materiel Readiness	Lt. Gen. Marvin D. Brailsford
Chief of Staff	Maj. Gen. William B. McGrath
Forces Command:	
Commander-in-Chief	Gen. Edwin H. Burba, Jr.
Commanding Generals:	
First United States Army	Lt. Gen. James H. Johnson, Jr.
Second United States Army	Lt. Gen. James W. Crysel
Third United States Army	Lt. Gen. John J. Yeosock
Fourth United States Army	Lt. Gen. James R. Hall, Jr.
Fifth United States Army	Lt. Gen. George R. Stotser
Sixth United States Army	Lt. Gen. William H. Harrison
I Corps	Lt. Gen. Calvin A.H. Waller
III Corps	Lt. Gen. H.G. Taylor
XVIII Corps	Lt. Gen. Gary E. Luck
Training and Doctrine Command:	
Commanding General	Gen. John W. Foss
Deputy Commanding General for Training	Maj. Gen. Craig A. Hagan
Deputy Commanding General for Combined Arms	Lt. Gen. Leonard P. Wishart
Deputy Commanding General for Logistics/Commanding General, LOG Center	Lt. Gen. Leon E. Salomon
Commander-in-Chief, United States Army Europe	Gen. Crosbie E. Saint
Deputy Commander-in-Chief	Lt. Gen. John M. Shalikashvili
Commanding Generals:	
21st TAACOM	Lt. Gen. William S. Flynn
V Corps	Lt. Gen. David M. Maddox
VII Corps	Lt. Gen. Frederick M. Franks, Jr.
Commanding General, Eighth United States Army	Gen. Robert W. Riscassi
Commanding General, United States Army Pacific	Lt. Gen. Claude M. Kicklighter
Commanding General, United States Army Japan/IX Corps	Lt. Gen. Jack D. Woodall
Commanding General, United States Army Alaska/6th Infantry Division	Maj. Gen. Samuel E. Ebbesen
Commanding General, United States Army South	Maj. Gen. William W. Hartzog

DEPARTMENT OF THE ARMY

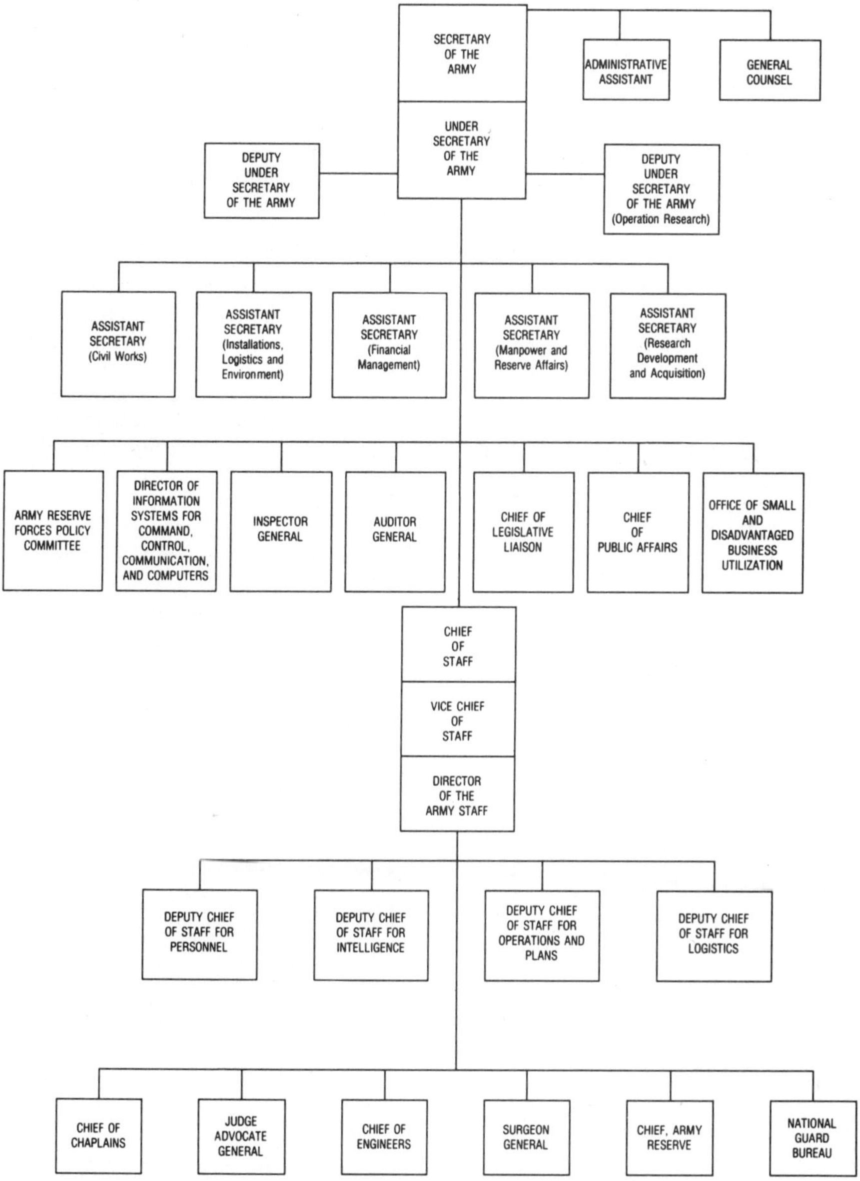

The American Continental Army, now called the United States Army, was established by the Continental Congress on June 14, 1775, more than a year before the Declaration of Independence.

The mission of the Department of the Army is to organize, train, and equip active duty and reserve forces for the preservation of peace, security, and the defense of our nation. It serves as part of our national military team, whose members include the Navy, Air Force, Marines, and Coast Guard. The Army's mission focuses on land operations; its soldiers must be trained with modern arms and equipment and be ready to respond quickly.

The Army also administers programs aimed at protecting the environment, improving waterway navigation, flood and beach erosion control, and water resource development. It provides military assistance to Federal, State, and local government agencies, including natural disaster relief assistance.

The Department of War was established as an executive department at the seat of government by act approved August 7, 1789. The Secretary of War was established as its head, and his powers were those entrusted to him by the President (10 U.S.C. 3012).

The National Security Act of 1947 (50 U.S.C. 401) created the National Military Establishment, and the Department of War was designated the Department of the Army. The title of its Secretary became Secretary of the Army (5 U.S.C. 171).

The National Security Act Amendments of 1949 (63 Stat. 578) established the Department of Defense as an executive department of the Government and provided that the Department of the Army be a military department within the Department of Defense.

The Army Organization Act (64 Stat. 263) provided the statutory basis for the internal organization of the Army and the Department of the Army. The act consolidated and revised the numerous earlier laws, incorporated various adjustments made necessary by the National Security Act of 1947 and other postwar enactments, and provided for the organization of the Department of the Army in a single comprehensive statute, with certain minor exceptions. In general, the act followed the policy of vesting broad organizational powers in the Secretary of the Army, subject to delegation by him, rather than specifying duties of subordinate officers (10 U.S.C. 3012, 3062).

The Goldwater-Nichols Department of Defense Reorganization Act of 1986 (10 U.S.C. 111 note) made significant changes within the Department of Defense. The Department was reorganized to strengthen civilian authority, to improve military advice to the President, to place clear responsibility on the commanders of the unified and specified combatant commands, and to provide a more efficient use of defense resources.

Command of the Army is exercised by the President through the Secretary of Defense and the Secretary of the Army, who directly represent him; and, under the law and decisions of the Supreme Court, their acts are the President's acts, and their directions and orders are the President's directions and orders.

Office of the Secretary of the Army

Secretary The Secretary of the Army is the head of the Department of the Army. Subject to the direction, authority, and control of the President as Commander in Chief and of the Secretary of Defense, the Secretary of the Army is responsible for and has the authority to conduct all affairs of the Department of the Army, including its organization, administration, operation, efficiency, and such other activities as may be prescribed by the President or the Secretary of Defense as authorized by law.

As a result of the 1986 Department of Defense reorganization, certain civilian functions, such as comptroller, acquisition, inspector general, auditing and information management, were transferred from the Army Staff to the Office of the Secretary of the Army. Additionally, the Secretary is responsible for civil functions, such as oversight of the Panama Canal Commission and execution of the Panama Canal Treaty; the civil works program of the Corps of Engineers; Arlington and Soldiers' Home National Cemeteries; and such other activities of a civil nature as may be prescribed by higher authority or authorized by law.

Principal Assistants Subject to the direction and control of the Secretary of the Army, the Under Secretary of the Army, Assistant Secretary of the Army (Civil Works), Assistant Secretary of the Army (Financial Management), Assistant Secretary of the Army (Installations, Logistics and Environment), Assistant Secretary of the Army (Manpower and Reserve Affairs), Assistant Secretary of the Army (Research, Development and Acquisition), Army Acquisition Executive, General Counsel, the Administrative Assistant, Director of Information Systems for Command, Control, Communications and Computers, the Inspector General, the Auditor General, Chief of Legislative Liaison, Chief of Public Affairs, and Director, Office of Small and Disadvantaged Business Utilization and Chairman, Army Reserve Forces Policy Committee are authorized and directed to act for the Secretary of the Army within their respective fields of responsibility and as further directed by the Secretary.

Army Policy Council The Council is the senior policy advisory council of the Department of the Army. It provides the Secretary of the Army and his principal civilian and military assistants with a forum for the discussion of Army subjects of significant policy interest and an opportunity for members to consult with other members on matters arising within their specific areas of responsibility.

For further information, call 202–695–7922.

Army Staff

The Army Staff, presided over by the Chief of Staff, is the military staff of the Secretary of the Army. The Army Staff renders professional advice and assistance to the Secretary of the Army, the Under Secretary of the Army, the Assistant Secretaries of the Army, and other officials of the Army Secretariat.

It is the duty of the Army Staff to: prepare for employment of the Army and for such recruiting, organizing, supplying, equipping, training, mobilizing, and demobilizing of the Army as will assist the execution of any power, duty, or function of the Secretary or the Chief of Staff; investigate and report upon the efficiency of the Army and its preparation for military operations; act as the agent of the Secretary of the Army and the Chief of Staff in coordinating the action of all organizations of the Department of the Army; and perform such other duties not otherwise assigned by law as may be prescribed by the Secretary of the Army.

Chief of Staff The Chief of Staff is the principal military adviser to the Secretary of the Army and is charged by him with the planning, development, execution, review, and analysis of the Army programs. The Chief of Staff, under the direction of the Secretary of the Army, supervises the members and organization of the Army and performs the duties prescribed for him by the National Security Act of 1947 (50 U.S.C. 401) and other laws. He is directly responsible to the Secretary of the Army for the efficiency of the Army, its state of preparation for military operations and plans therefor.

The Chief of Staff serves as the Army member of the Joint Chiefs of Staff and as a member of the Army Policy Council and the Armed Forces Policy Council. As a member of the Joint Chiefs of Staff, he is one of the military advisers to the President, the National Security Council, and the Secretary of Defense.

The Army Staff renders professional advice and assistance to the Secretary, the Under Secretary, the Assistant Secretaries of the Army, and other Secretariat officials in providing broad basic policies and plans for the guidance of the Department of the Army. The Army General Staff specifically assists the Secretary in the preparation and issuance of directives to implement plans and policies and in the supervision of the execution and implementation of these directives.

Department of the Army Program Areas

Military Operations and Plans Determination of requirements and priorities for, and the employment of, Army forces strategy formation; mid-range, long-range, and regional strategy application; arms control, negotiation and disarmament; national security affairs; joint service matters; net assessment; politico-military affairs; force mobilization and demobilization; force planning, programming structuring, development, analysis and management; operational readiness; overall roles and missions; collective security; individual and unit training; psychological operations; unconventional warfare; counterterrorism; operations security; signal security; military aspects of space and sea; special plans; table of equipment development and approval; electronic warfare; nuclear and chemical matters; civil affairs; military support of civil defense; civil disturbance; domestic actions; audiovisual activities; command and control; automation and communications programs and activities; management of the program for law enforcement, correction and crime prevention for military members of the Army; and physical security.

Personnel Management of military and civilian personnel for overall integrated support of the Army, including policies and programs for manpower utilization standards, allocation and documentation, career development, equal opportunity, leadership, alcohol and drug abuse control, welfare and morale, promotion, retention, and separation; military compensation, transportation and travel entitlements; the personnel aspects of military construction and housing management; research and development related to training personnel, manpower systems, and human factors; and management of civilian personnel training.

Reserve Components Management of individual and unit readiness and mobilization for Reserve Components, comprised of the Army National Guard and the U.S. Army Reserve.

Intelligence Management of Army intelligence and counterintelligence activities, personnel, equipment, systems, and organizations; Army cryptology, topography, and meteorology; coordination of Army requirements for mapping, charting, and geodesy; and Army industrial security.

Management-Comptrollership Review and analysis of Army programs and major Army commands; management information systems in the financial area, progress and statistical reporting, and reports control; financial management, budgeting, finance and accounting, cost analysis, economic analysis, military pay and allowances, resource management, and productivity and value improvement; regulatory policies and programs pertaining to the overall management of the Army; and legislative policies and programs pertaining to appropriation acts affecting the Army.

Research, Development, and Materiel Acquisition Management of Army research, development and materiel acquistion; planning, programming, budgeting and execution for the acquisition of materiel obtained by the procurement appropriations for the Army; materiel life cycle management from concept phase through acquisition; and international acquisition programs.

Information Management Automation, communications, audiovisual, records management, publications, and information management.

Logistics Management of Department of the Army logistical activities for the movement and maintenance of forces; logistical planning and support of Army and joint service operations; materiel and supply management and maintenance; security assistance; transportation; and Army interservice supply operations.

Engineering Management of Army engineering, construction, installations, family housing, real estate, facilities requirements and stationing, and real property maintenance activities; environmental preservation and improvement activities; applicable research and development activities for engineer missions to include environmental sciences; Army topographic and military geographic information activities; and engineer aspects of Army strategic and operational plans.

Civil Functions Civil functions of the Department of the Army include the Civil Works Program, the administration of Arlington and Soldiers' Home National Cemeteries, and other related matters. The Army's Civil Works Program, a responsibility of the Corps of Engineers under the direction and supervision of the Secretary of the Army, dates back to 1824 and is the Nation's major Federal water resources development activity and involves engineering works such as major dams, reservoirs, levees, harbors, waterways, locks, and many other types of structures. These works provide flood protection for cities and major river valleys, reduce the cost of transportation, supply water for municipal and industrial use, generate hydroelectric power, provide recreational opportunities for vast numbers of people, regulate the rivers for many purposes including the improvement of water quality, protect the shores of oceans and lakes, and provide other types of benefits. Planning assistance is also provided to States and other non-Federal entities for the comprehensive management of water resources, including pollution abatement works. In addition, through the Civil Works Program the Federal Government protects the navigable waters of the United States under legislation empowering the Secretary of the Army to prohibit activities that would reduce the value of such waters to the Nation.

Medical Management of health services for the Army and, as directed for other services, agencies, and organizations; health standards for Army personnel; health professional education and training; career management authority over commissioned and warrant officer personnel of the Army Medical Department; medical research, materiel development, testing and evaluation; policies concerning health aspects of Army environmental programs and prevention of disease; and planning, programming, and budgeting for Army-wide health services.

Inspection Management of inquiries, inspections, and reports on matters affecting the performance of mission and the state of discipline, efficiency, economy, and morale of the Department of the Army.

Religious Management of religious, moral and moral leadership, and chaplain support activities Army-wide; religious ministrations, religious education, pastoral care, and counseling for Army military personnel; liaison with the ecclesiastical agencies; chapel construction requirements and design approval; and career management of clergymen serving in the Chaplains Branch.

Legal Legal advisory services provided for all military personnel and agencies of the Army; review and take final action as designee of the Secretary of the Army on complaints of wrongs by service personnel submitted under the Uniform Code of Military Justice; administration of military justice and civil law matters pertaining to the Army; administration of Army claims and legal assistance services; operation of the legal system of appellate reviews of court-martial records as provided by the Uniform Code of Military Justice; general court-martial and real property records custodianship; records administration of proceedings of courts of inquiry and military commissions; liaison service with the Department of Justice and other Federal and State agencies on matters connected with litigation and legal proceedings concerning the Army; and career management of Judge Advocate General's Corps officers.

Public Affairs Public information, command information, and community relations services and preparation of information plans and programs in support of Army basic plans and programs.

History Advisory and coordination service provided on historical matters, including historical properties; formulation and execution of the Army Historical Program; and preparation and publication of histories required by the Army.

Major Army Commands [1]

United States Army Forces Command The Commanding General, United States Army Forces Command, commands all assigned active Army forces in the continental United States and the Continental United States Armies, and assigned United States Army Reserve Troop Program Units in the continental United States and Puerto Rico. He also commands those subordinate commands, installations, and activities assigned by Headquarters, Department of the Army, and, as directed, provides administrative and logistical support through his subordinate installation commanders to other Department of the Army, Department of Defense, or other Government agencies. He also serves as the Commander-in-Chief, Forces Command, a specified command, and as the Commander-in-Chief, Army Forces Atlantic Command, the Army component of the United States Atlantic Command, a unified command.

The Commanding General of each of the Continental United States Armies has the primary mission, under the Commanding General, United States Army Forces Command, to command the United States Army Reserve, plan for mobilization, coordinate domestic emergencies, and exercise training supervision over the Army National Guard. The five Army areas are as follows:

First United States Army (Headquarters, Fort George G. Meade, MD)—Connecticut, Delaware, the District of Columbia, Maine, Maryland, Massachusetts, New Hampshire, New Jersey, New York, Pennsylvania, Rhode Island, Vermont, Virginia, and West Virginia.

Second United States Army (Headquarters, Fort Gillem, GA)—Alabama, Florida, Georgia, Kentucky, Mississippi, North Carolina, Puerto Rico, South Carolina, and Tennessee.

Third United States Army (Headquarters, Fort McPherson, GA).

Fourth United States Army (Headquarters, Fort Sheridan, IL)—Illinois, Indiana, Iowa, Michigan, Minnesota, Ohio, and Wisconsin.

Fifth United States Army (Headquarters, Fort Sam Houston, TX)—Arkansas, Kansas, Louisiana, Missouri, Nebraska, New Mexico, Oklahoma, and Texas.

Sixth United States Army (Headquarters, Presidio of San Francisco, CA)—Arizona, California, Colorado, Idaho, Montana, Nevada, North Dakota, Oregon, South Dakota, Utah, Washington, and Wyoming.

For further information, call 404–669–5607.

United States Army Training and Doctrine Command The Commanding General, United States Army Training and Doctrine Command, prepares the Army

[1] Writeups on Defense Agencies and Defense Joint Service Schools begin on pages 237 and 257, respectively.

for war and acts as its architect for the future. The Commanding General accomplishes his duty through six related mission domains—doctrine, force design, materiel requirements, leader development, training, and mission support. He is responsible for conducting all concept and doctrine development not assigned by HQDA to other commands and agencies and integrates the Army's total doctrine development. He is further responsible for conducting all combat developments not assigned by HQDA to other commands and agencies. As the Army's principal combat developer, the Commanding General guides, coordinates, and integrates the Army's total combat development effort. Additionally, he develops, maintains, and supervises the training system by which the total Army trains to fight.

The Commanding General commands installations and activities as assigned by Headquarters, Department of the Army; and, as directed, provides administrative and logistical support through his assigned installation commanders to elements and agencies of the Department of the Army, the Department of Defense, or other Federal agencies that are tenants or satellites of the installation.

For further information, call 804–727–4465.

United States Army Materiel Command The Commanding General, United States Army Materiel Command, develops and provides materiel and related services to the Army, to Army elements of unified commands and specified commands, to Department of Defense agencies, and to other United States and foreign agencies as directed. His principal missions are to equip and sustain a trained, ready Army; to provide equipment and services to other nations through the security assistance program; to develop and acquire non-major systems and equipment; to provide development and acquisition support to program managers; to define, develop, and acquire superior technologies; to maintain the mobilization capabilities necessary to support the Army in emergencies; and to continue to improve productivity and quality of life.

For further information, call 703–274–9625.

United States Army Information Systems Command The Commanding General, United States Army Information Systems Command, is responsible for providing information systems and services to the Army and to other Department of Defense agencies and Government organizations as directed.

For further information, call 602–538–6161.

United States Army Intelligence and Security Command The Commanding General, United States Army Intelligence and Security Command, is responsible for worldwide support of the Army at echelons above corps through electronic warfare, intelligence collection, counterintelligence, and operations security.

For further information, call 202–706–1232.

United States Army Health Services Command The Commanding General, United States Army Health Services Command, performs health services for the Army within the United States and, as directed, for other governmental agencies and activities. He commands the Army hospital system within the United States and other organizations, units, and facilities as may be directed. He is responsible for the conduct of medical professional education for Army personnel. He is further responsible, under the guidance of the Commanding General, United States Training and Doctrine Command, for the development of medical doctrine, concepts, organizations, materiel requirements, and systems in support of the Army.

For further information, call 512–221–6313.

United States Army Criminal Investigation Command The Commanding General, USACIC, centrally commands and controls worldwide Army investigation of serious crime, provides the full range of investigative support to all Army elements, conducts sensitive and special interest investigations, and provides personal security for selected

Army and DOD officials. To support these missions, the Commanding General operates a forensic laboratory system and a crime records center. The investigative mission inherently includes devising investigative standards, procedures, and doctrinal policies; special agent accreditation/certification; collection/analysis of criminal intelligence; assisting the legal community (and the Department of Justice) in fraud-related actions; and operating a polygraph program.

For further information, call 202–756–1232.

Military Traffic Management Command The Commanding General, Military Traffic Management Command, is the Executive Director for military traffic management, land transportation, and common-user ocean terminal service within the continental United States, and for worldwide traffic management of the Department of Defense personal property moving and storage program. He provides transportation engineering services and support to all Department of Defense components. He administers Department of Defense activities pertaining to Highways for National Defense and Railroads for National Defense.

For further information, call 202–756–1724.

United States Army Military District of Washington The Commanding General, United States Army Military District of Washington, commands units, activities, and installations in the National Capital area as may be assigned by Headquarters Department of the Army (HQDA); provides base operation and other support to the Department of the Army, Department of Defense, or other Government activities that are tenants of or are located on their installations for such support; plans for and executes those missions peculiar to the needs of the seat of government as assigned by HQDA; and provides an organized and responsive defense of designated Department of Defense facilities.

For further information, call 202–475–0565.

United States Army Corps of Engineers The Commanding General, United States Army Corps of Engineers, serves as the Army's Real Property Manager, performing the full cycle of real property activities (requirements, programming, acquisition, operation, maintenance, and disposal); manages and executes engineering, construction, and real estate programs for the Army and the United States Air Force; and performs research and development in support of these programs. He manages and executes Civil Works Programs. These programs include research and development, planning, design, construction, operation and maintenance, and real estate activities related to rivers, harbors, and waterways; administration of laws for protection and preservation of navigable waters and related resources such as wetlands. He also assists in recovery from natural disasters.

For further information, call 202–272–0001.

Army Components of Unified Commands The missions of the commanding generals of the Army components of unified commands are set forth in directives of the Department of Defense. The Army components of unified commands are major commands of the Department of the Army and consist of such subordinate commands, units, activities, and installations as may be assigned to them by Headquarters, Department of the Army. In certain unified command areas—such as United States Atlantic Command—where the Army does not have a separate, single, and distinct component headquarters or commander, a designated Army commander in the area will be responsible for certain Army "component" functions that must be performed at his location.

COMMANDS:

United States Army Europe. Phone, 011–49–6221–57–8831.
United States Army Japan. Phone, 011–81–0462–51–1520.
Eighth United States Army (Pentagon Korean Liaison Office). Phone, 202–694–3475.
United States Army Western Command. Phone, 808–471–7471.
United States Army Special Operations Command. Phone, 919–432–7587.

United States Military Academy

West Point, NY 10996

Superintendent	LT. GEN. DAVE R. PALMER
Commandant of Cadets	BRIG. GEN. DAVE A. BRAMLETT
Dean of the Academic Board	BRIG. GEN. ROY K. FLYNT

The United States Military Academy is located at West Point, NY. The course is of 4 years' duration, during which the cadets receive, besides a general education, theoretical and practical training as junior officers. Cadets who complete the course satisfactorily receive the degree of Bachelor of Science and a commission as second lieutenant in the Army.

For further general information concerning the United States Military Academy, contact the Public Affairs Office, United States Military Academy, West Point, NY 10996. Phone, 914–938–4261. For information about Military Academy admission criteria and policies, contact the Office of the Registrar, United States Military Academy, West Point, NY 10996.

Sources of Information

Arlington and Soldiers' Home National Cemeteries For information write to the Superintendent, Arlington National Cemetery, Arlington, VA 22211–5003. Phone, 202–695–3175.

Army Historical Program For information concerning the Army Historical Program, write to the U.S. Army Center of Military History, HQDA (DAMH), Pulaski Building, Washington, DC 20314–0200. Phone, 202–272–0291.

Civilian Employment Employment inquiries and applications should be directed to the following: (1) For employment in the Washington, DC, metropolitan area—Personnel and Employment Service—Washington, Room 3D727, The Pentagon, Washington, DC 20310–6800 (phone, 202–695–3383); (2) For employment outside the Washington, DC, metropolitan area—address or apply directly to the Army installation where employment is desired, Attn: Civilian Personnel Office; (3) For employment overseas—U.S. Army Civilian Personnel Center, Attn: PECC-CSS, Hoffman II Building, 200 Stovall Street, Alexandria, VA 22332–0300 (phone, 202–325–8712).

Contracts Contract procurement policies and procedures are the responsibility of the Deputy for Procurement, Office of the Assistant Secretary of the Army (Research, Development and Acquisition), Room 2E661, The Pentagon, Washington, DC 20310–0103. Phone, 202–695–2488.

Environment Contact the Public Affairs Office, Office of the Chief of Engineers, Washington, DC 20314–1000, phone, 202–272–0010; or the nearest Corps of Engineers Division or District Office located in most major cities throughout the United States.

Films, videotapes, and videodiscs Requests for loan of Army-produced films, videotapes, and videodiscs should be addressed to the Visual Information Support Centers of Army installations. Army productions are available for sale from the National Audiovisual Center (NAC), Washington, DC 20409–3701. Department of the Army pamphlet 25–90, *Visual Information Products Catalog*, lists the products that have been cleared for public release.

Freedom of Information and Privacy Act Requests Requests should be addressed to the Information Management Officer of the Army installation or activity responsible for the requested information. If it is uncertain which Army activity has the information, requests may be submitted to the Army Freedom of Information and Privacy Act Division, Information Systems Command-Pentagon, Attn: ASQNS-OP-F, Room 1146, 2461 Eisenhower Avenue, Alexandria, VA 22331–0301. Phone, 202–325–6163.

Publications Requests should be addressed to the Information Management Officer of the Army activity that publishes the requested publication. Official publications published by Headquarters, Department of the Army, are available from the National Technical Information Service, Department of Commerce, Attn: Order Preprocessing Section, 5285 Port Royal Road, Springfield, VA 22161–2171. Phone, 703–487–4600. If it is uncertain which Army activity published the publication, requests should be addressed to the Publishing Division, U.S. Army Publications and Printing Command, Room 1050, 2461 Eisenhower Avenue, Alexandria, VA 22331–0301. Phone, 202–325–6292.

Reading Rooms The Pentagon Library is located in Room 1A518, The Pentagon, Washington, DC 20310–6000. Phone, 202–697–4301. The Discharge Review/Correction Boards Reading Room is located in Room 2E165, The Pentagon, Washington, DC 20319–1803. Phone, 202–695–3973. The Army Freedom of Information Act Reading Room is located in Room 1146, 2461 Eisenhower Avenue, Alexandria, VA 22331–0301. Phone, 202–325–6163.

Military Career and Training Opportunities

Information on all phases of Army enlistments and specialized training are available by writing the United States Army Recruiting Command, Fort Sheridan, IL 60037. Phone, 312–926–3322.

Army Health Professions For information concerning career opportunities in Army Health Professions, write to HQDA (SGPS-PD), Skyline No. 5, 5100 Leesburg Pike, Falls Church, VA 22041–3258. Phone, 703–756–8114.

Army ROTC The Army Reserve Officers' Training Corps is an educational program designed to develop college educated officers for the Active Army, the Army National Guard, and the Army Reserve. For information, write or contact the Professor of Military Science at the nearest college or university offering the program, or the Army ROTC Regional Headquarters in your area.

Army National Guard For information concerning individual training opportunities in the National Guard, contact the Army National Guard, ARO–OAC–ME, Edgewood, MD 21010–5420. Phone, 301–671–4789.

Chaplains Corps For information concerning career opportunities as a chaplain, write to the Chief of Chaplains, HQDA (DACH–ZA), Washington, DC 20310. Phone, 202–695–1133.

Commissioning Opportunities for Women All commissioning sources available to men are available to women.

Judge Advocate General's Corps For information concerning career opportunities as a lawyer, military and civilian, write to the Personnel, Plans, and Training Office, Office of the Judge Advocate General, Department of the Army, HQDA (DAJA–PT), Washington, DC 20310–2206. Phone, 202–695–1353.

Officer Candidate Schools Members of the Active Army may attend the 14-week course at Fort Benning, GA. Members of the Reserve Components may attend a short course at Fort Benning, GA.

United States Military Academy For information write to Director of Admissions, United States Military Academy, West Point, NY 10996. Phone, 914–938–4041.

Public Affairs and Community Relations For official Army information and community relations, contact the Office of the Chief of Public Affairs, Department of the Army, Washington, DC 20310–1508. Phone, 202–694–0741.

Research Industry may obtain information on long-range research and development plans concerning future materiel requirements and objectives from Commander, U.S. Army Materiel Command, Attn: AMCPA, 5001 Eisenhower Ave., Alexandria, VA 22333-0001. Phone, 703-274-8010.

Small Business Activities Aids to assist small businesses in obtaining defense procurement contracts are available through the Office of Small and Disadvantaged Business Utilization, Office of the Secretary of the Army, Room 2A712, The Pentagon, Washington, DC 20310-0106. Phone, 202-695-9800.

Speakers Civilian organizations desiring an Army speaker may contact a nearby Army installation or write or call the Community Relations Division, Office of the Chief of Public Affairs, Department of the Army, Washington, DC 20310-1508. Phone, 202-697-5720. Requests for Army Reserve speakers may be addressed to HQDA (DAAR-PA), Washington, DC 20310-2423, or the local Army Reserve Center. Organizations in the Washington, DC, area desiring chaplain speakers may contact the Chief of Chaplains, Department of the Army, Washington, DC 20310-2700. Phone, 202-695-1137. Information on speakers may be obtained by contacting the Public Affairs Office, Office of the Chief of Engineers, Washington, DC 20314, or the nearest Corps of Engineer Division or District Office.

For further information concerning the Department of the Army, contact the Office of the Chief of Public Affairs, Headquarters, Department of the Army, Washington, DC 20310-1508. Phone, 202-694-0741.

290-950 O 91 - 8

DEPARTMENT OF THE NAVY

The Pentagon, Washington, DC 20350
Phone, 202–545–6700

SECRETARY OF THE NAVY	H. LAWRENCE GARRETT III
Executive Assistant and Naval Aide	CAPT. M.N. MATTON, USN
Special Assistant and Marine Corps Aide	COL. D.B. HERBERT, USMC
Administrative Aide	COMDR. JOHN M. KENNY, USN
Director, Office of Program Appraisal	REAR ADM. N.W. RAY, USN
Deputy Director	CAPT. M.G. BELL, USN
Deputy for Marine Corps Matters	COL. W.R. BISHOP
Director, Navy Industrial Management Program	WILLIAM LINDAHL
Under Secretary of the Navy	J. DANIEL HOWARD
Executive Assistant and Naval Aide	CAPT. DOROTHY PROSE, USN
Special Assistant and Marine Corps Aide	COL. E. RITCHIE, USMC
Assistant for Administration	OLIVER R. ASHE
Assistant Deputy Under Secretary (Safety and Survivability)	JOSEPH K. TAUSSIG, JR.
Director, Small and Disadvantaged Business Utilization	D.L. HATHAWAY
Assistant to the Under Secretary for Total Quality Management	(VACANCY)
Director, DON Management Report Implementation Coordination Office	REBECCA D. PAULK
Office of Information, Chief of Information	REAR ADM. BRENT BAKER, USN
Deputy Chief of Information	CAPT. GORDON PETERSON, USN
Office of Legislative Affairs, Chief of Legislative Affairs	REAR ADM. W.J. FLANAGAN, USN
Deputy Chief	CAPT. JOSEPH R. MCCLEARY, USN
Naval Inspector General	REAR ADM. G.W. DAVIS, USN
Deputy Naval Inspector General	CAPT. JAMES D. CURRY, USN
Judge Advocate General of the Navy	REAR ADM. J.E. GORDON, JAGC, USN
Deputy Judge Advocate General	REAR ADM. W.L. SCHACHTE, JR., JAGC, USN
Auditor General of the Navy	RICHARD L. SHAFFER
Assistant Secretary of the Navy (Financial Management)	ROBERT C. MCCORMACK
Executive Assistant and Naval Aide	COMDR. RICHARD L. RODGERS, USN
Special Assistant and Marine Corps Aide	LT. COL. STEVEN QUENTMEYER, USMC
Comptroller of the Navy	ROBERT C. MCCORMACK
Deputy Comptroller of the Navy	CAPT. JOHN T. KAVANAUGH, USN
Director, Office of Budget and Reports	REAR ADM. RICHARD D. MILLIGAN, USN
Assistant Secretary of the Navy (Manpower and Reserve Affairs)	BARBARA SPYRIDON POPE

Executive Assistant and Naval Aide	CAPT. S.A. FRY, USN
Military Assistant and Marine Corps Aide	(VACANCY)
Deputy Assistant Secretary (Manpower)	DANIEL R. HEIMBACH
Deputy Assistant Secretary (Reserve Affairs)	DONALD C. MORENCY
Deputy Assistant Secretary (Force Support and Families)	MARIANNE B. DREW
Deputy Assistant Secretary (Civilian Personnel Policy/Equal Employment Opportunity)	DOROTHY M. MELETZKE
Director, Naval Council of Personnel Boards	CAPT. J.H. GROTENHUIS, USN
Deputy Director	COL. W.R. GAGE, USMC
Executive Director, Board for Correction of Naval Records	W. DEAN PFEIFFER
Deputy Executive Director	R. ZSALMAN
Assistant Secretary of the Navy (Installation and Environment)	JACQUELINE E. SCHAFER
Executive Assistant and Naval Aide	CAPT. RICHARD RICE, JR.
Special Assistant and Marine Aide	LT. COL. ALAN GENTEMAN
Principal Deputy	BEN ROSE
Administrative Aide	COMDR. JEFFERY GREENE
Environment and Safety	FRED STERNS, *Acting*
Installation and Facilities	FRED STERNS
Shore Resources	RICHARD O. THOMAS
Assistant Secretary of the Navy (Research, Development and Acquisition)	GERALD A. CANN
Executive Assistant/Naval Aide	CAPT. MARC PELAEZ, USN
Special Assistant/Marine Corps Aide	LT. COL. PERRY DUNN, USMC
Principal Deputy	GENIE MCBURNETT
Deputy Assistant Secretary (ASW Programs)	ARTHUR E. BISSON
Deputy Assistant Secretary (Air Programs)	WILLIAM J. SCHAEFER
Deputy Assistant Secretary (Communication, Command, Control, Computer, Intelligence (C^4I)/Electronic Warfare/Space Programs)	EDWARD C. WHITMAN
Deputy Assistant Secretary (Ship Programs)	RONALD K. KISS
Deputy for Acquisition Policy/Integrity Account Programs	REAR ADM. W.H. HAUENSTEIN, USN
Director, Procurement Policy	E. CAMMACK
Director, Product Integrity	W. WILLOUGHBY
Director, Workforce Education/Training	G. KEIGHTLEY
Competition Advocate General	REAR ADM. W.H. HAUENSTEIN, USN
Deputy for Expeditionary Force Programs	MAJ. GEN. RONALD L. BECKWITH
Director, Resources and Evaluation Programs	CAPT. G.W. RITCHEY, USN
Special Assistants	S. TRONIC; CAPT. G. DOWNER, USN; COMDR. G. BERRY, USN
Deputy Assistant Secretary (International Programs)	ALLAN CAMERON

Program Executive Officers	REAR ADM. J.F. CALVERT, USN; REAR ADM. W.L. VINCENT, USN; REAR ADM. W.C. BOWES, USN; REAR ADM. K.C. MALLEY, USN; D.E. PORTER; REAR ADM. D.C. VOLGENAU, USN; REAR ADM. J.T. HOOD, USN; REAR ADM. M.S. FIREBAUGH, USN; REAR ADM. L.E. BLOSE, USN
General Counsel	CRAIG S. KING
Principal Deputy General Counsel	CHESTER PAUL BEACH
Deputy General Counsel (Logistics)	HARVEY J. WILCOX
Associate General Counsel (Management)	FRED A. PHELPS
Associate General Counsel (Litigation)	C. JOHN TURNQUIST
Assistant General Counsel (Research, Development, and Acquisition)	ELWARD L. SAUL
Assistant General Counsel (Manpower and Reserve Affairs)	JOSEPH G. LYNCH
Assistant General Counsel (Installation and Environment)	ELSIE L. MUNSELL
Counsel, Comptroller of the Navy	PHILIP M. HITCH
Counsel, Commandant of the Marine Corps	P.M. MURPHY
Counsel, Naval Air Systems Command	MARGARET A. OLSEN
Counsel, Space and Naval Warfare Systems Command	HARVEY J. NATHAN
Counsel, Naval Facilities Engineering Command	MATTHEW K. MCELHANEY
Counsel, Naval Sea Systems Command	EUGENE P. ANGRIST
Counsel, Naval Supply Systems Command	CHARLES J. MCMANUS
Counsel, Military Sealift Command	RICHARD S. HAYNES
Counsel, Office of the Chief of Naval Research	SOPHIE A. KRASIK

U.S. Navy

Chief of Naval Operations	ADM. FRANK B. KELSO II, USN
Vice Chief of Naval Operations	ADM. J.L. JOHNSON, USN
Deputy Chief, Manpower, Personnel and Training and Chief of Naval Personnel	VICE ADM. J.M. BOORDA, USN
Assistant Chief, Undersea Warfare	VICE ADM. R.F. BACON, USN
Assistant Chief, Surface Warfare	VICE ADM. R.K. KIHUNE, USN
Deputy Chief, Logistics	VICE ADM. S. LOFTUS, USN
Assistant Chief, Air Warfare	VICE ADM. R.M. DUNLEAVY, USN
Deputy Chief, Plans, Policy and Operations	VICE ADM. L.W. SMITH, JR., USN
Deputy Chief, Naval Warfare	VICE ADM. J.D. WILLIAMS, USN
Deputy Chief, Navy Program Planning	VICE ADM. H.H. MAUZ, USN
Assistant Vice Chief of Naval Operations	REAR ADM. R.M. WALSH, USN
Director of Naval Nuclear Propulsion Program	ADM. B. DEMARS, USN
Director of Test and Evaluation and Technology Requirements	REAR ADM. J.G. REYNOLDS, USN
Director of Naval Intelligence	REAR ADM. T.A. BROOKS, USN
Director of Naval Medicine and Surgeon General of the Navy	VICE ADM. D.F. HAGEN, MC, USN
Director of Space and Electronic Warfare	VICE ADM. J.O. TUTTLE, USN

Director of Naval Reserve	REAR ADM. J.E. TAYLOR, USN
Oceanographer of the Navy	REAR ADM. G.L. CHESBROUGH, USN
Director of Religious Ministries and Chief of Chaplains of the Navy	REAR ADM. A.B. KOENEMAN, CHC, USN
Special Assistant for Public Affairs Support	REAR ADM. B. BAKER, USN
Special Assistant for Safety Matters	REAR ADM. J.H. FINNEY, USN
Special Assistant for Inspection Support	REAR ADM. G.W. DAVIS, USN
Special Assistant for Legal Services	REAR ADM. J.E. GORDON, JAGC, USN
Special Assistant for Legislative Support	REAR ADM. W.J. FLANAGAN, USN
Special Assistant for Naval Investigative Matters and Security	REAR ADM. D.M. WILLIAMS, JR., JAGC, USN
Special Assistant for Material Inspections and Surveys	REAR ADM. T.E. LEWIN, USN
Major Shore Commands:	
Director, Strategic Systems Program	CAPT. J.T. MITCHELL, USN
Commander, Naval Air Systems Command	VICE ADM. W.C. BOWES, USN
Commander, Space and Naval Warfare Systems Command	REAR ADM. R.H. AILES, USN
Commander, Naval Facilities Engineering Command	REAR ADM. D.E. BOTTORFF, CEC, USN
Commander, Naval Sea Systems Command	REAR ADM. W.H. CANTRELL, USN, *Acting*
Commander, Naval Supply Systems Command	REAR ADM. J.E. MILLER, SC, USN
Chief, Bureau of Medicine and Surgery	VICE ADM. D.F. HAGEN, MC, USN
Chief of Naval Personnel	VICE ADM. J.M. BOORDA, USN
Commander, Naval Military Personnel Command	REAR ADM. S.F. GALLO, USN
Commander, Naval Oceanography Command	REAR ADM. J.E. KOEHR, USN
Commander, Naval Computer and Telecommunications Command	CAPT. K. LAUGHTON, USN
Commander, Naval Intelligence Command	CAPT. J.A. FROST, USN
Commander, Naval Security Group Command	REAR ADM. I.C. COLE, USN
Chief of Naval Education and Training	VICE ADM. J.H. FETTERMAN, JR., USN
Commander, Naval Legal Service Command	REAR ADM. W.L. SCHACHTE, JR., JAGC, USN
Commander, Naval Investigative Service Command	REAR ADM. D.M. WILLIAMS, JR., JAGC, USN
Commander, Naval Space Command	REAR ADM. L.E. ALLEN, USN
Major Fleet Commands:	
Commander in Chief, U.S. Atlantic Fleet	ADM. P.D. MILLER, USN
Commander in Chief, U.S. Pacific Fleet	ADM. R.J. KELLY, USN
Commander in Chief, U.S. Naval Forces Europe	ADM. J.T. HOWE, USN
Commander, Military Sealift Command	VICE ADM. F.R. DONOVAN, USN
Commander, U.S. Naval Forces Central Command	REAR ADM. R. SUTTON, USN
Commander, Naval Special Warfare Command	REAR ADM. G.R. WORTHINGTON, USN
Commander, Naval Reserve Force	REAR ADM. J.E. TAYLOR, USN

Commander, Operational Test and Evaluation Force	REAR ADM. H.L. WEBSTER, USN
Commander, Mine Warfare Command	REAR ADM. S.E. BUMP, USN

U.S. Marine Corps

Commandant of the Marine Corps	GEN. C.E. MUNDY, JR., USMC
Military Secretary to the Commandant	COL. P.T. METZGER, USMC
Sergeant Major of the Marine Corps	SGT. MAJ. H.G. OVERSTREET, USMC
Assistant Commandant of the Marine Corps	GEN. J.R. DAILEY, USMC
Aide-de-Camp	LT. COL. S.C. TAGG, USMC
Secretary of the General Staff	COL. W.D. CARR, USMC
Director, Special Projects Directorate	COL. A.J. PONNWITZ, USMC
Counsel for the Commandant	P.M. MURPHY
Deputy Chief of Staff for Plans, Policies, and Operations	LT. GEN. J.P. HOAR, USMC
Director, Operations Division	BRIG. GEN. R.H. SUTTON, USMC
Director, Plans Division	MAJ. GEN. J.W. PEARSON III, USMC
Deputy Chief of Staff for Aviation	LT. GEN. D.A. WILLS, USMC
Assistant Deputy Chief of Staff for Aviation and Director, Aviation Plans, Policy and Requirements Division	BRIG. GEN. J.D. HOWELL, USMC
Deputy Chief of Staff for Manpower and Reserve Affairs	LT. GEN. N.H. SMITH, USMC
Assistant Deputy Chief of Staff for Manpower and Reserve Affairs for Reserve Affairs	MAJ. GEN. H.E. DAVISON, USMC
Deputy Chief of Staff for Manpower and Reserve Affairs	J.W. MARSH
Director, Personnel Management Division	MAJ. GEN. J.J. SHEENAN, USMC
Director, Manpower Plans and Policy Division	BRIG. GEN. R.I. NEAL, USMC
Director, Personnel Procurement Division	BRIG. GEN. G.E. BROWN, USMC
Director, Morale, Welfare, Recreation Support Activity	J.R. JOY
Director, Manpower Management Information Systems Division	LT. COL. R.L. CARTER, USMC
Director, Human Resources Division	COL. A.A. QUEBODEAUX, USMC
Deputy Chief of Staff for Installations and Logistics	LT. GEN. R.J. WINGLASS, USMC
Special Assistant	R.K. RIGGS
Director, Facilities and Services Division	BRIG. GEN. J.C. ARICK, USMC
Director, Contracts Division	P.E. ZANFAGNA, JR.
Director, Logistics Plans, Policies, and Strategic Mobility Division	COL. J.D. STEWART, USMC
Director, Programs and Financial Management Division	COL. F.C. WILLIAMS, JR., USMC
Deputy Chief of Staff for Requirements and Programs	MAJ. GEN. D.R. GARDNER, USMC
Assistant Deputy Chief of Staff	J.R. MASCIARELLI
Deputy Naval Inspector General for Marine Corps Matters/Inspector General of the Marine Corps	MAJ. GEN. H.E. DAVISON, USMC
Fiscal Director of the Marine Corps	E.T. COMSTOCK
Assistant Chief of Staff for Command, Control, Communications and Computer, Intelligence and Interoperability	MAJ. GEN. J.A. STUDDS, USMC
Deputy Assistant Chief of Staff	BRIG. GEN. G.L. MCKAY, USMC

Director of Intelligence	MAJ. GEN. J.A. STUDDS, USMC
Director, Command, Control, Communications, and Computer Division	BRIG. GEN. G.L. MCKAY, USMC
Legislative Assistant to the Commandant	BRIG. GEN. J.H. ADMIRE, USMC
Director of Public Affairs	BRIG. GEN. T.V. DRAUDE, USMC
Staff Judge Advocate to CMC	BRIG. GEN. G.L. MILLER, USMC
Director of Administration and Resource Management	L.J. KELLY
Director of Marine Corps History and Museums/President, Permanent Marine Corps Uniform Board	BRIG. GEN. E.H. SIMMONS, USMC (RET.)
The Medical Officer, U.S. Marine Corps	REAR ADM. R.I. RIDENOUR, MC, USN
The Dental Officer, U.S. Marine Corps	CAPT. A.E. BRANDT, DC, USN
The Chaplain, U.S. Marine Corps	CAPT. D.L. KRABBE, USN
Commanding General, Marine Corps Combat Development Command	LT. GEN. E.T. COOK, JR., USMC
Commanding General, Marine Corps Research Development and Acquisition Command	MAJ. GEN. R.A. TIEBOUT, USMC

[For the Department of the Navy statement of organization, see the *Code of Federal Regulations,* Title 32, Part 700]

The primary mission of the Department of the Navy is to protect the United States, as directed by the President or the Secretary of Defense, by the effective prosecution of war at sea including, with its Marine Corps component, the seizure or defense of advanced naval bases; to support, as required, the forces of all military departments of the United States; and to maintain freedom of the seas.

The United States Navy was founded on October 13, 1775, when Congress enacted the first legislation creating the Continental Navy of the American Revolution. The Department of the Navy and the Office of Secretary of the Navy were established by act of April 30, 1798 (10 U.S.C. 5011, 5031). For 9 years prior to that date, by act of August 7, 1789 (1 Stat. 49), the conduct of naval affairs was under the Secretary of War.

The National Security Act Amendments of 1949 established the Department of Defense as an executive department of the Federal Government, and provided that the Department of the Navy be a military department within the Department of Defense (63 Stat. 578).

The Secretary of the Navy is appointed by the President as the head of the Department of the Navy and is responsible to the Secretary of Defense for the operation and efficiency of the Navy (10 U.S.C. 5031).

The organization of the Department of the Navy is reflected in the organization chart and personnel listing. The Department of the Navy includes the U.S. Coast Guard when it is operating as a Service in the Navy.

DEPARTMENT OF THE NAVY

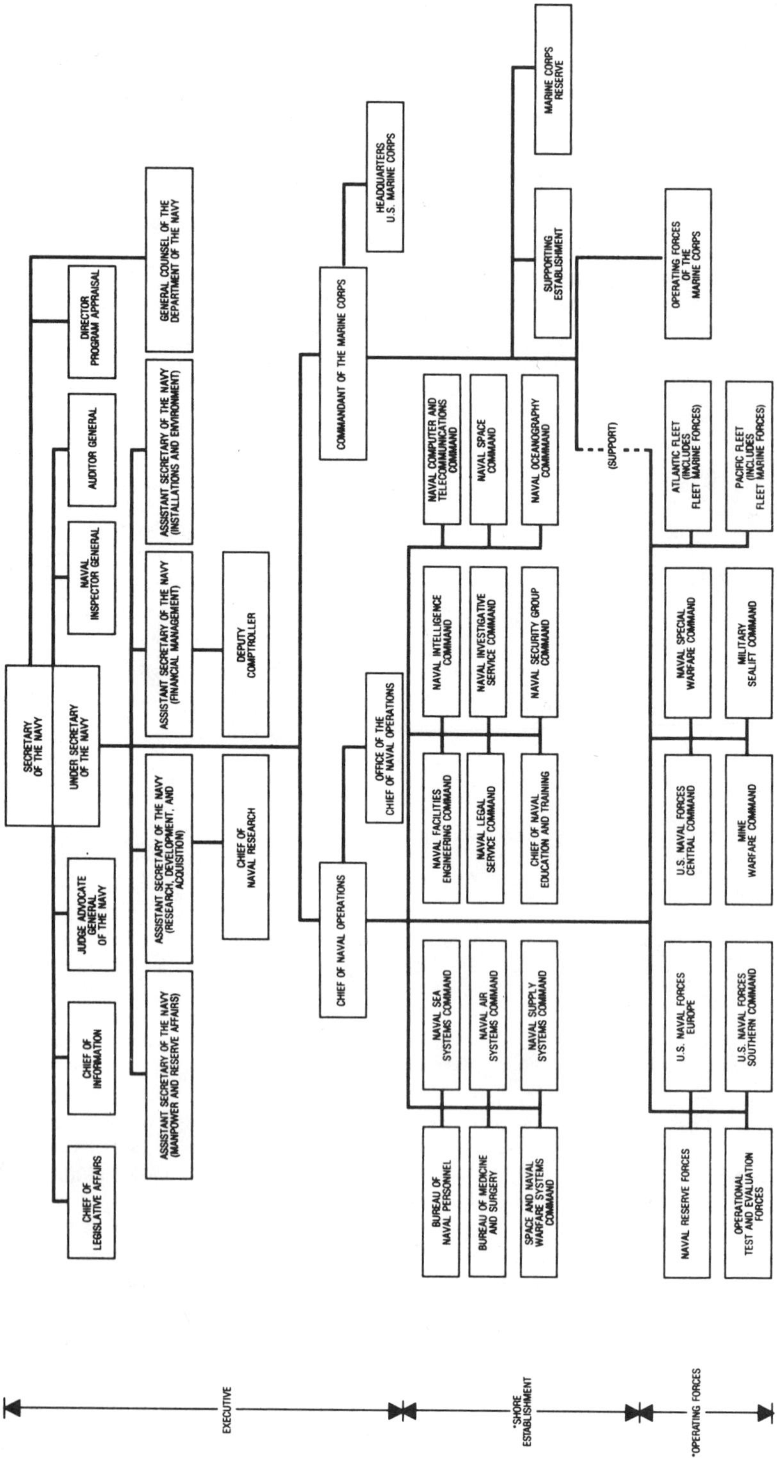

*ALSO INCLUDES OTHER DESIGNATED ACTIVITIES NOT SHOWN ON THE CHART WHICH ARE UNDER THE COMMAND OR SUPERVISION OF THE ORGANIZATIONS DEPICTED.

Office of the Secretary of the Navy

Secretary of the Navy

The Secretary of the Navy is the head of the Department of the Navy. Under the direction, authority, and control of the Secretary of Defense, the Secretary of the Navy is responsible for the policies and control of the Department of the Navy, including its organization, administration, functioning, and efficiency. The members of the Secretary's executive administration assist in the discharge of the responsibilities of the Secretary of the Navy.

During the temporary absence of the Secretary of the Navy, the Under Secretary of the Navy is next in succession to act as the Secretary of the Navy. The Under Secretary functions as deputy and principal assistant to the Secretary, and acts with full authority of the Secretary in the general management of the Department.

Civilian Executive Assistants

The Civilian Executive Assistants to the Secretary are the principal advisers and assistants to the Secretary of the Navy on the administration of the affairs of the Department of the Navy as a whole and are assigned departmentwide responsibilities for areas essential to the efficient administration of the Department of the Navy.

The Civilian Executive Assistants to the Secretary of the Navy are the Under Secretary of the Navy, the Assistant Secretaries of the Navy, and the General Counsel of the Navy. It is the policy of the Secretary to assign departmentwide responsibilities essential to the efficient administration of the Department of the Navy to the Civilian Executive Assistants.

Each Civilian Executive Assistant, within an assigned area of responsibility, is the principal adviser and assistant to the Secretary on the administration of the affairs of the Department of the Navy. The Civilian Executive Assistants carry out the duties in harmony with the statutory positions of the Chief of Naval Operations, who is the principal military adviser and executive to the Secretary regarding naval matters, and the Commandant of the Marine Corps, who is the principal military adviser and executive regarding Marine Corps matters. Each is authorized and directed to act for the Secretary within his assigned area of responsibility.

The Under Secretary of the Navy is designated as the deputy and principal assistant to the Secretary of the Navy to act with full authority of the Secretary in the general management of the Department and to supervise the offices and organizations as assigned by the Secretary.

The Assistant Secretary of the Navy (Financial Management) is the Comptroller of the Department of the Navy and is responsible for developing and maintaining policies, standards, and procedures for obtaining resources and operating financial systems throughout the Department to include budgeting, accounting, disbursing, financing, internal review, and statistical reporting.

The Assistant Secretary of the Navy (Manpower and Reserve Affairs) is responsible for the overall supervision of manpower and reserve component affairs of the Department, including policy and administration of affairs related to military (active and inactive) and civilian personnel, and supervision of offices and organizations as assigned by the Secretary, specifically the Naval Council of Personnel Boards and the Board for Correction of Naval Records.

The Assistant Secretary of the Navy (Installation and Environment) is responsible for policy and oversight of acquisition, construction, utilization, improvement, alteration, maintainence, and disposal of real estate and facilities, including capital equipment, utilities, housing, and public quarters; strategic homeporting; base closures; environmental protection, restoration, and compliance; natural resources management; control and minimization of hazardous material and hazardous waste; occupational safety and health for naval personnel; and commercial activities programs of the Navy shore establishment.

The Assistant Secretary of the Navy (Research, Development and Acquisition) is responsible for developing acquisition policy and procedures for all Department of the Navy research, development, production, shipbuilding and logistics support programs, and international technology transfers; overseeing the PEO/SYSCOM/PM compliance with procurement, product integrity, competition, and specification policy, procedures, and requirements; and matters concerning management, contract integrity and accountability.

The General Counsel provides legal advice, counsel, and guidance to the Secretary of the Navy and the other Civilian Executive Assistants and their staffs on any issue or matter involving the Department of the Navy. The Office of General Counsel provides legal services relating to general legal issues, litigation, business and commercial law, real and personal property, civilian personnel law, environmental law, patent law, and procurement of services.

The Staff Assistants

The Staff Assistants to the Secretary of the Navy are the Naval Inspector General, the Judge Advocate General of the Navy, the Comptroller of the Navy, the Auditor General of the Navy, the Chief of Information, and the heads of such other offices and boards as may be established by law or by the Secretary for the purpose of assisting the Secretary or one or more of the Civilian Executive Assistants in the administration of the Department of the Navy. Each supervises all functions and activities internal to that office and assigned shore activities, if any. Each is responsible to the Secretary or to one of the Civilian Executive Assistants for the utilization of resources by, and the operating efficiency of, all activities under their supervision. The duties of the individual Staff Assistants and their respective offices are provided by law or assigned by the Secretary.

Inspector General The duties of the Naval Inspector General are specified by 10 U.S.C. 5020. The Naval Inspector General, who is detailed from officers on active duty in the line and serving in the grade above Captain, inquires into and reports upon any matter that affects the discipline or military efficiency of the Department of the Navy and makes such inspections, investigations, and reports as the Secretary of the Navy or the Chief of Naval Operations directs. The Naval Inspector General cooperates fully with the Inspector General of the Department of Defense in connection with the performance of any duty or function by the Inspector General of the Department of Defense under 5 U.S.C. app. 2 and recommends additional inspections and investigations as may appear appropriate.

(Naval Inspector General, Building 200, Washington Navy Yard, Washington, DC 20374–2001. Phone, 202–433–2000.)

Judge Advocate General The Judge Advocate General, the senior officer and Chief of the Judge Advocate General's Corps, commands the Office of the Judge Advocate General. The Judge Advocate General provides or supervises the provision of all legal advice and related services throughout the Department of the Navy, except for the advice and services provided by the General Counsel. He also performs functions required or authorized by law; provides legal and policy advice to the Secretary of the Navy on military justice, administrative law, claims, environmental law, operational and international law and treaty interpretation, and litigation involving these issues; and acts on other matters as directed by the Secretary.

The Judge Advocate General also supervises the administration of military justice throughout the Department of the Navy, performs functions required or authorized by the Uniform Code of Military Justice, and provides technical supervision for the Naval Justice School at Newport, RI.

The Judge Advocate General maintains a close working relationship with the General Counsel on all matters of common interest and liaisons with other departments and agencies of the Government as appropriate.

The Deputy Judge Advocate General performs the duties of the Judge Advocate General when there is a vacancy in that office, or during the absence or disability of the Judge Advocate General. The Deputy Judge Advocate General is also Commander of the Naval Legal Service Command which includes 21 Naval Legal Service Offices, their detachments, and the Naval Justice School.

Officers of the Judge Advocate General's Corps and judge advocates of the Marine Corps provide a variety of legal services to both individual servicemembers and naval commands and activities. Legal assistance service to qualified servicemembers and their dependents includes advice on tax, adoption, divorce, contracts, and landlord/tenant matters. Individual servicemembers are provided personal representation for courts-martial, and may be provided assistance for nonjudicial punishment, complaints pursuant to Article 138 of the Uniform Code of Military Justice, and petitions to the Board for Correction of Naval Records.

Unified, specified, and naval commands are provided legal service on such diverse matters as investigations, claims, environmental law, admiralty, operational and international law and treaty interpretation, courts-martial, nonjudicial punishment, civilian personnel law at field activities (under the overall coordination and policy guidance of the Office of Civilian Personnel Management), military personnel law, Freedom of Information Act/Privacy Act, service of process, and the authority of installation commanders.

(Public Affairs Officer, Office of the Judge Advocate General, Department of the Navy, 200 Stovall Street, Alexandria, VA 22332–2400. Phone, 703–614–7420.)

Comptroller The Comptroller of the Navy is responsible for financial management of the Navy, including budgeting, accounting, progress and statistical reporting, administrative organization, and related managerial procedures.

Auditor General The Auditor General of the Navy is responsible for developing and implementing Navy internal audit policies, programs, and procedures within the framework of Government auditing standards and serving as Director of the Naval Audit Service.

The function of internal audit is to objectively evaluate and make recommendations concerning the integrity and reliability of financial and other data used to make management decisions; the adequacy of policies and procedures affecting the expenditure of funds, the safeguarding and efficient use of resources, and the accomplishment of management objectives and program results; and the extent of compliance with applicable policies, procedures, laws, and regulations.

Audits are accomplished through four Naval Audit Service regional offices with support from Naval Audit Service Headquarters.

(Auditor General of the Navy, Department of the Navy, 5611 Columbia Pike, Falls Church, VA 22041–0206. Phone, 703–756–2117.)

Information The Chief of Information is the direct representative of the Secretary of the Navy and of the Chief of Naval Operations in all public affairs and internal relations matters and is authorized to implement Navy public affairs and internal relations policies and to coordinate those Navy and Marine Corps activities that are of mutual interest.

The Chief of Information is responsible for keeping Navy commands informed of Department of Defense policies and requirements and is the only principal component within the Office of the Chief of Naval Operations authorized to deal directly with the Office of the Assistant Secretary of Defense (Public Affairs).

Principal functions of the Office of Information include making available accurate and timely information about the Navy so that the general public, the press, and Congress may understand and assess the Navy's programs, operations, and needs; coordination of Navy participation in community events; and supervision of the Navy's internal information programs.

Field activities of the Chief of Information include six Navy Information Offices, two Navy Public Affairs Centers, and one Fleet Home Town News Center.

(Office of Information, Department of the Navy, Washington, DC 20350–1200. Phone, 202–697–5342.)

Research and Technology The Office of Naval Research, established by act of August 1, 1946 (10 U.S.C. 5150–5153), is headed by the Chief of Naval Research, who is appointed by the President with the advice and consent of the Senate and who is authorized to act for the Secretary of the Navy on all assigned matters. Since that time, additional functions and responsibilities have been assigned to the Chief of Naval Research. To preserve the intent of the law that established the Office and to achieve optimum integration of resources for basic research and exploratory development, all headquarters management functions have been incorporated into one office now known as the Office of the Chief of Naval Research.

The Office of the Chief of Naval Research includes three lead offices: the Office of Naval Research, the Office of Naval Technology, and the Office of Advanced Technology.

(Office of the Chief of Naval Research, Ballston Tower No. 1, 800 North Quincy Street, Arlington, VA 22217–5000. Phone, 703–696–4258.)

Personnel Boards The Naval Council of Personnel Boards, comprised of the Naval Discharge Review Board, Naval Complaints Review Board, Naval Clemency and Parole Board, and the Physical Evaluation Board administers, under the Assistant Secretary of the Navy (Manpower and Reserve Affairs), personnel services and support as indicated by each component board's title.

The Naval Discharge Review Board reviews, pursuant to 10 U.S.C. 1553, upon its own motion or upon request by or on behalf of former Navy and Marine Corps members, the type and reason for discharge or dismissal received by that former member, except a discharge or dismissal by reason of the sentence of general court-martial. It determines whether, under reasonable standards of naval law and discipline, a discharge or dismissal should be changed and, if so, what change should be made.

The Naval Complaints Review Board reviews, upon request, decisional documents and/or index entries created by the Naval Discharge Review Board after April 1, 1977. The Naval Complaints Review Board determines whether decisional documents conform to those applicable regulations of the Department of Defense and the Department of the Navy.

The Naval Clemency and Parole Board reviews, pursuant to 10 U.S.C. 953–954, Navy and Marine Corps court-martial cases referred to it and grants or denies clemency; and, pursuant to 10 U.S.C. 952, reviews and directs that parole be granted or denied in cases referred to it for review.

The Physical Evaluation Board organizes and administers disability evaluations within the Department of the Navy, pursuant to 10 U.S.C., chapter 61, and other applicable provisions of law and regulation. It is comprised of the Record Review Panel, regional hearing panels at Bethesda, MD, and San Diego, CA, and disability evaluation system counselors located at major medical centers. The system considers evidence concerning disabilities of personnel and determines the appropriate disposition in each case.

(Naval Council of Personnel Boards, Department of the Navy, Room 905, 801 North Randolph Street, Arlington, VA 22203. Phone, 703–696–4356.)

Naval Records The Board for Correction of Naval Records is a statutory civilian board established, pursuant to the provisions of 10 U.S.C. 1552, to relieve the Congress of the burden and necessity of considering private relief legislation for the correction of errors and injustices suffered by members and former members of the Navy and Marine Corps. The Secretary of the Navy, acting through this board of civilians of the executive part of the Department, is authorized to take action consistent with law and regulation to correct naval or military records of the Department of the Navy where such action is necessary or appropriate to correct an error or to remove an injustice. The Board represents the highest echelon of review of administrative errors and injustices. The Board reviews, on application, actions taken by various boards and officials in the Department.

(Board for Correction of Naval Records, Department of the Navy, Room 2432, Navy Annex, Washington, DC 20370–5100. Phone, 202–694–1402.)

United States Navy [1]

Chief of Naval Operations

In the performance of his duties within the Department of the Navy, the Chief of Naval Operations takes precedence above all other officers of the naval service. He is the Navy member of the Joint Chiefs of Staff.

The Chief of Naval Operations, under the Secretary of the Navy, exercises command over certain central executive organizations, assigned shore activities, and the Operating Forces of the Navy.

The Chief of Naval Operations plans for and provides the manpower, material, weapons, facilities, and services to support the needs of the Navy, with the exception of the Fleet Marine Forces; maintains water transportation services, including sea transportation services for the Department of Defense; directs the Naval Reserve; and exercises authority for matters of naval administration, including matters related to customs and traditions of the naval service, security, intelligence, discipline, naval communications, and naval operations.

The Chief of Naval Operations exercises area coordination authority over all shore activities of the Department of the Navy to ensure that total efforts afford adequate support to the combatant forces and are coordinated among themselves to assure economy and efficiency of operation.

Operating Forces of the Navy

The Operating Forces of the Navy are responsible for naval operations necessary to carry out the Department of the Navy's role in upholding and advancing the national policies and interests of the United States. The Operating Forces of the Navy include the several fleets, seagoing forces, Fleet Marine Forces and other assigned Marine Corps forces, the Military Sealift Command, and other forces and activities as may be assigned by the President or the Secretary of the Navy. The Chief of Naval Operations is responsible for the command and administration of the Operating Forces of the Navy.

The Pacific Fleet is composed of ships, submarines, and aircraft operating throughout the Pacific and Indian Oceans.

The Atlantic Fleet is composed of ships, submarines, and aircraft that operate throughout the Atlantic Ocean and Mediterranean Sea.

The Naval Forces, Europe, includes forces assigned by the Chief of Naval Operations or made available from either the Pacific or Atlantic Fleet to operate in the European theater.

The Military Sealift Command provides ocean transportation (by Government-owned or commercial vessels) for personnel and cargo of all components of the Department of Defense and as authorized for other Federal agencies;

[1] Writeups on Defense Agencies and Defense Joint Service Schools begin on pages 237 and 257, respectively.

operates and maintains underway replenishment ships and other vessels providing mobile logistic support to elements of the combatant fleets; and operates ships in support of scientific projects and other programs for Federal agencies.

Other major commands of the Operating Forces of the Navy are the Commander, U.S. Naval Forces Central Command; Commander, Operational Test and Evaluation Force; Commander, Mine Warfare Command; Commander, Naval Special Warfare Command; and Commander, Naval Reserve Force.

Navy Command Structure

The Chief of Naval Operations manages and supports the Operating Forces of the Navy through the following executive and functional organization structure.

Chief of Naval Operations The Office of the Chief of Naval Operations is the headquarters of the Navy which advises and assists the Secretary, the Under Secretary, the Assistant Secretaries, and the Chief of Naval Operations in the discharge of their responsibilities. The Office of the Chief of Naval Operations was established basically in its present structure by Executive Order 9635 of September 29, 1945, and later by act of March 5, 1948 (10 U.S.C. 141, 171, 5036(b), 5081–5088). Additional changes in the organization and responsibilities of the Office of the Chief of Naval Operations were directed by the Goldwater-Nichols Department of Defense Reorganization Act of 1986 (Pub. L. 99–433 of Oct. 1, 1986, 10 U.S.C. 111 note).

Sea Systems The Commander, Naval Sea Systems Command, provides material support to the Navy and Marine Corps, and for mobilization purposes to the Department of Defense and Department of Transportation, for ships, submarines, and other sea platforms, shipboard combat systems and components, other surface and undersea warfare and weapons systems, and ordnance expendables not specifically assigned to other system commands.

(Commander, Naval Sea Systems Command, Washington, DC 20362-5101. Phone, 703–602–3328.)

Air Systems The Commander, Naval Air Systems Command, provides for the material support to the Navy and Marine Corps for aircraft, airborne weapon systems, avionics, related photographic and support equipment, ranges, and targets.

(Commander, Naval Air Systems Command, Washington, DC 20361–0001. Phone, 703–692–2260.)

Space and Naval Warfare Systems The Commander, Space and Naval Warfare Systems Command, provides technical and material support to the Department of the Navy for space systems; command, control, communications, and intelligence systems; and electronic warfare and undersea surveillance.

(Commander, Space and Naval Warfare Systems Command, Washington, DC 20363–5100. Phone, 703–602–8768.)

Supply Systems The Commander, Naval Supply Systems Command, provides for the material support to the Navy and Marine Corps for materials, supplies, and supporting services by providing supply management policies and methods and administering related support service systems.

(Commander, Naval Supply Systems Command, Washington, DC 20376–5000. Phone, 703–695–4009.)

Naval Facilities The Commander, Naval Facilities Engineering Command, provides for material and technical support to the Navy and Marine Corps for shore facilities, real property and utilities, fixed ocean systems and structures, transportation and construction equipment, energy, environmental and natural resources management, and support of the Naval Construction Forces.

(Commander, Naval Facilities Engineering Command, 200 Stovall Street, Alexandria, VA 22332–2300. Phone, 703–325–0589.)

Strategic Systems The Director, Strategic Systems Programs, provides for the development, production, and material support to the Navy for fleet ballistic missile and strategic weapon systems, including the missiles, platforms, and associated equipment; security, training of personnel, and the installation and direction of necessary supporting facilities.

(Director, Strategic Systems Programs, Department of the Navy, Washington, DC 20376–5002. Phone, 703–695–2158.)

Naval Personnel The Chief of Naval Personnel directs the procurement, distribution, administration, and career motivation of the military personnel of the regular and reserve components of the United States Navy to meet the quantitative and qualitative manpower requirements determined by the Chief of Naval Operations. He also directs the management and administration of the Navy Civilian Personnel/Equal Employment Opportunity Programs and develops servicewide programs for improved human resources management.

(Bureau of Naval Personnel, Department of the Navy, Federal Office Building No. 2, Washington, DC 20370–5000. Phone, 703–614–1271.)

Naval Medicine The Chief, Bureau of Medicine and Surgery:

—directs the provision of medical and dental services for Navy and Marine Corps personnel and other persons authorized by law;

—ensures that health care program policies are optimally executed through the acquisition and effective utilization of financial and manpower resources;

—maintains all assigned activities in a proper state of material and personnel readiness to fulfill assigned peacetime and contingency mission taskings;

—administers the execution and implementation of contingency support plans and programs that provide for an effective medical and dental readiness capability;

—acquires, trains, and maintains a force of professional and technical personnel;

—provides professional and technical medical and dental service to the Fleet, Fleet Marine Force, and shore activities of the Navy;

—ensures that assigned activities are able to achieve successful accreditation and recognition by appropriate governmental and civilian agencies and commissions; and

—ensures cooperation with civil authorities in matters pertaining to public health disasters and other emergencies, in conjunction with maintaining and safeguarding the health of Navy and Marine Corps personnel.

(Bureau of Medicine and Surgery, Department of the Navy, Twenty-third and E Streets NW., Washington, DC 20372–5120. Phone, 202–653–1327.)

Oceanography The Commander, Naval Oceanography Command, and the Superintendent, U.S. Naval Observatory, are responsible for the science, technology, engineering, operations, and those personnel and facilities associated with each, which are essential to explore the ocean and the atmosphere and to provide astronomical data and time for naval and related national objectives. Oceanography examines how naval operations are influenced by the physical environment and applies its findings to the development of technology and methods for improving naval operations.

The Naval Oceanographic Program embraces five major disciplines of physical science to investigate the nature and behavior of the ocean environment in which the Navy operates. They are:

Hydrography—to collect data for the charting of the oceans and to establish geodetic references for navigation;

Oceanography—to define the characteristics of the water volume for use in ocean reporting and prediction, and studies of underwater acoustics, water dynamics, corrosion, and other factors influencing the performance of naval systems;

Meteorology—to define the characteristics of the atmosphere for use in weather reporting and prediction, and studies of upper atmosphere winds and currents, refractive indices for radar performance, and similar factors;

Astrometry—to determine the position and motions of celestial bodies required for accurate navigation, operational support, and use in calculating precise geodetic positions and azimuth references on Earth; and

Precise Time—to determine, provide, and manage the distribution of precise time and time interval (frequency), both atomic and astronomical, for use in electronic navigation and command, control, and communications.

(Oceanographer of the Navy, U.S. Naval Observatory, Washington, DC 20392–1800. Phone, 202–653–1295. Commander, Naval Oceanography Command, Stennis Space Center, Bay St. Louis, MS 39529–5002. Phone, 601–688–4726. Superintendent, Naval Observatory, Washington, DC 20392–5100. Phone, 202–653–1541.)

Space Command The Commander, Naval Space Command, provides operational space systems support to naval forces worldwide and helps prepare the naval service for extended future involvement in space. The Command has operational responsibility for all Navy space-related systems, plus coordination responsibility with other operational activities so that the space capabilities are integrated into the Navy's operational plans. The Command identifies fleet operational requirements for space systems, which will be translated into specific program planning and budgeting. The Command has operational responsibility for the Navy Navigation Satellite System, the Naval Space Surveillance System, and elements supporting the Fleet Satellite Communications System.

The Command has administrative responsibility for the Fleet Surveillance Support Command and the Relocatable Over-the-Horizon Radar System, a broad area surveillance high-frequency radar that will have the capability to be relocated to prepared global sites to support naval forces.

(Commander, Naval Space Command, Department of the Navy, Dahlgren, VA 22448–5170. Phone, 703–663–7841.)

Legal Services The Commander, Naval Legal Service Command, under the command of the Chief of Naval Operations, is responsible for administering the legal services program within the Navy and providing command direction for all Naval Legal Service Command activities and resources.

(Commander, Naval Legal Service Command, 200 Stovall Street, Alexandria, VA 22332–2400. Phone, 703–325–9820.)

Computers and Telecommunications The Commander, Naval Computer and Telecommunications Command, performs functions to provide, operate, and maintain all Navy ashore communications resources and all non-tactical information and resources for command, control, and administration of the Navy and those elements of the Defense Communications System assigned to the Navy.

(Commander, Naval Computer and Telecommunications Command, 4401 Massachusetts Avenue NW., Washington, DC 20390–5290. Phone, 202–282–0357.)

Cryptology The Commander, Naval Security Group Command, performs cryptologic functions; provides, operates, and maintains an adequate Naval Security Group; approves requirements for the use of existing Naval Security Group capabilities and resources; and coordinates the execution of approved cryptologic programs.

(Commander, Naval Security Group Command, 3801 Nebraska Avenue NW., Washington, DC 20393–5210. Phone, 202–282–0272.)

Intelligence The Commander, Naval Intelligence Command, ensures the fulfillment of the intelligence requirements and responsibilities of the Department of the Navy.

(Commander, Naval Intelligence Command, Department of the Navy, 4600 Silver Hill Road, Washington, DC 20389–5000. Phone, 202–763–3552; hotline, 301–763–3557.)

Investigative Service Command The Commander, Naval Investigative Service Command, commands a worldwide organization with representation in more than 160 geographic locations to provide criminal investigative, counterintelligence, law enforcement and physical security, and information and personnel security support to the Navy and Marine Corps, both ashore and afloat. The Naval Investigative Service Command is comprised of law enforcement professionals who are investigators, crime laboratory technicians, technical investigative specialists, counterintelligence analysts, physical security specialists, and administrative support personnel.

(Commander, Naval Investigative Service, Department of the Navy, Washington, DC 20388–5000. For general information, call 202–433–8800, or contact the Operations Control Center/ Headquarters Duty Officer, 202–433–9323.)

Education and Training The mission of the Chief of Naval Education and Training is to:

—provide assigned shore-based education and training for Navy, certain Marine Corps, and other personnel in support of the Fleet, Naval Shore Establishment, Naval Reserve, Interservice Training Program, and Security Assistance Program;

—develop specifically designated education and training afloat programs for the Fleet;

—execute the Navy's responsibility for voluntary education and dependents education;

—participate with research and development activities in the development and implementation of the most effective teaching and training systems and devices for optimal education and training; and

—perform such other functions as directed.

(Chief of Naval Education and Training, Naval Air Station, Department of the Navy, Pensacola, FL 32508–5100. Phone, 904–452–4858.)

United States Marine Corps

Commandant of the Marine Corps,
Department of the Navy, Washington, DC 20380–0001
Phone, 703–614–2500

The United States Marine Corps was established on November 10, 1775, by resolution of the Continental Congress. The present composition, missions, and functions of the Marine Corps are set forth in the National Security Act of 1947, as amended (50 U.S.C. 401).

The primary mission of the Marine Corps is to provide Fleet Marine Forces of combined arms, together with supporting air components, for service with the Fleet in the seizure or defense of advanced naval bases and for the conduct of land operations essential to the prosecution of a naval campaign. Collateral functions of the Marine Corps are to provide detachments and organizations for service on armed vessels of the Navy and security detachments aboard naval stations and bases and other governmental installations. The Marine Corps is also responsible for developing, in coordination with the other military services, the tactics, doctrine, techniques, and equipment employed by landing forces in amphibious operations. Additionally, it prepares for wartime expansion, in accordance with joint mobilization plans, which may require activation of reserve forces when necessary. The Marine Corps mission also encompasses "performing such other duties as the President may direct."

Structure The National Security Act, as amended in 1978, reaffirms the Marine Corps as a separate service within the Department of the Navy and seats the Commandant of the Marine Corps as a full member of the Joint Chiefs of Staff.

The Marine Corps is composed of Operating Forces and a Supporting Establishment. The actual Operating Forces include three active divisions, one reserve division, three active aircraft wings, one reserve aircraft wing, two security force battalions (Atlantic and Pacific), three force service support groups, and one reserve force service support group. The largest of the Operating Forces is the Fleet Marine Force (Pacific), with major subordinate commands located on the west coast and in Hawaii and Japan.

Included under Fleet Marine Force (Pacific) are two Marine divisions, two Marine aircraft wings, and two Force Service Support Groups. In addition, the headquarters of two Marine Expeditionary Forces, two Marine Expeditionary Brigades, and three Marine Expeditionary Units are being permanently formed. The Fleet Marine Force (Atlantic) commands the Operating Forces located on the east coast. These forces consist of a Marine division, a Marine aircraft wing, a supporting Force Service Support Group, the permanent headquarters of a Marine Expeditionary Force, a Marine Expeditionary Brigade, and three Marine Expeditionary Units.

The Marine Corps is organized to fight as Marine Air Ground Task Forces (MAGTF's). There are four basic types of MAGTF's, which are task-organized to support national strategy and combatant CINC crisis response requirements. The range of MAGTF's includes: Marine Expeditionary Forces (MEF's), capable of prosecuting operational campaigns against the most capable adversarial threat; the rapidly deployable and employable Marine Expeditionary Brigades (MEB's); routinely forward deployed Marine Expeditionary Units (MEU's); and smaller Special Purpose Forces formed for specific missions or contingencies. All MAGTF's are task-organized to efficiently maximize combined arms effects through the integration of organic ground and air firepower with maneuver.

Activities The Marine Corps' top priority is combat readiness. Its traditional peacetime role is to serve as a force-in-readiness. The Marine Corps has a global outlook, and Marines stand ready to be deployed to any part of the world to carry out their assigned missions. The Marines emphasize physical fitness and intensive training. The Marine Corps continuously maintains forward deployed MEU's, Special Operations Capability MAGTF's, geo-pre-positioned equipment (Norway), maritime pre-positioned equipment and force elements, air contingency forces, and other MAGTF-deployed forces. The deployment of these forces is executed through the flexible use of strategic and tactical deployment resources.

Marine Corps Districts

District/Address	Telephone
1. 605 Stewart Ave., Garden City, NY 11530-4761	516-228-5652
4. Bldg. 75, Naval Base, Philadelphia, PA 19112-5000	215-897-6301
6. 1365 Peachtree St., NE., Atlanta, GA 30309-3117	404-347-7561
8. Bldg. 10, Naval Support Activity, New Orleans, LA 70146-5100	504-361-2619
9. 10000 W. 75th St., Shawnee Mission, KS 66204-2265	913-236-3302
12. Bldg. 7, Naval Station, Treasure Island, San Francisco, CA 94130-5059	415-765-5901

United States Naval Academy

Annapolis, MD 21402–5018
Phone, 1–800–638–9156 (Office of the Dean of Admissions—Candidate Guidance)

The United States Naval Academy is the undergraduate college of the naval service. Through its comprehensive 4-year program, which stresses excellence in academics, physical education, professional training, conduct, and honor, the Academy prepares young men and women morally, mentally, and physically to be professional officers in the Navy and Marine Corps. All graduates receive a bachelor of science degree in 1 of 18 majors.

For further information concerning the United States Naval Academy, contact the Superintendent, United States Naval Academy, Annapolis, MD 21402–5018.

Sources of Information

Astronomy The United States Naval Observatory provides the astronomical data and precise time required by the Navy and other components of the Department of Defense for navigation, precise positioning, and command, control, and communications. These data also are made available to other Government agencies and to the general public. To broaden the understanding of the mission, functions, and programs of the Naval Observatory, regular night tours and special group day tours are conducted. The night tours are open to the general public and are given every Monday night, except on Federal holidays. Information concerning activities of the observatory and public tours may be obtained by writing to the Superintendent, Naval Observatory, Washington, DC 20392-5100. Phone, 202-653-1543.

Civilian Employment Information about civilian employment opportunities within the Department of the Navy in the Washington, DC, metropolitan area can be obtained from the Office of Civilian Personnel Management, Northeast Region, Washington Detachment, 801 North Randolph Street, Arlington, VA 22203-1927 (phone, 703-696-4567); or the Commandant of the Marine Corps (ARCA), Headquarters, U.S. Marine Corps, Washington, DC 20380 (phone, 703-697-7474).

Consumer Activities Research programs of the Office of the Chief of Naval Research cover a broad spectrum of scientific fields, primarily for the needs of the Navy, but much information is of interest to the public. Inquiries on specific research programs should be directed to the Director, Office of Naval Research, ONR (Code 10), 800 North Quincy Street, Arlington, VA 22217-5000. Phone, 202-696-4517. Inquiries on specific technology programs should be directed to the Director, Office of Naval Technology, ONT (Code 20), 800 North Quincy Street, Arlington, VA 22217-5000. Phone, 202-696-5115.

Contracts and Small Business Activities Information in these areas can be obtained from the Assistant Secretary of the Navy (Installation and Environment), Department of the Navy, Washington, DC 20350 (phone, 703-602-2700); or from the Assistant Secretary of the Navy (Research, Engineering, and Systems), Department of the Navy, The Pentagon, Washington, DC 20350 (phone, 202-695-6315). Information pertaining specifically to the Marine Corps in the areas of small businesses, minority-owned businesses, and labor surplus activities can be obtained from the Marine Corps Small Business Specialist (LS), Installations and Logistics Department, Headquarters, U.S. Marine Corps, Washington, DC 20380. Phone, 703-696-1022.

Environment The Assistant Secretary of the Navy (Installation and Environment) is responsible for the conduct of the environmental protection and natural resources management programs of the Navy and Marine Corps, and serves as the focal point for the Department in establishing policy in environmental affairs. This is the contact for liaison at the highest level with other Federal and State agencies in addition to private agencies organized on a national level. All environmental impact statements that originate within the Navy and Marine Corps for submission to the Environmental Protection Agency, in compliance with the National Environmental Policy Act, are processed by the Assistant Secretary of the Navy (Installation and Environment). This Office maintains close liaison with the Council on Environmental Quality, the Environmental Protection Agency, and the Assistant Secretary of Defense (Production and Logistics) in the implementation of the environmental protection and natural resources management programs. Other responsible offices within the Department of the Navy are the Environmental Protection, Occupational Safety and Health Division in the Office of the Chief of Naval Operations, and the Office of the Deputy Chief of Staff for Installations and Logistics, Headquarters, U.S. Marine Corps.

General Inquiries Navy and Marine Corps recruiting offices, installation commanders, and Directors of Marine Corps Districts (see above) can answer general inquiries concerning the Navy and Marine Corps and their community and public information programs.

Military Career and Training Opportunities

Marine Corps The Marine Corps conducts enlisted and officer training programs requiring various lengths of service and provides the assurance of specialized skill training and other benefits.

The Marine Corps provides opportunities for training in a variety of technical skills that are necessary in support of ground and aviation combat operations. Radar operation and repair, meteorology, engineer equipment and automotive mechanics, artillery and armor repair, data processing, communications-electronics, jet aircraft repair, avionics, and air control are but a few specialized fields available.

The Marine Corps participates in the Naval Reserve Officers Training Corps Program for commissioning officers in the Marine Corps.

Platoon Leaders Class is a Marine Corps program for commissioning officers in the Marine Corps Reserve. Freshmen, sophomores, or juniors in an accredited college may apply. The Program provides financial assistance to undergraduates.

The Officer Candidate Class is another program for commissioning officers in the Marine Corps Reserve. Applicants must be college graduates or in their senior year.

Information on the above programs is available at most civilian educational institutions and Navy and Marine Corps recruiting stations. Local telephone directories list the address and telephone number of the Recruiting Station and Officer Selection Officer under U.S. Government. Interested persons also may write directly to the Commandant of the Marine Corps (M&RA), Washington, DC 20380–0001. Phone, 703–614–2914.

Information concerning Marine Corps Reserve opportunities can be obtained from local Marine Corps recruiting stations or Marine Corps Reserve Drill Centers. Interested persons may also write directly to the Commandant of the Marine Corps (M&RA, RA), Washington, DC 20380–0001.

Speakers and Films Information can be obtained on the following: speakers (phone, 202–697–8711); films (phone, 202–697–0866); and exhibits for Navy recruiting (phone, 202–433–3548). Information concerning the Navy can be obtained by writing the Office of Information, Department of the Navy, Washington, DC 20350 (phone, 202–695–0965); information on how to obtain Marine Corps speakers can be obtained by writing to the Legislative Assistant to the Commandant and Director of Public Affairs, Headquarters, U.S. Marine Corps, Washington, DC 20380–0001; or by contacting the Director of any Marine Corps District.

For further information concerning the Navy and Marine Corps, contact the Office of Information, Department of the Navy, Washington, DC 20350 (phone, 703–697–7391); or the Legislative Assistant to the Commandant and Director of Public Affairs, Headquarters, U.S. Marine Corps, Washington, DC 20380 (phone, 703–614–1492).

DEFENSE AGENCIES

Defense Advanced Research Projects Agency

3701 North Fairfax Drive, Arlington, VA 22203–1714
Phone, 703–614–5469

Director	VICTOR H. REIS
Deputy Director	GARY L. DENMAN
Deputy Director for Management	RONNIE H. REGISTER
General Counsel	RICHARD DUNN
Comptroller	GREG COLOCOTRONIS
Director, Advanced Systems Technology	RONALD MURPHY
Director, Computing Systems Technology	STEPHEN SQUIRES
Director, Contracts Management	R. TIMOTHY ARNOLD
Director, Defense Science	H. LEE BUCHANAN
Director, Electronic Systems Technology	LANCE GLASSER
Director, Land Systems	JAMES RICHARDSON
Director, Microelectronics Technology	ARATI PRABHAKAR
Director, Nuclear Monitoring Research	RALPH W. ALEWINE
Director, Security and Intelligence	ALLEN M. BROWN
Director, Software and Intelligent Systems Technology	BARRY W. BOEHM
Director, Special Projects	DONALD H. FOLEY
Director, Administration and Small Business	BUD DURAND
Director, Undersea Warfare	CHARLES STUART

The Defense Advanced Research Projects Agency is a separately organized agency within the Department of Defense under a Director appointed by the Secretary of Defense. The Agency, under the direction, authority, and control of the Under Secretary of Defense (Acquisition), engages in advanced basic and applied research and development projects essential to the Department of Defense, and conducts prototype projects that embody technology that may be incorporated into joint programs, programs in support of deployed U.S. forces, or selected Military Department programs and, on request, assists the Military Departments in their prototype efforts.

In this regard, the Agency arranges, manages, and directs the performance of work connected with assigned advanced projects by the Military Departments, other government agencies, individuals, private business entities, and educational or research institutions, as appropriate; recommends through the Under Secretary of Defense for Acquisition to the Secretary of Defense assignment of advanced projects to the Agency; keeps the Under Secretary, the Chairman of the Joint Chiefs of Staff, the Military Departments, and other Department of Defense agencies informed on significant new developments and technological advances within assigned projects; and performs other such functions as the Secretary of Defense or the Under Secretary may assign.

For further information, contact the Defense Advanced Research Projects Agency, 3701 North Fairfax Drive, Arlington, VA 22203–1714. Phone, 703–614–5469.

Defense Commissary Agency

Fort Lee, VA 23801–6300

Director	MAJ. GEN. J.P. DRESKA
Deputy Director	ROY C. SPEIGHT
Director, Pentagon Liaison Office	COL. TERRY FOWLER

The Defense Commissary Agency was established by direction of the Secretary of Defense on November 9, 1990, and operates under DOD Directive 5105.55 as a separate agency under the guidance, authority, and control of the Assistant Secretary of Defense (Production and Logistics).

The Agency is responsible for providing an efficient and effective worldwide system of commissaries for reselling groceries and household supplies at low, practical prices (consistent with quality) to members of the Military Services, their families, and other authorized patrons, while maintaining high standards of quality, facilities, products, and service. In addition, DeCA provides a peacetime training environment for food supply logisticians needed in wartime and, as circumstances dictate, troop issue subsistence support to military dining facilities consistent with Service needs.

For further information, contact the Director of Public Affairs, Fort Lee, VA 23801–6300. Phone, 804–734–2513 or –2492.

Defense Contract Audit Agency

Building 4, Cameron Station, Alexandria, VA 22304–6178
Phone, 703–274–6785

Director	WILLIAM H. REED
Deputy Director	FRED J. NEWTON
Executive Officer	PHILLIP E. ROGERS
Special Assistant for Quality	KEN KISHISHITA
General Counsel (Defense Legal Services)	JOHN J. QUILL
Assistant Director, Operations	ROY C. HEIDEMANN
Deputy Assistant Director, Operations	RUSSELL J. RICHARDS
Assistant Director, Policy and Plans	WILLIAM J. SHARKEY
Deputy Assistant Director, Policy and Plans	MICHAEL J. THIBAULT
Assistant Director, Resources	JOHN H. VAN SANTEN, JR.
Deputy Assistant Director, Resources	MICHAEL L. KOZA
Director of Personnel	DALE R. COLLINS
Chief, Financial Management Division	EDWARD J. MIGLIORE

The Defense Contract Audit Agency was established in 1965 and operates under Department of Defense Directive 5105.36 as a separate agency under the direction, authority, and control of the DOD Comptroller.

The Agency performs all necessary contract audit functions for the Department of Defense and provides accounting and financial advisory services to all Defense components responsible for procurement and contract administration. These services are provided in connection with the negotiation, administration, and settlement of contracts and subcontracts. They include evaluating the acceptability of costs claimed or proposed by contractors and reviewing the efficiency and economy of contractor operations. Other Government agencies may request the Agency's services under appropriate arrangements.

The Agency manages its operations through 6 regional offices responsible for approximately 153 field audit offices throughout the United States and overseas. Each region is responsible for the contract auditing function in its assigned area.

Regional Offices—Defense Contract Audit Agency

Region	Address	Director
CENTRAL—Arizona, Arkansas, Illinois, Iowa, Kansas, Minnesota, Missouri, Nebraska, New Mexico, North Dakota, Oklahoma, South Dakota, Texas, Wisconsin, and northern Louisiana	5615 High Point Dr., Suite 701, Irving, TX 75038-2414	(Vacancy)
EASTERN—Alabama, Florida, Georgia, Indiana, Kentucky, Louisiana, Mississippi, North Carolina, Ohio, Tennessee, Virginia, West Virginia, Central America, South America, Bermuda, Puerto Rico and nearby islands, and Mexico	Suite 103, 805 Walker St., Marietta, GA 30060-2731	Harvey Della Bernarda
MID-ATLANTIC—Delaware, District of Columbia, Maryland, southern New York, Pennsylvania, and northern Virginia	Rm. 4400, 4th Fl., 600 Arch St., Philadelphia, PA 19106-1604	William Kraft
NORTHEASTERN—Connecticut, Maine, Massachusetts, New Hampshire, Rhode Island, Vermont, Michigan (excluding the Upper Peninsula), northern New York, Africa and adjacent islands, Europe and adjacent islands, the Middle East and adjacent islands, Greenland, and Iceland	83 Hartwell Ave., Lexington, MA 02173-3163	Bernard Topf
SOUTHWESTERN—southern California	Suite 300, 16700 Valley View Ave., La Mirada, CA 90638-5830	Joel Valenzuela
WESTERN—Alaska, Colorado, Hawaii, Idaho, Montana, Nevada, Oregon, Utah, Washington, Wyoming, northern California, Pacific Ocean and Asian islands, Asia (excluding the Middle East), and Australia	Box 36116, 450 Golden Gate Ave., San Francisco, CA 94102-3563	Robert Matter

For further information, contact the Executive Officer, Defense Contract Audit Agency, Cameron Station, Alexandria, VA 22304–6178. Phone, 703–274–7319. Information regarding employment may be obtained from the regional offices.

Defense Finance and Accounting Service

Room 507, Crystal Mall 3, Arlington, VA 22202–4302
Phone, 703–695–5092

Director	ALBERT V. CONTE
Principal Deputy Director	JOHN P. SPRINGETT

The Defense Finance and Accounting Service was established by direction of the Secretary of Defense on November 26, 1990, and operates under DOD Directive 5118.5 as a separate agency under the guidance, authority, and control of the Comptroller of the Department of Defense.

The Service is responsible for standardizing financial and accounting information that will be accurate, comprehensive, and timely. To accomplish this, the Director of the Service shall direct finance and accounting requirements, systems, and functions for all appropriated, nonappropriated, working capital, revolving, and trust fund activities, including security assistance; establish and enforce requirements, principles, standards, systems, procedures, and practices necessary to comply with finance and accounting statutory and regulatory requirements applicable to DOD; provide finance and accounting services for DOD components and other Federal activities, as designated by the Comptroller of DOD; and, direct the consolidation, standardization, and integration of finance and accounting requirements, functions, procedures, operations, and systems within DOD to ensure their proper relationship with other DOD functional areas, such as budget, personnel, logistics, acquisition, and civil engineering.

For further information, contact the Public Affairs Office, Room 507, Crystal Mall 3, Arlington, VA 22202–4302. Phone, 703–695–5092.

Defense Information Systems Agency

Eighth Street and South Courthouse Road, Arlington, VA 22204
Phone, 703–692–9012

Director	LT. GEN. THURMAN D. RODGERS, USA
Vice Director	REAR ADM. ARLINGTON T. CAMPBELL, USN
Associate Director	DAVID T. SIGNORI
Chief of Staff	COL. EDWARD J. HENDERSON, USAF
General Counsel	M. SUSAN CHADICK
Chief Regulatory Counsel—Telecommunications (DOD)	CARL W. SMITH
Director, Equal Employment Office	GWENDOLYN V. BOWDEN
Director, Office of Small and Disadvantaged Business Utilization	GLEN C. MOORE
Chief, Vision 21/Total Quality Management Office	JAMES E. TATE
Director, Center for Agency Services	MICHAEL F. SLAWSON
Comptroller	GEORGE J. HOFFMAN
Director, Defense Network Systems Organization	BRIG. GEN. DENNIS BEASLEY, USAF
Director, Defense Systems Support Organization	E.W. HARDING
Deputy Manager, National Communications System	BENHAM E. MORRISS
Chief Information Officer	SARAH J. LEAGUE
Director, Acquisition Management Organization	DENNIS W. GROH
Director, Joint Tactical Command, Control, and Communications Agency	BRIG. GEN. RICHARD J. MALLION, USA
Director, Center for Information Management	DENIS BROWN

The Defense Communications Agency, established by direction of the Secretary of Defense on May 12, 1960, was renamed the Defense Information Systems Agency (DISA) by DOD Directive 5105.19 dated June 25, 1991. It is a combat support agency of the Department of Defense under the direction, authority, and control of the Assistant Secretary of Defense (Command, Control, Communications, and Intelligence). Guidance with regard to military and communications doctrine, operational policies, requirements, and procedures is furnished to the Director of the Agency by the Chairman of the Joint Chiefs of Staff.

The Agency is organized into a headquarters and field activities acting for the Director in assigned areas of responsibility. The field organizations include the White House Communications Agency; the Joint Tactical Command, Control, and Communications Agency; and the Defense Commercial Communications Office.

The mission of DISA is to:

—perform systems engineering for the Defense Communications System and ensure that it is planned, improved, operated, maintained, and managed effectively and efficiently;

—exercise program management responsibility over the activities of the Department of Defense Components that directly support the establishment and progressive improvement of the Communications System;

—provide technical and management advice and perform planning support, system engineering, and test and/or evaluation support through the design, development, deployment, and evolutionary phases of the Worldwide Military Command and Control System, which includes the National Military Command System and supporting communications, and manage, design, develop, maintain, test, and evaluate standard operating systems and applications software for the System;

—formulate the departmentwide Military Satellite Communications architecture and define system performance criteria for the systems;

—analyze user requirements and maintain the user data base;

—ensure the end-to-end interoperability of strategic and tactical command, control, and communications (C^3) and information systems used by the National Command Authority, Commanders-in-Chief, Military Departments, and Agencies for joint and combined operations through the development and maintenance of joint architectures, technical and procedural interface standards, specifications, protocols, and definitions, and through testing and/or verifying the interoperability of hardware and procedures;

—provide automated information systems, analytical, and other technical support for programs managed by the Chairman of the Joint Chiefs of Staff and the Office of the Secretary of Defense;

—assist in implementing configuration control over evolving information systems;

—develop systems architectures, provide systems engineering support, and conduct operational test and evaluation to ensure the evolution of integrated C^3 and information systems supporting the National Command Authority, Commanders-in-Chief, Services and Agencies to effectively employ weapon systems and forces;

—acquire commercial information systems services (e.g., long-haul C^3 circuits, facilities, networks, and associated equipment) for the Department of Defense and other Federal agencies as directed;

—initiate and manage actions relating to regulatory and tariff matters, including rates for communications services acquired by Department of Defense, and maintain the Communications Services Industrial Fund;

—execute tasks as Manager of the National Communications System as may be assigned by law or directed by the Secretary of Defense as Executive Agent for the System; and

—support national security emergency preparedness telecommunications functions of the National Communications System as prescribed by Executive Order 12472.

For further information, contact the Director, Defense Information Systems Agency, Eighth Street and South Courthouse Road, Arlington, VA 22204. Phone, 703–692–0018.

Defense Intelligence Agency

The Pentagon, Washington, DC 20340–0001
Phone, 703–695–7353

Director	LT. GEN. HARRY E. SOYSTER, USA
Executive Officer	COL. FRANCIS P. KEOUGH, USA
Executive Director	DENNIS M. NAGY

The Defense Intelligence Agency was established by DOD Directive 5105.21, effective October 1, 1961, under provisions of the National Security Act of 1947, as amended (50 U.S.C. 401 *et seq.*). The Agency operates under the direction, authority, and control of the Assistant Secretary of Defense (Command, Control, Communications and Intelligence). Additionally, the Agency's Director reports to the Chairman of the Joint Chiefs of Staff for the specific purposes of providing the military intelligence support required to perform their statutory and assigned responsibilities and of ensuring that the necessary intelligence support is available to the Unified and Specified Commands.

Under its Director, the Agency is responsible for producing and disseminating military intelligence to satisfy the intelligence requirements of the Secretary of Defense, the Chairman of the Joint Chiefs of Staff, major components of the Department of Defense, and other authorized requirements. It accomplishes this either by use of internal resources; through the management, control, and coordination of the intelligence functions of other Department activities; or through cooperation with other intelligence agencies.

The Agency provides military intelligence for U.S. foreign intelligence and counterintelligence products and staff support to the Chairman of the Joint Chiefs of Staff. It reviews and coordinates those Department intelligence functions retained by or assigned to the Military Departments. It also develops guidance for the conduct and management of such functions for review, approval, and promulgation by the Secretary of Defense.

For further information, contact the Defense Intelligence Agency, The Pentagon, Washington, DC 20340–1030. Phone, 703–695–7353.

Defense Investigative Service

Buzzard's Point, 1900 Half Street SW., Washington, DC 20324–1700
Phone, 202–475–0966

Director	JOHN F. DONNELLY
Special Assistant to the Director	WILLARD J. ISAACS, JR.
Deputy Director, Investigations	THOMAS E. EWALD
Deputy Director, Industrial Security	GREGORY GWASH
Deputy Director, Resources	MICHAEL G. NEWMAN

Inspector General	JAMES R. CONNOLLY
Chief, Information and Public Affairs	DALE L. HARTIG
Deputy Director, Information Systems and Planning	MELVIN B. DEGUZMAN
General Counsel	THOMAS N. WILLESS
Chief, Office of Security	JAMES L. PACKETT
Director, Personnel Investigations Center (Holabird Industrial Park, Baltimore, MD 21203–1211)	WILLIAM A. HUGHES, *Acting*
Director, Defense Industrial Security Clearance Office (Columbus, OH 43216–5006)	THOMAS J. RAINSFORD
Director of Equal Employment Opportunity, Office of Affirmative Action, and Equal Opportunity Policy	WARREN A. HEMPHILL, SR.

The Defense Investigative Service was established by the Secretary of Defense, effective January 1, 1972. The Service is chartered by Department of Defense Directive 5105.42, dated June 14, 1985, and operates under the direction, authority, and control of the Deputy Under Secretary of Defense for Policy.

The Service consists of a Headquarters, two Operations Centers, eight regional offices and their subordinate field offices and resident agencies located in the 50 States and Puerto Rico, the Office of Industrial Security, International-Europe, in Brussels, Belgium, and Mannheim, Federal Republic of Germany; and the Office of Industrial Security, International-Far East, in Yokohama, Japan, and Seoul, Korea.

The Service conducts all personnel security investigations for Department components and, when authorized, also conducts investigations for other U.S. Government activities. These include investigation of allegations of subversive affiliations, adverse suitability information, or any other situation that requires resolution to complete the personnel security investigation.

The Service is responsible for the three major programs involving industrial security: the Defense Industrial Security Program for Safeguarding Classified Information; the Key Assets Protection Program; and the Defense Sensitive Conventional Arms, Ammunition and Explosives Security Program.

The Service also manages the Defense Clearance and Investigations Index, a centralized list of all Defense components investigative files, and security clearance information pertaining to Department of Defense personnel.

Regional Offices—Defense Investigative Service

City	Director
Alexandria, VA 22331–1000	Charles A. Baldwin
Boston, MA 02210–2192	James B. Witkowski, Jr.
Cherry Hill, NJ 08034–1908	John N. Held
Chicago, IL 60607–4577	W. Graham Bell, Jr.
Irving, TX 75062	James S. Rogner
Long Beach, CA 90807–4013	David L. McDonald
San Francisco, CA 94129–7700	Alfred W. Hazen
Smyrna, GA 30080–7606	Joan J. Turner

For further information, contact the Chief, Office of Information and Public Affairs, Defense Investigative Service, 1900 Half Street SW., Washington, DC 20324–1700. Phone, 202–475–1062.

Defense Legal Services Agency

The Pentagon, Washington, DC 20301–1600
Phone, 703–695–3341

Director (General Counsel, Department of Defense)	TERRENCE O'DONNELL
Deputy Director (Deputy General Counsel)	LEONARD NIEDERLEHNER
Administrative Officer	ELIZABETH H. WHEELER
Director for Industrial Security Clearance Review	LEON J. SCHACHTER
Chief, Department Counsel	ROBERT S. BRADY
Director, Standards of Conduct Office	DAVID W. REAM
Director, Legislative Reference Service	SAMUEL BRICK

The Defense Legal Services Agency was established by Department of Defense Directive 5145.4, dated August 12, 1981. The Agency is under the direction, authority, and control of the General Counsel of the Department of Defense, who also serves as its Director.

The Agency provides legal advice and services for the Office of the Secretary of Defense, its field activities, and the Defense agencies. It provides technical support and assistance for development of the Department's Legislative program; coordinates positions on legislation and Presidential Executive orders; provides a centralized legislative and congressional document reference and distribution point for the Department; and maintains the Department's historical legislative files. The Agency administers the Defense Industrial Security Clearance Review program and the Standards of Conduct Ethics program.

For further information, contact the Administrative Officer, Defense Legal Services Agency, The Pentagon, Washington, DC 20301–1600. Phone, 703–697–8343.

Defense Logistics Agency

Cameron Station, Alexandria, VA 22304–6100
Phone, 703–274–6000 or –6001

Director	LT. GEN. C. MCCAUSLAND, USAF
Deputy Director	REAR ADM. B.M. COLE, SC, USN
Deputy Director, Acquisition Management	MAJ. GEN. C.R. HENRY, USA
Commander, Defense Contract Management Command	MAJ. GEN. C.R. HENRY, USA
Chief of Staff	COL. F.J. HACKLEMAN, USAF
Executive/Secretariat	LT. COL. W. ARBACAS, JR., USMC
Assistant Director, Policy and Plans	ROGER C. ROY
Deputy	CHRISTINE L. GALLO
Assistant Director, Telecommunications and Information Systems	T.J. KNAPP
Deputy	B.L. PARSONS
Staff Director, Public Affairs	LARRY J. WILSON
Staff Director, Congressional Affairs	G.C. FLESSATE
General Counsel	KARL W. KABEISEMAN

Deputy General Counsel	G.P. Quigley
Staff Director, Contracting Integrity	J.C. Cook
Comptroller	R.J. Connelly
Deputy Comptroller	H.T. McCoy
Command Security Officer	Col. H.J. Lenius, USA
Staff Director, Administration	Col. G.C. Tucker, USA
Deputy	R.A. Martinez
Staff Director, Civilian Personnel	Anthony W. Hudson
Deputy	A.C. Ressler
Staff Director, Military Personnel	Col. J.D. Winkelmann, USAF
Staff Director, Installation Services and Environmental Protection	Col. W.R. Andrews, Jr., USA
Staff Director, Small and Disadvantaged Business Utilization	L.C. Alderman
Deputy	S.C. Mitchell, *Acting*
Executive Director, Supply Operations	Rear Adm. J.P. Davidson, SC, USN
Deputy	James J. Grady, Jr.
Executive Director, Contracting	Raymond F. Chiesa
Deputy	Capt. H.O. Ruppmann, SC, USN
Executive Director, Technical and Logistics Services	H.A. Filippi
Deputy	Col. T.A. Klimas, USAF
Executive Director, Contract Management	William V. Gordon
Deputy	Capt. J.R. McNabnay, SC, USN
Executive Director, Quality Assurance	Brig. Gen. R.E. McCoy, USA
Deputy	E.D. Ellis
Executive Director, Program and Technical Support	Rear Adm. D.E. Hickman, SC, USN

The Defense Logistics Agency was established by the Secretary of Defense and operates under Department of Defense Directive 5105.22. The Agency is under the direction of the Under Secretary of Defense for Acquisition, and is subject to Department policies, directives, and instructions.

The Agency consists of a Director, a Deputy Director, a Deputy Director for Acquisition Management, a Headquarters establishment, and 23 primary level field activities and their subordinate activities. Some of the subordinate activities of the Defense Fuel Supply Center, the Defense Reutilization and Marketing Service, and the Defense Personnel Support Center operate in overseas areas. There also are a number of Headquarters management support offices that are controlled by Headquarters staff elements.

The mission of the Agency, as a combat support agency, is to provide effective and efficient worldwide logistic support to the Military Departments and the Unified and Specified Commands under conditions of peace or war, as well as to other Department of Defense components, Federal civilian agencies, foreign governments, and international organizations as assigned.

The Agency provides logistics services directly associated with furnishing materiel commodities and items of supply that have been determined to be appropriate for integrated management by a single agency on behalf of all Defense components or that have been otherwise specifically assigned. It administers departmentwide logistics management systems, programs, and activities, as assigned, including the provision of technical assistance, support services, and information.

Under the direction, authority, and operational control of its Director, the Agency is responsible for the performance of the following major functions:

—materiel management, including item management classification; cataloging; requirements determination; supply control; procurement; quality assurance; industrial responsiveness and mobilization planning; receipt, storage, inventory accountability, and distribution control; transportation; maintenance and manufacture; shelflife control; provisioning; technical logistics data and information; engineering support; value engineering; standardization; reutilization and marketing; and management of the strategic reserves;

—contract administration services provided in support of the Military Departments and other Department components, the National Aeronautics and Space Administration, other designated Federal and State agencies, foreign governments, and international organizations;

—operation of management information and technical report data banks; oversight of the management of contractor-operated Department Information Analysis Centers in selected fields of science and technology; and provision of scientific and technical information to Defense components, individuals, businesses, educational institutions, government laboratories and contractors, and others, consistent with policy guidance provided by the Director of Defense Research and Engineering;

—monitoring Defense supply relationships with the General Services Administration, performing systems analysis and design, procedural development, and maintenance for supply and service systems and other logistics matters assigned by the Secretary of Defense; and

—administering assigned Department of Defense programs including the Coordinated Procurement Program; Federal Catalog System; Industrial Plant Equipment; operating Military Parts Control Advisory Groups for standardization of parts at the system equipment design stage; Defense Automatic Addressing System; Defense Precious Metals Recovery; assigned aspects of Food Service Management; Defense Procurement Management Review; Defense Energy Information System; Centralized Referral System; Overseas Employment Referral; Automation Resources Management System; Depot Maintenance and Maintenance Support Cost Accounting and Production Reporting Information System; Shelflife Item Management; Scientific and Technical Information; Information Analysis Center; Hazardous Materials Information System; Hazardous Material Technology Development; Personal Property Utilization and Disposal; Industrial Resources Management; Integrated Material Manager for Bulk Petroleum; Specification Standardization; and the Defense National Stockpile.

Defense Contract Management Command The Defense Contract Management Command (DCMC) was established as a Defense Logistics Agency major subordinate Command reporting to the Director of the Agency, effective February 6, 1990. The Commander of DCMC is responsible for contract administration services currently performed worldwide by both the Agency and the military departments. Those services include contract management support, program and technical support, contractor payments, and quality assurance. Also, the Commander is authorized to organize, direct, manage, and control all functions and resources assigned to DCMC.

Primary Level Field Activities

Supply Centers The six supply centers are responsible for materiel management of assigned commodities and items of supply relating to food, clothing, textiles, medical, chemical, petroleum, industrial, construction, electronics, and general items. The Defense Fuel Supply Center is also responsible for contracting for commercial petroleum services and coal, as well as all crude oil and petroleum products for the Strategic Petroleum Reserve. Two of the supply centers have depots at the same location: Defense Depot Columbus is located with the Defense Construction Supply Center, and

Defense Depot Richmond is located with the Defense General Supply Center.

For further information, call 703–274–6000 or –6001.

Service Centers The seven service centers furnish varied support services as follows:

The Defense Logistics Services Center is responsible for maintenance of the Federal Cataloging System records including the development and dissemination of cataloging and item intelligence data to the Military Departments and other authorized customers.

The Defense Industrial Plant Equipment Center is responsible for the Department of Defense General Reserve of industrial plant equipment. The Center maintains visibility records of all Department equipment in use by government facilities and contractors and provides specified supply support of industrial plant equipment to the Military Departments.

The Defense Technical Information Center is responsible for the development, maintenance, and operation of the management information system in the field of scientific and technical information; acquisition, storage, announcement, retrieval, and provision of secondary distribution of scientific and technical reports; and primary distribution of foreign technical reports.

The Agency's Administrative Support Center provides administrative support and common service functions to Agency activities within the Washington, DC, metropolitan area.

The Defense Reutilization and Marketing Service is responsible for the integrated management of worldwide personal property disposal operations, including reutilization of serviceable assets, in support of the Military Departments and other authorized customers.

The Agency's Systems Automation Center is responsible for the operational execution of the Agency's Automated Data Processing and Telecommunications Programs.

The Defense National Stockpile Center is responsible for acquiring, upgrading, rotating, and disposing of stockpile materials. The Center conducts operations including storage, security, testing, contracting and quality studies, maintenance, and replacement of materials in the Defense National Stockpile. The Center directs the development of new or revised specifications and special instructions for existing and proposed strategic and critical materials to be stockpiled.

For further information, call 703–274–6000 or –6001.

Depots These activities are responsible for depot operations functions for assigned commodities.

Districts The five Defense Contract Management districts provide contract administration services including the performance of contract administration, production, quality assurance, and data and financial management activities, and small business/labor surplus programs, within the United States and such external areas as specifically authorized. A sixth district, Defense Contract Management Command International, is located in Dayton, OH, and performs the contract management function worldwide. These districts report to the newly established Defense Contract Management Command.

For further information, call 703–274–6000 or –6001.

Primary Level Field Activities—Defense Logistics Agency

Activity	Commander
DEFENSE SUPPLY CENTERS:	
Defense Construction Supply Center	Brig. Gen. R.A. Browning, USAF
Defense Electronics Supply Center	Brig. Gen. J.W. Oster
Defense Fuel Supply Center	Brig. Gen. J.E. Bickford, USA
Defense General Supply Center	Rear Adm. P.A. Bondi, SC, USN
Defense Industrial Supply Center	Brig. Gen. D.L. Walsh, USAF
Defense Personnel Support Center	Col. J.J. Cusick, USA

Primary Level Field Activities—Defense Logistics Agency—Continued

Activity	Commander
DEFENSE SERVICE CENTERS:	
Defense Technical Information Center	K.N. Molholm [1]
Defense Industrial Plant Equipment Center	Capt. D.W. Hall, SC, USN
Defense Logistics Services Center	Col. G. Kobernus, USAF
Defense Reutilization and Marketing Service	Col. R. Agnor, USAF
DLA Administrative Support Center	Col. G.C. Tucker, USA
DLA Systems Automation Center	Capt. D.J. Quirk, SC, USN
Defense National Stockpile Center	R.M. O'Brien, *Acting*
DEFENSE DEPOTS:	
Defense Distribution Region East	Col. T.W. Baker, USA
Defense Depot Memphis	Col. W.F. Murphy, USMC
Defense Depot Ogden	Capt. C.D. Correll, SC, USN
Defense Distribution Region West	Col. J.W. LaBounty, USA
Secondary Level Field Activities	
Defense Depot Columbus	Col. W.E. George, Jr., USAF
Defense Depot Richmond	Col. C.K. Childers, QM, USA
DEFENSE CONTRACT MANAGEMENT DISTRICTS:	
South	Col. V.G. Grosse, USAF
Northeast	Col. J.F. Cashman, USAF
North Central	Col. F.B. Holland, USA
West	Brig. Gen. K.G. Miller, USAF
Mid-Atlantic	Maj. Gen. H.C. Kammer, USA
Defense Contract Management Command International	Capt. L. Vincent, SC, USN

[1] Administrator

Sources of Information

Consumer Activities Any questions concerning this program or placement on the Department of Defense bidders list should be addressed to DOD Surplus Sales, P.O. Box 1370, Battle Creek, MI 49016. Phone, 616–962–6511, extension 6736 or 6737.

Employment For the Washington, DC, metropolitan area, inquiries and applications should be addressed to Defense Logistics Agency, DLA Administrative Support Center, Attn: DASC–KS, Room 6–214, Cameron Station, Alexandria, VA 22304–6100. Phone, 703–274–6041. For other areas, contact the local DLA field activity.

The Agency has a college recruitment program. Schools interested in participating should direct inquiries to Defense Logistics Agency, Attn: DLA–KS, Room 3D224, Cameron Station, Alexandria, VA 22304–6100. Phone, 703–274–6040.

Environment For information concerning the Agency's program, contact Defense Logistics Agency, Attn: DLA–WS, Room 4D415, Cameron Station, Alexandria, VA 22304–6100. Phone, 703–274–0995.

Films For information on films available for public showing, contact Headquarters, Defense Logistics Agency, Attn: DASC–T, Room 3C547, Cameron Station, Alexandria, VA 22304–6100. Phone, 703–274–6185.

Procurement and Small Business Activities For information, contact Staff Director, Small and Disadvantaged Business Utilization (DLA–U), Room 4B110, Cameron Station, Alexandria, VA 22304–6100. Phone, 703–274–6471.

Publications *An Identification of Commodities Purchased by the Defense Logistics Agency* is available free of charge from the Staff Director, Small and Disadvantaged Business Utilization (DLA–U), above address.

Reading Room Defense Logistics Agency Library, Room 4D120, Cameron Station, Alexandria, VA 22304–6100. Phone, 703–274–6055.

For further information, contact the Executive Officer, Defense Logistics Agency, Room 3A150, Cameron Station, Alexandria, VA 22304–6100. Phone, 703–274–6115.

Defense Mapping Agency

8613 Lee Highway, Fairfax, VA 22031–2139
Phone, 703–285–9368

Director	Maj. Gen. William K. James, USAF
Deputy Director	Brig. Gen. Joseph Pratt, USA
Deputy Director for Management and Technology	Penman R. Gilliam
Scientific Advisor for Hydrography	James E. Ayres
Chief of Staff	Col. Charles M. Rose, USAF, *Acting*
General Counsel	Edward J. Obloy
Public Affairs Officer	David L. Black
Inspector General	Col. Raymond L. Abrahamson, USAF
Deputy Director, Plans and Requirements Directorate	D.R. Barrowman
Deputy Director, Programs/Production and Operations Directorate	William N. Hogan
Deputy Director, Research and Engineering Directorate	Kenneth I. Daugherty
Deputy Director, Information Systems Directorate	Bill E. Robinson
Deputy Director, Transition Management Directorate	John P. Mendez
Comptroller	John Vaughn
Deputy Director, Human Resources Directorate	Curt L. Dierdorff
Director, Security Office	Stephen Earle
Director, Administration Office	Maj. S.D. Walker, USAF
Deputy Director, Acquisitions, Installations and Logistics Directorate	Mordecai Z. Labovitz
Protocol Officer	Margaret M. Burke

The Defense Mapping Agency (DMA) was established in 1972, when mapping, charting, and geodesy functions of the Defense Community were combined into this joint Department of Defense agency. The Agency operates as a combat support agency of DOD under the direction, authority, and control of the Assistant Secretary of Defense for Command, Control, Communications, and Intelligence.

The mission of the Agency is to:

—enhance national security and support the Office of the Secretary of Defense, the Chairman of the Joint Chiefs of Staff, Unified and Specified Commands, Military Departments, and other users, by producing and distributing timely and tailored mapping, charting, and geodetic products, services, and training, and advising on such matters;

—provide nautical charts and marine navigational data to worldwide merchant marine and private vessel operators; and

—maintain liaison with civil agencies and other national and international mapping, charting, and geodetic activities.

The Defense Mapping Agency has some 8,500 employees in more than 50 locations around the world.

Agency Components

The mapping, charting, and geodesy functions of the Agency are principally conducted by its two major production Centers. Aerospace products and support to aerospace manned and unmanned

290-950 O 91 - 9

weapons systems are provided to Department of Defense users primarily by the DMA Aerospace Center, which is located in St. Louis, MO. The DMA Hydrographic/Topographic Center, located in Brookmont, MD, primarily provides nautical products, topographic products, land combat support, and support to ground weapons and naval weapons systems.

A third production center, the DMA Reston Center, located in Reston, VA, was established in 1987. The Center will increase the volume of mapping, charting and geodetic products and data currently being produced by the Aerospace and Hydrographic/Topographic Centers.

The DMA Systems Center, located in Fairfax, VA, is responsible for advancing the capability of producing Agency products using softcopy or computerized production techniques.

The DMA Combat Support Center is primarily responsible for the distribution of Agency products to the Unified and Specified Commands, as well as other military and civilian users. Its headquarters is located in Brookmont, MD.

The Defense Mapping School, located at Fort Belvoir, VA, is responsible for providing personnel of the Army, Navy, Air Force, Marine Corps, and other Government agencies with training in all aspects of mapping, charting, and geodesy.

The DMA Technical Services Center, located in Fairfax, VA, provides overall operational direction and management supervision of Agency Telecommunications Systems and operates and maintains the long-haul systems linking major production centers and field activities.

Components—Defense Mapping Agency

Activity	Director
DMA Aerospace Center (3200 S. 2d St., St. Louis, MO 63118-3399)	Col. Marcus J. Boyle, USAF
DMA Combat Support Center (Washington, DC 20315-0010)	Capt. Craig A. Peterson, USN
DMA Hydrographic/Topographic Center (Washington, DC 20315-0030)	Col. Robert F. Kirby, USA
DMA Technical Services Center (Fairfax, VA 22031-2139)	Bill E. Robinson
DMA Reston Center (Reston, VA 22091-3414)	Col. Peter G. O'Neill, USA
DMA Systems Center (Fairfax, VA 22031-2138)	Kenneth I. Daugherty
Defense Mapping School (Fort Belvoir, VA 22060-5828)	Col. Samuel R. Schwartz, USA

Sources of Information

Contracts and Small Business Activities For information, contact the Small and Disadvantaged Business Utilization Office, Acquisition Office, Defense Mapping Agency, Building 56, U.S. Naval Observatory, Washington, DC 20305-3000. Phone, 202-653-1016.

Employment General employment applications and inquiries should be addressed to the following Personnel Offices:

Defense Mapping Agency: Attn: HRWAQ, 8613 Lee Highway, Fairfax, VA 22031-2137. Phone, 703-285-9461.

DMA Aerospace Center: Attn: PO, 3200 South Second Street, St. Louis, MO 63118-3399. Phone, 314-263-4965.

DMA Hydrographic/Topographic Center: Attn: PO, 6500 Brookes Lane, Washington, DC 20315-0030. Phone, 202-227-2050.

Public Sale of Maps and Charts The Agency produces aeronautical and hydrographic charts and topographic maps of foreign areas. For information on ordering products, contact the DMA Combat Support Center: Attn: PMA, Washington, DC 20315-0020. Phone, 202-227-2495 or toll-free, 1-800-826-0342.

Aeronautical products available to the public are listed in the *Defense Mapping Agency Aeronautical Public Sale Catalog,* which is free of charge.

Nautical charts available to the public and a list of DMA-authorized sales agents are included in the *DMA Catalog of Maps, Charts, and Related Products, Part 2—Hydrographic Products* (Volumes I-X). Detailed ordering instructions, as well as the sales agents list, are found in Volume X, *Miscellaneous and Special Purpose Navigational Charts, Sheets and Tables.* These volumes are available for $2.75 each.

Topographic maps available to the public are listed in the *Defense Mapping Agency Public Sale Catalog,* which is free of charge.

Domestic aeronautical charts are produced by the National Ocean Service and may be purchased from NOS sales agents established at the principal civil airports.

Nautical charts of coastal waterways of the continental United States, Hawaii, Alaska, and U.S. territories may be purchased from: National Ocean Service, Distribution Branch (N-CG33), Riverdale, MD 20737-1199. Phone, 301-436-6990.

Topographic maps of the continental United States and Hawaii may be purchased from: U.S. Geological Survey, Federal Center, P.O. Box 25286, Denver, CO 80255. Phone, 303-236-7477.

Defense Nuclear Agency

Washington, DC 20305-1000
Phone, 202-325-7095

Director	MAJ. GEN. GERALD G. WATSON, USA
Deputy Director	GEORGE W. ULLRICH
Chief of Staff	J.M. BACHKOSKY
Director, Operations Directorate	MAJ. GEN. WALTER E. WEBB, USAF
Director, Radiation Sciences Directorate	JOAN MA PIERRE
Director, Shock Physics Directorate	(VACANCY)
Director, Test Directorate	DON A. LINGER
Director, Command Services Directorate	CAPT. E. WILLIAM BALLER, USN
Director, Aquisition Management Office	DAVID G. FREEMAN
Equal Employment Opportunity Manager	NATHANIEL WILLIAMS
Inspector General	CAPT. G.M. ZORBACH, USN
Public Affairs Officer	LT. COL. JAY A. CRAIG, USA
General Counsel	ROBERT L. BRITTIGAN
Comptroller	PAUL H. CAREW
Director, Armed Forces Radiobiology Research Institute (Bethesda, MD 20014-5000)	COL. GEORGE W. IRVING III, USAF
Commander, Field Command	REAR ADM. MACK C. GASTON, USN

The Defense Nuclear Agency is responsible for developing nuclear weapon effects technology, expertise, and testing capabilities that are the foundation for the survivability and effectiveness of our deterrent forces. The authority for the Agency's activities is included in DOD Directive 5105.31. The Agency operates under the direction, authority, and control of the Director, Defense Research and Engineering.

Agency activities are focused on nuclear weapon effects research and testing. Emphasis is placed on developing technology to harden materials, electronics, structures, and man against blast, thermal, nuclear radiation, and other secondary nuclear effects. The Agency also develops simulation techniques to evaluate nuclear hardness and conducts DOD's underground nuclear tests to investigate nuclear weapons effects. The Agency advises the Assistant to the Secretary of Defense (Atomic Energy) on the adequacy of military service hardening programs for acquisition of major systems.

The Agency is the central DOD agency for coordination of nuclear weapons development and initial testing with the Department of Energy. It manages the Department of Defense nuclear weapons stockpile and its associated report system, conducts nuclear surety inspections, and provides logistical support for nuclear weapons in the field. The Agency provides emergency response support in the event of a nuclear weapons accident or incident, and also conducts technical investigations and field tests to enhance the safety and security of theater nuclear forces. In addition, it provides advice and assistance to the Chairman of the Joint Chiefs of Staff and the Military Departments on all nuclear matters, including site security, tactics, vulnerability, radiation effects, and biomedical effects. The Agency provides support to the Strategic Defense Initiative Organization, particularly in the areas of lethality, survivability, target hardening, and pulse power technology. The Agency also develops the technology necessary to verify arms control treaties through on-site inspection.

The Agency's headquarters is located at 6801 Telegraph Road in Alexandria, VA. The Field Command is at Kirtland Air Force Base, NM, and the Armed Forces Radiobiology Research Institute is in Bethesda, MD. The Agency retains management of Johnston Atoll in the Pacific to ensure its availability as a test site.

Sources of Information

Employment Inquiries should be directed as follows:

Headquarters—Defense Nuclear Agency, Attn: CVHR, 6801 Telegraph Road, Alexandria, VA 22310–2298. Phone, 703–325–7591.

Field Command—1606 Air Base Wing, Attn: MSSQ/MSC, Kirtland Air Force Base, NM 87115–5000. Phone, 505–844–9282 or 9281.

Armed Forces Radiobiology Research Institute—Attn: CPO, Bethesda, MD 20814–5000. Phone, 301–295–1426.

Procurement and Small Business Activities Contact the Defense Nuclear Agency, Attn: AM, 6801 Telegraph Road, Alexandria, VA 22310–3398. Phone, 703–325–5021.

For further information, contact the Public Affairs Office, Defense Nuclear Agency, 6801 Telegraph Road, Alexandria, VA 22310–3398. Phone, 703–325–7095.

Defense Security Assistance Agency

The Pentagon, Washington, DC 20301–2800
Phone, 703–695–3291

Director	Lt. Gen. Teddy G. Allen, USA
Deputy Director	Glenn A. Rudd
Comptroller	James R. Woods
Director for Operations	H. Diehl McKalip
Director for Plans	Diane L. Blundell
General Counsel	Jerome Silber
Director, Congressional Relations	Lt. Col. Carla Stucki, USAF

The Defense Security Assistance Agency was established on September 1, 1971, by DOD Directive 5105.38, dated August 11, 1971. The Agency operates under the direction, authority, and control of the Under Secretary of Defense for Policy.

The Agency directs, administers, and supervises the execution of approved security assistance plans and programs, such as military assistance, international military education and training, and foreign military sales. In so doing, it works closely with the U.S. Security Assistance offices worldwide.

For further information, contact the Defense Security Assistance Agency, The Pentagon, Washington, DC 20301–2800. Phone, 703–695–3291.

National Security Agency/Central Security Service

Fort George G. Meade, MD 20755–6000
Phone, 301–688–6311

Director	VICE ADM. WILLIAM O. STUDEMAN, USN
Deputy Director	ROBERT L. PRESTEL

The National Security Agency/Central Security Service is responsible for the centralized coordination, direction, and performance of highly specialized technical functions in support of U.S. Government activities to protect U.S. communications and produce foreign intelligence information. The National Security Agency was established by Presidential directive in 1952 as a separately organized agency within the Department of Defense. In this directive, the President designated the Secretary of Defense Executive Agent for the signals intelligence and communications security activities of the Government. The Agency was charged with an additional mission, computer security, in a 1984 Presidential directive, and with an operations security training mission in a 1988 Presidential directive.

In 1972 the Central Security Service was established, in accordance with a Presidential memorandum, to provide a more unified cryptologic organization within the Department of Defense and appointed the Director, National Security Agency, as Chief of the Central Security Service.

The Agency has three primary missions: an information systems security mission, an operations security training mission, and a foreign intelligence information mission. To accomplish these missions, the Director has been assigned the following responsibilities:

—prescribing certain security principles, doctrines, and procedures for the U.S. Government;

—organizing, operating, and managing certain activities and facilities for the production of foreign intelligence information;

—organizing and coordinating the research and engineering activities of the U.S. Government that are in support of the Agency's assigned functions;

—regulating certain communications in support of Agency missions; and

—operating the National Computer Security Center in support of the Director's role as national manager for telecommunications security and automated information systems security.

Executive Order 12333 of December 4, 1981, describes in more detail the responsibilities of the National Security Agency.

On-Site Inspection Agency

Washington, DC 20041–0498
Phone, 703–742–4449

Director	Brig. Gen. Roland Lajoie
Principal Deputy Director	Joerg Menzel
Deputy Director, International Negotiations	David Pabst
Deputy Director, Counterintelligence	Frank LoTurco
Chief of Staff	Col. Douglas Englund, USA
Director for Operations	Col. Ronald Forest, USA
Director for Operations Staff	Col. John Hadley, USAF
Chief, Portal Monitoring Division	Col. Laurence Burgess, USMC
Chief, Escort Division	Col. Gerald West, USAF
Chief, Inspections Division	Capt. John Williams, USN
Director for Support	Col. Stephen Huff, USAF
Chief, Manpower, Personnel, and Administration Division	Comdr. Margie Stevens, USN
Chief, Resource Management Division	Lt. Col. David Potter, USAF
Chief, Comptroller Division	Lt. Col. Joseph Nelson, USAF
Chief, Information Systems Management Division	Lt. Col. Gordon Aitken, USAF
Chief, Acquisition Management Office	Sharon Davie
Science Advisor	Roger Ide
Public Affairs Officer	Col. Arthur C. Forster, Jr., USAF
Security Officer	Donald Loos
Historian	Pat Harahan
General Counsel	Michael Ra'anan
Governmental Affairs Officer	K. Eileen Giglio
Implementation Requirements Officer	Col. James Loftus, USA
Director, OSIA—Europe	Col. Frederic Grossick, USAF
Chief, OSIA Field Office, Washington	Lt. Col. Robert Marshall, USA
Chief, OSIA Field Office, San Francisco	Lt. Col. Stephen Boyd, USAF
Chief, OSIA MAGNA Portal Detachment	Col. William McNally, USAF
Chief, OSIA ACIU Detachment, Moscow, U.S.S.R.	Col. David Giddens, USAF
Chief, OSIA Gateway, Yokota, Japan	Lt. Col. Gerald Heuer, USAF

The On-Site Inspection Agency was established by Presidential directive on January 15, 1988, to implement the on-site inspection provisions of the Treaty between the United States and the Soviet Union on the Elimination of Intermediate-Range Nuclear Forces (INF Treaty). The Agency was chartered as a Department of Defense agency on January 26, 1988, and reports to an executive committee composed of the Under Secretary of Defense for Acquisition, Under Secretary of Defense for Policy, and the Chairman of the Joint Chiefs of Staff.

The Agency's mission is to manage all INF-related, U.S. on-site inspection activities in the Soviet Union, Czechoslovakia, and the German Democratic Republic, and to coordinate all activities associated with the Soviet Union's inspection of American INF facilities in the United States and Western Europe. It is also responsible for continuous monitoring of the Soviet missile assembly facility at Votkinsk, U.S.S.R., and coordination of the Soviet Union's reciprocal monitoring of the U.S. missile production facility in Magna, Utah.

The Agency is permanently manned by military personnel from all of the armed services, as well as civilian technical experts and support personnel. It maintains close liaison with various interested government agencies, and it draws its three Deputy Directors from the U.S. Arms Control and Disarmament Agency, Department of State, and Federal Bureau of Investigation. The permanently assigned personnel are further augmented by a cadre of trained temporary-duty personnel who support the Agency on an as-required basis.

For further information, contact the On-Site Inspection Agency, Washington, DC 20041–0498. Phone, 703–742–4449.

Strategic Defense Initiative Organization

The Pentagon, Washington, DC 20301–7100
Phone, 703–697–4040

Director	HENRY F. COOPER
Deputy Director	MAJ. GEN. MALCOLM O'NEILL, USA
Systems Architect	EDWARD T. GERRY
General Counsel	WILLIAM CARROLL
Director, Small and Disadvantaged Business	STEPHEN MOSS
Director, International and External Programs	DAVID MARTIN
Director, Acquisition and Mission Operations	COL. KENNETH COLLINS, USAF
Director, Contracts	COL. CHARLES STEWART, USAF
Director, Management Operations	DEBORAH VINSON
Director, Security, Intelligence and Countermeasures	THOMAS WARD
Deputy for Program Operations	ROBERT SNYDER
Director, Financial Management	DONALD KOVAL
Director, Cost Estimating and Analysis	JAMES DRYDEN
Director, Information Systems	ELAINE LITMAN
Director, Planning and Control	COL. BILLY HORN, USA
Deputy for Strategic Defense	JAMES CARLSON
Director, National Defense Segment	COL. LAWRENCE BECKER, USA
Director, System Integration and Command and Control	COL. DAVID NAGY, USAF
Director, National Test Bed	COL. WILLIAM HECKER, JR., USA
Director, Global Defense Segment	COL. ROWLAND WORRELL, USAF
Deputy for Technology	MICHAEL GRIFFIN
Director, Directed Energy	COL. THOMAS MEYER, USAF
Director, Innovative Science and Technology	DWIGHT DUSTON
Director, Key Technologies	RICHARD VERGA
Director, Sensor Technology	COL. DANIEL HEITZ, USAF
Director, Test and Evaluation	COL. MICHAEL TOOLE, USA
Director, Interceptor Technology	MICK BLACKLEDGE

Deputy for Theater Missile Defense	Col. Raymond Ross, USA
Director, Sensors	Col. Carl Drews, Jr., USA
Director, Weapons	Lt. Col. Ernest Bubb, USA
Director, System Integration	Lt. Col. Richard Ritter, USAF

[For the Strategic Defense Initiative Organization statement of organization, see the *Code of Federal Regulations,* Title 32, Part 388]

The Strategic Defense Initiative Organization was established as a separate agency of the Department of Defense under the direction, authority, and control of the Secretary of Defense.

The agency's mission is to manage and direct the conduct of research through advanced technology programs that will provide the technological basis for an informed decision regarding feasibility of eliminating the threat posed by nuclear ballistic missiles of all ranges and increasing the contribution of defensive systems to U.S. and allied security. In the performance of its research, the agency utilizes the services of the Military Departments, the Department of Energy, private industries, and educational and research institutions.

For further information, contact the Manpower and Personnel Division (MO), Strategic Defense Initiative Organization, Washington, DC 20301–7100. Phone, 703–693–1500.

JOINT SERVICE SCHOOLS

Defense Intelligence College

Defense Intelligence Analysis Center, Washington, DC 20340–5485
Phone, 202–373–3344

Commandant	Lt. Gen. Charles J. Cunningham, Jr., USAF (Ret.)
Provost	Robert L. DeGross
Dean, School of Strategic Intelligence	James W. Lucas
Dean, School of Attaché Training	Col. Robert L. Helvey
Dean, School of Intelligence Information Systems	Joseph P. Longo
Director, Research Center	Robert O. Slater
Director, Institutional Plans and Academic Affairs	Hugo A. Keesing

The Defense Intelligence College, established January 1, 1963, is a joint-service, educational institution operating under the authority of the Director of the Defense Intelligence Agency. The College's mission is to assist in the career development and training of military and civilian personnel who are assigned to intelligence functions or who are pursuing broad careers in intelligence. The College also conducts academic research and prepares DOD and civilian personnel for duty in the Defense Attaché System.

The College conducts a 9-month, resident postgraduate course to prepare personnel for command, staff, and policymaking positions in national and international security activities, which can lead to the Master of Science of Strategic Intelligence degree. The College also conducts more than 45 other professional courses, ranging in length from 1 day to 12 weeks. More than 7,500 full- and part-time students attend various Defense Intelligence College courses each year. Accreditation is by the Middle States Association of Colleges and Schools.

The Defense Academic Research Support Program, managed by the College, sponsors contract studies and hosts roundtables, symposia, and conferences that bring together members of the intelligence and academic communities.

For further information, contact the Office of the Registrar, Defense Intelligence College, Washington, DC 20340–5485. Phone, 202–373–4545.

Defense Systems Management College

Fort Belvoir, VA 22060–5426
Phone, 703–664–6323

Commandant	Maj. Gen. Lynn Stevens, USA
Provost	Gregory Wierzbicki
Dean, Department of College Operations and Services	Col. Rudolph H. Ehrenberg, Jr., USA

Dean, School of Systems Acquisition Education	COL. FREDERICK AYER, USAF
Dean, Department of Research and Information	CAPT. RALPH W. ORTENGREN, JR., USN

The Defense Systems Management College, established July 1, 1971, is a joint service educational institution operating under the direction of the Defense Systems Management College Policy Guidance Council, which is chaired by the Under Secretary of Defense for Acquisition. The mission of the College is to conduct advanced courses of study that will prepare selected military officers and civilian personnel for assignments in program management; to conduct, research, and disseminate information concerning new methods and practices in program management; and, as Defense action agent, to provide oversight for Department of Defense education and training programs for the acquisition work force.

The College conducts a resident course to educate selected intermediate level military officers and civilian personnel in a broad spectrum of program management activities through formal studies, simulation exercises, and case studies. The College also conducts an executive refresher course in program management for senior-level managers and an orientation in systems acquisition for selected generals of the Army and Air Force, flag officers of the Navy, and supergrade civilians in each of the services and the Department of Defense. In addition, special courses are routinely scheduled to disseminate new concepts and methods in program management and respond to the needs of the Military Departments and Defense agencies. Most of the courses are available to selected persons from other Federal agencies and the defense industry on a space-available basis. The main campus is at Fort Belvoir, VA, but many courses are taught at the four regions: Boston, MA; St. Louis, MO; Los Angeles, CA; and Huntsville, AL.

For further information, contact the Office of the Registrar, Defense Systems Management College, Fort Belvoir, VA 22060. Phone, 703–664–2152.

National Defense University

Fort Lesley J. McNair, Fourth and P Streets SW., Washington, DC 20319–6000
Phone, 202–475–1966

President	LT. GEN. BRADLEY C. HOSMER, USAF
Vice President	AMBASSADOR ROBERT H. MILLER
Chief of Staff	COL. P. WAYNE GASKINS, USA

The National Defense University was established by the Department of Defense on January 16, 1976, thereby merging the Industrial College of the Armed Forces and the National War College to form a university. Because the two senior service colleges are located at Fort Lesley J. McNair, Washington, DC, their close affiliation reduces administrative costs, provides for the sharing of faculty expertise and educational resources and promotes a constructive dialog, which benefits both colleges. On August 16, 1981, the Armed Forces Staff College in Norfolk, VA, an institution educating mid-career officers, was incorporated into the National Defense University. This action united the Department of Defense's three joint colleges under one university and allowed coordination of the curricula and professional development of its students and the sharing of its resources.

In early 1982, the Secretary of Defense directed the establishment of three research centers at the University: a Strategic Concepts Development Center, a Mobilization Concepts Development Center, and a War Gaming and Simulation Center. Later in the year, two institutions became part of the University: the Institute for Higher Defense Studies and the Department of Defense Computer Institute.

The University's mission is threefold: to prepare selected military officers and civilian officials, in a joint environment, to fulfill responsibilities at the national level for national security policy and strategy, force generation, joint and combined operations, and resources management; to perform research and policy analysis for the Secretary of Defense and Chairman of the Joint Chiefs of Staff; and to coordinate professional military education for the Chairman of the Joint Chiefs of Staff.

The University is pursuing numerous initiatives designed to ensure that its curriculum focuses on critical issues associated with the Nation's current security posture. At the same time, increased emphasis has been placed on achieving a closer relationship between research and education. This is reflected in the studies programs of the two senior colleges. Basic improvements in the scope and thrust of the curricula of both colleges are designed to enrich the joint educational process while emphasizing the important role played by research in the University's mission.

For further information, contact the Administrative Office, National Defense University, Fort Lesley J. McNair, Fourth and P Streets SW., Washington, DC 20319–6000. Phone, 202–475–1966.

The National War College

Fort Lesley J. McNair, Fourth and P Streets SW., Washington, DC 20319–6000
Phone, 202–475–1776

Commandant	MAJ. GEN. GERALD P. STADLER, USA
Dean of Students and Executive Officer	CAPT. WARREN P. HUDSON, USN
Dean of Faculty and Academic Programs	COL. R.W. STAFFORD, USAF

The National War College provides education in national security policy to selected military officers and career civil service employees of Federal departments and agencies concerned with national security. It is the only senior service college with the primary mission of offering a course of study that emphasizes national security policy formulation and the planning and implementation of national strategy.

Its 10-month academic program is an issue-centered study in U.S. national security. It consists of a prescribed curriculum and an elective study program. The prescribed portion of the curriculum combines interwoven themes: international politics and the process and substance of security policy formulation. Emphasis is placed on the role of force in national security policy and strategy through the study of major issues likely to affect the national security of the United States. The elective program is designed to permit each student to tailor his academic experience to meet individual professional development needs. Electives include tutorial research, writing, and reading, in addition to individual courses offered at the National War College and the Industrial College of the Armed Forces.

For further information, contact the Department of Administration, The National War College, Fort Lesley J. McNair, Fourth and P Streets SW., Washington, DC 20319–6000. Phone, 202–475–1776.

Industrial College of the Armed Forces

Fort Lesley J. McNair, Fourth and P Streets SW., Washington, DC 20319–6000
Phone, 202–475–1832

Commandant	Maj. Gen. David M. Goodrich, USAF
Dean of Students and Chief of Staff	Col. Lloyd H. Barton, USAF
Dean of Faculty and Academic Programs	John H. Johns
Dean of Administration and Resources	Col. William D. Idell, USA

The Industrial College of the Armed Forces provides executive-level education to selected senior military and career Federal civil service employees. It is the only senior service college with the primary mission of offering a course of study pertaining to the resources component of national power and its integration into national security strategy for peace and war.

The College's 10-month academic program is organized into two semesters: The first deals with national security decisionmaking, history, political science, strategy and warfare, and regional security studies-national security strategy. The second covers economics, logistics, acquisition, mobilization, and defense industry studies-national resources. These core program courses are complemented by both individual research and elective courses offered within the National Defense University.

For further information, contact the Director of Administration, Industrial College of the Armed Forces, Fort Lesley J. McNair, Fourth and P Streets, SW., Washington, DC 20319–6000. Phone, 202–475–1832.

Armed Forces Staff College

Norfolk, VA 23511–6097
Phone, 804–444–5302

Commandant	Brig. Gen. Stanley Kwieciak, Jr., USA
Deputy Commandant	Col. John R. Vick, USAF

The Armed Forces Staff College (AFSC), a major component of the National Defense University, is an intermediate- and senior-level joint college in the professional military education system dedicated to the study of the principles, perspectives, and techniques of joint and combined operations.

The mission of AFSC is to prepare selected officers for joint and combined duty. The college accomplishes this mission through two schools: the Joint and Combined Staff Officer School (JCSOS) and the Joint Command, Control, and Electronic Warfare School (JCEWS). JCSOS consists of the

Intermediate-Level Phase II Program and the Senior-Level Phase II Program. The Dean of JCSOS is responsible for the development, preparation, and presentation of the JCSOS curriculum which emphasizes joint planning, operations, procedures, and perspectives. Faculty of JCSOS also teach three off-campus courses: the Joint Planning Orientation Course (JPOC), the Joint Planning and Execution Course (JPEC), and the Flag and General Officer Seminar on Joint Planning (FGOS). These courses are designed to update personnel on current joint planning procedures. The Dean of JCEWS is responsible for the development, preparation, and presentation of three separate resident courses: a 6-week Joint Command, Control, and Communications Staff and Operations Course that covers the C^2 process and C^3 systems at the national, strategic, and theater/tactical levels; a 2-week Joint Electronic Warfare (EW) Staff Officer course that covers the concepts, doctrine, procedures, and capabilities required by the Joint EW Staff Officer; and a 2-week Joint Command, Control, and Communications Countermeasures Staff Officer Course that details the concepts and procedures of C^3CM needed by the joint C^3CM staff officer. The Dean of JCEWS is also responsible for two off-campus courses: the Joint Electronic Warfare Orientation Course and the Joint Command, Control, and Communications Countermeasures Orientation Course. These courses are designed to enhance the knowledge of staff and operational personnel. Two departments, the Department of Academic Support and the Department of Academic Operations, support both schools.

For further information, contact the Department of Academic Operations, Armed Forces Staff College, 7800 Hampton Blvd., Norfolk, VA 23511–6097. Phone, 804–444–5074.

Information Resources Management College

Washington Navy Yard, Building 175, Washington, DC 20374
Phone, 202–433–2013

Dean — JOHN M. CARABELLO

The Information Resources Management College was established on March 1, 1990, as a full college of the National Defense University. Its mission and purpose is to:

—develop and teach Information Resources Management courses for National Defense University colleges;

—provide education and training to senior executives with Information Resources Management responsibilities;

—provide education, training, and technical assistance to Information Resources Management program managers and their staff;

—perform think-tank and applied research assignments related to Information Resources Management policy; and

—facilitate Information Resources Management research, scholarship, and intellectual exchange.

The College's Advanced Management Program is a 4-month graduate-level program for senior IRM personnel that encompasses the managerial, technical, operational, and financial areas of information resources management. The program topics include: information management, technical management, procurement management, financial management, national security policy management, project management, and the DOD Automated Information Systems life cycle management process. The program also addresses current Information Resources Management policy issues and trends and the essential management concepts and skills necessary to avoid past DOD information systems problems.

The College's courses are intensive classes covering areas of prime concern for effective management of DOD's information systems and life cycle activities. The courses range from 1-day senior executive seminars to 2-week classes in specific Information Resources Management disciplines.

The College's Technical Assistance Center supports program managers and Information Resources Management officials by performing life cycle management analysis, policy analysis, and management studies.

The Information Resources Management College's programs and courses are primarily for DOD military and civilian executives; however, courses are also open to other Federal, State, and local government employees, and, under some circumstances, to employees of private organizations.

For further information, contact the Administrative Officer, Information Resources Management College, Washington Navy Yard, Building 175, Washington, DC 20374. Phone, 202–433–2013.

Uniformed Services University of the Health Sciences

4301 Jones Bridge Road, Bethesda, MD 20814–4799
Phone, 202–295–3030

Chairman, Board of Regents	SAM A. NIXON, M.D.
Executive Secretary, Board of Regents	CHARLES R. MANNIX, JR.
President	JAY P. SANFORD, M.D.
Commandant	COL. B. WOLCOTT, USA
Dean, School of Medicine	JAY P. SANFORD, M.D.
Associate Dean, Academic Affairs	RANDALL K. HOLMES, M.D.
Associate Dean, Operations	KENNETH E. KINNAMON, D.V.M.
Associate Dean, Continuing and Graduate Education	JOHN W. BULLARD
Assistant Dean, Student Affairs	COL. RICHARD M. MACDONALD, MC, USA
Assistant Dean, Clinical Sciences	COL. RICHARD C. DIMOND, MC, USA
Assistant Dean, Graduate Medical Education Liaison	DOUGLAS R. KNAB, M.D.

Authorized by act of September 21, 1972 (10 U.S.C. 2112), the Uniformed Services University of the Health Sciences was established to educate career-oriented medical officers for the Military Departments. It is a separate agency of the Department of Defense, directly responsible to the Secretary of Defense (Department of Defense Directive 5105.45).

The University currently incorporates the F. Edward Hébert School of Medicine and graduate and continuing education programs. It is located on the Naval Medical Command reservation in Bethesda, MD.

Students are selected by procedures recommended by the Board of Regents and prescribed by the Secretary of Defense. The actual selection is carried out by a faculty committee on admissions and is based upon motivation and dedication to a career in the uniformed services and an overall appraisal of the personal and intellectual characteristics of the candidates without regard to sex, race, religion, or national origin. Applicants must be U.S. citizens. Matriculants will be commissioned officers in one of the uniformed services. They must meet the physical and personal qualifications for such a commission and must give evidence of a strong commitment to serving as a uniformed medical officer. The graduating medical student is required to serve a period of obligation of not less than 7 years.

Currently, there are approximately 650 officers training for their M.D. degrees in the University's F. Edward Hébert School of Medicine and approximately 120 individuals enrolled in one of the University's graduate programs in the basic sciences.

The University's graduate program is fully accredited and is available to both civilian and military applicants. Graduates may receive the Ph.D. degree in one of the biomedical sciences, the master of public health degree, or the master of tropical medicine and hygiene degree. In addition, the University serves as the focus for continuing medical education programs that support the Military Departments by providing unique training opportunities both at the University's Bethesda campus and at military bases around the world.

The Military Medicine Education Institute was established in 1988 to enhance wartime readiness training for active and reserve component health professionals. It is responsible for the Joint Medical Readiness Training Center with resident and nonresident Combat Casualty Care Courses, and other courses for reserve health professionals and active duty special operations medical sergeants.

For further information, contact the President, Uniformed Services University of the Health Sciences, 4301 Jones Bridge Road, Bethesda, MD 20814–4799. Phone, 202–295–3030.

DEPARTMENT OF EDUCATION

400 Maryland Avenue SW., Washington, DC 20202
Phone, 202–708–5366

SECRETARY OF EDUCATION	Lamar Alexander
Chief of Staff/Counselor to the Secretary	Stephen I. Danzansky
Director, Office of Public Affairs	Etta Fielek
Deputy Secretary	David T. Kearns
Deputy Under Secretary for Management	Gary J. Rasmussen, *Acting*
Director, Information Resources Management	(vacancy)
Controller	Michael R. Zysman, *Acting*
Director, Financial Management Service	Ronald C. Oleyar
Director, Grants and Contracts Service	Gary J. Rasmussen
Director, Financial and Management Control	James B. Holmberg
Administrator for Management Services	Neal Peden
Director, Personnel Management Service	Veronica D. Trietsch
Director, Administrative Resource Management Service	Arthur M. Love III
Deputy Under Secretary for Planning, Budget and Evaluation	Sally H. Christensen, *Acting*
Director, Budget Service	Sally H. Christensen
Director, Planning and Evaluation Service	Alan Ginsburg
Deputy Under Secretary for Intergovernmental and Interagency Affairs	William L. Smith, *Acting*
Director, Intergovernmental Affairs	John W. Barth
Director, Interagency Operations	Mary Witten Neal
Director, Hearing and Appeals	Dan R. DeLacy
Director, Center for Choice in Education	Jack Klenk
Inspector General	James B. Thomas, Jr.
Assistant Inspector General for Investigation Services	John L. Horn
Assistant Inspector General for Policy, Planning and Management Services	John P. Higgins, Jr., *Acting*
Assistant Inspector General for Audit Services	Mitchell L. Laine
Assistant Secretary for Legislation and Congressional Affairs	William D. Hansen, *Acting*
Director, Legislation and Congressional Affairs	Victor Klatt
General Counsel	Edward C. Stringer
Deputy General Counsel for Departmental Service	John M. Kristy, *Acting*
Deputy General Counsel for Program Service	Steven Y. Winnick
Assistant Secretary for Civil Rights	Michael L. Williams
Deputy Assistant Secretary for Operations	Richard Komer, *Acting*
Deputy Assistant Secretary for Policy	Richard Komer
Director, Analysis and Data Collection Service	Paul L. Fairley
Director, Operations Support Service	Maurice Clifford, *Acting*
Director, Policy and Enforcement Service	Frederick Cioffi, *Acting*

Assistant Secretary for Educational Research and Improvement	Bruno V. Manno, *Acting*
Deputy Assistant Secretary for Operations	Dick W. Hays
Director, Library Programs	Anne J. Matthews
Director, Programs for the Improvement of Practice	Nelson Smith
Director, Office of Research	Milton Goldberg
Director, Center for Education Statistics	Emerson J. Elliott
Assistant Secretary for Special Education and Rehabilitative Services	Robert Davila
Director, Special Education Programs	Judith Schrag
Director, National Institute on Disability and Rehabilitation Research	William H. Graves
Commissioner, Rehabilitation Services Administration	Nell C. Carney
Director, Office of Bilingual Education and Minority Languages Affairs	Rita Esquivel
Assistant Secretary for Elementary and Secondary Education	John T. MacDonald
Director, Compensatory Education Programs	Mary Jane LeTendre
Director, Impact Aid Programs	Charles E. Hansen
Director, School Improvement Programs	Alicia Coro
Director, Indian Education Programs	John W. Tippeconnic III
Director, Migrant Education	Francis Corrigan
Assistant Secretary for Vocational and Adult Education	Betsy Brand
Assistant Secretary for Postsecondary Education	Michael J. Farrell, *Acting*
Director, Debt Collection and Management Assistance Service	John S. Haines
Deputy Assistant Secretary for Higher Education Programs	John B. Childers
Director, Higher Education Program Management Service	W. Reed Saunders
Director, Center for International Education	John C.T. Alexander
Director, Higher Education Program Service	Richard D. Scarfo, *Acting*
Deputy Assistant Secretary for Student Financial Assistance	Ernest C. Canellos, *Acting*
Director, Student Financial Assistance Programs	William L. Moran
Director, Fund for the Improvement of Postsecondary Education	Charles Karelis

The Department of Education is the Cabinet-level department that establishes policy for, administers, and coordinates most Federal assistance to education.

The Department of Education was created by the Department of Education Organization Act (20 U.S.C. 3411), with the first Secretary of Education, appointed by the President with the advice and consent of the Senate, sworn in on December 6, 1979.

Office of the Secretary

Secretary The Secretary of Education advises the President on education plans, policies, and programs of the Federal Government. The Secretary directs Department staff in carrying out the

DEPARTMENT OF EDUCATION

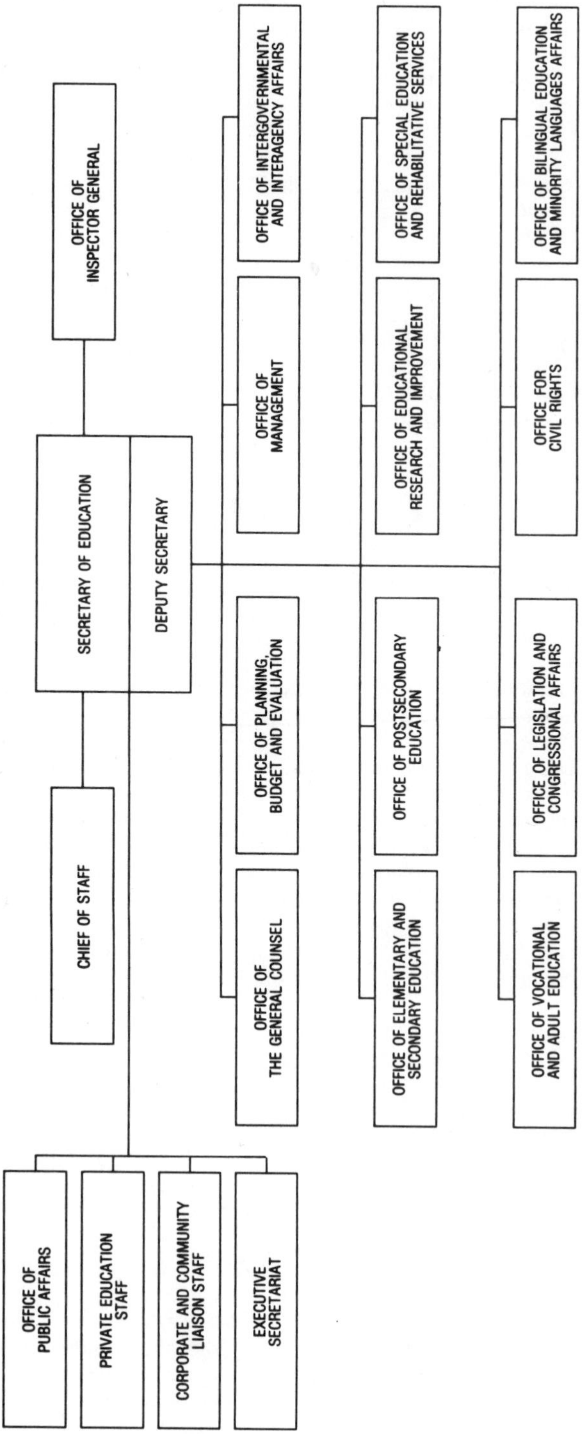

approved programs and activities of the Department and promotes general public understanding of the Department's goals, programs, and objectives. The Secretary also carries out certain Federal responsibilities for four federally aided corporations: the American Printing House for the Blind, Gallaudet University, Howard University, and the National Technical Institute for the Deaf. The Deputy Secretary, the Deputy Under Secretaries, the Assistant Secretaries, the Inspector General, and the General Counsel aid the Secretary in the overall management of the Department.

Deputy Secretary The Deputy Secretary serves as Acting Secretary in the absence of the Secretary and performs on behalf of the Secretary such functions and duties as the Secretary may designate and coordinates Federal-State relations.

Intergovernmental and Interagency Affairs The Deputy Under Secretary for Intergovernmental and Interagency Affairs is responsible for providing overall leadership in coordinating regional and field activities as well as establishing and directing intergovernmental and interagency services for the Department. The office is also responsible for hearings and appeals related to departmental programs.

Inspector General The Inspector General is responsible for conducting and supervising audits and investigations relating to programs and operations of the Department. The office provides leadership, coordination, and policy recommendations to promote economy, efficiency, and effectiveness; and to prevent and detect fraud and abuse in the administration of the Department's programs and operations.

General Counsel The General Counsel provides legal advice to the Secretary and to the components of the Department.

Bilingual Education The Director of the Office of Bilingual Education and Minority Languages Affairs ensures access to equal educational opportunity and improves the quality of programs for limited English proficiency and minority languages populations by providing support for programs, activities, and management initiatives meeting the special educational needs of those populations. The Office also provides assistance for the development, adoption, and implementation of plans for the desegregation of public schools.

Management The Deputy Under Secretary for Management provides advice and guidance to the Secretary on administrative and financial management and provides for the direction and coordination of these activities throughout the Department on a day-to-day basis. These activities include financial management, personnel, training, grants and procurement management, management evaluation, ADP, and other support functions.

Planning, Budget and Evaluation The Deputy Under Secretary for Planning, Budget and Evaluation coordinates Department activities in the preparation of the departmental budget, program analysis, and planning activities, and ensures that Department policy and program planning appropriately reflects the results of these activities.

Legislation and Congressional Affairs The Assistant Secretary for Legislation and Congressional Affairs serves as the principal adviser to the Secretary on matters concerning the Department's legislative program and congressional relations.

Civil Rights The Assistant Secretary for Civil Rights is responsible for the administration and enforcement of civil rights laws related to education and the handicapped. The office is responsible for ensuring compliance in programs and activities receiving Federal financial assistance and by employers holding Federal contracts.

Elementary and Secondary Education The Assistant Secretary for Elementary and Secondary Education formulates policy for, directs, and coordinates the activities relating to preschool, elementary, and secondary education in the Department. Included are programs of grants to State educational agencies and local school districts for Indian and migrant education, programs of financial and technical assistance to school districts to meet special needs incident to the elimination of racial segregation and discrimination, and grants for the education of neglected and delinquent students.

Educational Research and Improvement The Assistant Secretary for Educational Research and Improvement administers functions of the Department concerning research, statistics, development, demonstration, dissemination, and assessment. The office also administers a wide variety of discretionary grant programs to maximize individual program impact on school improvement.

Vocational and Adult Education The Assistant Secretary for Vocational and Adult Education administers grant, contract, and technical assistance programs for vocational-technical education and for adult education and literacy. The Office is also responsible for coordinating these programs with other Education Department and Federal programs supporting services and research for adult education, literacy, and occupational training.

Special Education and Rehabilitative Services The Assistant Secretary for Special Education and Rehabilitative Services is responsible for special education programs and services expressly designed to meet the needs and develop the full potential of handicapped children; and comprehensive rehabilitation service programs specifically designed to reduce human dependency, to increase self-reliance, and to fully utilize the productive capabilities of all handicapped persons. Programs include support for training of teachers and other professional personnel; grants for research; financial aid to help States initiate, expand, and improve their resources; and media services and captioned films for the deaf.

Postsecondary Education The Assistant Secretary for Postsecondary Education formulates policy and directs and coordinates programs for assistance to postsecondary educational institutions and students pursuing a postsecondary education. Programs include assistance for the improvement and expansion of American educational resources for international studies and services, grants to improve instruction in crucial academic subjects, and construction assistance for academic facilities. Also included are programs of student financial assistance, including Pell Grants, Supplemental Educational Opportunity Grants, Grants to States for State Student Incentives, Direct Loans to Students in Institutions of Higher Education, Work-Study, Cooperative Education, Insured Loans to Students in Health Professions Schools, and the Guaranteed Student Loan Program.

Regional Offices Each regional office serves as a center for the dissemination of information and provides technical assistance to State and local educational agencies and other institutions and individuals interested in Federal education activities. At present, offices are located in 10 cities: Atlanta, GA; Boston, MA; Chicago, IL; Dallas, TX; Denver, CO; Kansas City, MO; New York, NY; Philadelphia, PA; San Francisco, CA; and Seattle, WA.

Federally Aided Corporations

(These Corporations are supported in part by Federal funds appropriated in the budget of the Department of Education.)

American Printing House for the Blind

P.O. Box 6085, Louisville, KY 40206
Phone, 502–895–2405

President	TUCK TINSLEY
Chairman of the Board	JOSEPH B. WOODLIEF

The American Printing House for the Blind was incorporated by the Kentucky Legislature in 1858 to assist in the education of the blind by distributing Braille books, talking books, and educational aids without cost to educational institutions educating blind children pursuant to the act "To Promote the Education of the Blind," as amended (20 Stat. 467), adopted by Congress in 1879.

Gallaudet University

800 Florida Avenue NE., Washington, DC 20002
Phone, 202–651–5000

Chairman, Board of Trustees	PHIL BRAVIN
President, Gallaudet University	I. KING JORDAN
Provost	HARVEY CORSON
Dean of Graduate Studies and Research	MICHAEL KARCHMER
Vice President for Administration and Business	PAUL KELLY
Dean of College for Continuing Education	ROSLYN ROSEN
Dean of Pre-College Programs	MICHAEL DENNINGER

The Columbia Institution for the Instruction of the Deaf and Dumb, and the Blind was incorporated by act of February 16, 1857 (11 Stat. 161). An amendatory act of February 23, 1865 (13 Stat. 436), changed the name to the Columbia Institution for the Instruction of the Deaf and Dumb. The name was subsequently changed to Columbia Institution for the Deaf by act of March 4, 1911 (36 Stat. 1422). The act of June 18, 1954 (20 U.S.C. 691 *et seq.*), changed its name to Gallaudet College. The Education of the Deaf Act of 1986 (20 U.S.C. 4301) changed the name to Gallaudet University.

Gallaudet University was established to provide a liberal higher education for deaf persons who need special facilities to compensate for their loss of hearing. The primary purpose of the university is to afford its students the intellectual and spiritual development that can be acquired through a study of the liberal arts and sciences.

In addition to its undergraduate program, Gallaudet University operates a graduate program at the master's level for preparing teachers and other professional personnel to work with persons who are deaf, a research program focusing on problems related to deafness, and a preschool for young deaf children.

Accreditation Gallaudet University is accredited by the Middle States Association of Colleges and Secondary Schools, the National Council for Accreditation of Teacher Education, and the Council on Social Work Education.

Model Secondary School for the Deaf The school was established by act of October 15, 1966 (20 U.S.C. 693), when the Department of Health, Education, and Welfare entered into an agreement with Gallaudet College for the establishment and operation, including construction, of such a facility. It was established as an exemplary educational facility for deaf students of high school age from the District of Columbia, Maryland, Virginia, West Virginia, Pennsylvania, and Delaware. The school is to provide maximum flexibility in curricula and to encourage originality, imagination, and innovation needed to satisfy deaf students' high levels of aspirations.

The objectives of the school are to provide day and residential facilities for deaf youth of high school age, in order to prepare some for college and other advanced study and to provide terminal education for others; to prepare all students to the maximum extent possible to be independent, contributing members of society; and to stimulate the development of similar programs throughout the Nation.

Kendall Demonstration Elementary School The school, which is located on the campus of Gallaudet University and now serves approximately 200 students, became the Nation's first demonstration elementary school for the deaf by act of December 24, 1970 (20 U.S.C. 695), which authorized Gallaudet College to operate and maintain the school as a model that will experiment in techniques and materials, and to disseminate information from these and future projects to educational facilities for deaf children throughout the country.

For further information, contact the Division of Public Service, Gallaudet University, 800 Florida Avenue NE., Washington, DC 20002. Phone, 202–651–5505.

Howard University

2400 Sixth Street NW., Washington, DC 20059
Phone, 202–806–6100

President	FRANKLYN G. JENIFER

Howard University was established by act of March 2, 1867 (14 Stat. 438). It is governed by a 27-member self-perpetuating board of trustees. The University maintains a special relationship with the Federal Government through the Department of Education.

Howard University, jointly supported by congressional appropriations and private funds, is a comprehensive university organization offering instruction in 17 schools and colleges as follows: the college of liberal arts, the school of engineering, the school of architecture and planning, the school of business and public administration, the college of fine arts, the college of medicine, the college of dentistry, the college of pharmacy and pharmaceutical science, the school of law, the school of religion, the graduate school, the school of social work, the school of communications, the school of education, the college of nursing, the school of human ecology, the college of allied health sciences, and a summer school. In addition, Howard University has research institutes in the following areas: the arts and the humanities, urban affairs and research, drug abuse and addiction, minority business education, and the study of educational policy.

The University admits students of both sexes of every race, creed, color, and national origin, but it accepts and discharges a special responsibility for the admission and training of black students.

For further information, contact the Office of Public Information, Howard University, 2400 Sixth Street NW., Washington, DC 20001. Phone, 202–686–5400.

National Technical Institute for the Deaf

Rochester Institute of Technology

P.O. Box 9887, 1 Lomb Memorial Drive, Rochester, NY 14623
Phone, 716–475–6400 (Voice only)

President of Rochester Institute of Technology	M. RICHARD ROSE
Vice President for Government Affairs/Director of the National Technical Institute for the Deaf	WILLIAM E. CASTLE

The National Technical Institute for the Deaf (NTID) was established by act of June 8, 1965 (20 U.S.C. 681), and after several years of planning, programs began in 1968. Funded through the Department of Education, it is an integral part of a larger institution known as the Rochester Institute of Technology (RIT).

NTID's presence at RIT is the first effort to educate large numbers of deaf students within a college campus planned primarily for hearing students. Unique in the world, NTID is a vital part of RIT's main 1,300-acre campus in suburban Rochester, NY. It provides educational opportunities for qualified students from every State in the Nation and, through educational outreach, publications, and related service, serves deaf persons throughout the world. In addition, NTID conducts research to better understand the role of deafness in education and employment, and to develop innovative teaching techniques. It develops training activities for its faculty and staff, as well as for other professionals working with deaf persons across the country.

One of the major reasons for NTID's success in helping deaf students join the mainstream of American life is its close working relationship with other RIT colleges in developing career-oriented programs of study. One of RIT's main strengths over the years has been its ability to adapt its educational programs to technological and social change. NTID helps keep that RIT tradition alive and has served more than 5,362 deaf students since 1968.

Deaf graduates from RIT have found employment throughout the Nation or have moved on to advanced academic studies. Of those who pursued employment, more than 90 percent have been placed in jobs; 93 percent in jobs commensurate with their educational preparation. Of those employed, 80 percent work in business and industry, more than 11 percent in government, and the remainder in education.

An applicant for NTID at RIT must be a U.S. resident. An overall eighth grade achievement level or above is required, and, except under special circumstances, an applicant must have completed a secondary program. An applicant also must show evidence of need for special services because of hearing loss and have an unaided better ear average of 70dB ISO. References are requested.

Both Institutes are accredited by the Middle States Association of Colleges and Secondary Schools. RIT also has been accredited by the Engineers' Council for Professional Development; National Association of Schools of Art; Committee on Professional Training of American Chemical Society; Council on Social Work Education; and the National Accrediting Agency for Clinical Laboratory Sciences.

For further information, contact the Public Information Office, National Technical Institute for the Deaf, P.O. Box 9887, 1 Lomb Memorial Drive, Rochester, NY 14623. Phone, 716–475–6283.

Sources of Information

Office of the Secretary
Inquiries on the following information may be directed to the specified office, Department of Education, 400 Maryland Avenue SW., Washington, DC 20202.

Contracts and Small Business Activities Call or write the Office of Small and Disadvantaged Business Utilization. Phone, 202–708–9820.

Employment Inquiries and applications for employment, and inquiries regarding the college recruitment program, should be directed to the Personnel Management Service. Phone, 202–401–0553.

Organization and Internal Procedures Call or write the Director, Organizational and Policy Analysis Staff. Phone, 202–401–1790.

For further information concerning the Department of Education, contact the Information Center, Department of Education, Room 4608 (ROB3), 400 Maryland Avenue NW., Washington, DC 20202. Phone, 202–708–5366.

DEPARTMENT OF ENERGY

1000 Independence Avenue SW., Washington, DC 20585
Phone, 202–586–5000

SECRETARY OF ENERGY	JAMES D. WATKINS
Deputy Secretary	W. HENSON MOORE
Under Secretary	JOHN C. TUCK
General Counsel	STEPHEN A. WAKEFIELD
Inspector General	JOHN C. LAYTON
Assistant Secretary, Congressional and Intergovernmental Affairs	JACQUELINE KNOX BROWN
Assistant Secretary, International Affairs and Energy Emergencies	JOHN J. EASTON, JR.
Assistant Secretary, Environment, Safety and Health	PAUL L. ZIEMER
Assistant Secretary, Nuclear Energy	WILLIAM A. YOUNG
Assistant Secretary, Fossil Energy	ROBERT H. GENTILE
Assistant Secretary, Defense Programs	RICHARD A. CLAYTOR
Assistant Secretary, Conservation and Renewable Energy	J. MICHAEL DAVIS
Deputy Under Secretary, Policy, Planning and Analysis	LINDA G. STUNTZ
Administrator, Economic Regulatory Administration	CHANDLER L. VAN ORMAN, *Acting*
Administrator, Energy Information Administration	CALVIN A. KENT
Director of Administration and Human Resource Management	JOHN J. NETTLES, JR.
Director of Procurement, Assistance, and Program Management	SILAS B. FISHER
Director of Public Affairs	M.J. JAMESON
Director of Energy Research	JAMES F. DECKER, *Acting*
Director of Minority Economic Impact	MELVA G. WRAY
Director of Civilian Radioactive Waste Management	JOHN W. BARTLETT
Director of New Production Reactors	DOMINIC J. MONETTA
Director of Hearings and Appeals	GEORGE B. BREZNAY
Director, Office of Environmental Restoration and Waste Management	LEO P. DUFFY, *Acting*
Director, Office of Nuclear Safety	STEVEN M. BLUSH
Director, Office of Scientific and Engineering Recruitment, Training, and Development	RICHARD W. STAROSTECKI
Director, Office of Small and Disadvantaged Business Utilization	LEONEL V. MIRANDA
Chief Financial Officer	ELIZABETH E. SMEDLEY
Director of Intelligence	ROBERT W. DANIEL, JR.
Director of Security Affairs	WILLIAM L. BARKER, *Acting*
Director of Scheduling and Logistics	VICTORIA L. THORNTON
Director of Special Projects	PEGGY DUFOUR

Executive Director, Office of the Secretary of Energy Advisory Board	ROBERT M. SIMON
Chairman, Board of Contract Appeals	E. BARCLAY VAN DOREN
Chairman, Federal Energy Regulatory Commission	MARTIN L. ALLDAY

The Department of Energy provides the framework for a comprehensive and balanced national energy plan through the coordination and administration of the energy functions of the Federal Government. The Department is responsible for long-term, high-risk research and development of energy technology; the marketing of Federal power; energy conservation; the nuclear weapons program; energy regulatory programs; and a central energy data collection and analysis program.

The Department of Energy (DOE) was established by the Department of Energy Organization Act (42 U.S.C. 7131), effective October 1, 1977, pursuant to Executive Order 12009 of September 13, 1977. The act consolidated the major Federal energy functions into one Cabinet-level Department, transferring to DOE all the responsibilities of the Energy Research and Development Administration; the Federal Energy Administration; the Federal Power Commission; and the Alaska, Bonneville, Southeastern, and Southwestern Power Administrations, formerly components of the Department of the Interior, as well as the power-marketing functions of the Department of the Interior's Bureau of Reclamation. Also transferred to DOE were certain functions of the Interstate Commerce Commission and the Departments of Commerce, Housing and Urban Development, the Navy, and the Interior.

The Secretary, Deputy Secretary, and Under Secretary are the principal officers of the Department. They are responsible for the overall planning, direction, and control of departmental activities.

Supporting DOE in matters of departmentwide scope are support offices, including the Offices of the Assistant Secretaries for Environment, Safety and Health; International Affairs and Energy Emergencies; Congressional and Intergovernmental Affairs; the Deputy Under Secretary, Office of Policy, Planning and Analysis; the General Counsel; the Inspector General; the Executive Director, Office of the Secretary of Energy Advisory Board; the Director of Minority Economic Impact; the Director of Small and Disadvantaged Business Utilization; the Director of Hearings and Appeals; the Director of Administration and Human Resource Management; the Director of Procurement, Assistance, and Program Management; the Chief Financial Officer, Office of the Chief Financial Officer; the Director of Security Affairs; the Director of Intelligence; the Director of Public Affairs; the Director of Nuclear Safety; the Director of Scientific and Engineering Recruitment, Training, and Development; the Director of Special Projects; the Director of Scheduling and Logistics; and the Chairman of the Board of Contract Appeals.

Programs requiring large budget outlays are the responsibility of the Director of Energy Research; the Director of Civilian Radioactive Waste Management; the Director of New Production Reactors; the Director of Environmental Restoration and Waste Management; and four program Assistant Secretaries (Fossil Energy; Nuclear Energy; Conservation and Renewable Energy; and Defense Programs).

The Department's organization also includes the Economic Regulatory Administration, the Energy Information Administration, and the Federal Energy Regulatory Commission, which is an independent regulatory organization within the Department.

In addition to headquarters' components, the Department has an

DEPARTMENT OF ENERGY

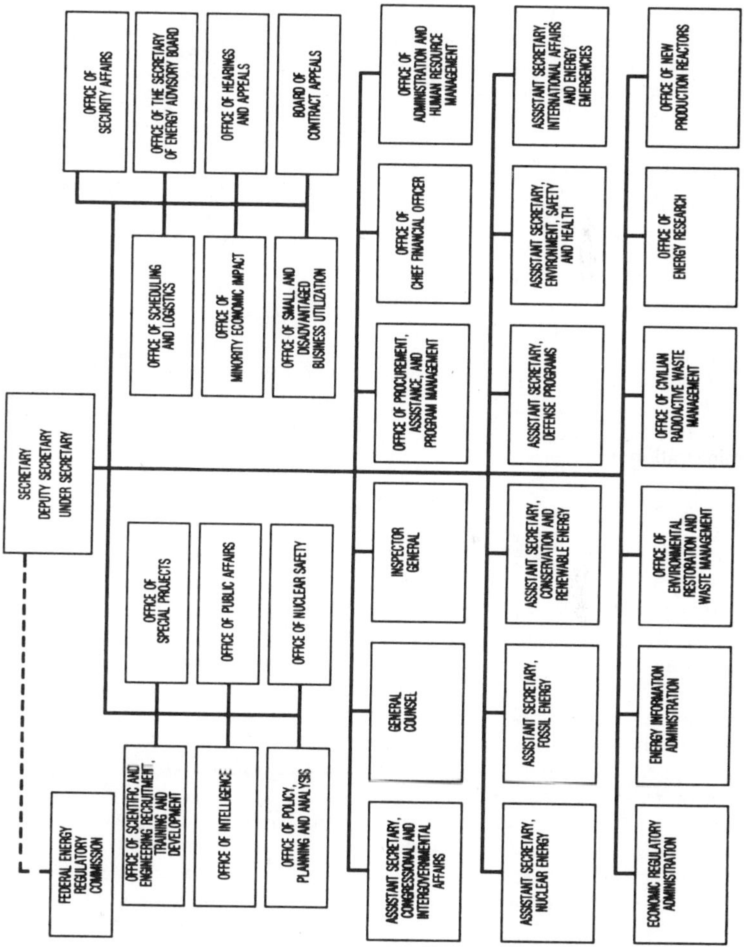

extensive field structure that plays an integral part in the implementation and management of departmental projects and programs.

Office of the Secretary

Secretary The Secretary directs and supervises the administration of the Department, decides major energy policy and planning issues, and acts as the principal spokesman for the Department. The Secretary is the principal adviser to the President on energy policies, plans, and programs.

In the absence of the Secretary, the Deputy Secretary acts for the Secretary and assists the Secretary in deciding major energy policy and planning issues and in representing the Department before Congress and the public. The Deputy Secretary has primary oversight responsibility for nuclear energy, energy research conservation and renewable energy, and fossil energy. The Under Secretary has primary responsibility for the Department's defense programs; security affairs; environmental, safety, and health programs; civilian radioactive waste management; new production reactors; environmental restoration and waste management; nuclear safety; and scientific and engineering recruitment, training, and development.

Staff Offices

General Counsel The General Counsel provides diverse legal services to the Secretary and the Department, including legal support and counseling for all Department activities, except for the Federal Energy Regulatory Commission; conducts the Department's patent and standards of conduct programs; and carries out traditional legal functions such as certain aspects of litigation and the development of legislative proposals.

Policy, Planning and Analysis The Office of Policy, Planning and Analysis formulates and recommends the overall national energy policy, coördinates the analysis and evaluation of policies and programs, and conducts a continuing assessment of the national energy situation.

The Office develops legislative proposals to support policy objectives and reviews program and management plans and budgets to ensure integration of new policy proposals. The Office also prepares the Department's proposed biennial National Energy Policy Plan to be transmitted by the President to the Congress.

Environment, Safety and Health The Assistant Secretary for Environment, Safety and Health ensures that departmental programs are in compliance with environmental safety and health regulations and that environmental and safety impacts of Department programs receive management review.

Administration and Human Resource Management The Director, Office of Administration and Human Resource Management, is the principal adviser to the Secretary of Energy on departmental organization and management and administrative management and support matters. The Office provides advice on program planning, personnel management, and policy matters; provides staff support to top policy officials and program offices to ensure the efficient and effective management and operation of the Department and its programs; undertakes special management-related projects for the Secretary; and provides management and administrative support services to all headquarters organizations, and overall policy direction and oversight of administrative activities in all field organizations. The Office is also responsible for the Department's personnel management programs; organization and management systems; equal employment and civil rights activities; automated data processing and telecommunications administration and acquisition; scientific and technical information management; information resources management; directives; and management of real and personal property.

Procurement, Assistance, and Program Management The Director, Office of Procurement, Assistance, and Program Management, is the Department's senior procurement official and functional manager for all procurement, grant, cooperative agreement, and financial assistance contracting activities; personal property management; industrial mobilization; and related business activities for the Department.

Chief Financial Officer The Office of the Chief Financial Officer ensures the financial integrity of the Department by developing and implementing the appropriate policies and procedures to provide control and assistance for the effective management of the Department's financial resources. The Office plans and performs departmentwide reviews to determine compliance with the requirements of the Federal Manager's Financial Integrity Act and DOE accounting and financial management policy; develops, maintains, and provides technical assistance for the program to reduce waste, fraud, and error; manages audit followup and liaison activities; plans, develops, and maintains departmental financial systems; provides departmental payroll services, departmentwide accounting and reporting functions, and all accounting functions for headquarters; and prepares the Secretary's Annual Report to Congress.

Congressional and Intergovernmental Affairs The Assistant Secretary for Congressional and Intergovernmental Affairs establishes policy and procedures for the conduct of relations with Congress, and serves as the principal point of departmental contact with the Congress and provides guidance to Department staff on congressional matters and interests. The Assistant Secretary also advises the Secretary on departmental relations with State, local, Indian, and territorial governments and labor organizations; provides policy direction for oversight of the consumer activities of the Department and responds to citizen-oriented energy initiatives; and ensures that all DOE policies and programs promote competition in the energy industry and that consumer impact is considered in decisionmaking.

Minority Economic Policy The Director of Minority Economic Impact advises the Secretary on the effects of energy policies, regulations, and other actions of the Department and its components on minorities, minority business enterprises, and minority educational institutions; and advises the Secretary on ways to ensure that minorities are afforded an opportunity to participate in energy programs of the Department.

Scientific and Engineering Recruitment, Training, and Development The Director, Office of Scientific and Engineering Recruitment, Training, and Development, reports directly to the Under Secretary and, working in concert with various Assistant Secretaries and program directors, is responsible for formulating and implementing scientific and engineering training, recruitment, and development programs.

Intelligence The Office of Intelligence ensures that intelligence information requirements of the Secretary and senior departmental policymakers are met and that the Department's technical, analytical, and research expertise is made available to the intelligence community in accordance with Executive Order 12333 of December 4, 1981. The Office provides threat assessments and support to DOE Headquarters and field offices.

International Affairs and Energy Emergencies The Assistant Secretary for International Affairs and Energy Emergencies develops, manages, and directs programs and activities relating to the international aspects of overall energy policy; ensures that U.S. international energy policies and programs conform to national goals, legislation, and treaty obligations; advises the Secretary on international energy negotiations; assesses world price and supply trends; and coordinates cooperative international energy programs with foreign governments and international organizations such as the International Energy Agency and the International Atomic Energy Agency.

The Assistant Secretary also directs and coordinates the Department's energy emergency preparedness and energy emergency operations efforts; develops contingency plans and tests and evaluates response plans; develops and maintains continuity of government and national emergency plans.

Inspector General The Office of Inspector General coordinates, supervises, and conducts inspections, investigations, and audits of all departmental internal activities, including those of the Federal Energy Regulatory Commission, to ensure honesty and efficiency. When necessary, these activities are coordinated with other Federal, State, and local agencies and with nongovernment entities. The Office also recommends corrective actions and identifies and refers for prosecution participants in fraud and abuse cases.

Hearings and Appeals The Office of Hearings and Appeals reviews and issues all final DOE orders of an adjudicatory nature, other than those involving matters over which the Federal Energy Regulatory Commission or the Energy Board of Contract Appeals exercises final jurisdiction. The Office is responsible for considering and issuing decisions on appeals from orders of a regulatory nature issued by DOE components and requests for exception or exemption from any regulatory or mandatory requirements.

Contract Appeals The Board of Contract Appeals hears and resolves appeals pertaining to contract-related matters. The Board may act as the Department's Contract Adjustment Board, the Financial Assistance Appeal Board, or the Invention Licensing Appeal Board.

Small and Disadvantaged Business Utilization The Office of Small and Disadvantaged Business Utilization is responsible for the policy, plans, and oversight of Department functions under sections 8 and 15 of the Small Business Act (15 U.S.C. 637, 644) relating to preferred programs for small businesses, disadvantaged businesses, labor surplus area concerns, and women-owned businesses. The Office also provides functional direction and oversight to headquarters and field personnel regarding implementation of these programs.

Secretary of Energy Advisory Board The Office of the Secretary of Energy Advisory Board provides administrative support and manages the activities of the Secretary of Energy Advisory Board (SEAB). The Office acts as a link between the Secretary and SEAB and other departmental advisory committees. The Office also acts as the Department's long-range planning group to provide the Secretary with advice on a wide spectrum of long-range scientific, environmental, international, and strategic matters.

Security Affairs The Office of Security Affairs establishes policies and procedures for the safeguarding and security of classified information and protection of departmental and DOE contractor facilities and installations. The Office also manages a personnel security program for sensitive positions within the Department.

Public Affairs The Office of Public Affairs manages press services, public affairs, and public information activities. The Office provides policy advice and support to the Secretary, Deputy Secretary, Under Secretary, and other secretarial officers on interacting with the news media. The Office serves as the chief spokesperson for the Secretary and the Department.

For further information, contact the Office of Public Affairs. Phone, 202–586–4940.

Programs

Energy Research The Office of Energy Research advises the Secretary on the physical and energy research and development programs of the Department, the use of multipurpose laboratories, education, and training for basic and applied research, and financial assistance and budgetary priorities for these activities.

The Office manages the basic energy sciences, high energy physics, and fusion energy research programs; administers DOE programs supporting university researchers; funds research in mathematical and computational sciences critical to the use and development of supercomputers; and administers a financial support program for research and development projects not funded elsewhere in the Department. The Office also manages a research program directed at determining the generic environmental, health, and safety aspects of energy technologies and programs.

The Office monitors DOE research and development programs for deficiencies or duplication of effort and, in conjunction with the Assistant Secretary for International Affairs and Energy Emergencies, monitors the international exchange of scientific and technical personnel.

For further information, contact the Deputy Director of Management. Phone, 301–353–4944.

Environmental Restoration and Waste Management The Director of the Office of Environmental Restoration and Waste Management provides program policy guidance and manages the assessment and cleanup of inactive waste sites and facilities, continues safe and effective waste management operations, and develops and implements an aggressively applied waste research and development program to provide innovative environmental technologies that yield permanent disposal solutions at reduced costs. The Director provides centralized management for the Department for waste management operations, environmental restoration, and applied research and development programs and activities, including environmental restoration and waste management program policy and guidance to DOE field offices in these areas.

For further information, contact the Office of Planning and Resource Management. Phone, 202–586–2661.

Fossil Energy The Assistant Secretary for Fossil Energy is responsible for research and development programs involving fossil fuels—coal, petroleum, and gas. The fossil energy program involves applied research, exploratory development, and limited proof-of-concept testing targeted to high-risk and high-payoff endeavors. The objective of the program is to provide the general technology and knowledge base that the private sector can use to complete development and initiate commercialization of advanced processes and energy systems. The program is principally executed through two Energy Technology Centers located in the field.

The Assistant Secretary also manages the Clean Coal Technology Program, the Strategic Petroleum Reserve, the Naval Petroleum and Oil Shale Reserves, and the Liquefied Gaseous Fuels Spill Test Facility.

For further information, contact the Deputy Assistant Secretary for Management, Fundamental Research and Cooperative Development. Phone, 301–353–2617.

Nuclear Safety The Office of Nuclear Safety provides independent oversight of line management performance, including self-assessment, to assure proper development and implementation of reactor and nonreactor nuclear facility safety policies and standards throughout the Department. The Office enforces the civil penalty and criminal referral provisions of the Price-Anderson Amendments Act of 1988.

For further information, contact the Office of Nuclear Safety. Phone, 202–586–2407.

Conservation and Renewable Energy The Assistant Secretary for Conservation and Renewable Energy is responsible for formulating and directing programs designed to increase the production and utilization of renewable energy (solar, biomass, wind, geothermal, alcohol fuels, etc.) and improving the energy efficiency of transportation, buildings, industrial systems, and related processes through support of long-term, high-risk research and development activities. The Assistant Secretary also has responsibility for administering statutorily mandated assistance programs that provide financial assistance for State energy planning, weatherization of housing owned by the poor and disadvantaged, and the implementation of energy conservation measures by schools and hospitals, local units of government, and public care institutions. In addition, the Office coordinates and oversees the operations of five power-marketing administrations.

For further information, contact the Director of Management and Resources. Phone, 202–586–6768.

Defense Programs The Assistant Secretary for Defense Programs directs the Nation's nuclear weapons research, development, testing, production, and surveillance program, as well as the production of the special nuclear materials used by the weapons program within the Department, and management of defense nuclear waste and byproducts.

The Office also manages research in inertial confinement fusion; the safeguards and security line management responsibilities of the Office and DOE field offices; classification, declassification, and reclassification of documents; unclassified controlled nuclear information; export control; test ban treaty verification and monitoring technology; and coordinates the Department's emergency management activities.

For further information, contact the Deputy Assistant Secretary for Planning and Resource Management. Phone, 202–586–2295

Nuclear Energy The Assistant Secretary for Nuclear Energy administers the Department's research and development programs associated with fission energy. This includes programs relating to nuclear reactor development, both civilian and naval; nuclear fuel cycle; space nuclear applications; and uranium enrichment. The Assistant Secretary also manages the Department's Remedial Action Program to treat or stabilize radioactive wastes and perform decontamination and decommissioning at DOE surplus sites. In addition, the Assistant Secretary conducts technical analyses and provides advice concerning nonproliferation; assesses alternative nuclear systems and new reactor and fuel cycle concepts; and evaluates proposed advanced nuclear fission energy concepts and technical improvements for possible application to nuclear powerplant systems.

For further information, contact the Director of Program Support. Phone, 202–586–1941.

Civilian Radioactive Waste Management The Office of Civilian Radioactive Waste Management was established by the Nuclear Waste Policy Act of 1982 (42 U.S.C. 10224). The Office has responsibility for the Nuclear Waste Fund and for the management of Federal programs for recommending, constructing, and operating repositories for disposal of high-level radioactive waste and spent nuclear fuel; interim storage of spent nuclear fuel; monitored retrievable storage; and research, development, and demonstration regarding disposal of high-level radioactive waste and spent nuclear fuel.

For further information, contact the Associate Director for Program and Resources Management. Phone, 202–586–9116.

New Production Reactors The Office of New Production Reactors manages and directs a program for the acquisition and construction of new production reactor capacity to meet national security requirements.

For further information, contact the Director of Business Management. Phone, 202–586–6456.

Administrations

Energy Information Administration The Energy Information Administration is responsible for the timely and accurate collection, processing, and publication of data in the areas of energy resource reserves, energy production, demand, consumption, distribution, and technology.

The Administration performs analyses of energy data to assist government and nongovernment users in understanding energy trends. Analyses are prepared on complex, long-term energy trends and the microeconomic and macroeconomic impacts of energy trends on regional and industrial sectors. Special purpose analyses are prepared involving competition within the energy industries, the capital/financial structure of energy companies, and interfuel substitution. Audits are conducted to ensure the validity of regulatory and other energy data.

The Administration provides data publication and distribution services within DOE, throughout the Government, and for the public. It is a clearinghouse for general information on energy and coordinates its activities with the Department's Technical Information Center.

For further information, contact the Director, National Energy Information Center. Phone, 202–586–2363; (TDD) 202–586–1181.

Economic Regulatory Administration The Economic Regulatory Administration administers the Department's regulatory programs other than those assigned to the Federal Energy Regulatory Commission.

For further information, contact the Director of Management and Information Systems. Phone, 202–586–4241.

Independent Commission

Federal Energy Regulatory Commission An independent, five-member commission within the Department of Energy, the Federal Energy Regulatory Commission has retained many of the functions of the Federal Power Commission, such as setting rates and charges for the transportation and sale of natural gas and for the transmission and sale of electricity and the licensing of hydroelectric power projects. In addition, the Commission establishes rates or charges for the transportation of oil by pipeline, as well as the valuation of such pipelines.

For further information, contact the Executive Director. Phone, 202–357–8300.

Field Structure

DOE Field Offices and Contractor-Operated Field Installations

The vast majority of the Department's energy research and development, uranium enrichment and nuclear weapons research and development, and testing and production activities are carried out by contractors who operate Government-owned facilities. Management and administration of Government-owned, contractor-operated facility contracts are the major responsibility of the Department's eight field offices.

The DOE field offices provide a formal link between Department headquarters and the field laboratories and other operating facilities. They also manage programs and projects as assigned from headquarters. Each DOE field office reports directly to a specific program Secretarial officer as follows: (1) DOE field offices in Albuquerque, NM; Las Vegas, NV; and Savannah River, SC; report to the Assistant Secretary for Defense Programs; (2) DOE field offices in Chicago, IL; and San Francisco, CA; report to the Director of Energy Research; (3) DOE field offices in Idaho Falls, ID; and Oak Ridge, TN; report to the Assistant Secretary for Nuclear Energy; and (4) the DOE field office in Richland, WA, reports to the Director of Environmental Restoration and Waste Management. Specific program direction for the DOE field offices is provided by the responsible Assistant Secretaries and the Director or the program officer.

Field Offices—Department of Energy

Office/Address	Telephone
Albuquerque, NM (P.O. Box 5400, 87115)	505–846–7231
Chicago, IL (9800 S. Cass Ave., Argonne, IL 60439)	708–972–2110
Idaho Falls, ID (785 Doe Pl.. 83402)	208–526–1322
Las Vegas, NV (P.O. Box 98518, 89193-8518)	702–295–3211
Oak Ridge, TN (P.O. Box 2001, 37831)	615–576–4444
Richland, WA (P.O. Box 550, 825 Jadwin Ave., 99352)	509–376–7395
San Francisco, CA (1333 Broadway, Oakland, CA 94612)	415–273–7111
Savannah River, SC (P.O. Box A, Aiken, SC 29808)	803–725–2277

Other Field Offices The Department also has several field offices concerned primarily with specific programs, such as the Strategic Petroleum Reserve Project Office, two offices involved with the

290-950 0 91 - 10

development of nuclear reactors for the Navy, and several offices devoted to the management of the Naval Petroleum and Oil Shale Reserves.

Regulatory Programs

The Department of Energy's enforcement program is conducted by the field staff under the supervision and direction of the Administrator of the Economic Regulatory Administration.

Power Administrations

The marketing and transmission of electric power produced at Federal hydroelectric projects and reservoirs is carried out by the Department's five Power Administrations. Management oversight of the Power Administrations is the responsibility of the Assistant Secretary for Conservation and Renewable Energy.

Bonneville Power Administration The Administration was created pursuant to the Bonneville Project Act of August 20, 1937, as amended (16 U.S.C. 832 *et seq.*). Through a regionwide, interconnecting transmission system it markets electric power and energy from Federal hydroelectric projects in the Pacific Northwest constructed and operated by the Army Corps of Engineers and the Department of the Interior's Bureau of Reclamation. Through interregional connections, it sells surplus power to areas outside the Pacific Northwest region and participates in exchanges of power.

The Administration markets power produced by the Federal Columbia River Power System at the lowest rates, consistent with sound business practices. Preference is given to public entities.

Power is sold at wholesale to utilities and directly to electroprocess industries and other Federal agencies. The Administration also exchanges electric power; prepares wholesale rates and repayment schedules; and constructs, operates, and maintains a transmission system that integrates Federal power projects and interconnects with non-Federal utility systems.

In addition, the Administration is responsible for energy conservation, renewable resource development, and fish and wildlife enhancement under the provisions of the Pacific Northwest Electric Power Planning and Conservation Act of 1980 (16 U.S.C. 839 note).

The Administration, in cooperation with the Corps of Engineers, represents the United States in implementing the provisions of the Columbia River Treaty with Canada.

By act of October 18, 1974 (16 U.S.C. 838), the Bonneville Power Administration has the authority, in lieu of appropriations, to use its revenues and to sell revenue bonds to the U.S. Treasury to finance its programs.

For further information, contact the Bonneville Power Administration, P.O. Box 3621, 1002 NE. Holladay Street, Portland, OR 97208. Phone, 503–230–5101.

Southeastern Power Administration The Administration was created by the Secretary of the Interior in 1950 to carry out functions assigned to the Secretary by the Flood Control Act of 1944 (58 Stat. 890), which pertain to the transmission and disposition of surplus electric power and energy generated at reservoir projects that are or may be under the control of the Department of the Army in the States of West Virginia, Virginia, North Carolina, South Carolina, Georgia, Florida, Alabama, Mississippi, Tennessee, and Kentucky. The Southeastern Power Administration was transferred from the Department of the Interior to the Department of Energy by the Department of Energy Organization Act (42 U.S.C. 7152), effective October 1, 1977.

The Administration transmits and disposes of the surplus electric power and energy generated at the Federal reservoir projects in such manner as to encourage the most widespread use. The Administration sets the lowest possible rates to consumers, consistent with sound business principles, and gives preference in the sale of such power and energy to public bodies and cooperatives.

The program of the Administration includes the negotiation, preparation, execution, and administration of contracts for the disposition of electric power; the preparation of wholesale rates and repayment schedules; the provision by construction, contract, or otherwise, of transmission and related facilities to interconnect reservoir projects and to serve contractual loads; and activities pertaining to the planning and operation of power facilities.

For further information, contact the Southeastern Power Administration, Elberton, GA 30635. Phone, 404–283–9917.

Alaska Power Administration The Administration is responsible for operating and marketing power for two Federal hydroelectric projects in Alaska. Legislative authorities for this work include the Eklutna Project Act (64 Stat. 382); the Snettisham Project authorization in the Flood Control Act of 1962 (76 Stat. 1193); the power-marketing provision of the Flood Control Act of 1944 (58 Stat. 890); the act of August 9, 1955, Investigation of Water Resources, Alaska; and section 201 of the Water Resources Development Act of 1976 (90 Stat. 2944).

Power operations and marketing functions involving the Eklutna and Snettisham Hydroelectric Projects include the projects' transmission systems serving the Anchorage and Juneau areas.

For further information, contact the Alaska Power Administration, Suite 2B, 2770 Sherwood Lane, Juneau, AK 99801. Phone, 907–586–7405.

Southwestern Power Administration The Administration was created by the Secretary of the Interior in 1943 to carry out the Secretary's responsibility for the sale and disposition of electric power and energy generated at certain projects constructed and operated by the Department of the Army. For these projects, the Administration carries out the functions assigned to the Secretary by the Flood Control Act of 1944 (16 U.S.C. 825s) in the States of Arkansas, Kansas, Louisiana, Missouri, Oklahoma, and Texas. Since October 1, 1977, the Southwestern Power Administration has been functioning under the direction of the Secretary of Energy, pursuant to section 302(a)(1) of the Department of Energy Organization Act (42 U.S.C. 7152).

The headquarters office is located at Tulsa, OK, and there are three area offices—Springfield, MO; Muskogee, OK; and Jonesboro, AR—four maintenance units, and two dispatching offices.

The Southwestern Power Administration transmits and disposes of the electric power and energy generated at Federal reservoir projects, supplemented by power purchased from public and private utilities, in such a manner as to encourage the most widespread and economical use. The Administration sets the lowest possible rates to consumers, consistent with sound business principles, and gives preference in the sale of power and energy to public bodies and cooperatives.

The Administration:

—develops, negotiates, and administers contracts for the sale and interchange of electric power and energy on a wholesale basis;

—prepares rate and repayment studies;

—designs and constructs transmission lines and related facilities to interconnect hydroelectric projects of the Administration's system and other systems, both public and private;

—operates and maintains the high-voltage transmission system to serve contractual loads, maintain reliable interconnections, and utilize excess capacity to provide transmission service to others;

—develops long-range marketing programs for maximum utilization of power from existing and proposed hydroelectric projects; and

—conducts and participates in the comprehensive planning of water resource development in the Southwest.

For further information, contact the Southwestern Power Administration, P.O. Box 1619, Tulsa, OK 74101. Phone, 918–581–7474.

Western Area Power Administration The Administration was established on December 21, 1977, pursuant to section 302 of the Department of Energy Organization Act (42 U.S.C. 7152). The Administration is responsible for the

Federal electric power-marketing and transmission functions in 15 central and western States, encompassing a geographic area of 1.3 million square miles. The Administration sells power to 532 customers, consisting of cooperatives, municipalities, public utility districts, private utilities, Federal and State agencies, and irrigation districts. The wholesale power customers, in turn, provide service to millions of retail consumers in the States of Arizona, California, Colorado, Iowa, Kansas, Minnesota, Montana, Nebraska, Nevada, New Mexico, North Dakota, South Dakota, Texas, Utah, and Wyoming.

The Administration is responsible for the operation and maintenance of 16,178 miles of transmission lines, 228 substations, and various auxiliary power facilities in the aforementioned geographic areas and also for planning, construction, and operation and maintenance of additional Federal transmission facilities that may be authorized in the future. Electric power marketed by the Administration is generated by the Bureau of Reclamation, the U.S. Army Corps of Engineers, and the International Boundary and Water Commission, which operates 47 hydropower generating plants in its service area. In addition, it markets the United States entitlement from the Navajo coal-fired plant near Page, AZ. The Administration's current installed generating capacity is 8,321 megawatts.

In carrying out the Federal power-marketing program, the Administration's organization consists of the Headquarters Office located in Golden, CO; five area offices—Billings, MT; Boulder City, NV; Loveland, CO; Sacramento, CA; and Salt Lake City, UT—five district offices, and one power systems operations office.

For further information, contact the Western Area Power Administration, P.O. Box 3402, Golden, CO 80401. Phone, 303–231–1513.

DEPARTMENT OF HEALTH AND HUMAN SERVICES

200 Independence Avenue SW., Washington, DC 20201
Phone, 202–619–0257

SECRETARY OF HEALTH AND HUMAN SERVICES	LOUIS W. SULLIVAN, M.D.
Executive Assistant to the Secretary	RONNY LANCASTER
Confidential Assistant to the Secretary	SHIRLEY DESAUSSURE
Deputy Secretary	CONSTANCE HORNER
Deputy Under Secretary for Policy and Administration	ANN AGNEW
Deputy Under Secretary for Intergovernmental Affairs, Boards and Commissions	SCHUYLER BAAB
Chief of Staff	MICHAEL CALHOUN
Executive Secretary	ROBIN CARLE
Inspector General	RICHARD P. KUSSEROW
Principal Deputy Inspector General	BRYAN B. MITCHELL
Assistant Inspector General for Management and Policy	JANE TEBBUTT
Deputy Inspector General for Audit Services	THOMAS D. ROSLEWICZ
Deputy Inspector General for Investigations	LARRY D. MOREY
Deputy Inspector General for Evaluation and Inspections	MICHAEL MANGANO
Director, Office for Civil Rights	EDWARD MERCADO
Deputy Director	CHARLES TAYLOR
Associate Deputy Director, Management Planning and Evaluation	PAUL R. KRETCHMAR
Deputy to the Associate Director, Management Planning and Evaluation	GUY E. WITCHER
Associate Deputy Director, Program Operations	RONALD COPELAND
Deputy to the Associate Deputy Director, Program Operations	PATRICIA MACKEY
Director, Policy and Special Projects Staff	MARCELLA HAYNES
Director, U.S. Office of Consumer Affairs	ANN WINDHAM WALLACE
Assistant Secretary (Public Affairs)	ALIXE REED GLEN
Deputy Assistant Secretary for Public Affairs (Policy and Communications)	DEBORAH MESSICK
Deputy Assistant Secretary for Public Affairs (Media)	JOHN GIBBONS
Director, News Division	P. CAMPBELL GARDETT
Assistant Secretary (Legislation)	STEVEN B. KELMAR
Confidential Assistant	VARRICK M. MCKEE
Principal Deputy Assistant Secretary	WENDY R. STRONG
Deputy Assistant Secretary (Congressional Liaison)	JUDI A. LINDSEY

Deputy Assistant Secretary (Health)	JAMES RICCIUTI
Deputy Assistant Secretary (Human Services)	LINDA E. TARPLIN
Assistant Secretary for Planning and Evaluation	MARTIN H. GERRY
Executive Assistant	(VACANCY)
Deputy Assistant Secretary for Health Policy	CHRISTOPHER BLADEN, *Acting*
Deputy Assistant Secretary for Program Systems	GERALD H. BRITTEN
Deputy Assistant Secretary for Income Security Policy	MICHAEL FISHMAN, *Acting*
Deputy Assistant Secretary for Social Services Policy	PATRICK FAGAN
General Counsel	MICHAEL J. ASTRUE
Principal Deputy General Counsel	GROVER G. HANKINS
Deputy General Counsel	BEVERLY DENNIS III
Special Assistant to the General Counsel	CAROLYN J. HARVEY
Deputy General Counsel (Legal Counsel)	SUSAN K. ZAGAME
Special Assistant to the General Counsel	DAVID V. FOSTER
Executive Officer	RONALD J. RUFFO
Associate General Counsel, Business and Administrative Law Division	SANDRA SHAPIRO
Associate General Counsel, Civil Rights Division	GEORGE LYON
Associate General Counsel, Family Support and Human Development	FRANK DELL'ACQUA
Associate General Counsel, Food and Drug Division	MARGARET PORTER
Associate General Counsel, Health Care Financing Division	DARREL GRINSTEAD
Associate General Counsel, Inspector General Counsel	D. MCCARTY THORNTON
Associate General Counsel, Legislation	FRANCES WHITE
Associate General Counsel, Public Health Division	RICHARD RISEBERG
Associate General Counsel, Social Security Division	DONALD GONYA
Assistant Secretary for Management and Budget	KEVIN E. MOLEY
Principal Deputy Assistant Secretary for Management and Budget	ELIZABETH M. JAMES
Deputy Assistant Secretary, Budget	DENNIS P. WILLIAMS
Deputy Assistant Secretary, Finance	DENNIS J. FISCHER
Deputy Assistant Secretary for Information Resources Management	NEIL STILLMAN
Deputy Assistant Secretary for Management and Acquisition	JAMES F. TRICKETT
Assistant Secretary for Personnel Administration and Director, Equal Employment Opportunity	THOMAS S. MCFEE
Deputy Assistant Secretary for Personnel Administration and Deputy Director, Equal Employment Opportunity	EUGENE KINLOW
Director, Office of Special Initiatives	CHARLES J. MCCARTY III
Chairman, Departmental Appeals Board	NORVAL (JOHN) D. SETTLE
Director, Office of Human Resource Information Management	THOMAS M. KING
Director, Office of Personnel Services	EVELYN KIRBY

Director, Office of Human Resources Programs	CHARLES J. MCCARTY III, *Acting*
Director, Office of Human Relations	LAFOREST FAULKNER
Commissioner, Administration on Aging	JOYCE T. BERRY

ADMINISTRATION FOR CHILDREN AND FAMILIES

370 L'Enfant Promenade SW., Washington, DC 20447
Phone, 202–401–9200

Assistant Secretary	JO ANNE B. BARNHART
Principal Deputy Assistant Secretary	DONNA N. GIVENS
Deputy Assistant Secretaries	LAURENCE J. LOVE
	ROBERT M. WILSON

Family Support Administraton

370 L'Enfant Promenade SW., Washington, DC 20447
Phone, 202–401–9200

Director, Office of Family Assistance	JASON TURNER
Director, Office of Child Support Enforcement	JO ANNE B. BARNHART
Director, Office of Community Services	EUNICE S. THOMAS
Director, Office of Refugee Resettlement	CHRISTOPHER GERSTEN
Associate Administrator, Office of Financial Management	MICHAEL STURMAN
Associate Administrator, Office of Program Evaluation	HOWARD ROLSTON
Associate Administrator, Office of Management and Information Systems	NAOMI B. MARR
Associate Administrator, Office of Communications	BARBARA A. CEBUHAR

Office of Human Development Services

200 Independence Avenue SW., Washington, DC 20201
Phone, 202–245–7246

Director, Office of Public Affairs	SUSAN G. LONG
Director, Office of Management Services	ROBERT E. STOVENOUR
Director, Office of Policy, Planning and Legislation	WILLIAM SCHAMBRA
Commissioner, Administration for Children, Youth and Families	WADE F. HORN
Commissioner, Administration for Native Americans	S. TIMOTHY WAPATO
Commissioner, Administration on Developmental Disabilities	DEBORAH MCFADDEN

PUBLIC HEALTH SERVICE

Office of the Assistant Secretary for Health

200 Independence Avenue SW., Washington, DC 20201
Phone, 202–619–1296

5600 Fishers Lane, Rockville, MD 20857
Phone, 301–443–2404

Assistant Secretary for Health	JAMES O. MASON
Principal Deputy Assistant Secretary for Health	AUDREY F. MANLEY
Surgeon General of the Public Health Service	ANTONIA C. NOVELLO
Deputy Assistant Secretary for Health (Communications)	PAUL B. SIMMONS
Deputy Assistant Secretary for Health (Disease Prevention and Health Promotion)	J. MICHAEL MCGINNIS
Deputy Assistant Secretary for Health (Intergovernmental Affairs)	SAMUEL LIN
Deputy Assistant Secretary for Health (Management Operations)	ANTHONY L. ITTEILAG
Deputy Assistant Secretary for Health (Science and Environment)	FRANK E. YOUNG
Deputy Assistant Secretary for Minority Health	WILLIAM A. ROBINSON
Deputy Assistant Secretary for Population Affairs	WILLIAM R. ARCHER III
Deputy Assistant Secretary for Public Health Policy	SANDRA K. MAHKORN
Executive Director, President's Council on Physical Fitness and Sports	WILLIAM D. MIZELL, SR.
Director, National AIDS Program Office	JAMES R. ALLEN
Director, National Vaccine Program Office	KENNETH J. BART
Director, Office of Adolescent Pregnancy Programs	PATRICIA FUNDERBURK
Director, Office of Emergency Preparedness	THOMAS P. REUTERSHAN
Director, Office of Equal Employment Opportunity	DAN RONDEAU
Director, Office of Family Planning	MARA DUFFY
Director, Office of Health Legislation	JAMES RICCIUTI
Director, Office of International Health	LINDA A. VOGEL, *Acting*
Director, Office of Management	WILFORD J. FORBUSH
Director, Office of Refugee Health	RICHARD B. CRAVENS
Director, Office of Scientific Integrity Review	LYLE W. BIVENS
Director, PHS Executive Secretariat	ROBERT A. RICKARD

Agency for Health Care Policy and Research

5600 Fishers Lane, Rockville, MD 20857
Phone, 301–443–4100

Administrator	J. JARRETT CLINTON
Director, Office of Planning and Resource Management	WILLARD B. EVANS, *Acting*
Director, Office of Science and Data Development	J. MICHAEL FITZMAURICE
Director, Office of the Forum for Quality and Effectiveness in Health Care	LAWRENCE E. WILLIAMS, *Acting*

Director, Office of Health Technology Assessment	THOMAS V. HOLOHAN
Director, Center for Medical Effectiveness Research	RICHARD J. GREENE, *Acting*
Director, Center for General Health Services Intramural Research	DONALD E. GOLDSTONE
Director, Center for General Health Services Extramural Research	NORMAN W. WEISSMAN
Director, Center for Research Dissemination and Liaison	MARGARET A. VANAMRINGE

Alcohol, Drug Abuse, and Mental Health Administration

5600 Fishers Lane, Rockville, MD 20857
Phone, 301–443–4797

Administrator	FREDERICK K. GOODWIN
Deputy Administrator	ROBERT L. TRACHTENBERG
Associate Administrator for Prevention	ELAINE M. JOHNSON
Associate Administrator for Management	JOSEPH R. LEONE
Associate Administrator for Communications and External Affairs	JAMES A. MILLER
Associate Administrator for Extramural Programs	MICHELE W. APPLEGATE
Associate Administrator for Policy Coordination	FRANK N. SULLIVAN, JR.
Associate Administrator for Treatment Improvement	BENY J. PRIMM
Director, National Institute of Mental Health	ALAN I. LESHNER, *Acting*
Director, National Institute on Alcohol Abuse and Alcoholism	ENOCH GORDIS
Director, National Institute on Drug Abuse	CHARLES R. SCHUSTER
Director, Office for Substance Abuse Prevention	ELAINE K. JOHNSON

Centers for Disease Control

1600 Clifton Road NE., Atlanta, GA 30333
Phone, 404–639–3311

Director	WILLIAM L. ROPER
Deputy Director	WALTER R. DOWDLE
Deputy Director (HIV)	GARY R. NOBLE
Assistant Director (Washington)	GEORGE E. HARDY, JR.
Deputy Director, CDC Washington Office	FRANCES LEE DE PEYSTER
Special Assistant to Assistant Director (CDC Washington Office)	ROBERT C. IRWIN
Assistant Director for Public Health Practice	DENNIS D. TOLSMA
Assistant Director for Science	CLAIRE V. BROOME
Assistant Director for International Health	JOE H. DAVIS
Assistant Director for Minority Health	RUEBEN C. WARREN
Associate Director for Policy Coordination	ELVIN R. HILYER
Equal Employment Opportunity Manager	B.J. FLOWERS, *Acting*
Director, Office of Program Support	GLENDA S. COWART
Director, Office of Health and Safety	JONATHAN Y. RICHMOND
Director, Office of Program Planning and Evaluation	MARTHA F. KATZ

Director, Office of Public Affairs	Donald A. Berreth
Director, Epidemiology Program Office	Stephen B. Thacker
Director, International Health Program Office	Joe H. Davis
Director, Public Health Practice Program Office	Edward L. Baker
Director, Center for Environmental Health and Injury Control	Vernon N. Houk
Director, Center for Chronic Disease Prevention and Health Promotion	Jeffrey P. Koplan
Director, Center for Infectious Diseases	Frederick A. Murphy
Director, Center for Prevention Services	Alan R. Hinman
Director, National Institute for Occupational Safety and Health	J. Donald Millar
Director, National Center for Health Statistics	Manning Feinleib

Agency for Toxic Substances and Disease Registry

1600 Clifton Road NE., Atlanta, GA 30333
Phone, 404–452–4111

Administrator	William L. Roper
Deputy Administrator	Walter R. Dowdle
Assistant Administrator	Barry L. Johnson
Deputy Assistant Administrator	William D. Adams

Food and Drug Administration

5600 Fishers Lane, Rockville, MD 20857
Phone, 301–443–1544

Commissioner of Food and Drugs	David A. Kessler
Deputy Commissioner	James S. Benson
Chief of Staff and Director, Executive Operations	Joseph A. Levitt
Associate Commissioner for Regulatory Affairs	Ronald G. Chesemore
Associate Commissioner for Management and Operations	Sharon Smith Holston
Associate Commissioner for Health Affairs	Stuart L. Nightingale
Director, Executive Secretariat	Dennis L. Myers
Associate Commissioner for Science	(vacancy)
Associate Commissioner for Planning and Evaluation	Gerald L. Barkdoll
Associate Commissioner for Legislative Affairs	Hugh C. Cannon
Associate Commissioner for Public Affairs	Jeffrey A. Nesbit
Associate Commissioner for Consumer Affairs	Alexander Grant
Director, Center for Food Safety and Applied Nutrition	Fred R. Shank
Director, Center for Biologics Evaluation and Research	Gerald V. Quinnan, Jr., *Acting*
Director, Center for Drug Evaluation and Research	Carl C. Peck
Director, Center for Veterinary Medicine	Gerald B. Guest
Director, Center for Devices and Radiological Health	Walter E. Gundaker, *Acting*
Director, National Center for Toxicological Research	Ronald W. Hart

Health Resources and Services Administration

5600 Fishers Lane, Rockville, MD 20857
Phone, 301–443–2086

Administrator	ROBERT G. HARMON
Deputy Administrator	JOHN H. KELSO
Associate Administrator for AIDS	SAMUEL C. MATHENY
Associate Administrator for Operations and Management	JAMES A. WALSH
Associate Administrator for Planning, Evaluation, and Legislation	RONALD H. CARLSON
Associate Administrator for Communications	SYLVIA W. SHAFFER
Associate Administrator for Extramural Affairs	FLORENCE B. FIORI
Associate Administrator for Policy Coordination	THOMAS D. HATCH
Associate Administrator for International Health	GEORGE B. DINES
Associate Administrator for Minority Health	(VACANCY)
Associate Administrator for Equal Opportunity and Civil Rights	J. CALVIN ADAMS
Director, Bureau of Health Professions	FITZHUGH M. MULLAN
Director, Maternal and Child Health Bureau	VINCE L. HUTCHINS
Director, Bureau of Health Resources Development	G. STEPHEN BOWEN
Director, Bureau of Health Care Delivery and Assistance	MARILYN H. GASTON

Indian Health Service

5600 Fishers Lane, Rockville, MD 20857
Phone, 301–443–1083

Director	EVERETT R. RHOADES
Deputy Director	MICHEL LINCOLN
Director of Headquarters Operations	ROBERT MARSLAND
Associate Director, Office of Administration and Management	GEORGE BUZZARD
Associate Director, Office of Planning, Evaluation, and Legislation	LUANA L. REYES
Associate Director, Office of Tribal Activities	DOUGLAS BLACK, *Acting*
Associate Director, Office of Environmental Health and Engineering	BILL F. PEARSON
Associate Director, Office of Information Resources Management	JACK N. MARKOWITZ, *Acting*
Associate Director, Office of Health Programs	CRAIG VANDERWAGEN, *Acting*
Associate Director, Office of Health Program Research and Development	ELEANORE ROBERTSON

National Institutes of Health

9000 Rockville Pike, Bethesda, MD 20892
Phone, 301–496–4000

Director	BERNADINE P. HEALY
Deputy Director	WILLIAM F. RAUB
Deputy Director for Intramural Research	JOSEPH E. RALL
Deputy Director for Extramural Research	JOHN W. DIGGS

Assistant Director for Program Coordination	VIDA H. BEAVEN
Associate Director for Research on Women's Health	RUTH L. KIRSCHSTEIN, *Acting*
Associate Director for Minority Programs	JOHN RUFFIN
Associate Director for AIDS Research	ANTHONY S. FAUCI
Associate Director for Administration	JOHN D. MAHONEY
Associate Director for Clinical Care	SAUL W. ROSEN, *Acting*
Associate Director for Communications	STORM WHALEY
Associate Director for Disease Prevention	JOHN H. FERGUSON, *Acting*
Associate Director for Extramural Affairs	GEORGE J. GALASSO
Associate Director for Intramural Affairs	PHILIP S. CHEN, JR.
Associate Director for Science Policy and Legislation	JAY MOSKOWITZ
Associate Director for Research Services	NORMAN D. MANSFIELD
Director, Office of Scientific Integrity	JULES V. HALLUM
Director, National Cancer Institute	SAMUEL BRODER
Director, National Heart, Lung, and Blood Institute	CLAUDE J.M. LENFANT
Director, National Institute of Diabetes and Digestive and Kidney Diseases	PHILLIP GORDEN
Director, National Library of Medicine	DONALD A.B. LINDBERG
Director, National Institute of Allergy and Infectious Diseases	ANTHONY S. FAUCI
Director, National Institute on Deafness and Other Communication Disorders	JAMES B. SNOW, JR.
Director, National Institute of Dental Research	HARALD A. LÖE
Director, National Institute of Neurological Disorders and Stroke	MURRAY GOLDSTEIN
Director, National Institute of General Medical Sciences	RUTH L. KIRSCHSTEIN
Director, National Institute of Child Health and Human Development	DUANE F. ALEXANDER
Director, National Institute of Environmental Health Sciences	DAVID G. HOEL, *Acting*
Director, National Eye Institute	CARL KUPFER
Director, National Institute on Aging	T. FRANKLIN WILLIAMS
Director, National Institute of Arthritis, Musculoskeletal and Skin Diseases	LAWRENCE E. SHULMAN
Director, Division of Research Grants	JEROME G. GREEN
Director, Clinical Center	SAUL W. ROSEN, *Acting*
Director, National Center for Research Resources	ROBERT A. WHITNEY, JR.
Director, Fogarty International Center	PHILIP E. SCHAMBRA
Director, Division of Computer Research and Technology	DAVID RODBARD
Director, National Center for Nursing Research	ADA SUE HINSHAW
Director, National Center for Human Genome Research	JAMES D. WATSON

HEALTH CARE FINANCING ADMINISTRATION

200 Independence Avenue SW., Washington, DC 20201
Phone, 202–245–6113

Administrator	GAIL R. WILENSKY
Deputy Administrator	J. MICHAEL HUDSON

Director, Office of Legislation and Policy	JEFFREY SANDERS
Director, Office of Coordinated Care Policy and Planning	EDMUND MOY
Director, Medicaid Bureau	CHRISTINE NYE
Director, Office of Executive Operations	KATHLEEN MEANS
Director, Office of Attorney Advisor	(VACANCY)
Associate Administrator for Communications	KEVIN ERBE
Deputy Associate Administrator for Communications	JOHN TROUT
Director, Office of Public Liaison	MATTHEW CROW, *Acting*
Director, Office of Public Affairs	MARIA FRIEDMAN
Associate Administrator for Management	ROBERT STREIMER
Deputy Associate Administrator for Management	RICHARD JOHN COTTER
Director, ıreau of Data Management and Strategy	REGINA MCPHILLIPS
Director, Office of the Actuary	ROLAND E. KING
Director, Equal Opportunity Office	ELAINE LAZAROFF
Director, Office of Budget and Administration	LEE MOSEDALE
Associate Administrator for Operations	LOUIS B. HAYS
Deputy Associate Administrator for Operations	DAVID BUTLER
Director, Office of Prepaid Health Care Operations and Oversight	WILLIAM BROGLIE
Director, Health Standards and Quality Bureau	THOMAS MORFORD
Director, Bureau of Program Operations	BARBARA GAGEL
Associate Administrator for Program Development	ROBERT EATON
Director, Bureau of Policy Development	KATHLEEN BUTO
Director, Office of Research and Demonstrations	JOSEPH ANTOS

SOCIAL SECURITY ADMINISTRATION

6401 Security Boulevard, Baltimore, MD 21235
Phone, 301–965–1234

Commissioner of Social Security	GWENDOLYN S. KING
Principal Deputy Commissioner	LOUIS D. ENOFF
Senior Executive Officer	RICHARD A. EISINGER
Director, Executive Operations	ANDRIA CHILDS
Director, Strategic Planning Staff	PAUL J. TRACY
Director, Office of Information Resources Management	GEORGE FAILLA, *Acting*
Counselor to the Commissioner	ANDREW YOUNG
Deputy Commissioner, Programs	(VACANCY)
Assistant Deputy Commissioner, Programs	GILBERT C. FISHER
Chief Actuary	HARRY C. BALLANTYNE
Associate Commissioner, Retirement and Survivors Insurance	SANDY CRANK
Associate Commissioner, Supplemental Security Income	RHODA M.G. DAVIS
Associate Commissioner, Disability	SUSAN B. PARKER
Associate Commissioner, Hearings and Appeals	(VACANCY)

Deputy Commissioner, Finance, Assessment and Management	John R. Dyer, *Acting*
Assistant Deputy Commissioner, Finance, Assessment and Management	Dale W. Sopper, *Acting*
Senior Financial Executive	Norman Goldstein, *Acting*
Associate Commissioner, Program and Integrity Reviews	Joseph A. Gribbin
Associate Commissioner, Financial Policy and Operations	Matthew G. Schwienteck
Associate Commissioner, Budget	Robert M. Rothenberg, *Acting*
Associate Commissioner, Acquisition and Grants	James M. Fornataro, *Acting*
Associate Commissioner, Facilities Management	Marilyn O'Connell, *Acting*
Director, Office of Publications and Logistics Management	Robert D. Marder
Deputy Commissioner, Operations	Janice L. Warden, *Acting*
Assistant Deputy Commissioner, Operations	Huldah Lieberman, *Acting*
Associate Commissioner, Public and Employee Services	Michael W. Grochowski, *Acting*
Associate Commissioner, Operations Management and Program Integration	Elliot A. Kirschbaum, *Acting*
Associate Commissioner, Automation Support	Winston M. Cobb, *Acting*
Director, Central Records Operations	Edward P. Arthur
Director, Disability and International Operations	Joseph R. Muffolett
Deputy Commissioner, Policy and External Affairs	Charles P. Maloney III
Assistant Deputy Commissioner, Policy and External Affairs	(vacancy)
Associate Commissioner, Public Affairs	Patricia Butler
Associate Commissioner, Policy	Sara A. Hamer
Associate Commissioner, Legislation and Congressional Affairs	Gayle J. Cozens
Director, Office of International Policy	James A. Kissko
Director, Office of Research and Statistics	Peggy S. Trout, *Acting*
Deputy Commissioner, Human Resources	Ruth A. Pierce, *Acting*
Assistant Deputy Commissioner, Human Resources	David L. Jenkins, *Acting*
Associate Commissioner, Personnel	(vacancy)
Director, Office of Labor-Management Relations	Paulette Weinrich, *Acting*
Director, Office of Training	Stephen C. Kennedy
Director, Office of Workforce Analysis	Kenneth D. Nibali, *Acting*
Director, Office of Civil Rights and Equal Opportunity	Miguel Torrado
Deputy Commissioner, Systems	Renato A. DiPentima, *Acting*
Assistant Deputy Commissioner, Systems	D. Dean Mesterharm, *Acting*
Associate Commissioner, Systems Operations	Thomas J. O'Hare, Jr.
Associate Commissioner, Systems Design and Development	Margaret Foertschbeck, *Acting*
Associate Commissioner, Systems Requirements	Eve Hilgenberg

Associate Commissioner, Information Management	RALPH J. DEANGELUS, *Acting*
Associate Commissioner, Telecommunications	MARTIN BAER, *Acting*
Director, Office of Systems Planning and Integration	F. CARY GREEN

The Department of Health and Human Services is the Cabinet-level department of the Federal executive branch most concerned with people and most involved with the Nation's human concerns. In one way or another—whether it is mailing out social security checks or making health services more widely available—HHS touches the lives of more Americans than any other Federal agency. It is literally a department of people serving people, from newborn infants to our most elderly citizens.

The Department of Health, Education, and Welfare was created on April 11, 1953. The Department was redesignated as the Department of Health and Human Services (HHS), effective May 4, 1980, by the Department of Education Organization Act (20 U.S.C. 3508).

Office of the Secretary

The Secretary of Health and Human Services advises the President on health, welfare, and income security plans, policies, and programs of the Federal Government. The Secretary directs Department staff in carrying out the approved programs and activities of the Department and promotes general public understanding of the Department's goals, programs, and objectives. The Secretary administers these functions through the Office of the Secretary and the four Operating Divisions, which include: the Social Security Administration, the Health Care Financing Administration, the Administration for Children and Families, and the Public Health Service.

The Deputy Secretary, the Assistant Secretaries, the General Counsel, the Inspector General, and other senior officials aid the Secretary with the overall management responsibilities of the Department.

Since the Secretary is accountable to the Congress and the public for the way the Department spends taxpayers' money, the Secretary and top staff spend a considerable amount of time testifying before committees of the Congress, making speeches before national organizations, and meeting with the press and the public to explain HHS actions. They also prepare special reports on national problems that are available to the public through the Department and the Government Printing Office. In addition, the Secretary submits to the President and the Congress periodic reports required by law that further explain how tax money was spent, progress was achieved, or social problems resolved.

Deputy Secretary The Deputy Secretary serves as Acting Secretary in the absence of the Secretary and performs on behalf of the Secretary such functions and duties as the Secretary may designate, coordinates regional and field activities, and coordinates Federal-State relations.

Inspector General The Office of Inspector General is responsible for conducting and supervising audits, investigations, and inspections relating to programs and operations of the Department. The Office provides leadership and coordination for, and recommends policies and corrective actions concerning activities designed to promote economy and efficiency in the administration of, and prevent and detect fraud and abuse in the Department's programs and operations. The Office

An up-to-date organizational chart, reflecting the latest major reorganization of the Department of Health and Human Services, was unavailable at the time of publication of this book.

provides a means for keeping the Secretary and Congress fully and currently informed about problems and deficiencies relating to the administration of such programs and operations, and the necessity of corrective action.

Civil Rights The Office for Civil Rights is responsible for the administration and enforcement of the following laws that prohibit discrimination in federally assisted health and human services programs:

—title VI of the Civil Rights Act of 1964;

—section 504 of the Rehabilitation Act of 1973, as amended;

—the Age Discrimination Act of 1975;

—title IX of the Education Amendments of 1972;

—section 407 of the Drug Offense and Treatment Act of 1972;

—section 321 of the Comprehensive Alcohol Abuse and Alcoholism Prevention, Treatment and Rehabilitation Act of 1970;

—the Equal Employment Opportunity provisions of the Communications Finance Act of 1934, as amended;

—titles VI and XVI of the Public Health Service Act;

—the nondiscrimination provisions of the Omnibus Budget Reconciliation Act of 1981;

—section 307(a) of the Family Violence Prevention and Services Act; and

—titles VII and VIII of the Public Health Service Act.

Consumer Affairs The U.S. Office of Consumer Affairs advises the White House and the Secretary of HHS on consumer-related policy and programs and is responsible for handling consumer matters; analyzes and coordinates implementation of all Federal activities in the area of consumer protection; and recommends ways in which governmental consumer programs can be made more effective. The Director of the Office also chairs the U.S. Consumer Affairs Council.

Public Affairs The Assistant Secretary (Public Affairs) serves as the Secretary's principal public affairs adviser; provides functional management of public affairs activities throughout the Department; reviews and approves all publications and audio visual material released throughout the Department; communicates on behalf of the Department with various segments of the public, special interest groups, news media, and other government agencies at all levels; and administers Freedom of Information Act and Privacy Act requests.

Legislation The Assistant Secretary (Legislation) serves as principal adviser to the Secretary in the development and implementation of the Department's legislative program and maintains liaison with the Members and committees of Congress and their staffs.

Planning and Evaluation The Office of the Assistant Secretary for Planning and Evaluation coordinates Department activities in economic and social analysis, program analysis and planning, and evaluation activities; and ensures that Department policy and program planning appropriately reflects the results of these activities.

General Counsel The General Counsel furnishes legal advice to the Office of the Secretary and to the Operating and Staff Components of the Department.

Management and Budget The Assistant Secretary for Management and Budget provides advice and guidance to the Secretary on administrative and financial management and directs and coordinates these activities throughout the Department on a day-to-day basis. The activities include: providing leadership and advice on management issues related to reorganizations, delegations of authority, space management, acquisition, grants, and real and personal property management; providing leadership and coordination in the design and development of HHS financial policies and systems, directing the review and negotiation of cost allocation plans and indirect cost rates, and operating the system which pays all of the Department's grantees; overseeing the preparation of the Department's budget estimates, forecasting resources required to support programs and activities of the Department, and managing the policy and procedures for allocating and controlling the Department's employment ceiling; and providing guidance and direction on policies pertaining to the use of information resources, administering the Department's Information Resource Management Strategic Plan, and overseeing the Department's activities to implement the Paperwork Reduction Act. In addition, the Assistant Secretary provides administrative and facilities management services to HHS components located in the Washington, DC, southwest complex, and manages the budget and equal employment opportunity and emergency preparedness functions for the Office of the Secretary.

Personnel Administration The Assistant Secretary for Personnel Administration promotes effective personnel management and personnel administration in the Department. The Assistant Secretary advises and acts for the Secretary on personnel management and training matters, formulating policies and plans for broad programs under which the personnel and training functions will be carried out; maintains cognizance of such policies and programs; and represents the Department on personnel and training matters with the Office of Personnel Management, other Federal agencies, the Congress, and the public. The Assistant Secretary for Personnel Administration also advises the Secretary on and provides departmentwide leadership and guidance to equal employment opportunity programs and activities and oversees the establishment, staffing, and operation of departmental advisory committees.

Administration on Aging The Administration on Aging is the principal agency designated to carry out the provisions of the Older Americans Act of 1965, as amended (42 U.S.C. 3001 *et seq.*). As the lead agency within HHS on all issues concerning aging, it advises the Secretary, Department components, and other Federal departments and agencies on the characteristics, circumstances, and needs of older people; develops policies, plans, and programs designed to promote their welfare and advocates for their needs in HHS program planning and policy development; administers a program of formula grants to States to establish State and community programs for older persons under title III of the act (45 CFR 1321); administers a program of grants to Indians, Alaskan Natives, and Native Hawaiians to establish programs for older Native Americans under title VI of the act (45 CFR 1328); provides policy, procedural direction, and technical assistance to States and Native American grantees to promote the development of community-based systems of comprehensive social, nutrition, and support services for older persons; and administers programs of training, research, and demonstration under title IV of the act.

For further information, contact the Commissioner on Aging. Phone, 202-619-0556.

Regional Offices The 10 Regional Directors of the Department of Health and Human Services are the Secretary's representatives in direct, official dealings with State and local government organizations. They provide a central focus in each region for departmental relations with Congress and promote general understanding of Department programs, policies, and objectives. They also advise the Secretary on the potential effects of decisions and provide administrative services and support to Department programs and activities in the regions.

Regional Offices—Department of Health and Human Services

(Areas included within each region are indicated on the map in Appendix A.)

Region/Address	Director	Telephone
1. John F. Kennedy Federal Bldg., Boston, MA 02203	Sue W. Davenport	617-565-1500
2. 26 Federal Plz., New York, NY 10278	Cleveland Johnson, Jr.	212-264-4600
3. 3535 Market St., Philadelphia, PA 19101	Alma R. Jacobs	215-596-6492
4. 101 Marietta Tower, Atlanta, GA 30323	Thomas T. Williams	404-331-2442

Regional Offices—Department of Health and Human Services—Continued

(Areas included within each region are indicated on the map in Appendix A.)

Region/Address	Director	Telephone
5. 105 W. Adams St., Chicago, IL 60603	Delilah Brummet-Flaum	312-353-5160
6. 1200 Main Tower, Dallas, TX 75202	Paulette Standefer	214-767-3301
7. 601 E. 12th St., Kansas City, MO 64106	Dana Petrowsky	816-426-2821
8. 1961 Stout St., Denver, CO 80294-3538	Jane E. Artist	303-844-3372
9. Federal Office Bldg., San Francisco, CA 94102	Deane Dana III	415-556-6746
10. Blanchard Plz. Bldg., 2201 6th Ave., Seattle, WA 98121	Bernard E. Kelly	206-553-0420

Administration for Children and Families

The Administration for Children and Families was created on April 15, 1991, under authority of section 6 of Reorganization Plan No. 1 of 1953 and pursuant to the authority vested in the Secretary of Health and Human Services. This newly created organization merged the Family Support Administration and the Office of Human Development Services.

The Administration is headed by the Assistant Secretary for Children and Families who reports to the Secretary of HHS and who retains the titles of Assistant Secretary for Family Support and Director of the Office of Child Support Enforcement.

Family Support Administration

[For the Family Support Administration statement of organization, see the *Federal Register* of Oct. 6, 1986, 51 FR 35561; June 24, 1988, 53 FR 24150, 24151; Sept. 1, 1988, 53 FR 33850–33853]

The Family Support Administration:

—serves as the adviser to the Secretary and Deputy Secretary on efforts to serve America's children and families, especially low-income families;

—provides leadership and direction to family support programs;

—recommends to the Secretary actions and strategies that improve coordination of family support programs among HHS programs, other Federal agencies, State and local governments, and private-sector organizations;

—manages and provides leadership in planning and developing programs; and

—supervises the use of research and evaluation funds and controls equal employment opportunity programs for the Administration.

The Office of the Assistant Secretary for the Family Support Administration provides executive direction to all Administration components and is the Director of the Office of Child Support Enforcement.

Family Assistance The Office of Family Assistance is the principal agency designated to carry out the Aid to Families with Dependent Children (AFDC) Program (title IV-A of the Social Security Act (42 U.S.C. 601)), a Federal-State program that helps needy families with children. The program subsidizes children who are deprived of the financial support of one of their parents due to death, disability, absence from the home, or, in some States, unemployment. The assistance payment programs are State and local programs administered by State welfare agencies under individual plans developed by each State in conformity with Federal requirements and regulations. This Office is also responsible for administering the Job Opportunities and Basic Skills (JOBS) Training Program, established by the Family Support Act of 1988 (Pub. L. 100–485).

For further information, contact the Office of Family Assistance, Family Support Administration, Department of Health and Human Services, 370 L'Enfant Promenade SW., Washington, DC 20447. Phone, 202–401–9275.

Child Support Enforcement The Office of Child Support Enforcement was established pursuant to act of January 4,

1975 (42 U.S.C. 651). Its mission is to provide leadership in the planning, development, management, and coordination of the Department's Child Support Enforcement programs and activities authorized and directed by title IV–D of the Social Security Act, as amended (42 U.S.C. 651), and other pertinent legislation. The general purpose of this legislation and the Child Support Enforcement programs is to require States to enforce support obligations owed by absent parents to their children by locating absent parents, establishing paternity when necessary, and obtaining child support.

For further information, contact the Child Support Information Officer, Office of Child Support Enforcement, Family Support Administration, Department of Health and Human Services, 370 L'Enfant Promenade SW., Washington, DC 20447. Phone, 202–401–9373.

Community Services The Office of Community Services was established within HHS by section 676 of the Omnibus Budget Reconciliation Act of 1981 (42 U.S.C. 9905).

The Office administers the community services block grant and discretionary grant programs established by sections 672 (42 U.S.C. 9901) and 681 (42 U.S.C. 9910) of the act and the community services transition project grants authorized by section 682 (42 U.S.C. 9911) for implementation during fiscal year 1982. The Office also carries out the Low Income Home Energy Assistance Program, which provides assistance to low-income households in meeting the costs of home energy. The program provides funds through block grants to States, Indian tribes, Puerto Rico, and the territories for their use in programs tailored to meet the unique requirements of their jurisdictions.

For further information, contact the Director, Office of Community Services, Family Support Administration, Department of Health and Human Services, 370 L'Enfant Promenade SW., Washington, DC 20447. Phone, 202–401–9333.

Refugee Resettlement The Office of Refugee Resettlement administers the Refugee Assistance Program, which is designed to assimilate refugees and Cuban and Haitian entrants into American society as quickly and effectively as possible (title IV of the Immigration and Nationality Act (8 U.S.C. 1521) and section 501 of the Refugee Education Assistance Act of 1980 (8 U.S.C. 1522 note). The Refugee Assistance Program provides a comprehensive program of cash and medical assistance and social services for refugees.

The Office of Refugee Resettlement also administers the State Legalization Impact Assistance Grant Program authorized by section 204 of the Immigration Reform and Control Act of 1986 (8 U.S.C. 1255a note). The program's purpose is to pay a portion of State and local costs associated with providing public assistance, public health, and educational services to eligible legalized aliens.

For further information, contact the Office of Refugee Resettlement, Family Support Administration, Department of Health and Human Services, 370 L'Enfant Promenade SW., Washington, DC 20447. Phone, 202–401–9246.

Financial Management The Office of Financial Management (OFM) is a staff office for the Family Support Administration (FSA). OFM develops, directs, and coordinates financial policies, budget, and controls necessary for FSA programs. The Office provides technical processing of grant awards and manages procedures for handling grant disallowances and appeals.

For further information, contact the Office of Financial Management, Family Support Administration, Department of Health and Human Services, 370 L'Enfant Promenade SW., Washington, DC 20447. Phone, 202–401–9238.

Communications The Office of Communications (OC) develops, directs, and coordinates public affairs and communication services for the Assistant Secretary of FSA. It provides leadership, direction, and oversight in promoting and marketing FSA's public affairs policies, programs, and initiatives.

For further information, contact the Office of Communication, Family Support Administration, Department of Health and Human Services, 370 L'Enfant Promenade SW., Washington, DC 20447. Phone, 202–401–9215.

Management and Information Systems The Office of Management and

Information Systems (OMIS), a staff office of FSA, advises the Assistant Secretary in the areas of internal administration and management, internal information systems, and external-state automated systems designed to support all FSA programs except the Child Support Enforcement program.

It establishes policy, requirements, standards, and guidelines for information systems for the Department to support programs funded under the Social Security Act and management improvement initiatives, such as Income Eligibility Verification Systems (IEVS) and Systematic Alien Verification for Entitlement (SAVE), involved in the administration and operation of federally funded programs. The Office provides leadership, guidance, and liaison throughout FSA on administrative policies, procedures, and activities, including: personnel management, employee development, management studies and assessments, facilities, telecommunications, material management, and similar supporting services. The Office serves as the focal point for liaison with FSA regional offices.

For further information, contact the Office of Management and Information Systems, Family Support Administration, Department of Health and Human Services, 370 L'Enfant Promenade SW., Washington DC 20447. Phone, 202–401–9257.

Program Evaluation The Office of Program Evaluation (OPE) is a staff office for FSA which is responsible for managing program evaluation, research and demonstration, legislation coordination, and special program initiatives. OPE plans, develops, and monitors strategies for promoting FSA program directions and analyzes the impact of programmatic alternatives, including fiscal impact.

It coordinates the development of priority areas for funding research and evaluation programs; manages crosscutting research demonstration and evaluation projects; recommends to and advises the Assistant Secretary of FSA on all programmatic matters having substantial impact on program direction, in the areas of program evaluation, program impact, cost efficiency and effectiveness, and internal organization and coordination.

For further information, contact the Office of Program Evaluation, Family Support Administration, Department of Health and Human Services, 370 L'Enfant Promenade SW., Washington, DC 20447. Phone, 202–401–9220.

Office of Human Development Services

[For the Office of Human Development Services statement of organization, see the *Federal Register* of Sept. 29, 1980, 45 FR 64253]

The Office of Human Development Services serves as the adviser to the Secretary and Deputy Secretary on human development services and provides leadership and direction to human services programs for the elderly, children and youth, families, Native Americans, persons living in rural areas, and people with disabilities. The Office:

—recommends to the Secretary actions and strategies that improve coordination of human services programs among HHS programs, other Federal agencies, State and local governments, and private-sector organizations;

—manages and provides leadership in planning and developing Office programs;

—supervises the use of research and impact evaluation funds;

—promotes the development of simplified and coherent human services delivery systems;

—provides support and coordination for key advisory bodies;

—controls the Office's equal employment opportunity and civil rights policies and programs; and

—directs public affairs, regional operations, and correspondence and assignment tracking activities.

Office of the Assistant Secretary for Human Development Services The Office of the Assistant Secretary for Human Development Services provides executive direction, leadership, and guidance to all HDS headquarters and regional components; and serves as the Director of Equal Employment

Opportunity for the Office of Human Development Services.

Administration for Children, Youth, and Families The Administration advises the Secretary, through the Assistant Secretary for Human Development Services, on matters relating to children, youth, and families, and:

—serves as the principal adviser at the Federal level concerning such matters and is the focal point in the Department to support and encourage the sound development of children, youth, and families by planning, developing, and implementing a broad range of activities;

—administers State grant programs under title IV, parts B and E, of the Social Security Act, as amended (42 U.S.C. 620 and 670);

—manages the adoption opportunities program;

—manages the temporary child care and crisis nurseries program;

—administers discretionary grant programs providing Head Start services and runaway youth facilities;

—administers a discretionary demonstration program of comprehensive family support services under the Augustus F. Hawkins-Robert T. Stafford Elementary and Secondary School Improvement Amendments of 1988 (20 U.S.C. 2701 note);

—administers provisions of the Child Abuse Prevention and Treatment Act (42 U.S.C. 5101 *et seq.*);

—supports and encourages services that prevent or remedy the effects of abuse and/or neglect of children and youth; and

—manages the national clearinghouse on child abuse and neglect and administers the child abuse and neglect State grant programs.

Together with other units of the Office of Human Development Services, the Administration:

—develops and implements research, demonstration, and evaluation strategies for discretionary funding of activities designed to improve and enrich the lives of children and youth and to strengthen families;

—administers child welfare services training and child welfare services research demonstration programs authorized by title IV, part B, of the Social Security Act (42 U.S.C. 620);

—administers the Runaway and Homeless Youth Act authorized by title III of the Juvenile Justice and Delinquency Prevention Act of 1974 (42 U.S.C. 5601 note);

—manages initiatives that involve the private and voluntary sectors in the areas of children, youth, and families;

—administers the Drug Abuse Prevention program for runaway and homeless youth, and the Youth Gang Drug Prevention program, as authorized by the Anti-Drug Abuse Act of 1988; and

—manages the Dependent Care Program as authorized by the Human Services Reauthorization Act (42 U.S.C. 9801 note).

For further information, contact the Commissioner, Administration for Children, Youth, and Families. Phone, 202–245–0347.

Administration for Native Americans The Administration represents the concerns of American Indians, Alaskan Natives, Native Hawaiians, and other Native American Pacific Islanders (including American Samoan Natives) and advises the Assistant Secretary for Human Development Services on their behalf.

The Administration:

—develops policy, legislative proposals, and guidance on matters involving the social and economic development and self-sufficiency of Native Americans;

—serves as departmental liaison with other Federal agencies on Native American affairs;

—administers a grant program to promote the social and economic development of Native Americans;

—provides technical assistance to Native American organizations to further these goals;

—explores new program concepts and methods;

—ensures that information about departmental services and benefits and eligibility criteria is conveyed to Native Americans;

—fosters self-determination in Native Americans and their operation of Native American programs and enterprises;

—serves as the primary agency within the Office of Human Development Services on all issues concerning Native Americans; and

—develops standards, provides technical assistance, issues best practices guidelines, and initiates policy relative to Office-funded services provided to Native Americans.

For further information, contact the Commissioner, Administration for Native Americans. Phone, 202–245–7776.

Administration on Developmental Disabilities The Administration assists States and public and private nonprofit agencies and organizations to assure that appropriate services, assistance, and opportunities are available to persons with developmental disabilities and that each State has in place a system to plan, coordinate, monitor, and evaluate the services to protect the legal and human rights of persons with developmental disabilities. The Administration:

—administers formula grants programs to address these goals and oversees project grants that provide administrative and operations support to interdisciplinary training programs for specialized personnel, services, and research and demonstration programs for people with developmental disabilities;

—administers grants for projects aimed at enabling persons with developmental disabilities to achieve their maximum potential through increased independence, productivity, and integration into the community;

—advises the Assistant Secretary for Human Development Services on the formulation, development, implementation, and review of legislation and policies affecting persons with developmental disabilities;

—serves as the primary agency within the Office of Human Development Services on all issues concerning people with developmental disabilities.

—advocates for the needs of people with disabilities in Office program planning and policy development; and

—develops standards, provides technical assistance, issues best practices guidelines, and initiates policy relative to Office programs for persons with developmental disabilities.

For further information, contact the Commissioner, Administration on Developmental Disabilities. Phone, 202–245–2890.

Regional Offices—Administration for Children and Families

Region/Address		Administrator	Telephone
I.	Boston, MA (Rm. 600, 6th Fl., John F. Kennedy Federal Bldg., 02203).	Hugh Galligan, *Acting*	508–565–2463
II.	New York, NY (Rm. 4048, 26 Federal Plz., 10278)	Ann Schreiber, *Acting*	212–264–2890
III.	Philadelphia, PA (P.O. Box 13716, 3535 Market St., 19104)	Richard Spitzborg, *Acting*	215–596–0351
IV.	Atlanta, GA (Suite 821, 101 Marietta Twr., 30323)	Suanne Brooks, *Acting*	404–331–5733
V.	Chicago, IL (20th Fl., 105 W. Adams St., 60606)	Marion Steffy, *Acting*	312–353–4237
VI.	Dallas, TX (1200 Main Tower Bldg., 75202)	Marvin Layne, *Acting*	214–767–4540
VII.	Kansas City, MO (Rm. 515, Federal Bldg., 601 E. 12th St., 64106).	Dwight High, *Acting*	816–426–2806
VIII.	Denver, CO (Rm. 1194, Federal Bldg., 1961 Stout St., 80294-3538).	David Chapa, *Acting*	303–844–2622
IX.	San Francisco, CA (MS. 351, 50 United Nations Plz., 94102)	Sharon Fujii, *Acting*	415–556–4415
X.	Seattle, WA (2201 6th Ave., 98121)	Edward Singler, *Acting*	206–442–2430

Public Health Service

[For the Public Health Service statement of organization, see the *Federal Register* of Dec. 2, 1977, 42 FR 61317]

The Public Health Service was established by act of July 16, 1798 (ch. 77, 1 Stat. 605), authorizing marine hospitals for the care of American merchant seamen. Subsequent legislation has vastly broadened the scope of its activities.

The Public Health Service Act of July 1, 1944 (42 U.S.C. 201), consolidated and revised substantially all existing legislation relating to the Public Health Service. The basic Public Health Service legal responsibilities have been broadened and expanded many times since 1944. Major organizational changes have occurred within the Public Health Service to support its mission to promote the protection and advancement of the Nation's physical and mental health. This is accomplished by:

—coordinating with the States to set and implement national health policy and pursue effective intergovernmental relations;

—generating and upholding cooperative international health-related agreements, policies, and programs;

—conducting medical and biomedical research;

—sponsoring and administering programs for the development of health resources, prevention and control of diseases, and alcohol and drug abuse;

—providing resources and expertise to the States and other public and private institutions in the planning, direction, and delivery of physical and mental health care services; and

—enforcing laws to assure the safety and efficacy of drugs and protection against impure and unsafe foods, cosmetics, medical devices, and radiation-producing projects.

The Office of the Assistant Secretary for Health consists of general and special staff offices that support the Assistant Secretary for Health and the Surgeon General plan and direct the activities of the Public Health Service.

Agency for Health Care Policy and Research The Agency was established by the Omnibus Budget Reconciliation Act of 1989 (42 U.S.C. 299) as the successor to the National Center for Health Services Research and Health Care Technology Assessment. The Agency is the Federal Government's focal point for health services research. To accomplish its mission of enhancing the quality of patient care services, the Agency promotes improvements in clinical practice and patient outcomes through more appropriate and effective health care services; improvements in the financing, organization, and delivery of health care services; and increased access to quality health care.

The Agency acquires, develops, and transfers new knowledge through a coordinated program of research, demonstrations, evaluations, and information dissemination activities. Generally, the Agency's primary functions are:

—developing a broad base of scientific research, methods, and databases through extramural research grants and contracts and intramural research activities;

—demonstrating and evaluating new ways to organize, finance, and direct health care services to improve the delivery, access to, and outcomes of such services;

—assessing technologies being considered for reimbursement by federally funded programs;

—facilitating the development of practice guidelines and standardized measures of quality care for use by physicians and other health care practitioners; and

—promoting the use of health services research findings through systematic, broad-based information dissemination.

The Agency supports research in medical treatment effectiveness and patient outcomes; assessment of health care technologies; medical malpractice and liability; delivery of health services in rural areas; availability, accessibility, and quality care for underserved populations; alternative delivery systems, providers, and practice patterns in primary care; and resource use, cost of care, and delivery of services to persons with human immunodeficiency virus-related (HIV) illnesses.

For further information, call 301–443–4100.

Alcohol, Drug Abuse, and Mental Health Administration

The mission of the Alcohol, Drug Abuse, and Mental Health Administration is to find scientifically based solutions to alcohol, drug abuse, and mental health problems and to provide a national focus for the Federal effort to increase knowledge and promote effective strategies to deal with health problems and issues associated with the use and abuse of alcohol and drugs and with mental illness and mental health.

In carrying out these responsibilities, the Administration:

—conducts and supports research on the biological, psychological, behavioral, and epidemiological aspects of alcoholism, drug abuse, and mental health and illness;

—conducts and supports research on the delivery of alcoholism, drug abuse, and mental health treatment and prevention services;

—supports the training of scientists to conduct research in the alcoholism, drug abuse, and mental health fields;

—gathers and analyzes data about the extent of alcohol, drug abuse, and mental health problems and the national response to these needs in terms of planning, establishing, and evaluating alcoholism, drug abuse, and mental health programs;

—administers the alcohol, drug abuse, and mental health services block grant program and collaborates with, provides assistance to, and encourages other Federal agencies and national, foreign, State, and local organizations, hospitals, and voluntary groups to facilitate and expand programs for the prevention and treatment of alcohol, drug abuse, and mental health problems; and

—provides information on alcoholism, drug abuse, and mental health to the public and to the scientific community.

For further information, call 301–443–3875.

Major Components

National Institute on Alcohol Abuse and Alcoholism The Institute provides a national focus for the Federal effort to increase knowledge and promote effective strategies to deal with health problems and issues associated with alcohol abuse and alcoholism. In carrying out these responsibilities, the Institute:

—conducts and supports research on alcohol-related disorders in its own laboratories and through extramural projects;

—supports epidemiological studies and national and community surveys to assess the risks for alcohol abuse among various population groups;

—plans, directs, supports, and evaluates research to identify new and improved alcoholism prevention, intervention, and treatment methods and techniques for application in the Nation's health care system;

—supports training and development of scientists for participation in alcohol research programs and activities;

—collaborates with other research institutes and Federal programs relevant to alcohol abuse and alcoholism and coordinates Federal alcohol abuse and alcoholism research activities;

—serves as a national resource for the collection, analysis, and dissemination of scientific findings and improved methods of alcoholism prevention and treatment services;

—maintains continuing relationships with institutions and professional associations and with international, national, State, and local officials and voluntary agencies and organizations engaged in alcohol-related work;

—conducts policy studies and activities which have broad implications for alcoholism treatment, prevention, and rehabilitation activities;

—performs data collections and analysis and provides technical assistance and technology transfer to State and local governments and community and voluntary organizations in the areas of policy development, program assessment, establishment of treatment standards, accreditation, and resource utilization; and

—supports public education activities to inform the public of the risks and consequences associated with alcohol abuse and alcoholism.

For further information, call 301–443–4373.

National Institute on Drug Abuse The Institute provides a national focus for the Federal effort to increase knowledge and promote effective strategies in dealing with health problems and issues associated with drug abuse. In carrying out these responsibilities, the Institute:

—conducts and supports research on the biological, psychological, and psychosocial aspects, epidemiology, treatment, and prevention of drug abuse and addiction;

—supports research training and career development of individuals and institutions that are training individuals for participation in drug abuse research programs and activities;

—works with States to provide technical assistance and national leadership in the areas of data collection, treatment, effectiveness, and health services research;

—collaborates with the Office for Substance Abuse Prevention and the Office for Treatment Improvement to encourage Federal agencies; national, foreign, and State and local organizations; hospitals; and volunteer groups to facilitate and extend programs for the prevention of drug abuse and addiction, and the care, treatment, and rehabilitation of drug abusers; and

—carries out administrative and financial management, policy and program development, planning and evaluation, and public information functions which are required to implement such programs.

For further information, call 301–443–6487.

National Institute of Mental Health The Institute provides a national focus for the Federal effort to increase knowledge and advance effective strategies to deal with health problems and issues in promoting mental health and preventing and treating mental illness.

In carrying out these responsibilities, the Institute:

—conducts and supports research and research training on the biological, psychological, behavioral, and epidemiological aspects of mental health and illness;

—maintains research on developing, executing, improving, and financing mental health services and prevention programs;

—collaborates with, and provides technical assistance and data to, State and local authorities to assist them in planning, establishing, maintaining, coordinating, and evaluating more effective mental health programs;

—collaborates with, provides assistance to, and encourages other Federal agencies; national, foreign, and State and local organizations; hospitals; professional associations; and volunteer groups to facilitate and extend programs to promote good mental health, prevent mental illness, and to provide for the care, treatment, and rehabilitation of mentally ill persons;

—collects, analyzes, and disseminates scientific data on the incidence, prevalence, and resources for the treatment of mental illness; and

—carries out administrative and financial management, policy development, planning and evaluation, and public information functions that are required to implement such programs.

For further information, call 301–443–3877.

Office for Substance Abuse Prevention The Office provides a national focus for the Federal effort to prevent alcohol abuse and other drug problems. In carrying out this responsibility, the Office:

—develops, implements, and reviews prevention and health promotion policy related to alcohol and drug abuse, analyzing the impact of Federal activities on State and local governments and private program activities;

—supports comprehensive, collaborative, community-based innovative prevention demonstration programs;

—operates a grant program for projects to demonstrate effective models for the prevention, early intervention, and treatment of drug and alcohol use or abuse among high-risk youth and other specific target populations;

—sponsors regional and national workshops and conferences on the prevention of drug and alcohol abuse;

—supports the training of sustance abuse counselors and other health professionals involved in drug and alcohol abuse education, prevention, and intervention;

—provides technical assistance to State and local authorities and other national organizations and groups in planning, establishing, and maintaining substance abuse prevention efforts;

—collects and compiles drug and alcohol abuse prevention literature and other materials and supports a clearinghouse to disseminate such materials among States, political subdivisions, educational agencies and institutions, health and drug treatment and rehabilitation networks, and the general public;

—serves as a national authority and resource for developing and analyzing information relating to alcohol and drug abuse prevention;

—participates in disseminating and implementing research findings by PHS agencies and other research institutes on the prevention of alcohol and drug abuse;

—collaborates with and encourages other Federal agencies, national, foreign, State, and local organizations in promoting substance abuse prevention activities;

—provides and promotes the evaluation of individual projects, as well as overall programs; and

—carries out administrative and financial management, policy and program development, planning and evaluation, and public information functions which are required to implement such programs.

For further information, call 301–443–5266.

Office for Treatment Improvement

The principal function of the Office is providing national leadership for the Federal effort enhancing approaches and programs focusing on the treatment of drug abusers as well as associated problems of alcoholism and mental illness among this population. In carrying out this responsibility, the Office:

—collaborates with States, communities, health care providers, and national organizations in upgrading the quality of drug treatment, in improving the effectiveness of drug treatment programs, and in expanding drug treatment capacity;

—provides financial assistance to targeted geographic areas in strengthening treatment programs for drug abuse and other related disorders (with emphasis on assistance for pregnant and post partum women and their infants, minorities, adolescents, and residents of public housing projects), and in strengthening the collaboration among members of the drug treatment community;

—provides a focus for addressing the treatment needs of individuals with multiple drug, alcohol, and mental problems;

—collaborates with the National Institute on Drug Abuse and the States to promote development of treatment outcome standards;

—collaborates with the Institutes and the Office for Substance Abuse Prevention in treatment data collection and training of health care providers;

—promotes the usage of treatment for alcohol and drug abuse and mental health problems as a general part of the health care system; and

—administers the Alcohol, Drug Abuse, and Mental Health Services block grant program and the homeless block grant program, including compliance reviews, technical assistance to States, territories, and Indian tribes, and application and reporting requirements related to the block grant programs.

For further information, call 301–443–6501.

Centers for Disease Control

The Centers for Disease Control, established as an operating health agency within the Public Health Service by the Secretary of Health, Education, and Welfare on July 1, 1973, is the Federal agency charged with protecting the public health of the Nation by providing leadership and direction in the prevention and control of diseases and other preventable conditions and responding to public health emergencies. It is composed of nine major operating components: Epidemiology Program Office, International Health Program Office, Public Health Practice Program Office, Center for Prevention Services, Center for Environmental Health and Injury Control, National Institute for Occupational Safety and Health, Center for Chronic Disease Prevention and Health Promotion, Center for Infectious Diseases, and the National Center for Health Statistics.

The Agency administers national programs for the prevention and control of communicable and vector-borne diseases and other preventable conditions. It develops and implements programs in chronic disease prevention and control, including consultation with State and local health departments. It develops and implements programs to deal with environmental health problems, including responding to environmental, chemical, and radiation emergencies.

The Agency directs and enforces foreign quarantine activities and regulations; provides consultation and assistance in upgrading the performance of public health and clinical laboratories; organizes and implements a National Health Promotion Program, including a nationwide program of research, information, and education in the field of smoking and health. It also collects, maintains, analyzes, and disseminates national data on health status and health services.

To ensure safe and healthful working conditions for all working people, occupational safety and health standards are developed, and research and other activities are carried out, through the National Institute for Occupational Safety and Health.

The Agency also provides consultation to other nations in the control of preventable diseases, and participates with national and international agencies in the eradication or control of communicable diseases and other preventable conditions.

For further information, call 404–639–3286.

Agency for Toxic Substances and Disease Registry

The Agency for Toxic Substances and Disease Registry was established as an operating agency within the Public Health Service by the Secretary of Health and Human Services on April 19, 1983. The Agency's mission is to carry out the health-related responsibilities of the Comprehensive Environmental Response, Compensation, and Liability Act of 1980 (42 U.S.C. 9601), as amended by the Superfund Amendments and Reauthorization Act of 1986, the Resource Conservation and Recovery Act (42 U.S.C. 6901), and provisions of the Solid Waste Disposal Act relating to sites and substances found at those sites and other forms of uncontrolled releases of toxic substances into the environment. The Agency provides leadership and direction to programs and activities designed to protect both the public and workers from exposure and/or the adverse health effects of hazardous substances in storage sites or released in fires, explosions, or transportation accidents.

To carry out this mission, the Agency, in cooperation with States and other Federal and local agencies:

—collects, maintains, analyzes, and disseminates information relating to serious diseases, mortality, and human exposure to toxic or hazardous substances;

—establishes appropriate registries necessary for long-term followup or specific scientific studies;

—establishes and maintains a complete listing of areas closed to the public or otherwise restricted in use because of toxic substance contamination;

—assists, consults, and coordinates with private or public health care providers in the provision of medical care and testing of exposed individuals;

—assists the Environmental Protection Agency in identifying hazardous waste substances to be regulated;

—develops scientific and technical procedures for evaluating public health risks from hazardous substance incidents and for developing recommendations to protect public health and worker safety and health in instances of exposure or potential exposure to hazardous substances; and

—arranges for program support to ensure adequate response to public health emergencies.

For further information, call 404–639–0727.

Food and Drug Administration

The name "Food and Drug Administration" was first provided by the Agriculture Appropriation Act of 1931 (46 Stat. 392), although similar law enforcement functions had been in existence under different organizational titles since January 1, 1907, when the Food and Drug Act of 1906 (21 U.S.C. 1–15) became effective.

The Food and Drug Administration's activities are directed toward protecting the health of the Nation against impure and unsafe foods, drugs and cosmetics, and other potential hazards.

Center for Drug Evaluation and Research The Center develops Administration policy with regard to the safety, effectiveness, and labeling of all drug products for human use and reviews and evaluates new drug applications and investigational new drug applications. It develops and implements standards for the safety and effectiveness of all over-the-counter drugs and monitors the quality of marketed drug products through product testing, surveillance, and compliance programs.

The Center coordinates with the Center for Biologics Evaluation and Research regarding activities for biological drug products, including research, compliance, and product review and approval, and develops and promulgates guidelines on Current Good Manufacturing Practices for use by the drug industry. It develops and disseminates information and educational material dealing with drug products to the medical community and the public in coordination with the Office of the Commissioner. It conducts research and develops scientific standards on the composition, quality, safety, and effectiveness of human drugs; collects and evaluates information on the effects and use trends of marketed drug products; monitors prescription drug advertising and promotional labeling to assure their accuracy and integrity; and analyzes data on accidental poisonings and disseminates toxicity and treatment information on household products and medicines.

In carrying out these functions, the Center cooperates with other components of the Administration, other Public Health Service organizations, governmental and international agencies, volunteer health organizations, universities, individual scientists, nongovernmental laboratories, and manufacturers of drug products.

For further information, call 301–443–2894.

Center for Biologics Evaluation and Research The Center administers regulation of biological products under the biological product control provisions of the Public Health Service Act and applicable provisions of the Federal Food, Drug, and Cosmetic Act. It provides dominant focus in the Administration for coordination of the Acquired Immune Deficiency Syndrome (AIDS) program, works to develop an AIDS vaccine and AIDS diagnostic tests, and conducts other AIDS-related activities. It inspects manufacturers' facilities for compliance with standards, tests products submitted for release, establishes written and physical standards, and approves licensing of manufacturers to produce biological products.

The Center plans and conducts research related to the development, manufacture, testing, and use of both new and old biological products to develop a scientific base for establishing standards designed to ensure the continued safety, purity, potency, and efficacy of biological products and coordinates with the Center for Drug Evaluation and Research regarding activities for biological drug products, including research, compliance, and product review and approval.

The Center plans and conducts research on the preparation,

preservation, and safety of blood and blood products, the methods of testing safety, purity, potency, and efficacy of such products for therapeutic use, and the immunological problems concerned with products, testing, and use of diagnostic reagents employed in grouping and typing blood.

In carrying out these functions, the Center cooperates with other components of the Administration, other Public Health Service organizations, governmental and international agencies, volunteer health organizations, universities, individual scientists, nongovernmental laboratories, and manufacturers of biological products.

For further information, call 301–496–3556.

Center for Food Safety and Applied Nutrition The Center conducts research and develops standards on the composition, quality, nutrition, and safety of food and food additives, colors, and cosmetics. It conducts research designed to improve the detection, prevention, and control of contamination that may be responsible for illness or injury conveyed by foods, colors, and cosmetics and coordinates and evaluates the Administration's surveillance and compliance programs relating to foods, colors, and cosmetics.

The Center also reviews industry petitions and develops regulations for food standards to permit the safe use of color additives and food additives; collects and interprets data on nutrition, food additives, and environmental factors affecting the total chemical result posed by food additives; and maintains a nutritional data bank.

For further information, call 202–245–8850.

Center for Veterinary Medicine The Center develops and conducts programs with respect to the safety and efficacy of veterinary preparations and devices; evaluates proposed use of veterinary preparations for animal safety and efficacy; and evaluates the Administration's surveillance and compliance programs relating to veterinary drugs and other veterinary medical matters.

For further information, call 301–443–3450.

Center for Devices and Radiological Health The Center develops and carries out a national program designed to control unnecessary exposure of humans to, and ensure the safe and efficacious use of, potentially hazardous ionizing and non-ionizing radiation. It develops policy and priorities regarding Administration programs relating to the safety, effectiveness, and labeling of medical devices for human use; conducts an electronic product radiation control program, including the development and administration of performance standards.

The Center plans, conducts, and supports research and testing relating to medical devices and to the health effects of radiation exposure; and reviews and evaluates medical devices premarket approval applications, product development protocols, and exemption requests for investigational devices. It develops, promulgates, and enforces performance standards for appropriate categories of medical devices and Good Manufacturing Practice regulations for manufacturers; provides technical and other nonfinancial assistance to small manufacturers of medical devices.

The Center develops regulations, standards, and criteria and recommends changes in Administration legislative authority necessary to protect the public health; provides scientific and technical support to other components within the Administration and other agencies on matters relating to radiological health and medical devices; and maintains appropriate liaison with other Federal, State, and international agencies, with industry, and with consumer and professional organizations.

For further information, call 301–443–4690 or 301–427–7163.

National Center for Toxicological Research The Center conducts research programs to study the biological effects of potentially toxic chemical substances found in the environment, emphasizing the determination of the health effects resulting from long-term, low-level exposure to chemical toxicants and the basic biological processes for chemical toxicants in animal organisms; develops improved methodologies and test protocols for evaluating the safety of chemical toxicants and the data that will facilitate the extrapolation of toxicological data from laboratory animals to man; and develops Center programs as a natural resource under the National Toxicology Program.

For further information, call 501–541–4000.

Regional Operations Field operations for the enforcement of the laws under the jurisdiction of the Food and Drug Administration are carried out by 6 Regional Field Offices located in the cities of the Department's Regional Offices, through 21 District Offices and 135 Resident Inspection Posts located throughout the United States and Puerto Rico.

For further information, call 301–443–1594. **For a listing of Consumer Affairs Offices see page 322.**

Health Resources and Services Administration The Administration has leadership responsibility in the Public Health Service for general health services and resource issues relating to access, equity, quality, and cost of care.

To accomplish this goal, the Administration:

—supports States and communities in their efforts to plan, organize, and deliver health care, especially to underserved area residents, migrant workers, mothers and children, the homeless, and other groups with special needs;

—participates in the Federal campaign against AIDS by funding service demonstration projects in major cities, establishing centers to train health professionals serving AIDS patients, supporting renovation of health facilities for AIDS patients, and awarding pediatric health care grants;

—provides leadership in improving the education, distribution, quality, and use of the health professionals needed to staff the Nation's health care system;

—tracks the supply of and requirements for health professionals and addresses their competence through the development of a health practitioner data bank;

—monitors developments affecting health facilities and ensures that previously aided institutions honor their commitments to provide uncompensated care;

—administers the National Organ Transplant Act by serving as an information resource on donation, procurement, and transplantation and by promoting other activities designed to increase the availability of organs and tissues;

—provides direct, personal health services for Hansen's disease patients and other designated beneficiaries;

—assists Federal managers to assure that employees and workplace health factors that increase the Government's productivity are raised to the highest practical level;

—monitors rural health issues and helps coordinate government and private efforts on behalf of rural health facilities;

—processes claims submitted under the National Vaccine Injury Compensation Program; and

—strengthens the public health system by working with State and local public health agencies;

—oversees management of the Federal initiative to combat infant mortality through grants to hard-hit communities working to overcome social and non-financial barriers to prenatal care; and

—coordinates health program activities that address the special needs and problems of minority populations.

For further information, contact the Associate Administrator for Communications. Phone, 301–443–2086.

Major Components

Bureau of Health Care Delivery and Assistance The Bureau serves as a national focus for efforts to ensure the availability and delivery of health care services in health manpower shortage areas, to medically underserved populations, and to special services populations.

To accomplish this goal, the Bureau:

—provides, through project grants to community-based organizations, funds to meet the health needs of populations in medically underserved areas by supporting the development of primary health care delivery capacity;

—provides, through project grants to State, local, voluntary, public, and private entities, funds to help them meet the health needs of special populations such as migrants, Alzheimer's disease patients, the homeless, AIDS victims, Pacific Basin inhabitants, Native Hawaiians, and victims of black lung disease;

—administers the National Health Service Corps Program, which recruits and places highly trained health care practitioners for health manpower shortage areas and populations;

—administers the National Health Service Corps Scholarship and Loan Repayment Programs, which provide financial assistance to medical, dental, and nursing students or former students in return for service in health manpower shortage areas;

—designates health manpower shortage and medically underserved areas and populations;

—provides leadership and direction for the Bureau of Prisons Medical Program, the National Hansen's Disease Program, and support for Health Unit No. 1 and the CHAMPUS Program;

—provides on a reimbursable basis comprehensive occupational health consultation and assistance to Federal agencies to enhance productivity and limit employment-related liability through the Federal Employee Occupational Health Program;

—administers a comprehensive health program for designated PHS beneficiaries, including active duty members of PHS and the National Oceanic and Atmospheric Administration.

For further information, contact the Director, Office of Management. Phone, 301–443–2330.

Bureau of Health Professions The Bureau provides national leadership in coordinating, evaluating, and supporting the development and utilization of the Nation's health personnel.

To accomplish this goal, the Bureau:

—serves as a focus for health care quality assurance activities, issues related to malpractice, and the operation of the National Practitioner Data Bank, and the Vaccine Injury Compensation Program;

—supports through grants health professions and nurse training institutions, targeting resources to areas of high national priority such as disease prevention, health promotion, bedside nursing, care of the elderly, and HIV/AIDS;

—funds regional centers that provide educational services and multidisciplinary training for health professions faculty and practitioners in geriatric health care;

—supports programs to increase the supply of primary care practitioners and to improve the distribution of health professionals;

—develops, tests, and demonstrates new and improved approaches to the development and utilization of health personnel within various patterns of health care delivery and financing systems;

—provides leadership for promoting equity in access to health services and health careers for the disadvantaged;

—administers several loan programs supporting students training for careers in the health professions and nursing;

—funds regional centers to train faculty and practicing health professionals in the counseling, diagnosis, and management of HIV/AIDS infected individuals;

—collects and analyzes data and disseminates information on the characteristics and capacities of U.S. health training systems;

—assesses the Nation's health personnel force and forecasts supply and requirements; and

—in coordination with the Office of the Administrator, Health Resources and Services Administration, serves as a focus for technical assistance activities in the international projects relevant to domestic health personnel problems.

For further information, contact the Information Officer. Phone, 301–443–2060.

Bureau of Health Resources Development The Bureau develops, coordinates, administers, directs, monitors, and supports Federal policy and programs pertaining to health care facilities; a national network of activities associated with organ donations, procurements, and transplants; and activities related to acquired immune deficiency syndrome (AIDS). This includes financial, capital, organizational, and physical matters.

To accomplish this goal, the Bureau:

—provides national leadership in supporting, identifying, and interpreting national trends and issues relative to the health status of persons with AIDS and HIV infections, including availability of facilities and services for AIDS and AIDS-related patients—as well as the needy and indigent; and administers block and discretionary grants, contracts, and funding arrangements designed to address those issues;

—administers grant, loan guarantee, and interest subsidy programs relating to the construction, modernization, conversion, and closure of health care organizations;

—develops long- and short-range program goals and objectives for health facilities and for specific health promotions, organ transplants, and AIDS activities (OPO's);

—develops, conducts, and maintains a program of grants to organ procurement organizations;

—serves as adviser to and coordinates activities with other Administration organizational elements, other Federal organizations within and outside the Department, State and local governments, and professional and scientific organizations;

—develops, promotes, and directs efforts to improve the management, operational effectiveness, and efficiency of health care systems, organizations, and facilities;

—provides technical assistance to OPO's and health care delivery systems and facilities in a wide variety of specific technical and technological systems;

—administers the Health Resources and Service Administration's regional facility engineering and construction activities; and

—maintains liaison and coordinates with non-Federal public and private entities to accomplish the Bureau's mission and objectives.

Maternal and Child Health Bureau

The Bureau develops, administers, directs, coordinates, monitors, and supports Federal policy and programs pertaining to health and related care for the Nation's mothers and children. Programs administered by the Bureau address the full spectrum of primary, secondary, and tertiary care services and related activities conducted in the public and private sector which impact upon maternal and child health.

To accomplish this goal, the Bureau:

—provides national leadership in supporting, identifying, and interpreting national trends and issues relating to the health needs of mothers, infants, and children, and administers State block and discretionary grants, contracts, and funding arrangements designed to address these issues;

—administers grant, contracts, and other funding arrangements and programs under title V of the Social Security Act, as amended, relating to implementation of State maternal and child health (MCH) service programs, research, training, and education programs located in institutions of higher learning and State and local health agencies and organizations involved in the care of mothers and children;

—administers grants, contracts, and other funding arrangements under title III of the Public Health Service Act for care and improvement of the health status of pediatric AIDS patients;

—administers grants, contracts, and other funding arrangements under title V of the Social Security Act, as amended, relating to the care of persons affected by hemophilia (regardless of age);

—administers grants and contracts under title XIX of the Public Health Service Act relating to pediatric emergency medical systems development and care improvement;

—develops, promotes, and directs efforts to improve the management, financing, operational effectiveness and efficiency of health care systems,

290-950 O 91 - 11

organizations, and providers of maternal and child health and related care;

—serves as the principal adviser to and coordinates activities with other Administration organizational elements, other Federal organizations within and outside the Department, and with State and local agencies and professional and scientific organizations;

—provides technical assistance and consultation to the full spectrum of primary, secondary, and tertiary MCH agencies and organizations in both the public and private sector; and

—maintains liaison and coordinates with non-Federal public and private entities to accomplish the Bureau's mission and objectives.

For further information, contact the Information Officer. Phone, 301-443-3376.

Indian Health Service

The Indian Health Service provides a comprehensive health services delivery system for American Indians and Alaska Natives with opportunity for maximum tribal involvement in developing and managing programs to meet their health needs. The Service's goal is to improve the health of the American Indian and Alaska Natives to the highest possible level.

To carry out its mission and to attain its goal, the Service:

—assists American Indian tribes in developing their health programs through activities including health management training, technical assistance, and human resource development;

—facilitates and assists Indian tribes in coordinating health planning, in obtaining and utilizing health resources available through Federal, State, and local programs, in operating comprehensive health programs, and in health program evaluation;

—provides comprehensive health care services, including hospital and ambulatory medical care, preventive and rehabilitative services, and development of community sanitation facilities; and

—serves as the principal Federal advocate for American Indians in the health field to assure comprehensive health services for American Indians and Alaska Natives.

For further information, contact the Information Coordinator. Phone, 301-443-1397.

National Institutes of Health

The National Institutes of Health (NIH) is the principal biomedical research agency of the Federal Government. By conducting, supporting, and promoting biomedical research, NIH seeks to improve the health of the American people through increasing the understanding of processes underlying human health, disability, and disease; advancing knowledge concerning the health effects of interactions between humans and the environment; developing methods of preventing, detecting, diagnosing, and treating disease; and disseminating research results for critical review and ultimately for medical application. In the pursuit of this mission, NIH supports biomedical and behavorial research domestically and abroad, conducts research in its own laboratories and clinics, trains promising young researchers, and promotes acquiring and distributing medical knowledge. Focal points have been established to assist in developing NIH-wide goals for health research and research training programs related to women and minorities, coordinating program direction, and ensuring that research pertaining to women's and minority health is identified and addressed through research activities conducted and supported by NIH. Research activities conducted by NIH will determine much of the quality of health care for the future and reinforce the quality of health care currently available.

Major Components

National Cancer Institute Research on cancer is a high priority program as a result of the National Cancer Act, which made the conquest of cancer a national goal. The Institute developed a National Cancer Program to expand existing scientific knowledge on cancer cause and prevention as well as on the diagnosis, treatment, and rehabilitation of cancer patients.

Research activities conducted in the Institute's laboratories or supported through grants or contracts include many investigative approaches to cancer, including chemistry, biochemistry, biology, molecular biology, immunology, radiation physics, experimental chemotherapy, epidemiology, biometry, radiotherapy, and pharmacology. Cancer research facilities are constructed with Institute support, and training is provided under university-based programs. The Institute, through its cancer control element, applies research findings as rapidly as possible in preventing and controlling human cancer.

For further information, call 301–496–5737.

National Heart, Lung, and Blood Institute The Institute provides leadership for a national program in diseases of the heart, blood vessels, blood, and lungs, and in the use of blood and the management of blood resources.

It conducts studies and research into the clinical use of blood and all aspects of the management of blood resources, and supports training of manpower in fundamental science and clinical disciplines for participation in basic and clinical research programs relating to heart, blood vessel, blood, and lung diseases.

It coordinates with other research institutes and with all Federal agency programs relating to the above diseases, including programs in hypertension, stroke, respiratory distress, and sickle cell anemia.

The Institute plans, conducts, fosters, and supports an integrated and coordinated program of research, investigations, clinical trials and demonstrations relating to the causes, prevention, methods of diagnosis and treatment (including emergency medical treatment) of heart, blood vessel, lung, and blood diseases through research performed in its own laboratories and through contracts and research grants to scientific institutions and to individual scientists.

The Institute also conducts educational activities, including the collection and dissemination of educational materials about these diseases, with emphasis on the prevention thereof, for health professionals and the lay public, and maintains continuing relationships with institutions and professional associations and with international, national, and State and local officials, and voluntary agencies and organizations working in these areas.

For further information, call 301–496–2411.

National Library of Medicine The Library, which serves as the Nation's chief medical information source, is authorized to provide medical library services and on-line bibliographic searching capabilities, such as MEDLINE, TOXLINE, and others, to public and private agencies and organizations, institutions, and individuals. It is responsible for the development and management of a Biomedical Communications Network, applying advanced technology to the improvement of biomedical communications, and operates a computer-based toxicology information system for the scientific community, industry, and other Federal agencies. Through its National Center for Biotechnology Information, the Library has a leadership role in developing new information technologies to aid in the understanding of the molecular processes that control health and disease. In addition, the Library acquires and makes available for distribution audiovisual instructional material, and develops prototype audiovisual communication programs for the health educational community. Through grants and contracts, the Library administers programs of assistance to the Nation's medical libraries that include support of a Regional Medical Library network, research in the field of medical library science, establishment and improvement of the basic library resources, and supporting biomedical scientific publications of a nonprofit nature.

For further information, call 308–496–6308.

National Institute of Diabetes and Digestive and Kidney Diseases The

Institute conducts, fosters, and supports basic and clinical research into the causes, prevention, diagnosis, and treatment of the various metabolic and digestive diseases. It covers the broad areas of diabetes, blood, endocrine, and metabolic diseases; digestive diseases and nutrition; and kidney and urologic diseases, joined with the Artificial Kidney/Chronic Uremia Program, through research performed in its own laboratories and clinics, research grants, individual and institutional research training awards, applied research and development programs through the contract mechanisms, field epidemiologic and clinical investigation studies on selected populations in the United States, and collection and dissemination of information on Institute programs.

For further information, call 301–496–5741.

National Institute of Allergy and Infectious Diseases The Institute conducts and supports broadly based research and research training on the causes, characteristics, prevention, control, and treatment of a wide variety of diseases believed to be attributable to infectious agents, including bacteria, viruses, and parasites, to allergies, or to other deficiencies or disorders in the responses of the body's immune mechanisms. Among areas of special emphasis are: asthma and allergic disease, clinical immunology, including organ transplantation, venereal diseases, hepatitis, influenza and other viral respiratory infections, disease control measures, research and development, antiviral substances, and hospital-associated infections.

For further information, call 301–496–5717.

National Institute of Child Health and Human Development The Institute conducts and supports biomedical and behavioral research on child and maternal health; on problems of human development, with special reference to mental retardation; and on family structure, the dynamics of human population, and the reproductive process. Specific areas of research include pediatric and maternal AIDS, genetic diseases, short stature, premature puberty, infertility, minority health, learning disabilities such as dyslexia, sexually transmitted diseases, and the causes of infant morbidity and mortality—including low birth weight, premature birth, and sudden infant death syndrome. The Institute recently added a National Center for Medical Rehabilitation Research, which conducts and supports research and research training related to the rehabilitation of people with physical disabilities. Research-related findings are disseminated to other researchers, medical practitioners, and the general public to improve the health of children and families.

For further information, call 301–496–5133.

National Institute on Deafness and Other Communication Disorders The Institute conducts and supports research and training with respect to disorders of hearing and other communication processes, including diseases affecting hearing, balance, voice, speech, language, taste, and smell through a diversity of research performed in its own laboratories; a program of research grants, individual and institutional research training awards, career development awards, center grants, and contracts to public and private research institutions and organizations.

For further information, call 301–496–7243.

National Institute of Dental Research The Institute supports and conducts clinical and laboratory research directed toward the ultimate eradication of tooth decay and of a broad array of oral-facial disorders.

For further information, call 301–496–6621.

National Institute of Environmental Health Sciences The Institute, located in Research Triangle Park, NC, conducts and supports fundamental research concerned with defining, measuring, and understanding the effects of chemical, biological, and physical factors in the environment on the health and well-being of man.

For further information, call 919–541–3212 or (FTS) 8–629–3211.

National Institute of General Medical Sciences The emphasis of the Institute's programs for support of research and research training is basic biomedical science. The activities range from cell biology to genetics to pharmacology and systemic response to trauma and anesthesia.

For further information, call 301–496–7714.

National Institute of Neurological Disorders and Stroke The Institute conducts and supports fundamental and applied research on human neurological disorders such as Parkinson's disease, epilepsy, multiple sclerosis, muscular dystrophy, head and spinal cord injuries, and stroke. The Institute also conducts and supports research on the development and function of the normal brain and nervous system in order to better understand normal processes relating to disease states.

For further information, call 301–496–5751.

National Eye Institute The Institute conducts and supports fundamental studies on the eye and visual system, and on the causes, prevention, diagnosis, and treatment of visual disorders.

For further information, call 301–496–7425.

National Institute on Aging The Institute conducts and supports biomedical and behavioral research to increase the knowledge of the aging process and associated physical, psychological, and social factors, resulting from advanced age. Incontinence, menopause, susceptibility to diseases, and memory loss are among the areas of special concern.

For further information, call 301–496–5345.

National Institute of Arthritis and Musculoskeletal and Skin Diseases The Institute conducts and supports fundamental research in the major disease categories of arthritis and musculoskeletal and skin diseases through: research performed in its own laboratories and clinics, epidemiologic studies, research contracts and grants, and cooperative agreements to scientific institutions and to individuals. It supports training of manpower in fundamental sciences and clinical disciplines, conducts educational activities, including the collection and dissemination of health educational materials on these diseases, and coordinates with the other research institutes and with all Federal health programs relevant activities in the categorical diseases.

For further information, call 301–496–4353.

Clinical Center The Center is designed to bring scientists working in the Center's laboratories into close proximity with clinicians caring for patients, so that they may collaborate on problems of mutual concern. The research institutes select patients, referred to the National Institutes of Health by physicians throughout the United States and overseas, for clinical studies of specific diseases and disorders. A certain percent of the patients are "normal volunteers," healthy persons who provide an index of normal body functions against which to measure the abnormal. Normal volunteers come under varied sponsorship, such as colleges, civic groups, and religious organizations.

For further information, call 301–496–3227.

Fogarty International Center The Center promotes discussion, study, and research on the development of science internationally as it relates to health and administers a number of international programs for advanced study in the health sciences.

For further information, call 301–496–4625.

National Center for Human Genome Research The Center advises the Director of NIH and senior staff on all aspects of genomic analysis; coordinates the integration, review, and planning of genomic analysis research; formulates research goals and long-range plans with the guidance of the NIH Program Advisory Committee on Complex Genomes; serves as a focal point for coordination within NIH and will be the HHS point of contact for Federal interagency coordination, collaboration with industry and academia, and international cooperation; fosters, conducts, supports, and administers research and research training programs directed at promoting the growth and quality of research relating to mapping and sequencing of complex genomes through: (a) research grants, contracts, and cooperative agreements with institutions and individuals, (b) individual and institutional research training awards, (c) promotion of closer interaction with other bases of genomic analysis research, and (d) collection and dissemination of research findings in these areas. The Center develops plans for the centralized, systematic-targeted effort to create detailed maps of the genomes of organisms; sponsors scientific meetings and symposia to promote progress through information sharing; and fosters national and international information exchanges with industry and academia concerning research on complex genomes.

For further information, call 301–496–0844.

National Center for Nursing Research The Center fosters, conducts, supports, and administers research and research training programs aimed at promoting the growth and quality of research related to nursing and patient care and expanding the pool of experienced nurse researchers.

For further information, call 301–496–0523.

Division of Computer Research and Technology The Division conducts an integrated research, developmental, and service program in computer-related physical and life sciences in support of Institute biomedical research programs.

For further information, call 301–496–5206.

National Center for Research Resources The Center administers, fosters, and supports research for the development and support of various research resources needed on an institutional, regional, or national basis for health-related research. Programs are carried out through research grants and individual and institutional research training awards; cooperation and collaboration with organizations and institutions engaged in multicategorical research resource activities; and collection and dissemination of information on research and findings in these areas. The Center oversees a centralized program of intramural research resources through the planning, performance, and reporting of research projects.

For further information, call 301–496–5605.

Division of Research Grants The Division provides staff support to the Office of the Director, National Institutes of Health, in the formulation of grant and award policies and procedures, central receipt of all Public Health Service applications for research and research training support, and makes initial referral to Service components.

For further information, call 301–496–7881.

Health Care Financing Administration

[For the Health Care Financing Administration statement of organization, see the *Federal Register* of March 25, 1991, 56 FR 12374]

The Health Care Financing Administration was established by the Secretary's reorganization of March 8, 1977, as a principal operating component of the Department. It places under one Administration the oversight of the Medicare and Medicaid Programs and related Federal medical care quality control staffs.

Medicare The Medicare Program is a Federal health insurance program for persons over 65 years of age and certain disabled persons. It is funded through social security contributions, premiums, and general revenue. The Administration develops and implements policies related to program recipients, the providers of services such as hospitals, nursing homes, physicians, and the contractors who process claims. It also coordinates with the States to develop departmental programs, activities, and organizations that are closely related to the Medicare Program.

Medicaid The Medicaid Program, through grants to States, provides medical services to the needy and the medically needy. The Administration is responsible for working with the States to develop approaches toward meeting the needs of those who cannot afford adequate medical care.

The Medicare/Medicaid Programs include a quality assurance focal point to carry out the quality assurance provisions of the Medicare and Medicaid Programs; the development and implementation of health and safety standards for providers of care in Federal health programs; and the implementation of the End Stage Renal Disease Program and the Professional Review provisions.

For further information, contact the Administrator, Health Care Financing Administration, Department of Health and Human Services, 200 Independence Avenue SW., Washington, DC 20201. Phone, 301–966–3000.

Social Security Administration

[For the Social Security Administration statement of organization, see the *Code of Federal Regulations,* Title 20, Part 422]

The Social Security Administration was established and its predecessor, the Social Security Board, was abolished by Reorganization Plan No. 2 of 1946 (5 U.S.C. app.), effective July 16, 1946.

By Reorganization Plan No. 1 of 1953 (5 U.S.C. app.), effective April 11, 1953, the Social Security Administration was transferred from the Federal Security Agency to the Department of Health, Education, and Welfare, later the Department of Health and Human Services.

The Office of the Commissioner of Social Security is directly responsible to the Secretary of Health and Human Services for all programs administered by the Administration.

The Social Security Administration, under the direction of the Commissioner of Social Security, administers a national program of contributory social insurance whereby employees, employers, and the self-employed pay contributions that are pooled in special trust funds. When earnings stop or are reduced because the worker retires, dies, or becomes disabled, monthly cash benefits are paid to partially replace part of the earnings the family has lost.

Part of the contributions go into a separate hospital insurance trust fund, so that when workers and their dependents become 65 years old they will have help with their hospital bills. They may also elect to receive help with doctor bills and other medical expenses by paying a percentage of supplementary medical insurance premiums, while the Federal Government pays the remainder. Together, these two programs are often referred to as "Medicare." Under certain conditions, Medicare protection also is provided to people who are receiving social security or railroad retirement monthly benefits based on a disability. The responsibility for the administration of the Medicare Program has been transferred to the Health Care Financing Administration. By agreement with the Department of Labor, the Administration is also involved in certain aspects of the administration of the black lung benefits provisions of the Federal Coal Mine Health and Safety Act of 1969, as amended (30 U.S.C. 901).

Principal programs include the Old Age Survivors and Disability Insurance Program, which provides monthly benefits to retired and disabled workers, their spouses and children, and to survivors of insured workers.

The agency administers the supplemental security income program for the aged, blind, and disabled. This basic Federal payment program is financed out of general revenue, rather than a special trust fund. Some States, choosing to provide payments to supplement the benefits, have agreements with Administration under which it administers the supplemental payments for the States.

In addition, the Administration, through a nationwide field organization of 10 regional offices, 6 processing centers, and over 1,300 local offices, guides and directs all aspects of the cash benefit program operations of the agency; and directs the activities of those offices responsible for various program operations, including retirement, survivors, and disability insurance, and supplemental security income.

The Social Security Administration also provides administrative direction to a national organization of administrative law judges, who conduct independent hearings and decide appealed determinations involving the benefit provisions of Administration programs. The Administration, through its Appeals Council, reviews such appealed determinations and renders the Secretary's final decision.

Social Security Administration operations are decentralized to provide appropriate services at the local level. The United States is divided into 10 regions, each headed by a Regional Commissioner. The Regional Commissioner is the principal agency representative at the regional level, responsible for effective Administration contact with HHS, other Federal agencies, State disability determination services, and State welfare agencies. Regional Commissioners implement national operational and management plans for providing services directly to the public and coordinate regional operations so that they are effective and consistent with national and regional requirements, as well as systems and policy directives.

Each region contains, under the overall direction of the Regional Commissioner, a network of district offices, branch offices, and teleservice centers, which serve as the contact between Administration and the public. These installations have responsibility for:

—informing people of the purposes and provisions of programs and their rights and responsibilities thereunder;

—assisting with claims filed for retirement, survivors, health, or disability insurance benefits, black lung benefits, or supplemental security income;

—developing and adjudicating claims;

—assisting certain beneficiaries in claiming reimbursement for medical expenses;

—conducting development of cases involving earnings records, coverage, and fraud-related questions;

—making rehabilitation service referrals; and

—assisting claimants in filing appeals on Administration determinations of benefit entitlement or amount.

For further information, contact the Office of Public Inquiries, Social Security Administration, Department of Health and Human Services, 6401 Security Boulevard, Baltimore, MD 21235. Phone, 301-965-7700.

Sources of Information

Office of the Secretary

Inquiries on the following information may be directed to the specified office, Department of Health and Human Services, Humphrey Building, 200 Independence Avenue SW., Washington, DC 20201.

Civil Rights For information on enforcement of civil rights laws, call or write the Office for Civil Rights, Cohen Building, Washington, DC 20201. Phone:

Washington, DC, metropolitan area (202-863-0100 or TDD, 202-863-0101). Outside Washington, DC, metropolitan area (1-800-368-1019 or TDD, 1-800-537-7697).

Consumer Activities Call or write the U.S. Office of Consumer Affairs. Phone, 202-634-4310.

Contracts and Small Business Activities For information concerning programs, call or write the Director, Office of Small and Disadvantaged Business Utilization. Phone, 202-245-7300.

Employment Inquiries regarding applications for employment and the college recruitment program should be directed to the Office of Personnel Services. Phone, 202-619-2560.

Locator Inquiries about the location and telephone numbers of HHS offices should be directed to the HHS locator, Room G-174, Wilbert H. Cohen Building, 330 Independence Avenue SW., Washington, DC 20201. Phone, 202-619-0257.

Publications Persons requiring a short history of the Department of Health and Human Services may request *A Common Thread of Service* from the Information Center.

Prenatal Care, Infant Care, Your Child from 1 to 6, Your Child From 6 to 12, No Smoking! Pamphlets for Parents, Teenagers, Grade School Children, Thinking About Drinking, and many others are available at various prices from the Superintendent of Documents, Government Printing Office, Washington, DC 20402.

Telephone Directory The Department of Health and Human Services telephone directory is available for sale by the Superintendent of Documents, Government Printing Office, Washington, DC 20402.

Office of Inspector General

General inquiries may be directed to the Office of Inspector General, Department of Health and Human Services, 330 Independence Avenue SW., Washington, DC 20201.

Hotline Individuals wishing to report fraud, waste, or abuse against Department programs should write to: OIG Hotline, P.O. Box 17303, Baltimore, MD 21203-7303. Phone, 800-368-5779 (toll-free).

Publications Single copies of most Office of Inspector General publications are available free of charge. Phone, 202-619-1142.

Office of Human Development Services

General inquiries may be directed to the Office of Human Development Services, Department of Health and Human Services, Washington, DC 20201.

Contracts Contact the Grants and Contract Management Division. Phone, 202-472-3243.

Information Center Public Information Office, Room 348F, Humphrey Building. Phone, 202-472-7257.

Mental Retardation Call or write the President's Committee on Mental Retardation, OHDS, for information on HHS mental retardation programs. Phone, 202-245-7634.

Public Health Service

Office of the Assistant Secretary for Health Inquiries on the following subjects should be directed to the specified office, Office of the Assistant Secretary for Health, 5600 Fishers Lane, Rockville, MD 20857.

Employment The majority of positions are in the Federal civil service. Inquiries should be addressed to the Office of Personnel Operations, Room 17A-07. Phone, 301-443-6900.

Many medical, scientific, and technical positions are filled through the Commissioned Corps of the Public Health Service, a uniformed service of the U.S. Government. Inquiries should be directed to the Division of Commissioned Personnel, Office of the Surgeon General, Room 4A-15. Phone, 301-443-3067.

Films, Publications, and Other Information Information concerning films, publications, and other specific information should be directed to the six health agencies that are listed below. All other inquiries about the Public Health Service should be directed to the Office of Communications, Room 712H, Hubert

H. Humphrey Building. Phone, 202-245-6867.

Agency for Health Care Policy and Research

Inquiries on the following subjects may be directed to the appropriate office at the Agency for Health Care Policy and Research, 5600 Fishers Lane, Rockville, MD 20857.

Grants Write to the Chief, Grants Management Branch. Phone, 301-443-4033.

Contracts Write to the Contracts Officer, Management Systems and Services Branch. Phone, 301-443-5690.

Employment Inquiries should be addressed to the Administrative Officer, Management Systems and Services Branch. Phone, 301-443-5690.

Publications Single copies of most publications produced by the Agency are available free of charge from the Publications Branch, Center for Research Dissemination and Liaison. Phone, 301-443-4100.

Alcohol, Drug Abuse, and Mental Health Administration

Inquiries on the following subjects may be directed to the specified office, Alcohol, Drug Abuse, and Mental Health Administration, 5600 Fishers Lane, Rockville, MD 20857.

Contracts Write to the Director, Division of Grants and Contracts Management. Phone, 301-443-4147.

Employment Inquiries should be addressed to the Director, Division of Personnel Management. Phone, 301-443-3408.

Publications Write to the Associate Administrator for Communications and External Affairs. Phone, 301-443-3783.

Centers for Disease Control

Inquiries on the following information may be directed to the office indicated at the Centers for Disease Control, 1600 Clifton Road NE., Atlanta, GA 30333.

Employment The majority of positions are in the Federal civil service. For information about positions, inquiries may be addressed to the Personnel Management Office.

Many medical, scientific, and technical positions are filled through the Commissioned Corps of the Public Health Service, a uniformed service of the U.S. Government. Inquiries may be addressed to Centers for Disease Control, Personnel Management Office (phone, 404-639-3276); or to Division of Commissioned Personnel, Office of the Surgeon General, Public Health Service, Department of Health and Human Services, 5600 Fishers Lane, Rockville, MD 20857.

Films Information concerning availability of audiovisual materials related to program activities may be obtained from the Office of Public Affairs. Phone, 404-639-3286.

Publications Single copies of most publications are available free of charge from the Management Analysis and Services Office, Centers for Disease Control. Phone, 404-639-3534.

Bulk quantities of publications may be purchased from the Superintendent of Documents, Government Printing Office, Washington, DC 20402.

Food and Drug Administration

Inquiries on the following subjects may be directed to the specified office, Food and Drug Administration, 5600 Fishers Lane, Rockville, MD 20857.

Consumer Activities FDA Consumer Affairs Offices are located in 32 cities across the country. Consumer phones in these same cities provide recorded messages of interest to the consumer. Phone, 301-443-5006.

Consumer Affairs Offices—Food and Drug Administration

Office	Address	Telephone
Atlanta, GA	60 8th St. NE., 30309	404-347-7355
Baltimore, MD	900 Madison Ave., 21201	301-962-3731
Boston, MA	1 Montvale Ave., Stoneham, MA 02180	617-279-1479
Brooklyn, NY	850 3d Ave., 11232	718-965-5043

Consumer Affairs Offices—Food and Drug Administration—Continued

Office	Address	Telephone
Buffalo, NY	599 Delaware Ave., 14202	716-846-4483
Chicago, IL	1222 Main Post Office Bldg. and 433 W. Van Buren St., 60607	312-353-7126
Cincinnati, OH	1141 Central Pkwy., 45202-1097	513-684-3501
Cleveland, OH	P.O. Box 838, 3820 Center Rd., Brunswick, OH 44212	216-273-1038
Dallas, TX	3032 Bryan St., 75204	214-767-5433
Denver, CO	P.O. Box 25087, Bldg. 20, Denver Federal Ctr., 80225-0087	303-236-3018
Detroit, MI	1560 E. Jefferson Ave., 48207	313-226-6274
West Orange, NJ	61 Main St., 07052	201-645-3265
Houston, TX	Suite 420, 1445 N. Loop West, 77008	713-229-2322
Indianapolis, IN	Rm. 693, 575 N. Pennsylvania St., 46204	317-269-6500
Kansas City, MO	1009 Cherry St., 64106	816-374-6366
Los Angeles, CA	1521 W. Pico Blvd., 90015-2486	213-252-7597
Minneapolis, MN	240 Hennepin Ave., 55401	612-334-4103
Nashville, TN	297 Plus Park Blvd., 37217	615-736-7277
New Orleans, LA	4298 Elysian Fields Ave., 70122	504-589-2420
Omaha, NE	200 S. 16th St., 68102	402-221-4676
Orlando, FL	Suite 120, 7200 Lake Ellenor Dr., 32809	305-855-0900
Philadelphia, PA	Rm. 900, 2d and Chestnut Sts., 19106	215-597-0837
San Antonio, TX	Rm. B-406, 727 E. Durango, 78206	512-229-6737
San Francisco, CA	Rm. 526, 50 United Nations Plz., 94102	415-556-1457
San Juan, PR	P.O. Box 5719, Puerta de Tierra Station, 00906-5719	809-729-6852
Seattle, WA	22201 23d Dr. SE., Bothell, WA 98021-4421	206-483-4953
St. Louis, MO	808 N. Collins Alley, 63102	314-425-5021

Contracts Contact the Director, Division of Contracts and Grants Management (HFA-500). Phone, 301-443-6890.

Employment The Administration uses various civil service examinations and registers in its recruitment for positions such as consumer safety officers, pharmacologists, microbiologists, physiologists, chemists, mathematical statisticians, physicians, dentists, animal caretakers, etc. Inquiries for positions in the Washington, DC, metropolitan area should be directed to the Personnel Officer (HFA-400). Phone, 301-443-2234.

Inquiries for positions outside the Washington, DC, area should be directed to the appropriate local FDA office.

Schools interested in the college recruitment program should write to the Personnel Officer (HFA-400). Phone, 301-443-6890.

Publications *FDA Consumer,* FDA's official magazine, is available from the Superintendent of Documents, Government Printing Office, Washington, DC 20402. Phone, 301-443-3220.

Reading Rooms Freedom of Information, Room 12A-30, phone, 301-443-1813; Hearing Clerk, Room 4-65, phone, 301-443-1751; and Press Office, Room 15-05 (or Room 3807, FB-8, 200 C Street SW., Washington, DC 20204), phone, 301-443-3285.

Speakers Available for presentations to private organizations and community groups. Requests should be directed to the local FDA office.

Health Resources and Services Administration

Inquiries on the following should be directed to the specified office, Health Resources and Services Administration, 5600 Fishers Lane, Rockville, MD 20857.

Employment The majority of positions are in the Federal civil service. For positions in the Washington, DC, metropolitan area, employment inquiries may be addressed to the Division of Personnel, Room 14A46. Phone, 301-443-5460.

Hiring in other areas is decentralized to the Regional Health Administrators in each of the 10 HHS regional offices. The U.S. Government listings in the appropriate commercial telephone directories will provide specific addresses.

Some health professional positions are filled through the Commissioned Corps of the Public Health Service, a uniformed service of the U.S. Government. Inquiries may be addressed to Division of

Commissioned Personnel, Office of the Surgeon General, Public Health Service, Parklawn Building, 5600 Fishers Lane, Rockville, MD 20857.

Films Information concerning the availability of audiovisual materials related to program activities, including films for recruiting minorities into health professions and women into dentistry, are available from the Office of Communications.

Publications Single copies of most publications are available free of charge. For a complete listing, request the catalog *Current Publications of the Health Resources and Services Administration* from the Office of Communications, Room 14–43. Bulk quantities of publications may be purchased from the Superintendent of Documents, Government Printing Office, Washington, DC 20402. Certain technical publications may be purchased from the National Technical Information Service, Department of Commerce, Springfield, VA 22151.

Indian Health Service

Inquiries on the following subjects should be directed to the specified office, Indian Health Service, 5600 Fishers Lane, Rockville, MD 20857.

Employment The majority of positions are in the Federal civil service. For positions in the Washington, DC, metropolitan area, employment inquiries may be addressed to the Division of Personnel Management, Room 5A–55. Phone, 301–443–6520.

Hiring in other areas is decentralized to the 11 area offices. The U.S. Government listings are in the commercial telephone directories for: Aberdeen, SD; Albuquerque, NM; Anchorage, AK; Bemidji, MN; Billings, MT; Nashville, TN; Oklahoma City, OK; Phoenix, AZ; Portland, OR; Sacramento, CA; and Window Rock, AZ. The area offices can be referenced for specific addresses. Some health professional positions are filled through the Commissioned Corps of the Public Health Service, a uniformed service of the U.S. Government. Inquiries may be addressed to the Indian Health Service, Commissioned Corp Management Branch, Room 6A–25, 5600 Fishers Lane, Rockville, MD 20857.

Publications Single pamphlet copies containing general information about the Indian Health Service are available free of charge. This information may be requested from the Indian Health Service, Office of Communications, Room 6–35, Parklawn Building, Rockville, MD 20857.

National Institutes of Health

Inquiries on the following subjects may be directed to the office indicated at the National Institutes of Health, Bethesda, MD 20892, or the address given.

Contracts For information on research and development contracts, contact the Division of Contracts and Grants. Phone, (FTS) 8–496–6431. For all other contracts, contact the Division of Procurement. Phone, (FTS) 8–496–3181.

Employment A wide range of civil service examinations and registers are used; staff fellowships are available to recent doctorates in biomedical sciences; college recruitment is conducted as necessary to meet requirements. Write to Division of Personnel Management for further information. Phone, 301–496–4197.

PHS Commissioned Officer Program For information on the Commissioned Officer programs at NIH and the program for early commissioning of senior medical students in the Reserve Corps of the Public Health Service, contact the Division of Personnel Management. Phone, (FTS) 8–496–4212 or 301–496–4212.

Environment Research on the biological effects of chemical, physical, and biological substances present in the environment are conducted and supported by the National Institute of Environmental Health Sciences, Research Triangle Park, NC 22709. Phone, (FTS) 8–629–3211.

Films Research and health-related films are available for loan from the National Library of Medicine, Collection Access Section, Bethesda, MD 20984. Films are available for purchase from the National

Audiovisual Center (General Services Administration), Washington, DC 20409.
Publications Publications, brochures, and reports on health and disease problems, medical research, and biomedical communications are available from the Division of Public Information, Office of Communications, National Institutes of Health, Bethesda, MD 20892 (phone, 301–496–4143); or Government Printing Office, Washington, DC 20402. Publications include: *Journal of National Cancer Institute; Environmental Health Perspectives; Scientific Directory and Annual Bibliography; NLM—Medline* (brochure); and *NIH Publications List.* Single copies of these publications are available from NIH. *Index Medicus, Cumulated Index Medicus Annual,* and *Research Grants Index* may be ordered from the Government Printing Office.

Health Care Financing Administration

Inquiries on the following subjects may be directed to the Health Care Financing Administration, Department of Health and Human Services, 6325 Security Boulevard, Baltimore, MD 21207.
Contracts and Small Business Activities Contact the Chief, Contract Administration and Grants Branch, Division of Contracts and Grants. Phone, 301–966–5157.
Employment Inquiries should be addressed to the Office of Human Resources. For information on employment in a regional office, contact the Regional Personnel Officer in the Office of the Regional Director for that region. Phone, 301–966–5489.
Publications For information on publications write to the Printing, Distribution, and Property Management Branch, Division of General Services. Phone, 301–966–3215.

Social Security Administration

Inquiries on the following subjects may be directed to the specified office, Social Security Administration, 6401 Security Boulevard, Baltimore, MD 21235.
Contracts and Small Business Activities Contact the Office of Acquisitions and Grants. Phone, 301–965–9457.
Employment A variety of civil service registers and examinations are used in hiring new employees. Specific employment information may be obtained from the Office of Human Resources. Phone, 301–965–4506.
Publications The Social Security Administration collects a substantial volume of economic, demographic, and other data in furtherance of its program mission. Basic data on employment and earnings, beneficiaries and benefit payments, utilization of health services and other items of program interest are published regularly in the *Social Security Bulletin,* its *Annual Statistical Supplement,* and in special releases and reports that appear periodically on selected topics of interest to the general public. Additional information may be obtained from the Publications Staff, Office of Research and Statistics, Room 209, 4301 Connecticut Avenue NW., Washington, DC 20008. Phone, 202–281–7136.

The Office of Public Affairs has published numerous pamphlets concerning Administration programs. Single copies may be obtained at any of over 1,300 local offices.
Reading Rooms Requests for information, for copies of records, or to inspect or copy records may be made at any local office or the Headquarters Contact Unit, Room G–44, Altmeyer Building. Phone, 1–800–2345–SSA (toll-free answering service).
Speakers and Films It is the Administration's policy to make speakers, films, and exhibits available to public or private organizations, community groups, schools, etc., throughout the Nation. Requests for this service should be directed to the nearest Social Security Office or the Office of Public Affairs.

For further information concerning the Department of Health and Human Services, contact the Information Center, Department of Health and Human Services, 200 Independence Avenue SW., Washington, DC 20201. Phone, 202–619–0257.

DEPARTMENT OF HOUSING AND URBAN DEVELOPMENT

451 Seventh Street SW., Washington, DC 20410
Phone, 202–708–1422

SECRETARY OF HOUSING AND URBAN DEVELOPMENT	Jack Kemp
Chief of Staff	Scott W. Reed
Senior Adviser to the Secretary	Sharon A. Zelaska
Special Assistant to the Secretary	Leah G. Levy
Assistant to the Secretary for Policy and Planning	William Dal Col
Executive Officer for Administrative Operations and Management	James R. Walker
Deputy Secretary	Alfred A. DelliBovi
Executive Assistant to the Deputy Secretary	Michael M. Jacobson
Assistant to the Secretary for Field Management	Linda Z. Marston
Assistant to the Secretary for Labor Relations	Joseph A. Scudero
Staff Offices:	
Special Assistant to the Secretary for Indian and Alaskan Native Programs	Joel E. Starr
Director, Office of Small and Disadvantaged Business Utilization	Jim E. Tarro, *Acting*
Chief, Office of Administrative Law Judges	Alan W. Heifetz
Chairperson, HUD Board of Contract Appeals	David T. Anderson
External Organizations:	
Executive Director, Interagency Council on the Homeless	Patricia A. Carlile
Chairperson, Federal Housing Finance Board	Daniel F. Evans, Jr.
General Counsel	Francis A. Keating II
Principal Deputy General Counsel	Clarence H. Albright, Jr.
Deputy General Counsel	Shelley A. Longmuir
Deputy General Counsel for Operations	George L. Weidenfeller
Associate Deputy General Counsel	Dorothy Brown, *Acting*
Associate General Counsel, Office of Equal Opportunity and Administrative Law	Carole Wilson
Associate General Counsel, Office of Insured Housing and Finance	John J. Daly
Associate General Counsel, Office of Assisted Housing and Community Development	Robert S. Kenison
Associate General Counsel, Office of Program Enforcement	John P. Kennedy

Associate General Counsel, Office of Litigation	JOHN W. HEROLD
Associate General Counsel, Office of Legislation and Regulations	EDWARD J. MURPHY, JR.
Chief Financial Officer	PHILLIP M. KANE
Deputy Chief Financial Officer for Financial Policy and Evaluation	(VACANCY)
Director, Office of Debt Collection, Cash, and Credit Management	(VACANCY)
Director, Office of Financial Policy and Evaluation	(VACANCY)
Deputy Chief Financial Officer for Operations	DONNA M. ABBENANTE
Director, Office of Financial Systems Integration	(VACANCY)
Director, Office of Internal Control and Audit Resolution	(VACANCY)
Assistant Secretary for Housing—Federal Housing Commissioner	ARTHUR J. HILL
General Deputy Assistant Secretary	RONALD A. ROSENFELD
Associate General Deputy Assistant Secretary	JAMES E. SCHOENBERGER
Housing-FHA Comptroller	ELEANOR M. CLARK
Director, Office of Evaluation	(VACANCY)
Deputy Housing-FHA Comptroller for Financial Systems Enhancements	THOMAS D. SHOLEDICE
Director, Office of Mortgage Insurance Accounting and Servicing	CHRISTOPHER PETERSON
Deputy Housing-FHA Comptroller for Policy and Planning	C. DUNCAN MACRAE
Deputy Assistant Secretary for Multifamily Housing Programs	PHILIP J. SALAMONE
Director, Office of Elderly and Assisted Housing	LAWRENCE GOLDBERGER
Director, Office of Insured Multifamily Housing Development	LINDA D. CHEATHAM, *Acting*
Director, Office of Multifamily Housing Management	DONALD A. KAPLAN
Director, Office of Multifamily Housing Preservation and Property Disposition	AUDREY HINTON, *Acting*
Deputy Assistant Secretary for Operations	DONALD P. MADDY
Director, Office of Management	C. SUE MITCHELL
Director, Office of Budget and Field Resource	JOHN R. AMBROGNE, JR.
Deputy Assistant Secretary for Single Family Housing	JUAN M. ACOSTA
Director, Office of Insured Single Family Housing	STEPHEN A. MARTIN
Director, Office of Lender Activities and Land Sales Registration	WILLIAM M. HEYMAN
Director, Office of Manufactured Housing and Regulatory Functions	DAVID C. NIMMER
Assistant Secretary for Community Planning and Development	S. ANNA KONDRATRAS
Deputy Assistant Secretary for Economic Development	PAUL R. BARDACK

Director, Office of Economic Development	(VACANCY)
Director, Office of Special Needs Assistance Programs	JAMES N. FORSBERG
CPD Comptroller	ALAN K. LOMBARD
Deputy Assistant Secretary for Grant Programs	RUSSELL K. PAUL
Director, Office of Block Grant Assistance	DON I. PATCH
Director, Office of Urban Rehabilitation	DAVID M. COHEN
Director, Office of Technical Assistance	SYLVESTER C. ANGEL
Deputy Assistant Secretary for Operations	(VACANCY)
Director, Office of Environment and Energy	RICHARD H. BROUN
Director, Office of Management	JO ANN W. STANTON
Executive Operations Staff:	
Director, Field Coordination Unit	FRANK DAVIS
Director, Policy Coordination Unit	CHRISTOPHER G. WYE
Assistant Secretary for Policy Development and Research	JOHN C. WEICHER
General Deputy Assistant Secretary	(VACANCY)
Deputy Assistant Secretary, Office of Policy Development	THOMAS M. HUMBERT
Deputy Assistant Secretary, Office of Economic Affairs	SUSAN E. WOODWARD
Deputy Assistant Secretary, Office of Research	JAMES W. STIMPSON
Assistant Secretary for Administration	JIM E. TARRO
Director, Office of Ethics	ARNOLD J. HAIMAN
Deputy Assistant Secretary for Resource Planning and Operations	MICHAEL F. HILL
Director, Office of Budget	HERBERT G. PERSIL
Director, Office of Management and Quality Assurance	HAROLD W. HENRY
Director, Office of Personnel and Training	ELMER LEE, *Acting*
Director, Office of Administrative and Management Services	MARIE P. KISSICK
Deputy Assistant Secretary for Finance and Management	JERRY R. PIERCE
Director, Office of Procurement and Contracts	ROOSEVELT JONES
Administration Comptroller/Director, Office of Finance and Accounting	WILLIAM H. EARGLE, JR.
Director, Office of Information Policies and Systems	DONALD C. DEMITROS
Deputy Assistant Secretary for Executive Services	(VACANCY)
Director, Office of Executive Scheduling	CAROL A. FLATLEY
Director, Executive Secretariat	GAIL L. LIVELY
Assistant Secretary for Congressional and Intergovernmental Relations	IVAN A. RANSOPHER, *Acting*
Deputy Assistant Secretary for Legislation	IVAN A. RANSOPHER
Deputy Assistant Secretary for Congressional Relations	JAMES L. BYNUM
Deputy Assistant Secretary for Intergovernmental Relations	STEPHEN A. GLAUDÉ

Assistant Secretary for Fair Housing and Equal Opportunity	GORDON H. MANSFIELD
Deputy Assistant Secretary for Fair Housing and Equal Opportunity/Enforcement and Compliance	LEONORA L. GUARRAI
Director, Office of Fair Housing Enforcement and Section 3 Compliance	JACQULYN SHELTON
Director, Office of HUD Program Compliance	PETER KAPLAN
Director, Office of Voluntary Compliance	FLORENCE L. MAULTSBY
Deputy Assistant Secretary for Operations and Management	JOHNNIE B. BOOKER
Director, Office of Management and Field Coordination	PAUL WILLIAMS
Director, Office of Program Standards and Evaluation	LAURENCE D. PEARL
Director, Office of Affirmative Action and Equal Employment Opportunity	WILLIAM O. ANDERSON
Assistant Secretary for Public Affairs	MARY S. BRUNETTE
Deputy Assistant Secretaries	ANTHONY F. MITCHELL FREDERICK L. AHEARN
Director, Office of Press Relations	ROBERT E. NIPP
Director, Office of Policy Support	CHARLES S. COGAN
Assistant Secretary for Public and Indian Housing	JOSEPH G. SCHIFF
General Deputy Assistant Secretary	MICHAEL B. JANIS
Deputy Assistant Secretary, Office of Resident Initiatives	DAVID L. CAPRARA
Director, Office of Management and Policy	CASIMIR BONKOWSKI
Director, Office of Construction, Rehabilitation, and Maintenance	JANICE RATTLEY
Director, Office of Public and Indian Housing Comptroller	BARBARA BURKHALTER
Director, Office of Indian Housing	DOMINIC A. NESSI
Director, Office of Management Operations	THOMAS SHERMAN
President, Government National Mortgage Association	ARTHUR J. HILL, *Acting*
Executive Vice President	ROBERT P. KALISH
Vice President, Office of Asset Management	GEORGE S. ANDERSON
Vice President, Office of Mortgage-Backed Securities	GUY S. WILSON
Corporate Secretary	ELTON A. PELLER
Vice President, Office of Finance	WILLIAM E. DOBRZYKOWSKI
Controller	ALBERT J. FULNER, JR.
Treasurer	VICTOR M. CORREA
Inspector General	PAUL A. ADAMS
Deputy Inspector General	JOHN J. CONNORS
Assistant Inspector General for Management and Policy	JACQULYN K. HOWARD
Assistant Inspector General for Investigation	PATRICK J. NERI
Assistant Inspector General for Audit	JOHN H. (CHRIS) GREER

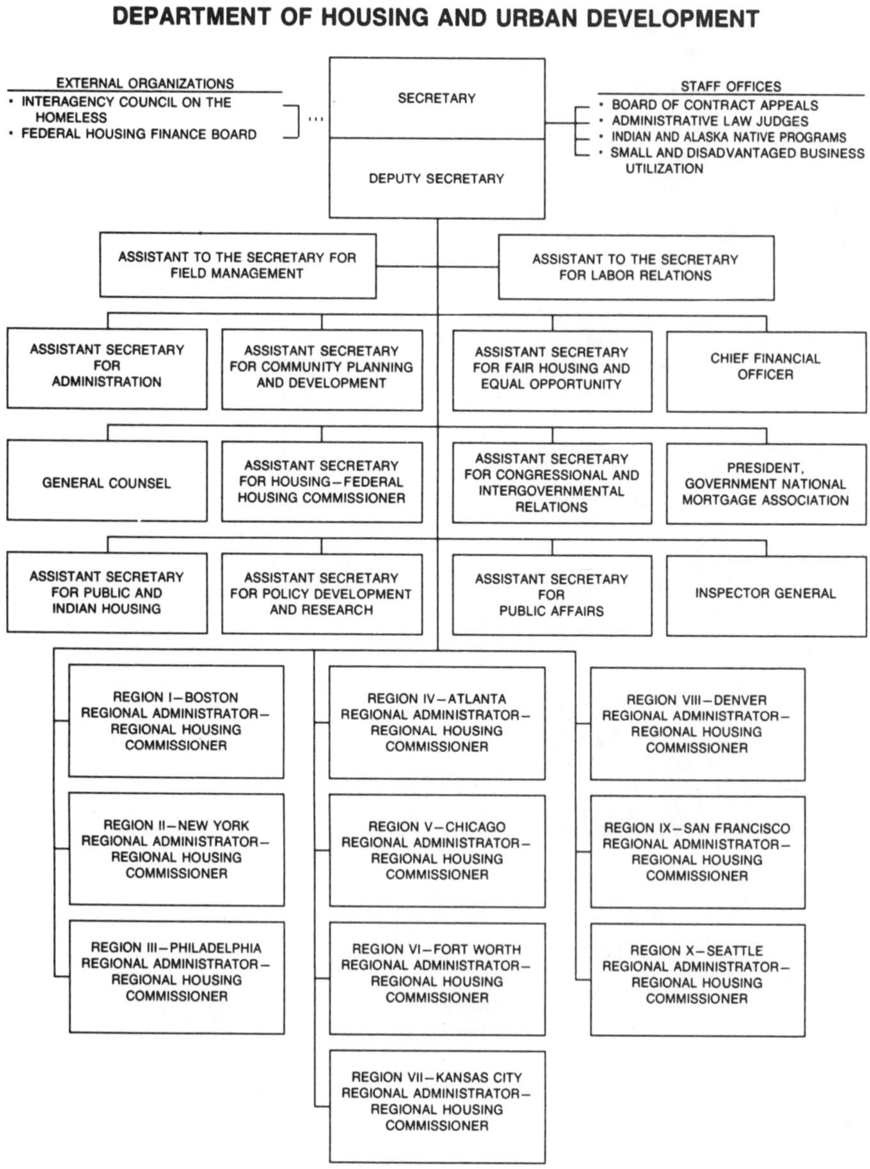
DEPARTMENT OF HOUSING AND URBAN DEVELOPMENT
EXTERNAL ORGANIZATIONS
• INTERAGENCY COUNCIL ON THE HOMELESS
• FEDERAL HOUSING FINANCE BOARD
SECRETARY
DEPUTY SECRETARY
STAFF OFFICES
• BOARD OF CONTRACT APPEALS
• ADMINISTRATIVE LAW JUDGES
• INDIAN AND ALASKA NATIVE PROGRAMS
• SMALL AND DISADVANTAGED BUSINESS UTILIZATION
ASSISTANT TO THE SECRETARY FOR FIELD MANAGEMENT
ASSISTANT TO THE SECRETARY FOR LABOR RELATIONS
ASSISTANT SECRETARY FOR ADMINISTRATION
ASSISTANT SECRETARY FOR COMMUNITY PLANNING AND DEVELOPMENT
ASSISTANT SECRETARY FOR FAIR HOUSING AND EQUAL OPPORTUNITY
CHIEF FINANCIAL OFFICER
GENERAL COUNSEL
ASSISTANT SECRETARY FOR HOUSING—FEDERAL HOUSING COMMISSIONER
ASSISTANT SECRETARY FOR CONGRESSIONAL AND INTERGOVERNMENTAL RELATIONS
PRESIDENT, GOVERNMENT NATIONAL MORTGAGE ASSOCIATION
ASSISTANT SECRETARY FOR PUBLIC AND INDIAN HOUSING
ASSISTANT SECRETARY FOR POLICY DEVELOPMENT AND RESEARCH
ASSISTANT SECRETARY FOR PUBLIC AFFAIRS
INSPECTOR GENERAL
REGION I—BOSTON REGIONAL ADMINISTRATOR—REGIONAL HOUSING COMMISSIONER
REGION II—NEW YORK REGIONAL ADMINISTRATOR—REGIONAL HOUSING COMMISSIONER
REGION III—PHILADELPHIA REGIONAL ADMINISTRATOR—REGIONAL HOUSING COMMISSIONER
REGION IV—ATLANTA REGIONAL ADMINISTRATOR—REGIONAL HOUSING COMMISSIONER
REGION V—CHICAGO REGIONAL ADMINISTRATOR—REGIONAL HOUSING COMMISSIONER
REGION VI—FORT WORTH REGIONAL ADMINISTRATOR—REGIONAL HOUSING COMMISSIONER
REGION VII—KANSAS CITY REGIONAL ADMINISTRATOR—REGIONAL HOUSING COMMISSIONER
REGION VIII—DENVER REGIONAL ADMINISTRATOR—REGIONAL HOUSING COMMISSIONER
REGION IX—SAN FRANCISCO REGIONAL ADMINISTRATOR—REGIONAL HOUSING COMMISSIONER
REGION X—SEATTLE REGIONAL ADMINISTRATOR—REGIONAL HOUSING COMMISSIONER

The Department of Housing and Urban Development is the principal Federal agency responsible for programs concerned with the Nation's housing needs, fair housing opportunities, and improvement and development of the Nation's communities.

In carrying out its responsibilities, the Department administers a wide variety of programs, including: Federal Housing Administration mortgage insurance programs that help families become homeowners and facilitate the construction and rehabilitation of rental units; rental assistance programs for lower-income families who otherwise could not afford decent housing; the Government National Mortgage Association mortgage-backed securities program that helps ensure an adequate supply of mortgage credit; programs to combat housing discrimination and affirmatively further fair housing; programs that aid community and neighborhood development and preservation; and programs to help protect the homebuyer in the marketplace. The Department also takes steps to encourage a strong private sector housing industry that can produce affordable housing, and to stimulate private sector initiatives, public/private sector partnerships, and public entrepreneurship.

The Department of Housing and Urban Development (HUD) was established by the Department of Housing and Urban Development Act (42 U.S.C. 3532–3537), effective November 9, 1965. It was created to:

—administer the principal programs that provide assistance for housing and for the development of the Nation's communities;

—assist the President in achieving maximum coordination of the various Federal activities that have a major effect upon community preservation and development;

—encourage the problem-solving of housing and community development through States and localities;

—encourage the maximum contributions that may be made by vigorous private homebuilding and mortgage lending industries, both primary and secondary, to housing, community development, and the national economy; and

—provide for full and appropriate consideration, at the national level, of the needs and interests of the Nation's communities and of the people who live and work in them.

Although HUD administers many programs, its major functions may be grouped into six categories, which include:

—insuring mortgages for single-family and multifamily dwellings and loans for home improvement and the purchase of mobile homes;

—channeling funds from investors into the mortgage industry through the Government National Mortgage Association;

—making direct loans for construction or rehabilitation of housing projects for the elderly and the handicapped;

—providing Federal housing subsidies for low- and moderate-income families;

—providing grants to States and communities for community development activities; and

—promoting and enforcing fair housing and equal housing opportunity.

Office of the Secretary

The Department is administered under the supervision and direction of a Cabinet-level Secretary. The Secretary formulates recommendations for basic policies in the fields of housing and community development, and works with other Federal agencies in establishing and maintaining housing and community development policies consistent with other economic and fiscal policies of the Government.

Secretary The Secretary:

—works with the Executive Office of the President and other Federal agencies to ensure that economic and fiscal policies in housing and community development are consistent with other economic and fiscal policies of the Government;

—encourages private enterprise to serve as large a part of the Nation's total housing and community development needs as possible;

—promotes the growth of cities and States, the efficient and effective use of housing and community and economic development resources by stimulating private sector initiatives, public/private sector partnerships, and public entrepreneurship;

—takes steps to ensure equal access to housing and to affirmatively prevent discrimination in housing; and

—develops the fullest cooperation with private enterprise in achieving the objectives of the Department. The Secretary also provides general oversight—as required by law—of the Federal National Mortgage Association.

Deputy Secretary The Deputy Secretary assists the Secretary in discharging Secretarial duties and responsibilities and serves as Acting Secretary in the absence of the Secretary.

Assistant to the Secretary for Field Management The Assistant to the Secretary for Field Coordination advises the Secretary, Deputy Secretary, and other principal staff on the effectiveness of regional and field operating policies and procedures and serves as the Secretary's principal focal point in all matters dealing with the regional and field offices.

Assistant to the Secretary for Labor Relations The Assistant to the Secretary for Labor Relations advises the Secretary, Deputy Secretary, and principal staff on all matters pertaining to organized labor, labor regulations, and related matters.

Staff Offices The Office of the Secretary also contains staff offices having departmentwide responsibility in specialized areas such as Indian and Alaskan Native programs, small and disadvantaged business utilization, administrative judicial proceedings, and contract appeals.

Special Assistant for Indian and Alaska Native Programs The Special Assistant coordinates all departmental housing and community development programs for Indian and Alaskan Natives.

Office of Small and Disadvantaged Business Utilization The Office oversees HUD's small and disadvantaged set-aside contracting activities and the Minority Business Enterprise Program.

Office of Administrative Law Judges The Office hears and decides Federal Housing Equal Opportunity cases, as well as cases under the Administrative Procedure Act.

HUD Board of Contract Appeals The Board issues binding decisions on all appeals of HUD actions in contracting, awarding grants, disciplining mortgagees, and offsetting tax refunds of people indebted to HUD.

External Organizations

Interagency Council on the Homeless The Council is responsible for reviewing and coordinating Federal programs and activities designed to help the homeless. The Council works with State and local governments on homeless-related efforts and collects and disseminates information on homeless activities. It is comprised of the heads of 10 Cabinet departments and 5 independent agencies.

Federal Housing Finance Board The Board oversees the Federal Home Loan Banks. It is the function of the Board to ensure that the Federal Home Loan Banks carry out their housing finance mission, remain adequately capitalized, and operate in a safe and sound manner.

Office of General Counsel The Office serves as the chief legal advisor to the Secretary and other principal staff on the effectiveness of regional and field operating policies and procedures and serves as the Secretary's principal focal point in all legal matters dealing with the regional and field offices.

The General Counsel provides legal opinions, advice, and services with respect to all programs and activities of the Department; and provides counsel and assistance in the development of the Department's programs and policies. The General Counsel supervises all staff assigned to the Headquarters office and provides professional guidance for staff assigned to the regional and field Counsel's offices.

Office of the Chief Financial Officer The Office oversees the financial management of the Department's programs, working with the Council of Comptrollers to develop, promulgate, and enforce a departmental body of financial policy; establishes policies and standards for the development, maintenance, operations, and evaluation of all departmental financial management systems; and advises the Secretary on all aspects of financial management, including directing the Department in establishing and meeting financial management goals.

Assistant Secretary for Administration The Assistant Secretary advises the Secretary and other departmental staff and is the chief officer of the Department for administrative management.

The Office of Ethics reports directly to the Assistant Secretary for Administration and manages ethics programs, standards of conduct, and review of financial disclosure reports.

Deputy Assistant Secretary for Resource Planning and Operations The Deputy Assistant Secretary functions through the following offices:

—Office of Budget, which prepares HUD budget, policy for formulation, presentation, execution, funding, and staffing controls;

—Office of Management and Quality Assurance, which prepares the Secretary's management reporting systems, Administration's participation in field performance reviews, management analysis, and consulting services;

—Office of Personnel and Training, which handles human resources management, staffing and classification, training, labor and employee relations, payroll, and leave management; and

—Office of Administrative and Management Services, which oversees building operations, space and communications management, printing and visual arts, directives and records management, safety and health services, and contract services (library, cafeteria, parking).

Deputy Assistant Secretary for Finance and Management The Deputy Assistant Secretary functions through the following offices:

—Office of Procurement and Contracts, which awards and administers contracts, purchase orders, grants, cooperative agreements, and interagency agreements;

—Office of Finance and Accounting/Administration Comptroller, which handles policy and coordination of financial and accounting systems and services (other than GNMA and MIAS); and

—Office of Information Policies and Systems, which oversees information management, ADP policy and services, systems development, and equipment operation.

Deputy Assistant Secretary for Executive Services The Deputy Assistant Secretary functions through the Office of Executive Scheduling, which schedules public appearances for top staff and prepares briefing papers; and the Executive Secretariat, which controls correspondence for the Secretary and Deputy Secretary, and Freedom of Information Act requests.

Assistant Secretary for Congressional and Intergovernmental Relations The Assistant Secretary works with the Office of General Counsel and program offices to develop HUD's position on all legislative matters. The Assistant Secretary oversees the progress of the Department's legislative and appropriations initiatives in the Congress; ensures that all testimony and responses to congressional inquiries are consistent with the Secretary's positions; and helps to resolve differences with the Office of Management and Budget on legislative issues.

The Deputy Assistant Secretary for Intergovernmental Relations serves as the principal point of contact with State and local governments and public and private interest groups on departmental intergovernmental policy; and advises the Secretary on policy matters affecting State and local governments.

Assistant Secretary for Public Affairs The Assistant Secretary provides advice to the Secretary and principal staff members on matters involving HUD's communication with the public and the media. Through the speechwriting and media relations sub-offices, this office is responsible for matters relating to public information, public opinion, and participation in public events.

Office of the Inspector General The Inspector General is appointed by the President and reports to the Congress and the Secretary in accordance with the provisions of the Inspector General Act of 1978 (5 U.S.C. app.).

This office conducts independent audits and investigations of departmental activities; advises the Secretary with respect to audits, investigations, and designated security services; and coordinates activities designed to promote economy, efficiency, and integrity of programs and operations. The HUD Hotline is maintained by OIG as a means for individuals to report activities involving fraud and waste due to mismanagement.

Hotline numbers are:

FTS—458-4200; 458-2451 (hearing impaired).

Headquarters/Commercial—202-708-4200; 202-708-2451 (hearing impaired).

Toll-free—1-800-347-3735.

Program Areas

Assistant Secretary for Housing—Federal Housing Commissioner This office underwrites single family, multifamily, property improvement, and manufactured home loans; administers special purpose programs designed specifically for the elderly, the handicapped, and the chronically mentally ill; administers assisted housing programs for low-income families who are experiencing difficulties affording standard housing; and protects consumers against fraudulent practices of land developers and promoters.

For further information, contact the Assistant Secretary for Housing—Federal Housing Commissioner. Phone, 202-708-3600.

Assistant Secretary for Community Planning and Development This office administers:

—Community Development Block Grants (CDBG's), which provide communities with funds to carry out a wide range of community development activities. These grants are authorized under title I of the Housing and Community Development Act of 1974, as amended. The Department's Block Grant Program legislatively consolidates a number of earlier categorical programs, including the model cities, urban renewal, and water and sewage programs. The Block Grant Program has three components: entitlement grants made on a formula basis to each State and eligible unit of local government; State block grants to assist small cities; and discretionary grants to assist Indian tribes, insular areas, and States needing technical assistance to plan, develop, and administer grant programs.

—Section 108 Loan Guarantees, a program under which HUD guarantees loans to communities to finance the acquisition and rehabilitation of real property;

—Urban Development Action Grants (UDAG's), which are made to encourage private investment in cities and urban counties experiencing severe economic distress, and to stimulate economic recovery (This program has not been refunded and therefore no new grants are being awarded.);

—rehabilitation loans (312 Loans), which are low-interest loans for rehabilitation of property, primarily for low- and moderate-income persons;

—Urban Homesteading Program, which provides homeownership opportunities for individuals and families using existing housing stock;

—Rental Rehabilitation Program, which provides funds to State and local governments to support rehabilitation of existing residential housing units and to provide rental assistance to low-income families;

—programs to assist States, communities, and nonprofit organizations in providing housing and support services for the homeless;

—title V of the McKinney Act establishes a procedure for the identification and use of vacant and underutilized Federal real property for facilities to assist the homeless;

—Supplemental Assistance for Facilities to Assist the Homeless (SAFAH) Program, which provides grants and interest-free advances to stimulate communitywide innovative efforts to assist homeless families and individuals;

—Supportive Housing Demonstration Program, which provides competitive grants funds to State and local governments, nonprofit organizations, and Indian tribes to stimulate communitywide innovative efforts to assist homeless families and individuals. The two components of this program are Transitional Housing Grants and Permanent Housing for the Handicapped Homeless Grants; and

—Neighborhood Development Demonstration Program, which provides grants to eligible neighborhood organizations to support their activities using cooperative efforts and monetary contributions from individuals, businesses, and nonprofit and other organizations located within established neighborhood boundaries.

For further information, contact the Assistant Secretary for Community Planning and Development. Phone, 202–708–2690.

Assistant Secretary for Policy Development and Research This office:

—evaluates and analyzes existing and proposed programs and policies;

—undertakes research, studies, testing, and demonstrations related to HUD's mission;

—provides the Secretary and program administrators with information for use in formulating policy, assessing alternative policies, and measuring their impact;

—develops a research agenda to reflect the overall policy needs of the Department; and

—conducts field studies and evaluates all major programs to determine their effectiveness and to analyze their costs and benefits; and

—provides the Secretary with economic, legal, and policy analyses of all issues related to the Department's oversight responsibilities over major housing finance institutions.

For further information, contact the Assistant Secretary for Policy Development and Research. Phone, 202–708–1600.

Assistant Secretary for Fair Housing and Equal Opportunity This office administers:

—fair housing laws and regulations prohibiting discrimination in public and private housing on the basis of race, color, religion, sex, national origin, handicap, or familial status;

—equal opportunity laws and regulations prohibiting discrimination in HUD-assisted housing and community development programs on the basis of race, handicap, sex, age, or national origin; and

—equal employment opportunity laws and regulations prohibiting discrimination on the basis of race, color, religion, sex, national origin, handicap, or age.

For further information, contact the Assistant Secretary for Fair Housing and Equal Opportunity. Phone, 202–708–4252.

Assistant Secretary for Public and Indian Housing This office:

—administers public and Indian housing programs, including rental and homeownership programs, and provides technical and professional assistance in planning, developing, and managing low-income housing projects;

—administers an operating subsidy program for public housing agencies (PHA's) and Indian housing authorities (IHA's), including operation and management of low-income housing projects;

—administers the Comprehensive Improvement Assistance Program for modernization of low-income housing projects to upgrade living conditions, correct physical deficiencies, and achieve operating efficiency and economy;

—administers the Resident Initiatives Program for resident participation, resident management, homeownership, economic development and supportive services programs, and drug-free neighbor programs; and

—protects tenants from the hazards of lead-based paint poisoning by requiring PHA's and IHA's to comply with HUD regulations for the removal of lead-based paint from low-income housing units.

For further information, contact the Office of Public and Indian Housing. Phone, 202-708-0950.

Government National Mortgage Association This office, also known as Ginnie Mae (GNMA), is a Government corporation. GNMA's purpose is to support the Government's housing objectives by establishing secondary market facilities for residential mortgages; guaranteeing mortgage-backed securities composed of FHA-insured or VA-guaranteed mortgage loans that are issued by private lenders and guaranteed by GNMA with the full faith and credit of the United States; and through its mortgage-backed securities programs, increasing the overall supply of credit available for housing by providing a vehicle for channeling funds from the securities market into the mortgage market.

For further information, contact the Government National Mortgage Association. Phone, 202-708-0926.

Field Structure

The regional offices of the Department have boundaries prescribed by the Secretary. Each regional office is headed by a Regional Administrator-Regional Housing Commissioner, who is responsible to the Secretary for the management of the offices within the region. The Regional Administrators are also responsible to each Assistant Secretary for their respective programs.

For information concerning the detailed jurisdiction of an office, contact the nearest regional office.

The field activities of the Office of the Inspector General (OIG) are carried out through the regional offices listed below:

Field Offices—Department of Housing and Urban Development

(Areas included within each region are indicated on the map in Appendix A.)

(R: Regional Administrator-Regional Housing Commissioner; A: Regional Inspector General for Audit; I: Regional Inspector General for Investigation)

Region/Address	Officer in Charge	Telephone/FTS
1. BOSTON, MA (Rm. 375, 10 Causeway St., 02222-1092)	John A. MastroDietro (R)	617-565-5234; 835-5234
	Ardashes DerAnanian, Jr. (A)	617-565-5259; 835-5259
	Raymond A. Carolan (I)	617-565-5293; 835-5293
2. NEW YORK, NY (26 Federal Plz., 10278-0068)	Anthony M. Villane, Jr. (R)	212-264-8053; 264-8068
	A. Paul Kane (A)	212-264-4174; 264-4174
	Garland L. Isdell (I)	212-264-8062; 264-8062
3. PHILADELPHIA, PA (105 S. 7th St., 19106-3392)	Harry W. Staller, *Acting* (R)	215-597-2560; 597-2560
	Edward F. Mornorella (A)	215-597-2461; 597-2461
	Robert J. Brickley (I)	215-597-2413; 597-2413
4. ATLANTA, GA (75 Spring St. SW., 30303-3388)	Raymond A. Harris (R)	404-331-5136; 841-5136
	Kathryn Kuhl-Inclan (A)	404-331-5195; 841-3369
	Emil J. Schuster (I)	404-331-5155; 841-5155
5. CHICAGO, IL (626 W. Jackson Blvd., 60606-5601)	Gertrude W. Jordan (R)	312-353-5680; 353-5680
	Thomas J. Bannon (A)	312-353-7832; 353-7832
	Thomas W. Boockmeier (I)	312-353-4196; 353-4196

Field Offices—Department of Housing and Urban Development—Continued

(Areas included within each region are indicated on the map in Appendix A.)

(R: Regional Administrator-Regional Housing Commissioner; A: Regional Inspector General for Audit; I: Regional Inspector General for Investigation)

Region/Address	Officer in Charge	Telephone/FTS
6. FORT WORTH, TX (P.O. Box 2905, 100 Throckmorton, 76113-2905)	Sam R. Moseley (R)	817-885-5401; 728-5401
	Wayne Cordell (A)	817-885-5551; 728-5551
	Larry Chapman (I)	817-885-5561; 728-5561
7. KANSAS CITY, KS (400 State Ave., 66101-2506)	William H. Brown (R)	913-236-2162; 757-2162
	Phillip L. Whitaker (A)	913-236-2870; 757-2870
	Alma L. Bahr (I)	913-236-2866; 757-2866
8. DENVER, CO (1405 Curtis St., 80202-2349)	Michael R. Chitwood (R)	303-844-4513; 564-4513
	D. Michael Beard (A)	303-844-3469; 564-4365
	Daniel G. Pifer (I)	303-844-2325; 564-2325
9. SAN FRANCISCO, CA (P.O. Box 36003, 450 Golden Gate Ave., 94102-3448)	Robert J. De Monte (R)	415-556-4752; 556-4752
(Suite 300, 1375 Sutter St., 94109)	Miguel P. Barrios, Jr. (A)	415-556-6895; 556-6895
	Richard L. Fix (I)	415-556-5490; 556-5490
10. SEATTLE, WA (1321 2d Ave., 98101-2058)	Richard Bauer (R)	206-442-5414; 399-5414
	George Tilley (A)	206-442-0270; 399-0270
	Noel A. Tognazzini (I)	206-422-0272; 399-0272

Sources of Information

Inquiries on the following subjects should be directed to the nearest regional office or to the Department of Housing and Urban Development, (specific Headquarters office), 451 Seventh Street SW., Washington, DC 20410. Phone, 202-708-1112 (voice); and 202-708-1455 (TDD). Telephone numbers are not toll-free.

Contracts Contact the Headquarters' Office of Procurement and Contracts, phone, 202-708-1290; or the nearest regional office's Administrative Services Division.

Property Disposition Contact the Headquarters' Management Branch, Office of Multifamily Housing Management, phone, 202-708-4280; or the nearest regional office.

Employment Inquiries and applications should be directed to the Headquarters' Office of Personnel, phone, 202-708-0408; or the nearest regional office's Personnel Division.

Program Information Center The Center provides viewing facilities for information regarding departmental activities and functions and publications and other literature to Headquarters visitors.

Freedom of Information Act (FOIA) Requests Persons interested in inspecting documents or records under the Freedom of Information Act should contact the Program Information Center. Phone, 202-708-1420.

Written requests should be directed to the Director, Executive Secretariat, U.S. Department of Housing and Urban Development, Room 10139, 451 Seventh Street SW., Washington, DC 20410.

DEPARTMENT OF THE INTERIOR

1849 C Street NW., Washington, DC 20240
Phone, 202–208–3171

SECRETARY OF THE INTERIOR	MANUEL LUJAN, JR.
Deputy Secretary	FRANK A. BRACKEN
Associate Deputy Secretary	DONALD R. KNOWLES
Executive Assistant to the Secretary	LUCY M. SALAZAR
Assistant to the Secretary and Director, Office of Public Affairs	I. STEVEN GOLDSTEIN
Assistant to the Secretary and Director, External Affairs	SELMA SIERRA
Assistant to the Secretary and Director, Office of Congressional and Legislative Affairs	JAMES F. SPAGNOLE
Solicitor	THOMAS L. SANSONETTI
Deputy Solicitor	MARTIN J. SUUBERG
Associate Solicitor (General Law)	DANIEL G. SHILLITO
Associate Solicitor (Conservation and Wildlife)	PAUL R. KRAUSE
Associate Solicitor (Indian Affairs)	(VACANCY)
Associate Solicitor (Energy and Resources)	(VACANCY)
Associate Solicitor (Surface Mining)	(VACANCY)
Associate Solicitor (Audit and Investigation)	THOMAS E. ROBINSON
Inspector General	JAMES R. RICHARDS
Deputy Inspector General	JOYCE N. FLEISCHMAN
Assistant Inspector General (Administration)	(VACANCY)
Assistant Inspector General (Investigations)	THOMAS I. SHEEHAN
Assistant Inspector General (Audits)	HAROLD BLOOM
Assistant Secretary (Water and Science)	JOHN M. SAYRE
Deputy Assistant Secretary for Science	HARLAN L. WATSON
Deputy Assistant Secretary	JOSEPH H. HUNTER
Director, Bureau of Mines	T S ARY
Director, Geological Survey	DALLAS L. PECK
Commissioner, Bureau of Reclamation	DENNIS B. UNDERWOOD
Assistant Secretary for Fish and Wildlife and Parks	MIKE HAYDEN
Principal Deputy Assistant Secretary	SCOTT SEWELL
Deputy Assistant Secretary	(VACANCY)
Director, United States Fish and Wildlife Service	JOHN F. TURNER
Director, National Park Service	JAMES M. RIDENOUR
Assistant Secretary (Indian Affairs)	EDDIE F. BROWN
Commissioner of Indian Affairs	(VACANCY)
Deputy Commissioner of Indian Affairs	(VACANCY)
Assistant Secretary (Land and Minerals Management)	DAVID C. O'NEAL
Deputy Assistant Secretaries	JENNIFER A. SALISBURY

	James M. Hughes
Director, Minerals Management Service	Barry A. Williamson
Director, Bureau of Land Management	D. Cy Jamison
Director, Office of Surface Mining	Harry M. Snyder
Assistant Secretary for Territorial and International Affairs	Stella G. Guerra
Deputy Assistant Secretaries	Donald J. Senese
	William Houston
Assistant Secretary (Policy, Management and Budget)	(vacancy)
Principal Deputy Assistant Secretary	C. Ed Kay
Director, Office for Equal Opportunity	Carmen Maymi
Director, Office of Hearings and Appeals	Roger E. Middleton
Director, Office of Small and Disadvantaged Business Utilization	(vacancy)
Director, Office of Historically Black Colleges and University Programs	Ira J. Hutchison
Director, Office of Construction Management	David J. Matheson
Deputy Assistant Secretary (Policy)	John E. Schrote
Director, Office of Program Analysis	Merritt Sprague
Director, Office of Environmental Affairs	Jonathan F. Deason
Director, Office of Management Improvement	Oscar W. Mueller, Jr.
Director of Budget and Program Resource Management	Philip G. Kiko
Director, Office of Budget	(vacancy)
Director, Office of Financial Management	William L. Kendig
Director, Office of Information Resources Management	James P. Jadlos
Director, Office of Acquisition and Property Management	Larry D. Cardwell
Director of Program Services	Barton R. House
Director, Office of Personnel	Morris A. Simms
Director, Office of Administrative Services	Albert C. Camacho
Director, Office of Aircraft Services	Robert L. Peterson

[For the Department of the Interior statement of organization, see the *Federal Register* of Apr. 14, 1978, 43 FR 15791]

As the Nation's principal conservation agency, the Department of the Interior has responsibility for most of our nationally owned public lands and natural resources. This includes fostering the wisest use of our land and water resources, protecting our fish and wildlife, preserving the environmental and cultural values of our national parks and historical places, and providing for the enjoyment of life through outdoor recreation. The Department assesses our mineral resources, works to ensure that their development is in the best interests of all our people, and promotes the goals of the Take Pride in America campaign by encouraging stewardship and citizen participation in their care. The Department also has a major responsibility for American Indian reservation communities and for people who live in island territories under United States administration.

DEPARTMENT OF THE INTERIOR

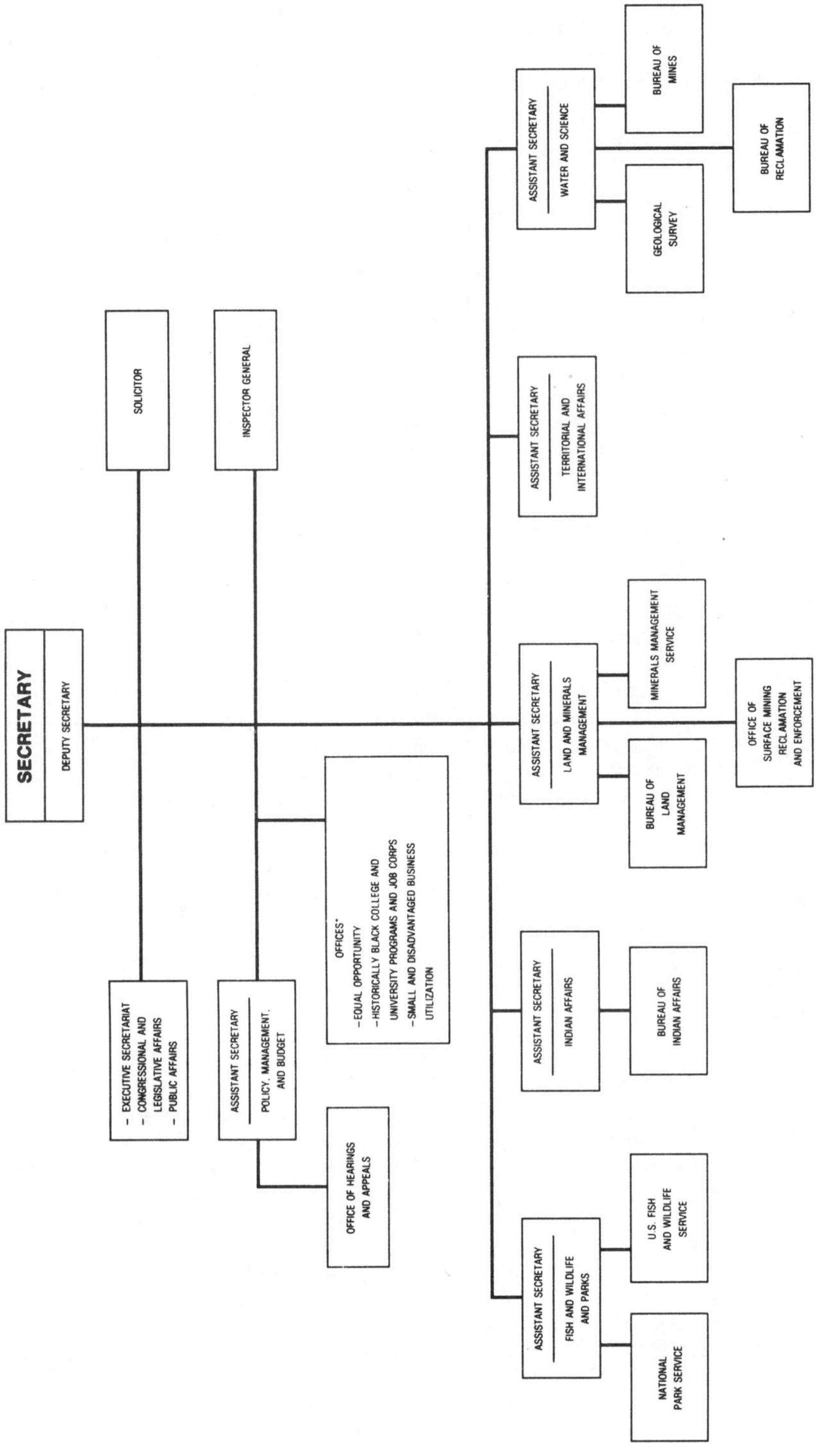

* Overseen for the Secretary by the Assistant Secretary—Policy, Management, and Budget.

The jurisdiction of the Department of the Interior includes:

—administration of over 500 million acres of Federal land, and trust responsibilities for approximately 50 million acres of land, mostly Indian reservations;

—conservation and development of mineral and water resources;

—conservation, development, and utilization of fish and wildlife resources;

—coordination of Federal and State recreation programs;

—preservation and administration of the Nation's scenic and historic areas;

—operation of Job Corps Conservation Centers and Youth Conservation Corps Camps, and coordination of other manpower and youth training programs;

—reclamation of arid lands in the West through irrigation; and

—management of hydroelectric power systems.

The Department of the Interior is also concerned with the social and economic development of the territories of the United States and in the Trust Territory of the Pacific Islands; and administers programs providing services to Indians and Alaska Natives.

The Department of the Interior was created by act of March 3, 1849 (43 U.S.C. 1451), which transferred to it the General Land Office, the Office of Indian Affairs, the Pension Office, and the Patent Office. The Department also had responsibility for supervision of the Commissioner of Public Buildings, the Board of Inspectors and the Warden of the Penitentiary of the District of Columbia, the census of the United States, and the accounts of marshals and other officers of the United States courts, and of lead and other mines in the United States.

Over the many years of its existence, other functions have been added and removed, so that its role has changed from that of general housekeeper for the Federal Government to that of custodian of the Nation's natural resources.

Office of the Secretary

Secretary The Secretary of the Interior, as the head of an executive department, reports directly to the President and is responsible for the direction and supervision of all operations and activities of the Department. The Secretary also has certain powers or supervisory responsibilities relating to Territorial governments.

Deputy Secretary The Deputy Secretary assists the Secretary in the discharge of Secretarial duties and serves as Acting Secretary in the absence of the Secretary. With the exception of certain matters reserved by the Secretary, the Deputy Secretary has the full authority of the Secretary.

Fish and Wildlife and Parks The Assistant Secretary for Fish and Wildlife and Parks discharges the duties of the Secretary with the authority and direct responsibility for programs associated with the development, conservation, and utilization of fish, wildlife, recreation, historical, and national park system resources. The Assistant Secretary represents the Department in the coordination of marine environmental quality and biological resources programs with other Federal agencies. The Assistant Secretary also exercises Secretarial direction and supervision over the United States Fish and Wildlife Service and the National Park Service.

Water and Science The Assistant Secretary (Water and Science) discharges the duties of the Secretary with the authority and direct responsibility to carry out the statutory mandate to manage and direct programs that support the development and implementation of water, mineral, and science policies and assist the development of economically and environmentally sound resource activities. The Assistant Secretary oversees the programs of the Bureau of Reclamation, the Bureau of Mines, and the Geological Survey. The Assistant Secretary's duties include:

—development, management, and conservation of the Nation's water supply and support of cost-sharing techniques for development and management of water supplies in the 17 Western States;

—oversight of the Department's irrigation drainage water quality program;

—assessment of the quantity, quality, and use of the Nation's water resources;
—fostering and encouraging the private sector in the orderly and economic development of domestic mineral resources;
—collection and analysis of mineral data;
—assessment of frontier area energy and mineral resources for long-term availability;
—direction of departmental research activities in geology, hydrology, topography, metallurgy, mining technology, and mine health and safety, including international work supporting long-term national objectives;
—geologic and mineral resource investigations;
—natural hazards research, including earthquakes, landslides, and floods;
—geographic information systems research; and
—remote sensing activities.

The Office of the Assistant Secretary provides scientific advice to the Secretary; coordinates Department activities with the Board on Geographic Names; and represents the Secretary on the interagency group for Arctic research, the National Acid Precipitation Assessment Program, the Senior Interagency Group—National Security Emergency Preparedness, and other interagency efforts as appropriate.

Land and Minerals Management The Assistant Secretary (Land and Minerals Management) discharges the duties of the Secretary with the authority and direct responsibility for programs associated with:
—public land management, including land use planning;
—onshore and offshore minerals management;
—development and management of effective fuel-related mineral data collection and analysis;
—surface mining reclamation and enforcement functions;
—operations management for minerals on the Outer Continental Shelf to the outer limits of the United States economic jurisdiction; and
—management of revenues from Federal mineral leases to ensure efficient collection of bonuses, rentals, and royalties.

The Assistant Secretary also serves as adviser to the Secretary in the Secretary's role as a member of the Cabinet Council on Domestic Policy. The Assistant Secretary exercises Secretarial direction and supervision over the Bureau of Land Management, the Minerals Management Service, and the Office of Surface Mining Reclamation and Enforcement.

Indian Affairs The Assistant Secretary (Indian Affairs) discharges the authority and responsibility of the Secretary for activities pertaining to Indians and Indian affairs. The Assistant Secretary is responsible for:
—providing the Secretary with detailed and objective advice on matters involving Indians and Indian affairs;
—identifying and acting on issues affecting Indian policy and programs;
—establishing policy on Indian affairs;
—maintaining liaison and coordination between the Department of the Interior and other Federal agencies that provide services or funding to Indians;
—representing the Department in transactions with Congress;
—monitoring and evaluating ongoing activities related to Indian affairs;
—undertaking or providing leadership in special assignments and projects for the Secretary; and
—exercising Secretarial direction and supervision over the Bureau of Indian Affairs.

Territorial and International Affairs The Office of the Assistant Secretary for Territorial and International Affairs was established by Secretarial Order No. 3046 of February 14, 1980. The Assistant Secretary discharges the authority and responsibility of the Secretary for activities pertaining to U.S. territorial areas and the Freely Associated States (Republic of the Marshall Islands and Federated States of Micronesia) and for the coordination of international affairs of the Department.

The Assistant Secretary is responsible for promoting the economic, social, and political development of the U.S. territories of Guam, American Samoa, the Virgin Islands, the Commonwealth of the Northern Mariana Islands, and the Trust Territory of the Pacific Islands (Republic of Palau). The degree to which the Office conducts activities to further these objectives in a specific territory depends on the status of the territorial government, its relationship to the Secretary of the Interior, and the extent of development already achieved within the territory.

In consultation with the Assistant Secretary of State for East Asian and Pacific Affairs, who is responsible for government-to-government relations with the Freely Associated States, the Assistant Secretary for Territorial and International Affairs is responsible for general oversight of all Federal programs provided to the Freely Associated States of the Republic of the Marshall Islands and the Federated States of Micronesia under the Compact of Free Association.

The Assistant Secretary also serves as the Department's focal point for analysis, development, and review of the Department's policy and programs pertaining to international activities and the opportunities for support of U.S. foreign policy through the use of the Department's natural resource and environmental expertise.

For further information, contact the Office of Territorial and International Affairs, Department of the Interior, Washington, DC 20240. Phone, 202-208-4822.

Policy, Management and Budget The Assistant Secretary (Policy, Management and Budget) discharges the authority of the Secretary for all phases of management and administrative activities and serves as the principal policy adviser to the Secretary. The Assistant Secretary's responsibilities include:

—providing advice on program planning, budget, and policy matters;

—developing and maintaining administrative policy, standards, objectives, and procedures for use throughout the Department;

—coordinating organizational aspects of proposed legislation with appropriate bureaus and offices;

—undertaking special management-related projects for the Secretary; and

—providing management and administrative support services for the Office of the Secretary.

The Assistant Secretary performs and supervises the following activities: hearings and appeals; ethics and audit; construction management; program analysis, environmental management; management improvements, directives and regulatory management; budget and financial management, management systems and information resources management, automated data processing and telecommunications; procurement, property, space, energy conservation, grants management, library and information services, business and economic development; emergency preparedness, aircraft services, law enforcement and security, drug-free workplace, health and safety; and personnel, equal opportunity, historically black colleges and universities, and job corps.

Office of the Solicitor

The Office of the Solicitor performs all of the legal work of the Department with the exception of that performed by the Office of Hearings and Appeals and the Office of Congressional and Legislative Affairs. The Solicitor is the principal legal advisor to the Secretary and the chief law officer of the Department.

The headquarters office, located in Washington, DC, consists of six Divisions. The Division of Conservation and Wildlife is responsible for legal matters involving the programs of the Assistant Secretary for Fish and Wildlife and Parks, the National Park Service, and the U.S. Fish and Wildlife Service. The Division of Energy and Resources is responsible for legal matters involving the programs of the Assistant Secretary (Water and Science), the Assistant Secretary (Land and Minerals Management), the Bureau of Land Management, the Bureau of Mines, the Geological Survey, the Bureau of Reclamation, and the Minerals Management Service. The Division of Indian Affairs is responsible for legal matters involving the programs of the

Assistant Secretary (Indian Affairs) and the Bureau of Indian Affairs. The Division of Surface Mining provides legal advice to the Assistant Secretary (Land and Minerals Management) on surface mining matters and to the Office of Surface Mining Reclamation and Enforcement. The Division of General Law is responsible for general administrative law and legal matters involving programs under the jurisdiction of the Assistant Secretary (Policy, Management and Budget), the Assistant Secretary for Territorial and International Affairs, and the Office for Equal Opportunity. The Division of Audit and Investigation is responsible for providing legal advice and services to the Office of Inspector General. Administrative and support services for the Office of the Solicitor are provided by the Division of Administration.

The field organization of the Office is divided into eight regions, each headed by a Regional Solicitor.

Regional Offices—Office of the Solicitor

Region	Address	Telephone
ALASKA—Alaska	222 W. 8th Ave., Anchorage, AK 99513-7584	907-271-4131
INTERMOUNTAIN—Arizona, Idaho, Utah	125 S. State St., Salt Lake City, UT 84138	801-524-5677
NORTHEAST—Connecticut, Delaware, Illinois, Indiana, Maine, Maryland, Massachusetts, Michigan, New Hampshire, New Jersey, New York, Ohio, Pennsylvania, Rhode Island, Vermont, Virginia, West Virginia, Wisconsin	1 Gateway Ctr., Newton Corner, MA 02158	617-965-5100
PACIFIC NORTHWEST—Minnesota, Montana, North Dakota, Oregon, South Dakota, Washington	500 NE. Multnomah St., Portland, OR 97232	503-231-2126
PACIFIC SOUTHWEST—California, Hawaii, Nevada, Pacific Territories	2800 Cottage Way, Sacramento, CA 95825	916-978.4821
ROCKY MOUNTAIN—Colorado, Iowa, Kansas, Missouri, Nebraska, Wyoming	Rm. D-105, P.O. Box 25007, Denver, CO 80225	303-236-8444
SOUTHEAST—Alabama, Florida, Georgia, Kentucky, Mississippi, North Carolina, Puerto Rico, South Carolina, Tennessee, Virgin Islands	75 Spring St. SW., Atlanta, GA 30303	404-331-4447
SOUTHWEST—Arkansas, Louisiana, New Mexico, Oklahoma, Texas	P.O. Box 3156, Tulsa, OK 74101	918-581-7502

For further information, contact the Administrative Officer, Office of the Solicitor, Department of the Interior, Washington, DC 20240. Phone, 202-208-6115.

Office of Inspector General

The Office of Inspector General provides policy direction and conducts, supervises, and coordinates all audits, investigations, and other activities in the Department designed to promote economy and efficiency or prevent and detect fraud and abuse. The Inspector General recommends policies for and conducts, supervises, or coordinates relations between the Department and other Federal, State, and local government agencies concerning matters that promote economy and efficiency, prevent and detect fraud and abuse, and identify and prosecute people involved in fraud or abuse.

In the Trust Territories of Guam, American Samoa, the Virgin Islands, the Commonwealth of Northern Mariana Islands, and the Trust Territory of the Pacific Islands (Palau), the Office performs the functions of government comptroller through audit of revenues and receipts and expenditure of funds and property pursuant to the Insular Areas Act of 1982 (48 U.S.C. 1422).

The Office also reviews existing and proposed legislation and regulations and makes recommendations to the Secretary and Congress regarding the impact such initiatives will have on the economy and efficiency of the Department's programs and operations and the prevention and detection of fraud and abuse in such programs; keeps the Secretary and the Congress fully informed about fraud, abuses, and deficiencies in Department programs and operations, and other serious problems; recommends corrective action and reports on the progress made in correcting the problem.

Regional Offices—Office of Inspector General

(A: Audits; I: Investigations)

Region/Headquarters	Address	Telephone
EASTERN:		
Arlington, VA (A)	Rm. 401, BT-1, 800 N. Quincy St., 22217	703-235-1506; 4359
Arlington, VA (I)	Rm. 1105, BT-3, 4015 Wilson Blvd., 22203	703-235-2446
CENTRAL:		
Lakewood, CO (A)	Suite 520, 134 Union Blvd., 80228	303-236-9243
Lakewood, CO (I)	Suite 540, 134 Union Blvd., 80228	303-236-8296
WESTERN:		
Sacramento, CA (A)	Rm. W2400, 2800 Cottage Way, 95825	916-978-4883
Sacramento, CA (I)	Rm. W2326, 2800 Cottage Way, 95825	916-978-4887
CARIBBEAN:		
St. Thomas, VI (A)	P.O. Box 7730, 00801	809-774-8300
NORTH PACIFIC:		
Agana, GU (A)	Suite 807, 238 Archbishop F.C. Flores St., 96910	671-472-7279

For further information, contact the Office of Inspector General, Department of the Interior, Washington, DC 20240. Phone, 202-208-4356.

Office of Hearings and Appeals

The Office of Hearings and Appeals was established by the Secretary on April 8, 1970, to consolidate related functions and to provide for more effective departmental appeals procedures.

The Office of Hearings and Appeals is responsible for departmental quasi-judicial and related functions. Administrative law judges and three formal boards of appeal render decisions in cases pertaining to contract disputes; Indian probate and administrative appeals; public and acquired lands and their resources; submerged offshore lands of the Outer Continental Shelf; surface coal mining control and reclamation; claims under the Alaska Native Claims Settlement Act; and enforcement of the importation and transportation of rare and endangered species. The Director of the Office of Hearings and Appeals may assign administrative law judges or other officials from the Office of Hearings and Appeals for the purpose of holding rulemaking hearings and may also assign administrative law judges or establish ad hoc boards of appeal to meet special requirements of disputes not falling under one of the previously listed categories. Board decisions are final for the Department.

The Office includes the headquarters organization and two field offices for departmental administrative law judges and seven field offices for Indian probate administrative law judges.

For further information, contact the Office of Hearings and Appeals, Department of the Interior, 4015 Wilson Boulevard, Arlington, VA 22203. Phone, 703-235-3810.

Bureaus

United States Fish and Wildlife Service

[For the United States Fish and Wildlife Service statement of organization, see the *Code of Federal Regulations*, Title 50, Subchapter A, Part 2]

The United States Fish and Wildlife Service's national responsibility in the service of fish, wildlife, and people reaches back over 115 years to the establishment in 1871 of a predecessor agency, the Bureau of Fisheries. First created as an independent agency, the

290-950 O 91 - 12

Bureau of Fisheries was later placed in the Department of Commerce. A second predecessor agency, the Bureau of Biological Survey, was established in 1885 in the Department of Agriculture.

The two Bureaus and their functions were transferred in 1939 to the Department of the Interior. They were consolidated into one agency and redesignated the Fish and Wildlife Service in 1940 by Reorganization Plan III (5 U.S.C. app.).

Further reorganization came in 1956 when the Fish and Wildlife Act (16 U.S.C. 742a) created the United States Fish and Wildlife Service and provided for it to replace and succeed the former Fish and Wildlife Service. The Act established two Bureaus within the new Service: the Bureau of Commercial Fisheries and the Bureau of Sport Fisheries and Wildlife.

In 1970, under Reorganization Plans 3 and 4 (5 U.S.C. app.), the Bureau of Commercial Fisheries was transferred to the Department of Commerce. The Bureau of Sport Fisheries and Wildlife, which remained in Interior, was renamed by an act of Congress in April 1974 (16 U.S.C. 742b) as the United States Fish and Wildlife Service.

The Service is composed of a headquarters office in Washington, DC; 7 regional offices in the lower 48 States and Alaska; a regional research structure; and a variety of field units and installations. These include 465 National Wildlife Refuges and 150 Waterfowl Production Areas comprising more than 90 million acres, 25 major fish and wildlife laboratories and centers, 36 cooperative research units at universities across the country, 76 National Fish Hatcheries, and a nationwide network of wildlife law enforcement agents.

The United States Fish and Wildlife Service is responsible for migratory birds, endangered species, certain marine mammals, inland sport fisheries, and specific fishery and wildlife research activities. Its mission is to conserve, protect, and enhance fish and wildlife and their habitats for the continuing benefit of the American people. Within this framework, the Service assists in the development of an environmental stewardship ethic for our society based on ecological principles, scientific knowledge of wildlife, and a sense of moral responsibility; works with the States to improve the conservation and management of the Nation's fish and wildlife resources; and administers a national program providing opportunities to the American public to understand, appreciate, and wisely use these resources.

In the area of resource management, the Service provides leadership for the protection and improvement of land and water environments (habitat preservation), which directly benefits the living natural resources and adds quality to human life. Activities include:

—biological monitoring through scientific research;

—surveillance of pesticides, heavy metals, and other contaminants;

—studies of fish and wildlife populations;

—ecological studies;

—environmental impact assessment, including hydroelectric dams, nuclear power sites, stream channelization, and dredge-and-fill permits; and

—environmental impact statement review.

The Service is responsible for improving and maintaining fish and wildlife resources by proper management of migratory birds and other wildlife. It also assists in fulfilling the public demand for recreational fishing while maintaining the Nation's fisheries at a level and in a condition that will ensure their continued survival. Specific wildlife and fishery resources programs include:

—migratory birds: wildlife refuge management for production, migration, and wintering; law enforcement; research, including bird banding, production, and harvest studies; breeding, migrating, and wintering surveys; and disease studies;

—mammals and nonmigratory birds: refuge management of resident species; law enforcement; research on disease and population distribution, including marine mammals and species transplants; and technical assistance;

—cooperative fish and wildlife research units: located at universities to conduct research and supervise graduate student research, complementing the Service's wildlife and fishery research programs;

—coastal anadromous fish: hatchery production, stocking, and research on nutrition, disease, and habitat requirements in 16 of the 24 coastal States;

—Great Lakes fisheries: hatchery production of lake trout; fishery management in cooperation with Canada and the States, and research; and

—other inland fisheries: hatchery production and stocking of Indian lands; technical assistance; and research on genetics, disease, nutrition, and taxonomy.

The Service provides national and international leadership in the area of identifying, protecting, and restoring endangered species of fish, wildlife, and plants. This program includes:

—development of the Endangered and Threatened Species List, conduct of status surveys, preparation of recovery plans, and coordination of efforts nationally and internationally;

—research on propagation methods, distribution, genetics, and behavior;

—operation of wildlife refuges;

—law enforcement;

—foreign importation enforcement; and

—consultation with foreign countries.

Public information programs include preparation of news releases, leaflets, and brochures; operation of environmental study areas on Service lands for use by school groups and teachers; operation of visitor centers, self-guided nature trails, observation towers, display ponds, and providing recreational activities, such as hunting, fishing, and wildlife photography.

The Service's Federal aid programs apportion funds to the States and territories for projects designed to conserve, develop, and enhance the Nation's fish and wildlife resources.

Regional Offices—United States Fish and Wildlife Service

Region	Address	Telephone
ALBUQUERQUE—Arizona, New Mexico, Oklahoma, Texas	P.O. Box 1306, Albuquerque, NM 87103	505-766-2321
ANCHORAGE—Alaska	1011 E. Tudor Rd., Anchorage, AK 99503	907-786-3542
ATLANTA—Alabama, Arkansas, Florida, Georgia, Kentucky, Louisiana, Mississippi, North Carolina, Puerto Rico, South Carolina, Tennessee, Virgin Islands	75 Spring St. SW., Atlanta, GA 30303	404-331-3588
BOSTON—Connecticut, Delaware, Maine, Maryland, Massachusetts, New Hampshire, New Jersey, New York, Pennsylvania, Rhode Island, Vermont, Virginia, West Virginia	Suite 700, 1 Gateway Ctr., Newton Corner, MA 02158	617-965-5100
DENVER—Colorado, Kansas, Montana, Nebraska, North Dakota, South Dakota, Utah, Wyoming	P.O. Box 25486, Denver, CO 80225	303-236-7920
PORTLAND—California, Hawaii, Idaho, Nevada, Oregon, Washington	Suite 1692, 500 NE. Multnomah St., Portland, OR 97232	503-231-6118
TWIN CITIES—Illinois, Indiana, Iowa, Michigan, Minnesota, Missouri, Ohio, Wisconsin	Federal Bldg., Fort Snelling, Twin Cities, MN 55111	612-725-3500
WASHINGTON, DC—(Research facilities nationwide)	1849 C St. NW., Washington, DC 20240	703-358-1801

For further information, contact the Office of Public Affairs, United States Fish and Wildlife Service, Department of the Interior, Washington, DC 20240. Phone, 202-208-5634.

National Park Service

The National Park Service was established in the Department of the Interior on August 25, 1916 (16 U.S.C. 1).

The National Park Service administers for the American people an extensive system of national parks, monuments, historic sites, and recreation areas. The objectives of the National Park Service are to administer the properties under its jurisdiction for the enjoyment and education of our citizens, to protect the natural environment of the areas, and to assist States, local governments, and citizen groups in the development of park areas, the protection of the natural environment, and the preservation of historic properties.

The National Park Service has a Service Center in Denver that provides planning, architectural, engineering, and other professional services; and a Center for production of interpretive exhibits, audiovisual materials, and publications in Harpers Ferry, WV. There are more than 350 units in the National Park System, including national parks and monuments of noteworthy natural and scientific value; scenic parkways, riverways, seashores, lakeshores, recreation areas, and reservoirs; and historic sites associated with important movements, events, and personalities of the American past.

Activities The National Park Service develops and implements park management plans and staffs the areas under its administration. It relates the natural values and historical significance of these areas to the public through talks, tours, films, exhibits, publications, and other interpretive media. It operates campgrounds and other visitor facilities and provides—usually through concessions—lodging, food, and transportation services in many areas.

The National Park Service also administers the following programs: the State portion of the Land and Water Conservation Fund, Nationwide Outdoor Recreation statistics and information and State comprehensive outdoor recreation planning, planning and technical assistance for the National Wild and Scenic Rivers System, and the National Trails System, natural area programs, the National Register of Historic Places, national historic landmarks, historic preservation, technical preservation services, Historic American Buildings Survey, Historic American Engineering Record, and interagency archeological services.

Regional Offices—National Park Service

Region	Address	Telephone
ALASKA--Alaska	2525 Gambell St., Anchorage, AK 99503	907-257-2696
MID-ATLANTIC—Delaware, Maryland, Pennsylvania, Virginia, West Virginia	143 S. 3d St., Philadelphia, PA 19106	215-597-3679
MIDWEST—Illinois, Indiana, Iowa, Kansas, Michigan, Minnesota, Missouri, Nebraska, Ohio, Wisconsin	1709 Jackson St., Omaha, NE 68102	402-221-3448
NATIONAL CAPITAL—Washington, DC, and nearby Maryland and Virginia	1100 Ohio Dr. SW., Washington, DC 20242	202-619-7222
NORTH ATLANTIC—Connecticut, Maine, New Hampshire, Massachusetts, New Jersey, New York, Rhode Island, Vermont	15 State St., Boston, MA 02109	617-223-5199
PACIFIC NORTHWEST—Idaho, Oregon, Washington	Suite 212, 83 S. King St., Seattle, WA 98104	206-442-5622
ROCKY MOUNTAIN—Colorado, Montana, North Dakota, South Dakota, Utah, Wyoming	P.O. Box 25287, Denver, CO 80225	303-969-2504
SOUTHEAST—Alabama, Florida, Georgia, Kentucky, Mississippi, North Carolina, Puerto Rico, South Carolina, Tennessee, Virgin Islands	75 Spring St. SW., Atlanta, GA 30303	404-331-4998
SOUTHWEST—Arkansas, Louisiana, New Mexico, Oklahoma, Texas	Box 728, Santa Fe, NM 87504	505-988-6375
WESTERN—Arizona, California, Guam, Hawaii, Nevada, Northern Mariana Islands	Suite 600, 600 Harrison St., San Francisco, CA 94107	415-744-3929

For further information, contact the Chief, Office of Public Affairs, National Park Service, Department of the Interior, P.O. Box 37127, Washington, DC 20013-7127. Phone, 202-208-6843.

Bureau of Mines

The Bureau of Mines was established July 1, 1910, in the Department of the Interior by the Organic Act of May 16, 1910, as amended (30 U.S.C. 1, 3, 5–7). The 1910 act has been supplemented by several statutes, including those authorizing production and sale of helium, and research on environmental problems associated with minerals.

The Bureau of Mines is primarily a research and factfinding agency. Its goal is to help ensure that the Nation has adequate supplies of nonfuel minerals for security and other needs. Research is conducted to provide the technology for the extraction, processing, use, and recycling of the Nation's nonfuel mineral resources at a reasonable cost without harm to the environment or the workers involved.

The Bureau also collects, compiles, analyzes, and publishes statistical and economic information on all phases of nonfuel mineral resource development, including exploration, production, shipments, demand, stocks, prices, imports, and exports. Special studies are frequently made on subjects of particular national interest, such as the effects of potential economic, technologic, or legal developments on resource availability. The effects of policy alternatives on mineral supply and demand are also analyzed.

For further information, contact the Office of Public Information, Bureau of Mines, Department of the Interior, 2401 E Street NW., Washington, DC 20241. Phone, 202–634–1004.

Geological Survey

The Geological Survey was established by act of March 3, 1879 (43 U.S.C. 31), which provided for "the classification of the public lands and the examination of the geological structure, mineral resources, and products of the national domain." The act of September 5, 1962 (43 U.S.C. 31(b)), expanded this authorization to include such examinations outside the national domain. Topographic mapping and chemical and physical research were recognized as an essential part of the investigations and studies authorized by act of March 3, 1879, and specific provision was made for them by act of October 2, 1888 (25 Stat. 526).

Provision was made in 1894 for gauging the streams and determining the water supply of the United States (28 Stat. 398). Authorizations for publication, sale, and distribution of material prepared by the Geological Survey are contained in several statutes (43 U.S.C. 41–45; 44 U.S.C. 260–262).

The Geological Survey's primary responsibilities are: investigating and assessing the Nation's land, water, energy, and mineral resources; conducting research on global change; investigating natural hazards such as earthquakes, volcanoes, landslides, floods, and droughts; and conducting the National Mapping Program. To attain these objectives, the Geological Survey prepares maps and digital and cartographic data; collects and interprets data on energy and mineral resources; conducts nationwide assessments of the quality, quantity, and use of the Nation's water resources; performs fundamental and applied research in the sciences and techniques involved; and publishes and disseminates the results of its investigations in thousands of new maps and reports each year.

For further information, contact the Public Affairs Officer, U.S. Geological Survey, Department of the Interior, 119 National Center, Reston, VA 22092. Phone, 703–648–4460.

Office of Surface Mining Reclamation and Enforcement

The Office of Surface Mining Reclamation and Enforcement (OSM) was established in the Department of the Interior by the Surface Mining Control and Reclamation Act of 1977 (30 U.S.C. 1211).

The Office's primary goal is to assist States in operating a nationwide program that protects society and the environment from the adverse effects of coal mining, while ensuring that surface coal mining can be done without permanent damage to land and water resources. The main objectives, now that most coal-mining States have assumed primary responsibility for regulating coal mining and reclamation activities within their borders, are to oversee mining and reclamation in States with primary responsibility, to assist States in meeting the objectives of the act, and to regulate mining and reclamation activities in those States choosing not to assume primary responsibility.

The Office's headquarters is located in Washington, DC. In addition, Assistant Directors in Pittsburgh (Eastern Support Center) and Denver (Western Support Center) provide technical support to the States and to OSM's 13 field offices and 8 area offices. The field offices interact with State and other Federal agencies, assisting the States in implementing their regulatory and reclamation programs. The Eastern and Western Support Centers also review mine plans and permit applications on Federal lands.

Activities The Office's major activities are carried out through the Office of the Director, assisted by two Deputy Directors and six Assistant Directors. The Director establishes national policy for the conduct of the surface mining control and reclamation program provided for in the act; reviews and approves amendments to previously approved State programs; and provides overall direction to the agency.

Supporting the immediate Office of the Director are staff offices providing assistance in the areas of congressional, public, and external affairs, equal opportunity, planning, analysis, correspondence control, and issues management.

The Deputy Director for Administration and Finance is responsible for the development and operation of an integrated and computerized financial management process that applies to the full range of collections, disbursements, and accounting for all OSM's funds and accounts. The Deputy Director for Administration and Finance is also responsible for implementing an operations evaluation program. Assisting this Deputy Director are three Assistant Directors.

The Assistant Director for Budget and Administration formulates policy and provides guidance for budget formulation and execution, personnel, administrative services, and records management.

The Assistant Director for Finance and Accounting:

—manages all financial systems, including the collection of civil penalties and abandoned mine land fees;

—audits abandoned mine land fee payments; and

—provides policy and direction for all financial programs.

The Assistant Director for Information Systems Management:

—provides policy guidance for automated data processing activities throughout the agency and oversees the implementation of all data processing contracts and procurements;

—oversees the design and management of the nationwide data processing systems needed to implement the agency's mission;

—analyzes the validity of program-related statistics;

—provides technical support to headquarters and field personnel using computer systems; and

—assures the agency's capability to support the computer technology requirements of the State regulatory authorities.

The Deputy Director for Operations and Technical Services is responsible for managing the field offices, which are located in Alabama, Illinois, Indiana, Kentucky, Missouri, New Mexico, Ohio, Oklahoma, Pennsylvania, Tennessee, Virginia, West Virginia, and Wyoming.

Also reporting to the Deputy Director for Operations and Technical Services is the Assistant Director for Reclamation and Regulatory Policy, who is responsible for establishing technical standards and regulatory policy for OSM's reclamation and enforcement efforts; providing guidance for environmental considerations, research, training, and technology transfer for State and Federal regulatory and abandoned mine land reclamation programs; and providing direction and leadership for the

Regulatory Programs, Abandoned Mine Lands, and Technical Services Divisions.

For further information, contact the Office of Public Affairs, Office of Surface Mining Reclamation and Enforcement, Department of the Interior, Washington, DC 20240. Phone, 202-208-2719.

Bureau of Indian Affairs

The Bureau of Indian Affairs was created as part of the War Department in 1824 and transferred to the Department of the Interior when the latter was established in 1849. The Snyder Act of 1921 (25 U.S.C. 13) provided substantive law for appropriations covering the conduct of activities by the Bureau of Indian Affairs. The scope and character of the authorizations contained in this act were broadened by the Indian Reorganization Act of 1934 (25 U.S.C. 461 *et seq.*), the Indian Self-Determination and Education Assistance Act of 1975 (25 U.S.C. 450), title XI of the Education Amendments of 1978 (20 U.S.C. 2701 note), and the Hawkins-Stafford Elementary and Secondary School Improvement Amendments of 1988 (20 U.S.C. 2701).

The principal objectives of the Bureau are to encourage and assist Indian and Alaska Native people to manage their own affairs under the trust relationship to the Federal Government; to facilitate, with maximum involvement of Indian and Alaska Native people, full development of their human and natural resource potential; to mobilize all public and private aids to the advancement of Indian and Alaska Native people for use by them; and to utilize the skill and capabilities of Indian and Alaska Native people in the direction and management of programs for their benefit.

Activities In carrying out these objectives, the Bureau works with Indian and Alaska Native people, tribal governments, Native American organizations, other Federal agencies, State and local governments, and other interested groups in the development and implementation of effective programs for their advancement.

The Bureau seeks for them adequate educational opportunities in public education systems, assists them in the creation and management of educational systems for their own benefit, or provides from Federal resources the educational systems needed; actively promotes the improvement of their social welfare by working with them to obtain and provide needed social and community development programs and services; works with them in the development and implementation of programs for their economic advancement and for full utilization of their natural resources consistent with the principles of resource conservation.

The Bureau also acts as trustee for their lands and moneys held in trust by the United States, assisting them to realize maximum benefits from such resources.

Area Offices—Bureau of Indian Affairs

Area	Address	Telephone
Aberdeen, SD	115 4th Ave. SE., 57401-4302	605-226-7343
Albuquerque, NM	P.O. Box 26567, 615 N. 1st St., 87125-6567	505-766-3170
Anadarko, OK	P.O. Box 368, 73005	405-247-6673
Billings, MT	316 N. 26th St., 58101-1397	406-657-6315
Eastern Area	Suite 260, 3701 N. Fairfax Dr., Arlington, VA 22203	703-235-2571
Juneau, AK	Box 3-8000, 99802-1219	907-586-7177
Minneapolis, MN	15 S. 5th St., 55401-1020	612-349-3631
Muskogee, OK	5th and W. Okmulgee St., 74401-4898	918-687-2296
Navajo Area	P.O. Box M, Window Rock, AZ 86515-0714	602-241-2305
Phoenix, AZ	P.O. Box 10, 1 N. 1st St., 85001-0010	505-863-9501
Portland, OR	1002 NE. Holladay St., 97232-4169	503-231-6702
Sacramento, CA	2800 Cottage Way, 95825-1884	916-978-4691

For further information, contact the Public Affairs Office, Bureau of Indian Affairs, Department of the Interior, Washington, DC 20240. Phone, 202-208-7315.

Minerals Management Service

The Minerals Management Service was established on January 19, 1982, by Secretarial Order No. 3071, under the authority provided by section 2 of Reorganization Plan No. 3 of 1950 (5 U.S.C. app.). All Outer Continental Shelf leasing responsibilities of the Department of the Interior were consolidated within the Service on May 10, 1982, by amendment 1 to Secretarial Order No. 3071. Amendment 2, dated May 26, 1982, set forth the basic organizational structure and provided for the transfer of administrative functions.

Secretarial Order No. 3087, dated December 3, 1982, and amendment 1, dated February 7, 1983, provided for the transfer of royalty and mineral revenue management functions, including collection and distribution, to the Minerals Management Service and transferred all onshore minerals management functions on Federal and Indian lands to the Bureau of Land Management.

The Service assesses the nature, extent, recoverability, and value of leasable minerals on the Outer Continental Shelf. It ensures the orderly and timely inventory and development, as well as the efficient recovery, of mineral resources; encourages utilization of the best available and safest technology; provides for fair, full, and accurate returns to the Federal Treasury for produced commodities; and safeguards against fraud, waste, and abuse.

Offshore Minerals Management The Service is responsible for resource evaluation and classification, environmental review, leasing activities (including public liaison and planning functions), lease management, and inspection and enforcement programs for Outer Continental Shelf lands.

Five-year oil and gas leasing programs are developed for leasing on the Outer Continental Shelf in consultation with the Congress, the 23 coastal States, local governments, environmental groups, industry, and the public.

The Service conducts extensive environmental studies and consultations with State officials prior to issuing leases. Once leases have been issued, inspectors conduct frequent inspections of offshore operations, and environmental studies personnel collect more data to ensure that marine environments are kept free of pollutants.

Royalty Management The Service is responsible for the collection of all royalty payments, rentals, bonus payments, fines, penalties, assessments, and other revenues due the Federal Government and Indian lessors as monies or royalties-in-kind from the extraction of mineral resources from Federal and Indian lands onshore and from the leasing and extraction of mineral resources on the Outer Continental Shelf.

The revenues generated by minerals leasing are one of the largest nontax sources of income to the Federal Government. As specified by law, these revenues are distributed to the States, to the general fund of the Treasury, and to Indian tribes and allottees.

The basic organization of the Service consists of a headquarters in Washington, DC, with program components located in Herndon, VA; the Royalty Management Program, headquartered in Lakewood, CO; four Outer Continental Shelf regional offices; and three administrative service centers.

Field Offices—Minerals Management Service

Office	Address	Telephone
ROYALTY MANAGEMENT PROGRAM	P.O. Box 25165, Lakewood, CO 80225	303-231-3058
	OCS Regional Offices	
ATLANTIC REGION	Suite 1109, 381 Elden St., Herndon, VA 22070	703-787-1113
ALASKA REGION	Rm. 110, 949 E. 36th Ave., Anchorage, AK 99508-4302	907-261-4010
GULF OF MEXICO REGION	1201 Elmwood Park Blvd., New Orleans, LA 70123-2394	504-736-0557

Field Offices—Minerals Management Service—Continued

Office	Address	Telephone
PACIFIC REGION	770 Paseo Camarillo, Camarillo, CA 93010	805-389-7502
Administrative Service Centers		
WESTERN SERVICE CENTER	P.O. Box 25165, Lakewood, CO 80225	303-236-2101
SOUTHERN SERVICE CENTER	1201 Elmwood Park Blvd., New Orleans, LA 70123-2394	504-736-2616

For further information, contact the Office of Public Affairs, Room 4245, (MS 4230), 1849 C Street NW., Washington, DC 20240-7000. Phone, 202-208-3983.

Bureau of Land Management

The Bureau of Land Management (BLM) was established July 16, 1946, by the consolidation of the General Land Office (created in 1812) and the Grazing Service (formed in 1934).

The Federal Land Policy and Management Act of 1976 (90 Stat. 2743) repealed and replaced many obsolete or overlapping statutes. It provides a basic mission statement for the Bureau and establishes policy guidelines and criteria for the management of public lands and resources administered by the Bureau.

The Bureau's basic organization consists of a headquarters in Washington, DC, a Service Center in Denver, CO, a Fire Center in Boise, ID, and a Training Center in Phoenix, AZ, which have BLM-wide support responsibilities; and a field organization of State, district, and resource area offices. The Bureau also utilizes a system of advisory councils to assist in the development of management plans and policies.

The Bureau is responsible for the total management of more than 270 million acres of public lands. These lands are located primarily in the West and Alaska; however, small scattered parcels are located in other States. In addition to minerals management responsibilities on the public lands, BLM is also responsible for subsurface resource management of an additional 300 million acres where mineral rights are owned by the Federal Government.

Resources managed by the Bureau include timber, solid minerals, oil and gas, geothermal energy, wildlife habitat, endangered plant and animal species, rangeland vegetation, recreation and cultural values, wild and scenic rivers, designated conservation and wilderness areas, and open space. Bureau programs provide for the protection (including fire suppression), orderly development, and use of the public lands and resources under principles of multiple use and sustained yield. Land use plans are developed with public involvement to provide orderly use and development while maintaining and enhancing the quality of the environment. The Bureau also manages watersheds to protect soil and enhance water quality; develops recreational opportunities on public lands; administers programs to protect and manage wild horses and burros; and, under certain conditions, makes land available for sale to individuals, organizations, local governments, and other Federal agencies when such transfer is in the public interest. Lands may be leased to State and local government agencies and to nonprofit organizations for certain purposes.

The Bureau oversees and manages the development of energy and mineral leases and ensures compliance with applicable regulations governing the extraction of these resources.

The Bureau has responsibility to issue rights-of-way, in certain instances, for crossing Federal lands under other agencies' jurisdiction. It also has general enforcement authority.

The Bureau is responsible for the survey of Federal lands and establishes and maintains public land records and records of mining claims. It administers a program of payments in lieu of taxes based on the amount of federally owned lands in counties and other units of local government.

Field Offices—Bureau of Land Management

State Office	Address	Telephone
ALASKA—Alaska	Box 13, 222 W. 7th Ave., Anchorage, AK 99513-7599	907-271-5076
ARIZONA—Arizona	P.O. Box 16563, 3707 N. 7th St., Phoenix, AZ 85011	602-640-5501
CALIFORNIA—California	Rm. E-2841, 2800 Cottage Way, Sacramento, CA 95825-1889.	916-978-4743
COLORADO—Colorado	2850 Youngfield St., Lakewood, CO 80215	303-239-3700
EASTERN STATES—All States bordering on and east of the Mississippi River.	350 S. Pickett St., Alexandria, VA 22304	703-461-1400
IDAHO—Idaho	3380 Americana Ter., Boise, ID 83706	208-384-3001
MONTANA—Montana, North Dakota, South Dakota.	P.O. Box 36800, 222 N. 32d St., Billings, MT 59107	406-255-2904
NEVADA—Nevada	P.O. Box 12000, 850 Harvard Way, Reno, NV 89520-0006.	702-785-6590
NEW MEXICO—New Mexico, Kansas, Oklahoma, Texas.	P.O. Box 1449, S. Federal Pl., Santa Fe, NM 87504-1449	505-988-6030
OREGON—Oregon, Washington	P.O. Box 2965, 1300 NE. 44th Ave., Portland, OR 97208-2965.	503-280-7024
UTAH—Utah	Coordinated Financial Ctr., 324 S. State St., Salt Lake City, UT 84111-2303.	801-539-4010
WYOMING—Wyoming, Nebraska	P.O. Box 1828, 2515 Warren Ave., Cheyenne, WY 82003	307-775-6001
	Service and Support Offices	
BOISE INTERAGENCY FIRE CENTER	3905 Vista Ave., Boise, ID 83705	208-389-2447
DENVER SERVICE CENTER	Denver Federal Center Bldg. 50, Denver, CO 80225	303-236-6452

For further information, contact the Office of Public Affairs, Bureau of Land Management, Department of the Interior, Washington, DC 20240. Phone, 202-208-3435.

Bureau of Reclamation

The Reclamation Act of 1902 (43 U.S.C. 371 *et seq.*) authorized the Secretary of the Interior to administer a reclamation program that would provide the arid and semiarid lands of the 17 contiguous Western States a secure, year-round water supply for irrigation. To perform the mission, the Reclamation Service was created within the U.S. Geological Survey. In 1907 the Reclamation Service was separated from the Survey, and in 1923 the name was changed to Bureau of Reclamation.

As the West grew and water resources needs increased, the Bureau of Reclamation's mission expanded as well. The Bureau now provides water for farms, towns, and industries, and is responsible for the generation of hydroelectric power, river regulation and flood control, outdoor recreation opportunities, and the enhancement and protection of fish and wildlife habitats.

The Bureau's functions include:

—development of plans for the conservation and wise use of water resources;

—design and construction of authorized projects;

—repair and rehabilitation of existing projects;

—operation and maintenance of many Bureau-constructed facilities;

—salinity control;

—groundwater management;

—administration of small loans to States and local entities for construction and rehabilitation of water supply systems;

—hazardous waste management;

—research to improve technology in support of its mission;

—safety evaluation of existing dams;

—water quality and environmental enhancement; and

—technical assistance to foreign countries for water resource development.

Through contracts with project beneficiaries, the Bureau arranges repayment to the Federal Treasury for construction, operation and maintenance costs. About 81 percent of all direct project costs are repaid to the Government.

At present, Reclamation project facilities in operation include 355 storage reservoirs, 254 diversion dams, 15,855 miles of canals, 1,380 miles of pipeline, 276 miles of tunnels, 17,000 miles of project drains, and 54 hydroelectric powerplants.

Major Offices—Bureau of Reclamation

Office	Address	Telephone
COMMISSIONER	Rm. 7654, Department of the Interior, Washington, DC 20240-0001.	202-208-4157
DEPUTY COMMISSIONER	Bldg. 67, Box 25007, Denver, CO 80225	303-236-9208
GREAT PLAINS REGION	Box 36900, 316 N. 26th St., Billings, MT 59107	406-657-6218
LOWER COLORADO REGION	Box 427, Nevada Hwy. and Park St., Boulder City, NV 89005.	702-293-8420
MID-PACIFIC REGION	2800 Cottage Way, Sacramento, CA 95825	916-978-4919
PACIFIC NORTHWEST REGION	Box 043, 550 W. Fort St., Boise, ID 83724	208-334-1938
UPPER COLORADO REGION	Box 11568, 125 S. State St., Salt Lake City, UT 84147	801-524-5403

For further information, contact the Office of Public Affairs, Bureau of Reclamation, Department of the Interior, Washington, DC 20240–0001. Phone, 202–208–4662.

Sources of Information

Inquiries on the following subjects should be directed to the specified office, Department of the Interior, Washington, DC 20240.

Contracts Contact the Office of Acquisition and Property Management, Room 5526. Phone, 202–208–6431.

Departmental Museum Provides information regarding departmental activities. Publications and other literature are available to the public free of charge. Located in Room 1238 (Museum), Main Interior Building. Phone, 202–208–2743.

Employment Direct general inquiries to the Office of Personnel or visit any of the field personnel offices.

Publications Most departmental publications are available from the Superintendent of Documents, Government Printing Office, Washington, DC 20402. All other inquiries regarding publications should be directed to the individual bureau or office's publications or public affairs office.

Information regarding bibliographies on select subjects is available from the Information Services Branch of the Natural Resources Library. Phone, 202–208–5815.

Reading Room Natural Resources Library, Main Interior Building. Phone, 202–208–5815.

Telephone Directory The Department of the Interior telephone directory is available for sale by the Superintendent of Documents, Government Printing Office, Washington, DC 20402.

United States Fish and Wildlife Service

Inquiries on the following subjects should be directed to the specified office, U.S. Fish and Wildlife Service, Department of the Interior, Washington, DC 20240.

Contracts Contact the Washington Office Division of Contracting and General Services, phone, 202–653–8703; or any of the regional headquarters locations.

Public and News Media Inquiries Specific information about the U.S. Fish and Wildlife Service and its activities is available from the Director, Office of Public Affairs (phone, 202–208–4131); or the public affairs officer in each of the Service's regional offices.

Publications The U.S. Fish and Wildlife Service has publications available on subjects ranging from the National Wildlife Refuge System to endangered species and fish and wildlife research. Some publications are only available as sales items from the Superintendent of Documents, Government Printing Office, Washington, DC 20402. Further information is available from the Publications Unit, U.S. Fish and Wildlife

Service, Washington, DC 20240. Phone, 703–358–1711.

National Park Service

Contracts Contact the nearest Regional Office, Administrative Services Division, National Park Service, P.O. Box 37127, Washington, DC 20013–7127 (phone, 202–523–0059); or the Denver Service Center, P.O. Box 25287, 12795 West Alameda Parkway, Denver, CO 80225 (phone, 303–969–2110).

Employment Employment inquiries and applications may be sent to the Personnel Office, National Park Service, Department of the Interior, Washington, DC, and to the Regional Offices and individual parks. Applications for seasonal employment (which must be received between September 1 and January 15) should be sent to the Division of Personnel Management, National Park Service, P.O. Box 37127, Washington, DC 20013–7127. Phone, 202–208–5093. Schools interested in the recruitment program should write to: Chief Personnel Officer, National Park Service, Department of the Interior, Washington, DC 20013–7127. Phone, 202–208–5093.

Films The National Park Service has many films on environmental and historical themes. For a list of these films and sales, and information on how to obtain them write: National Audiovisual Center, 8700 Edgeworth Drive, Capitol Heights, MD 20743. Phone, 301–763–1896.

Grants-in-Aid For information on grants authorized under the Land and Water Conservation Fund and the Historic Preservation Fund, write the National Park Service, P.O. Box 37127, Washington, DC 20013–7127. Phone, 202–343–3700.

Publications National Park Service publications of interest to the public, available from the Superintendent of Documents, Government Printing Office, Washington, DC 20402, include the following: *Access National Parks, a Guide for Handicapped Visitors; Lesser Known Areas of the National Park System;* a natural history series; a scientific monograph series; an official handbook series; and a Publications in Archaeology series. *National Parks of the United States* (guide and map) is available from the Consumer Information Center, Pueblo, CO 81009. For information on scientific, cultural, and technical publications, and publications on historic preservation, natural landmarks, and outdoor recreation, write the National Park Service, P.O. Box 37127, Washington, DC 20013–7127. Phone, 202–208–4747.

Bureau of Mines

Contracts Contact the Branch of Procurement, Bureau of Mines, Department of the Interior, 2401 E Street NW., Washington, DC 20241. Phone, 202–634–4704.

Employment For information on employment opportunities throughout the United States, contact the Chief, Division of Personnel, Bureau of Mines, Department of the Interior, 2401 E Street NW., Washington, DC 20241. Phone, 202–634–4710.

Films Requests for film loans should be directed to: Motion Pictures, Bureau of Mines, P.O. Box 18070, Cochrans Mill Road, Pittsburgh, PA 15236. Phone, 412–892–6845.

Publications *Reports of Investigation, Information Circulars, Mineral Industry Surveys* (monthly and quarterly), and *Mineral Commodity Summaries* (annual) can be obtained without charge from the Bureau of Mines, Publication Distribution Branch, P.O. Box 18070, Cochrans Mill Road, Pittsburgh, PA 15236. Phone, 412–892–4338. *The Minerals Yearbook* in 3 volumes (Vol. I—Metals and Minerals; Vol. II—Domestic; Vol. III—International) can be purchased from the Superintendent of Documents, Government Printing Office, Washington, DC 20402. Paper and microfiche copies of most publications issued after 1970 and many issued before then also are available from the National Technical Information Service, 5285 Port Royal Road, Springfield, VA 22161. Phone, 800–553–NTIS (toll-free); or 703–487–4650 (in Virginia and the District of Columbia only).

Geological Survey

Contracts, Grants, and Cooperative Agreements Write to the Administrative Division, Office of Procurement and Contracts, 205 National Center, 12201 Sunrise Valley Drive, Reston, VA 22092. Phone, 703-648-7373.

Employment Inquiries should be directed to one of the following Personnel Offices:

Recruitment and Placement, 215 National Center, 12201 Sunrise Valley Dr., Reston, VA 22092. Phone, 703-648-6131.

Personnel Office, Geological Survey, 75 Spring St. SW., Atlanta, GA 30303. Phone, 404-331-5494.

Personnel Office, Geological Survey, 1400 Independence Rd., Rolla, MO 65401. Phone, 314-341-0810.

Personnel Office, Geological Survey, Denver Federal Center, Bldg. 25, Denver, CO 80225. Phone, 303-236-5900.

Personnel Office, Geological Survey, 345 Middlefield Rd., Menlo Park, CA 94025. Phone, 415-329-4104.

Exhibits Exhibit displays and presentation materials illustrating and explaining technical and scientific aspects of the Geological Survey's activities are prepared for use at professional meetings, technical seminars, and similar gatherings. For information about exhibits write to: Branch of Visual Services, Geological Survey, 790 National Center, 12201 Sunrise Valley Drive, Reston, VA 22092. Phone, 703-648-4357.

Films Sound/color 16mm Earth sciences-related films are available for short-term loan to the general public. Film inquiries should be addressed to the Branch of Visual Services, Geological Survey, 790 National Center, 12201 Sunrise Valley Drive, Reston, VA 22092. Phone, 703-648-4357.

General Inquiries A network of 14 Earth Science Information Centers responds to requests for Earth science information that are made in person, by mail, or by telephone and assists in the selection and ordering of all Geological Survey products:

Rm. 101, 4230 University Dr., Anchorage, AK 99508-4664. Phone, 907-786-7011.

Rm. G-84, 605 W. 4th Ave., Anchorage, AK 99501. Phone, 907-271-2754.

7638 Federal Bldg., 300 N. Los Angeles St., Los Angeles, CA 90012. Phone, 213-894-2850.

Rm. 3128, Bldg. 3 (MS 532), 345 Middlefield Rd., Menlo Park, CA 94025. Phone, 415-329-4309.

504 Custom House, 555 Battery St., San Francisco, CA 94111. Phone, 415-705-1010.

169 Federal Bldg., 1961 Stout St., Denver, CO 80294. Phone, 303-844-4169.

Box 25046, (MS 504), Denver Federal Center, Denver, CO 80225. Phone, 303-236-5829.

Rm. 2650, Dept. of the Interior Bldg., 1849 C St. NW., Washington, DC 20240. Phone, 202-208-4047.

Bldg. 3101, Stennis Space Center, Bay St. Louis, MS 39529. Phone, 601-688-3544.

(MS 231), 1400 Independence Rd., Rolla, MO 65401. Phone, 314-341-0851.

8105 Federal Bldg., 125 S. State St., Salt Lake City, UT 84138. Phone, 801-524-5652.

Rm. 1C402, 507 National Center, 12201 Sunrise Valley Dr., Reston, VA 22092. Phone, 703-648-6045.

678 U.S. Courthouse, W. 920 Riverside Ave., Spokane, WA 99201. Phone, 509-353-2524.

EROS Data Center, Sioux Falls, SD 57198. Phone, 605-594-6151.

Maps Maps are sold by the Distribution Branch, Geological Survey, Map Distribution, Box 25286, Denver Federal Center, Denver, CO 80225; Alaska Distribution Section, Geological Survey, Box 12, New Federal Building, 101 Twelfth Avenue, Fairbanks, AK 99701; and the Earth Science Information Centers (see General Inquiries). Information about the status of Geological Survey mapping in any State and availability of maps by other Federal and State agencies can be obtained from the Earth Science Information Center, 507 National Center, 12201 Sunrise Valley Drive, Reston, VA 22092. Phone, 800-USA-MAPS; or in Virginia, 703-648-6045.

News Media The Public Affairs Office of the Geological Survey responds to news media inquiries, arranges interviews, and prepares news and feature releases and related visual material pertaining to Survey programs and activities for news media use. The headquarters office is located at 119 National Center, 12201 Sunrise Valley Drive, Reston, VA 22092. Phone, 703-648-4460. News media service also is available in Menlo Park—San Francisco. Phone, 415-329-4000.

Publications The Geological Survey publishes technical and scientific reports and maps, described in the monthly periodical *New Publications of the U.S. Geological Survey,* with yearly supplements; *Publications of the U.S. Geological Survey, 1879–1961; Publications of the Geological Survey, 1962–1970;* and a variety of nontechnical publications described in *General Interest Publications of the United States Geological Survey.*

Book publications are sold by the Geological Survey's Distribution Branch, Books and Open-file Reports Section, Denver Federal Center, Box 25425, Denver, CO 80225, and by the Geological Survey's Earth Science Information Centers (see General Inquiries).

Open-file reports, in the form of microfiche and/or black and white paper copies, are sold by the same facility that sells books. Phone 303–236–7476.

Single copies of a variety of nontechnical leaflets, technical reports, books, and special interest publications on Earth science subjects and Geological Survey activities are available to the public upon request from the Geological Survey, Books and Open-file Reports Section, Denver Federal Center, Box 25425, Denver, CO 80225. Phone, 303–236–7476. Bulk quantities may be purchased from the Superintendent of Documents, Government Printing Office, Washington, DC 20402.

The *Earth Science Data Directory* (ESDD) is an on-line service containing references to significant, publicly available Earth science data sets that are maintained by the Geological Survey, other governmental agencies, and academia. For further information, contact the ESDD manager, U.S. Geological Survey, 801 National Center, Reston, VA 22092. Phone, 703–648–7112.

Reading Rooms Facilities for examination of reports, maps, publications of the Geological Survey, and a wide selection of general Earth science information resources and historical documents are located at the Geological Survey's libraries at the National Center, 12201 Sunrise Valley Drive, Reston, VA 22092; Denver Federal Center, Building 20, Box 25046, Denver, CO 80225; 345 Middlefield Road, Menlo Park, CA 94025; and 2255 North Gemini Drive, Flagstaff, AZ 86001; and Earth Science Information Centers (see General Inquiries). Maps, aerial photographs, geodetic control data or index material, and cartographic data in digital form may be examined at the following Earth Science Information Centers:

Rm. 1C402, 507 National Center, 12201 Sunrise Valley Dr., Reston, VA 22092

1400 Independence Rd., Rolla, MO 65401

Bldg. 3101, Stennis Space Center, MS 39529

Box 25046, Bldg. 25, (MS 504), Lakewood Center, Denver Federal Center, Denver, CO 80225

345 Middlefield Rd., Menlo Park, CA 94025

4230 University Dr., Anchorage, AK 99508–4664

Spacecraft and aircraft remote sensor data may be examined at the EROS Data Center, Sioux Falls, SD 57198. Phone, 605–594–6511.

Water Data Information on the availability of and access to water data acquired by the Geological Survey and other local, State, and Federal agencies may be obtained from the National Water Data Exchange, 421 National Center, 12201 Sunrise Valley Drive, Reston, VA 22092. Phone, 703–648–5663.

Office of Surface Mining Reclamation and Enforcement

Contracts Contact the Procurement Branch, Office of Surface Mining, Department of the Interior, 1951 Constitution Avenue NW., Washington, DC 20240. Phone, 202–343–4685.

Employment For information on employment opportunities throughout the United States, contact the Chief, Division of Personnel, Office of Surface Mining, Department of the Interior, 1951 Constitution Avenue NW., Washington, DC 20240. Phone, 202–208–2965.

Bureau of Indian Affairs

Inquiries on the following subjects should be directed to the specified office, Bureau of Indian Affairs, Department of the Interior, Washington, DC 20240.

Contracts and Small Business Activities For information on doing business with the Bureau and its Small Business

Procurement Program, contact the Chief, Contracting and Grants Administration Staff. Phone, 202-208-2825.

Employment General employment inquiries may be directed to the Branch of Personnel Services. Phone, 202-208-2547.

Publications The following publications are among those available from the Superintendent of Documents, Government Printing Office, Washington, DC 20402: *Answers to Your Questions About American Indians; Indian Land Areas; Famous Indians; American Indian Calendar; The States and Their Indian Citizens.*

Reading Room Extensive material on Indians and Indian tribes and the relationship of the U.S. Government with Indians is available for inspection in the National Resources Library, Main Interior Building. Phone, 202-208-5815.

Speakers and Films Contact the Office of Public Affairs. Phone, 202-208-7315.

Minerals Management Service

Inquiries on specific subjects should be directed to the appropriate headquarters office at 381 Elden Street, Herndon, VA 22070 (phone, 202-208-3983), or to the appropriate Minerals Management Service field office.

Public and News Media Inquiries Specific information about the Minerals Management Service and its activities is available from the Chief, Office of Public Affairs, Room 4245, (MS 4230), 1849 C Street NW., Washington, DC 20240.

Bureau of Land Management

Contracts Contracts for public land projects are awarded by the Contracting Officer at the Denver Service Center. Phone, 303-969-6502.

Employment Initial appointments to the Bureau are made from registers established by the Office of Personnel Management as a result of examination announcements issued by area offices of the Office of Personnel Management throughout the country. The following Office of Personnel Management announcements are applicable to most professional positions within the Bureau. Announcement No. 421, Biological and Agricultural Sciences; Announcement No. 424, Engineering, Physical Sciences and Related Professions. The Mid-Level and Senior-Level registers are also used in a limited number of cases for social sciences professionals and other positions.

Inquiries should be directed to the Service Center, any Bureau of Land Management State Office, or to the Personnel Officer, Bureau of Land Management, Department of the Interior, Washington, DC, from whom the booklet *Career Opportunities in the BLM* is available.

General Inquiries The Bureau occasionally sells tracts of land, but generally by public auction and never for less than fair market value. It acts as the leasing agent for mineral rights on public and other federally administered lands. Information may be obtained from any of the State offices or from the Bureau of Land Management, Office of Public Affairs, Department of the Interior, Washington, DC 20240. Phone, 202-208-3435.

Publications The annual publication *Public Land Statistics,* which relates to public lands, is available from the Superintendent of Documents, Government Printing Office, Washington, DC 20402.

Reading Rooms All State offices provide facilities for individuals who wish to examine status records, tract books, or other records relating to the public lands and their resources.

Small Business Activities The Bureau has three major buying offices that provide contacts for small business activities. The Service Center Branch of Procurement (phone, 303-969-6502) is responsible for the western States' activities, except for Oregon (phone, 503-280-7216), which is a major buying office. All other small business contacts may be made to the Washington office of the Bureau. Phone, 202-208-4843.

Speakers Local Bureau offices will arrange for speakers to explain Bureau programs upon request from organizations within their areas of jurisdiction.

Bureau of Reclamation

Contracts The Advance Construction Bulletin and Advance Equipment Bulletin give information to contractors, manufacturers, and suppliers. Available from the Engineering and Research Center, Building 67, Denver Federal Center, Denver, CO 80225. Phone, 303-236-6914.

Employment Information on engineering and other positions is available from the Personnel Office, Denver (phone, 303-236-3820); or from the nearest regional office.

Publications Pamphlets listing publications available without charge and publications for sale are available from the Office of Public Affairs and from the Denver Office. Phone, 303-236-6741.

Speakers and Films A volunteer speaker service provides engineers and scientists for schools and civic groups in the Denver area. The Commissioner's office and the field offices provide speakers on Bureau programs and activities. Films are available on free loan. For speakers or films, contact the nearest field office or the Public Affairs Office. Phone, 202-208-4662.

DEPARTMENT OF JUSTICE

Constitution Avenue and Tenth Street NW., Washington, DC 20530
Phone: Locator, 202–514–2000 or TDD, 202–514–4019

ATTORNEY GENERAL OF THE UNITED STATES	DICK THORNBURGH
Assistants to the Attorney General	MURRAY G. DICKMAN, JOHN D. HUMPHREVILLE, WILLIAM G. MEYERS III, ROBERT S. ROSS, JR., ALVIN A. SCHALL, CUYLER H. WALKER, RICHARD C. WEATHERBEE
Special Assistant to the Attorney General	DREW J. BATAVIA
Deputy Assistant to the Attorney General	PAT M. WOODWARD, JR.
Deputy Attorney General	WILLIAM P. BARR
Associate Deputy Attorneys General	REX J. FORD, J. MARK GIDLEY, DANIEL B. LEVIN, KRISTINE M. MARCY, ANDREW G. MCBRIDE, TIMOTHY C. MURPHY, JOHN A. SMIETANKA, GEORGE J. TERWILLIGER III
Special Assistant to the Deputy Attorney General	MAURICE A. ROSS
Solicitor General	KENNETH W. STARR
Assistant Attorney General, Office of Legal Counsel	J. MICHAEL LUTTIG
Principal Deputy Assistant Attorney General	TIMOTHY E. FLANIGAN
Deputy Assistant Attorneys General	DOUGLAS R. COX, JOHN C. HARRISON, JOHN O. MCGINNIS
Assistant Attorney General, Office for Legislative Affairs	W. LEE RAWLS
Assistant Attorney General for Administration, Justice Management Division	HARRY H. FLICKINGER
Assistant Attorney General, Antitrust Division	JAMES F. RILL
Assistant Attorney General, Civil Division	STUART M. GERSON
Assistant Attorney General, Civil Rights Division	JOHN R. DUNNE
Assistant Attorney General, Criminal Division	ROBERT S. MUELLER III
Assistant Attorney General, Environment and Natural Resources Division	RICHARD B. STEWART
Assistant Attorney General, Tax Division	SHIRLEY D. PETERSON
Special Counsel for Immigration Related Unfair Employment Practices	ANDREW M. STROJNY, *Acting*
Assistant Attorney General, Office of Justice Programs	JIMMY GURULE
Director, Bureau of Justice Assistance	GERALD P. REGIER, *Acting*
Director, Bureau of Justice Statistics	STEVEN D. DILLINGHAM
Director, National Institute of Justice	CHARLES B. DEWITT
Administrator, Office of Juvenile Justice and Delinquency Prevention	ROBERT W. SWEET, JR.

Director, Office for Victims of Crime	JANE NADY BURNLEY
Director, Office of Policy Development	PAUL J. MCNULTY, *Acting*
Director, Office of International Affairs	(VACANCY)
Inspector General	RICHARD J. HANKINSON
Administrator, Drug Enforcement Administration	ROBERT C. BONNER
Commissioner, Immigration and Naturalization Service	GENE MCNARY
Director, Bureau of Prisons	J. MICHAEL QUINLAN
Director, United States Marshals Service	K. MICHAEL MOORE
Director, Community Relations Service	GRACE FLORES HUGHES
Chairman, United States Parole Commission	(VACANCY)
Vice Chairman, United States Parole Commission	(VACANCY)
Chairman, National Appeals Board	(VACANCY)
Chairman, Foreign Claims Settlement Commission of the United States	STANLEY J. GLOD
Director, Executive Office for Immigration Review	DAVID L. MILHOLLAN
Director, Office of Liaison Services	WILLIAM LUCAS
Director, Office of Public Affairs	(VACANCY)
Counsel, Office of Professional Responsibility	MICHAEL E. SHAHEEN, JR.
Pardon Attorney	DAVID C. STEPHENSON
Director, Executive Office for United States Attorneys	LAURENCE S. MCWHORTER
Counsel, Office of Intelligence Policy and Review	MARY C. LAWTON
Deputy Counsel for Intelligence Policy	A.R. CINQUEGRANA
Deputy Counsel for Operations	ALLAN N. KORNBLUM
Director Executive Office for United States Trustees	JOHN E. LOGAN
Associate Director	JEFFREY M. MILLER
General Counsel	MARTHA L. DAVIS
Assistant Director, Office of Review and Oversight	ALBERT T. ANNILLO
Executive Officer	EDWARD F. CINCINNATI

FEDERAL BUREAU OF INVESTIGATION

Ninth Street and Pennsylvania Avenue NW., Washington, DC 20535
Phone, 202–324–3000

Director, Federal Bureau of Investigation	WILLIAM S. SESSIONS
Deputy Director	FLOYD I. CLARKE
Associate Deputy Director (Investigation)	W. DOUGLAS GOW
Associate Deputy Director (Administration)	JAMES W. GREENLEAF
Assistant Director (Identification Division)	LAWRENCE K. YORK
Assistant Director (Training Division)	ANTHONY E. DANIELS
Assistant Director (Administrative Services Division)	WELDON L. KENNEDY
Assistant Director (Records Management Division)	G. NORMAN CHRISTENSEN
Assistant Director (Intelligence Division)	W. DOUGLAS GOW
Assistant Director (Criminal Investigative Division)	WILLIAM M. BAKER

Assistant Director (Laboratory Division)	John W. Hicks
Assistant Director (Technical Services Division)	William A. Bayse
Assistant Director (Legal Counsel Division)	Joseph R. Davis
Assistant Director (Inspection Division)	Delbert C. Toohey
Inspector in Charge (Office of Public Affairs)	Robert B. Davenport
Inspector-in-Charge (Congressional Affairs Office)	John E. Collingwood
Inspector-in-Charge (Office of Liaison and International Affairs)	John E. Guido
Equal Employment Opportunity Officer (Office of Equal Employment Opportunity Affairs)	James R. Perez

[For the Department of Justice statement of organization, see the *Code of Federal Regulations,* Title 28, Chapter I, Part 0]

As the largest law firm in the Nation, the Department of Justice serves as counsel for its citizens. It represents them in enforcing the law in the public interest. Through its thousands of lawyers, investigators, and agents, the Department plays the key role in protection against criminals and subversion, in ensuring healthy competition of business in our free enterprise system, in safeguarding the consumer, and in enforcing drug, immigration, and naturalization laws. The Department also plays a significant role in protecting citizens through its efforts for effective law enforcement, crime prevention, crime detection, and prosecution and rehabilitation of offenders.

Moreover, the Department conducts all suits in the Supreme Court in which the United States is concerned. It represents the Government in legal matters generally, rendering legal advice and opinions, upon request, to the President and to the heads of the executive departments. The Attorney General supervises and directs these activities, as well as those of the U.S. attorneys and U.S. marshals in the various judicial districts around the country.

The Department of Justice was established by act of June 22, 1870 (28 U.S.C. 501, 503), with the Attorney General as its head. Prior to 1870 the Attorney General was a member of the President's Cabinet, but not the head of a department, the office having been created under authority of act of September 24, 1789, as amended (28 U.S.C. 503).

The affairs and activities of the Department of Justice are generally directed by the Attorney General. The offices, divisions, bureaus, and boards of the Department are described below.

Offices

Attorney General The Attorney General, as head of the Department of Justice and chief law enforcement officer of the Federal Government, represents the United States in legal matters generally and gives advice and opinions to the President and to the heads of the executive departments of the Government when so requested. The Attorney General appears in person to represent the Government before the U.S. Supreme Court in cases of exceptional gravity or importance.

Deputy Attorney General The Deputy Attorney General advises and assists the Attorney General in formulating and

DEPARTMENT OF JUSTICE

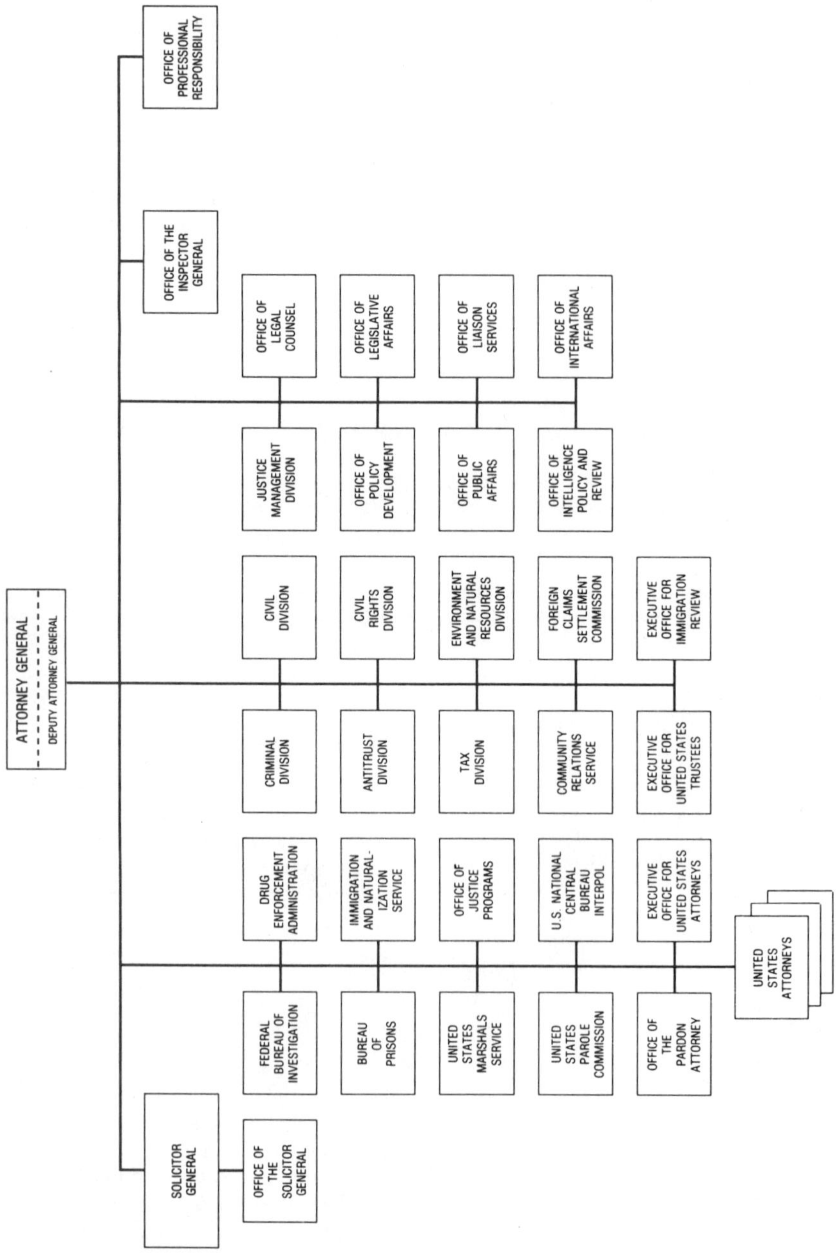

implementing Department policies and programs and in providing overall supervision and direction to all organizational units of the Department. The Deputy Attorney General is authorized to exercise all the power and authority of the Attorney General, except where such power or authority is prohibited by law from delegation or has been delegated to another official. In the absence of the Attorney General, the Deputy Attorney General acts as Attorney General.

Solicitor General The Solicitor General represents the U.S. Government in cases before the Supreme Court. He decides what cases the Government should ask the Supreme Court to review and what position the Government should take in cases before the Court. Also, he supervises the preparation of the Government's Supreme Court briefs and other legal documents and the conduct of the oral arguments in the Court. He or his staff argue most of the Government's cases in the Supreme Court. The Solicitor General's duties also include deciding whether the United States should appeal in all cases it loses before the lower courts.

Legal Counsel The Assistant Attorney General in charge of the Office of Legal Counsel assists the Attorney General in his function as legal adviser to the President and all the executive branch agencies. The Office drafts legal opinions of the Attorney General rendered in response to requests from the President and heads of the executive departments. It also provides its own written opinions and informal advice in response to requests from the various agencies of the Government as well as offices within the Department and from Presidential staff and advisers. Such requests typically deal with legal issues of particular complexity and importance about which two or more agencies are in disagreement or with pending legislation. The Office also is responsible for providing legal advice to the executive branch on all constitutional questions.

All Executive orders and proclamations proposed to be issued by the President are reviewed by the Office of Legal Counsel for form and legality, as are various other matters that require the President's formal approval.

In addition to serving as, in effect, outside counsel for the other agencies of the executive branch, the Office of Legal Counsel also functions as general counsel for the Department itself. It reviews all proposed orders of the Attorney General and all regulations requiring his approval.

The Office coordinates the work of the Department with respect to treaties, executive agreements, and international organizations. It performs a variety of special assignments referred by the Attorney General or the Deputy Attorney General.

The Office of Legal Counsel is not authorized to give legal advice to private persons.

Legislative Affairs The Assistant Attorney General in charge of the Office of Legislative Affairs is responsible for liaison between the Department and Congress. The Office prepares reports and recommendations with respect to pending legislation originating in the Department of Justice or elsewhere in the Government. The Office coordinates all departmental efforts to advise the Congress on departmental views, secure enactment of the Department's legislative agenda, and assist departmental and judicial nominees in the confirmation process.

Policy Development The Office of Policy Development was created in 1989 to enhance the central management of the Department of Justice by functioning as a focal point for the development and coordination of departmental policy.

Acting under the direction of the Attorney General, the Office develops and coordinates mid- and long-range planning and policy development within the Department, including legal research and analysis necessary to support major Department initiatives. The Office also coordinates the review of legislative and regulatory initiatives. In coordinating the development of policy positions within the Department, the Office of Policy Development functions to bring together the best ideas, programs, and policy initiatives from all areas of the

Department's responsibilities for consideration by the Attorney General and the Department's senior management.

Pardon Attorney The Office of the Pardon Attorney, in consultation with the Attorney General or his designee, assists the President in the exercise of Executive clemency as authorized under Article II, section 2, of the Constitution. Generally, all requests for Executive clemency are directed to the Pardon Attorney for investigation and review. Executive clemency may take several forms, including pardon, commutation, remission of fine, and reprieve.

Community Relations Service The Service was created by title X of the Civil Rights Act of 1964 (42 U.S.C. 2000g *et seq.*). It is under the general authority of the Attorney General and is headed by a Director, appointed by the President with the advice and consent of the Senate.

The Service fulfills its mission by providing onsite dispute resolution assistance through its field staff of mediators and conciliators working out of 10 regional offices and 3 field offices. Under its mandate it is not restricted to issues stemming from alleged violations of a particular antidiscrimination statute, but can offer assistance in resolving any dispute relating to race, color, or national origin discrimination. The Service not only aids in resolving disputes and difficulties as they erupt but also seeks to assist and support communities in developing local mechanisms to address future problems.

Primary activities of the Service include the use of conciliation and/or mediation processes to settle differences through mutual understanding and voluntary action. Each process is composed of certain specialized techniques designed to deal with complex racial and ethnic issues. The goal of each, however, is the immediate reduction of community tension and the establishment of viable alternatives for resolving difficulties, short of coercion, violence, or litigation.

In conciliation, trained Service experts serve as outside resources, providing an independent, objective perspective, as well as making recommendations for settlement of the issues involved. Mediation is a more formal process in which the professional mediator acts as a neutral facilitator for negotiations, assisting disputants to reach a mutually satisfactory settlement, with built-in, self-enforcing mechanisms. Inherent in both processes is the technical assistance that the Service provides. This ranges from conducting training in conflict resolution to providing resource materials, program tools, and models indicating how other community groups or agencies have dealt effectively with similar problems or issues.

The Service offers its assistance either on its own motion, when in its judgment peaceful relations among the citizens of a community are threatened, or upon request of State or local officials or other interested persons. The Service seeks the cooperation of appropriate State and local, public and private agencies in carrying out the agency's mission.

The Service also is responsible for continuing efforts to integrate into the United States almost 180,000 Cubans and Haitians who have entered the country since 1980 without documentation or imminent prospects of returning to their homelands. Effective March 6, 1983, it assumed responsibility for the Cuban/Haitian Reception Processing Program, substantially increasing its role in assisting with refugee-immigrant problems. This program was authorized by section 501(c) of the Refugee Education Assistance Act of 1980 (8 U.S.C. 1522 note) and was formerly administered by the Office of Refugee Settlement in the Department of Health and Human Services.

Regional Offices—Community Relations Service

(Areas included within each region are indicated on the map in Appendix A.)

	Region/Address	Director	Phone/FTS
I.	Boston, MA, (10 Causeway St., 02220-1032)	Martin A. Walsh	617-565-6830; 835-6830
II.	New York, NY (26 Federal Plz., 10278)	Patricia Glenn	212-264-0700; 264-0700
III.	Philadelphia, PA (2d and Chestnut Sts., 19106)	Jonathan Chace	215-597-2344; 597-2344
IV.	Atlanta, GA (75 Piedmont Ave. NE., 30303)	Ozell Sutton	404-331-6883; 841-6883
V.	Chicago, IL (175 W. Jackson Blvd., 60604)	Jesse Taylor	312-353-4391; 353-4391
VI.	Dallas, TX (1100 Commerce St., 75242)	John G. Perez	214-767-0824; 729-0824
VII.	Kansas City, MO (911 Walnut St., 64106)	Atkins Warren	816-426-2022; 867-2022
VIII.	Denver, CO (1244 Speer Blvd., 80204-3584)	Leo Cardenas	303-844-2973; 564-2973
IX.	San Francisco, CA (211 Main St., 94103)	Julian Klugman	415-744-6565; 484-6565
X.	Seattle, WA (915 2d Ave., 98101)	Robert Lamb, Jr.	206-442-4465; 399-4465

For further information, contact any regional office or the Director, Community Relations Service, Department of Justice, Suite 330, 5550 Friendship Boulevard, Chevy Chase, MD 20815. Phone, 301-492-5929.

Justice Management Division Under the direction of the Assistant Attorney General for Administration, the Division provides assistance to senior management officials relating to basic Department policy for evaluation, budget and financial management, personnel management and training, equal opportunity programs, automatic data processing and telecommunications, security, records management, procurement, real property and materiel management, and for all other matters pertaining to organization, management, and administration.

The Division provides direct administrative support services, such as personnel, accounting, payroll, procurement, budget, and facilities and property management to the offices, boards, and divisions of the Department and operates several central services such as automated data processing and payroll. The Division supplies automated litigation support as required to the Department of Justice and to other Federal agencies involved in litigation. It also oversees and coordinates the implementation of a Department of Justice case management system.

The Division develops and promulgates departmentwide policies, standards, and procedures for the management of automated information processing resources and for the directive system and reviews their implementation. The Division collects, organizes, and disseminates recorded information that is necessary for the Department to carry out its statutory mandate and provides general research and reference assistance regarding information to Department staff, other Government attorneys, and members of the public.

Professional Responsibility The Office of Professional Responsibility, which reports directly to the Attorney General, is responsible for investigating allegations of criminal or ethical misconduct by employees of the Justice Department. The Counsel on Professional Responsibility heads the Office, the role of which is to ensure that departmental employees continue to perform their duties in accordance with the high professional standards expected of the Nation's principal law enforcement agency.

All allegations against Department employees in attorney, criminal investigative, or law enforcement positions involving violations of law, departmental regulations, or departmental applicable standards of conduct, are reported to the Office of Professional Responsibility. At the Counsel's discretion, the Office frequently conducts its own investigations into those allegations.

The Office may also participate in or direct an investigation conducted by another component of the Department, or may simply monitor an investigation conducted by an appropriate agency having jurisdiction over the matter. In addition, the Office oversees the internal inspection operations of the Federal

Bureau of Investigation and Drug Enforcement Administration.

The Counsel submits an annual report to the Attorney General that reviews and evaluates the Department's internal inspection units. The Counsel makes recommendations to the Attorney General on the need for changes in policies or procedures that become evident during the course of internal inquiries reviewed or initiated by the Office.

Intelligence Policy and Review The Office of Intelligence Policy and Review, under the direction of the Counsel to the Attorney General for Intelligence Policy, is responsible for advising the Attorney General on all matters relating to the national security activities of the United States. The Office prepares and files all applications for surveillance under the Foreign Intelligence Surveillance Act of 1978, assists Government agencies by providing legal advice on matters of national security law and policy and represents the Department of Justice on a variety of interagency committees such as the National Foreign Intelligence Council. The Office also comments on and coordinates other agencies' views regarding proposed legislation affecting intelligence matters.

The Office serves as adviser to the Attorney General and various client agencies, including the Central Intelligence Agency, the Federal Bureau of Investigation, and the Defense and State Departments, concerning questions of law, regulation, and guidelines as well as the legality of domestic and overseas intelligence operations.

Liaison Services The Office of Liaison Services represents the Attorney General and the Department in matters concerning intergovernmental affairs and nongovernmental organizations interested in the justice field. At the same time, the Office provides those governments and organizations with a central point of communication with the Department.

Principal points of liaison for the Office include:

—State Governors, attorneys general, legislators, local elected officials, and the law enforcement community;

—local mayors, prosecutors, public safety directors, sheriffs, chiefs of police, and civil rights organizations;

—Federal, State, and local judicial conferences and judicial administrative bodies;

—foreign justice and police ministers and their departments;

—foreign judiciaries;

—the American Bar Association, the National District Attorneys Association, the Federalist Society, and other Federal, State, local, and foreign bar organizations;

—the International Association of Chiefs of Police and other societies of the law enforcement professions; and

—law schools and other academic institutions with substantive interests in justice fields.

Executive Office for United States Attorneys Under the supervision of the Deputy Attorney General and the direction of a Director, the Executive Office for United States Attorneys provides general executive assistance and nonlitigative oversight to the 94 offices of United States attorneys, including evaluating the performance of the offices of United States attorneys, making appropriate reports and taking corrective action where indicated, and coordinating and directing the relationships of the offices of the United States attorneys with other organizational units of the Department of Justice.

The Office supervises the operation of the Office of Legal Education, including the Attorney General's Advocacy Institute, the Legal Education Institute, and the Support Staff Training Office, which develops, conducts, and authorizes the training of Federal executive branch legal personnel. Administrative and logistic services, including the allocation of personnel, financial resources, and office automation equipment, are furnished to the offices of the United States attorneys. The Office supervises the implementation and administration of the Law Enforcement Coordination Program and of the Victim and Witness Protection Act. Administrative support to the Organized Crime Drug Enforcement Task

Force Program is provided by the Office, and direction and administrative support are provided to the Debt Collection Program and Debt Collection Criminal Fines.

The Office manages the appointment process of United States attorneys, assistant United States attorneys, and special assistant United States attorneys. The *United States Attorneys' Manual* and a *United States Attorneys' Bulletin* are published and maintained for the internal guidance of the United States attorneys' offices and those other organizational units of the Department concerned with litigation. The Office also provides legal opinions, interpretations, and advice to United States attorneys on topics such as budget, legislation, ethics, and Department guidelines.

The Office provides the Attorney General's Advisory Committee of United States Attorneys with such staff assistance and funds as are reasonably necessary to carry out the Committee's responsibilities. It is responsible for maintaining effective liaison and guidance in intergovernmental legal affairs, including congressional matters.

United States Attorneys and Marshals

(A: Attorney General appointment; C: Court appointment; I: Interim appointment)

District/Address	U.S. Attorney	U.S. Marshal
Alabama, Northern (Birmingham 35203)	Frank W. Donaldson	Thomas C. Greene
Alabama, Middle (Montgomery 36101)	James Eldon Wilson	Walter J. Bamberg
Alabama, Southern (Mobile 36602)	J.B. Sessions III	Howard V. Adair
Alaska (Anchorage 99513)	Wevley William Shea	John McKay
Arizona (Phoenix 85025)	Linda A. Akers	Donald W. Tucker
Arkansas, Eastern (Little Rock 72203)	Charles A. Banks	Donald R. Melton
Arkansas, Western (Fort Smith 72901)	J. Michael Fitzhugh	J.C. Patterson
California, Central (Los Angeles 90012)	Lourdes G. Baird	Craig L. Meacham
California, Eastern (Sacramento 95814)	Richard H. Jenkins	Arthur F. Van Court
California, Northern (San Francisco 94102)	William T. McGivern, Jr.	Reginald Boyd
California, Southern (San Diego 92189)	William Braniff (C)	Richard W. Cameron (I)
Colorado (Denver 80294)	Michael J. Norton	Jack Egnor
Connecticut (New Haven 06508)	Richard N. Palmer	William C. Andersen
Delaware (Wilmington 19801)	William C. Carpenter, Jr.	O. Evans Denney
District of Columbia (District Court, Washington 20001).	Jay B. Stephens	Herbert M. Rutherford III
District of Columbia (Superior Court, Washington 20001).		Todd W. Dillard
Florida, Middle (Tampa 33602)	Robert W. Genzman (C)	James A. Tassone
Florida, Northern (Tallahassee 32301)	Kenneth W. Sukhia	W.L. McLendon
Florida, Southern (Miami 33130)	Dexter W. Lehtinen (C)	Daniel J. Horgan
Georgia, Middle (Macon 31202)	Edgar Wm. Ennis, Jr.	William D. Breese
Georgia, Northern (Atlanta 30335)	Joe D. Whitley	Lynn H. Duncan
Georgia, Southern (Savannah 31412)	Hinton R. Pierce	Jimmy C. Carter
Guam (Agana 96910)	D. Paul Vernier	Jose R. Mariano
Hawaii (Honolulu 96850)	Daniel A. Bent	James L. Prepotnick
Idaho (Boise 83724)	Maurice O. Ellsworth	Michael L. Johnson
Illinois, Central (Springfield 62705)	J. William Roberts	James L. Fyke
Illinois, Northern (Chicago 60604)	Fred L. Foreman	John Adams (I)
Illinois, Southern (East St. Louis 62201)	Frederick J. Hess	Donald R. Brookshier
Indiana, Northern (Hammond 46320)	John F. Hoehner	J. Jerome Perkins
Indiana, Southern (Indianapolis 46204)	Deborah J. Daniels	Ralph D. Morgan
Iowa, Northern (Cedar Rapids 52407)	Charles W. Larson	James P. Jonker
Iowa, Southern (Des Moines 50309)	Gene W. Shepard	Terry A. Walker
Kansas (Wichita 67202)	Lee Thompson	Kenneth L. Perkarek
Kentucky, Eastern (Lexington 40591)	Louis G. DeFalaise	Sherman L. Hansford
Kentucky, Western (Louisville 40202)	Joseph M. Whittle	Ralph Boling
Louisiana, Eastern (New Orleans 70130)	Harry A. Rosenberg	James V. Serio, Jr.
Louisiana, Middle (Baton Rouge 70801)	P. Raymond Lamonica	Grover W. Garrison
Louisiana, Western (Shreveport 71101)	Joseph S. Cage, Jr.	Brian P. Joffrion
Maine (Portland 04104)	Richard S. Cohen	John F. Cooper
Maryland (Baltimore 21201)	Richard D. Bennett	Scott Sewell
Massachusetts (Boston 02109)	Wayne Budd	Robert T. Guiney
Michigan, Eastern (Detroit 48226)	Stephen Markman	James Y. Stewart
Michigan, Western (Grand Rapids 49503)	John A. Smietanka	John R. Kendall
Minnesota (Minneapolis 55401)	Jerome G. Arnold	Tony L. Bennett
Mississippi, Northern (Oxford 38655)	Robert Q. Whitwell	Dwight G. Williams
Mississippi, Southern (Jackson 39201)	George L. Phillips	Marvin E. Breazeale
Missouri, Eastern (St. Louis 63101)	Thomas E. Dittmeier	Willie Greason, Jr.

United States Attorneys and Marshals—Continued

(A: Attorney General appointment; C: Court appointment; I: Interim appointment)

District/Address	U.S. Attorney	U.S. Marshal
Missouri, Western (Kansas City 64106)	Jean Paul Bradshaw II	Larry J. Joiner
Montana (Billings 59103)	Doris Swords Poppler	Leo Giacometto
Nebraska (Omaha 68101)	Ronald D. Lahners	Thomas A. O'Hara, Jr.
Nevada (Las Vegas 89101)	Leland E. Lutfy	John H. Robinson
New Hampshire (Concord 03302)	Jeffrey R. Howard	Robert F. Gilbert
New Jersey (Newark 07102)	Michael Chertoff	Arthur Borinsky
New Mexico (Albuquerque 87103)	William L. Lutz	Alfonso Solis
New York, Eastern (Brooklyn 11201)	Andrew J. Maloney	Charles E. Healey
New York, Northern (Syracuse 13260)	Frederick J. Scullin, Jr.	Francis K. Peo
New York, Southern (New York 10007)	Otto G. Obermaier	Romolo J. Imundi
New York, Western (Buffalo 14202)	Dennis C. Vacco (C)	Daniel B. Wright
North Carolina, Eastern (Raleigh 27611)	Margaret P. Currin	William I. Berryhill, Jr.
North Carolina, Middle (Greensboro 27402)	Robert H. Edmunds, Jr.	George L. McBane
North Carolina, Western (Charlotte 28802)	Thomas J. Ashcraft (C)	Jesse R. Jenkins
North Dakota (Fargo 58108)	Stephen D. Easton	Errol L. Wood
Northern Mariana Islands (Saipan, MP 96950)	D. Paul Vernier	Jose R. Mariano
Ohio, Northern (Cleveland 44114)	Joyce J. George	Albert Moore
Ohio, Southern (Columbus 43215)	D. Michael Crites	Robert W. Foster
Oklahoma, Eastern (Muskogee 74401)	John W. Raley, Jr.	James L. Webb
Oklahoma, Northern (Tulsa 74103)	Tony M. Graham	Donald E. Crowl
Oklahoma, Western (Oklahoma City 78102)	Timothy D. Leonard	Stuart E. Earnest
Oregon (Portland 97205)	Charles H. Turner	Kernan H. Bagley
Pennsylvania, Eastern (Philadelphia 19106)	Michael Baylson (C)	Flavio Lorenzoni
Pennsylvania, Middle (Scranton 18501)	James J. West (C)	Gary E. Shovlin
Pennsylvania, Western (Pittsburgh 15219)	Thomas W. Corbett, Jr.	Eugene V. Marzullo
Puerto Rico (Hato Rey 00918)	Daniel F. Lopez-Romo	Herman Wirshing-Rodriguez
Rhode Island (Providence 02901)	Lincoln C. Almond	Donald W. Wyatt
South Carolina (Columbia 29202)	E. Bart Daniel	Lydia E. Glover
South Dakota (Sioux Falls 57101)	Philip N. Hogen	Gene G. Abdallah
Tennessee, Eastern (Knoxville 37901)	John W. Gill, Jr.	Bruce R. Montgomery
Tennessee, Middle (Nashville 37203)	Joe B. Brown	Charles F. Goggin III
Tennessee, Western (Memphis 38103)	Edward G. Bryant	John T. Callery
Texas, Eastern (Beaumont 77701)	Robert J. Wortham	J. Keith Gary
Texas, Northern (Fort Worth 76102)	Marvin Collins	W. Bruce Beaty
Texas, Southern (Houston 77208)	Ronald G. Woods	B.S. Baker
Texas, Western (San Antonio 78206)	Ronald F. Ederer	William J. Jonas, Jr.
Utah (Salt Lake City 84101)	Dee Benson	Eugene H. Davis
Vermont (Burlington 05402)	George J. Terwilliger III	Christian Hansen
Virgin Islands (St. Thomas 00801)	Terry Halpern (C)	John W. Washington
Virginia, Eastern (Alexandria 22314)	Henry E. Hudson	Roger Ray
Virginia, Western (Roanoke 24008)	E. Montgomery Tucker	Wayne D. Beaman
Washington, Eastern (Spokane 99210)	John E. Lamp	Paul R. Nolan
Washington, Western (Seattle 98104)	Mike McKay	Noreen Skagen
West Virginia, Northern (Wheeling 26003)	William A. Kolibash	Charles M. Adkins, Jr.
West Virginia, Southern (Charleston 25332)	Michael W. Carey	William L. Brookhart
Wisconsin, Eastern (Milwaukee 53202)	John E. Fryatt	Robert T. Keating
Wisconsin, Western (Madison 53703)	Grant C. Johnson	Frederick N. Falk
Wyoming (Cheyenne 82008)	Richard A. Stacy	Delaine Roberts

U.S. Trustee Program The Bankruptcy Reform Act of 1978 (11 U.S.C. 101 *et seq.*) established the U.S. Trustee Program as a pilot effort in 10 geographic areas encompassing 18 Federal judicial districts. The program was expanded nationwide by the Bankruptcy Judges, United States Trustee, and Family Farmer Act of 1986 (28 U.S.C. 581 note). The mission of the U.S. Trustees is to ensure compliance with the bankruptcy laws and to supervise the administration of bankruptcy cases and trustees, leaving traditional judicial functions as the sole concern of bankruptcy judges. The program is funded by the United States Trustee System Fund, which consists of fees assessed against those invoking the protections of the bankruptcy laws.

The U.S. Trustees administer three of the four types of bankruptcy proceedings defined under the Bankruptcy Code. These are:

—proceedings under chapter 7 in which the assets of the debtor are liquidated;

—reorganization proceedings under chapter 11 for rehabilitation of the business debtor; and

—adjustment of debts of an individual with regular income under chapter 13, pursuant to which an individual can discharge debts by arranging for payments over a period of time, usually not to exceed 36 months. The U.S. Trustee has no significant role in proceedings under chapter 9, which relates to the adjustment of debts of a municipality.

Specific responsibilities of the U.S. Trustees include:

—appointing and supervising the performance of private trustees in individual cases;

—appointing and convening creditors' committees in chapter 11 corporate reorganization cases;

—reviewing applications for the retention of professionals and the payment of fees;

—reviewing disclosure statements and submitting statements to the court regarding their adequacy;

—appointing trustees or examiners in such cases as needed;

—recommending court approval of trustees or examiners in such cases as needed;

—ensuring that the assets involved in bankruptcy cases are protected during the administration of cases;

—serving as trustees in chapter 7 and 13 cases where private trustees are unwilling to serve; and

—advocating matters relating to the Bankruptcy Code in court.

Executive Office for U.S. Trustees
The Attorney General is charged with the appointment, supervision, and coordination of the U.S. Trustees and Assistant U.S. Trustees. Day-to-day policy and legal direction, coordination, and control are provided by the Director of the Executive Office for U.S. Trustees. The Executive Office also provides administrative and management support to individual U.S. Trustee Offices.

U.S. Trustee Offices

Region	Address	U.S. Trustee	Telephone
1. Maine, Massachusetts, New Hampshire, and Rhode Island	Rm. 472, 10 Causeway St., Boston, MA 02222-1043	E. Franklin Childress	617-565-6360
2. Connecticut, New York, and Vermont	Rm. 534, 1 Bowling Green, New York, NY 10004	Harold D. Jones	212-480-3804
3. Delaware, New Jersey, and Pennsylvania	Rm. 607, 200 Chestnut St., Philadelphia, PA 19106	Thomas E. Ross	215-597-4411
4. District of Columbia, Maryland, North Carolina, South Carolina, Virginia, and West Virginia	Rm. 1108, 1835 Assembly St., Columbia, SC 29201	John E. Waites	803-765-5886
5. Louisiana and Mississippi	Suite 1820, 400 Poydras St., New Orleans, LA 70130	William F. Baity	504-589-4018
6. Northern and Eastern Districts of Texas	Rm. 9C60, 1100 Commerce St., Dallas, TX 75242	William T. Neary	214-767-8967
7. Southern and Western Districts of Texas	Suite 2500, 440 Louisiana St., Houston, TX 77002	Ben T. Head	713-653-3000
8. Kentucky and Tennessee	Suite 400, 200 Jefferson Ave., Memphis, TN 38103	E. Franklin Childress	901-544-3251
9. Michigan and Ohio	Suite 200, 113 St. Clair Ave. NE., Cleveland, OH 44114	Conrad J. Morgenstern	216-522-7800
10. Central and Southern Districts of Illinois and Indiana	Rm. 258, 46 E. Ohio St., Indianapolis, IN 46204	Kenneth C. Meeker	317-226-6101
11. Northern District of Illinois and Wisconsin	Rm. A-1335, 175 W. Jackson Blvd., Chicago, IL 60604	M. Scott Michel	312-886-5785
12. Iowa, Minnesota, North Dakota, and South Dakota	Rm. 675, 425 2d St. SE., Cedar Rapids, IA 52401	Wesley B. Huisinga	319-364-2211
13. Arkansas, Nebraska, and Missouri	Rm. 806, 911 Walnut St., Kansas City, MO 64106	John R. Stonitsch	816-426-7959
14. Arizona	Rm. 100, 320 N. Central Ave., Phoenix, AZ 85004	William T. Neary	602-379-3092
15. Southern District of California, Hawaii, Guam, and the Northern Mariana Islands	Suite 440, 101 W. Broadway, San Diego, CA 92101	Sandra J. Wittman	619-557-5013
16. Central District of California	Rm. 3101, 300 N. Los Angeles St., Los Angeles, CA 90012	Marcy J.K. Tiffany	213-894-6811
17. Eastern and Northern Districts of California and Nevada	Suite 2008, 601 Van Ness Ave., San Francisco, CA 94102	Anthony G. Sousa	415-556-7900

U.S. Trustee Offices—Continued

Region	Address	U.S. Trustee	Telephone
18. Alaska, Idaho, Montana, Oregon, and Washington	Rm. 600, 1200 6th Ave., Seattle, WA 98101	Mary Jo Heston	206-553-2000
19. Colorado, Utah, and Wyoming	Suite 300, 1845 Sherman St., Denver, CO 80203	David D. Bird	303-844-5188
20. Kansas, New Mexico, and Oklahoma	Rm. 180, 401 N. Market St., Wichita, KS 67202	John R. Stonitsch	316-269-6637
21. Alabama, Florida, Georgia, Puerto Rico, and Virgin Islands	Suite 1418, 75 Spring St. SW., Atlanta, GA 30303	Robert L. Coley	404-331-4437

For further information, contact the Executive Office for U.S. Trustees, Department of Justice, Room 812, 320 First Street NW., Washington, DC 20530. Phone, 202-307-1391.

Inspector General The Inspector General provides leadership and assists management in promoting economy, efficiency, and effectiveness within the Department. The Inspector General enforces fraud, waste, abuse, and integrity laws and regulations within the Department and identifies those individuals or organizations involved in financial, contractual, or criminal misconduct in its programs and operations.

The Office of the Inspector General (OIG) consists of an immediate office which is comprised of the Inspector General, Deputy Inspector General, Office of the General Counsel, and the Internal Control Unit; and four major components, each headed by an Assistant Inspector General. The four components are:

—the *Audit Division,* which conducts, reports on, and tracks the resolution of financial and performance audits of organizations, programs, and functions within the Department. Financial audits include financial statements and financial-related activities. Performance audits encompass economy, efficiency, and programmatic issues. Additionally, the Audit Divison monitors expenditures made under Department contracts, grants, and other agreements.

—the *Investigations Division,* which investigates violations of fraud, abuse, and integrity laws that govern the Department and the operations it finances. It also develops such allegations for criminal prosecution and civil or administrative action.

—the *Inspections Division,* which increases efficiency throughout the Department by performing short-term management reviews of the operations and programs within or financed by the Department.

—the *Management and Planning Division,* which provides the Inspector General with advice on administrative and fiscal policy. It provides services to the components of OIG in planning, budget, finance, quality assurance and evaluation, personnel, training, procurement, automated data processing and network communications, and general support.

Headquartered in Washington, DC, OIG's offices are located throughout the United States, with field offices in Arizona, California, Colorado, Florida, Georgia, Illinois, New York, Puerto Rico, Texas, and Washington.

Regional Field Offices—Office of the Inspector General

Region/Address	Inspector General	Telephone
Regional Audit Offices		
NORTHEAST (Suite 701, 4 Skyline Pl., 5113 Leesburg Pike, Falls Church, VA 22041).	Dominic A. Zazzaro	703-756-6294
WASHINGTON (Suite 701, 4 Skyline Pl., 5113 Leesburg Pike, Falls Church, VA 22041).	E. William Rine	703-756-6980
SAN FRANCISCO (Rm. 3522, 525 Market St., San Francisco, CA 94105)	M. Thomas Clark	415-744-6566
ATLANTA (Suite 2322, 101 Marietta St., Atlanta, GA 30323)	Clark F. Cooper	404-331-5037

Regional Field Offices—Office of the Inspector General—Continued

Region/Address	Inspector General	Telephone
CHICAGO (Suite A-1335, 175 W. Jackson Blvd., Chicago, IL 60604)	Robert C. Gruensfelder	312-353-1203
DALLAS (Rm. 334, 207 S. Houston St., Dallas, TX 75202)	George W. Stendall	214-939-6625
Field Investigation Offices		
WASHINGTON (Suite 401, 1400 L St. NW., Washington, DC 20537)	J. Jerome Bullock	202-786-5661
NEW YORK (Rm. 3400, 26 Federal Plz., New York, NY 10278)	Joseph A. Greco	212-264-7550
MIAMI (Suite 312, 3800 Inverrary Blvd., Fort Lauderdale, FL 33319)	Dimitrios J. Pappas	305-527-7142
CHICAGO (Rm. 276D, 1919 S. Highland Ave., Lombard, IL 60148)	Velia A. Youakim	708-495-4090
EL PASO (Suite 120, 3 Butterfield Trail Blvd., El Paso, TX 79906)	Stephen P. Beauchamp	915-540-7370
SAN DIEGO (Rm. 103, 815 E St., San Diego, CA 92112)	Ralph F. Paige	619-557-5970
SAN FRANCISCO (Suite 220, 1200 Bayhill Dr., San Bruno, CA 94066)	Gary Overby	415-876-9058

Divisions

Antitrust Division

The Assistant Attorney General in charge of the Antitrust Division is responsible for promoting and maintaining competitive markets by enforcing the Federal antitrust laws. Such enforcement, which is the principal function of the Division, involves investigating possible antitrust violations, conducting grand jury proceedings, preparing and trying antitrust cases, prosecuting appeals, and negotiating and enforcing final judgments. The antitrust laws affect virtually all industries and apply to every phase of business, including manufacturing, transportation, distribution, and marketing. They prohibit a variety of practices that restrain trade, such as price-fixing conspiracies, corporate mergers likely to reduce the competitive vigor of particular markets, and predatory acts designed to achieve or maintain monopoly power. The Division prosecutes serious and willful violations of the antitrust laws by filing criminal suits that can lead to large fines and jail sentences. Where criminal prosecution is not appropriate, the Division seeks a court order forbidding future violations of the law and requiring steps by the defendant to remedy the anticompetitive effects of past violations.

The Division also is responsible for acting as an advocate of competition within the Federal Government. This involves formal appearances in Federal administrative agency proceedings, development of legislative initiatives to promote deregulation and eliminate unjustifiable exemptions from the antitrust laws, participation on executive branch policy task forces, and publication of reports on regulated industry performance. The Division provides formal advice to other agencies on the competitive implications of proposed transactions requiring Federal approval, such as construction of nuclear powerplants and mergers of financial institutions. It also consults with Federal agencies on a variety of other matters, including the issuance of Federal coal and oil drilling leases and the disposition of surplus Government property.

In addition, the Antitrust Division represents the United States in judicial proceedings to review certain orders of the Interstate Commerce Commission, Federal Maritime Commission, Federal Communications Commission, and Nuclear Regulatory Commission, and provides direct court representation for the Secretary of the Treasury in certain Bureau of Alcohol, Tobacco and Firearms cases. It also participates in Federal Trade Commission cases before the Supreme Court.

In the international law area, the Division represents the United States on the Committee on Competition Law and Policy of the Organization for Economic Cooperation and Development, participates in the United Nations Conference on Trade and Development, and, through the Department of State, maintains liaison with foreign governments on antimonopoly laws and policies.

Field Offices—Antitrust Division

City	Address
Atlanta, GA	Russell Federal Bldg., 30303
Chicago, IL	Kluczynski Federal Bldg., 60604
Cleveland, OH	Plaza 9 Bldg., 44114
Dallas, TX	Earle Cabell Federal Bldg., 75242
New York, NY	26 Federal Plz., 10278-0096
Philadelphia, PA	Curtis Center Bldg., 19106
San Francisco, CA	450 Golden Gate Ave., 94102

For further information, contact the FOIA Unit, Antitrust Division, Department of Justice, Tenth Street and Pennsylvania Avenue NW., Washington, DC 20530. Phone, 202–514–2692.

Civil Division

The Civil Division represents the United States, its departments and agencies, Members of Congress, Cabinet officers, and other Federal employees. Its litigation reflects the diversity of government activities, involving, for example, the defense of challenges to Presidential actions; national security issues; benefit programs; energy policies; commercial issues such as contract disputes, banking, insurance, patents, fraud, and debt collection; all manner of accident and liability claims; and criminal violations of the immigration and consumer protection laws. Each year, Division attorneys handle thousands of cases that collectively involve billions of dollars in claims and recoveries. The Division confronts significant policy issues, which often rise to constitutional dimensions, in defending and enforcing various Federal programs and actions.

The Civil Division litigates cases in all Federal district courts, the U.S. Courts of Appeals, the U.S. Claims Court, other Federal and State courts, and the courts of foreign nations. Division attorneys either conduct this litigation directly or they supervise or assist the U.S. attorneys and foreign counsel to whom the Division refers the cases. The Division is composed of seven major groups: the Torts Branch, the Commercial Litigation Branch, the Federal Programs Branch, the Appellate Staff, the Office of Consumer Litigation, the Office of Immigration Litigation, and an Office of Management Programs.

Torts The Torts Branch is responsible for suits under the Federal Tort Claims Act, including medical malpractice, aviation disasters, environmental and occupational disease, and radiation and toxic substance exposure. It also handles maritime litigation and suits that seek personal money judgments against individual officers or employees.

Tort litigation more specifically includes the defense of all Federal Tort Claims Act suits against the United States or cost-plus-fixed-fee Government contractors, and the prosecution of suits in tort on behalf of the United States. Suits and administrative claims for death, personal injury, and property damage brought under the Tort Claims Act allege negligence on the part of Government employees acting within the scope of their employment and involve matters such as the operation of Government vehicles, the maintenance of Government premises, and the performance of Federal services and regulatory functions such as medical treatment, hospital care, and the control of civilian, military, and commercial air traffic. In addition, the Torts Branch defends petitions filed pursuant to the Vaccine Injury Compensation Program and is responsible for administering the Radiation Exposure Compensation Act.

Tort litigation also includes all legal proceedings involving the United States related to ships, shipping, navigable waters, and workmen's compensation. The Division's admiralty litigation includes suits for personal injury and property damage involving vessels, shore installations, and maritime personnel, equipment, and cargoes; suits arising out of contracts involving shipping, chartering of vessels, and the construction, repair, and salvaging of vessels; proceedings to enforce navigation and shipping laws; and litigation based on international maritime agreements.

Commercial Litigation The Commercial Litigation Branch is responsible for litigation associated with the Government's diverse financial involvements.

This litigation includes all monetary suits involving contracts, expressed or implied; actions to foreclose on Government mortgages and liens; bankruptcy and insolvency proceedings; and suits against guarantors and sureties.

Branch attorneys bring suit under the False Claims Act (31 U.S.C. 3729) and related statutes for the recovery of treble damages and civil penalties, or comparable remedies, upon proof of loss to the Government sustained through fraud in the award or performance of Government contracts, false claims presented in connection with Federal programs, the submission of false statements and vouchers to Government agencies, and the use of other fraudulent devices in transactions with the Government. They also bring suits to recover sums paid to bribe Government officials and kickbacks in Government procurement.

The Branch is responsible for all cases in the U.S. Court of International Trade, including suits brought by importers of merchandise to challenge the appraisement or classification of imported goods or other decisions of the U.S. Customs Service in its administration of the tariff laws and schedules.

The Branch has responsibility for all litigation in the U.S. Claims Court except for those cases assigned to the Environment and Natural Resources Division and the Tax Division. Included are:

—patent cases and suits arising out of construction, procurement, service contracts, and claims associated with contract terminations;

—claims involving freight rate disputes arising out of the transportation of Government property;

—claims for just compensation under the fifth amendment;

—claims for salary or retirement by civilian and military personnel; and

—cases assigned by congressional reference or special legislation.

Likewise, Branch attorneys handle the majority of cases before the Court of Appeals for the Federal Circuit. This litigation involves appeals of decisions made by the U.S. Claims Court, Boards of Contract Appeals, the Merit Systems Protection Board, and Federal district courts.

The Branch handles all litigation involving the rights, liabilities, and administrative functions of the Government with respect to patent, copyright, and trademark matters. This includes:

—defense of patent infringement suits based on the liability of the United States for infringements in connection with the performance of Government contracts;

—legal proceedings to establish Government priority of invention;

—suits for specific performance to require transfer of rights and title and payment of royalties;

—suits to cancel patents acquired by fraud upon the Patent Office;

—defense of administrative acts of the Register of Copyrights; and

—actions on behalf of the Government involving the use of trademarks.

The Branch is also responsible for all legal proceedings in foreign tribunals against diplomatic and consular agents of the United States and civilian or military personnel stationed abroad who are being sued for acts that they have performed in the course of their Government service. Additionally, the Branch renders international judicial assistance to foreign and international tribunals.

Federal Programs The Federal Programs Branch defends and asserts the programs, policies, and decisions of virtually all Federal departments and agencies, the President, Cabinet officers, Members of Congress, and other Government officials. It defends against constitutional challenges to statutes, suits to overturn Government policies and programs, and challenges to the legality of Government decisions. These suits typically seek injunctive and declaratory relief and range from objections to the way that the Government deals with its employees to allegations that the President has violated the Constitution or Federal law. The Branch also initiates suits to enforce regulatory statutes and to remedy or prevent statutory or regulatory violations.

The areas of litigation include:

—defense of suits against the heads of Federal departments and agencies and other government officials to enjoin official actions, as well as suits for judicial review of administrative decisions, orders, and regulations;

—defense and prosecution of suits involving national security, including suits to protect sensitive intelligence sources and materials;

—prosecution of suits to prevent interference with Government operations;

—litigation concerning the constitutionality of Federal legislation; and

—defense of suits involving specialized statutes, such as the Freedom of Information Act, the Federal Advisory Committee Act, and the Privacy Act.

Appellate Staff The Appellate Staff has primary responsibility for the litigation of Civil Division cases in the appellate courts. The Staff prepares Government briefs and presents oral argument for the cases. Additionally, the Appellate Staff participates in drafting all documents filed for these cases in the United States Supreme Court, including briefs on the merits, petitions for certiorari, and jurisdictional statements.

Consumer Litigation The Office of Consumer Litigation is responsible for litigation and related matters arising under various consumer protection statutes, including the Federal Food, Drug, and Cosmetic Act, the Federal Trade Commission Act, the Consumer Product Safety Act, the Hazardous Substances Act, and the Truth in Lending Act. The Office also serves as a liaison with other Federal agencies and with local enforcement agencies for the referral of consumer complaints outside the jurisdiction of the Department of Justice.

Immigration Litigation The Office of Immigration Litigation is responsible for conducting civil litigation under the Immigration and Nationality Act (8 U.S.C. 1101) and related laws and for representing the United States in civil litigation brought against employees of the Immigration and Naturalization Service. In addition, this Office handles district court litigation, deportation review proceedings, habeas corpus review and general advice, and immigration-related appellate matters. The Office is also responsible for cases pertaining to the issuance of visas and passports, and for litigation arising under the amnesty and employer sanctions provisions of the Immigration Reform and Control Act of 1986 (8 U.S.C. 1255a, 1324a).

Management Programs The Office of Management Programs provides management and administrative services to the Division, including policy analysis and planning, administrative management, budget formulation and execution, management information systems, office automation, and automated litigation support.

Field Offices—Civil Division

Branch	Address
COMMERCIAL LITIGATION BRANCH (International Trade)	26 Federal Plz., New York, NY 10007
TORTS BRANCH (Admiralty and Shipping Litigation)	26 Federal Plz., New York, NY 10007 450 Golden Gate Ave., San Francisco, CA 94102

For further information, contact the Office of the Assistant Attorney General, Civil Division, Department of Justice, Tenth Street and Pennsylvania Avenue NW., Washington, DC 20530. Phone, 202–514–3301.

Civil Rights Division

The Civil Rights Division, headed by an Assistant Attorney General, was established in 1957 in response to the need to secure effective Federal enforcement of civil rights.

This Division is responsible for enforcing Federal civil rights laws that prohibit discrimination on the basis of race, national origin, religion, and, in some instances, sex or handicap in the areas of voting, education, employment, housing, credit, the use of public facilities and public accommodations, and in the administration of federally assisted programs. The congressional statutes enforced are, *inter alia,* the Civil Rights Acts of 1957 (42 U.S.C. 1975), 1960 (42 U.S.C. 1971, 1974), 1964 (42 U.S.C. 2000a-h), and 1968 (42 U.S.C. 245, 42 U.S.C. 3601–3619, 3631), the Voting Rights Act of 1965, as amended (42 U.S.C. 1971, 1973), the Equal Educational Opportunities Act of 1974 (20 U.S.C. 1701–1720), the Equal Credit Opportunity Act, as amended in 1976 (15 U.S.C. 1691), the Civil Rights of Institutionalized Persons Act of 1980 (42 U.S.C. 1997), and the Americans with Disabilities Act of 1990 (42 U.S.C. 12101 note).

Additionally, the Division is responsible for the implementation of Executive Order 12250 of November 2, 1980, which requires coordination of efforts of executive agencies and departments to eliminate discrimination based on race, color, national origin, sex, religion, and handicap in programs receiving Federal financial assistance and discrimination based on handicap in federally conducted programs.

The Civil Rights Division also has the obligation to enforce specific criminal statutes including those concerning willful deprivation of constitutional rights under color of law or through conspiracy, involuntary servitude, and violent interference with federally protected activities (18 U.S.C. 241, 242, 245, 1584).

Finally, the Division is responsible for implementing section 105 of the Civil Liberties Act of 1988, which entitles many Japanese Americans who were interned or relocated during World War II to receive restitution.

The Civil Rights Division is composed of eight major organizational sections and an administrative component. Each of the eight litigating sections has jurisdiction over particular subject areas and related statutes, except for the appellate section, which handles most appeals involving all areas of Division litigation. With the approval of the Assistant Attorney General and, where necessary, the Attorney General and Solicitor General, each litigating section undertakes or authorizes investigations, conducts negotiations, and initiates and conducts litigation. One section is specifically responsible for coordinating Federal efforts as called for by Executive Order 12250, and for the implementation of titles II and III of the Americans with Disabilities Act of 1990.

For further information, contact the Executive Officer, Civil Rights Division, Department of Justice, Tenth Street and Pennsylvania Avenue NW., Washington, DC 20530. Phone, 202–514–4224.

Criminal Division

The Assistant Attorney General in charge of the Criminal Division formulates criminal law enforcement policies, and enforces and exercises general supervision over all Federal criminal laws except those specifically assigned to the Antitrust, Civil Rights, Land and Natural Resources, and Tax Divisions. The Criminal Division also supervises certain civil litigation incidental to Federal law enforcement activities.

Child Exploitation and Obscenity Section The Section spearheads and coordinates Federal obscenity and child exploitation prosecutions. It assists Federal, State, and local prosecutors with advice, training, and legal resource materials. The Section serves as the Department's contact office for the public and media on the issue of pornography and the sexual exploitation of women and children.

Organized Crime and Racketeering Section This Section investigates and prosecutes cases to suppress the illicit activities of organized criminal

290-950 O 91 - 13

syndicates. Cases handled in this Section typically focus on labor-management racketeering, loansharking, extortion, gambling, and prostitution. The Section also supervises the use of the Racketeer Influenced and Corrupt Organizations (RICO) statute throughout the Federal legal system and is responsible for identifying and targeting emerging organized criminal groups.

Narcotic and Dangerous Drug Section This Section investigates and prosecutes high-level drug traffickers and members of criminal organizations involved in the importation, manufacture, shipment, or distribution of illicit narcotics and dangerous drugs, with particular emphasis on litigation attacking the financial bases of those criminal organizations.

Internal Security Section This Section investigates and prosecutes cases affecting the national security, foreign relations, and the export of military and strategic commodities and technology. It also administers and enforces the Foreign Agents Registration Act of 1938 (22 U.S.C. 611) and related statutes. The Section has exclusive prosecutorial responsibility for criminal statutes regarding espionage, sabotage, neutrality, and atomic energy.

Fraud Section This Section directs and coordinates the Federal effort against fraud and white-collar crime, focusing primarily upon frauds against government programs and procurement, transnational and multidistrict fraud, the security and commodity exchanges, banking practices, and consumer victimization. It conducts investigations and prosecutes certain fraud cases of national significance or great complexity.

Public Integrity Section This Section investigates and prosecutes corruption cases involving public officials and the elective system at the Federal, State, and local levels.

Money Laundering Section This Section investigates and prosecutes high-level drug traffickers and members of other criminal organizations involved in money laundering activities. The Section analyzes and evaluates departmental policy concerning money laundering efforts, seeks to train Federal agents and prosecutors in money laundering practice and policy; and provides general advice and support to United States Attorneys' offices on money laundering matters.

Terrorism and Violent Crime Section This Section has primary responsibility for the prosecution of domestic and international terrorism cases. The Section also handles certain domestic violent crimes, including the criminal activity of gangs, and serves as the Department's authority in applying the death penalty in all Federal cases.

Appellate Section This Section assists the Office of the Solicitor General in obtaining favorable constitutional and statutory interpretations in criminal cases being heard on appeal before the United States Supreme Court and the 12 United States Courts of Appeals.

General Litigation and Legal Advice Section This Section investigates and prosecutes cases involving violations of approximately 75 percent of all Federal criminal statutes. The Section is responsible for application of the Computer Fraud and Abuse Act, crimes against the public and against Government operations, and offenses involving criminally enforceable regulations. The Section also handles certain civil matters, including the defense of suits challenging actions taken by the Bureau of Prisons and the Parole Commission, and provides extensive legal advice to officials of the Department, U.S. Attorneys' offices, and investigative agencies.

Office of International Affairs The Office supports the Department's legal divisions, the U.S. attorneys, and the State and local prosecutors regarding international criminal justice enforcement matters pursuant to treaties concerning extradition, mutual legal assistance, and prisoner exchange. It also engages in treaty negotiations with the State Department.

Office of Enforcement Operations The Office oversees the use of sensitive and sophisticated investigative tools, such as witness protection and electronic surveillance. It also assists and supports government prosecutors by reviewing requests for authorization to compel testimony (immunity) and responding to inquiries under the Freedom of Information and Privacy Acts.

Office of Legislation The Office develops legislative proposals, legal memoranda, and congressional testimony and prepares comments upon pending and proposed legislation affecting the Federal criminal justice system. It also provides legal support to the Advisory Committee on Criminal Rules of the Judicial Conference regarding the Federal rules of criminal procedure.

Office of Policy and Management Analysis The Office develops and recommends positions on policy and management issues for Department and Division officials, including developing priorities and objectives, program planning and evaluation, management improvement, and research liaison.

Office of Special Investigations The Office detects, identifies, and takes appropriate legal action leading to the denaturalization and/or deportation of Nazi war criminals in the United States who were involved in the atrocities committed against civilian populations during the Second World War and who subsequently entered the United States illegally.

Office of Administration The Office provides administrative support to the sections and offices of the Division, including personnel, automated data processing, procurement, the development of budget proposals, and the execution of financial plans.

Asset Forfeiture Office The Office develops uniform policies and assists in the prosecution of both civil and criminal asset forfeiture cases, particularly regarding narcotics trafficking and organized crime. It adjudicates all judicial petitions for remission or mitigation of forfeited assets and determines equitable sharing of judicially forfeited assets with State and local law enforcement agencies.

For further information, contact the Office of the Assistant Attorney General, Criminal Division, Department of Justice, Tenth Street and Pennsylvania Avenue NW., Washington, DC 20530. Phone, 202–514–2601.

Environment and Natural Resources Division

The Environment and Natural Resources Division represents the United States in litigation involving public lands and natural resources, environmental quality, Indian lands and claims, and wildlife resources. The fastest growing area of responsibility involves civil and criminal enforcement of environmental statutes. Although the cases filed by the Division in the area of hazardous chemical wastes are the most visible and complex, enforcement of the clean air and water laws is also a prominent part of the docket. Thus, the Division brings civil and criminal enforcement cases primarily on behalf of the Environmental Protection Agency for the control and abatement of pollution of air and water resources, the regulation and control of toxic substances, as well as the environmental hazards posed by hazardous wastes. In the hazardous waste area, most cases are brought under the Comprehensive Environmental Response, Compensation and Liability Act of 1980 (42 U.S.C. 9601), as amended by the Superfund Amendments and Reauthorization Act of 1986 (42 U.S.C. 9601 note), for the purposes of protecting public health and ensuring that responsible parties, rather than the public, bear the burden of abating hazardous waste pollution.

The various environmental enforcement statutes also generate a great deal of defensive litigation since many of the provisions of those laws also apply to Federal programs or activities. This litigation generally falls into one of two categories: suits by industry and environmental groups challenging agency regulations, or challenges to agency decisions relating to individual activities such as permits, grants, and variances.

The Division is also responsible for prosecuting and defending criminal and civil cases arising under the Federal wildlife laws and laws concerning the conservation and management of marine fish and mammals. Prosecutions focus on major smugglers of and black market dealers in protected species.

In addition, the Division represents the United States in cases where the Government supports rights claimed by individual Indians or Indian tribes. These include suits to establish water rights, to establish and protect hunting and fishing rights, to collect damages for trespassing on Indian lands, and to establish reservation boundaries and rights to land.

For much of the Division's 75-year history, its litigation has principally involved the management and development of the lands and resources owned by the United States. The Division acquires land for the Federal Government, either by direct purchase or condemnation proceedings, and seeks to implement the protections of the fifth amendment in a way that is fair to both property owners and taxpayers.

For further information, contact the Office of the Assistant Attorney General, Environment and Natural Resources Division, Department of Justice, Tenth Street and Pennsylvania Avenue NW., Washington, DC 20530. Phone, 202–514–2701.

Tax Division

The Tax Division represents the United States and its officers in all civil and criminal litigation arising under the internal revenue laws, other than proceedings in the United States Tax Court. While the Division's primary client is the Internal Revenue Service, it also represents Federal officials and employees in actions arising out of the performance of their official duties, as well as representing other Federal departments and agencies in their dealings with State and local tax authorities. In civil tax litigation the Division's responsibility involves cases in the United States District Courts, the United States Claims Court, the United States Courts of Appeals, and the United States Supreme Court, as well as cases in the State courts.

The Division represents the United States in many different types of disputes, both civil and criminal, dealing with the interpretation of Federal tax laws. For example, when the Internal Revenue Service challenges a tax return and determines a deficiency, the taxpayer may pay the full amount of tax assessed and then bring a suit against the Government for refund. The Division defends the Government in these refund actions.

Other areas of civil litigation in which the Tax Division is involved on behalf of the Federal Government include:

—suits brought by individuals to foreclose mortgages or to quiet title to property in which the United States is named as a party defendant because of the existence of a Federal tax lien on the property;

—suits brought by the United States to collect unpaid assessments, to foreclose Federal tax liens or determine the priority of such liens, to obtain judgments against delinquent taxpayers, to enforce summonses, and to establish tax claims in bankruptcy, receivership, or probate proceedings;

—proceedings involving mandamus, injunctions, and other specific writs arising in connection with internal revenue matters;

—suits against Internal Revenue Service employees for damages claimed because of alleged injuries caused in the performance of their official duties;

—suits against the Secretary of the Treasury, the Commissioner of Internal Revenue, or similar officials to test the validity of regulations or rulings not in the context of a specific refund action;

—suits brought by the United States to enjoin the promotion of abusive tax shelters and to enjoin activities relating to aiding and abetting the understatement of tax liabilities of others;

—suits brought by taxpayers for a judicial determination of the reasonableness of a jeopardy or termination assessment and the appropriateness of the amount;

—proceedings brought against the Tax Division and the Internal Revenue Service for disclosure of information under the Freedom of Information Act; and

—intergovernmental immunity suits in which the United States resists attempts to apply a State or local tax to some activity or property of the United States.

The Division also collects judgments in tax cases. To this end, the Division directs collection efforts and coordinates with, monitors the efforts of, and provides assistance to the various United States attorneys' offices in collecting outstanding judgments in tax cases.

With respect to criminal tax litigation, the Division prosecutes or supervises the prosecution of all criminal offenses committed under the internal revenue laws, including attempts to evade and defeat taxes, willful failure to file returns and to pay taxes, filing false returns and other deceptive documents, making false statements to revenue officials, and other miscellaneous offenses involving internal revenue matters. These duties include the institution of criminal proceedings and collaboration with U.S. attorneys in the conduct of litigation in the trial and appellate courts. Further, Tax Division attorneys frequently conduct grand jury investigations and actual trials of criminal tax cases, often as a result of requests for assistance by the appropriate U.S. attorney. In its efforts to deter willful deception through prosecution of criminal offenders, the Tax Division also plays a significant role in curbing organized crime, public corruption, narcotics trafficking, and most recently, financial institution fraud.

The primary functions of the Division are to aid the Internal Revenue Service in collecting the Federal revenue and to establish principles of law that will serve as guidelines to taxpayers and their representatives, as well as to the Internal Revenue Service, in the administration of the Internal Revenue Code. As a result, coordination with the Internal Revenue Service's administrative policies and the Treasury Department's legislative tax concerns in developing litigating postures is essential.

The Division also provides input into the preparation of reports to the Congress, the Office of Management and Budget, and the Office of Legislative Affairs on pending or proposed legislation and monitors congressional activities with respect to matters of interest to the Division.

In accordance with the Attorney General's program to enhance the litigating skills of Department attorneys, the Division conducts training programs for its attorneys, with special emphasis on matters unique to tax litigation and the development of advocacy skills.

For further information, contact the Office of the Assistant Attorney General, Tax Division, Department of Justice, Tenth Street and Pennsylvania Avenue NW., Washington, DC 20530. Phone, 202–514–2901.

Office of Special Counsel for Immigration Related Unfair Employment Practices

The Office of Special Counsel for Immigration Related Unfair Employment Practices was established pursuant to section 102 of the Immigration Reform and Control Act of 1986 (8 U.S.C. 1324b). The Special Counsel is responsible for investigating and prosecuting charges of national origin and citizenship status discrimination in hiring, firing, or recruitment. Jurisdiction over national origin charges is limited to those not covered by the Equal Employment Opportunity Commission. Jurisdiction over citizenship status is exclusive.

The Special Counsel files complaints before an administrative law judge based on charges filed with this Office, or on its own independent investigations. Appeals of administrative decisions are to the U.S. Courts of Appeals.

In addition, the Special Counsel coordinates with the Immigration and Naturalization Service, the Equal Employment Opportunity Commission, and other Federal agencies in promoting public awareness of the antidiscrimination provisions of the act, through employer and public interest conferences, public service announcements, and nationwide distribution of enforcement information.

For further information, contact the Executive Officer, Office of Special Counsel for Immigration Related Unfair Employment Practices, P.O. Box 65490, Washington, DC 20035–5490. Phone, (voice) 202–653–8430 or 800–255–7688 (toll-free); and (TDD) 202–296–0168 or 800–237–2515 (toll-free).

Bureaus

Federal Bureau of Investigation

Ninth Street and Pennsylvania Avenue NW., Washington, DC 20535. Phone, 202–324–3000

The Federal Bureau of Investigation (FBI) is the principal investigative arm of the United States Department of Justice. It is charged with gathering and reporting facts, locating witnesses, and compiling evidence in cases involving Federal jurisdiction.

The Federal Bureau of Investigation was established in 1908 by the Attorney General, who directed that Department of Justice investigations be handled by its own staff. The Bureau is charged with investigating all violations of Federal law except those that have been assigned by legislative enactment or otherwise to another Federal agency. Its jurisdiction includes a wide range of responsibilities in the criminal, civil, and security fields. Priority has been assigned to the six areas that affect society the most—organized crime, drugs, counterterrorism, white-collar crime, foreign counterintelligence, and violent crime.

On January 28, 1982, the Attorney General assigned concurrent jurisdiction for the enforcement of the Controlled Substances Act (21 U.S.C. 801) to the Bureau and the Drug Enforcement Administration (DEA). The DEA Administrator reports to the Attorney General through the FBI Director.

The Bureau also offers cooperative services such as fingerprint identification, laboratory examination, police training, and the National Crime Information Center to duly authorized law enforcement agencies.

The Bureau headquarters in Washington, DC, consists of 10 separate divisions, a Deputy Director, 2 Associate Deputy Directors, an Office of Public Affairs, a Congressional Affairs Office, an Office of Liaison and International Affairs, an Office of Equal Employment Opportunity Affairs, and a Director's staff.

The Bureau's investigations are conducted through 56 field offices. Most of its investigative personnel are trained at the FBI Academy in Quantico, VA.

Field Divisions—Federal Bureau of Investigation

Division	Address	Telephone
Albany, NY	5th Fl., U.S. Post Office and Courthouse, 445 Broadway, 12201-1219	518-465-7551
Albuquerque, NM	301 Grand Ave. NE., 87102	505-247-1555
Anchorage, AK	Suite 6, 222 W. 7th Ave., 99513-7598	907-276-4441
Atlanta, GA	77 Forsyth St. SW., 30303	404-521-3900
Baltimore, MD	7142 Ambassador Rd., 21207	301-265-8080
Birmingham, AL	Rm. 1400, 2121 Bldg., 35203	205-252-7705
Boston, MA	John F. Kennedy Federal Office Bldg., 02203	617-742-5533
Buffalo, NY	111 W. Huron St., 14202	716-856-7800
Charlotte, NC	6010 Kenley Lane, 28217	704-529-1030
Chicago, IL	219 S. Dearborn St., 60604	312-431-1333
Cincinnati, OH	550 Main St., 45202	513-421-4310
Cleveland, OH	1240 E. 9th St., 44199	216-522-1400
Columbia, SC	1835 Assembly St., 29201	803-254-3011
Dallas, TX	1801 N. Lamar, 75202	214-720-2200
Denver, CO	Rm. 1823, Federal Office Bldg., 80202	303-629-7171
Detroit, MI	477 Michigan Ave., 48226	313-965-2323
El Paso, TX	700 E. San Antonio Ave., 79901	915-533-7451
Honolulu, HI	300 Ala Moana Blvd., 96850	808-521-1411
Houston, TX	Suite 200, 2500 East T.C. Jester, 77008	713-868-2266
Indianapolis, IN	575 N. Pennsylvania St., 46204	317-639-3301
Jackson, MS	100 W. Capitol St., 39269	601-948-5000
Jacksonville, FL	7820 Arlington Expressway, 32211	904-721-1211
Kansas City, MO	300 U.S. Courthouse Bldg., 64106	816-221-6100
Knoxville, TN	710 Locust St., 37901	615-544-0751
Las Vegas, NV	700 E. Charleston Blvd., 89104	702-385-1281
Little Rock, AR	Suite 200, 2 Financial Ctr., 10825 Financial Pkwy., 72211	501-221-9100
Los Angeles, CA	11000 Wilshire Blvd., 90024	213-477-6565

Field Divisions—Federal Bureau of Investigation—Continued

Division	Address	Telephone
Louisville, KY	Rm. 500, 600 Martin Luther King Pl., 40202	502-583-3941
Memphis, TN	167 N. Main St., 38103	901-525-7373
Miami, FL	16320 NW. 2d Ave., N. Miami Beach, 33169	305-944-9101
Milwaukee, WI	517 E. Wisconsin Ave., 53202	414-276-4684
Minneapolis, MN	S-1100, 111 Washington Ave. S., 55401	612-376-3200
Mobile, AL	1 St. Louis St., 36602	205-438-3674
Newark, NJ	Gateway 1, Market St., 07102	201-622-5613
New Haven, CT	150 Court St., 06510	203-777-6311
New Orleans, LA	1250 Poydras St., 70112	504-522-4671
New York, NY	26 Federal Plz., 10278	212-335-2700
Norfolk, VA	200 Granby St., 23510	804-623-3111
Oklahoma City, OK	50 Penn Pl., 73118	405-842-7471
Omaha, NE	215 N. 17th St., 68102	402-348-1210
Philadelphia, PA	600 Arch St., 19106	215-629-0800
Phoenix, AZ	201 E. Indianola, 85012	602-279-5511
Pittsburgh, PA	1000 Liberty Ave., 15222	412-471-2000
Portland, OR	1500 SW. 1st Ave., 97201	503-224-4181
Quantico, VA	FBI Academy, 22135	703-640-6131
Richmond, VA	111 Greencourt Rd., 23228	804-261-1044
Sacramento, CA	2800 Cottage Way, 95825	916-481-9110
St. Louis, MO	1520 Market St., 63103	314-241-5357
Salt Lake City, UT	125 S. State St., 84138	801-355-7521
San Antonio, TX	615 E. Houston, 78205	512-225-6741
San Diego, CA	880 Front St., 92188	619-231-1122
San Francisco, CA	450 Golden Gate Ave., 94102	415-553-7400
San Juan, PR	Rm. 526, U.S. Courthouse, Hato Rey, 00918	809-754-6000
Seattle, WA	915 2d Ave., 98174	206-622-0460
Springfield, IL	400 W. Monroe St., 62704	217-522-9675
Tampa, FL	500 Zack St., 33602	813-228-7661
Washington, DC	FBI, Washington Metropolitan Field Office, 20535	202-324-3000

For further information, contact the Office of Public Affairs, Federal Bureau of Investigation, J. Edgar Hoover F.B.I. Building, Ninth Street and Pennsylvania Avenue NW., Washington, DC 20535. Phone, 202-324-3691.

Bureau of Prisons

320 First Street NW., Washington, DC 20534. Phone, 202-307-3198

The mission of the Bureau of Prisons is to protect society by carrying out the judgments of the Federal courts through providing confinement services to committed offenders and to provide program opportunities to all inmates who qualify and who wish to participate. This confinement function complements other sentencing options available to Federal judges.

The Bureau's mission includes the responsibility to maintain secure, safe, and humane correctional institutions for individuals placed in the care and custody of the Attorney General; develop and operate correctional programs that seek a balanced application of the concepts of punishment, deterrence, incapacitation, and rehabilitation; and provide, primarily through the National Institute of Corrections, assistance to State and local correctional agencies.

The Executive Office of the Director provides overall direction for agency operations. In addition to typical administrative functions performed by an agency head, the Offices of General Counsel and Internal Affairs are within the Office and report to the Director.

The Administration Division develops plans, programs, and policies concerning the acquisition, construction, and staffing of new facilities, as well as budget development, financial management, procurement, and contracting.

The Correctional Programs Division is responsible for managing the correctional services (security) operations in Bureau institutions, community corrections programs, and case and unit management, as well as religious and psychological services, and inmate systems.

Federal Prison Industries (trade name UNICOR) is a wholly-owned

Government corporation whose mission is to provide employment and training opportunities for inmates confined in Federal correctional facilities. UNICOR manufactures a wide range of items—from executive and systems furniture to electronics, textiles and graphics/signage. Services performed by UNICOR's inmates include data entry, printing, and furniture refinishing. The corporation funds selected preindustrial, vocational, and experimental training programs.

The Health Services Division has oversight responsibility for all medical programs and environmental, health, safety, and sanitation services in Bureau institutions. This Division also is responsible for food services, farm operations, and inmate accident compensation programs.

The Human Resources Division provides personnel, training, and labor management within the agency. Its functions also include pay and position management and recruitment.

The National Institute of Corrections provides advisory and technical support to State and local correctional agencies throughout the country. The Institute also operates the National Academy of Corrections, the Institute Information Center, and the National Jail Center, all of which are currently located in Boulder, CO. The Institute receives logistical support from the Bureau of Prisons but is a separate budget entity.

The Program Review Division is responsible for oversight of agency audit functions and manages an internal control branch for training of auditors and coordinating the year-end assurance statement to the Attorney General. This Division has a program analysis branch, coordinating in-depth analysis of audit outcomes and recommending necessary management changes in accord with those findings. The inmate grievance (administrative remedy) procedure is operated out of this division as well as strategic planning.

On February 20, 1991, the Attorney General established the Information, Policy and Public Affairs Division, encompassing the Bureau's Information Systems, Policy Review, Research and Evaluation, Security Technology, and Office of Public Affairs.

The establishment of the Community Corrections and Detention Division was also approved by the Attorney General on February 20, 1991. This Division is responsible for the Bureau's Community Corrections and Detention Programs, Contract Services, Administration, and Program Development.

The Bureau is subdivided into six geographic regions, each staffed with field-qualified personnel who are responsible for policy development and oversight, providing operational guidance to field locations, and providing support functions in areas such as auditing, technical assistance, budget, and personnel. Each regional office is headed by an experienced career Bureau manager who is a full member of the Bureau's Executive Staff.

Regional Offices—Bureau of Prisons

Region/Address	Director	Telephone
MID-ATLANTIC—Suite 100N, 10010 Junction Dr., Annapolis Junction, MD 20701.	Gilbert L. Ingram	301-317-7000
NORTH CENTRAL—10920 Ambassador Dr., Kansas City, MO 64153	Calvin Edwards	816-891-7007
NORTHEAST—7th Fl., 2d and Chestnut Sts., Philadelphia, PA 19106	George Wilkinson	215-597-6317
SOUTH CENTRAL—4211 Cedar Springs Rd., Dallas, TX 75219	Charles Turnbo	214-767-9700
SOUTHEAST—5213 McDonough Blvd. SE., Atlanta, GA 30315	Jerry Williford	404-624-5202
WESTERN—4th Fl., 1301 Shoreway Rd., Belmont, CA 94002	F.P. Samples	415-595-8160

Federal Penal and Correctional Institutions

U.S. Penitentiaries

U.S. Penitentiary, Atlanta, GA 30315
U.S. Penitentiary, Leavenworth, KS 66048
U.S. Penitentiary, Lewisburg, PA 17837
U.S. Penitentiary, Lompoc, CA 93436
U.S. Penitentiary, Marion, IL 62959
U.S. Penitentiary, Terre Haute, IN 47808

Federal Correctional Institutions

Federal Correctional Institution, Alderson, WV 24910
Federal Correctional Institution, Ashland, KY 41101
Federal Correctional Institution, Bastrop, TX 78602
Federal Correctional Institution, McKean, Bradford, PA 16701
Federal Correctional Institution, Danbury, CT 06811
Federal Correctional Institution, Camp Parks, Dublin, CA 94568
Federal Correctional Institution, El Reno, OK 73036
Federal Correctional Institution, Fairton, NJ 08320
Federal Correctional Institution, Fort Worth, TX 76119
Federal Correctional Institution, Grand Marsh, WI 53936
Federal Correctional Institutuon, Jesup, GA 31545
Federal Correctional Institution, La Tuna, TX 88021
Federal Correctional Institution, Littleton, CO 80123
Federal Correctional Institution, Lompoc, CA 93436
Federal Correctional Institution, Loretto, PA 15940
Federal Correctional Institution, Marianna, FL 32446
Federal Correctional Institution, Memphis, TN 38134
Federal Correctional Institution, Milan, MI 48160
Federal Correctional Institution, Minersville, PA 17954
Federal Correctional Institution, Morgantown, WV 26505
Federal Correctional Institution, Oakdale, LA 71463
Federal Correctional Institution, Oxford, WI 53952
Federal Correctional Institution, Petersburg, VA 23804-1000
Federal Correctional Institution, Phoenix, AZ 85027
Federal Correctional Institution, Ray Brook, NY 12977
Federal Correctional Institution, Safford, AZ 85546
Federal Correctional Institution, Sandstone, MN 55072
Federal Correctional Institution, Seagoville, TX 75159
Federal Correctional Institution, Sheridan, OR 97378
Federal Correctional Institution, Talladega, AL 35160
Federal Correctional Institution, Tallahassee, FL 32301
Federal Correctional Institution, Terminal Island, CA 90731
Federal Correctional Institution, Texarkana, TX 75501
Federal Correctional Institution, Three Rivers TX 78071
Federal Correctional Institution, Tucson, AZ 85706

Federal Prison Camps

Federal Prison Camp, Big Spring, TX 79720-7799
Federal Prison Camp, Boron, CA 93516
Federal Prison Camp, Bryan, TX 77803
Federal Prison Camp, Duluth, MN 55814
Federal Prison Camp, Eglin Air Force Base, FL 32542
Federal Prison Camp, El Paso, TX 79906
Federal Prison Camp, Seymour Johnson Air Force Base, Goldsboro, NC 27533
Federal Prison Camp, Homestead Air Force Base, Homestead, FL 33090
Federal Prison Camp, Leavenworth, KS 66048
Federal Prison Camp, Lewisburg, PA 17837
Federal Prison Camp, Maxwell Air Force Base, AL 36112
Federal Prison Camp, Millington, TN 38053
Federal Prison Camp, Allenwood, Montgomery, PA 17752
Federal Prison Camp, Nellis Air Force Base, NV 89191-5000
Federal Prison Camp, Tyndall Air Force Base, Panama City, FL 32403
Federal Prison Camp, Saufley Field, Pensacola, FL 32509
Federal Prison Camp, Yankton, SD 57078

Administrative Facilities

Federal Correctional Institution, Butner, NC 27509
Federal Medical Center, Carville, LA 70721
Metropolitan Correctional Center, Chicago, IL 60605 (71 W. Van Buren St.) [1]
Federal Correctional Institution, Lexington, KY 40511
Metropolitan Detention Center, Los Angeles, CA 90053
Metropolitan Correctional Center, Miami, FL 33177 (15801 SW. 137th Ave.) [1]
Federal Detention Center, Oakdale, LA 71463
Federal Correctional Institution, Otisville, NY 10963
Metropolitan Correctional Center, New York, NY 10007 (150 Park Row) [1]
Federal Medical Center, Rochester, MN 55903-4600
Metropolitan Correctional Center, San Diego, CA 92101 (808 Union St.) [1]
Metropolitan Detention Center, San Juan, PR 00902
U.S. Medical Center for Federal Prisoners, Springfield, MO 65808

Staff Training Centers

Federal Law Enforcement Training Center, Glynco, GA 31524 (Bldg. 21)
Food Management, c/o FCI, Fort Worth, TX 76119
Management and Specialty, Aurora, CO 80011 (Suite 300, 601 Chambers Rd.)
Trust Fund, c/o FCI, Fort Worth, TX 76119

For further information, contact the Public Information Officer, Bureau of Prisons, Department of Justice, Washington, DC 20534. Phone, 202-307-3198.

United States Marshals Service

600 Army Navy Drive, Arlington, VA 22202-4210. Phone, 202-307-9000

The United States Marshals Service is the Nation's oldest Federal law enforcement agency, having served as a vital link between the executive and judicial branches of the Government since 1789. Today, the Presidentially appointed marshals and their support staff of just over 3,000 deputy marshals and administrative personnel operate from 427 office locations in all 94 Federal judicial districts nationwide, from Guam to Puerto Rico, and from Alaska to Florida.

The Marshals Service performs tasks that are essential to the operation of virtually every aspect of the Federal justice system. The Service is responsible for:

---

[1] Male and female offenders.

—providing support and protection for the Federal courts, including security for 560 judicial facilities and nearly 1,900 judges and magistrates, as well as countless other trial participants such as jurors and attorneys;

—apprehending most Federal fugitives;

—operating the Federal Witness Security program, ensuring the safety of endangered government witnesses;

—maintaining custody of and transporting thousands of Federal prisoners annually;

—executing court orders and arrest warrants;

—seizing, managing, and selling property forfeited to the Government by drug traffickers and other criminals, and operating the Justice Department's National Asset Seizure and Forfeiture Program; and

—responding to emergency circumstances, including civil disturbances, terrorist incidents, and other crisis situations, through its Special Operations Group, and restoring order in riot and mob-violence situations.

The Director of the U.S. Marshals Service, who is appointed by the President, supervises the operations of the Service throughout the United States and its territories. The Deputy Director for Operations oversees the Service's enforcement, court security, witness protection, prisoner transportation, and asset seizure and forfeiture activities. The Deputy Director for Administration is responsible for personnel management; procurement and property management; space, transportation, and communications; information systems; and the U.S. Marshals Service Training Academy.

For further information, contact the Office of Congressional and Public Affairs, U.S. Marshals Service, Department of Justice, Suite 1260, 600 Army Navy Drive, Arlington, VA 22202. Phone, 202-307-9065.

United States National Central Bureau-International Criminal Police Organization

Washington, DC 20530. Phone, 202-272-8383

The U.S. National Central Bureau (USNCB) represents the United States in INTERPOL, the International Criminal Police Organization. Also known as Interpol-Washington, the USNCB provides an essential communications link between the U.S. police community and their counterparts in the foreign member countries.

INTERPOL is an association of 154 countries dedicated to promoting mutual assistance among law enforcement authorities in the prevention and suppression of international crime. With no police force of its own, INTERPOL has no powers of arrest or search and seizure. Instead, INTERPOL serves as a channel of communication among the police of the member countries, and provides a forum for discussions, working group meetings, and symposia to enable police to focus on specific areas of criminal activity affecting their countries.

United States participation in INTERPOL began in 1938 by congressional authorization, designating the Attorney General as the official representative to the organization. INTERPOL operations were interrupted during World War II, but resumed in 1947.

The Attorney General officially designated the Secretary of the Treasury as the U.S. representative to INTERPOL in 1958, and the U.S. National Central Bureau was established within the Treasury Department in 1969. In 1977, an arrangement was effected between Justice and Treasury officials establishing dual authority in administering the USNCB. This Memorandum of Understanding designates the Attorney General as the permanent representative to INTERPOL and the Secretary of the Treasury as the alternate representative.

The Bureau operates through cooperative efforts with Federal, State, and local law enforcement agencies. New programs and initiatives, such as the State Liaison Program, the Airport/Seaport Program, and the Canadian Interface Project, broaden the scope of U.S. investigative resources to include the international community, thus forming an integral part of the United

States efforts to confront the problem of international crime.

Federal and State law enforcement agencies represented at the USNCB include the Federal Bureau of Investigation; U.S. Marshals Service; Drug Enforcement Administration; Immigration and Naturalization Service; Criminal Division, U.S. Customs Service; U.S. Secret Service; Internal Revenue Service; Bureau of Alcohol, Tobacco and Firearms; Office of the Comptroller of the Currency; Office of the Inspector General, Department of Agriculture; U.S. Postal Inspection Service; Bureau of Diplomatic Security, Department of State; Naval Investigative Service; and the Illinois State Police.

Under the State Liaison Program, States establish an office within their own law enforcement community to serve as liaison to the USNCB. International leads developed in criminal investigations being conducted by a State or local police entity can be pursued through their Liaison Office, and criminal investigative requests from abroad are funneled through the relevant State liaison office for action by the appropriate State or local agency. All 50 States now participate in the liaison program, which is currently coordinated by a representative from the Illinois State Police.

The USNCB has three sub-bureaus which serve to more effectively address the law enforcement needs of U.S. territories. The sub-bureaus are located in San Juan, Puerto Rico; Pago Pago, American Samoa; and the U.S. Virgin Islands.

For further information, contact the U.S. National Central Bureau-INTERPOL, Washington, DC 20530. Phone, 202–272–8383.

Immigration and Naturalization Service

425 I Street NW., Washington, DC 20536. Phone, 202–514–4316, 4330, or 4354

[For the Immigration and Naturalization Service statement of organization, see the *Code of Federal Regulations,* Title 8, Part 100]

The Immigration and Naturalization Service was created by act of March 3, 1891 (8 U.S.C. 1551 note), and its purpose and responsibilities were further specified by the Immigration and Nationality Act, as amended (8 U.S.C. 1101 note), which charges the Attorney General with the administration and enforcement of its provisions.

Unique to the Service is the dual mission of providing information and service to the general public, while concurrently exercising its enforcement responsibilities.

Its mission is divided into four major areas of responsibility:

—facilitating the entry of persons legally admissible as visitors or as immigrants to the United States;

—granting benefits under the Immigration and Nationality Act, as amended, including providing assistance to those seeking permanent resident status or naturalization;

—preventing unlawful entry, employment, or receipt of benefits by those who are not entitled to them; and

—apprehending or removing those aliens who enter or remain illegally in the United States and/or whose stay is not in the public interest.

The Service also has a firm commitment to strengthen criminal investigations and seek the most effective deterrents to illegal immigration.

The Attorney General has delegated authority to the Commissioner of the Immigration and Naturalization Service to carry out a national immigration policy that will administer and enforce the immigration laws and promote and protect the public health and safety, economic welfare, national security, and humanitarian interests of this country.

The Immigration Act of 1990 (8 U.S.C. 1101 note) represents a major overhaul of immigration law, amending the Immigration and Nationality Act. Changes include revisions to the numerical limits and preference system regulating immigration, administrative naturalization empowering the Attorney General to issue final determinations on applications for U.S. citizenship, and administering the oath of citizenship and issuing certificates of naturalization.

Immigration and Naturalization Service

Regional Office	Address
EASTERN—Connecticut, Delaware, District of Columbia, Maine, Maryland, Massachusetts, New Hampshire, New Jersey, New York, Pennsylvania, Puerto Rico, Rhode Island, Vermont, Virgin Islands, Virginia, West Virginia	Elmwood Ave., Burlington, VT 05401
NORTHERN—Alaska, Colorado, Idaho, Illinois, Iowa, Indiana, Kansas, Michigan, Minnesota, Missouri, Montana, Nebraska, North Dakota, Ohio, Oregon, South Dakota, Wisconsin, Washington, Wyoming, Utah	Federal Bldg., Fort Snelling, Twin Cities, MN 55111
SOUTHERN—Alabama, Arkansas, Florida, Georgia, Kentucky, Louisiana, Mississippi, New Mexico, North Carolina, Oklahoma, South Carolina, Tennessee, Texas	311 N. Stemmons Freeway, Dallas, TX 75207
WESTERN—Arizona, California, Guam, Hawaii, Nevada	24000 Avila Rd., Laguna Niguel, CA 92677-8080

District Office	Address
Anchorage, AK	629 E. 10th Ave., 99513
Atlanta, GA	Rm. G-85, 77 Forsyth St. SW., 30303
Baltimore, MD	101 W. Lombard St., 21201
Boston, MA	John F. Kennedy Federal Bldg., 02203
Buffalo, NY	68 Court St., 14202
Chicago, IL	219 S. Dearborn St., 60604
Cleveland, OH	Rm. 1917, 1240 E. 9th St., 44199
Dallas, TX	Rm. 6A21, 1100 Commerce St., 75242
Denver, CO	Albrook Ctr., 4730 Paris St., 80239
Detroit, MI	333 Mt. Elliott St., 48207
El Paso, TX	700 E. San Antonio, 79901
Harlingen, TX	2102 Teege Rd., 78550
Helena, MT	Rm. 512, 301 S. Park, 59626-0036
Honolulu, HI	595 Ala Moana Blvd., 96813
Houston, TX	509 N. Belt, 77060
Kansas City, MO	9747 N. Conant Ave., 64153
Los Angeles, CA	300 N. Los Angeles St., 90012
Miami, FL	7880 Biscayne Blvd., 33138
New Orleans, LA	Rm. T-8005, 701 Loyola Ave., 70113
New York, NY	26 Federal Plz., 10278
Newark, NJ	970 Broad St., 07102
Omaha, NE	Rm. 1008, 106 S. 15th St., 68102
Philadelphia, PA	1600 Callowhill St. 19103
Phoenix, AZ	230 N. 1st Ave., 85025
Portland, ME	739 Warren Ave., 04103
Portland, OR	511 NW. Broadway, 97209
San Antonio, TX	Suite A301, 727 E. Durango, 78206
San Diego, CA	880 Front St., 92188
San Francisco, CA	630 Sansome St., 94111
San Juan, PR	GPO Box 5068, 00936
St. Paul, MN	2901 Metro Dr., Bloomington, 55425
Seattle, WA	815 Airport Way S., 98134
Washington, DC	4420 N. Fairfax Dr., Arlington, VA 22203

District Office	Address
Bangkok, Thailand	District Director, U.S. Immigration and Naturalization Service, c/o American Embassy, Bangkok, Thailand, Box 12, APO San Francisco, CA 96346-0001
Mexico City, Mexico	District Director, Mexico City, U.S. Immigration and Naturalization Service, c/o American Embassy, Mexico City, Mexico, Room 118, P.O. Box 3087, Laredo, TX 78044
Rome, Italy	District Director, U.S. Immigration and Naturalization Service, c/o American Embassy, Rome, Italy, APO New York, NY 09794-0007

For further information, contact the Office of Information, Immigration and Naturalization Service, Department of Justice, 425 I Street NW., Washington, DC 20536. Phone, 202-514-4316, 4330, or 4354.

Drug Enforcement Administration

600-700 Army Navy Drive, Arlington, VA 22202. Phone, 202-307-1000; FTS, 367-1000

The Drug Enforcement Administration is the lead Federal agency in enforcing narcotics and controlled substances laws and regulations. It was created in July 1973, by Reorganization Plan No. 2 of 1973 (5 U.S.C. app.), which merged four separate drug law enforcement agencies.

The Administration's priority mission is the long-term immobilization of major trafficking organizations through the removal of the leaders and assets upon which these organizations depend.

Its primary responsibilities include:

—investigation of major narcotic violators who operate at interstate and international levels;

—enforcement of regulations governing the legal manufacture, distribution, and dispensing of controlled substances;

—management of a national narcotics intelligence system;

—coordination with Federal, State, and local law enforcement authorities and cooperation with counterpart agencies abroad; and

—training, scientific research, and information exchange in support of drug traffic prevention and control.

The Administration manages the El Paso Intelligence Center, a 24-hour tactical and strategic drug intelligence center that includes all 50 States and 9 other Federal agencies.

The agency concentrates its efforts on high-level narcotics smuggling and distribution organizations in the United States and abroad, working closely with such agencies as the Customs Service, the Internal Revenue Service, and the Coast Guard. It also chairs the 11-agency National Narcotics Intelligence Consumers Committee, which develops an annual report on drug production, trafficking, and abuse trends.

Nearly 300 Administration compliance investigators enforce regulation of the legal manufacture and distribution of prescription drugs. The agency also maintains an active training program for narcotics officers in other Federal, State, and local agencies—as well as foreign police.

The Administration has offices throughout the United States and in 48 foreign countries.

Field Divisions—Drug Enforcement Administration

Division/Address	Telephone
Atlanta, GA (75 Spring St. SW., 30303)	404-331-4401
Boston, MA (John F. Kennedy Federal Bldg., 02203)	617-565-2800
Chicago, IL (219 S. Dearborn St., 60604)	312-353-7875
Dallas, TX (1880 Regal Row, 75235)	214-767-7151
Denver, CO (316 U.S. Customs House, 80201)	303-844-3951
Detroit, MI (231 W. Lafayette, 48226)	313-226-7290
Houston, TX (333 W. Loop St., 77024)	713-681-1771
Los Angeles, CA (350 S. Figueroa St., 90071)	213-894-2650
Miami, FL (8400 NW. 53d St., 33166)	305-591-4870
Newark, NJ (970 Broad St., 07102)	201-645-6060
New Orleans, LA (1661 Canal St., 70112)	504-585-5500
New York, NY (555 W. 57th St., 10019)	212-399-5151
Philadelphia, PA (600 Arch St., 19106)	215-597-9530
Phoenix, AZ (3010 N. 2d St., 85012)	602-640-5700
San Diego, CA (402 W. 35th St., 92050)	619-585-4200
San Francisco, CA (450 Golden Gate Ave., 94102)	415-556-7214
Seattle, WA (220 W. Mercer, 98119)	206-553-5443
St. Louis, MO (7911 Forsyth Blvd., 61305)	314-425-3241
Washington, DC (400 6th St. SW., 20024)	202-401-7834

For further information, contact the Office of Public Affairs, Drug Enforcement Administration, Department of Justice, Washington, DC 20537. Phone, 202-307-7977.

Office of Justice Programs

633 Indiana Avenue NW., Washington, DC 20531. Phone, 202-307-0781

The Office of Justice Programs (OJP) was established by the Justice Assistance Act of 1984 and reauthorized in 1988 to serve as the principal Federal agency responsible for maximizing efficiency and effectiveness in the Nation's criminal justice system. The Office is a small agency with an important mission: identifying emerging criminal justice issues; developing and testing promising approaches to address these issues; evaluating program results, and disseminating these findings and other information to State and local governments.

The Office is headed by an Assistant Attorney General who, by statute and delegation of authority from the Attorney General, guides, promotes, and coordinates policy; focuses efforts on the priorities established by the President and the Attorney General; and promotes coordination among the five major bureaus or offices within OJP. These are: Bureau of Justice Assistance, Bureau of Justice Statistics, National Institute of Justice, Office of Juvenile Justice and Delinquency Prevention, and Office for Victims of Crime.

Through the programs developed and financed by its bureaus and offices, OJP works to form partnerships among Federal, State, and local government officials to control drug abuse and trafficking, improve the administration of justice in America, meet the needs of crime victims, and find innovative ways to address problems such as gang violence, prison crowding, juvenile crime, and white-collar crime. The functions of each bureau or office are interrelated. For example, the statistics generated by the Bureau of Justice Statistics may drive the research that is conducted through the National Institute of Justice and the Office of Juvenile Justice and Delinquency Prevention. Research results may generate new programs that receive support from the Bureau of Justice Assistance and the Office of Juvenile Justice and Delinquency Prevention.

Although some research and technical assistance is provided directly by OJP's bureaus and offices, most of the work is accomplished through Federal financial assistance to scholars, practitioners, and State and local governments.

Program bureaus and offices award formula grants to State agencies, which, in turn, subgrant funds to units of State and local government. Formula grant programs—drug control and system improvement, juvenile justice, victims compensation, and victims assistance—are administered by State agencies designated by each State's Governor. Discretionary grant programs usually are announced in the *Federal Register,* and applications are made directly to the sponsoring Office of Justice Programs bureau or office.

Bureau of Justice Assistance The Bureau provides financial and technical assistance to State and local units of government to control drug abuse, drug trafficking, and violent crime to improve the criminal justice system.

The Anti-Drug Abuse Act of 1988 (42 U.S.C. 3750), which established the Edward Byrne Memorial State and Local Law Enforcement Assistance Programs, authorizes the Bureau to make grants for the purpose of enforcing State and local laws that establish offenses similar to those established in the Controlled Substances Act and to improve the functioning of the criminal justice system, with emphasis on violent crime and serious offenders. The States are required to prepare a statewide anti-drug and violent crime strategy as part of their applications for Formula Grant funds. Federal funds from fiscal year 1990 and prior fiscal years may be used for up to 75 percent of the total project costs. Fiscal year 1991 and subsequent year appropriations may be used for up to 50 percent of the total project costs.

The Bureau uses the Discretionary Grant program to provide State and local criminal justice agencies with state-of-the-art information on innovative and effective programs, practices, and techniques through demonstration projects, training, and technical assistance. For example, the Bureau is demonstrating effective ways of depriving drug traffickers of the profit of their activities through the seizure and forfeiture of drug-related assets, financial investigations, the use of civil statutes, and the denial of Federal Benefits Programs. Criminal justice agencies are provided assistance in addressing new issues and problems, such as the spread of "crack" cocaine, disruption of clandestine laboratories, and drug testing of criminal offenders. The Bureau also supports programs that are national or multistate in scope, such as the National Crime Prevention (McGruff) Campaign. Discretionary Grant funds are awarded directly by the Bureau and do not require matching funds.

Direct assistance is also provided by the Bureau through programs such as the Public Safety Officers' Death Benefits Program, the Emergency Federal Law Enforcement Assistance Program, the Regional Information Sharing System, the Mariel Cuban Reimbursement Program, the Federal Surplus Property Transfer Program, and the Prison Industry Certification Program.

Bureau of Justice Statistics The Bureau is responsible for collecting, analyzing, publishing, and disseminating statistical information about crime, its perpetrators and victims, and the operation of justice systems at the Federal, State, and local levels of government.

The Bureau also assists State governments in developing capabilities in criminal justice statistics and improving their criminal justice records and information systems.

The Bureau provides the President, the Congress, other officials, and the public with timely and accurate data about crime and the administration of justice. The Bureau's *Report to the Nation on Crime and Justice* presents comprehensive statistical information about crime and the justice system in a format suitable for the general public. It publishes concise *Special Reports* and periodic *Bulletins* that provide up-to-date information about various aspects of criminal justice. In addition, lengthier volumes present detailed analyses of specific topics.

The National Crime Survey is the largest ongoing statistical series currently conducted by the Bureau. Using interviews from a large sample of U.S. households, the Survey measures the rates at which the Nation's population is victimized by crimes of violence and theft.

Other statistical series cover prison and jail inmates, probation and parole, adjudication, processing offenders as they move through the criminal justice system, criminal justice expenditure and employment, and the Federal justice system.

The Bureau supports a statistical component in the National Criminal Justice Reference Service. The Justice Statistics Clearinghouse provides reference services for people requesting information, maintains a mailing list, and distributes Bureau publications. The Bureau may be contacted on 800–732–3277 (toll-free).

The Bureau also manages the Drugs and Crime Data Center and Clearinghouse which gathers and evaluates existing data on drugs and the justice system; identifies drug enforcement data gaps; operates a clearinghouse/reference center that serves as a single source for those in need of drug statistics; and prepares special reports and tabulations of existing drug data. The Drugs and Crime Data Center and Clearinghouse may be contacted on 800–666–3332 (toll-free).

National Institute of Justice The Institute is the primary Federal sponsor of research on crime and its control and is a central resource for information on innovative approaches in criminal justice. As mandated by the Justice Assistance Act of 1984, as amended (42 U.S.C. 3711 note), the National Institute sponsors and conducts research, evaluates policies and practices, demonstrates promising new approaches, provides training and technical assistance, assesses new technology for criminal justice, and disseminates its findings to State and local practitioners and policymakers.

The Institute emphasizes policy-relevant research that responds to the practical needs of those in the criminal justice system. Working with State and local practitioners and researchers across the country, the Institute sponsors research efforts through grants and contracts that are carried out by universities, private institutions, and State and local agencies. In addition, it directs a small in-house research program to provide quick, reliable data on emerging policy issues.

The Institute studies a wide spectrum of issues, ranging from drug treatment and prevention to drug arrests and interdiction. The National Institute's research reports and demonstration projects range from prison construction and user accountability punishments to innovations in science and technology.

Recent advances produced by Institute research hold the potential for:

—reducing demand for drugs among criminals through court-supervised drug testing;

—reducing victimizations through new police deployment strategies that lower crime rates and strengthen links to the community;

—cutting drug-related robberies and burglaries through police strategies to stop street-level drug traffickers; and

—applying modern construction technologies to corrections construction that, depending on local conditions, may save between $30,000 and $40,000 per cell.

The Institute also operates an international information clearinghouse, the National Criminal Justice Reference Service. The Service maintains a computerized data base of more than 85,000 books, reports, articles, and audiovisual materials. Its information specialists answer queries on a wide range of subjects and facilitate the exchange of information among criminal justice practitioners and researchers. The Service may be contacted on 301–251–5500 (Maryland and District of Columbia residents only); or nationwide on 800–851–3420 (toll-free).

To bring research findings to the people who can put them to use, the Institute carries out an active communications program. Research results are published in a variety of formats—from summaries to detailed guides and reports.

Office of Juvenile Justice and Delinquency Prevention The Office was created by the Juvenile Justice and Delinquency Prevention Act of 1974 (42 U.S.C. 5601) in response to national concern about juvenile crime. It is the primary Federal agency for addressing juvenile crime and delinquency and the problem of missing and exploited children. The Office is comprised of five divisions.

The State Relations and Assistance Division oversees the formula grants program. States can receive formula grants to help implement delinquency prevention and system improvement programs, including the mandates of the Juvenile Justice and Delinquency Prevention Act, as amended. These mandates include deinstitutionalizing status offenders, separating juveniles from adult offenders in institutions, and removing juveniles from adult jails and lockups.

The Special Emphasis Division provides funds directly to public and private nonprofit agencies and individuals to foster new approaches to delinquency prevention and control and the improvement of the juvenile justice system. The Division focuses on such areas as chronic juvenile offenders, gangs and drug-related juvenile crime, school crime, and the victimization of children.

The Research and Program Development Division sponsors research about national trends in juvenile delinquency and drug use, serious juvenile crime, the causes of delinquency, prevention strategies, and the juvenile justice system.

The Training and Technical Assistance Division sponsors training for juvenile justice practitioners and provides technical assistance in planning, funding, establishing, operating, and evaluating juvenile delinquency programs. It also applies this research to developing and testing state-of-the-art programs.

The Information Dissemination Unit conducts a wide variety of information dissemination activities for the Office in support of its statutory mandate to serve as a clearinghouse and information center for the preparation, publication, and dissemination of information on juvenile delinquency and missing children. This Unit also monitors the operations of the Juvenile Justice Clearinghouse, which collects, stores, and disseminates the Office's and other juvenile justice-related publications. The toll-free telephone number is 1–800–638–8736.

Two programs—the Concentration of Federal Efforts Program and the Missing Children's Program—are also under the Office's direction. The Concentration of Federal Efforts Program coordinates Federal programs dealing with juvenile delinquency and assists Federal agencies that have responsibility for delinquency prevention and treatment. It also promotes interagency cooperation in eliminating duplicate efforts and provides direction for the use of Federal resources in facilitating a comprehensive, unified Federal juvenile justice policy.

The Missing Children's Program was created in 1984 by the Missing Children's Assistance Act to provide Federal leadership in ensuring that every practical step is taken in recovering missing children, reuniting them with their families, and prosecuting abductors. The Program serves as a central focus for research, data collection, policy development, and information about missing and exploited children. It also funds the National Center for Missing and Exploited Children, which operates a national toll-free telephone line and serves as a national information clearinghouse.

Office for Victims of Crime The Office for Victims of Crime (OVC) serves as the Federal focal point for addressing the needs and improving the treatment of crime victims. This includes carrying out the activities mandated by the Victims of Crime Act of 1984 (VOCA), as amended (42 U.S.C. 10601 note); monitoring compliance with the provisions regarding assistance for Federal crime victims of the Victim and Witness Protection Act of 1982; and implementing the recommendations of the President's Task Force on Victims of Crime, the Attorney General's Task Force on Family Violence, and the President's Child Safety Partnership.

The act (VOCA) created a Crime Victims Fund in the U.S. Treasury to provide Federal financial assistance to State governments to compensate and assist victims of crime. Monies in the fund come from fines and penalties assessed on convicted Federal defendants. The Office awards grants to States to compensate crime victims for expenses, such as medical costs, resulting from their victimization. Grants also are awarded to State governments to support State and local programs that provide direct assistance to crime victims and their families. Priority for victim assistance funds is given to programs providing direct services to victims of sexual assault, spouse abuse, and child abuse. States also must use grant funds to assist previously underserved victim populations, such as victims of drunk drivers or the families of homicide victims.

A small portion of the Crime Victims Fund is available to support services for victims of Federal crimes. Programs under this initiative have focused on developing victim assistance services for Federal crime victims in indian country, creating an emergency fund for use by U.S. Attorneys Offices to pay for emergency services for Federal crime victims, and assisting Native American child abuse victims.

In collaboration with other agencies and groups, OVC administers numerous projects serving the victims of drug-related crimes. The Office also supports national programs to improve and coordinate services to crime victims and sponsors conferences and training for criminal justice practitioners, medical and mental health personnel, the clergy, and others who work with crime victims and their families. The National Victims Resource Center, which provides information concerning victims issues to victims advocates, criminal justice practitioners, and the public, is funded by OVC. The Center may be reached on 800–627–6872 (toll-free).

For further information, contact the Office of Congressional and Public Affairs, Office of Justice Programs, Department of Justice, 633 Indiana Avenue NW., Washington, DC 20531. Phone, 202–307–0781.

Boards

Executive Office for Immigration Review

Falls Church, VA 22041

The Attorney General is responsible for the administration and enforcement of the Immigration and Nationality Act of 1952 (8 U.S.C. 1101) and all other laws relating to the immigration and naturalization of aliens. The Attorney General has delegated certain aspects of his power and authority for the administration and interpretation of the immigration laws to the Executive Office for Immigration Review. The Executive Office for Immigration Review is completely independent of the Immigration and Naturalization Service, the body charged with the enforcement of the immigration laws. It includes the Board of Immigration Appeals, the Office of the Chief Immigration Judge, and the Office of the Chief Administrative Hearing Officer. It operates under the supervision of the Deputy Attorney General and is headed by a Director, who is responsible for the immediate supervision of the Board of Immigration Appeals, the Office of the Chief Immigration Judge, and the Office of the Chief Administrative Hearing Officer.

Board of Immigration Appeals The Board of Immigration Appeals is a quasi-judicial body composed of a Chairman, four members, and a Chief Attorney-Examiner, who is also an alternate Board member.

Located in Falls Church, VA, the Board hears oral argument only in that location. The Board is authorized a staff of attorney-advisers who assist the Board in the preparation of decisions.

The Board has been given nationwide jurisdiction to hear appeals from decisions entered by district directors of the Immigration and Naturalization Service and by immigration judges. In addition, the Board, with approval of the Attorney General, is responsible for suspension or barring from practice before the Service and the Board any representatives and attorneys when the public interest so requires.

Decisions of the Board are binding on all Service officers and immigration judges unless modified or overruled by the Attorney General, and are subject to judicial review in the Federal courts. The majority of appeals reaching the Board involves orders of deportation and applications for relief from deportation. Other cases before the Board include the exclusion of aliens applying for admission to the United States, petitions to classify the status of alien relatives for the issuance of preference immigrant visas, fines imposed upon carriers for the violation of the immigration laws, and motions for reopening and reconsideration of decisions previously rendered.

Upon the filing of an appeal by either party or certification of a case by the immigration judge or district director, the record of proceedings is forwarded to the Board. Following a review of the record and research into questions of law raised by the parties, the attorney-adviser drafts a proposed order for consideration of the Board members. He or she frequently confers with individual Board members concerning the proposed order. Attorney-advisers also assist in various administrative and support functions. In addition to developing expertise in the field of immigration law, the attorney-adviser is often called upon to analyze questions of constitutional law, State, Federal, and foreign civil and criminal law and to resolve questions relating to conflicts of law.

Office of the Chief Immigration Judge The Office of the Chief Immigration Judge is responsible for the general supervision and direction of the immigration judges in the performance of their duties. It establishes operational policies for the offices of the immigration judges and evaluates the performance of those offices.

Located in Falls Church, VA, the Office of the Chief Immigration Judge includes a headquarters staff of management and legal personnel.

Office of the Immigration Judge The offices of the immigration judges are responsible for presiding at formal, quasi-judicial deportation and exclusion proceedings. The immigration judges act independently in their decisionmaking capacity, and their decisions are administratively final unless appealed or certified to the Board of Immigration Appeals.

In exclusion proceedings, an immigration judge determines whether an individual arriving from a foreign country should be allowed to enter the United States or should be excluded and deported. Located throughout the United States, each judge has jurisdiction to consider various forms of relief available in exclusion proceedings, including applications for asylum and relief under section 243(h) of the Immigration and Nationality Act of 1952 (8 U.S.C. 101).

In deportation proceedings, the immigration judge determines whether an individual who has already entered the

United States is deportable from this country. In such proceedings the judge also adjudicates applications for the various forms of relief available under this country's immigration laws. These include applications for adjustment of status, suspension of deportation, voluntary departure, relief under section 212(c) of the act (8 U.S.C. 1182), and applications for asylum and withholding of deportation.

Office of the Chief Administrative Hearing Officer The Office of the Chief Administrative Hearing Officer is responsible for the general supervision of administrative law judges in the performance of their duties under 8 U.S.C. 1324a and 1324b. Administrative law judge proceedings are mandated by the Immigration Reform and Control Act of 1986 and concern allegations of unlawful employment of aliens and unfair immigration-related employment discrimination.

For further information, contact the Executive Officer, Executive Office for Immigration Review, Department of Justice, Falls Church, VA 22041. Phone, 703–756–6171.

United States Parole Commission

5550 Friendship Boulevard, Chevy Chase, MD 20815. Phone, 301–492–5990

The granting, denying, or revocation of parole for eligible Federal offenders rests in the discretion of the U.S. Parole Commission. The Commission will be abolished on November 1, 1997, 10 years after the implementation of the U.S. Sentencing Guidelines. (The Comprehensive Crime Control Act of 1984 abolished the U.S. Parole Commission and instituted mandatory sentencing for all offenders whose crimes were committed after November 1, 1987.) The Commission is also responsible for the supervision of paroled or otherwise released offenders until expiration of their terms and may discharge parolees early from supervision. Under the Labor Management Reporting and Disclosure Act of 1959 (29 U.S.C. 401 note), the Commission determines whether or not persons convicted of certain crimes may serve as officials in the field of organized labor or in labor-oriented management positions; likewise, under the Employment Retirement Income and Security Act of 1974, the Commission determines whether or not such persons may provide services to or be employed by employment benefit plans.

The Parole Commission consists of nine members, appointed by the President with the advice and consent of the Senate. It has sole authority to grant, modify, or revoke paroles of eligible U.S. prisoners serving sentences of more than 1 year and D.C. Code prisoners housed in Federal institutions. It is responsible for the supervision of parolees and prisoners released upon the expiration of their sentences with allowances for statutory good time, and the determination of supervisory conditions and terms. U.S. probation officers supervise parolees and mandatory releasees under the direction of the Commission.

The Anti-Drug Abuse Act of 1988 gave the Commission jurisdiction over all foreign transfer treaty cases beginning January 1, 1989. For offenses committed after November 1, 1987, the Commission is to apply the guidelines of the U.S. Sentencing Commission.

Regional Offices—U.S. Parole Commission

Region/Address	Commissioner
NORTH CENTRAL—Suite 220, 10920 Ambassador Dr., Kansas City, MO 64153	Carol Pavilack Getty
NORTHEAST—7th Fl., U.S. Customs House, 2d and Chestnut Sts., Philadelphia, PA 19106	(Vacancy)
SOUTH CENTRAL—Suite 820, 525 Griffin St., Dallas, TX 75202	Victor M.F. Reyes
SOUTHEAST—Suite 250, 1718 Peachtree St. NW., Atlanta, GA 30309	(Vacancy)
WESTERN—4th Fl., 1301 Shoreway Rd., Belmont, CA 94002	(Vacancy)

For further information, contact the Office of the Chairman, United States Parole Commission, Department of Justice, 5550 Friendship Boulevard, Chevy Chase, MD 20815. Phone, 301–492–5990.

Foreign Claims Settlement Commission of the United States

The Foreign Claims Settlement Commission of the United States is a quasi-judicial, independent agency within the Department of Justice which adjudicates claims of U.S. nationals against foreign governments, either under specific jurisdiction conferred by Congress or pursuant to international claims settlement agreements. Funds for payment of the Commission's awards are variously derived from congressional appropriations, international claims settlements, or liquidation of foreign assets in the United States by the Departments of Justice and the Treasury.

The Commission was created under Reorganization Plan No. 1 of 1954 (5 U.S.C. app.), effective July 1, 1954, and was transferred to the Department of Justice as a separate agency within the Department (22 U.S.C. 1622a), effective October 1, 1980.

Claims Programs Under authority of the Iran Claims Settlement Act, the Commission conducts a program for adjudication of some 3,100 claims of U.S. nationals against Iran, valued at less than $250,000 per claim, for uncompensated nationalization or other taking of property by the Iranian revolutionary government which took power in 1979. These claims were settled by agreement between the United States and Iran at the U.S.-Iranian Claims Tribunal at The Hague, Netherlands, on May 13, 1990. In addition, the Commission continues to have authority under the War Claims Act of 1948, as amended, to receive, determine, and provide for the payment of any further claims that may be filed for maltreatment of U.S. servicemen and civilians held as prisoners of war or interned by a hostile force in Southeast Asia during the Vietnam conflict.

The Commission also furnishes technical assistance and advice to other Federal agencies and offices in planning new claims adjudication programs and negotiating international claims settlement agreements. In addition, the Commission has responsibility for maintaining records and responding to inquiries relating to the various claims programs it has conducted under the International Claims Settlement Act of 1949, as amended, involving the Governments of Yugoslavia, Panama, Poland, Bulgaria, Hungary, Romania, Italy, the Soviet Union, Czechoslovakia, Cuba, the German Democratic Republic (East Germany), the People's Republic of China, Vietnam, Ethiopia, and Egypt, as well as those authorized under the War Claims Act of 1948 and other statutes.

For further information, contact the Office of the Chairman, Foreign Claims Settlement Commission of the United States, Department of Justice, Room 10000, 601 D Street NW., Washington, DC 20579. Phone, 202–208–7730.

Sources of Information

Controlled Substances Act Registration Information about registration under the Controlled Substances Act may be obtained from the Registration Section of the Drug Enforcement Administration, P.O. Box 28083, Central Station, Washington, DC 20038. Phone, 202–307–7255.

Employment Attorneys' applications: Director, Office of Attorney Personnel Management, Department of Justice, Room 4311, Tenth Street and Constitution Avenue NW., Washington, DC 20530. Phone, 202–633–3396. Assistant U.S. attorney applicants should apply to individual U.S. attorneys.

Federal Bureau of Investigation: Director, Washington, DC 20535, or any of the field offices or resident agencies whose addresses are listed in the front of most local telephone directories.

Immigration and Naturalization Service: Central Office, 425 I Street NW., Washington, DC 20536 (phone, 202–633–2690); or any regional or district office.

Drug Enforcement Administration: regional offices, laboratories, or

Washington Headquarters Office of Personnel.

Bureau of Prisons: Central Office, 320 First Street NW., Washington, DC 20534 (phone, 202-307-3082); or any regional or field office.

Office of Justice Programs, 633 Indiana Avenue NW., Washington, DC 20531. Phone, 202-307-0730.

Foreign Claims Settlement Commission: Attorneys: Office of the Chief Counsel, Room 400, 1111 Twentieth Street NW., Washington, DC 20579 (phone, 202-653-5883); Other: Administrative Officer, Room 400, 1111 Twentieth Street NW., Washington, DC 20579 (phone, 202-653-6155).

Reading Rooms Located in Washington, DC, at: Bureau of Prisons, 320 First Street NW., 20534 (phone, 202-307-3029); Immigration and Naturalization Service, 425 I Street NW., 20536 (phone, 202-633-2761, 4316, or 4330); Foreign Claims Settlement Commission, 1111 Twentieth Street NW., 20579 (phone, 202-653-5883). Also at the U.S. Parole Commission, 5550 Friendship Boulevard, Chevy Chase, MD 20815 (phone, 202-492-5959); Board of Immigration Appeals, Suite 1609, 5203 Leesburg Pike, Falls Church, VA 22015 (phone, 202-756-6183); some of the Immigration and Naturalization Service district offices; the U.S. attorneys principal offices beginning on page 369; and the National Institute of Justice, 9th Floor, 633 Indiana Avenue NW., Washington, DC 20531 (phone, 202-307-5883).

Publications and Films

The *FBI Law Enforcement Bulletin* and *Uniform Crime Reports—Crime in the United States* are available from the Superintendent of Documents, Government Printing Office, Washington, DC 20402.

The Annual Report of the Attorney General of the United States is published each year by the Department of Justice, Washington, DC 20530.

Approximately nine textbooks on citizenship, consisting of teachers manuals and student textbooks at various reading levels, are distributed free to public schools for applicants for citizenship and are on sale to all others from the Superintendent of Documents, Government Printing Office, Washington, DC 20402. Public schools or organizations under the supervision of public schools which are entitled to free textbooks should make their requests to the appropriate Immigration and Naturalization Service Regional Office (see appropriate section of this manual for mailing addresses). For general information, call 202-514-3946.

Guidelines for Effective Human Relations Commissions, Annual Report of the Community Relations Service, What Is CRS, Conflict Resolution Program, and *Activities Relating to the Desegregation of Public Schools* are available upon request from the Public Information Office, Community Relations Service, Department of Justice, Washington, DC 20530.

A limited number of drug educational films are available, free of charge, to civic, educational, private, and religious groups.

A limited selection of pamphlets and brochures is available. The most widely requested publication is *Drugs of Abuse,* an identification manual intended for professional use. Single copies are free.

Copies of the Foreign Claims Settlement Commission's semiannual (through December 1966) and annual (from January 1967) reports to the Congress concerning its activities are available at the Commission in limited quantities.

Reference Service All five OJP bureaus support the National Criminal Justice Reference Service, a clearinghouse of information and publications concerning OJP programs and other information of interest to the criminal justice community. The Office's National Institute of Justice, which has supported the clearinghouse for almost 20 years, provides most of the funding for the National Criminal Justice Reference Service. Police, corrections agencies, courts, criminal justice planners, juvenile justice practitioners, community crime prevention groups, and others needing information for planning and problem solving in criminal justice can refer to this international information service specially designed to assist the justice community.

The National Criminal Justice Reference Service provides information from its computerized data base system free or at a minimal cost to users through a variety of products and services including the bimonthly *NIJ Reports,* which contains abstracts of significant additions to the data base and pertinent information and a Calendar of Events announcing upcoming training courses and conferences; selected hardcopy documents upon request; three types of data base search packages; various microfiche products; and referrals to other information sources. Under contracts with OJP bureaus, the National Criminal Justice Reference Service also operates the Drugs and Crime Data Center and Clearinghouse, the Bureau of Justice Assistance Clearinghouse, the Justice Statistics Clearinghouse, the Juvenile Justice Clearinghouse, the National Victims Resource Center, the AIDS Clearinghouse, and the Construction Information Exchange. All the Service's clearinghouses may be contacted on 800–851–3420 (toll-free); or in the Washington, DC, metropolitan area on 301–251–5500.

Organizations and individuals may register to receive information from the National Criminal Justice Reference Service by writing or calling NCJRS, Box 6000, Rockville, MD 20850.

Small Business Activities Contract information for small businesses can be obtained from the Office of Small and Disadvantaged Business Utilization, Department of Justice, Tenth Street and Pennsylvania Avenue NW., Washington, DC 20530. Phone, 202–724–6271.

For further information concerning the Department of Justice, contact the Office of Public Affairs, Department of Justice, Tenth Street and Constitution Avenue NW., Washington, DC 20530. Phone, 202–514–2007 (voice); 202–786–5731 (TDD).

DEPARTMENT OF LABOR

200 Constitution Avenue NW., Washington, DC 20210
Phone, 202–523–8165

SECRETARY OF LABOR	LYNN M. MARTIN
Chief of Staff	FRANCES C. MCNAUGHT
Confidential Assistant to the Secretary	DEBORAH S. DITTMAR
Director, Executive Secretariat	RUTH E. MORGENSTERN
Deputy Secretary	RODERICK DEARMENT
Associate Deputy Secretaries	MICHAEL K. WYATT
	LAURA GENERO
Director, Office of Small and Disadvantaged Business Utilization	WALTER C. TERRY
Executive Director, Administrative Appeals	ELIZABETH CULBRETH
Chief Administrative Law Judge	NAHUM LITT
Chief Administrative Appeals Judge, Benefits Review Board	BETTY ROBERTS STAGE
Chairman, Employees Compensation Appeals Board	MICHAEL J. WALSH
Chairman, Wage Appeals Board	CHARLES E. SHEARER, JR.
Director, DOL Academy	NANCY FLYNN
Director, Women's Bureau	ELSIE VARTANIAN
Deputy Director	(VACANCY)
Inspector General	JULIAN W. DE LA ROSA
Deputy Inspector General	(VACANCY)
Assistant Secretary for Public Affairs	DALE T. TATE
Solicitor	ROBERT P. DAVIS
Deputy Solicitor, National Operations	DAVID S. FORTNEY
Deputy Solicitor, Regional Operations	RONALD G. WHITING
Deputy Solicitor, Planning and Coordination	JUDITH E. KRAMER
Director, Office of Management	LYDIA G. LEEDS
Associate Solicitor, Employment and Training Legal Services	CHARLES D. RAYMOND
Associate Solicitor, Fair Labor Standards	MONICA GALLAGHER
Associate Solicitor, Legislation and Legal Counsel	ROBERT A. SHAPIRO
Associate Solicitor, Labor-Management Laws	JOHN F. DEPENBROCK
Associate Solicitor, Black Lung Benefits	DONALD S. SHIRE
Associate Solicitor, Employee Benefits	CAROL DEDEO
Associate Solicitor, Occupational Safety and Health	CYNTHIA ATTWOOD
Associate Solicitor, Civil Rights	JAMES D. HENRY
Associate Solicitor, Plan Benefits Security	MARC I. MACHIZ
Associate Solicitor, Mine Safety and Health	EDWARD P. CLAIR
Associate Solicitor, Special Appellate and Supreme Court Litigation	ALLEN H. FELDMAN
Assistant Secretary for Congressional and Intergovernmental Affairs	FRANCES C. MCNAUGHT
Deputy Assistant Secretary	VIRGINIA LAMP THOMAS

Deputy Under Secretary for International Affairs	SHELLYN G. MCCAFFREY
Associate Deputy Under Secretary for Policy and Programs	(VACANCY)
Associate Deputy Under Secretary for Planning	BERTON J. BRALEY, JR., *Acting*
Director, Office of Management, Administration and Planning	EDWARD V. BOND
Assistant Secretary for Policy	DEBRA R. BOWLAND, *Acting*
Deputy Assistant Secretaries	DEBRA R. BOWLAND
	ROLAND G. DROITSCH
Assistant Secretary for Administration and Management	THOMAS C. KOMAREK
Deputy Assistant Secretary	BETTY BOLDEN
Comptroller for the Department	WILLIAM R. REISE
Director, National Capital Service Center	THOMAS K. DELANEY
Director, Information Resources Management	JOHN DINNEEN
Director, Civil Rights	ANNABELLE T. LOCKHART
Director, Administrative and Procurement Programs	JANICE SAWYER
Director, Personnel Management	LARRY GOODWIN
Director, Office of Safety and Health	FREDERICK DRAYTON
Assistant Secretary for Veterans' Employment and Training	THOMAS E. COLLINS
Deputy Assistant Secretary	JOHN V. MEYERS
Assistant Secretary for Employment and Training	ROBERTS T. JONES
Deputy Assistant Secretaries	DAVID O. WILLIAMS
	CAROLYN GOLDING
	JOHN FLOREZ
Administrator, Office of Job Training Programs	DOLORES BATTLE
Administrator, Office of Strategic Planning and Policy Development	RAYMOND J. UHALDE
Administrator, Office of Regional Management	DONALD J. KULICK
Administrator, Office of Work-Based Learning	JAMES VAN ERDEN
Director, Public and Intergovernmental Affairs	BONNIE FRIEDMAN
Deputy Under Secretary for Labor-Management Relations and Cooperative Programs	H. CHARLES SPRING, *Acting*
Assistant Secretary, Pension and Welfare Benefits Administration	DAVID GEORGE BALL
Deputy Assistant Secretaries	ANN L. COMBS
	ALAN D. LEBOWITZ
Assistant Secretary for Employment Standards	S.D. WALKER, *Acting*
Deputy Assistant Secretary	(VACANCY)
Director, Office of Public Affairs	ROBERT A. CUCCIA
Administrator, Wage and Hour Division	JOHN R. FRASER, *Acting*
Director, Office of Federal Contract Compliance Programs	CARI M. DOMINGUEZ
Director, Office of Workers' Compensation Programs	LAWRENCE W. ROGERS
Director, Office of Management, Administration and Planning	RICHARD A. STAUFENBERGER

Director, Office of Policy Management and Analysis	JUNE M. ROBINSON
Assistant Secretary for Occupational Safety and Health	GERARD F. SCANNELL
Deputy Assistant Secretaries	ALAN C. MCMILLAN
	CINDY DOUGLASS
Director, Office of Information and Consumer Affairs	JAMES F. FOSTER
Director, Office of Special Management Programs	FRED HAWKINS
Director, Office of Construction and Engineering	CHARLES CULVER
Director, Office of Statistics	STEPHEN NEWELL
Director, Policy	ROY CLASON
Director, Administrative Programs	DAVID C. ZEIGLER
Director, Federal/State Operations	BRUCE HILLENBRAND
Director, Field Programs	LEO CAREY
Director, Technical Support	THOMAS SHEPICH
Director, Compliance Programs	PATRICIA CLARK
Director, Health Standards Programs	CHARLES ADKINS
Director, Safety Standards Programs	ROGER CLARK
Commissioner of Labor Statistics	JANET L. NORWOOD
Director, Quick Response Policy Surveys and Analysis	DEBORAH P. KLEIN
Deputy Commissioner for Administration and Internal Operations	WILLIAM G. BARRON
Assistant Commissioner for Technology and Survey Processing	CARL J. LOWE
Director for Survey Processing	JOHN D. SINKS
Director for Technology and Computing Services	ARNOLD BRESNICK
Assistant Commissioner for Administration	DANIEL J. LACEY
Director, Quality and Information Management	WILLIAM D. STEAD
Associate Commissioner for Employment and Unemployment Statistics	THOMAS J. PLEWES
Deputy Associate Commissioner for Employment and Unemployment Statistics	(VACANCY)
Assistant Commissioner for Federal/State Programs	MARTIN ZIEGLER
Assistant Commissioner for Current Employment Analysis	JOHN E. BREGGER
Associate Commissioner for Prices and Living Conditions	KENNETH V. DALTON
Deputy Associate Commissioner for Prices and Living Conditions	(VACANCY)
Assistant Commissioner for Consumer Prices and Price Indexes	PAUL ARMKNECHT
Assistant Commissioner for Producer Prices and Price Indexes	THOMAS R. TIBBETTS
Assistant Commissioner for International Prices	KATRINA W. REUT
Associate Commissioner for Compensation and Working Conditions	GEORGE L. STELLUTO

Deputy Associate Commissioner for Compensation and Working Conditions	(VACANCY)
Assistant Commissioner for Safety, Health, and Working Conditions	WILLIAM E. EISENBERG
Assistant Commissioner for Compensation Levels and Trends	KATHLEEN MACDONALD
Associate Commissioner for Productivity and Technology	EDWIN R. DEAN
Associate Commissioner for Employment Projections	RONALD E. KUTSCHER
Associate Commissioner for Publications	DEBORAH P. KLEIN, *Acting*
Associate Commissioner for Field Operations	LAURA B. KING
Associate Commissioner for Research and Evaluation	WESLEY L. SCHAIBLE
Assistant Commissioner for Survey Methods Research	CATHRYN S. DIPPO
Assistant Commissioner for Economic Research	MARILYN E. MANSER
Assistant Secretary for Mine Safety and Health	WILLIAM J. TATTERSALL
Deputy Assistant Secretary for Policy	JOHN B. HOWERTON
Deputy Assistant Secretary for Operations	(VACANCY)
Administrator for Coal Mine Safety and Health	(VACANCY)
Administrator for Metal and Nonmetal Mine Safety and Health	MARVIN W. NICHOLS, JR.
Director of Technical Support	MADISON MCCULLOCH
Director of Educational Policy and Development	RICHARD L. BRECHBIEL
Director, Office of Standards, Regulations and Variances	PATRICIA W. SILVEY
Director, Office of Assessments	RICHARD G. HIGH, JR.
Director of Administration and Management	RUSSELL B. SWANSON
Director of Program Policy Evaluation	GEORGE M. FESAK, JR.
Director, Office of Information and Public Affairs	WAYNE E. VENEMAN
Chief, Office of Congressional and Legislative Affairs	(VACANCY)
Legislative Affairs Specialist	SYLVIA MILANESE
Assistant Secretary, Office of Labor-Management Standards	ROBERT M. GUTTMAN
Deputy Assistant Secretary	MARIO A. LAURO, JR., *Acting*
Director, Field Operations	MARIO A. LAURO, JR.
Director, Office of Elections, Trusteeships and International Union Audits	RICHARD G. HUNSUCKER
Director, Office of Program and Policy Support	JOHN KOTCH
Director, Office of Administration and Human Resources	JOSEPH T. O'NEILL

The purpose of the Department of Labor is to foster, promote, and develop the welfare of the wage earners of the United States, to improve their working conditions, and to advance their opportunities for profitable employment. In

DEPARTMENT OF LABOR

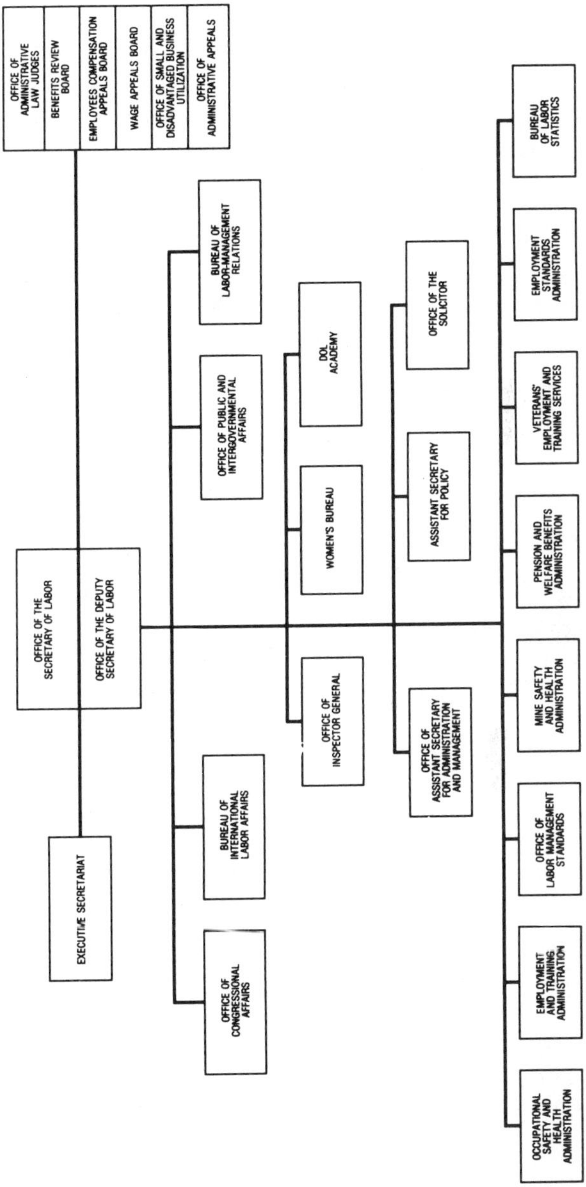

carrying out this mission, the Department administers a variety of Federal labor laws guaranteeing workers' rights to safe and healthful working conditions, a minimum hourly wage and overtime pay, freedom from employment discrimination, unemployment insurance, and workers' compensation. The Department also protects workers' pension rights; provides for job training programs; helps workers find jobs; works to strengthen free collective bargaining; and keeps track of changes in employment, prices, and other national economic measurements. As the Department seeks to assist all Americans who need and want to work, special efforts are made to meet the unique job market problems of older workers, youths, minority group members, women, the handicapped, and other groups.

The Department of Labor (DOL), ninth executive department, was created by act of March 4, 1913 (29 U.S.C. 551). A Bureau of Labor was first created by Congress in 1884 under the Interior Department. The Bureau of Labor later became independent as a Department of Labor without executive rank. It again returned to bureau status in the Department of Commerce and Labor, which was created by act of February 14, 1903 (15 U.S.C. 1501).

Office of the Secretary of Labor

Secretary The Secretary is the head of the Department of Labor and the principal adviser to the President on the development and execution of policies and the administration and enforcement of laws relating to wage earners, their working conditions, and their employment opportunities.

Inspector General The Office of Inspector General is responsible for providing comprehensive, independent, and objective audit and investigation programs to identify and report program deficiencies and improve the economy, efficiency, and effectiveness of operations. The Office also is responsible for ensuring employee and program integrity through prevention and detection of criminal activity, unethical conduct, and program fraud and abuse. The Office provides for departmental participation in investigations under the Department of Justice's Organized Crime Strike Force Program.

The Office also maintains a toll-free hotline telephone for complaints of fraud, waste, and abuse of Department resources. The number is 800–424–5409, or 202–357–0227 in the Washington, DC, metropolitan area.

Regional Offices—Office of Inspector General

(Areas included within each region are indicated on the map in Appendix A.)

Region/Address	Office of Audit	Office of Investigations
I, II. New York, NY (Rm. 877, 201 Varick St., 10014–4811)	212–337–2566	212–337–2300
III. Philadelphia, PA (Rm. 12100, 3535 Market St., 19104)	215–596–4024	215–596–4758
IV. Atlanta, GA (Rm. 231, 1371 Peachtree St. NE., 30367)	404–347–3256	404–347–3324
V, VII. Chicago, IL (Rm. 756, 230 S. Dearborn St., 60604)	312–353–2416	312–353–0509
VI, VIII. Dallas, TX (Rm. 414, 525 Griffin St., 75202)	214–767–6981	214–767–2925
IX, X. San Francisco, CA (Suite 700, 71 Stevenson St., 94105)	415–744–6664	415–744–6665

Office of Labor Racketeering

Field Office/Address	Telephone
Atlanta, GA (75 Spring St. SW., 30303)	404–331–7058
Chicago, IL (230 S. Dearborn St., 60604)	312–353–3164
Cleveland, OH (1621 Euclid Ave., 44115)	216–522–7373
Detroit, MI (231 W. Lafayette St., 48226)	313–226–3100
Kansas City, MO (Rm. 2505, 911 Walnut St., 64106)	816–426–5991
Miami, FL (P.O. Box 52–4143, 33152)	305–526–2530

Regional Offices—Office of Inspector General—Continued

Office of Labor Racketeering—Continued

Field Office/Address	Telephone
New York, NY (Rm. 849, 201 Varick St., 10014)	212-337-2550
Newark, NJ (970 Broad St., 07102)	201-645-3976
Newburgh, NY (Stewart Airport, Bldg. 702, D St., 12552-0154)	914-567-1941
Philadelphia, PA (615 Chestnut St., 19106)	215-597-3947
San Diego, CA (610 W. Ash St., 92131)	619-557-6870
San Francisco, CA (71 Stevenson St., 94105)	415-744-7078
Waltham, MA (Bldg. 138, W. 424 Trapelo Rd., 02154)	617-647-8888

Information and Public Affairs The Office of Information and Public Affairs is responsible for providing the Department with a comprehensive information program designed to inform the public about the Department's policies, programs, and actions. It plans, directs, coordinates, and carries out information activities to ensure that all Americans can have access to Department programs that affect them. The Assistant Secretary for Public Affairs advises the Secretary and other Department executives on information and public affairs matters. Regional Directors for Public Affairs in all 10 Federal regions conduct informational activities to inform the public in their regions.

Regional Information and Public Affairs Offices

(Areas included within each region are indicated on the map in Appendix A.)

Region/Address	Information Director
1. Boston, MA (John F. Kennedy Federal Bldg., 02203)	John Chavez
2. New York, NY (201 Varick St., 10014)	Chester Fultz
3. Philadelphia, PA (3535 Market St., 19104)	Jack Hord
4. Atlanta, GA (1371 Peachtree St., 30309)	Dan Fuqua
5. Chicago, IL (230 S. Dearborn St., 60604)	John Mellott
6. Dallas, TX (525 Griffin St., 75202)	Sherrie Moran
7. Kansas City, MO (911 Walnut St., 64106)	Patrick Hand
8. Denver, CO (1961 Stout St., 80294)	Ernest Sanchez
9. San Francisco, CA (71 Stevenson St., 94105)	Joe Kirkbride
10. Seattle, WA (1111 3d Ave. Bldg., 98101)	Mike Shimizu

Women's Bureau

The Women's Bureau is responsible for formulating standards and policies that promote the welfare of wage earning women, improve their working conditions, increase their efficiency, and advance their opportunities for profitable employment.

Regional Offices—Women's Bureau

(Areas included within each region are indicated on the map in Appendix A.)

Region/Address	Administrator
I. Boston, MA (1 Congress St., 02114)	Martha Izzi
II. New York, NY (201 Varick St., 10014)	Mary Murphree
III. Philadelphia, PA (3535 Market St., 19104)	Helen E. Sherwood
IV. Atlanta, GA (1371 Peachtree St. NE., 30367)	Delores L. Crockett
V. Chicago, IL (230 S. Dearborn St., 60604)	Sandra K. Frank
VI. Dallas, TX (525 Griffin Sq., 75202)	Evelyn F. Smith
VII. Kansas City, MO (911 Walnut St., 64106)	Rose A. Kemp
VIII. Denver, CO (1961 Stout St., 80294)	Oleta Crain
IX. San Francisco, CA (71 Stevenson St., 94105)	Madeline Mixer
X. Seattle, WA (111 3d Ave., 98101)	Lazelle S. Johnson

For further information, call 202-523-6611.

Office of the Deputy Secretary of Labor

Deputy Secretary The Deputy Secretary of Labor is the principal adviser to the Secretary. He serves as Acting Secretary in the Secretary's absence.

Employees' Compensation Appeals The Employees' Compensation Appeals Board consists of three members and three alternate members appointed by the Secretary of Labor, one of whom is designated as Chairman. The function of the Board is to consider and decide appeals from final decisions in cases arising under the Federal Employees' Compensation Act (5 U.S.C. 8101). The decisions of the Board are final and not subject to court review.

For further information, call 202–401–8600.

Administrative Appeals The Office of Administrative Appeals assists the Secretary, Deputy Secretary, and Assistant Secretary for Employment Standards in reviewing appeals from decisions of Administrative Law Judges under certain laws and programs. These appeals arise under the Service Contract Act, the Comprehensive Employment and Training Act, the Job Training Partnership Act, the Trade Act, the Surface Transportation Assistance Act, the Energy Reorganization Act, and several environmental laws, unemployment insurance conformity proceedings and cases brought by the Office of Federal Contract Compliance Programs.

For further information, contact the Director, Office of Administrative Appeals. Phone, 202–523–9728.

Office of Small and Disadvantaged Business Utilization This Office, under the direction of the Deputy Secretary of Labor, administers Department responsibilities under the Small Business Act (15 U.S.C. 631). The Director aids, counsels, and assists small businesses; ensures that small businesses, small disadvantaged businesses, and women-owned small businesses obtain a fair share of the Department's procurements; conducts surveillance reviews of Department contracting activities' small business programs; establishes and reviews departmental small business policies, procedures, and initiatives; manages the Department's Labor Surplus Area program; manages the Historically Black Colleges and Universities program; and develops and reviews legislative initiatives.

For further information, call 202–523–9148.

Office of Administrative Law Judges Administrative law judges preside over formal hearings to determine violations of minimum wage requirements, overtime payments, compensation benefits, employee discrimination, grant performance, alien certification, employee protection, and health and safety regulations set forth under numerous statutes, Executive orders, and regulations. With few exceptions, hearings are required to be conducted in accordance with the Administrative Procedure Act (5 U.S.C. note prec. 551).

For further information, contact the Administrative Officer. Phone, 202–653–5052.

Benefits Review The Benefits Review Board is a nine-member quasi-judicial body with exclusive jurisdiction to consider and decide appeals raising substantial questions of law or fact from decisions of Administrative Law Judges with respect to cases arising under the Longshoremen's and Harbor Workers' Compensation Act (33 U.S.C. 901) and its extensions and the Black Lung Benefits Act of 1972 (30 U.S.C. 801). The Board exercises the same review authority that the United States District Courts formerly held in these areas of the law prior to the 1972 amendments to both acts.

For further information, contact the Administrative Officer. Phone, 202–653–5060.

Wage Appeals The Wage Appeals Board acts on behalf of the Secretary of Labor in deciding appeals on questions of law and fact, taken in the discretion of the Board from wage determinations issued under the Davis-Bacon Act and its related prevailing wage statutes; debarments under the Department's regulations (29 CFR Part 5), which implement Reorganization Plan No. 14 of

1950 (5 U.S.C. app.); under the Department's regulations, part 5, disputes concerning the payment of prevailing wage rates or proper classifications that involve significant sums of money, large groups of employees, or novel or unusual situations; questions relating to coverage of the various acts; and recommendations by Federal agencies for appropriate adjustments of liquidated damages that are assessed under the Contract Work Hours and Safety Standards Act.

For further information, contact the Executive Secretary. Phone, 202-523-9039.

Department of Labor Academy The DOL Academy provides training and career development to DOL employees nationwide to enable them to perform at peak levels in their current jobs and to develop skills needed in the future. The Director of the DOL Academy reports to a Board of Governors chaired by the Deputy Secretary of Labor. The DOL Academy receives advice and policy oversight from the Board of Governors on Department of Labor training programs.

For further information, contact the Director, Department of Labor Academy. Phone, 202-523-7401.

The Solicitor of Labor

The Office of the Solicitor (SOL) provides the Secretary of Labor and departmental officials with the legal services required to accomplish the mission of the Department of Labor and the priority goals established by the Secretary. Through attorney staff in Washington and 16 field offices, the Solicitor directs a broad-scale litigation effort in the Federal courts pertaining to the statutes administered by the Department, including institution and prosecution of Civil Court actions under the Fair Labor Standards Act, the Employment Retirement Income Security Act of 1971, and the Migrant Seasonal Agricultural Worker Protection Act. The attorney staff also represents the Department in hearings under various laws including the Occupational Safety and Health Act of 1970, the Black Lung Benefits Reform Act, Federal Mine Safety and Health Act of 1977, and various Government contract labor standards laws. Appellate litigation is conducted by attorneys in the national headquarters, and trial litigation is carried out by attorneys under the direction of regional solicitors.

The Solicitor of Labor also coordinates the Department's legislative program; prepares testimony and reports on proposed legislation; provides legal advice to interagency groups responsible for U.S. trade matters; participates in international organizations including the International Labor Organization; reviews rules, orders, and regulations; and provides oral and written interpretations and opinions to client agencies and the public to clarify Department responsibilites.

For further information, contact the Office of Management, Office of the Solicitor, Department of Labor, 200 Constitution Avenue NW., Washington, DC 20210. Phone, 202-523-6863.

Regional Offices—Office of the Solicitor

(RS: Regional Solicitor; ARS: Associate Regional Solicitor)

Region	Address	Solicitor
1. Connecticut, Maine, Massachusetts, New Hampshire, Rhode Island, Vermont	1 Congress St., Boston, MA 02114	Albert H. Ross (RS)
2. New Jersey, New York, Puerto Rico, Virgin Islands	201 Varick St., New York, NY 10014	Patricia M. Rodenhausen (RS)
3. Delaware, District of Columbia, Maryland, Pennsylvania, Virginia, West Virginia	3535 Market St., Philadelphia, PA 19104	Marshall H. Harris (RS)
Branch Office	Rm. 516, 4015 Wilson Blvd., Arlington, VA 22203	James B. Leonard (ARS)
4. Alabama, Florida, Georgia, Kentucky, Mississippi, North Carolina, South Carolina, Tennessee	1371 Peachtree St. NE., Atlanta, GA 30367	Bobbye D. Spear (RS)

Regional Offices—Office of the Solicitor—Continued

(RS: Regional Solicitor; ARS: Associate Regional Solicitor)

Region	Address	Solicitor
Branch Offices	2015 2d Ave. N., Birmingham, AL 35203	George D. Palmer (ARS)
	2002 Richard Jones Rd., Nashville, TN 37215	Carl W. Gerig, Jr. (ARS)
	299 E. Broward Blvd., Ft. Lauderdale, FL 33301	Donald R. McCoy (ARS)
5. Illinois, Indiana, Michigan, Minnesota, Ohio, Wisconsin	230 S. Dearborn St., Chicago, IL 60604	John H. Secaras (RS)
Branch Office	1240 E. 9th St., Cleveland, OH 44199	William S. Kloepfer (ARS)
6. Arkansas, Louisiana, New Mexico, Oklahoma, Texas	525 S. Griffin St., Dallas, TX 75202	James E. White (RS)
7. Colorado, Iowa, Kansas, Missouri, Montana, Nebraska, North Dakota, South Dakota, Utah, Wyoming	911 Walnut St., Kansas City, MO 64106	Tedrick A. Housh (RS)
Branch Office	1961 Stout St., Denver, CO 80294	Henry C. Mahlman (ARS)
8. Alaska, Arizona, California, Hawaii, Idaho, Nevada, Oregon, Washington	71 Stevenson St., San Francisco, CA 94119	Daniel W. Teehan (RS)
Branch Offices	300 N. Los Angeles St., Los Angeles, CA 90012	John C. Nangle (ARS)
	1111 3d Ave., Seattle, WA 98101	Robert A. Friel (ARS)

Administration and Management

The Assistant Secretary for Administration and Management has responsibility for administrative policy; centralized management staff support and services to the Department's agencies in the areas of financial, organization, and personnel management; program review; labor-management relations; automated data processing systems development and services; administrative services; and equal employment opportunity.

Policy

The Assistant Secretary for Policy is responsible for coordinating and providing leadership to the Department's activities in economic policy issues, both short- and long-term program evaluation and economic research, bearing on the welfare of all American workers.

International Affairs

The Bureau of International Labor Affairs carries out the Department's international responsibilities under the direction of the Deputy Under Secretary for International Affairs, and assists in formulating international economic, trade, and immigration policies affecting American workers.

The Bureau represents the United States on delegations to multilateral and bilateral trade negotiations and on such international bodies as the General Agreement on Tariffs and Trade (GATT), the International Labor Organization (ILO), the Organization for Economic Cooperation Development, and other U.N. organizations. It also helps administer the U.S. labor attaché program at embassies abroad; carries out overseas technical assistance projects; monitors internationally recognized worker rights; and conducts labor study programs for foreign visitors to the United States.

The Deputy Under Secretary, a Presidential appointee, serves as Permanent Representative to the ILO governing body and as head of the tripartite U.S. delegation to the annual ILO June conference. During this period, the Deputy Under Secretary holds the rank of Ambassador. The Department of Labor is the lead agency on ILO matters in cooperation with the Departments of State and Commerce. The AFL–CIO represents American workers, and American employers are represented by the the U.S. Council for International Business. The President's Committee on the ILO, a Federal advisory committee chaired by the Secretary of Labor, was established to formulate and coordinate U.S. policy towards the ILO in order to promote continued reform and progress in that organization. Its other members are the Secretaries of State and Commerce, the Assistant to the President for National Security Affairs, and the

Presidents of the AFL–CIO and the U.S. Council for International Business. The Deputy Under Secretary serves as Counselor to the Committee, and the Bureau provides the necessary support for it.

Employment and Training Administration

The Employment and Training Administration, through a variety of programs, fulfills responsibilities assigned to the Secretary of Labor that relate to employment services, job training, and unemployment insurance. Component offices and services of the Administration administer a Federal-State employment security system; fund and oversee programs to provide work experience and training for groups having difficulty entering or returning to the work force; formulate and promote apprenticeship standards and programs; and conduct continuing programs of research, development, and evaluation.

The Assistant Secretary for Employment and Training directs the administration of agency programs and is responsible for ensuring that programs funded through the agency are free from unlawful discrimination, fraud, and abuse, and that they comply with constitutional, statutory, and regulatory provisions. It is the policy of the Administration to promote equal opportunity, affirmative action, and integrity in programs to which the Administration extends financial assistance.

The Administration has five major components that cover employment security, job training, planning and policy development, financial and administrative management, and regional management.

Federal Unemployment Insurance Service The Federal-State Unemployment Compensation Program, under provisions of the Social Security Act of 1935 (42 U.S.C. 1305), is the basic program of income support for the Nation's unemployed workers. With limited Federal intervention, unemployment insurance benefits are payable under laws of individual States. The Federal Unemployment Insurance Service provides leadership and policy guidance to State employment security agencies for the development, improvement, and operation of the Federal-State unemployment insurance system and of related wage-loss, worker dislocation, and adjustment assistance compensation programs, including to ex-service personnel and Federal civilian workers, and supplemental or extended benefits programs.

The Service reviews State unemployment insurance laws and their administration by the States to determine whether they are in conformity with Federal requirements; supervises the development of programs and methods for benefit, adjudication, appeals, tax collection, and trust fund management activities implemented by the State agencies; oversees the actuarial soundness of the level and relationship of State expenditures, revenues, and reserves, and of Federal appropriations for payment of benefits; and is implementing a quality control program to provide a diagnostic tool for States to identify and correct errors in benefit payments and tax collections and to raise program quality and integrity.

The Service also provides national leadership and direction in implementing its responsibilities under trade adjustment assistance, redwood park expansion, airline deregulation, and disaster unemployment assistance legislation.

For further information, call 202–535–0600.

United States Employment Service The Service, under the provisions of the Wagner-Peyser Act (29 U.S.C. 49 *et seq.*), provides assistance to States in establishing and maintaining a system of local public employment offices in the States and territories and interstate clearance of Labor. The State public employment service is responsible for providing unemployed individuals and

290-950 O 91 - 14

other jobseekers with job placement and other employment services and for providing employers with recruitment services and referrals of job-seeking applicants.

The Service administers the Work Incentive (WIN) program, which was authorized by the Social Security Amendments of 1967 (42 U.S.C. 1305 note) and 1971 (85 Stat. 802). WIN is jointly administered by the Departments of Labor and Health and Human Services and is designed to help persons receiving Aid to Families with Dependent Children (AFDC) become self-supporting.

The Service, through the State public employment service system, also provides subsidiary services which include:

—certifying aliens who seek to enter the United States for permanent employment as immigrants or as temporary workers;

—providing specialized recruitment assistance to employers;

—determining classifications of labor surplus area annually and for exceptional circumstance petitions;

—providing labor surplus area information to the general public and to other Federal or State agencies to meet various program responsibilities;

—disseminating labor market information;

—providing individuals with guidance, counseling, testing referral, and job opportunities;

—reviewing rural industrialization loan and grant certification applications under the Rural Development Act of 1972 (7 U.S.C. 1921);

—distributing airline job opening information for rehiring under the Airline Deregulation Act (49 U.S.C. app. 1301); and

—providing supportive services to employers and applicants through the Federal bonding program.

For further information, call 202–535–0157.

Office of Work-Based Learning The Office administers activities under several Federal laws regarding worker training and retraining. These include the dislocated worker program under the Economic Dislocation and Worker Adjustment Assistance Act (EDWAA) (Title III of the Job Training Partnership Act (JTPA)); Federal activities under the Worker Adjustment and Retraining Notification Act (WARN); Federal activities under the Apprenticeship Act; and the Trade Adjustment Assistance Program under the Trade Act. In addition, the Office carries out research and demonstration programs.

For further information, call 202–535–0540.

Office of Worker Retraining and Adjustment Programs The Office performs dislocated worker programs functions under the the Economic Dislocation and Worker Adjustment Assistance Act (Title III of JTPA), and Federal activities under the Worker Adjustment and Retraining Notification Act.

For further information, call 202–535–0525.

Office of Trade Adjustment Assistance The Office administers the Trade Adjustment Assistance program provisions of the Trade Act of 1974, as amended (19 U.S.C. 2101 *et seq.*), through agreements with the States. The program provides reemployment services such as training, job search and relocation allowances, and weekly cash payments to U.S. workers who are separated from employment because of foreign imports.

The Office receives petitions for adjustment assistance from either adversely affected workers, a duly recognized union, or an authorized representative of the workers and conducts factfinding investigations to develop necessary data on which certification determinations can be based. Determinations may involve approval, denial, or termination of worker groups' eligibility for trade adjustment assistance benefits.

The Office develops policies and prepares program directives to regional offices and State agencies on the administration and funding of reemployment services, and develops and maintains a system for allocating funds to those offices and agencies for reemployment services. It also directs and conducts industry studies of the number of workers in a domestic industry likely to be certified as eligible for adjustment assistance and of the extent to which existing training and employment programs may facilitate the workers' adjustment to import competition when an industry petitions the Federal Government that it is being injured because of import competition.

For further information, call 202-523-0555.

Bureau of Apprenticeship and Training The National Apprenticeship Act (29 U.S.C. 50) was passed in 1937 to enable the Department of Labor to formulate and promote the furtherance of labor standards necessary to safeguard the welfare of apprentices and cooperate with the States in the promotion of such standards and to bring together employers and labor for the formulation of programs of apprenticeship.

Sponsors and potential sponsors are encouraged and assisted in the development, expansion, and improvement of apprenticeship and other forms of allied industrial training. Technical information on training methods, public training facilities, and successfully executed systems are made available to industry. Through field representatives in States, the Bureau works closely with employers, labor unions, vocational schools, community planning groups, and others concerned with apprenticeship.

Programs must meet standards established by the Bureau or a recognized State Apprenticeship Council to be registered. Field compliance reviews are conducted to determine conformity with Federal equal employment opportunity and other standards for apprenticeship and training.

For further information, call 202-535-0540.

Job Training Partnership Act

The Office of Job Training Programs is responsible for the development and issuance of Federal procedures and policies pertaining to the operation of the Job Training Partnership Act (29 U.S.C. 1501 note) programs.

Under the act, the Secretary of Labor makes block grants to the 50 States, Guam, the Virgin Islands, Puerto Rico, the Commonwealth of the Northern Marianas, American Samoa, Republic of the Marshall Islands, Republic of Palau, Federated States of Micronesia, and the District of Columbia.

The goal of the act is to train or retrain and place eligible individuals in permanent, unsubsidized employment, preferably in the private sector. Eligible individuals are primarily economically disadvantaged individuals, in particular economically disadvantaged youth, dislocated workers, and others who face significant barriers to employment. The act also provides that a fixed percentage of the block grant be used for programs for older individuals.

The Job Training Partnership Act may be used for a variety of purposes including classroom instruction in occupational skills and other job-related training; on-the-job training; recruitment; orientation; counseling; testing; and placements and supportive services. In addition to the block grants, the act provides for national programs for special target groups such as Native Americans and migrant and seasonal farmworkers. It also provides authority for the Job Corps, a residential training program for disadvantaged youth.

The act is open-ended legislation and was signed into law on October 13, 1982. Implementing regulations for the act issued by the Department of Labor are contained in title 20 of the *Code of Federal Regulations,* Parts 626–636 and 675–684.

For further information, call 202-535-0236.

Senior Community Service Employment Program Authorized by title V of the Older Americans Act (42 U.S.C. 3056), the program makes subsidized, part-time job opportunities in community service activities available to low-income persons aged 55 and above. Project grants are made to national-level public and private nonprofit agencies and to units of State government. The distribution of funds among the States is governed by a statutory apportionment formula.

For further information, call 202–535–0500.

Planning and Policy Development

The Office of Strategic Planning and Policy Development formulates and recommends Administration policies, plans, and resource allocations; develops and maintains strategic and operational planning systems, and regulatory tracking system; develops and reviews legislative proposals relating to employment and training initiatives; administers the research, demonstration, and evaluation program; and develops and implements a nationwide system of legislatively mandated performance standards and program review and assessment procedures.

For further information, call 202–535–0662.

Financial and Administrative Management

Financial and Administrative Management is provided to the Employment and Training Administration through the Office of the Comptroller, the Office of Information Resources Management, the Office of Grants and Contract Management, and the Office of Management Support.

The Office of the Comptroller provides leadership and direction to ensure sound management of financial resources throughout the Employment and Training Administration; provides budget, accounting, and data analysis services for the agency; and plans, develops, promulgates, and executes policies, standards, and guidelines governing management information, budget, accounting, and financial procurement systems.

The Office of Information Resources Management plans, develops, implements, and operates the Administration's comprehensive management information system composed of integrated supplementary systems for collecting, processing, and communicating employment and training programs, and financial data.

The Office of Grants and Contract Management resolves audits, closes out contracts and grants, and seeks to satisfy extraordinary monetary claims; and applies sanctions against grantees and contractors who violate agency-administered laws or regulations.

The Office of Management Support provides centralized procurement services to the Administration's national office components; provides all administrative, personnel, organizational analysis, and property and engineering management services; directs the development, implementation, and administration of functions concerning the operational and financial integrity of agency programs; conducts inquiries, assessments, and reviews, including intra-agency and interagency investigations for the Assistant Secretary; and coordinates all activities associated with reviews of the Administration by the General Accounting Office, the Inspector General of the Department of Labor, the Department of Justice, and other agencies.

The Administration's internal control staff administers the Federal Managers' Financial Integrity Act of 1982 to ensure the adoption of safeguards to protect the Employment and Training Administration's resources, to produce information that is accurate and reliable, and to promote adherence to laws, regulations, and policy governing operational efficiency and economy. Pre-award clearance screening, internal control reviews of selected administrative and program activities, and administration of vulnerability assessments are the key responsibilities of this office.

For further information, call 202–535–0690.

Regional Management

The Office of Regional Management provides leadership to the Employment and Training Administration's regional offices that are located in 10 areas throughout the United States. The Office executes direct-line authority over Administration field activities (except the Bureau of Apprenticeship and Training and Job Corps) and provides a central point of contact at the headquarters level in connection with national office component dealings with regional staff.

Within its area of jurisdiction, each regional office is responsible for the oversight and grant administration of employment and training programs operated by State governments. Other public interest responsibilities include the coordination of Administration activities with Federal assistance programs of other agencies within the region; the implementation of employment training administrative policies on equal employment opportunity; and assistance to the States in carrying out operational responsibilities for employment and training programs at the State and local levels.

Regional Offices—Employment and Training Administration

(Areas included within each region are indicated on the map in Appendix A.)

Region/Address	Administrator
I. Boston, MA (John F. Kennedy Federal Bldg., 02203)	Robert Semler
II. New York, NY (201 Varick St., 10014)	Thomas E. Hill
III. Philadelphia, PA (P.O. Box 8796, 19101)	William J. Haltigan
IV. Atlanta, GA (1371 Peachtree St. NE., 30367)	Dan Lowry
V. Chicago, IL (230 S. Dearborn St., 60604)	Joseph C. Juarez
VI. Dallas, TX (525 Griffin Sq. Bldg., 75202)	Floyd E. Edwards
VII. Kansas City, MO (911 Walnut St., 64106)	Grace Kilbane
VIII. Denver, CO (1961 Stout St., 80294)	Luis Sepulveda
IX. San Francisco, CA (71 Stevenson St., 94102)	Don A. Balcer
X. Seattle, WA (909 1st Ave., 98174)	Armando Quiroz

For further information, call 202–535–0585.

Labor-Management Standards

The Office of Labor-Management Standards, formerly the Office of Labor-Management Standards Enforcement within the Labor-Management Services Administration, was created by Secretary's Order No. 3–84 of May 3, 1984, and is headed by the Assistant Secretary for Labor-Management Standards.

The Office administers provisions of the Labor-Management Reporting and Disclosure Act of 1959 (29 U.S.C. 401 note) and section 1209 of the Postal Reorganization Act (39 U.S.C. 1209), which affect labor organizations in the private sector and labor organizations composed of postal service employees, and section 701 of the Civil Service Reform Act (5 U.S.C. 7120) and section 1017 of the Foreign Service Act (22 U.S.C. 4117), which affect labor organizations composed of employees of most agencies of the executive branch of the Federal Government and certain other Federal agencies subject to similar standards of conduct. These provisions regulate certain internal union procedures and protect the rights of members in approximately 48,000 unions and govern the handling of union funds; the reporting and disclosure of certain financial transactions and administrative practices of unions, union officers and employees, surety companies, employers, and labor relations consultants; the election of union officers; the imposition and administration of trusteeships; and other matters.

Through technical assistance, the Office seeks to obtain voluntary compliance with the requirements of the law by labor organizations, employers, and other affected entities and individuals. Enforcement through the Federal courts also is available under the reporting and disclosure act procedures, while the standards of conduct are enforced by administrative action with a final decision by the Assistant Secretary.

For further information, call 202–523–7320.

Area Offices—Office of Labor-Management Standards

Area	Address	Administrator
ATLANTA—Alabama, Florida, Georgia, South Carolina	Suite 600, 1365 Peachtree St. NE., Atlanta, GA 30367	Ronald Lehman
BOSTON—Connecticut, Maine, Massachusetts, New Hampshire, New York (northern and western), Rhode Island, Vermont	Suite 801, J.W. McCormick Post Office and Courthouse, Boston, MA 02109	James Cannon
CHICAGO—Illinois (northern), Indiana (northern), Michigan, Minnesota, North Dakota, South Dakota, Wisconsin	Suite 774, 230 S. Dearborn St., Chicago, IL 60604-2773	John Beaty
CLEVELAND—Indiana (southern), Kentucky, Ohio	Suite 831, 1240 E. 9th St., Cleveland, OH 44199	Richard Crino
DALLAS—Arkansas, Louisiana, Mississippi, Oklahoma, Texas	Suite 300, 525 Griffin Sq. Bldg., Dallas, TX 75202	Stephen Jeroutek
KANSAS CITY—Colorado, Illinois (southern), Iowa, Kansas, Missouri, Montana, Nebraska, New Mexico, Utah, Wyoming	Suite 1606, 911 Walnut St., Kansas City, MO 64106	Kamil Bishara
NEW YORK—New Jersey, New York (southeastern and metropolitan areas)	Suite 878, 201 Varick St., New York, NY 10014	Patricia Thompson
PHILADELPHIA—Delaware, Pennsylvania, West Virginia	Suite 9452, 600 Arch St., Philadelphia, PA 19106	A. Lois Barksdale
SAN FRANCISCO—Alaska, Arizona, California, Hawaii, Idaho, Nevada, Oregon, Washington	Suite 725, 71 Stevenson St., San Francisco, CA 94105	C. Russell Rock
WASHINGTON, DC—District of Columbia, Maryland, North Carolina, Puerto Rico, Tennessee, Virginia	Suite 558, 1730 K St. NW., Washington, DC 20006	Robert L. Merriner

Pension and Welfare Benefits Administration

The Pension and Welfare Benefits Administration (PWBA) helps to protect the economic future and retirement security of working Americans, as required under the Employment Retirement Income Security Act of 1974 (ERISA) (29 U.S.C. 1001).

The act requires administrators of private pension and welfare plans to provide plan participants with easily understandable summaries of plans; to file those summaries with the agency; and to report annually on the financial operation of the plans and bonding of persons charged with handling plan funds and assets. Plan administrators must also meet strict fiduciary responsibility standards that are enforced by PWBA.

The Administration is charged with assuring responsible management of nearly 1 million pension plans and 4½ million health and welfare plans, and is the national guardian of a vast private retirement and welfare benefit system. Its major activities include: formulating current and future policy; conducting research; issuing regulations and technical guidance concerning ERISA requirements; enforcing ERISA requirements; and assisting and educating the employee benefits community about ERISA. The Administration is enforced through its 15 field offices nationwide and the national office in Washington, DC.

Vesting, participation, and funding standards are primarily administered by the Internal Revenue Service.

Field Offices—Pension and Welfare Benefits Administration

Area/Address	Director
Atlanta, GA (1371 Peachtree St. NE., 30367)	Howard Marsh
Boston, MA (J.W. McCormack Bldg., 02109)	James Benages
Chicago, IL (401 S. State St., 60605)	Kenneth M. Bazar
Dallas, TX (525 Griffin St., 75202)	Bruce Ruud
Fort Wright, KY (1885 Dixie Hwy., 41011)	Joseph Menez
Kansas City, MO (911 Walnut St., 64106)	Gregory Egan
Los Angeles, CA (3660 Wilshire Blvd., 90010)	David Ganz
New York, NY (1633 Broadway, 10019)	John Wehrum
Philadelphia, PA (3535 Market St., 19104)	Gerard Gumpertz
San Francisco, CA (71 Stevenson St., 94105)	Leonard Garofolo

For further information, call 202-523-8921.

Labor-Management Relations

The Bureau of Labor-Management Relations and Cooperative Programs offers a wide range of information and technical assistance services to employers, unions, academics, third-party neutrals, and other organizations and individuals sharing common interests in improving the practice of industrial relations, especially through joint labor and management efforts. The Bureau's activities include sponsoring conferences and other meetings on contemporary issues, publishing special reports on organizational experiences, preparing educational and training materials, and conducting research and evaluation studies in the areas of cooperative labor relations, collective bargaining, and quality of work life programs. The Bureau gathers and disseminates information about innovative policies and programs developed to enhance employee participation in shared decisionmaking with regard to issues such as work organization, the work environment, technological change, and plant closings and dislocated worker assistance.

The Bureau also reports on current and potentially critical dispute situations, analyzes collective bargaining data, and provides staff assistance to Presidential emergency boards and other boards and commissions dealing with major labor-management disputes.

In the field of labor-management policy development and research, the Bureau reviews collective bargaining relationships and their contribution to meeting the economic needs of the parties involved as well as the general public. The Bureau helps to develop policy for legislation and Executive orders, studies the impact of collective bargaining agreements, and coordinates labor-management relations research activities.

The Bureau administers employee protection provisions of various laws to ensure that workers' employment conditions covered by the laws are not adversely impacted by government actions.

For further information, call 202-523-6045.

Employment Standards Administration

The Assistant Secretary for Employment Standards has responsibility for administering and directing employment standards programs dealing with: minimum wage and overtime standards; registration of farm labor contractors; determining prevailing wage rates to be paid on Government contracts and subcontracts; nondiscrimination and affirmative action for minorities, women, veterans, and handicapped Government contract and subcontract workers; and workers' compensation programs for Federal and certain private employers and employees.

Wage and Hour Division

The Wage and Hour Administrator is responsible for planning, directing, and administering programs dealing with a variety of Federal labor legislation. These programs are designed to:

—protect low-wage incomes as provided by the minimum wage provisions of the Fair Labor Standards Act (29 U.S.C. 201);

—safeguard the health and welfare of workers by discouraging excessively long hours of work through enforcement of the overtime provisions of the Fair Labor Standards Act;

—prevent curtailment of employment and earnings for students, trainees, and handicapped workers;

—minimize losses of income and job rights caused by indebtedness; and

—direct a program of farm labor contractor registration designed to protect the health, safety, and welfare of migrant and seasonal agricultural workers; and

—administer and enforce a number of immigration-related programs (with INS) designed to safeguard the rights of both American and foreign workers and to prevent American workers similarly employed from being adversely affected by employment of alien workers.

The Wage and Hour Division is also responsible for predetermination of prevailing wage rates for Federal construction contracts and federally assisted programs for construction, alteration and repair of public works subject to the Davis-Bacon (40 U.S.C. 276a) and related acts, and a continuing program for determining wage rates under the Service Contract Act (41 U.S.C. 351). The Division also has enforcement responsibility in ensuring that prevailing wages and overtime standards are paid in accordance with the provisions of the Davis-Bacon and related acts: Service Contract Act, Public Contracts Act, and Contract Work Hours and Safety Standards Act.

For further information, contact the Office of the Administrator, Wage and Hour Division, Department of Labor, Room S-3502, 200 Constitution Avenue NW., Washington, DC 20210. Phone, 202-523-8305.

Federal Contract Compliance Programs

The Office of Federal Contract Compliance Programs is responsible for establishing policies and goals and providing leadership and coordination of the Government's program to achieve nondiscrimination in employment by Government contractors and subcontractors and in federally assisted construction programs.

The Office also is responsible for administering programs to assure affirmative action by government contractors to employ and advance in the employment of Vietnam-era veterans and handicapped workers; coordinating with the Equal Employment Opportunity Commission and the Department of Justice in matters relating to title VII of the Civil Rights Act of 1964 (42 U.S.C. 2000e); and maintaining liaison with other agencies having civil rights and equal employment opportunity activities.

For further information, contact the Office of the Director, Office of Federal Contract Compliance Programs, Department of Labor, Room C-3325, 200 Constitution Avenue NW., Washington, DC 20210. Phone, 202-523-9475.

Office of Workers' Compensation Programs

The Office of Workers' Compensation Programs is responsible for the administration of the three basic Federal workers' compensation laws: the Federal Employees' Compensation Act and related laws (the War Hazards Compensation Act and the War Claims Act), which provide workers' compensation for Federal employees and others; the Longshore and Harbor Workers' Compensation Act and its various extensions (the Defense Base Act, Outer Continental Shelf Lands Act, Nonappropriated Fund Instrumentalities Act, and District of Columbia

Compensation Act), which provide benefits to employees in private enterprise while engaged in maritime employment on navigable waters in the United States, and extend coverage to private employment in the District of Columbia for injuries that occurred prior to July 27, 1982; and the Black Lung Benefits Act, as amended, which extends benefits to coal miners who are totally disabled due to pneumoconiosis, a respiratory disease contracted after prolonged inhalation of coal mine dust, and to their survivors when the miner's death is due to pneumoconiosis.

Regional Administrators/Directors—Employment Standards Administration

(Areas included within each region are indicated on the map in Appendix A.)

Region Office/Address	Wage and Hour Administrator	Federal Contract Compliance Regional Director	Workers' Compensation Programs Regional Director
1. Boston, MA (1 Congress St., 02203)	Walter P. Parker	Brenda J. Joyce	Charity Benz
2. New York, NY (201 Varick St., 10014)	Dorris Wooten	Carmen McCulloch	Willis Nordlund
3. Philadelphia, PA (3535 Market St., 19104)	James W. Kight	Joseph J. Dubray, Jr.	Robert D. Lotz
4. Atlanta, GA (1375 Peachtree St. NE., 30367).	James L. Valin	Carol A. Gaudin	(Vacancy)
5. Jacksonville, FL (Suite 1006, 214 N. Hogan St., 32202).			Nancy L. Ricker
6. Chicago, IL (230 S. Dearborn St., 60604)	William Van Zanen,	Halcolm Holliman	Phyllis Crane
7. Dallas, TX (525 Griffin St., 75202)	Bill A. Belt	Joe C. Garcia	Carol L. Fleschute
8. Kansas City, MO (911 Walnut St., 64106)	Everett P. Jennings	Betty Robinson	Charles O. Ketcham, Jr.
9. Denver, CO (1961 Stout St., 80294)	Loren E. Gilbert	Irene N. Mee	Robert J. Mansanares
10. San Francisco, CA (71 Stevenson St., 84105).	William C. Buhl	Helene Haase	Donna Onodera
11. Seattle, WA (909 1st Ave., 98174)	Wilbur J. Olson	John Checkett	Thomas K. Morgan

District Offices—Workers' Compensation Programs

District/Address	FECA District Director	DLHWD District Director	DCMWC District Director
1. Boston, MA (1 Congress St., 02203)	Robert M. Sullivan	Frank Mahoney	
2. New York, NY (201 Varick St., 10014)	Colleen Coleman	Richard V. Robilotti	
3. Philadelphia, PA (3535 Market St., 19104)	Alonza Hart	John McTaggart	
4. Baltimore, MD (31 Hopkins Plz., 21201)		Bruno DiSimone	
5. Norfolk, VA (200 Granby Mall, 23510)		Basil E. Voultsides	
6. Johnstown, PA (Rm. 201, 319 Washington St., 15901).			Margaret R. Peterson
7. Greensburg, PA (1225 S. Main St., 15601			John Ciszek
8. Wilkes-Barre, PA (116 S. Main St., 18701)			Jack Geller
9. Charleston, WV (2 Hale St., 25301)			Robert Hardesty
10. Pikeville, KY (334 Main St., 41501)			Herb Koudry
11. Jacksonville, FL (214 N. Hogan St., 32202)	William C. Franson	Noella S. Kitchin	
12. New Orleans, LA (701 Loyola St., 70113)		Donette Glenn	
13. Houston, TX (12600 Featherwood Dr., 77004).		Marilyn Felkner	
14. Dallas, TX (525 Griffin St., 75202)	Frank Allen		
15. Chicago, IL (230 S. Dearborn St., 60604)	Richard Kadus	Thomas C. Hunter	
16. Cleveland, OH (1240 E. 9th St., 44199)	Deborah Sanford		
17. Columbus, OH (274 Marconi Blvd., 43215)			Robert Mitchell
18. Kansas City, MO (911 Walnut St., 64106)	Charles O. Ketcham, Jr..		
19. Denver, CO (1961 Stout St., 80294)	Robert J. Mansanares.		John Martin
20. San Francisco, CA (71 Stevenson St., 94102).	(Vacancy)	Deborah Oppenheim	
21. Honolulu, HI (300 Ala Moana Blvd., 96850)		Donald Reichart	
22. Seattle, WA (1111 3d Ave., 98101-3212)	William Howard	Karen Goodwin	

District Offices—Workers' Compensation Programs—Continued

District/Address	FECA District Director	DLHWD District Director	DCMWC District Director
23. Long Beach, CA (401 E. Ocean Blvd., 90807).	....	Edward Bounds........	

For further information, contact the Office of the Director, Office of Workers' Compensation Programs, Department of Labor, Room S–3524, 200 Constitution Avenue NW., Washington, DC 20210. Phone, 202–523–7503.

Occupational Safety and Health Administration

The Assistant Secretary for Occupational Safety and Health has responsibility for occupational safety and health activities.

The Occupational Safety and Health Administration, established pursuant to the Occupational Safety and Health Act of 1970 (29 U.S.C. 651 *et seq.*), develops and promulgates occupational safety and health standards; develops and issues regulations; conducts investigations and inspections to determine the status of compliance with safety and health standards and regulations; and issues citations and proposes penalties for noncompliance with safety and health standards and regulations.

Regional Offices—Occupational Safety and Health Administration

(Areas included within each region are indicated on the map in Appendix A.)

Region/Address	Administrator	Telephone
1. Boston, MA (133 Portland St., 02114)	John B. Miles	617–565–7159
2. New York, NY (201 Varick St., 10014)	James Stanley	212–337–2378
3. Philadelphia, PA (3535 Market St., 19104)	Linda R. Anku	215–596–1201
4. Atlanta, GA (1375 Peachtree St. NE., 30367)	R. Davis Layne	404–347–3573
5. Chicago, IL (230 S. Dearborn St., 60604)	Michael Connors	312–357–2220
6. Dallas, TX (555 Griffin Sq. Bldg., 75202)	Gilbert J. Saulter	214–767–4731
7. Kansas City, MO (911 Walnut St., 64106)	(Vacancy)	426–867–5861
8. Denver, CO (1961 Stout St., 80294)	Byron R. Chadwick	303–844–3061
9. San Francisco, CA (71 Stevenson St., 94105)	Frank Strasheim	415–744–6670
10. Seattle, WA (1111 3d Ave., 98101)	James W. Lake	206–442–5930

For further information, contact the Occupational Safety and Health Administration, Department of Labor, 200 Constitution Avenue NW., Washington, DC 20210. Phone, 202–523–8151.

Mine Safety and Health Administration

The Assistant Secretary of Labor for Mine Safety and Health has responsibility for safety and health in the Nation's mines.

The Federal Coal Mine Health and Safety Act of 1969 (30 U.S.C. 801 *et seq.*) gave the Administration strong enforcement provisions to protect the Nation's coal miners and, in 1977, the Congress passed amendments which strengthened the act, expanding its protections and extending its provisions to the noncoal mining industry.

The Administration develops and promulgates mandatory safety and health standards, ensures compliance with such standards, assesses civil penalties for violations, and investigates accidents. It cooperates with and provides assistance to the States in the development of effective State mine safety and health programs, improves and expands training programs in cooperation with the States and the mining industry, and, in coordination with the Department of Health and Human Services and the Department of the Interior, contributes to the improvement and expansion of mine safety and health research and development. All of these activities are aimed at preventing and reducing mine accidents and occupational diseases in the mining industry.

The statutory responsibilities of the Administration are administered by a headquarters staff located at Arlington, VA, reporting to the Assistant Secretary for Mine Safety and Health and by a field network of district, subdistrict, and field offices, technology centers, and the Approval and Certification Center.

For further information, contact the Office of Information and Public Affairs, Mine Safety and Health Administration, Department of Labor, Room 601, 4015 Wilson Boulevard, Arlington, VA 22203. Phone, 703–235–1452.

District Offices—Mine Safety and Health Administration

	District/Address	Telephone
	Coal Mine Safety and Health	
I.	Wilkes-Barre, PA (20 N. Pennsylvania Ave., 18701)	717–826–6321
II.	Pittsburgh, PA (4800 Forbes Ave., 15213)	412–578–3787
III.	Morgantown, WV (5012 Mountaineer Mall, 26505)	304–291–4277
IV.	Mt. Hope, WV (P.O. Box 112, 25880)	304–877–3906
V.	Norton, VA (P.O. Box 560, 24273)	703–679–0230
VI.	Pikeville, KY (219 Ratliff's Creek Rd., 41501)	606–432–0944
VII.	Barbourville, KY (HC 66, Box 1762, 40906)	606–546–5123
VIII.	Vincennes, IN (P.O. Box 418, 47591)	812–882–7617
IX.	Denver, CO (P.O. Box 25367, 80225–0367)	303–231–5458
X.	Madisonville, KY (P.O. Box 473, 42431)	502–821–4180
	Metal/Nonmetal Mine Safety and Health	
	Northeastern District (230 Executive Dr., Mars, PA 16046–9812)	412–772–2333
	Southeastern District (280 W. Valley Ave., Birmingham, AL 35209–4896)	205–731–1510
	North Central District (515 W. 1st St., Duluth, MN 55802–1302)	218–720–5448
	South Central District (1100 Commerce St., Dallas, TX 75242–0499)	214–767–8401
	Rocky Mountain District (P.O. Box 25367, Denver, CO 80225–0367)	303–236–2794
	Western District (620 Central Ave., Alameda, CA 94501)	415–273–7457

Labor Statistics

The Bureau of Labor Statistics is the principal data-gathering agency of the Federal Government in the broad field of labor economics. It has no enforcement or regulatory functions. The Bureau collects, processes, analyzes, and disseminates data relating to employment, unemployment, and other characteristics of the labor force; prices and consumer expenditures; wages, other worker compensation, and industrial relations; productivity and technological change; economic growth and employment projections; and occupational safety and health. Most of the data are collected in surveys conducted by the Bureau, the Bureau of the Census (on a contract basis), or on a cooperative basis with State agencies.

The Bureau strives to have its data satisfy a number of criteria, including: relevance to current social and economic issues, timeliness in reflecting today's rapidly changing economic conditions, accuracy and consistently high statistical quality, and impartiality in both subject matter and presentation.

The basic data—practically all supplied voluntarily by business establishments and members of private households—are issued in monthly, quarterly, and annual news releases; bulletins, reports, and special publications; and periodicals. Data are also made available through an electronic news service, magnetic tape, diskettes, and microfiche. Regional offices issue additional reports and releases usually presenting locality or regional detail.

Regional Offices—Bureau of Labor Statistics

Region/Address	Address	Commissioner
ATLANTA—Alabama, Florida, Georgia, Kentucky, Mississippi, North Carolina, South Carolina, Tennessee	1371 Peachtree St. NE., Atlanta, GA 30367	Janet S. Rankin
BOSTON—Connecticut, Maine, Massachusetts, New Hampshire, Rhode Island, Vermont	1603-B Federal Bldg., Boston, MA 02203	Anthony J. Ferrara
CHICAGO—Illinois, Indiana, Michigan, Minnesota, Ohio, Wisconsin	230 S. Dearborn St., Chicago, IL 60604	Lois Orr
DALLAS—Arkansas, Louisiana, New Mexico, Oklahoma, Texas	525 Griffin Sq. Bldg., Dallas, TX 75202	Bryan Richey
KANSAS CITY—Colorado, Iowa, Kansas, Missouri, Montana, Nebraska, North Dakota, South Dakota, Utah, Wyoming	911 Walnut St., Kansas City, MO 64106	Gunnan Engen
NEW YORK—New Jersey, New York, Puerto Rico, Virgin Islands, Canal Zone	201 Varick St., New York, NY 10014	Alan M. Paisner
PHILADELPHIA—Delaware, District of Columbia, Maryland, Pennsylvania, Virginia, West Virginia	3535 Market St., Philadelphia, PA 19104	Alvin I. Margulis
SAN FRANCISCO—Alaska, American Samoa, Arizona, California, Guam, Hawaii, Idaho, Nevada, Oregon, Trust Territory of the Pacific Islands, Washington	71 Stevenson St., San Francisco, CA 94119-3766	Sam M. Hirabayashi

For further information, contact the Associate Commissioner, Office of Publications, Bureau of Labor Statistics, Department of Labor, Room 2822, 441 G Street NW., Washington, DC. 20212. Phone, 202-523-1327.

Veterans' Employment and Training Service

The Veterans' Employment and Training Service is the component of the Department of Labor administered by the Assistant Secretary for Veterans' Employment and Training. The Assistant Secretary is the principal advisor to the Secretary of Labor in the formulation and implementation of all Departmental policies, procedures, and regulations affecting veterans and is responsible for administering veterans' employment and training programs and activities through the Service to ensure that legislative and regulatory mandates are accomplished.

The Service carries out its responsibilities for directing the Department's veterans' employment and training programs through a nationwide network that includes Regional Administrators, Directors (in each State) and Assistant Directors (one for each 250,000 veterans in each State) for Veterans' Employment and Training, Assistant Regional Administrators and Area Agents for Veterans' Reemployment Rights, Veterans' Program Specialists, and program support staff.

The Service field staff works closely with and provides technical assistance to State Employment Security Agencies and Job Training Partnership Act grant recipients to ensure that veterans are provided the priority services required by law. They also coordinate with employers, labor unions, veterans service organizations, and community organizations through planned public information and outreach activities. Federal contractors are provided management assistance in complying with their veterans affirmative action and reporting obligations.

Also administered by the Assistant Secretary through the Service is the Job Training Partnership Act, title IV, part C grant program designed to meet the employment and training needs of service-connected disabled veterans, Vietnam-era veterans, and veterans recently separated from military service. IV-C grants are awarded and monitored through the Service's national office and field staff.

Certain other Service staff also administer the veterans reemployment rights program. They provide assistance to help restore job, seniority, and pension rights to veterans following absences from work for active military service and to protect employment and retention rights of members of the Reserve or National Guard.

Regional Administrators/State Directors—Veterans' Employment and Training Service

(RA: Regional Administrator; D: Director)

(Areas included within each region are indicated on the map in Appendix A.)

Region/Address	Director	Telephone
REGION I		
Boston, MA (Rm. 506, John F. Kennedy Federal Bldg., 02203)	Jerome T. Underwood (D)	617-565-2080
	Richard Brennan (RA)	617-565-2080
Concord, NH (Rm. 325, 55 Pleasant St., 03301)	David Houle (D)	603-225-1424
Lewiston, ME (522 Lisbon St., 04243)	(Vacancy) (D)	207-783-5352
Montpelier, VT (Rm. 303, 87 State St., 05602)	Ronald R. Benoit (D)	802-828-4441
Providence, RI (Rm. 507, Federal Bldg. and Courthouse, 02903)	Arthur L. Dawson, Jr. (D)	401-528-5134
Wethersfield, CT (200 Folly Brook Blvd., 06601)	Robert B. Inman (D)	203-566-3326
REGION II		
Albany, NY (Rm. 578, Bldg. 12, Harriman State Campus, 12240)	James H. Hartman (D)	518-472-4415
New York, NY (Rm. 766, 201 Varick St., 10014)	H. Miles Sisson (RA)	212-337-2211
Santurce, PR (No. 505, Munoz Rivera Ave., 00918)	Hiram Gonzalez (D)	809-754-5391
Trenton, NJ (Rm. 200, 28 Yard Ave., CN-058, 08609)	Alan E. Grohs (D)	609-292-2930
REGION III		
Baltimore, MD (Rm. 205, 1100 N. Eutaw St., 21201)	Gary Lobdell (D)	301-333-5194
Charleston, WV (Rm. 212, 112 California Ave., 25305)	David L. Bush (D)	304-348-4001
Harrisburg, PA (Rm. 625, Labor and Industry Bldg., 17121)	Larry Babbitts (D)	717-787-5834
Newark, DE (Stockton Bldg., University Plz., 19702)	Joseph Hortiz (D)	302-368-6898
Philadelphia, PA (Rm. 240, U.S. Customs House, 2d & Chestnut Sts., 19160).	Elmer Sims (RA)	215-597-1664
Richmond, VA (Suite 1409, 701 E. Franklin St., 23219)	Benjamin I. Trotter, Jr. (D)	804-786-7269
Washington, DC (Rm. 108, 500 C St. NW., 20001)	George H. Joiner (D)	202-727-3342
REGION IV		
Atlanta, GA (Rm. 326, 1371 Peachtree St. NE., 30367)	William Bolls (RA)	404-347-3673
Atlanta, GA (Suite 640, Sussex Pl., 148 International Blvd. NE., 30303)	Eugene R. Wagner (D)	404-656-3138
Columbia, SC (Suite 101-A, 914 Richland St., 29201)	William C. Plowden, Jr. (D)	803-737-1717
Frankfort, KY (c/o Department for Employment Services, 275 E. Main St., 40621).	Charles R. Netherton (D)	502-564-7062
Jackson, MS (1520 W. Capitol St., 39215)	W.H. Cooper (D)	601-961-7588
Montgomery, AL (519 Industrial Relations Bldg., 36130)	(Vacancy) (D)	205-242-8115
Nashville, TN (Rm. 317, 301 James Robertson Pkwy., 37245-4000)	Clayton Lamberth, Jr. (D)	615-741-2135
Raleigh, NC (700 Wade Ave., 27605)	S. Marvin Burton (D)	919-733-7402
Tallahassee, FL (Suite 102, 1320 Executive Ctr. Dr., 32399-0676)	Lewis E. Waggoner (D)	904-877-4164
REGION V		
Chicago, IL (Rm. 1064, 230 S. Dearborn St., 60604)	Richard A. Mock (RA)	312-353-0970
Chicago, IL (2 North, 401 S. State St., 60605)	Samuel A. Parks (D)	312-793-3433
Columbus, OH (145 S. Front St., 43216)	Wesley Leggett (D)	614-466-2768
Detroit, MI (Suite 407, 7310 Woodward Ave., 48204)	John T. Kaarsberg (D)	313-876-5613
Indianapolis, IN (Rm. 203, 10 N. Senate Ave., 46204)	Bruce Redman (D)	317-232-6804
Madison, WI (Rm. 250, 201 E. Washington Ave., 53703)	James R. Gutowski (D)	608-266-3110
St. Paul, MN (1st Fl., 390 N. Robert, 55101)	Michael D. Graham (D)	612-296-3665
REGION VI		
Albuquerque, NM (401 Broadway NE., 87102)	Jacob Castillo (D)	505-766-2113
Austin, TX (Suite 516-T, TEC Bldg., 12th & Trinity Sts., 78701)	John McKinny (D)	512-463-2207
Baton Rouge, LA (Rm. 174, 1001 N. 23d St., 70804-9094)	Lester Parmenter (D)	504-389-0339
Dallas, TX (Rm. 204, 555 Griffin Sq. Bldg., Griffin and Young Sts., 75202).	Lester L. Williams, Jr. (RA)	214-767-4987
Little Rock, AR (Rm. G-12, Employment Security Bldg., State Capitol Mall, 72203).	Billy R. Threlkeld (D)	501-682-3786
Oklahoma City, OK (Rm. 301, Will Rogers Memorial Office Bldg., 73105).	Joseph Walden (D)	405-557-7189
REGION VII		
Des Moines, IA (1000 E. Grand Ave., 50319)	Leonard E. Shaw, Jr. (D)	515-281-5144

Regional Administrators/State Directors—Veterans' Employment and Training Service—Continued

(RA: Regional Administrator; D: Director)

(Areas included within each region are indicated on the map in Appendix A.)

Region/Address	Director	Telephone
REGION VII—**Continued**		
Jefferson City, MO (421 E. Dunklin St., 65104)	Jonas N. Matthews (D)	314-751-3921
Kansas City, MO (Rm. 803, 911 Walnut St., 64106)	Jack Titus (RA)	816-426-7151
Lincoln, NE (550 S. 16th St., 68509)	Robert T. Manifold (D)	402-437-5289
Topeka, KS (1309 Topeka Blvd., 66612)	John A. Hill (D)	913-296-5032
REGION VIII		
Aberdeen, SD (420 S. Roosevelt St., 57402-4730)	Earl R. Schultz (D)	605-226-7289
Bismarck, ND (1000 Divide Ave., 58502-1632)	Leo A. Swenson (D)	701-224-2865
Casper, WY (100 W. Midwest Ave., 82602)	Ernest E. Fender (D)	307-235-3281
Denver, CO (Rm. 375, 721 19th St., 80202-2516)	Ronald G. Bachman (RA)	303-866-4456
Denver, CO (Suite 900, 600 Grant St., 80203)	Mark A. McGinty (D)	303-866-1114
Helena, MT (515 N. Sanders, 59624)	Daniel P. Antonietti (D)	406-449-5431
Salt Lake City, UT (178 Social Hall Ave., 84111)	J. Dale Madsen (D)	801-524-5703
REGION IX		
Carson City, NV (500 E. 3d St., 89710)	Claude U. Shipley (D)	702-687-4632
Honolulu, HI (Rm. 232A, 830 Punch Bowl St., 96813)	Raymond S. Sumikawa (D)	808-541-1780
Phoenix, AZ (1300 W. Washington St., 85005)	Marco A. Valenzuela (D)	602-261-4961
Sacramento, CA (Rm. W1142, 800 Capitol Mall, 94280-0001)	Charles Martinez (D)	916-551-1422
San Francisco, CA (Suite 705, 71 Stevenson St. 94105)	John E. Giannelli, Jr. (RA)	415-744-6677
REGION X		
Boise, ID (Rm. 303, 317 Main St., 83735)	Robert M. Wilson (D)	208-334-6164
Juneau, AK (1111 W. 8th St., 99802)	Daniel Travis (D)	907-465-2723
Olympia, WA (605 Woodview Dr., SE., 98507)	Donald J. Hutt (D)	206-438-4600
Salem, OR (875 Union St. NE., 97311)	Rex A. Newell (D)	503-378-3338
Seattle, WA (Suite 800, 1111 3d Ave., 98101-3212)	Joseph J. Molinari (RA)	206-553-4831

For further information, contact the Assistant Secretary for Veterans' Employment and Training, Department of Labor, 200 Constitution Avenue NW., Washington, DC 20210. Phone, 202-523-9116.

Sources of Information

Contracts General inquiries may be directed to the Office of Procurement and Grants Management, OASAM, Room S-1522, 200 Constitution Avenue NW., Washington, DC 20210. Phone, 202-523-8904.

Inquiries on doing business with the Job Corps should be directed to the appropriate Job Corps Regional Director in the Employment and Training Administration regional office.

Employment Personnel Offices use lists of eligibles from the clerical, scientific, technical, and general examinations of the Office of Personnel Management.

Inquiries and applications may be directed to any of the eight personnel offices within the Department of Labor, 200 Constitution Avenue NW., Washington, DC 20210 (phone, 202-523-6666), or the nearest regional office.

Publications The Office of Information and Public Affairs distributes a brochure entitled *Department of Labor,* which describes the activities of the major agencies within the Department, and *Publications of the Department of Labor,* a subject listing of publications available from the Department.

The Employment and Training Administration issues periodicals such as *Area Trends in Employment and Unemployment* available by subscription through the Superintendent of Documents, Government Printing Office, Washington, DC 20402. Information about publications may be obtained from the Administration's Information Office. Phone, 202-523-6871.

The Office of Labor-Management Standards publishes the text of the Labor-Management Reporting and Disclosure Act (29 U.S.C. 401) and pamphlets that explain the reporting, election, bonding, and trusteeship provisions of the act. The pamphlets and reporting forms used by persons covered by the act are available free in limited quantities from the OLMS National Office at Room N–5616, 200 Constitution Avenue NW., Washington, DC 20210, and from OLMS field offices listed in the telephone directory under United States Government, Department of Labor.

The Pension and Welfare Benefits Administration distributes fact sheets, pamphlets, and booklets on employer obligations and employee rights under ERISA. A list of publications is available by writing: PWBA, Division of Public Information, Room N–5666, 200 Constitution Avenue NW., Washington, DC 20210. Phone, 202–523–8921.

The Bureau of Labor Statistics has an Information Office in the General Accounting Office Building, 441 G Street NW., Washington, DC 20212, phone, 202–523–1221. Periodicals include the *Monthly Labor Review, Consumer Price Index, Producer Prices and Price Indexes, Employment and Earnings, Current Wage Developments, Occupational Outlook Handbook,* and *Occupational Outlook Quarterly.* Publications are both free and for sale, but for-sale items must be obtained from the Superintendent of Documents, Government Printing Office. Inquiries may be directed to the Washington Information Office or to the Bureau's regional offices.

Publications of the Employment Standards Administration, such as *Handy Reference Guide to the Fair Labor Standards Act,* and *OFCCP, Making Affirmative Action Work,* are available from the nearest area office. Single copies are free.

Reading Rooms Department of Labor Library, Room N2439, Frances Perkins Building, 200 Constitution Avenue NW., Washington, DC 20210. Phone, 202–523–6988.

The Office of Labor-Management Standards maintains a Public Disclosure Room at Room N–5616, 200 Constitution Avenue NW., Washington, DC 20210. Reports filed under the Labor-Management Reporting and Disclosure Act may be examined there and purchased for 15 cents per page. Reports also may be obtained by calling the Public Disclosure Room at 202–523–7393, or by contacting an Office field office listed in the telephone directory under United States Government, Department of Labor.

The Pension and Welfare Benefits Administration maintains a Public Disclosure Room at Room N–5507, 200 Constitution Avenue NW., Washington, DC 20210. Reports filed under the Employee Retirement Income Security Act may be examined there and purchased for 10 cents per page or by calling the Public Disclosure Room on 202–523–8771.

For further information concerning the Department of Labor, contact the Office of Information and Public Affairs, Department of Labor, Room S–1032, 200 Constitution Avenue NW., Washington, DC 20210. Phone, 202–523–7316.

DEPARTMENT OF STATE

2201 C Street NW., Washington, DC 20520
Phone, 202–647–4000

SECRETARY OF STATE	James A. Baker III
Special Assistant to the Secretary	Caron S. Jackson
Chief of Protocol	Joseph Verner Reed
Special Assistant to the Secretary and Executive Secretary of the Department	Stapleton Roy
Special Assistant to the Secretary and Coordinator for International Labor Affairs	Anthony G. Freeman
Chairman, Foreign Service Grievance Board	Arthur Stark
Civil Service Ombudsman	John R. Byerly
Deputy Secretary of State	Lawrence S. Eagleburger
Under Secretary for Political Affairs	Robert Michael Kimmitt
Under Secretary for Economic and Agricultural Affairs	Richard T. McCormack
Under Secretary for International Security Affairs	Reginald Bartholomew
Under Secretary for Management	(vacancy)
Assistant Secretary for Administration	Arthur W. Fort
Assistant Secretary for Consular Affairs	Elizabeth Tamposi
Assistant Secretary for Diplomatic Security	Sheldon J. Krys
Director, Finance and Management Policy	Jill Kent
Director General and Director of Personnel	Edward Perkins
Director of the Foreign Service Institute	Brandon Grove
Medical Director, Department of State and the Foreign Service	Paul Goff, M.D.
Executive Secretary, Board of the Foreign Service	C. Edward Dickens
Director, Office of Foreign Missions	David Fields
Director, Refugee Programs	Princeton Lyman
Counselor of the Department	Robert B. Zoellick
Inspector General	Sherman M. Funk
Director, Policy Planning Staff	Dennis B. Ross
Assistant Secretary for Legislative Affairs	Janet G. Mullins
Assistant Secretary for Human Rights and Humanitarian Affairs	Richard Schifter
Legal Adviser	Edwin D. Williamson
Assistant Secretary for African Affairs	Herman J. Cohen
Assistant Secretary for East Asian and Pacific Affairs	Richard Solomon
Assistant Secretary for European and Canadian Affairs	Raymond G.H. Seitz
Assistant Secretary for Inter-American Affairs	Bernard W. Aronson
Permanent Representative of the United States of America to the Organization of American States	(vacancy)

Assistant Secretary for Near Eastern and South Asian Affairs	JOHN H. KELLY
Assistant Secretary for Economic and Business Affairs	EUGENE MCALLISTER
Assistant Secretary for Intelligence and Research	DOUGLAS P. MULHOLLAND
Assistant Secretary for International Organization Affairs	JOHN R. BOLTON
Assistant Secretary for Oceans and International Environmental and Scientific Affairs	E.U. CURTIS BOHLEN
Assistant Secretary for Public Affairs and Spokesman of the Department	MARGARET TUTWILER
Assistant Secretary, Bureau of Politico-Military Affairs	RICHARD A. CLARKE
Assistant Secretary for International Narcotics Matters	MELVYN LEVITSKY
Director, Bureau of International Communications and Information Policy	BRADLEY P. HOLMES

United States Mission to the United Nations [1]

799 United Nations Plaza, New York, NY 10017

United States Representative to the United Nations and Representative in the Security Council	THOMAS R. PICKERING
Deputy United States Representative to the United Nations	ALEXANDER F. WATSON
Deputy United States Representative in the Security Council	(VACANCY)
United States Representative on the Economic and Social Council	JONATHAN MOORE
Alternate Representative for Special Political Affairs in the United Nations	SHIRIN R. TAHIR-KHELI

[For the Department of State statement of organization, see the *Code of Federal Regulations,* Title 22, Part 5]

The Department of State advises the President in the formulation and execution of foreign policy. As Chief Executive, the President has overall responsibility for the foreign policy of the United States. The Department of State's primary objective in the conduct of foreign relations is to promote the long-range security and well-being of the United States. The Department determines and analyzes the facts relating to American overseas interests, makes recommendations on policy and future action, and takes the necessary steps to carry out established policy. In so doing, the Department engages in continuous consultations with the American public, the Congress, other U.S. departments and agencies, and foreign governments; negotiates treaties and agreements with foreign nations; speaks for the United States in the United Nations and in more than 50 major international organizations in which the United States participates; and represents the United States at more than 800 international conferences annually.

---

[1] For a description of the organization and functions of the United Nations, see page 799.

DEPARTMENT OF STATE

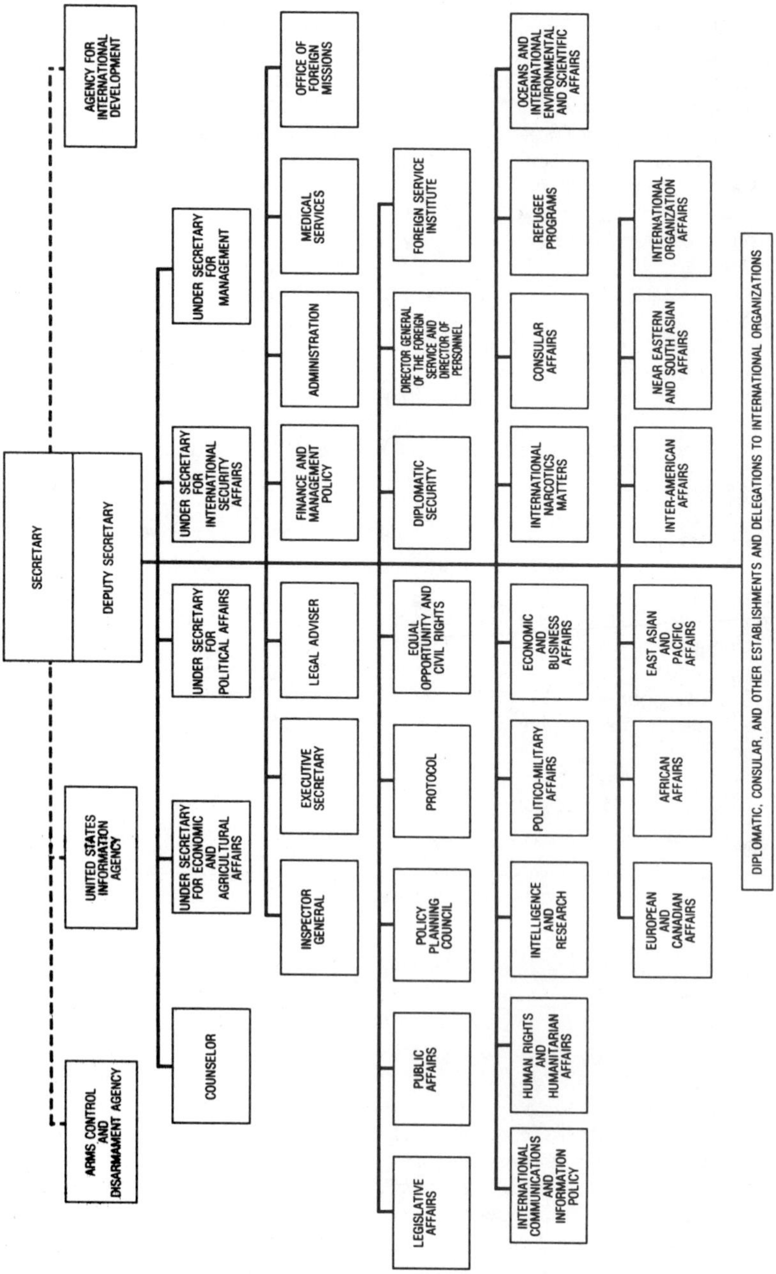

The Department of State, the senior executive department of the U.S. Government, was established by act of July 27, 1789 (1 Stat. 28) as the Department of Foreign Affairs and was renamed Department of State by act of September 15, 1789 (1 Stat. 68).

The Secretary of State is the principal official of the Department and performs duties enjoined or entrusted to the position by the President in accordance with the Constitution, relative to correspondence, commissions, or instructions to or with public ministers or consuls from the United States, or to negotiations with public ministers from foreign states or princes, or to memorials or other applications from foreign public ministers or other foreigners, or to such other matters respecting foreign affairs, as the President assigns to the Department; and, furthermore, the Secretary conducts the business of the Department in such manner as the President orders or instructs.

The act of September 15, 1789, provided that certain domestic duties, such as maintaining custody of The Great Seal of the United States and the publication of laws enacted by Congress, were entrusted to the Department. During the first few decades of the Republic, a large number of additional domestic functions were assigned to the Department, which for a time came to be the equivalent of the "home department" of the Government. Many of these responsibilities were eventually transferred to other Federal agencies as the U.S. Government grew in size and complexity during the 19th and 20th centuries.

The duties of the Department of State in the field of foreign affairs have not changed significantly in scope since the early years of the United States but have become far more detailed as the Nation has grown and its international commitments have multiplied.

Office of the Secretary

Secretary of State The Secretary of State, the principal foreign policy adviser to the President, is responsible for the overall direction, coordination, and supervision of U.S. foreign relations and for the interdepartmental activities of the U.S. Government overseas. The Secretary is the first-ranking member of the Cabinet, is a member of the National Security Council, and is in charge of the operations of the Department, including the Foreign Service.

Deputy Secretary of State The Deputy Secretary of State is the Secretary's principal deputy and serves as Acting Secretary in the Secretary's absence.

Political Affairs The Under Secretary for Political Affairs assists the Secretary and Deputy Secretary in the formulation and conduct of foreign policy and in the overall direction of the Department, including coordination of relations with other departments and agencies and interdepartmental activities of the U.S. Government overseas.

Counselor The Counselor is a principal officer of the Department, serving the Secretary as a special adviser and consultant on major problems of foreign policy. The Counselor conducts special international negotiations and consultations as directed by the Secretary and provides guidance to the appropriate bureaus with respect to such matters.

Economic and Agricultural Affairs The Under Secretary for Economic and Agricultural Affairs is principal adviser to the Secretary and Deputy Secretary in the formulation and conduct of foreign economic policy. Specific areas for which the Under Secretary is responsible include international trade, agriculture, energy, finance, transportation, and relations with developing countries.

International Security Affairs The Under Secretary for International Security Affairs is responsible for assuring the integration of all elements of the Foreign Assistance Program as an effective instrument of U.S. foreign policy and serves as Chairman of the Arms Transfer Management Group. The Under Secretary is also responsible for international scientific and technological issues, communications and information policy, and technology transfers.

Management The Under Secretary for Management is the principal management official of the Department.

The Under Secretary serves as the principal adviser to the Secretary and Deputy Secretary on management matters, including direction of all budgetary, administrative, and personnel policies of the Department and the Foreign Service. The Under Secretary also coordinates the activities of the Bureau of Personnel, the Bureau of Administration, the Bureau of Finance and Management Policy, the Bureau of Consular Affairs, the Bureau of Refugee Programs, the Office of Medical Services, the Bureau of Diplomatic Security, the Foreign Service Institute, the Family Liaison Office, the Curator of the Diplomatic Reception Rooms, and the Office of Foreign Missions. The Under Secretary for Management's principal concern is the reconciliation of resources, both fiscal and personnel, with policy requirements.

Inspector General The Office of the Inspector General of the Department of State and the Foreign Service arranges for, directs, and conducts inspections, investigations, and audits of Department offices and bureaus and its missions and posts overseas. The Office provides an independent and systematic assessment of how effectively foreign policy is being implemented and how the interests of the United States are being represented overseas, including a review of all activities, operations, and functions under the direction, coordination, and supervision of the chiefs of missions overseas. The Office also assesses the efficiency and economy of Department activities and operations, security standards and functions, and provides the coordination and leadership for inquiries into allegations of fraud, abuse, or other serious problems.

Regional Bureaus

Five Assistant Secretaries direct the activities of the geographic bureaus, which are responsible for our foreign affairs activities throughout the world. These are the Bureaus of African Affairs, European and Canadian Affairs, East Asian and Pacific Affairs, Inter-American Affairs, and Near Eastern and South Asian Affairs. The Assistant Secretaries for these bureaus are responsible for advising the Secretary regarding countries within their regional jurisdictions and for guiding the operation of the U.S. diplomatic establishments in the countries in their geographic areas. They also direct, coordinate, and supervise interdepartmental and interagency matters involving these regions. They are assisted in these duties by Deputy Assistant Secretaries and country Office Directors within their bureaus. The Office Directors and their staffs have specific responsibility for working-level management of U.S. relations with respect to their assigned countries. As the Washington focal point for the development of policy recommendations for coordination with other departments and agencies, and for transmission of guidance to Ambassadors in the field, these Office Directors are charged with assuring that all elements—both in Washington and within our missions abroad—jointly pursue U.S. foreign policy directives.

Each bureau also includes an executive office responsible for management issues including budget design and formulation, financial control, personnel administration, administrative support of overseas posts, implementation of data processing and other systems requirements, and coordination with other regional executive offices on departmentwide administrative questions.

The regional Assistant Secretaries also serve as Chairmen of Interdepartmental Groups in the National Security Council system. These groups discuss and decide issues that can be settled at the Assistant Secretary level, including those arising out of the implementation of National Security Council decisions. They prepare policy papers for consideration by the Council and contingency papers on potential crisis areas for Council review.

Functional Areas

Economic and Business Affairs The Bureau of Economic and Business Affairs has overall responsibility for formulating and implementing policy regarding foreign economic matters, including resource and food policy, international energy issues, trade and trade controls, international finance and development, aviation and maritime affairs.

For further information, call 202–647–2720.

Intelligence and Research The Bureau of Intelligence and Research coordinates programs of intelligence, research, and analysis for the Department and for other Federal agencies, and produces intelligence studies and current intelligence analyses essential to foreign policy determination and execution. In addition, the Bureau, through its Office of Research, maintains liaison with cultural and educational institutions and with other Federal agencies on a wide range of matters relating to Government contractual and private foreign affairs research.

For further information, call 202–647–1080.

International Communications and Information Policy The Bureau of International Communications and Information Policy is the principal adviser to the Secretary of State on international telecommunications policy issues affecting U.S. foreign policy and national security. The Bureau acts as coordinator with other U.S. Government agencies and the private sector in the formulation and implementation of international policies relating to a wide range of rapidly evolving communications and information technologies. The Bureau promotes U.S. telecommunications interests bilaterally and multilaterally.

For further information, call 202–647–5832.

International Narcotics Matters The Bureau of International Narcotics Matters is responsible for developing, coordinating, and implementing international narcotics control assistance activities of the Department of State as authorized under sections 481 and 482 of the Foreign Assistance Act of 1961, as amended (22 U.S.C. 2291, 2292). It is the principal point of contact and provides advice on international narcotics control matters for the Office of Management and Budget, the National Security Council, and the White House Office of National Drug Control Policy in ensuring implementation of U.S. policy in international narcotics matters.

The Bureau provides guidance on narcotics control matters to chiefs of missions and directs narcotics control coordinators at posts abroad; communicates or authorizes communication, as appropriate with foreign governments, on drug control matters including negotiating, concluding, and terminating agreements relating to international narcotics control programs as authorized by section 1(g)(3) of State Department Delegation of Authority No. 145 of February 4, 1980.

It also oversees and coordinates the international narcotics control policies and programs of all involved U.S. agencies.

The Bureau represents the United States at the United Nations Commission on Narcotic Drugs and at other international meetings and conferences on drugs, narcotics, and psychotropic substances.

International Organization Affairs The Bureau of International Organization Affairs provides guidance and support for United States participation in international organizations and conferences. It leads in the development, coordination, and implementation of United States multilateral policy. The Bureau formulates and implements United States policy toward international organizations, with particular emphasis on those organizations which make up the United Nations system.

For further information, call 202–647–6400.

Legal Adviser The Legal Adviser is the principal adviser to the Secretary and, through the Secretary, to the President on all matters of international law arising in the conduct of United States foreign relations. The Legal Adviser also provides general legal advice and services to the Secretary and other officials of the Department on matters with which the Department and overseas posts are concerned.

Legislative Affiars The Office of the Assistant Secretary for Legislative Affairs is responsible for supervising and coordinating all legislative activities, with the exception of administrative matters, between the Department of State, the Congress, and the other executive agencies.

The objectives of the Office are to assist in directing the Secretary's foreign policy legislative programs; providing advice and information to other areas of the Department on legislative matters; monitoring, processing, and transmitting all correspondence to the Congress; and serving as the initial point of contact for legislative inquiries.

The Office closely monitors all bills which affect the foreign affairs agencies; approves and schedules appearances by Department officers before congressional committees; coordinates the nominations process for ambassadors and other political officers requiring Senate confirmation; and administers all congressional travel overseas.

For further information, call 202–647–2163.

Medical Services The Office of Medical Services (MED) develops, manages, and staffs a worldwide primary health care system for American citizen employees, and eligible dependents, of the U.S. Government residing abroad. Agencies which participate in this medical program include the Department of State, the U.S. Information Service, the U.S. Agency for International Development, and over 45 other foreign affairs agencies and offices. In support of its overseas operations, MED approves and monitors the medical evacuation of patients, conducts pre-employment and in-service physical examinations, and provides clinical referral and advisory services. Domestically, MED offers occupational health care, as well as numerous health education and health maintenance programs.

For further informaion, call 202–647–3617.

Public Affairs The Bureau of Public Affairs provides information on U.S. foreign policy to the American people. It advises the Secretary on public opinion, plans and carries out domestic public affairs activities, and arranges continuing contacts between Department officials and private citizens and groups through conferences, briefings, and speaking and media engagements within the Department and across the country. The Assistant Secretary for Public Affairs is also the Spokesman of the Department, and the Bureau's Press Office conducts daily press briefings. The Bureau produces and distributes publications on U.S. foreign policy; publishes the diplomatic history of the United States, and answers public inquiries and replies to correspondence on foreign policy issues. The Bureau also serves as liaison between the State Department and State and local elected officials.

For further information, call 202–647–6575.

Consular Affairs The Bureau of Consular Affairs, under the direction of the Assistant Secretary, is responsible for the administration and enforcement of the provisions of the immigration and nationality laws, insofar as they concern the Department and the Foreign Service, for the issuance of passports and visas and related services, and for the protection and welfare of American citizens and interests abroad. Approximately 4 million passports a year are issued by the Passport Office of the Bureau, which has agencies in Boston, Chicago, Honolulu, Houston, Los Angeles, Miami, New Orleans, New York, Philadelphia, San Francisco, Seattle, Stamford, and Washington, DC.

For further information, see Sources of Information on pages 434, 436, and 437.

Politico-Military Affairs The Bureau of Politico-Military Affairs originates and develops policy guidance and provides general direction within the Department on issues that affect U.S. security policies, military assistance, nuclear policy, and arms control matters. In addition, the Bureau maintains liaison with the Department of Defense and other Federal agencies on a wide range of political/military affairs.

For further information, call 202–647–5104.

Oceans and International Environmental and Scientific Affairs The Bureau of Oceans and International Environmental and Scientific Affairs has principal responsibility for the Department's formulation and implementation of U.S. Government policies and proposals for the scientific and technological aspects of our relations with other countries and international organizations. It also has the management responsibility for a broad range of foreign policy issues and significant global problems related to environment, oceans, fisheries, population, nuclear technology, space and other fields of advanced technology, and for cooperative efforts dealing with the application and transfer of technology.

The Bureau:

—advises the Secretary where science and technology or the Bureau's functional responsibilities are concerned;

—represents the Department in international negotiations in its area of responsibility;

—provides policy guidance to the U.S. oceanic, environmental, scientific, and technological communities on activities and programs affecting foreign policy issues;

—assures effective coordination of policy responsibilities between the Department and the Agency for International Development in the field of science and technology; and

—directs the Environment Science and Technology Cone and the Overseas Counselor/Attaché Programs.

The Bureau develops and directs the carrying out of policy recommendations relative to U.S. participation in international science and technology programs; in bilateral cooperative programs related to its areas of interests; and in the activities of the International Fisheries Commissions of which the United States is a member.

For further information, call 202–647–3529.

Protocol The Office of the Chief of Protocol is the principal adviser for the U.S. Government, the President, the Vice President, and the Secretary of State on matters of diplomatic procedure governed by law or international custom and practice. The Office is responsible for:

—visits of foreign chiefs of state, heads of government, and other high officials to the United States;

—operation of the President's guest house, Blair House;

—delegations representing the President at official ceremonies abroad;

—conduct of official ceremonial functions and public events;

—accreditation of approximately 46,000 foreign embassy, consular, and international organization personnel throughout the United States;

—determining entitlement to diplomatic or consular immunity;

—publication of diplomatic, mission employee, and consular lists;

—resolution of problems arising out of diplomatic or consular immunity such as legal and police matters; and

—approving the opening of consular offices in conjunction with the Office of Foreign Missions.

For further information, call 202–647–2663.

Human Rights and Humanitarian Affairs The Bureau of Human Rights and Humanitarian Affairs has responsibility for the formulation and development and, in cooperation with other bureaus, the implementation of U.S. policy relating to the observance of human rights throughout the world. The Bureau maintains liaison with nongovernmental organizations active in the human rights field and is principally responsible for the preparation of the annual Department report on human rights practices in countries that are members of the United Nations or receive U.S. economic or military assistance. In addition, the Bureau provides the Department's advice to the

Immigration and Naturalization Service regarding applications for political asylum by foreign nationals.

For further information, call 202–647–2126.

Refugee Programs The Bureau for Refugee Programs is responsible for the operation of U.S. refugee programs overseas, carried out in cooperation with other governments, private and international organizations, and other U.S. Government agencies, including the Agency for International Development, the Immigration and Naturalization Service of the Department of Justice, and the Office of Refugee Resettlement of the Department of Health and Human Services. These programs include relief and repatriation of refugees; and the selection, processing, and training of refugees to be admitted into the United States, in consultation with the Congress and State and local governments. They are carried out through grants to private voluntary agencies and international organizations, including the Intergovernmental Committee for Migration, the United Nations High Commissioner for Refugees, and the United Nations Relief and Works Agency for Palestine Refugees.

For further information, call 202–663–1520.

Foreign Service

To a great extent the future of our country depends on the relations we have with other countries, and those relations are conducted principally by the United States Foreign Service. As of April 1990, representatives at 144 Embassies, 9 missions, 71 consulates general, 26 consulates, 1 branch office, and 23 consular agencies throughout the world report to the State Department on the multitude of foreign developments that have a bearing on the welfare and security of the American people. These trained representatives provide the President and the Secretary of State with much of the raw material from which foreign policy is made and with the recommendations that help shape it.

The Ambassador is the personal representative of the President and reports to the President through the Secretary of State. Ambassadors have full responsibility for implementing the U.S. foreign policy by any and all U.S. Government personnel within their country of assignment, except those under military commands. Their responsibilities include negotiating agreements between the United States and the host country, explaining and disseminating official U.S. policy, and maintaining cordial relations with that country's government and people.

A listing of Foreign Service posts, together with addresses and telephone numbers and key personnel, appears in *Key Officers of Foreign Service Posts—Guide for Business Representatives,* which is for sale by the Superintendent of Documents, Government Printing Office, Washington, DC 20402.

United States Diplomatic Offices—Foreign Service

(C: Consular Office; N: No Embassy or Consular Office)

Country/Embassy	Ambassador
Albania/Tirana	(Vacancy)
Algeria/Algiers	Mary Ann Casey
Antigua and Barbuda/St. Johns	Reginald J. McHugh (Chargé)
Argentina/Buenos Aires	Terence A. Todman
Australia/Canberra	Melvin F. Sembler
Austria/Vienna	Roy M. Huffington
Bahamas/Nassau	Carol B. Hallett
Bahrain/Manama	Charles W. Hostler
Bangladesh/Dacca	Willard Ames De Pree
Barbados/Bridgetown	(Vacancy)
Belgium/Brussels	Bruce S. Gelb
Belize/Belize City	Robert G. Rich, Jr.
Benin/Cotonou	Harriet Isom
Bolivia/La Paz	Robert S. Gelbard
Botswana/Gaborone	David Passage
Brazil/Brasilia	Richard Huntington Melton
Brunei Darussalam/Bandar Seri Begawan.	Christopher H. Phillips
Bulgaria/Sofia	Kenneth H. Hill
Burkina Faso/Ouagadougou	Edward Brynn
Burma/Rangoon	(Vacancy)
Burundi/Bujumbura	Cynthia Perry
Cameroon/Yaoundé	Frances Cook
Canada/Ottawa	Edward Ney
Cape Verde/Praia	Francis T. McNamara

United States Diplomatic Offices—Foreign Service—Continued

(C: Consular Office; N: No Embassy or Consular Office)

Country/Embassy	Ambassador
Central African Republic/Bangui	Daniel Simpson
Chad/N'Djamena	Richard Bogosian
Chile/Santiago	Charles A. Gillespie
China, People's Republic of/Beijing.	Stapleton Roy
Colombia/Bogotá	Thomas E. McNamara
Comoros, Federal and Islamic Republic of the/Moroni (N).	Kenneth Peltier
Congo, People's Republic of the/Brazzaville.	Leonard Grant Shurtleff
Costa Rica/San José	(Vacancy)
Cyprus/Nicosia	(Vacancy)
Czechoslovakia/Prague	Shirley Temple Black
Denmark/Copenhagen	Keith L. Brown
Djibouti, Republic of/Djibouti	Charles R. Baquet III
Dominica/Roseau (N)	(Vacancy)
Dominican Republic/Santo Domingo.	Paul D. Taylor
Ecuador/Quito	Richard N. Holwill
Egypt/Cairo	Robert H. Pelletreau
El Salvador/San Salvador	William G. Walker
Equatorial Guinea/Malabo	John E. Bennett
Ethiopia/Addis Ababa	Robert G. Houdek
Fiji/Suva	Evelyn I.H. Teegan
Finland/Helsinki	John G. Weinmann
France/Paris	Walter J. Gurley
Gabon/Libreville	Keith Wauchope
Gambia/Banjul	Arlene Render
Germany, Federal Republic of/Bonn.	Vernon A. Walters
Ghana/Accra	Raymond C. Ewing
Greece/Athens	Michael Sotirhos
Grenada/St. George's	John Ford Cooper (Chargé)
Guatemala/Guatemala	Thomas F. Stroock
Guinea/Conakry	Dane Smith
Guinea-Bissau, Republic of/Bissau.	William L. Jacobsen, Jr.
Guyana/Georgetown	Theresa Anne Tull
Haiti/Port-au-Prince	Alvin P. Adams
Holy See/Vatican City	Thomas P. Melady
Honduras/Tegucigalpa	Cresencio S. Arcos, Jr.
Hungary/Budapest	Charles H. Thomas II
Iceland/Reykjavik	Charles E. Cobb, Jr.
India/New Delhi	William Clark, Jr.
Indonesia/Jakarta	John C. Monjo
Iraq/Baghdad	April Catherine Glaspie
Ireland/Dublin	Richard A. Moore
Israel/Tel Aviv	William Andreas Brown
Italy/Rome	Peter Secchia
Ivory Coast/Abidjan	Keith L. Brown
Jamaica/Kingston	Glenn Holden
Japan/Tokyo	Michael H. Armacost
Jerusalem (C)	Philip Wilcox, Jr.
Jordan/Amman	Roscoe Seldon Suddarth
Kenya/Nairobi	Smith Hempstone
Kiribati, Republic of/Parawa (N)	Evelyn I.H. Teegan
Korea/Seoul	Donald P. Gregg
Kuwait/Kuwait	W. Nathaniel Howell
Laos/Vientiane	Charles B. Salmon, Jr. (Chargé)
Lebanon/Beirut	John T. McCarthy
Lesotho/Maseru	Leonard O. Spearman
Liberia/Monrovia	Peter J. DeVos
Libyan Arab Jamahiriya, Socialist People's/Tripoli.	(Vacancy)
Liechtenstein (N)	
Luxembourg/Luxembourg	Edward M. Rowell
Madagascar/Antananarivo	Howard Walker
Malawi/Lilongwe	George Michael T.F. Pistor
Malaysia/Kuala Lampur	Paul M. Cleveland
Maldives/Malé (N)	Marion V. Creekmore, Jr.
Mali/Bamako	Herbert D. Gelber
Malta/Valletta	Sally Johnson Novetze
Marshall Islands/Majuro	William Bodde, Jr.
Mauritania/Nouakchott	Gordon S. Brown
Mauritius/Port Louis	Penne Percy Korth
Mexico/Mexico, D.F.	John D. Negroponte
Micronesia/Kolonia	Aurelia E. Brazeal
Mongolia/Ulaanbaatar/	Joseph Edward Lake
Morocco/Rabat	E. Michael Ussery
Mozambique/Maputo	Townsend Friedman
Nauru/Yaren (N)	(Vacancy)
Nepal/Kathmandu	Julia Chang Bloch
Netherlands/The Hague	C. Howard Wilkins
New Zealand/Wellington	Della Newman
Nicaragua/Managua	(Vacancy)
Niger/Niamey	Jennifer C. Ward
Nigeria/Lagos	Lannon Walker
Norway/Oslo	Loret M. Ruppe
Oman/Muscat	Richard W. Boehm
Pakistan/Islamabad	Nicholas Platt
Panama/Panamá	Deane Roesch Hinton
Papua New Guinea/Port Moresby.	Robert William Farrand
Paraguay/Asunción	John D. Glassman
Peru/Lima	Anthony Cecil Eden Quainton
Philippines/Manila	Nicholas Platt
Poland/Warsaw	Thomas W. Simmons, Jr.
Portugal/Lisbon	Everett E. Briggs
Qatar/Doha	Mark G. Hambley
Romania/Bucharest	Alan Green, Jr.
Rwanda/Kigali	Robert A. Flaten
Sao Tome and Principe/Sao Tome (N).	Keith Wauchope
San Marino (N)	
Saudi Arabia/Jidda	Charles W. Freeman, Jr.
Senegal/Dakar	Katherine Shirley
Seychelles, Republic of/Victoria, Mahe.	Richard W. Carlson
Sierra Leone/Freetown	Johnny Young
Singapore/Singapore	Robert D. Orr
Solomon Islands/Honiara (N)	Daniel A. Vernon
Somali Democratic Republic/Mogadscio.	(Vacancy)
South Africa/Pretoria, Transvaal	William L. Swing
Spain/Madrid	Joseph Zappala
Sri Lanka/Colombo	Marion V. Creekmore, Jr.
St. Christopher and Nevis/Basseterre (N).	Reginald J. McHugh (Chargé)
St. Lucia/Castries (N)	(Vacancy)
St. Vincent and the Grenadines/Kingstown (N).	(Vacancy)
Sudan/Khartoum	James Cheek
Suriname/Paramaribo	Richard C. Howland
Swaziland/Mbabane	Stephen Rogers
Sweden/Stockholm	Charles E. Redman
Switzerland/Bern	Stephen Rogers
Syria/Damascus	Edward P. Djerejian
Tanzania/Dar es Salaam	Edmund DeJarnette
Thailand/Bangkok	Daniel A. O'Donohue
Togo/Lomé	Harmon E. Kirby
Tonga/Nuku'alofa (N)	Evelyn I.H. Teegan

United States Diplomatic Offices—Foreign Service—Continued

(C: Consular Office; N: No Embassy or Consular Office)

Country/Embassy	Ambassador
Trinidad and Tobago/Port-of-Spain.	Charles A. Gargano
Tunisia/Tunis	John T. McCarthy
Turkey/Ankara	Morton I. Abramowitz
Tuvalu/Funafuti (N)	Evelyn I.H. Teegan
Uganda/Kampala	Johnnie Carson
Union of Soviet Socialist Republics/Moscow.	Jack F. Matlock
United Arab Emirates/Abu Dhabi.	Edward S. Walker, Jr.
United Kingdom of Great Britain and Northern Ireland/London.	(Vacancy)
Uruguay/Montevideo	Malcolm Richard Wilkey
Vanuatu, Republic of/Port Vila (N).	Robert William Farrand
Venezuela/Caracas	(Vacancy)
Western Samoa/Apia (N)	William Francisco III (Chargé)
Yemen Arab Republic/Sanaa	Charles Franklin Dunbar
Yugoslavia/Belgrade	Warren Zimmermann
Zaire/Kinshasa	William Caldwell Harrop
Zambia/Lusaka	Gordon Streeb
Zimbabwe/Harare	(Vacancy)

Sources of Information

Audiovisual Materials The Bureau of Consular Affairs has a 12-minute videotape on the safety of international travel. "Traveling Abroad More Safely" provides general practical advice to U.S. citizen travelers on avoiding the hazards of foreign travel. It includes steps to take prior to departure, ways to protect against theft and legal problems, and ways U.S. embassies and consulates can assist U.S. citizens who encounter difficulty abroad. The tape is available for $9 in VHS and Beta and $12.50 in 3/4-inch format, plus a $3 mailing and handling fee from Video Transfer, Inc., 5710 Arundel Avenue, Rockville, MD 20552. Phone, 301–881–0270.

Conferences, Seminars, Speaking Engagements, Briefings The Department of State arranges a variety of programs, both in Washington, DC, and throughout the country, designed to bring officials into personal contact with the public. National foreign policy conferences for specific audiences—business leaders, educators, nongovernmental organizations—plus Executive and Media-Diplomat Seminars are held each year at the Department of State. These seminars consist of foreign policy briefings and roundtable discussions. Special briefings for national nongovernmental organizations and other visiting groups are also available on request.

Foreign policy specialists from the Department of State are available for speaking engagements outside Washington before nongovernmental organizations and institutions in the United States as well as to brief local editors and journalists and take part in local radio and TV call-in and current events programs. Regional foreign policy conferences also are held in cooperation with local sponsors in major cities throughout the country.

For information, write to the Office of Public Liaison, Bureau of Public Affairs, Department of State, Room 5831, Washington, DC 20520. Phone, 202–647–1433.

Contracts General inquiries may be directed to the Office of Acquisitions (A/OPR/ACQ), Department of State, Washington, DC 20520. Phone, 703–875–6000.

Diplomatic and Official Passports Department employees and administrative offices may use diplomatic and official passports only as long as they are retained in the position or status for which originally issued. Section 51.4 of title 22 of the *Code of Federal Regulations* states that such passports must be returned upon termination of the bearer's diplomatic or official status.

In accordance with the Department's *Foreign Affairs Manual* (3 FAM 784), it is the responsibility of administrative officers to ensure that Form DS-8A includes a record of the disposition of passports issued to separating or retiring employees and their dependents. This includes all diplomatic and official passports, as well as any tourist passports for which the employee has been reimbursed by the Department.

Because of the possibility of misuse of these documents, it is important that all offices establish and maintain effective control over passport use. These passports are normally destroyed; however, they may be cancelled and returned as mementos if requested.

Diplomatic passports may not be used by employees for strictly personal travel. Regulations permit their use for incidental personal travel related to an official assignment if the host government does not object. However, if employees or their dependents perfer to travel on a regular tourist passport in connection with official travel, they may apply by paying the regular passport fees and claiming reimbursement on their travel voucher.

Inquiries on these matters should be directed to Passport Services, Diplomatic and Congressional Travel Branch. Phone, 202-326-6234.

Employment Inquiries about employment in the Foreign Service should be directed to PER/REE/REC, P.O. Box 9317, Rosslyn Station, Arlington, VA 22209. Phone, 703-875-7247. Inquiries about civil service positions in the Department of State should be directed to PER/CSP/SSD, P.O. Box 18657, Washington, DC 20036-8657. The Department's Civil Service Employment Information Office is located in Room 2819 at the D Street (north) entrance of the Department of State Building, Washington, DC. Phone, 202-647-6132. The Civil Service Personnel Office maintains a 24-hour job information line which can be reached on 202-647-7284.

Freedom of Information Act and Privacy Act Requests Requests from the public for Department of State records should be addressed to the Director, Office of Freedom of Information Privacy and Classification Review, Department of State, 2201 C Street NW., Washington, DC 20520-1512. Phone, 202-647-8484. Individuals are requested to indicate on the outside of the envelope the statute under which they are requesting access: FOIA REQUEST or PRIVACY REQUEST.

Any identifiable Department of State document can be requested under the Freedom of Information Act (5 U.S.C. 552). Requesters should provide as much identifying information as possible about the document to assist the Department in locating it. Include subject matter, timeframe, originator of the information, or any other helpful data.

Only persons who are U.S. citizens or aliens who are lawfully admitted to the United States for permanent residence can request information under the Privacy Act (5 U.S.C. 552a). Under this act, individuals may request access to records that are maintained under the individual's name or some other personally indentifiable symbol. Descriptions of record systems from which documents can be retrieved by the individual's name are published in the *Federal Register,* copies of which are available from the Director, Office of Freedom of Information, Privacy and Classification Review. To expedite processing of requests, individuals should specify the system of records they wish to have searched and should provide the following identifying information: full name; aliases (if any); date and place of birth; and circumstances, including approximate time period, which would have led to the creation of the record.

A public reading room, where unclassified and declassified documents may be inspected, is located in the Department of State, 2201 C Street NW., Washington, DC. Phone, 202-647-8484. Directions to the reading room may be obtained from receptionists at public entrances to the Department.

Missing Persons, Emergencies, Deaths of Americans Abroad For information concerning missing persons, emergencies, travel advisories, and deaths of Americans abroad, contact the Citizens

Emergency Center, Department of State, 202-647-5225. Correspondence should be directed to the Overseas Citizens Services, Bureau of Consular Affairs, Department of State, Washington, DC 20520.

Passports For information concerning the issuance of U.S. passports, contact Passport Services, Bureau of Consular Affairs, 1425 K Street NW., Washington, DC 20524 (phone, 202-647-0518), or any of the field offices. Additional information concerning passport applications is available for sale by the Superintendent of Documents, Government Printing Office, Washington, DC 20402.

Field Offices—Passport Office

City	Address	Telephone
Boston, MA	Thomas P. O'Neill Federal Bldg., 02222	617-565-6990
Chicago, IL	Federal Bldg., 60604	312-353-7155
Honolulu, HI	Federal Bldg., 96850	808-541-1918
Houston, TX	1919 Smith St., 77002	713-653-3153
Los Angeles, CA	11000 Wilshire Blvd., 90024-3615	213-209-7075
Miami, FL	Federal Office Bldg., 33130	305-536-4681
New Orleans, LA	701 Loyola Ave., 70130	504-589-6161
New York, NY	Rockefeller Ctr., 10111-0031	212-541-7710
Philadelphia, PA	Federal Bldg., 19106	215-597-7482
San Francisco, CA	525 Market St., 94105-2773	415-974-9941
Seattle, WA	Federal Bldg., 98174	206-442-7945
Stamford, CT	1 Landmark Sq., 06901	203-325-3530
Washington, DC	1425 K St. NW., 20524-0002	212-647-0518

Publications The Department's Bureau of Public Affairs produces a variety of publications on the Department and foreign policy, including two official documentary series, *Foreign Relations of the United States* and *American Foreign Policy: Current Documents*; and *Background Notes.*

The series *Foreign Relations of the United States,* published since 1861 in over 300 volumes to date, constitutes the official documentary record of the foreign policy of the United States. It is the most extensive and most nearly current publication of diplomatic papers in the world. The Office of the Historian has published all but 4 of 27 triennial volumes of declassified documents covering the years 1955 through 1957 and has begun release of 18 print volumes for the years 1958 through 1960 (with up to 9 microfiche supplements). Selected volumes for the years 1961 through 1963 relating to Vietnam also have been released.

The *American Foreign Policy* annual volumes contain current official public expressions of policy that best convey the objectives of U.S. foreign policy. The series includes texts of major official messages, addresses, statements, reports, and communications by the White House, Department of State, and other Federal agencies involved in the foreign affairs process. Microfiche supplements, which include additional public documents, accompany the 1981 and subsequent annual volumes.

Background Notes provide brief, factual summaries concerning the people, history, government, economy, and foreign relations of about 170 countries (excluding the United States) and of selected international organizations. A free index is available from the Bureau of Public Affairs.

For information on these and other Department publications, write to the Public Information Center, Bureau of Public Affairs, Department of State, Room 5819, Washington, DC 20520. Phone, 202-647-6575.

Reading Room To review declassified Department documents, contact the receptionists at the public entrance to the Department of State, 2201 C Street NW., Washington, DC, for the specific location. Phone, 202-647-8484.

Telephone Directory The Department's telephone directory is available for sale by the Superintendent of Documents, Government Printing Office, Washington, DC 20402.

Tips for U.S. Travelers Abroad The following pamphlets from the Bureau of Consular Affairs are for sale for $1 by the Superintendent of Documents, U.S. Government Printing Office, Washington, DC 20402:

Travel Tips for Older Americans contains basic information on official documents, clothing, health, money, aid for serious problems, and other useful travel tips for senior citizens.

Your Trip Abroad contains basic information on official documents, vaccinations, unusual travel requirements, dual nationality, drugs, modes of travel, customs, legal requirements, and many other topics for the American tourist, business representative, or student traveling overseas.

A Safe Trip Abroad contains helpful precautions to minimize one's chances of becoming a victim of terrorism and also provides safety tips.

Tips for Americans Residing Abroad contains advice for more than 2 million Americans living in foreign countries.

Travel Warning on Drugs Abroad contains important facts on the potential dangers of being arrested for illegal drugs abroad and the type of assistance that U.S. consular officers can and cannot provide. This booklet is free from the Department of State, Room 5807, Consular Affairs/Political Affairs, Washington, DC 20520.

The Bureau of Consular Affairs also publishes a series of brochures on travel to specific areas of the world. Depending on the region, the brochures cover topics such as currency and customs regulations, entry requirements, dual nationality, and restrictions on the use of photography. Copies are available from the Government Printing Office for $1. Currently available are: *Tips for Travelers to the Caribbean; Tips for Travelers to Cuba; Tips for Travelers to Eastern Europe and Yugoslavia; Tips for Travelers to Mexico; Tips for Travelers to the Middle East and North Africa; Tips for Travelers to the People's Republic of China; Tips for Travelers to South Asia; Tips for Travelers to the USSR; Tips for Travelers to Central and South America,* and *Tips for Travelers to Sub-Saharan Africa.*

Foreign Entry Requirements contains visa and other entry requirements of foreign countries. Order for 50 cents from the Consumer Information Center, Pueblo, CO 81009.

Visas To obtain information on visas for foreigners wishing to enter the United States, call 202–647–0510.

For further information concerning the Department of State, contact the Office of Public Communication, Public Information Service, Bureau of Public Affairs, Department of State, Washington, DC 20520. Phone, 202–647–6575.

DEPARTMENT OF TRANSPORTATION

400 Seventh Street SW., Washington, DC 20590
Phone, 202–366–4000

SECRETARY OF TRANSPORTATION	SAMUEL K. SKINNER
Chief of Staff	JOHN A. GAUGHAN
Special Assistant to the Secretary	ELIZABETH R. MONRO
White House Liaison	KATHY WILLS
Special Assistant to the Secretary for Scheduling	SANDRA K. BUSHUE
Deputy Secretary	ELAINE L. CHAO
Counselor to the Secretary	D. CAMERON FINDLAY
Director for Drug Enforcement and Program Compliance	ROBERT A. KNISELY
Director, Executive Secretariat	RUTH DRINKARD KNOUSE
Chairman, Board of Contract Appeals	THADDEUS V. WARE
Director of Civil Rights	WILLIAM T. HUDSON
Director of Small and Disadvantaged Business Utilization	ALICIA L. CASANOVA
Director of Commercial Space Transportation	STEPHANIE LEE-MILLER
Associate Director for Program Affairs	CHARLES T. KLINE, JR.
Associate Director for Licensing Programs	NORMAN C. BOWLES
Associate Director for Industry Policy and Planning	RICHARD W. SCOTT, JR.
Director of Intelligence and Security	CLYDE E. ROBBINS
Deputy Director of Intelligence and Security	JACK A. RENWICK
Inspector General	A. MARY STERLING
Assistant Inspector General for Auditing	RAYMOND J. DECARLI
Deputy Assistant Inspector General for Auditing	LAWRENCE H. WEINTROB
Assistant Inspector General for Investigations	H. RAE SCOTT
Deputy Assistant Inspector General for Investigations	SEBASTIAN R. LORIGO
Assistant Inspector General for Policy, Planning, and Resources	JOHN W. LAINHART IV
General Counsel	(VACANCY)
Deputy General Counsel	ROSALIND A. KNAPP
Associate General Counsel	C. DEAN MCGRATH, JR.
Special Counsel	DIANE R. LIFF
Assistant General Counsel for Environmental, Civil Rights and General Law	ROBERTA D. GABEL
Deputy Assistants	JAMES R. DANN DAVID K. TOCHEN
Patent Counsel	OTTO M. WILDENSTEINER
Assistant General Counsel for International Law	DONALD H. HORN
Deputy Assistant	(VACANCY)
Assistant General Counsel for Litigation	PAUL M. GEIER
Deputy Assistant	MARY B. REED

Assistant General Counsel for Legislation	THOMAS W. HERLIHY
Deputy Assistant	CLARE R. DONELAN
Assistant General Counsel for Regulation and Enforcement	NEIL R. EISNER
Deputy Assistant	ROBERT C. ASHBY
Chief, Documentary Services Division	PHYLLIS T. KAYLOR
Chairman, Board for Correction of Military Records	ROBERT H. JOOST
Deputy Chairman	NANCY BATTAGLIA
Assistant General Counsel for Aviation Enforcement and Proceedings	SAMUEL PODBERESKY
Deputy Assistant	DAYTON LEHMAN, JR.
Assistant Secretary for Policy and International Affairs	JEFFREY N. SHANE
Deputy Assistant Secretaries	PATRICK MURPHY JOSEPH F. CANNY (VACANCY)
Director of Special Programs	PETER ROSENOW
Director, Management Staff	ALLEN TRUHAN
Director of Transportation Regulatory Affairs	DONALD R. TRILLING
Director of Economics	RICHARD WALSH
Director of International Transportation and Trade	ARNOLD LEVINE
Director of International Aviation	PAUL GRETCH
Director of Aviation Analysis	JOHN COLEMAN
Director of Safety Program Review	JAMES H. NEW
Assistant Secretary for Budget and Programs	KATE L. MOORE
Deputy Assistant Secretary	WALLACE D. BURNETT
Special Assistant	JOCELYN A. STEVENSON
Director of Programs and Evaluation	GEORGE W. MCDONALD
Director of Budget	KATHERINE E. COLLINS
Assistant Secretary for Administration	JON H. SEYMOUR
Deputy Assistant Secretaries	MELISSA J. ALLEN PAUL T. WEISS
Director of Personnel	DIANA L. ZEIDEL
Director of Management Planning	GLENDA M. TATE
Director of Information Resource Management	(VACANCY)
Director of Administrative Services and Property Management	RONALD D. KEEFER
Director, Office of Hearings	JOHN J. MATHIAS
Director of Acquisition and Grant Management	LINDA M. HIGGINS
Director of Security	(VACANCY)
Director of Financial Management	JOYCE D. SHELTON
Director of Departmental Accounting and Financial Information System Development and Implementation	EUGENE K. TAYLOR, JR.
Assistant Secretary for Governmental Affairs	GALEN J. RESER
Deputy Assistant Secretary	MARILYN RICHMOND
Director of Congressional Affairs	JOHN CLINE
Director of Intergovernmental and Industry Affairs	BETH ANN HANCOCK
Assistant Secretary for Public Affairs	MARION C. BLAKEY
Deputy Assistant Secretary	(VACANCY)

Special Assistant	CATHRYN C. LAYFIELD

UNITED STATES COAST GUARD

2100 Second Street SW., Washington, DC 20593–0001
Phone, 202–267–1587

Commandant	ADM. J. WILLIAM KIME, USCG
Vice Commandant	VICE ADM. MARTIN H. DANIELL, USCG
Chaplain	CAPT. JAMES G. GOODE, USCG
Chief Administrative Law Judge	(VACANCY)
Chairman, Marine Safety Council	REAR ADM. PAUL E. VERSAW, USCG
Chief, Congressional Affairs Staff	CAPT. JAMES D. HULL, USCG
Chief, Public Affairs Staff	CAPT. E.I. KILEY, USCG
Chief of Staff	REAR ADM. ROBERT T. NELSON, USCG
Deputy Chief of Staff	CAPT. NORMAN T. SAUNDERS, USCG
Resource Director/Comptroller	REAR ADM. RICHARD D. HERR, USCG
Chief, Office of Acquisitions	REAR ADM. KENT H. WILLIAMS, USCG
Chief, Office of Engineering and Development	REAR ADM. PETER A. BUNCH, USCG
Chief, Office of Civil Rights	WALTER R. SOMERVILLE
Chief, Office of Health and Safety	REAR ADM. MICHAEL P. HUDGINS, USPHS
Chief Counsel	REAR ADM. PAUL E. VERSAW, USCG
Chief, Office of Marine Safety, Security and Environmental Protection	REAR ADM. ARTHUR E. HENN, USCG
Chief, Office of Law Enforcement and Defense Operations	REAR ADM. WILLIAM P. LEAHY, USCG
Chief, Office of Navigation Safety and Waterway Services	REAR ADM. WILLIAM J. ECKER, USCG
Chief, Office of Personnel and Training	REAR ADM. GEORGE D. PASSMORE, JR., USCG
Chief, Office of Readiness and Reserve	(VACANCY)
Chief, Office of Command, Control and Communications	REAR ADM. RONALD M. POLANT, USCG

FEDERAL AVIATION ADMINISTRATION

800 Independence Avenue SW., Washington, DC 20591
Phone, 202–366–4000

Administrator	JAMES B. BUSEY IV
Deputy Administrator	BARRY L. HARRIS
Assistant Administrator for Airports	LEONARD L. GRIGGS
Deputy Assistant Administrator for Airports	QUENTIN S. TAYLOR
Director of Airport Planning and Programming	PAUL L. GALIS
Director of Airport Safety and Standards	LEONARD E. MUDD
Assistant Administrator for Aviation Safety	B. KEITH POTTS
Deputy Assistant Administrator for Aviation Safety	CHARLES H. HUETTNER
Director of Safety Analysis	CHARLES FLUET, *Acting*

Director of Safety Oversight	RICHARD WEISS, *Acting*
Director of Safety Quality Assurance	BILL HILL, *Acting*
Chief Counsel	KENNETH P. QUINN
Assistant Administrator for Civil Aviation Security	ORLO K. STEELE
Director of Civil Aviation Security Intelligence	JACK GREGORY
Director of Civil Aviation Security Operations	PATRICK MCDONNELL
Director of Civil Aviation Security Policy and Planning	LYNNE A. OSMUS, *Acting*
Director of Civil Aviation Security Program and Resource Management	ROBERT M. BLUNK, *Acting*
Assistant Administrator for Civil Rights	LEON C. WATKINS
Assistant Administrator for Government and Industry Affairs	BRENDA L. YAGER
Assistant Administrator for Policy, Planning and International Aviation	MICHAEL C. MOFFET
Deputy Assistant Administrator for Policy Planning and International Aviation	DALE E. MCDANIEL
Director of Aviation Policy and Plans	JOHN M. RODGERS
Director of Environment and Energy	JAMES E. DENSMORE
Director of International Aviation	JOAN W. BAUERLEIN
Assistant Administrator for Public Affairs	HUGH L. O'NEILL
Executive Director for Acquistion	JOHN BURT
Director of Acquisition Policy and Oversight	DAVID MORRISSEY
Director of Independent Operational Test and Evaluation Oversight	A. MARTIN PHILLIPS
Executive Director for Administration and Resource Management	(VACANCY)
Associate Administrator for Administration	BROOKS C. GOLDMAN
Deputy Associate Administrator for Appraisal	THERON A. GRAY
Director of Accounting	ERNEST M. KEELING
Director of Budget	NICHOLAS S. STOER
Director, Logistics Service	CAROLYN C. BLUM
Director of Management Systems	MICHAEL D. SHERWIN
Associate Administrator for Human Resource Management	HERBERT R. MCLURE
Deputy Associate Administrator for Human Resource Management	DOROTHY H. BERRY
Director of Human Resource Development	ANN ROSENWALD
Director of Labor and Employee Relations	JOSEPH W. NOONAN
Director of Personnel	KAY F. DOLAN
Director of Training and Higher Education	JOSEPH P. KISCIKI
Executive Director for Regulatory Standards and Compliance	(VACANCY)
Associate Administrator for Aviation Standards	MONTE R. BELGER
Deputy Associate Administrator for Aviation Standards	DARLENE FREEMAN
Director of Accident Investigation	WILLIAM R. HENDRICKS
Federal Air Surgeon	JON L. JORDAN, M.D., *Acting*
Associate Administrator for Regulation and Certification	ANTHONY J. BRODERICK, JR.
Deputy Associate Administrator for Regulation and Certification	(VACANCY)
Director, Aircraft Certification Service	MELVIN C. BEARD

290-950 O 91 - 15

Director, Flight Standards Service	DANIEL C. BEAUDETTE
Director of Rulemaking	CHRIS A. CHRISTIE
Director of Program and Resource Management	IRENE A. BARNETT
Executive Director for System Development	JOSEPH M. DEL BALZO
Associate Administrator for NAS Development	JOHN E. TURNER
Deputy Associate Administrator for NAS Development	ROBERT VALONE
Program Manager for Advanced Automation	MICHAEL PERIE
Program Director for Automation	TERRY R. HANNAH
Program Director for Navigation and Landing	ROD GILL, *Acting*
Program Director for Surveillance	CAREY L. WEIGEL
Program Director for Communications	(VACANCY)
Program Director for Weather and Flight Service Systems	ALVIN THOMAS
Associate Administrator for System Engineering and Development	MARTIN T. POZESKY
Deputy Associate Administrator for System Engineering and Development	JAMES G. CAIN
Facility System Engineering Service	ROBERT WEIN
NAS Program Management Service	J. ROBBINS TUCKER
NAS System Engineering Service	ROBERT E. BROWN
Operations Research Service	ANDRES ZELLWEGER
Research and Development Service	STEVEN ZAIDMAN
Executive Director for System Operations	(VACANCY)
Associate Administrator for Airway Facilities	ARNOLD AQUILANO
Deputy Associate Administrator for Airway Facilities	EDWARD M. KELLY
Director, NAS Transition and Implementation Service	STEVEN I. ROTHSCHILD
Director, System Maintenance Service	DAVID F. MORSE
Associate Administrator for Air Traffic	WILLIAM H. POLLARD
Deputy Associate Administrator for Air Traffic	NORBERT A. OWENS
Director, Air Traffic System Management	DAVID HURLEY
Director, Air Traffic Plans and Requirement Service	WALTER H. MITCHELL
Director of Air Traffic Program Management	NEIL PLANZER
Director, Air Traffic Rules and Procedures Service	L. LANE SPECK
Director of Air Traffic System Effectiveness	JOHN D. CANOLES
Director of System Capacity and Requirements	EDWARD T. HARRIS

FEDERAL HIGHWAY ADMINISTRATION

400 Seventh Street SW., Washington, DC 20590
Phone, 202–366–0660

Administrator	THOMAS D. LARSON
Deputy Administrator	EUGENE R. MCCORMICK
Executive Director	E. DEAN CARLSON
Chief Counsel	STEVEN E. WERMCRANTZ
Deputy Chief Counsel	EDWARD V.A. KUSSY
Director of Public Affairs	DAVID W. FREDERICKSON
Director of Civil Rights	EDWARD W. MORRIS, JR.

Director of Program Review	EMIL ELINSKY
Associate Administrator for Policy	STEPHEN C. LOCKWOOD
Director of Policy Development	MADELEINE S. BLOOM
Director of Highway Information Management	DAVID R. MCELHANEY
Director of International Programs	JOHN D. CUTRELL
Associate Administrator for Research and Development	CHARLES L. MILLER
Managing Director, Turner-Fairbank Highway Research Center	ROBERT J. BETSOLD
Director of the National Highway Institute	GEORGE M. SHRIEVES
Director of Engineering and Highway Operations Research and Development	THOMAS J. PASKO
Director of Safety and Traffic Operations Research and Development	ROBERT J. BETSOLD
Director of Research and Development Operations and Support	ROBERT J. KREKLAY
Associate Administrator for Program Development	ANTHONY R. KANE
Director of Engineering	THOMAS O. WILLETT
Director of Environment and Planning	KEVIN E. HEANUE
Director of Right-of-Way	BARBARA K. ORSKI
Associate Administrator for Safety and System Applications	DENNIS C. JUDYCKI
Director of Highway Safety	R. CLARKE BENNETT
Director of Traffic Operations and Intelligent Vehicle/Highway Systems	NORMAN J. VAN NESS
Director of Technology Applications	(VACANCY)
Associate Administrator for Motor Carriers	RICHARD P. LANDIS
Director of Motor Carrier Standards	JAMES E. SCAPELLATO
Director of Motor Carrier Information Management and Analysis	JOHN F. GRIMM
Director of Program Management Support	JOHN P. EICHER
Director of Motor Carrier Field Operations	MICHAEL F. TRENTACOSTE
Associate Administrator for Administration	GEORGE S. MOORE, JR.
Director of Personnel and Training	JERRY A. HAWKINS
Director of Management Systems	MICHAEL J. VECCHIETTI
Director of Fiscal Services	PETER J. BASSO
Director of Contracts and Procurement	M.K. MONCADA
Federal Lands Highway Program Administrator	THOMAS O. EDICK

FEDERAL RAILROAD ADMINISTRATION

400 Seventh Street SW., Washington, DC 20590
Phone, 202–366–4000

Administrator	GILBERT E. CARMICHAEL
Deputy Administrator	PERRY A. RIVKIND
Chief of Staff	NANCY L. BRUCE
Director, Office of Civil Rights	MILES S. WASHINGTON, JR.
Director, Office of Public Affairs	CLAIRE AUSTIN
Director, Office of Budget	KATHRYN B. MURPHY
Chief Counsel	S. MARK LINDSEY
Deputy Chief Counsel	MICHAEL T. HALEY

Assistant Chief Counsel, Commerce and Legal Services Division	(VACANCY)
Assistant Chief Counsel, Freight Economics and Finance Division	ROBERT S. VERMUT
Assistant Chief Counsel, Safety Division	GREGORY MCBRIDE
Associate Administrator for Administration	RAY ROGERS
Deputy Associate Administrator for Administration	THOMAS F. PROCTOR
Director, Office of Personnel	THOMAS F. PROCTOR, *Acting*
Director, Office of Management Systems	HEINZ (TED) KROHN
Director, Office of Procurement Services	JOSEPH KERNER
Director, Office of Financial Services	GERALD SCHOENAUER
Associate Administrator for Policy	WILLIAM J. WATT
Deputy Associate Administrator for Policy	THOMAS FERRARA
Chief, Defense and Special Programs Staff	JAMES BOONE
Director, Office of Economic Analysis	JANE H. BACHNER, *Acting*
Director, Office of Industry Finance Operations and Program Policy Evaluation	THOMAS HARTMAN, *Acting*
Director, Office of Policy Systems	RAPHAEL KEDAR
Associate Administrator for Safety	GRADY C. COTHEN, *Acting*
Deputy Associate Administrator for Safety	PHILIP OLEKSZYK
Chief, Communications and Training Staff	SHARON STINSON
Director, Office of Safety Enforcement	EDWARD R. ENGLISH
Director, Office of Safety Analysis	BRUCE FINE
Associate Administrator for Railroad Development	JAMES T. MCQUEEN
Deputy Associate Administrator for Railroad Services	ARRIGO MONGINI
Deputy Associate Administrator for Technology Development	ROBERT L. KRICK
Chief, Maglev and High Speed Technology Development Staff	JOHN HARDING
Director, Office of Freight Services	ROBERT C. HUNTER
Director, Office of Passenger Services	(VACANCY)
Director, Office of Research and Development	ROBERT L. KRICK, *Acting*
DOT Contact, Transportation Test Center, Pueblo, CO	GUNARS SPONS

NATIONAL HIGHWAY TRAFFIC SAFETY ADMINISTRATION

400 Seventh Street SW., Washington, DC 20590
Phone, 202–366–9550

Administrator	JERRY R. CURRY
Counselor to the Administrator	FREDERICK H. GRUBBE
Deputy Administrator	(VACANCY)
Executive Director	HOWARD M. SMOLKIN
Regional Coordinator	BRIAN MCLAUGHLIN
Director, Executive Correspondence	LINDA DIVELBISS
Director, Office of Civil Rights	HANLEY J. NORMENT
Chief Counsel	PAUL JACKSON RICE
Director, Office of Public and Consumer Affairs	SKIPP CALVERT
Associate Administrator for Plans and Policy	DONALD C. BISCHOFF

Director, Office of Standards Evaluation	FRANK EPHRAIM
Director, Office of Regulatory Analysis	(VACANCY)
Director, Office of Budget Planning and Policy Development	CARL E. NASH
Associate Administrator for Rulemaking	BARRY FELRICE
Director, Office of Vehicle Safety Standards	(VACANCY)
Director, Office of Market Incentives	STANLEY SCHEINER
Associate Administrator for Research and Development	GEORGE PARKER
Director, Office of Crash Avoidance Research	WILLIAM A. LEASURE
Director, Office of Crashworthiness	RALPH HITCHCOCK
Director, Vehicle Research and Test Center	JAMES HOFFERBERTH
Director, National Center for Statistics and Analysis	WILLIAM H. WALSH, JR.
Director, Office of Driver and Pedestrian Research	WILLIAM E. SCOTT
Associate Administrator for Enforcement	WILLIAM A. BOEHLY
Director, Office of Defects Investigation	MICHAEL BROWNLEE
Director, Office of Vehicle Safety Compliance	ROBERT F. HELLMUTH
Associate Administrator for Traffic Safety Programs	ADELE DERBY
Deputy Associate Administrator	ROBERT NICHOLSON
Director, Office of Occupant Protection	JAMES NICHOLS
Director, Office of Alcohol and State Programs	JAMES HEDLUND
Director, Office of Enforcement and Emergency Services	CLAYTON HALL
Associate Administrator for Administration	BARBARA D. KERNAN
Deputy Associate Administrator for Administration	PAULINE M. GINGRAS
Director, Office of Personnel	HERMAN SIMMS
Director, Office of Contracts and Procurement	THOMAS J. STAFFORD
Director, Office of Information Resource Management	L. DONALD TUCKER
Director, Office of Administrative Operations	ALEX R. LAWRENCE
Director, Office of Financial Management	CHARLES H. KENT

URBAN MASS TRANSPORTATION ADMINISTRATION

400 Seventh Street SW., Washington, DC 20590
Phone, 202–366–4043

Administrator	BRIAN W. CLYMER
Deputy Administrator	ROLAND J. MROSS
Chief Counsel	STEVEN A. DIAZ
Director, Executive Secretariat	(VACANCY)
Director, Office of Civil Rights	ROBERT G. OWENS
Director, Office of Public Affairs	JERRY BROWN
Associate Administrator for Budget and Policy	ROLAND J. MROSS, *Acting*
Associate Administrator for Grants Management	ROBERT H. MCMANUS

Associate Administrator for Technical Assistance and Safety	Lawrence L. Schulman
Associate Administrator for Administration	Thomas R. Hunt

MARITIME ADMINISTRATION

400 Seventh Street SW., Washington, DC 20590
Phone, 202–366–5807

Administrator	Capt. Warren G. Leback
Deputy Administrator	Robert E. Martinez
Deputy Administrator for Inland Waterways and Great Lakes	Penny Eastman
Secretary, Maritime Administration/Maritime Subsidy Board	James E. Saari
Director of External Affairs	Sandra T. Farrow
Chief Counsel	W. Patrick Morris
Deputy Chief Counsel	Robert J. Patton, Jr.
Director, Office of Maritime Labor and Training	Bruce J. Carlton
Associate Administrator for Policy and International Affairs	Reginald A. Bourdon
Deputy Associate Administrator for Policy and International Affairs	Nan K. Harllee
Director, Office of International Activities	James A. Treichel
Director, Office of Policy and Plans	Frank W. Pentti
Director, Office of National Security Plans	Thomas M.P. Christensen
Associate Administrator for Administration	Earnest Hawkins
Deputy Associate Administrator for Administration	John L. Mann, Jr.
Director, Office of Management Services	Michael E. Myrtle
Director, Office of Budget	Taylor E. Jones II
Director, Office of Accounting	John G. Hoban
Director, Office of Information Resources Management	Robert J. Curry
Director, Office of Personnel	William N. Turanin
Director, Office of Acquisition	Margaret D. Duncan
Associate Administrator for Maritime Aids	Richard E. Bowman
Deputy Associate Administrator for Maritime Aids	James J. Zok
Director, Office of Ship Financing	Mitchell D. Lax
Director, Office of Ship Operating Assistance	Arthur B. Sforza
Director, Office of Trade Analysis and Insurance	Edmond J. Fitzgerald
Director, Office of Financial Approvals	Richard J. McDonnell
Associate Administrator for Shipbuilding and Ship Operations	Harlan T. Haller
Director, Office of Ship Construction	Norman O. Hammer
Director, Office of Ship Operations	Michael Delpercio, Jr.
Associate Administrator for Marketing	Gary S. Misch
Director, Office of Domestic Shipping	Howard G. Norseth
Director, Office of Market Development	Lewis C. Paine
Director, Office of Port and Intermodal Development	John M. Pisani
Director, Office of Technology Assessment	Paul B. Mentz
Director, North Atlantic Region	Robert F. McKeon

Director, Great Lakes Region	ALPHA H. AMES, JR.
Director, Central Region	FRANK X. MCNERNEY
Director, South Atlantic Region	WILLAM S. CHAMBERS
Director, Western Region	ROBERT A. BRYAN
Superintendent, United States Merchant Marine Academy	PAUL L. KRINSKY

SAINT LAWRENCE SEAWAY DEVELOPMENT CORPORATION

Washington Office: 400 Seventh Street SW., Washington, DC 20590
Phone, 202–366–0091

Massena Office: 180 Andrews Street, Massena, NY 13662
Phone, 315–764–3200

Administrator	STANFORD E. PARRIS
Executive Assistant	DAVID G. SANDERS
Special Assistant	ROBERT J. LEWIS
Associate Administrator	ERMAN J. COCCI
Comptroller	EDWARD MARGOSIAN
Chief Counsel	MARC C. OWEN
Director of Communications	DENNIS E. DEUSCHL
Director of Engineering and Planning	STEPHEN C. HUNG
Director of Operations and Maintenance	THEODORE J. BRUE
Director of Personnel and Safety	JOHN F. SULLIVAN
Director of Trade and Traffic Development	STEPHEN J. RYBICKI

RESEARCH AND SPECIAL PROGRAMS ADMINISTRATION

400 Seventh Street SW., Washington, DC 20590
Phone, 202–366–4433

Administrator	TRAVIS P. DUNGAN
Deputy Administrator	DOUGLAS B. HAM
Executive Assistant	GEORGE L. DAVIS
Chief Counsel	JUDITH S. KALETA
Director, Office of Civil Rights	BERNICE D. VANDERVALK
Associate Administrator for Management and Administration	ROSE A. MCMURRAY
Associate Administrator for Pipeline Safety	GEORGE W. TENLEY, JR.
Associate Administrator for Hazardous Materials Safety	ALAN I. ROBERTS
Associate Administrator for Research, Technology and Analysis	MARK C. DOWIS
Director, Office of Emergency Transportation	LLOYD E. MILBURN
Director, Office of Research Policy and Technology Transfer	ALFONSO B. LINHARES
Director, Office of Airline Statistics	ROBIN A. CALDWELL
Director, Volpe National Transportation Systems Center	RICHARD R. JOHN
Director, Transportation Safety Institute	H. ALDRIDGE GILLESPIE

[For the Department of Transportation statement of organization, see the *Code of Federal Regulations,* Title 49, Part 1, Subpart A]

DEPARTMENT OF TRANSPORTATION

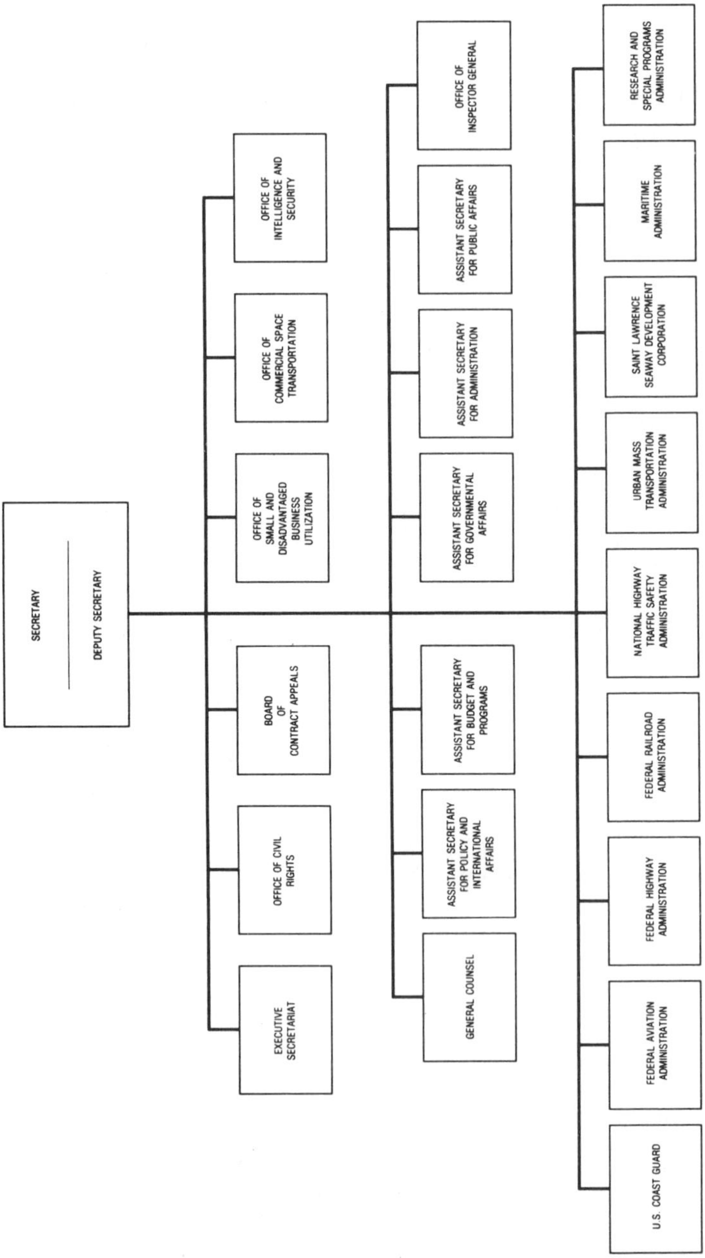

The U.S. Department of Transportation establishes the Nation's overall transportation policy. Under its umbrella there are nine administrations whose jurisdictions include highway planning, development, and construction; urban mass transit; railroads; aviation; and the safety of waterways, ports, highways, and oil and gas pipelines. Decisions made by the Department in conjunction with the appropriate State and local officials strongly affect other programs such as land planning, energy conservation, scarce resource utilization, and technological change.

The Department of Transportation (DOT) was established by act of October 15, 1966 (49 U.S.C. app. 1651 note), "to assure the coordinated, effective administration of the transportation programs of the Federal Government" and to develop "national transportation policies and programs conducive to the provision of fast, safe, efficient, and convenient transportation at the lowest cost consistent therewith." It became operational in April 1967 and was comprised of elements transferred from eight other major departments and agencies. It presently consists of the Office of the Secretary and nine operating administrations whose heads report directly to the Secretary and who have highly decentralized authority.

The central management concept of the Department is that operating programs are carried out by the operating administrations, which are organized generally by mode (e.g., air, rail, etc.). The Secretary and Deputy Secretary are responsible for the overall planning, direction, and control of all departmental activities, and the Office of the Secretary focuses its attention largely on policy formulation, resource allocation, interagency and intradepartmental coordination, evaluation of programs, and on matters of an intermodal nature requiring integration and balancing of modal interests. The Assistant Secretaries and the General Counsel are essentially staff officers, having one or more functional areas in which they assist the Secretary in matters of departmentwide scope. These officials do not exercise line control over the operating administrations.

Effective management of the Department is dependent for its efficient operation on a high degree of teamwork between the Assistant Secretaries and the heads of the operating administrations. Although operating generally within the standard regional boundaries, the field organizations of the various operating administrations differ widely in character primarily due to the nature of their work—some essentially providing funds to State and/or local governments for transportation undertakings such as road building and airport development, with others providing vital, nationwide public services such as air traffic control. The Department relies on Regional Representatives of the Secretary to coordinate the diverse programs of the Department in the field.

Office of the Secretary of Transportation

[For the Office of the Secretary of Transportation statement of organization, see the *Code of Federal Regulations*, Title 49, Part 1, Subpart B]

The Department of Transportation is administered by the Secretary of Transportation, who is the principal adviser to the President in all matters relating to Federal transportation programs. The Secretary is assisted in the administration of the Department by a Deputy Secretary of Transportation, who acts for and exercises the powers of the Secretary of Transportation and is responsible for the supervision and coordination of the activities of the Department as directed by the Secretary of Transportation.

Policy and International Affairs The Assistant Secretary for Policy and International Affairs is the Secretary's key officer for the development, review, and coordination of policy for domestic and international transportation. The Assistant Secretary:

—develops and evaluates public policy related to the transportation industries and their economic regulation;

—assures that the Department's regulatory programs remain consistent with established policy and maintains oversight of all departmental safety regulatory actions;

—proposes and coordinates transportation-related legislation involving the private sector;

—provides analyses of current and emerging transportation policy issues to assess their economic and institutional implications, particularly with regard to Federal assistance, public trust funds, user charges, nondiscrimination of the handicapped in the provision of public transportation services, and energy and environmental aspects;

—undertakes studies and analyses to aid in the resolution of safety problems;

—develops policies to support the Department in aviation and maritime multilateral and bilateral negotiations with foreign governments and participates on the U.S. negotiating delegations;

—develops policies on a wide range of international transportation and trade matters;

—furnishes guidance to the United States Trade Representative's Trade Policy Committee in efforts to improve the U.S. balance of payments;

—coordinates efforts to combat transport-related terrorist acts and drug smuggling;

—arranges and coordinates cooperative agreements with foreign governments for the exchange of state-of-the-art scientific and technical information;

—provides assistance to the Agency for International Development's transportation programs in developing countries; and

—participates on the U.S.-Saudi Arabian Joint Commission for Economic Cooperation.

The Assistant Secretary also:

—develops, coordinates, and carries out U.S. Government policy relating to the economic regulation of the airline industry, including licensing of U.S. and foreign carriers to serve in international air transportation and carrier fitness determinations;

—processes and resolves complaints concerning unfair competitive practices in international fares, rates, and tariff filings;

—establishes international and intra-Alaska mail rates; and

—determines the disposition of requests for approval and immunization from the antitrust laws of international aviation agreements.

The Assistant Secretary also administers the essential air service program, which involves:

—establishing appropriate subsidy levels for subsidized carriers;

—processing applications to terminate, suspend, or reduce air service below the defined essential level;

—determining which carrier among various applicants should be selected to provide subsidized service; and

—continuously reviewing essential air service definitions for each community.

For further information, call 202–366–4544.

Budget and Programs The Assistant Secretary for Budget and Programs is the principal staff adviser to the Secretary on the development, review, and presentation of the Department's budget resource requirements and on the evaluation and oversight of the Department's programs. The Assistant Secretary reviews the effectiveness of programs in achieving their objectives and advises the Secretary on major problem areas that impede attainment of departmental program objectives and on program and legislative changes necessary to resolve them. The Assistant Secretary also coordinates the impact on departmental resources of legislative and other proposals, establishes procedures for development of long-range budgetary resource planning, and makes recommendations on the budget and program aspects of proposals for acquisition of major new technical systems.

For further information, call 202-366-9191.

Administration The Department's management program includes formulating, prescribing, assuring compliance with, and evaluating the effectiveness of policies in the areas of personnel, staff utilization, financial and information management systems (including telecommunications and automated data processing management), acquisition and grants, administrative services and property management, and security. The program also includes the provision of comprehensive administrative services and computer support services to the Office of the Secretary and certain other components of the Department. These programs are under the direction and control of the Assistant Secretary for Administration, who also serves as the principal adviser to the Secretary and Deputy Secretary in matters involving the internal management of the Department. The Office of Hearings, under the Assistant Secretary for organizational and administrative purposes, conducts hearings in all formal Administrative Procedure Act proceedings under legislation vesting implementing responsibility in the Secretary.

Governmental Affairs The Office of Governmental Affairs is responsible for:

—maintaining liaison with the Congress, State and local governments, and public and private interest groups;

—coordinating matters of congressional concern within the Department;

—coordinating the presentation to the Congress of the Department's legislative program;

—ensuring effective communication and coordination with other Federal agencies and State and local governments with respect to DOT programs; and

—maintaining and assuring—as the Department's point of contact for public and private organizations and groups—that consumer preferences, awareness, and needs are brought into the decisionmaking process.

General Counsel The General Counsel is the chief legal officer of the Department and the final authority within the Department on questions of law; represents the Department in proceedings before regulatory agencies; supervises legal aspects of the Department's legislative program; and promotes and coordinates the efficient use of departmental legal resources.

Civil Rights The Director of the Office of Civil Rights is the principal adviser to the Secretary on civil rights and equal opportunity matters. The Director acts for and represents the Secretary to assure full and affirmative implementation of civil rights and equal opportunity precepts within the Department in all its official actions, including departmental employment practices, services rendered to the public, operation of federally assisted activities, and other programs and efforts involving departmental assistance, participation, or endorsement. This Office is also responsible for the implementation of Executive Order 12677 of April 28, 1989, on aid to historically black colleges and universities.

For further information, call 202-366-4648.

Public Affairs The Assistant Secretary for Public Affairs is the principal adviser to the Secretary on the dissemination of information to the public and news media concerning the Department's policies and programs. The Assistant Secretary is responsible for the overall public information program and supervises the information activities of the nine operating elements of the Department.

Small and Disadvantaged Business Utilization The Office of Small and Disadvantaged Business Utilization, established in July 1980, is responsible for the Department's implementation and execution of the functions and duties under sections 8 and 15 of the Small Business Act (15 U.S.C. 637, 644) for developing policies and procedures consistent with Federal statutes to provide policy direction for minority, women-owned, and small and disadvantaged business participation in the Department's procurement and Federal financial assistance activities. The Office is also responsible for setting the Department's goals for minority, women-owned, and small disadvantaged businesses, which includes monitoring and evaluating the accomplishments of these goals.

The Minority Business Resource Center, a division of the Office, is authorized under 49 U.S.C. 332 to design and conduct coordinated program activities directed at stimulating, promoting, and actively assisting minority and women-owned business participation in departmental procurement and Federal financial assistance activities. The Center's program consists of a Short-term Lending Program under which loans are available at prime interest rates and a Bonding Assistance Program which enables firms to obtain bonding in support of transportation-related contracts. The Center also operates several other program initiatives which provide technical assistance, outreach, and information dissemination involving minority chambers of commerce and trade associations, historically black colleges and universities, and a National Information Clearinghouse.

For further information, call 202–366–1930.

Contract Appeals The Contract Appeals Board conducts hearings and issues final decisions in appeals from contracting officer decisions under contracts awarded by the Department and its constituent administrations in accordance with the Contract Disputes Act of 1978 (41 U.S.C. 601); sits as the Contract Adjustment Board with plenary authority to grant extraordinary contractual relief under Public Law 85–804 (50 U.S.C. 1431); and hears and decides all contractor debarment cases pursuant to 41 CFR 12–1.604–1 (1984). Judges are designated as hearing officers to hear cases arising as a result of suspensions and debarments of participants in DOT financial assistance programs and perform such other adjudicatory functions assigned by the Secretary not inconsistent with the duties and responsibilities of the Board as set forth in the Contract Disputes Act of 1978.

For further information, contact the Contract Appeals Board, Department of Transportation, 400 Seventh Street SW., Washington, DC 20590. Phone, 202–366–4305.

Commercial Space Transportation
The Office of Commercial Space Transportation is the Government agency responsible for regulating and promoting the U.S. commercial space transportation industry. The Office licenses the private sector launching of space payloads on expendable launch vehicles and commercial space launch facilities. It also sets insurance requirements for the protection of persons and property and assures that space transportation activities are in compliance with U.S. domestic and foreign policy. In addition, the Office is charged with promoting and facilitating the industry and provides a focal point in the Federal Government for formulating and implementing consistent policies that enable the American space transportation industry to compete in domestic and international markets.

For further information, call 202–366–5770.

Inspector General The Department's Inspector General performs all audit functions, evaluates the effectiveness of programs to ensure uniform adherence to policy and procedures, promotes economy and efficiency in the administration of programs, and maintains a system of program review and followup on audit findings. The Inspector General performs all of the Department's investigative functions relating to waste, fraud, and abuse in Department programs and operations, including coordinating such matters with the Justice Department and other law enforcement agencies in accordance with the Inspector General Act of 1978, as amended (5 U.S.C. app.). The Inspector General also operates the Department's Hotline Complaint Center.

For further information, call 202–366–1461 or 800–424–9071 (toll-free).

United States Coast Guard

The Coast Guard, established by act of January 28, 1915 (14 U.S.C. 1), became a component of the Department of Transportation on April 1, 1967, pursuant to the Department of Transportation Act of October 15, 1966 (49 U.S.C. app. 1651 note). The Coast Guard is a branch of the Armed Forces of the United States at all times and is a service within the Department of Transportation except when operating as part of the Navy in time of war or when the President directs.

The predecessor of the Coast Guard, the Revenue Marine, was established in 1790 as a Federal maritime law enforcement agency. Many other major responsibilities have since been added.

Activities

Search and Rescue The Coast Guard maintains a system of rescue vessels, aircraft, and communications facilities to carry out its function of saving life and property in and over the high seas and the navigable waters of the United States. This function includes flood relief and removing hazards to navigation.

For further information, call 202–267–1948.

Maritime Law Enforcement The Coast Guard is the primary maritime law enforcement agency for the United States. It enforces or assists in the enforcement of applicable Federal laws and treaties and other international agreements to which the United States is party, on, over, and under the high seas and waters subject to the jurisdiction of the United States, and may conduct investigations into suspected violations of such laws and international agreements. The Coast Guard works with other Federal agencies in the enforcement of such laws as they pertain to the protection of living and nonliving resources and in the suppression of smuggling and illicit drug trafficking.

For further information, call 202–267–1890.

Marine Inspection The Coast Guard is charged with formulating, administering, and enforcing various safety standards for the design, construction, equipment, and maintenance of commercial vessels of the United States and offshore structures on the Outer Continental Shelf. The program includes enforcement of safety standards on foreign vessels subject to U.S. jurisdiction.

Investigations are conducted of reported marine accidents, casualties, violations of law and regulations, misconduct, negligence, and incompetence occurring on commercial vessels subject to U.S. jurisdiction. Surveillance operations and boardings are conducted to detect violations of law and regulations. The program also functions to facilitate marine transportation by admeasuring and administering the vessel documentation laws.

For further information, call 202–267–1464.

Marine Licensing The Coast Guard administers a system for evaluating and licensing of U.S. Merchant Marine personnel. This program develops safe manning standards for commercial vessels. The Coast Guard also maintains oversight and approval authority for the numerous mariner training programs.

For further information, call 202–267–0218.

Great Lakes Pilotage The Coast Guard administers the Great Lakes Pilotage Act of 1960 (46 U.S.C. 216), which regulates pilotage services on the Great Lakes.

For further information, call 202–267–0214.

Marine Environmental Response The Coast Guard is responsible for enforcing the Federal Water Pollution Control Act (33 U.S.C. 1251) and various other laws relating to the protection of the marine environment. Program objectives are to ensure that public health and welfare and the environment are protected when spills occur. Under these laws, U.S. and foreign vessels are prohibited from using U.S. waters unless they have insurance or other guarantees that potential pollution liability for cleanup and damages will be met.

Other functions include providing a National Response Center to receive reports of oil and hazardous substance spills, investigating spills, initiating subsequent civil penalty actions when warranted, encouraging and monitoring responsible party cleanups, and when necessary, coordinating federally funded spill response operations. The program also provides a National Strike Force to assist Federal On-Scene Coordinators in responding to pollution incidents.

For further information, call 202–267–0518.

Port Safety and Security This program is administered by the Coast Guard Captains of the Port. The Coast Guard is authorized to enforce rules and regulations governing the safety and security of ports and anchorages, and the movement of vessels and prevention of pollution in U.S. waters. Port safety and security functions include supervising cargo transfer operations, both storage and stowage, conducting harbor patrols and waterfront facility inspections, establishing security zones as required, and the control of vessel movement.

For further information, call 202–267–0489.

Waterways Management The Coast Guard has a significant role in the safe and orderly passage of cargo, people, and vessels on our nation's waterways. It has established Vessel Traffic Services in six major ports to provide for the safe movement of vessels at all times, but particularly during hazardous conditions, restricted visibility, or bad weather. The program's goal is to ensure the safe, efficient flow of commerce. The Coast Guard also regulates the installation of equipment necessary for vessel safety.

For further information, call 202–267–0980.

Aids to Navigation The Coast Guard establishes and maintains the U.S. aids to navigation system that includes lights, buoys, daybeacons, fog signals, marine radiobeacons, racons, and long-range radionavigation aids. Long-range radionavigation aids include loran-C, OMEGA, and the Global Positioning System (GPS). Aids are established in or adjacent to waters subject to the jurisdiction of the United States, although OMEGA provides global coverage, and loran-C coverage has been established in parts of the Western Pacific, Europe, and the Mediterranean to meet Department of Defense requirements. These aids are intended to assist a navigator to determine a position or plot a safe course or to warn the navigator of dangers or obstructions to navigation. Other functions related to navigation aids include broadcasting marine information and publishing Local Notice to Mariners and Light Lists.

For further information, call 202–267–1965.

Bridge Administration The Coast Guard administers the statutes regulating the construction, maintenance, and operation of bridges and causeways across the navigable waters of the United States to provide for safe navigation through and under bridges.

For further information, call 202–267–0368.

Ice Operations The Coast Guard operates the Nation's icebreaking vessels (icebreakers and ice-capable cutters), supported by aircraft, for ice reconnaissance, to facilitate maritime transportation and aid in prevention of flooding in domestic waters. Additionally, icebreakers support logistics to U.S. polar installations and also support scientific research in Arctic and Antarctic waters.

For further information, call 202–267–1450.

Deepwater Ports Under the provisions of the Deepwater Port Act of 1974 (33 U.S.C. 1501), the Coast Guard administers a licensing and regulatory program governing the construction, ownership (international aspects), and operation of deepwater ports on the high seas to transfer oil from tankers to shore.

For further information, call 202–267–0495.

Boating Safety The Coast Guard develops and directs a national boating safety program aimed at making the operation of small craft in U.S. waters both pleasurable and safe. This is accomplished by establishing uniform safety standards for recreational boats and associated equipment; encouraging State efforts through a grant-in-aid and liaison program; coordinating public education and information programs; administering the Coast Guard Auxiliary; and enforcing compliance with Federal laws and regulations relative to safe use and safety equipment requirements for small boats.

For further information, call 202–267–1077.

Coast Guard Auxiliary The Auxiliary is a nonmilitary volunteer organization of private citizens who own small boats, aircraft, or radio stations. Auxiliary members assist the Coast Guard by conducting boating education programs, patrolling marine regattas, participating in search and rescue operations, and conducting courtesy marine examinations.

For further information, call 202–267–1001.

Military Readiness As required by law, the Coast Guard maintains a state of readiness to function as a specialized service in the Navy in time of war, or as directed by the President. Coastal and harbor defense, including port security, are the most important military tasks assigned to the Coast Guard in times of national crisis.

For further information, call 202–267–2039.

Reserve Training The Coast Guard Reserve provides qualified individuals and trained units for active duty in time of war or national emergency and at such other times as the national security requires. In addition to its role in national defense, the Reserve augments the active service in the performance of peacetime missions during domestic emergencies and during routine and peak operations.

For further information, call 202–267–1240.

Marine Safety Council The Marine Safety Council acts as a deliberative body to consider proposed Coast Guard regulations and to provide a forum for the consideration of related problems.

For further information, call 202–267–1477.

District and Field Organizations—United States Coast Guard

Organization	Address	Commander	Telephone
ATLANTIC AREA	Governors Island, New York, NY 10004-5098	Vice Adm. Paul A. Welling, USCG	212-668-7196
Maintenance and Logistics Command—Atlantic	Governors Island, New York, NY 10004-5098	Rear Adm. John N. Faigle, USCG	212-668-7196
1st District—Connecticut, Maine, Massachusetts, New Hampshire, northern New Jersey, eastern New York, Rhode Island, Vermont	408 Atlantic Ave., Boston, MA 02210-2209	Rear Adm. Joel D. Sipes, USCG	617-223-8480
2d District—Arkansas, Colorado, Illinois, Indiana, Iowa, Kansas, Kentucky, Minnesota, Missouri, Nebraska, North Dakota, Ohio, Oklahoma, western Pennsylvania, South Dakota, Tennessee, West Virginia, Wisconsin, Wyoming	1222 Spruce St., St. Louis, MO 63103-2832	(Vacancy)	314-425-4601
5th District—Delaware, District of Columbia, Maryland, southern New Jersey, North Carolina, eastern Pennsylvania, Virginia	431 Crawford St., Portsmouth, VA 23704-5004	Rear Adm. Walter T. Leland, USCG	804-398-6287
7th District—Florida, Georgia, Puerto Rico, South Carolina, Virgin Islands	909 SE. 1st Ave., Miami, FL 33131-3050	Rear Adm. Robert E. Kramek, USCG	305-536-5654
8th District—Alabama, Louisiana, Mississippi, New Mexico, Texas	500 Camp St., New Orleans, LA 70130-3396	Rear Adm. James M. Loy, USCG	504-589-6298
9th District—Great Lakes area	1240 E. 9th St., Cleveland, OH 44199-2060	Rear Adm. Gregory A. Penington, USCG	216-522-3910
PACIFIC AREA	Coast Guard Island, Alameda, CA 94501-5100	Vice Adm. A. Bruce Beran, USCG	415-437-3196
Maintenance and Logistics Command—Pacific	Coast Guard Island, Alameda, CA 94501-5100	Rear Adm. Gerald F. Woolever, USCG	415-437-3196

District and Field Organizations—United States Coast Guard—Continued

Organization	Address	Commander	Telephone
11th District—Arizona, California, Nevada, Utah	400 Oceangate Blvd., Long Beach, CA 90822-5399	Rear Adm. Marshall E. Gilbert, USCG	213-499-5201
13th District—Idaho, Montana, Oregon, Washington	915 2d Ave., Seattle, WA 98174-1067	Rear Adm. Joseph E. Vorbach, USCG	206-442-5078
14th District—American Samoa, Guam, Hawaii, Pacific Islands	9th Fl., 300 Ala Moana Blvd., Honolulu, HI 96850-4982	Rear Adm. William C. Donnell, USCG	808-541-2051
17th District—Alaska	P.O. Box 3-5000, Juneau, AK 99802-1217	Rear Adm. David E. Ciancaglini, USCG	907-586-2680
U.S. COAST GUARD ACADEMY, SUPERINTENDENT	New London, CT 06320-4195	Rear Adm. Thomas T. Matteson, USCG	203-444-8444
NATIONAL POLLUTION FUNDS CENTER, COMMANDER	2100 2d St. SW., Washington, DC 20593-0001	Rear Adm. Richard A. Applebaum, USCG	202-267-6781

For further information, contact the Information Office, United States Coast Guard, Department of Transportation, 2100 Second Street SW., Washington, DC 20593. Phone, 202-267-2229.

Federal Aviation Administration

The Federal Aviation Administration, formerly the Federal Aviation Agency, was established by the Federal Aviation Act of 1958 (49 U.S.C. 106) and became a component of the Department of Transportation in 1967 pursuant to the Department of Transportation Act (49 U.S.C. app. 1651 note).

The Administration is charged with:

—regulating air commerce in ways that best promote its development and safety and fulfill the requirements of national defense;

—controlling the use of navigable airspace of the United States and regulating both civil and military operations in such airspace in the interest of safety and efficiency;

—promoting, encouraging, and developing civil aeronautics;

—consolidating research and development with respect to air navigation facilities;

—installing and operating air navigation facilities;

—developing and operating a common system of air traffic control and navigation for both civil and military aircraft; and

—developing and implementing programs and regulations to control aircraft noise, sonic boom, and other environmental effects of civil aviation.

Activities

Safety Regulation The Administrator issues and enforces rules, regulations, and minimum standards relating to the manufacture, operation, and maintenance of aircraft, as well as the rating and certification (including medical) of airmen and the certification of airports serving air carriers certified by the Office of Aviation Operations in the Office of the Secretary of Transportation.

The agency performs flight inspection of air navigation facilities in the U.S. and, as required, abroad. It also enforces regulations under the Hazardous Materials Transportation Act (49 U.S.C. app. 1801 note) applicable to shipments by air.

Airspace and Air Traffic Management The safe and efficient utilization of the navigable airspace is a primary objective of the agency. To meet this objective, it operates a network of airport traffic control towers, air route traffic control centers, and flight service stations. It develops air traffic rules and regulations and allocates the use of the airspace. It also provides for the security control of air traffic to meet national defense requirements.

Air Navigation Facilities The agency is responsible for the location, construction or installation, maintenance, operation, and quality assurance of Federal visual and electronic aids to air navigation. The agency operates and maintains voice/ data communications equipment, radar facilities, computer systems, and visual display equipment at flight service stations, airport traffic control towers, and air route traffic control centers.

Research, Engineering, and Development The research, engineering, and development activities of the agency are directed toward providing the systems, procedures, facilities, and devices needed for a safe and efficient system of air navigation and air traffic control to meet the needs of civil aviation and the air defense system. The agency also performs an aeromedical research function to apply knowledge gained from its research program and the work of others to the safety and promotion of civil aviation and the health, safety, and efficiency of agency employees. The agency also supports development and testing of improved aircraft, engines, propellers, and appliances.

Test and Evaluation The agency conducts tests and evaluations of specified items such as aviation systems, subsystems, equipment, devices, materials, concepts, or procedures at any phase in the cycle of their development from conception to acceptance and implementation, as well as assigned independent testing at key decision points.

Airport Programs The agency maintains a national plan of airport requirements, administers a grant program for development of public use airports to assure and improve safety and to meet current and future airport capacity needs, evaluates the environmental impacts of airport development, and administers an airport noise compatibility program with the goal of reducing noncompatible uses around airports. It also develops standards and technical guidance on airport planning, design, safety, and operations and provides grants to assist public agencies in airport system and master planning and airport development and improvement.

Registration and Recordation The agency provides a system for the registration of aircraft and recording of documents affecting title or interest in the aircraft, aircraft engines, propellers, appliances, and spare parts.

Civil Aviation Abroad Under the Federal Aviation Act of 1958 and the International Aviation Facilities Act (49 U.S.C. app. 1151), the agency promotes aviation safety and civil aviation abroad by exchanging aeronautical information with foreign aviation authorities; certifying foreign repair stations, airmen, and mechanics; negotiating bilateral airworthiness agreements to facilitate the import and export of aircraft and components; and providing technical assistance and training in all areas of the agency's expertise. It provides technical representation at international conferences, including participation in the International Civil Aviation Organization and other international organizations.

Other Programs The agency administers the aviation insurance and aircraft loan guarantee programs. It is an allotting agency under the Defense Materials System with respect to priorities and allocation for civil aircraft and civil aviation operations. The agency develops specifications for the preparation of aeronautical charts. It publishes current information on airways and airport service and issues technical publications for the improvement of safety in flight, airport planning and design, and other aeronautical activities. It serves as the executive administration for the operation and maintenance of the Department of Transportation automated payroll and personnel systems.

Major Field Organizations—Federal Aviation Administration

Region/Field Office	Address	Administrator/Director
ALASKAN—Alaska	P.O. Box 14, 701 C St., Anchorage, AK 99513	Ted R. Beckloff
CENTRAL—Iowa, Kansas, Missouri, Nebraska	601 E. 12th St., Kansas City, MO 64106	Stanley Rivers
EASTERN—Delaware, Maryland, New Jersey, New York, Pennsylvania, Virginia, West Virginia	Federal Bldg., JFK International Airport, Jamaica, NY 11430	Daniel J. Peterson
GREAT LAKES—Illinois, Indiana, Michigan, Minnesota, North Dakota, Ohio, South Dakota, Wisconsin	2300 E. Devon Ave., Des Plaines, IL 60018	Edward J. Phillips
NEW ENGLAND—Connecticut, Maine, Massachusetts, New Hampshire, Rhode Island, Vermont	12 New England Executive Park, Burlington, MA 01803	Arlene B. Feldman
NORTHWEST MOUNTAIN—Colorado, Idaho, Montana, Oregon, Utah, Washington, Wyoming	1601 Lind Ave. SW., Renton, WA 98055	Frederick M. Isaac
SOUTHERN—Alabama, Georgia, Florida, Kentucky, Mississippi, North Carolina, Puerto Rico, South Carolina, Tennessee	P.O. Box 20636, Atlanta, GA 30320	Garland P. Castleberry
SOUTHWEST—Arkansas, Louisiana, New Mexico, Oklahoma, Texas	P.O. Box 1689, Fort Worth, TX 76101	Clyde M. DeHart
WESTERN-PACIFIC—Arizona, California, Hawaii, Nevada	P.O. Box 92007, Los Angeles, CA 90009	Carl B. Schellenberg
AVIATION STANDARDS NATIONAL FIELD OFFICE	P.O. Box 25082, Oklahoma City, OK 73125	William H. Williams, *Acting*
EUROPE, AFRICA, and MIDDLE EAST OFFICE	15, Rue de la Loi B-1040, Brussels, Belgium	Patrick Poe
FAA TECHNICAL CENTER	Atlantic City, NJ 08405	Harvey B. Safeer
MIKE MONRONEY AERONAUTICAL CENTER	P.O. Box 25082, Oklahoma City, OK 73125	Homer C. McClure

For further information, contact the Office of Public Affairs (Public Information Center, APA–200), Federal Aviation Administration, Department of Transportation, 800 Independence Avenue SW., Washington, DC 20591. Phone, 202–267–3484.

Federal Highway Administration

The Federal Highway Administration became a component of the Department of Transportation in 1967 pursuant to the Department of Transportation Act (49 U.S.C. app. 1651 note). It administers the highway transportation programs of the Department of Transportation under pertinent legislation and the provisions of law cited in section 6(a) of the act (49 U.S.C. 104).

The Administration encompasses highway transportation in its broadest scope, seeking to coordinate highways with other modes of transportation to achieve the most effective balance of transportation systems and facilities under cohesive Federal transportation policies pursuant to the act.

The Administration is concerned with the total operation and environment of highway systems, including highway and motor carrier safety. In administering its highway transportation programs, it gives full consideration to the impacts of highway development and travel; transportation needs; engineering and safety aspects; social, economic, and environmental effects; and project costs. It ensures balanced treatment of these factors by utilizing a systematic, interdisciplinary approach in providing for safe and efficient highway transportation.

Activities

Federal-Aid Highway Program The Administration administers the Federal-aid highway program of financial assistance to the States for highway construction and improvement of efficiency in highway and traffic operations. This program provides for construction and preservation of the approximately 42,500-mile National System of Interstate and Defense Highways, financed generally on a 90-percent Federal, 10-percent State basis, and the improvement of approximately 800,000 miles of other Federal-aid primary, secondary, and urban roads and streets, with financing generally on a 75-percent Federal to 25-percent State basis. As existing sections of the Federal-aid highway systems age, certain repair, reconstruction, and rehabilitation projects become eligible for Federal aid.

The Administration also administers the Highway Bridge Replacement and Rehabilitation Program to assist in the inspection, analysis, and rehabilitation or replacement of bridges both on and off the Federal-aid highway systems. In addition, it administers an emergency program to assist in the repair or reconstruction of Federal-aid highways and certain Federal roads that have suffered serious damage by natural disasters over a wide area or catastrophic failures. The State highway agencies administer all Federal-aid highway projects and are responsible for planning, design, and construction. Revenues derived from special taxes on highway users are deposited into the general funds of the U.S. Treasury and credited to the Highway Trust Fund to meet, through the congressional authorization and appropriation processes, the Federal share of highway program costs.

Special emphasis is directed toward making highway improvements that are the highest priority needs in each State, adherence to environmental requirements, improving the safety design of new highways, correcting highway hazards on existing roads, reducing traffic congestion, and facilitating the flow of traffic. The Administration provides multidisciplinary expertise to States in assessing environmental impacts so that highways are located, designed, and constructed in harmony with environmental concerns. Severe environmental impacts are often avoided and proper mitigation measures are taken when avoidance is not possible.

The Federal-aid highway program also involves improving access for the handicapped, encouraging the joint use and development of highway corridors, acquiring real property for right-of-way, and providing relocation assistance to those displaced by highway construction, encouraging disadvantaged business enterprises to participate in highway construction, and preserving along highways the natural beauty of the countryside, public parks and recreation lands, wildlife and waterfowl refuges, and historic sites. The agency is responsible for developing and maintaining standards for traffic control devices used on all public streets and highways.

The Administration administers technology transfer and traffic engineering programs aimed at promoting the use and adoption of innovative highway engineering practices, an Intelligent Vehicle/Highway System Program to advance the application of electronic communications and control technologies for safer and more efficient highway travel, and a Rural Technical Assistance Program to help States and local areas meet the growing transportation demands placed on rural roads and bridges. The technical assistance includes funding university-based technology transfer centers, onsite demonstrations, microcomputer software development, workshops, user manuals and guidelines, and special studies that aid rural areas.

Highway Safety Programs The Administration is responsible for several of the highway safety programs undertaken by the Federal Government. Under the authority of the Federal-aid highway acts, highway construction programs to increase safety are administered through the Federal-Aid Highway Program. These safety construction programs fund activities that remove, relocate, or shield roadside obstacles, identify and correct hazardous locations, eliminate or reduce hazards at railroad crossings, and improve signing, pavement markings, and signalization.

Under the Highway Safety Act of 1966 (23 U.S.C. 402), the Federal Government is authorized to provide funding assistance in the form of matching grants to States establishing specific highway safety programs in accordance with national guidelines promulgated by the Secretary of Transportation. The agency administers highway-related safety guidelines providing for the identification and surveillance of accident locations; highway design, construction, and maintenance; traffic engineering services; and highway-related aspects of pedestrian safety. These guidelines form the foundation for the State and local programs dealing with street and highway safety.

Motor Carrier Programs Under the provisions of the Surface Transportation Assistance Act of 1982 (23 U.S.C. 101), the Administration was authorized to establish and maintain a National Network for trucks, review State truck size and weight enforcement programs, and assist in obtaining uniformity among the States in the area of commercial motor carrier registration and taxation reporting.

The National Network was established to provide an opportunity for larger commercial vehicles to travel long interstate distances without regard to individual State size and weight restrictions.

The agency, in an effort to reduce pavement damage by larger commercial motor vehicles, reviews State plans for truck size and weight enforcement and requires that States annually provide information on the number of trucks weighed, the number of fines and penalties issued for overweight violations, and the number of permits issued for overweight loads.

The Administration initiated the Interjurisdictional Trucking Program to promote simplified, more uniform State registration and taxation requirements.

Under the authority of the motor carrier safety provisions of title 49 of the United States Code, the agency exercises Federal regulatory jurisdiction over the safety performance of all commercial motor carriers engaged in interstate or foreign commerce. It deals with more than 210,000 carriers and approximately 25,000 shippers of hazardous materials. Reviews are conducted at the carrier's facilities to determine the safety performance of the carrier's over-the-road operations. These reviews may lead to prosecution or other sanctions against violators of the Federal motor carrier safety regulations or the hazardous materials transportation regulations. Additionally, the agency is responsible for establishing and enforcing the minimum levels of financial responsibility of motor carriers, section 30 of the Motor Carrier Act of 1980 (49 U.S.C. 10927 note) and section 18 of the Bus Regulatory Reform Act of 1982 (49 U.S.C. 10927 note).

Under the provisions of the Commercial Motor Vehicle Safety Act of 1986 (49 U.S.C. app. 2701 note), the Administration has established requirements for a single national commercial vehicle driver license for State issuance; a national information system clearinghouse for commercial driver license information; knowledge and skills tests for licensing commercial vehicle drivers; disqualification of drivers for serious traffic offenses, including alcohol and drug abuse; and administration of grants to the States to implement the commercial vehicle driver licensing program. It has responsibility for administering the Motor Carrier Safety Assistance Program under the provisions of sections 401–404 of the Surface Transportation Assistance Act of 1982 (49 U.S.C. app. 2301–2304).

The act provides for grants to qualified States for the development or implementation of programs for the enforcement of Federal or compatible State regulations applicable to commercial vehicle safety and hazardous materials transportation by highway. In fiscal year 1990, this partnership agreement between the States and the Federal Government resulted in approximately 1.6 million inspections being conducted, removing over 540,000 unsafe vehicles and 112,000 drivers from service for violations of the safety regulations.

Federal Lands Highway Program The Administration, through cooperative agreements with Federal land managing agencies, administers a coordinated Federal lands program consisting of forest highways, public lands highways, park roads and parkways, and defense access and Indian reservation roads. This program provides for the funding of more than 80,000 miles of federally owned roads or public authority-owned roads that are open for public travel and serve Federal lands. The agency's Federal Lands Highway Office provides for the program coordination and administration and directs transportation planning, engineering studies, design, and construction engineering assistance.

Research and Technology The Administration coordinates varied research, development, and technology transfer activities consisting of six principal programs: Intelligent Vehicle/Highway Systems, Highway Research and Development, Long-Term Pavement Performance, Technology Applications, Rural Technical Assistance, and the National Highway Institute. The Intelligent Vehicle/Highway Systems Program involves developing and deploying state-of-the-art vehicle and information systems to alleviate congestion on highways. Other programs focus on highway safety, structures, pavements, materials, environment, policy, and planning to discover ways to improve the quality and durability of highways and streets, to reduce construction and maintenance costs, and to offset the negative impact of highway transportation. A new effort is the Long-Term Pavement Performance Program, a massive evaluation of existing street and highway surfaces. A major effort of the agency is to transfer technology developed through research and other means to State, county, city, and other local highway jurisdictions. Through its National Highway Institute, the Administration develops and administers, in cooperation with State highway agencies, instructional training programs designed primarily for State and local highway agency employees engaged or about to be engaged in Federal-aid highway work. A separate program of Motor Carrier research investigates the special aspects of that function, such as the stopping capability of heavy vehicles, medical qualifications for commercial drivers, driver fatigue, and improving Motor Carrier management information systems.

International Programs To qualitatively advance the design, construction, and management of highways and bridges in the United States and around the world, the Administration supports and participates various international highway organizations, as well as joint projects with other countries. Such activities include international conferences, technical committee deliberations or studies, and assistance for study teams abroad; all fostering the international exchange of technical information and experiences.

Additional Programs The Administration administers a highway planning program, the highway beautification program, the highway construction phase of the Appalachian regional development program, and the territorial highway program; provides highway program support and technical assistance on an allocation/transfer basis for other Federal agencies. It administers civil rights programs pursuant to a variety of statutes. The programs have the aims of preventing discrimination in the impacts of programs and activities of recipients and subrecipients; providing equal employment opportunities and promoting diversity in public employment (Federal/State transportation agencies' motor carrier safety program and commercial driver's license program recipients and subrecipients) and private employment (contractors, subcontractors, material suppliers, vendors, and consultants) related to agency-funded projects; providing training opportunities for minorities and women in highway construction crafts; ensuring contracting opportunities for disadvantaged business enterprises and other historically underutilized businesses; increasing opportunities for historically black colleges and universities; providing technical assistance and training to State staffs; providing for supportive services to enhance the capabilities of disadvantaged business enterprises and on-the-job trainees; and determining compliance by States and contractors with the nondiscrimination and Equal Employment Opportunity provisions of assurances and contracts.

The administration is the lead agency in the Federal Government for implementation of the Uniform Relocation Assistance and Real Property Acquisition Policies Act. This act sets policy for the acquisition of property and relocation of the occupants for Federal and federally assisted projects.

Major Field Organizations—Federal Highway Administration

(Areas included within each region are indicated on the map in Appendix A.)

Region [1]	Address	Administrator	Telephone
1. Connecticut, Maine, Massachusetts, New Hampshire, New Jersey, New York, Puerto Rico, Rhode Island, Vermont	Rm. 719, Leo W. O'Brien Federal Bldg., Albany, NY 12207	John G. Bestgen, Jr.	518-472-6476
3. Delaware, District of Columbia, Maryland, Pennsylvania, Virginia, West Virginia	Rm. 1633, 31 Hopkins Plz., Baltimore, MD 21201	David S. Gendell	301-962-0093
4. Alabama, Florida, Georgia, Kentucky, Mississippi, North Carolina, South Carolina, Tennessee	Suite 200, 1720 Peachtree Rd. NW., Atlanta, GA 30367	Leon N. Larson	404-347-4078
5. Illinois, Indiana, Michigan, Minnesota, Ohio, Wisconsin	18209 Dixie Hwy., Homewood, IL 60430-2294	Herbert R. Teets	708-206-3206
6. Arkansas, Louisiana, New Mexico, Oklahoma, Texas	Rm. 8A00, 819 Taylor St., Fort Worth, TX 76102	W.S. Mendenhall, Jr.	817-334-3741
7. Iowa, Kansas, Missouri, Nebraska	6301 Rockhill Rd., Kansas City, MO 64141	Volmer K. Jensen	816-926-7563
8. Colorado, Montana, North Dakota, South Dakota, Utah, Wyoming	Rm. 400, 555 Zang St., Lakewood, CO 80228	Louis N. MacDonald	303-969-6722
9. Arizona, California, Hawaii, Nevada	Rm. 1100, 211 Main St., San Francisco, CA 94105	Edwin M. Wood	415-744-2639
10. Alaska, Idaho, Oregon, Washington	222 SW. Columbia St., Portland, OR 97201	Jerald P. Clark	503-326-2053

[1] Region 1 conforms to Standard Regions I and II.

For further information, contact the Office of Management Systems, Federal Highway Administration, Department of Transportation, 400 Seventh Street SW., Washington, DC 20590. Phone, 202-366-0630.

Federal Railroad Administration

The purpose of the Federal Railroad Administration is to promulgate and enforce rail safety regulations, administer railroad financial assistance programs, conduct research and development in support of improved railroad safety and national rail transportation policy, provide for the rehabilitation of Northeast Corridor rail passenger service, and consolidate government support of rail transportation activities.

The Federal Railroad Administration was created pursuant to section 3(e)(1) of the Department of Transportation Act of 1966 (49 U.S.C. app. 1652).

Activities

Railroad Safety The Administration administers and enforces the Federal laws and related regulations designed to promote safety on railroads; exercises jurisdiction over all areas of rail safety under the Rail Safety Act of 1970, such as track maintenance, inspection standards, equipment standards, and operating practices. It also administers and enforces regulations resulting from railroad safety legislation for locomotives, signals, safety appliances, power brakes, hours of service, transportation of explosives and other dangerous articles, and reporting and investigation of railroad accidents. Railroad and related industry equipment, facilities, and records are inspected and required reports reviewed.

Research and Development A ground transportation research and development program is administered to advance all aspects of intercity ground transportation and railroad safety pertaining to the physical sciences and engineering, in order to improve railroad safety and ensure that railroads continue to be a viable national transportation resource.

Transportation Test Center This 50-square-mile facility, located near Pueblo, CO, provides testing for advanced and conventional systems and techniques designed to improve ground transportation. The facility has been managed and staffed for the Administration by the Association of American Railroads since October 1, 1982. The United States and Canadian Governments and private industry use this facility to explore, under controlled conditions, the operation of both conventional and advanced systems. It is used by the Urban Mass Transportation Administration for testing of urban rapid transit vehicles.

For further information, contact the Transportation Test Center, Pueblo, CO 81001. Phone, 303–545–5660, ext. 5000.

Policy Program management for new and revised policies, plans, and projects related to railroad transportation economics, finance, system planning, and operations is provided; appropriate studies and analyses are performed; relevant tests, demonstrations, and evaluations are conducted; and labor/management programs are evaluated. Analyses of issues before regulatory agencies are carried out and recommendations are made to the Secretary as to the positions to be taken by DOT.

Passenger and Freight Services The Administration administers a program of Federal assistance for national, regional, and local rail services. Programs include rail freight service assistance programs; rail service continuation programs and State rail planning; and rail passenger service on a national, regional, and local basis.

The agency also administers programs to develop, implement, and administer rail system policies, plans, and programs for the Northeast Corridor in support of applicable provisions of the Railroad Revitalization and Regulatory Reform Act of 1976 (45 U.S.C. 801), the Rail Passenger Service Act (45 U.S.C. 501), and related legislation.

Major Field Organizations—Federal Railroad Administration

Region	Address	Regional Director of Railroad Safety
1. NORTHEASTERN—Connecticut, Maine, Massachusetts, New Hampshire, New Jersey, New York, Rhode Island, Vermont	10th Fl., 55 Broadway, Cambridge, MA 02142	Rolf Mowatt-Larssen
2. EASTERN—Delaware, District of Columbia, Maryland, Ohio, Pennsylvania, Virginia, West Virginia	Rm. 712, 841 Chestnut St., Philadelphia, PA 19107	John F. Megary
3. SOUTHERN—Alabama, Florida, Georgia, Kentucky, Mississippi, North Carolina, South Carolina, Tennessee	Suite 440, 1720 Peachtree Rd. NW., North Tower, Atlanta, GA 30309	Robert J. Farley
4. CENTRAL—Illinois, Indiana, Michigan, Minnesota, Wisconsin	14th Fl., 165 N. Canal St., Chicago, IL 60606	Mark H. McKeon
5. SOUTHWESTERN—Arkansas, Louisiana, New Mexico, Oklahoma, Texas	Rm. 7A35, 819 Taylor St., Fort Worth, TX 76102	Shafter H. Stotts, Jr.
6. MIDWESTERN—Colorado, Iowa, Kansas, Missouri, Nebraska	Rm. 1807, 911 Walnut St., Kansas City, MO 64106	Darrell J. Tisor
7. WESTERN—Arizona, California, Nevada, Utah	Rm. 1085, 211 Main St., San Francisco, CA 94105	Harry T. Paton
8. NORTHWESTERN—Alaska, Idaho, Montana, North Dakota, Oregon, South Dakota, Washington, Wyoming	Rm. 250, 1500 SW. 1st Ave., Portland, OR 97201	Richard M. McCord

For further information, contact the Public Affairs Officer, Federal Railroad Administration, Department of Transportation, 400 Seventh Street SW., Washington, DC 20590. Phone, 202–366–0881.

National Highway Traffic Safety Administration

[For the National Highway Traffic Safety Administration statement of organization, see the *Code of Federal Regulations*, Title 49, Part 501]

The National Highway Traffic Safety Administration was established by the Highway Safety Act of 1970 (23 U.S.C. 101). The Administration carries out programs relating to the safety performance of motor vehicles and related equipment, motor vehicle drivers and pedestrians, and a uniform nationwide speed limit under the National Traffic and Motor Vehicle Safety Act of 1966, as amended (15 U.S.C. 1381 *et seq.*), and the Highway Safety Act of 1966, as amended (23 U.S.C. 401 *et seq.*). Under the authority of the Motor Vehicle Information and Cost Saving Act, as amended (15 U.S.C. 1901 *et seq.*), the Administration carries out programs and studies aimed at reducing economic losses in motor vehicle crashes and repairs through general motor vehicle programs; administers the Federal odometer law; issues theft prevention standards; and promulgates average fuel economy standards for passenger and nonpassenger motor vehicles.

Under the authority of the Clean Air Amendments of 1970 (42 U.S.C. 7544(2)), the Administration certifies as to the consistency of Environmental Protection Agency State grants with any highway safety program developed pursuant to section 402 of title 23 of the United States Code.

The National Highway Traffic Safety Administration was established to carry out a congressional mandate to reduce the mounting number of deaths, injuries, and economic losses resulting from traffic accidents on the Nation's highways and to provide motor vehicle damage susceptibility and ease of repair information, motor vehicle inspection demonstrations, and protection of purchasers of motor vehicles having altered odometers, and to provide average standards for greater vehicle mileage per gallon of fuel for vehicles under 10,000 pounds (gross vehicle weight).

Activities—Rulemaking and Enforcement Programs

Motor Vehicle Safety Programs The Administration administers motor vehicle safety programs to:

—reduce the occurrence of highway crashes;

—reduce the severity of injuries in such crashes as do occur;

—improve survivability and injury recovery by better postcrash measures;

—reduce the economic losses in crashes;

—provide consumer information in the areas of vehicle crashworthiness and tire grading for treadwear, temperature resistance, and traction; and

—establish safeguards for the protection of purchasers of motor vehicles having altered or reset odometers.

Under the Administration's program, Federal Motor Vehicle Safety Standards are issued that prescribe safety features and levels of safety-related performance for vehicles and motor vehicle equipment. Damage susceptibility, crashworthiness, and theft prevention are to be studied and reported to the Congress and the public. The Administration establishes safeguards to protect purchasers of motor vehicles from vehicles with altered or reset odometers. The Administration conducts an intensive testing program to determine whether vehicles and equipment comply with applicable standards. It also investigates reports of safety-related defects. The Administration can require a manufacturer of motor vehicles or motor vehicle equipment to take corrective action.

The Energy Policy and Conservation Act, as amended (42 U.S.C. 6201 note), sets automotive fuel economy standards for passenger cars for model years 1985 and thereafter. The Administration has the option of altering the standards for the post-1985 period.

The Administration develops and promulgates mandatory fuel economy standards for light trucks for each model year and administers the fuel economy regulatory program. The Administration establishes rules for the collection and reporting of information required concerning manufacturers' technological alternatives and corporate economic capabilities in meeting fuel economy standards.

Traffic Safety Programs The law provides for Federal matching funds to assist States with their driver, pedestrian, and motor vehicle safety programs. The Administration has issued standards as guidelines and provides technical assistance to State and local community safety programs. Areas of primary emphasis are the implementation of countermeasures to reduce crashes and resultant deaths and injuries attributable to the use of alcohol and drugs, to increase occupant restraint usage, to improve emergency medical systems, and to control the aberrant driver.

The Administration maintains a register of persons who have had their operator's license withdrawn or revoked for more than 6 months.

Research and Development To provide a foundation for the development of motor vehicle and highway safety program standards, the Administration administers a broad-scale program of research, development, testing, demonstration, and evaluation of motor vehicles, motor vehicle equipment, Intelligent/Vehicle Highway Systems (IVHS), operator and pedestrian safety, and accident data collection and analysis.

The research program covers numerous areas affecting safety problems and includes provision for appropriate laboratory testing facilities to obtain necessary basic data. In this connection, research in both light and heavy vehicle crashworthiness and crash avoidance is being pursued. The objectives are to encourage industry to adopt advanced motor vehicle safety designs, stimulate public awareness of safety potentials, and provide a base for vehicle safety information. In addition, through a behavioral research program, the Administration addresses the fact that human error is the primary cause of motor vehicle crashes. The research seeks to find ways to change people's unsafe behavior, such as drinking and driving; failing to wear seatbelts; misuse of child restraints; not wearing motorcycle helmets; and speeding.

The Administration maintains a collection of scientific and technical information related to motor vehicle safety, and operates the National Center for Statistics and Analysis, whose activities include the development and maintenance of highway accident data collection systems and related analysis efforts. These comprehensive motor vehicle safety information resources serve as documentary reference points for Federal, State, and local agencies, as well as industry, universities, and the public.

Regional Offices—National Highway Traffic Safety Administration

(Areas included within each region are indicated on the map in Appendix A.)

Headquarters/Address	Administrator
I. Cambridge, MA (Kendall Sq., Code 903, 02142)	George A. Luciano
II. White Plains, NY (222 Mamaroneck Ave., 10605)	Tom Louizou
III. Hanover, MD (Suite L, 7526 Connelley Dr., 21076-1699)	Frank Altobelli
IV. Atlanta, GA (1720 Peachtree Rd. NW., 30309)	Tom Enright
V. Homewood Heights, IL (18209 Dixie Hwy., 60430)	Donald J. McNamara
VI. Fort Worth, TX (819 Taylor St., 76102-6177)	Georgia Jupinko
VII. Kansas City, MO (P.O. Box 412515, 64141)	Norman B. McPherson
VIII. Denver, CO (4th Fl., 555 Zang St., 80228)	Louis R. De Carolis
IX. San Francisco, CA (Suite 1000, 211 Main St., 94105)	Joseph M. Cindrich
X. Seattle, WA 98174 (915 2d Ave.)	Curtis A. Winston

For further information concerning the National Highway Traffic Safety Administration, contact the Office of Public and Consumer Affairs, National Highway Traffic Safety Administration, Department of Transportation, 400 Seventh Street SW., Washington, DC 20590. Phone, 202-366-9550. Additional information may be obtained by calling the Technical Reference Division, Office of Administrative Operations. Phone, 202-366-2768.

Urban Mass Transportation Administration

[For the Urban Mass Transportation Administration statement of organization, see the *Code of Federal Regulations,* Title 49, Part 601]

The Urban Mass Transportation Administration operates under the authority of the Urban Mass Transportation Act of 1964, as amended (49 U.S.C. 1601 *et seq.*). The Administration was established as a component of the Department of Transportation by section 3 of Reorganization Plan No. 2 of 1968 (5 U.S.C. app.), effective July 1, 1968.

The missions of the Administration are:

—to assist in the development of improved mass transportation facilities, equipment, techniques, and methods, with the cooperation of mass transportation companies both public and private;

—to encourage the planning and establishment of areawide urban mass transportation systems needed for economical and desirable urban development, with the cooperation of mass transportation companies both public and private; and

—to provide assistance to State and local governments and their instrumentalities in financing such systems, to be operated by public or private mass transportation companies as determined by local needs.

Programs

Discretionary Capital Grants Section 3 grants or loans are authorized to assist communities in acquiring or improving capital equipment and facilities needed for urban mass transit systems, both public and private. Only State, regional, or local governmental bodies and public agencies are eligible as applicants. Private transit operators may be assisted under the program through arrangements with an eligible public body.

The Federal grant is 75 percent of the net project cost. If the project is in an urbanized area, it must be part of a program for a unified or officially coordinated urban transportation system as a part of the comprehensive planned development of the area.

For further information, contact the Regional Office for the area concerned.

Urbanized Area Formula Grants
Section 9 is a formula-apportioned resource that has been available for capital, operating, and planning assistance since fiscal year 1984. Section 9 replaced an earlier formula assistance program, section 5, which was phased out with the passage of the Federal Public Transportation Act of 1982.

Recipients of funds in urbanized areas of over 200,000 population are jointly designated by the Governors of the respective States, local officials, and public transit operators. The Governor acts as recipient for urbanized areas with populations from 50,000 up to 200,000. Recipients must be State, regional, or local governmental bodies or public agencies. Private transit operators may be assisted under the program through arrangements with an eligible public body.

Grants may be made for 80 percent of the project cost for capital and planning activities and up to 50 percent for operating subsidies. Each year, potential grantees submit a proposed program of projects for funding based on the annual element of the Transportation Improvement Program, a technical document endorsed by the local metropolitan planning organization.

For further information, contact the Regional Office for the area concerned.

Nonurbanized Area Formula Grants
The section 18 program provides capital and operating assistance for public transportation in nonurbanized areas (under 50,000 population). Funds are allocated by formula to the Governor and the program is administered at the State level by the designated transportation agency. Eligible activities are operating assistance, planning, administrative and program development activities, coordination of public

transportation programs, vehicle acquisition, and other capital investments in support of general or special transit services, including services provided for the elderly and handicapped and other transit-dependent persons. A Rural Transit Assistance Program authorized under section 18(h) provides funding for training and technical assistance for transit operators in nonurbanized areas. Capital assistance is funded up to an 80-percent Federal share and operating assistance is funded with up to a 50-percent Federal share.

Elderly and Handicapped Assistance The section 16(b)(2) program provides capital assistance to private nonprofit organizations for transportation of elderly and handicapped persons, where services provided by public operators are unavailable, insufficient, or inappropriate. Funds are administratively allocated to the States; local organizations apply for funding through a designated State agency.

Technical Assistance The Administration provides funds for research, development, and demonstration projects in urban transportation for the purpose of increasing productivity and efficiency in urban and nonurban area transportation systems, improving mass transportation service and equipment, and assisting State and local governments in providing total urban transportation services in a cost-effective, safe manner, and expanding private-sector participation in all facets of urban transportation.

The Administration conducts a program of research, development, and demonstration addressing the following principal areas: urban and suburban mobility, human resources management, rail modernization, transportation systems evaluation, rural transportation and safety, and security.

Major project areas include:

—developing and demonstrating new approaches to involve employers, developers, local governments, and transportation providers in finding solutions to the problems of urban mobility, with special emphasis on institutional changes required to improve mobility in suburban areas and between suburbs and central city locations;

—encouraging management and organized labor to jointly seek opportunities for improving performance through upgrading of skills for nonmanagerial personnel;

—identifying, evaluating, and documenting significant cost-effective approaches to modernizing existing rail transit systems;

—encouraging participation by the private sector in the provision of transportation services and encouragement of joint public/private financing of transit capital investments;

—conducting a program of university research;

—providing guidance and training concerning long-term financial planning and leasing of capital assets;

—implementing a program of new model bus testing and test facility improvements;

—promoting the delivery of safe and effective public transportation in nonurbanized areas;

—assisting new safety and security initiatives, including safety training; and

—compiling information on costs, benefits, financial feasibility, and performance of new energy sources including nonpolluting fuels.

Projects are conducted under grants and cooperative agreements with public bodies, including State and local governments, or contracts with private organizations, both profit and nonprofit.

For further information, contact the Regional Office for the area concerned.

University Research and Training Grants Grants may be awarded to public and private nonprofit institutions of higher learning to assist in carrying out research activities on problems of urban mass transportation and in providing training for students and working professionals in the field of urban transportation analysis and operations. The objective is to encourage and support university research, education, and training that addresses and is responsive to Federal, State, and local transportation concerns, and advances the understanding and resolution of critical transportation problems.

Rural The Rural Transportation Assistance Program provides assistance for transit research, technical assistance, training, and related support activities in non-urbanized areas (less than 50,000 population). A portion of this is used at the national level for development of training materials, development and maintenance of a national clearing house on rural activities, and technical assistance through peer practitioners to promote exemplary techniques and practices.

For further information, call 202–366–4052.

Managerial Training Grants Grants to governmental bodies and agencies and operators of public transportation services provide fellowships for training in public or private training institutions for personnel employed in managerial, technical, and professional positions in the public transportation field. The assistance provided under this section is provided on a 50-50 funding match basis. Available funds will be used exclusively for single agency grants or for States submitting comprehensive applications on behalf of agencies within the State. A "block" type grant is awarded on the basis of comprehensive, agencywide training plans to support training activities for periods of up to 12 months. The Administration will allow 50 percent of the costs incurred by grantees for training and educational expenses which may include tuition, fees, books, or other training materials, excluding any equipment items.

For further information, call 202–366–4052.

Safety The Urban Mass Transportation Administration Safety Program is designed to support State and local agencies in fulfilling their responsibility for the safety and security of urban mass transportation facilities and services. The program accomplishes its objectives through the encouragement and sponsorship of safety and security planning, training, information collection and analysis, drug control programs, system/safety assurance reviews, generic research, and other cooperative government/industry activities.

For further information, call 202–366–2896.

Field Organization—Urban Mass Transportation Administration

(Regions included within each area are indicated on the map in Appendix A.)

Region/Address	Telephone
I. Cambridge, MA (Transportation Systems Center, Suite 920, Kendall Sq., 55 Broadway, 02142)	617–494–2055
II. New York, NY (Suite 2940, 26 Federal Plz., 10278)	212–264–8162
III. Philadelphia, PA (Suite 714, 841 Chestnut St., 19107)	215–597–8098
IV. Atlanta, GA (Suite 400, 1720 Peachtree Rd. NW., 30309)	404–347–3948
V. Chicago, IL (Rm. 1415, 55 E. Monroe St., 60603)	312–353–2789
VI. Fort Worth, TX (Suite 9A32, 819 Taylor St., 76102)	817–334–3787
VII. Kansas City, MO (Suite 303, 6301 Rockhill Rd., 64131)	816–926–5053
VIII. Denver, CO (Rm. 520, 1961 Stout St., 80294)	303–844–3242
IX. San Francisco, CA (Rm. 1160, 211 Main St., 94105)	415–974–7313
X. Seattle, WA (Suite 3142, 915 2d Ave., 98174)	206–442–4210

For further information, contact the area/regional office for the area concerned or contact the Office of Public Affairs, Urban Mass Transportation Administration, Department of Transportation, 400 Seventh Street SW., Washington, DC 20590. Phone, 202–366–4043. Technical information may be obtained by contacting the Transit Research Information Center. Phone, 202–366–9157.

Maritime Administration

The Maritime Administration was established by Reorganization Plan No. 21 of 1950 (5 U.S.C. app.), effective May 24, 1950. The Maritime Act of 1981 (46 U.S.C. 1601) transferred the Maritime Administration to the

Department of Transportation, effective August 6, 1981.

The Maritime Administration administers programs to aid in the development, promotion, and operation of the U.S. merchant marine. It is also charged with organizing and directing emergency merchant ship operations.

The Maritime Administration administers subsidy programs, through the Maritime Subsidy Board, under which the Federal Government, subject to statutory limitations, pays the difference between certain costs of operating ships under the U.S. flag and foreign competitive flags on essential services, and the difference between the costs of constructing ships in U.S. and foreign shipyards. It provides financing guarantees for the construction, reconstruction, and reconditioning of ships; and enters into capital construction fund agreements that grant tax deferrals on moneys to be used for the acquisition, construction, or reconstruction of ships.

The Administration constructs or supervises the construction of merchant type ships for the Federal Government. It helps industry generate increased business for U.S. ships and conducts programs to develop ports, facilities, and intermodal transport, and to promote domestic shipping.

The Administration conducts program and technical studies and administers a War Risk Insurance Program that ensures operators and seamen against losses caused by hostile action if domestic commercial insurance is not available.

Under emergency conditions the Maritime Administration charters Government-owned ships to U.S. operators, requisitions or procures ships owned by U.S. citizens, and allocates them to meet defense needs.

It maintains a National Defense Reserve Fleet of Government-owned ships that it operates through ship managers and general agents when required in national defense interests. An element of this activity is the Ready Reserve Force consisting of a number of ships available for quick-response activation.

It regulates sales to aliens and transfers to foreign registry of ships that are fully or partially owned by U.S. citizens. It also disposes of Government-owned ships found nonessential for national defense.

The Administration operates the U.S. Merchant Marine Academy, Kings Point, NY, where young people are trained to become merchant marine officers, and conducts training in shipboard firefighting at Earle, NJ, and Toledo, OH. It also administers a Federal assistance program for the maritime academies operated by California, Maine, Massachusetts, Michigan, New York, and Texas.

Field Organization—Maritime Administration

Region	Address	Telephone
CENTRAL REGION	Suite 2590, 365 Canal St., New Orleans, LA 70130-1137	504-589-6556
GREAT LAKES REGION	Suite 366, 2300 E. Devon Ave., Des Plaines, IL 60018-4605	708-298-4535
NORTH ATLANTIC REGION	Rm. 3737, 26 Federal Plz., New York, NY 10278	212-264-1300
SOUTH ATLANTIC REGION	Rm. 211, Bldg. 4D, 7737 Hampton Blvd., Norfolk, VA 23505	804-441-6393
U.S. MERCHANT MARINE ACADEMY	Kings Point, NY 11024-1699	516-773-5000
WESTERN REGION	Rm. 1112, 211 Main St., San Francisco, CA 94105	415-744-2580

For further information, contact the Office of External Affairs, Maritime Administration, Department of Transportation, 400 Seventh Street SW., Washington, DC 20590. Phone, 202-366-5807.

Saint Lawrence Seaway Development Corporation

The Saint Lawrence Seaway Development Corporation was established by act of May 13, 1954 (33 U.S.C. 981-990), as an operating administration of the Department of Transportation.

The Corporation, a wholly Government-owned enterprise, is responsible for the development, operation, and maintenance of that part of the St. Lawrence Seaway between the port of Montreal and Lake Erie, within the territorial limits of the United States.

It is the function of the Seaway Corporation to provide a safe, efficient, and effective water artery for maritime commerce, both in peacetime and in time of national emergency. The Seaway Corporation charges tolls in accordance with established rates for users of the Seaway that it negotiates with the St. Lawrence Seaway Authority of Canada. Beginning April 1, 1987, U.S. tolls are rebated to the user by the U.S. Treasury in accordance with the Water Resources Development Act of 1986 (33 U.S.C. 2201 note). The Corporation coordinates its activities with its Canadian counterpart, particularly with respect to overall operations, traffic control, navigation aids, safety, season extension, and related programs designed to fully develop the "fourth seacoast." The Corporation encourages the development of traffic through the Great Lakes/ Seaway system so as to contribute significantly to the comprehensive economic and environmental development of the entire region.

For further information, contact the Director of Communications, Saint Lawrence Seaway Development Corporation, Department of Transportation, 400 Seventh Street SW., Washington, DC 20590. Phone, 202–366–0091.

Research and Special Programs Administration

The Research and Special Programs Administration was established formally on September 23, 1977. The Administration currently consists of the Office of Hazardous Materials Transportation; the Office of Pipeline Safety; the Office of Civil Rights; the Office of the Chief Counsel; the Transportation Systems Center in Cambridge, Massachusetts; the Office of Emergency Transportation; the Office of Aviation Information Management; and the Office of Program Management and Administration.

Staff functions for the Administration are assigned to the Office of Program Management and Administration. The Office of the Chief Counsel provides the Administration with necessary legal support. The Administration is responsible for hazardous material transportation and pipeline safety, transportation emergency preparedness, safety training, and multimodal transportation research and development activities, and collection and dissemination of air carrier economic data.

Office of Hazardous Materials Transportation

400 Seventh Street SW., Washington, DC 20590. Phone, 202–366–0656

The Office of Hazardous Materials Transportation develops and issues regulations for the safe transportation of hazardous materials by all modes, excluding bulk transportation by water. The regulations cover shipping and carrier operations, packaging and container specifications, and hazardous materials definitions. The Office is also responsible for the enforcement of regulations other than those applicable to a single mode of transportation. It reviews and analyzes reports made by the industry and by field staffs bearing upon compliance with the regulations, and conducts training and education programs to support the Department's regulatory system and the program for shipper and container manufacturer inspection and compliance. The Office is the national focal point for coordination and control of the Department's multimodal hazardous materials regulatory program, ensuring uniformity of approach and action by all modal administrations.

Office of Pipeline Safety

400 Seventh Street SW., Washington, DC 20550. Phone, 202–366–4595

The Office of Pipeline Safety establishes and provides for enforcement of safety standards for the transportation of gas and hazardous liquids by pipeline.

Federal/State Program The Office administers a program whereby a State, when permitted by its statutes, can voluntarily assert safety regulatory jurisdiction over all or some of the intrastate pipeline facilities. The States' statutes must include adoption of the Federal Pipleline Safety standards. To enable States to initiate a safety program or to broaden an existing program, the Federal Government is authorized to pay a State agency grant-in-aid funds of up to 50 percent of the actual cost for carrying out a pipeline safety program. This payment assures that Federal and State regulation of pipelines is based on a common set of safety standards.

Information Dissemination The Administration publishes annual reports on the hazardous materials and pipeline safety programs, which are transmitted to Congress, State agencies, safety organizations, and to industry and the public upon request. It maintains a reporting system that gathers, processes, and analyzes accident and operator data from pipeline companies, carriers transporting hazardous materials by rail, highway, air and water, and from manufacturers of containers used in transporting hazardous materials.

Training The Office sponsors a number of training and information dissemination activities designed to familiarize industry personnel with the requirements of hazardous materials and pipeline safety regulations, and to educate Federal and State inspectors in inspection and enforcement procedures. These activities include in-depth classroom training at the Transportation Safety Institute, development of home-study training packages, regional and State seminars, and the distribution of a variety of information guides to those involved in hazardous materials and pipeline transportation.

Major Field Organizations—Office of Pipeline Safety

Region	Address	Chief
CENTRAL—Illinois, Indiana, Iowa, Kansas, Michigan, Minnesota, Missouri, Nebraska, North Dakota, Ohio, South Dakota, Wisconsin	Rm. 1811, 911 Walnut St., Kansas City, MO 64106	Ivan Huntoon
EASTERN—Connecticut, Delaware, District of Columbia, Maine, Maryland, Massachusetts, New Hampshire, New Jersey, New York, Pennsylvania, Puerto Rico, Rhode Island, Vermont, Virginia, West Virginia	Rm. 8321, 400 7th St. SW., Washington, DC 20590	Ralph Kubitz
SOUTHERN—Alabama, Florida, Georgia, Kentucky, Mississippi, North Carolina, South Carolina, Tennessee	Suite 504 N., 1720 Peachtree Rd. NW., Atlanta, GA 30309	Frederick Joyner
SOUTHWEST—Arkansas, Louisiana, New Mexico, Oklahoma, Texas	2320 LaBranch, Houston, TX 77074	James Thomas
WESTERN—Alaska, Arizona, California, Colorado, Hawaii, Idaho, Montana, Nevada, Oregon, Utah, Washington, Wyoming	555 Zang St., Lakewood, CO 80228	Edward Ondak

Transportation Systems Center

Kendall Square, Cambridge, MA 02142. Phone, 617–494–2224

The Transportation Systems Center (TSC), as part of the Research and Special Programs Administration (RSPA), provides research, analysis, and systems capability to the Department of Transportation (DOT) and other agencies requiring expertise in national transportation and logistics programs.

Integrated systems approaches are developed by TSC to address Federal transportation issues of national importance. It does not appear as a line item in the Federal budget, but is funded directly by its sponsors. TSC projects are therefore responsive to customer needs. The Center has come to be increasingly recognized by government, industry, and academia as a focal point for the assimilation, generation, and interchange of knowledge and understanding concerning national and international transportation and logistics systems. TSC is widely valued as a vital national resource for solving complex transportation and logistics problems.

Based on shifting national priorities and availability of its resources, TSC programmatic activities for DOT and other agencies vary from year-to-year. Currently, TSC's programs continue emphasis on enhancing transportation safety, while responding to changing national needs, including the modernization of federally operated transportation systems, such as the National Airspace System.

Activities

Major TSC programmatic activities can be grouped into four transportation and logistics areas: (1) Enhanced Safety and Security; (2) Infrastructure Modernization; (3) Upgrade of Management Support Systems; and (4) Institutional Support.

Safety and Security A number of projects supporting both regulatory and nonregulatory safety and security enhancement activities are carried out by TSC, including:

—assessment of the effect of human factors on transportation system safety performance, including impact of fatigue, design of vehicle controls, and pilot interaction with cockpit displays;

—assessment of the vulnerability of major Federal computer systems and identification of techniques for enhancing computer security;

—development of prototype explosives detection technology for passenger screening at critical transportation facilities; and

—application of structural analysis and inspection technology to assess metal fatigue in aging aircraft.

Infrastructure Modernization To upgrade and modernize Federal transportation operations, TSC has major programs under way such as:

—bridging civilian and defense transportation systems through information and database exchange for all modes of transportation;

—facility modernization projects in support of national ground and satellite-based radionavigation systems; and

—rehabilitation of federally operated rail lines at critical military reservations.

Management Support Systems The Transportation Systems Center is extensively involved in efforts to upgrade federally operated transportation and logistics management support systems. Major projects include:

—design, development, and implementation of information systems for aviation safety and inspection activities;

—management and operational support of telecommunications network planning and engineering, resource allocation, and performance analysis and improvement;

—research and systems analysis to integrate safely the needs and scheduling of air traffic for the shared use of airspace by civilian and military aircraft; and

—support the development of an advanced traffic management system for air traffic flow control and delay reduction.

Institutional Support The Department's formulation of domestic and international transportation policy is supported by TSC through collection and assessment of technical, economic, and other information, and performed by special investigations of critical transportation concerns requiring immediate attention. These activities include:

—support for congressionally mandated studies on the economic impacts of regulatory reform;

—continuing independent and objective "smart buyer" support for major transportation-related system acquisitions;

—support of departmental safety task forces; and

—organization of transportation colloquia to develop an awareness of and sensitivity to future transportation needs and opportunities within the public and private sectors.

For further information, contact the Transportation Systems Center, Kendall Square, Department of Transportation, Cambridge, MA 02142. Phone, 617–494–2224.

Office of Emergency Transportation

400 Seventh Street SW., Washington, DC 20590. Phone, 202–366–5270

The Office of Emergency Transportation provides the staff to administer and execute the Secretary of Transportation's statutory and administrative responsibilities in the area of transportation civil emergency preparedness. It is the primary element of the Department engaged in the development, coordination, and review of policies, plans, and programs for attaining and maintaining a high state of Federal transportation emergency preparedness. This Office oversees the effective discharge of the Secretary's responsibilities in all emergencies affecting the national defense and in national or regional emergencies, including those caused by natural disasters and other crisis situations.

For further information, contact the Office of Emergency Transportation, DET–1, Research and Special Programs Administration, Department of Transportation, 400 Seventh Street SW., Washington, DC 20590. Phone, 202–366–5270.

Office of Program Management and Administration

400 Seventh Street SW., Washington, DC 20590 Phone, 202–366–4347

The Office of Program Management and Administration provides staff and administrative support services for the Research and Special Programs Administration. In addition, it promotes safety and security management by designing and conducting training programs and plans and develops transportation statistics and data for the Department. The Office consists of three organizational elements: the Office of Administration, the Transportation Safety Institute, and the Office of Budget and Programs.

Activities

Administration The Office of Administration provides personnel management, organization planning, and contracting and procurement support for RSPA.

For further information, call 202–366–4347.

Transportation Safety Institute The Institute was established in 1971 by the Secretary of Transportation to support the Department's efforts to reduce the number and cost of transportation accidents. The Institute develops and conducts training programs for Federal, State, and local government as well as industry and foreign personnel in response to requests by the several departmental administrations in support of improved safety and security management of transportation functions.

For further information, contact the Transportation Safety Institute, Department of Transportation, 6500 South McArthur Boulevard, Oklahoma City, OK 73125. Phone, 405–747–3153.

Budget and Programs The Office of Budget and Programs provides planning and implementation for budget formulation. It also provides financial management and reporting, and develops, analyzes, and disseminates domestic and international transportation information and statistics.

For further information, call 202–366–4347.

Office of Aviation Information Management

400 Seventh Street SW., Washington, DC 20590. Phone, 202–366–9059

The Office of Aviation Information Management fulfills the Secretary's statutory responsibility to collect and disseminate economic aviation data. The data shows the financial and statistical results of air carrier operations in providing air transportation. The Office identifies the DOT program requirements for aviation data and arranges access. Where data collections are needed, the Office prescribes rules for air carrier accounting and reporting. It also receives the reports, validates and processes the

290-950 O 91 - 16

data, and generates a variety of end-product publications and data banks. Aviation data may be viewed in the Office's public reports facility or accessed through a variety of Government and private-sector services. Certain restrictions apply to public access to some of the data.

For information about access to public reports and information about Office functions, call 202-366-9059, DAI-1.

For further information, contact the Office of Administration, Research and Special Programs Administration, Department of Transportation, 400 Seventh Street SW., Washington, DC 20590. Phone, 202-366-4347.

Sources of Information

Inquiries for information on the following subjects should be directed to the specified office, Department of Transportation, Washington, DC 20590, or to the address indicated.

Coast Guard Career and Training Opportunities Inquiries for information on the U.S. Coast Guard Academy should be directed to the Director of Admissions, U.S. Coast Guard Academy, New London, CT 06320. Phone, 203-444-8444.

Information on the enlistment program and the Officer Candidate School may be obtained from the local recruiting offices or the Commandant (G-PRJ), U.S. Coast Guard, Washington, DC 20593. Phone, 202-267-1726.

Persons interested in joining the Coast Guard Auxiliary may obtain information from the Commandant (G-NAB), U.S. Coast Guard, Washington, DC 20593. Phone, 202-267-1077.

Consumer Activities For information about air travelers' rights or for assistance in resolving consumer problems with providers of commercial air transportation services, contact the Consumer Affairs Division (phone, 202-366-2220); for consumer assistance, to report possible boat safety defects, and to obtain information on boats and associated equipment involved in safety defect (recall) campaigns, call the U.S. Coast Guard's Boating Safety Hotline. Residents of Washington, DC, call 267-0780. Other residents nationwide, call 800-368-5647.

To report vehicle safety problems, obtain information on motor vehicle and highway safety, or to request consumer information publications, call the National Highway Traffic Safety Administration's 24-hour Auto Safety Hotline. Residents of Washington, DC, call 366-0123. Other residents nationwide (except Alaska and Hawaii) call toll free, 800-424-9393.

Contracts Contact the Office of Acquisition and Grant Management. Phone, 202-366-4285.

Employment Principal occupations in the Department are covered in the civil service examinations for air traffic controller, electronics maintenance technician, engineer (civil, aeronautical, automotive, electronic, highway, general), administrative/management, and clerical. For positions in Washington, DC, inquiries should be directed to the Central Employment Information Office, Office of Personnel, Room 9113, 400 Seventh Street SW., Washington, DC 20590 (phone, 202-366-9392). For employment outside of Washington, DC, inquiries may be directed to regional and district offices of the various administrations.

Schools interested in participating in the college recruitment program should address inquiries to the regional and district offices of the various administrations.

Environment Inquiries on environmental activities and programs should be directed to the Assistant Secretary for Policy and International Affairs, Office of Transportation Regulatory Affairs, Washington, DC 20590. Phone, 202-366-4366.

Films Many films on transportation subjects are available for use by educational institutions, community groups, private organizations, etc. Requests for specific films relating to a particular mode of transportation may be directed to the appropriate operating administration.

Fraud, Waste, and Abuse To report, contact the Office of Inspector General Hotline, P.O. Box 23178, Washington, DC 20024. Phone, 202-366-1461 or, toll-free, 800-424-9071.

Publications The Department and its operating agencies issue publications on a wide variety of subjects. Many of these publications are available from the issuing agency or for sale from the Government Printing Office and the National Technical Information Service, 5285 Port Royal Road, Springfield, VA 22151. Contact the Department or the specific agency at the addresses indicated in the text.

Reading Rooms Contact the Office of the General Counsel, Room 4107, Public Docket, Department of Transportation, 400 Seventh Street SW., Washington, DC 20590. Phone, 202-366-9322. Administrations and their regional offices maintain reading rooms for public use. Contact the specific administration at the address indicated in the text.

Other reading rooms include: Department of Transportation Library, Room 2200, 400 Seventh Street SW., Washington, DC 20590 (phone, 202-366-0746); Department of Transportation Law Library, Room 2215, 400 Seventh Street SW., Washington, DC 20590 (phone, 202-366-0749); Department of Transportation Library, FOB-10A Services Section, Room 930, 800 Independence Avenue SW., Washington, DC 20591 (phone, 202-267-3115); and U.S. Coast Guard Law Library, Room 4407, 2100 Second Street SW., Washington, DC 20593 (phone, 202-267-2536).

Speakers The Department of Transportation and its operating administrations and regional offices make speakers available for civic, labor, and community groups. Contact the specific agency or the nearest regional office at the address indicated in the text.

Telephone Directory The Department of Transportation telephone directory is available for sale by the Superintendent of Documents, Government Printing Office, Washington, DC 20402.

For further information concerning the Department of Transportation, contact the Office of the Assistant Secretary for Public Affairs, Department of Transportation, 400 Seventh Street SW., Washington, DC 20590. Phone, 202-366-5580.

DEPARTMENT OF THE TREASURY

1500 Pennsylvania Avenue NW., Washington, DC 20220
Phone, 202–566–2000

SECRETARY OF THE TREASURY	Nicholas F. Brady
Deputy Secretary of the Treasury	John E. Robson
Under Secretary (International Affairs)	David C. Mulford
Under Secretary (Finance)	Robert R. Glauber
Assistant Secretary (Domestic Finance)	Jerome H. Powell
Director, Office of Synthetic Fuels	Ralph L. Bayrer
Deputy Assistant Secretary (Federal Finance)	Michael E. Basham
Director, Office of Government Financing	Charles D. Haworth
Director, Office of Market Finance	Jill K. Ouseley
Director, Office of Federal Finance Policy Analysis	Norman K. Carleton
Deputy Assistant Secretary (Financial Institutions Policy)	John C. Dugan
Director, Office of Financial Institutions	Gordon Eastburn
Deputy Assistant Secretary (Corporate Finance)	J. French Hill
Director, Office of Corporate Finance	Michael Jacobs
Assistant Secretary (Economic Policy)	Sidney L. Jones
Deputy Assistant Secretary (Policy Analysis)	Bruce R. Bartlett
Director, Office of Policy Analysis	Maynard S. Comiez
Deputy Assistant Secretary (Policy Coordination)	Robert F. Gillingham
Director, Office of Financial Analysis	John H. Auten
Director, Office of Economic Analysis	John S. Greenlees
Assistant Secretary (Enforcement)	Peter K. Nunez
Deputy Assistant Secretary (Law Enforcement)	Nancy L. Worthington
Director, Office of Law Enforcement	Charles E. Brisbin, *Acting*
Director, Office of Financial Enforcement	Peter G. Djinis, *Acting*
Deputy Assistant Secretary (Regulatory, Tariff and Trade Enforcement)	John P. Simpson
Director, Office of Trade and Tariff Affairs	Dennis M. O'Connell
Director, Office of Operations	John W. Mangels
Director, Office of Foreign Assets Control	R. Richard Newcomb
Director, Financial Crimes Enforcement Network (FinCEN)	Brian M. Bruh
Fiscal Assistant Secretary	Gerald Murphy
Deputy Fiscal Assistant Secretary	Marcus W. Page
Assistant Fiscal Assistant Secretary	John A. Kilcoyne
Director, Office of Cash and Debt Management	Bartlett A. Derrick
Senior Advisor for Fiscal Management	Roger H. Bezdek
General Counsel	Jeanne S. Archibald
Deputy General Counsel	Dennis I. Foreman
Assistant General Counsel (Banking and Finance)	John E. Bowman
Assistant General Counsel (Enforcement)	Robert M. McNamara, Jr.

Assistant General Counsel (Administrative and General Law)	KEN R. SCHMALZBACH
Assistant General Counsel (International Affairs)	RUSSELL L. MUNK
Tax Legislative Counsel	ROBERT R. WOOTTON
International Tax Counsel	PHILIP D. MORRISON
Counsel to the Inspector General	ALEXANDRA B. KEITH
Inspector General	DONALD E. KIRKENDALL
Special Assistant to the Inspector General	KENNETH F. CLARKE
President's Council on Integrity and Efficiency Training Center Administrator	ANDREW J. PASDEN
Counsel to the Inspector General	ALEXANDRA B. KEITH
Deputy Inspector General	ROBERT P. CESCA
Assistant Inspector General for Investigations	CHARLES D. FOWLER III
Deputy Assistant Inspector General for Investigations	PAUL J. LILLIS
Assistant Inspector General for Audit	JAY M. WEINSTEIN
Deputy Assistant Inspector General for Audit (Operations)	(VACANCY)
Deputy Assistant Inspector General for Audit (Program Services)	(VACANCY)
Assistant Inspector General for Policy, Planning and Resources	GARY L. WHITTINGTON
Assistant Inspector General for Oversight and Quality Assurance	JOHN N. BALAKOS
Assistant Secretary (International Affairs)	(VACANCY)
Senior Deputy Assistant Secretary for International Economic Policy	JOHN M. NIEHUSS
Deputy Assistant Secretary for International Monetary Affairs	ROBERT M. BESTANI
Director, Office of Foreign Exchange Operations	JAMES M. LISTER
Director, Office of International Banking and Portfolio Investment	JAMES E. AMMERMAN
Director, Office of Industrial Nations and Global Analyses	DONALD C. TEMPLEMAN
Director, Office of International Monetary Policy	(VACANCY)
Director, Office of Balance of Payments Analysis	DAVID J. KLOCK
Deputy Assistant Secretary for Arabian Peninsula Affairs	CHARLES SCHOTTA
Director, Office of Regional and Resources Policy	DAVID S. CURRY
Director, Office of Data Management	THOMAS A. MCCOWN, JR.
Director, Office of Foreign Portfolio Investment Survey	WILLIAM L. GRIEVER
Director, U.S.-Saudi Arabian Joint Commission Program Office	JON M. GAASERUD
Deputy Assistant Secretary for Developing Nations	GEORGE A. FOLSOM
Director, Office of Developing Nations Finance	JAMES H. FALL III
Director, Office of Multilateral Development Banks	FRANK G. VUKMANIC

Director, Office of National Advisory Council	ALLEN E. CLAPP
Director, Office of Development Policy	MICHAEL D. O'CONNOR, *Acting*
Director, Office of International Debt Policy	MARY E. CHAVES
Deputy Assistant Secretary for Trade and Investment Policy	WILLIAM E. BARREDA
Director, Office of International Trade	(VACANCY)
Director, Office of International Investment	STEPHEN J. CANNER
Director, Office of East-West Economic Policy	JERRY M. NEWMAN
Director, Office of Trade Finance	WILLIAM L. MCCAMEY
Director, Office of Commodity Policy	DONALD NIEWIAROSKI, *Acting*
Director, Program Services	(VACANCY)
Assistant Secretary (Legislative Affairs)	MARY C. SOPHOS
Director, Office of Legislative Affairs	ANNA HOLMQUIST DAVIS
Deputy Assistant Secretary (Senate)	CAROLINE H. HAYNES
Deputy Assistant Secretary (House)	(VACANCY)
Assistant Secretary (Management)	DAVID M. NUMMY, *Acting*
Deputy to Assistant Secretary	WILLIAM H. GILLERS
Director, Office of Security	J. MARTIN FERRIS, *Acting*
Deputy Assistant Secretary for Departmental Finance and Management	DAVID M. NUMMY
Director, Financial Services Directorate	EDWIN A. VERBURG
Director, Office of Planning and Management Analysis	MICHAEL BLOOM
Comptroller	SAMUEL T. MOK
Director, Office of Finance	JOHN M. MURPHY
Director, Management Programs Directorate	THOMAS P. O'MALLEY
Director, Office of Procurement	PAUL A. DENETT
Director, Office of Management Support Systems	ROBERT T. HARPER
Director, Office of Automated Payroll and Personnel Systems	SUSAN M. HUBBARD
Director, Human Resources Directorate	CHARLENE J. ROBINSON
Director, Office of Personnel Policy	JACK R. HOWARD
Director, Equal Opportunity Programs	RONALD A. GLASER
Director, Treasury Executive Institute	PHILIP E. CAROLAN
Director, Treasury Integrated Management Information Systems (TIMIS)	EDWARD B. POWELL
Deputy Assistant Secretary for Administration	CHARLES B. RESPASS
Director, Automated Systems	G. DALE SEWARD
Director, Printing and Graphics	THOMAS E. MAY
Director, Facilities Management	JOHN D. ROBINSON
Director, Financial Management	MARY BETH SHAW
Director, Procurement Services	LLOYD W. PRATSCH
Director, Administrative Operations	GARY T. ENGELSTAD
Director, Personnel Resources	ROSEMARY DOWNING, *Acting*
Deputy Assistant Secretary for Information Systems	STEVEN W. BROADBENT
Director, Office of Information Resources Management	JANE L. SULLIVAN
Director, Telecommunications Management	JAMES J. FLYZIK

Assistant Secretary for Policy Management	HOLLIS S. MCLOUGHLIN
Executive Secretary to the Secretary	R. BLAIR DOWNING
Special Assistant to the Secretary (National Security)	MICHAEL L. ROMEY
Assistant Secretary (Public Affairs and Public Liaison)	DESIREE TUCKER-SORINI
Deputy Assistant Secretary for Public Affairs	(VACANCY)
Director, Office of Public Affairs	ARTHUR J. SIDDON
Deputy Assistant Secretary for Public Liaison	SARAH M. HILDEBRAND
Director, Office of Business Liaison	(VACANCY)
Director, Office of Intergovernmental Affairs	KATE T. BEACH
Director, Office of Consumer Affairs	DOLLY D. WELLS
Director, Office of Operations	ROSE CICALA
Assistant Secretary (Tax Policy)	KENNETH W. GIDEON
Deputy Assistant Secretary (Tax Policy)	MICHAEL J. GRAETZ
Tax Legislative Counsel	ROBERT R. WOOTTON
International Tax Counsel	PHILIP D. MORRISON
Deputy International Tax Counsel	(VACANCY)
Associate International Tax Counsel	MARLIN RISINGER
Benefits Tax Counsel	THOMAS D. TERRY
Deputy Assistant Secretary (Tax Analysis)	HARVEY S. ROSEN
Director, Office of Tax Analysis	LOWELL DWORIN
Treasurer of the United States	CATALINA V. VILLALPANDO
Deputy Treasurer	DAVID J. RYDER
Press Secretary	STEVAN W. GIBSON

BUREAU OF ALCOHOL, TOBACCO AND FIREARMS

650 Massachusetts Avenue NW., Washington, DC 20226
Phone, 202–566–7777

Director	STEPHEN E. HIGGINS
Deputy Directors	DANIEL M. HARTNETT
	DANIEL R. BLACK
Assistant to the Director (Equal Opportunity)	JOHN J. MCGUIRE
Chief Counsel	MARVIN J. DESSLER
Associate Director (Law Enforcement)	DANIEL M. HARTNETT
Associate Director (Compliance Operations)	DANIEL R. BLACK
Assistant Director (Administration)	ARTHUR J. LIBERTUCCI
Assistant Director (Internal Affairs)	JAMES K. BRIGHTWELL
Assistant Director (Congressional and Media Affairs)	JAMES O. PASCO

OFFICE OF THE COMPTROLLER OF THE CURRENCY

250 E Street SW., Washington, DC 20219
Phone, 202–874–5000

Comptroller	ROBERT L. CLARKE
Executive Assistant	R. JULIE OLSON
Deputy Comptroller, Communications	LEONORA S. CROSS
Senior Deputy Comptroller for Legislative and Public Affairs	FRANK MAGUIRE, JR.
Director, Communications	ELLEN STOCKDALE
Director, Congressional Liaison	CAROLYN Z. MCFARLANE

Director, Banking Relations	WILLIAM F. GRANT III
Director, Customer and Industry Affairs	JANICE A. BOOKER
Senior Deputy Comptroller for Bank Supervision Policy	SUSAN F. KRAUSE
Deputy Comptroller for Bank Supervision Policy	FRED D. FINKE
Deputy Comptroller for International Banking and Finance	JON HARTZELL
Chief National Bank Examiner	DONALD G. COONLEY
Deputy Comptroller for Compliance	(VACANCY)
Senior Deputy Comptroller for Bank Supervision Operations	STEPHEN STEINBRINK
Deputy Comptroller for Multinational Banking	(VACANCY)
Senior Deputy Comptroller for Corporate and Economic Programs	DANA COOK
Deputy Comptroller for Bank Organization and Structure	STEVEN J. WEISS
Deputy Comptroller for Economic and Policy Analysis	JAMES KAMIHACHI
Senior Deputy Comptroller for Administration	JUDITH A. WALTER
Deputy Comptroller for Systems and Financial Management	JERRY FISHER
Deputy Comptroller for Resource Management	GARY W. NORTON
Chief Counsel	WILLIAM BOWDEN, JR.
Deputy Chief Counsel (Policy)	ROBERT B. SERINO
Deputy Chief Counsel (Operations)	ROBERTA W. BOYLAN

UNITED STATES CUSTOMS SERVICE

1301 Constitution Avenue NW., Washington, DC 20229
Phone, 202–566–8195

Commissioner of Customs	CAROL B. HALLETT
Confidential Assistant	KIMBERLY BLECK
Executive Assistant to the Commissioner	JAMES PICARD
Deputy Commissioner	MICHAEL H. LANE
Assistant Commissioner (International Affairs)	JAMES W. SHAVER
Assistant Commissioner (Management)	EDWARD F. KWAS
Comptroller	FRANK PALMER
Assistant Commissioner (Information Management)	WILLIAM RILEY
Assistant Commissioner (Enforcement)	JOHN E. HENSLEY
Assistant Commissioner (Inspection and Control)	CHARLES W. WINWOOD
Assistant Commissioner (Commercial Operations)	SAMUEL H. BANKS
Assistant Commissioner (Internal Affairs)	GEORGE D. HEAVEY
Assistant Commissioner (Congressional and Public Affairs)	CHARLES R. PARKINSON
Chief Counsel	MICHAEL T. SCHMITZ
Special Assistant to the Commissioner (Equal Opportunity)	EARL MITCHELL

BUREAU OF ENGRAVING AND PRINTING

Fourteenth and C Streets SW., Washington, DC 20228
Phone, 202–447–0193

Director	Peter H. Daly
Associate Director (Chief Operating Officer)	Carl V. D'Alessandro
Associate Director (Chief Financial Officer)	L. Paul Blackmer, Jr.
Assistant Director (Technology)	Milton J. Seidel
Assistant Director (Management)	Joel C. Taub, *Acting*
Project Director (Facilities Planning and Development)	Eugenie E. Foster
Chief Counsel	Carrol H. Kinsey

FEDERAL LAW ENFORCEMENT TRAINING CENTER

Glynco, GA 31524
Phone, 912–267–2100; Washington, DC, 202–566–2951; FLETC-Marana Operations, 602–670–5305; Artesia Operations, 505–748–8000

Director	Charles F. Rinkevich
Deputy Director	R.J. Miller
Assistant Director (Administration)	William M. Kelso
Assistant Director (General Training)	Ray M. Rice
Assistant Director (Special Training)	Kenneth A. Hall
Assistant Director (State and Local Training)	Hobart M. Henson
Assistant Director (Washington Office)	John C. Dooher
Assistant Director (Artesia and Marana Operations)	David W. McKinley

FINANCIAL MANAGEMENT SERVICE

401 Fourteenth Street SW., Washington, DC 20227
Phone, 202–287–0669

Commissioner	William E. Douglas
Deputy Commissioner	Russell D. Morris
Director, Legislative and Public Affairs	Thomas Gillilland
Director, Planning Office	(vacancy)
Chief Counsel	David A. Ingold
Assistant Commissioner, Agency Services	Michael D. Serlin
Assistant Commissioner, Federal Finance	Michael T. Smokovich
Assistant Commissioner, Financial Information	Diane E. Clark
Assistant Commissioner, Information Resources	Ronald A. Nervitt
Assistant Commissioner, Management (CFO)	Bland T. Brockenborough
Assistant Commissioner, Regional Operations	Mitchell A. Levine

INTERNAL REVENUE SERVICE

1111 Constitution Avenue NW., Washington, DC 20224
Phone, 202–566–5000

Commissioner	Fred T. Goldberg, Jr.
Deputy Commissioner	Michael J. Murphy
Chief Financial Officer	John D. Johnson

Chief Operations Officer	DAVID G. BLATTNER
Chief Information Officer	HENRY H. PHILCOX
Assistant to Deputy Commissioner	MICHAEL KILLFOIL
Counselor to the Commissioner	THOMAS R. HOOD
Assistants to the Commissioner	GARY J. GASPER
	HUGH S. HATCHER
Assistant to the Commissioner (Taxpayer Ombudsman)	DAMON O. HOLMES
Assistant to the Commissioner (Equal Opportunity)	HELEN L. WHITE
Assistant to the Commissioner (Public Affairs)	ELLEN MURPHY
Assistant to the Commissioner (Legislative Liaison)	GAYLE G. MORIN
Assistant to the Commissioner (Quality)	ALVIN H. KOLAK
Director, Executive Secretariat	(VACANCY)
Assistant Commissioner (Collection)	RAYMOND P. KEENAN
Assistant Commissioner (Criminal Investigation)	INAR MORICS
Assistant Commissioner (Employee Plans and Exempt Organizations)	JOHN BURKE
Assistant Commissioner (Examination)	GEORGE O'HANLON
Assistant Commissioner (Finance)/Controller	C. MORGAN KINGHORN
Assistant Commissioner (Procurement)	GREGORY ROTHWELL
Assistant Commissioner (Human Resources and Support)	ROBERT T. JOHNSON
Assistant Commissioner (International)	REGINA DEANEHAN
Assistant Commissioner (Planning and Research)	ROBERT F. HILGEN
Assistant Commissioner (Taxpayer Services)	PHILIP BRAND
Assistant Commissioner (Returns Processing)	CHARLES J. PEOPLES
Assistant Commissioner (Information Systems Development)	MARK D. COX
Assistant Commissioner (Information Systems Management)	WALTER A. HUTTON, JR.
Chief Inspector	TEDDY R. KERN
Chief Counsel	ABRAHAM SHASHY, JR.
Deputy Chief Counsel	DAVE JORDAN
Associate Chief Counsel (Finance and Management)	RICHARD J. MIHELCIC
Associate Chief Counsel (International)	STEVEN R. LAINOFF
Associate Chief Counsel (Litigation)	JAMES J. KEIGHTLEY
Assocate Chief Counsel (Domestic)	STUART BROWN
National Director of Appeals	JAMES CASIMIR

UNITED STATES MINT

633 Third Street NW., Washington, DC 20220
Phone, 202-376-0560

Director of the Mint	DONNA POPE
Deputy Director	EUGENE H. ESSNER
Special Assistant to the Director	JON B. RAWLSON
Chief Counsel	KENNETH B. GUBIN
Chief, Security/Internal Review	WILLIAM F. DADDIO

Associate Director for Information and Management	ROBERT JENKINS, *Acting*
Associate Director for Finance	KENNETH J. WINTER, *Acting*
Associate Director for Operations	ANDREW COSGAREA, JR.
Associate Director for Marketing	DAVID PICKENS

BUREAU OF THE PUBLIC DEBT

999 E Street NW., Washington, DC 20239–0001
Phone, 202–376–4300

Commissioner	RICHARD L. GREGG
Deputy Commissioner	VAN ZECK
Director, Government Securities Regulation Staff	KENNETH R. PAPAJ
Chief Counsel	CALVIN NINOMIYA
Assistant Commissioner (Financing)	CARL M. LOCKEN, JR.
Assistant Commissioner (Securities and Accounting Services)	ELEANOR J. HOLSOPPLE
Assistant Commissioner (Administration)	KENNETH W. RATH
Assistant Commissioner (Automated Information Systems)	RICHARD T. MILLER
Assistant Commissioner (Savings Bond Operations)	ARTHUR A. KLASS, *Acting*
Assistant Commissioner (Public Debt Accounting)	MICHAEL D. PECOVISH

UNITED STATES SAVINGS BONDS DIVISION

1111 Twentieth Street NW., Washington, DC 20226
Phone, 202–634–5350

National Director	CATALINA V. VILLALPANDO
Executive Director	LELAND L. COGGAN
Deputy Executive Director (Operations)	DAWN R. HALEY
Deputy Executive Director (Sales)	RICHARD J. SCHEENBELI
Director of Administration	WILLIAM L. MCCARNEY
Director for Eastern Market Sales	SCOTT N. LUDRICK
Director for Western Market Sales	JAMES R. WYNN
Director of Program Support, Evaluation, and Policy Development	HOWARD PATTON
Director of Marketing and Communications	JAMES H. GIANFAGNA

UNITED STATES SECRET SERVICE

1800 G Street NW., Washington, DC 20223
Phone, 202–535–5708

Director	JOHN R. SIMPSON
Deputy Director	GUY P. CAPUTO
Assistant Director (Administration)	DAVID C. LEE
Assistant Director (Inspection)	GEORGE J. OPFER
Assistant Director (Protective Research)	H. TERRENCE SAMWAY
Assistant Director (Protective Operations)	HUBERT T. BELL
Assistant Director (Investigation)	RAYMOND A. SHADDICK

Assistant Director (Government Liaison and Public Affairs)	ROBERT R. SNOW
Assistant Director (Training)	DONALD A. EDWARDS
Chief Counsel	JOHN J. KELLEHER

OFFICE OF THRIFT SUPERVISION

1700 G Street NW., Washington, DC 20552
Phone, 202–906–6000; or Fax, 202–906–7494

Director	T. TIMOTHY RYAN, JR.
Special Assistants to the Director	KIMBERLY A. WYCHE
	MARK HURLEY
Associate Director for Resolution Trust Corporation Operations	DAVID KELSO
Associate Director for Federal Deposit Insurance Corporation Operations	WALTER B. MASON
Deputy Director for Washington Operations	JONATHAN L. FIECHTER
Deputy Director for Regional Operations	JOHN F. DOWNEY
Chief Counsel	HARRIS WEINSTEIN
Associate Director for Public Affairs	ROBERT P. SCHMERMUND
Associate Director for Congressional Affairs	STEPHANIE C. BLUHER

The Department of the Treasury performs four basic functions: formulating and recommending economic, financial, tax, and fiscal policies; serving as financial agent for the U.S. Government; enforcing the law; and manufacturing coins and currency.

The Treasury Department was created by act of September 2, 1789 (31 U.S.C. 1001). Many subsequent acts have figured in the development of the Department, delegating new duties to its charge and establishing the numerous bureaus and divisions that now comprise the Treasury.

Secretary

As a major policy adviser to the President, the Secretary has primary responsibility for formulating and recommending domestic and international financial, economic, and tax policy; participating in the formulation of broad fiscal policies that have general significance for the economy; and managing the public debt. The Secretary also oversees the activities of the Department in carrying out its major law enforcement responsibility; in serving as the financial agent for the U.S. Government; and in manufacturing coins, currency, and other products for customer agencies.

In addition, the Secretary has many responsibilities as chief financial officer of the Government. The Secretary serves as Chairman pro tempore of the Economic Policy Council and as U.S. Governor of the International Monetary Fund, the International Bank for Reconstruction and Development, the Inter-American Development Bank, and the African Development Bank.

Deputy Secretary

The Deputy Secretary assists the Secretary in the supervision and direction of the Department and its assigned programs, and acts for the Secretary in his absence, sickness, or unavailability.

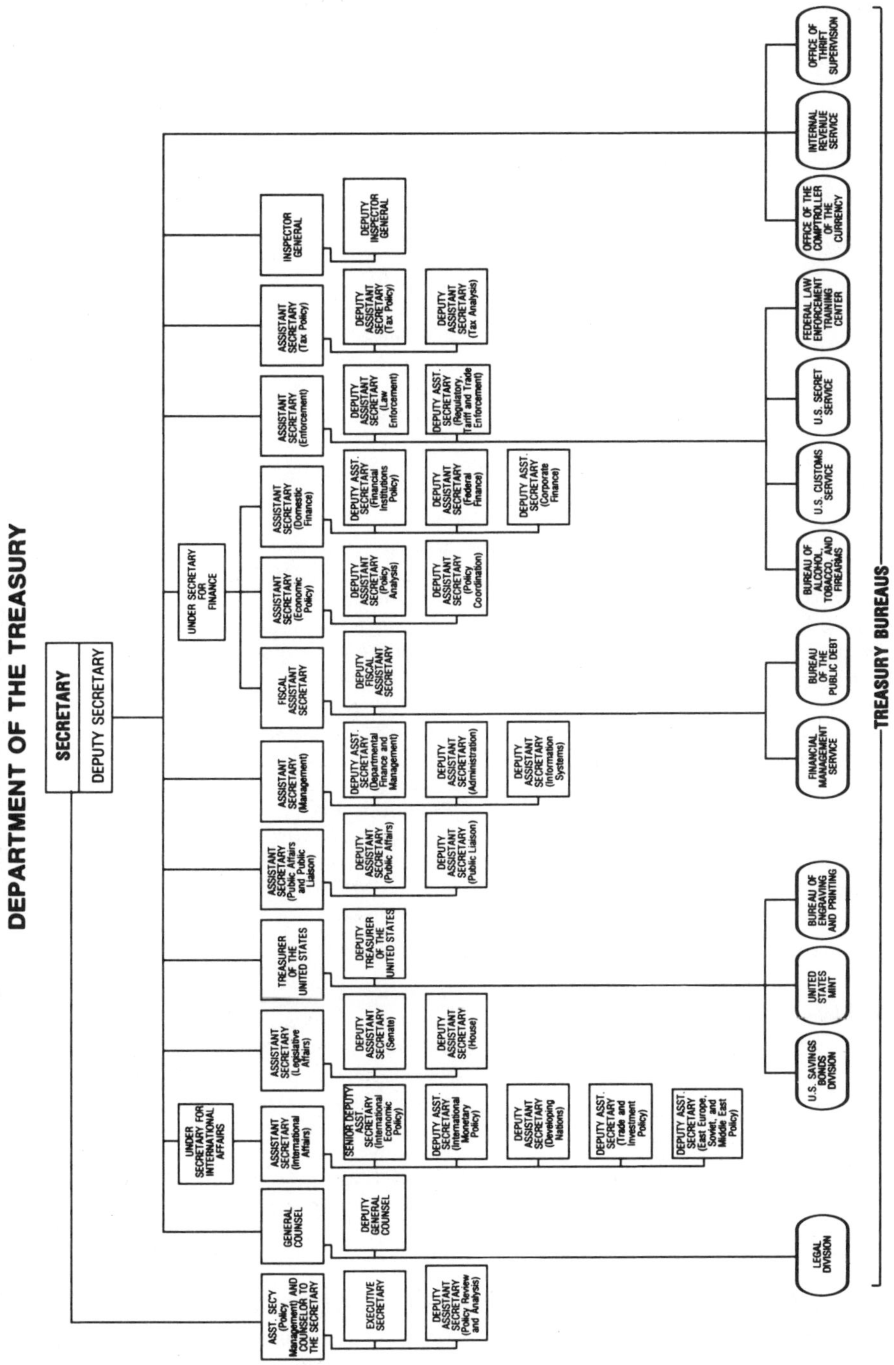
DEPARTMENT OF THE TREASURY
SECRETARY
DEPUTY SECRETARY
ASST. SEC'Y (Policy Management) AND COUNSELOR TO THE SECRETARY
EXECUTIVE SECRETARY
DEPUTY ASSISTANT SECRETARY (Policy Review and Analysis)
GENERAL COUNSEL
DEPUTY GENERAL COUNSEL
UNDER SECRETARY FOR INTERNATIONAL AFFAIRS
ASSISTANT SECRETARY (International Affairs)
SENIOR DEPUTY ASST. SECRETARY (International Economic Policy)
DEPUTY ASST. SECRETARY (International Monetary Policy)
DEPUTY ASSISTANT SECRETARY (Developing Nations)
DEPUTY ASST. SECRETARY (Trade and Investment Policy)
DEPUTY ASST. SECRETARY (East Europe, Soviet, and Middle East Policy)
ASSISTANT SECRETARY (Legislative Affairs)
DEPUTY ASSISTANT SECRETARY (Senate)
DEPUTY ASSISTANT SECRETARY (House)
TREASURER OF THE UNITED STATES
DEPUTY TREASURER OF THE UNITED STATES
ASSISTANT SECRETARY (Public Affairs and Public Liaison)
DEPUTY ASSISTANT SECRETARY (Public Affairs)
DEPUTY ASSISTANT SECRETARY (Public Liaison)
ASSISTANT SECRETARY (Management)
DEPUTY ASST. SECRETARY (Departmental Finance and Management)
DEPUTY ASSISTANT SECRETARY (Administration)
DEPUTY ASSISTANT SECRETARY (Information Systems)
UNDER SECRETARY FOR FINANCE
FISCAL ASSISTANT SECRETARY
DEPUTY FISCAL ASSISTANT SECRETARY
ASSISTANT SECRETARY (Economic Policy)
DEPUTY ASSISTANT SECRETARY (Policy Analysis)
DEPUTY ASSISTANT SECRETARY (Policy Coordination)
ASSISTANT SECRETARY (Domestic Finance)
DEPUTY ASST. SECRETARY (Financial Institutions Policy)
DEPUTY ASSISTANT SECRETARY (Federal Finance)
DEPUTY ASST. SECRETARY (Corporate Finance)
ASSISTANT SECRETARY (Enforcement)
DEPUTY ASSISTANT SECRETARY (Law Enforcement)
DEPUTY ASST. SECRETARY (Regulatory, Tariff and Trade Enforcement)
ASSISTANT SECRETARY (Tax Policy)
DEPUTY ASSISTANT SECRETARY (Tax Policy)
DEPUTY ASSISTANT SECRETARY (Tax Analysis)
INSPECTOR GENERAL
DEPUTY INSPECTOR GENERAL
LEGAL DIVISION
U.S. SAVINGS BONDS DIVISION
UNITED STATES MINT
BUREAU OF ENGRAVING AND PRINTING
FINANCIAL MANAGEMENT SERVICE
BUREAU OF THE PUBLIC DEBT
BUREAU OF ALCOHOL, TOBACCO, AND FIREARMS
U.S. CUSTOMS SERVICE
U.S. SECRET SERVICE
FEDERAL LAW ENFORCEMENT TRAINING CENTER
OFFICE OF THE COMPTROLLER OF THE CURRENCY
INTERNAL REVENUE SERVICE
OFFICE OF THRIFT SUPERVISION
TREASURY BUREAUS

Under Secretary for International Affairs

The Under Secretary for International Affairs advises and assists the Secretary and Deputy Secretary of the Treasury in the formulation and execution of U.S. international economic policy. These responsibilities include the development of policies and guidance of Department activities in the areas of international monetary affairs, trade and investment policy, international debt strategy, and U.S. participation in international financial institutions. The Under Secretary acts as the U.S. G-7 Deputy with responsibility for coordinating economic policies with finance ministers from seven industrial nations and preparing the President for the annual economic summits.

Under Secretary for Finance

The Under Secretary for Finance advises and assists the Secretary and Deputy Secretary of the Treasury in domestic, finance, banking, and economic matters. These responsibilities include the development of policies and guidance of Treasury Department activities in the areas of monetary affairs, management of public debt, financial institutions policy, and domestic fiscal and economic monetary matters.

General Counsel

The Office of the General Counsel furnishes legal advice to the Secretary with respect to his responsibilities as chief financial officer of the Government and overseer of the operating functions of the Treasury Department. The General Counsel is the chief law officer of the department and, as such, is the head of the Legal Division, which is composed of all attorneys providing legal service to all offices and bureaus of the Department.

Assistant Secretaries

Domestic Finance The Assistant Secretary (Domestic Finance) advises and assists the Secretary, Deputy Secretary, and Under Secretary for Finance on matters of Federal, State, and local finance, financial institutions policy, and synthetic fuels projects.

In the area of Federal finance, the Office is responsible for Government financing and debt management; determining interest rates for various Federal borrowing, lending, and investment purposes under pertinent statutes; and developing legislative and administrative principles and standards for Federal credit programs, loan asset sales, and the Federal Financing Bank.

The Office is also responsible for:

—issues involving the financing of State and local governments;

—oversight of the Office of Revenue Sharing, which returns specified amounts of federally collected funds to eligible units of general-purpose governments;

—coordinating the Treasury Department's legislative efforts with regard to financial institutions legislation and legislation affecting the Federal agencies that regulate financial institutions; and

—providing support to carry out the Department's responsibilities regarding the Securities Investor Protection Corporation, the Pension Benefit Guaranty Corporation, and synthetic fuels projects taken over from the Synthetic Fuels Corporation.

Economic Policy The Assistant Secretary (Economic Policy) informs the Secretary and other senior Treasury officials of current and prospective economic developments and assists in the determination of appropriate economic policies. The Assistant Secretary:

—reviews and analyses both domestic and international economic issues, as well as developments in the financial markets;

—participates with the Secretary in the Economic Policy Council and the Troika Forecasting Group, which develops official economic projections and advises the President on choices among alternative courses of economic policy; and

—works closely with officials of the Office of Management and Budget, the Council of Economic Advisers, and other Government agencies on the economic forecasts underlying the yearly budget process, and advises the Secretary on the economic effects of tax and budget policy.

Within the Office of Economic Policy, staff support is provided by the Office of Financial Analysis, the Office of Special Studies, the Office of Monetary Policy Analysis, and the Applied Econometric Staff.

Enforcement The Assistant Secretary (Enforcement) supervises the following operating bureaus: U.S. Secret Service; U.S. Customs Service; Federal Law Enforcement Training Center; and Alcohol, Tobacco and Firearms. In addition, the Assistant Secretary is responsible for the Office of Financial Enforcement, and the Office of Foreign Assets Control.

The Assistant Secretary coordinates Treasury law enforcement matters, including the formulation of policies for Treasury enforcement activities, and cooperates on law enforcement matters with other Federal agencies.

The important missions of protecting the President and other high Government officials and preventing counterfeiting of U.S. currency and theft and forgery of Government securities and checks are entrusted to the United States Secret Service. The U.S. Customs Service collects revenue from imports and enforces the customs laws. In addition, it interdicts contraband, including narcotics, along the land and sea borders of the United States. The Bureau of Alcohol, Tobacco and Firearms is charged with collecting excise taxes on alcoholic beverages and tobacco products; suppressing traffic in illicit distilled spirits and illegal use of explosives; and controlling the sale and registration of firearms. The Federal Law Enforcement Training Center provides law enforcement training for personnel of Federal agencies. The Office of Financial Enforcement assists in implementing the Bank Secrecy Act and administering related Treasury regulations. The Office of Foreign Assets Control assists U.S. foreign policy aims by controlling assets in the United States of "blocked" countries and the flow of funds and trade to them.

Fiscal Affairs The Office of the Fiscal Assistant Secretary was established pursuant to Reorganization Plan No. III of 1940 (5 U.S.C. app.). The Office supervises the administration of the Government's fiscal affairs. This includes the administration of Treasury financing operations; management of Treasury's cash balances in tax and loan investment accounts in commercial financial institutions and operating balances with Federal Reserve Banks; and the Department's participation in the Joint Financial Management Improvement Program for improvement of accounting in the Federal Government. Supervision and oversight over the functions and activities of the Financial Management Service and the Bureau of the Public Debt are also provided. The Fiscal Assistant Secretary is responsible for improved cash management, debt collection, and credit administration on a governmentwide basis under the umbrella of the Administration's Reform '88 initiative.

The Office:

—acts as liaison between the Secretary and other Government agencies with respect to their financial operations;

—manages the cash position of the Treasury; projects and monitors "debt subject-to-limit";

—directs the performance of the fiscal agency functions of the Federal Reserve Banks;

—conducts governmentwide accounting and cash management activities;

—exercises supervision over depositories of the United States; and

—provides management overview of investment practices for Government trust and other accounts.

International Affairs The Office of the Assistant Secretary (International Affairs) advises and assists the Secretary, Deputy Secretary, and Under Secretary for International Affairs in the formulation and execution of policies dealing with international monetary, financial, commercial, energy, and trade policies and programs. The work of the Office is organized into groups responsible for monetary affairs, developing nations, trade and investment policy, and Arabian Peninsula affairs.

These functions are performed by supporting staff offices, which:

—conduct financial diplomacy with industrial and developing nations and regions;

—work toward improving the structure and operations of the international monetary system;

—monitor developments in foreign exchange and other markets and official operations affecting those markets;

—facilitate structural monetary cooperation through the International Monetary Fund and other channels;

—oversee U.S. participation in the multilateral development banks and coordinate U.S. policies and operations relating to bilateral and multilateral development lending programs and institutions;

—formulate policy concerning financing of trade;

—coordinate policies toward foreign investments in the United States and U.S. investments abroad; and

—analyze balance of payments and other basic financial and economic data, including data on petroleum, affecting world payment patterns and the world economic outlook.

As part of those functions, the Office supports the Secretary in his role as co-Chairman of the U.S.-Saudi Arabian Joint Commission on Economic Cooperation, co-Chairman of the U.S.-Israel Joint Committee for Investment and Trade, co-Chairman of the U.S.-China Joint Economic Committee, and Chairman of the National Advisory Council on International Monetary and Financial Policies.

Legislative Affairs The Office of the Assistant Secretary (Legislative Affairs) advises the Secretary and all sub-Cabinet officers on congressional relations policy and serves as the principal contact and coordinator of all departmental contacts with Congress and with congressional relations activities in the White House and other departments.

Management The Office of the Assistant Secretary (Management) serves as the principal policy adviser to the Secretary and Deputy Secretary on the management of the annual planning and budget process and on matters involving the internal management of the Department and its bureaus. The Assistant Secretary oversees the Department's management programs, which include personnel and training and affirmative action and equal employment opportunity; management analysis; financial management; information systems; and property procurement and contracting. The Office also is responsible for the provision of comprehensive administrative services to the Office of the Secretary and certain other components of the Department.

Policy Management The Office of the Assistant Secretary (Policy Management) serves as senior adviser to the Secretary and oversees the Executive Secretary and the functions of the Executive Secretariat. As senior policy adviser, the incumbent supports the Secretary in the management of policies covering the full range of the Department's activities; identifies for the Secretary policy areas of the Department's requiring reexamination; and assists the Secretary in the review of such policies. In the oversight functions, the incumbent ensures the review of all materials submitted to the Secretary and Deputy Secretary for completeness, quality, and coordination with other offices; maintains direct liaison with the White House Staff Secretary, the Cabinet Secretary, and the Cabinet Councils; and coordinates execution of selected tasks involving various offices within the Department, as directed by the Secretary.

Public Affairs and Public Liaison The Office of the Assistant Secretary (Public Affairs and Public Liaison) advises the Secretary and his staff on the Department's relations with the news media, the White House Press Office, other Government agencies, businesses, trade and professional organizations, consumer groups, and the public. It establishes general policies for administering public affairs, business affairs, consumer affairs, and intergovernmental affairs programs in Treasury bureaus. This office designs and implements policies and programs that will increase the public's knowledge and understanding of Treasury's activities and services among the news media, business groups, consumer groups, other Government agencies, and the public.

Tax Policy The Office of the Assistant Secretary (Tax Policy) advises and assists the Secretary and the Deputy secretary in the formulation and execution of domestic and international tax policies and programs.

These functions, carried out by supporting staff offices, include:

—analysis of proposed tax legislation and tax programs;

—projections of economic trends affecting tax bases;

—studies of effects of alternative tax measures;

—preparation of official estimates of Government receipts for the President's annual budget messages;

—legal advice and analysis on domestic and international tax matters;

—assistance in the development and review of tax legislation and domestic and international tax regulations and rulings; and

—participation in international tax treaty negotiations and in maintenance of relations with international organizations on tax matters.

Inspector General

The Inspector General Act of 1978, as amended (5 U.S.C. app.), provides for an Inspector General within the Department of the Treasury. The Office of Inspector General is responsible for providing comprehensive, independent, and objective audit and investigation programs to identify and report program deficiencies and improve the economy, efficiency, and effectiveness of operations. The Office is also responsible for ensuring employee and program integrity through prevention and detection of criminal activity, unethical conduct, and program fraud and abuse. The Office is required to keep the Secretary of the Treasury and the Congress fully informed of problems and deficiencies in the administration of Treasury programs and operations. The Office maintains telephone services for complaints of fraud, waste, and abuse of Department resources. Phone, 800–826–0407 (toll-free hotline); or 202–566–7901 in the Washington, DC, metropolitan area.

Treasurer of the United States

The Office of the Treasurer of the United States was established on September 6, 1777. The Treasurer was originally charged with the receipt and custody of Government funds, but many of these functions have been assumed by different bureaus of the Department of the Treasury. In 1981, the Treasurer was assigned responsibility for oversight of the Bureau of Engraving and Printing, the United States Mint, and the United States Savings Bonds Division.

For further information concerning the Departmental Offices, contact the Public Affairs Office, Department of the Treasury, 1500 Pennsylvania Avenue NW., Washington, DC 20220. Phone, 202–566–2041.

Bureau of Alcohol, Tobacco and Firearms

The Bureau of Alcohol, Tobacco and Firearms was established by Treasury Department Order No. 221, effective July 1, 1972. The order transferred the functions, powers, and duties arising under laws relating to alcohol, tobacco, firearms, and explosives from the Internal Revenue Service to the Bureau. On December 5, 1978, Treasury Department Order No. 120–1 assigned to the Bureau responsibility for enforcing chapter 114 of title 18 of the United States Code (18 U.S.C. 2341 *et seq.*) relating to interstate trafficking in contraband cigarettes. With passage of the Anti-Arson Act of 1982, the Bureau was given the additional responsibility of addressing commercial arson nationwide.

Bureau headquarters is located in Washington, DC, but since the Bureau is decentralized, most of its personnel are stationed throughout the country where many of its operational functions are performed. The Director is appointed by the Secretary of the Treasury and is under the supervision of the Assistant Secretary (Enforcement).

The Bureau is responsible for enforcing and administering firearms and explosives laws, as well as those covering the production, use, and distribution of alcohol and tobacco products. The Bureau's objectives are to maximize compliance and investigate violations of these laws. To achieve these goals, the Bureau is divided into two basic functions: law enforcement and compliance operations.

The objectives of our law enforcement activity are to:

—eliminate illegal trafficking, possession and use of firearms, destructive devices, and explosives;

—impact arson-for-profit schemes;

—suppress the traffic in illicit distilled spirits;

—suppress interstate trafficking in contraband cigarettes; and

—assist Federal, State, and local law enforcement agencies in reducing crime and violence.

—investigate narcotics traffickers who use firearms and explosives as tools of their trade.

The compliance operations activity:

—determines and ensures full collection of revenue due from legal alcohol, tobacco, and firearms industries;

—fulfills the Bureau's responsibility in product integrity, health warning statements, the prevention of commercial bribery, consumer deception, and other improper trade practices in the beverage alcohol industry;

—assists other Federal, State, and local governmental agencies in the resolution of problems relating to revenue protection;

—ensures that persons prohibited by law from manufacturing, importing, or dealing in alcohol, tobacco, firearms, and explosives do not obtain a license or permit;

—ensures that storage facilities for explosives are safe and secure, to avoid presenting a hazard to the public, and that explosives are properly stored in such facilities; and

—ensures that the audit trail is preserved to permit the tracing of firearms used in the commission of crimes and full accountability for explosive materials.

Regional Offices—Compliance Operations

Region	Address	Director
MIDWEST—Illinois, Indiana, Kentucky, Michigan, Minnesota, North Dakota, Ohio, South Dakota, West Virginia, Wisconsin	15th Fl., 230 S. Dearborn St., Chicago, IL 60604	Wayne P. Moran
NORTH ATLANTIC— Connecticut, Delaware, District of Columbia, Maine, Maryland, Massachusetts, New Hampshire, New Jersey, New York, Pennsylvania, Rhode Island, Vermont	Rm. 620, 6 World Trade Ctr., New York, NY 10048	Bruce L. Weininger
SOUTHEAST—Alabama, Florida, Georgia, Mississippi, North Carolina, Puerto Rico, South Carolina, Tennessee, Virginia, Virgin Islands	2600 Century Pkwy., Atlanta, GA 30345	Larry Moore
SOUTHWEST—Arkansas, Colorado, Iowa, Louisiana, New Mexico, Oklahoma, Texas, Wyoming, Nebraska, Kansas, Missouri	7th Fl., 1114 Commerce St., Dallas, TX 75242	Harriet S. Bobo
WESTERN—Alaska, American Samoa, Arizona, California, Guam, Idaho, Montana, Nevada, Oregon, Pacific Islands, Utah, Washington, Hawaii	11th Fl., 221 Main St., San Francisco, CA 94105	Harry Alder

District Offices—Law Enforcement

District	Address	Special Agent in Charge
Atlanta, GA	Suite 406, 101 Marietta St. NW., 30303	Thomas W. Stokes
Birmingham, AL	Rm. 725, 2121 8th Ave., 35203	Paul M. Durham
Boston, MA	Rm. 701, 10 Causeway St., 02222-1081	Terence J. McArdle
Charlotte, NC	Suite 400, 4530 Park Rd., 28209	Paul J. Lyon
Chicago, IL	Rm. 250, 1 S. 450 Summit Ave., Oakbrook Terrace, 60181-1364	Joseph J. Vince, Jr.
Cleveland, OH	Rm. 300, 7251 Engle Rd., Middleburg Heights, OH 44130	William J. Wood
Dallas, TX	Rm. 718, 1114 Commerce St., 75242	Michael C. Huckaby
Detroit, MI	Rm. 533, 231 W. Lafayette St., 48226	Bernard LaForest
Houston, TX	Suite 263, 16630 Imperial Valley Dr., 77060-3411	Philip J. Chojnacki
Kansas City, MO	Rm. 106, 811 Grand Ave., 64106	George Rodriguez
Los Angeles, CA	Rm. 4354, 300 N. Los Angeles St., 90012	Andrew L. Vita
Louisville, KY	Suite 807, 510 W. Broadway, 40202	William A. Curley
Miami, FL	Suite 120, 8420 NW. 52d St., 33166	Robert J. Creighton
Nashville, TN	Suite 215-A, 215 Centerview Dr., Brentwood, TN 37027	Watson C. Beaty
New Orleans, LA	Rm. 309, 10001 Lake Forest Blvd., 70127	Peter B. Mastin II
New York, NY	Rm. 1016, 90 Church St., 10007	Charles R. Thomson
Philadelphia, PA	Rm. 504, 2d and Chestnut Sts., 19106	Henry J. Ballas
San Francisco, CA	Suite 1250, 221 Main St., 94105	Richard A. Rawlins
Seattle, WA	Rm. 806, 915 2d Ave., 98174	Nels C. Nelson
St. Louis, MO	Rm. 611, 1114 Market St., 63101	Daniel B. Hoggatt
St. Paul, MN	Rm. 658, 316 N. Robert St., 55101	Theodore B. Royster
Washington, DC	802 S. Tower, 7799 Leesburg Pike, Falls Church, VA 22043	David C. Troy

Office of the Comptroller of the Currency

[For the Office of the Comptroller of the Currency statement of organization, see the *Code of Federal Regulations,* Title 12, Part 4]

The Office of the Comptroller of the Currency was created by act of February 25, 1863 (12 Stat. 665), as an integral part of the national banking system.

The Comptroller, as the administrator of national banks, is responsible for the execution of laws relating to national banks and promulgates rules and regulations governing the operations of approximately 4,600 national and District of Columbia banks. Approval of the Comptroller is required for the organization of new national banks, conversion of State-chartered banks into national banks, consolidations or mergers of banks where the surviving institution is a national bank, and the establishment of branches by national banks.

The Office of the Comptroller exercises general supervision over the operations of national banks, including trust activities and overseas operations. Each bank is examined periodically through a nationwide staff of approximately 2,100 bank examiners under the immediate supervision of six district deputy comptrollers and six district administrators. These examinations operate in the public interest by assisting the Comptroller in appraising the financial condition of the banks, the soundness of their operations, the quality of their management, and their compliance with laws, rules, and regulations.

For further information, contact the Communications Division, Office of the Comptroller of the Currency, Department of the Treasury, 250 E Street SW., Washington, DC 20219. Phone, 202-874-5000.

United States Customs Service

The fifth act of the first Congress, passed on July 31, 1789 (1 Stat. 29), established customs districts and authorized customs officers to collect duties on goods, wares, and merchandise imposed by the second act of the first Congress, dated July 4, 1789 (1 Stat. 24). The Bureau of Customs was established as a separate agency under the Treasury Department on March 3, 1927 (19 U.S.C. 2071) and, effective August 1, 1973, was redesignated the United States Customs Service by Treasury Department Order 165-23 of April 4, 1973.

The Customs Service collects the revenue from imports and enforces customs and related laws. Customs also administers the Tariff Act of 1930, as amended (19 U.S.C. 1654), and other customs laws. Some of the responsibilities that Customs is specifically charged with are:

—assessing and collecting customs duties, excise taxes, fees, and penalties due on imported merchandise;

—interdicting and seizing contraband, including narcotics and illegal drugs;

—processing persons, carriers, cargo, and mail into and out of the United States;

—administering certain navigation laws; and

—detecting and apprehending persons engaged in fraudulent practices designed to circumvent customs and related laws; copyright, patent, and trademark provisions; quotas; and marking requirements for imported merchandise.

As the principal border enforcement agency, Customs' mission has been extended over the years to assisting in the administration and enforcement of some 400 provisions of law on behalf of more than 40 Government agencies. Today, in addition to enforcing the Tariff Act of 1930 and other customs statutes, the Customs Service:

—enforces export control laws and intercepts illegal high-technology exports to Soviet bloc countries;

—cooperates with other Federal agencies and foreign governments in suppressing the traffic of illegal narcotics and pornography;

—enforces reporting requirements of the Bank Secrecy Act; and

—collects international trade statistics.

Also, Customs enforces a wide range of requirements to protect the public, such as auto safety and emission control standards, radiation and radioactive material standards; counterfeit monetary instruments; flammable fabric restrictions; animal and plant quarantine requirements; and food, drug, and hazardous substance prohibitions.

Customs is extensively involved with outside commercial and policy organizations and trade associations, and with international organizations and foreign customs services. Customs is a member of the multinational Customs Cooperation Council, the Cabinet Committee to Combat Terrorism, and the International Narcotics Control Program. In addition, Customs participates in and supports the activities and programs of various international organizations and agreements, including the General Agreement on Tariffs and Trade, the International Civil Aviation Organization, and the Organization of American States.

Headquarters of the U.S. Customs Service is located in Washington, DC, under the supervision of the Commissioner of Customs, who is appointed by the Secretary of the Treasury.

The 50 States, plus the Virgin Islands and Puerto Rico, are divided into seven Customs Regions. Contained within these regions are 44 subordinate district or area offices under which there are approximately 240 ports of entry.

The foreign field offices of the Customs Service are located in Bangkok, Bonn, Dublin, Hermosillo, Hong Kong, London, Mexico City, Milan, Monterrey, Ottawa, Panama City, Paris, Rome, Seoul, Singapore, Tokyo, Vienna, and The

Hague. An attaché represents U.S. Customs in the U.S. Mission to the European Communities in Brussels.

The Customs Service also operates a Canine Enforcement Training Center at Front Royal, VA.

Regional Offices—U.S. Customs Service

(C: Commissioner; DC: Deputy Commissioner; RC: Regional Commissioner; DD: District Director; AD: Area Director)

Regional Headquarters/ District Offices	Address	Officer
MAIN HEADQUARTERS:		
Washington, DC	1301 Constitution Ave. NW., 20229	Carol B. Hallett (C)
		Michael H. Lane (DC)
NEW YORK:		
New York, NY	6 World Trade Ctr., 10048	Anthony M. Liberta (RC)
		Jean F. Maguire (AD)
	Kennedy Airport, 11430	Thomas Mattina (AD)
NORTH CENTRAL:		
Chicago, IL	55 E. Monroe St., 60603	Richard McMullen (RC)
	610 S. Canal St., 60607	Richard Roster (DD)
Cleveland, OH	55 Erie View Plz., 44114	John F. Nelson (DD)
Detroit, MI	477 Michigan Ave., 48226	William L. Morandini (DD)
Duluth, MN	209 Federal Bldg., 55802	Robert W. Nordness (AD)
Great Falls, MT	300 2d Ave. S., 59401	Donald Myhra (DD)
Milwaukee, WI	6269 Ace Industrial Dr., 53237	Richard L. Rudin (DD)
Minneapolis, MN	110 S. 4th St., 55401	Robert W. Nordness (AD)
Pembina, ND	Post Office Bldg., 58271	Raymond Hagerty, Jr. (DD)
St. Louis, MO	7911 Forsyth Bldg., 63105	Theodore Galantowicz (DD)
NORTHEAST:		
Baltimore, MD	40 S. Gay St., 21202	A. Robert Beikirch (DD)
Boston, MA	10 Causeway St., 02222	Philip Spayd (RC)
		John Linde (DD)
Buffalo, NY	111 W. Huron St., 14202	Carlton L. Brainard (DD)
Ogdensburg, NY	127 N. Water St., 13669	William Dietzel (DD)
Philadelphia, PA	2d & Chestnut Sts., 19106	Steve Knox (DD)
Portland, ME	312 Fore St., 04112	Emery W. Ingalls (DD)
Providence, RI	49 Pavilion Ave., 02905	Phillip A. Bernard (DD)
St. Albans, VT	Main & Stebbins Sts., 05478	Michael D'Ambrosio (DD)
SOUTH CENTRAL:		
Mobile, AL	150 N. Royal, 36602	David L. Willette (DD)
New Orleans, LA	423 Canal St., 70130	J. Robert Grimes (RC)
		Joel Mish (DD)
SOUTHEAST:		
Charleston, SC	200 E. Bay St., 29401	William Byrd (DD)
Miami, FL	909 SE. 1st Ave., 33131	George C. Corcoran, Jr. (RC)
	77 SE. 5th St., 33131	D. Lynn Gordon (DD)
Norfolk, VA	101 E. Main St., 23510	Dennis H. Murphy (DD)
San Juan, PR	U.S. Customhouse (P.O. Box 2112), 00903	Mamie Pollock (DD)
Savannah, GA	1 E. Bay St., 31401	Robert Richter (DD)
Tampa, FL	4430 E. Adams Dr., 33605	Diane Zwicker (DD)
Washington, DC	P.O. Box 17423, 20041	William Green (DD)
Wilmington, NC	1 Virginia Ave., 28401	John R. Babb (DD)
SOUTHWEST:		
Dallas/Fort Worth, TX	1205 Royal Ln., Dallas/Ft. Worth Airport, 75261	David Greenleaf (DD)
El Paso, TX	Bridge of the Americas (P.O. Box 9516), 79985	Mike Mack (DD)
Houston, TX	5850 San Felipe St., 77057	James Piatt (RC)
Houston/Galveston, TX	701 San Jacinto St., 77052	Patricia McCauley (DD)
Laredo, TX	Lincoln-Juarez Bridge, 78044	Joseph Castelland (DD)
Nogales, AZ	International and Terrace Sts., 85621	Frederick D. Lawrence (DD)
Port Arthur, TX	4550 75th Ave., 77642	Warnie Davis, *Acting* (DD)
PACIFIC:		
Anchorage, AK	605 W. 4th Ave., 99501	Duane Oveson (DD)
Honolulu, HI	335 Merchant St., 96806	George Roberts (DD)
Los Angeles, CA	Suite 705, 1 World Trade Ctr., Long Beach, CA 90831.	Quintin L. Villanueva, Jr. (RC)
Los Angeles/Long Beach, CA.	300 S. Ferry St., San Pedro, CA 90731	John Heinrich (DD)
Portland, OR	511 NW. Broadway, 97209	Thomas Hardy (DD)
San Diego, CA	880 Front St., 92188	Allan J. Rappoport (DD)
San Francisco, CA	555 Battery St., 94126	Paul Andrews (DD)

Regional Offices—U.S. Customs Service—Continued

(C: Commissioner; DC: Deputy Commissioner; RC: Regional Commissioner; DD: District Director; AD: Area Director)

Regional Headquarters/ District Offices	Address	Officer
Seattle, WA	909 1st Ave., 98174	Daniel C. Holland (DD)

For further information, contact the Public Affairs Office, U.S. Customs Service, Department of the Treasury, 1301 Constitution Avenue NW., Washington, DC 20229. Phone, 202–566–8195.

Bureau of Engraving and Printing

The Bureau of Engraving and Printing operates on basic authorities conferred by act of July 11, 1862 (31 U.S.C. 303) and additional authorities contained in past appropriations made to the Bureau that are still in force.

A working capital fund was established in accordance with the provisions of section 2 of act of August 4, 1950, as amended (31 U.S.C. 5142), which placed the Bureau on a completely reimbursable basis. The Bureau is headed by a Director, who is appointed by the Secretary of the Treasury.

The Bureau of Engraving and Printing designs, prints, and finishes a large variety of security products including Federal Reserve notes, U.S. postage stamps, Treasury securities, identification cards, and certificates. It also is responsible for advising and assisting Federal agencies in the design and production of other government documents that, because of their innate value or some other reason, require security or counterfeit-deterrence characteristics.

The Bureau is the largest printer of security documents in the world; over 40 billion security documents are printed annually. Total sales for fiscal year 1990 reached $275 million. The Bureau's headquarters are located in Washington, DC. In 1991, a second currency plant, located in Fort Worth, TX, began operating and will produce 25 percent of the U.S. currency requirement by 1995.

For further information, contact the Office of Public Affairs, Bureau of Engraving and Printing, Department of the Treasury, Room 104–18M, Fourteenth and C Streets SW., Washington, DC 20228. Phone, 202–447–0193.

Federal Law Enforcement Training Center

The Federal Law Enforcement Training Center was established by Treasury Department Order No. 217, effective March 2, 1970; Revision 1, effective June 30, 1970; and reaffirmed by Treasury Department Order No. 140–01 of January 13, 1987.

The Federal Law Enforcement Training Center is headed by a Director, who is appointed by the Secretary of the Treasury. The Center conducts operations at its training facility located at Glynco, GA. The Center also maintains a Washington office at 650 Massachusetts Avenue NW., Washington, DC 20226. Phone, 202–566–2951. In addition, the Center has two satellite operations located at Pinal Air Park, Marana, AZ 85653 (phone, 602–670–5305); and Artesia, NM 88210 (phone, 505–748–8000).

The Center is an interagency training facility serving 70 Federal law enforcement organizations. The major training effort is in the area of basic programs to teach common areas of law enforcement skills to police and investigative personnel. The Center also conducts advanced programs in areas of common need, such as white-collar crime, the use of microcomputers as an investigative tool, advanced law enforcement photography, international banking/money laundering, marine law enforcement, and several instructor training courses. In addition to the basic and common advanced programs, the Center provides the facilities and support services for participating organizations to conduct advanced training for their own law enforcement personnel. The Center offers selective, highly specialized training programs to State and local officers as an aid in deterring crime. These programs include a variety of areas such as fraud and financial investigations, cargo theft investigations, juvenile justice topics, marine law enforcement, and arson for profit.

The Center develops the curriculum content and training techniques for recruit training, and advises and assists the participating organizations in producing, formulating, and operating specialized training materials and equipment.

Administrative and financial activities are supervised by the Department of the Treasury. However, training policy, programs, criteria, and standards are governed by the interagency Board of Directors, comprised of senior officials from eight departments and independent agencies.

For further information, contact the Public Affairs Office, Federal Law Enforcement Training Center, Department of the Treasury, Glynco, GA 31524. Phone, 912-267-2447.

Financial Management Service

The mission of the Financial Management Service (FMS) is to improve the quality of Government financial management. Its commitment and responsibility is to help its Government customers achieve success. It does this by linking program and financial management objectives and by providing financial services, information, and advice to its customers. FMS serves taxpayers, the Treasury Department, Federal program agencies, and Government policymakers.

Working Capital Management The Service is responsible for programs to improve cash management, credit management, debt collection, and financial management systems governmentwide. For cash management, the Service issues guidelines and regulations and assists other agencies in managing financial transactions to maximize investment earnings and reduce the interest costs of borrowed funds. For credit management, the Service issues guidelines and regulations and assists program agencies with management of credit activities, including loan programs, to improve all parts of the credit cycle, such as credit extension, loan servicing, debt collection, and write-off procedures. The Service is presently working with other agencies to improve financial management systems and the way government handles its payments, collections, and receivables, and to take advantage of new automation technology.

Payments The Service issues approximately 500 million Treasury checks and close to 250 million electronic fund transfer payments annually for Federal salaries and wages, payments to suppliers of goods and services to the Federal Government, income tax refunds, and payments under major Government programs such as social security and veterans' benefits. The Service pays all Treasury checks and reconciles them against the accounts of government disbursing officers, receives and examines claims for checks that are cashed under forged endorsements or that are lost, stolen, or destroyed; and issues new checks on approved claims. The Service uses two electronic funds-transfer methods: the automated clearinghouses—for recurring payments such as Government benefits and salaries—and wire transfers through the Fedline System. The latter is a computer-to-computer link with the Federal Reserve System that allows for the electronic transfer of funds to virtually any financial institution in the United States.

Collections The Service supervises the collection of Government receipts and operates and maintains the systems for collecting these receipts. The Service is working with all Federal agencies to improve the availability of collected funds and the reporting of collection information to Treasury. Current collection systems include the Treasury General Account System, the Treasury Tax and Loan System for withholding and other Federal tax deposits, and the Treasury National Automated Lockbox System for accelerating the processing of agency receipts.

Central Accounting and Reporting The Service maintains a central system that accounts for the monetary assets and liabilities of the Treasury and tracks Government collection and payment operations. Periodic reports are prepared to show budget results, the Government's overall financial status, and other financial operations. These reports include the *Daily Treasury Statement,* the *Monthly Treasury Statement,* the *Quarterly Treasury Bulletin,* the annual *Treasury Report,* and the annual *Treasury Consolidated Financial Statement.*

Disbursing Centers—Financial Management Service

Center/Address	Director
Austin, TX (1619 Woodward St., 78741)	Gordon Hickam
Birmingham, AL (190 Vulcan Rd., 35209)	Zora T. Puckett
Chicago, IL (356 S. Clark St., 60605)	Ollice C. Holden
Kansas City, KS (2100 W. 36th Ave., 66103)	John H. Adams
Philadelphia, PA (5000 Wissahickon Ave., 19144)	Robert Langdon
San Francisco, CA (390 Main St., 94105)	Philip Belisle
Washington, DC (441 G St. NW., 20001)	Beverly Robinson

For further information, contact the Office of Legislative and Public Affairs, Financial Management Service, Department of the Treasury, Room 555, 401 Fourteenth Street SW., Washington, DC 20227. Phone, 202–287–0669.

Internal Revenue Service

The Office of the Commissioner of Internal Revenue was established by act of July 1, 1862 (26 U.S.C. 7802).

The Internal Revenue Service is responsible for administering and enforcing the internal revenue laws and related statutes, except those relating to alcohol, tobacco, firearms, and explosives. Its mission is to collect the proper amount of tax revenue at the least cost to the public, and in a manner that warrants the highest degree of public confidence in the Service's integrity, efficiency, and fairness. To achieve that purpose, the Service will:

—encourage and achieve the highest possible degree of voluntary compliance in accordance with the tax laws and regulations;

—advise the public of their rights and responsibilities;

—determine the extent of compliance and the causes of noncompliance;

—properly administer and enforce the tax laws; and

—continually search for and implement new, more efficient ways of accomplishing its mission.

Basic activities include:

—ensuring satisfactory resolution of taxpayer complaints, providing taxpayer service and education;

—determining, assessing, and collecting internal revenue taxes;

—determining pension plan qualifications and exempt organization status; and

—preparing and issuing rulings and regulations to supplement the provisions of the Internal Revenue Code.

The source of most revenues collected is the individual income tax and the social insurance and retirement taxes, with other major sources being the corporation income, excise, estate, and gift taxes. Congress first received authority to levy taxes on the income of individuals and corporations in 1913, pursuant to the 16th amendment of the Constitution.

Organization

Service organization is designed for maximum decentralization, consistent with the need for uniform interpretation of the tax laws and efficient utilization of resources. There are three organizational levels: the National Office; the Regional Offices; and the District Offices, Service Centers, and the Austin Compliance Center (in the Southwest Region). Districts may have local offices the number and location of which are determined by taxpayer and agency needs.

Headquarters Organization The National Office, located in Washington, DC, develops nationwide policies and programs for the administration of the internal revenue laws and provides overall direction to the field organization. The Martinsburg Computing Center in Martinsburg, WV, and the Detroit Computing Center in Detroit, MI, also are assigned to the National Office.

Field Organization

As a decentralized organization, most agency personnel and activities are assigned to field installations.

Regional Offices There are seven Regional Offices, each headed by a Regional Commissioner, which supervise and evaluate the operations of District Offices, Service Centers, and the Austin Compliance Center.

Regional Offices—Internal Revenue Service

Region	Address	Commissioner
CENTRAL—Indiana, Kentucky, Michigan, Ohio, West Virginia	550 Main St., Cincinnati, OH 45202	Leon Moore
MID-ATLANTIC—Delaware, Maryland, New Jersey, Pennsylvania, Virginia	841 Chestnut St., Philadelphia, PA 19107	Charles H. Brennan
MIDWEST—Illinois, Iowa, Minnesota, Missouri, Montana, Nebraska, North Dakota, South Dakota, Wisconsin	Gateway IV Bldg., 300 S. Riverside Plz., Chicago, IL 60606	Elmer Kletke
NORTH ATLANTIC—Connecticut, Maine, Massachusetts, New Hampshire, New York, Rhode Island, Vermont	90 Church St., New York, NY 10007	Cornelius J. Coleman
SOUTHEAST—Alabama, Arkansas, Georgia, Florida, Louisiana, Mississippi, North Carolina, South Carolina, Tennessee	401 W. Peachtree St. NE., Atlanta, GA 30365	Michael P. Dolan
SOUTHWEST—Arizona, Colorado, Kansas, New Mexico, Oklahoma, Texas, Utah, Wyoming	4050 Alpha Rd., Dallas, TX 75244-4203	Richard C. Voskuil
WESTERN—Alaska, California, Hawaii, Idaho, Nevada, Oregon, Washington	1650 Mission St., San Francisco, CA 94103	Thomas Coleman

District Offices There are 62 Internal Revenue districts, each administered by a District Director. Districts may encompass an entire State, or a certain number of counties within a State, depending on population. Programs of the District include taxpayer service, examination, collection, criminal investigation, resources management, and, in some districts, pension plans and exempt organizations. Functions performed are: assistance and service to taxpayers, determination of tax liability by examination of tax returns, determination of pension plan qualification, collection of delinquent returns and taxes, and investigation of criminal and civil violations of internal revenue laws (except those relating to alcohol, tobacco, firearms, and explosives). Directors are responsible for the deposit of taxes collected by the

District and for initial processing of original applications for admission to practice before the Internal Revenue Service and renewal issuances for those practitioners already enrolled. Local offices may be established to meet taxpayer needs and agency workload requirements.

Internal Revenue Districts—Internal Revenue Service

District	Address	Director
ALABAMA	500 22d St. S., Birmingham, 35233	Philip J. Sullivan
ALASKA	949 E. 36th Ave., Anchorage, 99508	Robert W. Brock
ARIZONA	2120 N. Central Ave., Phoenix, 85004	Prescott A. Berry
ARKANSAS	700 W. Capitol Ave., Little Rock, 72201	Lee R. Monks
CALIFORNIA:		
Laguna Niguel	24000 Avila Rd., 92677	Jesse Cota
Los Angeles	300 N. Los Angeles St., 90012	Michael Quinn
Sacramento	4330 Watt Ave., North Highland, CA 95660	Raymond Spillman
San Francisco	450 Golden Gate Ave., 94102	Francis Miceli
San Jose	55 S. Market St., 95113	Calvin Esselstrom
COLORADO	600 17th St., Denver, 80202	Gerald Swanson
CONNECTICUT	135 High St., Hartford, 06103	James E. Quinn
DELAWARE	844 King St., Wilmington, 19801	(vacancy)
DISTRICT OF COLUMBIA	(part of Baltimore District)	
FLORIDA:		
Fort Lauderdale	3d Fl., Bldg. B, 1 University Dr., 33324	Merlin W. Heye
Jacksonville	400 W. Bay St., 32202	James J. Ryan
GEORGIA	401 W. Peachtree St., Atlanta, 30365	Paul Williams
HAWAII	300 Ala Moana Blvd., Honolulu, 96850	Billy J. Brown
IDAHO	550 W. Fort St., Boise, 83724	Jack Cheskaty
ILLINOIS:		
Chicago	230 S. Dearborn St., 60604	Richard S. Wintrode
Springfield	320 W. Washington St., 62701	Daniel L. Black
INDIANA	575 N. Pennsylvania, Indianapolis, 46204	William Jacobs
IOWA	210 Walnut St., Des Moines, 50309	Curtis Jenkins
KANSAS	412 S. Main, Wichita, 67202	Bruce R. Thomas
KENTUCKY	601 W. Broadway, Louisville, 40202	William E. Palzkill
LOUISIANA	500 Camp St., New Orleans, 70130	John C. Wendorff
MAINE	68 Sewall St., Augusta, 04330	Richard E. Simko
MARYLAND	31 Hopkins Plz., Baltimore, 21201	Herma Hightower
MASSACHUSETTS	John F. Kennedy Federal Bldg., Boston, 02203	Gerard Esposito
MICHIGAN	477 Michigan Ave., Detroit, 48226	John Hummel
MINNESOTA	316 N. Robert St., St. Paul, 55101	C. Dudley Switzer
MISSISSIPPI	100 W. Capitol St., Jackson, 39269	Robert Douthitt
MISSOURI	1114 Market St., St. Louis, 63101	Ralph F. Shilling
MONTANA	301 S. Park Ave., Helena, 59626	Arnold D. Wiley
NEBRASKA	106 S. 15th St., Omaha, 68102	James A. Grant
NEVADA	4750 W. Oakey Blvd., Las Vegas, 89102	Robert E. Withers
NEW HAMPSHIRE	80 Daniel St., Portsmouth, 03801	Paul Harrington
NEW JERSEY	970 Broad St., Newark, 07102	John J. Jennings
NEW MEXICO	517 Gold Ave. SW., Albuquerque, 87102	Herbert Huff
NEW YORK:		
Albany	Clinton Ave. and N. Pearl St., 12207	Jean K. Pope
Brooklyn	35 Tillary St., 11201	Eugene Alexander
Buffalo	111 W. Huron St., 14202	Donald Mitgang
Manhattan	120 Church St., New York, 10007	Robert Mirsberger
NORTH CAROLINA	320 Federal Pl., Greensboro, 27401	J.R. Starkey
NORTH DAKOTA	653 2d Ave. N., Fargo, 58102	Audrey Saari
OHIO:		
Cincinnati	550 Main St., 45202	Harold M. Browning
Cleveland	1240 E. 9th St., 44199	Jack Chivatero
OKLAHOMA	200 NW. 4th St., Oklahoma City, 73102	Kenneth J. Sawyer
OREGON	1220 SW. 3d Ave., Portland, 97204	Carolyn Leonard
PENNSYLVANIA:		
Philadelphia	600 Arch St., 19106	Gary H. Matthews
Pittsburgh	1000 Liberty Ave., 15222	Robert Brauer
PUERTO RICO	Stop 27½, Ponce de Leon Ave., Hato Rey, 00917	Ramon Rivera [1]
RHODE ISLAND	380 Westminster Mall, Providence, 02903	Malcolm A. Liebermann
SOUTH CAROLINA	1835 Assembly St., Columbia, 29201	Donald L. Breihan
SOUTH DAKOTA	115 4th Ave. SE., Aberdeen, 57401	David Reizes
TENNESSEE	801 Broadway, Nashville, 37203	Glenn Cagle
TEXAS:		
Austin	300 E. 8th St., 78701	Richard R. Orosco
Dallas	1100 Commerce St., 75242	Gary O. Booth
Houston	1919 Smith St., 77002	Arturo A. Jacobs
UTAH	465 S. 4th East, Salt Lake City, 84111	Carol M. Fay

Internal Revenue Districts—Internal Revenue Service—Continued

District	Address	Director
VERMONT	199 Main St., Burlington, 05402	Stephen L. Daige
VIRGINIA	400 N. 8th St., Richmond, 23240	Jack G. Petrie
WASHINGTON	915 2d Ave., Seattle, 98174	Woodrow D. Malone
WEST VIRGINIA	425 Juliana St., Parkersburg, 26101	Jack Schroeder
WISCONSIN	310 W. Wisconsin Ave., Milwaukee, 53203	John Ader
WYOMING	308 W. 21st St., Cheyenne, 82001	Conrad L. Clapper

Overseas Taxpayers

Office	Address
DISTRICT OF COLUMBIA	Office of Taxpayer Service and Compliance, 950 L'Enfant Plaza SW. (IN:C), 20024

[1] Director's Representative

Service Centers Under the supervision of the Regional Commissioner having jurisdiction over the area of their location are 10 Service Centers, located at Andover, MA; Austin, TX; Brookhaven, NY; Chamblee, GA; Covington, KY; Fresno, CA; Kansas City, MO; Memphis, TN; Ogden, UT; and Philadelphia, PA. Each Service Center processes tax returns and related documents and maintains accountability records for taxes collected. Programs include the processing, verification, and accounting control of tax returns; the assessment and certification of refunds of taxes; and administering assigned examination, criminal investigation, and collection functions.

The Austin Compliance Center, located in Austin, TX, administers the examination, criminal investigation, and collection functions formerly assigned to the Austin Service Center.

For further information, contact any District Office or the Internal Revenue Service Headquarters, Department of the Treasury, 1111 Constitution Avenue NW., Washington, DC 20224. Phone, 202–566–5000.

United States Mint

The Mint of the United States was established by act of April 2, 1792 (1 Stat. 246). The Bureau of the Mint was established by act of February 12, 1873 (17 Stat. 424) and recodified on September 13, 1982 (31 U.S.C. 304, 5131). The name was changed to United States Mint by Secretarial order dated January 9, 1984.

The primary mission of the Mint is to produce sufficient circulation coinage for the Nation's commerce. The Mint also produces and sells numismatic coins, American Eagle gold and silver bullion coins, and national medals. Further, the Mint safeguards the Treasury Department's gold and silver reserves.

The U.S. Mint maintains public exhibit and sales areas at the Philadelphia and Denver Mints, the Old Mint in San Francisco, and Union Station in Washington, DC. Admission is free.

Field Facilities

(S: Superintendent; O: Officer in Charge)

Facility/Address	Facility Head
United States Mint, Philadelphia, PA 19106	John T. Martino (S)
United States Mint, Denver, CO 80204	Barbara E. McTurk (S)

Field Facilities—Continued

(S: Superintendent; O: Officer in Charge)

Facility/Address	Facility Head
United States Mint, San Francisco, CA 94102 and the Old Mint, San Francisco, CA 94103	Carol M. Marshall (S)
United States Mint, West Point, NY 10996	Bert W. Corneby (S)
United States Bullion Depository, Fort Knox, KY 40121	James M. Curtis (O)

For further information, contact the United States Mint, Department of the Treasury, Judiciary Square Building, 633 Third Street NW., Washington, DC 20220. Phone, 202–376–0837.

Bureau of the Public Debt

The Bureau of the Public Debt was established on June 30, 1940, pursuant to the Reorganization Act of 1939, and recodified on September 13, 1982 (31 U.S.C. 306). The Bureau's mission is to borrow the money needed to operate the Federal Government and to account for the resulting public debt.

The Bureau administers the public debt by borrowing money through the sale of United States Treasury securities; manages and directs the offering and auction of marketable securities (Treasury bills, bonds, and notes); supervises and participates in the issuing, servicing, and retirement of U.S. Savings Bonds; settles claims for lost, stolen, destroyed, or mutilated bonds; and makes daily and other periodic reports on the balance and composition of the debt. It also implements regulations for the Government securities market. These rules are designed to protect investors while maintaining a fair and liquid securities market.

The Bureau's principal office is located in Washington, DC. It also maintains an office in Parkersburg, WV, which handles public debt operations related to U.S. Savings Bonds and automated information systems.

For further information, contact the Public Affairs Officer, Office of the Commissioner, Bureau of the Public Debt, Department of the Treasury, Washington, DC 20239–0001. Phone, 202–376–4302.

United States Savings Bonds Division

Under Treasury Order 62, dated December 26, 1945, the Savings Bonds Division became successor to the War Finance Division, War Savings Staff, and Defense Savings Staff created originally by Treasury Order 39, dated March 19, 1941. The United States Savings Bonds Division promotes the sale and retention of U.S. Savings Bonds.

The promotional staff's major functions are the installation and maintenance of the payroll savings plan by employees and the promotion of bond sales through financial institutions that act as issuing agents. Financial institutions and businesses, and labor, farm, school, media, and community leaders are contacted to enhance awareness and understanding of the savings bonds program. A continuing effort is made to enlist volunteer support to further the sale of savings bonds. Volunteer commitment is a factor in the success of the program.

The Division, headquartered in Washington, DC, has field offices throughout the United States under the direction of 18 district offices.

District Offices—United States Savings Bonds Division

District	Address [1]	Director
ATLANTA—Florida, Georgia	Suite 242, 1720 Peachtree St. NW., Atlanta, GA 30309 [1]	David Heinrich
BIRMINGHAM—Alabama, Louisiana, Mississippi, Tennessee	Suite 750, 600 Beacon Pkwy. W., Birmingham, AL 35209 [1]	David W. Davis
BOSTON—Connecticut, Maine, Massachusetts, New Hampshire, Rhode Island, Vermont	Rm. 463, 10 Causeway St., Boston, MA 02222-1090 [1]	John A. Williams, Jr.
CHICAGO—northern Illinois	Rm. 530, 230 S. Dearborn St., Chicago, IL 60604-1594 [1]	Douglas Youngren
CLEVELAND—Kentucky, Ohio	Suite 580, 55 Erieview Plz., Cleveland, OH 44114 [1]	Robert Urbanek
DALLAS—Texas	Suite 130-LB-6, 7701 Stemmons Fwy., Dallas, TX 75247-9998 [1]	Don R. Carter
DETROIT—Indiana, Michigan	Suite 1745, 477 Michigan Ave., Detroit, MI 48226-2577 [1]	Edward G. Lynch
GREENSBORO—North Carolina, South Carolina	Suite 211, 2302 W. Meadowview Rd., Greensboro, NC 27407 [1]	Richard Jones
LOS ANGELES—Arizona, New Mexico, southern California, southern Nevada	Suite 9120, 11000 Wilshire Blvd., Los Angeles, CA 90024 [1]	Thomas Madara
MANHATTAN—New York City	Rm. 3046, 26 Federal Plz., New York, NY 10278 [1]	John Ahearn
MINNEAPOLIS—Iowa, Minnesota, Nebraska, North Dakota, South Dakota, Wisconsin	Rm. 301, 220 2d St., S. Bridgeplace, Minneapolis, MN 55401 [1]	George Clarke
NEW YORK—New York State	Rm. 320, 6 World Trade Ctr., New York, NY 10048 [1]	Frank K. Riley
NEWARK—New Jersey	Suite 303, 810 Bear Tavern Rd. W., Trenton, NJ 08628 [1]	Dorothy Ender
PITTSBURGH—Delaware, Pennsylvania	Rm. 832, 1000 Liberty Ave., Pittsburgh, PA 15222 [1]	Murray H. Birnbaum
SAN FRANCISCO—northern California, northern Nevada, Utah	Rm. 107, Bldg. 2E, 620 Cental Ave., Alameda, CA 94501 [1]	George P. Masot
SEATTLE—Alaska, Colorado, Hawaii, Montana, Oregon, Washington, Wyoming	Suite 123, 121 107th NE., Bellevue, WA 98004 [1]	Dan Schipper
ST. LOUIS—Arkansas, Kansas, Missouri, Oklahoma, southern Illinois	Rm. 1.208, 1222 Spruce St., St. Louis, MO 63101 [1]	(vacancy)
WASHINGTON, DC—District of Columbia, Maryland, Virginia, West Virginia	Suite 400A, 5500 Friendship Blvd., Chevy Chase, MD 20815 [1]	Kim Treat

[1] Address must include "U.S. Savings Bonds Division, Department of Treasury" or mail will not be delivered.

For further information, contact the Office of Public Affairs, United States Savings Bonds Division, Department of the Treasury, 1111 Twentieth Street NW., Washington, DC 20226. Phone, 202–634–5389.

United States Secret Service

Pursuant to certain sections of titles 3 and 18 of the United States Code, the mission of the Secret Service includes the authority and responsibility:

—to protect the President, the Vice President, the President-elect, the Vice-President-elect, and members of their immediate families; major Presidential and Vice Presidential candidates; former Presidents and their spouses, except that protection of a spouse shall terminate in the event of remarriage; minor children of a former President until the age of 16; visiting heads of foreign states or governments; other distinguished foreign visitors to the United States; and official representatives of the United States performing special missions abroad, as directed by the President;

—to provide security at the White House complex and other Presidential offices, the temporary official residence of the Vice President in the District of Columbia, and foreign diplomatic missions in the Washington, DC, metropolitan area and throughout the United States, its territories and possessions, as prescribed by statute;

—to detect and arrest any person committing any offense against the laws of the United States relating to currency, coins, obligations, and securities of the United States or of foreign governments;

—to suppress the forgery and fraudulent negotiation or redemption of Federal Government checks, bonds, and other obligations or securities of the United States;

—to conduct investigations relating to certain criminal violations of the Federal Deposit Insurance Act (12 U.S.C. 1811 note), the Federal Land Bank Act, and the Government Losses in Shipment Act (40 U.S.C. 721 note); and

—to detect and arrest offenders of laws pertaining to electronic funds transfer frauds, credit and debit card frauds, false identification documents or devices, computer access fraud, and U.S. Department of Agriculture food coupons, including authority to participate cards.

District Offices—United States Secret Service

District	Address	Telephone
Albany, GA	Suite 221, 235 Roosevelt Ave., 31701	912-430-8442
Albany, NY	Rm. 244, 445 Broadway, 12207	518-472-2884
Albuquerque, NM	Suite 1700, 505 Marquette St. NW., 87102	505-766-3336
Anchorage, AK	Rm. 526, 222 W. 7th Ave., 99513-7592	907-271-5148
Atlanta, GA	Suite 1100, 100 Peachtree St. NE., 30303	404-331-6111
Atlantic City, NJ	Rm. 200, Illinois and Pacific Aves., 08401	609-347-0772
Austin, TX	Suite 972, 300 E. 8th St., 78701	512-482-5103
Baltimore, MD	Rm. 7100, 101 W. Lombard St., 21201	301-962-2200
Baton Rouge, LA	Rm. 1502, 1 American Pl., 70825	504-389-0763
Birmingham, AL	Suite 203, 500 S. 22d St., 35233	205-731-1144
Bismarck, ND	Rm. 432, Federal Bldg., 58501	701-255-3294
Boise, ID	Rm. 732, 550 Fort St., 83702	208-334-1403
Boston, MA	Suite 791, 10 Causeway St., 02222	617-565-5640
Buffalo, NY	Rm. 1208, 111 W. Huron St., 14202	716-846-4401
Canton, OH	P.O. Box 490, Rm. 211, 201 Cleveland Ave. SW., 44701	216-489-4400
Charleston, SC	Suite 630, 334 Meeting St., 29403	803-724-4691
Charleston, WV	Suite 910, 1 Valley Sq., 25301	304-347-5188
Charlotte, NC	Suite 226, Parkwood Bldg., 4350 Park Rd., 28209	704-523-9583
Chattanooga, TN	Rm. 204, M.L. King Blvd. and Georgia Ave., 37401	615-752-5125
Cheyenne, WY	Suite 3026, 2120 Capitol Ave., 82001	307-772-2380
Chicago, IL	Suite 1200 N., 300 S. Riverside Plz., 60606	312-353-5431
Cincinnati, OH	Rm. 6118, 550 Main St., 45202	513-684-3585
Cleveland, OH	Rm. 440, 6100 Rockside Woods Blvd., 44131-2334	216-522-4365
Columbia, SC	P.O. Box 245, 29201	803-765-5446
Columbus, OH	Rm. 460, 85 Marconi Blvd., 43215	614-469-7370
Concord, NH	Rm. 337, 55 Pleasant St., 03302	603-225-1615
Corpus Christi, TX	Suite 1800, 802 N. Carancahua, 78470	512-888-3401
Dallas, TX	Suite 900, 525 S. Griffin St., 75202	214-767-8021
Dayton, OH	P.O. Box 743, 200 W. 2d St., 45402	513-222-2013
Denver, CO	Suite 1430, 1660 Lincoln St., 80264	303-844-3027
Des Moines, IA	637 Federal Bldg., 210 Walnut St., 50309	515-284-4565
Detroit, MI	Suite 477, Michigan Ave., 48226	313-226-6400
El Paso, TX	Rm. 301, 4100 Rio Bravo St., 79902	915-540-7546
Fort Worth, TX	Suite 2755, 801 Cherry St., 76102	817-334-2015
Fresno, CA	1130 O St., 93721	209-487-5204
Grand Rapids, MI	Rm. 326, 110 Michigan Ave. NW., 49503	616-456-2276
Great Falls, MT	P.O. Box 3063, 59403	406-452-8515
Greenville, SC	P.O. Box 10676, 29603	803-233-1490
Harrisburg, PA	P.O. Box 1244, 17108	717-782-4811
Honolulu, HI	P.O. Box 50046, Rm. 6309, 300 Ala Moana Blvd., 96850	808-541-1912
Houston, TX	P.O. Box 61607, 77208-1607	713-229-2755
Indianapolis, IN	Suite 211, 575 N. Pennsylvania St., 46204	317-226-6444
Jackson, MS	Suite 840, 100 W. Capitol St., 39269	601-965-4436
Jacksonville, FL	Suite 500, 7820 Arlington Expy., 32211	904-724-4530
Kansas City, MO	P.O. Box 2574, 64142	816-426-5022
Knoxville, TN	P.O. Box 97, 37901	615-673-4527
Las Vegas, NV	P.O. Box 16027, 89101	702-388-6446
Lexington, KY	P.O. Box 13310, 40583	606-233-2453
Little Rock, AR	Suite 640, 320 W. Capitol, 72201	501-378-6241
Los Angeles, CA	Rm. 4324, 300 N. Los Angeles St., 90012	213-894-4830
Louisville, KY	Rm. 439, 601 W. Broadway, 40202	502-582-5171
Lubbock, TX	P.O. Box 2975, 79048	806-743-7347
Madison, WI	P.O. Box 2154, 53701	608-264-5191
Melville, NY	Rm. 201, 560 Broad Hollow Rd., 11747	516-249-0404
Memphis, TN	Suite 831, 167 N. Main St., 38103	901-544-3568
Miami, FL	Suite 201, 8375 NW. 53d St., 33166	305-591-3660
Milwaukee, WI	Rm. 572, 517 E. Wisconsin Ave., 53202	414-297-3587
Minneapolis, MN	Rm. 218, 110 S. 4th St., 55401	612-348-1800
Mobile, AL	Suite 1100, 107 St. Francis St., 36602	205-690-2851

District Offices—United States Secret Service—Continued

District	Address	Telephone
Montgomery, AL	Suite 605, 1 Commercial St., 36104	205-223-7601
Morristown, NJ	7th Fl., 1 Speedwell Ave., West Tower, 07960-3990	201-645-2334
Nashville, TN	658 U.S. Courthouse, 801 Broadway St., 37203	615-736-5841
New Haven, CT	P.O. Box 45, 06501	203-865-2449
New Orleans, LA	Rm. 807, 501 Magazine St., 70130	504-589-4041
New York, NY	Rm. 623, 6 World Trade Ctr., 10048-0953	212-466-4400
Norfolk, VA	Rm. 400, Federal Bldg., 23510	804-441-3200
Oklahoma City, OK	Suite 926, 200 NW. 5th St., 73102	405-231-4476
Omaha, NE	P.O. Box 1375, Downtown Station, 68101	402-221-4671
Orlando, FL	Rm. 212, 80 N. Hughey Ave., 32801	407-648-6333
Philadelphia, PA	7236 Federal Bldg., 600 Arch St., 19106	215-597-0600
Phoenix, AZ	Suite 2180, 3200 N. Central Ave., 85012	602-640-5580
Pittsburgh, PA	Rm. 835, 1000 Liberty Ave., 15222	412-644-3384
Portland, ME	Rm. 2053, 151 Forest Ave., 04104	207-780-3493
Portland, OR	Suite 1330, 121 SW. Salmon St., 97204	503-326-2162
Providence, RI	Suite 343, 380 Westminster St., 02903	401-331-6456
Raleigh, NC	P.O. Box 26296, 27611	919-790-2834
Reno, NV	Suite 850, 100 Liberty St., 89501	702-784-5354
Richmond, VA	P.O. Box 10028, 23240	804-771-2274
Riverside, CA	P.O. Box 1525, 92502	714-276-6781
Roanoke, VA	P.O. Box 2885, 24001	703-982-6208
Rochester, NY	Rm. 606, 100 State St., 14614	716-263-6830
Sacramento, CA	Suite 530, 501 J St., 95814	916-551-2802
Saginaw, MI	Suite 200, 301 E. Genesee Ave., Saginaw, MI 48607	313-234-7223
St. Louis, MO	Rm. 924, 1114 Market St., 63101	314-539-2238
Salt Lake City, UT	Rm. 412, 350 S. Main St., 84101	801-524-5910
San Antonio, TX	Rm. B410, 727 E. Durango Blvd., 78206	512-229-6175
San Diego, CA	Suite 4-S-1, 880 Front St., 92188	619-557-5640
San Francisco, CA	Box 36037, 450 Golden Gate Ave., 94102	415-556-6800
San Jose, CA	Suite 2050, 280 S. 1st St., 95113	408-291-7233
San Juan, PR	Rm. 539, Carlos E. Chardon Ave., Hato Rey, PR 00918	809-766-5539
Santa Barbara, CA	Suite 309, 222 E. Carrillo St., 93101	805-963-9391
Savannah, GA	P.O. Box 8043, 31412	912-944-4401
Scranton, PA	Rm. 304, Washington and Linden Sts., 18501	717-346-5781
Seattle, WA	Rm. 890, 915 2d Ave., 98174	206-442-5495
Shreveport, LA	8A20 Federal Bldg., 500 Fannin St., 71101	318-226-5299
Sioux Falls, SD	208 E. 13th St., 57102	605-331-4565
Spokane, WA	761 U.S. Courthouse, 920 W. Riverside Ave., 99201	509-353-2532
Springfield, IL	Suite 414, 1 W. Old Capitol Plz., 62701	217-492-4033
Springfield, MO	P.O. Box 2233, 65801	417-864-8340
Syracuse, NY	Post Box 7006, Federal Station, 13261	315-423-5338
Tampa, FL	Suite 740, 700 Twiggs St., 33602	813-228-2636
Toledo, OH	Rm. 305, 234 Summit St., 43604	419-259-6434
Tucson, AZ	Box FB-56, 300 W. Congress St., 85701	602-670-6823
Tulsa, OK	Suite 400, 125 W. 15 St., 74119	918-581-7272
Tyler, TX	Suite 395, 6101 S. Broadway, 75703	214-534-2933
Washington, DC	Suite 1000, 1050 Connecticut Ave. NW., 20036-5305	202-634-5100
West Palm Beach, FL	Suite 231, 701 Clematis St., 33401	407-659-0184
White Plains, NY	Rm. 202, 300 Hamilton Ave., 10601-1877	914-682-8181
Wichita, KS	Rm. 225, 225 N. Market, 67202	316-267-1452
Wilmington, DE	Rm. 414, 920 King St., 19801	302-573-6188
Wilmington, NC	P.O. Box 120, 28401	919-343-4411

District Offices Overseas—United States Secret Service

District	Address	Telephone
London, England	Box 28, American Embassy/USSS, FPO New York, NY 09509-8400	011-44-1-499-9000
Paris, France	Rm. D-306, American Embassy/USSS, APO New York, NY 09777-9200.	9-0-1133-14-296-1202
Rome, Italy	American Embassy Rome, APO New York, NY 09794-0007	46741 Ext. 2736

For further information, contact any District Office or the Office of Public Affairs, United States Secret Service, Department of the Treasury, 1800 G Street NW., Washington, DC 20223. Phone, 202-535-5708.

Office of Thrift Supervision

The Office of Thrift Supervision (OTS) was established as a bureau of the Treasury Department in August 1989 and became operational in October 1989 as part of a major reorganization of the thrift regulatory structure mandated by the Financial Institutions Reform, Recovery and Enforcement Act. In that Act, Congress gave OTS authority to charter Federal thrift institutions and serve as the primary regulator of approximately 2,600 Federal and State-chartered thrifts belonging to the Savings Association Insurance Fund (SAIF). The Office carries out this responsibility by adopting regulations governing the savings and loan industry, by examining and supervising thrift institutions and their affiliates, and by taking whatever action is necessary to enforce their compliance with Federal law and regulations. In addition to overseeing thrift institutions, OTS also regulates, examines, and supervises companies that own thrifts and controls the acquisition of thrifts by such holding companies.

The Office is headed by a Director appointed by the President and confirmed by the Senate to serve a 5-year term. The Director also serves on the boards of the Federal Deposit Insurance Corporation and the Resolution Trust Corporation and, in addition, is a Director of the Neighborhood Reinvestment Corporation.

To carry out its mission, OTS is organized into five main divisions:

Washington Operations includes supervisory operations, policy, information resources management, and the administration program areas of OTS. This division develops national policy guidelines to enhance statutes and regulations; establishes programs to implement new policies and laws; develops and maintains surveillance systems that monitor the condition of the industry and assist in identifying emerging supervisory problem areas; develops and maintains financial management and information systems; maintains human resources programs; processes thrift institution applications; provides special supervision of selected thrift institutions; and performs other related functions.

Regional Operations examines and supervises thrift institutions in the five OTS regions to ensure the safety and soundness of the industry. It also oversees the training and development of Federal thrift regulators through accredited programs. The regional offices are headquartered in Jersey City, NJ; Atlanta, GA; Chicago, IL; Dallas, TX; and San Francisco, CA.

Chief Counsel provides a full range of legal services to the Agency, including drafting regulations, representing the agency in court, and taking enforcement actions against savings institutions that violate laws or regulations. This office also processes corporate filings required by the Securities and Exchange Act of 1934.

Congressional Affairs interacts with members of Congress, congressional staff, and committee members on behalf of OTS as well as executive-level personnel at other Federal agencies to accomplish the legislative objectives of the Agency. This division disseminates information to the Congress pertaining to the OTS supervisory, regulatory, and enforcement activities and policies, and manages congressional-liaison programs.

Public Affairs oversees dissemination of information concerning OTS regulations, policies, and key developments within the Agency. It convenes press conferences and distributes news releases to the public. It communicates and explains policy directives, objectives, and actions of the Agency by establishing and maintaining effective liaisons with the media, the general public, the thrift industry, all Government agencies, and other key constituencies.

This division provides a full range of audiovisual services, including creation of original designs for agency publications, graphics, desktop publishing, and editorial and production assistance. The division also maintains an archive of business records and documented actions of OTS and its predecessor, the

Federal Home Loan Bank Board; responds to Freedom of Information requests; and maintains a public reference room for viewing securities filing and other public documents.

The Office is a nonappropriated agency and thus uses no tax money to fund its operations. Its expenses are met by fees and assessments on the thrift institutions it regulates.

For further information, contact the Communications Division, Office of Thrift Supervision, 1700 G Street NW., Washington, DC 20552. Phone, 202–906–6913.

Sources of Information

Departmental Offices

Contracts Write to the Director, Office of Procurement, Room 6101, Main Treasury Annex, Washington, DC 20220. Phone, 202–566–9616.

Environment Environmental statements prepared by the Department are available for review in the Departmental Library. Information on Treasury environmental matters may be obtained from the Office of the Assistant Secretary of the Treasury (Management), Treasury Department, Washington, DC 20220. Phone, 202–377–9165.

General Inquiries For general information about the Treasury Department, including copies of news releases and texts of speeches by high Treasury officials, write to the Office of the Assistant Secretary (Public Affairs and Public Liaison), Room 3430, Departmental Offices, Treasury Department, Washington, DC 20220. Phone, 202–566–5252.

Reading Room The Reading Room is located in the Treasury Library, Room 5030, Main Treasury Building, 1500 Pennsylvania Avenue NW., Washington, DC 20220. Phone, 202–566–2777.

Small and Disadvantaged Business Activities Write to the Director, Office of Small and Disadvantaged Business Utilization, Room 6101, Main Treasury Annex, Washington, DC 20220. Phone, 202–566–9616.

Tax Legislation Information on tax legislation may be obtained from the Assistant Secretary (Tax Policy), Departmental Offices, Treasury Department, Washington, DC 20220. Phone, 202–566–5561.

Telephone Directory The Treasury Department telephone directory is available for sale by the Superintendent of Documents, Government Printing Office, Washington, DC 20402.

Office of the Comptroller of the Currency

Contracts Contact the procurement officer at 250 E Street SW., Washington, DC 20219. Phone, 202–874–5000.

Employment Civil service registers are used. A college recruitment program is conducted for positions of assistant national bank examiner. Descriptive literature and information are available from the Director for Human Resources, 250 E Street SW., Washington, DC 20219. Phone, 202–874–5000.

United States Customs Service

Address inquiries on the following subjects to the specified office, U.S. Customs Service, 1301 Constitution Avenue NW., Washington, DC 20229. Phone, 202–566–8195.

Contracts Write to the National Logistics Center, 6026 Lakeside Boulevard, Indianapolis, IN 46278.

Employment The U.S. Customs Service recruits from the Treasury Enforcement Agent examination. Employment inquiries may be addressed to the Director, Office of Human Resources in Washington, DC.

Forms Available from any district director's office. (There is a nominal charge for large quantities of certain forms.)

General Inquiries Contact the nearest district director's office for information regarding customs regulations and procedures for all persons entering the United States and the entry and clearance of imported merchandise.

290-950 O 91 - 17

Publications The U.S. Customs Service issues publications of interest to the general, importing, and traveling public that can be obtained from any of the District Directors' offices, or by writing to the Public Services and Information Materials Division in Washington, DC. Single copies of many of these publications are available at no charge to the public.

Reading Rooms Located at the headquarters library and in each of the seven regional offices.

Speakers Speakers are available for private organizations or community groups throughout the country. Contact any local customs officer or the Public Affairs Office in Washington, DC.

Bureau of Engraving and Printing

Address inquiries on the following subjects to the specified office, Bureau of Engraving and Printing, Fourteenth and C Streets SW., Washington, DC 20228.

Contracts and Small Business Activities Information relating to contracts and small business activity may be obtained by contacting the Office of Procurement Management on 202-447-9449 or 9391.

Employment The Bureau, as the world's largest security printer, employs personnel in a multitude of different craft, administrative, and professional fields. Competitive job opportunities may be available in the printing crafts, maintenance trades/crafts, engineering, electro-machinists, research, chemistry, data processing/computers, quality assurance, personnel, procurement, financial management, and other administrative fields. Due to the high level of security required, the Bureau also employs its own police force and a range of security specialists.

The Bureau participates in co-op and stay-in-school programs that enable students to gain work experience while pursuing their education. Periodically, apprenticeship programs may be announced in selected crafts.

Information regarding employment opportunities and required qualifications is available from the Employment and Classification Division, Office of Industrial Relations. Phone, 202-447-0275.

Freedom of Information Act Requests Inquiries should be directed to the Bureau Disclosure Officer, Office of Management Services, Room 321-12A. Phone, 202-447-0851.

General Inquiries Requests for information about the Bureau, its products, or numismatic and philatelic interests should be addressed to the Office of Public Affairs, Room 104-18M. Phone, 202-447-0193.

Product Sales Uncut sheets of currency, engraved Presidential portraits, historical engravings of national landmarks, and other similar products are available for purchase in the Visitors' Center or through the mail. The Visitors' Center sales area, located in the Fifteenth Street Lobby of the main building, is open from 8:30 a.m. to 3:30 p.m. on the same days as tours. Information and order forms for sales items may be obtained by writing to the Office of Public Affairs, Room 104-18M, or by calling 202-447-0193.

Financial Management Service

Inquiries on the following subjects should be directed to the specified office, 401 Fourteenth Street SW., Washington, DC 20227.

Contracts Write to the Director, Acquisition Management Division, Room 112 LC. Phone, 202-287-0838.

Employment Inquiries may be directed to the Personnel Management Division, Room 120 LC. Phone, 202-287-0834.

Internal Revenue Service

Audiovisual Materials Films, some of which are available in Spanish, provide information on the American tax system, examination and appeal rights, and the tax responsibilities of running a small business. The films can be obtained by contacting any District Office.

Also available are audio and video cassette tapes that provide step-by-step instructions for preparing basic individual income tax forms. These tapes are available in many local libraries.

Contracts Write to Internal Revenue Service, 1111 Constitution Avenue NW. (HR:C), Washington, DC 20224 (phone, 202–535–4804); or Chief, Facilities Management Branch, at any of the Internal Revenue regional offices.

Educational Programs The Service provides, free of charge, general tax information publications and booklets on specific tax topics. Taxpayer information materials also are distributed to major television networks and many radio and television stations, daily and weekly newspapers, magazines, and specialized publications. Special educational materials and films are provided for use in high schools and colleges. Individuals starting a new business are given specialized materials and information at small business workshops, and community colleges provide classes based on material provided by the Service. The Community Outreach Tax Assistance program provides agency employees to assist community groups at mutually convenient times and locations.

Through the Volunteer Income Tax Assistance program and the Tax Counseling for the Elderly program, the Service recruits, trains, and supports volunteers who offer free tax assistance to low-income, elderly, military, and non-English-speaking taxpayers.

Materials, films, and information on the educational programs can be obtained by contacting any District Office.

Employment Almost every major field of study has some application to the work of the Service. A substantial number of positions are filled by persons whose major educational preparation was accounting, business administration, finance, economics, criminology, and law. There are, however, a great number of positions that are filled by persons whose college major was political science, public administration, education, liberal arts, or other fields not directly related to business or law. Extensive use is made of competitive registers and examinations in selecting employees. Schools interested in participating in the extensive recruitment program, or anyone considering employment with the Service, may direct inquiries to the Recruitment Coordinator at any of the Regional or District Offices.

Problem Resolution Program Each District has a Problem Resolution Officer who attempts to resolve taxpayers' complaints not satisfied through regular channels.

Publications *The Annual Report—Commissioner of Internal Revenue* (Pub. 55), as well as periodic reports of Statistics of Incomes, which present statistical tabulations concerning various tax returns filed, are available from the Superintendent of Documents, Government Printing Office, Washington, DC 20402. *Audit of Returns, Appeal Rights, and Claims for Refund* (Pub. 556), *Your Federal Income Tax* (Pub. 17), *Farmers Tax Guide* (Pub. 225), *Tax Guide for Small Business* (Pub. 334), and other publications are available at Internal Revenue Service offices free of charge.

Reading Rooms Public reading rooms are located in the National Office and in each Regional Office or, in some cases, a District Office located in a Regional Office building.

Speakers Speakers on provisions of the tax law and operations of the Internal Revenue Service for professional and community groups may be obtained by writing to the District Directors or, for national organizations only, to the Public Affairs Division at the IRS national headquarters in Washington, DC.

Taxpayer Service The Internal Revenue Service provides year-round tax information and assistance to taxpayers, primarily through its toll-free telephone system. Taxpayers requesting information about the tax system, their rights and obligations under it, and the tax benefits available to them can call the number listed in their local telephone directory and in the tax form packages mailed to them annually. This service allows taxpayers anywhere in the United States to call the service without paying a long-distance charge. Special toll-free telephone assistance also is available to deaf and hearing-impaired taxpayers who have access to a teletypewriter or television/phone. These special numbers are included in the annual tax form packages and also are available from any agency office.

Taxpayers may also visit agency offices for help with their tax problems. The Service provides return preparation assistance to taxpayers by guiding groups of individuals line by line on the preparation of their returns. Individual preparation is available for handicapped or other individuals unable to use the group preparation method.

Foreign language tax assistance also is available at many locations.

United States Mint

Contracts and Employment Inquiries should be directed to the facility head of the appropriate field office or to the Director of the Mint.

Numismatic Services The United States Mint maintains public exhibit and sales areas at the Philadelphia and Denver Mints, the Old Mint in San Francisco, CA, and Union Station in Washington, DC. Information and order forms for proof sets, medals, and other numismatic items may also be obtained by writing to the United States Mint, 10001 Aerospace Road, Lanham, MD 20706. Phone, 301-436-7400. Also, for a 24-hour recording with additional information, call 202-447-9916.

Publications *The Annual Report of the Director of the Mint* and *World Coinage Report* are available from the United States Mint, Washington, DC, and the Superintendent of Documents, Government Printing Office, Washington, DC 20402. A current price list of medals and a brochure of official coins and medals sold by the United States Mint are available free of charge from the United States Mint, Washington, DC 20220.

Bureau of the Public Debt

Employment General employment inquiries should be addressed to the Bureau of the Public Debt, Division of Personnel Management, Employment Branch, Washington, DC 20239-0001. Phone, 202-447-1410.

Savings Bonds Requests for information relating to holdings of all series of savings bonds, savings notes, and retirement plan or individual retirement bonds should be addressed to the Bureau of the Public Debt, Department of the Treasury, 200 Third Street, Parkersburg, WV 26106-1328. Phone, 304-420-6112, extension 6274.

Treasury Securities Information inquiries regarding the purchase of Treasury bills, bonds, and notes should be addressed to your local Federal Reserve Bank or branch, or to the Bureau of the Public Debt, Department F, Washington, DC 20239-1200. Phone, 202-287-4113.

United States Savings Bonds Division

Savings Bonds Savings bonds are continuously on sale at more than 40,000 financial institutions and their branches in virtually every locality in the United States. Information about bonds is provided by such issuing agents.

Free informational materials are available from Savings Bonds District Offices (see page 501), and from the Office of Public Affairs, U.S. Savings Bonds Division, Department of the Treasury, Washington, DC 20226. Phone, 202-634-5389.

Current rate information is available toll-free by calling 800-US-BONDS.

United States Secret Service

Information about employment opportunities and publications and general public information may be obtained by contacting the nearest Secret Service field office or the Office of Government Liaison and Public Affairs, 1800 G Street NW., Washington, DC 20223. Phone, 202-535-5708.

For further information concerning the Department of the Treasury, contact the Public Affairs Office, Department of the Treasury, 1500 Pennsylvania Avenue NW., Washington, DC 20220. Phone, 202-566-2041.

DEPARTMENT OF VETERANS AFFAIRS

810 Vermont Avenue NW., Washington, DC 20420
Phone, 202–233–2300

SECRETARY OF VETERANS AFFAIRS	Edward J. Derwinski
Deputy Secretary of Veterans Affairs	Anthony J. Principi
Director, Operations and Policy Staff	Richard Pell, Jr.
White House Liaisons	Diane Landis
	Thomas L. Ryan
Counselor to the Department	Irwin Pernick
Executive Secretary to the Department	Alan Sinclair
Inspector General	Stephen A. Trodden
Chairman, Board of Contract Appeals	Guy H. McMichael III
Director, Office of Small and Disadvantaged Business Utilization	Scott F. Denniston
General Counsel	Raoul L. Carroll
Deputy General Counsel	Robert E. Coy
Chairman, Board of Veterans Appeals	Charles L. Cragin
Executive Assistant to the Chairman	Mary M. Sabulsky
Special Management Assistant	Ronald R. Aument
Special Legal Assistant	Steven L. Keller
Special Assistant, Litigation Support	Bettina S. Callaway
Special Assistant, Legal Affairs	Clarence H. Witt
Vice Chairman	Roger K. Bauer
Deputy Vice Chairman	Richard B. Standefer
Director, Administrative Service	Stuart E. Bossom
Chief Medical Director, Veterans Health Administration	James W. Holsinger, Jr., M.D.
Executive Assistant	Dennis Smith
Medical Inspector	Lewis Mantel, M.D.
Staff Director	Charles Koerber
Deputy Chief Medical Director	John T. Farrar, M.D.
Executive Assistant	Lydia Mavridis
Deputy Chief Medical Director for Administration and Operations	C. Wayne Hawkins
Associate Chief Medical Director for Operations	(vacancy)
Deputy Associate Chief Medical Director for Operations	David I. Given, *Acting*
Regional Director (Region 1—Eastern)	Donald Burnette
Director, Field Support	George H. Gray, Jr.
Regional Director (Region 2—Central)	Al Zamberlan
Director, Field Support	Alan T. Maurer
Regional Director (Region 3—Southern)	Richard Miller
Director, Field Support	Jonathan Gardner
Regional Director (Region 4—Western)	Clark R. Doughty
Director, Field Support	David I. Given
Associate Deputy Chief Medical Director	John T. Farrar, M.D., *Acting*

Deputy Chief Medical Director for Management	(VACANCY)
Associate Chief Medical Director for Clinical Affairs	ROBERT H. ROSWELL, M.D.
Associate Chief Medical Director for Research and Development	FRANKLIN J. ZIEVE, M.D., *Acting*
Associate Chief Medical Director for Academic Affairs	PETER F. REGAN III, M.D.
Associate Chief Medical Director for Dentistry	CHESTER P. PACZKOWSKI, D.D.S., *Acting*
Associate Chief Medical Director for Geriatrics and Extended Care	THOMAS T. YOSHIKAWA, M.D.
Associate Chief Medical Director for Environmental Medicine	SUSAN H. MATHER, M.D.
Director, Readjustment Counseling Service	ARTHUR S. BLANK, JR., M.D.
Assistant Chief Medical Director for Quality Management	GALEN BARBOUR, M.D.
Assistant Chief Medical Director for Administration	C.V. YARBROUGH
Director, Administrative Services	ALLINE L. NORMAN
Director, Medical Information Resources Management Office	DAVID VAN HOOSER
Director, Management Support Office	THOMAS J. HOGAN
Director, Health Care Staff Development and Retention Office	GREG HAAG
Director, Medical Care Cost Recovery Office	WALTER BESECKER
Assistant Chief Medical Director for Resource Management	JOHN R. FEARS
Director, Budget Office	C.R. WICHLACZ
Director, Strategic Planning and Policy Office	JAMES M. GREGG
Director, Management Review and Control Office	MAUREEN S. BALTAY
Director, Facilities Liaison Office	LINDA KURZ
Assistant Chief Medical Director for External Relations	JOSEPH G. GRAY
Director, Medical Sharing Office	ARTHUR S. HAMERSCHLAG
Director, Emergency Medical Preparedness Office	RAYMOND C. BONNABEAU, JR., M.D., *Acting*
Director, Legislative Liaison and Public Affairs Office	WILLIAM RAMSEY, *Acting*
Chief Benefits Director, Veterans Benefits Administration	D'WAYNE GRAY
Deputy Chief Benefits Director	BILL PEARSON
Chief of Staff	HAROLD F. GRACEY
Director, Personnel Assistance Staff	JOHN P. COGHLAN
Director, Budget and Finance Staff	GEORGE WOLOHOJIAN
Director, Program Analysis and Evaluation Staff	STANLEY R. SINCLAIR
Director, Administrative Support Staff	THOMAS WAGNER
Director, Debt Management Staff	DANIEL D. OSENDORF
Public Affairs Officer	CHARLES E. LUCAS
Assistant Chief Benefits Director for Planning	WILLIAM STINGER

Assistant Chief Benefits Director for Information Resources Management	Rhoda R. Mancher
Director, Eastern Area	Raymond H. Avent
Director, Central Area	Stephen L. Lemons
Director, Southern Area	James A. Maye
Director, Western Area	David M. Walls
Director, Compensation and Pension Service	J. Gary Hickman
Director, Education Service	Grady W. Horton
Director, Loan Guaranty Service	Keith Pedigo
Director, Veterans Assistance Service	David A. Brigham
Director, Vocational Rehabilitation Service	Dennis R. Wyant
Director, Insurance Service	Paul Koons
Director, National Cemetery System	Roger R. Rapp, *Acting*
Director, Field Operations	Fred L. Watson, *Acting*
Director, Office of Budget and Planning	Dorothy M. Mackay
Director, Office of Executive Communications and Administration	Alexander Havas
Director, Management and Support	Vincent L. Barile
Director, State Cemetery Grants Program	Harold F. Graber
Director, Public and Consumer Affairs Staff	William Jayne
Director, Information Systems Office	Mark P. Durocher
Director, Monument Service	Patrick J. Gartland
Directors, National Cemetery Area Offices:	
Philadelphia, PA	Thomas Balsanek
Atlanta, GA	Thomas W. Creed
Denver, CO	Donnell S. Mohr
Assistant Secretary for Finance and Information Resources Management	S. Anthony McCann
Deputy Assistant Secretary for Budget	D. Mark Catlett
Deputy Assistant Secretary for Financial Management	Frank Derville
Deputy Assistant Secretary for Information Resources Management	Robert J. Woods
Assistant Secretay for Policy and Planning	H. David Burge, *Acting*
Executive Officer	Raymond S. Blunt
Deputy Assistant Secretary for Policy	Dean E. Sharp
Associate Deputy Assistant Secretary for Policy	(vacancy)
Deputy Assistant Secretary for Planning	H. David Burge
Assistant Deputy Assistant Secretary for Planning	Renald Morani
Assistant Secretary for Human Resources and Administration	Ronald E. Ray
Deputy Assistant Secretary for Personnel and Labor Relations	Ronald E. Cowles
Deputy Assistant Secretary for Equal Employment Opportunity	Gerald K. Hinch
Deputy Assistant Secretary for Administration	Robert W. Schultz
Assistant Secretary for Public and Intergovernmental Affairs	Edward T. Timperlake
Deputy Assistant Secretary for Public Affairs	Dennis R. Boxx
Deputy Assistant Secretary for Intergovernmental Affairs	Wilmer Mizell
Assistant Secretary for Acquisition and Facilities	David E. Lewis

Principal Deputy Assistant Secretary for Acquisition and Facilities	C. Dale Duvall
Deputy Assistant Secretary for Facilities	Lester M. Hunkele III
Deputy Assistant Secretary for Acquisition and Materiel Management	H. Robert Saldivar
Assistant Secretary for Congressional Affairs	Dennis Duffy, *Acting*
Deputy Assistant Secretary for Congressional Liaison	Dennis Duffy, *Acting*
Deputy Assistant Secretary for Legislative Affairs	Jo Sherman

---

The Department of Veterans Affairs operates programs to benefit veterans and members of their families. Benefits include compensation payments for disabilities or death related to military service; pensions; education and rehabilitation; home loan guaranty; burial; and a medical care program incorporating nursing homes, clinics, and medical centers.

The Department of Veterans Affairs (VA) was established as an executive department by the Department of Veterans Affairs Act (38 U.S.C. 201 note). The Department's predecessor, the Veterans Administration, had been established as an independent agency under the President by Executive Order 5398 of July 21, 1930, in accordance with the act of July 3, 1930 (46 Stat. 1016). This act authorized the President to consolidate and coordinate the U.S. Veterans Bureau, the Bureau of Pensions, and the National Home for Volunteer Soldiers.

The Department of Veterans Affairs comprises three organizations that administer veterans programs: the Veterans Health Administration, the Veterans Benefits Administration, and the National Cemetery System. Each organization has field facilities and a Central Office component. The Central Office also includes separate offices that provide support to the top organizations' operations as well as to top VA executives. Top Central Office managers report to the highest level of Department management, which consists of the Secretary of Veterans Affairs and the Deputy Secretary.

Assistant Secretaries Six Assistant Secretaries provide policy guidance, operational support, and managerial oversight to the Secretary and Deputy Secretary, the administrations, and other top offices.

The Assistant Secretary for Finance and Information Resources Management is VA's Chief Financial Officer and manages the Department's budget process and fiscal operations. The Assistant Secretary also oversees VA's information resources management programs, which include integration and acquisition of automated data processing and telecommunications activities and information analysis.

The Assistant Secretary for Policy and Planning is responsible for managing the Secretary's policy analysis and planning processes and integrating both into the Secretary's Strategic Management Process.

The Assistant Secretary for Acquisition and Facilities provides management oversight of departmentwide capital facilities and real property programs, acquisition and materiel management activities, retail and food resale activities, and environmental affairs programs. The Assistant Secretary also serves as VA's senior procurement executive in accordance with Executive Order 12352 of March 17, 1982.

The Assistant Secretary for Human Resources and Administration provides direction and oversight of the Department's personnel and labor

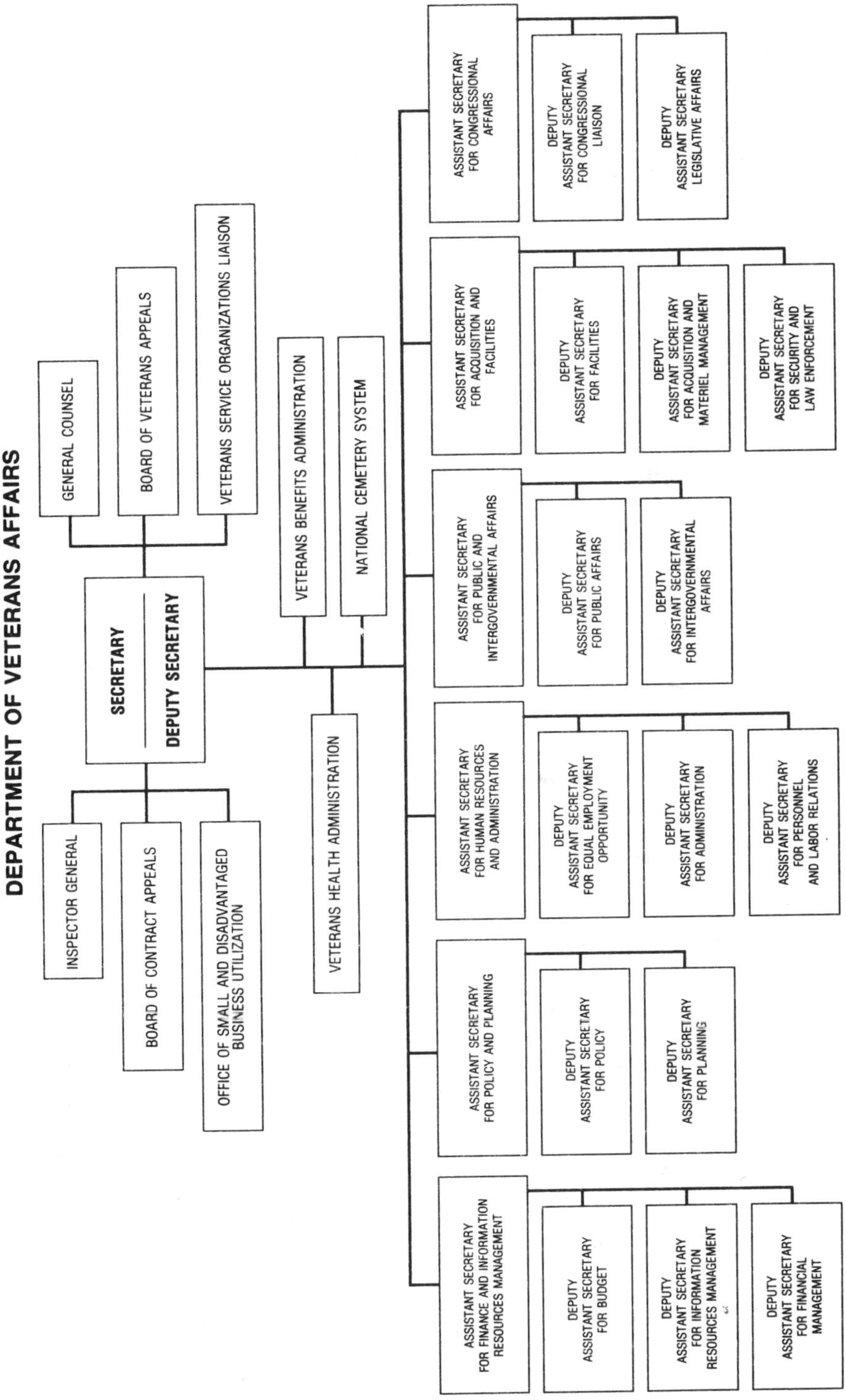
DEPARTMENT OF VETERANS AFFAIRS
SECRETARY
DEPUTY SECRETARY
GENERAL COUNSEL
BOARD OF VETERANS APPEALS
VETERANS SERVICE ORGANIZATIONS LIAISON
INSPECTOR GENERAL
BOARD OF CONTRACT APPEALS
OFFICE OF SMALL AND DISADVANTAGED BUSINESS UTILIZATION
VETERANS BENEFITS ADMINISTRATION
NATIONAL CEMETERY SYSTEM
VETERANS HEALTH ADMINISTRATION
ASSISTANT SECRETARY FOR CONGRESSIONAL AFFAIRS
DEPUTY ASSISTANT SECRETARY FOR CONGRESSIONAL LIAISON
DEPUTY ASSISTANT SECRETARY LEGISLATIVE AFFAIRS
ASSISTANT SECRETARY FOR ACQUISITION AND FACILITIES
DEPUTY ASSISTANT SECRETARY FOR FACILITIES
DEPUTY ASSISTANT SECRETARY FOR ACQUISITION AND MATERIEL MANAGEMENT
DEPUTY ASSISTANT SECRETARY FOR SECURITY AND LAW ENFORCEMENT
ASSISTANT SECRETARY FOR PUBLIC AND INTERGOVERNMENTAL AFFAIRS
DEPUTY ASSISTANT SECRETARY FOR PUBLIC AFFAIRS
DEPUTY ASSISTANT SECRETARY FOR INTERGOVERNMENTAL AFFAIRS
ASSISTANT SECRETARY FOR HUMAN RESOURCES AND ADMINISTRATION
DEPUTY ASSISTANT SECRETARY FOR EQUAL EMPLOYMENT OPPORTUNITY
DEPUTY ASSISTANT SECRETARY FOR ADMINISTRATION
DEPUTY ASSISTANT SECRETARY FOR PERSONNEL AND LABOR RELATIONS
ASSISTANT SECRETARY FOR POLICY AND PLANNING
DEPUTY ASSISTANT SECRETARY FOR POLICY
DEPUTY ASSISTANT SECRETARY FOR PLANNING
ASSISTANT SECRETARY FOR FINANCE AND INFORMATION RESOURCES MANAGEMENT
DEPUTY ASSISTANT SECRETARY FOR BUDGET
DEPUTY ASSISTANT SECRETARY FOR INFORMATION RESOURCES MANAGEMENT
DEPUTY ASSISTANT SECRETARY FOR FINANCIAL MANAGEMENT

relations, equal employment opportunity, and security and law enforcement programs. The Assistant Secretary also provides direction and oversight of Central Office administration and serves as the Department's designated safety and health official.

The Assistant Secretary for Public and Intergovernmental Affairs provides executive management for coordination of the information that VA communicates to the general public through the news media and provisions of policy guidance in public and intergovernmental affairs.

The Assistant Secretary for Congressional Affairs is responsible for coordinating the Department's relations and activities with the legislative branch; serves as the focal point for all departmental interaction, management, and coordination of congressional affairs activities; and is the primary point of contact on all policy matters with Congress and on all actions between the Offices of the Secretary and the Deputy Secretary and Members of Congress and their staffs.

Inspector General The Office of Inspector General was established on January 1, 1978, to consolidate audit, investigation, and related operations into a cohesive, independent organization. The Office is headed by an Inspector General who reports directly to the Secretary of Veterans Affairs. The Inspector General has the authority to inquire into all VA programs and activities of persons or parties performing under grants, contracts, or other agreements. The Inspector General is required to keep the Secretary and Congress fully informed about the problems and deficiencies in VA programs and operations and the need for corrective action.

General Counsel The General Counsel is the Department's chief legal officer on all matters of law, litigation, and legislation. The General Counsel prepares, for the Secretary's approval, legislative initiatives for submission to OMB and Congress. The General Counsel interprets all laws pertaining to the Department, has final legal authority in issuing Department regulations implementing those laws, holds responsibility for the conduct of litigation—both independently and in coordination with the Justice Department—in State and Federal courts, the U.S. Court of Veterans Appeals, the Federal Circuit Court of Appeals, and the U.S. Supreme Court.

Board of Veterans Appeals The Board of Veterans Appeals (BVA) conducts the appellate program for the Secretary of Veterans Affairs with statutory jurisdiction to make final VA decisions on appeals involving all benefits administered by VA under 38 United States Code 4001–4010. The Board is headed by a Chairman, who is a Presidential appointee confirmed by the Senate, and is directly responsible to the Secretary of Veterans Affairs. There are 66 Board members who are appointees of the Secretary and under the control and supervision of the Chairman. Each BVA decision is signed by approximately three Board members acting as agents of the Secretary. The mission of BVA is to ensure that appellants are afforded due process of law and receive all benefits to which they are entitled in nonadversarial proceedings. Final BVA decisions are appealable to the United States Court of Veterans Appeals.

Board of Contract Appeals The Board of Contract Appeals was established on March 1, 1979, pursuant to the Contract Disputes Act of 1978 (41 U.S.C. 601–613). The Board is a statutory, quasi-judicial tribunal that hears and decides appeals from decisions of Contracting Officers on claims relating to contracts awarded by VA, or by any other agency when such agency or the Administrator for Federal Procurement Policy has designated the Board to decide the appeal.

In August 1985, the Board's jurisdiction was expanded to include applications for attorney fees and expenses under the Equal Access to Justice Act, as amended (5 U.S.C. 504 note). Board decisions are final within VA, but may be appealed, either by the Government or by the contractor, to the United States Court of Appeals for the Federal Circuit.

Health Services

The Veterans Health Administration, formerly the Veterans Health Services and Research Administration, provides hospital, nursing home, and domiciliary care, and outpatient medical and dental care to eligible veterans of military service in the Armed Forces. It operates 172 medical centers, 27 domiciliaries, 260 outpatient clinics, 122 nursing home care units, and 198 Vietnam Veteran Outreach Centers in the United States, the Commonwealth of Puerto Rico, and the Republic of the Philippines, and provides for similar care under VA auspices in non-VA hospitals and community nursing homes and for visits by veterans to non-VA physicians and dentists for outpatient treatment. It also supports veterans under care in hospitals, nursing homes, and domiciliaries operated by 35 States. Under the Civilian Health and Medical Program, dependents of certain veterans are provided with medical care supplied by non-VA institutions and physicians.

The Administration conducts both individual medical and health-care delivery research projects and multihospital research programs. It assists in the education of physicians and dentists, and with training of many other health care professionals through affiliations with educational institutions and organizations. These programs are all conducted as prescribed by the Secretary of Veterans Affairs pursuant to sections 4101–4115 of title 38 of the United States Code and other statutory authority and regulations.

Veterans Benefits

The Veterans Benefits Administration, formerly the Department of Veterans Benefits, conducts an integrated program of veterans benefits.

Compensation and Pension The Compensation and Pension Service has responsibility for:

—claims for disability compensation and pension;

—automobile allowances and special adaptive equipment;

—claims for specially adapted housing;

—special clothing allowances;

—emergency officers' retirement pay;

—eligibility determinations based on military service for other VA benefits and services or those of other Government agencies;

—survivors' claims for death compensation, dependency and indemnity compensation, death pension, burial and plot allowance claims;

—claims for accrued benefits;

—forfeiture determinations;

—claims for adjusted compensation in death cases; and

—claims for reimbursement for headstone or marker.

Education The Education Service has responsibility for: the Montgomery GI Bill—Active Duty and Selected Reserve (chapters 30 and 106); the Post Vietnam Era Veterans' Educational Assistance Program (chapter 32); the Survivors' and Dependents' Educational Assistance Program (chapter 35); the Section 901 Test Program; and school approvals and compliance surveys.

Vocational Rehabilitation The Vocational Rehabilitation Service has responsibility for: outreach, motivation, evaluation, counseling, training, employment, and other rehabilitation services to disabled veterans (chapters 31 and 15); evaluation, counseling, and miscellaneous services to veterans and servicepersons (chapter 30) and other VA education programs; evaluation, counseling, and miscellaneous services to sons, daughters, and spouses of totally and permanently disabled veterans and to surviving orphans, widows, or widowers of certain deceased veterans, including rehabilitation services to certain handicapped dependents (chapter 35); and affirmative action activities.

Loan Guaranty Loan guaranty operations include: appraising properties to establish their values; supervising the construction of new residential properties; passing on the ability of a veteran to repay a loan and the credit risk; servicing and liquidating defaulted loans; and disposing of real estate acquired as the consequence of defaulted loans. There are also substantial operations involved in managing and realizing loan assets.

Insurance Life insurance operations are for the benefit of service members, veterans, and their beneficiaries. The day-to-day processing of all matters related to individual insurance accounts is handled by the Regional Office and Insurance Centers in Philadelphia, PA, and St. Paul, MN. These two centers provide the full range of functional activities necessary for a national life insurance program. Activities include the complete maintenance of individual accounts, underwriting functions, and life and death insurance claims awards, as well as any other insurance-related transactions.

The Department is also responsible for the administration of the Veterans Mortgage Life Insurance program for those disabled veterans who receive a VA grant for specially adapted housing. Accounts are maintained at the Regional Office and Insurance Center in St. Paul, MN.

In addition, the Department is responsible for supervising the Servicemen's Group Life Insurance (SGLI) and Veterans Group Life Insurance (VGLI) programs. Both programs are handled through the Office of Servicemen's Group Life Insurance, 231 Washington Street, Newark, NJ 07102.

Veterans Assistance Through the Veterans Assistance Service, information, advice, and assistance are provided to veterans, their dependents and beneficiaries, representatives, and others in applying for benefits administered by the Department of Veterans Affairs. In addition, the Veterans Assistance Service cooperates with the Department of Labor and other Federal, State, and local agencies in developing employment opportunities for veterans, and referral for assistance in resolving socioeconomic, housing, and other related problems.

The Service is responsible for maintaining a benefits protection program (fiduciary activities) for minors and incompetent adult beneficiaries. It also provides field investigative services for other VA components. It ensures compliance by schools and training institutions with VA directives. It also ensures compliance with title VI of the Civil Rights Act of 1964 (42 U.S.C. 2000d); title IX of the Education Amendments of 1972 (20 U.S.C. 1681); section 504 of the Rehabilitation Act of 1973 (29 U.S.C. 794); and the Age Discrimination Act of 1975, as amended (42 U.S.C. 6101). The programs of the Service are provided through VA regional offices, VA medical centers, itinerant visits to communities, and a special toll-free telephone service available in all 50 States, the District of Columbia, and Puerto Rico.

The Veterans Assistance Service also has the responsibility of providing information regarding veterans benefits to the various branches of the Armed Forces here and abroad and to veterans residing in foreign countries through United States embassies and consular offices, and of coordinating veterans' activities with foreign governments.

For further information, contact the Public Affairs Officer, Veterans Benefits Administration. Phone, 202–233–5210.

National Cemetery System

The National Cemetery System (NCS) provides services to veterans and their families by operating national cemeteries; furnishing headstones and markers for the graves of U.S. veterans worldwide; awarding grants to aid States in developing, improving, and expanding veterans cemeteries; and serving as the operations element for the Presidential Memorial Certificate Program.

Field Facilities

Insurance Centers Two field sites house all individual insurance records covering service members and veterans under the Government-administered programs: WW I United States Government Life Insurance; WW II National Service Life Insurance; Post-Korean Conflict; Veterans Reopened Insurance for the disabled of WW II and Korea; and Service-Disabled Veterans Insurance, the only Government-administered program open for new issues to disabled veterans only.

The two field locations are the VA Regional Office and Insurance Centers in Philadelphia, PA, and St. Paul, MN. All World War I insurance accounts, accounts for which the premium is paid by allotment from military service pay, and those paid by deduction from VA compensation or preauthorized debit are located at Philadelphia. All remaining insurance accounts are geographically distributed between the two VA Centers—with the Mississippi River serving as the approximate line of division. The Philadelphia Veterans Affairs Center is also responsible for formulating policy for the veterans insurance programs.

The insurance functions performed by the two field stations include the total range of insurance operations to provide individual policy, underwriting, and life and death insurance claims service for service members, veterans, and their beneficiaries.

Regional Office Department of Veterans Affairs regional offices:

—grant benefits and services provided by law for veterans, their dependents, and beneficiaries within an assigned territory;

—furnish information regarding VA benefits and services;

—adjudicate claims and makes awards for disability compensation and pension;

—supervise the payment of VA benefits to incompetent beneficiaries;

—aid, guide, and prescribe vocational rehabilitation training and administer educational benefits;

—guarantee loans for purchase of manufactured homes and lots and condominium units, purchase or construction or alteration of homes and farm residences, and under certain conditions, guarantee refinancing loans;

—process grants for specially adapted housing;

—process death claims;

—assist the veteran in exercising rights to benefits and services; and

—supervise VA offices under their jurisdiction.

The offices are also responsible for veterans assistance activities, including coordination of efforts of participating agencies in an "outreach" program to assist returning service members, particularly those who are educationally disadvantaged.

Services to U.S. veterans in most foreign countries normally are provided by the VA Regional Office, District of Columbia. The Honolulu Regional Office serves the Islands of American Samoa, the Commonwealth of the Northern Mariana Islands, Guam, Wake, and Midway and the Trust Territory of the Pacific Islands. U.S. veterans in the Virgin Islands and Mexico are served by the San Juan and Houston offices, respectively. Service is provided in cooperation with embassy staffs of the Department of State.

Department of Veterans Affairs Regional Office, District of Columbia The Department of Veterans Affairs Regional Office, District of Columbia, is a typical regional office with additional functions. It has global jurisdiction and grants benefits and services provided by law for veterans and their beneficiaries and dependents residing outside the territorial limits of the United States, and it adjudicates certain unusual claims and actions not common to all regional offices, such as WW I adjusted compensation death cases, forfeiture cases, and benefits under special enactments provided by the Congress. It also maintains liaison with the Treasury Department on types and methods of payments to recipients in foreign countries.

VA Office The VA office provides veterans assistance and such other services as cannot be conveniently provided to veterans, their dependents and beneficiaries, and others in a given locality by a regional office or center.

Medical Center Veterans Affairs Medical Centers provide eligible beneficiaries with medical and other health care services equivalent to those provided by private-sector institutions, augmented in many instances by services to meet the special requirements of veterans. One hundred and thirty-three VA medical facilities are affiliated with 104 medical facilities for residency training; 72 VA medical facilities are affiliated with 59 dental schools; and all centers cooperate with one or more educational institutions in programs of nursing, associated health professions and occupations, and administrative training and related research, both in individual projects and in association with other VA medical centers in broad cooperative studies. There are 106 nursing home care units associated with VA medical centers to provide skilled nursing care and related medical services to patients who are no longer in need of hospital care.

VA Regional Office and Insurance Center Veterans Affairs Regional Office and Insurance Centers combine a regional office and an insurance center under the jurisdiction of one director.

VA Medical and Regional Office Center Veterans Affairs Medical and Regional Office Centers combine a regional office and a medical center or a regional office, medical center, and domiciliary under the jurisdiction of one director.

Domiciliary Veterans Affairs Domiciliaries provide the least intensive level of inpatient medical care. This includes necessary ambulatory medical treatment, rehabilitation, and support services in a structured environment to veterans who are unable because of their disabilities to provide adequately for themselves in the community.

Outpatient Clinic Veterans Affairs Outpatient Clinics provide eligible beneficiaries with ambulatory care.

VA National Cemetery Veterans Affairs National Cemeteries are the final resting place for burial of the remains of veterans, their spouses, and certain eligible dependents. Memorial markers for veterans whose remains are not available for burial may also be placed in a national cemetery. These cemeteries are designated as national shrines created in tribute to the sacrifices of all Americans who have served in the U.S. Armed Forces.

National Facilities—Department of Veterans Affairs

Address	Type of facility	Director
National Facilities Under the Veterans Health Administration, Veterans Benefits Administration, and National Cemetery System—Centers, Domiciliaries, Medical Centers, Medical and Regional Office Centers, Outpatient Clinics, Insurance Centers, Regional Offices, Supply Activities, and National Cemeteries		
ALABAMA:		
Birmingham, 35233 (700 S. 19th St.)	Medical Center	William Mountcastle
Mobile, 36604 (1202 Virginia St.) (Mail: Barrancas National Cemetery, FL).	National Cemetery	Sandra Beckley
Montgomery, 36193 (215 Perry Hill Rd.)	Medical Center	John R. Rowan
Montgomery, 36104 (474 S. Court St.)	Regional Office	Sam Maraman
Seale, 36875 (Rte. 3, Box 195) (Fort Mitchell National Cemetery).	National Cemetery	Jimmy Jackson
Tuscaloosa, 35404	Medical Center	Robert P. Blair
Tuskegee, 36083	...do	Jimmie L. Clay
ALASKA:		
Anchorage, 99501	Outpatient Clinic	W. David Smith
Anchorage, 99501 (235 E. 8th Ave.)	Regional Office	John J. Conway
Fort Richardson, 99505 (P.O. Box 5-498)	National Cemetery	David G. Dimmick
Sitka, 99835 (P.O. Box 1065) (Mail: Fort Richardson National Cemetery, AK).	...do	David G. Dimmick
ARIZONA:		
Phoenix, 85012 (7th St. and Indian School Rd.).	Medical Center	Ray L. Bourne
Phoenix, 85012 (3225 N. Central Ave.)	Regional Office	Robert Schloendorn
Phoenix, 85024 (23029 N. Cave Creek Rd.) (National Memorial Cemetery of Arizona).	National Cemetery	William E. Rodgers, Jr.
Prescott, 86313	Medical Center (medical and domiciliary)	Alfonzo Estrada, Jr.
Prescott, 86313 (VA Medical Center)	National Cemetery	Maintained by VAMC
Tucson, 85723	Medical Center	R.E. Lindsey, Jr.
ARKANSAS:		
Fayetteville, 72701	...do	Richard F. Robinson
Fayetteville, 72701 (700 Government Ave.)	National Cemetery	Karen Browne
Fort Smith, 72901 (522 Garland Ave. and S. 6th St.).	...do	Candice Underwood
Little Rock, 72206 (2523 Confederate Blvd.)	...do	Douglas Miner
Little Rock, 72205 (300 Roosevelt Rd.) (John L. McClellan Memorial Veterans Hospital).	Medical Center	Robert Patton

National Facilities—Department of Veterans Affairs—Continued

Address	Type of facility	Director
Little Rock Division		
North Little Rock Division		
(Mail: Little Rock)		
North Little Rock, 72155, (P.O. Box 1280, Bldg. 65, Fort Root).	Regional Office	Kay Roberts
CALIFORNIA:		
Bell, 90201 (Federal Service Center, Bldg. 701, 5600 Rickenbacker Rd.).	Supply Depot	Henry A. Wilbur
Fresno, 93703 (2615 Clinton Ave.)	Medical Center	Wayne C. Tippets
Livermore, 94550	......do	Marvin E. O'Rear
Loma Linda, 92357 (11201 Benton St.) (Jerry L. Pettis Memorial Veterans Hospital).	......do	Charles Clark
Long Beach, 90822 (5901 E. 7th St.)	......do	Dean R. Stordahl
West Los Angeles, 90073	Medical Center (medical and domiciliary)	William K. Anderson
Los Angeles, 90013 (425 S. Hill St.)	Outpatient Clinic	Lee Nackman
Los Angeles, 90024 (11000 Wilshire Blvd.)	Regional Office	Henry W. Gresham
Los Angeles, 90049 (950 S. Sepulveda Blvd.)	National Cemetery	Helen B. Szumylo
Martinez, 94553 (150 Muir Rd.)	Medical Center	Jule Moravec
Palo Alto, 94304 (3801 Miranda Ave.)	......do	James C. De Niro
Menlo Park Division		
Palo Alto Division		
Riverside, 92508 (22495 Van Buren Blvd.)	National Cemetery	Therese Bush
San Bruno, 94066 (1300 Sneath Lane) (Golden Gate National Cemetery).	......do	Cynthia Nunez
San Diego, 92161 (3350 La Jolla Village Dr.)	Medical Center	Thomas A. Trujillo
San Diego, 92108 (2022 Camino Del Rio N.)	Regional Office	(Vacancy)
San Diego, 92106 (Point Loma, P.O. Box 6237) (Fort Rosecrans National Cemetery).	National Cemetery	Jack D. Shaw
San Francisco, 94121 (4150 Clement St.)	Medical Center	Lawrence C. Stewart
San Francisco, 94105 (211 Main St.)	Regional Office	Leo C. Wurschmidt
San Francisco, 94129 (P.O. Box 29012, Presidio of San Francisco).	National Cemetery	Matt Cornett
Sepulveda, 91343	Medical Center	Norman E. Hensley
COLORADO:		
Denver, 80225 (P.O. Box 25126, 44 Union Blvd.).	Regional Office	Jack McReynolds
Denver, 80220 (1055 Clermont St.)	Medical Center	Fred F. Salas
Denver, 80225 (Denver Federal Center)	Prosthetics Distribution Center	Robert A. Shields
Denver, 80235 (3698 S. Sheridan Blvd.) (Fort Logan National Cemetery).	National Cemetery	Jimmy Adamson
Fort Lyon, 81038	Prosthetics Distribution Center	Robert E. Lee, D.P.M.
Fort Lyon, 81038 (VA Medical Center)	National Cemetery	Maintained by VAMC
Fort Lyon, 81038	Medical Center	Billy J. Campbell
Grand Junction, 81501	Prosthetics Distribution Center	(Vacancy)
Grand Junction, 81501	Medical Center	Robert R. Rhyne, D.D.S.
CONNECTICUT:		
Hartford, 06103 (450 Main St.)	Regional Office	Thomas Brownell
Newington, 06111 (555 Willard Ave.)	Medical Center	Robert Perreault
West Haven, 06516 (W. Spring St.)	......do	Norman E. Brown
DELAWARE:		
Wilmington, 19805 (1601 Kirkwood Hwy.)	Medical and Regional Office Center	Michael B. Phaup
DISTRICT OF COLUMBIA:		
Washington, 20422 (50 Irving St. NW.)	Medical Center	Timothy B. Williams
Washington, 20421 (941 N. Capitol St. NE.)	Regional Office	Paul Ising
FLORIDA:		
Bay Pines, 33504 (1000 Bay Pines Blvd. N.)	Medical Center (medical and domiciliary)	Raymond J. Vogel
Bay Pines, 33504 (P.O. Box 477)	National Cemetery	Jeffrey Teas
Bushnell, 33513 (P.O. Box 337) (Florida National Cemetery).	......do	Fred I. Haselbarth, Jr.
Gainesville, 32602 (1601 SW. Archer Rd.)	Medical Center	J. Malcom Randall
Lake City, 32055 (801 S. Marion St.)	......do	Thomas F. Wheaton
Miami, 33125 (1201 NW. 16th St.)	......do	Thomas C. Doherty
Pensacola, 32508 (Naval Air Station) (Barrancas National Cemetery).	National Cemetery	Sandra Beckley
St. Augustine, 32084 (104 Marine St.) (Mail: Florida National Cemetery, FL).	......do	Fred I. Haselbarth, Jr.
St. Petersburg, 33731 (P.O. Box 1437)	Regional Office	Carlos Rainwater
Tampa, 33612 (13000 Bruce B. Downs Blvd.) (James A. Haley Veterans Hospital).	Medical Center	Richard A. Silver
GEORGIA:		
Atlanta, 30308 (730 Peachtree St. NE.)	Regional Office	Charles Wickes
Augusta, 30910 (2460 Wrightsboro Rd. (10))	Medical Center	Thomas L. Ayres

National Facilities—Department of Veterans Affairs—Continued

Address	Type of facility	Director
Forest Hills Division		
Lenwood Division		
Decatur, 30033 (1670 Clairmont Rd.)	......do	Glenn Alred, Jr.
Dublin, 31021	Medical Center (medical and domiciliary)	William O. Edgar
Marietta, 30060 (500 Washington Ave.)	National Cemetery	Douglas W. Smith, Sr.
HAWAII:		
Honolulu, 96850 (P.O. Box 50188)	Regional Office	(Vacancy)
Honolulu, 96813 (2177 Puowaina Dr.) (National Memorial Cemetery of the Pacific).	National Cemetery	Gene E. Castagnetti
Honolulu, 96813	Outpatient Clinic	Barry Raff
IDAHO:		
Boise, 83724 (550 W. Fort St.)	Regional Office	David A. Barrett
Boise, 83702 (5th and Fort Sts.)	Medical Center	James A. Goff
ILLINOIS:		
Alton, 62003 (600 Pearl St.) (Mail: Jefferson Barracks National Cemetery, MO).	National Cemetery	Ralph E. Church
Chicago, 60611 (333 E. Huron St.)	Medical Center	Joseph L. Moore
Chicago, 60680 (820 S. Damen Ave.)	......do	Paul R. Stanford, Jr.
Chicago, 60680 (P.O. Box 8136)	Regional Office	Samuel Holmes
Danville, 61832	Medical Center	Donald E. Riedl
Danville, 61832 (1900 E. Main St.)	National Cemetery	Richard J. Pless
Hines, 60141 (Edward Hines, Jr. Hospital)	Medical Center	Joan E. Cummings, M.D.
Hines, 60141 (P.O. Box 76)	Marketing Center	James R. Johnson
Hines, 60141 (P.O. Box 27)	Supply Depot	Earl N. Hill
Marion, 62959 (2401 W. Main St.)	Medical Center	Sidney M. Ford
Mound City, 62963 (Junction-Highway 37 and 51) (Mail: Jefferson Barracks National Cemetery, MO).	National Cemetery	Ralph E. Church
North Chicago, 60064	Medical Center	Alfred S. Pate
Quincy, 62301 (36th and Main Sts.) (Mail: Keokuk National Cemetery, IA).	National Cemetery	Dane B. Freeman
Rock Island, 61299 (Rock Island Arsenal)	......do	Arthur L. Conklin
Springfield, 62707 (R.R. #1) (Camp Butler National Cemetery).	......do	Kurt Rotar
INDIANA:		
Fort Wayne, 46805 (1600 Randalia Dr.)	Medical Center	Jonathan D. Hawk
Indianapolis, 46202 (1481 W. 10th St.)	......do	Terrence L. Johnson
Cold Spring Road Division		
Tenth Street Division		
(Mail: 1481 W. 10th St., Indianapolis)		
Indianapolis, 46204 (575 N. Pennsylvania St.)	Regional Office	Roy Bailey
Indianapolis, 46208 (700 W. 38th St.) (Crown Hill National Cemetery) (Mail: Marion National Cemetery, IN).	National Cemetery	Gerald Vitela
Marion, 46952	Medical Center	Jon E. Crisman
Marion, 46952 (VA Medical Center)	National Cemetery	Gerald Vitela
New Albany, 47150 (1943 Ekin Ave.) (Mail: Zachary Taylor National Cemetery, KY).	......do	Gary D. Peak
IOWA:		
Des Moines, 50309 (210 Walnut St.)	Regional Office	Norman W. Bauer
Des Moines, 50310 (30th and Euclid Ave.)	Medical Center	Archie Bourrett
Iowa City, 52240 (Highway 6 W.)	......do	Gary L. Wilkinson
Keokuk, 52632 (1701 J St.)	National Cemetery	Dane B. Freeman
Knoxville, 50138	Medical Center	Donald D. Ziska
KANSAS:		
Fort Leavenworth, 66048 (Mail: Leavenworth National Cemetery, KS).	National Cemetery	Velva Melton
Fort Scott, 66701 (P.O. Box 917)	......do	Velva Melton
Leavenworth, 66048	Medical Center (medical and domiciliary)	James H. Cuer
Leavenworth, 66048 (P.O. Box 1694)	National Cemetery	Velva Melton
Topeka, 66622 (2200 Gage Blvd.)	Medical Center	Paul K. Kennedy
Wichita, 67218 (5500 E. Kellogg)	Medical Center	Jerry E. Mayhall
Wichita, 67211 (901 George Washington Blvd.).	Regional Office	Jerry E. Mayhall
KENTUCKY:		
Danville, 40442 (377 N. 1st St.) (Mail: Camp Nelson National Cemetery, KY).	National Cemetery	Eileen Harrison
Lebanon, 40033 (R.R. #1, Box 616)	......do	Gary D. Peak
Lexington, 40511	Medical Center	Dexter D. Dix
Cooper Drive Division		
Leestown Division		
Lexington, 40508 (833 W. Main St.) (Mail: Camp Nelson National Cemetery, KY).	National Cemetery	Eileen Harrison

National Facilities—Department of Veterans Affairs—Continued

Address	Type of facility	Director
Louisville, 40202 (600 Federal Pl.)	Regional Office	John W. Hagan, Jr.
Louisville, 40202 (800 Zorn Ave.)	Medical Center	Larry J. Sander
Louisville, 40204 (701 Baxter Ave.) (Cave Hill National Cemetery) (Mail: Zachary Taylor National Cemetery, KY).	National Cemetery	Gary D. Peak
Louisville, 40207 (4701 Brownsboro Rd.) (Zachary Taylor National Cemetery).	......do	Gary D. Peak
Nancy, 42544 (R.R. #2, P.O. Box 172) (Mill Springs National Cemetery) (Mail: Camp Nelson National Cemetery, KY).	......do	Eileen Harrison
Nicholasville, 40356 (6980 Danville Rd.) (Camp Nelson National Cemetery).	......do	Eileen Harrison
LOUISIANA:		
Alexandria, 71301	Medical Center	Charles Freeman
Baton Rouge, 70806 (220 N. 19th St.) (Mail: Port Hudson National Cemetery, LA).	National Cemetery	Virgil M. Wertenberger
New Orleans, 70146 (1601 Peridido St.)	Medical Center	John D. Church, Jr.
New Orleans, 70113 (701 Loyola Ave.)	Regional Office	Anthony R. Lentini
Pineville, 71360 (209 Shamrock Ave.) (Alexandria National Cemetery).	National Cemetery	Kimberly M. Wright
Shreveport, 71130 (510 E. Stoner Ave.)	Medical Center	Robert Dawson, Jr.
Zachary, 70791 (20978 Port Hickey Rd.) (Port Hudson National Cemetery).	National Cemetery	Virgil M. Wertenberger
MAINE:		
Togus, 04330	Medical and Regional Office Center	Jack Simms
Togus, 04330 (VA Medical and Regional Office Center).	National Cemetery	Maintained by VAMC
MARYLAND:		
Annapolis, 21401 (800 W. St.) (Mail: Baltimore National Cemetery, MD).	National Cemetery	Arthur E. Bath
Baltimore, 21201 (31 Hopkins Plz.)	Regional Office	Newell Quinton
Baltimore, 21218 (3900 Loch Raven Blvd.)	Medical Center	Barbara L. Gallagher
Baltimore, 21228 (5501 Frederick Ave.)	National Cemetery	Arthur E. Bath
Baltimore, 21229 (3445 Frederick Ave.) (Loudon Park National Cemetery) (Mail: Baltimore National Cemetery, MD).	......do	Arthur E. Bath
Fort Howard, 21052	Medical Center	Kenneth H. Misrach
Perry Point, 21902	......do	Wilfred E. Kingsley
MASSACHUSETTS:		
Bedford, 01730 (200 Springs Rd.) (Edith Nourse Rogers Memorial Veterans Hospital).	......do	Michael J. Kane
Boston, 02130 (150 S. Huntington Ave.)	......do	Smith Jenkins, Jr.
Boston, 02203 (John F. Kennedy Federal Bldg.).	Regional Office	Robert Moakley
Boston, 02108 (17 Court St.)	Outpatient Clinic	combined VA Boston
Bourne, 02532 (Massachusetts National Cemetery).	National Cemetery	Gary W. Smith
Northampton, 01060	Medical Center	Mary W. Forsyth
West Roxbury, 02132 (1400 Veterans of Foreign Wars Pkwy.).	......do	William Kelleher
MICHIGAN:		
Allen Park, 48101	Medical Center	James H. Stephens
Ann Arbor, 48105 (2215 Fuller Rd.)	......do	Edward Gamache
Augusta, 49012 (15501 Dickman Rd.) (Fort Custer National Cemetery).	National Cemetery	Eugene Chambers
Battle Creek, 49106	Medical Center	Stephen J. Musser
Detroit, 48226 (477 Michigan Ave.)	Regional Office	Gordon W. Clowney
Iron Mountain, 49801	Medical Center	Helen K. Cornish
Saginaw, 48602 (1500 Weiss St.)	......do	Krista Ludenia
MINNESOTA:		
Minneapolis, 55417 (1 Veterans Dr.)	......do	Thomas P. Mullon
Minneapolis, 55450 (7601 34th Ave., S.) (Fort Snelling National Cemetery).	National Cemetery	William D. Napton
St. Cloud, 56301 (4801 8th St. N.)	Medical Center	Thomas A. Holthaus
St. Paul, 55111 (Bishop Henry Whipple Federal Bldg., Fort Snelling). Remittances: P.O. Box 1820.	Regional Office and Insurance Center	Morris B. Nooner, Jr.
MISSISSIPPI:		
Biloxi, 39531 Biloxi Hospital and Domiciliary Division Gulfport Hospital Division (Mail: Biloxi, MS)	Medical Center (medical and domiciliary)	James H. Caldwell, Jr.
Biloxi, 39535 (P.O. Box 4968)	National Cemetery	Jeffrey S. Barnes

National Facilities—Department of Veterans Affairs—Continued

Address	Type of facility	Director
Corinth, 38834 (1551 Horton St.)	do	(Vacancy)
Jackson, 39216 (1500 E. Woodrow Wilson Ave.).	Medical Center	James L. Warnock
Jackson, 39269 (100 W. Capitol St.)	Regional Office	Larry Woodard
Natchez, 39120 (61 Cemetery Rd.)	National Cemetery	(Vacancy)
MISSOURI:		
Columbia, 65201 (800 Hospital Dr.) (Harry S. Truman Memorial Veterans Hospital).	Medical Center	Joseph L. Kurzejeski
Jefferson City, 65101 (1024 E. McCarty St.) (Mail: Jefferson Barracks National Cemetery, MO).	National Cemetery	Ralph E. Church
Kansas City, 64128 (4801 Linwood Blvd.)	Medical Center	William Wright
Poplar Bluff, 63901	do	John Presley
Springfield, 65804 (1702 E. Seminole St.)	National Cemetery	Curtis E. Hardamon
St. Louis, 63125 John J. Cochran Division Jefferson Barracks Division	Medical Center	John T. Carson
St. Louis, 63115 (P.O. Box 5020)	Records Processing Center	Robert Adams
St. Louis, 63103 (1520 Market St.)	Regional Office	Donald R. Ramsey
St. Louis, 63125 (101 Memorial Dr.) (Jefferson Barracks National Cemetery).	National Cemetery	Ralph E. Church
MONTANA:		
Fort Harrison, 59636	Medical and Regional Office Center	Charles A. Milbrandt
Miles City, 59301	Medical Center	James A. Huff
NEBRASKA:		
Grand Island, 68801	do	Margaret Etheridge
Lincoln, 68510 (600 S. 70th St.)	do	Max L. Lybarger
Lincoln, 68508 (100 Centennial Mall N.)	Regional Office	Ronald Henke
Maxwell, 69151 (HCO 1, Box 67) (Fort McPherson National Cemetery).	National Cemetery	Robert E. Poe
Omaha, 68105 (4101 Woolworth Ave.)	Medical Center	Roderick L. Turcotte
NEVADA:		
Henderson (Las Vegas), 89015 (102 Lake Mead Dr.).	Outpatient Clinic	Ralph L. Fullwood
Reno, 89520 (1000 Locust St.)	Medical Center	Kenneth Clark
Reno, 89520 (1201 Terminal Way)	Regional Office	Eileen Straub
NEW HAMPSHIRE:		
Manchester, 03104 (718 Smyth Rd.)	Medical Center	Eugene Ochocki
Manchester, 03103 (275 Chestnut St.)	Regional Office	Edward Hubbard
NEW JERSEY:		
Beverly, 08010 (R.D. #1, Bridgeboro Rd.)	National Cemetery	Delores T. Blake
East Orange, 07019	Medical Center	Peter Baglio
Lyons, 07939	do	A. Paul Kidd
Newark, 07102 (20 Washington Pl.)	Regional Office	Robert P. Van Sprang
Salem, 08079 (R.F.D. #3, Fort Mott Rd., Box 542) (Finn's Point National Cemetery) (Mail: Beverly National Cemetery, NJ).	National Cemetery	Delores T. Blake
Somerville, 08876	Supply Depot	Anthony Borneo
NEW MEXICO:		
Albuquerque, 87108 (2100 Ridgecrest Dr. SE.)	Medical Center	R. Michael Harwell
Albuquerque, 87102 (500 Gold Ave. SW.)	Regional Office	Joseph S. Cordova
Fort Bayard, 88036 (P.O. Box 189) (Fort Bayard National Cemetery) (Mail: Fort Bliss National Cemetery, TX).	National Cemetery	Oakland deMoss
Santa Fe, 87504 (P.O. Box 88, 501 N. Guadalupe St.).	do	Gloria C. Gamez
NEW YORK:		
Albany, 12208 (113 Holland Ave.)	Medical Center	Fred Malphurs
Batavia, 14020	do	William Manley
Bath, 14810	Medical Center (medical and domiciliary)	Mel A. Gores
Bath, 14810 (VA Medical Center)	National Cemetery	William L. Livingston
Bronx, 10468 (130 W. Kingsbridge Rd.)	Medical Center	James S. Dooley
Brooklyn, 11209 (800 Poly Pl.) Brooklyn Division St. Albans Division	do	James J. Farsetta
Brooklyn, 11205 (35 Ryerson St.)	Outpatient Clinic	James J. Farsetta
Brooklyn, 11208 (625 Jamaica Ave.) (Cypress Hills National Cemetery) (Mail: Long Island National Cemetery, NY).	National Cemetery	Dennis E. Kuehl
Buffalo, 14202 (111 W. Huron St.)	Regional Office	Thomas E. Zamary
Buffalo, 14215 (3495 Bailey Ave.)	Medical Center	Richard S. Droske
Calverton, 11933 (210 Princeton Blvd.)	National Cemetery	Floyd J. Parker
Canandaigua, 14424	Medical Center	Mike Lawson

National Facilities—Department of Veterans Affairs—Continued

Address	Type of facility	Director
Castle Point, 12511	......do	Ronald F. Lipp
Elmira, 14901 (1825 Davis St.) (Woodlawn National Cemetery) (Mail: Bath National Cemetery, NY).	National Cemetery	William L. Livingston
Farmingdale, 11735 (Long Island National Cemetery).	......do	Dennis E. Kuehl
Montrose, 10548 (Franklin Delano Roosevelt Hospital).	Medical Center	(Vacancy)
New York, 10001 (252 7th Ave. at 24th St.)	Regional Office	Joseph Thompson
New York, 10001 (1st Ave. at E. 24th St.)	Medical Center	Sanford M. Garfunkel
Northport, Long Island, 11768	......do	Alice Wood
Syracuse, 13210 (Irving Ave. and University Pl.).	......do	Clyde H. Corsaro
NORTH CAROLINA:		
Asheville, 28805	......do	James A. Christian
Durham, 27705 (508 Fulton St. and Erwin Rd.)	......do	Barbara A. Small
Fayetteville, 28301 (2300 Ramsey St.)	......do	Anthony G. Branch
New Bern, 28560 (1711 National Ave.)	National Cemetery	Karen J. Duhart
Raleigh, 27610 (501 Rock Quarry Rd.)	......do	Richard Anderson
Salisbury, 28144 (1601 Brenner Ave.)	Medical Center	R. Eugene Konik
Salisbury, 28144 (202 Government Rd.)	National Cemetery	Malcus L. Richards
Wilmington, 28403 (2011 Market St.) (Mail: New Bern National Cemetery, NC).	......do	Karen J. Duhart
Winston-Salem, 27102 (251 N. Main St.)	Regional Office	Kenneth E. McDonald
NORTH DAKOTA:		
Fargo, 58102 (655 1st Ave. N.)	Medical and Regional Office Center	Donald C. Colston
OHIO:		
Chillicothe, 45601	Medical Center	Troy E. Page
Cincinnati, 45220 (3200 Vine St.)	......do	Donald L. Ziegenhorn
Cleveland, 44106 (10701 East Blvd.)	......do	Carl J. Gerber, M.D.
Becksville Division		
Wade Park Division		
Cleveland, 44199 (1240 E. 9th St.)	Regional Office	Phillip J. Ross
Columbus, 43221 (2090 Kenny Rd.)	Outpatient Clinic	Robert Sellers
Dayton, 45428	Medical Center (medical and domiciliary)	Edgar Thorsland
Dayton, 45428 (VA Medical Center, 4100 W. 3d St.).	National Cemetery	Richard L.R. Boyd
OKLAHOMA:		
Fort Gibson, 74434 (Route 2, Box 47)	......do	Carla S. Williams
Muskogee, 74401 (Memorial Station, Honor Heights Dr.).	Medical Center	Jerry Baxter
Muskogee, 74401 (125 S. Main St.)	Regional Office	Jerry G. McRae
Oklahoma City, 73104 (921 NE. 13th St.)	Medical Center	Steve J. Gentling
OREGON:		
Eagle Point, 97524 (2763 Riley Rd.)	National Cemetery	Gilbert Gallo
Portland, 97201 (3710 SW. U.S. Veterans Hospital Rd.).	Medical Center	Barry L. Bell
Portland, 97204 (1220 SW. 3d Ave.)	Regional Office	Joseph Williams
Portland, 97266 (11800 SE. Mt. Scott Blvd., P.O. Box 66147) (Williamette National Cemetery).	National Cemetery	Billy D. Murphy
Roseburg, 97470	Medical Center	Perry C. Norman
Roseburg, 97470 (VA Medical Center)	National Cemetery	Maintained by VAMC
White City, 97501	Domiciliary	Frank A. Drake
PENNSYLVANIA:		
Altoona, 16603	Medical Center	John J. Ruff
Annville, 17003 (P.O. Box 187) (Indiantown Gap National Cemetery).	National Cemetery	Willie Crosby
Aspinwall (see Pittsburgh, 15240)		
Butler, 16001	Medical Center	Reginald L. Mosior
Coatesville, 19320	......do	Richard Meiler
Erie, 16501 (135 E. 38th St. Blvd.)	......do	Jack D. Graham
Lebanon, 17042	......do	Leonard Washington, Jr.
Philadelphia, 19101 (5000 Wissahickon Ave.) (Insurance remittances: P.O. Box 7787). (Mail: P.O. Box 8079).	Regional Office and Insurance Center	Thomas M. Lastowka
Philadelphia, 19104 (University and Woodland Aves.).	Medical Center	Robert F. Stott
Philadelphia, 19138 (Haines St. and Limekiln Pike) (Mail: Beverly National Cemetery, NJ).	National Cemetery	Delores T. Blake
Pittsburgh, 15222 (1000 Liberty Ave.)	Regional Office	Harold T. Bushey
Pittsburgh, 15206 (Highland Dr.)	Medical Center	Reedes Hurt
Pittsburgh, 15240 (University Dr. C)	......do	Thomas A. Gigliotti

National Facilities—Department of Veterans Affairs—Continued

Address	Type of facility	Director
Aspinwall Division		
Pittsburgh Division		
(Mail: University Drive, Pittsburgh)		
Wilkes-Barre, 18711 (1111 East End Blvd.)	......do	Michael M. Linder
PHILIPPINE REPUBLIC:		
Manila (1131 Roxas Blvd.) (A.P.O., San Francisco, CA, 96528).	Regional Office and Outpatient Clinic	Daniel H. Emer
PUERTO RICO:		
Bayamon, 00619 (P.O. Box 1298) (Puerto Rico National Cemetery).	National Cemetery	Rafael B. Acosta
Hato Rey (U.S. Courthouse and Federal Bldg., Carlos E. Chardon St., 00918).		
San Juan (Barrio Monacillos G.P.O., Box 4867, 00936).	Medical Center	Edward Valenzuela
San Juan (Barrio Monacillos G.P.O. Box 4867, 00936).	Regional Office	Mary Leyland
RHODE ISLAND:		
Providence, 02903 (380 Westminster Mall)	Regional Office	John Montgomery
Providence, 02908 (Davis Park)	Medical Center	Edward H. Seiler
SOUTH CAROLINA:		
Beaufort, 29902 (1601 Boundary St.)	National Cemetery	Ramona Vaughn
Charleston, 29403 (109 Bee St.)	Medical Center	Jerry Boyd
Columbia, 29201 (William Jennings Bryan Dorn Veterans Hospital).	......do	Robert M. Athey
Columbia, 29201 (1801 Assembly St.)	Regional Office	R. Stedman Sloan, Jr.
Florence, 29501 (803 E. National Cemetery Rd.).	National Cemetery	Kenneth LaFevor
SOUTH DAKOTA:		
Fort Meade, 57741	Medical Center	(Vacancy)
Fort Meade, 57785 (VA Medical Center) (Mail: Black Hills National Cemetery, SD).	National Cemetery	Daniel Nelson
Hot Springs, 57747	Medical Center (medical and domiciliary)	James Dudley
Hot Springs, 57747 (VA Medical Center)	National Cemetery	Maintained by VAMC
Sioux Falls, 57107 (Royal C. Johnson Veterans Memorial Hospital).	Medical Center and Regional Office	R. Vincent Crawford
Sturgis, 57785 (P.O. Box 640) (Black Hills National Cemetery).	National Cemetery	Daniel Nelson
TENNESSEE:		
Chattanooga, 37404 (1200 Bailey Ave.)	......do	James Wallace
Knoxville, 37917 (939 Tyson St., NW.)	......do	Rodney Dunn
Madison, 37115 (1420 Gallatin Rd. S.) (Nashville National Cemetery).	......do	Kevin Taylor
Memphis, 38104 (1030 Jefferson Ave.)	Medical Center	Kenneth L. Mulholland
Memphis, 38122 (3568 Townes Ave.)	National Cemetery	David M. Cariota
Mountain Home, 37601 (Johnson City)	Medical Center (medical and domiciliary)	Jonathan F. Fitts
Mountain Home, 37684 (P.O. Box 8)	National Cemetery	Rodney L. Dunn
Murfreesboro, 37130	Medical Center	Brian Heckert
Nashville, 37203 (1310 24th Ave. S.)	......do	Larry E. Deters
Nashville, 37203 (110 9th Ave. S.)	Regional Office	Robert S. Bielak
TEXAS:		
Amarillo, 79106 (6010 Amarillo Blvd. W.)	Medical Center	Edward J. Sherwood, M.D.
Big Spring, 79720	Medical Center	Conrad Alexander
Bonham, 75418 (Sam Rayburn Memorial Veterans Center).	Medical Center (medical and domiciliary)	Billy M. Valentine
Dallas, 75216 (4500 S. Lancaster Rd.)	Medical Center	Alan Harper
El Paso, 79925 (5919 Brook Hollow Dr.)	Outpatient Clinic	Frank Caldwell
Fort Bliss, 79906 (P.O. Box 6342)	National Cemetery	Oakland deMoss
Houston, 77211 (2002 Holcombe Blvd.)	Medical Center	John V. Sheehan
Houston, 77054 (2515 Murworth Dr.)	Regional Office	Theodore W. Myatt
Houston, 77038 (10410 Veterans Memorial Dr.).	National Cemetery	Ronald R. Pemberton
Kerrville, 78028	Medical Center	Arnold E. Mouish
Kerrville, 78028 (VA Medical Center, 3600 Memorial Blvd.).	National Cemetery	Maintained by VAMC
Marlin, 76661	Medical Center	Melvin Baker
San Antonio, 78285 (7400 Merton Minter Blvd.) (Audi L. Murphy Memorial Veterans Hospital).	......do	Jose R. Coronado
San Antonio, 78202 (517 Paso Hondo St.) (Mail: Fort Sam Houston National Cemetery, TX).	National Cemetery	Donald H. Fritz

National Facilities—Department of Veterans Affairs—Continued

Address	Type of facility	Director
San Antonio, 78209 (1520 Harry Wurzbach Rd.) (Fort Sam Houston National Cemetery).	......do	Donald H. Fritz
Temple, 76504 (Olin E. Teague Veterans Center).	Medical Center (medical and domiciliary)	Eugene A. Borrell
Waco, 76711 (4800 Memorial Dr.)	Medical Center	Wallace M. Hopkins
Waco, 76799 (1400 N. Valley Mills Dr.)	Regional Office	Stephen L. Lemons
UTAH:		
Salt Lake City, 84147 (125 S. State St.)	Regional Office	Douglas B. Wadsworth
Salt Lake City, 84148 (500 Foothill Blvd.)	Medical Center	William L. Hodson, Jr.
VERMONT:		
White River Junction, 05001	Medical and Regional Office Center	Gary DeGasta
VIRGINIA:		
Alexandria, 22314 (1450 Wilkes St.) (Mail: Quantico National Cemetery, VA).	National Cemetery	Patricia K. Novak
Culpeper, 22701 (305 U.S. Ave.)	......do	David R. Wells
Danville, 24541 (721 Lee St.) (Mail: Salisbury National Cemetery, NC).	......do	Malcus L. Richards
Hampton, 23667	Medical Center (medical and domiciliary)	Allan S. Goss
Hampton, 23669 (Cemetery Rd. at Marshall Ave., VA).	National Cemetery	Homer D. Hardamon
Hampton, 23669 (VA Medical Center) (Mail: Cemetery Rd. at Marshall Ave., VA).	......do	Homer D. Hardamon
Hopewell, 23860 (10th Ave. and Davis St.) (City Point National Cemetery) (Mail: Richmond National Cemetery, VA).	......do	Leon B. Murphy
Leesburg, 22075 (Balls Bluff National Cemetery) (Mail: Culpeper National Cemetery, VA).	......do	David R. Wells
Mechanicsville, 23111 (Route 156 N.) (Cold Harbor National Cemetery) (Mail: Richmond National Cemetery, VA).	......do	Leon B. Murphy
Richmond, 23249 (1201 Broad Rock Rd.)	Medical Center	James Dudley
Richmond, 23231 (1701 Williamsburg Rd.)	National Cemetery	Leon B. Murphy
Richmond, 23231 (8620 Varina Rd.) (Fort Harrison National Cemetery) (Mail: Richmond National Cemetery, VA).	......do	Leon B. Murphy
Richmond, 23231 (8301 Willis Church Rd.) (Glendale National Cemetery) (Mail: Richmond National Cemetery, VA).	......do	Leon B. Murphy
Roanoke, 24011 (210 Franklin Rd. SW.)	Regional Office	Samuel A. Tiano
Salem, 24153	Medical Center	Clark C. Graninger
Sandston, 23150 (400 E. Williamsburg Rd.) (Seven Pines National Cemetery) (Mail: Richmond National Cemetery, VA).	National Cemetery	Leon B. Murphy
Staunton, 24401 (901 Richmond Ave.) (Mail: Culpeper National Cemetery, VA).	......do	David R. Wells
Triangle, 22172 (P.O. Box 10) (Quantico National Cemetery).	......do	Patricia K. Novak
Winchester, 22601 (401 National Ave.) (Mail: Culpeper National Cemetery, VA).	......do	David R. Wells
WASHINGTON:		
American Lake, Tacoma, 98493	Medical Center	Frank Taylor
Seattle, 98174 (915 2d Ave.)	Regional Office	Richard F. Murphy
Seattle, 98108 (4435 Beacon Ave., S.)	Medical Center	James T. Krajeck
Spokane, 99208 (N. 4815 Assembly St.)	......do	Edwin J. Mack
Walla Walla, 99362 (77 Wainwright Dr.)	......do	Mary Ann Coffey
WEST VIRGINIA:		
Beckley, 25801 (200 Veterans Ave.)	......do	Domenic R. Pisegna
Clarksburg, 26301	......do	E.L. McNeil, Jr.
Grafton, 26354 (431 Walnut St.)	National Cemetery	Terry Ellison
Pruntytown, 26354 (West Virginia National Cemetery) (Mail: Grafton National Cemetery, WV).	......do	Terry Ellison
Huntington, 25701 (1540 Spring Valley Dr.)	Medical Center	Phillip S. Elkins
Huntington, 25701 (640 4th Ave.)	Regional Office	Greg Mason
Martinsburg, 25401	Medical Center (medical and domiciliary)	Thomas H. Weaver
WISCONSIN:		
Madison, 53705 (2500 Overlook Ter.) (William S. Middleton Memorial Veterans Hospital).	Medical Center	Nathan L. Geraths
Milwaukee, 53193 (5000 W. National Ave.)	Medical Center (medical and domiciliary)	Russell E. Struble
Milwaukee, 53295 (P.O. Box 6)	Regional Office	Jon A. Baker
Milwaukee, 53295 (P.O. Box 79) (Wood National Cemetery).	National Cemetery	Elmer D. Nygaard
Tomah, 54660	Medical Center	(Vacancy)

National Facilities—Department of Veterans Affairs—Continued

Address	Type of facility	Director
WYOMING:		
Cheyenne, 82001 (2360 E. Pershing Blvd.)	Medical and Regional Office Center	George H. Andries
Sheridan, 82801	Medical Center	John Brinkers

Sources of Information

Audiovisuals Persons interested in the availability of VA motion pictures or exhibits for showing outside VA may write the Director, Audio Visuals Service (037), Department of Veterans Affairs, 810 Vermont Avenue NW., Washington, DC 20420. Phone, 202-233-2715.

Contracts and Small Business Activities Persons seeking to do business with the Department of Veterans Affairs may contact the Director, Acquisition Policy and Review Service (95), 810 Vermont Avenue NW., Washington, DC 20420. Phone, 202-233-3296. A brochure *Doing Business With the Department of Veterans Affairs,* which describes acquisition opportunities and contact points, is available upon request. Persons seeking information regarding special contracting and subcontracting programs for small, disadvantaged, 8(a) certified, and women- and veteran-owned businesses may contact the Director, Office of Small and Disadvantaged Business Utilization (005SB). Phone, 202-376-6996.

Employment The Department of Veterans Affairs employs physicians, dentists, podiatrists, optometrists, nurses, nurse anesthetists, physician assistants, expanded-function dental auxilliaries, registered respiratory therapists, certified respiratory technicians, licensed physical therapists, occupational therapists, pharmacists, and licensed practical or vocational nurses under VA's excepted merit system. This system does not require civil service eligibility. Other professional, technical, administrative, and clerical occupations exist in VA that do require civil service eligibility. Persons interested in employment should contact the Personnel Officer at their nearest VA facility.

Freedom of Information Act Requests Inquiries should be directed to the Assistant Secretary for Information Resources Management, Records Management Service (723), Room 1036, McPherson Square Building, Washington, DC 20420. Phone, 202-233-3616.

Medical Center (Hospital) Design, Construction, and Related Services VA projects requiring services for design, construction, and other related services are advertised in the *Commerce Business Daily*. Architectural/engineering firms interested in designing VA medical center construction projects may write to the Director, A/E Evaluation Staff (087G). Phone, 202-233-3181. Construction contractors should address their inquiries to the Chief, Administrative Services Division, (082C). Phone, 202-233-3308. Contact either office at the Department of Veterans Affairs Central Office, 810 Vermont Avenue NW., Washington, DC 20420; or write to the Chief, Supply Service, at any VA medical center or regional office center beginning on page 518.

News Media Representatives of the media outside Washington, DC, may contact VA through the nearest area Office of Public Affairs:

Atlanta (404-347-3236)
Chicago (312-353-4076)
Dallas (214-372-7084)
Denver (303-980-2995)
Los Angeles (213-824-4497)
New York (212-620-6525)

National and Washington, DC, media may contact the Office of Public Affairs in the VA Central Office, 810 Vermont Avenue NW., Washington, DC 20420. Phone, 202-535-8300.

Publications *Annual Report of the Secretary of Veterans Affairs* may be obtained (in single copies), without charge, from the Analysis and Reports Service (742), 810 Vermont Avenue NW., Washington, DC 20420.

The January 1991 VA IS-1 fact sheet, *Federal Benefits for Veterans and*

Dependents, is for sale by the Superintendent of Documents, Government Printing Office, Washington, DC 20402.

Board of Veterans Appeals Index I–01–1, an index to appellate decisions, is available in annual cumulation from July 1977 to the present on microfiche only. The quarterly indexes may be purchased for $7 and the annual cumulative index for $12.50. The VADEX/CITATOR of Appellate Research Materials is a complete quarterly looseleaf-bound cumulation of research material which may be purchased for $110. These publications may be obtained from Promisel and Korn, Inc., Suite 480, 7201 Wisconsin Avenue, Bethesda, MD 20814.

VA Pamphlet 27–82–2, *A Summary of Department of Veteran Affairs Benefits,* may be obtained, without charge, from any VA regional office.

VA NCS-IS-1, a list of *Department of Veterans Affairs National Cemeteries* showing those with and without available grave space, and information on procedures and eligibility for burial in a National Cemetery, may be obtained, without charge, from the National Cemetery System (40H), 810 Vermont Avenue NW., Washington, DC 20420.

Persons may obtain a construction research report listing from the Director, Management and Budget Staff (O82), Office of Facilities, Department of Veterans Affairs, 810 Vermont Avenue NW., Washington, DC 20420. Phone, 202–233–3481.

Reading Room Persons visiting Central Office, Washington, DC, to inspect, obtain information from, or copy VA records available to the public should go to Room 132, 810 Vermont Avenue NW., for referral. Phone, 202–233–2356. Assistance at field stations may be obtained by inquiring of local personnel.

For further information, contact the Office of Public Affairs, Department of Veterans Affairs, 810 Vermont Avenue NW., Washington, DC 20420. Phone, 202–535–8300.

Independent Establishments and Government Corporations

ACTION

1100 Vermont Avenue NW., Washington, DC 20525
Phone, 202–634–9380

Director	Jane A. Kenny
Deputy Director	(vacancy)
General Counsel	Frank Stilwell
Director, Legislative Affairs	Nora Manning, *Acting*
Associate Director, Office of Policy and Research	Roland Goodman
Associate Director, Management and Budget	Gary Kowalczyk, *Acting*
Associate Director for Domestic and Anti-Poverty Operations	Richard V. Bertain
Assistant Director, Older American Volunteer Programs	Constance M. Burns
Assistant Director, VISTA and Student Community Service	Patricia Rodgers
Director, Public Affairs	Nancy Yde

ACTION mobilizes Americans for voluntary service throughout the United States through programs that help meet basic human needs and support the self-help efforts of low-income individuals and communities.

ACTION is the principal agency in the Federal Government for administering volunteer service programs. It was created as an independent agency under the provisions of Reorganization Plan No. 1 of 1971 (5 U.S.C. app.), effective July 1, 1971, and Executive Order 11603 of June 30, 1971, with legislative authority provided by the Domestic Volunteer Service Act of 1973, as amended (42 U.S.C. 4951).

ACTION administers and coordinates the domestic volunteer programs sponsored by the Federal Government, which are linked by a commitment to a "bottom-up," locally initiated development process fostering self-reliance and utilizes available human and economic resources to overcome conditions of poverty. Through special demonstration grants and programs, ACTION also tests new ways of bringing volunteer resources to bear on human,

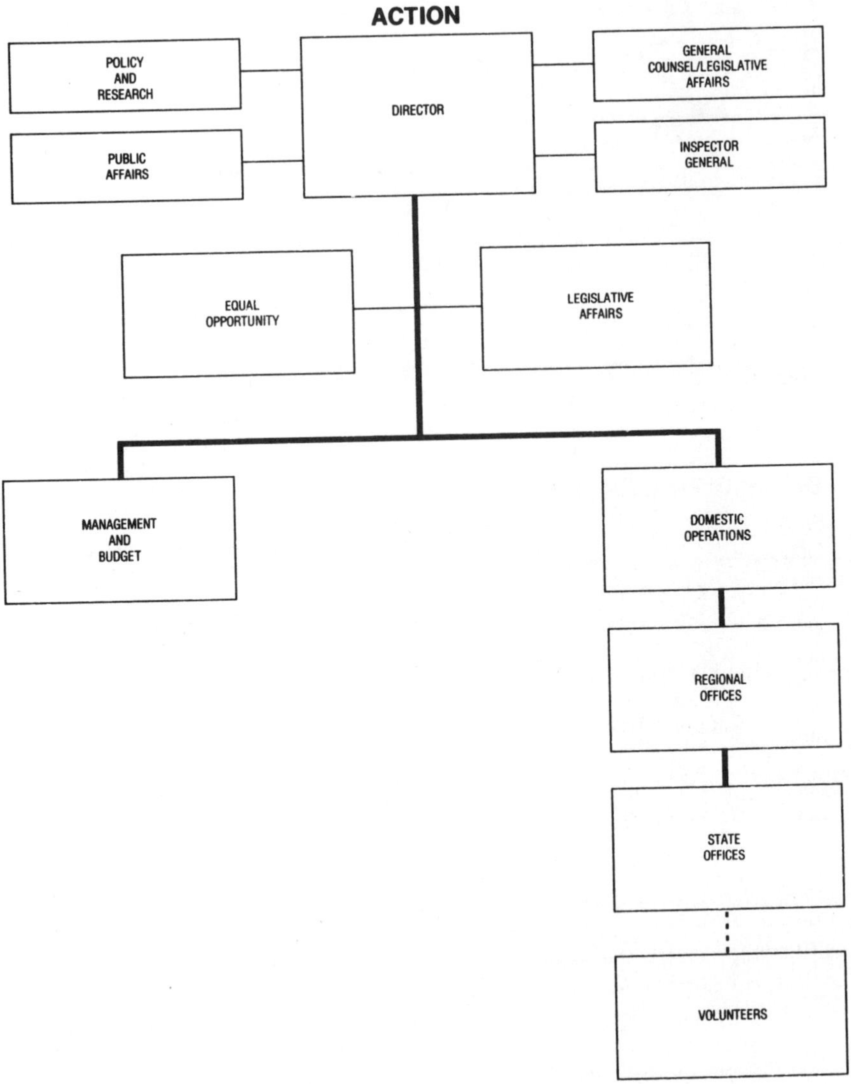
ACTION
POLICY AND RESEARCH
PUBLIC AFFAIRS
DIRECTOR
GENERAL COUNSEL/LEGISLATIVE AFFAIRS
INSPECTOR GENERAL
EQUAL OPPORTUNITY
LEGISLATIVE AFFAIRS
MANAGEMENT AND BUDGET
DOMESTIC OPERATIONS
REGIONAL OFFICES
STATE OFFICES
VOLUNTEERS

social, and economic problems. It identifies and develops the widest possible range of volunteer service opportunities for Americans of all ages and ethnic backgrounds. The Agency actively encourages private-sector involvement in support of its goals and programs.

ACTION includes Volunteers in Service to America (VISTA), the Foster Grandparent Program (FGP), the Retired Senior Volunteer Program (RSVP), the Senior Companion Program (SCP), the Demonstration Grant Program, the Mini-Grant Program, the Technical Assistance Program, and the State offices of voluntarism.

ACTION consists of a Washington, DC, headquarters and 9 regional offices, supporting 45 individual State offices and Puerto Rico.

Domestic Regional Offices—ACTION

(Areas included within each region are indicated on the map in Appendix A.)

	Region/Address	Regional Director	Telephone
1.	Boston, MA 02222-1039 (Rm. 473, 10 Causeway St.)	John Torian	617-565-7001
2.	New York, NY 10048-0206 (Rm. 758, 6 World Trade Ctr.)	Suzanne Tufts	212-466-3481
3.	Philadelphia, PA 19106-2912 (Rm. 108, 2d and Chestnut Sts.)	Margaret Matisko	215-597-9972
4.	Atlanta, GA 30323-2301 (Suite 1003, 101 Marietta St. NW.)	Marcus Bell	404-841-[illegible]360
5.	Chicago, IL 60604-3964 (10 W. Jackson Blvd.)	Jeanne Bradner	312-363-[illegible]107
6.	Dallas, TX 75242-0696 (Rm. 6B11, 1100 Commerce St.)	Beth Anderson	214-767-9494
8.	Denver, CO 80202-2349 (Suite 2930, 1405 Curtis St.)	Joyce Emerson	303-844-2671
9.	San Francisco, CA 94105-1914 (Rm. 503, 211 Main St.)	Teresa Keeshan	415-744-3046
10.	Seattle, WA 98174-1103 (Suite 3039, 909 1st Ave.)	John Keller	206-442-4520

Domestic Programs and Activities

Foster Grandparents The Foster Grandparent Program was created in 1965 and offers older men and women opportunities for close relationships with children having special or exceptional needs. It is an opportunity for older Americans to continue serving their communities and themselves in an active and meaningful capacity.

Foster Grandparents are low-income persons at least 60 years of age and come from various backgrounds. They receive both preservice orientation and inservice instruction. Volunteers serve 20 hours per week, receive a nontaxable stipend of $2.35 per hour, as well as provisions for reimbursement of travel costs, a meal each day they serve, accident and liability insurance coverage, and a yearly physical examination. Under certain conditions, nonstipended volunteers may be enrolled in the program.

Foster Grandparents serve in schools and hospitals for mentally retarded, disturbed, and handicapped children; in care centers, hospital wards, and corrections institutions; in homes for disadvantaged, dependent, or neglected children; and other settings within the community. An increased percentage of Foster Grandparents are being encouraged to serve in settings dealing with literacy, drug abuse, and runaway youth, including some inhome placements.

The Foster Grandparents' main purpose is to help provide for the emotional, mental, and physical well-being of children by affording them close, personal, and continuing relations with an adult. They furnish a renewed sense of love and intimacy often missing in institutional environments. They also may assist in feeding and dressing the children, reading, playing games, telling them stories, and aiding in speech and physical therapy and other care-giving activities that tend to maximize the functional capabilities of these children.

For further information, call 202-634-9349.

Retired Senior Volunteers The purpose of the Retired Senior Volunteer Program is to create a variety of significant opportunities for persons of retirement age to participate more fully in the life of their communities through volunteer service.

The program's projects are planned, organized, and operated at the local level and developed under the auspices of an established organization able to generate local program and financial support.

Volunteers must be at least 60 years of age and willing and able to serve on a regular basis. There are no income or educational restrictions. Volunteers perform various services, according to community need and their own preferences, in a variety of settings, including schools, courts, and health care, rehabilitation, day care, youth, and other community centers. They also serve in outreach roles within their community.

For further information, call 202–634–9353.

Senior Companions The Senior Companion Program provides meaningful part-time volunteer opportunities for low-income, older persons to render, in a mutually beneficial relationship, supportive person-to-person services to adults, especially older people, with special needs in health-, education-, and welfare-related settings.

Under the sponsorship and supervision of an approved agency, the Senior Companion serves in and through a variety of settings such as hospitals, social service agencies, or home and health care agencies. Over 80 percent of the Senior Companions are serving older persons in their own homes in order to prevent or delay inappropriate institutionalization. Senior Companions receive the same benefits as Foster Grandparents for 20 hours of service per week. Under certain conditions, nonstipended volunteers may be enrolled in the program.

For further information, call 202–634–9349.

Volunteers in Service to America The creation of Volunteers in Service to America was authorized by Congress in 1964 to provide constructive opportunities for Americans to work on a full-time basis with locally sponsored projects designed to increase the capability of low-income people to improve the condition of their own lives. Volunteers are assigned to local sponsors, which may be Federal or State agencies or private, nonprofit organizations located in the United States, Puerto Rico, the Virgin Islands, and Guam. Volunteers serve for 1 year. More than half of the program's resources focus upon illiteracy, unemployment, hunger, and homelessness.

Volunteers live and work among the poor in urban or rural areas or on Indian reservations. They share their skills and experience in fields such as drug abuse prevention, education, literacy, runaway youth, refugee resettlement, community design, weatherization, economic development, and emergency food and shelter. Most volunteers are recruited locally for community projects. Approximately 20 percent of the volunteers are age 55 and over. A volunteer must be a resident of the United States or one of its territories. A physical disability does not disqualify a volunteer, providing placement can be made on a project.

Volunteers participate in orientation and training sessions conducted by ACTION and sponsor personnel at the beginning of and during service. Volunteers receive a basic subsistence allowance, which covers housing, food, and incidentals. Health insurance also is provided. An additional $90 a month is paid as a stipend upon completion of service.

For further information, call the Director, VISTA and Student Service. Phone, 202–634–9445.

Student Community Service Projects Student Community Service Projects are designed to encourage students to undertake volunteer service in their communities in such a way as to enhance the educational value of the service experience through participation in activities which address poverty-related problems. Student volunteers must be enrolled in secondary, secondary vocational, or postsecondary schools on an in-school or out-of-school basis. They serve part-time and do not receive stipends.

The service opportunities must result in student volunteers gaining learning experiences through service in low-income communities, whether or not they receive academic credit.

The intent of Student Community Service Projects is to join community, school, and youth in developing the scope and nature of volunteer experiences that serve the needs of impoverished communities while securing resources by which the effort can be continued and expanded, if needed, after Federal support ends.

Local communities determine what their problems are and how best to solve them. ACTION resources may be made available to assist in helping communities solve some of their problems through fostering student volunteer service. The community must generate increasing resources to enable the project to continue once ACTION grant funds are no longer provided. Technical assistance and training in project management, fundraising, and recruiting will be provided by ACTION as required.

For further information, contact the Student Community Service Projects. Phone, 202–634–9424.

Program Demonstration and Development Division

The programs in the Program Demonstration and Development Division were developed to provide links at national, State, and local levels among public and private organizations to encourage volunteer activity in solving social problems.

Demonstration Projects The Division is responsible for the development of special emphasis and demonstration programs that focus on certain areas of concern where volunteers can make a special contribution in ameliorating human and social problems. These volunteer demonstration programs test models that, if successful, may form the basis of the agency's programming or may be adopted by the private sector and State or local governments.

Drug Alliance Office The Office coordinates the Agency's drug abuse prevention and education activities, awards grants that strengthen and expand local volunteer activities combating drug use among youth and the misuse of prescription and over-the-counter drugs by the elderly, provides training and technical assistance, and conducts public awareness and education efforts.

Mini-Grants The Mini-Grant Program offers one-time, 1-year seed money grants to support volunteer projects and enhance volunteer activities that show potential for providing long-term solutions to community problems. All projects must show substantial local support and respond to funding priorities established and publicized yearly. The program offers access to nonprofit groups of small grants through streamlined procedures.

Technical Assistance The Technical Assistance Program provides referrals and technical resources to organizations that work with volunteers and occasionally provides funds for the development of training and technical assistance material.

Volunteer Efforts Government's Involvement in Volunteer Efforts (GIVE) programs promote increased Federal employee voluntarism in nearly all Federal departments and agencies.

National Volunteer Week National Volunteer Week, designated in April of each year by the President, promotes special recognition of volunteers and their achievements among Federal agencies, State and local governments, and private organizations that use volunteers nationwide.

For further information, contact the Program Demonstration and Development Division. Phone, 202–634–9757.

Sources of Information

In all cases, information or assistance may be obtained by directing inquiries to or contacting ACTION's Washington headquarters or any of its regional and recruiting offices. Frequently, information is available from local post offices. Address specific inquiries as indicated below.

Publications For general literature and recruitment material, write to the Division of Public Affairs, ACTION, Washington, DC 20525. Phone, 202–634–9108.

Resource Center The Resource Center, including the library and computer data-bank, collects, processes, and disseminates information on ACTION policy and programs, national and Federal resources for voluntarism, legislation pertaining to voluntarism, and training for volunteers and administrators.

Volunteer Recruitment
Persons interested in volunteering for service in ACTION programs may contact any regional office, or write to the ACTION program office, Washington, DC 20525.
RSVP/FGP/SCP Information may be obtained from ACTION regional offices, or by writing to ACTION/RSVP, ACTION/SCP, or ACTION/FGP, Washington, DC 20525.
NCSL Write ACTION/National Center for Service Learning, Washington, DC 20525.

For further information, contact the Office of the Director, ACTION, Washington, DC 20525. Phone, 202–634–9380.

ADMINISTRATIVE CONFERENCE OF THE UNITED STATES

2120 L Street NW., Washington, DC 20037
Phone, 202–254–7020

Chairman	MARSHALL J. BREGER
Executive Director	WILLIAM J. OLMSTEAD
Research Director	JEFFREY S. LUBBERS
General Counsel	GARY J. EDLES
Council:	
Vice Chairman	(VACANCY)
Members	PHILLIP D. BRADY, RICHARD C. BREEDEN, HAROLD R. DEMOSS, JR., WALTER GELLHORN, TRUDI M. MORRISON, CONSTANCE BERRY NEWMAN, ROBERT S. ROSS, JR., R. CARTER SANDERS, EDWARD L. WEIDENFELD

[For the Administrative Conference of the United States statement of organization, see the *Code of Federal Regulations,* Title 1, Part 301]

The Administrative Conference develops recommendations for improving the procedures by which Federal agencies administer regulatory, benefit, and other Government programs. Conference members are agency heads, other Federal officials, private lawyers, university professors, and other experts in administrative law and government who meet to consider studies of selected problems involving administrative procedures. They combine their experience and judgment in cooperative efforts toward improving the fairness and effectiveness of agency procedures.

The Administrative Conference of the United States was established as a permanent independent agency by the Administrative Conference Act (5 U.S.C. 571–576) enacted in 1964. The statutory provisions prescribing the organization and activities of the Conference are based in part upon the experience of two temporary Conferences called by the President in 1953 and 1961, each of which operated for 18 months.

Membership

The Chairman of the Administrative Conference of the United States is appointed by the President with the advice and consent of the Senate for a 5-year term. The Council, which is the executive board, consists of the Chairman and 10 other members appointed by the President for 3-year terms. Federal officials named to the Council may constitute no more than one-half of the total Council membership. In addition to the Chairman and the Council, the membership of the Administrative Conference is composed of 50 high-level officials designated from 47 departments and agencies of the Federal Government and 40 private lawyers, university faculty members, and others specially informed in law and government. Members representing the private sector are appointed by the Chairman, with the approval of the Council, for 2-year terms. The Chairman is the only full-time compensated member.

The entire membership is divided into committees, each assigned a broad area of interest such as adjudication, administration, governmental processes, judicial review, regulation, or rulemaking. The membership meeting in plenary session is called the Assembly of the Administrative Conference, which by statute must meet at least once, and customarily meets twice, each year.

Activities

Subjects for inquiry are developed by the Chairman and approved by the Council. The committees, with staff assistance, conduct thorough studies of these subjects, propose recommendations, and prepare supporting reports. Recommendations are evaluated by the Council and, if ready for Assembly consideration, are distributed to the membership with the supporting reports and placed on the agenda of the next plenary session. The Assembly has complete authority to approve, amend, remand, or reject recommendations presented by the committees. The deliberations of the committees and Assembly are public.

The Chairman is authorized to encourage the departments and agencies to adopt the recommendations of the Conference and is required to transmit to the President and to Congress an annual report and interim reports concerning the activities of the Conference, including reports on the implementation of its recommendations.

Recommendations adopted by the Conference may call for new legislation or for action on the part of affected agencies. A substantial number of recommendations have been implemented and others are in the process of implementation.

The Chairman may make independent inquiries into procedural matters, including matters proposed by individuals inside or outside the Government. The purpose of such inquiries into such individual problems is to determine whether the problems should be made the subject of Conference study in the interest of developing fair and effective procedures for such cases.

Upon the request of the head of a department or agency, the Chairman is authorized to furnish advice and assistance on matters of administrative procedure. The Conference may collect information and statistics from departments and agencies and publish such reports as it considers useful for evaluating and improving administrative processes. The Conference also serves as a forum for the interchange among departments and agencies of information that may be useful in improving administrative practices and procedures.

Sources of Information

The Conference furnishes upon request copies of its recent recommendations and reports. It also maintains a library where copies of all official Conference documents are available for public inspection. Recommendations of the Conference appear in title 1, part 305, of the *Code of Federal Regulations.*

For further information, contact the Information Officer, Administrative Conference of the United States, 2120 L Street NW., Washington, DC 20037. Phone, 202–254–7020.

AFRICAN DEVELOPMENT FOUNDATION

1400 Eye Street NW., Washington, DC 20005
Phone, 202–673–3916

Chairman of the Board	F. EDWARD JOHNSON
Vice Chairman	WILLIAM H.G. FITZGERALD
President	GREGORY ROBESON SMITH
Vice President	CARROLL BOUCHARD

[For the African Development Foundation statement of organization, see the *Code of Federal Regulations,* Title 22, Part 1501]

The African Development Foundation assists and supports indigenous community-based, self-help grassroots organizations in their efforts to solve their own development problems.

The African Development Foundation was established by the African Development Foundation Act (22 U.S.C. 290h), as a nonprofit, Government corporation to support the self-help efforts of poor people in African countries. The Foundation became operational in 1984 and is governed by a seven-member Board of Directors appointed by the President with the advice and consent of the Senate. By law, five Board members are from the private sector and two are from the Government.

The purposes of the Foundation are to:

—strengthen the bonds of friendship and understanding between the people of Africa and the United States;

—support self-help development activities at the local level designed to promote opportunities for community development;

—stimulate and promote the effective and expanding participation of Africans in their development process; and

—encourage the establishment and growth of development institutions that are indigenous to particular countries in Africa and that can respond to the requirements of the poor in those countries.

To carry out its purposes, the Foundation makes grants, loans, and loan guarantees to any African private group, association, or other entity engaged in peaceful activities that enable the people of Africa to develop more fully.

For further information, contact the Public Affairs Officer, African Development Foundation, 10th Floor, 1400 Eye Street NW., Washington, DC 20005. Phone, 202–673–3916.

CENTRAL INTELLIGENCE AGENCY

Washington, DC 20505
Phone, 703–482–1100

Director of Central Intelligence	WILLIAM H. WEBSTER
Deputy Director of Central Intelligence	RICHARD J. KERR

[For the Central Intelligence Agency statement of organization, see the *Code of Federal Regulations,* Title 32, Part 1900]

The Central Intelligence Agency collects, evaluates, and disseminates the vital information on political, military, economic, scientific, and other developments abroad needed to safeguard national security.

The Central Intelligence Agency was established under the National Security Council by the National Security Act of 1947, as amended (50 U.S.C. 401 *et seq.*). It now functions under that statute, Executive Order 12333 of December 4, 1981, and other laws, regulations, and directives.

The Director of Central Intelligence heads both the Intelligence Community and the Central Intelligence Agency and is the President's principal adviser on intelligence matters. The Director and Deputy Director of Central Intelligence are appointed by the President with the advice and consent of the Senate.

The Central Intelligence Agency, under the direction of the President or the National Security Council:

—advises the National Security Council in matters concerning such intelligence activities of the Government departments and agencies as relate to national security;

—makes recommendations to the National Security Council for the coordination of such intelligence activities of the departments and agencies of the Government as relate to the national security;

—correlates and evaluates intelligence relating to the national security and provides for the appropriate dissemination of such intelligence within the Government;

—performs for intelligence agencies such additional services of common concern as the National Security Council determines can be more efficiently accomplished in the Agency;

—collects, produces, and disseminates counterintelligence and foreign intelligence, including information not otherwise obtainable. The collection of counterintelligence or foreign intelligence within the United States shall be coordinated with the Federal Bureau of Investigation as required by procedures agreed upon by the Director of Central Intelligence and the Attorney General;

—collects, produces, and disseminates intelligence on foreign aspects of narcotics production and trafficking;

—conducts counterintelligence activities outside the United States and, without assuming or performing any internal security functions, conducts counterintelligence activities within the United States in coordination with the Bureau as required by procedures agreed upon by the Director of Central Intelligence and the Attorney General;

—coordinates counterintelligence activities and the collection of information not otherwise obtainable when conducted outside the United States by other departments and agencies;

—conducts special activities approved by the President. No agency, except the Central Intelligence Agency (or the Armed Forces of the United States in time of war declared by Congress or during any period covered by a report from the President to the Congress under the War Powers Resolution (50 U.S.C. 1541 *et seq.*)), may conduct any special activity unless the President determines that another agency is more likely to achieve a particular objective;

290-950 O 91 - 18

—carries out or contracts for research, development, and procurement of technical systems and devices relating to authorized functions;

—protects the security of its installations, activities, information, property, and employees by appropriate means, including such investigations of applicants, employees, contractors, and other persons with similar associations with the Agency, as are necessary;

—conducts such administrative and technical support activities within and outside the United States as are necessary to perform its functions, including procurement and essential cover and proprietary arrangements; and

—performs such other functions and duties relating to intelligence that affect the national security as the National Security Council may from time to time direct.

The Agency has no police, subpoena, or law enforcement powers or internal security functions.

For further information, contact the Central Intelligence Agency, Washington, DC 20505. Phone, 703–482–1100.

COMMISSION ON THE BICENTENNIAL OF THE UNITED STATES CONSTITUTION

808 Seventeenth Street NW., Washington, DC 20006
Phone, 202–USA–1787

Chairman	WARREN E. BURGER
Members	FREDERICK K. BIEBEL, LINDY (MRS. HALE) BOGGS, HERBERT BROWNELL, LYNNE V. CHENEY, PHILIP M. CRANE, DENNIS DECONCINI, WILLIAM J. GREEN, MARK O. HATFIELD, EDWARD VICTOR HILL, CORNELIA G. KENNEDY, EDWARD M. KENNEDY, HARRY M. LIGHTSEY, JR., BETTY SOUTHARD MURPHY, THOMAS H. O'CONNOR, PHYLLIS SCHLAFLY, BERNARD H. SIEGAN, OBERT C. TANNER, STROM THURMOND, RONALD H. WALKER, CHARLES E. WIGGINS, CHARLES ALAN WRIGHT
Staff Director	HERBERT M. ATHERTON

[For the Commission on the Bicentennial of the United States Constitution statement of organization, see the *Code of Federal Regulations,* Title 45, Part 2000]

The Commission on the Bicentennial of the United States Constitution promotes, coordinates, and develops activities to commemorate the bicentennial of the Constitution, which was adopted at the Constitutional Convention on September 17, 1787.

The Commission was established by act of September 29, 1983 (97 Stat. 719), and extended through 1991 by Congress (100 Stat. 3063). The Commission is composed of 23 members, 20 of whom are appointed by the President. The

Chief Justice of the United States, the President pro tempore of the Senate, and the Speaker of the House of Representatives, or their designees, are also members. The Chairman is designated by the President.

One of the chief responsibilities of the Commission is to encourage private organizations and State and local governments to organize and participate in bicentennial activities that commemorate and examine the drafting, ratification, and history of the Constitution.

The Commission seeks cooperation, advice, and assistance from both private and governmental agencies and organizations in carrying out its responsibilities and also delegates authority to State advisory commissions to assist in this effort. Additionally, the Commission serves as a clearinghouse for the collection and dissemination of information about bicentennial events and plans.

The celebration of the 200th anniversary of the Constitution will continue through 1991. Every State, city, town, organization, family, and individual in the Nation will be invited to participate, and each community will be encouraged to conduct its own commemoration.

For further information, contact the Commission on the Bicentennial of the United States Constitution, 808 Seventeenth Street NW., Washington, DC 20006. Phone, 202–USA–1787.

COMMISSION ON CIVIL RIGHTS

1121 Vermont Avenue NW., Washington, DC 20425
Phone, 202–376–8177

Chairman	Arthur A. Fletcher
Vice Chairman	Charles Pei Wang
Commissioners	William B. Allen, Carl A. Anderson, Mary Frances Berry, Esther G. Buckley, Blandina C. Ramirez, Russell Redenbaugh
Staff Director	Wilfredo J. Gonzalez
General Counsel	Carol McCabe Booker
Solicitor	Emma Monroig
Assistant Staff Director for Programs, Policy and Research	James S. Cunningham
Chief, Civil Rights Evaluation	James S. Cunningham, *Acting*
Assistant Staff Director for Management	(vacancy)
Director, Congressional and Public Affairs	Barbara Brooks
Chief, Regional Programs Coordination	Carol-Lee Hurley
Director, Eastern Regional Division	John I. Binkley
Director, Central Regional Division	Melvin L. Jenkins
Director, Midwestern Regional Division	Constance D. Davis
Director, Rocky Mountain Regional Division	William Muldrow

Director, Southern Regional Division	BOBBY DOCTOR
Director, Western Regional Division	PHILIP MONTEZ

[For the Commission on Civil Rights statement of organization, see the *Code of Federal Regulations*, Title 45, Part 701]

The Commission on Civil Rights collects and studies information on discrimination or denials of equal protection of the laws because of race, color, religion, sex, age, handicap, national origin, or in the administration of justice in such areas as voting rights, enforcement of Federal civil rights laws, and equality of opportunity in education, employment, and housing.

The Commission on Civil Rights was first created by the Civil Rights Act of 1957, as amended, and reestablished by the United States Commission on Civil Rights Act of 1983, as amended (42 U.S.C. 1975).

Activities

The Commission makes findings of fact but has no enforcement authority. Findings and recommendations are submitted to the President and Congress, and many of the Commission's recommendations have been enacted, either by statute, Executive order, or regulation. The Commission evaluates Federal laws and the effectiveness of Government equal opportunity programs. It also serves as a national clearinghouse for civil rights information.

Regional Programs The Commission maintains six regional divisions.

Regional Divisions—Commission on Civil Rights

Region/Address	Telephone
Central—Rm. 3103, 911 Walnut St., Kansas City, MO 64106	816-426-5253
Eastern—Rm. 710, 1121 Vermont Ave. NW., Washington, DC 20425	202-523-5264
Midwestern—Suite A-1331, 175 W. Jackson St., Chicago, IL 60604	312-353-8311
Rocky Mountain—P.O. Drawer 3584, Suite 1366, 1961 Stout St., Denver, CO 80294	303-844-6716
Southern—Rm. 2402, 101 Marietta St., Atlanta, GA 30303	404-730-2476
Western—Rm. 810, 3660 Wilshire Blvd., Los Angeles, CA 90010	213-894-3437

Sources of Information

Complaints Complaints alleging denials of civil rights may be reported to Complaints Referral, 1121 Vermont Avenue NW., Washington, DC 20425. Phone, 202-376-8513; 800-552-6843 (toll-free).

Employment Personnel Office, Room 600, 1121 Vermont Avenue NW., Washington, DC 20425. Phone, 202-376-8364.

Publications Commission publications are made available on request from the Administrative Services and Clearinghouse Division, Room 600, 1121 Vermont Avenue NW., Washington, DC 20425. Phone, 202-376-8105. A catalog of publications may be obtained from this office.

Reading Room The National Civil Rights Clearinghouse Library is located in Room 709, 1121 Vermont Avenue NW., Washington, DC 20425. Phone, 202-376-8110.

For further information, contact the Congressional and Public Affairs Unit, Commission on Civil Rights, 1121 Vermont Avenue NW., Washington, DC 20425. Phone, 202-376-8312; hearing-impaired (TTY), 202-376-8116 .

COMMODITY FUTURES TRADING COMMISSION

2033 K Street NW., Washington, DC 20581
Phone, 202–254–6387

Chairman	WENDY L. GRAMM
Commissioners	JOSEPH B. DIAL
	FOWLER C. WEST
	WILLIAM P. ALBRECHT
	SHELIA C. BAIR
General Counsel	JOANNE T. MEDERO
Executive Director	EWEN M. WILSON

[For the Commodity Futures Trading Commission statement of organization, see the *Code of Federal Regulations*, Title 17, Part 140]

The Commodity Futures Trading Commission promotes healthy economic growth, protects the rights of customers, and ensures fairness and integrity in the marketplace through regulation of futures trading. To this end it also engages in the analysis of economic issues affected by or affecting futures trading.

The Commodity Futures Trading Commission, the Federal regulatory agency for futures trading, was established by the Commodity Futures Trading Commission Act of 1974 (7 U.S.C. 4a). The Commission began operation in April 1975, and its authority to regulate futures trading was renewed by Congress in 1978, 1982, and 1986.

The Commission consists of five Commissioners who are appointed by the President with the advice and consent of the Senate. One Commissioner is designated by the President to serve as Chairman. The Commissioners serve staggered 5-year terms, and by law no more than three Commissioners can belong to the same political party.

There exist five major operating components in the Commission: the divisions of enforcement, economic analysis, trading and markets, and the offices of the executive director and the general counsel.

Activities

The Commission regulates trading on the 14 U.S. futures exchanges, which offer active futures and options contracts. It also regulates the activities of numerous commodity exchange members, public brokerage houses (futures commission merchants), Commission-registered futures industry salespeople and associated persons, commodity trading advisers, and commodity pool operators. Some off-exchange transactions involving instruments similar in nature to futures contracts also fall under Commission jurisdiction.

The Commission's regulatory and enforcement efforts are designed to ensure that the futures trading process is fair and that it protects both the rights of customers and the financial integrity of the marketplace. It approves the rules under which an exchange proposes to operate and monitors exchange enforcement of those rules. It reviews the terms of proposed futures contracts, and registers companies and individuals who handle customer funds or give trading advice. The Commission also protects the public by enforcing rules that require that customer funds be kept in bank accounts separate from accounts maintained by firms for their own use, and that such customer accounts be marked to present market value at the close of trading each day.

Futures contracts for agricultural commodities were traded in the United States for more than 100 years before

COMMODITY FUTURES TRADING COMMISSION

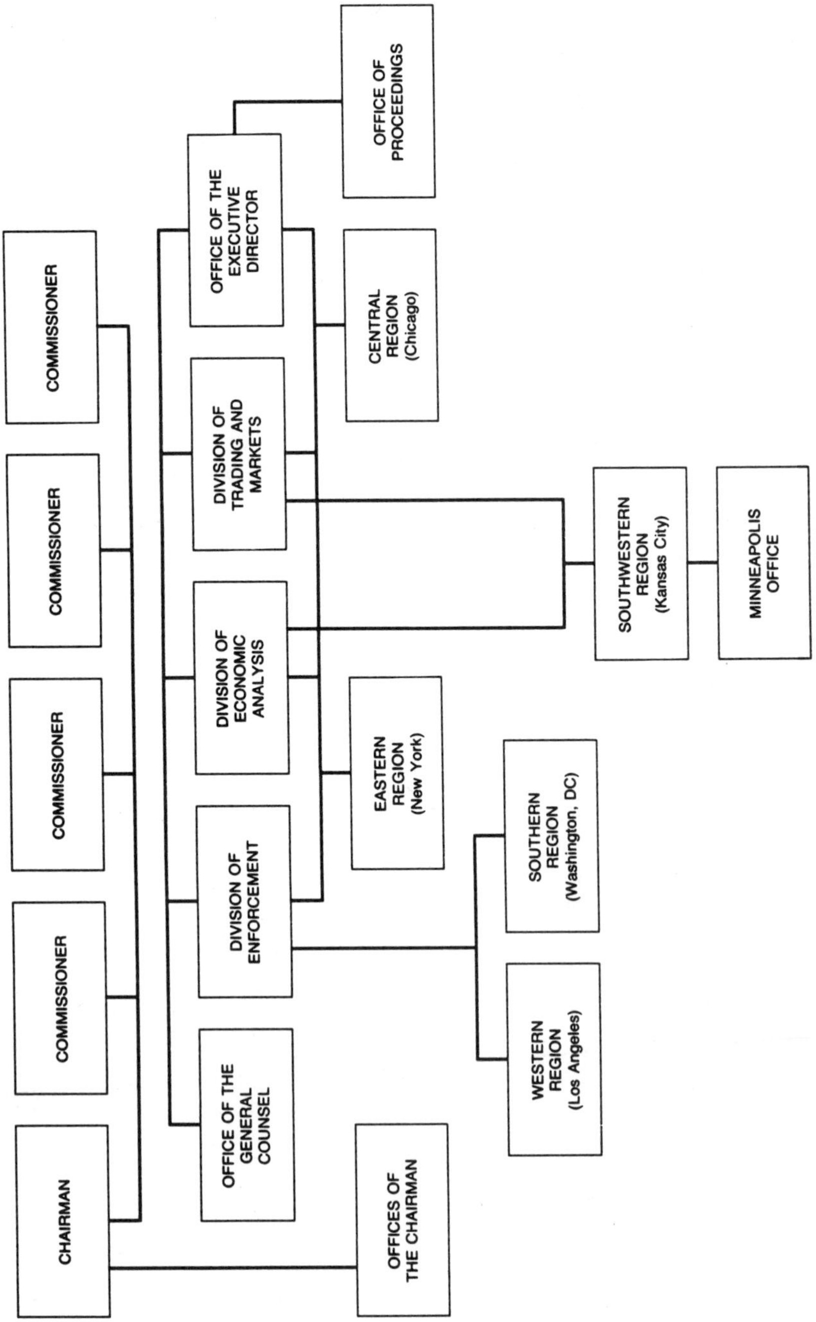

futures trading was diversified to include trading in contracts for precious metals, raw materials, foreign currencies, commercial interest rates, and U.S. Government and mortgage securities. Contract diversification has grown in exchange trading in both traditional and newer commodities.

Large regional offices are maintained in Chicago, IL, and New York, NY, where many of the Nation's futures exchanges are located. Smaller regional offices are located in Kansas City, MO, and Los Angeles, CA. A suboffice of the Kansas City regional office is located in Minneapolis, MN.

For further information, contact the Office of Communication and Education Services, Commodity Futures Trading Commission, 2033 K Street NW., Washington, DC 20581. Phone, 202–254–8630.

CONSUMER PRODUCT SAFETY COMMISSION

5401 Westbard Avenue, Bethesda, MD 20207
Phone, 301–492–6580

Chairman	JACQUELINE JONES-SMITH
Commissioners	CAROL G. DAWSON
	ANNE GRAHAM
	(2 VACANCIES)
General Counsel	CLEMENT D. ERHARDT III
Director, Office of Congressional Relations	EDWARD D. HARRILL
Director, Office of the Secretary	SADYE E. DUNN
Freedom of Information Officer	TODD A. STEVENSON
Director, Office of Equal Employment Opportunity and Minority Enterprise	JOHN W. BARRETT, JR.
Executive Director	ERIC C. PETERSON
Deputy Executive Director	THOMAS W. MURR, JR.
Inspector General	THOMAS F. STEIN
Director, Office of Planning and Evaluation	NICHOLAS V. MARCHICA
Director, Office of Information and Public Affairs	DANIEL L. RUMELT, *Acting*
Director, Office of the Budget	EDWARD E. QUIST
Associate Executive Director for Administration	MAUNA V. KAMMER, *Acting*
Associate Executive Director for Field Operations	ALFRED L. ROMA
Assistant Executive Director for Compliance and Enforcement	DAVID SCHMELTZER
Assistant Executive Director for Hazard Identification and Reduction	DOUGLAS L. NOBLE
Associate Executive Director for Engineering Sciences	WILLIAM W. WALTON, JR.
Associate Executive Director for Health Sciences	ANDREW G. ULSAMER

Associate Executive Director for Epidemiology	ROBERT D. VERHALEN
Director, National Injury Clearinghouse	JOEL I. FRIEDMAN
Associate Executive Director for Economic Analysis	WARREN J. PRUNELLA

[For the Consumer Product Safety Commission statement of organization, see the *Code of Federal Regulations,* Title 16, Part 1000]

The Consumer Product Safety Commission protects the public against unreasonable risks of injury from consumer products; assists consumers in evaluating the comparative safety of consumer products; develops uniform safety standards for consumer products and minimizes conflicting State and local regulations; and promotes research and investigation into the causes and prevention of product-related deaths, illnesses, and injuries.

The Consumer Product Safety Commission is an independent Federal regulatory agency established by the Consumer Product Safety Act (15 U.S.C. 2051).

In addition to the authority created by the Consumer Product Safety Act, the Commission has responsibility for implementing provisions of the Flammable Fabrics Act (15 U.S.C. 1191), the Poison Prevention Packaging Act of 1970 (15 U.S.C. 1471), the Federal Hazardous Substances Act (15 U.S.C. 1261), and the act of August 2, 1956 (15 U.S.C. 1211), which prohibits the transportation of refrigerators without door safety devices.

Activities

To help protect the public from unreasonable risks of injury associated with consumer products, the Commission:

—requires manufacturers to report defects in products that could create substantial hazards;

—requires, where appropriate, corrective action with respect to specific substantially hazardous consumer products already in commerce;

—collects information on consumer product-related injuries and maintains a comprehensive Injury Information Clearinghouse;

—conducts research on consumer product hazards;

—encourages and assists in the development of voluntary standards related to the safety of consumer products;

—establishes, where appropriate, mandatory consumer product standards;

—bans, where appropriate, hazardous consumer products; and

—conducts outreach programs for consumers, industry, and local governments.

Offices

The Consumer Product Safety Commission headquarters is located at 5401 Westbard Avenue, Bethesda, MD 20207. Regional offices are located in Chicago, IL; New York, NY; and San Francisco, CA. Field offices are maintained in various cities.

Sources of Information

Consumer Information The Commission operates a toll-free Consumer Product Safety Hotline, 800-638-CPSC, and a teletypewriter for the hearing-impaired, 800-638-8270 (in Maryland only, 800-492-8104).

General Inquiries Information on Commission activities may be obtained from the Office of Information and Public Affairs, Consumer Product Safety Commission, Washington, DC 20207. Phone, 301-492-6580.

Reading Room A public reading room is maintained in the Office of the Secretary.

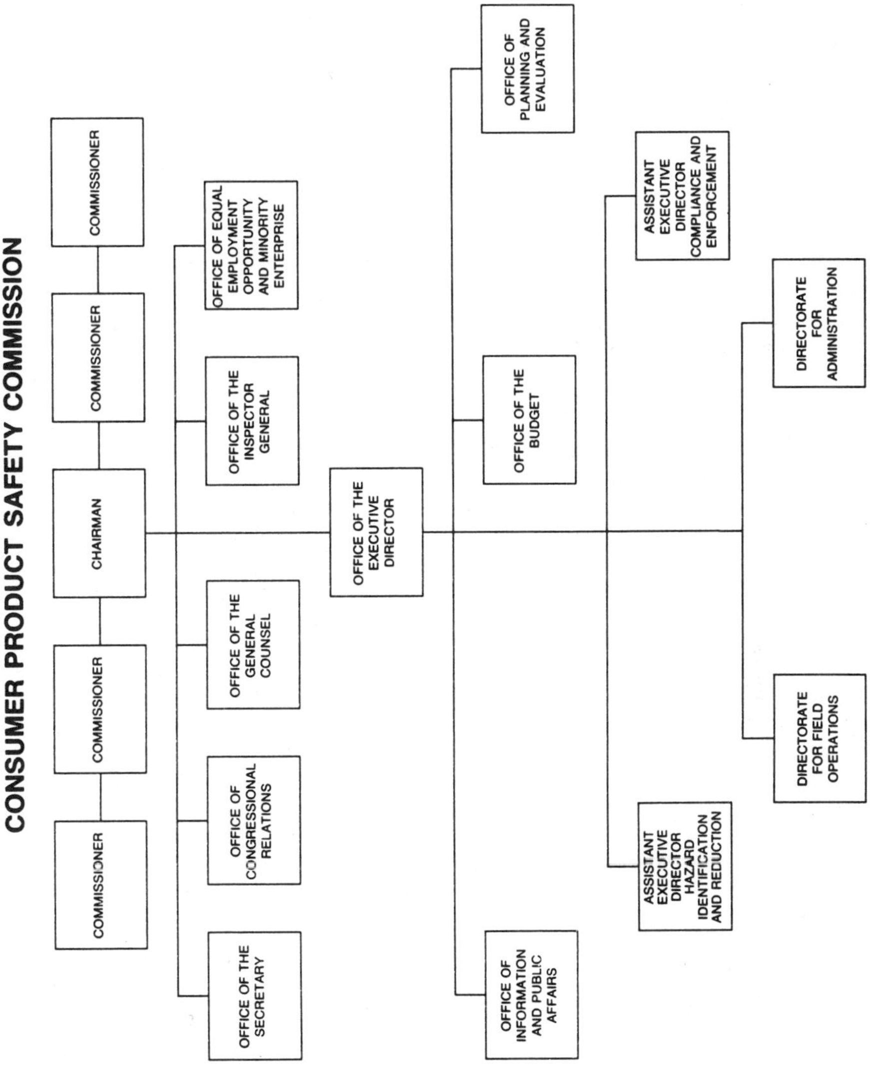
CONSUMER PRODUCT SAFETY COMMISSION
COMMISSIONER
COMMISSIONER
CHAIRMAN
COMMISSIONER
COMMISSIONER
OFFICE OF THE SECRETARY
OFFICE OF CONGRESSIONAL RELATIONS
OFFICE OF THE GENERAL COUNSEL
OFFICE OF THE INSPECTOR GENERAL
OFFICE OF EQUAL EMPLOYMENT OPPORTUNITY AND MINORITY ENTERPRISE
OFFICE OF THE EXECUTIVE DIRECTOR
OFFICE OF INFORMATION AND PUBLIC AFFAIRS
OFFICE OF THE BUDGET
OFFICE OF PLANNING AND EVALUATION
ASSISTANT EXECUTIVE DIRECTOR HAZARD IDENTIFICATION AND REDUCTION
ASSISTANT EXECUTIVE DIRECTOR COMPLIANCE AND ENFORCEMENT
DIRECTORATE FOR FIELD OPERATIONS
DIRECTORATE FOR ADMINISTRATION

For further information, contact the Office of Information and Public Affairs, Consumer Product Safety Commission, 5401 Westbard Avenue, Bethesda, MD, 20207. Phone, 301–492–6580.

DEFENSE NUCLEAR FACILITIES SAFETY BOARD

Suite 700, 625 Indiana Avenue NW., Washington, DC 20004
Phone, 202–208–6400

Chairman	JOHN T. CONWAY
Vice Chairman	A.J. EGGENBERGER
Members	EDSON G. CASE
	JOHN W. CRAWFORD, JR.
	HERBERT J.C. KOUTS
General Counsel	ROBERT M. ANDERSEN
General Manager	KENNETH M. PUSATERI
Technical Director	GEORGE W. CUNNINGHAM

The Defense Nuclear Facilities Safety Board reviews and evalutes the content and implementation of standards relating to the design, construction, operation, and decommissioning of defense nuclear facilities of the Department of Energy (DOE).

The Defense Nuclear Facilities Safety Board was established as an independent agency on September 29, 1988, by the Atomic Energy Act of 1954, as amended (42 U.S.C. 2286–2286i).

The Board is composed of five members appointed by the President, with the advice and consent of the Senate, from among United States citizens who are respected experts in the field of nuclear safety.

Activities

The Defense Nuclear Facilities Safety Board reviews and evaluates the content and implementation of standards for defense nuclear facilities of DOE; investigates any event or practice at these facilities which may adversely affect public health and safety; and reviews and monitors the design, construction, and operation of facilities. The Board makes recommendations to the Secretary of Energy concerning DOE defense nuclear facilities to ensure adequate protection of public health and safety. In the event that any aspect of operations, practices, or occurrences reviewed by the Board is determined to present an imminent or severe threat to public health and safety, the Board transmits its recommendations directly to the President.

For further information, contact the Defense Nuclear Facilities Safety Board, Suite 700, 625 Indiana Avenue NW., Washington, DC 20004. Phone, 202–208–6400.

ENVIRONMENTAL PROTECTION AGENCY

401 M Street SW., Washington, DC 20460
Phone, 202–382–2090

Administrator	WILLIAM K. REILLY
Deputy Administrator	F. HENRY HABICHT II
Staff Offices:	
Associate Administrator for Regional Operations and State/Local Relations	THOMAS DUNNE, *Acting*

Associate Administrator for Communications and Public Affairs	LEWIS P. CRAMPTON
Associate Administrator for Congressional and Legislative Affairs	PATRICK H. QUINN
Director, Office of Executive Support	DIANE N. BAZZLE
Chief, Office of Administrative Law Judges	HENRY FRAZIER III
Director, Office of Civil Rights	NATHANIEL SCURRY
Director, Office of Small and Disadvantaged Business Utilization	JOHN M. ROPES
Director, Science Advisory Board	DONALD G. BARNES
Program Offices:	
Assistant Administrator for Administration and Resources Management	CHARLES GRIZZLE
Deputy Assistant Administrator for Administration and Resources Management	EDWARD J. HANLEY
Associate Assistant Administrator for Administration and Resources Management	KELLY SINCLAIR
Director, Office of the Comptroller	DAVID P. RYAN
Director, Office of Human Resources Management	KENNETH F. DAWSEY
Director, Office of Administration	JOHN C. CHAMBERLIN
Director, Office of Information Resources Management	ALVIN M. PESACHOWITZ
Director, Office of Administration and Resources Management—Research Triangle Park, NC	WILLIS GREENSTREET
Director, Office of Administration—Cincinnati, OH	WILLIAM HENDERSON
Assistant Administrator for Enforcement	RAY LUDWISZEWSKI
Deputy Assistant Administrator—Civil	EDWARD REICH
Deputy Assistant Administrator—Criminal	ALBERICO PASQUALE, *Acting*
Director, Resource Conservation and Recovery Act Enforcement Division	KATHY STEIN
Director, Superfund Enforcement Division	WILLIAM WHITE, *Acting*
Associate Enforcement Counsel, Air Enforcement Division	MICHAEL S. ALUSHIN
Associate Enforcement Counsel, Water Enforcement Division	FREDERICK F. STIEHL
Associate Enforcement Counsel, Pesticides and Toxic Substances Enforcement Division	MICHAEL S. WALKER
Director, National Enforcement Investigations Center—Denver, CO	FRANK COVINGTON
General Counsel	E. DONALD ELLIOTT
Deputy General Counsel	GERALD H. YAMADA
Assistant Administrator for Policy, Planning and Evaluation	J. CLARENCE DAVIES
Deputy Assistant Administrator for Policy, Planning and Evaluation	DAN BEARDSLEY
Director, Office of Policy Analysis	RICHARD D. MORGENSTERN

Director, Office of Pollution Prevention	Stanley L. Laskowski
Director, Office of Regulatory Management and Evaluation	Thomas E. Kelley
Inspector General	John C. Martin
Deputy Inspector General	Anna H. Virbick
Assistant Inspector General, Office of Audit	Kenneth A. Konz
Deputy Assistant Inspector General, Office of Audit	James O. Rauch, *Acting*
Assistant Inspector General, Office of Investigations	John E. Barden
Deputy Assistant Inspector General, Office of Investigations	Daniel S. Sweeney
Assistant Inspector General, Office of Management and Technical Assessment	John C. Jones
Assistant Administrator for Water	Lajuana Wilcher
Deputy Assistant Administrator for Water	Martha G. Prothro
Director, Office of Ground Water and Drinking Water	James Elder
Director, Office of Wastewater Enforcement and Compliance	Michael Cook
Director, Office of Science and Technology	Tudor T. Davies
Director, Office of Wetlands, Oceans and Watersheds	Robert Wayland
Assistant Administrator for Solid Waste and Emergency Response	Don R. Clay
Deputy Assistant Administrator for Solid Waste and Emergency Response	Henry L. Longest II, *Acting*
Director, Office of Solid Waste	Sylvia Lowrance
Director, Office of Emergency and Remedial Response	Timothy Fields, Jr.
Director, Office of Waste Programs Enforcement	Bruce Diamond
Director, Office of Underground Storage Tanks	David Ziegele, *Acting*
Assistant Administrator for Air and Radiation	William G. Rosenberg
Deputy Assistant Administrator for Air and Radiation	Michael H. Shapiro
Director, Office of Air Quality Planning and Standards	John Seitz
Director, Office of Mobile Sources	Richard D. Wilson
Director, Office of Radiation Programs	Richard J. Guimond
Assistant Administrator for Pesticides and Toxic Substances	Linda Fisher
Deputy Assistant Administrator for Pesticides and Toxic Substances	Victor Kimm
Director, Office of Pesticide Programs	Douglas D. Campt
Director, Office of Toxic Substances	Mark Greenwood
Director, Office of Compliance Monitoring	Connie Musgrove, *Acting*
Assistant Administrator for Research and Development	David Kleffman
Deputy Assistant Administrator for Research and Development	John Skinner, *Acting*
Director, Office of Technology Transfer and Regulatory Support	Peter Preuss

Director, Office of Research Program Management	CLARENCE MAHAN
Director, Office of Exploratory Research	ROGER S. CORTESI
Director, Office of Environmental Engineering and Technology Demonstration	ALFRED LINDSEY
Director, Office of Environmental Processes and Effects Research	COURTNEY RIORDAN
Director, Office of Modeling, Monitoring Systems, and Quality Assurance	RICK LINTHURST
Director, Office of Health Research	KEN SEXTON
Director, Office of Health and Environmental Assessment	WILLIAM H. FARLAND

[For the Environmental Protection Agency statement of organization, see the *Code of Federal Regulations,* Title 40, Part 1]

The Environmental Protection Agency protects and enhances our environment today and for future generations to the fullest extent possible under the laws enacted by Congress. The Agency's mission is to control and abate pollution in the areas of air, water, solid waste, pesticides, radiation, and toxic substances. Its mandate is to mount an integrated, coordinated attack on environmental pollution in cooperation with State and local governments.

The Environmental Protection Agency was established in the executive branch as an independent agency pursuant to Reorganization Plan No. 3 of 1970 (5 U.S.C. app.), effective December 2, 1970.

The Environmental Protection Agency was created to permit coordinated and effective governmental action on behalf of the environment. It endeavors to abate and control pollution systematically, by proper integration of a variety of research, monitoring, standard setting, and enforcement activities. As a complement to its other activities, the Agency coordinates and supports research and antipollution activities by State and local governments, private and public groups, individuals, and educational institutions. It also reinforces efforts among other Federal agencies with respect to the impact of their operations on the environment, and it is specifically charged with publishing its determinations when those hold that a proposal is unsatisfactory from the standpoint of public health or welfare or environmental quality. In all, the Environmental Protection Agency is designed to serve as the public's advocate for a livable environment.

Activities

Air and Radiation The air activities of the Agency include:

—development of national programs, technical policies, and regulations for air pollution control;

—enforcement of standards;

—development of national standards for air quality, emission standards for new stationary and mobile sources, and emission standards for hazardous pollutants;

—technical direction, support, and evaluation of regional air activities; and

—provision of training in the field of air pollution control.

Related activities include technical assistance to States and agencies having radiation protection programs, including radon mitigation programs; a national surveillance and inspection program for measuring radiation levels in the environment.

For further information, call 202–382–7400.

ENVIRONMENTAL PROTECTION AGENCY

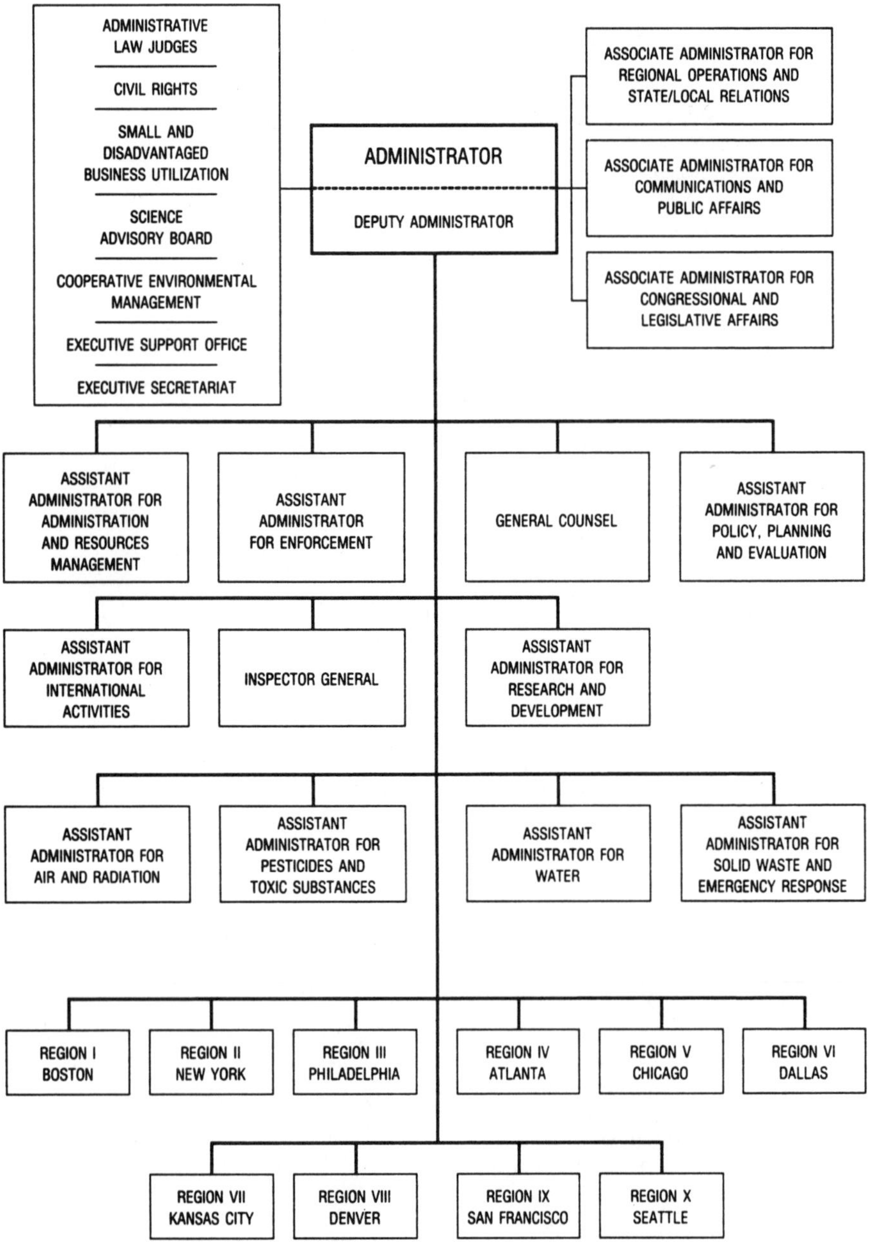

Water The Agency's water quality activities represent a coordinated effort to restore the Nation's waters. The functions of this program include:

—development of national programs, technical policies, and regulations for water pollution control and water supply;

—ground water protection;

—marine and estuarine protection;

—enforcement of standards;

—water quality standards and effluent guidelines development;

—technical direction, support, and evaluation of regional water activities;

—development of programs for technical assistance and technology transfer; and

—provision of training in the field of water quality.

For further information, call 202–382–5700.

Solid Waste and Emergency Response The Office of Solid Waste and Emergency Response provides policy, guidance, and direction for the Agency's hazardous waste and emergency response programs. The functions of these programs include:

—development of policies, standards, and regulations for hazardous waste treatment, storage, and disposal;

—national management of the Superfund toxic waste cleanup program;

—development of guidelines for the emergency preparedness and "Community Right to Know" programs;

—development of guidelines and standards for underground storage tanks;

—enforcement of applicable laws and regulations;

—analysis of technologies and methods for the recovery of useful energy from solid waste; and

—provision of technical assistance in the development, management, and operation of waste management activities.

For further information, call 202–382–4610.

Pesticides and Toxic Substances The Office of Pesticides and Toxic Substances is responsible for:

—developing national strategies for the control of toxic substances;

—directing the pesticides and toxic substances enforcement activities;

—developing criteria for assessing chemical substances, standards for test protocols for chemicals, rules and procedures for industry reporting and regulations for the control of substances deemed to be hazardous to man or the environment; and

—evaluating and assessing the impact of existing chemicals, new chemicals, and chemicals with new uses to determine the hazard and, if needed, develop appropriate restrictions.

Additional activities include:

—controlling and regulating pesticides and reducing their use to ensure human safety and protection of environmental quality;

—establishing tolerance levels for pesticides that occur in or on food;

—monitoring pesticide residue levels in food, humans, and nontarget fish and wildlife and their environments; and

—investigating pesticide accidents.

It also coordinates activities under its statutory responsibilities with other agencies for the assessment and control of toxic substances and pesticides.

For further information, call 202–382–2902.

Research and Development The Office of Research and Development is responsible for a national research program in pursuit of technological controls of all forms of pollution. It directly supervises the research activities of the Agency's national laboratories and gives technical policy direction to those laboratories that support the program responsibilities of the regional offices. Close coordination of the various research programs is designed to yield a synthesis of knowledge from the biological, physical, and social sciences that can be interpreted in terms of total human and environmental needs.

General functions include management of selected demonstration programs, planning for Agency environmental quality monitoring programs, coordination of Agency monitoring efforts with those of other Federal agencies, the States, and other public bodies, and dissemination of Agency research, development, and demonstration results.

For further information, call 202–382–7676.

Regional Offices

The Agency's 10 regional offices represent its commitment to the development of strong local programs for pollution abatement. The Regional Administrators are the Agency's principal representatives in the regions in contacts and relationships with Federal, State, interstate and local agencies, industry, academic institutions, and other public and private groups. They are responsible for accomplishing within their regions the national program objectives established by the Agency. They develop, propose, and implement an approved regional program for comprehensive and integrated environmental protection activities.

Regional Offices—Environmental Protection Agency

(Areas included within each region are indicated on the map in Appendix A.)

Region/Address	Administrator
I. Boston, MA (John F. Kennedy Federal Bldg., 02203)	Julie D. Belaga
II. New York, NY (26 Federal Plz., 10278)	Constantine Sidamon-Eristoff
III. Philadelphia, PA (841 Chestnut St., 19107)	Edwin B. Erickson
IV. Atlanta, GA (345 Courtland St. NE., 30365)	Greer C. Tidwell
V. Chicago, IL (230 S. Dearborn St., 60604)	Valdas V. Adamkus
VI. Dallas, TX (1445 Ross Ave., 75202)	Robert Layton
VII. Kansas City, KS (726 Minnesota Ave., 66101)	Morris Kay
VIII. Denver, CO (999 18th St., 80202)	James Scherer
IX. San Francisco, CA (1235 Mission St., 94103)	Daniel W. McGovern
X. Seattle, WA (1200 6th Ave., 98101)	Robie G. Russell

Sources of Information

Inquiries for information on the following subjects should be directed to the specified office of the Environmental Protection Agency, 401 M Street SW., Washington, DC 20460.

Contracts and Procurement Procurement and Contracts Management Division. Phone, 202–382–5020.

Employment Personnel Management Division. Phone, 202–382–3144.

Freedom of Information Act Requests Freedom of Information Officer. Phone, 202–382–4048.

Reading Room Information Management and Services Division. Phone, 202–382–5921. Public Reading Room—2430 Mall.

Telephone Directory Available for sale by the Superintendent of Documents, Government Printing Office, Washington, DC 20402.

For further information, contact the Office of Public Affairs, Environmental Protection Agency, 401 M Street SW., Washington, DC 20460 (phone, 202–382–4361); or write to the Public Information Office of the nearest regional office.

EQUAL EMPLOYMENT OPPORTUNITY COMMISSION

1801 L Street NW., Washington, DC 20507
Phones: 202–663–4900; 800–USA–EEOC (toll-free)

Chairman	EVAN J. KEMP, JR.
Chief of Staff	ROBERT J. FUNK
Special Assistant	KEN MASUGI
Attorney Advisors	SHERRY J. POWERS
	ISIAH SMITH
	PEGGY MASTROIANNI
Special Assistant	PHILIP LYONS

Executive Officer, Office of the Executive Secretariat	FRANCES HART
Vice Chairman	R. GAULL SILBERMAN
Special Assistants	GARY HOZEMPA
	SUSAN MURPHY
Commissioner	TONY E. GALLEGOS
Executive Assistant	MICHAEL BALDONADO
Special Assistant	GLADYS COLLAZO-VALENCIA
Commissioner	JOY CHERIAN
Executive Assistant	RAJ GUPTA
Special Assistant	BYRON SPEARS
Commissioner	JOYCE E. TUCKER
General Counsel	DONALD R. LIVINGSTON, *Acting*
Director, Office of Communications and Legislative Affairs	JAMES C. LAFFERTY
Director, Office of Equal Employment Opportunity	LOUIS W. JONES
Director, Legal Counsel	THOMASINA ROGERS
Director, Office of Management	R. EDISON ELKINS
Director, Office of Program Operations	JAMES TROY
Director, Office of Federal Operations	DOLORES L. ROZZI
Inspector General	WILLIAM D. MILLER

The purpose of the Equal Employment Opportunity Commission is to eliminate discrimination based on race, color, religion, sex, national origin, or age in hiring, promoting, firing, setting wages, testing, training, apprenticeship, and all other terms and conditions of employment. The Commission conducts investigations of alleged discrimination; makes determinations based on gathered evidence; attempts conciliation when reasonable allegations of discrimination has taken place; files lawsuits; and provides voluntary assistance programs for employers, unions, and community organizations. The Commission also has oversight responsibility for all compliance and enforcement activities relating to equal employment opportunity among Federal employees and applicants, including discrimination against individuals with disabilities.

The Equal Employment Opportunity Commission (EEOC) was created by title VII of the Civil Rights Act of 1964 (42 U.S.C. 2000e), and became operational July 2, 1965. Title VII was amended by the Equal Employment Opportunity Act of 1972 and the Pregnancy Discrimination Act of 1978 (42 U.S.C. 2000e).

Executive Order 12067 of June 30, 1978, abolished the Equal Employment Opportunity Coordinating Council and transferred its duties to the Commission with responsibility for providing coherence and direction to the Government's equal employment opportunity efforts. The same Executive order required that strong uniform enforcement standards be applied throughout the Government, and it provided for standardized data collection procedures and joint training programs, the sharing of enforcement-related data among agencies, and the development of methods and priorities for complaint and compliance reviews.

Reorganization Plan No. 1 of 1978 (5 U.S.C. app.) effective January 1, 1979, transferred Federal equal employment functions from the Civil Service Commission to the EEOC. Authorities for transferred functions include:

—section 717 of title VII (42 U.S.C. 2000e–16), which prohibits discrimination in employment in the

Federal Government on the basis of race, color, religion, sex, or national origin;

—Executive Order 11478 of August 8, 1969, which sets forth the U.S. policy of providing for equal employment opportunity in the Federal Government through affirmative action programs in Federal departments and agencies;

—the Equal Pay Act of 1963 (29 U.S.C. 206) in the Federal sector;

—the Age Discrimination in Employment Act of 1967, as amended (29 U.S.C. 621) in the Federal sector; and

—section 501 of the Rehabilitation Act of 1973 (29 U.S.C. 791), which pertains to employment discrimination against handicapped persons in the Federal Government.

On July 1, 1979, responsibility for enforcement—in private industry as well as in State and local governments—of the Equal Pay Act of 1963 and the Age Discrimination in Employment Act of 1967 was transferred from the Department of Labor to the Commission. The former act prohibits sex-based pay differences where substantially equal work performed in the same establishment under similar working conditions is of equal skill, effort, and responsibility, and the latter prohibits employment discrimination against workers or applicants 40 years of age or older. In addition to employers, the age discrimination act covers activities of employment agencies, and both acts cover activities of labor organizations.

The Americans with Disabilities Act of 1990 (42 U.S.C. 12101 *et seq.*) was approved on July 26, 1990. Title I of the act will be enforced by EEOC and becomes effective on July 26, 1992, and July 26, 1994, on a phase-in basis. Title I covers private employers, State and local governments, employment agencies, labor organizations, and joint labor-management committees. The act prohibits employment discrimination against qualified individuals with disabilities and requires that employers make reasonable allowances for their physical and mental limitations. These provisions are only relaxed when their enforcement would adversely affect the operations of a business.

The Americans with Disabilities Act of 1990 specifically incorporates the powers, remedies, and procedures contained in title VII of the Civil Rights Act of 1964. After July 26, 1992, employment discrimination charges based on disability may be filed at any of the Commission's field offices. The Commission will investigate and attempt to conciliate the charges using the same procedures it uses to investigate and conciliate charges filed under title VII. The litigation procedures under this title will also apply to charges filed under the act.

The Commission operates through 50 field offices, each of which processes complaints and performs various legal functions.

Activities

Enforcement The Commission's field offices receive written charges of job discrimination under title VII and the equal pay and age discrimination in employment acts. They also receive written or oral charges and complaints under the acts, and field offices may initiate investigations to find violations of the acts. Members of the Commission also may initiate charges alleging that a violation of title VII has occurred. Section 501 of the Rehabilitation Act of 1973 covers Federal employees and applicants only.

Charges Under Title VII Title VII prohibits employment discrimination based on race, color, religion, sex, or national origin by private employers, State and local governments, and educational institutions with 15 or more employees, or by the Federal Government, private and public employment agencies, labor organizations, and joint labor-management committees for apprenticeship and training.

Charges of title VII violations outside of the Federal sector must be filed with the Commission within 180 days of the alleged violation (or up to 300 days in a State or locality in which a fair employment practices agency is located), and the Commission is responsible for notifying persons so charged within 10 days of the receipt of a new charge. Before investigation, charges must be deferred for 60 days to a State or local fair employment practices agency in States and municipalities where an enforceable fair employment practices law exists. The deferral period is 120 days if the agency has been operating less than 1 year. Under worksharing agreements executed between the Commission and State and local fair employment practices agencies, the Commission routinely will assume jurisdiction over certain charges of discrimination and proceed with its investigation rather than wait for the expiration of the deferral period.

If there is reasonable cause to believe the charge is true, the district, area, or local office attempts to remedy the alleged unlawful practices through informal methods of conciliation, conference, and persuasion. If an acceptable conciliation agreement is not secured, the case is submitted to the Commission for possible litigation. If litigation is approved, the Commission will bring suit in an appropriate Federal district court.

Under title VII, the Attorney General brings suit when a State or local government, or political subdivision is involved. If the Commission or the Attorney General does not approve litigation or if a finding of no reasonable cause is made, at the conclusion of the administrative procedures (or earlier at the request of the charging party) a Notice of Right-to-Sue is issued that allows the charging party to proceed within 90 days in a Federal district court. In appropriate cases, the Commission may intervene in such civil action if the case is of general public interest. The investigation and conciliation of charges having an industrywide or national impact are coordinated or conducted by Systemic Investigations and Individual Compliance Programs, Office of Program Operations.

Under the provisions of title VII, section 706(f)(2), as amended by section 4 of the Equal Employment Opportunity Act of 1972 (42 U.S.C. 2000e-5), if it is concluded after a preliminary investigation that prompt judicial action is necessary to carry out the purposes of the act, the Commission or the Attorney General, in a case involving a State or local government, governmental agency or political subdivision, may bring an action for appropriate temporary or preliminary relief pending final disposition of a charge.

Age Discrimination in Employment or Equal Pay Act Complaints The age discrimination in employment and equal pay acts cover most employees and job applicants in private industry and Federal, State, and local governments.

An age discrimination charge must be filed with the Commission within 180 days of the alleged violation or, in a case where the alleged discriminatory action took place in a State which has its own age discrimination law and authority administering that law, within 300 days of the alleged violation or 30 days after the receipt of a notice of termination of State proceedings, whichever is earlier. A lawsuit must be filed within 2 years of the discriminatory act or 3 years in cases of a willful violation of the law. The Commission will attempt to eliminate the unlawful practice through informal methods of conciliation, conference, and persuasion. A lawsuit may be brought by the Commission if conciliation fails, or individuals may file suit on their own behalf 60 days after filing a charge with the Commission and the appropriate State agency. Should the Commission take legal action, an individual covered by such action may not file a private suit. If an individual files a complaint of age discrimination, his or her name will be kept confidential, but the individual filing the complaint cannot bring a private suit unless he or she elects to file a charge first in accordance with the above requirements. If the Commission determines there is no reasonable cause to believe the charge or complaint is true, the charging party has the right to request a review of the determination.

A lawsuit under the Equal Pay Act of 1963 may be filed by the Commission or by the complainants. There are no prerequisites to individual actions under this law. Back wages can be recovered for a period of up to 2 years prior to the filing of a suit, except in the case of willful violation, where 3 years backpay may be recovered. The name of the individual filing the complaint may be kept confidential at the administrative level.

Complaints Against the Federal Government The administrative processing of Federal sector discrimination complaints is governed by Commission regulations in part 1613 of title 29 of the *Code of Federal Regulations.* Federal employees or job applicants who want to file complaints of job discrimination based on race, color, national origin, sex, religion, age, or physical or mental handicap must first consult an equal employment opportunity counselor within their agency within 30 calendar days of the alleged discriminatory event or the effective date of the alleged discriminatory personnel action. If the complaint cannot be resolved informally, the person may file a formal complaint within 15 calendar days after the date of receipt of the notice of the right to file a complaint.

An accepted complaint is investigated by the Agency and there is a right to a hearing before an EEOC administrative judge before the Agency issues its final decision. An individual who wishes to file a complaint under the Equal Pay Act of 1963 need not follow these procedures. Such complaints may be filed directly with the Commission—within 2 years of the alleged violation—and can be kept confidential. An individual may also elect to file suit under the Equal Pay Act of 1963 without prior resort to the agency or to the Commission.

A complaint under the Age Discrimination in Employment Act of 1967 against a Federal agency or department must be filed with the head of the agency, director of equal employment opportunity, head of a field installation, or such other officials as the agency may designate. Federal-sector age discrimination complainants may bypass the administrative complaint process and file a civil action directly in a U.S. district court by first notifying the Commission within 180 calendar days of the alleged discriminatory act and thereafter waiting 30 calendar days before filing suit.

Federal employees may file appeals of final agency decisions or decisions of an arbitrator or the Federal Labor Relations Authority with the Commission's Office of Federal Operations at any time up to 20 calendar days after receipt of the agency notice of final decision. A petition for review of a Merit Systems Protection Board decision may be filed within 30 days of the date that the Board decision becomes final. A request for reopening and reconsideration of any decision of the Commission should be made in writing within 30 days of receipt of such decision. Office of Federal Operations decisions are issued in writing to the complainant, complainant's representative, and the agency. The Office monitors and ensures compliance by Federal agencies with Commission orders and appellate decisions, and provides technical assistance and training to other Federal agencies.

The Commission also publishes data on the employment and status of minorities and women. Using employers' surveys, it tabulates and stores data on the ethnic, racial, and gender characteristics of employees. Research information is made available for use by Federal agencies and the public.

Other Activities A distinct activity of the Commission is the Voluntary Assistance Program. This outreach program is designed to provide educational and technical assistance to small and midsize employers and unions—through 1-day seminars on equal employment opportunity laws—about their rights and obligations under all the statutes that the Commission enforces.

Another activity initiated by the Commission is the Expanded Presence Program, which is designed to make the Commission accessible in areas identified as underserved by Commission offices. The district offices send contact teams to these sites on a rotating basis to provide information to the public regarding their rights and responsibilities under the laws enforced by the Commission.

The Commission also provides assistance and guidance to Federal agencies in processing complaints and in resolving disputes. In addition to conducting on-site consultations, EEOC co-hosts an annual Federal Dispute Resolution Conference which provides a forum for Federal agencies to meet and exchange ideas on resolving disputes.

The Commission participates in the development of the employment discrimination law through the issuance of guidelines, publication of significant Commission decisions, and involvement in litigation brought under title VII and related statutes, and the Equal Pay Act of 1963 and the Age Discrimination in Employment Act of 1967.

The Commission has direct liaison with Federal, State, and local governments, employers and union organizations, trade associations, civil rights organizations, and other agencies and organizations concerned with employment of minority group members and women. The Commission engages in and contributes to the cost of research and other mutual interest projects with State and local agencies charged with the administration of fair employment practices laws. Furthermore, the Commission enters into contracts and worksharing agreements with the State and local agencies in order to avoid duplication of effort by identifying specific charges to be investigated by the respective agencies.

The Commission is also a major publisher of data on the employment status of minorities and women. Through six employment surveys (EEO–1 through EEO–6) covering private employers, apprenticeship programs, labor unions, State and local governments, elementary and secondary schools, and colleges and universities, the Commission tabulates and stores data on the ethnic, racial, and sex characteristics of employees at all job levels within the reported groups.

Research information thus collected is shared with selected Federal agencies, such as the Department of Health and Human Services, the Department of Labor, and others. It is also made available, in appropriate form, for public use.

Field Offices—Equal Employment Opportunity Commission

(DO: District Office; AO: Area Office; LO: Local Office; FO: Field Office)

Office	Address	Director	Telephone
Albuquerque, NM (AO)	Suite 1105, 505 Marquette NW., 87102	Andrew Lopez	505–766–2061
Atlanta, GA (DO)	Suite 1100, 75 Piedmont Ave., NE., 30335	Harris A. Williams	404–331–6093
Baltimore, MD (DO)	Suite 4000, 111 Market Pl., 21202	Chris Roggerson	301–962–3932
Birmingham, AL (DO)	Suite 101, 1900 3d Ave. N., 35203	Warren Bullock	205–731–0082
Boston, MA (AO)	Rm. 100, 10th Fl., 1 Congress St., 02114	Charles L. Looney	617–565–3200
Buffalo, NY (LO)	Rm. 301, 28 Church St., 14202	Jon Patterson	716–846–4441
Charlotte, NC (DO)	5500 Central Ave., 28212	Curtiss Todd, *Acting*	704–567–7100
Chicago, IL (DO)	Rm. 930-A, 536 S. Clark St., 60605	John Rowe	312–353–2713
Cincinnati, OH (AO)	Rm. 7015, 550 Main St., 45202	Earl Haley	513–684–2851
Cleveland, OH (DO)	Rm. 600, 1375 Euclid Ave., 44115	Harold Ferguson	216–522–2001
Dallas, TX (DO)	8303 Elmbrook Dr., 75247	Jacqueline Bradley	214–767–7015
Denver, CO (DO)	2d Fl., 1845 Sherman St., 80203	Francisco J. Flores	303–866–1300
Detroit, MI (DO)	Rm. 1540, 477 Michigan Ave., 48226	A. William Schukar	313–226–7636
El Paso, TX (LO)	Suite 100, Bldg. C, The Commons, 79902	Eliazar Salinas	915–534–6550
Fresno, CA (LO)	Suite 103, 1313 P St., 93721	David Rodriguez	209–487–5793
Greensboro, NC (LO)	Rm. B-27, 324 W. Market St., 27402	Daisy Crenshaw	919–333–5174
Greenville, SC (LO)	Suite B41, 300 E. Washington St., 29601	Joseph M. D'Arcangelo	803–233–1791
Honolulu, HI (LO)	Suite 404, 677 Ala Moana Blvd., 96813	Linda K. Kreis	808–541–3120
Houston, TX (DO)	7th Fl., 1919 Smith St., 77002	Harriet J. Ehrlich	713–653–3320
Indianapolis, IN (DO)	Rm. 456, 46 E. Ohio St., 46204	Thomas P. Hadfield	317–226–7212
Jackson, MS (AO)	207 W. Amite St., 39269	Henrene P. Matthews	601–965–4537
Kansas City, MO (AO)	10th Fl., 911 Walnut, 64106	Joseph P. Doherty	816–426–5773
Little Rock, AR (AO)	Suite 621, 320 W. Capitol Ave., 72201	W.P. Brown	501–378–5060
Los Angeles, CA (DO)	5th Fl., 3660 Wilshire Blvd., 90010	Dorothy Porter	213–251–7278
Louisville, KY (AO)	Rm. 613, 601 W. Broadway, 40202	Clifford J. Johnson	502–582–6082
Memphis, TN (DO)	Suite 621, 1407 Union Ave., 38104	Walter Grabon	901–722–2617
Miami, FL (DO)	6th Fl., 1 NE. 1st St., 33132	Federico Costales	305–536–4491
Milwaukee, WI (DO)	Suite 800, 310 W. Wisconsin Ave., 53203	Chester Bailey	414–297–1111
Minneapolis, MN (LO)	Rm. 108, 220 2d St. S., 55401	Michael Bloyer	612–370–3330
Nashville, TN (AO)	Suite 202, 50 Vantage Way, 37228	John A. Pahmeyer	615–736–5820
Newark, NJ (AO)	Rm. 301, 60 Park Pl., 07102	Corrado Gigante	201–645–6383

Field Offices—Equal Employment Opportunity Commission—Continued

(DO: District Office; AO: Area Office; LO: Local Office; FO: Field Office)

Office	Address	Director	Telephone
New Orleans, LA (DO)	Suite 600, 701 Loyola Ave., 70113	Patricia F. Bivins	504-589-2329
New York, NY (DO)	Rm. 1501, 90 Church St., 10007	Spencer H. Lewis, Jr.	212-264-7161
Norfolk, VA (AO)	1st Fl., SMA Bldg., 252 Monticello Ave., 23510.	Kathryne Stokes	804-441-3470
Oakland, CA (LO)	Rm. 430, 1333 Broadway, 94612	Glenn E. Cochran	415-273-7588
Oklahoma City, OK (AO)	531 Couch Dr., 94612	Jerry E. Jensen	405-231-4911
Philadelphia, PA (DO)	10th Fl., 1421 Cherry St., 19102	Johnny J. Butler	215-597-7784
Phoenix, AZ (DO)	Suite 300, 4520 N. Central Ave., 85012	Charles D. Burtner	602-640-5000
Pittsburgh, PA (AO)	Rm. 2038-A, 1000 Liberty Ave., 15222	Eugene V. Nelson	412-644-3444
Raleigh, NC (AO)	1309 Annapolis Dr., 27601	Richard E. Walz	919-856-4064
Richmond, VA (AO)	2d Fl., 3600 Broad St., 23240	Gloria Underwood	804-771-2692
San Antonio, TX (DO)	Suite 200, 5410 Fredericksburg Rd., 78229	Pedro Esquivel	512-229-4810
San Diego, CA (LO)	Rm. 4S-21, 880 Front St., 92188	Patrick Matarazzo	619-557-6288
San Francisco, CA (DO)	Suite 500, 901 Market St., 94103	Paula Montanez	415-744-6500
San Jose, CA (LO)	96 N. 3d St., 95113	Charles Carattini	408-291-7352
Savannah, GA (LO)	Suite B, 10 Whitaker St., 31401	Gloria Barnett-Mentor	912-944-4234
Seattle, WA (DO)	Suite 500, 2815 2d Ave., 98121	Jeanette M. Leino	206-553-0968
St. Louis, MO (DO)	5th Fl., 625 N. Euclid St., 63108	Lynn Bruner	314-425-6523
Tampa, FL (AO)	10th Fl., 501 E. Polk St., 33602	James D. Packwood, Jr.	813-228-2310
Washington, DC (FO)	2d Fl., 1400 L St. NW., 20005	Susan Reilly	202-275-7377

Sources of Information

Employment The Commission selects its employees from various examinations and registers, including mid- and senior-level registers; various secretarial, typing, and stenographic registers; and the Equal Opportunity Specialist register. Employment inquiries or applications for positions in the headquarters office should be directed to the Personnel Office, Equal Employment Opportunity Commission, 1801 L Street NW., Washington, DC 20507 (phone, 202-663-4306), or contact the appropriate district office for district office positions.

General Inquiries A nationwide toll-free telephone number puts callers in touch with a tape bank where information about programs and activities may be acquired and the caller directed to the appropriate field office where charges may be filed. Phone, 800-USA-EEOC; 800-800-3302 (TDD).

Information About Survey Forms (EEO-1, 2, 3, 4, 5, and 6). Phone, 202-663-4958.

Media Inquiries Office of Communications and Legislative Affairs, 1801 L Street NW., Washington, DC 20507. Phone, 202-663-4900.

Publications Nationwide toll-free telephone number, 800-USA-EEOC.

Reading Room EEOC Library, 1801 L Street NW., Washington, DC 20507. Phone, 202-663-4630.

Speakers Office of Communications and Legislative Affairs, 1801 L Street NW., Washington, DC 20507. Phone, 202-663-4900.

For further information, contact the Equal Employment Opportunity Commission, 1801 L Street NW., Washington, DC 20507. Phone, 202-663-4900.

EXPORT-IMPORT BANK OF THE UNITED STATES

811 Vermont Avenue NW., Washington, DC 20571
Phone, 202-566-8990

President and Chairman	John D. Macomber
First Vice President and Vice Chairman	Eugene K. Lawson

Directors	RICHARD C. HOUSEWORTH
	RITA M. RODRIGUEZ
	CECIL B. THOMPSON
General Counsel	HART FESSENDEN
Executive Vice President	JAMES R. SHARPE
Vice President—Asia	RAYMOND J. ALBRIGHT
Vice President—Public Affairs and Publications	JENI B. FALKIEWICZ
Vice President—Latin America	RICHARD D. CRAFTON
Vice President—United States	JAMES W. CRIST
Vice President—Policy and Planning	JAMES C. CRUSE
Vice President—Country Risk Analysis	DANIEL L. BOND
Vice President—Information Management	CANDELARIO TRUJILLO, JR.
Corporate Secretary	JOAN P. HARRIS
Treasurer—Controller	JAMES K. HESS
Vice President—Marketing and Program Development	ROBERT J. KAISER
Vice President—Europe and Canada	THOMAS E. MORAN
Vice President—Africa and Middle East	ARTHUR PILZER
Vice President—Congressional and External Affairs	FREDERICK A. RUTH
Vice President—Claims and Recoveries	STEPHEN D. PROCTOR
Administrative Officer	HELENE H. WALL
Vice President—Insurance	ROBERT L. CHARAMELLA
Vice President—Engineering	JOHN W. WISNIEWSKI
Director—Personnel	TAMZEN C. REITAN
Manager—Contract Administration	LEILANI NEWTON

[For the Export-Import Bank of the United States statement of organization, see the *Code of Federal Regulations*, Title 12, Part 401]

The Export-Import Bank of the United States facilitates and aids in financing exports of U.S. goods and services. The Bank has implemented a variety of programs to meet the needs of the U.S. exporting community. These programs take the form of direct lending or the issuance of guarantees and insurance so that exporters and private banks can extend appropriate financing without taking undue risks.

The Export-Import Bank of Washington was authorized in 1934 as a banking corporation organized under the laws of the District of Columbia by Executive Order 6581 of February 2, 1934. The Bank was continued as an agency of the United States by acts of Congress in 1935, 1937, 1939, and 1940. It was made an independent agency of the U.S. Government by the Export-Import Bank Act of 1945 (12 U.S.C. 635), subsequently amended in 1947 to reincorporate the Bank under Federal charter. The name was changed to Export-Import Bank of the United States (Eximbank) by the act of March 13, 1968 (12 U.S.C. 635 note).

The principal legislation governing the Bank's operations is the Export-Import Bank Act of 1945, as amended.

The mission of the Bank is to help American exporters meet government-supported competition from other countries and to correct market imperfections so that commercial export financing can take place. In 1987 Congress appropriated $100 million for use as grants in combination with regular export loans.

The Export-Import Bank will consider aiding in the export financing of U.S. goods and services when there is a reasonable assurance of repayment. Eximbank is not to compete with private financing, but supplement it when

EXPORT—IMPORT BANK OF THE UNITED STATES

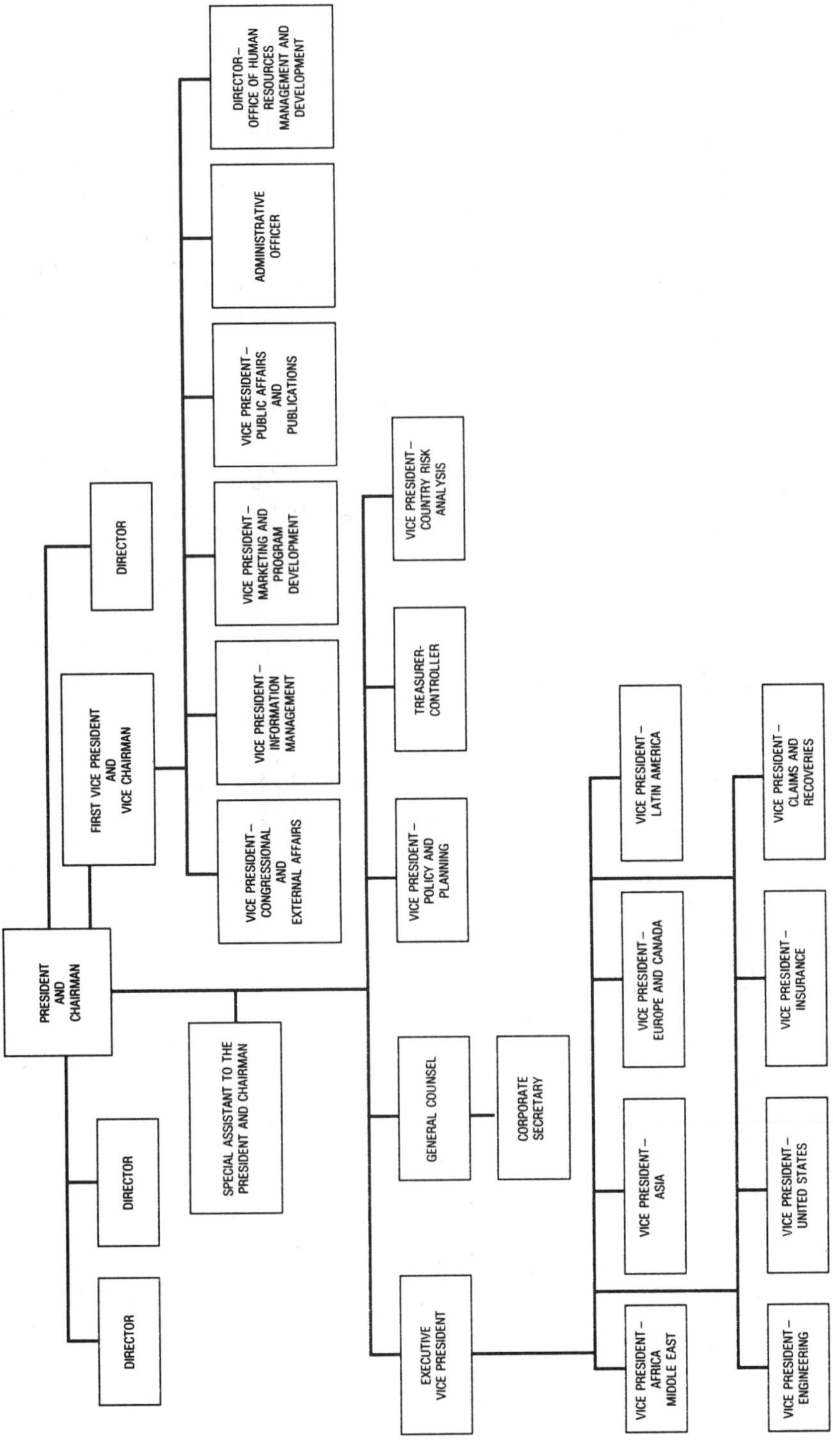

adequate funds are not available in the private sector.

Activities

The Bank is authorized to have outstanding at any one time dollar loans, guarantees, and insurance in aggregate amount not in excess of $40 billion. The Bank also is authorized to have a capital stock of $1 billion and to borrow from the United States Treasury up to $6 billion outstanding at any one time.

Important changes inaugurated in fiscal year 1987 make it easier for the Bank's programs to support U.S. exports. For example, Eximbank now has essentially one loan program and one guarantee program for both medium- and long-term export transactions. Both programs, providing up to 85-percent financing, operate on the basis of preliminary and final commitments and are open to any responsible party. Eximbank loans also carry the minimum interest rate allowed by the Organization for Economic Cooperation and Development. Other changes, including a restructuring of fee schedules based on risk, will help make Eximbank programs more accessible to financial institutions and to exporters.

Eximbank acts to reduce the risks of buyer default for American exporters under a variety of insurance programs administered by the Foreign Credit Insurance Association, an association of U.S. insurance companies organized by Eximbank in 1961. The Association sells and services export credit insurance policies under agency and reinsurance agreements with Eximbank. Its policies insure against risks of default in export transactions and are available in a variety of insurance plans that are tailored to the special needs of different types of exporters and financial institutions.

Other Eximbank programs include the Working Capital Guarantee Program, a loan guarantee program designed to provide eligible exporters with access to working capital loans from commercial lenders, and the Engineering Multiplier Program, which provides financing in support of project-related design services or feasibility studies with potential for generating further procurement of American exports.

For further information, contact the Public Affairs Office, Export-Import Bank of the United States, 811 Vermont Avenue NW., Washington, DC 20571. Phone, 202-566-8990.

FARM CREDIT ADMINISTRATION

1501 Farm Credit Drive, McLean, VA 22102-5090
Phone, 703-883-4000

Farm Credit Administration Board:	
Chairman	HAROLD B. STEELE
Staff Director	ROBERT R. ANDROS
Members of the Board	BILLY ROSS BROWN
	(VACANCY)
Secretary to the Board	CURTIS M. ANDERSON
Staff:	
Director, Office of Congressional and Public Affairs	MARY KAY THATCHER
General Counsel	NANCY E. LYNCH, *Acting*
Associate General Counsel, Corporate and Regulatory Law Division	NANCY E. LYNCH
Associate General Counsel, Litigation and Enforcement Division	VICTOR A. COHEN, *Acting*

Inspector General	ELDON W. STOEHR
Director, Office of Examination and Chief Examiner	DAVID C. BAER
Director, Office of Regulatory Enforcement	MICHAEL L. YOUNG
Director, Office of Resources Management	MICHAEL A. BRONSON

[For the Farm Credit Administration statement of organization, see the *Code of Federal Regulations,* Title 12, Parts 600 and 611]

The Farm Credit Administration is responsible for ensuring the safe and sound operation of the banks, associations, affiliated service organizations, and other entities that collectively comprise what is known as the Farm Credit System, and for protecting the interests of the public and those who borrow from Farm Credit institutions or invest in Farm Credit securities.

The Farm Credit Administration is an independent financial regulatory agency in the executive branch of the Federal Government. The Administration carries out its responsibilities by conducting examinations of the various Farm Credit lending institutions, which are Farm Credit Banks, Banks for Cooperatives, the National Bank for Cooperatives, Federal Land Bank Associations, Production Credit Associations, Agricultural Credit Associations, and Federal Land Credit Associations. It also examines the service organizations owned by the Farm Credit lending institutions.

The lending institutions of the Farm Credit System were established to provide adequate and dependable credit and closely related services to farmers, ranchers, and producers or harvesters of aquatic products; persons engaged in providing on-the-farm services; rural homeowners; and to associations of farmers, ranchers, and producers or harvesters of aquatic products, or federations of such associations that operate on a cooperative basis and are engaged in marketing, processing, supply, or business service functions for the benefit of their members. Initially capitalized by the United States Government, the Farm Credit lending institutions are organized as cooperatives and are completely owned by their borrowers. The loan funds provided to borrowers by these institutions are obtained primarily through the sale of securities to investors in the Nation's capital markets.

The Administration administers regulations under which Farm Credit institutions operate. These regulations implement the Farm Credit Act of 1971, as amended, and have the force and effect of law. Similar to other Federal regulators of financial institutions, the Administration's authorities include the power to issue cease-and-desist orders, to levy civil monetary penalties, to remove officers and directors of Farm Credit institutions, and to establish financial and operating reporting requirements. Although it is prohibited from participation in routine management or operations of Farm Credit institutions, the Administration is authorized to become involved in these institutions' management and operations when the Farm Credit Act or its regulations have been violated, when taking an action to correct an unsafe or unsound practice, or when assuming a formal conservatorship over an institution.

Management of the agency is vested in the Farm Credit Administration Board, whose three full-time members are appointed to terms of 6 years by the President with the advice and consent of the Senate. One member of the Board is designated by the President as Chairman and serves as the Administration's chief executive officer. The Board is responsible for approving rules and regulations, providing for the examination and regulation of and reporting by Farm

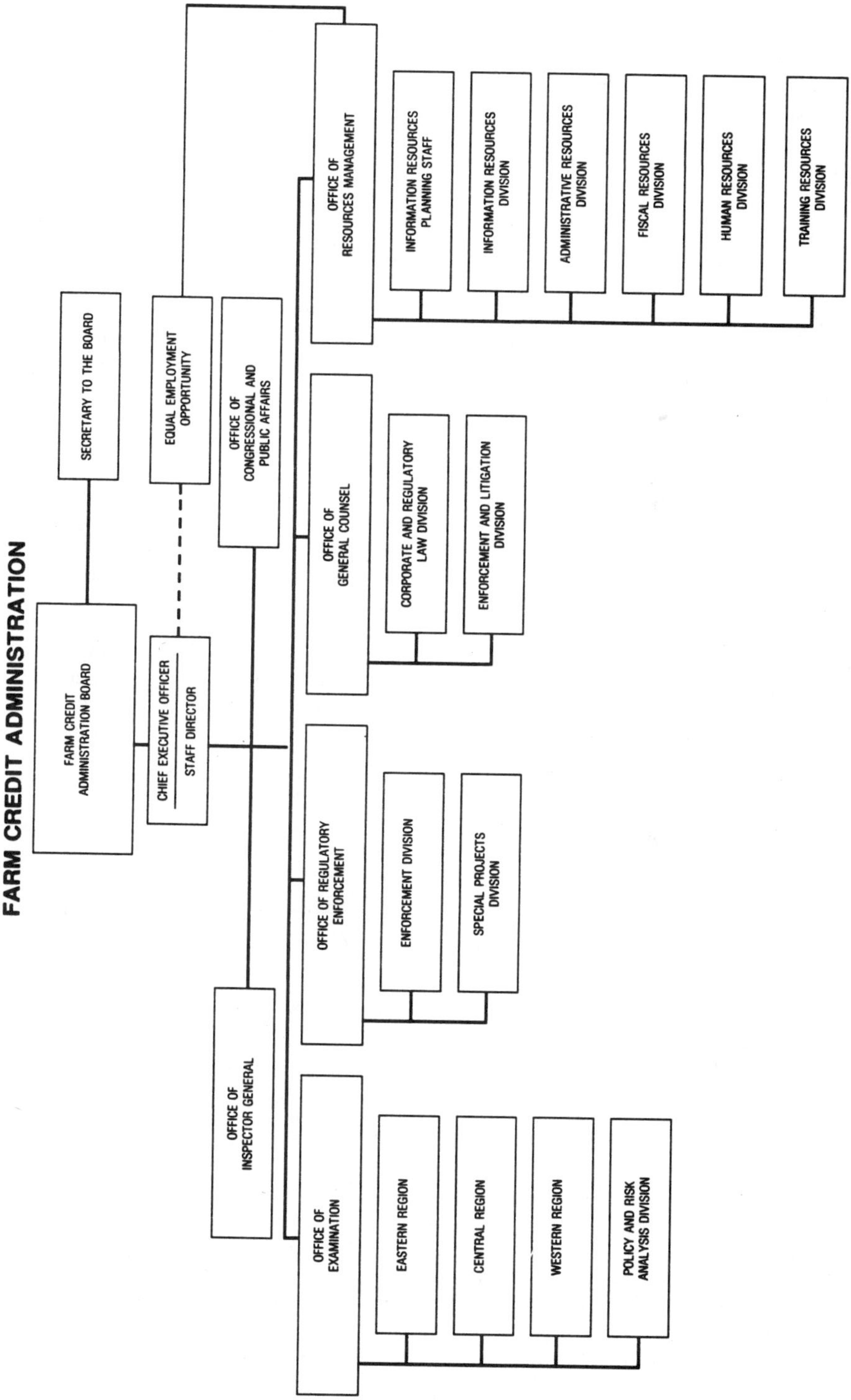
FARM CREDIT ADMINISTRATION
FARM CREDIT ADMINISTRATION BOARD
SECRETARY TO THE BOARD
CHIEF EXECUTIVE OFFICER
STAFF DIRECTOR
EQUAL EMPLOYMENT OPPORTUNITY
OFFICE OF CONGRESSIONAL AND PUBLIC AFFAIRS
OFFICE OF INSPECTOR GENERAL
OFFICE OF RESOURCES MANAGEMENT
INFORMATION RESOURCES PLANNING STAFF
INFORMATION RESOURCES DIVISION
ADMINISTRATIVE RESOURCES DIVISION
FISCAL RESOURCES DIVISION
HUMAN RESOURCES DIVISION
TRAINING RESOURCES DIVISION
OFFICE OF GENERAL COUNSEL
CORPORATE AND REGULATORY LAW DIVISION
ENFORCEMENT AND LITIGATION DIVISION
OFFICE OF REGULATORY ENFORCEMENT
ENFORCEMENT DIVISION
SPECIAL PROJECTS DIVISION
OFFICE OF EXAMINATION
EASTERN REGION
CENTRAL REGION
WESTERN REGION
POLICY AND RISK ANALYSIS DIVISION

Credit institutions, and establishing the policies under which the Administration operates.

The Administration does not operate on funds appropriated by Congress. Its income is derived from assessments collected from the institutions it regulates and examines. In addition to the headquarters office located in McLean, VA, the Administration maintains 11 field offices. They are located in Albany, NY; Aurora, CO; Bloomington, MN; Irving, TX; Louisville, KY; Marietta, GA; Oklahoma City, OK; Omaha, NE; Sacramento, CA; Spokane, WA; and St. Louis, MO. Field offices in Louisville, KY; Omaha, NE; and Spokane, WA; will close August 31, 1991.

Authority for the organization and activities of the institutions comprising the cooperative Farm Credit System and that operate under the regulation of the Farm Credit Administration may be found in the Farm Credit Act of 1971, as amended (12 U.S.C. 2001).

Sources of Information

Inquiries for information on the following subjects may be directed to the specified office, Farm Credit Administration, 1501 Farm Credit Drive, McLean, VA 22102-5090.

Contracts and Procurement Inquiries regarding the Administration's procurement and contracting activities should be directed in writing to Contracting and Procurement. Phone, 703-883-4149.

Employment The Farm Credit Administration has an ongoing college recruitment program. Inquiries regarding employment with the Administration should be directed to the Human Resources Division. Phone, 703-883-4139.

Freedom of Information Requests Requests for agency records must be submitted in writing, clearly identified with "FOIA Request" and addressed to the Office of Congressional and Public Affairs. Phone, 703-883-4056.

Publications Publications and information on the Farm Credit Administration may be obtained by writing the Office of Congressional and Public Affairs. Phone, 703-883-4056.

For further information, contact the Office of Congressional and Public Affairs, Farm Credit Administration, 1501 Farm Credit Drive, McLean, VA 22102-5090. Phone, 703-883-4056.

FEDERAL COMMUNICATIONS COMMISSION

1919 M Street NW., Washington, DC 20554
Phones, 202-632-7000; 202-632-6999 (TDD number for the hearing impaired)

Chairman	Alfred C. Sikes
Commissioners	James H. Quello
	Sherrie P. Marshall
	Andrew C. Barrett
	Ervin S. Duggan
Managing Director	Andrew S. Fishel
General Counsel	Robert L. Pettit
Chief Engineer	Thomas P. Stanley
Director, Office of Public Affairs	Lorrie A. Secrest
Director, Office of Legislative Affairs	Linda Townsend Solheim
Director, Office of International Communications	Walda Roseman
Inspector General	James Warwick
Chief, Office of Plans and Policy	Robert M. Pepper
Chairman, Review Board	Joseph A. Marino

Chief, Office of Administrative Law Judges	JOSEPH STIRMER
Chief, Mass Media Bureau	ROY J. STEWART
Chief, Common Carrier Bureau	RICHARD M. FIRESTONE
Chief, Field Operations Bureau	RICHARD M. SMITH
Chief, Private Radio Bureau	RALPH A. HALLER

[For the Federal Communications Commission statement of organization, see the *Code of Federal Regulations*, Title 47, Part 0]

The Federal Communications Commission regulates interstate and foreign communications by radio, television, wire, satellite, and cable. It is responsible for the orderly development and operation of broadcast services and the provision of rapid, efficient nationwide and worldwide telephone and telegraph services at reasonable rates. Its responsibilities also include the use of communications for promoting safety of life and property and for strengthening the national defense.

The Federal Communications Commission was created by the Communications Act of 1934 (15 U.S.C.; 21 U.S.C.; 47 U.S.C. 35, 151) to regulate interstate and foreign communications by wire and radio in the public interest. It was assigned additional regulatory jurisdiction under the provisions of the Communications Satellite Act of 1962 (47 U.S.C. 701–744). The scope of its regulation includes radio and television broadcasting; telephone, telegraph, and cable television operation; two-way radio and radio operators; and satellite communication.

The Commission is composed of five members, who are appointed by the President with the advice and consent of the Senate. One of the members is designated by the President as Chairman.

In administering the programs necessary to carry out its regulatory responsibility, the Commission is assisted by a General Counsel who, in addition to regular duties, represents the Commission before the United States Courts of Appeals; a Managing Director; a Director of Public Affairs; a Director of Legislative Affairs; a Director of International Communications, who ensures that the coordination and integration of the Commission's international policy activities are uniform and consistent, assumes the principal role for representing the Commission in international fora, and serves as the general focus for coordinating and directing international activities; an Inspector General, who is responsible for coordinating and conducting all audits and investigations relating to the programs and operations of the agency; a Chief Engineer; a Chief of Plans and Policy; and the Chiefs of four bureaus, to whom certain licensing and grant authority has been delegated.

To assist the Commission in exercising its responsibility in the adjudicatory process, there is a Review Board to review initial decisions and write decisions and an Adjudication Division in the Office of the General Counsel to assist the Commission and individual Commissioners in the disposition of matters arising in cases of adjudication (as defined in the Administrative Procedure Act (5 U.S.C. note prec. 551)) that have been designated for hearings. There also is a corps of administrative law judges, qualified and appointed pursuant to the requirements of the Administrative Procedure Act, who conduct evidentiary adjudicatory hearings and write initial decisions.

Activities

Mass Media The Mass Media Bureau administers the regulatory program for the following services: amplitude modulation (AM), frequency modulation (FM), television, low-power TV, translators, instructional TV fixed, related broadcast auxiliary services, direct

FEDERAL COMMUNICATIONS COMMISSION

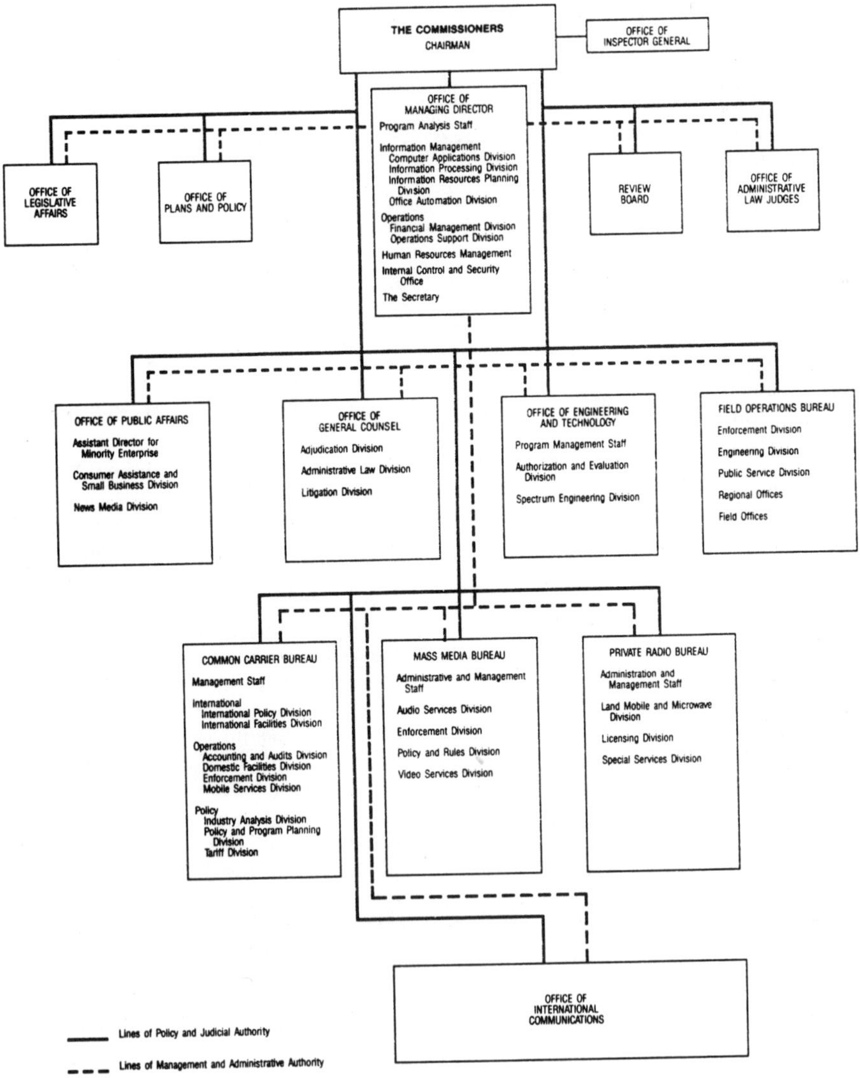

broadcast satellite, cable TV, microwave radio relay, and registration of new cable TV systems. The Bureau issues construction permits, operating licenses, and renewals or transfers of such broadcast licenses; and processes registrations, notifications, and petitions for cable TV systems. The Bureau also oversees compliance by broadcasters and cable TV system operators with statutes and Commission policies, and is responsible for maintaining relations with State and local authorities who share responsibility for the regulation of cable TV systems.

For further information, contact the Mass Media Bureau. Phone, 202–632–6460.

Common Carrier Communications
The Common Carrier Bureau administers the regulatory program for interstate and international common carrier communications by telephone, telegraph, radio, and satellite. Common carriers include companies, organizations, or individuals providing communications services to the public for hire, who must serve all who wish to use them at established rates. In providing interstate and foreign communications services, common carriers may employ landline wire or electrical or optical cable facilities, point-to-point microwave radio (signals relayed by stations spaced at given intervals), land mobile radio (two-way telephone or one-way signaling communications between base and mobile units), cellular systems, or satellite systems. Communications services between the United States and overseas points by common carriers are provided by ocean cable, high frequency radio, and satellite communications.

For further information, contact the Common Carrier Bureau. Phone, 202–632–6910.

Private Radio Communications The Private Radio Bureau regulates the use of the radio spectrum to fulfill the communications needs of businesses, State and local governments, aircraft, ships, and individuals. Over 2.5 million licensees use radio to promote safety of life and property, to increase productivity, and to advance the science of telecommunications. The Private Radio Bureau regulates and licenses two broad groups of radio services: the private land mobile and microwave radio services, and the special radio services. Private land mobile and microwave radio services are used by public safety entities (police, fire, local government), industrial entities (businesses of all types, including public utilities), and land transportation entities (buses, railroads, taxicabs). Special radio services include the aviation service, the marine service, the Alaska fixed service, and the personal radio services (amateur and general mobile). While two personal radio services, citizens (CB) and radio control (R/C), are regulated, licenses are not required. The Bureau also implements the compulsory provisions of laws and treaties covering the use of radio for the safety of life and property at sea and in the air.

For further information, contact the Private Radio Bureau. Phone, 202–632–6940.

Engineering and Technology The Office of Engineering and Technology administers the Experimental Radio Service and the Equipment Authorization Program. The Experimental Radio Service permits the public to experiment with new uses of radio frequencies. This allows development of radio equipment and exploration of new radio techniques prior to licensing under other regulatory programs. The Equipment Authorization Program includes several specific procedures by which the agency approves radio equipment as a prerequisite to importation, marketing, or use. The procedures range from Commission testing of an equipment sample for compliance with applicable standards, through FCC review of applications and accompanying test reports submitted by the applicants, to a self-authorization procedure whereby a manufacturer certifies that the product complies with the standards.

For further information, contact the Office of Engineering and Technology. Phone, 202–653–8103.

Enforcement Much of the investigative and enforcement work of the

Commission is carried out by its field staff. The Field Operations Bureau has 6 regional offices and 36 field offices. It also operates a nationwide fleet of mobile radio direction-finding vehicles for technical enforcement purposes. The field staff, in effect, are the Commission's "eyes and ears" in detecting radio violations and enforcing rules and regulations. Continuous surveillance of the radio spectrum is maintained to detect unlicensed operation and activities or nonconforming transmissions, and to furnish radio bearings on ships and planes in distress.

Public Service The Field Operations Bureau (FOB) administers public service programs aimed at educating Commission licensees, industry, and the general public to improve compliance with FCC rules and regulations. FOB also provides liaison with other licensing bureaus to ensure that the public is aware of current FCC rules and policies. Other functions of FOB's public service program are to provide interference resolution and to ensure compliance with obstruction marking and lighting of radio antenna towers.

Radio Operators The commercial radio operator program is administered by the Field Operations Bureau. The Private Radio Bureau administers the amateur operator program.

For further information, contact the Field Operations Bureau. Phone, 202-632-6980.

Regional and Field Offices—Federal Communications Commission

Field Operations Bureau

Regional Office	Address	Regional Director
Atlanta, GA	Suite 320, Koger Center-Gwinnett, 3575 Koger Blvd., Duluth, GA 30136.	Carl E. Pyron
Bellevue, WA	Rm. 414, 3605 132d Ave. SE., 98006	William E. Johnson
Kansas City, MO	Rm. 320, Brywood Office Twr., 8800 E. 63d St., 64133	Dennis P. Carlton
Park Ridge, IL	Rm. 306, Park Ridge Office Ctr., 1550 Northwest Hwy., 60068.	Russell D. Monie
Quincy, MA	NFPA Bldg., 1 Batterymarch Pk., 02169	Joseph P. Casey
San Francisco, CA	Rm. 420, 3777 Depot Rd., Hayward, CA 94545-2756	Kent Crawford

Field Office	Address	Engineer in Charge
Allegan, MI	P.O. Box 89, 49010	Melvyn H. Hyman
Anchorage, AK	6721 W. Raspberry Rd., 99502	Marlene Windel
Atlanta, GA	Rm. 320, 3575 Koger Blvd., Duluth, GA, 30136	Fred L. Broce
Baltimore, MD	Rm. 1017, 31 Hopkins Plz., 21201	Robert M. Mroz
Belfast, ME	P.O. Box 470, 04915	Barry A. Bohac
Bellevue, WA	Rm. 414, 3605 132d Ave. SE., 98006	Gary P. Soulsby
Buffalo, NY	Rm. 1307, 111 W. Huron St., 14202	David A. Viglione
Cerritos, CA	Rm. 660, 1800 Studebaker Rd., 90701	James R. Zoulek
Custer, WA	1330 Loomis Trail Rd., 98240	Jack W. Brazhaw
Dallas, TX	Rm. 1170, 9330 LBJ Freeway, 75243	James D. Wells
Denver, CO	Rm. 860, 165 Union Blvd., 80228	Robert D. Weller
Douglas, AZ	P.O. Box 6, 85608	Stephen Y. Tsuya
Farmington Hills, MI	24897 Hathaway St., 48331-4361	Irby C. Tallant
Grand Island, NB	P.O. Box 1588, 68802	James H. Berrie, Jr.
Hato Rey, PR	Rm. 747, Federal Bldg., 00918	William C. Berry
Hayward, CA	Rm. 402, 3777 Depot Rd., 94545-2756	Serge Matri-Volkoff
Honolulu, HI	P.O. Box 1030, 96797	Jack Shedletsky
Houston, TX	Rm. 900, 1225 N. Loop West, 77008	Loyd P. Perry
Kansas City, MO	Rm. 320, 8800 E. 63d St., 64133	James A. Dailey
Kingsville, TX	P.O. Box 632, 78363-0632	Oliver K. Long
Langhorne, PA	Rm. 404, 2300 E. Lincoln Hwy., 19047	John Rahtes
Laurel, MD	P.O. Box 250, Columbia, MD, 21045	Robert J. Douchis
Livermore, CA	P.O. Box 311, 94551-0311	Thomas N. Stavern
Miami, FL	Rm. 310, 8390 NW. 53d St., 33166	John L. Theimer
New Orleans, LA	Rm. 505, 800 W. Commerce Rd., 70123	James C. Hawkins
New York, NY	201 Varick St., 10014-4870	Alexander J. Zimney
Norfolk, VA	1200 Communications Cir., 23455-3725	J. Jerry Freeman
Park Ridge, IL	Rm. 306, 1550 Northwest Hwy., 60068	Phillip Bradford
Portland, OR	Rm. 1782, 1220 SW. 3d Ave., 97204	Charles W. Craig
Powder Springs, GA	P.O. Box 85, 30073	Donald E. Taylor
Quincy, MA	1 Batterymarch Pk., 02169	Vincent F. Kajunski

Field Office	Address	Engineer in Charge
St. Paul, MN	Rm. 693, 316 N. Robert St., 55101	Albert S. Jarratt
San Diego, CA	Rm. 370, 4542 Ruffner St., 92111-0311	William H. Grisby
Tampa, FL	Rm. 1215, 2203 N. Lois Ave., 33607-2356	Ralph M. Barlow
Vero Beach, FL	P.O. Box 1730, 32961-1730	Robert C. McKinney
	Common Carrier Bureau	
New York, NY	Rm. 1309X, 90 Church St., 10007	Beatrice Shapiro, Chief

Sources of Information

Inquiries for information on the special subjects listed in the following paragraphs and those concerning licensing/grant requirements in the various services may be directed to the person or office specified or to the Chief of the Bureau or Office listed below as having responsibility for the service: Federal Communications Commission, 1919 M Street NW., Washington, DC 20554.

Licensing/Grant Responsibility—Federal Communications Commission

Service	Bureau or Office
All broadcasting (radio and television) Cable television relay radio Registration of cable systems	Mass Media Bureau
Common carrier radio Section 214 of FCC Act Satellite	Common Carrier Bureau
Experimental radio	Office of Engineering and Technology
Equipment approval services: Certification Type acceptance Type approval Notification Verification	Office of Engineering and Technology
Amateur radio Aviation radio Industrial radio Land transportation Marine radio Private microwave radio Public safety radio	Private Radio Bureau
Commercial radio operators	Field Operations Bureau

Advisory Committee Management Direct inquiries to the Chief, Program Analysis Staff. Phone, 202-632-0923.

Consumer Assistance Inquiries concerning general information on how the Commission works and how the public can participate in the decisionmaking process should be addressed to the Office of Public Affairs, Consumer Assistance and Small Business Division, Room 254, 1919 M Street NW., Washington, DC 20554. Phone, 202-632-7000.

Contracts and Procurement Direct inquiries to the Chief, Procurement Branch. Phone, 202-634-1528.

Employment and Recruitment The Commission's programs require attorneys, electronics engineers, economists, accountants, administrative management and computer specialists, and clerical personnel. Requests for employment information should be directed to the Chief, Personnel Resources Branch. Phone, 202-632-7104. Schools interested in participating in the college recruitment programs of the Commission should direct their inquiries to the Associate Managing Director, Human Resources Management. Phone, 202-632-7120.

Equal Employment Practices by Industry Direct inquiries to the Chief, Consumer Assistance and Small Business Division. Phone, 202-632-7000.

Ex-Parte Presentations Information concerning ex-parte presentations should be directed to the Commission's Managing Director. Phone, 202-632-6390.

Fee Collection Inquiries concerning the Commission's Fee Collection Program should be addressed to the Office of Public Affairs, Consumer Assistance and Small Business Division, Room 254, 1919 M Street NW., Washington, DC 20554. Phone, 202-632-FEES.

Information Available for Public Inspection At the Commission's headquarters office in Washington, DC, dockets concerning rulemaking and adjudicatory matters, copies of applications for licenses and grants, and reports required to be filed by licensees

290-950 O 91 - 19

and cable system operators are maintained in the public reference rooms—some reports are by law held confidential. In addition to the information available at the Commission, each broadcasting station makes available for public reference certain information pertaining to the operation of the station, a current copy of the application filed for license, and nonconfidential reports filed with the Commission. Special requests for inspection of records at the Commission's offices should be directed to the Managing Director. Phone, 202-632-6390. The Library has on file Commission rules and regulations. Phone, 202-632-7100. The News Media Division distributes publications, public notices, and press releases. Phone, 202-632-5050.

For further information, contact the Office of Public Affairs, Consumer Assistance and Small Business Division, Federal Communications Commission, 1919 M Street NW., Washington, DC 20554. Phone, 202-632-7000.

FEDERAL DEPOSIT INSURANCE CORPORATION

550 Seventeenth Street NW., Washington, DC 20429
Phone, 202-393-8400

Board of Directors:	
Chairman	L. William Seidman
Vice Chairman	Andrew C. (Skip) Hove, Jr.
Directors	C.C. Hope, Jr.
(Comptroller of the Currency)	Robert L. Clarke
(Director of the Office of Thrift Supervision)	T. Timothy Ryan, Jr.
Officials:	
Deputy to the Chairman	John F. Bovenzi
Deputy to the Director (Comptroller of the Currency)	Thomas E. Zemke
Deputy to the Director	Robert V. Shumway
Executive Secretary	Hoyle L. Robinson
General Counsel	Alfred J.T. Byrne
Executive Director, Division of Resolutions and Supervision	Paul G. Fritts
Director, Division of Resolutions	Harrison Young
Director, Division of Supervision	John W. Stone
Director, Division of Liquidation	Steven A. Seelig
Director, Division of Accounting and Corporate Services	Stanley J. Poling
Director, Corporate Communications	Alan J. Whitney
Director, Legislative Affairs	Alice C. Goodman, *Acting*
Director, Research and Statistics	William Roger Watson
Director, Budget and Planning	J. Russell Cherry
Inspector General	Robert D. Hoffman
Director, Consumer Affairs	Janice M. Smith
Director, Personnel Management	Alfred P. Squerrini
Director, Equal Employment Opportunity	Mae Culp
Director, Training and Educational Services	Jane Sartori

FEDERAL DEPOSIT INSURANCE CORPORATION

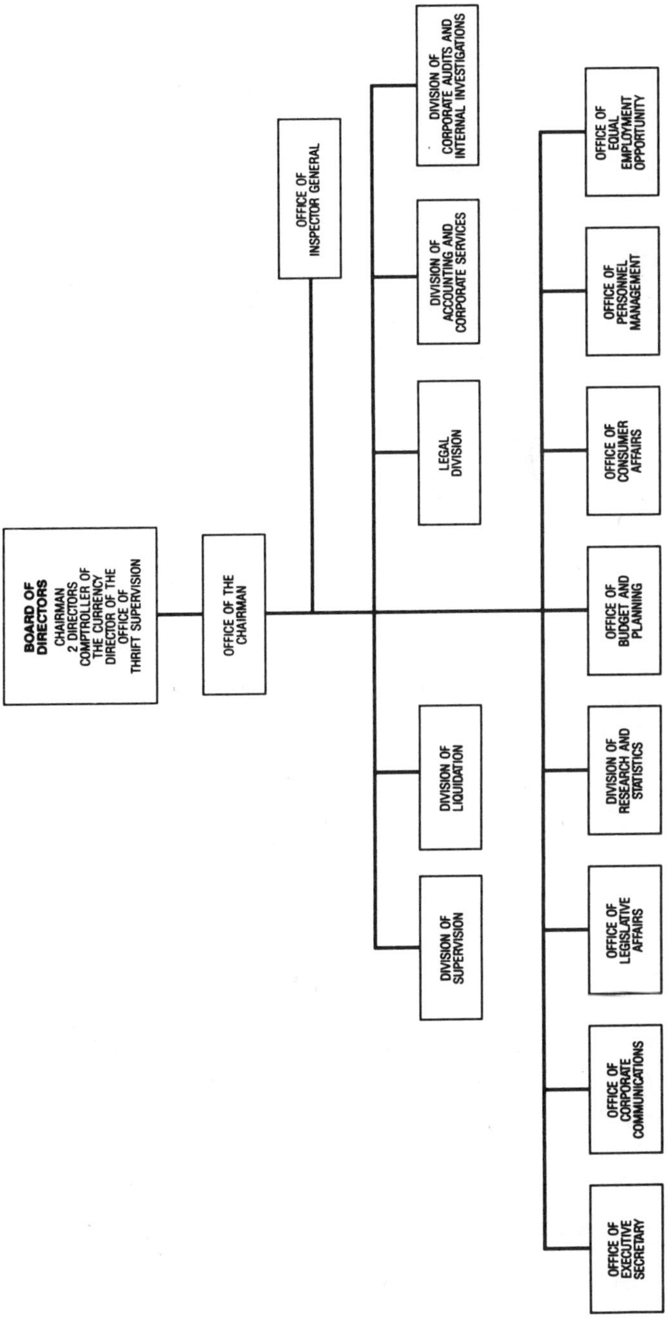

The Federal Deposit Insurance Corporation was established in 1933 to promote and preserve public confidence in banks and to protect the money supply through provision of insurance coverage for bank deposits and periodic examinations of insured State-chartered banks that are not members of the Federal Reserve System.

The Federal Deposit Insurance Corporation (FDIC) is an independent agency of the Government. Management is vested in a Board of Directors consisting of five members, one of whom is the Comptroller of the Currency, one of whom is the Director of the Office of Thrift Supervision, and three of whom are appointed by the President with the advice and consent of the Senate. Appointive members serve 6-year terms, and one is elected by the members of the Board as Chairman of the Board of Directors. The headquarters office is located in Washington, DC, and there are Division of Liquidation and Division of Supervision regional offices in the field with directors in charge of each. Most FDIC field employees are bank examiners or liquidators.

The Corporation does not operate on funds appropriated by Congress. Its income is derived from assessments on deposits held by insured banks and from interest on the required investment of its surplus funds in Government securities. It also has authority to borrow from the Treasury up to $5 billion for insurance purposes, although it has never used that authority.

The Corporation was organized under authority of section 12B of the Federal Reserve Act (12 U.S.C. 264), approved June 16, 1933. On September 21, 1950, section 12B of the Federal Reserve Act, as amended (12 U.S.C. 1811–1831), was withdrawn as part of the Federal Reserve Act and made a separate law known as the Federal Deposit Insurance Act. The act also made numerous amendments to the former deposit insurance statutes.

The Corporation also administers the Savings Association Insurance Fund (SAIF), which was established on August 9, 1989, under the authority of the Financial Institutions Reform, Recovery, and Enforcement Act of 1989. The SAIF replaces the Federal Savings and Loan Insurance Corporation as the insurer of deposits in savings and loan associations.

Activities

The Corporation insures, up to the statutory limitation, the deposits in national banks, in State banks that are members of the Federal Reserve System, State banks that apply for Federal Deposit Insurance and meet certain prescribed qualifications, and savings and loans which are members of the SAIF. In the event of a bank failure, the claim of each depositor (up to $100,000) is promptly paid upon assignment to the Corporation of the depositor's rights to recoveries to the extent of his or her insured deposits.

The Corporation may make loans to or purchase assets from insured depository institutions in order to facilitate mergers or consolidations, when such action for the protection of depositors will reduce risks or avert threatened loss to the agency. It will make possible the reopening of a closed insured depository institution or prevent the closing of an insured depository institution when it considers the continued operation of such institution essential to providing adequate banking services in the community.

The Federal Deposit Insurance Act authorizes the Corporation to terminate the insured status of a depository institution that continues, after notice and hearing, to engage in unsafe and unsound banking practices or in violation of law or regulations; publish notice of such termination; and regulate the manner in which the depository institution shall give the required notice of such termination to depositors (whose deposits in the bank at the time of termination continue to be insured for 2 years).

The Corporation acts as receiver for all national banks placed in receivership and for State banks placed in receivership when it is appointed by State authorities.

To inform the public that the deposits of certain depository institutions are insured, the Corporation prescribes rules and regulations relating to the use of its name and symbol in advertising.

Other functions and activities performed in relation to insured State banks that are not members of the Federal Reserve System, except banks in the District of Columbia, are to:

—examine such banks periodically to determine their condition for insurance purposes;

—approve or disapprove mergers, consolidations, acquisitions, and assumption transactions between insured banks where the resulting banks are to be insured nonmember State banks;

—approve or disapprove a proposal by a bank to establish and operate a new branch or move its main office or any branch from one location to another;

—issue cease-and-desist orders to a bank or to a banker with respect to specific violations or practices or, in situations involving personal dishonesty, suspend or remove bank personnel responsible for such actions, when corrective action is not obtainable by the State supervisory authority;

—require reports of changes in the ownership of outstanding voting stock of a bank that will result in a change in control of the bank, and reports of any loan secured by 25 percent or more of the stock;

—require reports of condition, income, and other data of banks;

—require banks to install, maintain, and operate a level of security designed to discourage robbery, burglary, and larceny and to assist in the identification and apprehension of persons who commit such acts; and

—require compliance of banks with the Federal Reserve Regulations pertaining to truth in lending, cost disclosure on consumer credit, and related areas.

Regional Offices—Federal Deposit Insurance Corporation

Region/Address	Director	Telephone
Supervision		
Atlanta, GA (Suite 1200, 245 Peachtree Ctr. Ave. NE., 30303)	A. David Meadows	404-525-0308
Boston, MA (160 Gould St., Needham, MA 02194)	Paul H. Wiechman	617-449-9080
Chicago, IL (Suite 3100, 30 S. Wacker Dr., 60606)	George J. Masa	312-207-0210
Dallas, TX (Suite 1900, 1910 Pacific Ave., 75201)	Kenneth L. Walker	214-220-3342
Kansas City, MO (Suite 1500, 2345 Grand Ave., 64108)	Charles E. Thacker	816-234-8000
Memphis, TN (Suite 1900, 5100 Poplar Ave., 38137)	Bill C. Houston	901-685-1603
New York, NY (21st Fl., 452 5th Ave., 10018)	Nicholas J. Ketcha, Jr.	212-704-1200
San Francisco, CA (Suite 2300, 25 Ecker St., 94105)	John R. Sexton	415-546-0160
Liquidation		
Chicago, IL (32d Fl., 30 S. Wacker Dr., 60606)	Bart L. Federici	312-207-0200
Dallas, TX (Suite 1600, 1910 Pacific Ave., 75201)	G. Michael Newton	214-754-0098
New York, NY (21st Fl., 452 5th Ave., 10018)	Thomas A. Beshara	212-704-1200
San Francisco, CA (Suite 1900, 25 Ecker St., 94105)	Keith W. Siebold	415-546-1810

Sources of Information

Inquiries for information on the following subjects may be directed to the specified office, Federal Deposit Insurance Corporation, 550 Seventeenth Street NW., Washington, DC 20429.

Bank Depositors and Customers It is easiest for bank depositors and customers to obtain information about deposit insurance at any insured bank, where explanatory material is available. This is also true with respect to certain aspects of the truth-in-lending legislation that the Corporation administers in part. Each bank regulatory agency has established a division of consumer affairs to deal with questions of interest to bank depositors and customers. In this connection, inquiries may be directed to the Director, Office of Consumer Affairs, or the agency's toll-free consumer hotline, 1-800-424-5485.

Contracts and Procurement
Individuals seeking to do business with the Corporation may obtain detailed information from the Support Services Section, Division of Accounting and Corporate Services. Phone, 202-898-3661.

Employment The Corporation has a continuing college recruitment program. Information about this program, employment inquiries and applications, and related requests should be directed to the Director, Office of Personnel Management. Phone, 202-898-8890.

General Inquiries Inquiries regarding types of records available to the public (including records available under the Freedom of Information Act) should be directed to 1 of 12 regional offices, or to the Office of the Executive Secretary. Phone, 202-898-3811.

For further information, contact the Corporate Communications Office, Federal Deposit Insurance Corporation, 550 Seventeenth Street NW., Washington, DC 20429. Phone, 202-898-6996.

FEDERAL ELECTION COMMISSION

999 E Street NW., Washington, DC 20463
Phone, 202-376-3120 or toll-free, 800-424-9530

Chairman	JOHN WARREN MCGARRY
Vice Chairman	JOAN D. AIKENS
Commissioners	LEE ANN ELLIOTT
	THOMAS J. JOSEFIAK
	DANNY L. MCDONALD
	SCOTT E. THOMAS
Secretary of the Senate (*ex officio*)	WALTER J. STEWART
Clerk of the House of Representatives (*ex officio*)	DONNALD K. ANDERSON
Statutory Officers:	
Staff Director	JOHN C. SURINA
General Counsel	LAWRENCE M. NOBLE

The Federal Election Commission exercises exclusive jurisdiction in the administration and civil enforcement of laws regulating the acquisition and expenditure of campaign funds to ensure compliance by participants in the Federal election campaign process. Its chief mission is to provide public disclosure of campaign finance activities and effect voluntary compliance by providing the public with information on the laws and regulations concerning campaign finance.

The Federal Election Commission is an independent agency established by section 309 of the Federal Election Campaign Act of 1971, as amended (2 U.S.C. 437c). It is composed of six Commissioners appointed by the President with the advice and consent of the Senate and two *ex officio,* nonvoting members—the Secretary of the Senate and the Clerk of the House of Representatives. The act also provides for two statutory officers—the Staff Director and the General Counsel—who are appointed by the Commission.

Activities

The Commission administers and enforces the Federal Election Campaign Act of 1971, as amended (2 U.S.C. 431 *et seq.*), and the Revenue Act (26 U.S.C. 1 *et seq.*). These laws provide for the public funding of Presidential elections, public disclosure of the financial activities of political committees involved in Federal elections, and limitations and prohibitions on contributions and expenditures made to influence Federal elections (Presidency, Senate, and House).

Public Funding of Presidential Elections The Commission oversees the public financing of Presidential elections by certifying Federal payments to primary candidates, general election nominees, and national nominating conventions. It also audits recipients of Federal funds and may require repayments to the U.S. Treasury if a committee makes nonqualified campaign expenditures.

Disclosure The Commission ensures the public disclosure of the campaign finance activities reported by political committees supporting Federal candidates. Committee reports, filed regularly, disclose where campaign money comes from and how it is spent. The Commission places reports on the public record within 48 hours after they are received and computerizes the data contained in the reports.

Contribution Limits and Prohibitions The Commission administers and enforces the law with respect to limits and prohibitions on contributions and expenditures made to influence Federal elections.

Voluntary Compliance The Commission seeks voluntary compliance with the above provisions of the law by providing information through a toll-free telephone line, publications, seminars, regulations (which clarify the law), and advisory opinions (which interpret the law in specific factual situations).

Enforcement The Commission has exclusive jurisdiction with respect to the civil enforcement of the campaign finance laws. Possible violations of the law are brought to the Commission's attention either internally (through report review procedures and audits) or externally (through complaints filed by the public or referrals from other government agencies). The Commission seeks to resolve compliance matters through conciliation and may bring suit when conciliation fails. It also defends the law in court.

Sources of Information

Clearinghouse on Election Administration The Clearinghouse compiles and disseminates election administration information related to Federal elections. It also conducts independent contract studies on the administration of elections. For further information, call 202–376–5670 or, toll-free, 800–424–9530.

Congressional Affairs Office This Office serves as primary liaison with Congress and executive branch agencies. The Office is responsible for keeping Members of Congress informed about Commission decisions and, in turn, for informing the Commission on legislative developments. For further information, call 202–376–5136 or, toll-free, 800–424–9530.

Employment Inquiries regarding employment opportunities should be directed to the Director, Personnel and Labor Management Relations. Phone, 202–376–5290 or, toll-free, 800–424–9530.

General Inquiries The Information Services Division provides information and assistance to Federal candidates, political committees, and the general public. This division answers questions on campaign finance laws, conducts workshops and seminars on the law, and provides publications and forms. Those who seek information or materials should call 202–376–3120 or, toll-free, 800–424–9530.

Media Inquiries The Press Office answers inquiries from print and broadcast media sources around the country, issues press releases on Commission actions and statistical data, responds to informational requests, and distributes other materials. All persons representing media should direct inquiries to the Press Office. For further information, call 202–376–3155 or, toll-free, 800–424–9530.

Public Records The Office of Public Records, located at 999 E Street NW., Washington, DC, provides space for public inspection of all reports and statements relating to campaign finance since 1972. It is open weekdays from 9 a.m. to 5 p.m. and has extended hours during peak election periods. The public is invited to visit the Office or obtain information by calling 202–376–3140 or, toll-free, 800–424–9530.

Reading Room The library contains a collection of basic legal research resources, with emphasis on political campaign financing, corporate and labor political activity, and campaign finance reform. It is open to the public on weekdays between 9 a.m. and 5 p.m. For further information, call 202–376–5312 or, toll-free, 800–424–9530.

For further information, contact Information Services, Federal Election Commission, 999 E Street NW., Washington, DC 20463. Phone, 202–376–3120 or, toll-free, 800–424–9530.

FEDERAL EMERGENCY MANAGEMENT AGENCY

500 C Street SW., Washington, DC 20472
Phone, 202–646–4600

Director	Wallace E. Stickney
Deputy Director	Jerry D. Jennings
Associate Director, National Preparedness	Antonio Lopez
Associate Director, State and Local Programs and Support	Grant C. Peterson
Associate Director, External Affairs	Thomas F. Kranz
Deputy Associate Director	Steven M. Gaddy
Assistant Associate Director, Public and Intergovernmental Affairs	Peg Maloy
Assistant Associate Director, Congressional Affairs	David Cole
Administrator, Federal Insurance Administration	C.M. (Bud) Schauerte
Administrator, U.S. Fire Administration	Olin L. Greene, Jr.
Inspector General	Russel F. Miller
Executive Director, Office of Management Services	Thomas R. McQuillan
Director, Regional Liaison Office	Robert McFerren, *Acting*
General Counsel	George Watson, *Acting*
Comptroller	George H. Orrell
Director, Personnel and Equal Opportunity	Katherine H. Shannon
Director, Administrative Support	Wesley C. Moore
Director, Acquisition Management	Kenneth J. Brzonkala
Director, Security	Jack R. Lilley II
Director, Program Analysis and Evaluation	Lynn Smith

[For the Federal Emergency Management Agency statement of organization, see the *Code of Federal Regulations,* Title 44, Part 2]

The Federal Emergency Management Agency is the focal point within the Federal Government for emergency planning, preparedness, mitigation, response, and recovery. The Agency works closely with State and local governments by funding emergency programs and providing technical guidance and training. These coordinated activities at the Federal, State, and local levels ensure a broad-based emergency program to protect public safety and property.

The Federal Emergency Management Agency (FEMA) was established in the executive branch as an independent agency pursuant to Reorganization Plan No. 3 of 1978 (5 U.S.C. app.) and Executive Orders 12127 of March 31, 1979 (effective April 1, 1979), and 12148 of July 20, 1979 (effective July 15, 1979).

Activities

National Preparedness Capability The National Preparedness Directorate develops and coordinates the national policy and facilities necessary for attaining and maintaining the Federal Government's capability to deliver effective emergency management during all phases of national security emergencies.

The Directorate coordinates national security emergency management and preparedness responsibilities with Federal departments and agencies. To enable the civil government to respond to national security and/or catastrophic domestic emergencies, the Directorate is responsible for:

—developing, coordinating, and evaluating procedures that provide for effective operation of the Government;

—creating and coordinating concepts and systems to improve the mobilization of industrial and Federal sectors;

—formulating concepts and systems to assure the availability of resources required to fulfill defense and critical civilian needs;

—developing Presidential emergency action documents;

—serving as the civil/military interface; and

—managing the 24-hour National Emergency Coordination Center for the collection of emergency information and notification of key emergency management officials.

The Directorate provides for planning, operation, and management of NATO civil communications for departments and agencies and is responsible for coordinating the design, development, operation, and maintenance of fixed and transportable facilities; maintaining capabilities and resources for day-to-day and emergency telecommunications, information processing, and warning systems requirements; and administering the National Defense Executive Reserve Program.

For further information, call 202–646–4600.

State and Local Programs The State and Local Programs and Support Directorate administers support programs to State and local governments that are designed to improve emergency planning, preparedness, mitigation, response, and recovery capabilities at the State and local levels in an all-hazards context—natural, technological, and attack-related.

The Directorate is also responsible for:

—assisting in the development of plans for Federal response to natural and technological catastrophic occurrences;

—administering the President's Disaster Relief Program, which provides supplemental Federal assistance in declared disasters and emergencies;

—developing and administering policy and guidance that ensures the effective implementation of relief programs to help individuals, as well as State and local governments, in recovering from the effects of disasters and emergencies and to mitigate or prevent losses after disasters or emergencies; and

—assisting State and local governments and the private sector in maximizing the survival of the population and other vital resources in the event of a national security emergency.

The Directorate also encompasses the Emergency Management Institute, which provides training in the areas of national security, technological and natural hazards, and emergency processes.

For further information, call 202–646–3692.

Federal Insurance The Federal Insurance Administration administers the National Flood Insurance Program, which makes flood insurance available to participating communities on an equitable basis and works closely with government officials at all levels to help reduce future flood damage through floodplain management.

For further information, call 202–646–4362.

Fire Policy The United States Fire Administration is responsible for the coordination and conduct of the Federal Government's response to the Nation's fire problem. Its mission is carried out through a series of offices in the following areas: fire policy and coordination, firefighter health and safety, fire data and analysis, and fire prevention and arson control.

The Administration encompassses the National Fire Academy, which provides training in fire prevention management, fire prevention and loss control, and fire service technology.

The Administration, as a focal point, works closely with the Nation's fire service organizations; Federal, State, and local governments; and the private sector in developing and implementing programs aimed at lowering fatalities and property loss due to fire.

For further information, call 202–646–2449.

External Affairs The External Affairs Directorate serves as the focal point of contact for those outside the Agency. Major program activities are aimed at external audiences, including the public, the media, public interest groups, State and local government organizations, the Congress, and foreign governments.

The Directorate provides advice to the Director, his staff, and program directorates and develops and executes programs in the areas of congressional affairs and public and intergovernmental affairs. Also, the Directorate coordinates NATO Senior Civil Emergency Planning Committee activities within the Federal Government.

For further information, call 202–646–4600.

Regional Offices

The 10 regional offices primarily carry out FEMA's programs at the State and local levels. The Regional Directors are the Agency Director's principal representatives in contacts and relationships with Federal, State, regional, and local agencies; industry; and other public and private groups. The Regional Directors are responsible for accomplishing within their regions the national program objectives established by FEMA. They also work in conjunction with the Director in developing national policy.

For further information, call 202–646–3631.

Regional Offices—Federal Emergency Management Agency

(Areas included within each region are indicated on the map in Appendix A.)

	Region/Address	Director	Telephone
I.	Boston, MA (Rm. 442, J.W. McCormack Bldg., 02109)	Richard H. Strome	617-223-9540
II.	New York, NY (Rm. 1338, 26 Federal Plz., 10278)	Stephen Kempf, Jr.	212-225-7209
III.	Philadelphia, PA (105 S. 7th St., 19106)	Paul P. Giordano	215-931-5500
IV.	Atlanta, GA (Suite 700, 1371 Peachtree St. NE., 30309)	Major P. May	404-853-4200
V.	Chicago, IL (4th Fl., 175 W. Jackson Blvd., 60606)	Arlyn F. Brower	312-408-5500
VI.	Denton, TX (Rm. 206, Federal Regional Ctr., 60606)	Bradley M. Harris	817-898-5399
VII.	Kansas City, MO (Rm. 300, 911 Walnut St., 64106)	S. Richard Mellinger	816-283-7061
VIII.	Denver, CO (Bldg. 710, Federal Regional Ctr., 80225)	Marian L. Olson	303-235-4811
IX.	San Francisco, CA (Bldg. 105, Presidio of San Francisco, 94129)	William M. Medigovich	415-923-7100
X.	Bothell, WA (130 228th St. SW., 98021)	Kim Whitman	206-487-8800

Sources of Information

Inquiries on the following subjects should be directed to the specified office of the Federal Emergency Management Agency, 500 C Street SW., Washington, DC 20472.

Contracts and Procurement Office of Acquisition Management. Phone, 202–646–3744.

Employment Office of Personnel. Phone, 202–646–3964.

Freedom of Information Act Requests Office of the General Counsel. Phone, 202–646–3840.

For further information, contact the Office of Public Affairs, Federal Emergency Management Agency, 500 C Street SW., Washington, DC 20472. Phone, 202–646–4600.

FEDERAL HOUSING FINANCE BOARD

1777 F Street NW., Washington, DC 20006
Phone, 202–408–2500

Board of Directors:

Chairman	DANIEL F. EVANS, JR.
Members:	
(Secretary of Housing and Urban Development, *ex officio*)	JACK KEMP
	MARILYN R. SEYMANN
	LAWRENCE U. COSTIGLIO
	WILLIAM C. PERKINS

Officials:

Executive Director	J. STEPHEN BRITT
Special Assistants	JOHN M. BARGER
	KATHLEEN S. BRUEGER
Executive Secretariat	ELAINE L. BAKER
Inspector General	GEORGE WOLOSHYN
Director, District Bank Directorate	PHILIP L. CONOVER
General Counsel	BETH L. CLIMO
Director of Public Affairs	CHARLES POWERS
Director, Office of Strategic Planning	MICHAEL J. HIGGINS
Director, Office of Administration	PATRICK PIZZELLA
Director, House Finance Directorate	SYLVIA C. MARTINEZ
Director of Congressional Affairs	J. TIMOTHY O'NEILL

The Federal Housing Finance Board is responsible for the administration and enforcement of the Federal Home Loan Bank Act, as amended.

The Federal Housing Finance Board (Finance Board) was established on August 9, 1989, by the Federal Home Loan Bank Act, as amended by the Financial Institutions Reform, Recovery, and Enforcement Act of 1989 (FIRREA) (12 U.S.C. 1421 *et seq.*), as an independent regulatory agency in the executive branch. The Finance Board succeeded the Federal Home Loan Bank Board for those functions transferred to it by FIRREA.

The Finance Board is governed by a five-member Board of Directors. Four members are appointed by the President with the advice and consent of the Senate for 7-year terms; one of whom is designated as Chairman. The Secretary of the Department of Housing and Urban Development is the fifth member and serves in an *ex officio* capacity.

The Finance Board supervises the Federal Home Loan Banks created by the Federal Home Loan Bank Act and issues regulations and orders for carrying out the purposes of the provisions of that act. Savings associations and other institutions specified in section 4 of the act that make long-term home-mortgage loans are eligible to become members of a Federal Home Loan Bank. The Finance Board supervises the Federal Home Loan

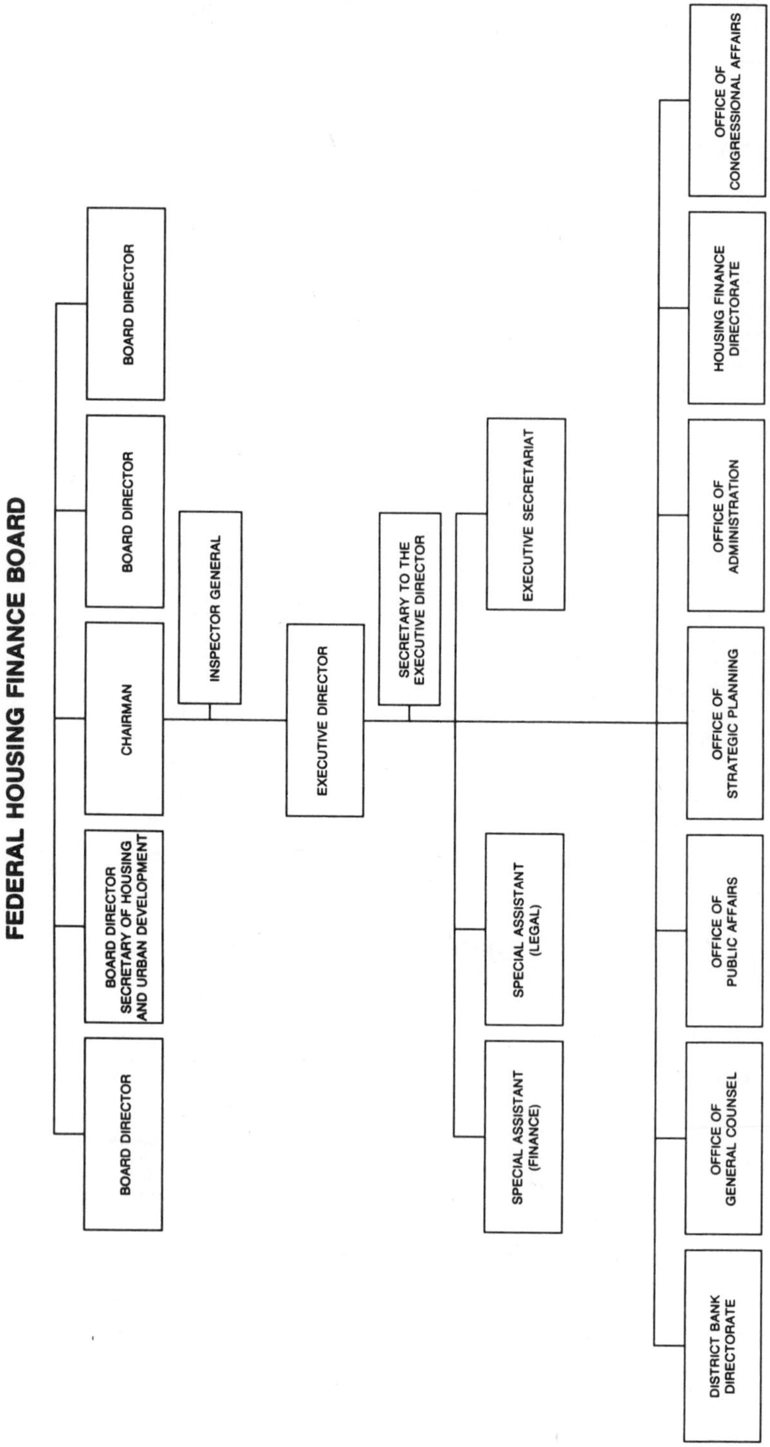
FEDERAL HOUSING FINANCE BOARD
BOARD DIRECTOR
BOARD DIRECTOR
CHAIRMAN
BOARD DIRECTOR SECRETARY OF HOUSING AND URBAN DEVELOPMENT
BOARD DIRECTOR
INSPECTOR GENERAL
EXECUTIVE DIRECTOR
SECRETARY TO THE EXECUTIVE DIRECTOR
EXECUTIVE SECRETARIAT
SPECIAL ASSISTANT (LEGAL)
SPECIAL ASSISTANT (FINANCE)
OFFICE OF CONGRESSIONAL AFFAIRS
HOUSING FINANCE DIRECTORATE
OFFICE OF ADMINISTRATION
OFFICE OF STRATEGIC PLANNING
OFFICE OF PUBLIC AFFAIRS
OFFICE OF GENERAL COUNSEL
DISTRICT BANK DIRECTORATE

Banks and ensures that they carry out their housing finance mission, remain adequately capitalized and able to raise funds in the capital markets, and operate in a safe and sound manner. The functions of the Finance Board with respect to the Banks and their members include: implementing community-oriented mortgage lending and affordable housing advance programs; prescribing rules and conditions upon which a Bank shall be authorized to borrow; issuing consolidated Federal Home Loan Bank bonds, notes, or debentures which are the joint and several obligations of all Federal Home Loan Banks; requiring an annual financial audit of each Bank; appointing six directors to the board of directors of each Bank and conducting the election of the remaining directors by the members; approving dividends paid to each Bank; and acting on applications for Bank membership.

The Finance Board is not subject to the appropriation process. Its funds are neither appropriated nor derived from Government funds, and are not subject to apportionment. The expenses of the Finance Board are paid by assessment against the regional Federal Home Loan Banks, which are deposited in a special account in the Treasury.

Financing Corporation

The Financing Corporation (FICO) was created by the Federal Home Loan Bank Act as amended by the Competitive Equality Banking Act of 1987 (12 U.S.C. 1441), as a mixed-ownership Government corporation. FICO has a three-member directorate, consisting of the director of the Office of Finance and two Federal Home Loan Bank presidents.

FICO operates under the authority of the Federal Housing Finance Board. It issues debt securities in the capital markets and purchases capital certificates of the Federal Savings and Loan Corporation Resolution Fund.

Federal Home Loan Bank System

In 1932, the Federal Home Loan Bank Act created and authorized the Federal Home Loan Bank System to provide a flexible credit reserve for member savings institutions engaged in home mortgage lending.

Regional Banks The System includes 12 regional Federal Home Loan Banks that are mixed-ownership Government corporations. A board of directors, six of whom are appointed by the Finance Baord, manages the Banks. The Finance Board conducts the election of the remaining directors.

Capital and Funds Member institutions, each of which is required to purchase stock, own the capital stock of the Federal Home Loan Banks. The Banks obtain other lendable funds through the issuance of consolidated obligations in the money and capital markets, through time and demand deposits accepted from member institutions and from other Federal Home Loan Banks.

Operations The Federal Home Loan Banks fulfill the responsibility of Congress and the Finance Board by providing appropriate loans, referred to as advances, to their members as a supplement to savings flows in meeting recurring variations in the supply of, and demand for, residential mortgage credit. Such loans, within the context of national housing goals, aid in stabilizing those sectors of the housing and mortgage markets served by the savings industry. The Banks also provide various services to member institutions pursuant to the statutory authority contained in the Federal Home Loan Bank Act.

The Office of Finance, located in Washington, DC, authorizes the Banks to perform their debt marketing operations, liquidity portfolio management, and financial forecasting. The Office also coordinates financial planning for the Bank System.

Eligible Institutions The types of institutions eligible to become members of the Federal Home Loan Banks are savings, building and loan, and homestead associations; savings and cooperative banks; insurance companies; and other insured depository institutions that satisfy the statutory requirements.

Power to Borrow Consolidated Federal Home Loan Bank obligations, which are the joint and several liabilities of all the

Banks, are issued by the Finance Board in the form of notes or bonds. Although the Banks are instrumentalities of the United States, such securities are not obligations of, and are not guaranteed by, the United States.

Sources of Information

Requests for information relating to human resources and procurement should be sent to the Office of Administration, Federal Housing Finance Board, 1777 F Street NW., Washington, DC 20006. Freedom of Information Act and any other information requests should be directed to the Executive Secretariat at the same address.

For further information, contact the Executive Secretariat, Federal Housing Finance Board, 1777 F Street NW., Washington, DC 20006. Phone, 202–408–2837.

FEDERAL LABOR RELATIONS AUTHORITY

500 C Street SW., Washington, DC 20424
Phone, 202–382–0711

Chairman	Jean McKee
Chief Counsel	Susan D. McCluskey
Public Affairs Specialist	Francisco Martinez-Alvarez
Director of Case Control	Alicia N. Columna
Member	Tony Armendariz
Chief Counsel	Steven H. Svartz
Executive Assistant	(vacancy)
Member	Pamela Talkin
Chief Counsel	Barbara B. Franklin
Executive Assistant	(vacancy)
Chief Administrative Law Judge	John H. Fenton
Solicitor	William E. Persina
Executive Director	Solly J. Thomas, Jr.
Director of Information Resources and Research Services	Harold D. Kessler
Director of Administration	Clyde B. Blandford, Jr.
Inspector General	Paul D. Miller
Office of the General Counsel	
General Counsel	Kathleen Day Koch
Executive Assistant	Robert S. Murphy
Deputy General Counsel and Director of Operations	Michael W. Doheny
Assistant General Counsel, Legal Policy and Advice	David L. Feder
Deputy Director of Operations, Field Management	Nancy A. Speight
Assistant General Counsel, Appeals	Michael D. Nossaman
Deputy Director of Operations, Program Analysis	Leonard F. Slobodin
Federal Service Impasses Panel	
Chairman	Roy M. Brewer

Members	EDWIN D. BRUBECK, N. VICTOR GOODMAN, CHARLES A. KOTHE, DANIEL H. KRUGER, SUSAN S. ROBFOGEL, JOHN R. VAN DE WATER
Executive Director	LINDA A. LAFFERTY
Foreign Service Labor Relations Board	
Chairman	JEAN MCKEE
Members	TIA SCHNEIDER DENENBERG
	MARCIA L. GREENBAUM
General Counsel	KATHLEEN DAY KOCH
Foreign Service Impasse Disputes Panel	
Chairman	MARGERY R. GOOTNICK
Members	JULIUS BALOG, JR., DIANNE BLANE, N. VICTOR GOODMAN, ANTHONY M. KERN

The Federal Labor Relations Authority oversees the Federal service labor-management relations program. It administers the law that protects the right of employees of the Federal Government to organize, bargain collectively, and participate through labor organizations of their own choosing in decisions affecting them. The Authority also ensures compliance with the statutory rights and obligations of Federal employees and the labor organizations that represent them in their dealings with Federal agencies.

The Federal Labor Relations Authority was created as an independent establishment by Reorganization Plan No. 2 of 1978 (5 U.S.C. app.), effective January 1, 1979, pursuant to Executive Order 12107 of December 28, 1978, to consolidate the central policymaking functions in Federal labor-management relations. Its duties and authority are specified in title VII (Federal Service Labor-Management Relations) of the Civil Service Reform Act of 1978 (5 U.S.C. 7101–7135).

Activities

The Authority provides leadership in establishing policies and guidance relating to the Federal service labor-management relations program. In addition, it determines the appropriateness of bargaining units, supervises or conducts representation elections, and prescribes criteria and resolves issues relating to the granting of consultation rights to labor organizations with respect to internal agency policies and governmentwide rules and regulations. It also resolves negotiability disputes, unfair labor practice complaints, and exceptions to arbitration awards. The Chairman of the Authority serves as the chief executive and administrative officer.

The General Counsel of the Authority investigates alleged unfair labor practices, files and prosecutes unfair labor practice complaints before the Authority, and exercises such other powers as the Authority may prescribe.

The Federal Service Impasses Panel, an entity within the Authority, is assigned the function of providing assistance in resolving negotiation impasses between agencies and unions. After investigating an impasse, the Panel can either recommend procedures to the parties for the resolution of the impasse or assist the parties in resolving the impasse through whatever methods and procedures, including factfinding and recommendations, it considers appropriate. If the parties do not arrive at a settlement after assistance by the Panel, the Panel may hold hearings and take whatever action is necessary to resolve the impasse.

The Foreign Service Labor Relations Board and the Foreign Service Impasse Disputes Panel administer provisions of chapter 2 of the Foreign Service Act of 1980 (22 U.S.C. 3921), concerning labor-management relations. This chapter establishes a statutory labor-management relations program for Foreign Service employees of the United States Government. Administrative and staff support is provided by the Federal Labor Relations Authority and the Federal Service Impasses Panel.

Regional Offices—Federal Labor Relations Authority

City/Address	Director	Telephone
Atlanta, GA (Suite 122, 1371 Peachtree St. NE., 30367)	Brenda M. Robinson	404-347-2324
Boston, MA (Rm. 1017, 10 Causeway St., 02222)	Edward S. Davidson	617-565-7280
Chicago, IL (Suite 1359-A, 175 W. Jackson Blvd., 60604)	William E. Washington	312-353-6306
Dallas, TX (Suite 926, 525 Griffin St., 75202)	James Petrucci	214-767-4996
Denver, CO (Suite 100, 1244 Speer Blvd., 80204)	Marjorie K. Thompson	303-844-5224
San Francisco, CA (Suite 220, 901 Market St., 94103)	Ronald T. Smith	415-744-4000
Washington, DC (P.O. Box 33758, Rm. 700, 1111 18th St. NW., 20033)	S. Jesse Reuben	202-653-8500

Sources of Information

Employment Employment inquiries and applications may be sent to the Director of Personnel. Phone, 202-382-0751.

Publications The Authority will assist in arranging reproduction of documents and ordering transcripts of hearings. Requests for publications should be submitted to the Printing Officer. Phone, 202-382-0724.

Reading Room Anyone desiring to inspect formal case documents or read agency publications may use facilities of the Authority's offices.

Speakers To give agencies, labor organizations, and other interested persons a better understanding of the Federal service labor-management relations program and the Authority's role and duties, its personnel participate as speakers or panel members before various groups. Requests for speakers or panelists should be submitted to the Office of the Chairman (phone, 202-382-0900); or the Deputy General Counsel (phone, 202-382-0842).

For further information, contact the Director of Information Resources and Research Services, Federal Labor Relations Authority, 500 C Street SW., Washington, DC 20424. Phone, 202-382-0715.

FEDERAL MARITIME COMMISSION

1100 L Street NW., Washington, DC 20573-0001
Phone, 202-523-5707

Chairman	Christopher L. Koch
Commissioners	William D. Hathaway
	Ming C. Hsu
	Francis J. Ivancie
	Donald R. Quartel, Jr.
General Counsel	Robert D. Bourgoin
Secretary	Joseph C. Polking
Director, Office of Informal Inquiries, Complaints, and Informal Dockets	Joseph T. Farrell
Chief Administrative Law Judge	Charles E. Morgan
Director, Office of Equal Employment Opportunity	Mary A. Jackson

Inspector General	Tony P. Kominoth
Managing Director	Edward Patrick Walsh
Deputy Managing Director	Bruce A. Dombrowski
Director, Bureau of Trade Monitoring	Austin Schmitt
Director, Bureau of Domestic Regulation	Robert G. Drew

The Federal Maritime Commission regulates the waterborne foreign and domestic offshore commerce of the United States, assures that United States international trade is open to all nations on fair and equitable terms, and protects against unauthorized, concerted activity in the waterborne commerce of the United States. This is accomplished through maintaining surveillance over steamship conferences and common carriers by water; assuring that only the rates on file with the Commission are charged; reviewing agreements between persons subject to the Shipping Act of 1984 and the Shipping Act, 1916; guaranteeing equal treatment to shippers, carriers, and other persons subject to the shipping statutes; and ensuring that adequate levels of financial responsibility are maintained for indemnification of passengers.

The Federal Maritime Commission was established by Reorganization Plan No. 7 of 1961 (5 U.S.C. app.), effective August 12, 1961. It is an independent agency that regulates shipping under the following statutes: the Shipping Act of 1984 (46 U.S.C. app. 1701–1720); the Shipping Act, 1916 (46 U.S.C. app. 801 *et seq.*); the Merchant Marine Act, 1920 (46 U.S.C. app. 861 *et seq.*); the Intercoastal Shipping Act, 1933 (46 U.S.C. app. 843 *et seq.*); the Merchant Marine Act, 1936 (46 U.S.C. app. 1101 *et seq.*); and certain provisions of the act of November 6, 1966 (46 U.S.C. app. 817(d) and 817(e)).

Activities

Agreements The Commission reviews for legal sufficiency agreements filed under section 15 of the Shipping Act, 1916 (46 U.S.C. app. 814), or section 5 of the Shipping Act of 1984 (46 U.S.C. app. 1704), including conference, interconference, and cooperative working agreements between common carriers, terminal operators, and other persons subject to the shipping statutes. The Commission also monitors activities under all effective (1984 act) or approved (1916 act) agreements for compliance with the provisions of law and its rules, orders, and regulations.

Tariffs The Commission accepts or rejects tariff filings, including filings dealing with service contracts, of common carriers engaged in the foreign and domestic offshore commerce of the United States, or conferences of such carriers. The Commission regulates rates of carriers in the domestic offshore trades. Special permission applications may be submitted for relief from statutory and/or Commission tariff requirements. The Commission monitors the activities of controlled carriers under section 9 of the Shipping Act of 1984 (46 U.S.C. app. 1708, 1709, 1714).

Licenses The Commission issues licenses to persons, partnerships, corporations, or associations desiring to engage in ocean freight forwarding activities.

Passenger Indemnity The Commission administers the passenger indemnity provisions of the act of November 6, 1966, which requires shipowners and operators to obtain certificates of financial responsibility to pay judgments for personal injury or death or to refund fares in the event of nonperformance of voyages.

Informal Complaints The Commission reviews alleged or suspected violations of the shipping statutes and rules and regulations of the Commission and may take administrative action to institute

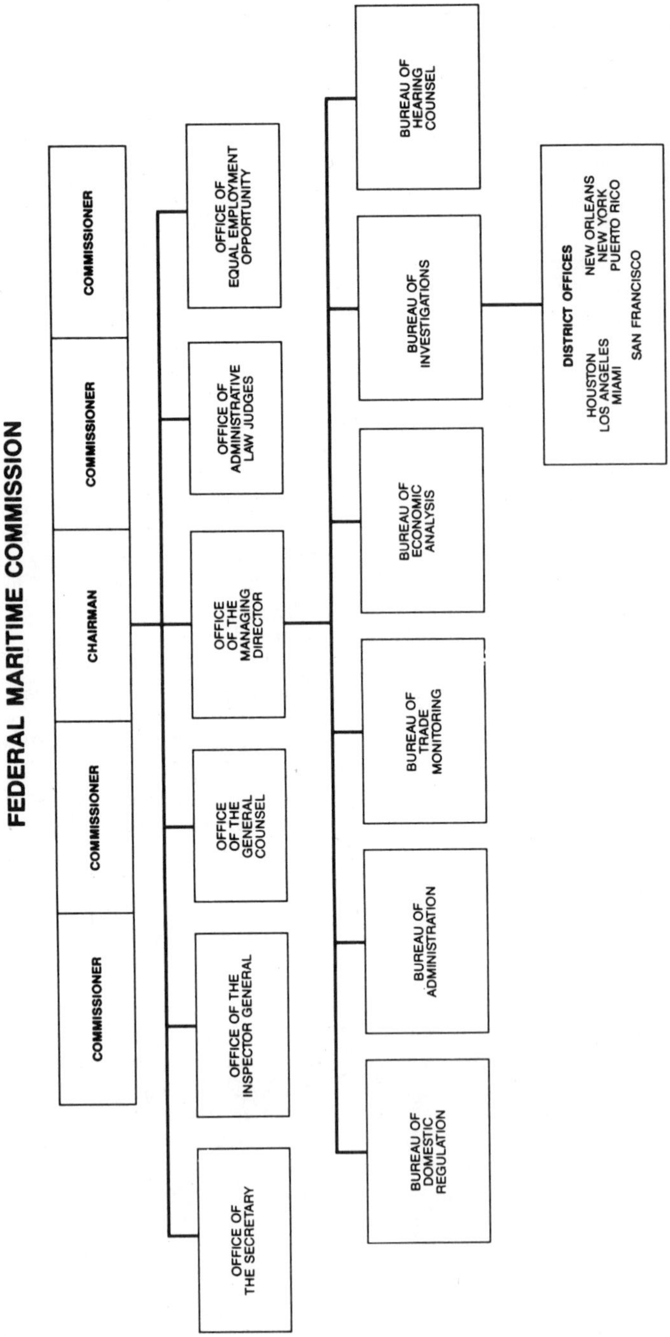
FEDERAL MARITIME COMMISSION
COMMISSIONER
COMMISSIONER
CHAIRMAN
COMMISSIONER
COMMISSIONER
OFFICE OF EQUAL EMPLOYMENT OPPORTUNITY
OFFICE OF ADMINISTRATIVE LAW JUDGES
OFFICE OF THE MANAGING DIRECTOR
OFFICE OF THE GENERAL COUNSEL
OFFICE OF THE INSPECTOR GENERAL
OFFICE OF THE SECRETARY
BUREAU OF HEARING COUNSEL
BUREAU OF INVESTIGATIONS
BUREAU OF ECONOMIC ANALYSIS
BUREAU OF TRADE MONITORING
BUREAU OF ADMINISTRATION
BUREAU OF DOMESTIC REGULATION
DISTRICT OFFICES
HOUSTON
LOS ANGELES
MIAMI
NEW ORLEANS
NEW YORK
PUERTO RICO
SAN FRANCISCO

formal proceedings, to refer matters to the Department of Justice, or to bring about voluntary agreement between the parties.

Formal Adjudicatory Procedure The Commission conducts formal investigations and hearings on its own motion and adjudicates formal complaints pursuant to the Administrative Procedure Act (5 U.S.C. note prec. 551).

Rulemaking The Commission promulgates rules and regulations to interpret, enforce, and ensure compliance with shipping and other statutes of common carriers by water and other persons subject to the statutes.

Investigation, Audit, and Financial and Economic Analyses The Commission prescribes and administers programs to ensure compliance with the provisions of the shipping statutes. These programs include the submission of information; field investigations and audits of activities and practices of common carriers; conferences; terminal operators, freight forwarders, and other persons subject to the shipping statutes; and rate analyses, studies, and economic reviews of current and prospective trade conditions, the extent and nature of competition in various trade areas, commodities carried, and future commodity trends.

International Affairs The Commission, in conjunction with the Department of State, conducts activities to effect the elimination of discriminatory practices on the part of foreign governments against United States-flag shipping and to achieve comity between the United States and its trading partners.

District Offices—Federal Maritime Commission

District	Address	Officer in Charge
Houston	Suite 102, 4141 E. Beltway 8, Houston, TX 77032	Donald H. Butler
Los Angeles	Suite 270, 11 Golden Shore, Long Beach, CA 90802	Michael A. Murphy
Miami	Rm. 115, 1001 North America Way, Miami, FL 33132	Richard L. Larson
New Orleans	Suite 440, World Trade Ctr., 2 Canal St., New Orleans, LA 70130	David M. Johnson
New York	Suite 614, 6 World Trade Ctr., New York, NY 10048-0949	Martin J. Keenaghan
Puerto Rico	Rm. 762, U.S. District Courthouse, Carlos Chardon St., Hato Rey, PR 00918-2254.	Lorraine Jiménez
San Francisco	Suite 3510, 525 Market St., San Francisco, CA 94105	Carlos D. Niemyer

Sources of Information

Employment Employment inquiries may be directed to the Office of Personnel, Federal Maritime Commission, 1100 L Street NW., Washington, DC 20573. Phone, 202-523-5773.

Informal complaints Phone, 202-523-5807.

Publications Recent publications of the Federal Maritime Commission are: *Twenty-Ninth Annual Report (1990)* and volume 23 of *Commission Decisions,* covering the period July 1980–June 1981; available from the Government Printing Office.

For further information, contact the Office of the Secretary, Federal Maritime Commission, 1100 L Street NW., Washington, DC 20573. Phone, 202-523-5725.

FEDERAL MEDIATION AND CONCILIATION SERVICE

2100 K Street NW., Washington, DC 20427
Phone, 202-653-5290

Director	Bernard E. DeLury
Deputy Director	Brian L. Flores

The Federal Mediation and Conciliation Service represents the public interest by promoting the development of sound and stable labor-management relationships; preventing or minimizing work stoppages by assisting labor and management to settle their disputes through mediation; advocating collective bargaining, mediation, and voluntary arbitration as the preferred processes for settling issues between employers and representatives of employees; developing the art, science, and practice of dispute resolution; and fostering constructive joint relationships of labor and management leaders to increase their mutual understanding and solution of common problems.

The Federal Mediation and Conciliation Service was created by the Labor Management Relations Act, 1947 (29 U.S.C. 172). The Director is appointed by the President with the advice and consent of the Senate.

Activities

The Federal Mediation and Conciliation Service helps prevent disruptions in the flow of interstate commerce caused by labor-management disputes by providing mediators to assist disputing parties in the resolution of their differences. Mediators have no law enforcement authority and rely wholly on persuasive techniques.

The Service offers its facilities in labor-management disputes in any industry affecting interstate commerce, either upon its own motion or at the request of one or more of the parties to the dispute, whenever in its judgment such dispute threatens to cause a substantial interruption of commerce. The Labor Management Relations Act requires that parties to a labor contract must file a dispute notice if agreement is not reached 30 days in advance of a contract termination or reopening date. The notice must be filed with the Service and the appropriate State or local mediation agency. The Service is required to avoid the mediation of disputes that would have only a minor effect on interstate commerce if State or other conciliation services are available to the parties.

For further information, contact one of the district offices listed below.

Mediation The mediator's efforts are directed toward the establishment of sound and stable labor-management relations on a continuing basis. In this work the mediator has a more basic function: encouraging and promoting better day-to-day relations between labor and management, thereby helping to reduce the incidence of work stoppages. Issues arising in negotiations may then be faced as problems to be settled through mutual effort rather than issues in dispute.

For further information, contact the Office of Public and International Affairs. Phone, 202–653–5290.

Arbitration The Service, on the joint request of employers and unions, will also assist in the selection of arbitrators from a roster of private citizens who are qualified as neutrals to adjudicate matters in dispute.

For further information, contact the Office of Arbitration Services. Phone, 202–653–5280.

District Offices—Federal Mediation and Conciliation Service

District/Address	Director	Telephone
1. 2d Fl., 1633 Broadway, New York, NY 10019	Kenneth C. Kowalski	202-399-5038
2. Rm. 3456, 600 Arch St., Philadelphia, PA 19106	John F. McDermott	215-597-7690
3. Suite 318, 1720 Peachtree St. NW., Atlanta, GA 30309	Leon E. Groves	404-347-2473
4. Suite 200, 3505 E. Royalton Rd., Broadview Heights, OH 44147	W. Kenneth Evans	216-522-4800
5. Rm. 310, 2001 6th Ave., Seattle, WA 98121	Norman A. Lee	206-442-5800
6. Suite 3950, 1300 Godward St., Minneapolis, MN 55413	Donovan Mayne	612-370-3300
7. Suite 203, 908 N. Elm St., Hinsdale, IL 60521	Daniel O'Leary	708-887-4750

District Offices—Federal Mediation and Conciliation Service—Continued

District/Address	Director	Telephone
8. Suite 325, 12140 Woodcrest Executive Dr., St. Louis (Creve Coeur), MO 63141.	James G. Kelly	314-576-3922
9. Suite 210, 4221 Wilshire Blvd., Los Angeles, CA 90010	Floyd Wood	213-965-3814

For further information, contact the Office of Public and International Affairs, Federal Mediation and Conciliation Service, 2100 K Street NW., Washington, DC 20427. Phone, 202-653-5290.

FEDERAL MINE SAFETY AND HEALTH REVIEW COMMISSION

1730 K Street NW., Washington, DC 20006
Phone, 202-653-5625

Chairman	RICHARD V. BACKLEY
Commissioners	JOYCE A. DOYLE
	ARLENE HOLEN
	L. CLAIR NELSON
	(VACANCY)
Chief Administrative Law Judge	PAUL MERLIN
General Counsel	L. JOSEPH FERRARA
Executive Director	RICHARD L. BAKER
Administrative Officer	REGINA M. CLARKE

The Federal Mine Safety and Health Review Commission is an independent, quasi-judicial agency established by the Federal Mine Safety and Health Act of 1977 (30 U.S.C. 801 *et seq.*). That act, enforced by the Secretary of Labor through the Mine Safety and Health Administration, governs compliance with occupational safety and health standards in the Nation's surface and underground mines, both coal and metal/nonmetal.

The Commission consists of five members who are appointed by the President with the advice and consent of the Senate and who serve staggered, 6-year terms. The Chairman, who is selected from among the Commissioners, serves at the pleasure of the President.

The Commission and its Office of Administrative Law Judges are charged with deciding cases brought pursuant to the act by the Mine Safety and Health Administration, mine operators, and miners or their representatives. These cases generally involve review of the Administration's enforcement actions including citations, mine closure orders, and proposals for civil penalties issued for violations of the act or the mandatory safety and health standards promulgated by the Secretary. The Commission also has jurisdiction over discrimination complaints filed by miners or their representatives in connection with their safety and health rights under the act, and over complaints for compensation filed on behalf of miners who have been idled through the enforcement of mine closure orders issued by the Administration.

Activities

Cases brought before the Commission are assigned to the Office of Administrative Law Judges, and hearings are conducted pursuant to the requirements of the Administrative Procedure Act (5 U.S.C. 554, 556) and the Commission's procedural rules (29 CFR Part 2700).

A judge's decision becomes a final but nonprecedential order of the Commission 40 days after issuance unless the Commission has directed the case for review in response to a petition or on its own motion. If a review is conducted, a decision of the Commission becomes final 30 days after issuance unless a party adversely affected seeks review in the U.S. Circuit Court of Appeals for the District of Columbia or the Circuit within which the mine subject to the litigation is located.

As far as practicable, hearings are held at locations convenient to the affected mines. The Office of Administrative Law Judges operates from two locations: the Falls Church Office, 2 Skyline, 5203 Leesburg Pike, Falls Church, VA 22041; and the Denver Office, Colonnade Center, Room 280, 1244 Speer Boulevard, Denver, CO 80204.

For further information, contact the Executive Director, Sixth Floor, 1730 K Street NW., Washington DC 20006. Phone, 202–653–5625.

FEDERAL RESERVE SYSTEM

Board of Governors of the Federal Reserve System
Twentieth Street and Constitution Avenue NW., Washington, DC 20551
Phone, 202–452–3000

Board of Governors

Chairman	ALAN GREENSPAN
Vice Chairman	(VACANCY)
Members	DAVID W. MULLINS, JR.
	WAYNE D. ANGELL
	EDWARD W. KELLEY, JR.
	JOHN P. LAWARE
	(VACANCY)
Official Staff:	
Assistants to the Board	JOSEPH R. COYNE
	DONALD J. WINN
General Counsel	J. VIRGIL MATTINGLY, JR.
Secretary	WILLIAM W. WILES
Associate Secretary	JENNIFER J. JOHNSON
Director, Division of Consumer and Community Affairs	GRIFFITH L. GARWOOD
Staff Director, Division of Banking Supervision and Regulation	WILLIAM TAYLOR
Associate Director (Bank Holding Companies)	DON E. KLINE
Associate Director (Regulation)	FREDERICK M. STRUBLE
Director, Division of Monetary Affairs	DONALD L. KOHN
Director, Division of Research and Statistics	MICHAEL J. PRELL
Deputy Director	EDWARD C. ETTIN
Staff Director, Division of International Finance	EDWIN M. TRUMAN
Senior Associate Director	LARRY J. PROMISEL
Staff Adviser	ROBERT F. GEMMILL
Senior Associate Director	CHARLES J. SIEGMAN

Staff Director, Office of Staff Director for Management	S. DAVID FROST
Director, Office of the Director for Information Resources Management	STEPHEN R. MALPHRUS
Director, Division of Applications Development and Statistical Services	WILLIAM R. JONES
Director, Division of Hardware and Software Systems	BRUCE M. BEARDSLEY
Director, Division of Human Resources Management	DAVID L. SHANNON
Associate Director	JOHN R. WEIS
Controller	GEORGE E. LIVINGSTON
Inspector General, Office of the Inspector General	BRENT L. BOWEN
Director, Division of Support Services	ROBERT E. FRAZIER
Staff Director, Office of Staff Director for Federal Reserve Bank Activities	THEODORE E. ALLISON
Director, Division of Federal Reserve Bank Operations and Payment Systems	CLYDE H. FARNSWORTH, JR.
Deputy Director, Payments and Automation	BRUCE J. SUMMERS
Deputy Director, Finance and Control	DAVID L. ROBINSON

Officers of the Federal Reserve Banks

Chairmen and Federal Reserve Agents:	
Boston	RICHARD N. COOPER
New York	CYRUS R. VANCE
Philadelphia	PETER A. BENOLIEL
Cleveland	JOHN R. MILLER
Richmond	ANNE MARIE WHITTEMORE
Atlanta	LARRY L. PRINCE
Chicago	CHARLES S. MCNEER
St. Louis	H. EDWIN TRUSHEIM
Minneapolis	DELBERT W. JOHNSON
Kansas City	FRED W. LYONS, JR.
Dallas	HUGH G. ROBINSON
San Francisco	ROBERT F. ERBURU
Presidents:	
Boston	RICHARD F. SYRON
New York	E. GERALD CORRIGAN
Philadelphia	EDWARD G. BOEHNE
Cleveland	W. LEE HOSKINS
Richmond	ROBERT P. BLACK
Atlanta	ROBERT P. FORRESTAL
Chicago	SILAS KEEHN
St. Louis	THOMAS C. MELZER
Minneapolis	GARY H. STERN
Kansas City	ROGER GUFFEY
Dallas	ROBERT D. MCTEER, JR.
San Francisco	ROBERT T. PARRY

Federal Open Market Committee

Chairman	ALAN GREENSPAN
Vice Chairman	E. GERALD CORRIGAN

Members	Wayne D. Angell, Robert P. Black, Robert P. Forrestal, Silas Keehn, Edward W. Kelley, Jr., John P. LaWare, David W. Mullins, Jr., Robert T. Parry, Martha R. Seger
Official Staff:	
Secretary and Economist	Donald L. Kohn
Deputy Secretary	Normand R.V. Bernard
Assistant Secretaries	Joseph R. Coyne
	Gary P. Gillum
General Counsel	J. Virgil Mattingly, Jr.
Deputy General Counsel	Ernest T. Patrikis
Economists	Michael J. Prell
	Edwin M. Truman
Manager for Domestic Operations, System Open Market Account	Peter D. Sternlight
Manager for Foreign Operations, System Open Market Account	Sam Y. Cross
President, Federal Advisory Council	Paul Hazen
Chairman, Consumer Advisory Council	James W. Head
President, Thrift Institutions Advisory Council	Marion O. Sandler

The Federal Reserve System, the central bank of the United States, is charged with administering and making policy for the Nation's credit and monetary affairs. Through its supervisory and regulatory banking functions, the Federal Reserve helps to maintain the banking industry in sound condition, capable of responding to the Nation's domestic and international financial needs and objectives.

The Federal Reserve System was established by the Federal Reserve Act (12 U.S.C. 221), approved December 23, 1913. The System serves as the Nation's central bank. The powers of central banks vary widely, but their major responsibility is in the execution of monetary policy. Central banks typically perform a number of other functions, such as the transfer of funds, handling Government deposits and debt issues, supervising and regulating banks, and acting as lender of last resort.

It is the responsibility of the Federal Reserve System to contribute to the strength and vitality of the U.S. economy. By influencing the lending and investing activities of depository institutions and the cost and availability of money and credit, the Federal Reserve System can help promote the full use of human and capital resources, the growth of productivity, relatively stable prices, and equilibrium in the Nation's international balance of payments. Through its supervisory and regulatory banking functions, the Federal Reserve System helps maintain a commercial banking system that is responsive to the Nation's financial needs and objectives.

The System consists of six parts: the Board of Governors in Washington, DC; the 12 Federal Reserve Banks and their 25 branches and other facilities situated throughout the country; the Federal Open Market Committee; the Federal Advisory Council; the Consumer Advisory Council; the Thrift Institutions Advisory Council; and the Nation's financial institutions, including commercial banks, savings and loan associations, mutual savings banks, and credit unions.

Board of Governors

Broad supervisory powers are vested in the Board of Governors, which has its offices in Washington. The Board is composed of seven members appointed by the President with the advice and consent of the Senate. The Chairman of the Board of Governors is, by Executive Order 11269 of February 14, 1966, a member of the National Advisory Council on International Monetary and Financial Policies.

The Board determines general monetary, credit, and operating policies for the System as a whole and formulates the rules and regulations necessary to carry out the purposes of the Federal Reserve Act. The Board's principal duties consist of monitoring credit conditions; supervising the Federal Reserve Banks, member banks, and bank holding companies; and regulating the implementation of certain consumer credit protection laws.

Power To Influence Credit Conditions Pursuant to the Depository Institutions Deregulation and Monetary Control Act of 1980, referred to as the Monetary Control Act of 1980 (12 U.S.C. 226 note), the Board is given the power, within statutory limitations, to fix the requirements concerning reserves to be maintained by depository institutions on transaction accounts or nonpersonal time deposits. Another important instrument of credit control is found in open market operations. The members of the Board of Governors also are members of the Federal Open Market Committee, whose work and organization are described below. The Board of Governors reviews and determines the discount rate charged by the Federal Reserve Banks. For the purpose of preventing excessive use of credit for the purchase or carrying of securities, the Board is authorized to regulate the amount of credit that may be initially extended and subsequently maintained on any security (with certain exceptions).

Supervision of Federal Reserve Banks The Board is authorized to make examinations of the Federal Reserve Banks, to require statements and reports from such Banks, to supervise the issue and retirement of Federal Reserve notes, to require the establishment or discontinuance of branches of Reserve Banks, and to exercise supervision over all relationships and transactions of those Banks with foreign branches. The Board of Governors reviews and follows the examination and supervisory activities of the Federal Reserve Banks aimed at further coordination of policies and practices.

Supervision of Bank Holding Companies The Bank Holding Company Act of 1956 gave to the Federal Reserve the primary responsibility for supervising and regulating the activities of bank holding companies. This act was designed to achieve two basic objectives: to control the expansion of bank holding companies by avoiding the creation of monopoly or restraining trade in banking; and to limit the expansion of bank holding companies to those nonbanking activities that are closely related to banking, thus maintaining a separation between banking and commerce. A company that seeks to become a bank holding company must obtain the prior approval of the Federal Reserve. Any company that qualifies as a bank holding company must register with the Federal Reserve System and file reports with the System. To preserve the traditional separation of banking and commerce, the Congress amended the Bank Holding Act in December 1970. Primarily as a result of this new legislation, the number of bank holding companies increased. The number has continued to increase steadily and totaled 6,474 at the end of 1988, when 91 percent of all deposits of domestic banking organizations were held by bank subsidiaries of holding companies. The number of applications received in 1988 totaled 1,337.

Supervision of Member Banks The Board has jurisdiction over the admission of State banks and trust companies to membership in the Federal Reserve System, the termination of membership of such banks, the establishment of branches by such banks, and the approval of bank mergers and consolidations where the resulting institution will be a State member bank. It receives copies of condition reports submitted by them to the Federal Reserve Banks. It has power to examine all member banks and the affiliates of member banks and to require condition reports from them. It has authority to require periodic and other public disclosure of information with respect to an equity security of a State member bank that is held by 500 or more persons. It establishes minimum standards with respect to installation, maintenance, and operation of security devices and procedures by State member banks. It has authority to issue cease-and-desist orders in connection with violations of law or unsafe or unsound banking practices by State member banks and to remove directors or officers of such banks in certain circumstances, and it may, in its discretion, suspend member banks from the use of the credit facilities of the Federal Reserve System for making undue use of bank credit for speculative purposes or for any other purpose inconsistent with the maintenance of sound credit conditions.

The Board may grant authority to member banks to establish branches in foreign countries or dependencies or insular possessions of the United States, to invest in the stocks of banks or corporations engaged in international or foreign banking, or to invest in foreign banks. It also charters, regulates, and supervises certain corporations that engage in foreign or international banking and financial activities.

The Board is authorized to issue general regulations permitting interlocking relationships in certain circumstances between member banks and organizations dealing in securities or between member banks and other banks.

Other Activities Under the Change in Bank Control Act of 1978 (12 U.S.C. 1817(j)), the Board is required to review other bank stock acquisitions.

Under the Truth in Lending Act (15 U.S.C. 1601), the Board is required to prescribe regulations to ensure a meaningful disclosure by lenders of credit terms so that consumers will be able to compare more readily the various credit terms available and will be informed about rules governing credit cards, including their potential liability for unauthorized use.

Under the International Banking Act of 1978 (12 U.S.C. 3101), the Board has authority to impose reserve requirements and interest rate ceilings on branches and agencies of foreign banks in the United States, to grant loans to them, to provide them access to Federal Reserve services, and to limit their interstate banking activities.

The Board also is the rulemaking authority for the Equal Credit Opportunity Act, the Home Mortgage Disclosure Act, the Fair Credit Billing Act, the Expedited Funds Availability Act, and certain provisions of the Federal Trade Commission Act as they apply to banks.

Expenses To meet its expenses and pay the salaries of its members and its employees, the Board makes semiannual assessments upon the Reserve Banks in proportion to their capital stock and surplus.

Federal Open Market Committee

The Federal Open Market Committee is comprised of the Board of Governors and five of the presidents of the Reserve Banks. The Chairman of the Board of Governors is traditionally the Chairman of the Committee. The president of the Federal Reserve Bank of New York serves as a permanent member of the Committee. Four of the twelve Reserve Bank presidents rotate annually as members of the Committee.

Open market operations of the Reserve Banks are conducted under regulations adopted by the Committee and pursuant to specific policy directives issued by the Committee, which meets in Washington at frequent intervals. Purchases and sales of securities in the open market are undertaken to supply bank reserves to support the credit and money needed for long-term economic growth, to offset cyclical economic swings, and to accommodate seasonal demands of businesses and consumers for money and credit. These operations are carried out principally in U.S. Government obligations, but they also include purchases and sales of Federal agency obligations and bankers' acceptances. All operations are conducted in New York, where the primary markets for these securities are located; the Federal

Reserve Bank of New York executes transactions for the Federal Reserve System Open Market Account in carrying out these operations.

Under the Committee's direction, the Federal Reserve Bank of New York also undertakes transactions in foreign currencies for the Federal Reserve System Open Market Account. The purposes of these operations include helping to safeguard the value of the dollar in international exchange markets and facilitating growth in international liquidity in accordance with the needs of an expanding world economy. The Federal Reserve has, in particular, entered into a network of mutual currency arrangements with other central banks providing for the right to draw foreign exchange within specified limits and for specified periods.

Federal Reserve Banks

The 12 Federal Reserve Banks are located in Atlanta, Boston, Chicago, Cleveland, Dallas, Kansas City, Minneapolis, New York, Philadelphia, Richmond, San Francisco, and St. Louis. Branch banks are located in Baltimore, Birmingham, Buffalo, Charlotte, Cincinnati, Denver, Detroit, El Paso, Helena, Houston, Jacksonville, Little Rock, Los Angeles, Louisville, Memphis, Miami, Nashville, New Orleans, Oklahoma City, Omaha, Pittsburgh, San Antonio, Portland, Salt Lake City, and Seattle.

Directors and Officers of Reserve Banks The Board of Directors of each Reserve Bank is composed of nine members, equally divided into three designated classes: class A, class B, and class C. Directors of class A are representative of the stockholding member banks. Directors of class B must be actively engaged in their districts in commerce, agriculture, or some other industrial pursuit, and may not be officers, directors, or employees of any bank. Class C directors may not be officers, directors, employees, or stockholders of any bank. The six class A and class B directors are elected by the stockholding member banks, while the three class C directors are appointed by the Board of Governors. The terms of office of the directors are so arranged that the term of one director of each class expires each year.

One of the class C directors appointed by the Board of Governors is designated as Chairman of the Board of Directors of the Reserve Bank and as Federal Reserve agent, and in the latter capacity he is required to maintain a local office of the Board of Governors on the premises of the Reserve Bank. Another class C director is appointed by the Board of Governors as deputy chairman.

Each Reserve Bank has as its chief executive officer a president appointed for a term of 5 years by its Board of Directors with the approval of the Board of Governors. There are also a first vice president, appointed in the same manner, and other officers appointed by the Board of Directors.

Reserves on Deposit In accordance with provisions of the Monetary Control Act of 1980 (12 U.S.C. 226 note), the Reserve Banks receive and hold on deposit the reserve or clearing account deposits of depository institutions. These banks are permitted to count their vault cash as part of their required reserve.

Extensions of Credit The Monetary Control Act of 1980 (12 U.S.C. 226 note) directs the Federal Reserve to open its discount window to any depository institution that is subject to Federal Reserve reserve requirements on transaction accounts or nonpersonal time deposits.

Discount window credit provides for Federal Reserve lending to eligible depository institutions under two basic programs. One is the adjustment credit program; the other supplies more extended credit for certain limited purposes.

Short-term adjustment credit is the primary type of Federal Reserve credit. It is available to help borrowers meet temporary requirements for funds. Borrowers are not permitted to use adjustment credit to take advantage of any spread between the discount rate and market rates.

Extended credit is provided through three programs designed to assist depository institutions in meeting longer term needs for funds. One provides seasonal credit—for periods running up to 9 months—to smaller depository institutions that lack access to market funds. A second program assists institutions that experience special difficulties arising from exceptional circumstances or practices involving only that institution. Finally, in cases where more general liquidity strains are affecting a broad range of depository institutions—such as those whose portfolios consist primarily of longer term assets—credit may be provided to address the problems of particular institutions being affected by the general situation.

Currency Issue The Reserve Banks issue Federal Reserve notes, which constitute the bulk of money in circulation. These notes are obligations of the United States and are a prior lien upon the assets of the issuing Federal Reserve Bank. They are issued against a pledge by the Reserve Bank with the Federal Reserve agent of collateral security including gold certificates, paper discounted or purchased by the Bank, and direct obligations of the United States.

Other Powers The Reserve Banks are empowered to act as clearinghouses and as collecting agents for depository institutions in the collection of checks and other instruments. They are also authorized to act as depositories and fiscal agents of the United States and to exercise other banking functions specified in the Federal Reserve Act. They perform a number of important functions in connection with the issue and redemption of United States Government securities.

Federal Advisory Council

The Federal Advisory Council acts in an advisory capacity, conferring with the Board of Governors on general business conditions.

The Council is composed of 12 members, one from each Federal Reserve district, being selected annually by the Board of Directors of the Reserve Bank of the district. The Council is required to meet in Washington at least four times each year, and more often if called by the Board of Governors.

Consumer Advisory Council

The Consumer Advisory Council confers with the Board of Governors several times each year on the Board's responsibilities in the field of consumer credit protection. The Council was established by Congress in 1976 at the suggestion of the Board and replaced the Advisory Committee on Truth in Lending that was established by the 1968 Truth in Lending Act.

The Council is composed of 30 members from all parts of the country. Its membership includes a broad representation of consumer and creditor interests. It advises the Board on its responsibilities under such laws as Truth in Lending, Equal Credit Opportunity, and Home Mortgage Disclosure.

Thrift Institutions Advisory Council

The Thrift Institutions Advisory Council is an advisory group established by the Board in 1980 made up of representatives from nonbank depository thrift institutions, which includes savings and loans, mutual savings bankers, and credit unions. The Council meets at least four times each year with the Board of Governors to discuss developments relating to thrift institutions, the housing industry and mortgage finance, and certain regulatory issues.

Sources of Information

Employment Inquiries regarding employment should be addressed to the Director, Division of Personnel, Board of Governors of the Federal Reserve System, Washington, DC 20551.

Procurement Firms seeking business with the Board should address their inquiries to the Director, Division of Support Services, Board of Governors of the Federal Reserve System, Washington, DC 20551.

Publications Among the publications issued by the Board are *The Federal Reserve System—Purposes and*

Functions, and a series of pamphlets including *Guide to Business Credit and the Equal Credit Opportunity Act; Consumer Handbook; Making Deposits: When Will Your Money Be Available;* and *When Your Home Is On the Line: What You Should Know About Home Equity Lines of Credit.* Copies of these pamphlets are available free of charge. Information regarding publications may be obtained in Room MP-510 (Martin Building) of the Board's headquarters. Phone, 202-452-3244.

Reading Room A reading room where persons may inspect records that are available to the public is located in Room B-1122 at the Board's headquarters, Twentieth and C Streets NW., Washington, DC. Information regarding the availability of records may be obtained by calling 202-452-3684.

For further information, contact the Office of Public Affairs, Board of Governors, Federal Reserve System, Washington, DC 20551. Phone, 202-452-3204 or 202-452-3215.

FEDERAL RETIREMENT THRIFT INVESTMENT BOARD

805 Fifteenth Street NW., Washington, DC 20005
Phone, 202-523-4511

Chairman	ROGER W. MEHLE
Members	JAMES H. ATKINS
	STEPHEN E. BELL
	J. DAVID DAVENPORT
	RICHARD H. HEADLEE
Officials:	
Executive Director	FRANCIS X. CAVANAUGH
Special Assistant	LUCILLE DICKINSON
General Counsel	ROBERT BLOOM
Assistant General Counsel (Administration)	JOHN J. O'MEARA
Assistant General Counsel (Programs)	JAMES B. PETRICK
Director of Accounting	DAVID L. BLACK
Director of Administration	STRAT D. VALAKIS
Director of Automated Systems	JOHN W. WITTERS
Director of Benefits and Program Analysis	ALISONE M. CLARKE
Director of Communications	VEDA R. CHARROW
Director of External Affairs	THOMAS J. TRABUCCO
Director of Investments	PETER B. MACKEY

The Federal Retirement Thrift Investment Board administers the Thrift Savings Plan, which provides Federal employees the opportunity to save for additional retirement security.

The Federal Retirement Thrift Investment Board was established as an independent agency by the Federal Employees' Retirement System Act of 1986 (5 U.S.C. 8472). The act vests responsibility for the agency in six named fiduciaries: the five Board members and the Executive Director. The five members of the Board, one of whom is designated as Chairman, are appointed by the President with the advice and consent of the Senate and serve on the Board on a part-time basis. The members appoint the Executive

Director, who is responsible for the management of the agency and the Plan.

Activities

The Thrift Savings Plan is a tax-deferred, defined contribution plan that was established as one of the three parts of the Federal Employees' Retirement System. For employees covered under the System, savings accumulated through the Plan make an important addition to the retirement benefits provided by Social Security and the System's Basic Annuity. Civil Service Retirement System employees can also take advantage of the Plan to supplement their annuities.

The Board operates the Thrift Savings Plan and manages the investments of the Thrift Savings Fund solely for the benefit of participants and their beneficiaries. As part of these responsibilities, the Board maintains an account for each Plan participant, makes loans, purchases annuity contracts, and provides for the payment of benefits.

For further information, contact the Director of External Affairs, Federal Retirement Thrift Investment Board, 805 Fifteenth Street NW., Washington, DC 20005. Phone, 202–523–5660.

FEDERAL TRADE COMMISSION

Pennsylvania Avenue at Sixth Street NW., Washington, DC 20580
Phone, 202–326–2222 (Public Reference Branch)

Chairman	JANET D. STEIGER
Executive Assistant	JAMES C. HAMILL
Commissioners	MARY L. AZCUENAGA
	DENNIS A. YAO
	DEBORAH K. OWEN
	ROSCOE B. STARK III
Executive Director	ROBERT S. WALTON III
Deputy Executive Director for Management	ROSEMARIE STRAIGHT
Deputy Executive Director for Planning and Information	ALAN PROCTOR
Director, Bureau of Competition	KEVIN J. ARQUIT
Deputy Director	MARY LOU STEPTOE
Director, Bureau of Consumer Protection	BARRY J. CUTLER
Deputy Director	GERALD M. CAPLAN
Director, Bureau of Economics	JOHN L. PETERMAN
Associate Director for Special Projects	RONALD S. BOND
General Counsel	JAMES M. SPEARS
Deputy General Counsel	JAY C. SHAFFER
Director, Office of Congressional Relations	WILLIAM B. PRENDERGAST
Director, Office of Public Affairs	BONNIE JANSEN, *Acting*
Director, Office of Consumer and Competition Advocacy	RICHARD F. FIELDING
Secretary of the Commission	DONALD S. CLARK
Chief Administrative Law Judge	LEWIS F. PARKER
Inspector General	FREDERICK J. ZIRKEL

[For the Federal Trade Commission statement of organization, see the *Code of Federal Regulations,* Title 16, Part 0]

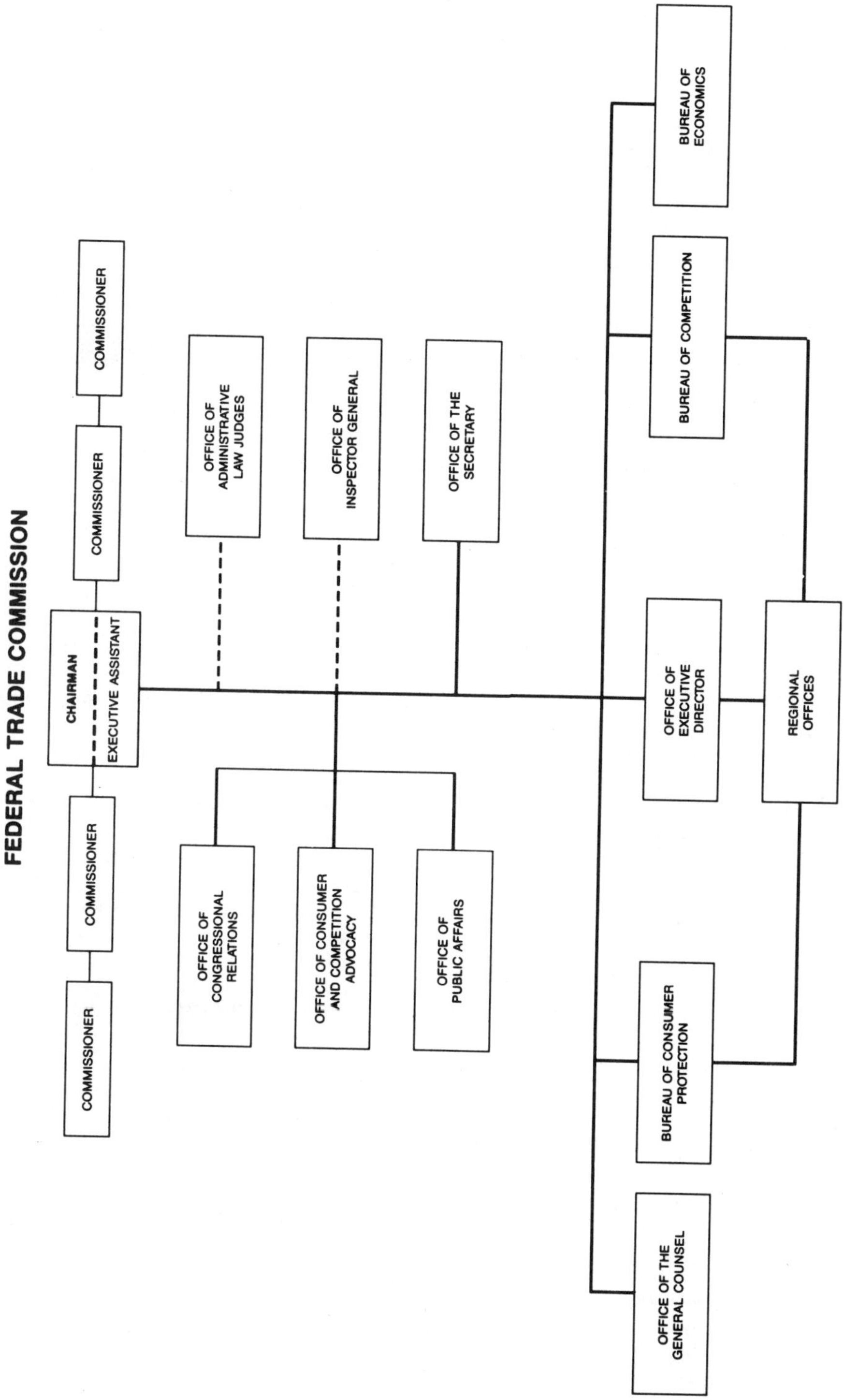
FEDERAL TRADE COMMISSION
COMMISSIONER
COMMISSIONER
CHAIRMAN
EXECUTIVE ASSISTANT
COMMISSIONER
COMMISSIONER
OFFICE OF ADMINISTRATIVE LAW JUDGES
OFFICE OF INSPECTOR GENERAL
OFFICE OF THE SECRETARY
OFFICE OF CONGRESSIONAL RELATIONS
OFFICE OF CONSUMER AND COMPETITION ADVOCACY
OFFICE OF PUBLIC AFFAIRS
BUREAU OF ECONOMICS
BUREAU OF COMPETITION
OFFICE OF EXECUTIVE DIRECTOR
REGIONAL OFFICES
BUREAU OF CONSUMER PROTECTION
OFFICE OF THE GENERAL COUNSEL

The objective of the Federal Trade Commission is to maintain competitive enterprise as the keystone of the American economic system. Although the duties of the Commission are many and varied, the foundation of public policy underlying all these duties is essentially the same: to prevent the free enterprise system from being fettered by monopoly or restraints on trade or corrupted by unfair or deceptive trade practices. In brief, the Commission is charged with keeping competition both free and fair.

The purpose of the Federal Trade Commission is expressed in the Federal Trade Commission Act (15 U.S.C. 41–51) and the Clayton Act (15 U.S.C. 12), both passed in 1914 and both successively amended in the years that have followed. The Federal Trade Commission Act prohibits the use in commerce of "unfair methods of competition" and "unfair or deceptive acts or practices." The Clayton Act outlaws specific practices recognized as instruments of monopoly. As an administrative agency, acting quasi-judicially and quasi-legislatively, the Commission was established to deal with trade practices on a continuing and corrective basis. It has no authority to punish; its function is to "prevent," through cease-and-desist orders and other means, those practices condemned by the law of Federal trade regulation; however, court-ordered civil penalties up to $10,000 may be obtained for each violation of a Commission order or trade regulation rule.

The Federal Trade Commission was organized as an independent administrative agency in 1914 pursuant to the Federal Trade Commission Act. Related duties subsequently were delegated to the Commission by the Wheeler-Lea Act, the Trans-Alaska Pipeline Authorization Act, the Clayton Act, the Export Trade Act, the Wool Products Labeling Act, the Fur Products Labeling Act, the Textile Fiber Products Identification Act, the Fair Packaging and Labeling Act, the Lanham Trade-Mark Act of 1946, the Consumer Credit Protection Acts, the Robinson-Patman Act, the Hobby Protection Act, the Magnuson-Moss Warranty-Federal Trade Commission Improvement Act, the Federal Trade Commission Improvements Act of 1980, and the Smokeless Tobacco Health Education Act of 1986.

The Commission is composed of five members. Each member is appointed by the President, by and with the advice and consent of the Senate, for a term of 7 years. Not more than three of the Commissioners may be members of the same political party. One Commissioner is designated by the President as Chairman of the Commission and is responsible for its administrative management.

Activities

The Commission's principal functions are to:

—promote competition in or affecting commerce through the prevention of general trade restraints such as price-fixing agreements, boycotts, illegal combinations of competitors, and other unfair methods of competition;

—safeguard the public by preventing the dissemination of false or deceptive advertisements of consumer products generally, and food, drug, cosmetics, and therapeutic devices, particularly, as well as other unfair or deceptive practices;

—prevent pricing discrimination; exclusive-dealing and tying arrangements; corporate mergers, acquisitions, or joint ventures, when such practices or arrangements may substantially lessen competition or tend to create a monopoly; interlocking directorates that may restrain competition; the payment or receipt of illegal brokerage; and discrimination among competing customers in the furnishing of or the payment for services or facilities used to promote the resale of a product;

—bring about truthful labeling of textile, wool, and fur products;

—regulate packaging and labeling of certain consumer commodities within the purview of the Fair Packaging and Labeling Act so as to prevent consumer deception and to facilitate value comparisons;

—supervise the registration and operation of associations of American exporters engaged in export trade;

—achieve accurate credit cost disclosure by consumer creditors (retailers, finance companies, non-Federal credit unions, and other creditors not specifically regulated by another Government agency) as called for in the Truth in Lending Act to ensure a meaningful basis for informed credit decisions, and to regulate the issuance of and liability for the use of credit cards so as to prohibit their fraudulent use in or affecting commerce;

—protect consumers against circulation of inaccurate or obsolete credit reports and ensure that consumer reporting agencies exercise their responsibilities in a manner that is fair and equitable and in conformity with the Fair Credit Reporting Act, the Fair Credit Billing Act, the Equal Credit Opportunity Act, and the Fair Debt Collection Practices Act; and

—gather and make available to the Congress, the President, and the public, factual data concerning economic and business conditions.

Enforcement The Commission's law enforcement work falls into two general categories: actions to foster voluntary compliance with the law, and formal administrative litigation leading to mandatory orders against offenders.

For the most part, compliance with the law is obtained through voluntary and cooperative action by way of staff level advice, which is not binding on the Commission, advisory opinions by the Commission, and through issuance of guides delineating legal requirements as to particular business practices.

The formal litigation is similar to that in Federal courts. Cases are instituted by issuance of a complaint charging the respondent—a person, partnership, or corporation—with violation of one or more of the statutes administered by the Commission. Cases may be settled by consent orders. If the charges are not contested, or if the charges are found to be true after a hearing in a contested case, a cease-and-desist order is issued requiring discontinuance of the unlawful practices.

Legal Case Work Cases before the Commission may originate through complaint by a consumer or a competitor; the Congress; or from Federal, State, or municipal agencies. Also, the Commission itself may initiate an investigation into possible violation of the laws it administers. No formality is permitted in submitting a complaint. A letter giving the facts in detail, accompanied by all supporting evidence in possession of the complaining party, is sufficient. It is the general policy of the Commission not to disclose the identity of any complainant, except as permitted by law or Commission rules.

Upon receipt of a complaint, various criteria are applied in determining whether the particular matter should be investigated. Within the limits of its resources, investigations are initiated that are considered to best support the Commission's goals of maintaining competition and protecting consumers.

On completion of an investigation, there will be a staff recommendation for final Commission action. The staff may recommend that the matter be closed. If that recommendation is approved, a closing letter is sent to the individual or company that was the subject of the investigation. The staff may instead recommend that the Commission approve the informal settlement of a case, usually by acceptance of an agreement containing a consent order to cease and desist. If such a consent order is worked out, it customarily provides that the respondent does not admit any violation of the law, but agrees to be bound by an order requiring the discontinuance of the challenged practices.

If the Commission determines that some action other than closing the investigation is appropriate, but no consent agreement can be negotiated, the Commission may issue a formal complaint alleging that the respondent has violated one or more of the laws

290-950 O 91 - 20

administered by the Commission. The respondent is served with a copy of the complaint, often accompanied by a proposed cease-and-desist order to be used if the allegations of law violations are proved. The Commission's counsel supporting the complaint and respondents may negotiate a consent agreement after the issuance of the formal complaint. Otherwise, the case is heard by an administrative law judge, who conducts a trial that is open to the public and issues an initial decision.

The initial decision becomes the decision of the Commission at the end of 30 days unless the respondent or the counsel supporting the complaint appeals the decision to the Commission, or the Commission by order stays the effective date or places the case on its own docket for review. In the Commission's decision on such an appeal or review, the initial decision may be sustained, modified, or reversed. If the complaint is sustained or modified, a cease-and-desist order is issued. If an initial decision dismissing a complaint is sustained, no cease-and-desist order is issued.

Under the Federal Trade Commission Act, an order to cease and desist or to take other corrective action—such as affirmative disclosure, divestiture, or restitution—becomes final 60 days after date of service upon the respondent, unless within that period the respondent petitions an appropriate United States court of appeals to review the order. The court has power to affirm, modify, or set the order aside. Either party, on writ of certiorari, may apply to the Supreme Court for review of the action of the court of appeals. In case of review, the order of the Commission becomes final after affirmation by the court of appeals or by the Supreme Court of the United States, if taken to that court on certiorari. Violations of a cease-and-desist order, after it becomes final, subject the offender to suit by the Government in a United States district court for the recovery of a civil penalty of not more than $10,000 for each violation and, where the violation continues, each day of its continuance is a separate violation.

In addition to the administrative proceeding initiated by a formal complaint, the Commission may, in some cases, request that a United States district court issue a preliminary or permanent injunction to halt the use of allegedly unfair or deceptive practices or to prevent an anticompetitive merger from taking place. The Commission may also bring suit in a United States district court to enforce a subpoena or civil investigative demand issued by the Commission.

The Commission also has specific authority to ask the United States district court to enjoin the dissemination of advertisements of food, drugs, cosmetics, and devices intended for use in the diagnosis, prevention, or treatment of disease, whenever it has reason to believe that such a proceeding would be in the public interest. Preliminary injunctions remain in effect until a cease-and-desist order is issued and becomes final, or until the complaint is dismissed by the Commission or the order is set aside by the court on review.

Further, the dissemination of a false advertisement of a food, drug, device, or cosmetic, where the use of the commodity advertised may be injurious to health or where there is intent to defraud or mislead, constitutes a misdemeanor. Conviction subjects the offender to a fine of not more than $5,000, or imprisonment of not more than 6 months, or both. Succeeding convictions may result in a fine of not more than $10,000, or imprisonment for not more than 1 year, or both. The statute provides that the Commission shall certify this type of case to the Attorney General for institution of appropriate court proceedings.

Compliance Activities Through systematic and continuous review, the Commission obtains and maintains compliance with its cease-and-desist orders. All respondents against whom such orders have been issued are required to file reports with the Commission to substantiate their compliance. In the event compliance is not obtained, or if the order is subsequently violated, civil penalty proceedings may be instituted. Violation of a court decree obtained by the

Commission makes the respondent further subject to contempt proceedings.

Trade Regulation Rules The Commission is authorized to issue trade regulation rules specifically defining acts or practices that are unfair or deceptive. A rule may also specify steps to prevent such practices from occurring. Such rules may be limited to certain industries or be applicable to all businesses within the Commission's jurisdiction. Rules are promulgated under specific procedures providing for participation of interested parties, including oral hearings and comments. The Commission's decision to issue a rule may be appealed to a United States court of appeals. Once a rule has become final, the Commission can institute a civil proceeding in a United States district court for knowing violations of the rule and seek civil penalties of up to $10,000 per violation and consumer redress.

Cooperative Procedures In carrying out the statutory directive to "prevent" the use in commerce of unfair practices, the Commission makes extensive use of voluntary and cooperative procedures. Through these procedures business and industry may obtain authoritative guidance and a substantial measure of certainty as to what they may do under the laws administered by the Commission.

Whenever it is practicable, the Commission will furnish an advisory opinion as to whether a proposed course of conduct, if pursued, would be likely to result in further action by the Commission. Such opinions are binding on the Commission but are subject to the right of the Commission to reconsider and rescind the opinion should the public interest require. Information submitted will not be used as the basis for a proceeding against the requesting party without prior notice and opportunity to discontinue the course of action pursued in good faith in reliance upon the Commission's advice.

Industry guides are administrative interpretations in laymen's language of laws administered by the Commission for the guidance of the public in conducting its affairs in conformity with legal requirements. They provide the basis for voluntary and simultaneous abandonment of unlawful practices by members of a particular industry or industry in general. Failure to comply with the guides may result in corrective action by the Commission under applicable statutory provisions.

Consumer Protection Consumer protection is one of the two main missions of the Commission. In addition to preventing the use of unfair or deceptive advertising and marketing practices generally, the Commission enforces a number of specific laws that help consumers.

One of the laws the Commission enforces is the Consumer Credit Protection Act, which establishes, among other things, rules for the use of credit cards, the disclosure of the terms on which open- and closed-end credit is granted, and the disclosure of the reasons a business uses in determining not to grant credit.

The Truth in Lending Act is one part of the Consumer Credit Protection Act. Its purpose is to ensure that every customer who has need for consumer credit is given meaningful information with respect to the cost of that credit. In most cases the credit cost must be expressed in the dollar amount of finance charges, and as an annual percentage rate computed on the unpaid balance of the amount financed. Other relevant credit information must also be disclosed so that the customer may compare the credit terms of different sources and avoid the uninformed use of credit. The act further provides a customer the right, in certain circumstances, to cancel a credit transaction involving a lien on his or her residence. The Truth in Lending Act was amended in October 1970 to regulate the issuance, holder's liability, and the fraudulent use of credit cards. New credit cards may be issued only in response to a request or application by the person who is to receive the card. Also, the liability to the cardholder for unauthorized use of a credit card is specifically limited to $50 if the cardholder has taken reasonable steps to notify the card issuer of the loss or theft.

The act also establishes penalties for the fraudulent use of credit cards in interstate or foreign commerce when the aggregate retail value is $5,000 or more. The Commission enforces the requirements of the Truth in Lending Act over finance companies, retailers, non-Federal credit unions, and other creditors not specifically regulated by another Government agency, and persons or their agents who issue credit cards.

The Fair Credit Reporting Act, another part of the Consumer Credit Protection Act, represents the first Federal regulation of the vast consumer reporting industry, covering all credit bureaus, investigative reporting companies, detective and collection agencies, lenders' exchanges, and computerized information reporting companies. The purpose of this act is to ensure that consumer reporting activities are conducted in a manner that is fair and equitable, upholding the consumer's right to privacy as against the informational demands of others. The consumer is given several important new rights, including the right to notice of reporting activities, the right to access to information contained in consumer reports, and the right to correction of erroneous information that may have been the basis for a denial of credit, insurance, or employment.

Under the Wool Products Labeling Act, the Textile Fiber Products Identification Act, and the Fur Products Labeling Act, the Commission engages in compliance investigations, inspections, and industry counseling; issues registered identification numbers; and records continuing guaranties. The Commission has published rules and regulations under these statutes, together with illustrations of acceptable labeling, which supply full information concerning their requirements. In connection with the Fur Act, the Commission has issued a register of animal names, known as the *Fur Products Name Guide,* for use in properly describing furs and fur products.

Economic Competition (Antitrust) The second major mission of the Commission is to encourage competitive forces in the American economy. Under the Federal Trade Commission Act, the Commission seeks to prevent unfair practices that may keep one company from competing with others. Under the Federal Trade Commission Act and the Clayton Act, the Commission attempts to prevent mergers of companies if the result may be to lessen competition. Under some circumstances, companies planning to merge must first give notice to the Commission and the Department of Justice's Antitrust Division and provide certain information concerning the operations of the companies involved.

The Commission also enforces the provisions of the Robinson-Patman Act, a part of the Clayton Act prohibiting companies from discriminating among other companies that are its customers in terms of price or other services provided.

Economic Factfinding The Commission makes economic and statistical studies of conditions and problems affecting competition in the economy. Reports of this nature may be in support of legislative proposals, in response to requests of the Congress and statutory directions, or for the information and guidance of the Commission and the executive branch of the Government as well as the public. The reports have provided the basis for significant legislation and, by spotlighting poor economic or otherwise objectionable trade practices, they have also led to voluntary changes in the conduct of business, with resulting benefits to the public.

Advocacy Activities (Intervention) To promote competition, consumer protection, and the efficient allocation of resources, the Commission has an active program designed to advocate the consumer interest in a competitive marketplace by encouraging courts, legislatures, and government administrative bodies to consider efficiency and consumer welfare as important elements in their deliberations. This is accomplished by appearances before legislative, judicial, or regulatory bodies at the local, State, or Federal level of government when the decisions of these bodies may have implications affecting competition, efficiency, and consumer welfare.

The Commission uses these opportunities to support procompetitive means of regulating the Nation's economy, including the elimination of anticompetitive regulations that reduce the welfare of consumers and the implementation of regulatory programs that protect the public and preserve as much as possible the discipline of competitive markets. The competition and consumer advocacy program relies on persuasion rather than coercion. It is intended to help legislators and government officials better understand the consumer welfare implications of proposed actions in the belief that this understanding will result in policy decisions that benefit consumers and the economy.

Regional Offices—Federal Trade Commission

Region	Address	Director
ATLANTA—Alabama, Florida, Georgia, Mississippi, North Carolina, South Carolina, Tennessee, Virginia	Rm. 1000, 1718 Peachtree St. NW., Atlanta, GA 30367	Paul K. Davis
BOSTON—Connecticut, Maine, Massachusetts, New Hampshire, Rhode Island, Vermont	Rm. 1184, 10 Causeway St., Boston, MA 02222-1073	Phoebe D. Morse
CHICAGO—Illinois, Indiana, Iowa, Kentucky, Minnesota, Missouri, Wisconsin	Suite 1437, 55 E. Monroe St., Chicago, IL 60603	C. Steven Baker
CLEVELAND—Delaware, Maryland, Michigan, Ohio, Pennsylvania, West Virginia	Suite 520-A, 668 Euclid Ave., Cleveland, OH 44114	Mark Kindt
DALLAS—Arkansas, Louisiana, New Mexico, Oklahoma, Texas	Suite 500, 100 N. Central Expressway, Dallas, TX 75201	Thomas B. Carter
DENVER—Colorado, Kansas, Montana, Nebraska, North Dakota, South Dakota, Utah, Wyoming	Suite 2900, 1405 Curtis St., Denver, CO 80202-2393	Claude C. Wild III
LOS ANGELES—Arizona, southern California	Suite 13209, 11000 Wilshire Blvd., Los Angeles, CA 90024	Eileen Harrington, *Acting*
NEW YORK—New Jersey, New York	Suite 13, 150 William St., New York, NY 10038	Michael J. Bloom
SAN FRANCISCO—Northern California, Hawaii, Nevada	Suite 570, 901 Market St., San Francisco, CA 94103	Jeffrey A. Klurfeld
SEATTLE—Alaska, Idaho, Oregon, Washington	2806 Federal Bldg., 915 2d Ave., Seattle, WA 98174	Charles A. Harwood

Sources of Information

Contracts and Procurement Persons seeking to do business with the Federal Trade Commission should contact the Division of Procurement and General Services, Federal Trade Commission, Washington, DC 20580. Phone, 202-326-2275.

Employment Civil service registers are used in filling positions for economists, accountants, consumer protection specialists, and other professional, administrative, and clerical personnel. The Federal Trade Commission employs a sizable number of attorneys under the excepted appointment procedure. All employment inquiries should be directed to the Director of Personnel, Federal Trade Commission, Washington, DC 20580. Phone, 202-326-2022.

General Inquiries Persons desiring information on consumer protection, restraint of trade questions, or to register a complaint, should contact the nearest Federal Trade Commission regional office.

Publications A copy of the *Federal Trade Commission—"Best Sellers,"* which lists a number of publications of interest to the general public, is available free upon request from the Public Reference Section, Federal Trade Commission, Washington, DC 20580. Phone, 202-326-2222.

For further information, contact the Director, Office of Public Affairs, Federal Trade Commission, Pennsylvania Avenue at Sixth Street NW., Washington, DC 20580. Phone, 202-326-2180.

GENERAL SERVICES ADMINISTRATION

General Services Building, Eighteenth and F Streets NW., Washington, DC 20405
Phone, 202–708–5082

Administrator of General Services	Richard G. Austin
Deputy Administrator	John P. Hiler
Special Assistant to the Deputy Administrator	Victor Arnold-Bik
Director of Regional Operations	Larrilyn Bertocchio
Chief of Staff	James A. Lobmaster
Deputy Chief of Staff	Anthony Artigliere
Special Counsel for Ethics and Civil Rights	Allie B. Latimer
Director of the Executive Secretariat	E. Madeline Smith
Director of Small and Disadvantaged Business Utilization	John F. Wynn, Jr.
Director of Child Care and Development Programs	Allaire D. Williams
Associate Administrator for Congressional and Intergovernmental Affairs	Lonnie P. Taylor
Associate Administrator for Policy Analysis	J. Christopher Brady
Associate Administrator for Public Affairs	Kathryn L. Gaddy
Associate Administrator for Business, Industry, and Governmental Affairs	Donald C.J. Gray
Deputy Associate Administrator	Tom Catlin, *Acting*
GSA Ombudsman	(vacancy)
Director of Governmental Affairs	Tom Catlin
Director of Business and Industry Affairs	(vacancy)
Associate Administrator for Administration	Carlene Bawden
Deputy to the Associate Administrator	Frank P. Pugliese
Executive Assistant	Mickey Femino
Director of Personnel	Donald P. Heffernan, *Acting*
Director of Management Controls and Evaluation	John H. Davenjay
Director of Administrative Programs and Support	Jon R. Halsall
Director of Quality Management and Training	Gregory L. Knott
Executive Director	David M. Millane
Director, Committee Management Secretariat	James L. Dean
Inspector General	William R. Barton
Deputy Inspector General	Edward F. Hefferon
Assistant Inspector General for Auditing	William E. Whyte, Jr.
Assistant Inspector General for Investigations	James E. Henderson
Assistant Inspector General for Quality Management	Lawrence J. Dempsey
Assistant Inspector General for Administration	William J. Frost
Counsel to the Inspector General	Joel S. Gallay
Chairman, GSA Board of Contract Appeals	Leonard J. Suchanek
Personal Assistant to the Chairman	Lisa Binckes
Executive Assistant	Nancy L. Winkler
Vice Chairman, Judicial Division	Vincent A. LaBella
Board Counsel	Wilbur Miller
Executive Director	James F. Neary
Clerk of the Board	Beatrice Jones

Director, Information Security Oversight Office	STEVEN GARFINKEL
Comptroller	WILLIAM B. EARLY, JR., *Acting*
Deputy Comptroller for Budget	NANCY L. POTTER, *Acting*
Deputy Comptroller for Finance	LEROY P. BOUCHER
Deputy Comptroller for Financial Management Systems	DAVID M. MITCHELL
Associate Administrator for Acquisition Policy	RICHARD H. HOPF III
Multiple Awards Schedule Coordinator	CAROLYN HARRIS
Executive Assistant	A. TONI LEWIS
Special Assistant for Contractor Integrity	JAMES DRUMMOND
Director of Contract Review	ARTHUR E. RONKOVICH
Director of GSA Acquisition Policy	IDA USTAD
Director of Federal Acquisition Policy	ALBERT VICCHIOLLA
Director, Federal Acquisition Institute	JACK LIVINGSTON, *Acting*
General Counsel	ROBERT C. MACKICHAN, JR.
Deputy General Counsel	FREDERICK P. HINK
Associate Deputy General Counsel	ARTHUR TROILO III
Special Counsel to the General Counsel	MICHAEL J. WOOTTEN
Associate General Counsel for General Law	LAWRENCE HARRINGTON, *Acting*
Associate General Counsel for Personal Property	VINCENT CRIVELLA
Associate General Counsel for Real Property	MELVILLE H. VALKENBURG

INFORMATION RESOURCES MANAGEMENT SERVICE

General Services Building, Eighteenth and F Streets NW., Washington, DC 20405
Phone, 202–501–1000

Commissioner, Information Resources Management Service	THOMAS J. BUCKHOLTZ
Deputy Commissioner	G. MARTIN WAGNER
Controller	VINCETTE L. GOERL
Assistant Commissioner for Federal Information Resources Management	FRANCIS A. MCDONOUGH
Deputy Assistant Commissioner for Information Resources Management Policy	FRED L. SIMS
Assistant Commissioner for Telecommunications Services	MICHAEL L. CORRIGAN
Deputy Assistant Commissioner for Regional Telecommunications Services	DON HARDESTY
Deputy Assistant Commissioner for Network Services	WILLIAM P. CUNNANE
Assistant Commissioner for GSA Information Resources Management	JUDITH PARKS
Assistant Commissioner for Technical Assistance	LAWRENCE S. COHAN, *Acting*
Director of Federal Systems Integration and Management	CHARLES A. SELF
Director of Software Development and Information Technology	CHARLES A. SELF, *Acting*
Assistant Commissioner for Information Resources Procurement	C. ALLEN OLSON

FEDERAL SUPPLY SERVICE

1941 Jefferson Davis Highway, Arlington, VA; Mailing address: Washington, DC 20406
Phone, 703–557–8667

Commissioner, Federal Supply Service	Roger D. Daniero
Deputy Commissioner	Ruben T. Morgan
Controller	Leonard Yonkler
Director of Transportation Audits	Ronald W. Piasecki
Assistant Commissioner for Distribution Management	Brian Freeman
Assistant Commissioner for Transportation and Property Management	Allan W. Beres
Assistant Commissioner for Customer Service and Marketing	William B. Foote
Assistant Commissioner for Strategic Business Planning	James Gilbert, *Acting*
Assistant Commissioner for Quality and Contract Administration	Charles Hulick
Assistant Commissioner for Commodity Management	James L. DeProspero

PUBLIC BUILDINGS SERVICE

General Services Building, Eighteenth and F Streets NW., Washington, DC 20405
Phone, 202–501–1100

Commissioner, Public Buildings Service	William C. Coleman
Deputy Commissioner	Wolfgang J. Zoellner
Controller	Michael C. Bielski, *Acting*
Assistant Commissioner for Real Property Development	Robert J. DiLuchio
Assistant Commissioner for Real Property Management and Safety	Thomas H. Walker
Assistant Commissioner for Facility Planning	David L. Bibb
Assistant Commissioner for Procurement	Brian K. Polly
Assistant Commissioner for Governmentwide Real Property Relations	John J. Landers
Assistant Commissioner for Physical Security and Law Enforcement	Gary DeYulia
Assistant Commissioner for PBS Information Systems	James A. Williams

FEDERAL PROPERTY RESOURCES SERVICE

General Services Building, Eighteenth and F Streets NW., Washington, DC 20405
Phone, 202–501–0210

Commissioner, Federal Property Resources Service	Earl E. Jones
Deputy Commissioner	(vacancy)

Controller	MARVIN L. STEFFEN
Assistant Commissioner for Real Estate Policy and Sales	JOHN V. NEALE

[For the General Services Administration statement of organization, see the *Code of Federal Regulations,* 41 CFR 105-53]

The General Services Administration establishes policy for and provides economical and efficient management of Government property and records, including construction and operation of buildings, procurement and distribution of supplies, utilization and disposal of property; transportation, traffic, and communications management; and management of the Governmentwide automatic data processing resources program.

The General Services Administration is organized much like a large corporation doing business in a number of different fields and might well be termed a conglomerate. It consists of operating services and support staff offices, with functions carried out at three levels of organization: the central office, regional offices, and field activities.

The General Services Administration was established by section 101 of the Federal Property and Administrative Services Act of 1949 (40 U.S.C. 751).

Business, Industry, and Governmental Affairs The Office of Business, Industry, and Governmental Affairs implements GSA's initiatives promoting GSA as a full-service, customer-oriented agency. The Office manages the GSA Ombudsman Program, facilitating communications between GSA and customer agencies and private industry. It coordinates the Customer Outreach Program and recommends the establishment of advisory groups such as the Client Advisory Board and the Business Advisory Board. The Office also coordinates activities with State, local, and foreign governments in areas of common interest.

Acquisition Policy The Office of Acquisition Policy plans, directs, and coordinates a comprehensive, agencywide acquisition policy program, including the establishment of major agency acquisition goals and objectives.

The Office of Acquisition Policy has a major role in developing, maintaining, issuing, and administering the Federal Acquisition Regulation (FAR), which is applicable to all Federal agencies. It chairs the Civilian Agency Acquisition Council and provides administrative support through the FAR Secretariat. The Office develops GSA implementing and supplementing regulations required by FAR, which is published as the General Services Administration Acquisition Regulation.

The Office manages the Agency's internal system for the suspension and debarment of nonresponsive contractors and a Governmentwide system for exchanging information on debarred, suspended, and ineligible parties; reviews selected major contract awards proposed by the Agency prior to award; coordinates GSA's Multiple Awards Schedule Program; and performs onsite intra-agency and interagency procurement management reviews. The Office also is responsible for overseeing the Agency's acquisition information system and serves as agency coordinator for the Federal Procurement Data System.

The Office's Federal Acquisition Institute fosters and promotes Governmentwide career management and training programs to develop a professional work force and coordinates Governmentwide studies to improve the procurement process.

In addition, Acquisition Policy establishes standards and requirements for the development of programs to enhance the recruitment, training,

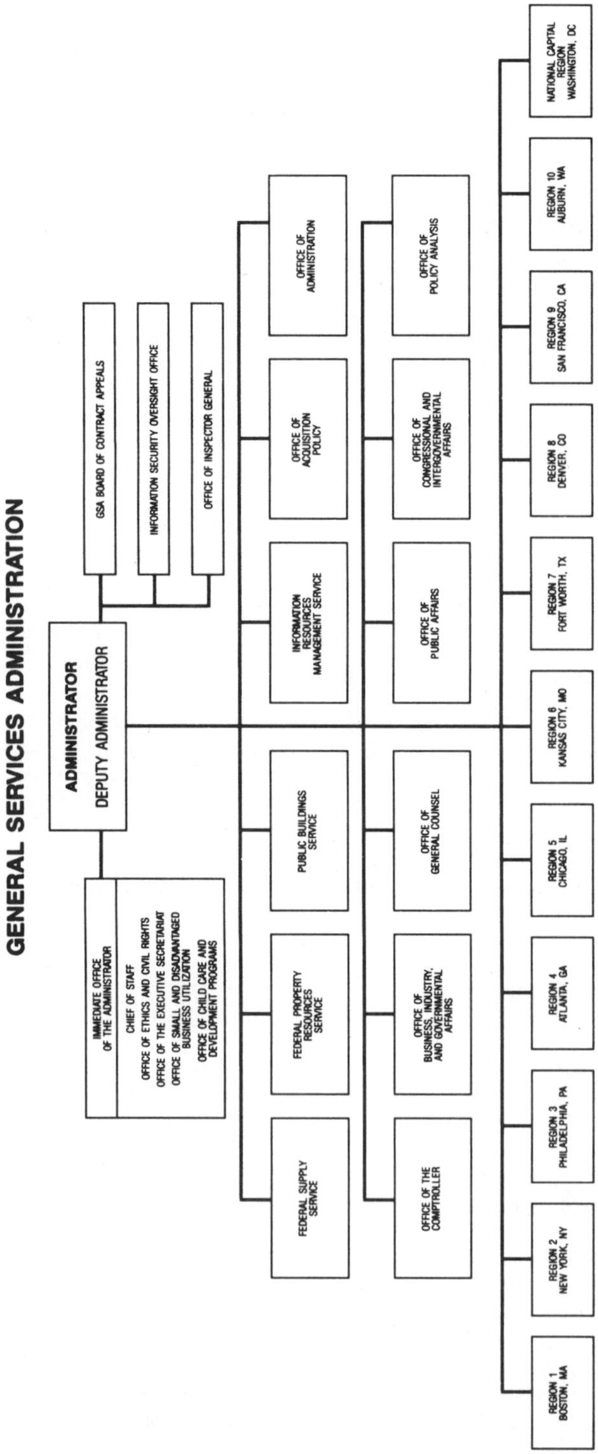
GENERAL SERVICES ADMINISTRATION
ADMINISTRATOR
DEPUTY ADMINISTRATOR
GSA BOARD OF CONTRACT APPEALS
INFORMATION SECURITY OVERSIGHT OFFICE
OFFICE OF INSPECTOR GENERAL
IMMEDIATE OFFICE OF THE ADMINISTRATOR
CHIEF OF STAFF
OFFICE OF ETHICS AND CIVIL RIGHTS
OFFICE OF THE EXECUTIVE SECRETARIAT
OFFICE OF SMALL AND DISADVANTAGED BUSINESS UTILIZATION
OFFICE OF CHILD CARE AND DEVELOPMENT PROGRAMS
FEDERAL SUPPLY SERVICE
FEDERAL PROPERTY RESOURCES SERVICE
PUBLIC BUILDINGS SERVICE
INFORMATION RESOURCES MANAGEMENT SERVICE
OFFICE OF ACQUISITION POLICY
OFFICE OF ADMINISTRATION
OFFICE OF THE COMPTROLLER
OFFICE OF BUSINESS, INDUSTRY, AND GOVERNMENTAL AFFAIRS
OFFICE OF GENERAL COUNSEL
OFFICE OF PUBLIC AFFAIRS
OFFICE OF CONGRESSIONAL AND INTERGOVERNMENTAL AFFAIRS
OFFICE OF POLICY ANALYSIS
REGION 1 BOSTON, MA
REGION 2 NEW YORK, NY
REGION 3 PHILADELPHIA, PA
REGION 4 ATLANTA, GA
REGION 5 CHICAGO, IL
REGION 6 KANSAS CITY, MO
REGION 7 FORT WORTH, TX
REGION 8 DENVER, CO
REGION 9 SAN FRANCISCO, CA
REGION 10 AUBURN, WA
NATIONAL CAPITAL REGION WASHINGTON, DC

certification, and career development of employees engaged in the acquisition process.

For further information, call 202–501–1043.

Small and Disadvantaged Business Utilization The Office of Small and Disadvantaged Business Utilization plans, implements, and evaluates comprehensive agencywide procurement preference programs. Included among these are the Small Business Program; the Women in Business Program; the Socially and Economically Disadvantaged Business Program; the Subcontracting Program; the Labor Surplus Area Program; the Javits/Wagner-O'Day Program; the Federal Prison Industry Program; and the Rural Area Development Program.

The Office coordinates and develops policies that regulate the operation and the implementation of the Small Business Programs under sections 8 and 15 of the Small Business Act (15 U.S.C. 637, 644).

The Office provides assistance, information, and counseling to small business persons interested in pursuing Federal Government contracts and conducts outreach, liaison, source listing, and seminars for small and disadvantaged businesses. This is accomplished through the Business Service Center Program.

Business Service Centers are located in major metropolitan areas. Service center counselors travel within their regions lecturing on the Federal procurement process. They also provide information on the new item introduction program and buying programs of other agencies. The Centers are also responsible for receiving and safeguarding bids (maintaining the integrity of the bid process).

Business Service Centers assist agency procurement officers by identifying potential suppliers. In doing this, they rely not only on "walk-in" contacts at reception areas but actively seek out business concerns which may be able to supply the Government's needs. They also operate bid rooms where vendors' offers are publicly opened and posted.

Special emphasis is placed on outreach programs that counsel small, small disadvantaged, minority, and women business owners.

For further information, call 202–501–1021.

Business Service Center Directory

(Areas included within each region are indicated on the map in Appendix A.)

	Region/Address	Telephone
	National Capital Region, Washington, DC (7th and D Sts. SW., 20407)	202–708–5804
1.	Boston, MA (10 Causeway St., 02222)	617–565–8100
2.	New York, NY (26 Federal Plz., 10278)	212–264–1234
3.	Philadelphia, PA (9th and Market Sts., 19107)	215–597–9613
4.	Atlanta, GA (75 Spring St. SW., 30303)	404–331–5103
5.	Chicago, IL (230 S. Dearborn St., 60604)	312–353–5383
6.	Kansas City, MO (1500 E. Bannister Rd., 64131)	816–926–7203
7.	Fort Worth, TX (819 Taylor St., 76102)	817–334–3284
8.	Denver, CO (Denver Federal Ctr., 80225)	303–236–7408
9.	San Francisco, CA (525 Market St., 94105)	415–744–5050
	Los Angeles, CA (300 N. Los Angeles St., 90012)	213–894–3210
10.	Auburn, WA (GSA Ctr., 98001)	206–931–7957

Child Care and Development Programs The Office of Child Care and Development Programs is responsible for developing and implementing the Governmentwide Child Care and Dependent Care Program to address the needs of Federal employees. The Office also develops and implements the Volunteerism Program and other employee programs, as directed by the Administrator.

The Office provides management advice and technical assistance to existing centers and child care organizing committees on the establishment of a developmentally appropriate curriculum and safe physical environment, recruitment and retention of staff, and training for boards of directors. The Office assists child care centers operating in GSA space to address the components of quality care.

The Office assists all Federal agencies in determining the types of child care and other dependent care services their employees need, and aids in the establishment of necessary services.

For further information, call 202–501–3965.

Contract Appeals The General Services Administration Board of Contract Appeals is responsible for resolving disputes arising out of contracts with the General Services Administration, the Department of the Treasury, the Department of Education, the Department of Commerce, and other independent Government agencies. The Board is also empowered to hear and decide bid protests arising out of automated data processing procurements Governmentwide. Although the Board is functionally located within the Agency, it is an independent tribunal.

Additionally, the Board hears and decides protests filed under section 2713 of the Competition in Contracting Act of 1984 involving procurements conducted under section 759 of title 40, United States Code.

Each of the Board's judges has extensive experience in Government contract law and is empowered, under the Contract Disputes Act of 1978 (41 U.S.C. 601 note), to grant the same relief as would be available in the United States Claims Court. In addition, contractors may elect to have their appeals processed under the Board's accelerated procedure if the claim is $50,000 or less, or under the small claims procedure if the claim is $10,000 or less. These provide for resolution of the appeal within 180 and 120 days, respectively, whenever possible. Contractors may also request that a hearing be held at a location convenient to them. With the exception of small claims decisions, Government agencies and contractors may appeal adverse Board decisions to the United States Court of Appeals for the Federal Circuit.

For further information, contact the Board of Contract Appeals (G), General Services Administration, Washington, DC 20405. Phone, 202–501–0116.

Information Security Oversight The Information Security Oversight Office is responsible for overseeing executive branch agencies' actions to implement Executive Order 12356, which prescribes a uniform system for classifying, declassifying, and safeguarding national security information. The Office's annual reports to the President on the status of this program are available upon request.

For further information, contact the Information Security Oversight Office (Z), General Services Administration, Suite 530, 750 Seventeenth Street NW., Washington, DC 20006. Phone, 202–634–6150.

Inspector General The Office of Inspector General is responsible for conducting and supervising audits and investigations relating to the programs and operations of the Agency. The Office recommends policies and corrective actions concerning activities designed to promote economy and efficiency, and prevent and detect fraud, waste, and mismanagement in Agency programs and operations. The Office provides a means for keeping the Administrator and Congress fully informed about problems and deficiencies in the administration of such programs and operations and the necessity for corrective action. This includes such activities as receiving and investigating employee complaints and reviewing proposed legislation and regulations. The Office maintains a toll-free telephone number for complaints concerning fraud, waste, and mismanagement in Agency programs. The number is 800–424–5210, or in the Washington, DC, metropolitan area, call 202–501–1780.

For further information, call 202–501–0335.

Administration The Office of Administration participates in the executive leadership of the Agency, providing advice on major policies and procedures, particularly those of a critical or controversial nature, to the Administrator and the Deputy Administrator. The Office plans and administers programs in organization, personnel services, audit and inspection reports, management controls, and agencywide administrative services that includes providing and outfitting State and district offices for Members of the Senate and House of Representatives. The Office is responsible as the Agency's point of contact for matters involving the Office of Special Counsel and the Merit Systems Protection Board. It provides positive leadership for the Agency's commitment to excellence in management practices and techniques in interactions with the Congress, other Federal agencies, and the private sector. The Office is also responsible for providing support to the Cooperative Administrative Support Program, and coordinating and administering the President's Quality and Productivity Improvement Program and the personnel, document, industrial, and physical security programs.

Within the Office of Administration is the Committee Management Secretariat, which is responsible for administration of the Federal Advisory Committee Program and prepares the annual report of the President to the Congress on the status of these committees, including recommendations on improving their operations.

For further information, call 202–501–0945.

Comptroller The Office of the Comptroller plans and administers the development and execution of all budgeting and financial management requirements.

The Office of Budget carries out responsibilities in centralized budget administration to ensure maximum utilization of available resources. Also, it develops and manages GSA's commercial activities programs.

The Office of Finance is responsible for the design, development, maintenance, and operation of the Agency's accounting systems. Additionally, it provides accounting expertise and reports on Indian Tribal Claims pending before the U.S. Court of Claims as assigned by the Department of Justice and provides cross-servicing to 50 commissions and small agencies.

The Office of Financial Management Systems oversees the development of the Agency's financial management systems and reviews financial operations to ensure the quality of Agency financial information. It manages the Agency's executive information system, directs its strategic planning process, and coordinates setting its annual goals and objectives.

For further information, call 202–501–1721.

Ethics and Civil Rights The Office of Ethics and Civil Rights is responsible for developing and directing the Agency's programs governing employee standards of ethical conduct and equal employment opportunity.

For further information, call 202–501–0765.

Information Resources Management Service

The Information Resources Management Service is responsible for the coordination and direction of a comprehensive, Governmentwide program for the management, procurement, and utilization of automated data processing and telecommunications equipment and services; planning and directing programs for improving Federal records and information management practices; and managing and operating the Federal Information Centers.

Governmentwide Information Resources Management The General Services Administration provides Governmentwide programs to assist Federal agencies in managing their information resources. The Office of Technical Assistance provides technical and contracting assistance in software, hardware, data communications, planning, and office automation.

The software program provides assistance in all areas of conversion, improvement and engineering of software as well as tools to improve programmer productivity.

The hardware program provides assistance in workload and requirements definition, capacity management, and performance evaluation.

The data communications program provides assistance in network design, evaluation, and implementation.

The planning program assists agencies in establishing strategic, tactical, and operational information resources management planning programs as well as providing information planning assistance.

The office automation program assists agencies in the effective acquisition and use of automation to improve clerical and professional productivity in the office.

The Service also administers the Contract Services Program, which is a nationwide program of requirements contracts under which Federal agencies are provided automated data processing services through regional contracts with private-sector vendors. The program allows the Service to consolidate relatively small, quick-reaction, technical services project requirements for other agencies in order to reduce costs.

For further information, contact the Office of Technical Assistance, Suite 400, 5203 Leesburg Pike, Falls Church, VA 22041. Phone, 703–756–4100.

Agency Management Assistance The Service conducts several management assistance programs that assist agencies in improving their information-related functions and activities. Among these are an Agency Liaison Officer Program that helps Federal agencies prepare for major acquisitions, a review program that evaluates agency information resource procurement and management activities, and an agency-directed program of triennial review. The Service prepares and generates recommendations to agencies on information resource management, which may result in varied procurement authority for information technology, and publishes handbooks related to information management practices and systems.

For further information, contact the Office of Information Resources Management Policy. Phone, 202–501–0202.

Information Resources Management Policy The Service is responsible for coordinating policymaking activities related to information functions and authorities; developing, coordinating, and issuing Governmentwide automated data processing and telecommunications acquisition management and use regulations; evaluating policy, regulatory, and legislative proposals from sources outside of the Service; developing guidance documents relating to records management and technology acquisition; issuing delegations of procurement authority to agencies; and reviewing agency information resource activities.

For further information, contact the Office of Information Resources Management Policy. Phone, 202–501–0202.

Information Resources Procurement The Service plays a major role in the Governmentwide procurement of automated data processing and telecommunications hardware, software, and services. In providing its acquisition services, the Agency seeks out and obtains the best buys; obtains the best leasing and/or purchase price arrangements; when possible, utilizes excess equipment to fill procurement requests; negotiates long-term procurement actions to achieve cost reductions; and continually strives to improve Federal procurement practices.

For further information, contact the Office of Information Resources Procurement. Phone, 202–501–1072.

Telecommunications Service The Service operates the Federal Telecommunications System (FTS), a comprehensive voice data system procured, operated, and maintained for use by Federal agencies. It includes local and long-distance telephone service for use among Federal agencies, with access to the general public. The System also includes Department of Defense-approved communications security transmissions with related worldwide support services.

The long-distance portion of the System was replaced by FTS2000 in June 1990. FTS2000 is a comprehensive network service that provides switched-voice, packet-switched, switched-data, video transmission, and dedicated service arrangements. These services may be integrated under a Switched Digital Integrated Service using common switches and facility arrangements.

The Service also develops policies and procedures and defines standards for the General Service Administration Local Service Program. Under this program, the Agency provides telephone services to Federal agencies at those locations where it is economically beneficial.

The Service is presently moving forward with an Aggregated Systems Procurement Program that will replace the Tariffed Local Telephone Service and upgrade service nationwide. It is implementing the replacement of the large tariffed system in the Nation's Capital with the Washington Interagency Telecommunications System and have placed purchase-of-telephone-and-services contracts nationwide except for the New England area and the States of Alaska and Hawaii to satisfy the Government's requirements for customer-provided telephone equipment and services. These requirements can be satisfied in New England using the Aggregated Systems Procurement Program contract and in Alaska and Hawaii using other telecommunications contracts. In addition, Purchase of Telephone and Services contracts will be implemented in Alaska and Hawaii during 1991 and 1992.

The Service implements and manages the Federal Secure Telephone Service, providing worldwide secure voice transmission for the Federal Government. It manages and administers the National Security Emergency Preparedness Telecommunications Program activities. It ensures that the Agency supports Governmentwide national security and domestic emergency plans, including those promulgated by the National Communications System.

For further information, contact the Office of Telecommunications Services. Phone, 202–501–0308.

Internal Information Systems Management In addition to its Governmentwide responsibilities, the Service develops internal agency policy governing the acquisition, development, and use of automated information systems equipment and facilities, including office automation equipment; prepares the Agency's 5-year Information Resources Management Plan and monitors performance against the plan; develops standards and procedures; provides support to end-users including those requiring special accommodations; and provides for common-use automated data processing and data communications facilities.

For further information, contact the Office of GSA Information Systems. Phone, 202–501–1800.

Federal Information Center Program

The Federal Information Center Program, a clearinghouse for information about the Federal Government, can eliminate the maze of referrals that people have experienced in contacting the Federal Government. Persons with questions about a Government program or agency, and who are unsure of which office can help, may call or write the Center. A specialist will either answer the question or locate an expert who can.

Residents of more than 70 key cities have direct access to a Center via local or toll-free (800) telephone service, and callers in four States—Iowa, Kansas, Missouri, and Nebraska—have statewide toll-free service. Users of telecommunications devices for the deaf (TDD/TTY) may call a nationwide toll-free number: 800–326–2996.

Written inquiries may be addressed to the Federal Information Center, P.O. Box 600, Cumberland, MD 21502–0600.

For further information, contact the Federal Information Center in your area.

Federal Information Centers—General Services Administration

(If your metropolitan area or State is not listed, please call 301–722–9098. TDD/TTY users, please call 800–326–2996.)

State/City	Telephone
ALABAMA:	
Birmingham	800–366–2998
Mobile	800–366–2998
ALASKA: Anchorage	800–729–8003
ARIZONA: Phoenix	800–359–3997
ARKANSAS: Little Rock	800–366–2998
CALIFORNIA:	
Los Angeles	800–726–4995

Federal Information Centers—General Services Administration—Continued

(If your metropolitan area or State is not listed, please call 301-722-9098. TDD/TTY users, please call 800-326-2996.)

State/City	Telephone
Sacramento	916-973-1695
San Diego	800-726-4995
San Francisco	800-726-4995
Santa Ana	800-726-4995
COLORADO:	
Colorado Springs	800-359-3997
Denver	800-359-3997
Pueblo	800-359-3997
CONNECTICUT:	
Hartford	800-347-1997
New Haven	800-347-1997
FLORIDA:	
Ft. Lauderdale	800-347-1997
Jacksonville	800-347-1997
Miami	800-347-1997
Orlando	800-347-1997
St. Petersburg	800-347-1997
Tampa	800-347-1997
West Palm Beach	800-347-1997
GEORGIA: Atlanta	800-347-1997
HAWAII: Honolulu	800-733-5996
ILLINOIS: Chicago	800-366-2998
INDIANA:	
Gary	800-366-2998
Indianapolis	800-347-1997
IOWA: From all points	800-735-8004
KANSAS: From all points	800-735-8004
KENTUCKY: Louisville	800-347-1997
LOUISIANA: New Orleans	800-366-2998
MARYLAND: Baltimore	800-347-1997
MASSACHUSETTS: Boston	800-347-1997
MICHIGAN:	
Detroit	800-347-1997
Grand Rapids	800-347-1997
MINNESOTA: Minneapolis	800-366-2998
MISSOURI:	
St. Louis	800-366-2998
From elsewhere in Missouri	800-735-8004
NEBRASKA:	
Omaha	800-366-2998
From elsewhere in Nebraska	800-735-8004
NEW JERSEY:	
Newark	800-347-1997
Trenton	800-347-1997
NEW MEXICO: Albuquerque	800-359-3997
NEW YORK:	
Albany	800-347-1997
Buffalo	800-347-1997
New York	800-347-1997
Rochester	800-347-1997
Syracuse	800-347-1997
NORTH CAROLINA: Charlotte	800-347-1997
OHIO:	
Akron	800-347-1997
Cincinnati	800-347-1997
Cleveland	800-347-1997
Columbus	800-347-1997
Dayton	800-347-1997
Toledo	800-347-1997
OKLAHOMA:	
Oklahoma City	800-366-2998
Tulsa	800-366-2998
OREGON: Portland	800-726-4995
PENNSYLVANIA:	
Philadelphia	800-347-1997
Pittsburgh	800-347-1997
RHODE ISLAND: Providence	800-347-1997
TENNESSEE:	
Chattanooga	800-347-1997
Memphis	800-366-2998
Nashville	800-366-2998
TEXAS:	
Austin	800-366-2998
Dallas	800-366-2998
Ft. Worth	800-366-2998
Houston	800-366-2998
San Antonio	800-366-2998
UTAH: Salt Lake City	800-359-3997
VIRGINIA:	
Norfolk	800-347-1997
Richmond	800-347-1997
Roanoke	800-347-1997
WASHINGTON:	
Seattle	800-726-4995
Tacoma	800-726-4995
WISCONSIN: Milwaukee	800-366-2998

Federal Information Relay Service (FIRS) The Federal Information Relay Service allows nationwide telephone communications between hearing and hearing- and speech-impaired individuals with and within the Federal Government. By using specially trained relay operators, FIRS translates conversations between hearing individuals using standard telephone handsets, and hearing- and speech-impaired individuals using telecommunications devices for the deaf (TDD's). FIRS also encourages direct telecommunications by maintaining an on-line bulletin board and by publishing an annual directory of Federal TDD telephone numbers.

To utilize the Federal Information Relay Service (voice or TDD), call 202-708-9300 or 800-877-8339.

To access the Federal Information Relay Service bulletin board, call 202-708-9320 or 800-877-8845.

For a free copy of the directory, write to: U.S. Government TDD Directory, Customer Information Center, Pueblo, CO 81009.

For further information, contact the Liaison Office, Office of Telecommunications Services. Phone, 202-501-0308 (voice) or 202-501-2860 (TDD).

Specialized Data Centers The Service operates several programs that collect and maintain information on equipment of interest to the public and the private sector.

The Federal Procurement Data Center provides information regarding goods and services bought by the Federal Government. The Center is a unique source of consolidated information about Federal purchases, and the data is readily available through reports prepared by the Center.

The Federal Equipment Data Center operates the Automatic Data Processing Equipment Data System Program, which collects and maintains information regarding general-purpose processing equipment being used by the Federal Government. Information is collected and disseminated on federally operated domestic assistance programs, such as grants, and is available in an annual catalog and through a nationally accessible computer system.

For further information, contact the Automated External Information Division. Phone, 703–235–2870.

Domestic Assistance Catalog The Federal Domestic Assistance Catalog Program collects and disseminates information on all federally operated domestic assistance programs such as grants, loans, and insurance. This information is published annually in the Catalog of Federal Domestic Assistance, and is available through the Federal Assistance Programs Retrieval System, a nationally accessible computer system.

For further information, contact the Federal Domestic Assistance Catalog staff. Phone, 202–708–5126.

Federal Supply Service

The Federal Supply Service (FSS) provides quality goods and services required by Federal departments and agencies to assure that their needs are efficiently and effectively met, at the least possible cost to the taxpayer. Towards this goal, FSS operates a worldwide supply system to contract for and distribute personal property and services to Federal agencies. FSS manages Governmentwide transportation and travel services and regulations, including transportation audits; operates a vehicle fleet program; and administers a Governmentwide property management program for the utilization of excess personal property and the donation and/or sale of surplus property. The Service provides over $8 billion annually in common-use goods and services.

As a provider of supplies, FSS determines the method of supply that is most economical and effective from among its Stock, Special Order, and Federal Supply Schedule Programs. Through the FSS Stock Program, Federal workers are able to perform their functions by using over 17,000 commercial items which are received, stored, and issued through its wholesale distribution system. Under the Special Order Program supplies or services, for which demand is limited or related to special needs, are purchased by FSS for direct shipment from the vendor to the user. The Federal Supply Schedule Program is utilized when Federal requirements are widely diversified and/or there is a rapidly evolving state of technology present with the product lines or services.

To eliminate unnecessary expenditures and maximize the utilization of federally owned personal property, FSS directs and coordinates, on a worldwide basis, a Government property management program. Under this program, excess personal property is transferred to other agencies and, ultimately, is donated to eligible recipients or disposed of through competitive public sales.

The Federal Supply Service administers Governmentwide programs for transportation and travel management, transportation audits, and fleet management to meet the requirements of Federal agencies. Through the travel management program, contracts are established with travel agencies, airline companies, and Diners Club. Negotiations are then arranged with hotels and motels, so that FSS can offer Federal employees greatly reduced rates while on official travel.

To provide agencies with economical fleet management services, FSS operates an interagency fleet management system comprised of 130,000 vehicles. In conjunction with the Department of

Energy, FSS is introducing alternative fuel vehicles into the Federal fleet. These vehicles are being acquired under the auspices of the Alternative Motor Fuels Act of 1988 (42 U.S.C. 6201 *et seq.*). The first vehicles—65 sedans capable of operating on methanol, unleaded gasoline, or any combination of both—are already in use.

In addition, as the Government's civilian freight manager, FSS provides rating and routing services to customer agencies at 20–50 percent off commercial rates, as well as small package overnight delivery service at a savings of 70 percent below commercial rates.

For further information, contact the Federal Supply Service, Washington, DC 20406. Phone, 703–557–8646.

Public Buildings Service

The Public Buildings Service (PBS) is responsible for the design, building or leasing, appraisal, repair, operation, protection, and maintenance of most of the federally controlled buildings in the Nation. It has responsibility for 250 million square feet of space, excluding outside parking areas, in about 7,200 federally owned and leased buildings, in addition to approximately $5.5 billion in construction projects currently underway. The President issued Executive Order 12512 of April 29, 1985, which gave PBS the responsibility to provide leadership in the development and maintenance of needed property management information systems for the Government.

The Public Buildings Act of 1959 (40 U.S.C. 601–615) gave PBS authority over the construction of most Federal public buildings nationwide. This act was expanded by the Public Buildings Amendments of 1972, establishing a new method of funding PBS operations through a special fund to be financed from user charges paid by agencies using agency-controlled space.

The Public Buildings Cooperative Use Act of 1976 (90 Stat. 2505) was signed into law by the President on October 18, 1976. This legislation changes the way PBS manages Federal buildings by allowing occupancy of space by commercial tenants. The law also encourages renovation and conversion to Federal use of older buildings of historic or cultural value.

For further information, call 202–501–1100.

Design and Construction As a Federal construction agency, PBS plans and executes a major design and construction program to expand and modernize its nationwide inventory of buildings for housing Federal agencies. New construction projects are undertaken for long-term housing needs—either to meet new space requests or to replace leaseholds with more economically owned space. Repair and alteration projects are performed as necessary to keep the buildings safe, efficient, and serviceable. Architectural and engineering studies and other consultation services are performed to support other functional areas within PBS. Such services, as well as construction management services, are provided to other agencies. The program is executed by eight regional offices, predominately through contracting with private sector design and construction professionals.

The Public Buildings Service conducts applied research to develop and maintain facility standards and criteria based on state-of-the-art technology for application in its design and construction program. Emphasis in other areas such as energy conservation, handicapped accessibility, historic preservation, and art-in-architecture are actively pursued.

For further information, contact the Office of Real Property Development. Phone, 202–501–1025.

Real Estate The Public Buildings Service is responsible for managing the acquisition, assignment, and utilization of general-purpose, Government-owned and -leased space for Federal agencies. A nationwide organization of real estate professionals executes this task through eight regional offices as well as a number of facility support centers. Professional standards, practices, and techniques, including professional space planning and programming and computer-aided design, are used to assist client agencies in determining requirements and developing technical specifications for leasing, construction, or alteration of space. A key goal is to deliver the optimum amount of quality workspace to support agency activities at a minimum cost to the Government. The real estate organization oversees execution of a $1.5 billion leasing budget as well as a building purchase program that buys commercial office buildings to meet Federal space needs.

For further information, contact the Office of Real Property Development. Phone, 202–501–1025.

Real Property Management and Safety The objective of PBS is to provide an attractive, well-maintained, and safe setting in which Federal employees will feel stimulated and proud to work. The management of federally owned and leased buildings encompasses such activities as the operation, maintenance, repair, and alteration of the structures, as well as safety, energy conservation, and concessions programs.

The comprehensive fire, occupational safety, health, and environmental programs further enhance the work environment for employees in GSA-controlled facilities. PBS' environmental responsibilities are particularly focused on recycling and energy conservation programs. In addition, it oversees the operations and management of GSA-controlled facilities which have been delegated to other agencies.

For further information, contact the Office of Real Property Management and Safety. Phone, 202–501–0971.

Physical Security and Law Enforcement The Public Buildings Service is responsible for law enforcement and security services that are provided to occupants and visitors on property under the Agency's charge and control. These services encompass preventive patrolling and timely responses to criminal occurrences, incidents, and life-threatening events; investigation of crimes and violations of Federal statutes; implementation of crime prevention activities, including tenant awareness programs; coordination of a comprehensive occupant emergency program; installation and maintenance of perimeter security devices and systems; performance of physical security surveys and vulnerability assessments of all properties on a recurring basis; and a wide range of physical security advisory and consulting services.

For further information, contact the Office of Physical Security and Law Enforcement. Phone, 202–501–0887.

Planning An integral part of PBS' space provision activities is the planning effort that provides the framework for project development. The planning process ensures that long-range housing requirements of the Federal work force are satisfied in the most economic and effective manner by analyzing and comparing the cost and impacts of various housing alternatives, including construction, direct acquisition, alteration of existing facilities, and leasing. Housing alternatives are analyzed at both the nationwide and community level. Plans are developed with tenant agency participation to ensure that they are housed in locations and facilities that maximize their operational efficiency and delivery of services to the public. Planning is vitally concerned with the socioeconomic and cultural conditions of the nation's communities and makes every effort to have a positive impact through PBS activities. The Service promotes and encourages intergovernmental cooperation and coordination with State and local governments and their planning, land use, zoning, historic preservation, and environmental programs. In addition, PBS conducts environmental impact analyses which are coupled with economic and technical project analyses to ensure that environmental considerations are included in the project development effort.

The Service's planning process provides the framework for more than just project development; it provides guidance and direction for all policy and program development. This is accomplished through its strategic planning effort which includes full participation by all PBS elements.

For further information, contact the Office of Planning. Phone, 202–501–0638.

Procurement The Service plans, directs, and coordinates on a servicewide basis a comprehensive program of contracting and management, including the development and administration of procurement policies, regulations, and procedures; construction, architecture, and engineering services; building management services; and repair and alteration procurements. Its major objectives include developing, establishing, and monitoring major acquisitions, and executing and administering assigned Federal grants. An oversight responsibility ensures compliance with acquisition policies, regulations, and procedures.

For further information, contact the Office of Procurement. Phone, 202–501–0907.

Public Utilities Management In managing the public utilities program, PBS reviews public utility rate schedules to determine the adequacy of the rates in respect to the Government as a consumer; negotiates utility rates and contracts for general Government use and for numerous special situations; and on behalf of Federal agencies, provides advice and expert testimony in proceedings before regulatory bodies when the Government's interest as a consumer needs to be protected. In addition, Governmentwide standards concerning the procurement, use, and conservation of utilities are issued to regulate and furnish management guidance in this area.

For further information, contact the Office of Procurement. Phone, 202–501–0907.

Governmentwide Real Property Relations The Service develops, directs, and administers comprehensive programs in the following areas:

—Governmentwide real property asset management reforms (pursuant to Executive Order 12512 of April 29, 1985);

—client outreach to ensure excellent relations and proper communications between the Service and client agencies;

—art and historic preservation;

—management of worldwide real property inventory systems;

—coordination of client agency space plans required under the asset management reform initiative; and

—coordination with Federal agencies on initiatives having Governmentwide application for which PBS has a role, such as physical fitness and ridesharing.

For further information, contact the Office of Governmentwide Real Property Relations. Phone, 202–501–0856.

Federal Property Resources Service

The Federal Property Resources Service maintains an extensive program to provide for the proper utilization and disposal of Government real property. The goal of this program is to provide for the efficient and economical utilization of Federal real property and the disposal of any real property surplus to Federal requirements.

In furtherance of this goal, the Service directs a continuing survey of Federal real properties to determine if they are not utilized, underutilized, or being put to their optimum use. Property worth millions of dollars has been reported excess to the Agency for further Federal utilization or disposal as a direct result of the survey program.

Property no longer needed by a Federal agency is reported as excess to the Service for disposal. Excess property may be transferred to another Federal agency for its use in lieu of acquiring additional facilities.

Property that is not needed by any Federal agency is determined surplus and may be made available for local public purposes specified by law where the highest and best use of the property is for such purposes and the use has exceptional merit. Such properties are also made available to homeless providers for homeless assistance purposes when determined suitable by the Department of Housing and Urban

Development under the Stewart B. McKinney Homeless Assistance Act.

Properties not needed for Federal purposes and not transferred to a local public body for authorized public uses are generally disposed of through negotiated or public competitive sale.

The Service also conducts sales, on a reimbursable basis, for other agencies having their own disposal authority.

For further information, contact the Office of Real Estate Policy and Sales. Phone, 202-501-0084.

Regional Offices Regional offices are located in 11 U.S. cities. Within its area of jurisdiction, each regional office is responsible for executing assigned programs.

Regional Offices—General Services Administration

(Areas included within each region are indicated on the map in Appendix A.)

Headquarters/Address	Administrator
1. Boston, MA (10 Causeway St., 02222)	(Vacancy)
2. New York, NY (26 Federal Plz., 10278)	William J. Diamond
3. Philadelphia, PA (9th and Market Sts., 19107)	George P. Cordes
4. Atlanta, GA (75 Spring St. SW., 30303)	Gary C. Cason
5. Chicago, IL (230 S. Dearborn St., 60604)	Donald L. Zito
6. Kansas City, MO (1500 E. Bannister Rd., 64131)	Delwyn D. Stromer
7. Ft. Worth, TX (819 Taylor St., 76102)	Hollis V. Rutledge, Jr.
8. Denver, CO (Denver Federal Ctr., 80225-0006)	Eric Lee
9. San Francisco, CA (525 Market St., 94105)	Edwin W. Thomas, Jr.
10. Auburn, WA (GSA Ctr., 98002)	Bob Eberle
National Capital Region, Washington, DC (7th and D Sts. SW., 20407)	James C. Handley

For further information, contact the Office of Regional Operations. Phone, 202-501-0397.

Sources of Information

Consumer Information Center Organized under the Office of Public Affairs is the Consumer Information Center, a program that assists Federal agencies in the release of relevant and useful consumer information and generates increased public awareness of this information. The Center publishes quarterly the *Consumer Information Catalog,* which is free to the public and lists more than 200 free or low-cost Federal consumer interest publications. Topics include health, food, nutrition, money management, employment, Federal benefits, the environment, and education. The *Catalog* is widely distributed through congressional offices, Federal facilities, educators, State and local governmental consumer offices, and private nonprofit organizations. For a free copy of the *Catalog,* write to Consumer Information Catalog, Pueblo, CO 81009. Phone, 719-943-4000. Bulk copies are free to nonprofit organizations.

Contracts Individuals seeking to do business with the General Services Administration may obtain detailed information from the Business Service Centers listed on page 611. Inquiries concerning programs to assist small business should be directed to one of the Business Service Centers.

Employment Inquiries and applications should be directed to the Personnel Operations Division (CPS), Office of Personnel, General Services Administration, Washington, DC 20405. Schools interested in the recruitment program should contact the Personnel Operations Division (CPS), Office of Personnel, Washington, DC 20405 (phone, 202-501-0370), and/or the appropriate regional office listed on this page.

Freedom of Information and Privacy Act Requests Inquiries concerning policies pertaining to Freedom of Information Act and Privacy Act matters should be addressed to the General Services Administration (CAIR), Attn: GSA FOIA or Privacy Act Officer, Room 7102, Washington, DC 20405. Phone, 202-501-2691. TDD callers may use the Federal Information Relay Service (phone, 202-708-9300; fax, 202-501-2727). FOIA or Privacy Act requests concerning GSA regions should be directed to the FOIA or Privacy Act officers for the particular region. See the listing on this page.

Public and News Media Inquiries The Office of Public Affairs is responsible for the coordination of responses to inquiries from both the general public and news media, as well as for maintaining an information network with agency employees with regard to items of interest to the Federal worker. The Office, through its Office of Media Relations, issues news releases. Its Office of Communications is responsible for printing the *GSA Update,* a weekly bulletin of noteworthy items designed to keep agency employees apprised of pertinent issues, and *GSA Today,* a bimonthly employee newspaper.

Publications Many publications are available at moderate prices through the bookstores of the Government Printing Office or from customer supply centers. Others may be obtained free or at production cost from a Business Service Center or a Federal Information Center. The telephone numbers and addresses of the Federal Information Centers and of the Government Printing Office bookstores are listed in local telephone directories. If a publication is not distributed by any of the centers or stores, inquiries should be directed to the originating agency service or office. The addresses for inquiries are:

Public Buildings Service (P), General Services Administration, Washington, DC 20405

Federal Supply Service (F), General Services Administration, Washington, DC 20406

Office of Finance (BC), General Services Administration, Washington, DC 20405

Information Resources Management Service (K), General Services Administration, Washington, DC 20405

Federal Property Resources Service (D), General Services Administration, Washington, DC 20405

Those who would like a brief index of publications or who are not certain of the service or office of origin should write to the Director of Publications, Office of Communications (XS), General Services Administration, Washington, DC 20405. Phone, 202-501-1235.

Small Business Activities Inquiries concerning programs to assist small business should be directed to one of the Business Centers listed on page 611.

Speakers Inquiries and requests for speakers should be directed to the Office of Public Affairs, General Services Administration, Washington, DC 20405 (phone, 202-501-0705); or contact the nearest regional office.

For further information concerning the General Services Administration, contact the Office of Public Affairs (X), General Services Administration, Washington, DC 20405. Phone, 202-501-0705.

INTER-AMERICAN FOUNDATION

1515 Wilson Boulevard, Rosslyn, VA 22209
Phone, 703-841-3800

Board of Directors:

Chairman	FRANK D. YTURRIA
Vice Chairman	NORTON STEVENS
Directors	JAMES R. WHELAN
	LYNDA A. BARNESS
	BERNARD W. ARONSON
	JAMES H. MICHEL
	(3 VACANCIES)

Staff:

President	BILL K. PERRIN
Vice President for Programs	STEPHEN G. VETTER
Vice President for Learning and Dissemination	CHARLES A. REILLY
General Counsel	CHARLES M. BERK

The Inter-American Foundation is an independent Government corporation that supports social and economic development in Latin America and the Caribbean. It makes grants primarily to private, indigenous organizations that carry out self-help projects benefiting poor people.

The Inter-American Foundation was created by Congress in 1969 (22 U.S.C. 290f) as a public corporation to support the self-help efforts of poor people in Latin America and the Caribbean. The Foundation was established because of congressional concern that traditional programs of development assistance were not reaching poor people. Instead of working through governments, the Foundation responds directly to the initiatives of the poor by supporting local and private organizations. Approximately one-half of the Foundation's funds come from congressional appropriations and the remainder from the Social Progress Trust Fund of the Inter-American Development Bank.

The Foundation was created as an independent agency so that its operations would not be affected by short-term U.S. foreign policy considerations. It is governed by a nine-member Board of Directors appointed by the President with the advice and consent of the Senate. By law, six members of the Board are from private organizations and three are from the Government.

The Foundation has made 2,918 grants, totaling over $292 million in 36 countries of Latin America and the Caribbean. Most grants are made to private, grassroots organizations, including community associations and small urban enterprises or to larger organizations that work with local groups and provide them with credit, technical assistance, training, and marketing services. A small number of grants each year are made to centers in Latin America and the Caribbean for research on the problems of poor people and grassroots development.

For further information, contact the Office of the President, Inter-American Foundation, 1515 Wilson Boulevard, Rosslyn, VA 22209. Phone, 703–841–3810.

INTERSTATE COMMERCE COMMISSION

Twelfth Street and Constitution Avenue NW., Washington, DC 20423
Phone, 202–275–7119

Chairman	EDWARD J. PHILBIN
Vice Chairman	EDWARD M. EMMETT
Commissioners	J.J. SIMMONS III
	GAIL C. MCDONALD
	KAREN B. PHILLIPS
Director, Office of Congressional Affairs	SPOFFORD H. CANFIELD IV
Special Assistant to the Director	SANDY K. BARUAH
Deputy Director, Congressional Affairs	JOY C. BELEW
Director, Office of External Affairs	PEGGY M. VENABLE
Deputy Director, Public Affairs	A. DENNIS WATSON
Director, Office of Human Relations	ALEXANDER W. DOBBINS
Managing Director	H.J. RHODES
Director, Office of Personnel	RICHARD H. MOOERS
Chief, Budget and Fiscal Office	ANTHONY JACOBIK, JR.
Chief, Section of Administrative Services	VIRGIL L. SHULTZ
Chief, Section of Systems Development	EDWARD F. WELKENER

Inspector General, Office of the Inspector General	JAMES J. MCKAY
Secretary	SIDNEY L. STRICKLAND, JR.
Assistant Secretary	KATHLEEN M. KING
Chief, Service Section	ELLEN R. KEYS, *Acting*
Chief, Public Records	EDWARD C. FERNANDEZ
General Counsel	ROBERT S. BURK
Deputy General Counsel	HENRI F. RUSH
Associate General Counsel	ELLEN D. HANSON
Deputy Associate General Counsels	CRAIG M. KEATS JOHN J. MCCARTHY, JR.
Director, Office of Public Assistance	DAN G. KING, *Acting*
Chief Administrative Law Judge	PAUL S. CROSS
Director, Office of Economics	HOWARD K. FACE
Assistant to the Director for Administration	AUBREY H. HERNDON, JR.
Assistant to the Director for Policy Review	LESLIE J. SELZER
Deputy Director of Economics (Accounts)	EDWARD J. GUTHRIE
Chief, Section of Auditing and Accounting	WILLIAM F. MOSS III
Chief, Section of Financial Analysis	WARD L. GINN, JR.
Chief, Section of Rail Costing	WILLIAM T. BONO
Chairman, Accounting and Valuation Board	WILLIAM F. MOSS III
Deputy Director of Economics	LELAND L. GARDNER, *Acting*
Chief, Section of Research and Analysis	MICHAEL A. REDISCH
Chief, Section of Energy and Environment	ELAINE K. KAISER
Chief, Section of Rail Services Planning	MICHAEL E. SULLIVAN
Director, Office of Proceedings	DAVID M. KONSCHNIK
Deputy Director, Motor Section	RICHARD B. FELDER
Deputy Director, Rail Section	JOSEPH H. DETTMAR
Director, Office of Compliance and Consumer Assistance	BERNARD GAILLARD
Associate Director	WILLIAM J. LOVE
Deputy Director, Section of Operations	HEBER P. HARDY
Deputy Director, Section of Enforcement	CHARLES E. WAGNER
Director, Bureau of Traffic	NEIL S. LLEWELLYN
Chief, Section of Tariffs	CHARLES E. LANGYHER III
Chief, Section of Rates and Informal Cases	LAWRENCE C. HERZIG
Chief, Tariff Examining Branch	THOMAS A. MONGELLI
Chief, Enforcement and Adjudication Support	JAMES E. MANNING
Chief, Informal Rate Cases	JOEL W. KING

[For the Interstate Commerce Commission statement of organization, see the *Code of Federal Regulations*, Title 49, Part 1011]

The Interstate Commerce Commission regulates interstate surface transportation, including trains, trucks, buses, water carriers, household goods transporters, freight forwarders, transportation brokers, and pipelines that are not regulated by the Federal Energy Regulatory Commission. The regulatory laws vary depending on the type of transportation; however, they generally involve certification of carriers seeking to provide transportation for the public and regulation of their rates, adequacy of service, and carrier consolidations. The Commission assures that the public receives shipping rates and services that are fair and reasonable.

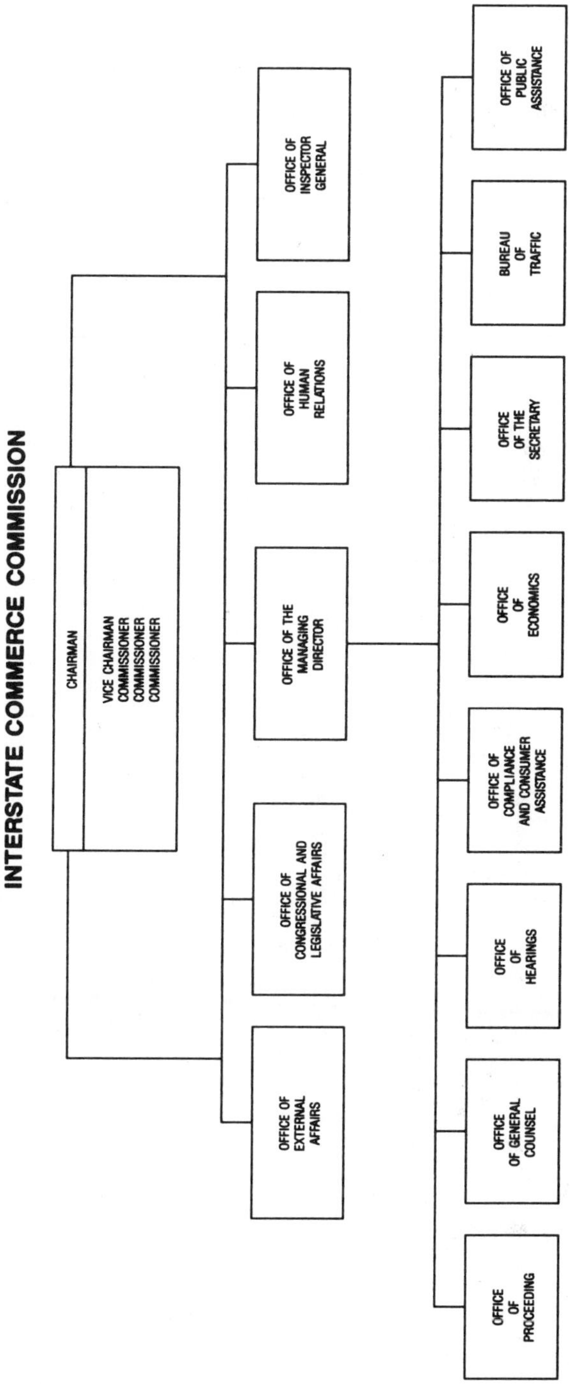
INTERSTATE COMMERCE COMMISSION
CHAIRMAN
VICE CHAIRMAN COMMISSIONER COMMISSIONER COMMISSIONER
OFFICE OF EXTERNAL AFFAIRS
OFFICE OF CONGRESSIONAL AND LEGISLATIVE AFFAIRS
OFFICE OF THE MANAGING DIRECTOR
OFFICE OF HUMAN RELATIONS
OFFICE OF INSPECTOR GENERAL
OFFICE OF PROCEEDING
OFFICE OF GENERAL COUNSEL
OFFICE OF HEARINGS
OFFICE OF COMPLIANCE AND CONSUMER ASSISTANCE
OFFICE OF ECONOMICS
OFFICE OF THE SECRETARY
BUREAU OF TRAFFIC
OFFICE OF PUBLIC ASSISTANCE

The Interstate Commerce Commission was created as an independent regulatory agency by act of February 4, 1887 (49 U.S.C. 10101 *et seq.*), now known as the Interstate Commerce Act.

The Commission's responsibilities include regulation of carriers engaged in transportation in interstate commerce and in foreign commerce to the extent that it takes place within the United States. Surface transportation under the Commission's jurisdiction includes railroads, trucking companies, bus lines, household goods transporters, freight forwarders, water carriers, transportation brokers, and pipelines that are not regulated by the Federal Energy Regulatory Commission.

The Commission's authority has been strengthened and its jurisdiction broadened by subsequent legislation, such as the Hepburn Act, the Panama Canal Act, the Motor Carrier Act of 1935, and the Transportation Acts of 1920, 1940, and 1958.

However, in more recent legislation, beginning with the Railroad Revitalization and Regulatory Reform Act of 1976 (45 U.S.C. 801), the Commission's statutory mandate has been altered to provide for less regulation over carrier rates and practices. This fundamental shift in national transportation policy has proceeded in the Motor Carrier Act of 1980, the Staggers Rail Act of 1980, the Household Goods Transportation Act of 1980, the Bus Regulatory Reform Act of 1982, and the Surface Freight Forwarder Deregulation Act of 1986. These measures provided for a sharply reduced Federal role in regulating the trucking, railroad, and bus industries.

The Chairman is designated by the President from among the Commissioners. The Commissioners elect their own Vice Chairman annually and may delegate certain duties and functions to individual Commissioners or to boards consisting of not less than three eligible employees.

Field offices are maintained in various cities to monitor the utilization of railroad freight cars in order to avoid severe shortages, investigate violations of the Interstate Commerce Act and related laws, and provide assistance to the public in its use of regulated carriers that provide transportation by railroad, highway, and waterway.

Activities

In broad terms and within prescribed legal limits, Commission regulations encompass transportation economics and service.

In the transportation economics area, the Commission settles controversies over rates and charges among regulated carriers, shippers, receivers of freight, passengers, and others. It rules upon applications for mergers, consolidations, and acquisitions of control. It prescribes accounting rules, awards reparations, and administers laws relating to railroad bankruptcy. It acts to prevent unlawful discrimination, destructive competition, and rebating. It also has jurisdiction over the use, control, supply, movement, distribution, exchange, interchange, and return of railroad equipment. Under certain limited conditions, it is authorized to direct the handling and movement of traffic over a railroad and its distribution over other lines of railroads.

In the transportation service area, the Commission grants the right to operate to railroads, trucking companies, bus lines, household goods transporters, freight forwarders, water carriers, and transportation brokers. It also approves applications to construct and abandon railroad lines.

Although public hearings on matters before the Commission may be held at any point throughout the country, final decisions are made at the Washington, DC, headquarters in all formal proceedings. These cases include rulings upon rate changes, applications to engage in for-hire transport, carrier mergers, adversary proceedings on complaint actions, and punitive measures taken in enforcement matters.

Consumer protection programs involve ensuring that the public obtains full measure of all transportation services to which entitlement is guaranteed by the Interstate Commerce Act. This law ensures that rates will be fair and service will be reasonable. Discrimination, preferential treatment, or prejudicial actions by carriers are illegal, and instances of such violations should be brought to the attention of the Commission at its headquarters or any field office.

The Office of Special Counsel was created by the Commission in November 1978 to help determine the public interest in proceedings subject to Commission jurisdiction. The Office can participate as a party or as an aid in the establishment of a record in those proceedings in which the public interest would be otherwise inadequately represented. The Office has authority to appear before the Commission, other agencies, and the courts. It is now part of the Office of Public Assistance.

The Regional Rail Reorganization Act of 1973 created in early 1974 a Rail Services Planning Office to ensure that public interest is represented in the restructuring and revitalization of railroads in the Northeast and Midwest. The Office was given permanent status by the Railroad Revitalization and Regulatory Reform Act of 1976 and is now part of the Office of Economics. In addition to its other responsibilities, it provides planning support for the Commission.

Regional Offices—Interstate Commerce Commission

Headquarters/Address	Director
CENTRAL—Rm. 1304, 219 S. Dearborn St., Chicago, IL 60604	William Redmond, Jr.
EASTERN—Rm. 16400, 3535 Market St., Philadelphia, PA 19104	Richard M. Biter
WESTERN—Suite 500, 211 Main St., San Francisco, CA 94105	John H. Kirkemo

Sources of Information

Consumer Affairs The Commission maintains a staff at each of its regional offices to handle complaints from the public regarding the transportation services provided by carriers.

Among the many consumer-oriented services are a series of advisory bulletins alerting the public and prospective transportation users to the existence of certain transportation problems. There is also a regulation requiring household goods carriers to furnish an information bulletin to each prospective customer. These public advisories may be obtained from the Office of Compliance and Consumer Assistance, Interstate Commerce Commission, Washington, DC 20423. Phone, 202-275-7849.

Contracts and Procurement Inquiries regarding the Commission's procurement and contracting activities should be addressed to the Chief, Procurement and Contracting Branch, Interstate Commerce Commission, Washington, DC 20423. Phone, 202-275-0890.

Employment Applications for employment may be sent to the Director of Personnel, Interstate Commerce Commission, Washington, DC 20423. Phone, 202-275-7288.

Publications A complete list of publications, including explanatory material on the operation and activities of the Interstate Commerce Commission, and on special consumer-related fields such as household goods movements and small shipments, is available. This list may be obtained from Public Affairs, Office of External Affairs, Room 4136, Interstate Commerce Commission, Washington, DC 20423. Phone, 202-275-7252.

Reading Rooms The library and several rooms at ICC headquarters are available for records inspection and copying. Requests for access to public records should be made at the Office of the Secretary, Room 2215, ICC Building; or write to the Secretary, Interstate Commerce Commission, Washington, DC 20423. Phone, 202-275-7428.

Small Business Activities The Commission maintains an Office of Public Assistance to help the small business owner or transportation firm in such matters as how to file protests on rates, how to file for new operating authority or extensions, or how to get adequate service where there is none. Inquiries should be addressed to the Office of Public Assistance, Room 3119, Interstate Commerce Commission, Washington, DC 20423. Phone, 202-275-7597.

Speakers Requests for speakers to discuss subjects relating to the Commission's organization, operations, procedures, and regulations should be directed to Public Affairs, Office of External Affairs, Room 4136, Interstate Commerce Commission, Washington, DC 20423. Phone, 202–275–7252.

For further information, contact Public Affairs, Office of External Affairs, Interstate Commerce Commission, Room 4136, Twelfth Street and Constitution Avenue NW., Washington, DC 20423. Phone, 202–275–7252. For consumer assistance, contact the Office of Compliance and Consumer Assistance, Interstate Commerce Commission, Room 4412, Twelfth Street and Constitution Avenue NW., Washington, DC 20423. Phone, 202–275–7849.

MERIT SYSTEMS PROTECTION BOARD

1120 Vermont Avenue NW., Washington, DC 20419
Phone, 202–653–7124

Chairman	Daniel R. Levinson
Counsel to the Chairman for Legal Policy	Garry M. Ewing
Counsel to the Chairman	Cameron P. Quinn
Inspector General	T. Paul Riegert
General Counsel	Llewellyn M. Fischer
Deputy General Counsel and Legislative Counsel	Mary L. Jennings
Deputy Legislative Counsel	Susan L. Williams
Director, Office of Equal Employment Opportunity	Janice E. Fritts
Vice Chairman	Antonio C. Amador
Chief Counsel	Mark Kelleher
Executive Assistant	Robert Hernandez
Member	Jessica L. Parks
Legal Counsel	Anne E. Broker
Executive Assistant	Linda L. Bowdoin
Special Advisor	Mary Ann Kane
Executive Director	Lucretia F. Myers
Deputy Executive Director	Michael W. Crum
Director, Office of Regional Operations	Thomas J. Lamphear
Director, Office of Management Analysis	Paul D. Mahoney
Director, Office of Appeals Counsel	William H. DuRoss III
Administrative Law Judge	Edward J. Reidy
Director, Office of Administration	Darrell L. Netherton
Director, Financial and Administrative Management	Robert W. Lawshe
Director, Information Resources Management	Stephen M. Beckman, *Acting*
Director, Human Resources Management	Marsha E. Scialdo
Director, Office of Policy and Evaluation	Evangeline W. Swift
Clerk of the Board	Robert E. Taylor

[For the Merit Systems Protection Board statement of organization, see the *Code of Federal Regulations,* Title 5, Part 1200]

MERIT SYSTEMS PROTECTION BOARD

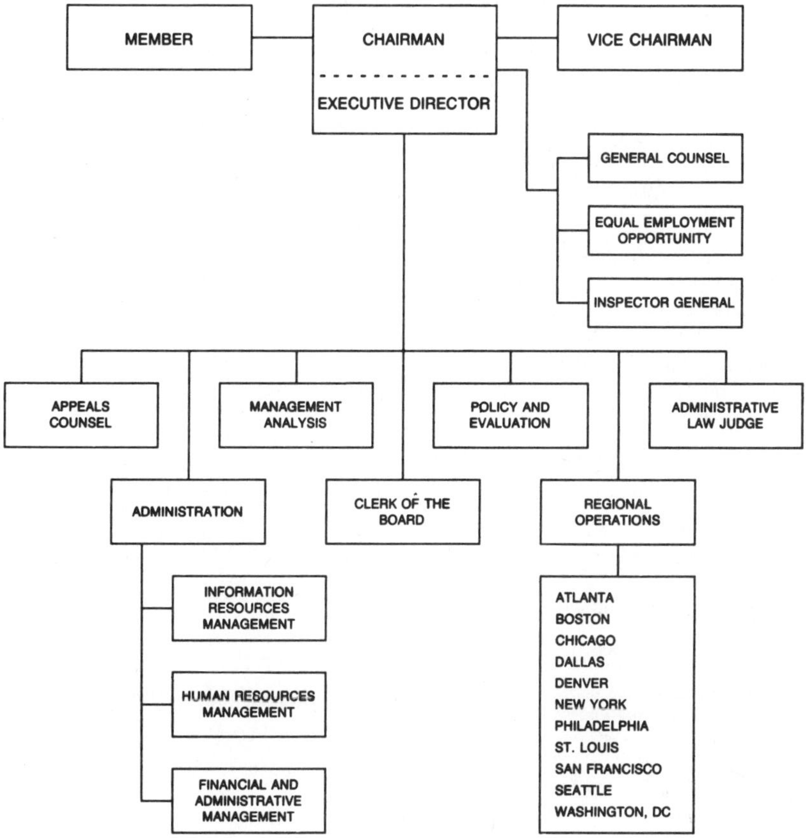

The Merit Systems Protection Board protects the integrity of Federal merit systems and the rights of Federal employees working in the systems. In overseeing the personnel practices of the Federal Government, the Board conducts special studies of the merit systems, hears and decides charges of wrongdoing and employee appeals of adverse agency actions, and orders corrective and disciplinary actions when appropriate.

The Merit Systems Protection Board is a successor agency to the United States Civil Service Commission, established by act of January 16, 1883 (22 Stat. 403). Reorganization Plan No. 2 of 1978 (5 U.S.C. app.), effective January 1, 1979, pursuant to Executive Order 12107 of December 28, 1978, redesignated part of the Commission as the Merit Systems Protection Board. The Board's duties and authority are specified in 5 U.S.C. 1201 through 1206.

Activities

The Board has responsibility for hearing and adjudicating appeals by Federal employees of adverse personnel actions, such as removals, suspensions, and demotions. It also resolves cases involving reemployment rights, the denial of periodic step increases in pay, actions against administrative law judges, and charges of prohibited personnel practices, including charges in connection with whistleblowing. The Board has the authority to enforce its decisions and to order corrective and disciplinary actions. An employee or applicant for employment involved in an appealable action that also involves an allegation of discrimination may ask the Equal Employment Opportunity Commission to review a Board decision. Final decisions and orders of the Board can be appealed to the U.S. Court of Appeals for the Federal Circuit.

The Board reviews regulations issued by the Office of Personnel Management and has the authority to require agencies to cease compliance with any regulation that could constitute a prohibited personnel practice. It also conducts special studies of the civil service and other executive branch merit systems and reports to the President and the Congress on whether the Federal work force is being adequately protected against political abuses and prohibited personnel practices.

Regional Offices—Merit Systems Protection Board

Region/Address	Director	Telephone
Atlanta, GA (401 W. Peachtree St. NW., 30308)	R.J. Payne	404–730–2751
Boston, MA (Suite 1078, 10 Causeway St., 02222)	William Carroll	617–565–6650
Chicago, IL (31st Fl., 230 S. Dearborn St., 60604)	Martin W. Baumgaertner	312–353–2923
Dallas, TX (Rm. 6F20, 1100 Commerce St., 75242)	Paula A. Latshaw	214–767–0555
Denver, CO (730 Simms St., 80225)	Gail E. Skaggs	303–231–5200
Falls Church, VA (Suite 1109, 5203 Leesburg Pike, 22041)	P.J. Winzer	703–756–6250
New York, NY (Rm. 3137, 26 Federal Plz., 10278)	Sean P. Walsh	212–264–9372
Philadelphia, PA (Rm. 501, 2d and Chestnut Sts., 19106)	Lonnie L. Crawford, Jr.	215–597–9960
San Francisco, CA (Rm. 2800, 525 Market St., 94105)	Denis Marachi	415–774–3081
Seattle, WA (Rm. 1840, 915 2d Ave., 98174)	Carl Berkenwald	206–442–0394
St. Louis, MO (Suite 615, 911 Washington Ave., 63101)	Earl A. Witten	314–425–4295

For further information, contact the Merit Systems Protection Board, 1120 Vermont Avenue NW., Washington, DC 20419. Phone, 202–653–7124.

NATIONAL AERONAUTICS AND SPACE ADMINISTRATION

600 Independence Avenue SW., Washington, DC 20546
Phone, 202–453–1000

Administrator	Richard H. Truly
Deputy Administrator	James R. Thompson, Jr.
Associate Deputy Administrator	Samuel W. Keller
Assistant Deputy Administrator	John E. O'Brien
Executive Officer	Jessie J. Harris
NASA Comptroller	Thomas Campbell
Deputy Comptroller	Gary B. Allison
Assistant Administrator for Commercial Programs	James T. Rose
Deputy Assistant Administrator	Ray T. Arnold
Deputy Assistant Administrator (Programs)	Frank E. Penaranda
Deputy Assistant Administrator (Special Projects)	Jon Michael Smith
Special Assistant for Industry Development	Clarence W. Pittman
Public Affairs Officer	Barbara Selby
Director, Program Support Office	Thomas D. Brown
Director, Commercial Development Division	Richard H. Ott
Director, Technology Utilization Division	Frank E. Penaranda, *Acting*
Director, Plans, Policy and Evaluation Division	Barbara A. Stone
Director, Small Business Innovation Division	Harry W. Johnson
Assistant Administrator for Headquarters Operations	Benita A. Cooper
Deputy Assistant Administrator	Michael D. Christensen
Assistant Administrator for Legislative Affairs	Martin P. Kress
Deputy Assistant Administrator (Operations)	Lynn W. Henninger
Deputy Assistant Administrator (Policy)	C. Everett Southwick
Director, Congressional Liaison	Mary D. Kerwin
Director, Legislation	Michael A. Maguire
Director, Congressional Inquiries	Lawrence E. Medway
Associate Administrator for Space Science and Applications	Lennard A. Fisk
Deputy Associate Administrator	A.V. Diaz
Assistant Associate Administrator (Science and Applications)	Joseph K. Alexander
Assistant Associate Administrator (Institutions)	Kathryn S. Schmoll
General Counsel	Edward A. Frankle
Deputy General Counsel	Gary L. Tesch
Associate General Counsel, General Law	George E. Reese
Associate General Counsel, Contracts	David Forbes
Associate General Counsel, Intellectual Property	Robert F. Kempf
Assistant General Counsel	June W. Edwards
Assistant Administrator for Procurement	Stuart J. Evans
Deputy Assistant Administrator	Don G. Bush, *Acting*
Director, Program Operations Division	Walker L. Evey

Director, Procurement Policy Division	William J. Maraist
Director, Procurement Management Division	A. Foster Fournier
Director, Contract Pricing and Finance Division	Thomas S. Luedtke
Director, Advanced Procurement Planning Division	Daniel R. Clough
Director, Competition Advocacy and Value Engineering	Bruce C. King
Director, Headquarters Contracts and Grants Division	John E. Horvath
Director, Space Station Freedom Procurement	Ronald E. Crider
Director, Office of Small and Disadvantaged Business Utilization	Eugene D. Rosen
Associate Administrator for Public Affairs	William Sheehan
Deputy Associate Administrator	Sue Richard
Director, Media Services Division	James W. McCulla
Director, Public Services Division	James Funkhouser
Director, Television Development Division	Robert J. Shafer
Associate Administrator for Space Flight	William B. Lenoir
Deputy Associate Administrator	Thomas E. Utsman
Deputy Associate Administrator (Space Shuttle)	Robert L. Crippen
Deputy Associate Administrator (Space Station Freedom)	Richard H. Kohrs
Deputy Associate Administrator (Flight Systems)	Michael T. Lyons
Deputy Associate Administrator (Institutions)	I. Duke Stanford
Associate Administrator for Management	C. Howard Robins, Jr.
Deputy Associate Administrator	Elmer T. Brooks
Chairperson, Inventions and Contributions Board	Carroll C. Dicus, Jr.
Chairperson, Board of Contract Appeals	Carroll C. Dicus, Jr.
Chairperson, Contract Adjustment Board	(vacancy)
Assistant Associate Administrator for Human Resources Management	Ann P. Bradley
Assistant Associate Administrator for Information Resources Management	Wallace O. Keene
Assistant Associate Administrator for Facilities Engineering	Billie J. McGarvey
Director, Management Operations Office	John W. Gaff III
Director, Logistics, Aircraft, and Security Office	Jeffrey E. Sutton
Director, Industrial Relations Office	Allan D. Harding
Director, Automated Information Management Program Office	Russell S. Rice, *Acting*
Associate Administrator for Safety and Mission Quality	George A. Rodney
Deputy Associate Administrator	James H. Ehl
Associate Administrator for Aeronautics, Exploration and Technology	Arnold D. Aldrich
Deputy Associate Administrator	Robert Rosen

Special Assistant to the Associate Administrator for Aeronautics Exploration and Technology	George W.S. Abbey
Director for Space	Lana M. Couch, *Acting*
Director for Aeronautics	Cecil C. Rosen III
Director for Institutions	Martin Stein
Associate Administrator for Space Operations	Charles T. Force
Deputy Associate Administrator	Jerry J. Fitts
Assistant Associate Administrator (Plans)	Albert R. Miller
Director, Administration and Resources Management Division	Ronald R. Dapice
Director, Communications and Data Systems Division	Charles F. Fuechsel
Director, Ground Networks Division	Robert M. Hornstein
Director, Space Network Division	Eugene Ferrick
Assistant Administrator for Equal Opportunity Programs	Harriett G. Jenkins
Deputy Assistant Administrator	Lewin S. Warren
Director, Affirmative Action and Evaluation Division	Alfonso J. Ludi
Director, Discrimination Complaints Division	Oceola S. Hall
Director, Minority University Research and Education Programs Division	(vacancy)
Inspector General	Bill D. Colvin
Deputy Inspector General	Lewis D. Rinker
Assistant Inspector General for Auditing	Richard J. Pelletier
Assistant Inspector General for Investigations	William D. Hager
Assistant Inspector General for Management	Danny P. Danigan
Associate Administrator for External Relations	Margaret G. Finarelli
Deputy Associate Administrator	John D. Shumacher
Special Assistant	Carl R. Praktish
Director, Defense and Intergovernmental Relations Division	Conrad O. Forsythe
Director, Educational Affairs Division	Robert W. Brown
Director, Management Support Office	Lynn A. Marra
Director, Industry Relations Division	David L. Stottlemyer
Director, International Relations Division	Peter G. Smith

Field Installations

Director, Ames Research Center	Dale L. Compton
Director, George C. Marshall Space Flight Center	Thomas J. Lee
Director, Goddard Space Flight Center	John M. Klineberg
Manager, NASA Resident Office, Jet Propulsion Laboratory	Fred W. Bowen
Director, John F. Kennedy Space Center	Forrest S. McCartney
Director, Langley Research Center	Richard H. Petersen
Director, Lewis Research Center	Lawrence J. Ross
Director, Lyndon B. Johnson Space Center	Aaron Cohen
Director, John C. Stennis Space Center	Roy S. Estess

[For the National Aeronautics and Space Administration statement of organization, see the *Code of Federal Regulations,* Title 14, Part 1201]

290-950 O 91 - 21

NATIONAL AERONAUTICS AND SPACE ADMINISTRATION

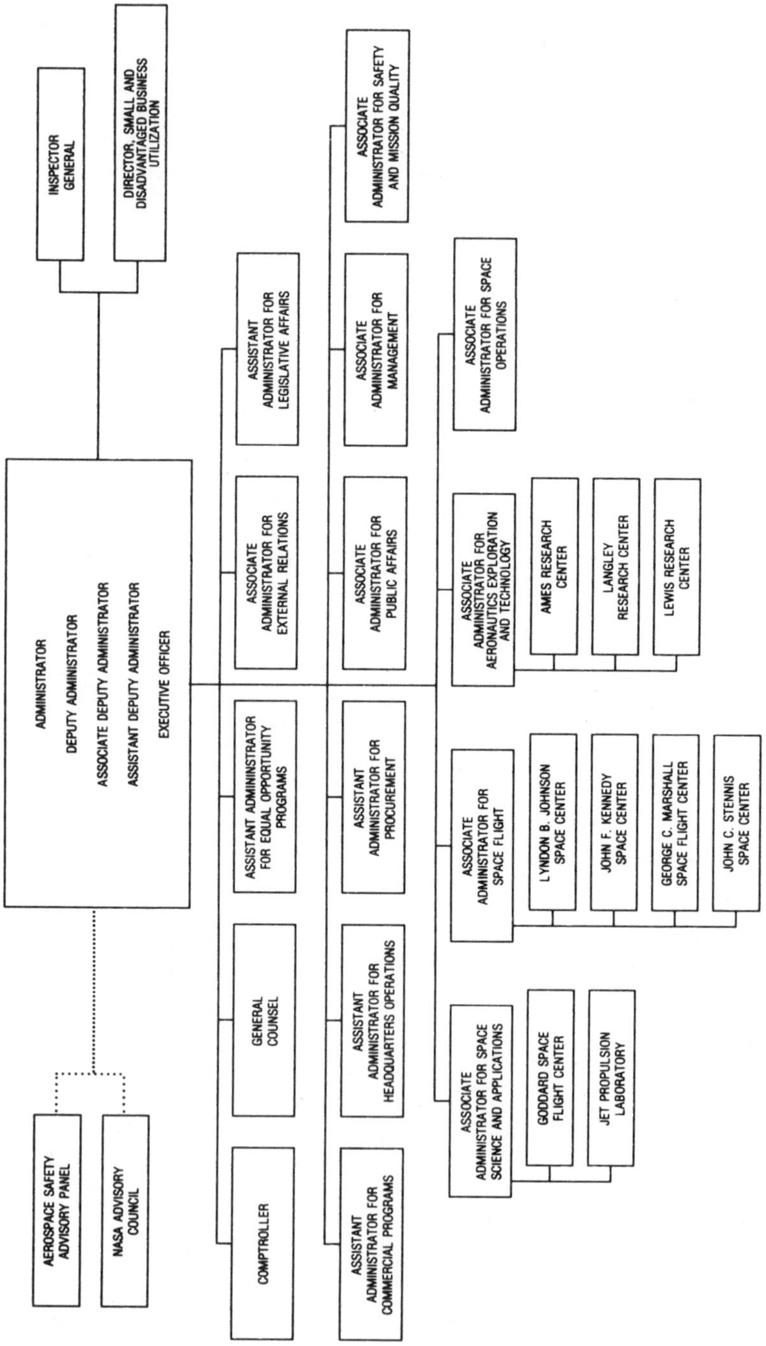

The National Aeronautics and Space Administration conducts research for the solution of problems of flight within and outside the Earth's atmosphere and develops, constructs, tests, and operates aeronautical and space vehicles. It conducts activities required for the exploration of space with manned and unmanned vehicles and arranges for the most effective utilization of the scientific and engineering resources of the United States with other nations engaged in aeronautical and space activities for peaceful purposes.

The National Aeronautics and Space Administration was established by the National Aeronautics and Space Act of 1958, as amended (42 U.S.C. 2451 *et seq.*).

NASA Headquarters

Planning, coordination, and control of Administration programs are vested in Headquarters. Directors of Field Installations are responsible for execution of agency programs, largely through contracts with research, development, and manufacturing enterprises. A broad range of research and development activities are conducted in field installations by Government-employed scientists, engineers, and technicians to evaluate new concepts and phenomena and to maintain the competence required to manage contracts with private enterprises.

Planning, direction, and management of research and development programs are the responsibility of four program offices, all of which report to and receive overall guidance and direction from the Administrator. The overall planning and direction of institutional operations at the field installations and management of agencywide institutional resources are the responsibility of the appropriate Institutional Associate Administrator under the overall guidance and direction of the Administrator.

Aeronautics, Exploration and Technology The Office of Aeronautics, Exploration and Technology is responsible for the conduct of programs to develop advanced technology to enable and enhance an aggressive pursuit of national objectives in aeronautics, space, and transatmospherics, including the National Aero-Space Plane Program; to demonstrate the feasibility of this advanced technology in ground, flight, and in-space facilities to ensure its early utilization; and to ensure the application of agency capabilities and facilities to programs of other agencies and the U.S. aerospace industry. The Office is the focal point for the Space Exploration Initiative, a long-term program of robotic and human exploration which will include sending humans to the Moon early in the 21st century to establish a permanent outpost and conducting human missions to the planet Mars. In addition, the Office is responsible for managing the Ames, Langley, and Lewis Research Centers.

For further information, call 202–453–2693.

Space Science and Applications The Office of Space Science and Applications is responsible for the Administration's efforts to understand the origin, evolution, and structure of the universe, the solar system, and the integrated functioning of the Earth. The Office conducts space application activities, such as remote sensing of the Earth, developing and understanding microgravity processes, and developing and testing advanced space communications as well as basic and applied science to facilitate life in space. The Office also is responsible for managing the Goddard Space Flight Center and the Jet Propulsion Laboratory and maintaining contacts with the Space Studies Board of the National Academy of Sciences, the Space Applications Board, and other science advisory boards and committees.

The Office coordinates its program with various government agencies, foreign interests, and the private sector. Its objectives are accomplished through research and development in astrophysics, life sciences, Earth sciences and applications, solar system exploration, space physics, and microgravity science and applications, and communications and information systems. The Office also utilizes the space shuttle, expendable launch vehicles, automated spacecraft, human-occupied spacecraft, sounding rockets, balloons, aircraft, and ground-based research to conduct its programs.

For further information, call 202–453–1409.

Space Flight The Office of Space Flight (OSF) is responsible for providing U.S. Government civil space transportation and manned space-based facilities and operations in support of the NASA mission. In fulfilling its responsibilities, OSF develops, operates, and maintains manned space-based facilities and space transportation systems and services. It is also responsible for managing the Johnson Space Center, Marshall Space Flight Center, Kennedy Space Center, and John C. Stennis Space Center. In further executing its responsibilities, the Office plans, directs, and executes the development, acquisition, testing, and operation of all elements of the Space Shuttle Program; plans, directs, and manages execution of prelaunch, launch, flight, landing, post-flight operations, and payload assignments; maintains and upgrades the design of ground and flight systems throughout the operational period; procures recurring system hardware; manages all U.S. Government civil launch capabilities, including expendable launch vehicles and spacelab development, procurement, and operations; develops and implements necessary policy with other government and commercial users of the Space Shuttle; and coordinates all associated research.

The Office of Space Flight is also responsible for managing and directing all aspects of the Space Station Freedom Program and achieving the goals established by the President. These goals include developing a permanently manned space station by the mid-1990's involving other countries in the program, and promoting scientific research, technology development, and private-sector investment in space. The Johnson Space Center, the Marshall Space Flight Center, and the Lewis Research Center are responsible for developing major elements of the space station, all of which will be launched by the Kennedy Space Center.

The concept of the Space Station Freedom Program is to provide a manned base, with growth to a permanent support crew of four, which will initially have crew present only during shuttle visits, and eventual increase in station resources and crew size.

For further information, call 202–453–2959.

Space Operations The Office of Space Operations is responsible for an array of functions critical to the operations of the Nation's space programs. They include spacecraft operations and control centers, ground and space communications, data acquisition and processing, flight dynamics and trajectory analyses, spacecraft tracking, and applied research and development of new technology. The Space Transportation System, Tracking and Data Relay Satellite System, Deep Space Network, Spaceflight Tracking and Data Network, and various other facilities currently provide for the requirements for NASA's space missions. A global communications system links tracking sites, control centers, and data processing facilities that provide real-time data processing for mission control, orbit and attitude determination, and routine processing of telemetry data for space missions.

For further information, call 202–453–2019.

Field Installations

Ames Research Center The Center, which is located at Moffett Field, CA, manages a diverse program of research and technology development in support of the Nation's aeronautics and astronautics programs and maintains unique research and test facilities including wind tunnels, simulators, supercomputers, aircraft, and flight test ranges. Current areas of emphasis include the development of aerospace vehicle concepts through synergistic application of the Center's complete capabilities, ranging from computation and experimentation (in wind tunnels and simulators) to flight testing; research in support of human adaptation and productivity in the microgravity environment; and research and development of human/machine interfaces and levels of automation to optimize the operation of future aerospace systems, as well as future hypersonic vehicles and probes. Specifically, the Center's major program responsibilities are concentrated in computational and experimental fluid dynamics and aerodynamics; fluid and thermal physics; rotocraft, power-lift, and high-performance aircraft technology; flight simulation and research; control and guidance; aerospace human factors; automation sciences; space and life sciences; airborne sciences and applications; space biology and medicine; atmospheric and earth sciences; and ground and flight projects in support of aeronautics and space technology. In addition to these major program responsibilities, the Center provides support for military programs and major agency projects such as the Space Transportation System, Space Station, and the National Aero-Space Plane.

Goddard Space Flight Center The Center, which is located in Greenbelt, MD, conducts Earth-orbital spacecraft and experiment development and flight operations. It develops and operates tracking and data acquisition systems and conducts supporting mission operations. It also develops and operates Spacelab payloads; space physics research programs; Earth science and applications programs; life science programs; information systems technology; sounding rockets and sounding rocket payloads; launch vehicles; balloons and balloon experiments; planetary science experiments; and sensors for environmental monitoring and ocean dynamics.

Jet Propulsion Laboratory The Laboratory, which is operated under contract by the California Institute of Technology in Pasadena, CA, develops spacecraft and space sensors and conducts mission operations and ground-based research in support of solar system exploration, Earth science and applications, Earth and ocean dynamics, space physics and astronomy, and life science and information systems technology. The Laboratory also is responsible for the operation of the Deep Space Network in support of NASA projects.

Lyndon B. Johnson Space Center The Center, which is located in Houston, TX, manages the development and operation of the space shuttle, a manned space transportation system developed for the United States by NASA. The shuttle is designed to reduce the cost of using space for commercial, scientific, and defense needs. This Center is responsible for development, production, delivery, and flight operation of the orbiter vehicle, that portion of the space shuttle that is designed to take crew and experiments into space, place satellites in orbit, retrieve ailing satellites, etc. The shuttle crew (up to seven people) includes pilots, mission specialists, and payload specialists. Crew personnel (other than payload specialists) are recruited, selected, and trained by the Center. It is also responsible for design, development, and testing of spaceflight payloads and associated systems for manned flight; for planning and conducting manned spaceflight missions; and for directing medical, engineering, and scientific experiments that are helping man understand and improve the environment. For the space station program, the Johnson Space Center is responsible for developing the main structure of the station and for several distributed systems such as data management, gudiance and control, and thermal control. In addition, the Center supports overall program management with a number of system engineering and integration tasks.

John F. Kennedy Space Center The Center in Florida designs, constructs, operates, and maintains space vehicle facilities and ground support equipment for launch and recovery operations. The Center is also responsible for prelaunch operations, launch operations, and payload processing for the space shuttle and expendable launch vehicle programs, and landing operations for the space shuttle orbiter; also recovery and refurbishment of the reusable solid rocket booster.

Langley Research Center The Center, located in Hampton, VA, performs research in long-haul aircraft technology; general aviation commuter aircraft technology; military aircraft and missile (systems) technology; National Aero-Space Plane; fundamental aerodynamics; computational fluid dynamics; propulsion/airframe integration; unsteady aerodynamics and aeroelasticity; hypersonic propulsion; aerospace acoustics; aerospace vehicle structures and materials; computational structural mechanics; space structures and dynamics; controls/structures interaction; aeroservoelasticity; interdisciplinary research; aerothermodynamics; aircraft flight management and operating procedures; advanced displays; computer science; electromagnetics; automation and robotics; reliable, fault-tolerant systems and software; aircraft flight control systems; advanced space vehicle configurations; advanced space station development; technology experiments in space; remote sensor and data acquisition and communication technology; space electronics and control systems; planetary entry technology; nondestructive evaluation and measurements technology; atmospheric sciences; Earth radiation budget; atmospheric dynamics; space power conversion and transmission; space environmental effects; and systems analysis of advanced aerospace vehicles.

Lewis Research Center The Center, located in Cleveland, OH, manages the design and development of the power generation, storage, and distribution system for Space Station Freedom. The Lewis Research Center is also responsible for conducting research and technology activities in the following areas: air-breathing propulsion systems, including those needed for the National Aero-Space Plane; turbomachinery thermodynamics and aerodynamics; fuel and combustion; aero and space propulsion systems; power transmission; tribology; internal engine computational fluid dynamics; materials; structural analysis; instrumentation; controls; space electronics; cryogenics; high-temperature engine instrumentation; space communications, including design and development of the Advanced Communications Technology Satellite, which is scheduled for launch on the space shuttle in 1992; design and development of approximately 12 microgravity flight experiments scheduled to be flown on board the space shuttle over the next few years; management of a complementary microgravity ground-based research program; and management of commercial launch services for medium-class expendable launch vehicles. In addition, the Center provides research and technology support to the Department of Defense and assists the private sector in identifying potential industrial applications and commercialization of NASA-developed technology.

George C. Marshall Space Flight Center The Center, which is located in Huntsville, AL, manages, develops, and tests the external tank, solid rocket booster, and main engines, which are major portions of the space shuttle project; oversees the development of the U.S. Spacelab; and conducts research in structural systems, materials science engineering, electronics, guidance, navigation, and control.

For the Space Station Freedom Program, the Marshall Space Flight Center is responsible for the pressurized laboratory and habitation modules, and the logistics module's elements supplied by the United States. In addition, the Center is responsible for systems integration of these modules.

John C. Stennis Space Center The Center, which is located in Bay St. Louis, MS, plans and manages research and development activities in the field of space and terrestrial applications; space flight; research in oceanography, meteorology, and environmental sciences.

Sources of Information

Contracts and Small Business Activities Inquiries regarding contracting or small business opportunities with the Administration should be directed to the Director of Small and Disadvantaged Business Utilization, NASA Headquarters, Federal Building 10-B, Washington, DC 20546. Phone, 202-453-2088.

Employment Direct all inquiries to the Personnel Director of the nearest field installation or, for the Washington, DC, metropolitan area, to the Director, HQ Human Resources Management Division, NASA Headquarters, Washington, DC 20546. Phone, 202-453-8478.

Publications, Speakers, Films, and Exhibit Services Several publications concerning these services can be obtained by contacting the Public Affairs Officer of the nearest agency installation. Publications include *NASA Directory of Services for the Public, NASA Film List,* and *NASA Educational Publications List.* The Headquarters telephone directory and certain publications and picture sets are available for sale from the Superintendent of Documents, Government Printing Office, Washington, DC 20402. Telephone directories for field installations are available only from the installations. Publications and documents not available for sale from the Superintendent of Documents or the National Technical Information Service (Springfield, VA 22151) may be obtained from installation Information Centers in accordance with the Administration regulation concerning freedom of information (14 CFR, part 1206).

Reading Room NASA Headquarters Information Center, Federal Building 10-B (Lobby), Washington, DC 20546. Phone, 202-453-1000.

For further information, contact the Headquarters Information Center, National Aeronautics and Space Administration, Washington, DC 20546. Phone, 202-453-1000.

NATIONAL ARCHIVES AND RECORDS ADMINISTRATION

Seventh Street and Pennsylvania Avenue NW., Washington, DC 20408
Phone, 202-501-5400

Archivist of the United States	DON W. WILSON
Deputy Archivist of the United States	CLAUDINE J. WEIHER
Assistant Archivist for Management and Administration	JAMES C. MEGRONIGLE
Executive Director, National Historical Publications and Records Commission	GERALD W. GEORGE
Assistant Archivist for Federal Records Centers	DAVID F. PETERSON
Assistant Archivist for Public Programs	LINDA N. BROWN
Director of the Federal Register	MARTHA L. GIRARD
Assistant Archivist for Presidential Libraries	JOHN T. FAWCETT
Assistant Archivist for Records Administration	JAMES W. MOORE
Assistant Archivist for the National Archives	TRUDY H. PETERSON
Inspector General	LAWRENCE A. OBERG

[For the National Archives and Records Administration statement of organization, see the *Federal Register* of June 25, 1985, 50 FR 26278]

NATIONAL ARCHIVES AND RECORDS ADMINISTRATION

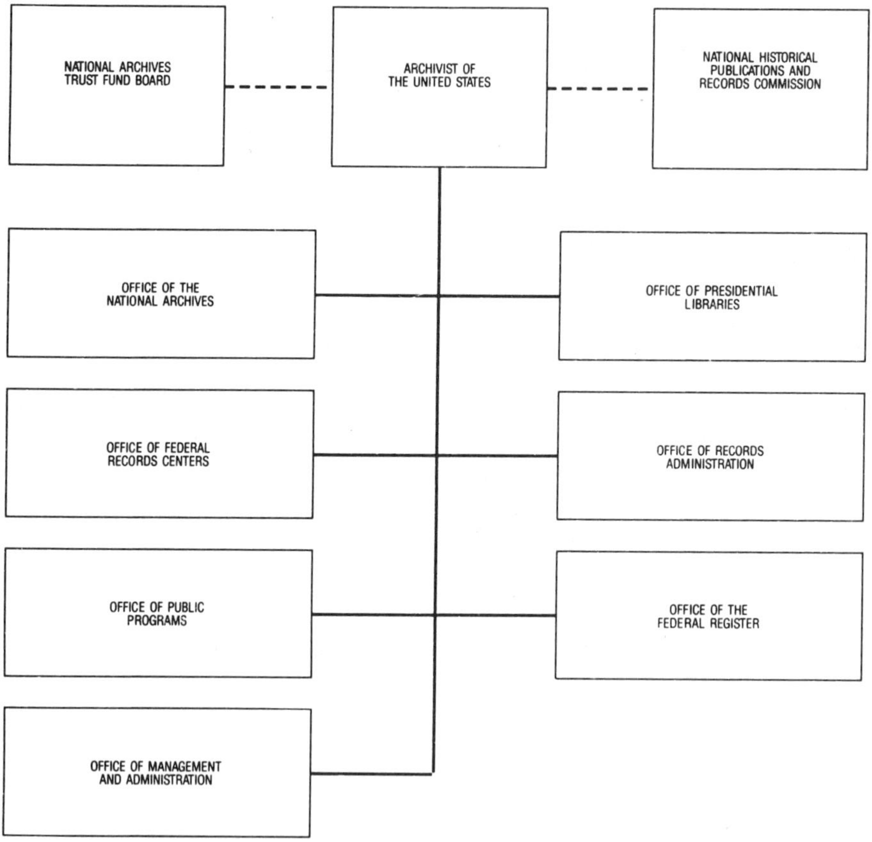

The National Archives and Records Administration establishes policies and procedures for managing U.S. Government records. The National Archives assists Federal agencies in documenting their activities, administering records management programs, scheduling records, and retiring noncurrent records to Federal Records Centers. The Agency also accessions, arranges, describes, preserves, and makes available to the public the historically valuable records of the three branches of Government; manages the Presidential Libraries system; assists the National Historical Publications and Records Commission in its grant program for State and local records and edited publications of the papers of prominent Americans; and publishes the laws, regulations, and Presidential and other public documents.

The National Archives and Records Administration was established by act of October 19, 1984 (44 U.S.C. 2101 *et seq.*), effective April 1, 1985, as an independent agency in the executive branch of the Government. It is the successor agency to the National Archives Establishment, which was created by act of June 19, 1934 (48 Stat. 1122), and subsequently incorporated into the General Services Administration as the National Archives and Records Service by section 104 of the Federal Property and Administrative Services Act of 1949 (63 Stat. 381), approved June 30, 1949.

Activities

Archival Program The National Archives maintains the historically valuable records of the U.S. Government dating from the Revolutionary War era to the recent past; arranges and preserves records and prepares finding aids to facilitate their use; makes records available for use in research rooms in all of its facilities; answers written and oral requests for information contained in its holdings; and, for a fee, provides copies of records. In addition, many important records are available on microfilm. Most of the historically valuable records in the Agency's custody are maintained in the Washington, DC, area. Records that are primarily of regional or local interest are, however, maintained in 12 regional archives, the locations of which are listed below.

Regional Archives—National Archives and Records Administration

City/Address	Director	Telephone
Anchorage, AK (654 W. 3d Ave., 99501)	Thomas C. Wiltsey	907-271-2441
Bayonne, NJ (Military Ocean Terminal, 07002)	Robert Morris	201-823-7545
Chicago, IL (7358 S. Pulaski Rd., 60629)	Peter W. Bunce	312-581-7816
Denver, CO (Denver Federal Ctr., 80225)	Joel Barker	303-236-0818
East Point, GA (1557 St. Joseph Ave., 30344)	Gayle P. Peters	404-763-7477
Fort Worth, TX (501 W. Felix St., 76115)	Kent Carter	817-334-5525
Kansas City, MO (2312 E. Bannister Rd., 64131)	Diana L. Duff	816-926-6272
Laguna Niguel, CA (24000 Avila Rd., 92677)	Diane Nixon	714-643-4241
Philadelphia, PA (9th and Market Sts., 19107)	Robert J. Plowman	215-597-3000
San Bruno, CA (1000 Commodore Dr., 94066)	Waverly Lowell	415-876-9009
Seattle, WA (6125 Sand Point Way NE., 98115)	Phillip E. Lothyan	206-526-6347
Waltham, MA (380 Trapelo Rd., 02154)	James K. Owens	617-647-8100

For further information concerning documents in the National Archives, contact the Reference Services Branch. Phone, 202-501-5400.

Presidential Libraries Through the Presidential Libraries, which are located at sites selected by the Presidents and built with private funds, the Agency preserves and makes available the records and personal papers of a particular President's administration. In addition to providing reference services on Presidential documents, each library prepares documentary and descriptive publications and operates a museum to exhibit documents, historic objects, and other memorabilia of interest to the public.

The records of each President since Herbert Hoover are administered by the Agency. Once considered personal papers, all Presidential records created on or after January 20, 1981, are declared by law to be owned and controlled by the United States and are required to be transferred to the National Archives at the end of the administration, pursuant to the Presidential Records Act of 1978 (44 U.S.C. 2201 *et seq.*).

Presidential Libraries—National Archives and Records Administration

Library	Address	Director	Telephone
Herbert Hoover Library	West Branch, IA 52358	Richard N. Smith	319-643-5301
Franklin D. Roosevelt Library	Hyde Park, NY 12538	Francis M. Seeber, *Acting*	914-229-8114
Harry S. Truman Library	Independence, MO 64050	Benedict K. Zobrist	816-833-1400
Dwight D. Eisenhower Library	Abilene, KS 67410	Daniel D. Holt	913-263-4751
John F. Kennedy Library	Boston, MA 02125	Charles V. Daly	617-929-4500
Lyndon B. Johnson Library	Austin, TX 78705	Harry J. Middleton	512-482-5137
Gerald R. Ford Library	Ann Arbor, MI 48109	Frank H. Mackaman	313-668-2218
Gerald R. Ford Museum	Grand Rapids, MI 49504	James R. Kratsas	616-456-2675
Nixon Presidential Materials Staff	Washington, DC 20408	Clarence Lyons, *Acting*	703-756-6498
Jimmy Carter Library	Atlanta, GA 30307	Donald B. Schewe	404-331-3942
Reagan Presidential Materials Staff	Simi Valley, CA 93065	Ralph C. Bledsoe	805-522-8444

For further information, contact the Office of Presidential Libraries. Phone, 202-501-5700.

Federal Records Centers Federal agencies retire certain noncurrent records to low-cost storage in Federal Records Centers in accordance with established disposition schedules. The Centers provide reference services, including loan or return of records to the agency of origin; prepare authenticated reproductions of documents; and furnish information from records. The Federal Records Centers dispose of records of transitory value and transfer to the Office of the National Archives those that have enduring value. The Centers also offer technical assistance workshops and advice on file maintenance, storage, records disposition practices, and vital records. Reimbursable microfilming services are available from most centers.

Federal Records Centers—National Archives and Records Administration

City/Address	Director	Telephone
Bayonne, NJ (Bldg. 22, Military Ocean Terminal, 07002)	Lee Romero	201-823-7161
Chicago, IL (7358 S. Pulaski Rd., 60629)	Robert Hutchinson	312-352-0164
Dayton, OH (3150 Springboro Rd., 45439)	Denis Pauskauskas	513-225-2878
Denver, CO (Bldg. 48, Denver Federal Ctr., 80225)	Robert Svenningsen	303-236-0804
East Point, GA (1557 St. Joseph Ave., 30344)	Thomas G. Hudson	404-763-7476
Fort Worth, TX (Bldg. 1, Ft. Worth Federal Ctr., 76115)	James W. Mouat	817-334-5515
Kansas City, MO (2312 E. Bannister Rd., 64131)	John J. Allshouse	816-926-7271
Laguna Niguel, CA (24000 Avila Rd., 92677)	Sharon L. Roadway	714-643-4220
Philadelphia, PA (5000 Wissahickon Ave., 19144)	David S. Weber	215-951-5588
San Bruno, CA (1000 Commodore Dr., 94066)	David D. Drake	415-876-9015
Seattle, WA (6125 Sand Point Way NE., 98115)	Steven M. Edwards	206-526-6501
St. Louis, MO (National Personnel Records Ctr., 9700 Page Blvd., 63132)	David L. Petree	314-263-7201
Suitland, MD (Washington National Records Ctr., 4205 Suitland Rd., 20409)	Ferris Stovel	301-763-7000
Waltham, MA (380 Trapelo Rd., 02154)	Clifford G. Amsler	617-647-8745

For further information, contact the Office of Federal Records Centers. Phone, 202-653-8450.

Records Administration The Agency develops standards and guidelines for the management and disposition of recorded information to ensure proper documentation of the organization, policies, and activities of the Government. It appraises Federal records and approves records disposition schedules. It also monitors archival records not in the Agency's custody, inspects agency records and records management practices, develops records management training programs, and provides guidance and assistance with respect to proper records management.

For further information, contact the Office of Records Administration. Phone, 202–501–6000.

Laws, Regulations, and Presidential Documents The Agency prepares and publishes a wide variety of public documents. Upon issuance, acts of Congress are published immediately in slip law (pamphlet) form and then cumulated and published for each session of Congress in the *United States Statutes at Large.*

Each Federal working day, the *Federal Register* publishes current Presidential proclamations and Executive orders, Federal agency regulations having general applicability and legal effect, proposed agency rules, and documents that are required by statute to be published. All Federal regulations in force are published annually in codified form in the *Code of Federal Regulations.*

Presidential speeches, news conferences, messages, and other materials made public by the White House are published each week in the *Weekly Compilation of Presidential Documents* and annually in the *Public Papers of the Presidents.*

The *Codification of Presidential Proclamations and Executive Orders* furnishes in one comprehensive source proclamations and Executive orders having general applicability and continuing legal effect, with currently effective amendments incorporated into their texts.

The *United States Government Manual,* published annually, serves as the official handbook of the Federal Government, providing extensive information on agencies of the legislative, judicial, and executive branches.

For further information, contact the Office of the Federal Register. Phone, 202–523–5240.

Public Programs The Agency has an extensive exhibits program. The Declaration of Independence, Constitution, and Bill of Rights are on permanent display in the National Archives Building. The 1297 Magna Carta, on indefinite loan, is also on display. The Agency exhibits numerous other documents on a variety of historical themes in its other facilities.

For further information, contact the Office of Public Programs. Phone, 202–501–5200.

Other Activities

National Archives Trust Fund Board The National Archives Trust Fund Board receives monies from the sale of reproductions of historic documents, audiovisual materials, and publications about the records, as well as gifts to the Administration. The Board invests these funds and uses income to support archival functions such as the preparation of publications that make information about historic records more widely available. Members of the Board are the Archivist of the United States, the Secretary of the Treasury, and the Chairman of the National Endowment for the Humanities.

For further information, contact the Secretary, National Archives Trust Fund Board. Phone, 202–501–5155.

National Historical Publications and Records Commission The Agency supports the initiatives of this statutory commission in making plans, estimates, and recommendations for historical works and in cooperating with and encouraging various non-Federal agencies and institutions in gathering and publishing papers and other documents important for the study of American history. The Commission awards grants to promote a variety of historically oriented projects, such as archival programs, documentary publications projects, and archival and editorial education.

The Publications Program provides grant money for printed and microfilm publications of the papers of important American diplomats, politicians, reformers, scientists, labor figures, as well as corporate and organizational records. A subsidy program provides grants to nonprofit presses to help support publication costs of sponsored editions.

The Records Program makes grants to State and local governments, historical societies, archives, libraries, and associations for the preservation, arrangement, and description of historical records.

Education programs sponsored by the Commission include an institute to train scholars in documentary editing and fellowships in the fields of documentary editing and archival administration.

For further information, contact the National Historical Publications and Records Commission. Phone, 202-501-5600.

Sources of Information

Calendar of Events The National Archives Calendar of Events is published monthly. To be added to the mailing list, call 202-501-5525. For a recorded announcement of events at the National Archives Building, call 202-501-5000.

Speakers and Presentations Community and school outreach programs are presented upon request. Interested groups in the Washington, DC, area should call 202-501-5205. Groups outside the Washington, DC, area should contact the regional archive or Presidential library in their area (see listings on pages 641 and 642).

Secondary education specialists present workshops at regional and national conferences of social studies professionals and as in-service training for teachers. For further information, contact the Education Branch by calling 202-724-0456.

Publications Agency publications, including facsimiles of certain documents, finding aids to the records, microfilm copies of many important records, and *Prologue,* a scholarly journal published quarterly, are available from Publications Services, National Archives and Records Administration, Washington, DC 20408. Phone, 202-501-5481. Records management publications are available from the Office of Records Administration by calling 202-501-6040.

Teaching Aids Secondary education specialists have developed low-cost documentary teaching materials for classroom use. Each kit deals with an historical event or theme and includes document facsimiles and teaching aids. For further information, contact the Education Branch by calling 202-724-0456.

Tours Individuals or groups may request general or specialty tours behind the scenes at the National Archives Building. The tours are given by reservation only, and individuals are requested to make reservations at least 2 weeks in advance. The tours are given at 10:15 a.m. or 1:15 p.m., Monday through Friday. Call 202-501-5205 between 9 a.m. and 4 p.m., Monday through Friday, to make reservations.

Audiovisual Sales and Rentals The National Audiovisual Center has motion pictures, film strips, slide sets, and video and audio tapes for sale or rent, depending on the item, to individuals, to schools, and to educational, civic, and community groups. The Center's inventory includes vocational, educational, documentary, and military audiovisuals made by and for Federal agencies. For additional information, contact the National Audiovisual Center, National Archives and Records Administration, 8700 Edgeworth Drive, Capitol Heights, MD 20743-3701. Phone, 301-763-1896.

Museum Shops Publications, document facsimiles, and souvenirs are available for sale in the National Archives Building, at each Presidential Library, and at some Regional Archives.

Educational Opportunities Several courses are offered on archival and records management principles and on using the resources of the institution.

The Modern Archives Institute is a 2-week course for archivists that introduces students to the principles and techniques of archival work. It is offered twice a year, in February and June, for a fee. Students are advised to register 3 months in advance. Inquiries should be sent to the Office of Public Programs, National Archives and Records Administration, Washington, DC 20408. Phone, 202-501-5212.

"Going to the Source: An Introduction to Research in Archives," is a 4-day, annual course on doing research in primary sources. The course provides experience with documents, microfilm, finding aids, and research methodology to researchers from such varied positions as public policy analysts, museum curators, and historical novelists. For further information, contact the Education Branch by calling 202-724-0456.

"Introduction to Genealogy" is a 4-day course offered annually to introduce genealogists to the records in the National Archives that can further their research in family history. There are also several half-day workshops each month that focus on specific aspects of genealogical research. For further information, contact the Education Branch, 202-724-0457.

The secondary school program annually offers an 8-day workshop, "Primarily Teaching," to introduce educators to the holdings of the National Archives and provide strategies for teaching with primary sources. For further information, contact the Education Branch by calling 202-724-0454.

A 2-day Files Improvement Workshop and a 3-day Records Disposition Workshop are designed for any Federal Government employee with responsibility for the records creation, filing, and disposition process. For further information, contact the Agency Services Division. Phone, 202-501-6000. Similar training is offered by the Federal Records Centers for agency field employees. For further information, contact any Federal Records Center listed on page 642.

A half-day program is offered by the Office of the Federal Register to provide public instruction on how to research Federal regulations that directly affect them. The program, "The Federal Register: What It Is And How To Use It," is conducted in Washington, DC, and in major regional cities. For further information, call 202-523-5240.

The National Historical Publications and Records Commission Institute for the Editing of Historical Documents is held for 2 weeks each summer at the University of Wisconsin, Madison. Admission is competitive and applicants should hold a masters degree in American history or American studies or have equivalent training. Tuition is $350. The Commission also offers three fellowships annually in advanced documentary editing and two fellowships in mid-level archival administration. The editorial fellows work with document publication projects supported or endorsed by the Commission. The archival fellows work at a historical records repository in such areas as appraisal, collection development, personnel administration, budget preparation, and external affairs. The fellows receive stipends and fringe benefits for a 9- to 10-month period. The fellowships are jointly funded by the Commission and the Andrew W. Mellon Foundation. For further information, contact the National Historical Publications and Records Commission, National Archives and Records Administration, Washington, DC 20408. Phone, 202-501-5600.

Volunteer Service Opportunities A wide variety of opportunities are available for volunteers. At the National Archives Building volunteers conduct tours, provide information in the Exhibit Hall, work with staff archivists in processing historic documents, and serve as genealogical aides in the genealogical orientation room. For further information, call 202-501-5205. Similar opportunities exist in the Presidential libraries and at some of the regional archives.

Congressional and External Affairs The Congressional and External Affairs Staff maintains contact with congressional offices, responds to news media inquiries, and issues news releases and other literature. For inquiries regarding congressional matters, call

202-501-5515; for news media inquiries, call 202-501-5525.

Reading Rooms Records are available for research purposes at the National Archives Building, Seventh Street and Pennsylvania Avenue NW., Washington, DC; at the Washington National Records Center in Suitland, MD; and at each Presidential library, Federal records center, and regional archives. In addition, cartographic materials are available at the Pickett Street Annex, 841 Pickett Street, Alexandria, VA 22304. Phone, 202-756-6700.

The Nixon Presidential Materials Staff also has a reading room at the Pickett Street Annex, although it is accessed through a different entrance and street address (845 Pickett Street, Alexandria, VA 22304). Phone, 703-756-6498. Some Nixon materials are available for public inspection, but researchers are advised to contact the staff in advance to ascertain the availability of materials before visiting the facility. Requests for additional information should be directed to the Reference Services Branch, National Archives and Records Administration, Washington, DC 20408. Phone, 202-501-5400.

Freedom of Information Act Requests Requests should be directed as follows:

Administrative records of the National Archives and Records Administration: Policy and Program Analysis Division, National Archives and Records Administration, Washington, DC 20408. Phone, 202-501-5110.

Historical records in the custody of the Office of the National Archives: Office of the National Archives, National Archives and Records Administration, Washington, DC 20408. Phone, 202-501-5300.

Historical records in the custody of a Presidential library: the library that has custody of the records (see page 642 for addresses).

Records in the custody of the Federal Records Centers: the Federal agency that transferred the records to the Federal Records Center.

Contracts Individuals seeking to do business with the Agency may obtain detailed information from the Acquisitions Management Branch, National Archives and Records Administration, Washington, DC 20408. Phone, 202-501-5920.

Employment For job opportunities nationwide, contact the nearest Agency facility or the Personnel Operations Branch, Room 2002, 9700 Page Boulevard, St. Louis, MO 63132. Phone, 800-634-4898.

Records Administration Information Center Upon request, the Records Administration Information Center provides individualized assistance in answering records management questions. For further information, call 202-501-6025.

For further information, write or visit the National Archives and Records Administration, Seventh Street and Pennsylvania Avenue NW., Washington, DC 20408.

NATIONAL CAPITAL PLANNING COMMISSION

Suite 301, 801 Pennsylvania Avenue NW., Washington, DC 20576
Phone, 202-724-0174

Chairman	Glen T. Urquhart
Members	William E. Baumgaertner
	W. Don MacGillivray
	Robert J. Nash
	Patricia Elwood
Ex Officio:	
(Secretary of the Interior)	Manuel Lujan, Jr.
(Secretary of Defense)	Dick Cheney

(Administrator of General Services)	Richard G. Austin
(Chairman, Senate Committee on Governmental Affairs)	John Glenn
(Chairman, House of Representatives Committee on the District of Columbia)	Ronald V. Dellums
(Mayor of the District of Columbia)	Sharon Pratt Dixon
(Chairman, Council of the District of Columbia)	John A. Wilson

Staff:

Executive Director	Reginald W. Griffith
Executive Assistant	Priscilla A. Brown
Assistant Executive Director for Intergovernmental and Public Affairs	Joseph Mancias, Jr.
Assistant Executive Director for Operations	Robert E. Gresham
Executive Officer	Connie M. Harshaw
General Counsel	Linda Dodd-Major
Secretariat	Rae N. Allen
Director, Long-Range Planning Division	Edward C. Hromanik
Director, Technical Planning Services Division	George H.F. Oberlander
Director, Planning Review and Implementation Division	Ronald E. Wilson

[For the National Capital Planning Commission statement of organization, see the *Code of Federal Regulations,* Title 1, Part 456.2]

The National Capital Planning Commission is the central agency for conducting planning and development activities for the Federal Government in the National Capital region. The region includes the District of Columbia and all land areas within the boundaries of Montgomery and Prince Georges Counties in Maryland and Fairfax, Loudoun, Prince William, and Arlington Counties in Virginia.

The National Capital Planning Commission was created as an independent establishment by the National Capital Planning Act of 1952 (40 U.S.C. 71a; D.C. Code 1-1001-1013).

The Commission is composed of five appointed and seven *ex officio* members. Three citizen members, including the Chairman, are appointed by the President and two by the mayor of the District of Columbia. Presidential appointees include one resident each from Maryland and Virginia and one from anywhere in the United States; however, the two mayoral appointees must be District of Columbia residents.

Activities

The Commission has three primary functions: comprehensive planning to ensure the orderly development of the Federal Establishment and protection of Federal interests in the National Capital region, plan and program review, and preparation of the Federal Capital Improvements Program.

Comprehensive Planning The Comprehensive Plan is a statement of policies dealing with the growth and development of the National Capital and consists of both Federal and District elements. It is an important planning tool that provides a framework for policy decisions regarding physical development

NATIONAL CAPITAL PLANNING COMMISSION

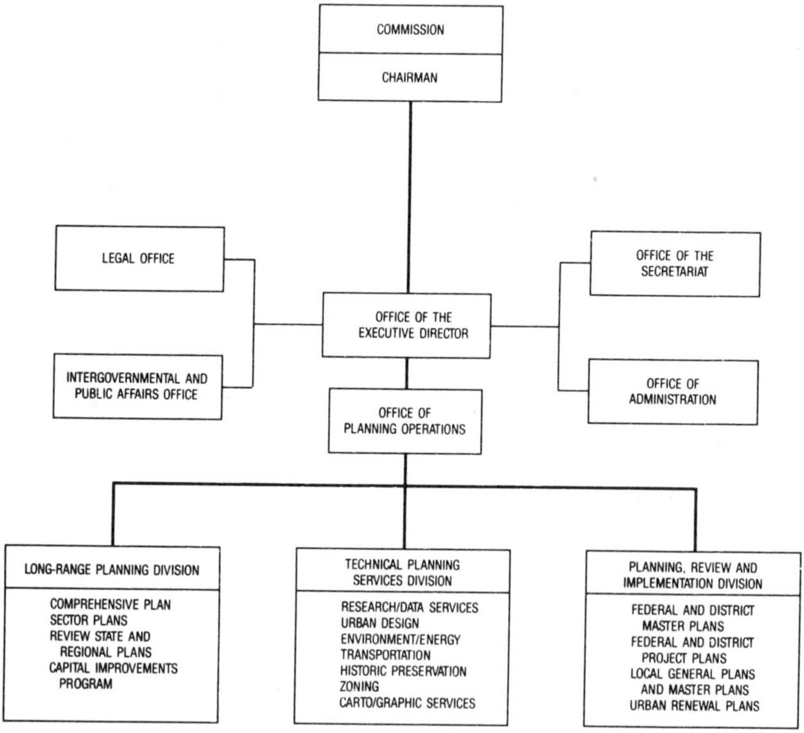

proposed by Federal, State, local, and regional agencies.

The Commission's comprehensive planning function involves preparation and adoption of Federal elements of the Comprehensive Plan for the National Capital as well as review, for Federal interests, of District or non-Federal elements of the Comprehensive Plan that are prepared by the mayor and adopted by the Council of the District of Columbia. If any District element is determined to have a negative impact on Federal interests, the Commission may veto it.

Plan and Program Review The Commission's plan and program review function consists of reviewing plans and programs proposed by Federal, State, regional, and local agencies or jurisdictions in the National Capital region. This function provides the Commission with an opportunity to coordinate plan and program proposals.

Following this review the Commission, with regard to certain types of projects, provides the sponsoring agency with comments and recommendations. Approval by the Commission must be obtained prior to construction of Federal public buildings in the District of Columbia and District of Columbia buildings in the central area of the District.

Each Federal or District project comes to the Commission for review at several stages. The first submission by an agency may be a master plan for an entire installation or facility. Plans for construction of individual projects implementing a master plan are submitted to the Commission at both the preliminary and the final stages.

Federal Capital Improvements Programming Another comprehensive planning activity is the preparation, adoption, and updating of the Five-Year Federal Capital Improvements Program, a "budget" schedule for Federal physical improvements throughout the National Capital region. It is prepared by the Commission in order to systematically review proposed Federal agency projects with regard to timing, location, and financing, and to coordinate agency development plans throughout the region.

A Federal Capital budget represents the first year of the 5-year program and consists of capital outlay requests for the region contained in the President's fiscal year Federal budget transmitted to Congress. The program for the second through fifth years incorporates Commission recommendations to Federal agencies and the Office of Management and Budget for subsequent budget submissions to Congress.

Additional Activities Other Commission responsibilities include review of all proposed zoning regulations, map changes, and amendments to the District of Columbia zoning ordinance in order to ensure consistency of zoning regulations with Federal interests and with the Comprehensive Plan.

The Commission also:

—adopts urban renewal area boundaries;

—prepares, adopts, and modifies urban renewal plans;

—approves the Permanent System of Highways Plan;

—makes recommendations on proposed street and alley closings;

—approves transfers of jurisdiction between Federal and District agencies;

—approves the sale of surplus property and park land; and

—acquires land for parks and parkways in the National Capital region.

The Commission serves the entire National Capital region by coordinating Federal planning and development with the planning activities of State, local, and regional agencies and jurisdictions.

For further information, contact the Public Affairs Officer, National Capital Planning Commission, Suite 301, 801 Pennsylvania Avenue NW., Washington, DC 20576. Phone, 202–724–0174.

NATIONAL CREDIT UNION ADMINISTRATION

1776 G Street NW., Washington, DC 20456
Phone, 202–682–9600

Chairman	ROGER W. JEPSEN
Vice Chairman	(VACANCY)
Member of the Board	ROBERT H. SWAN
Executive Director	DONALD E. JOHNSON
Secretary to the Board	BECKY BAKER
Special Assistant to the Chairman	SUSAN NELOWET
Special Assistant to the Vice Chairman	(VACANCY)
General Counsel	ROBERT M. FENNER
President, Central Liquidity Facility	ROBERT J. LAPORTE
Director, Office of Public and Congressional Affairs	ROBERT E. LOFTUS
Chief Economist	CHARLES BRADFORD
Director, Office of Examination and Insurance	D. MICHAEL RILEY
Director, Office of Information Systems	JOSEPH VISCONTI
Inspector General	JOAN PERRY
Controller	HERBERT YOLLES
Budget Officer	WILLIAM POLING
Director, Office of Administration	BENNY R. HENSON
Director, Office of Personnel	DOROTHY FOSTER

[For the National Credit Union Administration statement of organization, see the *Code of Federal Regulations*, Title 12, Part 720]

The National Credit Union Administration Board is responsible for chartering, insuring, supervising, and examining Federal credit unions and administering the National Credit Union Share Insurance Fund. The Board also manages the Central Liquidity Facility, a mixed-ownership Government corporation whose purpose is to supply emergency loans to member credit unions.

The National Credit Union Administration was established by act of March 10, 1970 (12 U.S.C. 1752), and reorganized by act of November 10, 1978 (12 U.S.C. 226), as an independent agency in the executive branch of the Federal Government. It regulates and insures all Federal credit unions and insures State-chartered credit unions that apply and qualify for share insurance.

Activities

Chartering The Administration's Board grants Federal credit union charters to groups sharing a common bond of occupation or association, or groups within a well-defined neighborhood, community, or rural district. A preliminary investigation is made to determine if certain minimum standards are met before granting a Federal charter.

For further information, contact the appropriate regional office listed in the table on page 639.

Supervision Supervisory activities are carried out through annual examiner contacts and through periodic policy and regulatory releases from the Administration. The Administration also maintains a warning system designed to identify emerging problems as well as to monitor operations between examinations.

Examinations The Administration conducts annual examinations of Federal credit unions to determine their solvency and compliance with laws and regulations and to assist credit union management and operations.

For further information, contact the Director, Office of Examination and Insurance. Phone, 202–682–9640.

Share Insurance The act of October 19, 1970 (12 U.S.C. 1781 *et seq.*), provides for a program of share insurance. The insurance is mandatory for Federal credit unions and for State-chartered credit unions in many States and is optional for other State-chartered credit unions that meet Administration standards. Credit union members' accounts are insured up to $100,000. The National Credit Union Share Insurance Fund requires each insured credit union to place and maintain a 1-percent deposit of its insured savings with the Fund.

For further information, contact the Director, Office of Examination and Insurance. Phone, 202-682-9640.

Regional Offices—National Credit Union Administration

Region	Address	Director	Telephone
1. ALBANY—Connecticut, Maine, Massachusetts, New Hampshire, New Jersey, New York, Puerto Rico, Rhode Island, Vermont, Virgin Islands	9 Washington Sq., Washington Ave. Ext., Albany, NY 12205	Layne L. Bumgardner	518-472-4554
2. CAPITAL—Delaware, District of Columbia, Maryland, Pennsylvania, Virginia, West Virginia	Suite 800, 1776 G St. NW., Washington, DC 20006	Daniel L. Murphy	202-682-1900
3. ATLANTA—Alabama, Arkansas, Canal Zone, Florida, Georgia, Kentucky, Louisiana, Mississippi, North Carolina, South Carolina, Tennessee	Suite 1600, 7000 Central Pkwy., Atlanta, GA 30328	H. Allen Carver	404-396-4042
4. CHICAGO—Illinois, Indiana, Michigan, Missouri, Ohio, Wisconsin	Suite 155, 300 Park Blvd., Itasca, IL 60143	Nicholas Veghts	708-250-6000
5. AUSTIN—Arizona, Colorado, Iowa, Kansas, Minnesota, Nebraska, New Mexico, North Dakota, Oklahoma, South Dakota, Texas, Utah, Wyoming	4807 Stillhouse Canyon #5, Spicewood Springs Rd., Austin, TX 78759	John S. Ruffin	512-482-4500
6. SAN FRANCISCO—Alaska, American Samoa, California, Guam, Hawaii, Idaho, Montana, Nevada, Oregon, Washington	2300 Clayton Rd., #1350, Concord, CA 94520	Foster C. Bryan	415-825-6125

Sources of Information

Consumer Complaints The Administration investigates the complaints of members who are unable to resolve problems with their Federal credit union when these problems relate to a possible violation of the Federal Credit Union Act or consumer protection regulations. Complaints should be sent directly to the appropriate regional office.

Employment Inquiries and applications for employment should be directed to the Personnel Officer, National Credit Union Administration, Washington, DC 20456. Phone, 202-682-9720.

Federally Insured Credit Unions A master list of the names and addresses of all federally insured credit unions is available for public scrutiny in the Washington, DC, and regional offices. Copies of the list may be obtained at a nominal cost by writing to the Freedom of Information Officer, National Credit Union Administration, Washington, DC 20456. Phone, 202-682-9700.

Publications Copies of the following publications may be obtained for a nominal fee by writing to the National Credit Union Administration, Washington, DC 20456: *Federal Credit Unions, Your Insured Funds, Chartering and Field of Membership Manual, Federal Credit Union Handbook, Federal Credit Union Act, Annual Report of the National Credit Union Administration, Annual Report of the CLF,* and the *Annual Report of the Share Insurance Fund.*

Starting a Federal Credit Union Groups interested in forming a Federal credit union may obtain free information by writing to the appropriate regional office.

For further information concerning the National Credit Union Administration, contact the Office of Public and Congressional Affairs, National Credit Union Administration, 1776 G Street NW., Washington, DC 20456. Phone, 202-682-9650.

NATIONAL FOUNDATION ON THE ARTS AND THE HUMANITIES

NATIONAL ENDOWMENT FOR THE ARTS

1100 Pennsylvania Avenue NW., Washington, DC 20506
Phone, 202–682–5400

Chairman	JOHN E. FROHNMAYER
Senior Deputy Chairman	ANNE RADICE
General Counsel	JULIE DAVIS
Director, Office of Policy, Planning, and Research	MARGARET WYSZOMIRSKI
Director, Public Affairs	JACK LICHTENSTEIN
Director, Office of Inspector General	LEON LILLY
Director, Congressional Liaison	ROSE DINAPOLI
Deputy Chairman for Programs	RANDY MCAUSLAND
Director, Program Coordination	ANA STEELE
Director, Challenge and Advancement	JEANNE HODGES
Director, Dance	SALI ANN KRIEGSMAN
Director, Design Arts	MINA BERRYMAN, *Acting*
Director, Expansion Arts	A.B. SPELLMAN
Director, Folk Arts	BESS LOMAX HAWES
Director, Inter-Arts	LENWOOD SLOAN
Director, Literature	JOE DAVID BELLAMY
Director, Media Arts	BRIAN O'DOHERTY
Director, Museums	ANDREW OLIVER, JR.
Director, Music	ANTOINETTE HANDY-MILLER
Director, Opera Musical Theater	TOMAS HERNANDEZ
Director, Theater	BEN CAMERON, *Acting*
Director, Visual Arts	SUSAN LUBOWSKY
Deputy Chairman for Public Partnership	(VACANCY)
Director, Arts in Education	DAVID O'FALLON
Director, International	MERIANNE GLICKMAN
Director, Locals	RICHARD HUFF
Director, States	EDWARD A. DICKEY
Deputy Chairman for Management	CYNTHIA RAND
Assistant Director for Administration	D. KEITH STEPHENS
Director, Administrative Services Division	MURRAY R. WELSH
Director, Arts Administration Fellows Program	ANYA NYKYFORIAK
Director, Budget Division	AARON FINEMAN
Director, Civil Rights Division	JUNE HARRISON
Director, Contracts and Procurement Division	WILLIAM HUMMEL
Director, Council and Panel Operations	YVONNE SABINE
Director, Finance Division	MARVIN MARKS
Director, Grants Division	LAURENCE M. BADEN

Director, Information Management Division	RUTH REED
Director, Management Systems Division	OWEN M. JONES
Director, Personnel Division	STEVEN M. KLINK

NATIONAL ENDOWMENT FOR THE HUMANITIES

1100 Pennsylvania Avenue NW., Washington, DC 20506
Phone, 202–786–0438

Chairman	LYNNE V. CHENEY
Deputy Chairman	CELESTE COLGAN
General Counsel and Congressional Liaison	ANNE D. NEAL
Director, Office of Planning and Budget	STEPHEN F. CHERRINGTON
Director, Office of Publications and Public Affairs	CLAIRE DEL REAL
Assistant Chairman for Programs and Policy	JERRY L. MARTIN
Director, Division of Fellowships and Seminars	MARJORIE A. BERLINCOURT
Director, Division of Education Programs	JAMES HERBERT
Director, Division of Public Programs	DONALD D. GIBSON
Director, Division of Research Programs	GUINEVERE L. GRIEST
Director, Division of State Programs	CAROLE WATSON, *Acting*
Director, Office of Challenge Grants	HAROLD CANNON
Director, Office of Preservation	GEORGE FARR
Assistant Chairman for Operations	THOMAS KINGSTON
Accounting Officer	D. RAY GLEASON
Administrative Services Officer	BARRY MAYNES
ADP Systems Officer	WILLIAM J. KINSELLA
Equal Employment Opportunity Officer	MARGARET V. HORNE
Grants Officer	DAVID WALLACE
Director of Personnel	TIMOTHY G. CONNELLY
Inspector General	SHELDON BERNSTEIN

INSTITUTE OF MUSEUM SERVICES

Room 510, 1100 Pennsylvania Avenue NW., Washington, DC 20506
Phone, 202–786–0536

Director	SUSANNAH S. KENT
Director, Policy, Planning, and Budget	LINDA BELL
Public Information Officer and Congressional Liaison	MAMIE BITTNER
Executive Assistant, National Museum Services Board and Administrative Assistant	S. WILLIAM LANEY
Program Director	REBECCA DANVERS

[For the National Foundation on the Arts and the Humanities statement of organization, see the *Code of Federal Regulations*, Title 45, Part 1100]

NATIONAL ENDOWMENT FOR THE ARTS

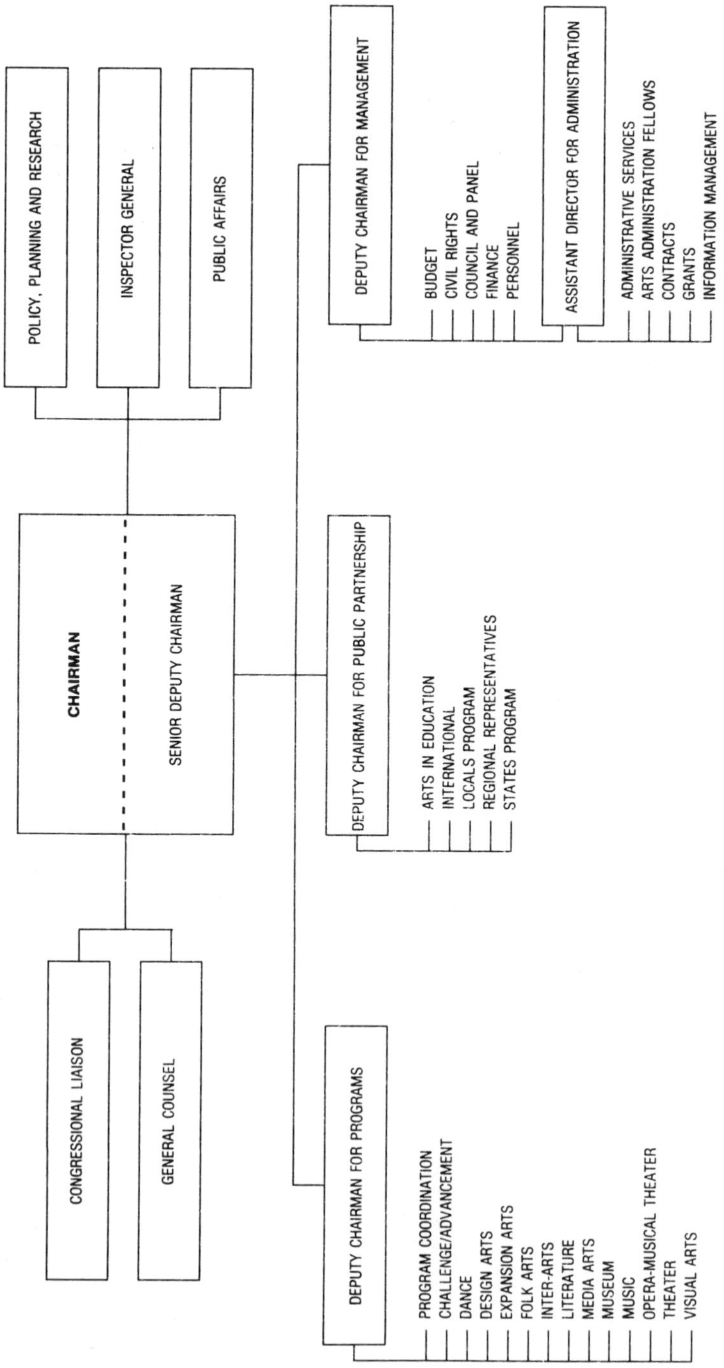

NATIONAL ENDOWMENT FOR THE HUMANITIES

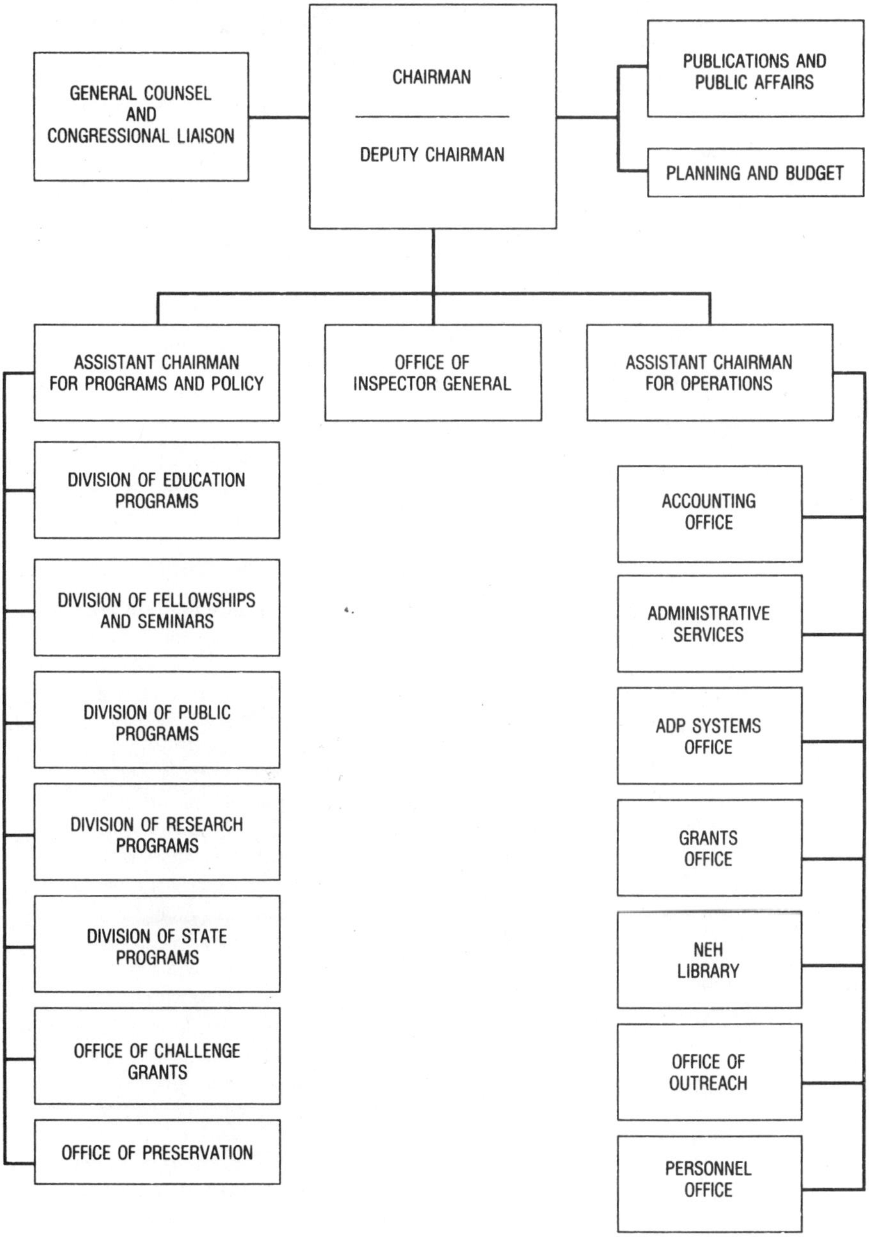

The National Foundation on the Arts and the Humanities encourages and supports national progress in the humanities and the arts.

The National Foundation on the Arts and the Humanities was created as an independent agency by the National Foundation on the Arts and the Humanities Act of 1965 (20 U.S.C. 951). The Foundation consists of a National Endowment for the Arts, a National Endowment for the Humanities, a Federal Council on the Arts and the Humanities, and an Institute of Museum Services. Each Endowment has its own Council, composed of the Endowment Chairman and 26 other members appointed by the President, which advises the Chairman with respect to policies and procedures and reviews applications for financial support while making recommendations thereon.

The Federal Council on the Arts and Humanities consists of 20 members, including the two Endowment Chairmen and the Director of the Institute of Museum Services, and is designed to coordinate the activities of the two Endowments and related programs of other Federal agencies. Four members are excluded from the Federal Council when it is considering matters under the Arts and Artifacts Indemnity Act (20 U.S.C. 971).

National Endowment for the Arts

The National Endowment for the Arts fosters, nurtures, and sustains artistic excellence in America and creates a climate in which the arts may flourish and be experienced and enjoyed by the public.

The Endowment awards grants to individuals, State and regional arts agencies, and nonprofit organizations representing the highest quality in the fields of design arts, dance, expansion arts, folk arts, literature, media arts (film, radio, and television), museums, music, opera-musical theater, theater, and the visual arts.

The programs of the National Endowment for the Arts have five basic goals: to foster individual creativity and excellence; to foster institutional creativity and excellence; to preserve the artistic birthright of present and future generations of Americans by supporting survival of the best of all art forms that reflect the American heritage in its full range of cultural and ethnic diversity; to ensure that all Americans have a true opportunity to make an informed, educated choice to have the arts of high quality touch their lives; and with responsiveness to the needs of the field, to provide leadership on behalf of the arts.

Sources of Information

Grants Persons interested in applying for a grant in the arts should contact the appropriate Program Director at the National Endowment for the Arts for further information.

Publications A report of the National Endowment for the Arts is issued annually and may be obtained from the Superintendent of Documents, Government Printing Office, Washington, DC 20402.

A Program Announcement containing information for prospective applicants may be obtained by writing to the National Endowment for the Arts, requesting the publication entitled *Guide to Programs,* Washington, DC 20506.

Employment Information The Office of Personnel Management registers from which employees are most often appointed are Clerk-Typist, Mid-Level Administrative Examination, and Senior-Level Examination.

For further information, contact the Public Information Office, National Endowment for the Arts, 1100 Pennsylvania Avenue NW., Washington, DC 20506. Phone, 202-682-5400.

National Endowment for the Humanities

The National Endowment for the Humanities is an independent, grant-making agency established by Congress in 1965 to support research, education, and public programs in the humanities.

According to the agency's authorizing legislation, the term "humanities" includes, but is not limited to, the study of the following: language, both modern and classical; linguistics; literature; history; jurisprudence; philosophy; archeology; comparative religion; ethics; the history, criticism, and theory of the arts; and those aspects of the social sciences that employ historical or philosophical approaches.

The Endowment makes grants to individuals, groups, or institutions—schools, colleges, universities, museums, public television stations, libraries, public agencies, and nonprofit private groups—to increase understanding and appreciation of the humanities. Its grant-making is conducted through five operating divisions—Education Programs, Fellowships and Seminars, General Programs, Research Programs, and State Programs—and two offices—Challenge Grants and Preservation.

Education Grants Grants in the Division of Education Programs support efforts in elementary and secondary schools as well as in institutions of higher education to improve instruction in humanities disciplines and to disseminate results of exemplary education programs.

For further information, call 202–786–0373.

Fellowships and Seminars Programs in the Division of Fellowships and Seminars offer support to individual scholars, teachers, and other interpreters of the humanities for full-time, independent study or research and for seminars that provide for collegial interaction.

For further information, call 202–786–0458.

Research Projects of longer duration, often involving collaboration between scholars, fall within the domain of the Division of Research Programs, which awards grants for the preparation for publication of important texts in the humanities, the organization of collections and the preparation of reference materials, the conduct of collaborative or coordinated research, and the development of potential research through specific regrant programs.

For further information, call 202–786–0200.

General Grants The Division of Public Programs strives to fulfill the Endowment's mandate "to increase public understanding of the humanities" by supporting those institutions and organizations that develop and present humanities programming for general audiences.

For further information, call 202–786–0267.

State Grants Humanities committees in each of the 50 States, the Virgin Islands, Puerto Rico, and the District of Columbia receive annual grants from the Division of State Programs, which they then regrant to support humanities programs at the local level.

For further information, call 202–786–0254.

Challenge Grants Through its Office of Challenge Grants, the Endowment supports cultural institutions and organizations so that they may increase their financial stability and preserve or improve the quality of their humanities programs.

For further information, call 202–786–0361.

Preservation The Office of Preservation expands Endowment support in attacking the problem of deteriorating humanities resources. Cooperative projects set in a national framework with an emphasis on the preservation of America's past and the work of American scholars, using both Federal and private funds, are particularly encouraged.

For further information, call 202–786–0570.

Special Initiatives All divisions at the Endowment are participating in the following special initiatives:

In anticipation of the international observance of the Columbian Quincentenary, the anniversary of Christopher Columbus' discovery of the New World, the Endowment invites proposals for original scholarship on related topics and for the dissemination of new and existing scholarship. For further information, call 202-786-0438.

Sources of Information

Employment The Office of Personnel Management registers from which employees are most often appointed are: Clerk-Typist, Mid-Level Administrative Register, and Senior-Level Register.

Grants Those interested in applying for a grant in the humanities should request information, guidelines, and application forms from the Endowment's Office of Publications and Public Affairs, Room 406, 1100 Pennsylvania Avenue NW., Washington, DC 20506. Phone, 202-786-0438.

Publications An annual report for the National Endowment for the Humanities is issued annually and may be obtained from the Endowment's Office of Publications and Public Affairs, Room 406, 1100 Pennsylvania Avenue NW., Washington, DC 20506. Phone, 202-786-0438.

Overview of Endowment Programs, which contains information for prospective applicants, may be obtained by writing to the Office of Publications and Public Affairs at the address given above.

Humanities, a bimonthly review of issues in the humanities published by the Endowment, is available by subscription through the Superintendent of Documents, Government Printing Office, Washington, DC 20402.

For further information, contact the Office of Publications and Public Affairs, National Endowment for the Humanities, Room 406, 1100 Pennsylvania Avenue NW., Washington, DC 20506. Phone, 202-786-0438.

Institute of Museum Services

The Institute of Museum Services is an independent, grant-making agency established by Congress in 1976 to assist museums in maintaining, increasing, and improving their services to the public.

The Institute of Museum Services (IMS) was created by the Museum Services Act (20 U.S.C. 961 note). In December 1981, pursuant to title II of act of Dec. 23, 1981 (20 U.S.C. 961, 962), the Institute was established as an independent agency within the National Foundation on the Arts and the Humanities. The Institute's Director is appointed by the President with the advice and consent of the Senate, and is authorized to make grants to museums subject to policy directives and priorities set by the National Museum Services Board. The Board is comprised of 15 Presidentially appointed nonvoting members and 5 *ex officio* nonvoting members.

The Institute awards grants on a competitive basis to support the efforts of museums to conserve the Nation's historic, scientific, and cultural heritage; to maintain and expand their educational role; and to ease the financial burden borne by museums as a result of their increasing use by the public. The Institute awards grants to all types of museums, including but not limited to art, history, general, children's, natural history, science and technology, historic houses, zoos and aquariums, botanical gardens and arboretums, nature centers, and planetariums.

The Institute currently makes grants in four categories: General Operating Support, Conservation Project Support,

Museum Assessment Program, and Professional Services Program. General Operating Support grants are annual competitive awards that maintain or improve the operations of museums. Conservation Project Support grants are annual competitive awards, for projects lasting up to 2 years, that provide funds for various conservation efforts. Museum Assessment Program grants are one-time awards made to museums to provide for an independent, professional assessment of their programs and operations. Professional Services Program grants provide funding to national, regional, State, or local private, nonprofit professional museum organizations and associations for proposals designed to strengthen museum services.

Sources of Information

Grants, Contracts, and Cooperative Agreements Those interested in applying for Institute of Museum Services funding should contact the Program Office, Institute of Museum Services, Room 609, 1100 Pennsylvania Avenue NW., Washington, DC 20506. Phone, 202-786-0539.

For further information, contact the Program Director, Institute of Museum Services, Room 609, 1100 Pennsylvania Avenue NW., Washington, DC 20506. Phone, 202-786-0539.

NATIONAL LABOR RELATIONS BOARD

1717 Pennsylvania Avenue NW., Washington, DC 20570
Phone, 202-254-8064 (Central Locator); 202-634-1669 (TDD)

Chairman	JAMES M. STEPHENS
Members	MARY MILLER CRACRAFT
	DENNIS M. DEVANEY
	CLIFFORD R. OVIATT, JR.
	JOHN N. RAUDABAUGH
Executive Secretary	JOHN C. TRUESDALE
Solicitor	JOHN E. HIGGINS, JR.
Inspector General	BERNARD LEVINE
Director, Division of Information	DAVID B. PARKER
Chief Administrative Law Judge	MELVIN J. WELLES
General Counsel	JERRY M. HUNTER
Deputy General Counsel	D. RANDALL FRYE, *Acting*
Director, Equal Employment Opportunity	BARBARA T. GAINEY
Associate General Counsel, Division of Enforcement Litigation	(VACANCY)
Associate General Counsel, Division of Operations Management	JOSEPH E. DESIO
Associate General Counsel, Division of Advice	ROBERT E. ALLEN
Director, Division of Administration	GLORIA J. JOSEPH

[For the National Labor Relations Board statement of organization, see the *Federal Register* of June 14, 1979, 44 FR 34215]

The National Labor Relations Board administers the Nation's principal labor law, the National Labor Relations Act. The Board is vested with the power to prevent and remedy unfair labor practices committed by private sector employers and unions and to safeguard employees' rights to organize and determine, through secret ballot elections, whether to have unions as their bargaining representative.

The National Labor Relations Board is an independent agency created by the National Labor Relations Act of 1935 (Wagner Act) (29 U.S.C. 167), as amended by acts of 1947 (Taft-Hartley Act), 1959 (Landrum-Griffin Act), and 1974.

The act affirms the right of employees to self-organization and collective bargaining through representatives of their own choosing, to engage in other protected, concerted activities, or to refrain from such activities. The act prohibits certain unfair labor practices by employers and labor organizations or their agents. It authorizes the Board to designate appropriate units for collective bargaining and to conduct secret ballot elections to determine whether employees desire representation by a labor organization.

As of July 1, 1971, the Postal Reorganization Act (39 U.S.C. note prec. 101) conferred jurisdiction upon the Board over unfair labor practice charges and representation elections affecting U.S. Postal Service employees. As of August 25, 1974, jurisdiction over all privately operated health care institutions was conferred on the Board by an amendment to the act (29 U.S.C. 152 *et seq.*).

Activities

Under the act, the Board has two principal functions: preventing and remedying unfair labor practices by employers and labor organizations or their agents, and conducting secret ballot elections among employees in appropriate collective-bargaining units to determine whether or not they desire to be represented by a labor organization in bargaining with employers about their wages, hours, and working conditions. The Board also conducts secret ballot elections among employees who have been covered by a union-security agreement to determine whether or not they wish to revoke their union's authority to make such agreements. In jurisdictional disputes between two or more unions, the Board determines which competing group of workers is entitled to perform the work involved. The Board conducts secret ballot elections among employees concerning employers' final settlement offers in national emergency labor disputes.

In unfair labor practice cases, the General Counsel has final authority to investigate charges, issue complaints, and prosecute such complaints before administrative law judges and the Board. The General Counsel, on behalf of the Board, prosecutes injunction proceedings; handles courts of appeals proceedings to enforce or review Board decisions and orders; participates in miscellaneous court litigation; and obtains compliance with Board orders and court judgments. The General Counsel is responsible for supervising personnel who process unfair labor practice charges and election petitions.

Under the general supervision of the General Counsel, 33 regional directors and their staffs process representation, unfair labor practice, and jurisdictional dispute cases. (Some regions have subregional or resident offices.) They issue complaints in unfair labor practice cases; seek settlement of unfair labor practice charges; obtain compliance with Board orders and court judgments; and petition district courts for injunctions to prevent or remedy unfair labor practices. The regional directors direct hearings in representation cases; conduct elections pursuant to the agreement of the parties or the decision-making authority delegated to them by the Board or pursuant to Board directions; and issue certifications of representatives when unions win or certify the results when unions lose employee elections. They process petitions for bargaining unit clarification, for amendment of certification, and for rescission of a labor organization's authority to make a union-shop agreement. They also conduct national emergency employee referendums.

The Board can act only when it is formally requested to do so. Individuals, employers, or unions may initiate cases by filing charges of unfair labor practices or petitions for employee representation elections with the Board field offices serving the area where the case arises.

In the event that a regional director declines to proceed on a representation petition, the party filing the petition may appeal to the Board. When a regional director declines to proceed on an unfair labor practice charge, the charging party may appeal to the General Counsel. For details concerning filing such appeals with those Washington, DC, offices, parties may contact the field office most convenient to them. Field office addresses and telephone numbers are listed below. Administrative law judges conduct hearings in unfair labor practice cases, make findings of fact and conclusions of law, and recommend remedies for violations found. Their decisions can be reviewed by the Board if exceptions to the decision are filed.

Field Offices—National Labor Relations Board

(RD: Regional Director; OC: Officer-in-Charge; RO: Resident Officer)

Office/Address	Director/Officer	Telephone
Albany, NY (Clinton Ave. at N. Pearl St., 12207)	Thomas J. Sheridan (RO)	518-472-2215
Albuquerque, NM (505 Marquette Ave. NW., 87102)	Robert A. Reisinger (RO)	505-766-3800
Anchorage, AK (222 W. 7th Ave., 99513)	Robert H. Wettleson (RO)	907-271-5015
Atlanta, GA (101 Marietta St. NW., 30323)	Martin M. Arlook (RD)	404-331-2896
Baltimore, MD (109 Market Pl., 21202)	Louis J. D'Amico (RD)	301-962-2822
Birmingham, AL (2025 3d Ave. N., 35203)	C. Douglas Marshall (RO)	205-731-1492
Boston, MA (10 Causeway St., 02222)	Rosemary Pye (RD)	617-565-6700
Brooklyn, NY (75 Clinton St., 11201)	Alvin P. Blyer (RD)	718-330-7713
Buffalo, NY (111 W. Huron St., 14202)	Richard L. Ahearn (RD)	716-846-4931
Chicago, IL (200 W. Adams St., 60606)	Elizabeth Kinney (RD)	312-353-7570
Cincinnati, OH (550 Main St., 45202)	(Vacancy) (RD)	513-684-3686
Cleveland, OH (1240 E. 9th St., 44199)	Frederick Calatrello (RD)	216-522-3715
Denver, CO (600 17th St., 80202)	Arthur L. DePalma (RD)	303-844-3551
Des Moines, IA (210 Walnut St., 50309)	Morris E. Petersen (RO)	515-284-4391
Detroit, MI (477 Michigan Ave., 48226)	Bernard Gottfried (RD)	313-226-3200
El Paso, TX (700 E. San Antonio Ave., 79901)	Laureano A. Medrano (RO)	915-534-6434
Fort Worth, TX (819 Taylor St., 76102)	Michael Dunn (RD)	817-334-2921
Grand Rapids, MI (82 Ionia NW., 49503)	David L. Basso (RO)	616-456-2679
Hartford, CT (1 Commercial Plz., 06103)	Peter B. Hoffman (RD)	203-240-3522
Hato Rey, PR (Carlos E. Chardon Ave., 00918)	Mary Zelma Asseo (RD)	809-766-5347
Honolulu, HI (300 Ala Moana Blvd., 96850)	Thomas W. Cestare (OC)	808-541-2814
Houston, TX (440 Louisiana St., 77002)	Curtis A. Wells (RO)	713-220-2365
Indianapolis, IN (575 N. Pennsylvania St., 46204)	William T. Little (RD)	317-226-7430
Jacksonville, FL (400 W. Bay St., 32202)	James L. McDonald (RO)	904-791-3768
Las Vegas, NV (600 Las Vegas Blvd. S., 89101)	Kenneth A. Rose (RO)	702-388-6416
Little Rock, AR (303 W. Capital St., 72201)	Thomas H. Smith, Jr. (RO)	501-324-6311
Los Angeles, CA (Region 31) (11000 Wilshire Blvd., 90024)	Roger W. Goubeaux (RD)	213-575-7352
Los Angeles, CA (Region 21) (811 Wilshire Blvd., 90017)	Victoria E. Aguayo (RD)	213-894-5200
Memphis, TN (1407 Union Ave., 38104)	Gerald P. Fleischut (RD)	901-722-2725
Miami, FL (51 SW. 1st Ave., 33130)	Hector O. Nava (RO)	305-536-5391
Milwaukee, WI (310 W. Wisconsin Ave., 53203)	Joseph A. Szabo (RD)	414-291-3861
Minneapolis, MN (110 S. 4th St., 55401)	Ronald M. Sharp (RD)	612-348-1794
Mission, KS (5799 Broadmoor, 66202)	F. Rozier Sharp (RD)	913-236-2777
Nashville, TN (801 Broadway, 37203)	Alton W. Barksdale (RO)	615-736-5922
Newark, NJ (970 Broad St., 07102)	William A. Pascarell (RD)	201-645-2100
New Orleans, LA (1515 Poydras St., 70112)	Hugh Frank Malone (RD)	504-589-6361
New York, NY (26 Federal Plz., 10278)	Daniel Silverman (RD)	212-264-0300
Oakland, CA (2201 Broadway, 94612)	James S. Scott (RD)	415-273-7200
Peoria, IL (411 Hamilton Blvd., 61602)	Glenn A. Zipp (RD)	309-671-7080
Philadelphia, PA (615 Chestnut St., 19106)	Peter W. Hirsch (RD)	215-597-7601
Phoenix, AZ (234 N. Central Ave., 85004)	Roy H. Garner (RD)	602-261-3361
Pittsburgh, PA (1000 Liberty Ave., 15222)	Gerald Kobell (RD)	412-644-2977
Portland, OR (222 SW. Columbia St., 97201)	Delano D. Eyer (OC)	503-326-3085
San Antonio, TX (727 E. Durango Blvd., 78206)	Guadalupe Ruiz (RO)	512-229-6140
San Diego, CA (555 W. Beech St., 92101)	Claude R. Marston (RO)	619-557-6184
San Francisco, CA (901 Market St., 94103)	Robert H. Miller (RD)	415-744-6810
Seattle, WA (915 2d Ave., 98174)	John D. Nelson (RD)	206-553-4532
St. Louis, MO (611 N. 10th St., 63101)	Joseph H. Solien (RD)	314-425-4167
Tampa, FL (700 Twiggs St., 33602)	Francis E. Dowd (RD)	813-228-2641
Tulsa, OK (440 S. Houston Ave., 74127)	Saundria Bordone (RO)	918-581-7951
Washington, DC (2120 L St. NW., 20037)	Steven L. Shuster (RO)	202-254-7612
Winston-Salem, NC (251 N. Main St., 27101)	Willie L. Clark, Jr. (RD)	919-631-5201

Sources of Information

Contracts Prospective suppliers of goods and services may inquire about agency procurement and contracting practices by writing to the Chief, Procurement and Facilities Branch, National Labor Relations Board, Washington, DC 20570. Phone, 202-634-4019.

Employment The Board appoints administrative law judges from a register established by the Office of Personnel Management. The agency hires attorneys, stenographers, and typists for all its offices; field examiners for its field offices; and administrative personnel for its Washington office. Inquiries regarding college and law school recruiting programs should be directed to the nearest regional office. Employment inquiries and applications may be sent to any regional office or the Washington personnel office.

Publications Anyone desiring to inspect formal case documents or read agency publications may use facilities of the Washington or field offices. The agency will assist in arranging reproduction of documents and order transcripts of hearings. The Board's offices offer free explanatory leaflets: *The National Labor Relations Board and YOU (Unfair Labor Practices), The National Labor Relations Board and YOU (Representation Cases), Your Government Conducts an Election for You on the Job,* and *The National Labor Relations Board—What It Is, What It Does.* The Superintendent of Documents, Government Printing Office, Washington, DC 20402, sells *A Guide to Basic Law and Procedures Under the NLRA,* the *Annual Report,* the *Classified Index of National Labor Relations Board Decisions and Related Court Decisions,* volumes of Board decisions, and a number of subscription services, including the *NLRB Casehandling Manual* (in three parts), the *Weekly Summary of NLRB Cases,* and the *NLRB Election Report.*

Speakers To give the public and persons appearing before the agency a better understanding of the National Labor Relations Act and the Board's policies, procedures, and services, Washington and regional office personnel participate as speakers or panel members before bar associations, labor, educational, civic, or management organizations, and other groups. Requests for speakers or panelists may be made to Washington officials or to the appropriate regional director.

For further information, contact the Information Division, National Labor Relations Board, 1717 Pennsylvania Avenue NW., Washington, DC 20570. Phone, 202-632-4950.

NATIONAL MEDIATION BOARD

1425 K Street NW., Washington, DC 20572
Phone, 202-523-5920

Chairman	PATRICK J. CLEARY
Members	KIMBERLY A. MADIGAN
	JOSHUA M. JAVITS
Executive Director	WILLIAM A. GILL, JR.
Assistant Executive Director	(VACANCY)
Administrative Officer	MARY CATHERINE MAIONE-PRICCI
Director, Research and Information Management	DONALD L. WEST
General Counsel	RONALD M. ETTERS
Hearing Officer/Assistant to General Counsel	JOYCE M. KLEIN

Senior Hearing Officers/Legal Counsels	MARY L. JOHNSON
	ROLAND WATKINS
Public Information Officer	THORNTON L. TOWNSEND

National Railroad Adjustment Board

Room A931, 175 West Jackson Boulevard, Chicago, IL 60604
Phone, 312–886–7300

Staff Director/Grievances	ROY J. CARVATTA

The National Mediation Board, in carrying out the provisions of the Railway Labor Act, assists in maintaining a free flow of commerce in the railroad and airline industries by resolving disputes that could disrupt travel or imperil the economy. The Board also handles railroad and airline employee representation disputes and maintains financial supervision of the National Railroad Adjustment Board, which handles rail grievances relating to the interpretation and application of existing contracts.

The National Mediation Board was created on June 21, 1934, by an act amending the Railway Labor Act, as amended (45 U.S.C. 151–158, 160–162, 1181–1188).

The Board's major responsibilities include the mediation of disputes over wages, hours, and working conditions that arise between rail and air carriers and organizations representing their employees; and the investigation of representation disputes and certification of employee organizations as representatives of crafts or classes of carrier employees.

Disputes arising out of grievances or interpretation or application of agreements concerning rates of pay, rules, or working conditions in the railroad industry are referable to the National Railroad Adjustment Board. This Board is divided into four divisions and consists of an equal number of representatives of the carriers and of national organizations of employees. In deadlocked cases the National Mediation Board is authorized to appoint a referee to sit with the members of the division for the purpose of making an award.

In the airline industry no national airline adjustment board has been established for settlement of grievances. Over the years the employee organizations and air carriers with established bargaining relationships have agreed to grievance procedures with final jurisdiction resting with a system board of adjustment. The Board is frequently called upon to name a neutral referee to serve on a system board when the parties are deadlocked and cannot agree on such an appointment themselves.

Activities

Mediation Disputes The National Mediation Board is charged with mediating disputes between carriers and labor organizations relating to initial contract negotiations or subsequent changes in rates of pay, rules, and working conditions. When the parties fail to reach accord in direct bargaining either party may request the Board's services or the Board may on its own motion invoke its services. Thereafter, negotiations continue until the Board determines that its efforts to mediate have been unsuccessful, at which time it seeks to induce the parties to submit the dispute to arbitration. If either party refuses to arbitrate, the Board issues a notice stating that the parties have failed to resolve their dispute through mediation. This notice commences a 30-day cooling-off period after which self-help is normally available to either or both parties.

Employee Representation If a dispute arises among a carrier's employees as to who is to be the representative of such employees, it is the Board's duty to investigate such dispute and to determine by secret-ballot election or other appropriate means whether or not and to whom a representation certification should be issued. In the course of making this determination, the Board must determine the craft or class in which the employees seeking representation properly belong.

Additional Duties Additional duties of the Board include the interpretation of agreements made under its mediatory auspices; the appointment of neutral referees when requested by the National Railroad Adjustment Board; the appointment of neutrals to sit on system boards and special boards of adjustment; and finally, the duty of notifying the President when the parties have failed to reach agreement through the Board's mediation efforts and that the labor dispute, in the judgment of the Board, threatens substantially to interrupt interstate commerce to a degree such as to deprive any section of the country of essential transportation service. In these cases, the President may, at his discretion, appoint an Emergency Board to investigate and report to him on the dispute. Self-help is barred for 60 days after appointment of the Emergency Board.

Section 9A of the Railway Labor Act (45 U.S.C. 159a) provides emergency dispute procedures covering publicly funded and operated commuter railroads and their employees. That section attempts to resolve contract disputes between the parties through a series of emergency board procedures with a maximum 8-month status quo period. Section 9A is invoked only after all other procedures under the act have been exhausted.

Sources of Information

Publications Available for public distribution are the following documents: *Determinations of the National Mediation Board* (17 volumes); *Interpretations Pursuant to Section 5, Second of the Act* (2 volumes); Annual Reports of the National Mediation Board including the Report of the National Railroad Adjustment Board; *The Railway Labor Act at Fifty;* and *The National Mediation Board at Fifty—Its Impact on Railroad and Airline Labor Disputes.*

Reading Room At the Board's headquarters in Washington, DC, copies of collective-bargaining agreements between labor and management of various rail and air carriers are available for public inspection, by appointment, during office hours (8:30 a.m. to 5 p.m., Monday through Friday).

For further information, contact the Executive Director, National Mediation Board, 1425 K Street NW., Washington, DC 20572. Phone, 202-523-5920.

NATIONAL RAILROAD PASSENGER CORPORATION (AMTRAK)

60 Massachusetts Avenue NE., Washington, DC 20002
Phone, 202-906-3000

Board of Directors:

Chairman	W. GRAHAM CLAYTOR, JR.
Members	HALEY R. BARBOUR, EUGENE R. CROISANT, DAVID F. GIRARD-DICARLO, CHARLES LUNA, GOV. TOMMY G. THOMPSON, CARL W. VOGT, PAUL M. WEYRICH
Secretary of Transportation (*ex officio*)	SAMUEL K. SKINNER

Officers:

President and Chairman	W. GRAHAM CLAYTOR, JR.

Executive Vice President and Chief Operating Officer	DENNIS F. SULLIVAN
Executive Vice President	WILLIAM S. NORMAN
Vice President, Law	HAROLD R. HENDERSON
Vice President, Finance and Administration	CHARLES W. HAYWARD
Controller	ROBERT L. LEWIS III
Vice President, Corporate Planning and Development	ELYSE G. WANDER
Corporate Secretary	WILLIAM ERKELENZ
Assistant Vice President, Government and Public Affairs	THOMAS J. GILLESPIE, JR.
Vice President, Information Systems	NORRIS W. OVERTON
Assistant Vice President, Labor Relations	JOHN P. LANGE
Vice President, Passenger Marketing	TIMOTHY P. GARDNER
Vice President, Passenger Services	EUGENE N. EDEN
Assistant Vice President, Personnel	NEIL D. MANN
Vice President, Real Estate and Operations Development	ANTHONY DEANGELO
Vice President, Sales	ROBERT E. GALL
Vice President, Transportation	ROBERT C. VANDERCLUTE
Vice President, Engineering	PETER A. CANNITO
Treasurer	RICHARD I. KLEIN

The National Railroad Passenger Corporation was established to develop the potential of modern rail service in meeting the Nation's intercity passenger transportation needs.

The National Railroad Passenger Corporation (Amtrak) was created by the Rail Passenger Service Act of 1970, as amended (45 U.S.C. 541), and was incorporated under the laws of the District of Columbia to provide a balanced national transportation system by developing, operating, and improving U.S. intercity rail passenger service.

Amtrak is governed by a nine-member board of directors: The Secretary of Transportation serves as an *ex officio* member and Amtrak's president serves as Chairman; three members (representing labor, State Governors, and the business community) are appointed by the President with the advice and consent of the Senate; two members represent commuter authorities; and two members are selected by the preferred stockholder. The Corporation is managed by its president along with 2 executive vice presidents, 10 vice presidents, and 3 assistant vice presidents.

Amtrak operates an average of 210 trains per day, serving over 500 station locations, over a system of approximately 24,000 route miles. Of this route system, Amtrak now owns a right-of-way of 2,611 track miles in the Northeast Corridor (Washington-New York-Boston; New Haven-Springfield; Philadelphia-Harrisburg), and several small track segments in the East, purchased pursuant to the Regional Rail Reorganization Act of 1973 (45 U.S.C. 701 *et seq.*) and the Railroad Revitalization and Regulatory Reform Act of 1976 (45 U.S.C. 801 *et seq.*).

Amtrak owns or leases its stations and owns its own repair and maintenance facilities. The Corporation employs a total work force of approximately 24,000 and provides all reservation, station, and on-board service staffs, as well as train and engine operating crews. Outside the Northeast Corridor, Amtrak has historically contracted with 21 privately owned railroads for the right to operate over their track and has compensated each railroad for its total package of services. Under contract, these railroads are responsible for the condition of the roadbed and for coordinating the flow of traffic.

290-950 O 91 - 22

In fiscal year 1990, Amtrak transported over 22.4 million people more than 6 billion passenger miles. In addition, under contracts with several transit agencies, Amtrak carried over 18 million commuters.

Although Amtrak's basic route system was originally designated by the Secretary of Transportation in 1971, modifications have been made to the Amtrak system and to individual routes that have resulted in more efficient and cost-effective operations. Currently, in the face of ongoing budget constraints, new service will only be added if a State agrees to share any losses associated with the service or if the new service does not substantially add to Amtrak's need for Federal assistance.

Amtrak began operation in 1971 with an antiquated fleet of equipment inherited from private railroads; some cars were nearly 30 years old. Since then, the fleet has been modernized and new state-of-the-art single- and bi-level passenger cars and locomotives have been added.

Systemwide ridership is steadily rising, and Amtrak is finding it increasingly difficult to meet the demands of increased travel patterns with its limited passenger fleet. To ease these equipment constraints, the Corporation is working to identify innovative funding sources in order to acquire additional passenger cars and locomotives.

There is no rail passenger system in the world that makes a profit; Amtrak is no exception. However, Amtrak has made significant progress in reducing its dependence on Federal support while at the same time improving the quality of service. Every year Amtrak moves further toward increasing the ratio of its earned revenue to total costs. The Corporation has gone from covering 48 percent of its total costs in fiscal year 1981 to 72 percent in fiscal year 1990. As a result, Amtrak's appropriation for the current fiscal year is 57 percent below that for fiscal year 1978 (in constant dollars). One of Amtrak's highest priorities is to make the Corporation even more self-sufficient in the future.

For further information, contact the Public Affairs Department, Amtrak, 60 Massachusetts Avenue NE., Washington, DC 20002. Phone, 202–906–3860.

NATIONAL SCIENCE FOUNDATION

1800 G Street NW., Washington, DC 20550
Phone, 202–357–5000

National Science Board

Chairman	MARY L. GOOD
Vice Chairman	THOMAS B. DAY

Members	PERRY L. ADKISSON, WARREN J. BAKER, ARDEN L. BEMENT, FREDERICK P. BROOKS, JR., BERNARD F. BURKE, W. GLENN CAMPBELL, F. ALBERT COTTON, DANIEL C. DRUCKER, JAMES J. DUDERSTADT, MARYE ANN FOX, PHILLIP A. GRIFFITHS, JOHN C. HANCOCK, JAMES B. HOLDERMAN, CHARLES L. HOSLER, JAIME OAXACA, JAMES L. POWELL, PETER H. RAVEN, FRANK H.T. RHODES, ROLAND W. SCHMITT, BENJAMIN S. SHEN, HOWARD E. SIMMONS, WALTER E. MASSEY (*ex officio*), (VACANCY)
Executive Officer	THOMAS UBOIS
Inspector General	LINDA G. SUNDRO
Counsel to Inspector General	PHILIP L. SUNSHINE
Assistant Inspector General for External Audit	CLIFFORD L. BENNETT
Assistant Inspector General for Internal Audit and Investigation	CHELTON T. GIVENS
Assistant Inspector General for Oversight	JAMES J. ZWOLENIK
Officials:	
Director	WALTER E. MASSEY
Deputy Director	FREDERICK M. BERNTHAL
Assistant to the Director	WILLIAM C. HARRIS
Executive Assistant to the Director	MARJORIE J. MAC FARLANE
General Counsel	CHARLES H. HERZ
Deputy General Counsel	LAWRENCE RUDOLPH
Director, Office of Legislative and Public Affairs	RAYMOND E. BYE, JR.
Director, Division of Public Affairs	ALAN M. LEVITT
Director, Division of Legislative Affairs	JOEL M. WIDDER
Controller, Office of Budget and Control	SANDRA D. TOYE
Director, Budget Division	JOSEPH L. KULL
Director, Program Evaluation Staff	JAMES M. MCCULLOUGH
Head, Special Data Group	ROBERT P. ABEL
Director, Office of Information Systems	CONSTANCE K. MCLINDON
Director, Information Management Division	ALBERT A. MUHLBAUER
Director, Information Technologies Division	FREDERIC J. WENDLING
Director, Office of Science and Technology Infrastructure	WILLIAM C. HARRIS
Assistant Director for Mathematical and Physical Sciences	DAVID A. SANCHEZ
Executive Officer	M. KENT WILSON
Director, Division of Physics	MARCEL BARDON
Director, Division of Chemistry	KENNETH G. HANCOCK
Director, Division of Materials Research	JAGDISH A. NARAYAN
Director, Division of Mathematical Sciences	JUDITH S. SUNLEY
Director, Division of Astronomical Sciences	JULIE A. LUTZ
Assistant Director for Geosciences	ROBERT W. CORELL
Executive Officer	KURT G. SANDVED
Director, Division of Atmospheric Sciences	EUGENE W. BIERLY

Director, Division of Earth Sciences	JAMES F. HAYS
Director, Division of Ocean Sciences	M. GRANT GROSS
Director, Division of Polar Programs	PETER E. WILKNISS
Assistant Director for Biological, Behavioral and Social Sciences	MARY E. CLUTTER
Executive Officer	W. FRANKLIN HARRIS
Director, Division of Instrumentation and Resources	JOHN C. WOOLEY
Director, Division of Molecular Biosciences	JAMES H. BROWN
Director, Division of Cellular Biosciences	BRUCE L. UMMINGER
Director, Division of Biotic Systems and Resources	PATRICIA A. WERNER
Director, Division of Behavioral and Neural Sciences	RICHARD T. LOUTTIT
Director, Division of Social and Economic Sciences	ROBERTA B. MILLER
Assistant Director for Engineering	JOHN A. WHITE
Deputy Assistant Director for Engineering	RAY M. BOWEN
Director, Division of Engineering Infrastructure Development	WILBUR L. MEIER, JR.
Director, Division of Engineering Centers	MARSHALL M. LIH
Director, Division of Electrical and Communications Systems	IRENE C. PEDEN
Director, Division of Chemical and Thermal Systems	HENRY A. MCGEE
Director, Division of Mechanical and Structural Systems	BRANIMIR VON TURKOVICH
Director, Division of Design and Manufacturing Systems	BRANIMIR VON TURKOVICH
Director, Division of Biological and Critical Systems	WILLIAM A. ANDERSON, *Acting*
Assistant Director for Computer and Information Science and Engineering	CHARLES N. BROWNSTEIN, *Acting*
Executive Officer	MELVYN CIMENT, *Acting*
Head, Office of Cross-Disciplinary Activities	HARRY A. HEDGES
Director, Division of Advanced Scientific Computing	THOMAS A. WEBER
Director, Division of Computer and Computation Research	RICHARD A. DEMILLO
Director, Division of Information, Robotics, and Intelligent Systems	YI-TZUU CHIEN
Director, Division of Microelectronic Information Processing Systems	BERNARD CHERN
Director, Division of Networking and Communications Research and Infrastructure	STEPHEN S. WOLFF
Assistant Director for Scientific, Technological, and International Affairs	F. KARL WILLENBROCK
Executive Officer	GERARD R. GLASER
Director, Office of Experimental Programs to Stimulate Competitive Research	JOSEPH G. DANEK
Director, Office of Small Business Research and Development	DONALD SENICH
Director, Office of Small and Disadvantaged Business Utilization	DONALD SENICH

Director, Division of Policy Research and Analysis	PETER W. HOUSE
Director of Science Resources Studies	KENNETH BROWN
Director, Division of International Programs	RICHARD R. RIES
Director, Division of Industrial Science and Technological Innovation	DONALD SENICH
Assistant Director for Education and Human Resources	LUTHER S. WILLIAMS
Deputy Assistant Director	JANE T. STUTSMAN
Executive Officer	PETER E. YANKWICH
Head, Office of Studies, Evaluation and Dissemination	KENNETH J. TRAVERS
Director, Division of Undergraduate Science, Engineering and Mathematics Education	ROBERT F. WATSON
Director, Division of Teacher Preparation and Enhancement	CHARLES R. PUGLIA
Director, Division of Research Career Development	TERENCE L. PORTER
Director, Division of Materials Development, Research, and Informal Science Education	JOAN R. LEITZEL
Director, Division of Human Resource Development	JOSEPH G. DANEK
Assistant Director for Administration	JEFF M. FENSTERMACHER
Executive Officer	WILLIAM COLE
Director, Office of Equal Opportunity	BRENDA M. BRUSH
Director, Division of Financial Management	KENNETH B. FOSTER
Director, Division of Grants and Contracts	WILLIAM S. KIRBY
Director, Division of Personnel and Management	MARGARET L. WINDUS
Director, Division of Administrative Services	ROBERT E. SCHMITZ

[For the National Science Foundation statement of organization, see the *Federal Register* of May 29, 1990, 55 FR 21807.]

The National Science Foundation promotes the progress of science and engineering through the support of research and education programs. Its major emphasis is on high-quality, merit-selected research—the search for improved understanding of the fundamental laws of nature upon which our future well-being as a nation depends. Its educational programs are aimed at ensuring increased understanding of science and engineering at all educational levels, maintaining an adequate supply of scientists and engineers to meet our country's needs.

The National Science Foundation, an independent agency, was established as an independent agency by the National Science Foundation Act of 1950 (42 U.S.C. 1861–1875), and was given additional authority by the Science and Engineering Equal Opportunities Act (42 U.S.C. 1885–1885d), title I of the Education for Economic Security Act (20 U.S.C. 3911–3922), the Academic Research Facilities Modernization Act of 1988 (42 U.S.C. 1862a–1862d), and parts of the Excellence in Mathematics, Science, and Engineering Education Act of 1990 (20 U.S.C. 5311–5364).

The purposes of the Foundation are: to increase the Nation's base of scientific and engineering knowledge and strengthen its ability to conduct research in all areas of science and engineering; to develop and help implement science and engineering education programs that can better prepare the Nation for meeting the challenges of the future; and to promote international cooperation through science and engineering. In its role as a leading Federal supporter of science and engineering, the agency also has an important role in national policy planning.

The Foundation consists of a National Science Board and a Director. The National Science Board is composed of 24 part-time members and the Director *ex officio.* Members are appointed by the President with the advice and consent of the Senate for 6-year terms. They are selected because of their distinguished service in science, medicine, engineering, agriculture, education, public affairs, research management, or industry. They are chosen in such a way as to be representative of the scientific and engineering leadership in all areas of the Nation.

Both the Director and the Deputy Director are appointed by the President with the advice and consent of the Senate, the former to a 6-year term and the latter to an unspecified term.

The National Science Foundation Act assigns policymaking functions to the National Science Board, and the administration of the Foundation to the Director. The policies of the Board in support of science and engineering and development of scientific and engineering personnel are implemented throughout the various programs of the Foundation.

The Inspector General of the Foundation is appointed by the National Science Board and, under section 8E of the Inspector General Act of 1978 (5 U.S.C. app. 3) is responsible for conducting and supervising audits, inspections, and investigations relating to the programs and operations of the Foundation, including allegations of misconduct in science.

Activities

The National Science Foundation initiates and supports fundamental, long-term, merit-selected research in all the scientific and engineering disciplines. This support is made through grants, contracts, and other agreements awarded to universities, university consortia, and nonprofit and other research organizations. Most of this research is directed toward the resolution of scientific and engineering questions concerning fundamental life processes, natural laws and phenomena, fundamental processes influencing the human environment, and the forces affecting people as members of society as well as the behavior of society as a whole.

The Foundation supports fundamental research on computing and information processing, provides U.S. research and education communities with advanced computing and communications capabilities, and encourages innovative use of sophisticated computing in science and engineering research.

The Foundation encourages cooperative efforts by universities, industries, and government. It also promotes the application of research and development for better products and services that improve the quality of life, create employment opportunities, stimulate economic growth, and increase productivity and foreign trade.

The Foundation promotes the development of research talent through support of precollege, undergraduate, and graduate students, as well as postdoctoral associates. It administers special programs to identify and encourage participation by groups underrepresented in science and technology and to strengthen research capability at smaller institutions, small businesses, undergraduate colleges, universities, and geographic regions.

The Foundation supports major national and international science and engineering activities, including the U.S. Antarctic Program, the Ocean Drilling Program, global geoscience studies, and others. Cooperative scientific and engineering research activities support exchange programs for American and foreign scientists and engineers, execution of jointly designed research projects, participation in the activities of international science and engineering organizations, and travel to international conferences.

Support is provided through contracts and cooperative agreements with national centers where large facilities are made available for use by qualified scientists and engineers. Among the types of centers supported by the Foundation are astronomy and atmospheric sciences, biological and engineering research, science and technology, supercomputers, and long-term ecological research sites.

The Foundation provides competitively awarded grants for repair, renovation, or, in exceptional cases, replacement of facilities used for research and research training at academic and nonprofit institutions.

The Foundation's science and engineering education activities include grants for research and development activities directed to model instructional materials for students and teachers and the application of advanced technologies to precollege education. Grants also are available for precollege teacher preparation and enhancement, and informal science education activities. At the undergraduate level, funding is provided for college science instrumentation, course and curriculum improvement, faculty and student activities, and minority resource centers. In addition, studies of the status of math, science, and engineering education are supported.

The Foundation supports research aimed at formulating national policy through analysis of existing and emerging issues that have significant scientific and engineering content. It defines options and supplies analysis directed toward enhancing the contribution of science and engineering to national goals. It also develops and disseminates information relating to the Nation's available human and financial resources for scientific and engineering activities.

The National Science Foundation presents annually the Alan T. Waterman Award to an outstanding young scientist or engineer for support of research and study. Periodically the National Science Board presents the honorary Vannevar Bush Award to a person who, through public service activities in science and technology, has made an outstanding contribution toward the welfare of mankind and the Nation. The two awards are designed to encourage individuals to seek to achieve the Nation's objectives in scientific and engineering research and education.

The Foundation also provides support for the President's Committee on the National Medal of Science.

Sources of Information

Board and Committee Minutes Summary minutes of the open meetings of the Board may be obtained from the National Science Board Office. Phone, 202–357–9582. Summary minutes of the Foundation's advisory groups may be obtained from the contacts listed in the notice of meetings published in the *Federal Register.* General information about the Foundation's advisory groups may be obtained from the Division of Personnel and Management, Room 208, Washington, DC 20550. Phone, 202–357–9520.

Contracts The Foundation publicizes contracting and subcontracting opportunities in the *Commerce Business Daily* and other appropriate publications. Organizations seeking to undertake contract work for the Foundation should contact either the Division of Grants and Contracts (phone, 202–357–7880) or the Division of Administrative Services (phone, 202–357–7922), National Science Foundation, Washington, DC 20550.

Employment Inquiries may be directed to the Division of Personnel and Management, National Science Foundation, Room 208, Washington, DC 20550. Phone, 202–357–9859, or, for the hearing impaired (TDD), 202–357–7492.

Fellowships Consult *NSF Guide to Programs* and appropriate announcements and brochures for postdoctoral fellowship opportunities that may be available through some Foundation divisions. Beginning graduate and minority graduate students wishing to apply for fellowships should contact the Directorate for Education and Human Resources. Phone, 202–357–7856.

Freedom of Information Act Requests Requests for agency records should be submitted in accordance with the

Foundation FOIA regulation at 45 CFR, part 612. Such requests should be clearly identified with "FOIA REQUEST" and be addressed to the Office of Legislative and Public Affairs, National Science Foundation, Room 527, Washington, DC 20550. Phone, 202–357–9498.

Grants Individuals or organizations who plan to submit grant proposals should refer to the *NSF Guide to Programs, Grants for Research and Education in Science and Engineering (GRESE),* and appropriate program brochures and announcements that may be obtained as indicated in the reference to publications, below.

Office of Inspector General General inquiries may be directed to the Office of Inspector General, National Science Foundation, Room 1241, Washington, DC 20550. Phone, 202–357–9457.

Privacy Act Requests Requests for personal records should be submitted in accordance with the Foundation Privacy Act regulation at 45 CFR, part 613. Such requests should be clearly identified with PRIVACY ACT REQUEST and be addressed to the Privacy Act Officer, National Science Foundation, Room 208, Washington, DC 20550. Phone, 202–357–7335.

Publications The National Science Board assesses the status and health of science and its various disciplines, including such matters as national resources and manpower, in reports submitted to the President for submission to the Congress. The most recent report is *Science and Engineering Indicators, 1989.*

Detailed brochures are issued by the Foundation which announce and describe new programs, critical dates, and application procedures for competitions. These and other materials are available online through the Science and Technology Information System (STIS) as listed:

Internet: STIS@NSF.GOV
Bitnet: STIS@NSF
Dial-in: 202–357–0359, 0360
Parity: even
Data bits: 7
Duplex: full
Emulation: VT-100

Single copies of these materials, including the booklet *Publications of the National Science Foundation,* are available by phone (202–357–7668) or electronically via Internet: PUBS@NSF.GOV and Bitnet: PUBS@NSF. Copies can also be obtained by writing to: National Science Foundation, Forms and Publications, Room 232, 1800 G Street NW., Washington, DC 20550.

Other publications include: *NSF Annual Report, Grant Policy Manual* (NSF 88–47), which contains comprehensive statements of Foundation grant administration policy, procedures, and guidance; *Guide to Programs,* which summarizes information about support programs; *Mosaic,* the Foundation magazine; and the quarterly *Antarctic Journal of the United States* (plus an annual review issue). These publications are available from the Superintendent of Documents, Government Printing Office, Washington, DC 20402.

Reading Room A collection of Foundation policy documents and staff instructions, as well as current indexes, are available to the public for inspection and copying during regular business hours, 8:30 a.m. to 5:00 p.m., Monday through Friday, in the National Science Foundation Library, Room 248, Washington, DC 20550. Phone, 202–357–7811.

Small Business Activities The Office of Small Business Research and Development provides information on opportunities for Foundation support to small businesses with strong research capabilities in science and technology. Phone, 202–357–7464. The Office of Small and Disadvantaged Business Utilization oversees agency compliance with the provisions of the Small Business Act and the Small Business Investment Act of 1958, as amended (15 U.S.C. 631, 661, 683). Phone, 202–357–7464.

For further information, contact the Office of Legislative and Public Affairs, National Science Foundation, 1800 G Street NW., Washington, DC 20550. Phone, 202–357–9498, or, for the hearing impaired (TDD), 202–357–7492.

NATIONAL TRANSPORTATION SAFETY BOARD

800 Independence Avenue SW., Washington, DC 20594
Phone, 202–382–6600

Chairman	James L. Kolstad
Vice Chairman	Susan M. Coughlin
Members	John K. Lauber
	John A. Hammerschmidt
	Christopher A. Hart
Managing Director	Terry L. Baxter
Deputy Managing Director for Management and Policy	Lloyd F. Miller
Deputy Managing Director for Program Operations	Herbert W.R. Banks
Director, Office of Congressional and Intergovernmental Relations	Brenda Meister
Director, Office of Public Affairs	Brent N. Bahler
Deputy Director	Alan M. Pollock
General Counsel	Daniel D. Campbell
Deputy General Counsel	Ronald S. Battocchi
Director, Office of Aviation Safety	Timothy P. Forté
Deputy Director	William G. Laynor
Director, Office of Research and Engineering	Bernard S. Loeb
Deputy Director	Vernon Ellingstad
Director, Office of Safety Recommendations	Barry M. Sweedler
Deputy Director	Richard Van Woerkom
Director, Office of Surface Transportation Safety	George Reagle
Deputy Director	Ralph E. Johnson
Director, Office of Administration	B. Michael Levins
Chief Administrative Law Judge	William W. Fowler, Jr.

[For the National Transportation Safety Board statement of organization, see the *Code of Federal Regulations*, Title 49, Part 800]

The National Transportation Safety Board seeks to assure that all types of transportation in the United States are conducted safely. The Board investigates accidents, conducts studies, and makes recommendations to Government agencies, the transportation industry, and others on safety measures and practices.

The National Transportation Safety Board was established as an independent agency of the Federal Government on April 1, 1975, by the Independent Safety Board Act of 1974 (49 U.S.C. app. 1901).

The Safety Board consists of five Board members appointed by the President with the advice and consent of the Senate for 5-year terms. The President designates two of these members as Chairman and Vice Chairman of the Board for 2-year terms. The designation of the Chairman is made with the advice and consent of the Senate.

The mission of the National Transportation Safety Board is to promote transportation safety by conducting independent investigations of accidents and other safety problems and by formulating safety improvement recommendations.

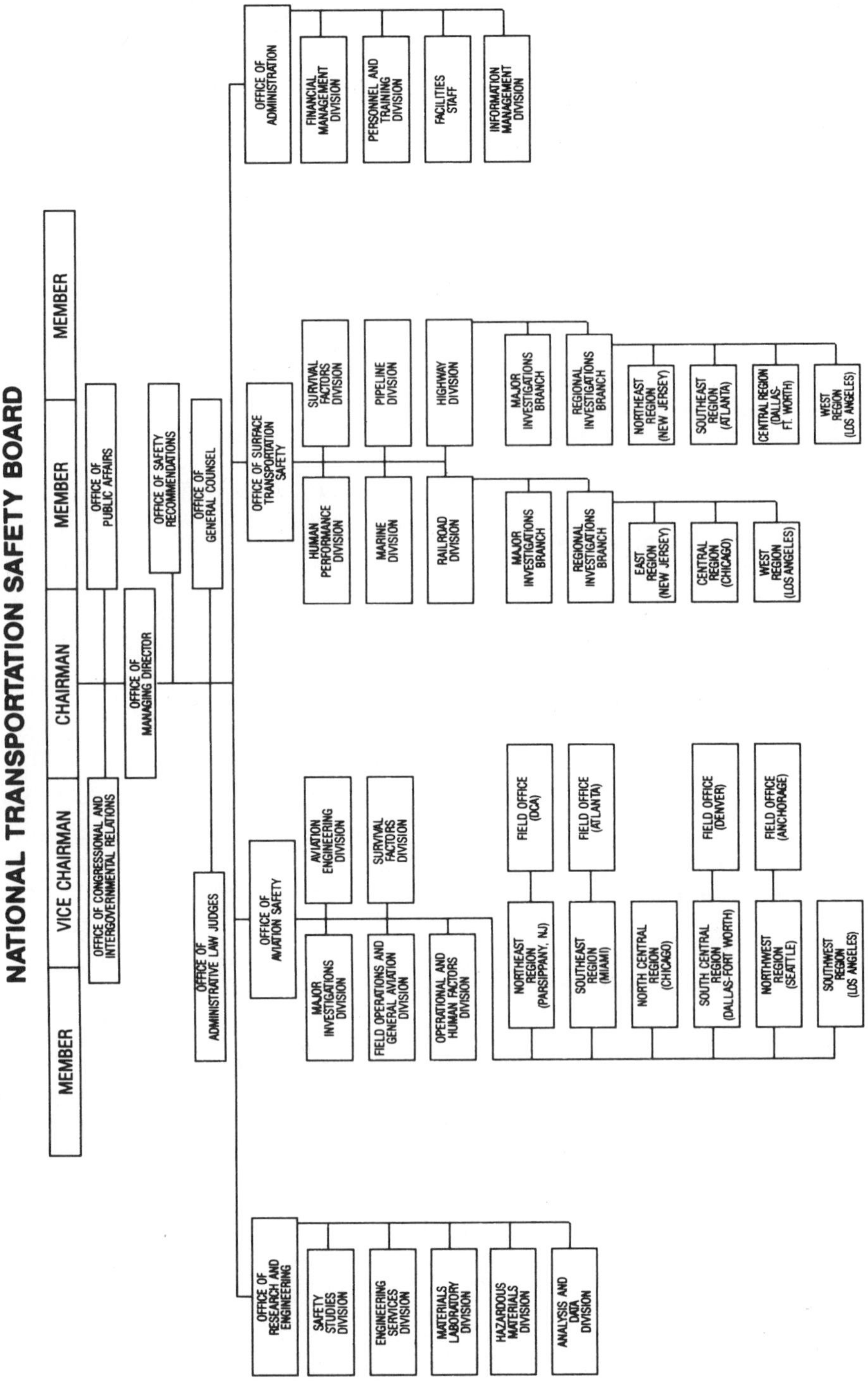
NATIONAL TRANSPORTATION SAFETY BOARD
MEMBER
VICE CHAIRMAN
CHAIRMAN
MEMBER
MEMBER
OFFICE OF CONGRESSIONAL AND INTERGOVERNMENTAL RELATIONS
OFFICE OF PUBLIC AFFAIRS
OFFICE OF MANAGING DIRECTOR
OFFICE OF SAFETY RECOMMENDATIONS
OFFICE OF GENERAL COUNSEL
OFFICE OF ADMINISTRATIVE LAW JUDGES
OFFICE OF RESEARCH AND ENGINEERING
SAFETY STUDIES DIVISION
ENGINEERING SERVICES DIVISION
MATERIALS LABORATORY DIVISION
HAZARDOUS MATERIALS DIVISION
ANALYSIS AND DATA DIVISION
OFFICE OF AVIATION SAFETY
AVIATION ENGINEERING DIVISION
SURVIVAL FACTORS DIVISION
MAJOR INVESTIGATIONS DIVISION
FIELD OPERATIONS AND GENERAL AVIATION DIVISION
OPERATIONAL AND HUMAN FACTORS DIVISION
FIELD OFFICE (DCA)
FIELD OFFICE (ATLANTA)
FIELD OFFICE (DENVER)
FIELD OFFICE (ANCHORAGE)
NORTHEAST REGION (PARSIPPANY, NJ)
SOUTHEAST REGION (MIAMI)
NORTH CENTRAL REGION (CHICAGO)
SOUTH CENTRAL REGION (DALLAS-FORT WORTH)
NORTHWEST REGION (SEATTLE)
SOUTHWEST REGION (LOS ANGELES)
OFFICE OF SURFACE TRANSPORTATION SAFETY
SURVIVAL FACTORS DIVISION
PIPELINE DIVISION
HIGHWAY DIVISION
HUMAN PERFORMANCE DIVISION
MARINE DIVISION
RAILROAD DIVISION
MAJOR INVESTIGATIONS BRANCH
REGIONAL INVESTIGATIONS BRANCH
NORTHEAST REGION (NEW JERSEY)
SOUTHEAST REGION (ATLANTA)
CENTRAL REGION (DALLAS-FT. WORTH)
WEST REGION (LOS ANGELES)
MAJOR INVESTIGATIONS BRANCH
REGIONAL INVESTIGATIONS BRANCH
EAST REGION (NEW JERSEY)
CENTRAL REGION (CHICAGO)
WEST REGION (LOS ANGELES)
OFFICE OF ADMINISTRATION
FINANCIAL MANAGEMENT DIVISION
PERSONNEL AND TRAINING DIVISION
FACILITIES STAFF
INFORMATION MANAGEMENT DIVISION

Activities

Accident Investigation The Board is responsible for investigating, determining probable cause, making safety recommendations, and reporting the facts and circumstances of:

—all U.S. civil aviation accidents;

—all railroad accidents in which there is a fatality or substantial property damage, or that involve a passenger train;

—all pipeline accidents in which there is a fatality or substantial property damage;

—highway accidents, including railroad grade-crossing accidents, which the Board selects in cooperation with the States;

—major marine casualties, and marine accidents involving a public vessel and a nonpublic vessel, in accordance with regulations prescribed jointly by the Board and the U.S. Coast Guard; and

—other transportation accidents that are catastrophic, involve problems of a recurring character, or otherwise should be investigated in the judgment of the Board.

Safety Problem Identification In addition, the Board makes recommendations on matters pertaining to transportation safety and is a catalyst for transportation accident prevention by conducting safety studies and special investigations, assessing techniques of accident investigation and publishing recommended procedures for accident investigations, establishing regulatory requirements for reporting accidents, evaluating the transportation safety consciousness and efficacy of other Government agencies in the prevention of accidents, evaluating the adequacy of safeguards and procedures concerning the transportation of hazardous materials and the performance of other Government agencies charged with ensuring the safe transportation of such materials, and reporting annually to the Congress on its activities.

Certificate or License Appeal The Board also reviews on appeal the suspension, amendment, modification, revocation, or denial of any certificate or license issued by the Secretary or an Administrator of the Department of Transportation.

Inquiries may be directed to the Office of Administrative Law Judges, National Transportation Safety Board, Suite 505, 1951 Kidwell Drive, Vienna, VA 22182. Phone, 703-506-9280.

Regional/Field Offices—National Transportation Safety Board

(R: Regional Director; FC: Field Chief)

Region/Field Office	Address	Officer
AVIATION:		
North Central Region	31 W. 775 North Ave., West Chicago, IL 60185	Carl Dinwiddie (R)
South Central Region	Suite 3007, 1200 Copeland Rd., Arlington, TX 76011	Tommy McFall (R)
South Central Field	Suite 500, 4760 Oakland St., Denver, CO 80239	Norm Wiemeyer (FC)
Southwest Region	P.O. Box 6117, Federal Bldg., 15000 Aviation Blvd., Lawndale, CA 90261.	Gary Mucho (R)
Southeast Region	Suite B-103, 8405 NW. 53d St., Miami, FL 33166	Jorge Prellezo (R)
Southeast Field	1720 Peachtree St. NW., Atlanta, GA 30309	Preston Hicks (FC)
Northeast Region	Suite 203, 2001 Rte. 46, Parsippany, NJ 07054	Barry Trotter (R)
Northeast Field	800 Independence Ave. SW., Washington, DC 20594	Dennis Jones (FC)
Northwest Region	Rm. 201, 19518 Pacific Hwy. S., Seattle, WA 98188	Keith McGuire (R)
Northwest Field	Box 11, Rm. 142, 222 W. 7th Ave., Anchorage, AK 99513	Jim Michelangelo (FC)
RAILROAD:		
Central Region	31 W. 775 North Ave., West Chicago, IL 60185	Russ Seipler (R)
Western Region	P.O. Box 6117, Federal Bldg., 15000 Aviation Blvd., Lawndale, CA 90261.	David Watson (R)
Eastern Region	Suite 203, 2001 Rte. 46, Parsippany, NJ 07054	Mark Garcia (R)
HIGHWAY:		
Central Region	Suite 300, 1200 Copeland Rd., Arlington, TX 76011	Kennith Rogers (R)
Western Region	P.O. Box 6117, Federal Bldg., 15000 Aviation Blvd., Lawndale, CA 90261.	William Klassen (R)
Southeast Region	1720 Peachtree St. NW., Atlanta, GA 30309	Jay Golden (R)
Northeast Region	Suite 203, 2001 Rte. 46, Parsippany, NJ 07054	Frank Ghiorsi (R)

Regional/Field Offices—National Transportation Safety Board—Continued

(R: Regional Director; FC: Field Chief)

Region/Field Office	Address	Officer
OTHER:		
Slated for Closing:		
Kansas City Field	Suite 109, 8725 Rosehill St., Lenexa, KS 66215	William Klassen (FC)

Sources of Information

Contracts and Procurement Inquiries regarding the Board's procurement and contracting activities should be addressed to the Chief, Operations and Facilities Division, National Transportation Safety Board, Washington, DC 20594. Phone, 202–382–6725.

Employment Send applications for employment to the Personnel and Training Division, National Transportation Safety Board, Washington, DC 20594. Phone, 202–382–6717; or Fax, 202–382–6007.

Publications Publications are provided free of charge to the following categories of subscribers: Federal, State, or local transportation agencies; international transportation organizations or foreign governments; educational institutions or public libraries; nonprofit public safety organizations; and the news media. Persons in these categories who are interested in receiving copies of Board publications should contact the Public Inquiries Section, National Transportation Safety Board, Washington, DC 20594. Phone, 202–382–6735.

All other persons interested in receiving publications must purchase them from the National Technical Information Service, 5285 Port Royal Road, Springfield, VA 22161. Orders may be placed by telephone to the Subscription Unit, 703–487–4630, or to their sales desk on 703–487–4650.

Reading Room The Public Reference Room of the Board is available for record inspection or copying. It is located in Room 805F at the Board's Washington, DC, headquarters. Requests for access to public records should be made in person at Room 805F, or by writing the National Transportation Safety Board, Public Inquiries Section, Washington, DC 20594. Phone, 202–382–6735.

For further information, contact the Office of Public Affairs, National Transportation Safety Board, 800 Independence Avenue SW., Washington, DC 20594. Phone, 202–382–6600.

NUCLEAR REGULATORY COMMISSION

Washington, DC 20555
Phone, 301–492–7000

Chairman	Ivan Selin
Executive/Legal Assistant	Stephen G. Burns
Legal Assistant	Karen D. Cyr
Commissioner	Kenneth C. Rogers
Legal Assistant	Myron Karman
Commissioner	James R. Curtiss
Executive/Legal Assistant	Joseph R. Gray
Commissioner	Forrest J. Remick
Executive/Legal Assistant	Steven F. Crockett
Commissioner	(vacancy)
Legal Assistant	(vacancy)

Chairman, Advisory Committee on Reactor Safeguards	CARLYLE MICHELSON
Chairman, Advisory Committee on Nuclear Waste	DADE W. MOELLER
Chief Administrative Judge, Atomic Safety and Licensing Board Panel	B. PAUL COTTER, JR.
Chairman, Atomic Safety and Licensing Appeal Panel	CHRISTINE N. KOHL
Inspector General	DAVID C. WILLIAMS
General Counsel	WILLIAM C. PARLER
Secretary of the Commission	SAMUEL J. CHILK
Director, Office of Governmental and Public Affairs	HAROLD R. DENTON
Director, Congressional Affairs	DENNIS K. RATHBUN
Director, State Programs	CARLTON KAMMERER
Director, Public Affairs	JOSEPH J. FOUCHARD
Director, International Programs	JAMES R. SHEA
Administrator, Office of the Licensing Support System Administrator	LLOYD J. DONNELLY
Executive Director for Operations	JAMES M. TAYLOR
Deputy Executive Director for Nuclear Reactor Regulation, Regional Operations and Research	JAMES H. SNIEZEK
Deputy Executive Director for Nuclear Materials Safety, Safeguards and Operations Support	HUGH L. THOMPSON, JR.
Assistant for Operations	JAMES L. BLAHA
Regional Administrator, Region I (King of Prussia, PA)	THOMAS T. MARTIN
Regional Administrator, Region II (Atlanta, GA)	STEWART D. EBNETER
Regional Administrator, Region III (Glen Ellyn, IL)	A. BERT DAVIS
Regional Administrator, Region IV (Arlington, TX)	ROBERT D. MARTIN
Regional Administrator, Region V (Walnut Creek, CA)	JOHN B. MARTIN
Director, Office of Investigations	BEN B. HAYES
Director, Office of Enforcement	JAMES LIEBERMAN
Director, Office of Consolidation	MICHAEL S. SPRINGER
Controller, Office of the Controller	RONALD M. SCROGGINS
Director, Office of Administration	PATRICIA G. NORRY
Director, Office of Information Resources Management	PATRICIA G. NORRY, *Acting*
Director, Office of Small and Disadvantaged Business Utilization and Civil Rights	WILLIAM B. KERR
Director, Office for Analysis and Evaluation of Operational Data	EDWARD JORDAN
Director, Office of Personnel	PAUL E. BIRD
Director, Office of Nuclear Material Safety and Safeguards	ROBERT M. BERNERO
Deputy Director, Office of Nuclear Material Safety and Safeguards	GUY A. ARLOTTO
Director, Division of Safeguards and Transportation	ROBERT F. BURNETT

Director, Division of Industrial and Medical Nuclear Safety	RICHARD E. CUNNINGHAM
Director, Division of High-Level Waste Management	BILLY J. YOUNGBLOOD
Director, Division of Low-Level Waste Management and Decommissioning	RICHARD L. BANGART
Director, Office of Nuclear Reactor Regulation	THOMAS E. MURLEY
Deputy Director, Office of Nuclear Reactor Regulation	FRANK J. MIRAGLIA
Associate Director for Projects	JAMES G. PARTLOW
Director, Division of Reactor Projects—I/II	STEVEN A. VARGA
Director, Division of Reactor Projects—III/IV/V	BRUCE A. BOGER
Director, Advanced Reactors and Special Projects	DENNIS M. CRUTCHFIELD
Associate Director for Inspection and Technical Assessment	WILLIAM T. RUSSELL
Director, Division of Engineering Technology	JAMES E. RICHARDSON
Director, Division of Systems Technology	ASHOK C. THADANI
Director, Division of Operational Events Assessment	CHARLES E. ROSSI
Director, Division of Reactor Inspection and Safeguards	BRIAN K. GRIMES
Director, Division of Radiation Protection and Emergency Preparedness	FRANK J. CONGEL
Director, Division of Licensee Performance and Quality Evaluation	JACK W. ROE
Director, Office of Nuclear Regulatory Research	ERIC S. BECKJORD
Deputy Director for Research	THEMIS P. SPEIS
Deputy Director for Generic Issues Rulemaking	CLEMENS J. HELTEMES, JR.
Director, Division of Engineering	LAWRENCE C. SHAO
Director, Division of Safety Issue Resolution	WARREN MINNERS
Director, Division of Systems Research	BRIAN W. SHERON
Director, Division of Regulatory Applications	BILL M. MORRIS

[For the Nuclear Regulatory Commission statement of organization, see the *Code of Federal Regulations,* Title 10, Part I]

The Nuclear Regulatory Commission licenses and regulates civilian use of nuclear energy to protect public health and safety and the environment. This is achieved by licensing persons and companies to build and operate nuclear reactors and other facilities and to own and use nuclear materials. The Commission makes rules and sets standards for these types of licenses. It also carefully inspects the activities of the persons and companies licensed to ensure that they do not violate the safety rules of the Commission.

The Nuclear Regulatory Commission was established as an independent regulatory agency under the provisions of the Energy Reorganization Act of 1974 (42 U.S.C. 5801) and Executive Order 11834 of January 15, 1975, effective January 19, 1975. Transferred to the Commission were all licensing and related regulatory functions formerly assigned to the Atomic Energy Commission, which was

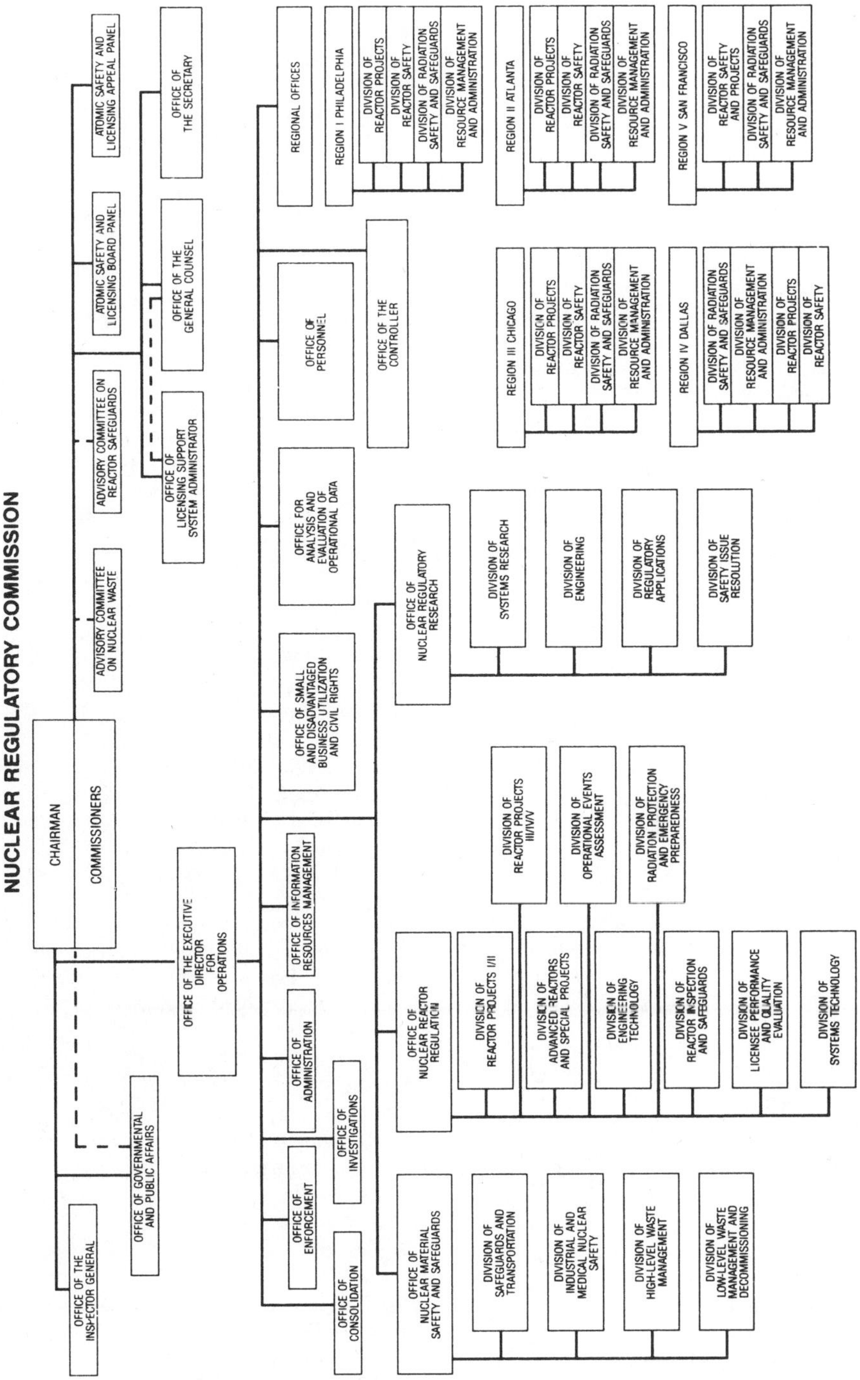
NUCLEAR REGULATORY COMMISSION
CHAIRMAN
COMMISSIONERS
ADVISORY COMMITTEE ON NUCLEAR WASTE
ADVISORY COMMITTEE ON REACTOR SAFEGUARDS
ATOMIC SAFETY AND LICENSING BOARD PANEL
ATOMIC SAFETY AND LICENSING APPEAL PANEL
OFFICE OF LICENSING SUPPORT SYSTEM ADMINISTRATOR
OFFICE OF THE GENERAL COUNSEL
OFFICE OF THE SECRETARY
OFFICE OF THE INSPECTOR GENERAL
OFFICE OF GOVERNMENTAL AND PUBLIC AFFAIRS
OFFICE OF THE EXECUTIVE DIRECTOR FOR OPERATIONS
OFFICE OF CONSOLIDATION
OFFICE OF ENFORCEMENT
OFFICE OF INVESTIGATIONS
OFFICE OF ADMINISTRATION
OFFICE OF INFORMATION RESOURCES MANAGEMENT
OFFICE OF SMALL AND DISADVANTAGED BUSINESS UTILIZATION AND CIVIL RIGHTS
OFFICE FOR ANALYSIS AND EVALUATION OF OPERATIONAL DATA
OFFICE OF PERSONNEL
OFFICE OF THE CONTROLLER
REGIONAL OFFICES
REGION I PHILADELPHIA
DIVISION OF REACTOR PROJECTS
DIVISION OF REACTOR SAFETY
DIVISION OF RADIATION SAFETY AND SAFEGUARDS
DIVISION OF RESOURCE MANAGEMENT AND ADMINISTRATION
REGION II ATLANTA
DIVISION OF REACTOR PROJECTS
DIVISION OF REACTOR SAFETY
DIVISION OF RADIATION SAFETY AND SAFEGUARDS
DIVISION OF RESOURCE MANAGEMENT AND ADMINISTRATION
REGION III CHICAGO
DIVISION OF REACTOR PROJECTS
DIVISION OF REACTOR SAFETY
DIVISION OF RADIATION SAFETY AND SAFEGUARDS
DIVISION OF RESOURCE MANAGEMENT AND ADMINISTRATION
REGION IV DALLAS
DIVISION OF RADIATION SAFETY AND SAFEGUARDS
DIVISION OF RESOURCE MANAGEMENT AND ADMINISTRATION
DIVISION OF REACTOR PROJECTS
DIVISION OF REACTOR SAFETY
REGION V SAN FRANCISCO
DIVISION OF REACTOR SAFETY AND PROJECTS
DIVISION OF RADIATION SAFETY AND SAFEGUARDS
DIVISION OF RESOURCE MANAGEMENT AND ADMINISTRATION
OFFICE OF NUCLEAR MATERIAL SAFETY AND SAFEGUARDS
DIVISION OF SAFEGUARDS AND TRANSPORTATION
DIVISION OF INDUSTRIAL AND MEDICAL NUCLEAR SAFETY
DIVISION OF HIGH-LEVEL WASTE MANAGEMENT
DIVISION OF LOW-LEVEL WASTE MANAGEMENT AND DECOMMISSIONING
OFFICE OF NUCLEAR REACTOR REGULATION
DIVISION OF REACTOR PROJECTS I/II
DIVISION OF ADVANCED REACTORS AND SPECIAL PROJECTS
DIVISION OF ENGINEERING TECHNOLOGY
DIVISION OF REACTOR INSPECTION AND SAFEGUARDS
DIVISION OF LICENSEE PERFORMANCE AND QUALITY EVALUATION
DIVISION OF SYSTEMS TECHNOLOGY
DIVISION OF REACTOR PROJECTS III/IV/V
DIVISION OF OPERATIONAL EVENTS ASSESSMENT
DIVISION OF RADIATION PROTECTION AND EMERGENCY PREPAREDNESS
OFFICE OF NUCLEAR REGULATORY RESEARCH
DIVISION OF SYSTEMS RESEARCH
DIVISION OF ENGINEERING
DIVISION OF REGULATORY APPLICATIONS
DIVISION OF SAFETY ISSUE RESOLUTION

established by the Atomic Energy Act of 1946 (60 Stat. 755), as amended by the Atomic Energy Act of 1954, as amended (42 U.S.C. 2011 *et seq.*).

The Commission's major program components are the Office of Nuclear Reactor Regulation, the Office of Nuclear Material Safety and Safeguards, and the Office of Nuclear Regulatory Research, which were created by the Energy Reorganization Act of 1974. Headquarters offices are located in suburban Maryland, and there are five regional offices.

The Commission ensures that the civilian uses of nuclear materials and facilities are conducted in a manner consistent with the public health and safety, environmental quality, national security, and the antitrust laws. The major share of the Commission's effort is focused on regulating the use of nuclear energy to generate electric power.

Activities

The Commission fulfills its responsibilities through a system of licensing and regulation that includes:

—licensing the construction and operation of nuclear reactors and other nuclear facilities and the possession, use, processing, handling, and disposal of nuclear materials;

—regulating licensed activities including assurance that measures are taken for the physical protection of facilities and materials;

—developing and implementing of rules and regulations governing licensed nuclear activities;

—inspecting licensee facilities and activities;

—investigating nuclear incidents and allegations concerning any matter regulated by NRC;

—enforcing NRC licenses and regulations by the issuance of orders, civil penalties, and other types of actions;

—conducting public hearings on nuclear and radiological safety, environmental concerns, common defense and security, and antitrust matters; and

—developing effective working relationships with the States regarding the regulation of nuclear materials.

This relationship includes the assurance that adequate regulatory programs are maintained by those States that exercise, by agreement with the Commission, regulatory control over certain nuclear materials within their respective borders. In addition, a systematic review of operational data, including reports of accidents and other events, from nuclear powerplants is performed in order to detect trends that will better enable the agency to forecast and solve safety problems. Inspection of Commission-licensed activities is carried out from five regional offices. In addition, resident inspectors have been assigned to reactor sites.

The Commission also contracts for research deemed necessary for performing licensing and related regulatory functions.

Sources of Information

Contracts and Procurement Detailed information on how to do business with the Commission and on programs to assist small business is available from the Director, Division of Contracts and Property Management, Nuclear Regulatory Commission, Washington, DC 20555. Phone, 301–492–4347.

Employment The Commission's employment activities are exempt from civil service requirements and are conducted under an independent merit system. However, employees receive Federal employee benefits (retirement, group life insurance, and health benefits) on the same basis as other Federal employees. Applicants with veterans preference are accorded the preference granted to them by the Veterans' Preference Act of 1944 (58 Stat. 387).

Recruitment is continual, and applications from individuals qualified for Commission needs are accepted whenever they are received. In addition to receiving applications from candidates at all grade levels throughout the year, the agency recruits annually from colleges as appropriate to fill needs for interns and entry-level professionals.

Employment inquiries, applications, and requests from schools for participation in the recruitment program may be directed to the Director, Office of Personnel, Nuclear Regulatory Commission, Washington, DC 20555. Phone, 301-492-4661.

Freedom of Information Act Requests Inquiries should be directed to the Director, Division of Freedom of Information and Publication Services, Nuclear Regulatory Commission, Washington, DC 20555. Phone, 301-492-7211.

Publications *The Annual Report* provides a summary of major agency activities for the year. Subscription service for NUREG-0540, consisting of 12 consecutive monthly issues, is available from the Government Printing Office. *Nuclear Regulatory Commission Issuances* (monthly, quarterly, and semiannual indexes), a compilation of adjudications and other issuances for the Commission, including Atomic Safety and Licensing Boards and the Atomic Safety and Licensing Appeal Boards, is available for sale from the Printing Office, either on subscription or on a single-issue basis. Hard-bound semiannual issuances and indexes are also available from the Printing Office. Other subscription items available from the Government Printing Office include: *Licensed Operating Reactors-Status Summary Report* (monthly), NUREG-0020; *Licensee, Contractor and Vendor Inspection Status Report* (quarterly), NUREG-0040; *Report to Congress on Abnormal Occurrences* (quarterly), NUREG-0090; *Regulatory and Technical Reports* (quarterly), NUREG-0304; *U.S. Nuclear Regulatory Commission Rules and Regulations; U.S. NRC Telephone Directory; Information Report on State Legislation* (monthly), NUREG/BR-0025; and the *Weekly Information Report.* Pricing and ordering information may be obtained by writing to the Superintendent of Documents, Government Printing Office, P.O. Box 37082, Washington, DC 20013-7082. Phone, 202-275-2060.

The Commission produces a variety of scientific, technical, and administrative information publications dealing with licensing and regulating civilian nuclear power. Information on agency publications can be obtained from *Title List of Documents Made Publicly Available,* NUREG-0540. This document, published monthly, includes docketed material associated with civilian nuclear powerplants and other uses of radioactive materials, and nondocketed material received and generated by the Commission pertinent to its role as a regulatory agency. Subscription service for the *Standard Review Plan,* NUREG-0800, is handled exclusively by the National Technical Information Service. Single copies of monthly issues of NUREG-0540 are available for purchase from the Government Printing Office and from the National Technical Information Service, Springfield, VA 22161. Phone, 703-487-4600.

Active *Regulatory Guides* may be purchased from the Government Printing Office or on standing orders as they are issued from the National Technical Information Service. These *Regulatory Guides* are published in 10 subject areas: Power Reactors, Research and Test Reactors, Fuels and Materials Facilities, Environmental and Siting, Material and Plant Protection, Products, Transportation, Occupational Health, Antitrust Review, and General.

Single copies of some publications, such as *Draft Environmental Statements* and *Draft Regulatory Guides,* are available without charge, depending on supply, from Nuclear Regulatory Commission Publication Services, Washington, DC 20555. Interested persons may be placed on a Commission mailing list for *Draft Regulatory Guides* by writing to the Document Control Branch, NRC, Washington, DC 20555.

Nuclear Regulatory Commission Regulatory Agenda (published in the *Federal Register* each April and October) are available in January, April, July, and October from the Director, Division of Freedom of Information and Publication Services, Office of Administration, Nuclear Regulatory Commission, Washington, DC 20555. Persons may obtain information regarding the status of any regulation or petition for rulemaking before the Commission by calling toll-free, 800–368–5642.

Reading Rooms The Commission maintains its principal Public Document Room at 2120 L Street NW., Washington, DC 20555. Phone, 202–634–3273. Documents pertain to the licensing of source material, production and utilization facilities, special nuclear material, transportation of radioactive materials, research and technical assistance reports, reports on generic technical issues, rules and regulations, Commission correspondence, transcripts of Commission meetings, minutes and reports of the Commission's advisory committees, and other material relating to the regulatory responsibilities and operation of the Commission.

Members of the public may visit the Public Document Room and examine any document in the collection, or phone or write in requests. The services offered include reference assistance, copying services, and microfiche reader-printers. Manual and on-line indexes and Daily Accession Listings providing bibliographic descriptions of documents in the collection also are available.

In addition, the Commission has approximately 100 local public document rooms around the country. The document rooms are typically located in libraries in cities and towns near proposed and actual nuclear plant sites and contain detailed information specific to the nearby facilities, which are either licensed or under regulatory review. A list of these local public document rooms is available from the Director, Division of Freedom of Information and Publication Services, Nuclear Regulatory Commission, Washington, DC 20555. To obtain specific information about the availability of documents at the local public document rooms, NRC's Local Public Document Room branch may be contacted directly by calling toll-free, 800–638–8081.

Records Freedom of Information Act inquiries should be directed to the Director, Division of Freedom of Information and Publication Services, Nuclear Regulatory Commission, Washington, DC 20555. Phone, 301–492–7211.

For further information, contact the Office of Governmental and Public Affairs, Nuclear Regulatory Commission, Washington, DC 20555. Phone, 301–492–0240.

OCCUPATIONAL SAFETY AND HEALTH REVIEW COMMISSION

1825 K Street NW., Washington, DC 20006
Phone, 202–634–7943

Chairman	Edwin G. Foulke, Jr.
Commissioners	Donald G. Wiseman
	Velma Montoya
Executive Director	Jan S. Collins
Chief Administrative Law Judge	(vacancy)
General Counsel	Earl R. Ohman, Jr.
Executive Secretary	Ray H. Darling, Jr.
Public Affairs Specialist	Linda A. Whitsett

OCCUPATIONAL SAFETY AND HEALTH REVIEW COMMISSION

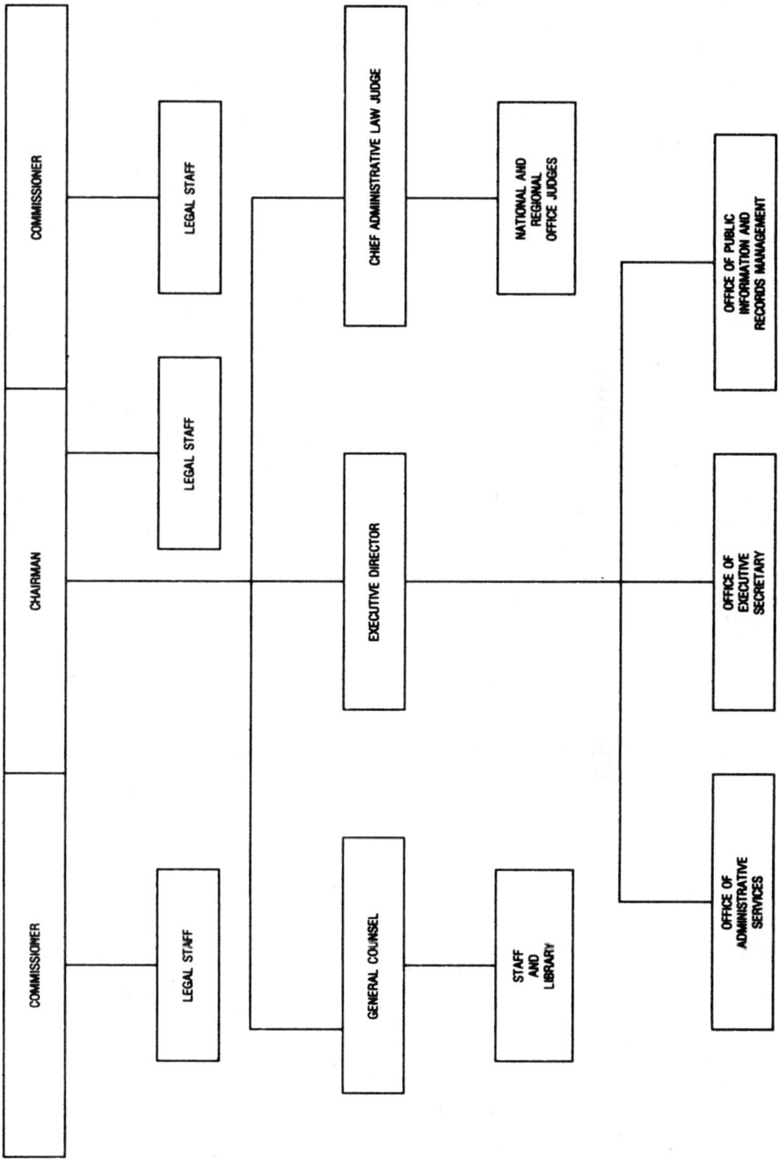

The Occupational Safety and Health Review Commission works to ensure the timely and fair resolution of cases involving the alleged exposure of American workers to unsafe or unhealthy working conditions.

The Occupational Safety and Health Review Commission is an independent, quasi-judicial agency established by the Occupational Safety and Health Act of 1970 (29 U.S.C. 651–678).

The Commission is charged with ruling on cases forwarded to it by the Department of Labor when disagreements arise over the results of safety and health inspections performed by the Department's Occupational Safety and Health Administration. Employers have the right to dispute any alleged job safety or health violation found during the inspection by the Administration, the penalties it proposed, and the time given by the agency to correct any hazardous situation. Employees and representatives of employees may initiate a case by challenging the propriety of the time the Administration has allowed for correction of any violative condition.

The Occupational Safety and Health Act covers virtually every employer in the country. Enforced by the Secretary of Labor, the act is an effort to reduce the incidence of personal injuries, illness, and deaths among working men and women in the United States that result from their employment. It requires employers to furnish to each of their employees employment and a place of employment free from recognized hazards that are causing or likely to cause death or serious physical harm to the employees and to comply with occupational safety and health standards promulgated under the act.

Activities

The Commission was created to adjudicate enforcement actions initiated under the act when they are contested by employers, employees, or representatives of employees. A case arises when a citation is issued against an employer as the result of an Occupational Safety and Health Administration inspection and it is contested within 15 working days.

The Commission is more of a court system than a simple tribunal, for within the Commission there are two levels of adjudication. All cases that require a hearing are assigned to an administrative law judge, who decides the case. Ordinarily the hearing is held in the community where the alleged violation occurred or as close as possible. At the hearing, the Secretary of Labor will generally have the burden of proving the case. After the hearing, the judge must issue a decision, based on findings of fact and conclusions of law.

A substantial number of the decisions of the judges become final orders of the Commission. However, each decision is subject to discretionary review by the three members of the Commission upon the direction of any one of the three, if done within 30 days of the filing of the decision. When that occurs, the Commission issues its own decision.

Once a case is decided, any person adversely affected or aggrieved thereby may obtain a review of the decision in the United States Courts of Appeals.

The principal office of the Commission is in Washington, DC. There are also four regional offices where Commission judges are stationed.

Review Commission Judges—Occupational Safety Review Commission

City/Address	Telephone
Atlanta, GA (1365 Peachtree St. NE., 30309)	404-347-4197
Boston, MA (John W. McCormack Post Office and Courthouse, 02110)	617-223-9746
Dallas, TX (1100 Commerce St., 75242)	214-767-5271
Denver, CO (1050 17th St., 80265)	303-844-2281

Sources of Information

Speakers To give the public and persons appearing before the

Commission a better understanding of the act and the Commission's procedures and decisions, members and officials participate as speakers or panel members before bar associations, safety councils, labor organizations, management associations, and educational, civic, and other groups. Requests for speakers, panelists, or publications may be made to the Commission's Washington office.

For further information, contact the Public Affairs Specialist, Occupational Safety and Health Review Commission, 1825 K Street NW., Washington, DC 20006. Phone, 202–634–7943.

OFFICE OF GOVERNMENT ETHICS

Suite 500, 1201 New York Avenue NW., Washington, DC 20005–3917
Phone, 202–523–5757

Director	STEPHEN D. POTTS
Deputy Director	DONALD E. CAMPBELL
General Counsel	F. GARY DAVIS
Deputy General Counsel	JANE S. LEY
Associate Director for Administration	ROBERT E. LAMMON
Associate Director for Education	STUART C. GILMAN
Associate Director for Monitoring and Compliance	JACK COVALESKI

[For the Office of Government Ethics statement of organization, see the *Code of Federal Regulations*, Title 5, Part 2600]

The Office of Government Ethics provides overall direction of executive branch policies in preventing conflicts of interest on the part of officers and employees of all executive agencies. The Office is the principal agency for administering the Ethics in Government Act for the executive branch.

The Office of Government Ethics, previously a part of the Office of Personnel Management, was established as a separate executive agency on October 1, 1989, under the Ethics in Government Act of 1978, as amended (5 U.S.C. app. 401).

The Director of the Office is appointed by the President with the advice and consent of the Senate for a 5-year term, and is required to submit to Congress a biennial report concerning the implementation of the Director's functions and responsibilities.

Activities

The chief responsibilities of the Office are:

—developing, in consultation with the Attorney General and the Office of Personnel Management, rules and regulations to be promulgated by the President or the Director of the Office of Government Ethics pertaining to standards of conduct of executive agencies and the identification and resolution of conflicts of interest;

—monitoring and investigating compliance with the executive branch financial disclosure requirements of the Ethics in Government Act of 1978, as amended;

—conducting periodic reviews of the ethics programs of executive agencies;

—ordering corrective action on the part of agencies and employees that the Director of the Office deems necessary, including orders to establish or modify an agency's ethics program; and

—providing guidance on and promoting understanding of ethical standards in executive agencies through an extensive program of Government ethics advice, education, and training.

Sources of Information

The Office of Government Ethics provides advisory letters and formal advisory opinions in an annually updated publication, *The Informal Advisory Letters and Memoranda and Formal Opinions of the United States Office of Government Ethics,* available from the Government Printing Office. In addition, the Office publishes a quarterly newsletter on Government ethics and has available an ethics handbook and instructional videotapes. The Office also maintains a public reading room and, upon request, provides copies of executive branch public financial disclosure reports in accordance with the ethics act and the Office's regulations.

For further information, contact the Office of Government Ethics, Suite 500, 1201 New York Avenue NW., Washington, DC 20005–3917. Phone, 202–523–5757.

OFFICE OF PERSONNEL MANAGEMENT

1900 E Street NW., Washington, DC 20415–0001
Phone, 202–606–1800

Director	CONSTANCE BERRY NEWMAN
Deputy Director	BILL R. PHILLIPS
General Counsel	JAIME RAMON
Director, Office of Congressional Relations	MARK VALENTE III
Director, Office of Communications	PAUL S. CLARK
Director, Office of International Affairs	DINAH LIN CHENG
Inspector General	PATRICK E. MCFARLAND
Chairman, Federal Prevailing Rate Advisory Committee	ANTHONY F. INGRASSIA
Associate Director for Personnel Systems and Oversight	CLAUDIA COOLEY
Associate Director for Investigations	FRANCES A. SCLAFANI
Associate Director for Retirement and Insurance	CURTIS J. SMITH
Associate Director for Career Entry	LEONARD R. KLEIN
Associate Director for Administration	JAMES B. LANCASTER, JR.
Director, Human Resources Development	DONA WOLF
Director, Washington Area Service Center	RICHARD B. POST

[For the Office of Personnel Management statement of organization, see the *Federal Register* of Jan. 5, 1979, 44 FR 1501]

The Office of Personnel Management administers a merit system for Federal employment that includes recruiting, examining, training, and promoting people on the basis of their knowledge and skills, regardless of their race, religion, sex, political influence, or other nonmerit factors. The Office's role is to ensure that the Federal Government provides an array of personnel services to applicants and employees. Through a range of programs designed to develop and encourage the effectiveness of the Government employee, the Office supports Government program managers in their personnel management responsibilities and provides benefits to employees and to retired employees and their survivors.

OFFICE OF PERSONNEL MANAGEMENT

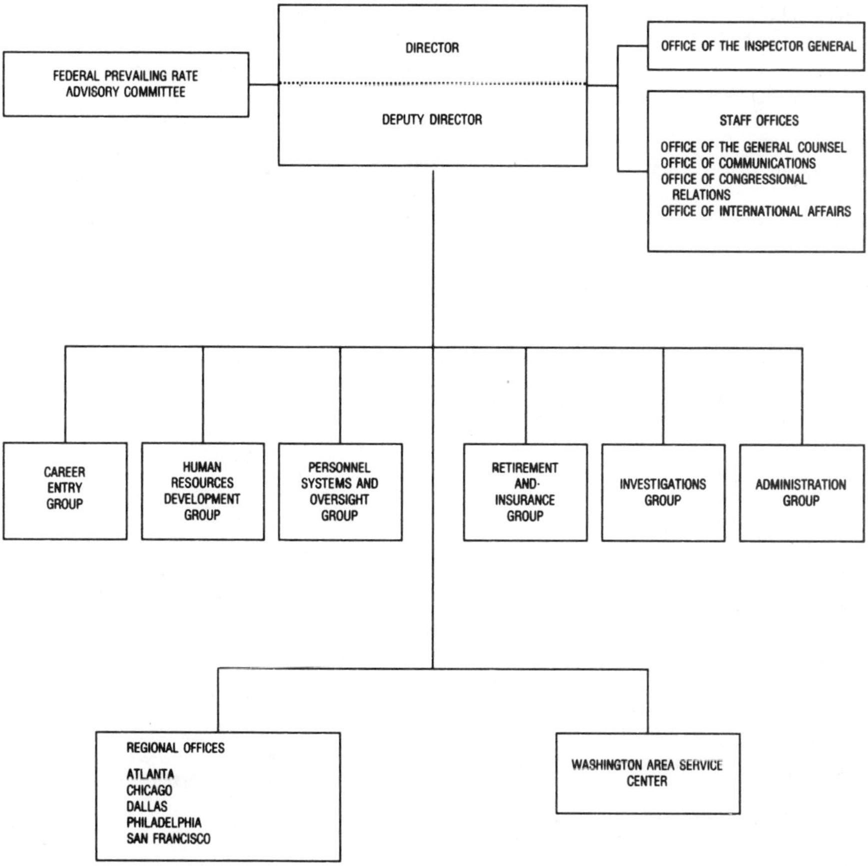

The Office of Personnel Management was created as an independent establishment by Reorganization Plan No. 2 of 1978 (5 U.S.C. app.), effective January 1, 1979, pursuant to Executive Order 12107 of December 28, 1978. Transferred to OPM were many of the functions of the former United States Civil Service Commission. The Office's duties and authority are specified in the Civil Service Reform Act of 1978 (5 U.S.C. 1101).

The five regional offices carry out programs in the field. In addition the Office has area offices in key locations, Federal job information and testing centers, and other field duty stations.

Office of the Inspector General The Office of the Inspector General provides agencywide audit functions to identify and correct management and administrative deficiencies from which fraud, mismanagement, or waste could arise. It provides for the detection and investigation of improper and illegal activities involoving agency programs, personnel, and operations, especially in the area of Federal employees retirement and insurance programs.

For further information, contact the Office of the Inspector General. Phone. 202–606–1200.

Activities

Recruiting and Examining The Office of Personnel Management is responsible for the nationwide recruiting and examining of applicants for competitive positions in the Federal civil service at General Schedule grades 1 through 15 and for Wage Grade positions. The Office also administers the Qualifications Review Board examining process for career Senior Executive Service appointments and conducts a competitive examination of applicants for administrative law judge positions.

Personnel Investigations Personnel investigations are used in support of the selection and appointment processes. They serve several purposes:

—to determine the suitability of applicants under consideration for appointment;

—to check on applicants or employees under consideration for appointment to positions having either national security and/or public trust requirements; and

—to enforce civil service regulations.

Affirmative Recruiting and Employment The Office provides leadership, direction, and policy for Governmentwide recruiting programs. These programs include general recruiting, college relations, and mobility and are designed to assist interns, students, disabled persons, veterans, women, and minorities. Specific policy, guidance, and technical assistance is provided to agencies in implementing the following programs: Disabled Veterans Affirmative Action, Federal Equal Opportunity Recruitment, Presidential Management Intern, Intergovernmental Personnel Act, Veterans Readjustment Appointment, and other recruiting programs. It is responsible for assuring that affirmative recruiting and employment practices are integral parts of all Federal personnel management activities.

Employee Development and Training The Office plans, promotes, sets standards, and evaluates Governmentwide programs and policies for the development and training of Federal employees. It offers a wide variety of training and development management services such as career development programs and contractual access to the private sector for courses and instructional technology application. It also provides training and development information and coordination services. Through a nationwide network of interagency training centers, a European center, Executive Seminar Centers, and the Federal Executive Institute, it offers a broad range of Government-related courses.

Personnel Systems The Office sets policy for, administers, and provides leadership and guidance to agencies on systems to support the manager's personnel management responsibilities. These include:

—blue and white collar pay systems, including Senior Executive Service pay and special rates to address recruitment and retention problems;

—annual and sick leave;

—performance management, covering appraisal systems, performance pay, and awards, including administration of the Presidential Rank Awards Program for Senior Executives, as well as incentive awards for suggestions, inventions, and special acts;

—research and demonstration projects to explore potential improvements in personnel systems and better and simpler ways to manage Federal personnel;

—classification policy and standards for agencies to assign series and grade to Federal jobs;

—labor-management relations, including responsibility for consulting with unions on Governmentwide issues;

—dealing with problem employees;

—quality of worklife initiatives, such as employee health and fitness, dependent care, AIDS in the workplace, and employee assistance programs; and

—information systems to support and improve Federal personnel management decisionmaking, including Governmentwide instructions for creation and maintenance of personnel records and for release of personnel data under the Freedom of Information Act and the Privacy Act.

Oversight The Office assesses agencies' effectiveness in personnel management at the Governmentwide, agency, and installation level to ensure compliance with personnel laws and regulations, enhance agency capability for self-evaluation, and assist agencies in operating personnel programs which effectively support accomplishment of their primary missions.

Employee Benefits The Office also manages numerous activities that directly affect the well-being of the Federal employee and indirectly enhance employee effectiveness. These include health benefits, life insurance, and retirement benefits.

Other Personnel Programs The Office administers the Senior Executive Service and is responsible for oversight and providing assistance on a variety of Governmentwide executive personnel management matters. It coordinates the temporary assignment of employees between Federal agencies and State, local, and Indian tribal governments; institutions of higher education; and other eligible organizations for up to 2 years, for work of mutual benefit to the participating organizations. It administers the Presidential Management Intern Program, which provides 2-year, excepted appointments with Federal agencies to recipients of graduate degrees in appropriate disciplines. In addition, the Office of Personnel Management administers the Federal Merit System Standards, which apply to certain grant-aided State and local programs.

Regional Offices—Office of Personnel Management

Region	Address	Director
ATLANTA—Alabama, Florida, Georgia, Mississippi, North Carolina, South Carolina, Tennessee, Virginia	75 Spring St. SW., Atlanta, GA 30303-3109	Ronald E. Brooks
CHICAGO—Illinois, Indiana, Iowa, Kansas, Kentucky, Michigan, Minnesota, Missouri, Nebraska, North Dakota, Ohio, South Dakota, West Virginia, Wisconsin,	230 S. Dearborn St., Chicago, IL 60604	Steven R. Cohen
DALLAS—Arizona, Arkansas, Colorado, Louisiana, Montana, New Mexico, Oklahoma, Texas, Utah, Wyoming	1100 Commerce St., Dallas, TX 75242	Edward Vela, Jr.
PHILADELPHIA—Connecticut, Delaware, Maine, Maryland, Massachusetts, New Hampshire, New Jersey, New York, Pennsylvania, Puerto Rico, Rhode Island, Vermont, Virgin Islands	600 Arch St., Philadelphia, PA 19106-1596	Frederick A. Kistler
SAN FRANCISCO—Alaska, California, Hawaii, Idaho, Nevada, Oregon, Washington, Pacific Ocean area	7th Fl. 211 Main St., San Francisco, CA 94105	Joseph S. Patti

Sources of Information

Contracts Contact the Assistant Director, Office of Procurement Services, Administration Group, Office of Personnel Management, Washington, DC 20415–0001 (phone, 202–606–2240); or the Administrative Officer of the appropriate regional office.

Employment A network of area offices and Federal Job Test Centers, located in major metropolitan areas, provides Federal employment information. To obtain the appropriate telephone number, check the blue pages under U.S. Government, Office of Personnel Management.

Publications The Office issues publications addressed to a variety of audiences ranging from applicants for employment to the heads of Federal agencies.

The Chief, Issuance System Office, Administration Group, can provide information about Federal personnel management publications, particularly those in the Federal Personnel Manual system. For further information, call 202-606-1973.

Reading Room The Office of Personnel Management Library maintains collections of historical and current information on personnel management and the Federal civil service, including legislative information. The Library also serves as a reading room for those interested in Office publications available to the public. The Superintendent of Documents, Government Printing Office, Washington, DC 20402, sells subscriptions to *Personnel Literature.*

For further information, contact the Office of Communications, Office of Personnel Management, 1900 E Street NW., Washington, DC 20415–0001. Phone, 202–606–1800.

OVERSIGHT BOARD

Suite 600, 1777 F Street NW., Washington, DC 20232
Phone, 202–786–9661

Chairman	NICHOLAS F. BRADY
Board of Directors:	
Secretary of the Treasury	NICHOLAS F. BRADY
Chairman of the Board of Governors of the Federal Reserve System	ALAN GREENSPAN
Secretary of Housing and Urban Development	JACK KEMP
Independent Members	PHILIP C. JACKSON
	ROBERT C. LARSON
President	PETER MONROE
General Counsel	RICHARD FARINA
Vice Presidents:	
Congressional Affairs	ROBERT VASTINE
Public Affairs	ARTHUR J. SIDDON
Finance and Management	LLOYD CHAISSON
Oversight and Evaluation	KURT WIERSCHEM

The Oversight Board is responsible for the general oversight of the Resolution Trust Corporation and the Resolution Funding Corporation. The Board is required, in consultation with the Resolution Trust Corporation, to develop and establish overall strategies, policies, and goals for the Corporation's activities, including the Corporation's overall financial goals, plans, and budgets. The Board is also required to review the overall performance of the Resolution Trust Corporation on a periodic basis, including its work, management activities, and internal controls and

OVERSIGHT BOARD FOR THE RESOLUTION TRUST CORPORATION

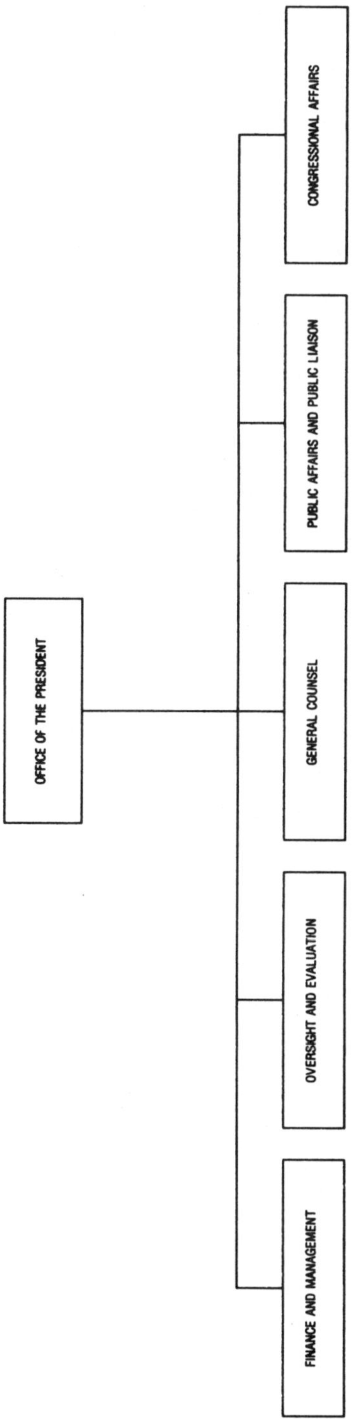

the performance of the Corporation relative to approved budget plans pursuant to the terms of the Financial Institutions Reform, Recovery, and Enforcement Act of 1989.

The Oversight Board for the Resolution Trust Corporation was established as an instrumentality of the United States on August 9, 1989, by the Financial Institutions Reform, Recovery, and Enforcement Act of 1989 (12 U.S.C. 1441a).

The Board is governed by a five-member Board of Directors consisting of the Secretary of the Treasury, who is the Chairman of the Board; the Chairman of the Board of Governors of the Federal Reserve System; the Secretary of Housing and Urban Development (HUD); and two independent members appointed by the President with the advice and consent of the Senate for 3-year terms.

The day-to-day operations of the Board are conducted through the President and Chief Executive Officer and other officers and staff members. The Board is required to make periodic reports to the President and to the Congress detailing operations, activities, receipts, and expenditures relating to the Resolution Trust Corporation (RTC), as well as operations relating to the Resolution Funding Corporation (REFCORP).

Activities

With respect to RTC, the Oversight Board:

—develops overall strategies, policies, and goals, in consultation with RTC, for management and disposition of the assets of failed depository institutions;

—considers periodic financing requests developed by RTC;

—reviews and authorizes regulations and other procedures relating to RTC's powers and activities as conservator or receiver to ensure consistency with the Federal Deposit Insurance Act, except those activities involving individual resolutions, asset liquidations, or day-to-day operations of the RTC;

—reviews overall performance of RTC on a periodic basis, including its work, management, internal controls, and budget;

—establishes national and regional advisory boards;

—authorizes the use of proceeds of funds provided by the Treasury to ensure consistency with approved budgetary plans;

—evaluates audits by the Inspector General or other congressionally mandated audits; and

—authorizes, as appropriate, RTC's sale of capital certificates to REFCORP.

With respect to REFCORP, the Oversight Board:

—prescribes the time and manner in which the Federal Home Loan Banks will invest in REFCORP;

—prescribes regulations, orders, and directions it deems appropriate to carry out the purposes of REFCORP;

—selects two members of the REFCORP directorate from among the Federal Home Loan Bank presidents;

—selects the chairperson of the REFCORP directorate from among its three members;

—ensures that the aggregate amount of funds to capitalize the Corporation is sufficient to purchase non-interest bearing instruments that are direct obligations of the United States and which at maturity will equal the aggregate amount of principal on the obligations of REFCORP; and

—approves the formula for determining each bank's pro rata share of the administrative and custodial expenses of REFCORP.

For further information, contact the Vice President of Public Affairs, Oversight Board for the Resolution Trust Corporation, Suite 700, 1777 F Street NW., Washington, DC 20232. Phone, 202–786–9672.

PANAMA CANAL COMMISSION

Room 550, 2000 L Street NW., Washington, DC 20036–4996
Phone, 202–634–6441

Official in Washington:

Secretary	MICHAEL RHODE, JR.

Officials in the Republic of Panama:

Administrator	GILBERTO GUARDIA
Deputy Administrator	RAYMOND P. LAVERTY

[For the Panama Canal Commission statement of organization, see the *Code of Federal Regulations,* Title 35, Part 9]

The Panama Canal Commission operates, maintains, and improves the Panama Canal to provide efficient, safe, and economical transit service for the benefit of world commerce.

The Panama Canal Commission was established as an independent agency by the Panama Canal Act of 1979 (22 U.S.C. 3601).

The Commission is supervised by a nine-member Board: five members who are nationals of the United States and four members who are nationals of the Republic of Panama. All members of the Board are appointed by the President; the members who are United States nationals are appointed with the advice and consent of the Senate.

Activities

The Commission was established by Congress on October 1, 1979, to carry out the responsibilities of the United States with respect to the Panama Canal under the Panama Canal Treaty of 1977. In fulfilling these obligations, the Commission manages, operates, and maintains the Canal, its complementary works, installations, and equipment, and provides for the orderly transit of vessels through the Canal. This U.S. agency will perform these functions until the treaty terminates on December 31, 1999, at which time the Republic of Panama will assume full responsibility for the Canal.

Sources of Information

Marine Operations Director, Marine Bureau, Panama. Phone, 011–507–52–4500.

Economic and Marketing Information Director, Office of Executive Planning, Panama. Phone, 011–507–52–7961.

Procurement Office of Logistical Support, 4400 Dauphine Street, New Orleans, LA 70146–6800. Phone, 504–948–5299.

Panama Canal Commission APO Miami, 34011–5000. Telex, 3034 PCCAMRM PG.

For further information, contact the Office of the Secretary, Panama Canal Commission, Room 550, 2000 L Street NW., Washington, DC 20036. Phone, 202–634–6441.

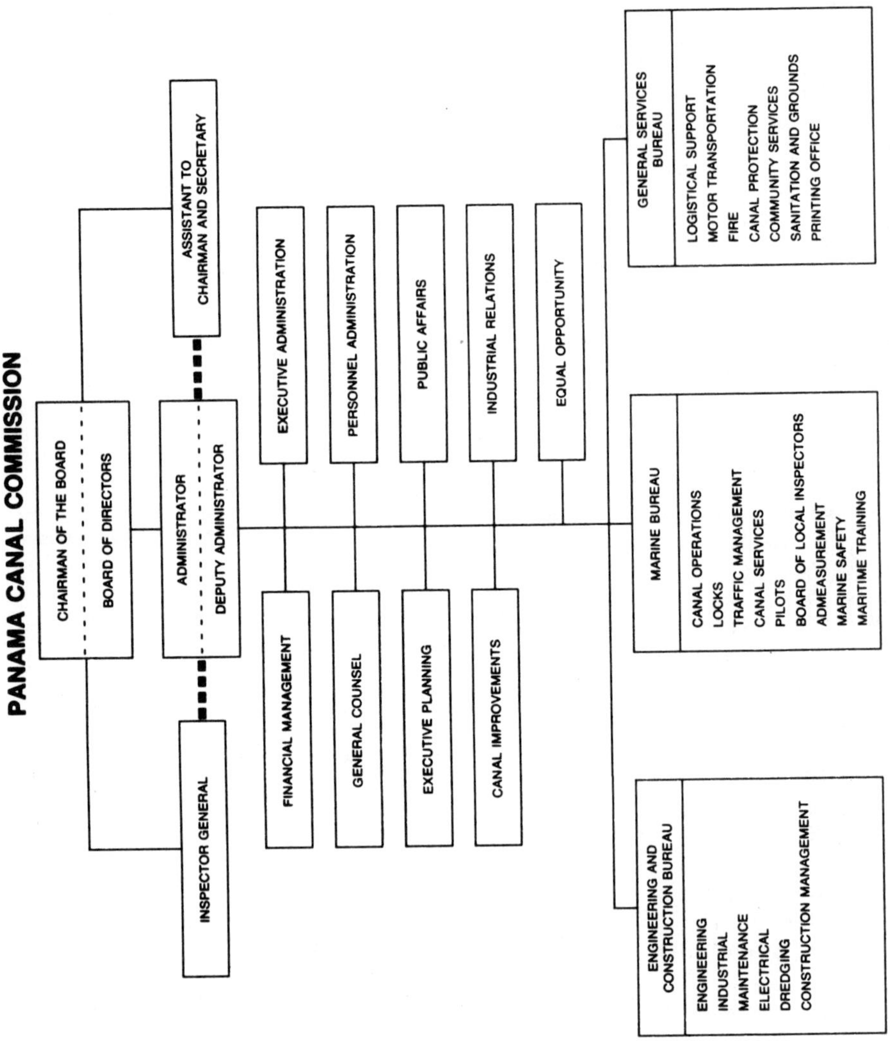
PANAMA CANAL COMMISSION
CHAIRMAN OF THE BOARD
BOARD OF DIRECTORS
ASSISTANT TO CHAIRMAN AND SECRETARY
INSPECTOR GENERAL
ADMINISTRATOR
DEPUTY ADMINISTRATOR
EXECUTIVE ADMINISTRATION
PERSONNEL ADMINISTRATION
PUBLIC AFFAIRS
INDUSTRIAL RELATIONS
EQUAL OPPORTUNITY
FINANCIAL MANAGEMENT
GENERAL COUNSEL
EXECUTIVE PLANNING
CANAL IMPROVEMENTS
GENERAL SERVICES BUREAU
LOGISTICAL SUPPORT
MOTOR TRANSPORTATION
FIRE
CANAL PROTECTION
COMMUNITY SERVICES
SANITATION AND GROUNDS
PRINTING OFFICE
MARINE BUREAU
CANAL OPERATIONS
LOCKS
TRAFFIC MANAGEMENT
CANAL SERVICES
PILOTS
BOARD OF LOCAL INSPECTORS
ADMEASUREMENT
MARINE SAFETY
MARITIME TRAINING
ENGINEERING AND CONSTRUCTION BUREAU
ENGINEERING
INDUSTRIAL
MAINTENANCE
ELECTRICAL
DREDGING
CONSTRUCTION MANAGEMENT

PEACE CORPS

1990 K Street NW., Washington, DC 20526
Phones—Locator: 202-606-3886; FAX: 202-606-3108; Toll-free: 1-800-424-8580

Director	PAUL D. COVERDELL
Deputy Director	BARBARA ZARTMAN
Chief of Staff	JODY OLSEN
General Counsel	JOHN SCALES
Inspector General	GERARD A. ROY
Director of Administrative Support	MARY ALDEN DYE
Director of Planning and Budget	RON PASSERO
Director of Congressional Relations	EDWIN E. CAIN
Director of Creative Services	FELICE PELOSI
Director of Communications	LEE RAUDONIS
Press Officer	(VACANCY)
Director of Private Sector Relations	PAMLA PROCHNOW
Director of Intergovernmental Affairs	ERIC TANENBATT
Executive Secretariat	SARALEE BOTELER
Director of World Wise Schools	SHIRLEY PUCHALSKI
Director of Africa Operations	(VACANCY)
Director of Inter-American Operations	EARL MCCLURE
Director of Pacific, Asian, Central Europe and Mediterranean Operations	JERRY LEACH
Director of International Research and Development	JON W. KEETON
Director of Training and Program Support	MARY KILLEEN
Special Assistant for Executive Personnel	LILIANE WILLENS
Associate Director for Management	COLLINS REYNOLDS
Director of Personnel Management	ORINDA NELSON
Director of Volunteer Services	LAVERNE PIERCE
Director of Information Resources Management	FERNANDO BURBANO
Director of Financial Services	YVONNE VAUGHAN
Director of Contracts	JOSEPH RADFORD
Director of Administrative Services	DANIEL GARCIA
Associate Director for Volunteer Recruitment and Selection	(VACANCY)
Director of Recruitment	JAMES SCANLON
Director of Placement	S. BROOKE FINN

[For the Peace Corps statement of organization, see the *Code of Federal Regulations,* Title 22, Part 302]

The Peace Corps purpose is to promote world peace and friendship, to help other countries in meeting their needs for trained manpower, and to help promote understanding between the American people and other peoples served by the Peace Corps. The Peace Corps Act emphasizes the Peace Corps' commitment toward programming to meet the basic needs of those living in the poorest countries in which it operates.

The Peace Corps was established by the Peace Corps Act of 1961, as amended (22 U.S.C. 2501), and was made an independent agency by title VI of the International Security and Development

PEACE CORPS

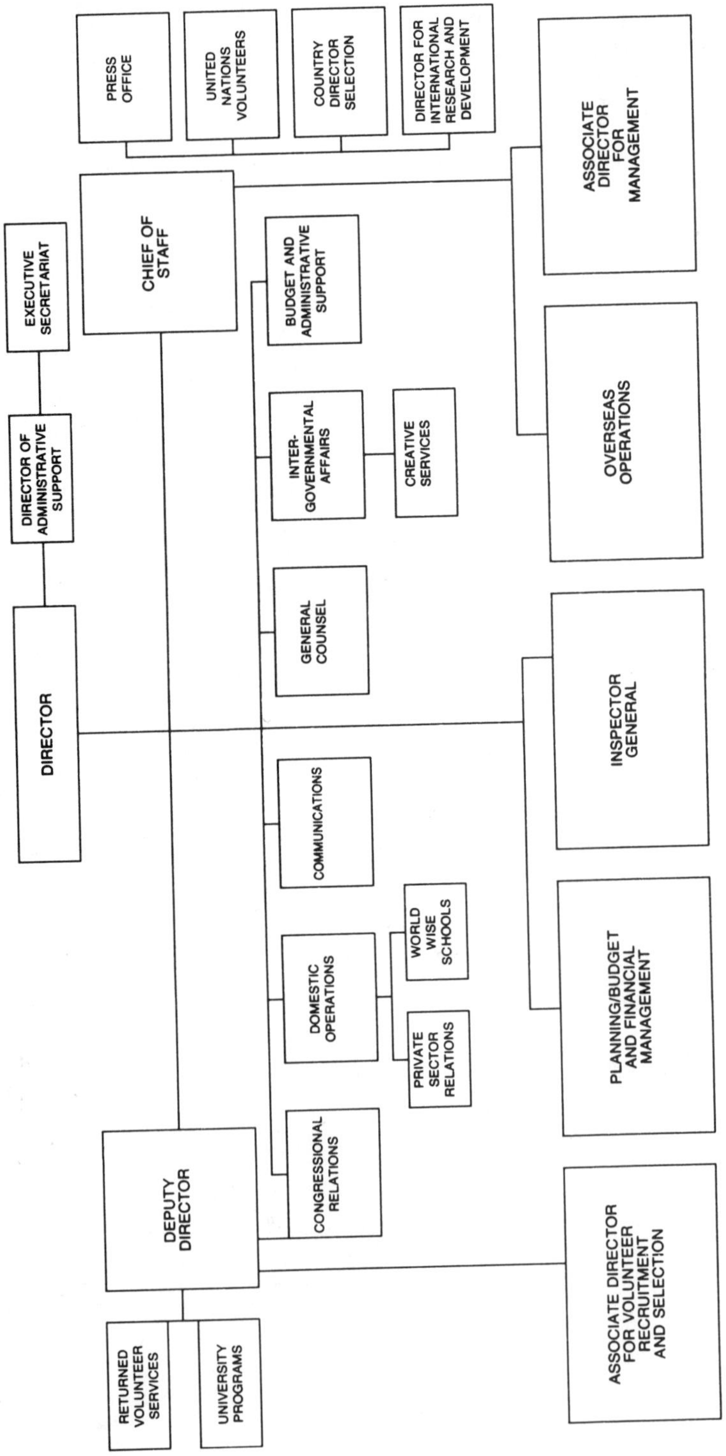
DIRECTOR
DIRECTOR OF ADMINISTRATIVE SUPPORT
EXECUTIVE SECRETARIAT
CHIEF OF STAFF
PRESS OFFICE
UNITED NATIONS VOLUNTEERS
COUNTRY DIRECTOR SELECTION
DIRECTOR FOR INTERNATIONAL RESEARCH AND DEVELOPMENT
ASSOCIATE DIRECTOR FOR MANAGEMENT
BUDGET AND ADMINISTRATIVE SUPPORT
INTER-GOVERNMENTAL AFFAIRS
CREATIVE SERVICES
GENERAL COUNSEL
COMMUNICATIONS
DOMESTIC OPERATIONS
WORLD WISE SCHOOLS
PRIVATE SECTOR RELATIONS
CONGRESSIONAL RELATIONS
OVERSEAS OPERATIONS
INSPECTOR GENERAL
PLANNING/BUDGET AND FINANCIAL MANAGEMENT
DEPUTY DIRECTOR
RETURNED VOLUNTEER SERVICES
UNIVERSITY PROGRAMS
ASSOCIATE DIRECTOR FOR VOLUNTEER RECRUITMENT AND SELECTION

Cooperation Act of 1981 (22 U.S.C. 2501–1).

The Peace Corps consists of a Washington, DC, headquarters; 16 area recruitment offices; and overseas operations in more than 70 countries. Its presence in foreign countries fluctuates as programs are added or withdrawn.

Activities

To fulfill the Peace Corps mandate, men and women are trained for a 9- to 14-week period in the appropriate local language, the technical skills necessary for their particular job, and the cross-cultural skills needed to adjust to a society with traditions and attitudes different from their own. Volunteers serve for a period of 2 years, living among the people with whom they work. Volunteers are expected to become a part of the community and to demonstrate, through their voluntary service, that people can be an important impetus for change.

Thousands of volunteers serve throughout Latin America, Africa, the Near East, Asia, the Pacific, and Eastern Europe and work in six program areas, including: education, agriculture, health, small business development, urban development, and the environment. Projects are designed to match the skills and community-level approach of the volunteers with the resources of host-country agencies and other international assistance organizations to help solve specific development problems, often in conjunction with private volunteer organizations.

In the United States, the Peace Corps is working to promote an understanding of peoples in other countries. Through a new program called *World Wise Schools,* volunteers are matched with elementary and junior high schools in the United States to encourage an exchange of letters, pictures, music, and artifacts. Participating students increase their knowledge of geography, languages, and different cultures, as well as gain an appreciation for volunteerism.

The Peace Corps offers an education initiative which involves former volunteers, universities, local public school systems, and private businesses and foundations in a partnership to help solve some of our most serious domestic problems. It is working to implement this initiative throughout the United States.

To help support efforts such as *World Wise Schools,* the Fellows/U.S.A. program, and community needs overseas, the Peace Corps Office of Private Sector Relations works with schools, civic groups, businesses, and neighborhood and youth organizations in the United States to facilitate their support of Peace Corps initiatives here and abroad.

Recruiting Area Offices—Peace Corps

Office	Address	Telephone
NEW YORK (Connecticut, New York, northern New Jersey)	Rm. 1317, 90 Church St., New York, NY 10007	212-264-6981
BOSTON (Maine, Massachusetts, New Hampshire, Rhode Island, Vermont)	Rm. 450, 10 Causeway St., MA 02222-1099	617-565-5555
PHILADELPHIA (Delaware, Pennsylvania, southern New Jersey)	Rm. 102-A, 2d and Chestnut Sts., Philadelphia, PA 19106	215-597-7044
WASHINGTON, DC (District of Columbia, Maryland, North Carolina, Virginia, West Virginia)	Rm. 5400, 1990 K St. NW., Washington, DC 20526	202-254-4940
CHICAGO (Illinois, Indiana)	Suite 300, 50 E. Washington St., Chicago, IL 60602	312-353-4990
ATLANTA	Rm. 2207, 101 Marietta St. NW., Atlanta, GA 30323	404-331-2932
Miami sub-office	Rm. 420, 330 Biscayne Blvd., Miami FL 33132	305-536-5273
Puerto Rico sub-office	Rm. 710, Mercantile Plz., Hato Rey, PR 00918	809-753-4694
MINNEAPOLIS (Minnesota, Wisconsin)	Rm. 420, 330 2d Ave. S., Minneapolis, MN 55401	612-334-4040
KANSAS CITY (Iowa, Kansas, Missouri, Nebraska)	Suite 512, 5799 Broadmoor St., Mission, KS 66202	913-236-2700

290-950 0 91 - 23

Recruiting Area Offices—Peace Corps—Continued

Office	Address	Telephone
DETROIT (Michigan, Ohio)	Rm. M-74, 477 Michigan Ave., Detroit, MI 48226	313-226-7928
SAN FRANCISCO (Hawaii, Nevada, northern California)	Rm. 533, 211 Main St., San Francisco, CA 94105	415-744-2677
LOS ANGELES (Arizona, southern California)	Rm. 8104, 11000 Wilshire Blvd., West Los Angeles, CA 90024	213-209-7444
SEATTLE (Arizona, eastern Washington, Idaho, Oregon)	Rm. 1776, 2001 6th Ave., Seattle, WA 98121	206-442-5490
DALLAS (Arkansas, Louisiana, New Mexico, Oklahoma, Texas)	Rm. 230, 400 N. Ervay St., P.O. Box 638 Dallas, TX 75201	214-767-5435
DENVER (Colorado, Montana, North Dakota, South Dakota, Utah, Wyoming)	Rm. 103, 1845 Sherman St., Denver, CO 80203	303-866-1057

Sources of Information

Becoming a Peace Corps Volunteer Persons interested in becoming a Peace Corps volunteer should write to: Peace Corps, Office of Volunteer Services, Washington, DC 20526 (phone, 202–606–3336), or contact any Peace Corps recruitment office.

Employment Persons interested in employment with the Peace Corps should address inquiries to Peace Corps, Office of Personnel Management, Washington, DC 20526. Phone, 202–606–3336. For recorded employment opportunities, call 202–775–2214.

General Inquiries In all cases, information or assistance may be obtained by contacting the Peace Corps' Washington, DC, headquarters or any of its recruiting offices. Frequently, information is available from local post offices.

A complete list of countries with specific addresses for Peace Corps operations is available upon request from the Director of Media Relations, at the address below.

For further information, contact the Office of Media Relations, Peace Corps, 1990 K Street NW., Washington, DC 20526. Phone, 202–606–3010.

PENNSYLVANIA AVENUE DEVELOPMENT CORPORATION

Suite 1220 North, 1331 Pennsylvania Avenue NW., Washington, DC 20004–1703
Phone, 202–724–9091

Board of Directors:	
Chairman	RICHARD A. HAUSER
Directors	EDWARD E. ALLISON, CATHERINE M. BOUCREE, ELEANOR LYONS WILLIAMS, PETER TERPELUK, JR., ELLEN M. WRIGHT, JAYNE B. IKARD, WALTER J. GANZI, JR.
Officials:	
Executive Director	M.J. BRODIE
Assistant Director, Legal	ROBERT E. MCCALLY
Assistant Director, Development	JERRY M. SMEDLEY
Director, Finance and Administration	ALEXANDER K. MILIN

Director, Public Improvements	RICHARD SITEK
Director, Design	JAN F. FRANKINA
Administrative Officer/Secretary, Board of Directors	DIANE G. SMITH
Director, Corporate Affairs and Congressional Relations	ANNE P. HARTZELL

The Pennsylvania Avenue Development Corporation is a Federal agency charged with responsibility for revitalizing Pennsylvania Avenue between the White House and the Capitol. A comprehensive plan, prepared by the agency and approved by Congress in 1975, guides development in a 21-block section of Pennsylvania Avenue and the adjacent blocks north of the avenue.

The Pennsylvania Avenue Development Corporation was established as a wholly owned Federal corporation by act of October 27, 1972, as amended (40 U.S.C. 871 *et seq.*).

The Corporation is governed by a 15-member Board of Directors. Eight members are appointed by the President from the private sector for 6-year terms; seven serve by virtue of their positions in the Federal or District of Columbia Governments. There also are eight nonvoting members representing Federal and District organizations with expertise in cultural, planning, and architectural matters.

Activities

The Corporation's activities to revitalize Pennsylvania Avenue take two forms. First, using funds appropriated by Congress, the Corporation undertakes projects which improve the public areas and ambience of Pennsylvania Avenue. These projects include repaving and landscaping the Avenue and adjacent areas, facilitating traffic patterns, and preserving the designated historic landmarks. It also has completed five parks and open spaces along the Avenue and sponsors people-oriented activities within the area.

The second part of the Corporation's activity involves a partnership with the private sector to develop projects compatible with the Pennsylvania Avenue Plan. It uses funds borrowed from the United States Treasury to assemble land for housing, office buildings, retail uses, hotels, and community arts space. It makes public offerings of development opportunities on sites, and either sells the property or enters into long-term leases with developers selected to carry out individual projects. The proceeds from the leases or sales are used to retire the agency's debt to the Treasury.

In carrying out the plan, the Corporation works closely with a number of Federal agencies, including the Commission of Fine Arts, the National Capital Planning Commission, the Advisory Council on Historic Preservation, and the National Park Service. It also works closely in the implementation of the plan with relevant agencies of the District of Columbia government.

In 1987 the Congress enacted and the President signed the Federal Triangle Development Act. The act gave the Corporation the authority to plan and implement, in consultation with the General Services Administration and the International Cultural Trade Center Commission, the development of a 3.1-million-square-foot complex to include the Center and Federal office space.

Sources of Information

Publications The *Pennsylvania Avenue Plan* (1974), as approved by Congress in May 1975, and *Amendments to the Pennsylvania Avenue Plan* (November 1990) describes the program for comprehensive revitalization of the

PENNSYLVANIA AVENUE DEVELOPMENT CORPORATION

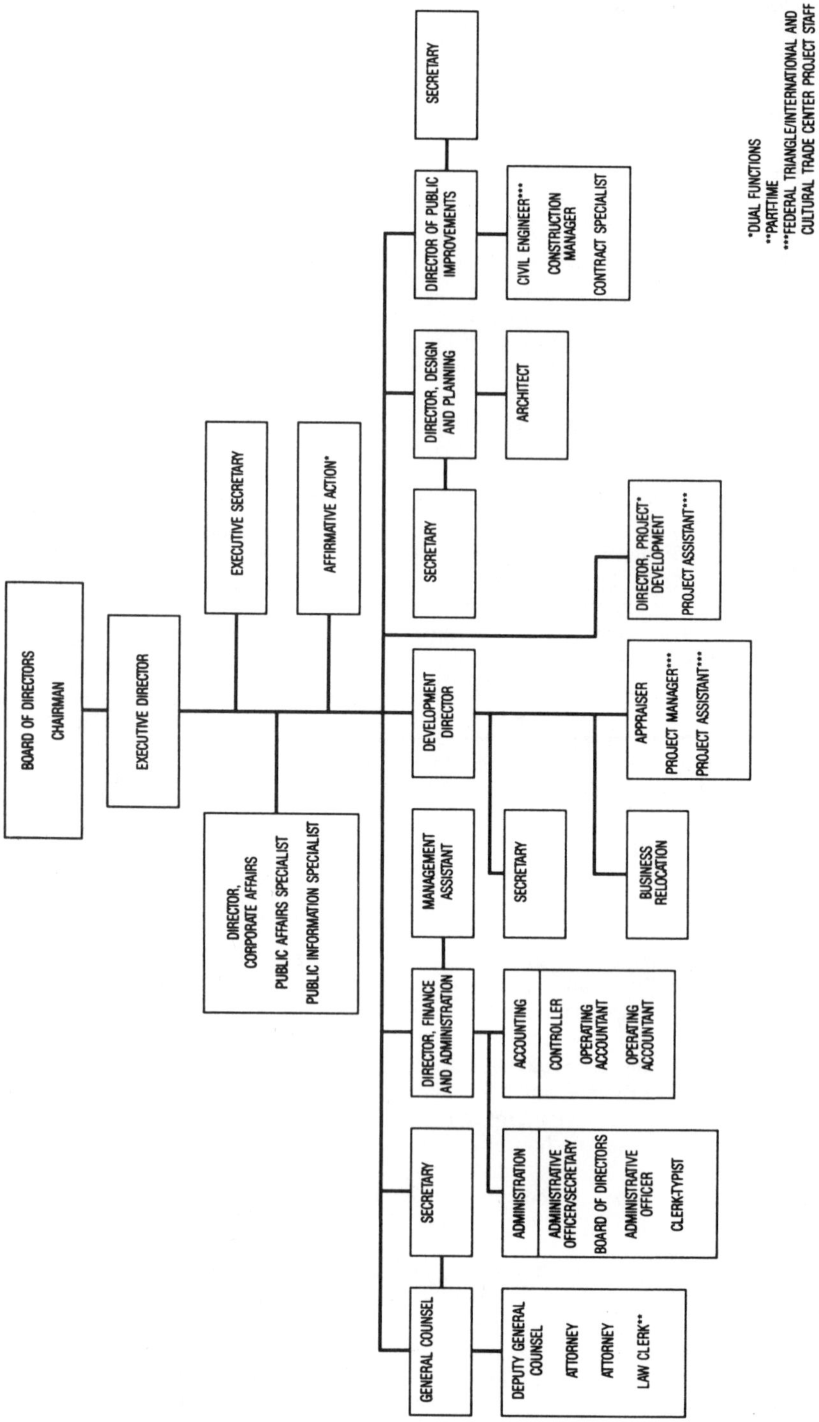

designated area. Copies of these documents, as well as the Corporation's annual report and other supplementary materials, are available upon request.

For further information, contact the Director of Corporate Affairs, Pennsylvania Avenue Development Corporation, Suite 1220 North, 1331 Pennsylvania Avenue NW., Washington, DC 20004–1703. Phone, 202–724–9073.

PENSION BENEFIT GUARANTY CORPORATION

2020 K Street NW., Washington, DC 20006
Phone, 202–778–8800

Board of Directors:

Chairman (Secretary of Labor)	LYNN M. MARTIN
Members:	
(Secretary of the Treasury)	NICHOLAS F. BRADY
(Secretary of Commerce)	ROBERT A. MOSBACHER

Officials:

Executive Director	JAMES B. LOCKHART III
Deputy Executive Director and Chief Negotiator	DIANE E. BURKLEY
Deputy Executive Director and Chief Operating Officer	WILLIAM M. DEHARDE
Deputy Executive Director and Chief Financial Officer	JAMES L. WOLBARSHT
Director, Communications and Public Affairs Department	JUDITH E. BEKELMAN
Director, Corporate Management and Budget Department	HENRY R. THOMPSON
Director, Corporate Finance and Negotiations Department	STEVEN M. HILL, *Acting*
Director, Corporate Policy and Research Department	DAVID C. LINDEMAN
Director, Financial Operations Department	LAWRENCE MASLAN
General Counsel	CAROL C. FLOWE
Director, Human Resources and Support Services Department	ROBERT E. GEIGER
Director, Information Resources Management Department	JON H. BAAKE
Inspector General	WAYNE R. POLL
Director, Insurance Operations Department	STEPHEN J. FAHERTY, SR., *Acting*
Director, Participant and Employer Appeals Department	CHARLES E. SKOPIC

The Pension Benefit Guaranty Corporation guarantees payment of nonforfeitable pension benefits in covered private sector-defined benefit pension plans.

Title IV of the Employee Retirement Income Security Act of 1974 (29 U.S.C. 1301–1461) established the Pension Benefit Guaranty Corporation, which is a

PENSION BENEFIT GUARANTY CORPORATION

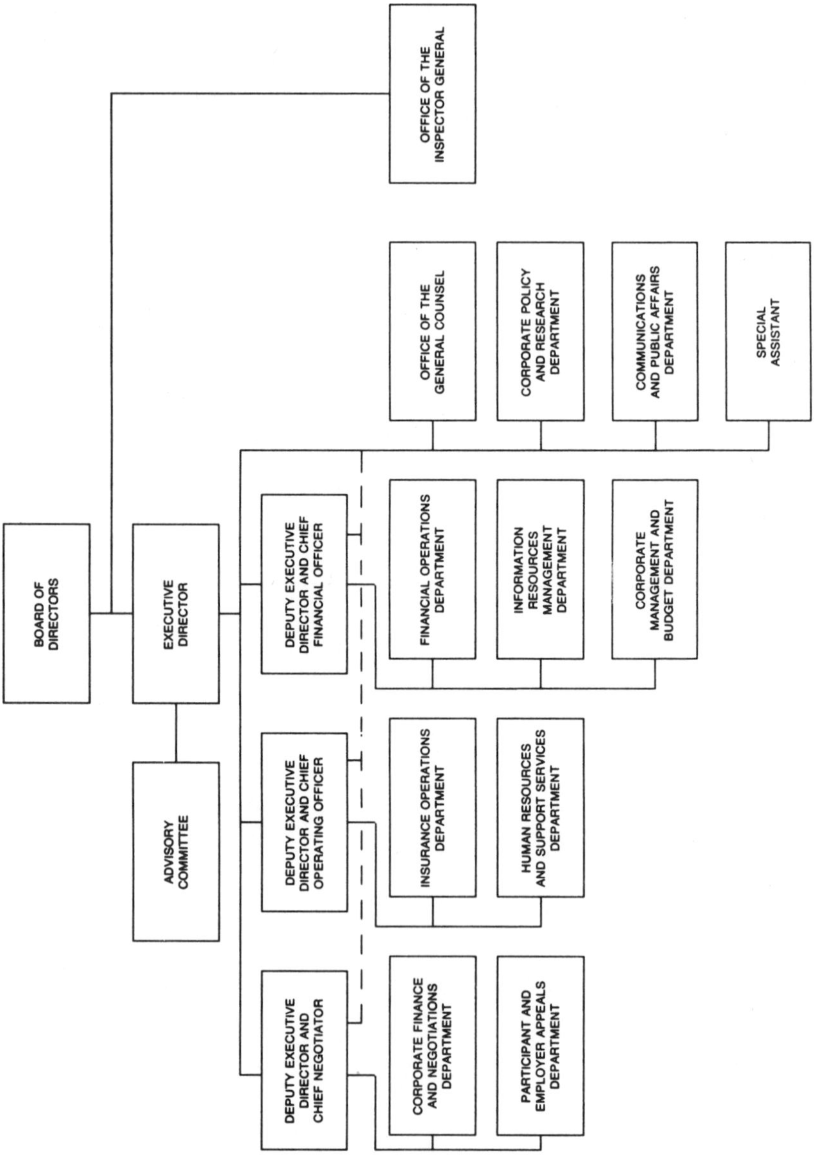

self-financing, wholly owned Government corporation subject to the provisions of the Government Corporation Control Act (31 U.S.C. 9101–9109). The Corporation is governed by a Board of Directors consisting of the Secretaries of Labor, Commerce, and the Treasury. The Secretary of Labor is Chairman of the Board. A seven-member Advisory Committee, composed of two labor, two business, and three public members appointed by the President, advises the agency on various matters.

Activities

Coverage Title IV provides for coverage of most private sector-defined benefit pension plans that provide a benefit based on factors such as age, years of service, and average or highest salary.

The Corporation administers two benefit insurance programs separately covering single-employer and multiemployer plans. Nearly 40 million workers participate in approximately 95,000 covered plans.

Single-Employer Insurance Under the single-employer program, the Corporation guarantees payment of a covered plan's nonforfeitable benefits if that plan terminates without sufficient assets to pay those guaranteed benefits. However, title IV limits the total monthly benefit that the agency may guarantee for one individual to $2,250 per month for a plan terminating during 1991, and requires that it guarantee recent benefit increases on a phased-in basis. Under the 1987 amendments to title IV, the Corporation also pays a portion of the benefits above the guaranteed amount, based on the percentage of the value of its recovery of termination liability.

A plan administrator may terminate a single-employer plan in a "standard" or "distress" termination if certain procedural and legal requirements are met. In either termination, the plan administrator must inform participants in writing at least 60 days prior to the date the administrator proposes to terminate the plan. Only a plan which has sufficient assets to fund all benefit liabilities may terminate in a standard termination. The Corporation also may institute termination proceedings upon the occurrence of certain events specified in title IV.

Multiemployer Insurance Under title IV, as originally enacted, the Corporation guaranteed nonforfeitable benefits for multiemployer plans in a similar fashion as for single-employer plans. However, until August 1, 1980, the payment of guaranteed benefits under multiemployer plans was at the agency's discretion.

The Multiemployer Pension Plan Amendments Act of 1980 revised title IV as applicable to multiemployer pension plans by changing the insurable event from plan termination to plan insolvency. In accordance with the act, the Corporation provides financial assistance to plans that are unable to pay nonforfeitable benefits. The plans are obligated to repay such assistance. The act also made employers withdrawing from a plan liable to the plan for a portion of its unfunded vested benefits.

Premium Collections All defined benefit pension plans covered by title IV of Employee Retirement Income Security Act are required to pay premiums under prescribed rates to the Corporation. The annual premium per plan participant for multiemployer pension plans is $2.60 for plan years beginning after September 26, 1988. As of January 1, 1991, the basic premium for all single-employer plans was $19 per participant per year. Single-employer plans must also pay an additional premium equal to $9 per $1,000 of unfunded nonforfeitable benefits. The total single-employer premium is capped at $72 per participant.

For further information, contact the Pension Benefit Guaranty Corporation, 2020 K Street NW., Washington, DC 20006–1860. Phone, 202–778–8800.

POSTAL RATE COMMISSION

1333 H Street NW., Washington, DC 20268-0001
Phone, 202-789-6800

Chairman	GEORGE W. HALEY
Special Assistant	IRVIN H. BROMALL
Special Assistant to the Commission	GERALD E. CERASALE
Vice Chairman	HENRY R. FOLSOM
Special Assistant	(VACANCY)
Commissioner	PATTI BIRGE TYSON
Special Assistant	(VACANCY)
Commissioner	JOHN W. CRUTCHER
Special Assistant	LEONARD MEREWITZ
Commissioner	W.H. TREY LEBLANC III
Special Assistant	JOHN O. BOVARD
Chief Administrative Officer and Secretary	CHARLES L. CLAPP
General Counsel	DAVID F. STOVER
Assistant General Counsel	STEPHEN L. SHARFMAN
Director, Office of Technical Analysis and Planning	ROBERT COHEN
Assistant Director, Office of Technical Analysis and Planning	WILLIAM FERGUSON
Director, Office of the Consumer Advocate	STEPHEN A. GOLD
Personnel Officer	CYRIL J. PITTACK

[For the Postal Rate Commission statement of organization, see the *Code of Federal Regulations,* Title 39, Part 3002]

The major responsibility of the Postal Rate Commission is to submit recommended decisions to the Unites States Postal Service Governors on postage rates, fees, and mail classifications. In addition, the Commission may issue advisory opinions at the Service's request on proposed nationwide changes in postal services; initiate studies and submit recommendations for changes in the mail classification schedule; initiate studies on postal matters, such as cost theory and operations; receive, study, and conduct hearings and issue recommended decisions and reports to the Service on complaints received from interested persons relating to postage rates, postal classifications, and problems of national scope regarding postal services; and act on appeals of the closing or consolidation of post offices.

The Postal Rate Commission is an independent agency created by the Postal Reorganization Act, as amended (39 U.S.C. 3601-3604).

The Commission promulgates rules and regulations, establishes procedures, and takes other actions necessary to carry out its obligations. Acting upon requests from the U.S. Postal Service, or on its own initiative, the Commission recommends to the Board of Governors of the U.S. Postal Service changes in rates or fees in each class of mail or type of service. It submits recommended decisions on establishing or changing the mail classification schedule, and holds such hearings on the record as are required by law and are necessary to arrive at sound and fair recommendations. The Commission has appellate jurisdiction to review Postal Service determinations to close or consolidate small post offices.

Sources of Information

Employment The Commission's programs require attorneys, economists, statisticians, accountants, industrial engineers, marketing specialists, and administrative and clerical personnel. Requests for employment information should be directed to the Personnel Officer.

Reading Room Facilities for inspection and copying of records that are available to the public are located in Suite 300, 1333 H Street NW., Washington, DC. The room is open from 8 a.m. to 4:30 p.m., Monday through Friday, except legal holidays.

Rules of Practice and Procedure The Postal Rate Commission's Rules of Practice and Procedure governing the conduct of proceedings before the Commission may be found in part 3001 of title 39 of the *Code of Federal Regulations.*

For further information, contact the Secretary, Postal Rate Commission, 1333 H Street NW., Washington, DC 20268–0001. Phone, 202–789–6840.

RAILROAD RETIREMENT BOARD

844 Rush Street, Chicago, IL 60611
Phone, 312–751–4776

Washington Legislative/Liaison Office: 2000 L Street NW., Washington, DC 20036
Phone, 202–653–9540

Chairman	Glen L. Bower
Labor Member	C.J. Chamberlain
Management Member	Andrew F. Reardon
Inspector General	William J. Doyle III
Chief Executive Officer	Kenneth P. Boehne
General Counsel and Director of Legal and Administrative Services	Dale G. Zimmerman
Deputy General Counsel	Steven A. Bartholow
Legislative Counsel	David D. Lucci
Chief Actuary	Maynard I. Kagen
Chief Financial Officer	Peter A. Larson
Director, Retirement and Survivor Programs	Robert S. Kaufman
Director, Retirement Benefits	Kenneth J. Zoll
Director, Survivor Benefits	Stanley A. Wyse
Director, Unemployment and Sickness Insurance	Robert J. Duda
Director, Field Service	Ronald J. Dammon
Director, Data Processing	Barry R. Hemphill
Director, Systems Initiatives	Edward A. Haney
Director, Taxation	John L. Thoresdale
Director, Research and Employment Accounts	Bobby V. Ferguson
Director, Disability and Medicare Operations	John R. Feldheim
Equal Employment Officer	Samuel Lyons
Director, Hearings and Appeals	Grace Koester
Director, Information Resources Management	Ronald J. Hodapp
Director, Personnel	John F. Malich
Director, Public Affairs	William G. Poulos

Director, Quality Assurance	MARY KAY SHUTT
Director, Supply and Service	HENRY M. VALIULIS

[For the Railroad Retirement Board statement of organization, see the *Code of Federal Regulations,* Title 20, Part 200]

The Railroad Retirement Board administers comprehensive retirement-survivor and unemployment-sickness benefit programs for the Nation's railroad workers and their families, under the Railroad Retirement and Railroad Unemployment Insurance Acts.

The Railroad Retirement Board administers the Railroad Retirement and Railroad Unemployment Insurance Acts and participates in the administration of the Social Security Act and the Health Insurance for the Aged Act insofar as they affect railroad retirement beneficiaries.

The Board derives statutory authority from the Railroad Retirement Act of 1974 (45 U.S.C. 231–231v) and the Railroad Unemployment Insurance Act (45 U.S.C. 351–368).

The Board is composed of three members appointed by the President with the advice and consent of the Senate—one upon recommendations of representatives of employees; one upon recommendations of carriers; and one, the Chairman, as a public member.

Field Organization The Board maintains field offices located in centers of railroad population that are grouped into regions.

Regional Offices—Railroad Retirement Board

City/Address	Director
Atlanta, GA (Suite 2304, 101 Marietta St., 30323)	(Vacancy)
Cleveland, OH (Rm. 493, 1240 E. 9th St., 44199)	Kevin B. McCrone
Kansas City, MO (Rm. 257, 601 E. 12th St., 64106)	Daniel H. Hauser
Philadelphia, PA (Suite 670, 1421 Cherry St., 19102)	Richard D. Baird
San Francisco, CA (Rm. 370, 211 Main St., 94105)	William W. Robe

Activities

The Railroad Retirement Act provides for the payment of annuities to individuals who have completed at least 10 years of creditable service and have ceased compensated service upon their attainment of specified ages, or at any age if permanently disabled for all employment. In some circumstances occupational disability annuities or supplemental annuities are provided for longer term or career employees.

A spouse's annuity is provided, under certain conditions, for the wife or husband of an employee annuitant. Divorced spouses may also qualify.

Survivor annuities are awarded to the qualified spouses, children, and parents of deceased career employees. Various lump-sum benefits are also provided under certain conditions.

Benefits are provided under the Railroad Unemployment Insurance Act to individuals who are unemployed in a benefit year, but who are ready and willing to work, and to individuals who are unable to work because of sickness or injury, based on qualifying railroad earnings in a preceding one-year period.

The Board maintains, through its field offices, a placement service for unemployed railroad personnel.

Sources of Information

Employment Inquiries and applications for employment should be directed to the Director of Personnel, Railroad Retirement Board, 844 Rush Street, Chicago, IL 60611.

Publications The Board provides general information pamphlets on its benefit programs. Inquiries should be directed to the Director of Public Affairs at the above address.

Telecommunications Devices for the Deaf (TDD) The Board provides TDD

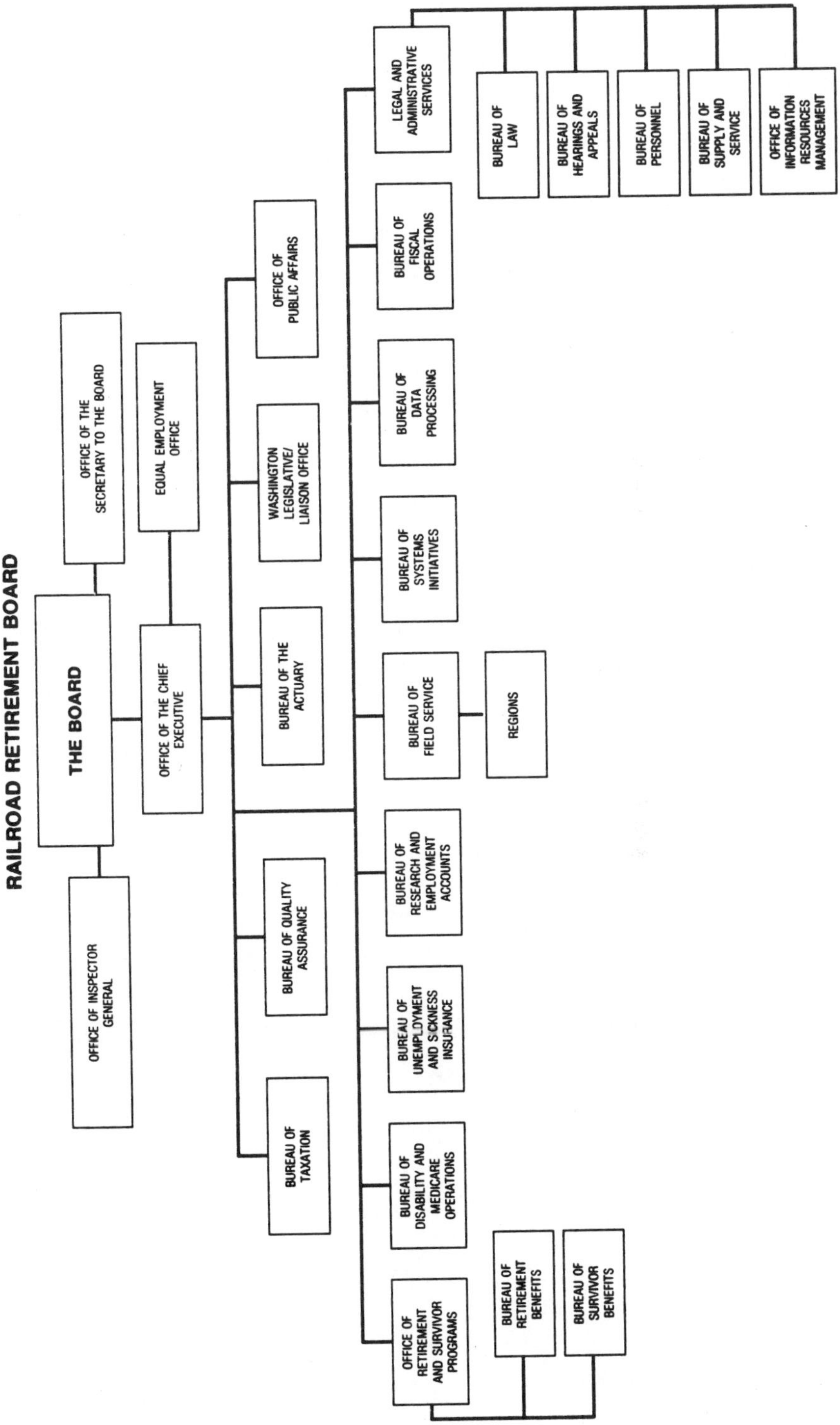
RAILROAD RETIREMENT BOARD
THE BOARD
OFFICE OF THE SECRETARY TO THE BOARD
OFFICE OF INSPECTOR GENERAL
EQUAL EMPLOYMENT OFFICE
OFFICE OF THE CHIEF EXECUTIVE
OFFICE OF PUBLIC AFFAIRS
WASHINGTON LEGISLATIVE/ LIAISON OFFICE
BUREAU OF THE ACTUARY
BUREAU OF QUALITY ASSURANCE
BUREAU OF TAXATION
LEGAL AND ADMINISTRATIVE SERVICES
BUREAU OF LAW
BUREAU OF HEARINGS AND APPEALS
BUREAU OF PERSONNEL
BUREAU OF SUPPLY AND SERVICE
OFFICE OF INFORMATION RESOURCES MANAGEMENT
BUREAU OF FISCAL OPERATIONS
BUREAU OF DATA PROCESSING
BUREAU OF SYSTEMS INITIATIVES
BUREAU OF FIELD SERVICE
REGIONS
BUREAU OF RESEARCH AND EMPLOYMENT ACCOUNTS
BUREAU OF UNEMPLOYMENT AND SICKNESS INSURANCE
BUREAU OF DISABILITY AND MEDICARE OPERATIONS
OFFICE OF RETIREMENT AND SURVIVOR PROGRAMS
BUREAU OF RETIREMENT BENEFITS
BUREAU OF SURVIVOR BENEFITS

services from 9 a.m. to 3:30 p.m. (CST/CDT) daily. Beneficiary inquiries: phone, 312-751-4701; FTS, 386-4701.

Employment inquiries: phone, 312-751-4334; FTS, 386-4334.

For further information, contact the Chief Executive Officer, Railroad Retirement Board, 844 Rush Street, Chicago, IL 60611. Phone, 312-751-4930.

RESOLUTION TRUST CORPORATION

801 Seventeenth Street NW., Washington, DC 20434
Phone, 202-416-6900

Chairperson	L. WILLIAM SEIDMAN
Directors:	
(Comptroller of the Currency)	ROBERT L. CLARKE
(Director of the Office of Thrift Supervision)	T. TIMOTHY RYAN, JR.
(Independent Members)	C.C. HOPE, JR.
	ANDREW C. (SKIP) HOVE, JR.
Executive Director	DAVID C. COOKE

The Resolution Trust Corporation was established to manage and resolve failed savings associations that were insured by the Federal Savings and Loan Insurance Corporation before the enactment of the Financial Institutions Reform, Recovery, and Enforcement Act of 1989, and for which a conservator or receiver is appointed between January 1, 1989, and August 9, 1992.

The Resolution Trust Corporation (Corporation) was established on August 9, 1989, by the Financial Institutions Reform, Recovery, and Enforcement Act of 1989 (12 U.S.C. 1441a). The Corporation will terminate all functions no later than December 31, 1996.

The Corporation is an agency of the United States for purposes of subchapter II, chapters 5 and 7, of title 5 of the United States Code, when it is acting as a corporation. When the Corporation is acting as a conservator or receiver of an insured depository institution, it is deemed to be a Federal agency to the same extent as the Federal Deposit Insurance Corporation when acting in the same capacity.

The Corporation is a mixed-ownership Government corporation for purposes of 31 U.S.C. 9105, 9107, and 9108, notwithstanding the fact that no Federal funds are permitted to be invested in the Corporation.

The Board of Directors and the Chairman of the Federal Deposit Insurance Corporation serve as the Board of Directors and Chairperson of the Resolution Trust Corporation. The Corporation has no employees of its own, but the Federal Deposit Insurance Corporation is authorized to perform all the responsibilities of the Corporation.

Under the general supervision of the Oversight Board and through the Federal Deposit Insurance Corporation, the duties of the Corporation include:

—managing and resolving all cases involving depository institutions, the accounts of which were insured by the former Federal Savings and Loan Insurance Corporation prior to August 9, 1989, and which have been or will be in conservatorship or receivership as of January 1, 1989, through August 9, 1992;

RESOLUTION TRUST CORPORATION

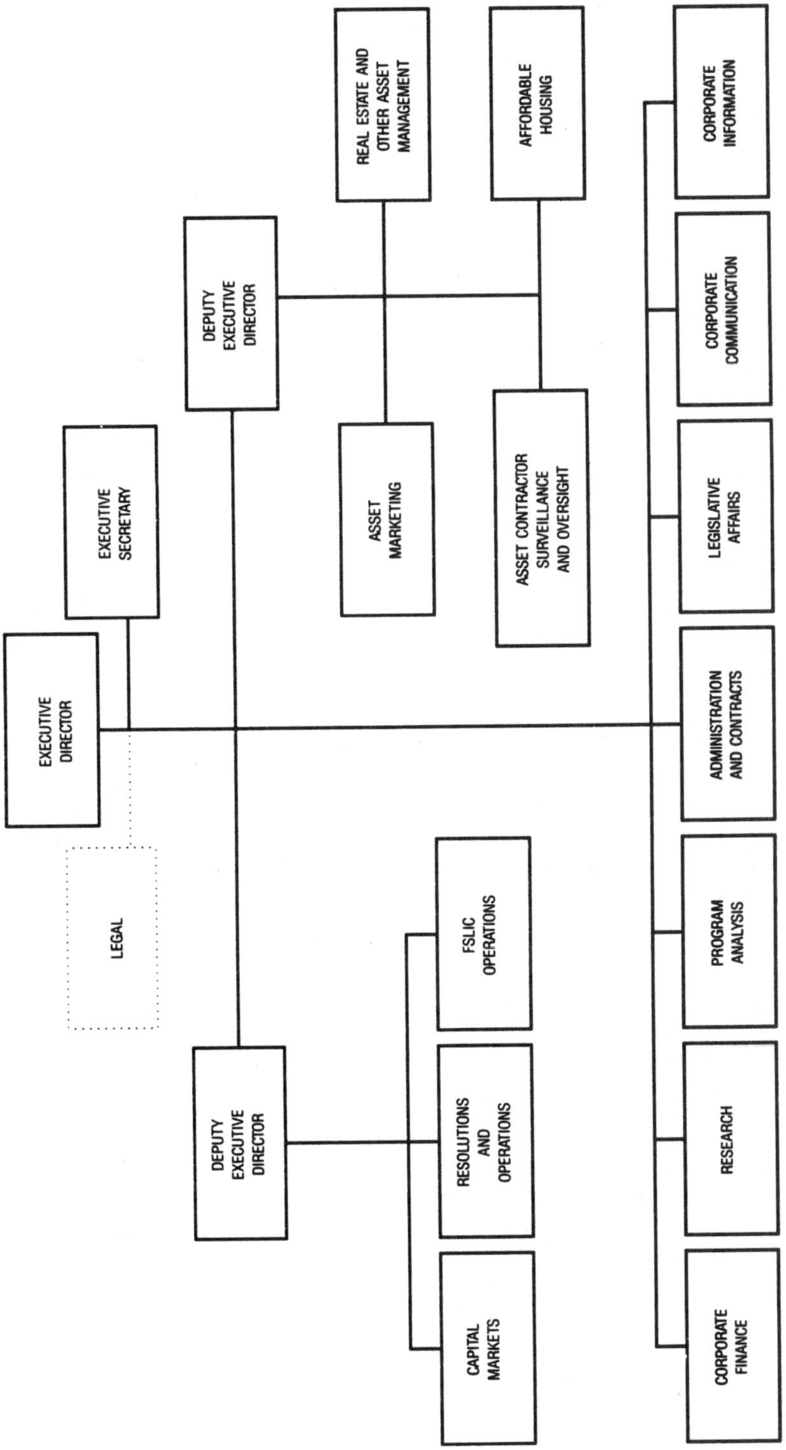

—conducting the operations of the Corporation in such a way as to maximize the return of value from the sale or other disposition of depository institutions or their assets, while minimizing the impact on real estate and financial markets and minimizing losses to the Government;

—making efficient use of funds provided by the Resolution Funding Corporation or the Treasury; and

—maximizing the availability and affordability of residential real property for low- and moderate-income individuals.

For further information, contact the Corporate Communications Office, Resolution Trust Corporation, 801 Seventeenth Street NW., Washington, DC 20434. Phone, 202-416-7557.

SECURITIES AND EXCHANGE COMMISSION

450 Fifth Street NW., Washington, DC 20549
Phone, 202-272-3100

Chairman	Richard C. Breeden
Commissioners	Edward H. Fleischman
	Mary L. Schapiro
	Richard Y. Roberts
	(vacancy)
Secretary	Jonathan G. Katz
Executive Director	James M. McConnell
Deputy Executive Director	Kenneth A. Fogash
Executive Assistant to the Chairman	Barbara J. Green
General Counsel	James R. Doty
Director, Division of Corporation Finance	Linda C. Quinn
Director, Division of Enforcement	William R. McLucas
Director, Division of Investment Management	Marianne K. Smythe
Director, Division of Market Regulation	William H. Heyman
Chief Accountant	(vacancy)
Chief Administrative Law Judge	Warren E. Blair
Comptroller	Lawrence H. Haynes
Director, Office of Information Systems Management	Gregory W. Jones, Sr.
Chief Economist	(vacancy)
Deputy Chief Economist	Jeffry L. Davis
Director, Office of International Affairs	Michael D. Mann
Director, Personnel	John Innocenti
Director, Office of Public Affairs	Mary M. McCue
Director, Office of Administrative Services	Richard J. Kanyan
Director, Office of Filings, Information and Consumer Services	Wilson A. Butler
Director, Office of Legislative Affairs	Kathryn Fulton
Director, Office of EDGAR Management	John O. Penhollow
Inspector General	Walter Stachnik

[For the Securities and Exchange Commission statement of organization, see the *Code of Federal Regulations*, Title 17, Part 200]

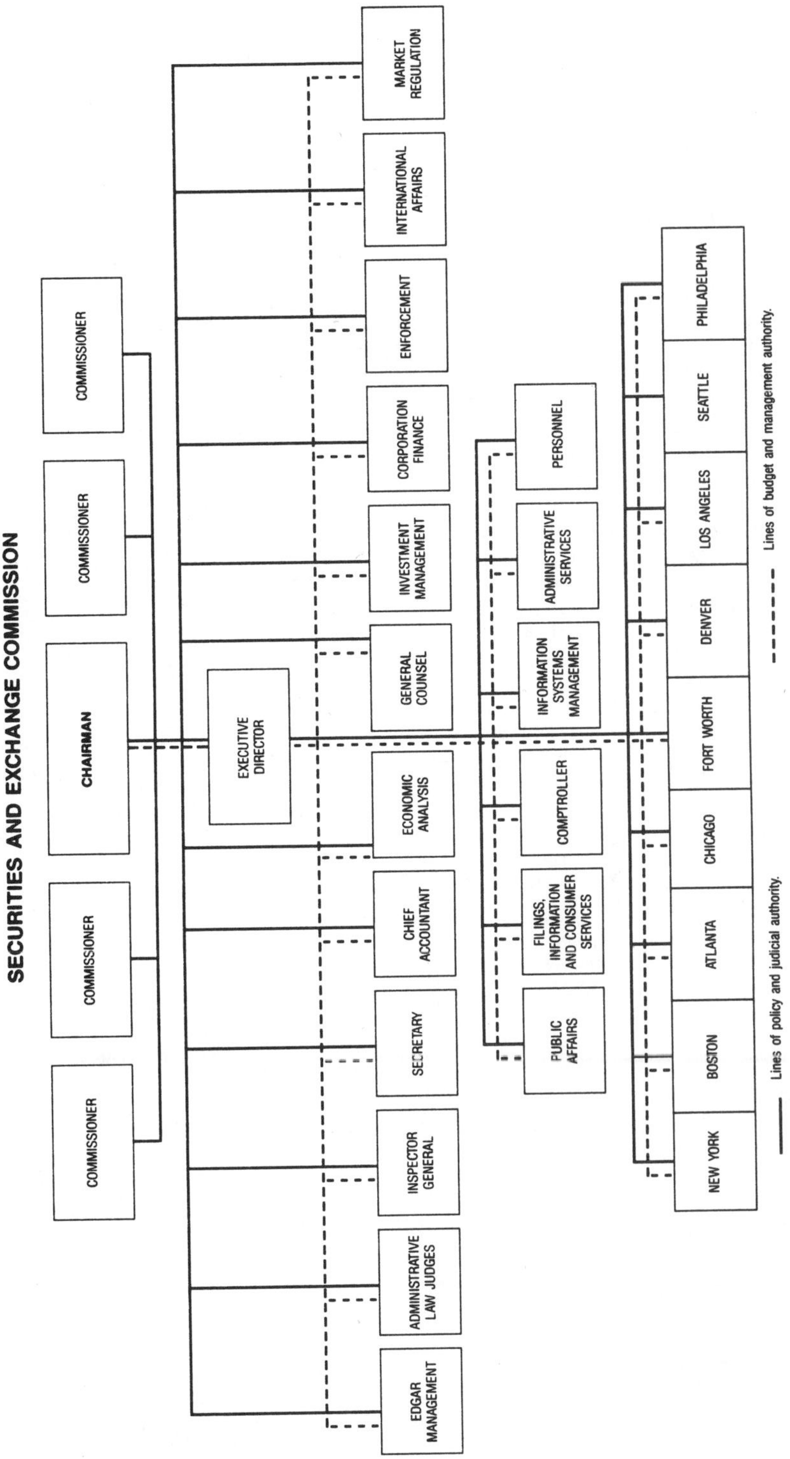
SECURITIES AND EXCHANGE COMMISSION
COMMISSIONER
COMMISSIONER
CHAIRMAN
COMMISSIONER
COMMISSIONER
EXECUTIVE DIRECTOR
MARKET REGULATION
INTERNATIONAL AFFAIRS
ENFORCEMENT
CORPORATION FINANCE
INVESTMENT MANAGEMENT
GENERAL COUNSEL
ECONOMIC ANALYSIS
CHIEF ACCOUNTANT
SECRETARY
INSPECTOR GENERAL
ADMINISTRATIVE LAW JUDGES
EDGAR MANAGEMENT
PERSONNEL
ADMINISTRATIVE SERVICES
INFORMATION SYSTEMS MANAGEMENT
COMPTROLLER
FILINGS, INFORMATION AND CONSUMER SERVICES
PUBLIC AFFAIRS
PHILADELPHIA
SEATTLE
LOS ANGELES
DENVER
FORT WORTH
CHICAGO
ATLANTA
BOSTON
NEW YORK
Lines of budget and management authority.
Lines of policy and judicial authority.

The Securities and Exchange Commission administers Federal securities laws that seek to provide protection for investors; to ensure that securities markets are fair and honest; and, when necessary, to provide the means to enforce securities laws through sanctions.

The Securities and Exchange Commission was created under authority of the Securities Exchange Act of 1934 (15 U.S.C. 78a–78jj) and was organized on July 2, 1934. The Commission serves as adviser to United States district courts in connection with reorganization proceedings for debtor corporations in which there is a substantial public interest. The Commission also has certain responsibilities under section 15 of the Bretton Woods Agreements Act of 1945 (22 U.S.C. 286k–1) and section 851(e) of the Internal Revenue Code of 1954 (26 U.S.C. 851(e)).

The Commission is vested with quasi-judicial functions. Persons aggrieved by its decisions in the exercise of those functions have a right of review by the United States Courts of Appeals.

Activities

Full and Fair Disclosure The Securities Act of 1933 (15 U.S.C. 77a) requires issuers of securities and their controlling persons making public offerings of securities in interstate commerce or through the mails, directly or by others on their behalf, to file with the Commission registration statements containing financial and other pertinent data about the issuer and the securities being offered. It is unlawful to sell such securities unless a registration statement is in effect. There are limited exemptions, such as Government securities, nonpublic offerings, and intrastate offerings, as well as certain offerings not exceeding $1,500,000. The effectiveness of a registration statement may be refused or suspended after a public hearing if the statement contains material misstatements or omissions, thus barring sale of the securities until it is appropriately amended.

Registration of securities does not imply approval of the issue by the Commission or that the Commission has found the registration disclosures to be accurate. It does not insure investors against loss in their purchase, but serves rather to provide information upon which investors may make an informed and realistic evaluation of the worth of the securities.

Persons responsible for filing false information with the Commission subject themselves to the risk of fine or imprisonment or both, and persons connected with the public offering may be liable in damages to purchasers of the securities if the disclosures in the registration statement and prospectus are materially defective. Also, the above act contains antifraud provisions that apply generally to the sale of securities, whether or not registered (15 U.S.C. 77a *et seq.*).

Regulation of Securities Markets The Securities Exchange Act of 1934 assigns to the Commission broad regulatory responsibilities over the securities markets, the self-regulatory organizations within the securities industry, and persons conducting a business in securities. Persons who execute transactions in securities generally are required to register with the Commission as broker-dealers. Securities exchanges and certain clearing agencies are required to register with the Commission, and associations of brokers or dealers are permitted to register with the Commission. The act also provides for the establishment of the Municipal Securities Rulemaking Board to formulate rules for the municipal securities industry.

The Commission oversees the self-regulatory activities of the national securities exchanges and associations, registered clearing agencies, and the Municipal Securities Rulemaking Board. In addition, the Commission regulates industry professionals, such as securities brokers and dealers, certain municipal securities professionals, government securities brokers and dealers, and transfer agents.

The act authorizes national securities exchanges, national securities associations, clearing agencies, and the Municipal Securities Rulemaking Board to adopt rules that are designed, among other things, to promote just and equitable principles of trade and to protect investors. The Commission is required to approve or disapprove most proposed rules of these self-regulatory organizations and has the power to abrogate or amend existing rules of the national securities exchanges, national securities associations, and the Municipal Securities Rulemaking Board.

In addition, the Commission has broad rulemaking authority over the activities of brokers, dealers, municipal securities dealers, securities information processors, and transfer agents. The Commission may regulate such securities trading practices as short sales and stabilizing transactions. It may regulate the trading of options on national securities exchanges and the activities of members of exchanges who trade on the trading floors. The Commission may adopt rules governing broker-dealer sales practices in dealing with investors. The Commission also is authorized to adopt rules concerning the financial responsibility of brokers and dealers and reports made by them.

The act also requires the filing of registration statements and annual and other reports with national securities exchanges and the Commission by companies whose securities are listed upon the exchanges, and by companies that have assets of $5 million or more and 500 or more shareholders of record. In addition, companies that distributed securities pursuant to a registration statement declared effective by the Commission under the Securities Act of 1933 must also file annual and other reports with the Commission. Such applications and reports must contain financial and other data prescribed by the Commission as necessary or appropriate for the protection of investors and to ensure fair dealing. In addition, the solicitation of proxies, authorizations, or consents from holders of such registered securities must be made in accordance with rules and regulations prescribed by the Commission. These rules provide for disclosures to securities holders of information relevant to the subject matter of the solicitation.

Disclosure of the holdings and transactions by officers, directors, and large (10-percent) holders of equity securities of companies also is required, and any and all persons who acquire more than 5 percent of certain equity securities are required to file detailed information with the Commission and any exchange upon which such securities may be traded. Moreover, any person making a tender offer for certain classes of equity securities is required to file reports with the Commission if, as a result of the tender offer, such person would own more than 5 percent of the outstanding shares of the particular class of equity security involved. The Commission also is authorized to promulgate rules governing the repurchase by a corporate issuer of its own securities.

Regulation of Mutual Funds and Other Investment Companies The Investment Company Act of 1940 (15 U.S.C. 80a-1—80a-64) requires investment companies to register with the Commission and regulates their activities to protect investors. The regulation covers sales load, management contracts, composition of boards of directors, and capital structure.

The act prohibits investment companies from engaging in various transactions, including transactions with affiliated persons, unless the Commission first determines that such transactions are fair. In addition, the act provides a somewhat parallel but less stringent regulation of business development companies.

Under the act, the Commission may institute court action to enjoin the consummation of mergers and other plans of reorganization of investment companies if such plans are unfair to security holders. It also may impose sanctions by administrative proceedings against investment company management for violations of the act and other Federal securities laws and file court actions to enjoin acts and practices of management officials involving breaches of fiduciary duty and personal misconduct and to disqualify such officials from office.

Regulation of Companies Controlling Utilities The Public Utility Holding Company Act of 1935 (15 U.S.C. 79—79z-6) provides for regulation by the Commission of the purchase and sale of securities and assets by companies in electric and gas utility holding company systems, their intrasystem transactions and service and management arrangements. It limits holding companies to a single coordinated utility system and requires simplification of complex corporate and capital structures and elimination of unfair distribution of voting power among holders of system securities.

The issuance and sale of securities by holding companies and their subsidiaries, unless exempt (subject to conditions and terms that the Commission is empowered to impose) as an issue expressly authorized by the State commission in the State in which the issuer is incorporated, must be found by the Commission to meet certain statutory standards.

The purchase and sale of utility properties and other assets may not be made in contravention of rules, regulations, or orders of the Commission regarding the consideration to be received, maintenance of competitive conditions, fees and commissions, accounts, disclosure of interest, and similar matters. In passing upon proposals for reorganization, merger, or consolidation, the Commission must be satisfied that the objectives of the act generally are complied with and that the terms of the proposal are fair and equitable to all classes of security holders affected.

Regulation of Investment Advisers The Investment Advisers Act of 1940 (15 U.S.C. 80b-1—80b-21) provides that persons who, for compensation, engage in the business of advising others with respect to securities must register with the Commission. The act prohibits certain fee arrangements, makes fraudulent or deceptive practices on the part of investment advisers unlawful, and requires, among other things, disclosure of any adverse personal interests the advisers may have in transactions that they effect for clients. The act authorizes the Commission, by rule, to define fraudulent and deceptive practices and prescribe means to prevent those practices.

Rehabilitation of Failing Corporations Chapter 11, section 1109(a), of the Bankruptcy Code (11 U.S.C. 1109) provides for Commission participation as a statutory party in corporate reorganization proceedings administered in Federal courts. The principal functions of the Commission are to protect the interests of public investors involved in such cases through efforts to ensure their adequate representation, and to participate in legal and policy issues that are of concern to public investors generally.

Representation of Debt Securities Holders The interests of purchasers of publicly offered debt securities issued pursuant to trust indentures are safeguarded under the provisions of the Trust Indenture Act of 1939 (15 U.S.C. 77aaa-77bbbb). This act, among other things, requires the exclusion from such indentures of certain types of exculpatory clauses and the inclusion of certain protective provisions. The independence of the indenture trustee, who is a representative of the debt holder, is assured by proscribing certain relationships that might conflict with the proper exercise of his duties (15 U.S.C. 77aaa-77bbbb).

Enforcement Activities The Commission's enforcement activities are designed to secure compliance with the Federal securities laws administered by the Commission and the rules and regulations adopted thereunder. These activities include measures to:

—compel obedience to the disclosure requirements of the registration and other provisions of the acts;

—prevent fraud and deception in the purchase and sale of securities;

—obtain court orders enjoining acts and practices that operate as a fraud upon investors or otherwise violate the laws;

—suspend or revoke the registrations of brokers, dealers, and investment companies and investment advisers who willfully engage in such acts and practices;

—suspend or bar from association persons associated with brokers, dealers, investment companies and investment advisers who have violated any provision of the Federal securities laws; and

—prosecute persons who have engaged in fraudulent activities or other willful violations of those laws.

In addition, attorneys, accountants, and other professionals who violate the securities laws face possible loss of their privilege to practice before the Commission.

To this end, private investigations are conducted into complaints or other indications of securities violations. Evidence thus established of law violations is used in appropriate administrative proceedings to revoke registration or in actions instituted in Federal courts to restrain or enjoin such activities. Where the evidence tends to establish criminal fraud or other willful violation of the securities laws, the facts are referred to the Attorney General for criminal prosecution of the offenders. The Commission may assist in such prosecutions.

Regional Offices—Securities and Exchange Commission

Region	Address	Administrator	Telephone
1. New Jersey, New York	75 Park Pl., New York, NY 10007	(Vacancy)	212-264-1636
2. Connecticut, Maine, Massachusetts, New Hampshire, Rhode Island, Vermont	90 Devonshire St., Boston, MA 02109	Douglas Scarff	617-223-9900
3. Alabama, Georgia, Florida, Louisiana (southeastern portion only), Mississippi, North Carolina, Puerto Rico, South Carolina, Tennessee, Virgin Islands	1375 Peachtree St. NE., Atlanta, GA 30367	Richard P. Wessel	404-347-4768
4. Illinois, Indiana, Iowa, Kentucky, Michigan, Minnesota, Missouri, Ohio, Wisconsin	219 S. Dearborn St., Chicago, IL 60604	William D. Goldsberry	312-353-7390
5. Arkansas, Kansas, Louisiana (except southeastern portion), Oklahoma, Texas	411 W. 7th St., Fort Worth, TX 76102	T. Christopher Browne	817-334-3821
6. Colorado, Nebraska, New Mexico, North Dakota, South Dakota, Utah, Wyoming	410 17th St., Denver, CO 80202	Robert H. Davenport	303-844-2071
7. Arizona, California, Guam, Hawaii, Nevada	5757 Wilshire Blvd., Los Angeles, CA 90036	(Vacancy)	213-965-3998
8. Alaska, Idaho, Montana, Oregon, Washington	915 2d Ave., Seattle, WA 98174	Jack H. Bookey	206-442-7990
9. Delaware, District of Columbia, Maryland, Pennsylvania, Virginia, West Virginia	601 Walnut St., Philadelphia, PA 19106	James C. Kennedy	215-597-3100

Sources of Information

Inquiries regarding the following matters should be directed to the appropriate office, Securities and Exchange Commission, 450 Fifth Street NW., Washington, DC 20549.

Consumer Activities Publications detailing the Commission's activities, which include material of assistance to the potential investor, are available from the Publications Unit. In addition, the Office of Filings, Information and Consumer Services answers questions from investors, assists investors with specific problems regarding their relations with broker-dealers and companies, and advises the Commission and other offices and divisions regarding problems frequently encountered by investors and possible regulatory solutions to such problems. Phone, 202-272-7440.

Contracts Contact the Office of Administrative Services. Phone, 202–272–7000.

Employment With the exception of the attorney category, positions are in the competitive civil service and are filled generally by selection from lists of eligibles established as a result of appropriate civil service examinations. The Commission operates a college and law school recruitment program, including on-campus visitations for interview purposes. Inquiries should be directed to the Director of Personnel. Phone, 202–272–2519.

Investor Information and Protection Complaints and inquiries may be directed to the home office or to any regional or branch office. Registration statements and other public documents filed with the Commission are available for public inspection in the public reference room at the home office. Much of the information also is available at the New York and Chicago regional offices. Copies of the public material may be purchased from the Commission's contract copying service at prescribed rates.

Publications *Official Summary*—A monthly summary of securities transactions and holding of officers, directors, and principal stockholders ($69.00 per year) is available through the Superintendent of Documents, Government Printing Office, Washington, DC 20402.

Reading Rooms The Commission maintains a public reference room (phone, 202–272–7450) and also a library (phone, 202–272–2618) where additional information may be obtained.

Small Business Activities Information on security laws that pertain to small businesses in relation to securities offerings may be obtained from the Commission. Phone, 202–272–2644.

For further information, contact the Office of Public Affairs, Securities and Exchange Commission, 450 Fifth Street NW., Washington, DC 20549. Phone, 202–272–2650.

SELECTIVE SERVICE SYSTEM

National Headquarters, Washington, DC 20435
Phone, 202–724–0820

Director	Robert W. Gambino
Deputy Director	Cipriano F. Guerra, Jr.
Executive Director	H.W. Walls
General Counsel	Henry N. Williams
Inspector General	Donna L. Bahls
Associate Director for Operations	Richard S. Flahavan
Associate Director for Information Management	Kenneth L. Johnsen
Associate Director for Resource Management	Ronald E. Redmon
Assistant Director for Congressional and Intergovernmental Affairs	John S. Rivers
Assistant Director for Public Affairs	Lewis C. Brodsky
Controller	G. Huntington Banister

[For the Selective Service System statement of organization, see the *Code of Federal Regulations,* Title 32, Part 1605]

SELECTIVE SERVICE SYSTEM

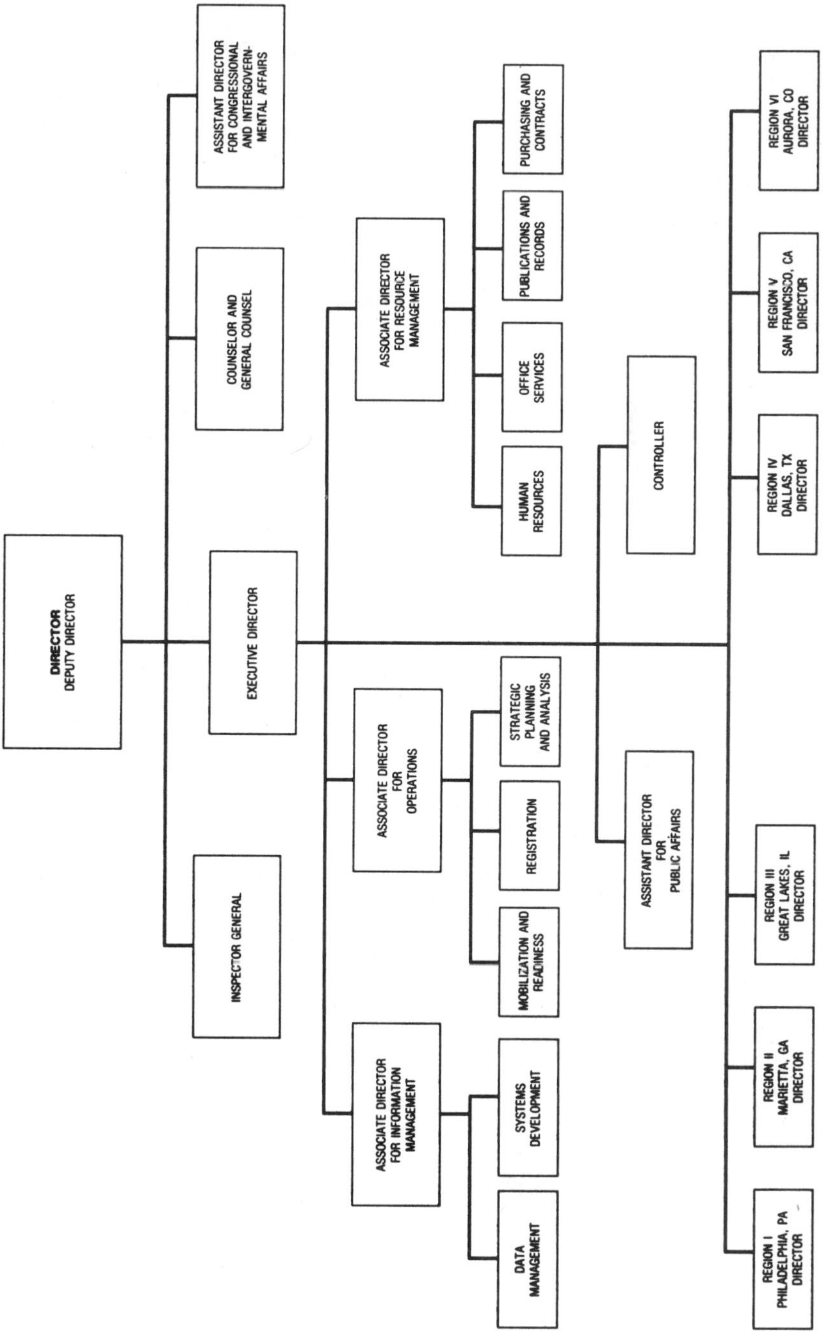

The purpose of the Selective Service System is to be prepared to supply to the Armed Forces human resources adequate to ensure the security of the United States, with concomitant regard for the maintenance of an effective national economy.

The Selective Service System was established by the Military Selective Service Act (50 U.S.C. app. 451–471a). The act authorizes the registration of male citizens of the United States and all other male persons who are in the United States and who are between the ages of 18 to 26 years. The act exempts members of the active Armed Forces and foreign diplomatic and consular personnel from registration and liability for training and service. Likewise exempted are nonimmigrant aliens. Proclamation 4771 of July 2, 1980, requires male persons born after January 1, 1960, and who have attained age 18 to register. Registration is conducted at post offices within the United States and at United States Embassies and consulates outside the United States.

The act imposes liability for training and service in the Armed Forces upon registrants who are between the ages of 18½ to 26 years, except those who are exempted or deferred. Persons who have been deferred remain liable for training and service until age 35. Aliens are not liable for training and service until they have remained in the United States for more than 1 year. Conscientious objectors who are found to be opposed to any service in the Armed Forces are required to perform civilian work in lieu of induction into the Armed Forces.

The authority to induct registrants, including doctors and allied medical specialists, expired July 1, 1973.

Regional Offices—Selective Service System

Region/Address	Telephone
I. Philadelphia, PA (Rm. 207, Bldg. 75, U.S. Navy Base, 19112)	215-897-6653
II. Marietta, GA (Rm. 118A, 805 Walker St., 30060)	404-590-6602
III. Great Lakes, IL (Bldg. 1, 60088)	708-688-4540
IV. Dallas, TX (1st Fl., Bldg. 1239, Naval Air Station, 75211)	214-266-6713
V. San Francisco, CA (Rm. 160, Bldg. 7, Treasure Island, 94130)	415-556-3411
VI. Aurora, CO (Bldg. T-318, Fitzsimons Army Medical Ctr., Harlow St., 80045)	303-361-8155

Sources of Information

Employment Inquiries and applications should be directed to the Director, Selective Service System, Attn: RMH, Washington, DC 20435. Phone, 202-724-0435.

Procurement Inquiries should be directed to the Director, Selective Service System, Attn: RMC, Washington, DC 20435. Phone, 202-724-0731.

Publications Selective Service Regulations appear in chapter XVI of title 32 of the *Code of Federal Regulations.*

Requirements of Law Persons desiring information concerning the requirements of the Military Selective Service Act should contact the National Headquarters of the Selective Service System.

For further information, contact the Office of Public Affairs, Selective Service System, Washington, DC 20435. Phone, 202-724-0790.

SMALL BUSINESS ADMINISTRATION

409 Third Street SW., Washington, DC 20416

Phones: Personnel locator, 202–205–6600; Answer desk, 800–U–ASK–SBA (toll-free); Fraud-waste, 202–205–7151

Administrator	PATRICIA F. SAIKI
Deputy Administrator	JUNE NICHOLS, *Acting*
Chief of Staff	SANDRA L. ULSAKER
Chief Counsel for Advocacy	MARK S. HAYWARD, *Acting*
Inspector General	JAMES F. HOOBLER
General Counsel	SALLY B. NAREY
Assistant Administrator for Congressional and Legislative Affairs	MICHAEL P. FORBES
Assistant Administrator for Public Communications	MARY M. CRAWFORD
Assistant Administrator for Hearings and Appeals	JOHN H. BARNETT
Associate Administrator for Management and Administration	FRANK M. RAMOS
Assistant Administrator for Information Resources Management	LAWRENCE E. BARRETT
Director, Equal Employment Opportunity and Compliance	GEORGE H. ROBINSON
Director of Personnel	RICHARD L. OSBOURN
Director, Program Analysis and Quality Assurance	JAMES P. GALLOGLY, *Acting*
Comptroller	LAWRENCE R. ROSENBAUM
Assistant Administrator for Administration	JEANNE M. SCLATER, *Acting*
Associate Deputy Administrator for Special Programs	CATHERINE S. MARSCHALL
Associate Administrator for Business Development	(VACANCY)
Director, Veterans Affairs	LEON J. BECHET
Director, Women's Business Ownership	LINDSEY L. JOHNSON
Director, Private Sector Initiatives	DAVID J. KIRKER
Director, International Trade	ANTONY KORENSTEIN
Director, National Advisory Councils Staff	JEAN M. NOWAK
Associate Administrator for Small Business Development Centers	JOHNNIE L. ALBERTSON
Assistant Administrator for Innovation, Research and Technology	RICHARD J. SHANE
Associate Deputy Administrator for Finance, Investment and Procurement	(VACANCY)
Assistant Administrator for Financial Assistance	CHARLES R. HERTZBERG
Assistant Administrator for Disaster Assistance	ALFRED E. JUDD
Associate Administrator for Investment	BERNARD KULIK, *Acting*
Assistant Administrator for Surety Guarantees	DOROTHY D. KLEESCHULTE
Associate Administrator for Procurement Assistance	ROBERT J. MOFFITT

Associate Administrator for Minority Small Business and Capital Ownership Development	(VACANCY)

[For the Small Business Administration statement of organization, see the *Code of Federal Regulations,* Title 13, Part 101]

The fundamental purposes of the Small Business Administration are to aid, counsel, assist, and protect the interests of small business; ensure that small business concerns receive a fair portion of Government purchases, contracts, and subcontracts, as well as of the sales of Government property; make loans to small business concerns, State and local development companies, and the victims of floods or other catastrophes, or of certain types of economic injury; and license, regulate, and make loans to small business investment companies.

The Small Business Administration (SBA) was created by the Small Business Act of 1953 and derives its present existence and authority from the Small Business Act (15 U.S.C. 631 *et seq.*). It also derives its authority from the Small Business Investment Act of 1958 (15 U.S.C. 661). The Secretary of Commerce has delegated to the Administration certain responsibilities and functions under section 202 of the Public Works and Economic Development Act of 1965 (42 U.S.C. 3142) and is further authorized to delegate to the Administrator certain responsibilities and functions under chapter 3 of the Trade Act of 1974 (19 U.S.C. 2101).

Activities

Financial Assistance The Administration provides guaranteed, direct, or immediate participation loans to small business concerns to help them finance plant construction, conversion, or expansion; and acquire equipment, facilities, machinery, supplies, or materials. It also provides them with working capital. Since enactment of the act of June 4, 1976 (90 Stat. 663), farming enterprises are included within the term "small business concerns."

The Administration is authorized to make direct loans to handicapped individuals and nonprofit organizations employing the handicapped in the production of goods or services. Direct loans are also available to Vietnam and disabled veterans and to eligible section 8(a) contractors. The Administration may provide loans to finance residential or commercial construction or rehabilitation for sale; loans to small business concerns located in urban or rural areas with high proportions of unemployed or low-income individuals or owned by low-income individuals; extensions and revolving lines of credit for export purposes to enable small business concerns to develop foreign markets and obtain pre-export financing; and guarantee loans to qualified employee trusts with respect to small business concerns. The Administration may finance small firms that manufacture, sell, install, service, or develop specific energy measures including engineering, architectural, consulting, or other professional services connected with eligible energy measures.

Under provisions of sections 501–504 of the Small Business Investment Act (15 U.S.C. 695, 696), loans are made to State and local development companies, which, in turn, assist small business concerns.

For further information, contact the Office of Financial Assistance. Phone, 202–205–6497.

Disaster Assistance The Administration also lends money to help the victims of floods, riots, or other catastrophes repair or replace most disaster-damaged property. Direct loans with subsidized interest rates are made to assist small businesses and small agricultural cooperatives without credit elsewhere that have sustained substantial economic injury resulting from natural disasters.

For further information, contact the Office of Disaster Assistance. Phone, 202–205–6734.

Investment The Administration licenses, regulates, and provides financial assistance to small business investment companies, and section 301(d) licensees (formerly minority enterprise small business investment companies). The sole function of these investment companies is to provide venture capital in the form of equity financing, long-term loan funds, and management services to small business concerns.

For further information, contact the Investment Division. Phone, 202–205–6510.

Surety Bonds Through its Surety Bond Guarantee Program, the Administration helps to make the contract bonding process accessible to small and emerging contractors who find bonding unavailable. It will guarantee to reimburse a qualified surety up to 90 percent of losses incurred under bid, payment, or performance bonds issued to small contractors on contracts valued up to $1.25 million. The contracts may be for construction, supplies, manufacturing, or services provided by either a prime or subcontractor for governmental or nongovernmental work.

For further information, contact the Office of Surety Guarantee. Phone, 202–205–6540.

Procurement Assistance The Administration works closely with purchasing agencies of the Federal Government and with the Nation's leading contractors in developing policies and procedures that will increase the number of contracts going to small business.

The Administration provides a wide range of services to small firms to help them obtain and fulfill Government contracts and subcontracts. It sets aside suitable Government purchases for competitive award to small business concerns and provides an appeal procedure for a low-bidding small firm whose ability to perform a contract is questioned by the contracting officer. The Administration develops subcontract opportunities for small businesses by maintaining close contact with prime contractors and referring qualified small firms to them. It cooperates with Federal agencies in setting procurement goals for small businesses, small disadvantaged businesses, and small women-owned businesses for prime contracts and subcontracts.

The Administration maintains a computerized small business source referral system that provides qualified sources for Federal Government and large business procurements. It cooperates with Government agencies in ensuring that small firms have an opportunity to procure a fair share of Government property, such as timber, royalty oil, strategic materials, and mineral leases, that is sold to the private sector. The Administration also works with Federal agencies to ensure that small firms have a fair opportunity to acquire surplus Government property.

For further information, contact the Office of Procurement Assistance. Phone, 202–205–6460.

Business Development The Administration develops and cosponsors courses and conferences, prepares informational leaflets and booklets, and encourages research into the operations of small business concerns. It counsels and conducts management workshops and courses for established as well as prospective businesspersons, and enlists the volunteer aid of retired and active executives in assisting small businesses with management and technical services. Also, it contracts with college and university schools of business for counseling services by qualified students.

For further information, contact the Office of Business Development. Phone, 202–205–6665.

Minority Small Business Development Sections 7(j) and 8(a) of the Small Business Act provide the authority for the Minority Small Business and Capital Ownership Development Program. The Development Program is a multi-faceted program designed to promote business ownership by socially and economically disadvantaged persons. Its components include the 8(a) program, the 7(j) management and technical assistance program, and the minority outreach program.

Participation in the 8(a) program is available to small businesses that are at least 51 percent unconditionally owned, controlled, and managed by one or more individuals determined by SBA to be socially and economically disadvantaged. In order to gain approval for participation in the 8(a) program, the firms must sell goods and/or services that the Federal Government purchases, and demonstrate the potential for successful business development.

Program participants receive a wide variety of services from SBA including management and technical assistance, loans, and Federal contracts. Under 8(a) program authority, SBA contracts with Federal Government entities to provide goods and services and, in turn, subcontracts the performance of these contracts to 8(a) program participants.

Information regarding the program and 8(a) program applications are provided by SBA's district offices. The Administration's Division of Program Certification and Eligibility addresses issues related to 8(a) program eligibility. The Division of Program Development handles matters related to 8(a) contract awards and the business development of 8(a) participant firms.

Under section 7(j) program authority, SBA provides management and technical assistance to section 8(a) program participants, other socially and economically disadvantaged persons, and those businesses operating in low-income or high-unemployment areas. The Administration enters into cooperative agreements and contracts with qualified organizations and individuals, including businesses, State and local governments, educational institutions, Indian tribes, and nonprofit organizations to provide this assistance. At the local level, services are provided on a one-to-one basis in the areas of bookkeeping and accounting services, production, engineering and technical advice, feasibility studies, marketing analysis and advertising expertise, legal services, and specialized management training. At the regional and national levels, SBA funds innovative programs to provide for services in such areas as transition management for 8(a) firms, competitive marketing strategies, financing, comprehensive business plans, and financial management services. The Administration's Division of Management and Technical Assistance administers the 7(j) program.

The minority outreach program provides a broad range of assistance to firms owned by socially and economically disadvantaged individuals by providing information and networking opportunities through a variety of programs. The Administration has combined its efforts with those of private industry, banks, local communities, and other Federal agencies to provide this assistance. The Administration's outreach efforts include publishing a newsletter, entering into cooperative agreements with major corporations to establish an information network with SBA regarding contracting opportunities for firms owned by disadvantaged individuals. The network would provide an electronic bulletin board to disseminate information about potential Federal and private sector contracting opportunities, and would sponsor numerous events designed to foster business development for economically disadvantaged firms. The Division of Minority Small Business Outreach, working in conjunction with other program divisions, is responsible for the Administration's outreach efforts.

For further information, contact the Office of Minority Small Business and Capital Ownership Development. Phone, 202–205–6410.

Advocacy The Office of Advocacy evaluates the impact on small businesses of legislative proposals and other public policy issues by preparing policy papers and by conducting research having an impact on small business. The Office conducts economic and statistical research into matters affecting the competitive strength of small business. The Office also researches the effect of Federal laws, programs, and regulations on small business and makes recommendations to Federal agencies for appropriate adjustments to meet the needs of small business.

The Chief Counsel for Advocacy is the Government's principal advocate of small business. The Office promotes the position of small business with Federal agencies and State and local governments; maintains liaison with trade and professional organizations; and serves as the major source of information about the Government for small business.

The Chief Counsel for Advocacy has specific responsibilities for monitoring the performance of Federal agencies under the Regulatory Flexibility Act (5 U.S.C. 601) and the patent and trademark laws amendments (35 U.S.C. 301).

For further information, contact the Office of Advocacy. Phone, 202–205–6533.

Women's Business Ownership The Women's Business Ownership Program, with a constituency of more than 4.5 million women business owners generating over $81 billion in gross receipts, was formed to implement a national policy to support women entrepreneurs. It operates under the authority and mandate of Executive Order 12138 of May 18, 1979, and the Small Business Act (15 U.S.C. 631). Its functions are carried out by the Office of Women's Business Ownership and their network of district and regional representatives.

The Office develops and coordinates a national program to increase the strength, profitability, and visibility of women-owned businesses while making maximum use of existing government and private-sector resources. It provides advice, assistance, and support to the Interagency Committee on Women's Business Enterprise in fulfilling its mandate to promote, coordinate, and monitor the efforts of the Federal Government to establish, preserve, and strengthen women-owned businesses. It serves as principal liaison with non-Federal business, educational organizations, and community resources to assist the growth and development of women-owned businesses.

The Office develops and recommends national pilot programs in the private sector to provide training and counseling in the initiation, management, and financing of women-owned businesses. It encourages access to capital formation through trade organizations and management consultants who provide financial education and counseling tailored to the needs of women business owners. The Office seeks out and adapts existing small business skills development programs to the needs of potential and actual women business owners and encourages delivery through existing private-sector organizations, SCORE, ACE, and SBA regional and district offices throughout the country.

The Women's Business Ownership Act of 1988 (15 U.S.C. 631 note) provides $10 million for demonstration projects over a 3-year period and a guaranteed loan program for loans not exceeding $50,000. It also established a National Women's Business Council, whose mission is to submit annual recommendations to the President and Congress on ways to improve opportunities for women-owned businesses, and to develop a long-range strategy for supporting such businesses.

In addition, the Office is responsible for negotiating with Federal agencies to set annual Governmentwide goals to increase Federal prime contracts with women-owned businesses. It is responsible for increasing and monitoring the number of women in the Administration-operated Procurement Automated Source System from which Government agencies and major corporations extract profiles of potential bidders.

To accomplish this mainstreaming approach, the Office cooperates with existing Administration programs to develop, implement, and evaluate all activities to ensure equal access for women business owners.

For further information, contact the Office of Women's Business Ownership. Phone, 202–205–6673.

Veterans Affairs The main objective of the Veterans Affairs program is to advocate for assistance to veterans in business or those who wish to start businesses. The Office of Veterans Affairs monitors and reviews the Administration's financial, procurement, and management assistance programs for "special consideration" for veterans. These efforts include the development and implementation of procurement and other specialized training, consultant services, and conferences tailored to the special needs of veterans. The Office also maintains liaison with Federal agencies, State and local governments, and private organizations to ensure maximum use of existing programs to assist veterans, and it advocates new and more effective programs to benefit veteran small business.

For further information, contact the Office of Veterans Affairs. Phone, 202–205–6773.

Private-Sector Initiatives The major objective of the private-sector initiatives program is to utilize the private sector to obtain maximum leverage from all programs in achieving agency goals and in meeting the needs of the small business community. The Office of Private Sector Initiatives serves as a focal point within the agency to foster and coordinate those elements of agency programs involving partnership with the private sector. The Office solicits maximum cooperation from State and local government entities in all agency program efforts in order to utilize local initiatives to the fullest and avoid costly duplication. The Office proposes legislative initiatives aimed toward increasing private-sector involvement in small business assistance and other agency programs.

For further information, contact the Office of Private Sector Initiatives. Phone, 202–205–6730.

Innovation, Research and Technology The Office of Innovation, Research and Technology has authority and responsibility for coordinating and monitoring the governmentwide activities of the Small Business Innovation Research Program. In accordance with the Small Business Innovation Development Act of 1982, as amended (15 U.S.C. 631 note), the Office develops and issues policy directives for the general conduct of the programs within the Federal Government and maintains a source file and information program to provide each interested and qualified small business concern with opportunities to compete for program awards. The Office also coordinates with each participating Federal agency in developing a master release schedule of all program solicitations; publishes the *Presolicitation Announcement* quarterly, which contains pertinent facts on upcoming solicitations; and surveys and monitors program operations within the Federal Government and reports on the progress of the program each year to Congress.

The program has four main objectives: to stimulate technology innovation, use small business concerns to meet Federal research and development needs, encourage participation by minority and disadvantaged persons in technological innovation, and increase private-sector commercialization of innovations derived from Federal research and development.

For further information, contact the Office of Innovation, Research and Technology. Phone, 202–205–6450.

International Trade The Office of International Trade develops and recommends agency policy regarding the International Trade Program. To this end, the Office develops plans, operating procedures, and standards to effectively strengthen and improve the agency's International Trade Program for small business; develops new methods and techniques for assisting small businesses entering international markets; and plans, develops, and implements programs to encourage small business participation in international trade. To assure that adequate consideration is given to small business interests in the Federal Government's export expansion program, the Office coordinates the Administration's International Trade Program with the Departments of Commerce and Agriculture, the Export-Import Bank of the United States, the Agency for International Development, and with other Federal and State agencies and private organizations concerned with international trade.

The Office also develops programs in cooperation with operating units of the Department of Commerce and other Federal and State agencies to assure that small businesses will be afforded maximum opportunities and benefits from participation in trade shows, fairs, and missions, and other domestic and overseas export development activities.

For further information, contact the Office of International Trade. Phone, 202–205–6720.

Small Business Development Centers The Office of Small Business Development Centers develops national policies and goals in accordance with the Small Business Development Center Act of 1980 (15 U.S.C. 631 note). It establishes standards for the selection and performance of Centers; develops alternative forms of Centers involving State governmental bodies and private, nonprofit organizations; and implements new approaches to improve operations of existing Centers.

The Office is responsible for coordinating program efforts with other internal activities of the Administration as well as with the activities of other Federal agencies, and maintains liaison with other Federal, State, and local agencies and private organizations whose activities relate to Small Business Development Centers. It also assesses the impact on the program of substantive developments in programs and policies in other areas of the agency, in other government agencies, and in the private sector.

For further information, contact the Office of Small Business Development Centers. Phone, 202–205–6766.

Field Offices—Small Business Administration

(RO: Regional Office; DO: District Office; BO: Branch Office; PD: Post of Duty)

Office	Address	Officer in Charge	Telephone
REGION I			
Augusta, ME (DO)	Rm. 512, 40 Western Ave., 04330	Leroy G. Perry	207–622–8378
Boston, MA (RO)	9th Fl., 155 Federal St., 02110	Mary Brennen Lukens	617–451–2023
Boston, MA (DO)	Rm. 265, 10 Causeway St., 02222-1093	Joseph D. Pelligrino	617–565–5590
Concord, NH (DO)	Rm. 210, 55 Pleasant St., 03302-1257	William K. Phillips	603–225–1400
Hartford, CT (DO)	2d Fl., 330 Main St., 06106	Michael McHale	203–240–4700
Montpelier, VT (DO).	Rm. 205, 87 State St., 05602	Kenneth Silvia	802–828–4474
Providence, RI (DO).	380 Westminister Mall, 02903	Anthony McMahon	401–528–4561
Springfield, MA (BO).	Rm. 212, 1550 Main St., 01103	Harold Webb	413–785–9484
REGION II			
Buffalo, NY (DO)	Rm. 1311, 111 W. Huron St., 14202	Franklin J. Sciortino	716–846–4305
Camden, NJ (PD)	2600 Mt. Ephrain, 08104	Cesar A. Ballester	609–757–4511
Elmira, NY (BO)	333 E. Water St., 14901	James J. Cristofaro	607–734–1571
Hato Rey, PR (DO)	Rm. 691, Federal Bldg., Carlos Chardon Ave., 00918.	Carlos E. Chardon	8–809–766–5003
Melville, NY (BO)	Rm. 102E, 35 Pinelawn Rd., 11747	Walter Leavitt	516–454–0764
New York, NY (RO)	Rm. 31–08, 26 Federal Plz., 10278	Charles Freeman	212–264–1450
New York, NY (DO)	Rm. 3100, 26 Federal Plz., 10278	Bert X. Haggerty	212–264–1318
Newark, NJ (DO)	4th Fl., 60 Park Pl., 07102	Stanley Salt	201–645–3580
Rochester, NY (BO).	Rm. 601, 100 State St., 14614	Peter Filhan	716–263–6700
St. Croix, VI (PD)	Rm. 7, United Shopping Plz., 4C&D State Sion Farm Christiansted, 00820.	Carl Christensen	809–778–5380
St. Thomas, VI (PD).	Rm. 283, Federal Office Bldg., Veterans Dr., 00801	Lionel Baptiste	809–774–8530
Syracuse, NY (DO)	Rm. 1071, 100 S. Clinton St., 13260	J. Wilson Harrison	315–423–5371
REGION III			
Baltimore, MD (DO)	3d Fl., 10 N. Calvert St., 21202	Charles J. Gaston	301–962–2054
Charleston, WV (BO).	Rm. 309, 550 Eagan St., 25301	Edward G. Zimmerman	304–347–5220
Clarksburg, WV (DO).	5th Fl., 168 W. Main St., 26301	Marvin P. Shelton	304–623–4317
Harrisburg, PA (BO)	Rm. 309, 100 Chestnut St., 17101	Kenneth J. Olson	717–782–3846
King of Prussia, PA (RO).	Suite 201, 475 Allendale Rd., 19406	Catherine Killian	215–962–3710
King of Prussia, PA (DO).	Suite 201, 475 Allendale Rd., 19406	Willam T. Gennetti	215–962–3801
Pittsburgh, PA (DO)	5th Fl., 960 Penn Ave., 15222	Joseph M. Kopp	412–644–4306
Richmond, VA (DO)	Rm. 3015, 400 N. 8th St., 23240	Dratin Hill, Jr.	804–771–2741
Washington, DC (DO).	6th Fl., 1111 18th St. NW., 20036	James O. Gordon	202–634–1805

Field Offices—Small Business Administration—Continued

(RO: Regional Office; DO: District Office; BO: Branch Office; PD: Post of Duty)

Office	Address	Officer in Charge	Telephone
Wilkes-Barre, PA (BO).	Rm. 2327, 20 N. Pennsylvania Ave., 18701	Frank H. Hamilton	717-826-6446
Wilmington, DE (BO).	Rm. 412, 920 N. King St., 19801	Fred B. Trescher, Jr	302-573-6295
REGION IV			
Atlanta, GA (RO)	5th Fl., 1375 Peachtree St. NE., 30367	June Nichols	404-347-4999
Atlanta, GA (DO)	6th Fl., 1720 Peachtree Rd. NW., 30309	Wilfred A. Stone	404-347-4749
Birmingham, AL (DO).	Suite 200, 2121 8th Ave. N., 35203	James C. Barksdale	205-731-1341
Charlotte, NC (DO)	Rm. 300, 222 S. Church St., 28202	Gary A. Keel	704-371-6561
Columbia, SC (DO)	Rm. 358, 1835 Assembly St., 29202	Elliott Cooper	803-253-5339
Coral Gables, FL (DO).	Suite 501, 1320 S. Dixie Hwy., 33136	John L. Carey	305-536-5533
Gulfport, MS (BO)	Suite 1001, 1 Hancock Plz., 39501	Charles Gillis	601-863-4449
Jackson, MS (DO)	Suite 322, 101 W. Capitol St., 39269	Jack K. Spradling	601-965-4363
Jacksonville, FL (DO).	Suite 100-B, 7825 Bay Meadows Way, 32202	Thomas Short	904-443-1900
Louisville, KY (DO)	Rm. 188, 600 M.L. King, Jr., Pl., 40202	William Federhofer	502-582-5976
Nashville, TN (DO)	Suite 201, 50 Vantage Way, 37228	Robert M. Hartman	615-736-5850
Statesboro, GA (PD).	Rm. 225, 52 N. Main St., 30458	Ralph T. Clark	912-489-8719
Tampa, FL (PD)	Rm. 607, 700 Twiggs St., 33602	Earl N. Moore	813-228-2594
West Palm Beach, FL (PD).	Suite 402, 5601 Corporate Way, 33407	Roderick Young	305-689-3922
REGION V			
Chicago, IL (RO)	Rm. 510, 230 S. Dearborn St., 60604	Edward Murnane	312-353-0359
Chicago, IL (DO)	Rm. 437, 219 S. Dearborn St., 60604	John L. Smith	312-353-4528
Cincinnati, OH (BO)	Rm. 5028, 550 Main St., 45202	David E. Gray	513-684-2814
Cleveland, OH (DO).	Rm. 317, 1240 E. 9th St., 44199	Norma Nelson	216-522-4180
Columbus, OH (DO).	Rm. 512, 85 Marconi Blvd., 43215	Frank D. Ray	614-469-7310
Detroit, MI (DO)	Rm. 515, 477 Michigan Ave., 48226	Raymond L. Harshman	313-226-7240
Indianapolis, IN (DO).	Rm. 578, 575 N. Pennsylvania St., 46204	Robert D. General	317-226-7275
Madison, WI (DO)	Rm. 213, 212 E. Washington Ave., 53703	Curtis A. Charter	608-264-5268
Marquette, MI (BO)	300 S. Front St.	Paul Jacobson	906-225-1108
Milwaukee, WI (BO)	Suite 400, 310 W. Wisconsin Ave., 53203	(Vacancy)	414-291-1094
Minneapolis, MN (DO).	610-C Butler Sq., 100 N. 6th St., 55403	Edward A. Daum	612-370-2306
Springfield, IL (BO)	Suite 302, 511 W. Capitol St., 62704	D.I. Brookhart	217-492-4232
REGION VI			
Albuquerque, NM (DO).	Suite 320, 5000 Marble Ave. NE., 87110	Tommy W. Dowell	505-262-6339
Austin, TX (PD)	Rm. 520, 300 E. 8th St., 78701	Arvan Holder	512-482-5288
Corpus Christi, TX (BO).	Suite 403, 400 Mann St., 78401	Gail Goodloe	512-888-3301
Dallas, TX (RO)	Bldg. C, 8625 King George Dr., 75235	Lejeune Wilson	214-767-7611
Dallas, TX (DO)	Rm. 3C-36, 1100 Commerce St., 75242	James S. Reed	214-767-0600
El Paso, TX (DO)	Suite 320, 10737 Gateway W., 79935	John Scott	915-540-5676
Fort Worth, TX (BO).	Rm. 10A27, 819 Taylor St., 76102	(Vacancy)	817-334-3673
Harlingen, TX (DO)	Suite 500, 222 E. Van Buren, 78550	Miguel Cavazos	512-427-8533
Houston, TX (DO)	Suite 112, 2525 Murworth, 77054	Rodney Martin	713-660-4401
Little Rock, AR (DO).	Suite 601, 320 W. Capitol Ave., 72201	Donald Libbey	501-378-5277
Lubbock, TX (DO)	Suite 200, 1611 10th St., 79401	Walter Fronstin	806-743-7462
Marshall, TX (PD)	Rm. 103, 500 E. Travis, 75670	George Lewis	214-935-5257
New Orleans, LA (DO).	Suite 2000, 1661 Canal St., 70112	Abby Carter	504-589-2744
Oklahoma City, OK (DO).	Suite 670, 200 NW. 5th St., 73102	(Vacancy)	405-231-5237
San Antonio, TX (DO).	Suite 200, 7400 Blanco Rd., 78216	(Vacancy)	512-229-4501
Shreveport, LA (PD).	Rm. 8A-08, 500 Fannin St., 71101	Bobby Boling	318-226-5196
REGION VII			
Cedar Rapids, IA (DO).	Rm. 100, 373 Collins Rd. NE., 52402	James Thomson	319-399-2571
Des Moines, IA (DO).	Rm. 749, 210 Walnut St., 50309	Conrad E. Lawlor	515-284-4567

Field Offices—Small Business Administration—Continued

(RO: Regional Office; DO: District Office; BO: Branch Office; PD: Post of Duty)

Office	Address	Officer in Charge	Telephone
Kansas City, MO (RO).	13th Fl., 911 Walnut St., 64106	Gary Nodler	816-426-3316
Kansas City, MO (DO).	Suite 501, 323 W. 8th St., 64105	Harold Nossaman	816-374-6760
Omaha, NE (DO)	11145 Mill Valley Rd., 68154	Glenn Davis	402-221-3620
Springfield, MO (BO).	Suite 110, 620 S. Glenstone St., 65802	Dean Cotton	417-864-7670
St. Louis, MO (DO)	Rm. 242, 815 Olive St., 63101	Robert L. Andrews	314-539-6600
Wichita, KS (DO)	1st Fl., 110 E. Waterman St., 67202	Gary Cook	316-269-6566
REGION VIII			
Casper, WY (DO)	Rm. 4001, 100 East B St., 82602	Paul Nemetz	307-261-5761
Denver, CO (RO)	Suite 701, 999 18th St., 80202	Gilbert M. Cisneros	303-294-7021
Denver, CO (DO)	Rm. 407, 721 19th St., 80201	Dratin Hill, Jr.	303-844-6501
Fargo, ND (DO)	Rm. 218, 657 2d Ave. N., 58108	James L. Stai	701-239-5131
Helena, MT (DO)	Rm. 528, 301 S. Park, 59626	John R. Cronholm	406-449-5381
Salt Lake City, UT (DO).	Rm. 2237, 125 S. State St., 84138	Stan Nakano	801-524-5804
Sioux Falls, SD (DO).	Suite 101, 101 S. Main Ave., 57102	Chester Leedom	605-330-4231
REGION IX			
Agana, GU (BO)	Rm. 508, Pacific Daily News Bldg., 96910	Jose M.L. Lujan	671-472-7277
Fresno, CA (DO)	2719 N. Air Fresno Dr., 93727	Peter Bergin	209-487-5791
Honolulu, HI (DO)	Rm. 2213, 300 Ala Moana, 96850	Charles Lum	808-541-2990
Las Vegas, NV (DO).	301 E. Stewart, 89125	Patrick Allison	702-388-6611
Los Angeles, CA (DO).	Suite 1200, 330 N. Brand Blvd., Glendale, 91203	M. Hawley Smith	213-894-2977
Phoenix, AZ (DO)	5th Fl., 2005 N. Central Ave., 85004	James P. Guyer	602-379-3737
Reno, NV (PD)	P.O. Box 3216, Rm. 238, 50 S. Virginia St., 89505	Art Ereckson	702-784-5268
Sacramento, CA (BO).	Suite 215, 660 J St., 95814	Roberta L. Conner	916-551-1445
San Diego, CA (DO).	Suite 4-S-29, 880 Front St., 92188	George P. Chandler, Jr.	619-557-7252
San Francisco, CA (RO).	20th Fl., 71 Stevenson St., 94105	Oscar Wright	415-774-6402
San Francisco, CA (DO).	4th Fl., 211 Main St., 94105	Michael R. Howland	415-744-6801
Santa Ana, CA (DO).	Rm. 160, 901 W. Civic Center Dr.	John S. Waddell	714-836-2494
Tucson, AZ (PD)	Rm. 3V, 300 W. Congress St., 85701	Ivan P. Hankins	602-629-6715
Ventura, CA (PD)	Suite 10, Bldg. C-1, 6477 Telephone Rd., 93003	Teddy Lutz	805-642-1866
REGION X			
Anchorage, AK (DO).	Rm. A36, No. 67, 222 W. 8th Ave., 99501	Frank Cox	907-271-4022
Boise, ID (DO)	Suite 290, 1020 Main St., 83702	(Vacancy)	208-334-9641
Portland, OR (DO)	Suite 500, 220 SW. Columbia St., 97204	John L. Gilman	503-326-5221
Seattle, WA (RO)	Rm. 440, 2615 4th Ave., 98121	Harold E. Wolf	206-553-5534
Seattle, WA (DO)	Rm. 1792, 915 2d Ave., 98174	Robert P. Meredith	206-553-2786
Spokane, WA (DO)	10th Fl. E., W. 601 1st Ave., 99210	Robert Wiebe	509-353-2807

For further information, contact the Office of Public Communications, Small Business Administration, 409 Third Street SW., Washington, DC 20416. Phone, 202-205-6533.

TENNESSEE VALLEY AUTHORITY

400 West Summit Hill Drive, Knoxville, TN 37902
Phone, 615–632–2101

Room 300, 412 First Street SE., Washington, DC 20444–2003
Phone, 202–479–4412

Chairman	MARVIN RUNYON
Directors	JOHN B. WATERS
	WILLIAM H. KENNOY
Vice President and General Counsel	EDWARD S. CHRISTENBURY
Inspector General	NORMAN A. ZIGROSSI
Senior Vice President and Chief Financial Officer	WILLIAM F. MALEC
Vice President, Human Resources	ROBERT E. SCHUETT
Vice President, Minority Resources	TONY CRESWELL
Vice President, Communications	MARY L. CARTWRIGHT
Washington Representative	TOM PRICE
Vice President, Information Services	LOU GRANDE
Vice President, Corporate Architect	(VACANCY)
Senior Vice President, Chief Quality Officer	ROBERT S. STEFFY
President, Resource Group	WILLIAM F. WILLIS
Senior Vice President, National Fertilizer and Environmental Research Center	JOHN T. SHIELDS
President, River Basin Operations	BILLY BOND
Vice President, Valley Resource Center	JOHN G. STEWART
President, Customer Group	MARY SHARP HAYES
Vice President, Transmission	STEVE WHITLEY
Vice President, Customer Planning	JIMMY L. CROSS
President, Generating Group	OLIVER D. KINGSLEY
Senior Vice President, Fossil and Hydro Generations	(VACANCY)
Vice President, Fossil Fuels	JOHN W. THOMPSON
Vice President, Fossil and Hydro Construction Engineering	WILLIAM M. BIVENS
Vice President, Hydro Operations	(VACANCY)
Vice President, Fossil Operations	(VACANCY)

The Tennessee Valley Authority is a Government-owned corporation that conducts a unified program of resource development for the advancement of economic growth in the Tennessee Valley region. The Authority's program of activities includes flood control, navigation development, electric power production, fertilizer development, recreation improvement, and forestry and wildlife development. While its power program is financially self-supporting, other programs are financed primarily by appropriations from Congress.

The Tennessee Valley Authority is a corporation created by act of May 18, 1933 (16 U.S.C. 831–831dd). All functions of the Authority are vested in its Board of Directors, the members of which are appointed by the President with the consent of the Senate. Offices of the Board and General Manager are in Knoxville, TN.

The Authority is wholly owned by the U.S. Government. While its electric power program is required to be

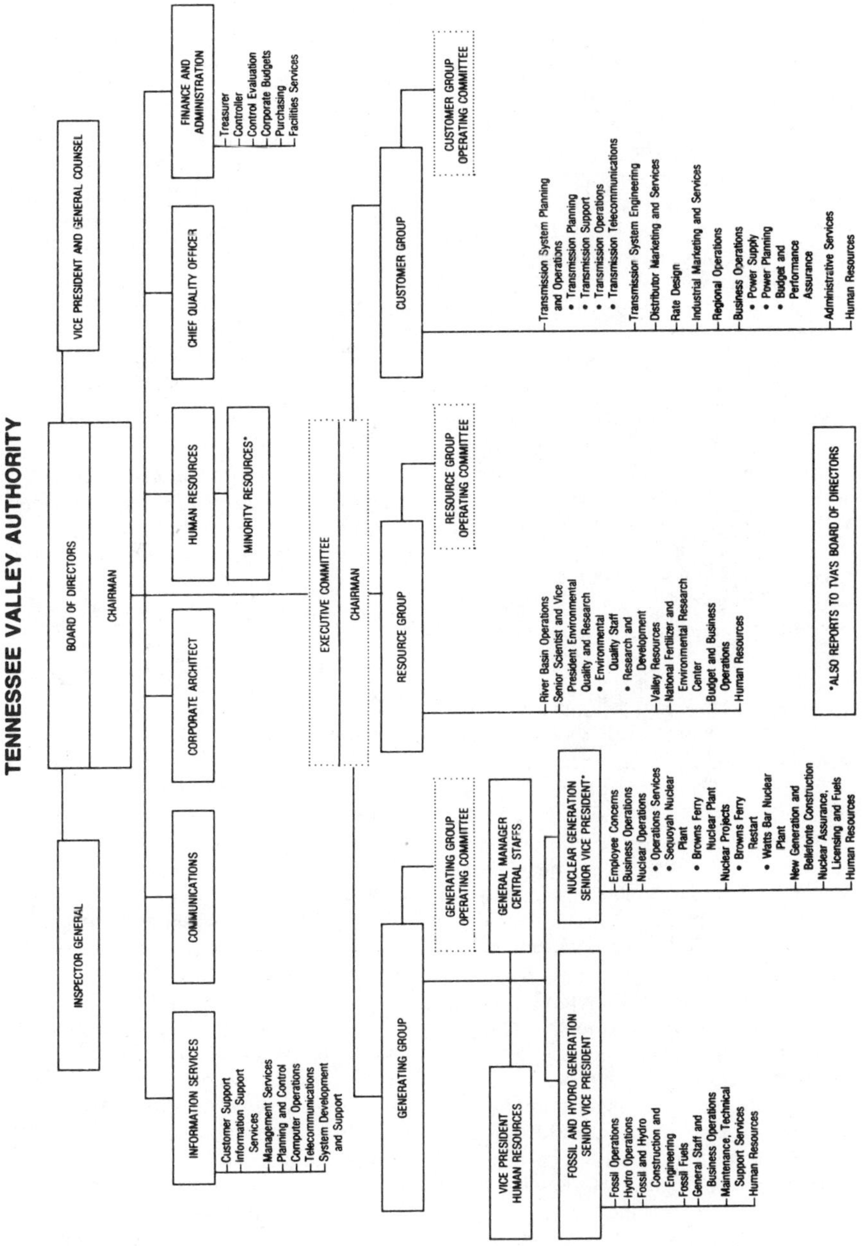
TENNESSEE VALLEY AUTHORITY
BOARD OF DIRECTORS
CHAIRMAN
INSPECTOR GENERAL
VICE PRESIDENT AND GENERAL COUNSEL
INFORMATION SERVICES
Customer Support
Information Support Services
Management Services
Planning and Control
Computer Operations
Telecommunications
System Development and Support
COMMUNICATIONS
CORPORATE ARCHITECT
HUMAN RESOURCES
MINORITY RESOURCES*
CHIEF QUALITY OFFICER
FINANCE AND ADMINISTRATION
Treasurer
Controller
Control Evaluation
Corporate Budgets
Purchasing
Facilities Services
EXECUTIVE COMMITTEE
CHAIRMAN
GENERATING GROUP
GENERATING GROUP OPERATING COMMITTEE
GENERAL MANAGER CENTRAL STAFFS
VICE PRESIDENT HUMAN RESOURCES
FOSSIL AND HYDRO GENERATION SENIOR VICE PRESIDENT
Fossil Operations
Hydro Operations
Fossil and Hydro Construction and Engineering
Fossil Fuels
General Staff and Business Operations
Maintenance, Technical Support Services
Human Resources
NUCLEAR GENERATION SENIOR VICE PRESIDENT*
Employee Concerns
Business Operations
Nuclear Operations
• Operations Services
• Sequoyah Nuclear Plant
• Browns Ferry Nuclear Plant
Nuclear Projects
• Browns Ferry Restart
• Watts Bar Nuclear Plant
New Generation and Bellefonte Construction
Nuclear Assurance, Licensing and Fuels
Human Resources
RESOURCE GROUP
RESOURCE GROUP OPERATING COMMITTEE
River Basin Operations
Senior Scientist and Vice President Environmental Quality and Research
• Environmental Quality Staff
• Research and Development
Valley Resources
National Fertilizer and Environmental Research Center
Budget and Business Operations
Human Resources
CUSTOMER GROUP
CUSTOMER GROUP OPERATING COMMITTEE
Transmission System Planning and Operations
• Transmission Planning
• Transmission Support
• Transmission Operations
• Transmission Telecommunications
Transmission System Engineering
Distributor Marketing and Services
Rate Design
Industrial Marketing and Services
Regional Operations
Business Operations
• Power Supply
• Power Planning
• Budget and Performance Assurance
Administrative Services
Human Resources
*ALSO REPORTS TO TVA'S BOARD OF DIRECTORS

financially self-supporting, other programs are financed primarily by appropriations.

A system of dams built by the Authority on the Tennessee River and its larger tributaries provides flood regulation on the Tennessee and contributes to regulation of the lower Ohio and Mississippi Rivers. The system maintains a continuous 9-foot-draft channel for navigation for the length of the 650-mile Tennessee River main stream, from Paducah, KY, to Knoxville, TN. The dams harness the power of the rivers to produce electricity. They also provide other benefits, including a major asset for outdoor recreation.

The Authority operates the river control system and provides assistance to State and local governments in reducing local flood problems. It also works with cooperating agencies to encourage full and effective use of the navigable waterway by industry and commerce.

The Authority is the wholesale power supplier for many local municipal and cooperative electric systems serving customers in parts of seven States. It supplies power to several Federal installations and industries whose power requirements are large or unusual. Power to meet these demands is supplied from dams, coal-fired powerplants, nuclear powerplants, combustion turbine installations, and a pumped-storage hydroelectric project operated by the Authority, U.S. Corps of Engineers dams in the Cumberland Valley; and Aluminum Company of America dams, whose operation is coordinated with the Authority's system.

In economic and community development programs, the Authority provides technical assistance in areas including industrial development, regional waste management, tourism promotion, community preparedness, and vanpool organization. It works with local communities and groups to develop maximum use of available area resources. Working with regional learning centers, businesses, and industries, the agency has identified skills that are needed in the high-technology job market and has set up training centers.

At Muscle Shoals, AL, the Authority operates a national laboratory for development of new and improved fertilizers and processes. Research results are made available to industry. Fertilizers produced in the demonstration facilities are distributed for use in research and educational programs, principally farm test-demonstrations and demonstrations conducted through cooperative and wholesale fertilizer distributors. It also conducts a major bioenergy research program.

In cooperation with other agencies, the Authority conducts research and development programs in forestry, fish and game, watershed protection, health services related to its operations, and economic development of Tennessee Valley communities.

In the western part of Kentucky and Tennessee, the Authority operates Land Between the Lakes—a demonstration project in outdoor recreation, environmental education, and natural resource management.

Sources of Information

Citizen Participation Regional Communications, ET PB 25H, 400 West Summit Hill Drive, Knoxville, TN 37902-1499. Phone, 615-632-8000.

Contracts Division of Purchasing, CST 17N 08B, P.O. Box 11127, 605 Chestnut Street, Chattanooga, TN 37401-2127. Phone, 615-751-2624. This office will direct inquiries to the appropriate procurement officer.

Electric Power Supply and Rates Power Group, LP 2S 180G, 1101 Market Street, Chattanooga, TN 37402-2801. Phone, 615-751-8678 or 3531.

Employment Human Resources Services, ET 5D 93U, 400 West Summit Hill Drive, Knoxville, TN 37902-1499 (and personnel offices at other major locations and construction projects). Phone, 615-632-3341.

Environmental and Energy Education/Information TVA Energy Education/Information Programs, Forestry Building, Ridgeway Road, Norris, TN 37828. Phone, 615-632-1599.

Environmental Quality Resource Development, SPB 2S 201P, 309 Walnut Street, Knoxville, TN 37902-1499. Phone, 615-632-6578.
Fertilizer and Agriculture National Fertilizer and Environmental Research Center, Muscle Shoals, AL 35660-1010. Phone, 205-386-2593.
Local Economic Development and Regional Planning Valley Resource Center, OCH 2E 62E, 601 Summit Hill Drive, Knoxville, TN 37902-1499 (phone, 615-632-4400); Minority Economic Development, 601 Summit Hill Drive, OCH E 3B 7B, Knoxville, TN 37902-1499 (phone, 615-632-4405).
Maps Maps and Surveys Department, HB 2N 200A, 311 Broad Street, Chattanooga, TN 37402-2801. Phone, 615-751-2133.
Medical Program Medical Services, EB 6W 4A, 20 East Eleventh Street, Chattanooga, TN 37402-2801. Phone, 615-751-2091.
Publications Regional Communications, ET PB 25H, 400 West Summit Hill Drive, Knoxville, TN 37902-1499. Phone, 615-632-8000.
Recreation, Shoreline Development, Regulation of Floating Structures, and Land and Land Rights Land Resources, Forestry Building, Ridgeway Road, Norris, TN 37828. Phone, 615-632-1802.
Technical Library Services Technical Library, WT 2D 15B, 400 West Summit Hill Drive, Knoxville, TN 37902-1499 (phone, 615-632-3033); Chattanooga Office Complex, SP 1N 30A, 1101 Market Street, Chattanooga, TN 37402-2801 (phone, 615-751-4913); National Fertilizer and Environmental Research Center, Room A100, NFD 1A 100E, Muscle Shoals, AL 35660-1010 (phone, 205-386-2871); Land Between the Lakes, 100 Van Morgan Drive, Golden Pond, KY 42211-9001 (phone, 502-924-5602).

For further information, contact Regional Communications, Tennessee Valley Authority, 400 West Summit Hill Drive, Knoxville, TN 37902-1499 (phone, 615-632-8000); or the Washington Office, 412 First Street SE., Washington, DC 20444-2003 (phone, 202-479-4412).

UNITED STATES ARMS CONTROL AND DISARMAMENT AGENCY

320 Twenty-first Street NW., Washington, DC 20451
Phone, 202-647-8677

Director	RONALD F. LEHMAN II
Deputy Director	STEPHEN READ HANMER, JR.
Executive Assistant	COMDR. MARINER G. COX, USN
Special Assistant	BRENDA HUDSON
Senior Policy Advisor	MICHELE MARKOFF
Executive Assistant	BARBARA STARR
Senior Military Advisor	COL. DONALD SELLERS, USAF
Chairman, General Advisory Committee	COMDR. ROBERT MEISSNER, USN
Special Advisor for Arms Control and Disarmament	(VACANCY)
U.S. Commissioner, Standing Consultative Commission	ROBERT JOSEPH
U.S. Negotiator for Strategic Offensive Arms	LINTON BROOKS, *Acting*
U.S. Negotiator for Defense and Space	DAVID SMITH
U.S. Representative to the Conference on Disarmament	STEPHEN LEDOGAR

U.S. Representative to European Conventional Arms Negotiations	R. James Woolsey
Head, Special Verification Committee	Steven Steiner
U.S. Negotiator for Nuclear Testing Talks	C. Paul Robinson
Assistant Director, Nonproliferation Policy Bureau	Bradley Gordon
Assistant Director, Multilateral Affairs Bureau	Michael Moodie
Assistant Director, Strategic and Nuclear Affairs	Susan Koch
Assistant Director, Verification and Implementation Bureau	Manfred Eimer
General Counsel	Thomas Graham, Jr.
Director of Congressional Affairs	Richard Holwill
Director of Public Affairs	Barry Daniel
Administrative Director	William J. Montgomery

[For the United States Arms Control and Disarmament Agency statement of organization, see the *Code of Federal Regulations,* Title 22, Part 601]

The United States Arms Control and Disarmament Agency formulates and implements arms control and disarmament policies that will promote the national security of the United States and its relations with other countries. At present, to effectively carry out its responsibilities, it prepares and participates in discussions and negotiations with the Soviet Union and other countries on such issues as strategic arms limitations, conventional force reductions in Europe, prevention of the spread of nuclear weapons to countries that do not now possess them, prohibition on chemical weapons, and the international arms trade.

The United States Arms Control and Disarmament Agency was established by act of September 26, 1961 (22 U.S.C. 2561), in response to congressional feeling that our country's arms control and disarmament policy could best be formed and carried out in a manner promoting the national security by a central organization charged by law with primary responsibility for arms control and disarmament.

Activities

The Agency conducts studies and provides advice relating to arms control and disarmament policy formulation; prepares for and manages United States participation in international negotiations in the arms control and disarmament field; disseminates and coordinates public information about arms control and disarmament; and prepares for, operates, or directs, as needed, U.S. participation in international control systems that may result from United States arms control or disarmament activities.

In addition to directing the Agency activities as described above, the Director functions as the principal adviser to the President, the National Security Council, and the Secretary of State in arms control and disarmament matters. Under the direction of the Secretary of State, the Director also has primary responsibility within the Government for such matters.

In support of its activities, the Agency conducts research and studies or, through contracts and agreements, makes arrangements for their conduct by private or public institutions or persons. It also coordinates such efforts by or for other Government agencies, and analyzes selected defense programs for their arms control implications.

The Arms Control and Disarmament Act also provides for the establishment of a General Advisory Committee, not to exceed 15 members, appointed by the President with the advice and consent of the Senate, to advise the President, the Secretary of State, and the Director of

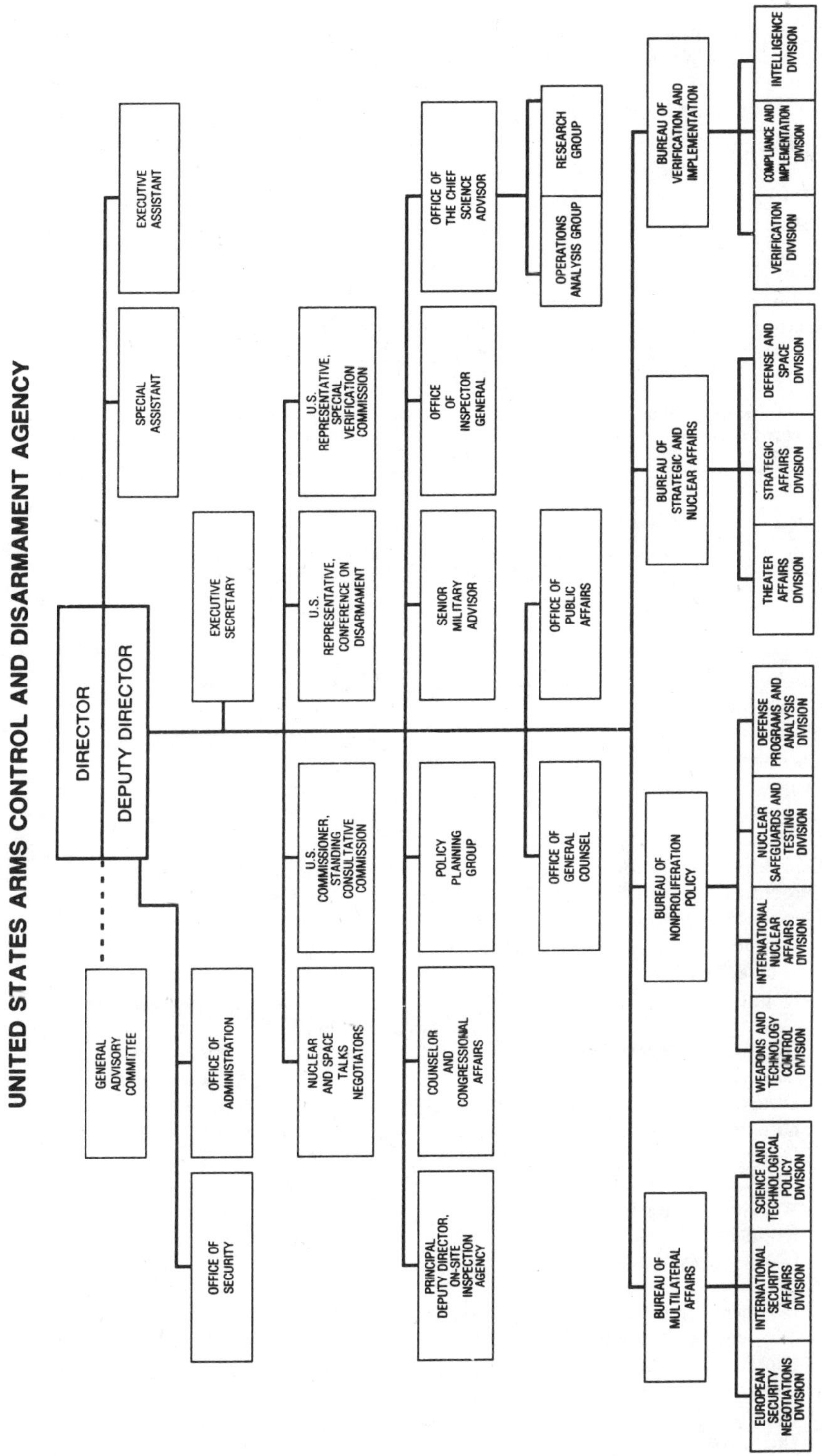
UNITED STATES ARMS CONTROL AND DISARMAMENT AGENCY
DIRECTOR
DEPUTY DIRECTOR
GENERAL ADVISORY COMMITTEE
SPECIAL ASSISTANT
EXECUTIVE ASSISTANT
EXECUTIVE SECRETARY
OFFICE OF ADMINISTRATION
OFFICE OF SECURITY
NUCLEAR AND SPACE TALKS NEGOTIATORS
U.S. COMMISSIONER, STANDING CONSULTATIVE COMMISSION
U.S. REPRESENTATIVE, CONFERENCE ON DISARMAMENT
U.S. REPRESENTATIVE, SPECIAL VERIFICATION COMMISSION
PRINCIPAL DEPUTY DIRECTOR, ON-SITE INSPECTION AGENCY
COUNSELOR AND CONGRESSIONAL AFFAIRS
POLICY PLANNING GROUP
SENIOR MILITARY ADVISOR
OFFICE OF INSPECTOR GENERAL
OFFICE OF THE CHIEF SCIENCE ADVISOR
OPERATIONS ANALYSIS GROUP
RESEARCH GROUP
OFFICE OF GENERAL COUNSEL
OFFICE OF PUBLIC AFFAIRS
BUREAU OF MULTILATERAL AFFAIRS
EUROPEAN SECURITY NEGOTIATIONS DIVISION
INTERNATIONAL SECURITY AFFAIRS DIVISION
SCIENCE AND TECHNOLOGICAL POLICY DIVISION
BUREAU OF NONPROLIFERATION POLICY
WEAPONS AND TECHNOLOGY CONTROL DIVISION
INTERNATIONAL NUCLEAR AFFAIRS DIVISION
NUCLEAR SAFEGUARDS AND TESTING DIVISION
DEFENSE PROGRAMS AND ANALYSIS DIVISION
BUREAU OF STRATEGIC AND NUCLEAR AFFAIRS
THEATER AFFAIRS DIVISION
STRATEGIC AFFAIRS DIVISION
DEFENSE AND SPACE DIVISION
BUREAU OF VERIFICATION AND IMPLEMENTATION
VERIFICATION DIVISION
COMPLIANCE AND IMPLEMENTATION DIVISION
INTELLIGENCE DIVISION

the Agency on matters affecting arms control, disarmament, and world peace.

Sources of Information

Contracts Individuals seeking to do business with the Agency or obtain information on research contracts may contact the Contracting Office (phone, 703–235–3288) at the address shown below.

Publications Copies of publications such as *World Military Expenditures* (annual series), *Documents on Disarmament* (annual series), *Arms Control and Disarmament Agreements,* and the Agency's Annual Report may be ordered from the Superintendent of Documents, Government Printing Office, Washington, DC 20402, or from the Office of Public Affairs (phone, 202–647–8677) at the address shown below.

Speakers Officers of the Agency will address audiences in all parts of the country if speaking engagements can be fitted into their work schedules. Phone, 202–647–4800.

For further information, contact the United States Arms Control and Disarmament Agency, 320 Twenty-first Street NW., Washington, DC 20451. Phone, 202–647–8677.

UNITED STATES INFORMATION AGENCY

301 Fourth Street SW., Washington, DC 20547
Phone, 202–619–4700

Director	Henry Catto
Counselor	McKinney Russell
Assistant Director	Walter Raymond, Jr.
Coordinator, President's U.S.-Soviet Exchange	Greg Guroff
Inspector General	George F. Murphy, Jr.
General Counsel	Alberto J. Mora
Director, Office of Congressional Liaison	Martha Johnston
Director, Office of Public Liaison	Leslie A. Goodman
Director, Office of Research	Ronald H. Hinckley
Deputy Director	Stephen M. Shaffer
Associate Director for Broadcasting and Director, Voice of America	Richard W. Carlson
Deputy Associate Director	Robert T. Coonrod
Director, Office of Administration	Dennis D. Sokol
Director, Office of Personnel	Janice H. Brambilla
Director, Office of Programs	Sidney A. Davis
Director, Office of Policy	Steve Munson
Director, Office of External Affairs	Joseph D. O'Connell, Jr.
Director, Office of Engineering and Technical Operations	Walter La Fleur
Associate Director for Programs	Michael D. Schneider, *Acting*
Deputy Associate Director	Michael D. Schneider
Chief, Policy Guidance Staff	Robert Bemis
Chief, Media Reaction Staff	Ray H. Burson
Director, Office of Program Coordination and Development	Victoria A. Hughes
Director, Exhibits Service	William H. Jones
Director, Foreign Press Centers	Carol E. Ludwig
Director, Press and Publications Service	Mort Smith
Executive Officer	Thomas P. Gratto

Associate Director for Educational and Cultural Affairs	William P. Glade
Deputy Associate Director	Warren J. Obluck
Executive Director, Cultural Property Staff	Ann Guthrie-Hingston
Staff Director, J. William Fulbright Foreign Scholarship Board	Ralph H. Vogel
Director, Office of Cultural Centers and Resources	Carl A. Howard
Director, Office of Citizen Exchanges	Judith B. Fox
Director, Office of International Visitors	William Codus
Director, Office of Academic Programs	Guy S. Brown
Director, Office of Arts America	Robert E. McDowell
Executive Officer	Thomas G. Leydon
Associate Director for Management	Henry Hockeimer
Deputy Associate Director	Herwald H. Morton
Director, Office of Administration	Eileen Keane Binns
Director, Office of Technology	Daniel S. Campbell
Director, Office of Personnel	Harlan F. Rosacker
Comptroller, Office of the Comptroller	Stanley M. Silverman
Director, Office of Security	Bernard C. Dowling
Director, Office of Equal Employment Opportunity	Marilyn B. Thompson
Director, Office of Contracts	Phillip R. Rogers
Executive Officer	Cathy T. Chikes
Director, Washington Relocation Project	Richard L. Roth
Director, Television and Film Service	Stephen E. Murphy
Deputy Director	William E. Eames
Director, Office of Programs	Sigmund M. Cohen
Director, Office of WORLDNET Production	Donald J. Cuozzo
Executive Officer	Daniel D. Dunning
Director, Office of Cuba Broadcasting	Antonio Navarro
Director, Radio Marti	Rolando Bonachea
Director, TV Marti	(vacancy)
Director, Office of African Affairs	Robert R. Gosende
Deputy Director	Michael O'Brien
Director, Office of American Republics Affairs	Stanley A. Zuckerman
Deputy Director	(vacancy)
Director, Office of East Asian and Pacific Affairs	David I. Hitchcock
Deputy Director	Wesley D. Stewart
Director, Office of European Affairs	Victor B. Olason
Deputy Director (Western Europe and Canada)	Mary E. Gawronski
Deputy Director (USSR, Eastern and Southern Europe)	Csaba Chikes
Director, Office of North African, Near Eastern and South Asian Affairs	William A. Rugh
Deputy Director	C. Edward Bernier

[For the United States Information Agency statement of organization, see the *Code of Federal Regulations*, Title 22, Part 504]

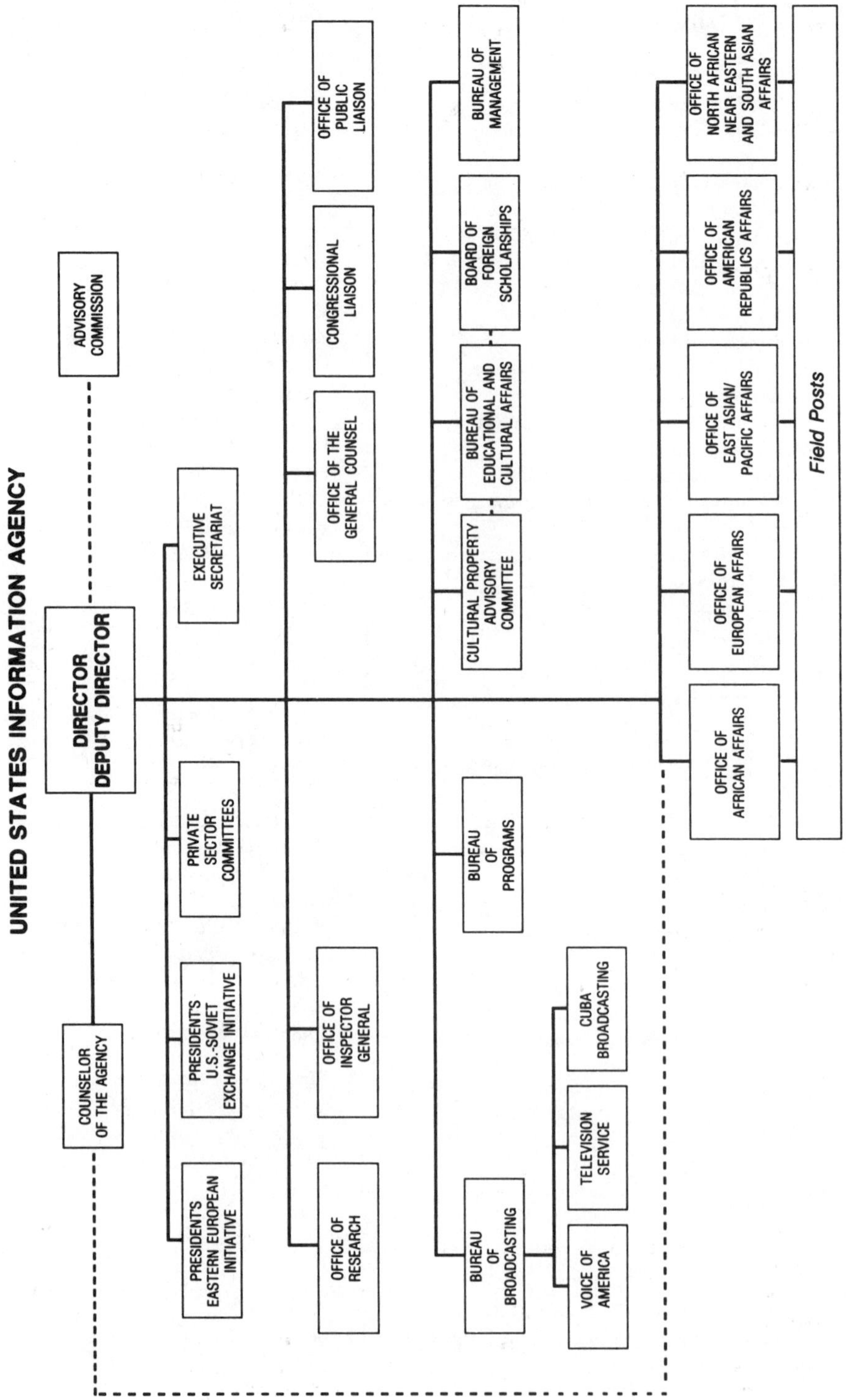
UNITED STATES INFORMATION AGENCY
DIRECTOR
DEPUTY DIRECTOR
ADVISORY COMMISSION
COUNSELOR OF THE AGENCY
EXECUTIVE SECRETARIAT
PRIVATE SECTOR COMMITTEES
PRESIDENT'S U.S.-SOVIET EXCHANGE INITIATIVE
PRESIDENT'S EASTERN EUROPEAN INITIATIVE
OFFICE OF PUBLIC LIAISON
CONGRESSIONAL LIAISON
OFFICE OF THE GENERAL COUNSEL
OFFICE OF INSPECTOR GENERAL
OFFICE OF RESEARCH
BUREAU OF MANAGEMENT
BOARD OF FOREIGN SCHOLARSHIPS
BUREAU OF EDUCATIONAL AND CULTURAL AFFAIRS
CULTURAL PROPERTY ADVISORY COMMITTEE
BUREAU OF PROGRAMS
BUREAU OF BROADCASTING
CUBA BROADCASTING
TELEVISION SERVICE
VOICE OF AMERICA
OFFICE OF NORTH AFRICAN NEAR EASTERN AND SOUTH ASIAN AFFAIRS
OFFICE OF AMERICAN REPUBLICS AFFAIRS
OFFICE OF EAST ASIAN/ PACIFIC AFFAIRS
OFFICE OF EUROPEAN AFFAIRS
OFFICE OF AFRICAN AFFAIRS
Field Posts

The United States Information Agency (USIA) is responsible for the U.S. Government's overseas information and cultural programs, including the Voice of America. The Agency, which is known overseas as the U.S. Information Service, conducts a wide variety of communication activities—from academic and cultural exchanges to press, radio, television, film, seminar, library, and cultural center programs abroad—in order to strengthen foreign understanding of American society, obtain greater support of U.S. policies, and increase understanding between the United States and other countries. The Agency reports to the President and the Secretary of State on worldwide public opinion as it is relevant to the formulation and conduct of U.S. foreign policy.

The legislative mandates of the United States Information Agency derives from the United States Information and Educational Exchange Act of 1948 (22 U.S.C. 1431), and the Mutual Educational and Cultural Exchange Act of 1961 (22 U.S.C. 2451). The U.S. Information and Educational Exchange Act's purpose is to increase mutual understanding between the people of the United States and the people of other countries. It prohibits, with certain exceptions approved by Congress, dissemination within the United States of materials produced by the Agency for distribution overseas. It also requires the Agency to make its overseas program materials available for public inspection at its Washington, DC, headquarters. The Mutual Educational and Cultural Exchange Act authorizes educational and cultural exchanges between the United States and other countries as well as United States participation in international fairs and expositions abroad.

Activities

The Agency's objectives are to:

—strengthen foreign understanding and support for U.S. policies and actions;

—advise the President, the Secretary of State, members of the National Security Council, and other key officials on the implications of foreign opinion for present and contemplated United States policies;

—counter attempts to distort the objectives and policies of the United States;

—promote and administer educational and cultural exchange programs in the national interest and in order to bring about greater understanding between the people of the United States and the peoples of the world;

—cooperate with the American private sector to enhance the quality and range of America's overseas information and cultural efforts;

—assist in the development of a comprehensive policy on the free flow of information and international communications; and

—conduct negotiations on information and educational and cultural exchanges with other governments.

To accomplish its purposes, the Agency conducts a variety of activities overseas—educational and cultural exchanges, English-teaching programs, television, radio, and film programs, Wireless File, magazine and book distribution, exhibits, and library and cultural center programs. The Agency offers facilitation to foreign press and television journalists working overseas and in the United States and to American journalists overseas.

The Agency conducts programs for the international exchange of students, teachers, and other educators. It brings leaders in government, politics, social welfare, and other professional fields to the United States to consult with their counterparts, observe American society and institutions, convey an understanding of their own cultures, and develop their particular fields of interest. Through all these programs, the Agency seeks to enlarge the circle of those able to serve as influential interpreters between the United States and other nations, encourage key institutions to strengthen their contacts across national boundaries, and reduce impediments to the exchange of ideas and information. It administers a program through which American groups and individuals in the performing arts and athletics are sent abroad to perform, advise, and consult with their professional colleagues in other societies.

The Agency also is charged with advising the President, the President's representatives abroad, and the various departments and agencies on the implications of foreign opinion for present and contemplated United States policies, programs, and official statements.

Abroad, the head of each Agency post, the Public Affairs Officer, provides the Ambassador and other members of the U.S. diplomatic mission with professional advice and expertise on all matters relating to the work of the Agency.

Functional Elements

The four major functional elements of the Agency are: the Bureaus of Broadcasting (includes the Voice of America), Programs, Educational and Cultural Affairs, and Management.

The Bureau of Broadcasting consists of the Voice of America, the Office of Cuba Broadcasting, and the Television and Film Service.

The *Voice of America (VOA)* is the Bureau of Broadcasting's functional element for worldwide radio broadcasting. VOA operates under a charter from Congress which requires that it serve as a consistently reliable, authoritative, accurate, objective, and comprehensive news source. It must present a balanced and comprehensive projection of significant American thought and institutions. VOA produces and broadcasts radio programs in English and 44 foreign languages for overseas audiences. Its programming includes news, reports from correspondents on the scene, analyses of events from Washington, feature programs, music, and editorials.

The *Office of Cuba Broadcasting* is located within the Voice of America. It oversees all programming broadcast for Cuba on VOA's Radio Marti and TV Marti programs. In keeping with the principles of the VOA charter, both services offer their audiences accurate and objective news reports and features on American culture and opinion. Radio Marti broadcasts on medium and shortwave frequencies. TV Marti is available on VHF (very high frequency) and international satellite.

The *Television and Film Service* is responsible for organizing and directing the Bureau of Broadcasting's worldwide television and film activities. The areas of responsibility encompass: producing programs and interactive press conferences for the WORLDNET satellite delivery system; producing and acquiring films and videotapes for direct projection or placement overseas; providing facilitative assistance to visiting foreign television and film producers; operating television news bureaus at foreign press centers; providing assistance to foreign broadcasters in the production and telecast of cooperative television programs; serving as the Bureau's primary point of contact with American motion picture and television industries; and coordinating with other U.S. and foreign government agencies on the dissemination of information overseas through motion pictures and television.

The Bureau of Programs consists of the Agency's Policy Guidance Staff, the Media Reaction Staff, and four major offices.

The Policy Guidance Staff provides fast daily and in-depth guidance for operating elements of the Agency on U.S. foreign policy issues. This staff also reviews field and Washington program proposals to assure consistency with policy and represents USIA in inter-agency meetings on pulbic affairs issues.

The Foreign Media Reaction Staff prepares daily reports on foreign media reaction to senior Agency management and other policymakers in the White House, National Security Council, Department of State, Department of Defense and other Federal agencies.

The Office of Program Coordination and Development recruits American speakers to explain U.S. policies and society to overseas audiences, both in person and via electronic media from the United States. The speakers address a wide variety of political, economic, and social subjects. The Office of Programs also sends sports experts abroad to assist foreign sports organizations.

The Exhibits Service is responsible for developing, producing, and managing major national exhibitions in the USSR and Eastern Europe; U.S. Government participation in Bureau of International Exposition—sanctioned events outside the United States; and Political Presence exhibits at international trade fairs in Third World countries. The larger exhibitions, such as those developed under exchange agreements, often include American guides, a library, brochures, and specialists who conduct seminars both at the exhibition and off site.

The Foreign Press Centers in Washington, DC, and New York, along with the Media Liaison Office in Los Angeles, provide facilitative services and conduct thematic working tours and policy briefings for foreign correspondents assigned to or visting the U.S., all of which contribute to a better understanding of American policies and motives.

The Press and Publications Service supports U.S. foreign policy objectives overseas through a variety of press articles, periodicals, pamphlets, photos, and other visual materials. It produces the Wireless File which transmits (7 days a week) to overseas posts texts of major speeches and official government statements, analytical and background articles explaining foreign policy and domestic developments, selected materials from U.S. publications, and reports from correspondents on developments pertinent to foreign audiences. The Wireless File is produced in English, Arabic, French, and Spanish. The Press and Publications Service also produces special thematic pamphlets and 6 magazines in over 11 different languages. Additionally, the Press and Publications Service manages printing and translation facilities in Manila, Mexico, and Tunis.

The Bureau of Educational and Cultural Affairs administers programs authorized by the Mutual Educational and Cultural Exchange Act of 1961 (the Fulbright-Hays Act), including academic exchanges, short-term professional exchanges, youth exchanges, cooperative projects with private organizations; and overseas book, library and English teaching programs. It also provides staff support for the Presidentially appointed J.William Fulbright Foreign Scholarship Board and for the Cultural Property Advisory Committee. The Bureau consists of five major offices.

The Office of Academic Programs develops and coordinates a wide variety of academic educational exchange programs. It oversees the administration of more than 7,000 grants each year to U.S. citizens to study, teach, and conduct research abroad, and for foreign nationals to conduct similar activities in the United States. The best known of the exchanges supported by this office is the Fulbright Program which operates in more than 120 countries. The Office of Academic Programs also supports a worldwide information network about education opportunities in the United States, and programs which enchance the experiences of foreign students enrolled in U.S. colleges and universities. The Office also encourages and supports American studies at foreign universities and other institutions of higher learning.

The Office of International Visitors arranges informative visits to the United States of more than 5,000 influential foreign leaders each year in such fields as government, labor, journalism, the arts, and education. Selected individuals, who are nominated by United States Information Service posts, travel throughout the country meeting counterparts in their fields of interest. They also meet with Americans in their homes or other informal settings. The Office also manages the Agency's three reception centers; administers educational and cultural exchange programs for young people ages 15 to 30; serves as the Agency's liaison with the large network of public and private organizations involved in the international visitor program; and arranges programs in the United States for United Nations fellows and foreign government trainees.

The Office of Citizen Exchanges is responsible for developing cooperative projects with private-sector institutions to support, complement, and enhance the goals and objectives of the Agency. These projects are designed to promote a better understanding of the United States abroad by means of educational and cultural exchange between Americans and citizens of other nations. The Office may provide selective assistance, encouragement, and grant support to activities of tax-exempt organizations and institutions that satisfy this purpose, with special emphasis on international educational and cultural exchanges. The Office also administers the Artistic Ambassadors program; provides grant support for creative arts projects; and consolidates, plans, and manages other arts activities of the Agency.

The Office of Cultural Centers and Resources provides policy direction, program support, and professional guidance and materials to United States Information Service libraries and binational centers overseas; provides library services to domestic Agency offices; promotes the publication of American books translated and reprinted in English; provides grants and operates a donated-books program; and supports English-teaching programs abroad.

The Office of Arts America administers fine and performing arts programs, sending performing arts groups and large fine arts exhibitions on overseas tours. Arts America identifies and recruits speakers and specialists in the fields of literature, film, and the plastic and performing arts to speak at or work with host country institutions in their fields of expertise. Arts America also represents the Agency in the Fund for U.S. Artists at International Festivals and Exhibitions.

The Bureau of Management is responsible for planning, organizing, directing, and controlling the Agency's administrative and management operations. The Bureau's offices provide support services in the areas of administration, advanced technology, personnel and training, budget and fiscal operations, management analysis, security, equal employment opportunity, contracts, and procurement.

Executive Level Offices

The five executive level offices of the Agency are the Office of Public Liaison, Office of the General Counsel, Office of Congressional Liaison, Office of the Inspector General, and the Office of Research.

The Office of Public Liaison is charged with increasing awareness of and support for USIA in the United States, within the framework of agency legislation. Its mandate covers three principal functions: press/media relations, external affairs, and publications/internal communications. The Office is responsible for planning, directing, coordinating, and evaluating USIA's domestic public affairs program. The Director of Public Liaison serves as the official spokesperson for the Agency within the United States and is the principal public affairs advisor to the agency Director.

The Office of General Counsel:

—provides general legal support, assistance, and representation to the Director and all elements of the Agency, both domestic and overseas, in all aspects of Agency operations;

—carries out the designation and supervisory authority of the Director with respect to international educational and cultural exchange visitor program sponsors;

—makes recommendations on requests of alien exchange visitors for waiver of the 2-year home-country residence requirement of section 212(e) of the Immigration and Nationality Act, as amended (8 U.S.C. 1182), and passes on all requests made under the Freedom of Information and Privacy Acts; and

—makes determinations to implement the act of October 19, 1965 (22 U.S.C. 2459), to render cultural objects imported for temporary exhibition immune from judicial seizure.

The Office of Congressional Liaison serves as the primary contact with Members and committees of the Congress and their staffs.

The Inspector General, who reports to the Director, is authorized under the Inspector General Act of 1978 to supervise and coordinate audits and investigations relating to the programs and operations of the Agency. The Office also conducts inspections of foreign posts and domestic elements to assess the effectiveness, efficiency, and economy with which resources are employed in fulfilling Agency program objectives. The Inspector General provides leadership and coordination and directs Office of Inspector General resources to promote economy, efficiency, and effectiveness, and to prevent and detect fraud and abuse in the administration of the Agency's programs and operations. Further, the Inspector General refers possible violations of criminal or civil laws to the Attorney General. The Inspector General also receives, evaluates, and investigates employee "whistleblower" complaints.

The Office of Research, reporting to the Director, conducts assessments of foreign attitudes, foreign media commentary, and communications issues. These activities are carried out in support of the Director's statutory role as adviser to the President, the Secretary of State, and the National Security Council on assessments of the impact of United States foreign policy decisions on public opinion abroad. To provide program guidance on Agency activities, the Office also evaluates Agency programs at the request of the Director or Agency elements.

Research memos, reports, briefing papers, and foreign media analyses are sent to the White House, foreign affairs agencies, and other interested Government departments.

Counselor The Counselor of the Agency reports to the Director and Deputy Director. As the senior career officer in the Agency, the Counselor assists in the overall direction of the Agency and shares responsibility for establishing broad Agency policies and assuring their effective execution. The Counselor oversees the activities of the five Area Directors and directly supervises the Agency Secretariat and Operations Center.

Geographic Areas The five geographic area offices are the principal Agency contacts with its overseas posts. They provide broad managerial oversight of the posts and programs abroad, providing Agency direction to the posts and, in return, relaying area and post needs and perspectives to the executive policy group and to functional offices of the Agency.

Overseas Posts

Principally an overseas agency, the USIA's work is carried out by its foreign service officers assigned to American missions abroad. Overseas posts engage in political advocacy of American foreign policy objectives and conduct communication, cultural, and educational exchange activities on behalf of the U.S. Government. The Agency maintains 204 posts in 127 countries.

Sources of Information

Administrative Regulations Inquiries regarding administrative staff manuals and instructions to staff affecting members of the public that were issued, adopted, or promulgated on or after July 5, 1967, should be directed to the Management Plans and Analysis Staff, United States Information Agency, Washington, DC 20547. Phone, 202-619-4700.

Contracts Contact the Office of Contracts, United States Information Agency, Washington, DC 20547. Phone, 202-485-6398.

Employment For information concerning employment opportunities, contact the Special Recruitment Staff, Office of Personnel, United States Information Agency, Washington, DC 20547. Phone, 202-619-5618. For Voice of America employment information, contact the Voice of America, Office of Personnel, United States Information Agency, Washington, DC 20547. Phone, 202-619-3763.

International Audiovisual Programs For information concerning a certification program under international agreement to facilitate the export and import of qualified visual and auditory materials of an educational, scientific, and cultural character, contact the Chief Attestation Officer of the United States, United States Information Agency, Washington, DC 20547. Phone, 202-501-7775.

For further information, contact the Office of Public Liaison, United States Information Agency, Washington, DC 20547. Phone, 202–619–4355.

UNITED STATES INTERNATIONAL DEVELOPMENT COOPERATION AGENCY

320 Twenty-first Street NW., Washington, DC 20523–0001
Phone, 202–663–1449

Director, U.S. International Development Cooperation Agency	RONALD W. ROSKENS, *Acting*
Deputy Director	MARK L. EDELMAN, *Acting*

AGENCY FOR INTERNATIONAL DEVELOPMENT

320 Twenty-first Street NW., Washington, DC 20523–0001
Phone, 202–647–9620

Administrator	RONALD W. ROSKENS
Deputy Administrator	MARK L. EDELMAN
Executive Secretary	DAVID G. MEIN
Assistant Administrator for Program and Policy Coordination	REGINALD J. BROWN
Assistant Administrator for Science and Technology	RICHARD E. BISSELL
Assistant Administrator for Legislative Affairs	R. RAY RANDLETT
Assistant Administrator for Africa	SCOTT M. SPANGLER
Assistant Administrator for Asia and Private Enterprise	HENRIETTA HOLSMAN FORE
Assistant Administrator for Europe and the Near East	CAROL C. ADELMAN
Assistant Administrator for Latin America and the Caribbean	JAMES H. MICHEL
Assistant Administrator for Food for Peace and Voluntary Assistance	JOHN F. HICKS, *Acting*
Assistant to the Administrator for Management Services	MICHAEL DOYLE
Director, Office of External Affairs	STEPHEN D. HAYES
Director, Office of U.S. Foreign Disaster Assistance	ANDREW S. NATSIOS
Director, Office of Small and Disadvantaged Business Utilization	JOHN L. WILKINSON
Director, Office of Equal Opportunity Programs	JESSALYN L. PENDARVIS
Inspector General	HERBERT L. BECKINGTON
General Counsel	HOWARD M. FRY

TRADE AND DEVELOPMENT PROGRAM

Room 309, State Annex 16, Washington, DC 20523–1602
Phone, 703–875–4357

Director	Priscilla Rabb Ayres
Deputy Director	Nancy Frame
Assistant Director for Management Operations	Deirdre Curley
General Counsel	Lisa DeSoto
Regional Officer/East and Southern Africa, Middle East, Czechoslovakia, Yugoslavia, Southern Europe, Bulgaria	Geoffrey Jackson
Regional Officer/Francophone, North and Central Africa, Eastern Europe (Poland and Hungary)	Fred Eberhart
Regional Officer/Latin America and the Caribbean, India, Pakistan, Indonesia, Bangladesh, Nepal, Sri Lanka	Daniel Stein
Regional Officer/Thailand, Malaysia, Singapore, Taiwan, South Korea, Philippines, Brunei, Pacific Islands	Jack Williamson
Regional Officer/Special Projects	Barbara Bradford
Program Analyst	(vacancy)
Financial Officer	David Fields
Computer Specialist	(vacancy)
Contract Specialist	Della Glenn
Information Specialist	Carol Stillwell
Personnel Specialist	(vacancy)

OVERSEAS PRIVATE INVESTMENT CORPORATION

1615 M Street NW., Washington, DC 20527
Phone, 202–457–7200

President and Chief Executive Officer	Fred M. Zeder
Executive Vice President	James D. Berg
Vice President and General Counsel	Howard L. Hills
Vice President and Treasurer	Mildred O. Callear
Vice President, Finance	Robert O. Draggon
Vice President, Insurance	Felton McL. Johnston
Vice President, Investment Development	Kevin R. Callwood
Vice President, Management Services	Richard K. Childress
Chairman of the Board	Ronald W. Roskens
Manager, Public Affairs	Daven Oswalt

[For the Agency for International Development statement of organization, see the *Federal Register* of Aug. 26, 1987, 52 FR 32174]

The International Development Cooperation Agency's function is policy planning, policymaking, and policy coordination on international economic issues affecting developing countries. The Agency's mission is twofold: first, to ensure that development goals are taken fully into account in all executive branch decisionmaking on trade, financing and monetary affairs, technology, and other economic policy issues affecting the less-developed nations; and second, to provide

UNITED STATES INTERNATIONAL DEVELOPMENT COOPERATION AGENCY

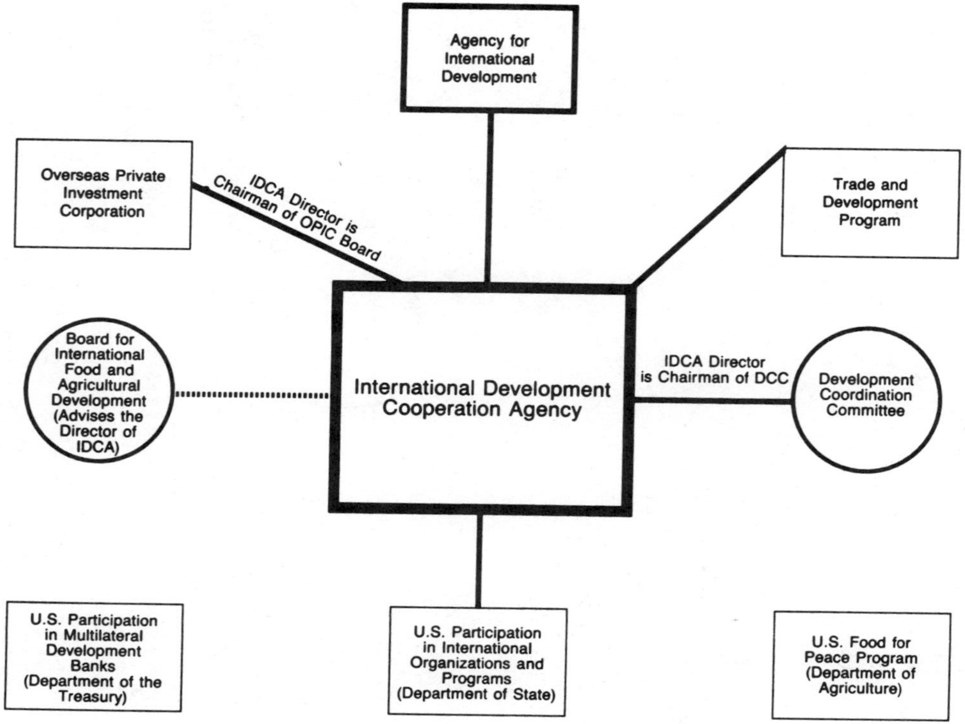

strong direction for U.S. economic policies toward the developing world and a coherent development strategy through the effective use of U.S. bilateral development assistance programs and U.S. participation in multilateral development organizations.

The International Development Cooperation Agency was established by Reorganization Plan No. 2 of 1979 (5 U.S.C. app.), effective October 1, 1979, to be a focal point within the U.S. Government for economic matters affecting U.S. relations with developing countries.

The Director of the Agency serves as the principal international development adviser to the President and to the Secretary of State, subject to guidance concerning the foreign policy of the United States from the Secretary of State.

The Director has a wide range of authorities to assist in the pursuit of the Agency's mission. The Agency for International Development is a component of the International Development Cooperation Agency, and its Administrator currently serves as the Agency's Acting Director. The Trade and Development Program and the Overseas Private Investment Corporation are component agencies of the Agency, and the Agency's Director serves as Chairman of the Board of Directors of the Corporation.

Activities

The Agency plays an important role in the implementation of the U.S. Economic Support Fund and a number of other development-related activities and programs.

The Director and senior agency staff chair and participate in a wide range of interagency committees. The Director is a member of the National Advisory Committee on International and Monetary Affairs, the Trade Policy Committee, and the Advisory Committee on Agricultural Assistance.

The Director chairs the Development Coordination Committee, a broad interagency body that coordinates development and development-related policies and programs. As Chair of this Committee, the Director annually prepares and submits to the Congress a report on development issues. This report reviews the efforts undertaken by the U.S. Government in the past year to promote international economic development, and it discusses key issues facing policymakers in the development field.

The Agency has responsibility for policy instructions for a number of U.S. programs affecting developing countries. The Director provides policy guidelines for the bilateral assistance program to use in developing projects and programs. The Director also works with other agencies in formulating the position the United States will take in international conferences or negotiations on many issues of concern to developing countries.

International Development Cooperation Agency staff functions are currently being performed by Agency for International Development personnel.

Agency for International Development

[For the Agency for International Development statement of organization, see the *Federal Register* of Aug. 26, 1987, 52 FR 32174]

The Agency for International Development administers economic assistance programs that combine an American tradition of international concern and generosity with the active promotion of America's national interest. The Agency assists developing countries in realizing their full national potential through the development of open and democratic societies and the dynamism of free markets and individual initiative. It also assists nations throughout the world in improving the quality of human life and in expanding the range of individual opportunities by reducing poverty, ignorance, and malnutrition.

The Agency meets these objectives through a worldwide network of country missions which develop and implement programs guided by six principles: support for free markets and broad-based economic growth; concern for individuals and the development of their economic and social well-being; support for democracy; responsible environmental policies and prudent management of natural resources; support for lasting solutions to transnational problems; and humanitarian assistance to those who suffer from natural or manmade disasters.

The Agency functions under an Administrator, who also currently serves as the Director of the International Development Cooperation Agency. The Administrator directs U.S. foreign and economic assistance operations in more than 80 countries.

Programs

The Foreign Assistance Act of 1961, as amended (22 U.S.C. 2151 note), authorizes the Agency to administer, normally on a bilateral basis, two kinds of foreign assistance: development assistance and economic support funds.

In addition, the Agency, in cooperation with the Departments of Agriculture and State, carries out the provisions of the Agricultural Trade Development and Assistance Act of 1954, as amended (7 U.S.C. 1691 *et seq.*) which includes the donation of agricultural commodities (title II), and the provision of food under the Food for Development Program (title III). The direction of the Food for Peace Program (7 U.S.C. 1691 *et seq.*) is a shared responsibility of the Agency and the Department of Agriculture.

The Agency also conducts humanitarian relief activities in support of those who suffer from natural calamities such as earthquakes, famine, floods, and drought. Programs are conducted, often in conjunction with those of other nations and private charitable organizations, to quickly alleviate the effects of disaster and reduce human suffering.

The Agency emphasizes the importance of stimulating rapid, sustained, broad-based economic growth. It helps developing countries develop democratic societies, adopt more market-oriented policies, liberalize their trade regimes, and put in place other progrowth programs.

Specifically, it administers programs under the Foreign Assistance Act within the following major categories of assistance:

Development Assistance The Agency focuses its development assistance programs on critical problem areas in those functional sectors that affect the majority of the people in the developing countries. The areas of concentration are:

—agriculture, rural development, and nutrition: to increase the incomes of the poor majority and to expand the availability and consumption of food, while maintaining and enhancing the natural resource base;

—health: to lower infant and child mortality rates through child survival programs and improve community and family health, in general, through primary health care programs; to reduce the incidence of serious communicable diseases; and assist developing countries in effectively managing the allocation of financial and human resources so that preventive and curative health services are sustained and more equitably distributed;

—population planning: to extend voluntary family planning services to the village level through programs that provide or promote safe, effective, affordable, acceptable family planning services;

—child survival: to increase the availability of both oral rehydration therapy and immunization programs to the children of developing countries;

—AIDS: to help control the further development of HIV and to monitor the epidemic and its effects on development through support to the World Health Organization and bilateral programs;

—education and human resource development: to expand access to basic education, particularly for the rural poor, through programs which improve the education systems management, the quality of primary education and the cost-effectiveness of resources used; to encourage the use of mass media and communications technology, and the development of informal education and training approaches for rural families and workers in agriculture, nutrition, health, and family planning; and to provide advanced training as needed for technicians, scientists, and managers at all levels;

—private-sector, environment, and energy activities: to support selected development activities that deal with a wide range of development concerns that do not fall within the above functional sectors; for example, projects directed toward assisting developing countries with their energy and natural resource problems and projects that provide for the transfer and adaptation of appropriate technology and lessen the problems of rapid urbanization, including employment and income problems. These activities place high priority on greater involvement of the private sector of both the United States and less developed countries in development, including greater reliance on private and voluntary organizations;

—private enterprise: to assist in shaping a market-oriented, developmental strategy, both directly and in collaboration with the U.S. and indigenous private sectors. Private sector resources in the U.S. and developing countries can be the main impetus for growth in these countries. As such, they are an important supplement and complement to existing bilateral and multilateral aid programs. Private investment, both local and foreign, can make a vital contribution to development through job creation, increased productivity, transferred technology, management know-how, and the generation of additional and diversified products to meet internal demand and expand export capacity; and

—Development Fund for Africa: to provide flexible grant financing for programs in sub-Saharan Africa, including the Sahel. This specific form of development assistance supports Africa's efforts to overcome constraints to more rapid growth of production and incomes, reduce the continent's vulnerability to economic reversals and its dependence on foreign food and financing, and lay the groundwork for longer term development. Assistance provided from the Development Fund for Africa can be in any of the above areas of focus but emphasizes programs to make African economies more competitive, more efficient, and more self-sustaining.

Economic Support The primary objective of the Economic Support Fund is to support U.S. economic, political, and security interests and to advance U.S. foreign policy goals. It provides resources that stem the spread of economic and political disruption and that help friends and allies in dealing with threats to their security and independence.

The Fund is flexible economic assistance provided on a grant basis and may be used to sustain economic activity and restore financial equilibrium, to address basic development needs, or to improve infrastructure. In administering the Fund, consideration is given to policy guidance that underlies the provision of development assistance. This would include, for example, assisting developing countries in building and maintaining social and economic institutions necessary for self-sustaining and equitable growth, providing opportunities to improve the quality of everyday life and meeting basic human needs.

For further information, contact the Office of Policy Development and Program Review, Bureau for Program and Policy Coordination. Phone, 202–647–8594.

Specific Programs

American Schools and Hospitals Abroad This competitive program provides grants to private U.S. nonprofit organizations that have founded or sponsor American schools and hospitals abroad for citizens of other countries. The purpose is to strengthen institutions demonstrating American ideas and practices in education and medicine.

For further information, contact the Office of American Schools and Hospitals Abroad, Bureau for Food for Peace and Voluntary Assistance. Phone, 202–663–2650.

International Disaster Assistance The Office of U.S. Foreign Disaster Assistance administers the Agency's overseas disaster assistance program. The Office draws upon other U.S. Government agencies, voluntary and international organizations, and the U.S. private sector to meet the demands of disaster relief, rehabilitation, preparedness, early warning, and mitigation in countries stricken or threatened by natural or manmade disasters. It provides technical assistance and training for the development of host government disaster assistance programs, technology transfer for improved prediction and warning systems, and material and personnel resources for emergency relief and rehabilitation. The Agency's Administrator serves as the President's Special Coordinator for International Disaster Assistance.

For further information, contact the Office of U.S. Foreign Disaster Assistance. Phone, 202–647–8924.

Housing Guaranty The Agency's Housing Guaranty Program facilitates private financing for shelter and urban services for lower income families in developing countries by guaranteeing repayment to U.S. lenders for projects requested by these countries. It seeks to finance innovative programs that promote individual initiative, local institutional development, and rational policy formulation for the delivery of serviced urban land and shelter solutions affordable to lower income households. Examples of program elements may include squatter settlement upgrading, servicing of urban lots with credit extended to families to construct their own dwelling units, construction of economic support infrastructure such as community markets, municipal management training programs, support to develop a market-oriented national housing finance system, and simplified approaches to local land cadastre and titling.

Programs are designed to promote affordable home ownership for lower income households, increase the participation of the private sector in the financing and delivery of low-cost shelter and urban services, support improved housing finance and land and infrastructure development policies, and strengthen local government institutions to manage the operation and development of cities.

The Office of Housing and Urban Programs also supports a program of research and technical assistance in urban development that emphasizes the development and application of new tools for analyzing urban issues and urban investment strategies and assists in strengthening urban investment strategies and urban and financial management policies and practices.

For further information, contact the Office of Housing and Urban Programs, Bureau for Asia and Private Enterprise. Phone, 202–663–2530.

Food for Peace In cooperation with the Department of Agriculture, the Agency administers programs pursuant to titles II and III of the Agricultural Trade Development and Assistance Act of 1954 (7 U.S.C. 1701) to encourage economic development, assist in combating hunger and malnutrition, and for other purposes.

Under title II, the Agency donates agricultural commodities to meet famine or other urgent or extraordinary relief requirements, to combat malnutrition, to promote economic and community development and policy reform, and for needy persons and nonprofit school lunch and preschool feeding programs outside the United States.

The Agency also administers the title III Food for Development Program, under which agricultural commodities are donated to least developed countries for direct distribution activities, the establishment of emergency food reserves, or sale with the foreign currency proceeds being used for specific economic development purposes.

The Agency supports the use of food aid in ways that promote rather than hinder the growth of food production and associated policy and program initiatives by the host government.

For further information, contact the Office of Food for Peace, Bureau for Food for Peace and Voluntary Assistance. Phone, 202–647–0263.

Science and Technology In recognition of the higher priority that developing countries are placing on science and technology, the Agency is focusing on more innovative and collaborative approaches to the problems and processes of development research and technology transfer. This program includes both support of research to explore the potential uses of emerging technologies for development and innovative approaches to strengthen the capacity of less developed countries to take advantage of these new technologies.

For further information, contact the Office of the Assistant Administrator, Bureau for Science and Technology. Phone, 202–647–1827.

Women in Development In recognition of the fact that women in developing countries play a significant role in economic production, family support, and the overall development process of the national economies of such countries, Congress requires that U.S. bilateral aid be administered so that programs, projects, and activities fully integrate women as participants and beneficiaries, thus improving their status and assisting the total development effort. The Agency implements this congressional mandate with leadership by the Office of Women in Development.

For further information, contact the Office of Women in Development, Bureau for Program and Policy Coordination. Phone, 202–647–3992.

Overseas Organizations

Agency country organizations are located in countries where the Agency is carrying out bilateral economic assistance programs.

Agency country organizations are subject to the coordinative direction and guidance of the chief U.S. diplomatic representative in the country, such as the Ambassador, and the direction and supervision of the Agency's Assistant Administrator of the geographic bureau that has responsibility for the economic assistance program to the country in which the organization is located. Some programs and program support activities of Agency country organizations are subject to the coordinative direction of the geographic and other Agency bureaus or offices.

Overseas Organizations—Agency for International Development

Missions, Offices, or Sections of Embassy

Country	Officer in Charge [1]
Bangladesh/Dhaka	Mary C. Kilgour (MD)
Belize/Belize City	Mosina H. Jordan (OR)
Bolivia/La Paz	Carl H. Leonard (MD)
Botswana/Gaborone	Howard Handler (MD)
Brazil/Brasilia	Howard B. Helman (OR)
Burkina Faso/Ouagadougou	Wilbur G. Thomas (MD)
Burundi/Bujumbura	Glenn G. Slocum, Jr. (OR)
Cameroon/Yaounde	Jay P. Johnson (MD)
Cape Verde/Praia	Thomas C. Luche (OR)
Caribbean/Bridgetown, Barbados.	Aaron S. Williams (RD)
Chad/N'Djamena	Bernard D. Wilder (OR)
Chile/Santiago	Paul W. Fritz (OR)
Colombia/Bogotá	James F. Smith (OR)
Costa Rica/San Jose	Ronald F. Venezia (MD)
Dominican Republic/Santo Domingo.	Raymond F. Rifenburg (MD)
Ecuador/Quito	Charles E. Costello (MD)
Egypt/Cairo	Marshall D. Brown (MD)
El Salvador/San Salvador	Henry H. Bassford (MD)
Ethiopia/Addis Ababa	Willard J. Pearson, Jr. (OR)
Fiji/Suva	John B. Woods (RD)
Gambia/Banjul	Jimmie M. Stone (OR)
Ghana/Accra	Joseph B. Goodwin (OR)
Guatemala/Guatemala City	Terrence J. Brown (MD)
Guatemala (ROCAP)	Irenemaree Castillo (RD)
Guinea/Conakry	William G. Kaschak (MD)
Guinea-Bissau/Bissau	Michael F. Lukomski (OR)
Haiti/Port-au-Prince	David A. Cohen (MD)
Honduras/Tegucigalpa	John A. Sanbrailo (MD)
India/New Delhi	Walter Bollinger (MD)
Indonesia/Jakarta	Lewis P. Reade (MD)
Jamaica/Kingston	Robert S. Queener (MD)
Jordan/Amman	(Vacancy) (MD)
Kenya/Nairobi	John R. Westley (MD)
Lebanon/Beirut	(Vacancy) (OR)
Lesotho/Maseru	Furman G. Towery (MD)
Liberia/Monrovia	(Vacancy) (MD)
Madagascar/Antananarivo	Phyllis Dichter-Forbes (MD)
Malawi/Lilongwe	Carol A. Peasley (MD)
Mali/Bamako	Dennis J. Brennan (MD)
Mexico/Mexico City	Gerald R. Bowers (OR)
Morocco/Rabat	Dennis M. Chandler (MD)
Mozambique/Maputo	Julius P. Schlotthauer (MD)
Namibia/Windhoek	Richard L. Shortlidge, Jr. (OR)
Nepal/Kathmandu	Kelly Kammerer (MD)
Nicaragua/Managua	Janet C. Ballantyne (MD)
Niger/Niamey	George T. Eaton (MD)
Nigeria/Lagos	Eugene Chiavaroli (AAO)
Oman/Muscat	Duncan R. Miller (MD)
Pakistan/Islamabad	James A. Norris (MD)
Pakistan/Islamabad (Afghan Affairs).	Robert N. Bakley (OR)
Panama/Panama City	Thomas W. Stukel, Jr. (MD)
Paraguay/Asuncion	(Vacancy) (OR)

[1] MD: Mission Director; D: Director; AD: Associate Director; OR: Office of the AID Representative; AAO: AID Affairs Officer for Section of Embassy; RDO: Regional Development Officer; DO: Development Officer; RD: Regional Director.

Overseas Organizations—Agency for International Development—Continued

Missions, Offices, or Sections of Embassy

Country	Officer in Charge [1]
Peru/Lima	Craig G. Buck (MD)
Philippines/Manila	Malcolm Butler (MD)
Poland/Warsaw	William R. Joslin (OR)
Rwanda/Kigali	James A. Graham (MD)
Senegal/Dakar	Julius E. Coles (MD)
Somalia/Mogadishu	(Vacancy) (MD)
South Africa/Pretoria	Dennis P. Barrett (MD)
Sri Lanka/Colombo	Richard M. Brown (MD)
Sudan/Khartoum	Frederick E. Machmer (MD)
Swaziland/Mbabane	Roger D. Carlson (MD)
Tanzania/Dar es Salaam	Joseph F. Stepanek (MD)
Thailand/Bangkok	Thomas H. Reese III (MD)
Thailand/Bangkok (Khmer Affairs).	William B. Erdahl (OR)
Togo/Lomé	Mark G. Wentling (OR)
Tunisia/Tunis	George Carner (MD)
Uganda/Kampala	Keith W. Sherper (MD)
Uruguay/Montevideo	Peter R. Orr (OR)
Yemen/Sanaa	(Vacancy) (MD)
Zaire/Kinshasa	Charles W. Johnson (MD)
Zambia/Lusaka	Fred E. Winch (MD)
Zimbabwe/Harare	Ted D. Morse (MD)

[1] MD: Mission Director; D: Director; AD: Associate Director; OR: Office of the AID Representative; AAO: AID Affairs Officer for Section of Embassy; RDO: Regional Development Officer; DO: Development Officer; RD: Regional Director.

Overseas Organizations—Agency for International Development

(Selected Regional Organizations)

(RD: Regional Director)

Country	Officer in Charge
Regional Economic Development Services Offices	
Kenya/Nairobi (REDSO/ESA)	Fred C. Fischer (RD)
Ivory Coast/Abidjan (REDSO/WSA)	Frederick E. Gilbert (RD)
U.S. Missions to International Organizations	
Office of the U.S. Representative to the Development Assistance Committee of the Organization for Economic Cooperation and Development—Paris, France.	Martin V. Dagata
Office of the AID Coordinator/Office of Food and Agriculture—Rome, Italy	Richard M. Seifman
Office of the AID Representative, Association of South East Asian Nations—Bangkok, Thailand.	Lawrence J. Ervin

Trade and Development Program

The Trade and Development Program was established on July 1, 1980, as a component organization of the International Development Cooperation Agency. The Omnibus Trade and Competitiveness Act of 1988 made the organization an independent agency within the International Development Cooperation Agency. The Agency's mandate is to promote economic development in, and simultaneously export U.S. goods and services to, Third World and middle-income developing countries. It funds feasibility studies for high-priority development projects that will be financed by the World Bank or other international financial institutions, or from the host country's own resources. The studies are performed only by U.S. firms.

The Agency operates under the authority of sections 607(a) and 661 of the Foreign Assistance Act of 1961 (22 U.S.C. 2357, 2421). Under section 607(a) of the act, it serves as the coordinating and authorizing agency for the provision of government-to-government technical assistance on a fully reimbursable basis.

Under section 661 of the act, the Agency funds planning services, including feasibility studies, orientation visits, and trade-related training to assist U.S. firms in becoming involved in development projects having substantial U.S. export potential in project implementation.

Overseas Private Investment Corporation

[For the Overseas Private Investment Corporation statement of organization, see the *Code of Federal Regulations,* Title 22, Chapter VII]

The Overseas Private Investment Corporation (OPIC) is a self-sustaining, Government agency whose purpose is to promote economic growth in developing countries by encouraging U.S. private investment in those nations. The Corporation assists American investors in three principal ways: financing investment projects through direct loans and/or guaranties; insuring investment projects against a broad range of political risks; and providing a variety of investor services including investor counseling, country and regional information kits, computer-assisted project and investor matching, and investment missions. All of these programs are designed to reduce the perceived stumbling blocks and risks associated with overseas investment.

Organized as a corporation and structured to be responsive to private business, OPIC's mandate is to mobilize and facilitate the participation of U.S. private capital and skills in the economic and social development of less-developed friendly countries and areas. Currently, OPIC programs are available for new business enterprises or expansion in 118 countries and areas worldwide. Assistance is not available for projects that adversely affect U.S. employment, are financially unsound, or do not promise significant benefits to the social and economic development of the host country or area.

The Corporation is governed by a 15-member Board of Directors—8 appointed from the private sector and 7 from the Federal Government.

Activities

By reducing or eliminating certain perceived political risks for investors and providing financing and assistance not otherwise available, the Corporation helps to reduce the unusual risks and problems that can make investment opportunities in the developing areas less attractive than in advanced countries. At the same time, it reduces the need for government-to-government lending programs by involving the U.S. private sector in establishing capital-generation and strengthening private-sector economies in developing countries.

The Corporation insures U.S. investors against the political risks of expropriation, inconvertibility of local currency holdings, and damage from war, revolution, insurrection, or civil strife. It also offers a special insurance policy to U.S. contractors and exporters against arbitrary drawings of letters of credit posted as bid, performance, or advance payment guaranties. Other special programs are offered for minerals exploration, oil and gas exploration, and development and leasing operations.

The Corporation offers U.S. lenders protection against both commercial and political risks by guaranteeing payment of principal and interest on loans (up to $50 million) made to eligible private enterprises.

Its Direct Investment Fund loans, offered to small- and medium-sized businesses, generally cover terms of from 7 to 12 years, and usually range from $500,000 to $6 million with varying interest rates, depending on assessment of the risks of the project financed.

Programs are available only for a new facility, expansion or modernization of an existing plant, or new inputs of technology or services in order to encourage new investment which will produce significant new benefits for host countries.

The Corporation also offers several preinvestment assistance programs. These include the Investor Information Service, an investment data clearinghouse; the Opportunity Bank, a computerized investor-project matching service; the Investment Missions Program, which provides senior U.S. business executives the opportunity to discuss investment opportunities with host country officials and businesses; and investor counseling.

Sources of Information

U.S. International Development Cooperation Agency

General Inquiries Inquiries may be directed to the Office of External Affairs, International Development Cooperation Agency, Washington, DC 20523. Phone, 202-647-1850.

Agency for International Development

Congressional Affairs Congressional inquiries may be directed to the Bureau for Legislative Affairs, Agency for International Development, Washington, DC 20523. Phone, 202-647-8264.
Employment For information regarding employment opportunities, contact the Recruitment Staff, Office of Human Resources Development and Management, Agency for International Development, Washington, DC 20523. Phone, 202-663-1290.
General Inquiries General inquiries may be directed to the Office of Public Inquiries, Agency for International Development, Washington, DC 20523. Phone, 202-647-1850.
News Media Press inquiries should be directed to the Office of Press Relations, Agency for International Development, Washington, DC 20523. Phone, 202-647-4274.

Trade and Development Program

General Inquiries Trade and Development Program inquiries may be directed to the Director, Trade and Development Program, Room 309, State Annex 16, Washington, DC 20523. Phone, 703-875-4357. Please convey the geographic region of interest.

Overseas Private Investment Corporation

General Inquiries Inquiries may be directed to the Information Office, Overseas Private Investment Corporation, Washington, DC 20527. Phone, 202-457-7010.
Publications OPIC programs are further detailed in the following publications available without charge: *Corporate Brochure; Annual Report; OPIC Programs for Contractors and Exporters; Country and Area List; Investment Insurance Handbook; Investment Financing Handbook; OPIC Programs for Insurance Brokers; OPIC Investment Mission Program; OPIC Opportunity Bank Program;* and *Investor Information Service.*
Small Business Activities For program information, call toll-free (outside the Washington, DC, area), 800-424-OPIC.

UNITED STATES INTERNATIONAL TRADE COMMISSION

500 E Street SW., Washington, DC 20436
Phone, 202-252-1000

Chairman	(VACANCY)
Vice Chairman	ANNE E. BRUNSDALE
Commissioners	SEELEY G. LODWICK
	DAVID B. ROHR
	DON E. NEWQUIST
	(VACANCY)
Director of Operations	CHARLES E. ERVIN
Director of Investigations	LYNN FEATHERSTONE
General Counsel	LYN SCHLITT
Executive Liaison	WILLIAM T. HART

Congressional Liaison	(VACANCY)
Chief Administrative Law Judge	JANET D. SAXON
Secretary	KENNETH R. MASON
Inspector General	JANE ALTENHOFEN
Director, Public and Consumer Affairs	EDWARD G. CARROLL, JR.
Director, Office of Economics	JOHN SUOMELA
Director, Office of Industries	ROBERT ROGOWSKY
Division Chief, Agriculture, Fisheries and Forest Products	DAVID L. INGERSOLL
Division Chief, Minerals and Metals	LARRY L. BROOKHART
Division Chief, Energy and Chemicals	JOHN J. GERSIC
Division Chief, Machinery and Equipment	AARON CHESSER
Division Chief, General Manufactures	WALTER S. TREZEVANT
Division Chief, Textiles, Leather Products and Apparel	DENNIS RUDY
Division Chief, Services and Electronic Technology	NORMAN MCLENNAN
Director, Office of Tariff Affairs and Trade Agreements	EUGENE A. ROSENGARDEN
Director, Office of Unfair Import Investigations	LYNN LEVINE
Director, Trade Remedy Assistance Office	WOODLEY L. TIMBERLAKE, *Acting*
Director, Office of Administration	LORIN GOODRICH

The United States International Trade Commission furnishes studies, reports, and recommendations involving international trade and tariffs to the President, the Congress, and other Government agencies. In this capacity, the Commission conducts a variety of investigations, public hearings, and research projects pertaining to the international policies of the United States.

The United States International Trade Commission is an independent agency created by act of September 8, 1916 (39 Stat. 795), and originally named the United States Tariff Commission. The name was changed to the United States International Trade Commission by section 171 of the Trade Act of 1974 (19 U.S.C. 2231). The Commission's present powers and duties are provided for largely by the Tariff Act of 1930 (19 U.S.C. 1654); the Agricultural Adjustment Act (7 U.S.C. 601); the Trade Expansion Act of 1962 (19 U.S.C. 1801); the Trade Act of 1974 (19 U.S.C. 2101); the Trade Agreements Act of 1979 (19 U.S.C. 2501); and the Omnibus Trade and Competitiveness Act of 1988 (19 U.S.C. 2901).

Six Commissioners are appointed by the President with the advice and consent of the Senate, for 9-year terms, unless appointed to fill an unexpired term. The Chairman and Vice Chairman are designated by the President for 2-year terms, and succeeding Chairmen may not be of the same political party. The Chairman generally is responsible for the administration of the Commission. Not more than three Commissioners may be members of the same political party (19 U.S.C. 1330).

Activities

The Commission performs a number of functions pursuant to the statutes referred to above. Under the Tariff Act of 1930, the Commission is given broad powers of investigation relating to the customs laws of the United States and foreign countries; the volume of importation in comparison with domestic production and consumption; the conditions, causes, and effects relating to competition of foreign industries with those of the United States; and all other factors affecting competition between articles of the United States and imported articles. The Commission is required to make available to the President and to the Committee on Ways and Means of the

House of Representatives and to the Committee on Finance of the Senate, whenever requested, all information at its command and is directed to make such investigations and reports as may be requested by the President or by either of said committees or by either branch of the Congress. The Omnibus Trade and Competitiveness Act of 1988 amended several of the statutes administered by the Commission and, in addition, required the Commission to conduct several industry competitiveness investigations.

In order to carry out these responsibilities, the Commission is required to engage in extensive research, conduct specialized studies, and maintain a high degree of expertise in all matters relating to the commercial and international trade policies of the United States.

Advice Concerning Trade Negotiations The Commission advises the President as to the probable economic effect on the domestic industry and consumers of modification of duties and other barriers to trade that may be considered for inclusion in any proposed trade agreement with foreign countries (19 U.S.C. 2151).

Generalized System of Preferences The Commission advises the President with respect to every article that may be considered for preferential removal of the duty on imports from designated developing countries as to the probable economic effect the preferential removal of duty will have on the domestic industry and on consumers (19 U.S.C. 2151, 2163).

Industry Adjustment to Import Competition The Commission conducts investigations upon petition on behalf of an industry, a firm, a group of workers, or other entity representative of an industry to determine whether an article is being imported in such increased quantities as to be a substantial cause or threat of serious injury to the domestic industry producing an article like or directly competitive with the imported article (19 U.S.C. 2251–2254). If the Commission's finding is affirmative, it recommends to the President the action that would address such injury and be most effective in facilitating positive adjustment by the industry to import competition. The President has discretion to take action that could be in the form of an increase in duties, imposition of a quota, negotiation of orderly marketing agreements, or provision of adjustment assistance to groups of workers, firms, or communities. If the President does not provide relief in the form recommended by the Commission, and if a joint resolution disapproving the action of the President is enacted by Congress, then the President is required to provide the relief recommended by the Commission (19 U.S.C. 2251–2254).

The Commission reports with respect to developments within an industry that has been granted import relief and advises the President of the probable economic effect of the reduction or elimination of the tariff increase that has been granted. The President may continue, modify, or terminate the import relief previously granted.

East-West Trade Monitoring System The Commission monitors imports into the United States from nonmarket-economy countries and makes a report at least once each calendar quarter on the effect of such imports on the production of like or directly competitive articles in the United States and on employment within the industry (19 U.S.C. 2240).

Market Disruption From Communist Countries The Commission conducts investigations to determine whether increased imports of an article produced in a Communist country are causing market disruption in the United States (19 U.S.C. 2436). If the Commission's determination is in the affirmative, the President may take the same action as in the case of serious injury to an industry, except that the action would apply only to imports of the article from the Communist country.

Investigations Relating to Imported Articles Subsidized or Sold at Less Than Fair Value The Commission conducts preliminary investigations under the Tariff Act of 1930 to determine whether there is reasonable indication of material injury to, threat of material injury to, or material retardation of the establishment of an industry in the United States by reason of imports of foreign merchandise allegedly being subsidized or sold at less than fair value (19 U.S.C. 1671, 1673, 1675). If the Commission's determination is affirmative, and the Secretary of Commerce further determines that the foreign merchandise is being subsidized or is being, or is likely to be, sold at less than its fair value, or there is reason to believe or suspect such unfair practices are occurring, then the Commission conducts final investigations to determine whether a U.S. industry is materially injured or threatened with material injury, or its establishment is materially retarded by reason of such imports.

If the Secretary of Commerce determines to suspend an investigation upon acceptance of an agreement to eliminate the injurious effect of subsidized imports or imports sold at less than fair value, the Commission may conduct an investigation to determine whether the injurious effect of imports of the merchandise that was the subject of the suspended investigation is eliminated completely by the agreement. The Commission also conducts investigations to determine whether in light of changed circumstances such a suspension agreement continues to eliminate completely the injurious effect of imports of the merchandise.

The Commission conducts investigations to determine whether changed circumstances exist that indicate that an industry in the United States would not be threatened with material injury, or the establishment of such an industry would not be materially retarded, if the countervailing duty order or antidumping order resulting from affirmative final determinations by the Commission and Secretary of Commerce were modified or revoked.

With regard to imports of articles from countries not party to the Agreement on Interpretation and Application of Articles VI, XVI, and XXIII of the General Agreement on Tariffs and Trade, the Commission determines, with respect to any such duty-free article that the Secretary of Commerce has determined is being subsidized, whether an industry in the United States is materially injured or threatened with material injury, or its establishment is materially retarded by reason of such imports (19 U.S.C. 1303).

Import Interference With Agricultural Programs The Commission conducts investigations at the direction of the President to determine whether any articles are being or are practically certain to be imported into the United States under such conditions and in such quantities as to render or tend to render ineffective, or to materially interfere with, programs of the Department of Agriculture for agricultural commodities or products thereof, or to reduce substantially the amount of any product processed in the United States from such commodities or products, and makes findings and recommendations (7 U.S.C. 624). The President may restrict the imports in question by imposition of either import fees or quotas.

Unfair Practices in Import Trade The Commission applies U.S. statutory and common law of unfair competition to the importation of products into the United States and their sale (19 U.S.C. 1337). The statute declares unlawful unfair methods of competition and unfair acts in the importation or sale of products in the United States, the threat or effect of which is to destroy or substantially injure a domestic industry, prevent the establishment of such an industry, or restrain or monopolize trade and commerce in the United States. The statute also declares as unlawful per se infringement of a valid and enforceable U.S. patent, copyright, registered trademark, or maskwork; no resulting injury need be found. If the Commission determines that there is a violation of the statute, it is to direct that the articles involved be excluded from entry into the United States, or it may issue cease-and-desist orders directing the person engaged in such violation to cease and desist from engaging in such unfair methods or acts.

Provision is made for the Commission to make certain public interest determinations that could result in the withholding of an exclusion or cease and desist order. Provision is made also for the President to intervene within 60 days after the issuance of a Commission order to terminate the order for policy reasons. Commission determinations of violation are subject to court review.

Uniform Statistical Data The Commission, in cooperation with the Secretary of the Treasury and the Secretary of Commerce, establishes for statistical purposes an enumeration of articles imported into the United States and exported from the United States, and seeks to establish comparability of such statistics with statistical programs for domestic production (19 U.S.C. 1484).

In conjunction with such activities, the three agencies are to develop concepts for an international commodity code for reporting transactions in international trade and to report thereon to the Congress (19 U.S.C. 1484).

Harmonized Tariff Schedule of the United States, Annotated The Commission issues a publication containing the U.S. tariff schedules and related matters and considers questions concerning the arrangement of such schedules and the classification of articles (19 U.S.C. note prec. 1202, 1332a, 1484e).

International Trade Studies The Commission conducts studies, investigations, and research projects on a broad range of topics relating to international trade, pursuant to requests of the President, the House Ways and Means Committee, the Senate Finance Committee, either branch of the Congress, or on its own motion (19 U.S.C. 1332). Public reports of these studies, investigations, and research projects are issued in most cases.

The Commission also keeps informed of the operation and effect of provisions relating to duties or other import restrictions of the United States contained in various trade agreements (19 U.S.C. 2482). Occasionally the Commission is required by statute to perform specific trade-related studies.

Tariff Summaries The Commission prepares and publishes, from time to time, a series of summaries of trade and tariff information (19 U.S.C. 1332). These summaries contain descriptions (in terms of the Tariff Schedules of the United States) of the thousands of products imported into the United States, methods of production, and the extent and relative importance of U.S. consumption, production, and trade, together with certain basic factors affecting the competitive position and economic health of domestic industries.

Sources of Information

Inquiries should be directed to the specific organizational unit or to the Secretary, U.S. International Trade Commission, 500 E Street SW., Washington, DC 20436. Phone, 202-252-1000.

Contracts The Chief, Contracting and Procurement Division, has responsibility for contract matters. Phone, 202-252-1730.

Employment Information on employment can be obtained from the Director, Office of Personnel. Personnel employed include international economists, attorneys, accountants, commodity and industry specialists and analysts, and clerical and other support personnel. Phone, 202-252-1653.

Publications The Commission publishes results of investigations concerning various commodities and subjects; it also publishes a series of reports on chemicals. Other publications include *Summaries of Trade and Tariff Information;* an annual report to the Congress on the operation of the trade agreements program; and an annual report to the Congress of Commission activities. Specific information regarding these publications can be obtained from the Office of the Secretary.

Reading Rooms Reading rooms are open to the public in the Office of the Secretary and in the Commission Library.

For further information, contact the Secretary, United States International Trade Commission, 500 E Street SW., Washington, DC 20436. Phone, 202-252-1000.

UNITED STATES OFFICE OF SPECIAL COUNSEL

Suite 1100, 1120 Vermont Avenue NW., Washington, DC 20005
Phones: Locator, 202-653-7188; Toll-free, 1-800-872-9855

Special Counsel	Mary F. Wieseman
Deputy Special Counsel	Erin McDonnell
Associate Special Counsel for Prosecution	William E. Reukauf
Associate Special Counsel for Investigation	Robert D. L'Heureux
Director for Management	William Larry Dean
Director, Legislative and Public Affairs	William G. Cinnamond

The United States Office of Special Counsel investigates allegations of certain activities prohibited by civil service laws, rules, or regulations and litigates before the Merit Systems Protection Board.

Activities

The United States Office of Special Counsel (OSC) was established on January 1, 1979, by Reorganization Plan No. 2 of 1978 (5 U.S.C. app.). The Civil Service Reform Act of 1978 (5 U.S.C. 1101 note), which became effective on January 11, 1979, enlarged its functions and powers. Pursuant to provisions of the Whistleblower Protection Act of 1989 (5 U.S.C. 1201 note), OSC functions as an independent investigative and prosecutorial agency within the executive branch which litigates before the Merit Systems Protection Board.

The primary role of OSC is to protect employees, former employees, and applicants for employment from prohibited personnel practices, especially reprisal for whistleblowing. OSC's basic areas of statutory responsibility are:

—receiving and investigating allegations of prohibited personnel practices and other activities prohibited by civil service law, rule, or regulation and, if warranted, initiating corrective or disciplinary action;

—providing a secure channel through which information evidencing a violation of any law, rule, or regulation, gross mismanagement, gross waste of funds, abuse of authority, or substantial and specific danger to public health or safety may be disclosed without fear of retaliation and without disclosure of identity, except with the employee's consent; and

—enforcing the provisions of the Hatch Act.

Sources of Information

Field offices are located in Dallas, TX (Room 7C30, 1100 Commerce Street, 75242; phone, 214-767-8871) and San Francisco, CA (Suite 121, 50 United Nations Plaza, 94102; phone, 415-556-9450).

For further information, contact the United States Office of Special Counsel, Suite 1100, 1120 Vermont Avenue NW., Washington, DC 20005. Phone, 202-653-7188; or toll-free, 1-800-872-9855.

UNITED STATES POSTAL SERVICE

475 L'Enfant Plaza SW., Washington, DC 20260–0010
Phone, 202–268–2000

Board of Governors:	
Chairman of the Board	NORMA PACE
Vice Chairman of the Board	JOHN N. GRIESEMER
Secretary of the Board	DAVID F. HARRIS
Governors	SUSAN E. ALVARADO, LEGREE S. DANIELS, IRA D. HALL, TIRSO DEL JUNCO, M.D., BERT H. MACKIE, CROCKER NEVIN, ROBERT SETRAKIAN
Postmaster General	ANTHONY M. FRANK
Deputy Postmaster General	MICHAEL S. COUGHLIN
Management:	
Postmaster General	ANTHONY M. FRANK
Executive Assistant to the Postmaster General	MICHAEL J. SHINAY
Assistant Postmaster General, Planning Department	FRANK R. POWER
Senior Assistant Postmaster General, Finance Group	COMER S. COPPIE
Assistant Postmaster General, Rates and Classification Department	FRANK R. HESELTON
Assistant Postmaster General, Department of the Controller	M. RICHARD PORRAS
Treasurer	STEPHEN M. KEARNEY
Chief Postal Inspector	CHARLES R. CLAUSON
Assistant Chief Inspector, Criminal Investigations	KENNETH M. HEARST
Assistant Chief Inspector, Administration	MICHAEL A. GUMP
Assistant Chief Inspector, Audit	THOMAS J. KOERBER
Assistant Chief Inspector, International	LOTHAR F. KINZLER
General Counsel, Law Department	HAROLD J. HUGHES
Deputy General Counsel	FRED EGGLESTON
Senior Assistant Postmaster General, Quality	DAVID H. CHARTERS
Deputy Postmaster General	MICHAEL S. COUGHLIN
Assistant Postmaster General, Automation Implementation Management Department	STEPHEN E. MILLER
Senior Assistant Postmaster General, Operations Support Group	WILLIAM R. CUMMINGS
Assistant Postmaster General, Delivery, Distribution and Transportation Department	ALLEN R. KANE
Assistant Postmaster General, Operations Systems and Performance Department	ARTHUR I. PORWICK
Assistant Postmaster General, Engineering and Technical Support Department	WILLIAM J. DOWLING
Regional Postmaster General, Northeast	PETER A. JACOBSON
Regional Postmaster General, Eastern	SAMUEL GREEN, JR.
Regional Postmaster General, Southern	JERRY K. LEE, SR.

Regional Postmaster General, Central	JOHN G. MULLIGAN
Regional Postmaster General, Western	JOSEPH R. CARAVEO
Associate Postmaster General	KENNETH J. HUNTER
Consumer Advocate	ANN MCK. ROBINSON
Assistant Postmaster General, Technology Resource Department	KAREN T. UEMOTO
Senior Assistant Postmaster General, Human Resources Group	JOSEPH J. MAHON, JR.
Assistant Postmaster General, Employee Relations Department	JOEL S. TROSCH
Assistant Postmaster General, Labor Relations Department	SHERRY A. CAGNOLI
Assistant Postmaster General, Training and Development Department	ELWOOD A. MOSLEY
Senior Assistant Postmaster General, Administrative Services Group	MITCHELL H. GORDON
Assistant Postmaster General, Facilities Department	STANLEY W. SMITH
Assistant Postmaster General, Procurement and Supply Department	JOHN J. DAVIN
Assistant Postmaster General, Information Resource Management Department	RICHARD D. WEIRICH
Associate Postmaster General	EDWARD E. HORGAN, JR.
Assistant Postmaster General, Communications Department	DEBORAH K. BOWKER
Judicial Officer	JAMES A. COHEN
Assistant Postmaster General, Government Relations Department	WILLIAM T. JOHNSTONE
Assistant Postmaster General, International Postal Affairs Department	THOMAS E. LEAVEY
Senior Assistant Postmaster General, Marketing and Customer Service Group	RICHARD J. STRASSER, JR.
Assistant Postmaster General, Marketing	JOHN R. WARGO
Assistant Postmaster General, Philatelic and Retail Services Department	GORDON C. MORISON

[For the United States Postal Service statement of organization, see the *Code of Federal Regulations,* Title 39, Parts 221–226]

The United States Postal Service provides mail processing and delivery services to individuals and businesses within the United States. The Service is committed to the development of efficient mail-handling systems and operates its own planning and engineering programs. It is also the responsibility of the Postal Service to protect the mails from loss or theft and to apprehend those who violate postal laws.

The Postal Service was created as an independent establishment of the executive branch by the Postal Reorganization Act (39 U.S.C. 101 *et seq.*), approved August 12, 1970. The United States Postal Service commenced operations on July 1, 1971.

The Postal Service has more than 760,000 employees and handles more than 166 billion pieces of mail annually. The chief executive officer of the Postal Service, the Postmaster General, is appointed by the nine Governors of the Postal Service, who are appointed by the President with the advice and consent of

UNITED STATES POSTAL SERVICE

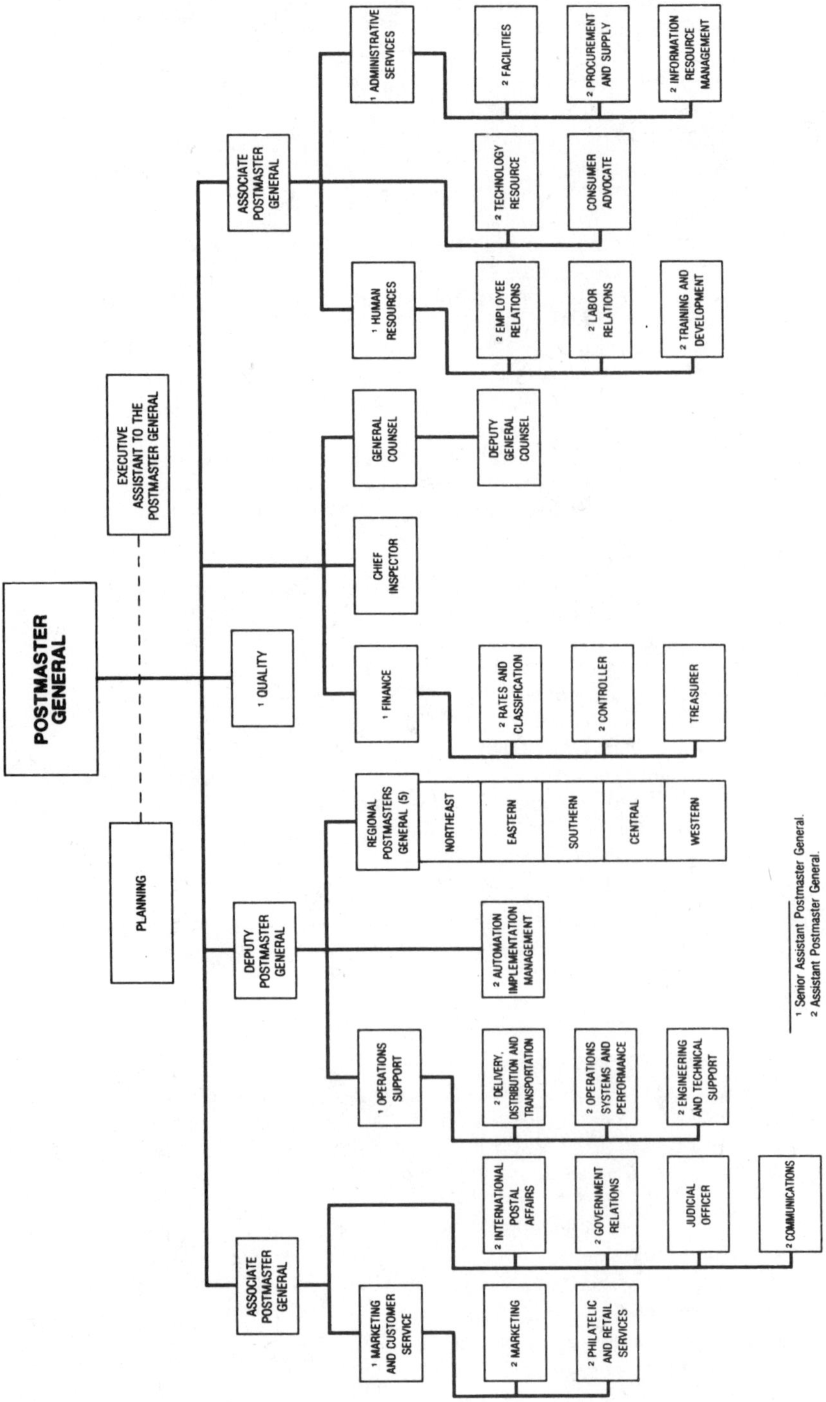

[1] Senior Assistant Postmaster General.
[2] Assistant Postmaster General.

the Senate for overlapping 9-year terms. The 9 Governors and the Postmaster General appoint the Deputy Postmaster General, and these 11 people constitute the Board of Governors.

In addition to the national headquarters, there are regional and field division offices supervising more than 40,000 post offices, branches, stations, and community post offices throughout the United States.

Activities

In order to expand and improve service to the public, the Postal Service is engaged in customer cooperation activities, including the development of programs for both the general public and major customers. The Consumer Advocate, a postal ombudsman, represents the interest of the individual mail customer in matters involving the Postal Service by bringing complaints and suggestions to the attention of top postal management and solving the problems of individual customers. To provide postal services responsive to public needs, the Postal Service operates its own planning, research, engineering, real estate, and procurement programs specially adapted to postal requirements, and maintains close ties with international postal organizations.

A fundamental commitment of the Postal Service is to provide swift and reliable mail delivery. Activities designed to facilitate postal operations include design and maintenance of the postal rate structure, development of mail classification standards, and generation of internal information necessary for effective management of the postal enterprise.

The Postal Service is the only Federal agency whose employment policies are governed by a process of collective bargaining. Labor contract negotiations, affecting all bargaining unit personnel, as well as personnel matters involving employees not covered by collective bargaining agreements, are administered by the Human Resources Group.

The Postal Inspection Service operates as the inspector general for the Postal Service and is its law enforcement arm. Duties include protecting the mails, postal funds, and property; investigating internal conditions and needs that may affect postal security and effectiveness; apprehending those who violate the postal laws; and auditing financial and nonfinancial operations.

There is a Regional Chief Inspector in each of the five postal regions. Information and complaints of postal violations should be presented to the nearest Postal Inspector in charge.

There are five Regional Postmasters General, each managing postal activities in a geographical area as indicated below.

Postal Regions—United States Postal Service

Region	Address	Telephone
CENTRAL—Colorado, Illinois, Indiana (except ZIP Codes 420, 423, 424, 470, 476, 477), Iowa, Kansas, Michigan, Minnesota, Missouri, Nebraska, North Dakota, South Dakota, Wisconsin, Wyoming	433 W. Van Buren St., Chicago, IL 60699–0100	312-765-5000
EASTERN—Delaware, District of Columbia, Indiana (ZIP Codes 420, 423, 424, 476, 477), Kentucky, Maryland, New Jersey (ZIP Codes 080–084), North Carolina, Ohio, Pennsylvania, South Carolina, Virginia, West Virginia	P.O. Box 8601, Philadelphia, PA 19197–0100	215-931-5001
NORTHEAST—Connecticut, Maine, Massachusetts, New Hampshire, New Jersey (ZIP Codes 070–079, 085–089), New York, Puerto Rico, Rhode Island, Vermont, Virgin Islands	6 Griffin Park Rd., North Windsor, CT 06006–0100	203-285-7001
SOUTHERN—Alabama, Arkansas, Florida, Georgia, Louisiana, Mississippi, Oklahoma, Tennessee, Texas (except ZIP Codes 797–799 and 885)	1407 Union Ave., Memphis, TN 38166–0100	901-722-7333

290-950 O 91 - 25

Postal Regions—United States Postal Service—Continued

Region	Address	Telephone
WESTERN—Alaska, Arizona, California, Hawaii, Idaho, Montana, Nevada, New Mexico, Oregon, Texas (ZIP Codes 797–799 and 885), Utah, Washington, Pacific Possessions and Trust Territories	850 Cherry Ave., San Bruno, CA 94099-0100	415–742–4922

Postal Inspection Service—United States Postal Service

Postal Region/Divisional Office	Address	Telephone
CENTRAL	Main Post Office Bldg., Chicago, IL 60607–5401	312–765–4605
Chicago, IL	433 W. Van Buren St., 60669–2201	312–765–4500
Denver, CO	P.O. Box 329, 80201–0329	303–297–6220
Des Moines, IA	P.O. Box 566, 50302–0566	515–253–9060
Detroit, MI	P.O. Box 330119, 48232–6119	313–226–8184
Indianapolis, IN	7188 Lakeview Pkwy. W. Dr., 46268–4101	317–328–2500
Kansas City, MO	P.O. Box 411606, 64141–1606	816–932–0400
Milwaukee, WI	P.O. Box 788, 53201–0788	414–291–2475
St. Louis, MO	1106 Walnut St., 63199–2201	314–539–9300
St. Paul, MN	P.O. Box 64558, 55164–2201	612–293–3202
EASTERN	1 Bala Cynwyd Plz., Bala Cynwyd, PA 19004–3609	215–668–4784
Baltimore, MD	P.O. Box 1856, 21203–1856	301–347–3480
Charlotte, NC	2901 I–85 S., 28228–3000	704–393–4470
Cincinnati, OH	P.O. Box 14487, 45250–0487	513–684–5700
Cleveland, OH	P.O. Box 5726, 44101–0726	216–443–4000
Harrisburg, PA	P.O. Box 3535, 17105–3535	717–257–2330
Philadelphia, PA	P.O. Box 7500, 19101–9000	215–895–8450
Pittsburgh, PA	1001 California Ave., 15290–9000	412–359–7900
Richmond, VA	P.O. Box 25009, 23260–5009	804–775–6267
Washington, DC	P.O. Box 96096, 20066–6096	202–636–2339
NORTHEAST	Gateway No. 2, McCarter Hwy. & Market St., Newark, NJ 07175–0001	201–621–5500
Boston, MA	P.O. Box 2217, 02202–2217	617–654–5825
Buffalo, NY	685 Ellicott Sq., 14203–2545	716–856–3674
Hartford, CT	P.O. Box 2169, 06145–2169	203–646–6060
Newark, NJ	P.O. Box 509, 07101–5901	201–596–5450
New York, NY	P.O. Box 555, James Farley Bldg., 10116–0555	212–330–3844
San Juan, PR	P.O. Box 3667, 00936–9614	809–753–2856
SOUTHERN	10th Fl., 1407 Union Ave., Memphis, TN 38161–0001	901–722–7700
Atlanta, GA	P.O. Box 16489, 30321–0489	404–765–7369
Birmingham, AL	P.O. Box 2767, 35202–2767	205–521–0270
Fort Worth, TX	P.O. Box 162929, 76161–2929	817–885–1111
Houston, TX	P.O. Box 1276, 77251–1276	713–236–7000
Memphis, TN	P.O. Box 3180, 38173–0180	901–576–2077
Miami, FL	P.O. Box 520772, 33152–0772	305–591–0379
New Orleans, LA	P.O. Box 51690, 70151–1690	504–589–1200
Tampa, FL	P.O. Box 22526, 33622–2526	813–228–2481
WESTERN	850 Cherry Ave., San Bruno, CA 94098–0100	415–742–4411
Pasadena, CA	P.O. Box 2000, 91102–2000	818–405–1200
Phoenix, AZ	P.O. Box 20666, 85036–0666	602–223–3660
Portland, OR	Suite 790, 921 SW., Washington, 97205–2898	503–294–2263
San Diego, CA	P.O. Box 2110, 92112–2110	619–233–0610
San Francisco, CA	P.O. Box 882000, 94188–2000	415–550–5602
Seattle, WA	P.O. Box 400, 98111–4000	206–442–6300

Sources of Information

Inquiries on the following information should be directed to the specified office, U.S. Postal Service, Washington, DC 20260, or to the appropriate regional office or post office, as indicated above.

Consumer Information Contact the Consumer Advocate. Phone, 202–268–2284. Information on specific products and services is available from the Marketing Department. Phone, 202–268–2205. Information on past and present schemes used to defraud the public is available through the Public Affairs Branch, Postal Inspection Service. Phone, 202–268–4293.

Contracts and Small Business Activities Contact the Procurement and Supply Department. Phone, 202–268–4633.

Employment General information about jobs such as clerk, letter carrier, etc., including information about programs for veterans, may be obtained by contacting the nearest post office.

Individuals interested in working at the Postal Headquarters in Washington, DC, may obtain information by calling 202-268-3218.

Information about Inspection Service employment may be obtained from the Chief Postal Inspector. Phone, 202-268-4267.

Films Contact the Communications Department for films available for loan to the public. Phone, 202-268-2189.

Philatelic Information Contact the Philatelic and Retail Services Department. Phone, 202-268-2312.

Philatelic Sales Contact the Philatelic Sales Branch, Kansas City, MO 64144-9998. Phone, 816-455-0970.

Publications Pamphlets on mailability, postage rates and fees, and many other topics may be obtained free of charge from the nearest post office.

Most postal regulations are contained in Postal Service manuals covering domestic mail, international mail, postal operations, administrative support, employee and labor relations, financial management, and procurement (Publication 41). These manuals and other publications including the *National ZIP Code and Post Office Directory* (Publication 65) may be purchased from the Superintendent of Documents, Government Printing Office, Washington, DC 20402-0001. (The *National ZIP Code and Post Office Directory* is also available through local post offices.)

Reading Rooms Located on 11th Floor North, Library Division. Phone, 202-268-2900.

Speakers Contact the Assistant Postmaster General, Communications Department, to schedule speakers and to coordinate Postal Service participation in meetings of national organizations and associations. Phone, 202-268-3653. Speakers for meetings that are regional or local in nature are scheduled by the appropriate Regional Postmaster General's office or the Regional Chief Inspector's office.

For further information, contact the U.S. Postal Service, Washington, DC 20260. Phone, 202-268-2000.

Boards, Commissions, and Committees

Note: This is a listing of Federal boards, centers, commissions, councils, panels, study groups, task forces, etc., not listed elsewhere in the *Manual,* which were established by congressional or Presidential action, whose functions are not strictly limited to the internal operations of a parent department or agency, and which are authorized to publish documents in the *Federal Register.* While the editors have attempted to compile a complete and accurate listing, suggestions for improving coverage of this guide are welcome. Please address your comments to the Office of the Federal Register, National Archives and Records Administration, Washington, DC 20408. Phone, 202–523–5230.

Federal advisory committees, as defined by the Federal Advisory Committee Act, as amended (5 U.S.C. app.), have not been included here. A complete listing of these committees can be found in the *Nineteenth Annual Report of the President on Federal Advisory Committees for Fiscal Year 1990.* For further information on Federal advisory committees and this report, contact the Committee Management Secretariat, General Services Administration, Room 6206, General Services Building (CTM), Washington, DC 20405. Phone, 202–501–4884.

Administrative Committee of the Federal Register

National Archives Building, Washington, DC 20408. Phone, 202–523–5240.

Advisory Commission on Intergovernmental Relations

Suite 2000, Vanguard Building, 1111 20th Street NW., Washington, DC 20575. Phone, 202–653–5540.

Advisory Council on Historic Preservation

Room 809, 1100 Pennsylvania Avenue NW., Washington, DC 20004. Phone, 202–786–0503.

American Battle Monuments Commission

Room 5127, Pulaski Building, 20 Massachusetts Avenue NW., Washington, DC 20314. Phone, 202–272–0533.

Appalachian Regional Commission

1666 Connecticut Avenue NW., Washington, DC 20235. Phone, 202–673–7893.

Architectural and Transportation Barriers Compliance Board

Suite 501, 1111 18th Street NW., Washington, DC 20036–3894. Phone, 202–653–7834.

Arctic Research Commission

Suite 6333, Interstate Commerce Commission Building, 12th Street and Constitution Avenue NW., Washington, DC 20423. Phone, 202–371–9631.

Arthritis and Musculoskeletal Interagency Coordinating Committee

National Institutes of Health, Room 4C32, Building 31, Bethesda, MD 20892. Phone, 301–496–4353.

Barry M. Goldwater Scholarship and Excellence in Education Foundation

Suite 405, 499 South Capitol Street SW., Washington, DC 20003–4013. Phone, 202–755–2312.

Board for International Broadcasting

Suite 400, 1201 Connecticut Avenue NW., Washington, DC 20036. Phone, 202–254–8040.

Christopher Columbus Quincentenary Jubilee Commission

Third Floor, 1801 F Street NW., Washington, DC 20006. Phone, 202–632–1992.

Citizens' Stamp Advisory Committee

Stamp Administration and Advisory Branch, United States Postal Service, Room 5670, 475 L'Enfant Plaza SW., Washington, DC 20260–6753. Phone, 202–268–6600.

Commission of Fine Arts

Suite 312, Pension Building, 441 F Street NW., Washington, DC 20001. Phone, 202–504–2200.

Committee on Foreign Investment in the United States

Room 5100, Main Treasury Building, 15th Street and Pennsylvania Avenue NW., Washington, DC 20220. Phone, 202–566–2386.

Committee for the Implementation of Textile Agreements

Department of Commerce, Room 3100, 14th Street and Constitution Avenue NW., Washington, DC 20230. Phone, 202–377–3737.

Committee for Purchase from the Blind and Other Severely Handicapped

Suite 1107, Crystal Square 5, 1755 Jefferson Davis Highway, Arlington, VA 22202–3509. Phone, 703–557–1145.

Coordinating Council on Juvenile Justice and Delinquency Prevention

Office of Juvenile Justice and Delinquency Prevention, Department of Justice, 633 Indiana Avenue NW., Washington, DC 20531. Phone, 202–307–0668.

Delaware River Basin Commission

Office of the United States Commissioner: Department of the Interior, Room 5113, 1100 L Street NW., Washington, DC 20240. Phone, 202–343–5761.

Office of the Executive Director: P.O. Box 7360, West Trenton, NJ 08628. Phone, 609–883–9500; (FTS) 483–2077.

Development Coordination Committee

Agency for International Development, Room 5942, 320 21st Street NW., Washington, DC 20523. Phone, 202–647–9620.

Endangered Species Committee

Department of the Interior, Room 4412, 1849 C Street NW., Washington, DC 20240. Phone, 202–208–4077.

Export Administration Review Board

Room 3886C, Herbert C. Hoover Building, 14th Street and Constitution Avenue NW., Washington, DC 20230. Phone, 202–377–3775.

Federal Financial Institutions Examination Council

Suite 850B, 1776 G Street NW., Washington, DC 20006. Phone, 202–357–0177.

Federal Financing Bank

Room 3054, Main Treasury Building, 15th Street and Pennsylvania Avenue NW., Washington, DC 20220. Phone, 202–566–2468.

Federal Interagency Committee on Education

Department of Education, Room 3061, Federal Office Building 6, 400 Maryland Avenue SW., Washington, DC 20202. Phone, 202–401–3669.

Federal Laboratory Consortium for Technology Transfer

Pacific Northwest Laboratory, P.O. Box 999, K1-34, Richland, WA 99352. Phone, 509-375-2559.

Federal Library and Information Center Committee

Library of Congress, Room 1026C, John Adams Building, Washington, DC 20540. Phone, 202-707-6055.

Franklin Delano Roosevelt Memorial Commission

H2347 House Office Building Annex No. 2, Washington, DC 20515. Phone, 202-226-2491.

Harry S Truman Scholarship Foundation

712 Jackson Place NW., Washington, DC 20006. Phone, 202-395-4831.

Illinois and Michigan Canal National Heritage Corridor Commission

15701 South Route 53, Lockport, IL 60441. Phone, 815-740-2047.

Indian Arts and Crafts Board

Department of the Interior, Room 4004, Main Interior Building, Washington, DC 20240. Phone, 202-208-3773.

Information Security Oversight Office

Suite 530, 750 17th Street NW., Washington, DC 20006. Phone, 202-634-6150.

Interagency Committee on Handicapped Employees [1]

Federal Sector Programs, Equal Employment Opportunity Commission, Room 5604, 1801 L Street NW., Washington, DC 20507. Phone, 202-663-4568; or (TDD) 202-663-4844.

Interagency United States Savings Bonds Committee

Suite 400A, 5550 Friendship Boulevard, Chevy Chase, MD 20815. Phone, 301-492-5797.

J. William Fulbright Foreign Scholarship Board

United States Information Agency, Room 247, 301 Fourth Street SW., Washington, DC 20547. Phone, 202-619-4290.

Japan-United States Friendship Commission

Room 3416, 1200 Pennsylvania Avenue NW., Washington, DC 20004. Phone, 202-275-7712.

Joint Board for the Enrollment of Actuaries

Department of the Treasury, Washington, DC 20220. Phone, 202-535-6787.

Mailers' Technical Advisory Committee

United States Postal Service, Marketing Department, Room 5410, 475 L'Enfant Plaza SW., Washington, DC 20260-6345. Phone, 202-268-2341.

Marine Mammal Commission

Room 512, 1825 Connecticut Avenue NW., Washington, DC 20009. Phone, 202-653-6237.

Migratory Bird Conservation Commission

622 ARLSQ, 18th and C Streets NW., Washington, DC 20240. Phone, 703-358-1716.

Mississippi River Commission

Lower Mississippi Valley Division, United States Army Corps of Engineers, P.O. Box 80, Vicksburg, MS 39181-0080. Phone, 601-634-5000.

National Advisory Council on International Monetary and Financial Policies

Room 5410, Main Treasury Building, 15th Street and Pennsylvania Avenue NW., Washington, DC 20220. Phone, 202-566-8170.

National Archives Trust Fund Board

Room G-5, National Archives Building, Seventh Street and Pennsylvania Avenue NW., Washington, DC 20408. Phone, 202-501-5155.

---

[1] *Also known as* Interagency Committee on Employment of People with Disabilities.

National Commission on Libraries and Information Science

Suite 310, 1111 18th Street NW., Washington, DC 20036. Phone, 202-254-3100.

National Communications System

Office of the Manager, Washington, DC 20305-2010. Phone, 703-692-3760.

National Council on Disability

Suite 814, 800 Independence Avenue SW., Washington, DC 20591. Phone, 202-267-3846; or (TDD) 202-267-3232.

National Historical Publications and Records Commission

Room 607, National Archives Building, Seventh Street and Pennsylvania Avenue NW., Washington, DC 20408. Phone, 202-501-5600.

National Occupational Information Coordinating Committee

Suite 156, 2100 M Street NW., Washington, DC 20037. Phone, 202-653-5665.

National Park Foundation

Suite 1008, 1101 17th Street NW., Washington, DC 20036. Phone, 202-785-4500.

Office of the Federal Inspector, Alaska Natural Gas Transportation System

FA-1, Room 3G064, 1000 Independence Avenue SW., Washington, DC 20585. Phone, 202-586-4669.

Office of Navajo and Hopi Indian Relocation

P.O. Box KK, Flagstaff, AZ 86002. Phone, 602-779-2721.

Office of Women's Business Ownership

Sixth Floor, 409 Third Street SW., Washington, DC 20416. Phone, 202-205-6673.

Pacific Northwest Electric Power and Conservation Planning Council

Suite 1100, 851 Southwest Sixth Avenue, Portland, OR 97204-1348. Phone, 503-222-5161.

Permanent Committee for the Oliver Wendell Holmes Devise

Manuscript Division, Library of Congress, Washington, DC 20540. Phone, 202-707-5383.

Physician Payment Review Commission

Suite 510, 2120 L Street NW., Washington, DC 20037. Phone, 202-653-7220.

President's Committee on Employment of People With Disabilities

Suite 636, 1111 20th Street NW., Washington, DC 20036. Phone, 202-653-5044; or (TDD) 202-653-5050.

President's Council on Integrity and Efficiency

Office of Management and Budget, Room 10221, New Executive Office Building, Washington, DC 20503. Phone, 202-395-6911.

President's Foreign Intelligence Advisory Board

Room 340, Old Executive Office Building, Washington, DC 20500. Phone, 202-456-2352.

President's Intelligence Oversight Board

Room 331, Old Executive Office Building, Washington, DC 20500. Phone, 202-456-2530.

Prospective Payment Assessment Commission

Suite 301B, 300 Seventh Street SW., Washington, DC 20024. Phone, 202-401-8986.

Regulatory Information Service Center

Suite 500, 750 17th Street NW., Washington, DC 20006. Phone, 202-634-6220.

Susquehanna River Basin Commission

Office of the United States Commissioner: Department of the Interior, Room 5113, 1100 L Street NW.,

Washington, DC 20240. Phone, 202–343–4091.

Office of the Executive Director: 1721 North Front Street, Harrisburg, PA 17102. Phone, 717–238–0422 (non-FTS).

Textile Trade Policy Group

Room 300, Winder Building, 600 17th Street NW., Washington, DC 20506. Phone, 202–395–3026.

Trade Policy Committee

Office of Policy Coordination, Room 517, Winder Building, 600 17th Street NW., Washington, DC 20506. Phone, 202–395–7210.

United States Holocaust Memorial Council

Suite 588, 2000 L Street NW., Washington, DC 20036. Phone, 202–653–9220.

United States Nuclear Waste Technical Review Board

Suite 910, 1100 Wilson Boulevard, Arlington, VA 22209. Phone, 703–235–4473.

United States Sentencing Commission

Suite 1400, 1331 Pennsylvania Avenue NW., Washington, DC 20004. Phone, 202–662–8800.

Veterans Day National Committee

Department of Veterans Affairs, Room 600, 810 Vermont Avenue NW., Washington, DC 20420. Phone, 202–233–7851.

White House Commission on Presidential Scholars

Room 2189, Federal Office Building 6, 400 Maryland Avenue SW., Washington, DC 20202. Phone, 202–401–0113.

QUASI–OFFICIAL AGENCIES

Note: This section contains organizations that are not Executive agencies under the definition in 5 U.S.C. 105 but that are required by statute to publish certain information on their programs and activities in the *Federal Register.*

LEGAL SERVICES CORPORATION

400 Virginia Avenue SW., Washington, DC 20024–2751
Phone, 202–863–1820

President	DAVID H. MARTIN
Vice President and General Counsel	(VACANCY)
Secretary	PATRICIA BATIE
Comptroller/Treasurer	DAVID RICHARDSON
Director, Office of Monitoring, Audit and Compliance	EMILIA DISANTO
Director, Office of Policy Development and Communications	ALAN SEVERSON
Director, Office of Field Services	ELLEN SMEAD
Inspector General	DAVID WILKINSON
Counsel to the Board	KENNETH F. BOEHM

[For the Legal Services Corporation statement of organization, see the *Code of Federal Regulations,* Title 45, Part 1601]

The Legal Services Corporation makes quality legal assistance for noncriminal proceedings available to those who would otherwise be unable to afford such assistance.

The Legal Services Corporation is a private, nonprofit organization established by the Legal Services Corporation Act of 1974, as amended (42 U.S.C. 2996), to provide financial support for legal assistance in noncriminal proceedings to persons financially unable to afford legal services.

The Corporation is governed by an 11-member Board of Directors, appointed by the President with the advice and consent of the Senate. The President of the Corporation, appointed by the Board of Directors, is the chief executive officer and serves as an *ex officio* Board member.

The Corporation provides financial assistance to qualified programs furnishing legal assistance to eligible clients and makes grants to and contracts with individuals, firms, corporations, and organizations for the purpose of providing legal assistance to these clients.

The Corporation establishes maximum income levels for clients based on family size, urban and rural differences, and cost-of-living variations. Using these maximum income levels and other financial factors, the Corporation's recipient programs establish criteria to determine the eligibility of clients and priorities of service based on an appraisal of the legal needs of the eligible client community.

The Corporation also conducts research and technical assistance activities.

For further information, contact the Division of Public Affairs, Legal Services Corporation, 400 Virginia Avenue SW., Washington, DC 20024–2751. Phone, 202–863–1820.

SMITHSONIAN INSTITUTION

1000 Jefferson Drive SW., Washington, DC 20560
Phone, 202–357–1300

The Establishment

The President of the United States
The Vice President of the United States
The Chief Justice of the United States
The Secretary of State
The Secretary of the Treasury
The Secretary of Defense
The Attorney General
The Secretary of the Interior
The Secretary of Agriculture
The Secretary of Commerce
The Secretary of Labor
The Secretary of Health and Human Services
The Secretary of Housing and Urban Development
The Secretary of Transportation
The Secretary of Energy
The Secretary of Education

Board of Regents:

The Chief Justice of the United States (*Chancellor*)	WILLIAM H. REHNQUIST
The Vice President of the United States	DAN QUAYLE
Members of the Senate	JAKE GARN
	DANIEL PATRICK MOYNIHAN
	JIM SASSER
Members of the House of Representatives	JAMIE L. WHITTEN
	IRA MICHAEL HEYMAN
	NORMAN Y. MINETA
Citizen Members	ANNE L. ARMSTRONG, MURRAY GELL-MANN, DAVID C. ACHESON, JEANNINE SMITH CLARK, SAMUEL C. JOHNSON, WILLIAM G. BOWEN, BARNABAS MCHENRY, HOMER A. NEAL, R. JAMES WOOLSEY

Officials:

The Secretary	Robert McC. Adams
Executive Assistant to the Secretary	James M. Hobbins
Special Assistant to the Secretary	Kathy Boi
General Counsel	Peter G. Powers
Under Secretary	Carmen Turner
The Inspector General	Thomas D. Blair
Assistant Secretary for Finance and Administration	Nancy Suttenfield
Director, Office of Sponsored Projects	Ardelle Foss
Director, Management Analysis Office	John G. Motheral
Director, Office of Equal Opportunity	Will Douglas, Jr.
Director, Office of Human Resources	Marilyn S. Marton
Director, Office of Printing and Photographic Services	James H. Wallace, Jr.
Director, Office of Planning and Budget	Mary J. Rodriguez, *Acting*
Director, Office of Contracting and Property Management	Robert P. Perkins
Director, Travel Services Office	Judith Petroski
Director of Facilities Services	Richard Siegle
Director, Office of Design and Construction	Robert Dillman
Director, Office of Plant Services	Michael R. League
Director, Office of Protection Services	Robert B. Burke
Director, Office of Information Resource Management	Vincent J. Marcalus
Director of Merchandising, Mail Order Division	John Giesecke
Director, Museum Shops	Edward Sullivan
Director, Office of Congressional Liaison	Margaret C. Gaynor
Director, Office of Architectural History and Historic Preservation	Cynthia R. Field
Director, Office of Environmental Management and Safety	F. William Billingsley
Treasurer	Rick Johnson, *Acting*
Comptroller, Office of Accounting and Financial Services	Shireen Dodson
Director, Office of Risk Management	Phillip H. Babcock
Business Manager, Office of Business Management	James J. Chmelik
Concessions Administrator	Roland Banscher
Director, Office of Product Development and Licensing	Lisa Stevenson
Director, Office of Financial Management and Planning	John Wilson, *Acting*
Director, Office of Sponsored Projects	Ardelle Foss
Assistant Secretary for Museums	Tom L. Freudenheim
Director, Archives of American Art	Richard Wattenmaker
Director, Cooper-Hewitt Museum	Dianne Pilgrim
Director, Freer Gallery of Art and Arthur M. Sackler Gallery	Milo C. Beach
Director, Hirshhorn Museum and Sculpture Garden	James T. Demetrion
Director, National Museum of African Art	Sylvia Williams

Associate Director for Collections and Research (NMAFA)	Roy Sieber
Director, National Museum of American Art	Elizabeth Broun
Curator in Charge, Renwick Gallery	Michael W. Monroe
Director, National Museum of American History	Roger G. Kennedy
Director, National Museum of the American Indian	W. Richard West, Jr.
Director, National Portrait Gallery	Alan M. Fern
Director, National Air and Space Museum	Martin O. Harwit
Director, National Museum of Natural History	Frank H. Talbot
Director, Office of Exhibits Central	(vacancy)
Assistant Directors, Office of Exhibits Central	Karen Fort Walter Sorrell
Director, Office of Museum Programs	James E. Sims, *Acting*
Registrar	Mary Case
Director, Office of Horticulture	Kathryn Meehan, *Acting*
Director, Smithsonian Institution Traveling Exhibition Service	Anna R. Cohn
Director, Anacostia Museum	Steven Newsome
Director, Office of Institutional Studies	Zahava Doering
Assistant Secretary for Research	Robert S. Hoffmann
Deputy Assistant Secretary for Research	Ross B. Simons
Editor, Joseph Henry Papers	Marc Rothenberg
Director, American Studies Program	Wilcomb E. Washburn
Director, National Zoological Park	Michael H. Robinson
Director, Office of Fellowships and Grants	Roberta Rubinoff
Director, Smithsonian Environmental Research Center	David L. Correll
Director, Smithsonian Astrophysical Observatory	Irwin I. Shapiro
Director, Smithsonian Tropical Research Institute	Ira Rubinoff
Director, Conservation Analytical Laboratory	Lambertus Van Zelst
Deputy Director, Conservation Analytical Laboratory	Alan W. Postlethwaite
Director, Office of Quincentenary Programs	Alicia Gonzalez
Director, Smithsonian Institution Libraries	Barbara Smith
Director, Smithsonian International Exchange Service	Thomas J. Matthews
Director, Museum Support Center	Vincent Wilcox
Director, Office of Interdisciplinary Studies	Ross B. Simons
Coordinator, International Environmental Science Program	Rita Jordan
Director, Office of Environmental Awareness	Judith Gradwohl
Director, Smithsonian Institution Archives	William Moss
Assistant Secretary for Public Service	James Early, *Acting*
Director, Office of Conference Services	Cheryl LaBerge
Director, Office of Elementary and Secondary Education	Ann Bay
Director, Visitor Information and Associates' Reception Center	Mary Grace Potter
Director, Office of Folklife Programs	Richard Kurin

Director, Office of Public Affairs	MADELEINE JACOBS
Director, National Science Resources Center	DOUGLAS LAPP
Director, Office of Wider Audience Development	MARSHALL WONG
Assistant Secretary for External Affairs	THOMAS E. LOVEJOY
Deputy Assistant Secretary for External Affairs	MARC PACHTER
Special Assistant, Office of the Assistant Secretary for External Affairs	E. JEFFREY STANN
Director, Office of International Relations	FRANCINE BERKOWITZ
Coordinator, International Center	FRANCINE BERKOWITZ
Program Manager for Smithsonian Man and the Biosphere Program	FRANCISCO DALLMEIER
Director, Office of Telecommunications	PAUL B. JOHNSON
Director, Smithsonian Institution Press	FELIX C. LOWE
Deputy Director	VINCENT L. MACDONNELL
Editor, Smithsonian Magazine	DONALD B. MOSER
Publisher, Smithsonian Magazine	RON WALKER
Director, Office of Development	MARIE MATTSON
Director, Resident Associate Program	JANET W. SOLINGER
Associate Director for Programs, Resident Associate Program	EDMUND H. WORTHY, JR.
Director, National Associate Program	JOSEPH CARPER
Director, Office of Special Events	BARBARA H. SPRAGGINS
Assistant Secretary for Institutional Initiatives	ALICE GREENE BURNETT

The John F. Kennedy Center for the Performing Arts [1]

Chairman	JAMES D. WOLFENSOHN

National Gallery of Art [1]

President	JOHN R. STEVENSON
Director	J. CARTER BROWN

Woodrow Wilson International Center for Scholars [1]

Director	CHARLES BLITZER
Deputy Director	SAMUEL WELLS
Deputy Director for Planning and Management	DEAN W. ANDERSON
Chairman, Board of Trustees	WILLIAM J. BAROODY, JR.

The Smithsonian Institution is an independent trust instrumentality of the United States that fosters the increase and diffusion of knowledge. History, technology, science, and the arts are represented in exhibits through the conduct of research, publication of studies, and participation in cooperative international programs of scholarly exchange.

[1] Administered under a separate Board of Trustees.

SMITHSONIAN INSTITUTION

Under Separate Boards of Trustees

JOHN F. KENNEDY CENTER FOR THE PERFORMING ARTS

NATIONAL GALLERY OF ART

WOODROW WILSON INTERNATIONAL CENTER FOR SCHOLARS

Secretariat•

Office of Inspector General

BOARD OF REGENTS

THE SECRETARY•

UNDER SECRETARY•

BOARDS AND COMMISSIONS

Advisory Council on Education
Archives of American Art Board of Trustees
Arthur M. Sackler Gallery Visiting Committee
Cooper-Hewitt National Museum of Design Advisory Board
Cultural Education Committee
Folklife Advisory Council
Freer Gallery of Art Visting Committee
Hirshhorn Museum and Sculpture Garden Board of Trustees
National Air and Space Museum Advisory Board
National Museum of African Art Commission
National Museum of American Art Commission
National Museum of the American Indian, Board of Trustees
National Council of the National Museum of Natural History
National Portrait Gallery Commission
National Science Resources Center Advisory Board
Smithsonian Council
Smithsonian National Board
Women's Committee of the Smithsonian Associates

GENERAL COUNSEL•

ASSISTANT SECRETARY FOR FINANCE AND ADMINISTRATION•

Office of the Treasurer•
Business Management Office
Office of Accounting and Financial Services
Office of Financial Management and Planning
Office of Planning and Budget
Office of Contracting and Property Management
Office of Risk Management
Office of Sponsored Projects

Management Analysis Office
Office of Equal Opportunity
Office of Facilities Services
Office of Architectural History and Historic Preservation
Office of Design and Construction
Office of Environmental Management and Safety
Office of Plant Services
Office of Protection Services

Office of Human Resources
Office of Information Resource Management
Office of Printing and Photographic Services
Travel Services Office

ASSISTANT SECRETARY FOR INSTITUTIONAL INITIATIVES•

ASSISTANT SECRETARY FOR RESEARCH•

International Environmental Science Program
National Zoological Park••
Office of Environmental Awareness
Office of Fellowships and Grants
Office of Interdisciplinary Studies
Office of Quincentenary Programs
Smithsonian Astrophysical Observatory
Smithsonian Environmental Research Center
Smithsonian Institution Archives
Smithsonian Institution Libraries
Smithsonian Tropical Research Institute

ASSISTANT SECRETARY FOR MUSEUMS•

Anacostia Museum••
Archives of American Art••
Arthur M. Sackler Gallery and Freer Gallery of Art••
Conservation Analytical Laboratory••
Cooper-Hewitt National Museum of Design••
Hirshhorn Museum and Sculpture Garden••
International Gallery
National Air and Space Museum••
National Museum of African Art••
National Museum of American Art••
Renwick Gallery••
National Museum of American History••
National Museum of the American Indian••
National Museum of Natural History/ National Museum of Man••
Museum Support Center••
National Portrait Gallery••
Office of Exhibits Central
Office of Horticulture
Office of Institutional Studies
Office of Museum Programs
Office of the Registrar
Smithsonian Institution Traveling Exhibition Service

ASSISTANT SECRETARY FOR PUBLIC SERVICE•

National Science Resources Center
Office of Conference Services
Office of Elementary and Secondary Education
Office of Folklife Programs
Office of Public Affairs
Office of Wider Audience Development
Visitor Information and Associates' Reception Center

ASSISTANT SECRETARY FOR EXTERNAL AFFAIRS•

Office of Development•
Office of Government Relations•
Office of International Relations
Office of Special Events
Office of Telecommunications
Smithsonian Institution Press
Smithsonian Magazine
Air and Space Magazine
Smithsonian National Associate Program
Smithsonian Resident Associate Program

•Secretary's Management Committee.
••The assistant secretaries for research and museums collaborate in the oversight of scholarly and presentational activities in these bureaus and offices.

The Smithsonian Institution was created by act of August 10, 1846 (20 U.S.C. 41 *et seq.*), to carry out the terms of the will of James Smithson of England, who in 1829 had bequeathed his entire estate to the United States "to found at Washington, under the name of the Smithsonian Institution, an establishment for the increase and diffusion of knowledge among men." On July 1, 1836, Congress accepted the legacy and pledged the faith of the United States to the charitable trust.

After accepting the trust property for the United States, Congress vested responsibility for administering the trust in the Smithsonian Board of Regents, composed of the Chief Justice, the Vice President, three Members of the Senate, three Members of the House of Representatives, and nine citizen members appointed by joint resolution of Congress.

To carry out Smithson's mandate, the Institution:

—performs fundamental research;

—publishes the results of studies, explorations, and investigations;

—preserves for study and reference some 137 million items of scientific, cultural, and historical interest;

—maintains exhibits representative of the arts, American history, technology, aeronautics and space exploration, and natural history;

—participates in the international exchange of learned publications; and

—engages in programs of education and national and international cooperative research and training, supported by its trust endowments and gifts, grants and contracts, and funds appropriated to it by Congress.

Activities

Anacostia Museum The Museum is located in the historic Fort Stanton neighborhood of southeast Washington. The Museum serves as a national resource for exhibitions, scholarly and applied research, historical documentation, and interpretive and educational programs relating to African American history and culture. The African-American church, the Harlem Renaissance, African-American inventors, and works by renowned artists such as Sam Gilliam have been the subjects of exhibitions by the Museum.

The Research Department, open for use by scholars, supports exhibition design and educational programs. It conducts independent studies of African-American history, minority and ethnic studies, and the history of Anacostia and Washington, DC.

The Education Department designs, prepares, and schedules programs that enhance current exhibitions and develops independent programs and activities to serve the needs and interests of the immediate neighborhood, as well as the broader community. These activities include guided tours, demonstrations, lectures, storytelling, teacher seminars, family workshops, conservation seminars, and performing arts programs.

For further information, contact the Anacostia Museum, 1901 Fort Place SE., Washington, DC 20020. Phone, 202–287–3369.

Archives of American Art The Archives contains the Nation's largest collection of documentary materials reflecting the history of visual arts in the United States. The Archives gathers, preserves, and microfilms the papers of artists, craftsmen, collectors, dealers, critics, museums, and art societies. These papers consist of manuscripts, letters, notebooks, sketchbooks, business records, clippings, exhibition catalogs, tape-recorded interviews, and photographs of artists and their work. The extensive microfilm holdings of the archives also include bodies of materials not belonging to the archives but recorded by it with permission of the owner.

The Archives' chief processing and reference center is in the Smithsonian's Museum of American Art and Portrait Gallery Building. The Archives has administrative offices in both Washington and New York. Regional branch offices, each with a complete set of microfilm duplicating the archives' collections, are located in Boston, Detroit, Los Angeles, New York, and San Francisco.

For further information, contact the Archives of American Art, Smithsonian Institution, Washington, DC 20560. Phone, 202-357-2781.

Arthur M. Sackler Gallery The museum of Asian art opened to the public September 1987 on the National Mall. Changing exhibitions drawn from major collections in the United States and abroad, as well as from the permanent holdings of the Sackler Gallery, are displayed in the distinctive new museum. The Gallery's permanent collection is founded on a group of 1,000 art objects from China, South and Southeast Asia, and the ancient Near East that was given by the late Arthur M. Sackler, a medical researcher, publisher, and art collector. Highlights include Chinese jades and bronzes, ancient Near Eastern gold and silver, and Persian manuscripts. Programs at the Gallery include loan exhibitions and major international shows offering both surveys of distinctive Asian traditions and comparative exhibitions showing the art of different centuries, geographic areas, and types of patronage. Many exhibitions are accompanied by public programs and scholarly symposia.

For further information, contact the Arthur M. Sackler Gallery, 1050 Independence Avenue SW., Washington, DC 20560. Phone, 202-357-4880.

Conservation Analytical Laboratory The Laboratory provides a focus within the Smithsonian Institution for conservation of the millions of artifacts in the collections. It provides chemical analyses to curators for cataloging purposes, and to conservators for establishing the nature of a particular example of deterioration and for determining whether commercial materials proposed for use in prolonged contact with artifacts are truly safe. It treats many hundreds of artifacts each year and, upon request, supports other conservators in the Institution with advice and specialized materials. It collaborates with archeologists, curators, and university and government laboratories in archeometric studies.

For further information, contact the Director, Conservation Analytical Laboratory, Museum Support Center, 4210 Silver Hill Road, Suitland, MD 20560. Phone, 301-238-3700.

Cooper-Hewitt Museum, the Smithsonian Institution's National Museum of Design The Museum is located in New York City. Its collection consists of more than 165,000 items. It maintains a reference library of about 50,000 volumes relating to design, ornament, and architecture, and a picture library of several million photographs and clippings, as well as a series of archives devoted to color material and industrial design. The Museum is not only a major assemblage of decorative art materials but also a research laboratory serving professionals and students of design. The regularly changing exhibitions always relate to some aspect of design. The museum is open daily except Mondays and major holidays.

For further information, contact the Cooper-Hewitt Museum, 2 East Ninety-First Street, New York, NY 10128. Phone, 212-860-6868.

Freer Gallery of Art The building, the original collection, and an endowment fund were the gift of Charles Lang Freer. The Gallery houses one of the world's most renowned collections of oriental art as well as an important group of ancient Egyptian glass, early Christian manuscripts, and the works of James McNeill Whistler together with other late 19th and early 20th century American painters.

Over 10,000 objects in the oriental section represent the arts of the Far East, the Near East, Indochina, and India, including paintings, manuscripts, scrolls, screens, pottery, metalwork, glass, jade, lacquer, and sculpture. Members of the staff conduct research on objects in the collection and publish results in scholarly journals and books. They arrange special exhibitions and present lectures in their field of specialization.

The Gallery is closed for renovation and expansion until 1992.

For further information, contact the Freer Gallery of Art, Twelfth Street and Jefferson Drive SW., Washington, DC 20560. Phone, 202-357-4880.

Hirshhorn Museum and Sculpture Garden The Museum houses major collections of art consisting primarily of American and European painting and sculpture of the past 100 years. The nucleus of the collection is the gift of more than 6,000 works of art presented in 1966 to the people of the United States by Joseph H. Hirshhorn (1899–1981).

Supplementing the permanent collection are loan exhibitions focusing on contemporary painting and sculpture as well as on art movements of the modern era. There is an active program of public service and education, including docent tours through the Museum to introduce visitors to the collections, lectures on contemporary art and artists, films of historic and artistic interest, and others. The Museum houses a collection research facility, a specialized 10,000-volume art library, and a photographic archive—available for consultation by prior appointment.

For further information, contact the Hirshhorn Museum and Sculpture Garden, Eighth Street and Independence Avenue SW., Washington, DC 20560. Phone, 202–357–3091.

National Museum of African Art This is the only art museum in the United States dedicated exclusively to portraying the rich, creative heritage of Africa.

Established in 1964 and incorporated as a bureau of the Smithsonian in 1979, the Museum opened its new location on the National Mall in September 1987. Its research components, collection, exhibitions, and public programs establish the Museum as a primary source for the examination and discovery of the arts and culture of sub-Saharan Africa. In recent years, works of outstanding aesthetic quality have been added to a collection numbering about 6,000 works in wood, metal, fired clay, ivory, and fiber. Examples of sub-Saharan traditional art include a wooden figure of a Zairian Yombe carver; a Lower Niger Bronze Industry vessel, with chameleons; and a memorial grave figure of a colonial officer from the Cameroon Grassfields.

The Eliot Elisofon Photographic Archives includes some 100,000 slides, photos, and film segments on Africa. There is also a specialized library of 18,000 volumes and periodicals.

For further information, contact the Museum of African Art, 950 Independence Avenue SW., Washington, DC 20560. Phone, 202–357–4600.

National Air and Space Museum Created to memorialize the development of aviation and space flight, the Museum collects, displays, and preserves aeronautical and space flight artifacts of historical significance as well as documentary and artistic materials related to air and space. The exhibitions and study collections record human conquest of the air from its tentative beginnings to recent achievements by high altitude aircraft, guided missiles, rockets, satellites, and manned space flight. The principal areas in which work is concentrated include flight craft of all types, manned and unmanned, space flight vehicles, and propulsion systems.

The Langley Theater, with a giant screen presentation, and the 70-foot domed Einstein Planetarium are featured.

For further information, contact the National Air and Space Museum, Seventh Street and Independence Avenue SW., Washington, DC 20560. Phone, 202–357–1745.

National Museum of American Art This museum is devoted to American painting, sculpture, folk art, photography, and graphic art from the 18th century to the present. A portion of the Museum's permanent collection of over 35,000 works is exhibited in its extensive galleries, and the remainder is available for study by scholars. Various aspects of American art are examined through numerous temporary exhibitions, accompanied by carefully documented publications. The Department of Educational Programs conducts tours for schoolchildren, university students, and the general public. It also has a program for junior interns. A research program for visiting scholars, both predoctoral and postdoctoral, is maintained, and training for university interns in all aspects of museum operations, including conservation, is carried on under staff supervision.

The Renwick Gallery presents special exhibitions of contemporary American crafts, with accompanying publications, as well as a selection of objects, dating from 1900 to the present, from its permanent collection. It also maintains an active film and lecture program.

Guided tours of the galleries, and special educational programs for schools and organizations are provided.

For further information, contact the National Museum of American Art, Eighth and G Streets NW., Washington, DC 20560. Phone, 202–357–1959.

National Museum of American History The Museum's exhibits offer a unique view of the American experience. Important elements of the collections present the European background, but emphasis is placed upon the growth of the United States, upon the men and women who have shaped our heritage, upon science and the arts, and upon the remaking of our world through technology.

Exhibits draw upon strong collections in the sciences and engineering, agriculture, manufacturing, transportation, medicine, printing, photography, ceramics, coins and stamps, and glass. Outstanding holdings include Whitney's cotton gin, Morse's telegraph, the John Bull locomotive, and a great variety of scientific instruments. Political, social, military, and cultural history are also well represented. Recent major installations treat everyday life in America just after the Revolutionary War, the American Industrial Revolution, and the diverse origins of the American people. The Museum offers changing exhibits on a wide range of subjects including news reporting, information technology, American music, and American cars and trains. Demonstrations, films, and performances highlight many aspects of the museum.

Scholars may be aided in the use of the Museum's research collections and specialized library facilities by appointment.

For further information, contact the National Museum of American History, Twelfth Street and Constitution Avenue NW., Washington, DC 20560. Phone, 202–357–2510.

National Museum of the American Indian The Museum was established by act of November 28, 1989 (20 U.S.C. 80q *et seq.*), and will eventually be located in a facility to be built on the National Mall in Washington, DC, near the end of the decade. In the meantime, some of the Museum's collections are on view at 155th Street and Broadway, New York City, until another exhibition area is opened to the public in the Custom House in New York City around 1993. The Musuem, whose collections were transferred from the former Museum of the American Indian, Heye Foundation, in New York City, is dedicated to the collection, preservation, study, and exhibition of the culture and history of the native peoples of the Americas.

Highlights include Northwest Coast carvings; Eskimo masks; Kachina dolls from the Southwest; painted hides and garments from the Plains; goldwork from Colombia, Mexico, and Peru; and Amazonian featherwork.

For information on hours and admission fees, call 212–283–2420 (in New York City) or 202–357–2700 (in Washington, DC).

For further information, contact the National Museum of the American Indian, Room 3161, 900 Jefferson Drive SW., Washington, DC 20560. Phone, 202–786–2784.

National Museum of Natural History This museum serves as a national and international center for the natural sciences. Among the exhibits are halls devoted to the Ice Age; the rise of Western civilization; mammals; birds; human biology; dinosaurs and other extinct animals and plants; sea life; South American, Asian, African, and Pacific cultures; gems and minerals; and American Indians. Notable attractions include a 3,000-gallon tank containing a living coral reef; a live-insect zoo; a discovery room, where persons of all ages may touch and handle natural history specimens; and a naturalist center designed to provide a quiet library atmosphere for amateur naturalists.

The Museum maintains the largest natural history reference collections in the Nation available to qualified researchers. Systematic and biological studies at the museum are providing new information that is of use in conservation, monitoring pollution, food production, improvement of medical knowledge, and other problems.

A Global Volcanism Network notifies scientists throughout the world of volcanic eruptions, earthquakes, meteorite falls and finds, and bright fireballs. The Museum also administers the Oceanographic Sorting Center, which sorts and distributes collections of marine animals to international researchers and the Smithsonian Marine Station at Link Port, which conducts marine biological research along the Florida coast.

The Museum staff participates in joint educational programs with universities by teaching courses, training graduate students, and conducting science seminars.

For further information, contact the National Museum of Natural History, Tenth Street and Constitution Avenue NW., Washington, DC 20560. Phone, 202-357-2664.

National Portrait Gallery The Gallery was established by act of April 27, 1962 (20 U.S.C. 75a), as a museum of the Smithsonian Institution "for the exhibition and study of portraiture depicting men and women who have made significant contributions to the history, development, and culture of the people of the United States." It is housed in one of the oldest Government structures in Washington—the former U.S. Patent Office Building, constructed between 1836 and 1867—on the very site that Pierre L'Enfant, in his original plan for the city, had designated for a pantheon to honor the Nation's immortals.

The first floor of the Gallery is devoted to major loan exhibitions, changing exhibitions from the Gallery's collection of paintings, sculpture, prints, photographs, and drawings as well as several galleries with special portrait collections. On the second floor are featured the permanent collection of portraits of eminent Americans and the Hall of Presidents containing portraits and associative items of our Chief Executives. The two-story Victorian Renaissance Great Hall on the third floor is used for special events and exhibitions.

Publications include richly illustrated catalogs for major shows, an illustrated checklist of portraits in the collection, and educational materials designed to be used as teaching guides.

A 45,000-volume library is shared with the National Museum of American Art. The education department offers outreach programs for elementary and secondary schools, senior citizen groups, hospitals, and nursing homes; walk-in or group tours; and programs for handicapped audiences.

For general information and descriptive brochures on the Gallery's activities, contact the Public Affairs Office, National Portrait Gallery, Eighth and F Streets NW., Washington, DC 20560. Phone, 202-357-1915.

National Zoological Park The Park covers an area of approximately 165 acres of parkland along Rock Creek, 2 miles north of the center of Washington. In addition, it operates a 3,000-acre conservation and research center near Front Royal, VA. Its collection is outstanding, and comprises about 5,000 living mammals, birds, amphibians, and reptiles of about 500 species. Research objectives include investigations in animal behavior, ecology, nutrition, reproductive physiology, pathology, and clinical medicine. Conservation-oriented studies cover maintenance of wild populations and long-term captive breeding and care of endangered species.

For further information, contact the National Zoological Park, 3001 Connecticut Avenue NW., Washington, DC 20008. Phone, 202-673-4721.

American Studies Program This office conducts a graduate program in the material aspects of American civilization for graduate students enrolled in cooperating universities. Interested students should apply to the American studies departments of the George Washington University or the University of Maryland or the Office of American Studies, Smithsonian Institution, Washington, DC 20560.

For further information, contact the Office of American Studies, Barney Studio House, Smithsonian Institution, Washington, DC 20560. Phone, 202-673-4872.

Office of Fellowships and Grants This office develops and administers the numerous Smithsonian programs designed to assist scholars and students from the United States and throughout the world in utilizing the Institution's unique resources. These academic programs, which include long- and short-term appointments, are an important complement to those offered by universities and support participants' research in art, history, and science.

Predoctoral, postdoctoral, and graduate student fellowship programs provide scholars and students the opportunity to conduct research on independently conceived projects at Smithsonian facilities in conjunction with the Institution's research staff.

Internship programs provide undergraduate and graduate students the opportunity to participate in ongoing research projects with the Smithsonian's research staff. In addition to these programs, the Office administers other research opportunity programs for many of the Smithsonian bureaus.

For further information, contact the Office of Fellowships and Grants, Suite 7300, 955 L'Enfant Plaza SW., Washington, DC 20560. Phone, 202-287-3271.

Office of Folklife Programs This office is responsible for research, documentation, and presentation of American folklife traditions. It prepares publications based on the papers, films, tapes, and other materials amassed during previous Festivals of American Folklife and directs the planning, development, and presentation of future folklife programs.

For further information, contact the Office of Folklife Programs, Suite 2600, 955 L'Enfant Plaza, Washington, DC 20560. Phone, 202-287-3424.

Office of Interdisciplinary Studies This office brings together the Smithsonian's own professional staff, visiting investigators, and distinguished figures from many areas of intellectual accomplishment in interdisciplinary symposia, colloquia, and seminars. It develops the Institution's international symposia series at which leading scholars and specialists from all over the world examine themes of contemporary concern and significance. These programs consist of closed scholarly working sessions and special presentations for the interested public; an important feature is the publication by the Smithsonian Institution Press of a book based on each symposium's overall activities.

Consultative colloquia and seminars are organized regularly on a smaller scale within the spectrum of Smithsonian research interests. The Office works closely with the many bureaus of the Institution in bridging the sciences and humanities for the benefit of specialists and nonspecialists from the United States and other countries.

For further information, contact the Office of Interdisciplinary Studies, 905 L'Enfant Plaza SW., Washington, DC 20560. Phone, 202-287-3657.

International Center The International Center supports Smithsonian activities abroad and coordinates the Smithsonian's international interests, particularly those that do not fall within the scope of a single Smithsonian bureau or museum. The International Center provides a meeting place and an organizational channel to bring together the world's scholars, museum professionals, decisionmakers, and the general public, to attend and participate in conferences, public forums, lectures, performances, exhibitions, films, and workshops. Through the International Center, the Smithsonian seeks to encourage a broadening of public understanding of the histories, cultures, and natural environments of regions throughout the world.

For further information, contact the Office of International Relations, Room 3123, 1100 Jefferson Drive SW., Washington, DC 20560. Phone, 202-357-4281.

Office of Museum Programs This office provides professional guidance and technical assistance to museums on collections and their management, exhibition techniques, educational activities, and operational methods. It conducts training programs for museum professionals and administers a central intern referral and placement service. The Office also supports programs in museum careers. It cooperates with American and foreign museums and governmental agencies on museum matters and houses the Museum Reference Center, the Nation's only museological library.

For further information, contact the Office of Museum Programs, 900 Jefferson Drive SW., Washington, DC 20560. Phone, 202–357–3101.

Smithsonian International Exchange Service This office is set up to distribute the publications of the Smithsonian Institution to scientific and learned institutions abroad.

The staff accepts addressed packages of publications from libraries, scientific societies, and educational institutions in the United States for transmission to similar organizations in foreign countries, and in return receives addressed publications from foreign sources for distribution in the United States.

For further information, contact the Smithsonian International Exchange Service, 1111 North Capitol Street, Washington, DC 20560. Phone, 202–357–1964.

Smithsonian Archives The Archives, which is open by appointment to the scholarly community and the general public, is the official depository for the Institution's records. These records are essential to an understanding of the growth of the Institution. They are equally significant for their documentation of the development of science and art in America, particularly during the 19th century, a process in which the Smithsonian played a major part. In addition to its official records, the archives holds a substantial number of private papers that further document the Smithsonian's role through the lives of eminent scientists, such as Joseph Henry, Spencer F. Baird, Samuel P. Langley, Charles D. Walcott, and Charles Greeley Abbot. Holdings are described in the *Guide to Smithsonian Archives,* Smithsonian Institution Press, 1978.

For further information, contact the Smithsonian Archives, 900 Jefferson Drive SW., Washington, DC 20560. Phone, 202–357–1420.

Smithsonian Astrophysical Observatory The Observatory is located in Cambridge, MA, on the grounds of the Harvard College Observatory. Since 1973, the observatories have coordinated research activities under a single director in a cooperative venture known as the Harvard-Smithsonian Center for Astrophysics.

The Center's research activities are organized in seven divisions, as follows: atomic and molecular physics, radio and geoastronomy, high-energy astrophysics, optical and infrared astronomy, planetary sciences, solar and stellar physics, and theoretical astrophysics.

Data-gathering facilities include a major observatory in Arizona, field stations to observe artificial satellites, an optical and radio astronomy facility in Massachusetts, and a radio astronomy and millimeter-wave facility in Texas. The Smithsonian Astrophysical Observatory's observational capabilities are complemented by library, computation, and laboratory facilities in Cambridge.

Research results are published in the *Center Preprint Series, Smithsonian Contributions to Astrophysics,* the *SAO Special Reports* series, and other technical and nontechnical bulletins, and distributed to scientific and educational institutions around the world. As a further service to international science, Smithsonian Astrophysical Observatory serves as the headquarters for the International Astronomical Union's Central Telegram Bureau and the Minor Planet Center. The Central Telegram Bureau provides rapid international dissemination of news about the discovery of comets, novae, and other astronomical phenomena. The Minor Planet Center is the principal source for all positional observations of asteroids as well as for establishing their orbits and ephemerides.

The Public Affairs Office coordinates an extensive public education program. A variety of "open nights" are held in Cambridge and at other facilities.

Information about these activities and other general materials for students and teachers may be obtained from the Information Officer, Smithsonian Astrophysical Observatory, 60 Garden Street, Cambridge, MA 02138. Phone, 617–495–7461.

Smithsonian Environmental Research Center The Center measures physical, chemical, and biological interactions in the environment and determines how these interactions control biological responses. This research is carried out in a 2,600-acre facility in Edgewater, MD, where the ecology of land/water interactions is studied for an estuary and its adjacent watersheds.

For further information, contact the Smithsonian Environmental Research Center, P.O. Box 28, Edgewater, MD 21037. Phone, 301-261-4190.

Smithsonian Institution Libraries The libraries of the Smithsonian Institution include approximately 1,078,935 volumes with strengths in natural history, museology, history of science, and humanities. The systems' administrative services and Central Reference and Loan are located in the National Museum of Natural History with branch libraries located in each of the major Smithsonian museums and research units including the Cooper-Hewitt Museum, New York City; the Smithsonian Astrophysical Observatory, Cambridge, MA; and the Smithsonian Tropical Research Institute, Republic of Panama. Inquiries on special subjects or special collections should be addressed to the appropriate branch library or to the Central Reference and Loan.

For further information, contact the Smithsonian Institution Libraries, Tenth Street and Constitution Avenue NW., Washington, DC 20560. Phone, 202-357-2240.

Smithsonian Institution Traveling Exhibition Service The purpose of the Service is to provide to educational, scientific, and cultural institutions exhibitions and other services that will enrich their programs and enable them to offer a greater variety of cultural experiences to their audiences. The Service circulates the best possible exhibits at the lowest possible rental fees.

More than 130 exhibitions of paintings, sculptures, prints, drawings, decorative arts, history, children's art, natural history, photography, science, and technology are circulated every year. Lists of available exhibitions and information for future bookings can be obtained directly from the Smithsonian Institution Traveling Exhibition Service, Washington, DC 20560.

For further information, contact the Smithsonian Institution Traveling Exhibition Service, Room 3146, 1100 Jefferson Drive SW., Washington, DC 20560. Phone, 202-357-3168.

Smithsonian Tropical Research Institute The Institute, a research organization devoted to the study and support of tropical biology, education, and conservation, focuses broadly on the evolution of patterns of behavior and ecological adaptations. The tropics offer a rich natural laboratory for these purposes. Panama further offers its unique zoogeographic characteristics—landbridge to terrestrial life forms of two continents and water barriers to marine life of two oceans.

The Institute provides a base of operations and an intellectual center for exploring the frontiers of biology across the varied land and seascapes of the tropical world. It operates the Barro Colorado Nature Monument, a 12,000-acre tropical forest research preserve including Barro Colorado Island and adjacent peninsulas in Gatun Lake, Republic of Panama. The Institute also maintains a research and conference center in Ancon, including one of the world's finest tropical biology libraries. In addition, there are two marine biology laboratories, one on the Atlantic side of the isthmus at Galeta Island and the other at Fort Amador on the Pacific side. The Institute's scientific staff conducts research in these areas as well as in other parts of Central and South America, the Pacific, Asia, and Africa, where comparative studies are clarifying the distinctive biological role of the tropics.

For a brochure describing the Institute's activities and illustrating some of the facilities and habitats available, contact the Director, Smithsonian Tropical Research Institute, APO Miami, FL 34002. Phone, 507-62-3049 (international operator assistance required).

The John F. Kennedy Center for the Performing Arts The Center, the sole official memorial in Washington to President Kennedy, is an independent bureau of the Smithsonian Institution, administered by a 42-member Board of Trustees.

Since its opening in 1971, the Center has presented a year-round program of the finest in music, dance, and drama from the United States and abroad. Facilities include the Opera House, the Eisenhower Theater, the Terrace Theater, the Theater Lab, and the Concert Hall, home of the Center's affiliate, the National Symphony Orchestra. By special arrangement, the Center also houses the American Film Institute Theater.

The Center's Education Department includes the nationwide American College Theater Festival, Theater for Young People, the National Symphony Orchestra Education Program, and the Alliance for Arts Education, designed to increase participation by students throughout the country in Center activities and to establish the Center as a focal point for strengthening the arts in education at all levels.

The Kennedy Center box offices are open daily, and general information and tickets may be obtained by calling 202–467–4600. Full-time students, senior citizens over the age of 65, enlisted personnel of grade E–4 and below, fixed low-income groups, and the disabled may purchase tickets for most performances at a 50-percent discount through the Specially Priced Ticket Program. This program is designed to make the Center accessible to all, regardless of economic circumstance.

Visitor services are provided by the Friends of the Kennedy Center. The National Park Service maintains a portion of the Center as a Presidential memorial while the Center's Board of Trustees is wholly responsible for theater programming and maintenance. Tours are available free of charge between 10 a.m. and 1 p.m. daily.

National Gallery of Art The National Gallery of Art is governed by a Board of Trustees composed of five Trustees and the Secretary of State, the Secretary of the Treasury, the Chief Justice of the United States, and the Secretary of the Smithsonian Institution. It houses one of the finest collections in the world, illustrating Western man's achievements in painting, sculpture, and the graphic arts. The collections, beginning with the 13th century, are rich in European old master paintings and French, Spanish, Italian, American, and British 18th- and 19th-century paintings; sculpture from the late Middle Ages to the present; Renaissance medals and bronzes; Chinese porcelains; and over 75,000 works of graphic art from the 12th to the 20th centuries. The collections continue to be built by private donation rather than by the expenditure of government funds, which serve solely to operate and maintain the building and its collections.

The National Gallery's West Building, designed by John Russell Pope in neoclassical style, was a gift to the Nation from Andrew W. Mellon, who also bequeathed his collection to the gallery in 1937. On March 17, 1941, President Franklin D. Roosevelt accepted the completed building and works of art on behalf of the people of the United States of America.

The National Gallery's East Building, designed by I.M. Pei, was accepted by President Jimmy Carter in June of 1978 as a gift of Paul Mellon and the late Ailsa Mellon Bruce, son and daughter of the gallery's founder, and the Andrew W. Mellon Foundation. The East Building provides space for temporary exhibitions, the gallery's growing collections, the Center for the Advanced Study in the Visual Arts, including greatly expanded library and photographic archives, and administrative and curatorial offices.

A professor-in-residence position is filled annually by a distinguished scholar in the field of art history; graduate and postgraduate research is conducted under a fellowship program; programs for schoolchildren and the general public are conducted daily; and an Extension Service distributes loans of audiovisual materials, including films, slide lectures, and slide sets throughout the world. Publications, slides, and reproductions may be obtained through the Publications Service.

For general information on the National Gallery of Art and its activities, call 202–737–4215.

Woodrow Wilson International Center for Scholars The Center, located in Washington, DC, is the Nation's official memorial to its 28th President. The Center's special mandate is to unite the world of learning with the world of public affairs. Through meetings and conferences, the Center brings scholars together with Members of Congress, Government officials, business leaders, and other policymakers. Through publication of books and the *Wilson Quarterly* and a nationally broadcast radio program, the results of the Center's research and meetings are made publicly available.

The Center awards approximately 40 residential fellowships annually to individuals with project proposals representing the entire range of superior scholarship, with a strong emphasis on the humanities and social sciences. Where appropriate, fellows may be associated with one of the Center's six programs: the Asia Program; the East and West European Program; the International Studies Program; the Kennan Institute for Advanced Russian Studies Program; the Latin American Program; or the United States Program.

Applications from any country are welcome. Persons with outstanding capabilities and experience from a wide variety of backgrounds (including government, the corporate world, academia, and other professions) are eligible for appointment. For academic participants, eligiblity is limited to the postdoctoral level.

The Center prefers its fellows to be in residence for the academic year—September to May or June—although a few fellowships are available for shorter or longer periods. The residence requirement is a minimum of 4 months and a maximum of 12 months.

The Center holds one round of competitive selection per year. The deadline for the receipt of applications by the Center for the annual cycle is October 1, and decisions on appointments are announced by March of the following year.

For further information, contact the Fellowship Office, Woodrow Wilson Center, Washington, DC 20560. Phone, 202–357–2841; FAX, 202–357–4439.

Sources of Information

Contracts and Small Business Activities Information may be obtained from the Director, Office of Contracting and Property Management, Smithsonian Institution, Washington, DC 20560, regarding procurement of supplies; contracts for construction, services, exhibits, research, etc.; and property management and utilization services for all Smithsonian Institution organizations except as follows: The Building Director, John F. Kennedy Center for the Performing Arts, Washington, DC 20566; Supply Officer, National Gallery of Art, Sixth Street and Constitution Avenue NW., Washington, DC 20565. Phone, 202–287–3343.

Education and Research See statements on the Office of Fellowships and Grants, the American Studies Program, the Office of Folklife Programs, the Woodrow Wilson International Center for Scholars, and other offices. For information, write to the Directors of these offices at the Smithsonian Institution, Washington, DC 20560.

Employment Employment information for the Washington, DC, metropolitan area may be obtained from the Office of Human Resources, Smithsonian Institution, Suite 2100, 955 L'Enfant Plaza SW., Washington, DC 20560. Phone, 202–287–3100. Employment information for the following locations may be obtained by contacting the organizations directly as follows: the Cooper-Hewitt Museum, 2 East 91st Street, New York, NY 10028 (phone, 212–860–6868); Smithsonian Astrophysical Observatory, Personnel Department, 160 Concord Avenue, Cambridge, MA 02138 (phone, 617–495–7371); National Gallery of Art, Fourth Street and Constitution Avenue NW., Washington, DC 20565 (phone, 202–842–6282); and the John F. Kennedy Center for the Performing Arts, Washington, DC 20566 (phone, 202–416–8000).

Films The National Gallery of Art circulates films, slide lectures, and slide sets to schools and civic organizations throughout the country. Contact the Extension Service, National Gallery of Art, Washington, DC 20565. Phone, 202-737-4215.

Memberships For information about membership in the Smithsonian Resident Associate Program, write the Resident Associate Program, Room 3077, 1100 Jefferson Drive SW., Washington, DC 20560. Phone, 202-357-3030. Resident members are entitled to the following benefits: free exhibition previews, films, behind-the-scenes museum tours, lectures, and outdoor festivals; guided tours with Smithsonian and guest specialists; courses for adults—an extensive range in the arts, humanities, sciences, and studio arts; lectures, seminars, and performing arts events; classes, workshops, films, and events for young people; family activities; substantially reduced fees and priority of admission for all paid events; *Smithsonian,* the monthly magazine of the arts, sciences, and history; *The Smithsonian Associate,* a monthly newsletter describing Resident Associate activities; free parking in the west lot of the National Museum of Natural History for members participating in Resident Associate activities on weeknights and on weekends one-half hour before the announced starting time of the event, evening and weekend parking discounts at nearby commercial lots with valid membership card. In addition, members 60 and over receive reduced rates on many activity fees; discounts on museum shop purchases, *Wilson Quarterly* subscriptions, and *Air and Space/Smithsonian* magazine; restaurant privileges daily in the Associates' Court; special services for handicapped persons; domestic and international travel opportunities; and volunteer programs.

For information about membership in the Smithsonian National Associate Program, write the Associates Reception Center, 1000 Jefferson Drive SW., Washington, DC 20560. Phone, 202-357-2700. National members receive the *Smithsonian* magazine, information services from the Associates Reception Center, foreign and domestic study tours, selected studies seminars, dining privileges in the Associates' Court, and discounts on museum shop purchases.

For information about higher category contributing memberships, write Contributing Membership, National Associate Program, 1100 Jefferson Drive SW., Washington, DC 20560. Phone, 202-357-1699.

Information about the national and local activities of Friends of the Kennedy Center (including the bimonthly *Kennedy Center News* for members) is available at the Information Desks within the Center or by writing to Friends of the Kennedy Center, Washington, DC 20566.

Information about activities of the Friends of the National Zoo and their magazine, *The Zoogoer,* is available by writing to them at the National Zoological Park, Washington, DC 20008. Phone, 202-673-4960.

Photographs Color and black and white photographs and slides (including illustrated slide lectures) are available to Government agencies, research and educational institutions, publishers, and the general public from the Smithsonian. Subjects include photographs of the Smithsonian's scientific, technological, historical, and art collections as well as pictures dating back more than 130 years taken from its photographic archives. Information, order forms, and price lists may be obtained from Photographic Services, Smithsonian Institution, Washington, DC 20560. Phone, 202-357-1933.

Publications The Smithsonian Institution Press publishes *Smithsonian Year,* the Institution's annual report, along with a supplement that lists current titles. The Press also publishes books and studies related to the sciences, technology, history, air and space, and the arts at a wide range of prices. A book catalog and a list of studies are available from Publications Sales, Smithsonian Institution Press, 1111 N. Capitol Street, Washington, DC 20002. Phone, 202-287-3738.

A monthly Calendar of Events, which appears on the next-to-last Friday of the month, is published in the Washington Post by the Office of Public Affairs.

A brief guide to the Smithsonian Institution, published in English and six foreign languages; a guide for handicapped visitors; the *Smithsonian Institution Research Reports* (containing news of current research projects in the arts and sciences that are being conducted by Smithsonian staff); and *Smithsonian Runner* (a newsletter for Native Americans) are available from the Office of Public Affairs, 900 Jefferson Drive SW., Washington, DC 20560. Phone, 202–357–2627.

For the monthly Calendar of Events of the National Museum of American Art and the Renwick Gallery, which also gives information on museum publications, write the Office of Public Affairs, National Museum of American Art, Smithsonian Institution, Washington, DC 20560. Phone, 202–357–2247.

The Publications Service, National Gallery of Art, makes available quality reproductions and publications about the gallery's collections. The Information Office provides a monthly Calendar of Events and several brochures including *Brief Guide to the National Gallery of Art* and *An Invitation to the National Gallery of Art* (the latter in several foreign languages). Contact the appropriate office listed above at the National Gallery of Art, Washington, DC 20565. Phone, 202–842–6355.

Radio and Telephone *Radio Smithsonian* produces award-winning radio series and specials about the arts, sciences, and human culture for national broadcast on public radio. *Folk Masters,* a series of thirteen 1-hour programs featuring performers of traditional music recorded live in Carnegie Hall's Weill Recital Hall, can be heard on 130 public radio stations. Check local listings.

Dial-A-Museum, 202–357–2020; a taped telephone message with daily announcements on new exhibits and special events.

Smithsonian Skywatchers Report, 202–357–2000; taped telephone message with weekly announcements on stars, planets, and worldwide occurrences of short-lived natural phenomena.

Speakers The Bureau maintains a roster of staff and volunteers available to speak about the Center and its activities. Contact the Speakers Bureau, Friends of the Kennedy Center, Washington, DC 20566. Phone, 202–416–8440.

Education Office, National Gallery of Art, Fourth Street and Constitution Avenue NW., Washington, DC 20565. (They provide gallery talks and lectures.) Phone, 202–842–6246.

Museum aides give slide and musical presentations in area schools and senior citizen facilities. National Portrait Gallery, Eighth and F Streets NW., Washington, DC 20560. Phone, 202–357–2920.

Special Functions Inquiries regarding the use of Kennedy Center facilities for special functions may be directed to the Office of Special Events, John F. Kennedy Center for the Performing Arts, Washington, DC 20566. Phone, 202–416–8000.

Theater Operations Inquiries regarding the use of the Kennedy Center's theaters may be addressed to the Booking Coordinator, John F. Kennedy Center for the Performing Arts, Washington, DC 20566. Phone, 202–416–8000.

Tours For tour information, contact the appropriate office listed below:

Education, Anacostia Museum, 1901 Fort Place SE., Washington, DC 20020. Phone, 202–287–3369.

Division of Museum Programs, National Museum of American Art, Smithsonian Institution, Washington, DC 20560. Phone, 202–357–3111.

Curator of Education, National Portrait Gallery, Eighth and F Streets NW., Washington, DC 20560. Phone, 202–357–2920.

Friends of the National Zoo, National Zoological Park, 3000 Connecticut Avenue NW., Washington, DC 20008. Phone, 202–673–4960.

Tour Information, Friends of the Kennedy Center, Washington, DC 20566. Phone, 202–416–8000.

Education Office, National Gallery of Art, Washington, DC 20565. Phone, 202–846–6246.

Office of Education, National Museum of Natural History, Tenth Street and

Constitution Avenue NW., Washington, DC 20560. Phone, 202–357–3045.

Office of Public Programs (tour scheduling), National Museum of American History, Fourteenth Street and Constitution Avenue NW., Washington, DC 20560. Phone, 202–357–1481; or for the hearing-impaired (TDD), 202–357–1563.

Office of Education, Hirshhorn Museum and Sculpture Garden, Eighth Street and Independence Avenue SW., Washington, DC 20560. Phone, 202–357–3235.

Department of Education, Smithsonian Environmental Research Center, RR4, Box 28, Edgewater, MD 21037. Phone, 202–261–4190, ext. 42.

Membership Department, Cooper-Hewitt Museum, 2 East 91st Street, New York, NY 10028. Phone, 212–860–6868.

Office of Volunteer Services (tour scheduling), National Air and Space Museum, Seventh Street and Independence Avenue SW., Washington, DC 20560. Phone, 202–357–1400.

Department of Education, National Museum of African Art, 950 Independence Avenue SW., Washington, DC 20560. Phone, 202–357–4600.

For the newsletter *Art to Zoo* for teachers from fourth through eighth grades, write to the Office of Elementary and Secondary Education, Room 1163, Arts and Industries Building, Washington, DC 20560. Phone, 202–357–2425.

Visitor Information The Smithsonian Information Center, located in the original Smithsonian building, provides a general orientation and assistance for members and the public relative to the national collections, museum events, and programs. Write to the Smithsonian Information Center, 1000 Jefferson Drive SW., Washington, DC 20560. Phone, 202–357–2700; or for the hearing impaired (TDD), 202–357–1729.

Volunteer Service Opportunities The Smithsonian Institution welcomes volunteers and offers a variety of service opportunities. Persons may serve as tour guides or information volunteers, or may participate in an independent program in which their educational and professional backgrounds are matched with curatorial or research requests from within the Smithsonian. For information, write to the Visitor Information and Associates' Reception Center, 1000 Jefferson Drive SW., Washington, DC 20560. Phone, 202–357–2700; or for the hearing-impaired (TDD), 202–357–1729.

For information about volunteer opportunities at the Kennedy Center, write to Friends of the Kennedy Center, Washington, DC 20566. Phone, 202–416–8000.

For further information, members of the press may contact the Office of Public Affairs, Smithsonian Institution, 900 Jefferson Drive SW., Washington, DC 20560. Phone, 202–357–2627. All other inquiries should be directed to the Smithsonian Visitor Information Center, 1000 Jefferson Drive SW., Washington, DC 20560. Phone, 202–357–2700; or for the hearing impaired (TDD), 202–357–1729.

STATE JUSTICE INSTITUTE

Suite 600, 1650 King Street, Alexandria, VA 22314
Phone, 703–684–6100

Board of Directors:

Chairman	C.C. Torbert, Jr.
Vice Chairman	John F. Daffron, Jr.

Secretary	JANICE GRADWOHL
Members	TERRENCE B. ADAMSON, CARL F. BIANCHI, JAMES DUKE CAMERON, VIVI L. DILWEG, MALCOLM M. LUCAS, KEITH MCNAMARA, DANIEL J. MEADOR, SANDRA A. O'CONNOR
Officers:	
Executive Director	DAVID I. TEVELIN
Deputy Director	RICHARD VAN DUIZEND

The State Justice Institute was established to further the development and adoption of improved judicial administration in the State courts of the United States.

The State Justice Institute was created by the State Justice Institute Act of 1984 (42 U.S.C. 10701) as a private, nonprofit corporation to further the development and improvement of judicial administration in the State courts.

The Institute is supervised by a Board of Directors consisting of 11 members appointed by the President with the advice and consent of the Senate. The Board is statutorily composed of six judges, a State court administrator, and four members of the public, of whom no more than two can be of the same political party.

The goals of the Institute are to:

—direct a national program of assistance to ensure that all U.S. citizens have ready access to a fair and effective judicial system;

—foster coordination and cooperation with the Federal Judiciary;

—serve as a clearinghouse and information center for the dissemination of information regarding State judicial systems; and

—encourage education for judges and support personnel of State court systems.

To accomplish these broad objectives, the Institute is authorized to provide funds, through grants, cooperative agreements, and contracts, to State courts and organizations that can assist in the achievement of improving judicial administration of the State courts.

Sources of Information

Inquiries concerning the following programs and activities should be directed to the specified office of the State Justice Institute, Suite 600, 1650 King Street, Alexandria, VA 22314. Phone, 703-684-6100.

Grants—Director/Program Division.

Publications, Consumer Information—Publications Coordinator/Office of the Executive Director.

Speakers, Privacy Act/Freedom of Information Act Requests—Assistant to the Executive Director/Office of the Executive Director.

Employment/Personnel—Personnel Specialist/Office of Finance and Management.

For further information, contact the Publications Coordinator, State Justice Institute, Suite 600, 1650 King Street, Alexandria, VA 22314. Phone, 703-684-6100.

UNITED STATES INSTITUTE OF PEACE

1550 M Street NW., Washington, DC 20005–1708
Phone, 202–457–1700; FAX, 202–429–6063

Board of Directors:

Public Members:	
Chairman	JOHN NORTON MOORE
Vice Chairman	ELSPETH DAVIES ROSTOW
Members	DENNIS L. BARK, WILLIAM R. KINTNER, EVRON M. KIRKPATRICK, MORRIS I. LEIBMAN, SIDNEY LOVETT, RICHARD JOHN NEUHAUS, MARY LOUISE SMITH, W. SCOTT THOMPSON, ALLEN WEINSTEIN
Ex Officio Members:	
Director, U.S. Arms Control and Disarmament Agency	RONALD F. LEHMAN II
Assistant Secretary of State for Human Rights and Humanitarian Affairs	RICHARD SCHIFTER
President, National Defense University	J.A. BALDWIN
Assistant Secretary of Defense for International Security Policy	STEPHEN J. HADLEY
Officials:	
President	SAMUEL W. LEWIS
Executive Vice President	CHARLES E. NELSON
General Counsel	CHARLES DURYEA SMITH
Director of Education and Training	STEVEN SCHLESINGER
Director, Research and Studies Program	KENNETH M. JENSEN
Director, Grants Program	HRACH GREGORIAN
Director, Jennings Randolph Fellowship Program for International Peace	MICHAEL LUND
Director, Jeannette Rankin Library Program	JEANNE BOHLEN
Director of Public Affairs and Information	GREGORY MCCARTHY
Senior Scholar for Religion, Ethics, and Human Rights	DAVID LITTLE
Director of Administration	BERNICE CARNEY

The United States Institute of Peace was established to strengthen the Nation's capacity to promote international peace and the peaceful resolution of conflicts among the peoples and nations of the world.

The United States Institute of Peace is an independent, nonprofit, Government corporation created and wholly funded by Congress to develop and disseminate knowledge about international peace and conflict resolution. The Institute addresses this mandate in three principal ways:

—by expanding basic and applied knowledge about the origins, nature, and processes of peace and war, encompassing the widest spectrum of approaches and insights;

—by disseminating this knowledge to officials, policymakers, diplomats, and others engaged in efforts to promote international peace; and

—by supporting education and training programs and providing information for secondary and university-level teachers and students and the general public.

The Institute's primary activities are grantmaking, fellowships, in-house research projects, public education activities, publications, and library services.

The Grants Program provides financial support for research, information services, education, and training. Eligible grantees include nonprofit organizations; official public institutions, including public schools, colleges, universities, libraries, and State, and local agencies; and individuals, whether or not they are associated with nonprofit or official public institutions.

The Jennings Randolph Program for International Peace provides fellowships to scholars, practitioners, and other professionals to undertake research and other appropriate forms of work on issues of international peace and the management of international conflicts. The Fellowship Program has three levels: Distinguished Fellows, persons whose careers show extraordinary accomplishment; Peace Fellows, mid-career persons also of accomplishment; and Peace Scholars, persons working on doctoral dissertations.

The Jeannette Rankin Library Program has four main components: a specialized research library; a network with and support for other libraries, both private and public; an oral history resource; and bibliographic as well as other data bases.

The Public Affairs Office fulfils requests for speakers, media services, and general inquiries. Institute-directed projects under the Education and Training Program include educational video programs and a National Peace Essay Contest for high school students. The in-house Research and Studies Program conducts seminars and study groups on issues of short- and long-term significance. Institute publications include the *Biennial Report to Congress and the President;* a newsletter, the *United States Institute of Peace Journal;* short-issue papers, *In Brief;* and monographs, books, and reports generated from Institute-supported activities.

For further information, contact the Office of Public Affairs and Information, United States Institute of Peace, Suite 700, 1550 M Street NW., Washington, DC 20005–1708. Phone, 202–457–1700.

SELECTED MULTILATERAL ORGANIZATIONS

MULTILATERAL INTERNATIONAL ORGANIZATIONS IN WHICH THE UNITED STATES PARTICIPATES

Explanatory note: Descriptions of most of the organizations listed below may be found in the publication entitled *United States Contributions to International Organizations, Fiscal Year 1989* (Department of State Publication 9666).

The United States participates in the organizations named below in accordance with the provisions of treaties, other international agreements, congressional legislation, or executive arrangements. In some cases, no financial contribution is involved.

Various commissions, councils, or committees subsidiary to the organizations listed here are not named separately on this list. These include the international bodies for narcotics control, which are subsidiary to the United Nations.

I. United Nations, Specialized Agencies, and International Atomic Energy Agency

United Nations
Food and Agricultural Organization
International Maritime Organization
International Atomic Energy Agency
International Civil Aviation Organization
International Fund for Agricultural Development (IFAD)
International Labor Organization
International Telecommunication Union
United Nations Industrial Development Organization (UNIDO)
Universal Postal Union
World Health Organization
World Intellectual Property Organization
World Meteorological Organization

II. Peacekeeping

United Nations Forces in Cyprus
United Nations Disengagement Observer Force (UNDOF) and UNIFIL
Multinational Force and Observers

III. Inter-American Organizations

Organization of American States
Inter-American Indian Institute
Inter-American Institute for Cooperation on Agriculture
Inter-American Tropical Tuna Commission
Pan American Health Organization (PAHO)
Pan American Institute of Geography and History
Pan American Railway Congress Association
Postal Union of the Americas and Spain

IV. Regional Organizations

NATO
North Atlantic Assembly
Colombo Plan for Cooperative Economic and Social Development in Asia and the Pacific
Organization for Economic Cooperation and Development (OECD)
South Pacific Commission

290-950 O 91 - 26

V. Other International Organizations

Bureau of International Expositions
Commission for the Conservation of Antarctic Marine Living Resources
Customs Cooperation Council (CCC)
Fund for the Protection of the World Cultural and Natural Heritage
General Agreement on Tariffs and Trade (GATT)
Hague Conference on Private International Law
International Agency for Research on Cancer
International Agreement on the Maintenance of Certain Lights in the Red Sea
International Bureau of the Permanent Court of Arbitration
International Bureau for the Publication of Customs Tariffs
International Bureau of Weights and Measures
International Center for the Study of the Preservation and the Restoration of Cultural Property (ICCROM)
International Coffee Organization (ICO)
International Commission for the Conservation of Atlantic Tunas
International Cotton Advisory Committee
International Council for the Exploration of the Seas (ICES)
International Council of Scientific Unions and Its Associated Unions (20)
International Criminal Police Organization (INTERPOL)
International Hydrographic Organization
International Institute for Cotton
International Institute for the Unification of Private Law
International Jute Organization
International Lead and Zinc Study Group
International Natural Rubber Organization
International North Pacific Fisheries Commission
International Office of Epizootics
International Office of Vine and Wine
International Organization for Legal Metrology
International Rubber Study Group
International Seed Testing Association
International Sugar Organization
International Tropical Timber Organization
International Union for the Protection of New Varieties of Plants (UPOV)
International Whaling Commission
International Wheat Council
Interparliamentary Union
North Atlantic Ice Patrol
North Atlantic Salmon Conservation Organization
Permanent International Association of Navigation Congresses
World Tourism Organization (WTO)

VI. Special Voluntary Programs

Colombo Plan Drug Advisory Program
Consultative Group on International Agricultural Research
Convention on International Trade in Endangered Species of Wild Fauna and Flora (CITES)
International Organization for Migration (IOM)
International Atomic Agency Technical Assistance and Cooperation Fund
OAS Special Cultural Fund
OAS Special Development Assistance Fund
OAS Special Multilateral Fund (Education and Science)
OAS Special Projects Fund (Mar del Plata)
PAHO Special Health Promotion Funds
United Nations Capital Development Fund (UNCDF)
United Nations Center for Human Settlements (Habitat) (UNCHS)
United Nations Children's Fund (UNICEF)
United Nations Development Fund for Women (UNIFEM)
United Nations Development Program (UNDP)
United Nations Educational and Training Program for South Africa
United Nations Environment Program (UNEP)
United Nations/Food and Agricultural Organization World Food Program (WFP)
United Nations Fund for Drug Abuse Control (UNFDAC)
United Nations High Commissioner for Refugees Program (UNHCR)
United Nations Relief and Works Agency (UNRWA)
United Nations Trust Fund for South Africa
United Nations Volunteers (UNV)
WHO Special Programs
WMO Voluntary Cooperation Program

African Development Bank

Headquarters: Abidjan, Ivory Coast

President: Babacar N'Diaye

The African Development Bank (AFDB) was formed in 1963 by 33 independent African countries to contribute, individually and jointly, to the economic and social progress of its regional members. In 1973, non-African countries joined with AFDB to establish the African Development Fund (AFDF) as the concessional lending affiliate of AFDB. The Fund loans only to the poorest African countries. Membership in the Bank was limited to 50 African nations until late 1982 when nonregional countries began to join the institution.

The United States became a member of AFDF in 1976 by virtue of the African Development Fund Act (22 U.S.C. 290g note), and in February 1983 the United States became a member of AFDB by virtue of the African Development Bank Act (22 U.S.C. 290i note).

Asian Development Bank

Headquarters: 6 ADB Avenue, 1501 Mandaluyong, Metro Manila, Philippines. Phone, 632-711-3851

President. Kimimasa Tarumizu

The Agreement establishing the Asian Development Bank came into effect on August 22, 1966, when it was ratified by 15 governments. The Bank commenced operations on December 19, 1966. The United States became a member by virtue of the Asian Development Bank Act of March 16, 1966 (22 U.S.C. 285).

The purpose of the Bank is to foster economic growth and contribute to the acceleration of economic development of the developing member countries in Asia, collectively and individually.

Correspondence to the Asian Development Bank can be mailed to P.O. Box 789, 1099 Manila, Philippines.

Inter-American Defense Board

2600 Sixteenth Street NW., Washington, DC 20441. Phone, 202-939-6600

Chairman: Maj. Gen. Bernard Loeffke, USA

The Inter-American Defense Board is a permanently constituted, international organization, autonomous within the inter-American system, composed of army, navy, and air officers appointed by the governments of American Republics. Its constitutional sources are: Resolution XXXIX of the Meeting of Foreign Ministers at Rio de Janeiro in January 1942; Resolution XXXIV of the Ninth International Conference of American States held in Bogotá, Colombia, in April 1948; and Resolution III of the Fourth Meeting of Consultation of Ministers of Foreign Affairs, held in Washington, DC, March–April 1951.

The Board studies and recommends to the governments of the American Republics measures necessary for close military collaboration in preparation for the collective self-defense of the American continents.

Inter-American Development Bank

Headquarters: 1300 New York Avenue NW., Washington, DC 20577. Phone, 202-623-1000

President: Enrique V. Iglesias

The Inter-American Development Bank (IDB) is an international financial institution established in 1959 to help accelerate economic and social development in Latin America and the Caribbean. It is based in Washington, DC.

The Bank has 27 member countries in the Western Hemisphere and 17 outside of the region.

In its 30 years of operations, IDB has helped to provide, secure, and organize financing for projects that represent a total investment of more than $122 billion. The Bank has also fostered a more equitable distribution of the benefits of development, and has been a pioneer in financing social projects.

The Bank's highest authority is its Board of Governors, on which each member country is represented. Its 12-member Board of Executive Directors is responsible for the conduct of the Bank's operations.

The Bank's field offices represent its dealings with local authorities and borrowers and supervise the implementation of Bank-supported projects.

International Bank for Reconstruction and Development

Headquarters: 1818 H Street NW., Washington, DC 20433. Phone, 202–477–1234

President: Barber B. Conable

The International Bank for Reconstruction and Development (IBRD), also called the World Bank, officially came into existence on December 27, 1945, when the Articles of Agreement, formulated at the United Nations Monetary and Financial Conference held at Bretton Woods, NH, in July 1944, were signed in Washington, DC, by 28 governments. As of March 1991, 155 countries were members of IBRD.

IBRD's purpose is to promote economic and social progress in developing nations by raising productivity so that their people may live a better and fuller life. It does this by lending funds, providing advice and serving as a catalyst to stimulate outside investments. IBRD's resources come primarily from funds raised in the world capital markets, its retained earnings, and repayments on its loans.

International Development Association The International Development Association (IDA) came into existence on September 24, 1960, as an affiliate of IBRD. Membership of IDA is open to all member countries of IBRD, and by March 1991, 138 countries had become members. IDA's resources consist of subscriptions and supplementary resources in the form of general replenishments, mostly from its 33 more industrialized and developed members; special contributions by its richer members; and transfers from the net earnings of IBRD.

IDA's purposes are to promote economic development, increase productivity, and raise the standard of living in the least developed areas of the world. It does this by financing their developmental requirements on concessionary terms, which are more flexible and bear less heavily on the balance of payments than those of conventional loans, thereby furthering the objectives of IBRD and supplementing its activities.

International Finance Corporation

Headquarters: 1818 H Street NW., Washington, DC 20433. Phone, 202–477–1234

President: Barber B. Conable
Executive Vice President: Sir William Ryrie
Vice President: José E. Camacho
Vice President: Makarand V. Dehejia
Vice President: Richard H. Frank
Vice President: Wilfried E. Kaffenberger
Vice President: Judhvir Parmar

The International Finance Corporation (IFC), an affiliate of the World Bank, was established in July 1956 to promote productive private enterprise in the developing countries. Membership is open to all countries that are members of the World Bank. All powers are vested in IFC's Board of Governors, with one Governor from each member country. Responsibility for conduct of IFC's general operations is vested in a Board of Directors made up of the 22 Executive Directors of the World Bank. The President of the World Bank is *ex officio* Chairman of the IFC Board of Directors, which has appointed him President of IFC. The Corporation's Executive Vice President is responsible for overall management operations.

As of March 30, 1991, IFC had 140 member countries, adequate subscribed capital and general reserves, and authority to borrow from the World Bank and other sources up to four times its unimpaired capital and surplus. Its capital is subscribed by its member countries.

The Corporation pursues its objective principally through direct investments in projects that either establish new businesses or expand, modify, or diversify existing businesses. It achieves this goal by providing finance of its own, either by loan or equity subscription or a combination of both, and by recruiting finance from other foreign and local sources. Advisory services and technical assistance are also provided by IFC to developing member countries in areas such as capital market development, privatization, corporate restructuring, and foreign direct investment.

International Monetary Fund

700 Nineteenth Street NW., Washington, DC 20431. Phone, 202-623-7000

Managing Director and Chairman of the Executive Board: Michel Camdessus

The Final Act of the United Nations Monetary and Financial Conference, signed at Bretton Woods, NH, on July 22, 1944, set forth the original Articles of Agreement of the International Monetary Fund. The Agreement became effective on December 27, 1945, when the President, authorized by the Bretton Woods Agreements Act (22 U.S.C. 286) accepted membership for the United States in the Fund, the Agreement having thus been accepted by countries having approximately 80 percent of the quotas. The inaugural meeting of the Board of Governors was held in March 1946, and the first meeting of the Executive Directors was held May 6, 1946.

On May 31, 1968, the Board of Governors approved a proposed amendment to the Articles of Agreement for the establishment of a facility based on Special Drawing Rights (SDR's) in the Fund and for modification of certain rules and practices of the Fund. The amendment became effective on July 28, 1969, and the Special Drawing Account became operative on August 6, 1969. The United States acceptance of the amendment and participation in the Special Drawing Account were authorized by the Special Drawing Rights Act (22 U.S.C. 286 *et seq.*).

On April 30, 1976, the Board of Governors approved a proposed second amendment to the Articles of Agreement, which entered into force on April 1, 1978. United States acceptance of this amendment was authorized by the Bretton Woods Agreements Act Amendments (22 U.S.C. 286e–5). Under this amendment two separate accounts are continued as departments: a General Department through which the Fund carries on its operations and transactions in currencies and gold, as in the past, and a Special Drawing Rights Department for functions related to SDRs, which serve as a supplement to gold and foreign exchange as a component of the international reserves of participant countries. The amendment introduces new and flexible provisions dealing with exchange arrangements, including provision for Fund surveillance over the exchange rate policies of members, and changes in the characteristics and uses of the SDR intended to enhance its status.

On June 28, 1990, the Board of Governors approved a proposed third amendment to the Articles of Agreement, under which a member's voting rights and certain related rights may be suspended by a 70-percent majority of the executive board if the member, having been declared ineligible to use the general resources of the Fund, persists in its failure to fulfill any of its obligations under the Articles.

The purposes of the Fund are to promote international monetary cooperation through a permanent institution that provides the machinery for consultation and collaboration on international monetary problems; to facilitate the expansion and balanced growth of international trade; to promote exchange stability; to assist in the establishment of a multilateral system of payments for current transactions between members; and to give confidence to members by making the Fund's resources temporarily available to them under adequate safeguards.

In accordance with these purposes, the Fund seeks to shorten the duration and lessen the degree of imbalance in the international balances of payments of members.

For further information, contact the Chief Information Officer, External Relations Department, International Monetary Fund, 700 Nineteenth Street NW., Washington, DC 20431. Phone, 202–623–7100.

International Organization for Migration

Headquarters: 17 Route des Morillons, Grand-Saconnex, Geneva; mailing address—P.O. Box 71, CH1211, Geneva 19, Switzerland

Director General: James N. Purcell, Jr.

Washington Office: Suite 1110, 1750 K Street NW., Washington, DC 20006. Phone, 202-862-1826

Chief of Mission: Frances E. Sullivan

New York Office: Room 717, 1123 Broadway, New York, NY 10010. Phone, 212-463-4822

Chief of Mission: Richard E. Scott

California Office: Suite 1225, 114 Sansome Street, San Francisco, CA 94104. Phone, 415-391-9832

Chief of Mission: James Gildea

The International Organization for Migration (IOM), formerly the Intergovernmental Committee for Migration (ICM), was created in 1951 at a conference in Brussels sponsored by the Governments of the United States and Belgium.

IOM is a technical, nonpolitical organization that plans and operates refugee resettlement, national migration, and emergency relief programs at the request of its member states and in cooperation with other international organizations.

IOM has four major objectives: the processing and movement of refugees to countries offering them permanent resettlement opportunities; the promotion of orderly migration to meet the specific needs of both emigration and immigration countries; the transfer of technology through migration in order to promote the economic, educational, and social advancement of countries in the process of development, particularly in Latin America and Africa; and the provision of a forum to states and other partners to discuss experiences, exchange views, and devise measures to promote cooperation and coordination of efforts on migration issues.

IOM has a membership of 35 governments; 22 other governments have observer status. Operational offices are located in 47 countries, including some nonmember countries.

Organization of American States

General Secretariat: Seventeenth Street and Constitution Avenue NW., Washington, DC 20006. Phone, 202-458-3000

Secretary General: João Clemente Baena Soares

Assistant Secretary General: Christopher Thomas

Executive Secretary for Economic and Social Affairs: Augusto Galli

Executive Secretary for Education, Science, and Culture: Juan Carlos Torchia-Estrada, *Acting*

Assistant Secretary for Management: Robert M. Sayre

Assistant Secretary for Legal Affairs: Hugo Caminos

The Organization of American States (OAS) is a regional, intergovernmental organization whose primary purposes are to preserve peace and security and to promote, by cooperative action, the integral development of the member states. Organized in its present form in 1948, its roots date from 1890, making it the oldest regional, international organization in the world.

The OAS member states are Argentina, Antigua and Barbuda, Barbados, Belize, Bolivia, Brazil, Canada, Chile, Colombia, Commonwealth of the Bahamas, Commonwealth of Dominica, Costa Rica, Cuba, Dominican Republic, Ecuador, El Salvador, Grenada, Guatemala, Guyana, Haiti, Honduras, Jamaica, Mexico, Nicaragua, Panama, Paraguay, Peru, St. Kitts and Nevis, St. Lucia, St. Vincent and the Grenadines, Suriname, Trinidad and Tobago, the United States of America, Uruguay, and Venezuela. The present Government of Cuba is excluded from participation by a decision of the Eighth Meeting of Consultation of Ministers of Foreign Affairs in 1962. Twenty-five nonmember countries and the European Community are Permanent Observers.

The principal organs of the OAS are:

—the General Assembly, which is normally composed of the foreign ministers of the member states and meets at least once a year to decide the general action and policy of the Organization;

—the Meeting of Consultation of Ministers of Foreign Affairs, which meets on call to consider urgent matters of common interest or threats to the peace and security of the hemisphere;

—the Permanent Council, which meets twice a month at OAS headquarters; and

—the Inter-American Economic and Social Council and the Inter-American Council For Education, Science, and Culture, which meet once a year.

For further information, contact the Director, Department of Public Information, Organization of American States, Seventeenth Street and Constitution Avenue NW., Washington, DC 20006. Phone, 202–458–3760.

United Nations

United Nations, New York, NY 10017. Phone, 212–963–1234; FAX, 202–289–4267

Secretary-General: Javier Perez de Cuellar

United Nations Office at Geneva: Palais des Nations, Geneva, Switzerland

Director-General: Jan Martenson

United Nations Office at Vienna: Vienna International Centre, Vienna, Austria

Director-General: Margaret J. Anstee

Washington, DC, Office: U.N. Information Centre, 1889 F Street NW., Washington, DC 20006. Phone, 202–289–8670; FAX, 202–289–4267

Director: (Vacancy)

The United Nations is an international organization that was set up in accordance with the Charter [1] drafted by governments represented at the Conference on International Organization meeting at San Francisco. The Charter was signed on June 26, 1945, and came into force on October 24, 1945, when the required number of ratifications and accessions had been made by the signatories. Amendments increasing membership of the Security Council and the Economic and Social Council came into effect on August 31, 1965.

The United Nations now consists of 160 member states of which 51 are founding members.

Purpose The purposes of the United Nations set out in the Charter are: to maintain international peace and security; to develop friendly relations among nations; to achieve international cooperation in solving international problems of an economic, social, cultural, or humanitarian character and in promoting respect for human rights; and to be a center for harmonizing the actions of nations in the attainment of these common ends.

Organization

The principal organs of the United Nations are:

General Assembly All states that are members of the United Nations are members of the General Assembly. Its functions are to consider and discuss any matter within the scope of the Charter of the United Nations and to make recommendations to the members of the United Nations and other organs. It approves the budget of the organization, the expenses of which are borne by the members as apportioned by the General Assembly.

The General Assembly may call the attention of the Security Council to situations likely to endanger international peace and security, may initiate studies, and may receive and consider reports from other organs of the United Nations. Under the "Uniting for Peace" resolution adopted by the General Assembly in November 1950, if the Security Council fails to act on an apparent threat to or breach of the peace or act of aggression because of lack of unanimity of its five permanent members, the Assembly itself may take up the matter within 24 hours—in emergency special session—and recommend collective measures, including, in case of a breach of the peace or act of aggression, use of armed force when necessary to maintain or restore international peace and security.

[1] Charter of the United Nations, together with the Statute of the International Court of Justice (Department of State Publication No. 2353, International Organization and Conference Series III, 21), June 26, 1945. Available for sale from the Superintendent of Documents, Government Printing Office, Washington, DC 20402 (87 pages).

The General Assembly has held to date 40 regular sessions, 12 special sessions, and 9 emergency special sessions. It normally meets in regular annual session in September.

Security Council The Security Council consists of 15 members of which 5—the People's Republic of China, France, the Union of Soviet Socialist Republics, the United Kingdom, and the United States of America—are permanent members and are elected each year. The 10 nonpermanent members are elected for 2-year terms by the General Assembly. The primary responsibility of the Security Council is to act on behalf of the members of the United Nations in maintenance of international peace and security. Measures that may be employed by the Security Council are outlined in the Charter.

The Security Council, together with the General Assembly, also elects the judges of the International Court of Justice and makes a recommendation to the General Assembly on the appointment of the Secretary General of the organization.

The Security Council first met in London on January 17, 1946, and is so organized as to be able to function continuously.

Economic and Social Council This organ is responsible, under the authority of the General Assembly, for the economic and social programs of the United Nations. Its functions include making or initiating studies, reports, and recommendations on international economic, social, cultural, educational, health, and related matters; promoting respect for and observance of human rights and fundamental freedoms for all; calling international conferences and preparing draft conventions for submission to the General Assembly on matters within its competence; negotiating agreements with the specialized agencies and defining their relationship with the United Nations; coordinating the activities of the specialized agencies; and consulting with nongovernmental organizations concerned with matters within its competence. The Council consists of 54 members of the United Nations elected by the General Assembly for 3-year terms; 18 are elected each year.

The Council usually holds two regular sessions a year. It has also held a number of special sessions.

Trusteeship Council The Trusteeship Council was initially established to consist of any member states that administer trust territories, permanent members of the Security Council that do not administer trust territories, and enough other nonadministering countries elected by the General Assembly for 3-year terms to ensure that membership would be equally divided between administering and nonadministering members. At present, the participating members of the Council are the United Kingdom, China, France, the Union of Soviet Socialist Republics, and the United States.

Of the original 11 trust territories, all except the Trust Territory of the Pacific Islands, which is administered by the United States, have attained the goals of the trusteeship system, either as independent states or as parts of such states.

The Council functions under authority of the General Assembly. It considers reports from the member administering the Trust Territory, examines petitions from inhabitants of the Trust Territory, and provides for periodic inspection visits to the Trust Territory. The Council has held 52 regular sessions and a number of special sessions; it now holds one regular session a year.

International Court of Justice The International Court of Justice is the principal judicial organ of the United Nations. It has its seat at The Hague, the Netherlands. All members of the United Nations are *ipso facto* parties to the Statute of the Court. Nonmembers of the United Nations may become parties to the Statute of the Court on conditions prescribed by the General Assembly on the recommendation of the Security Council.

The jurisdiction of the Court comprises all cases that the parties refer to it and all matters specially provided for in the Charter of the United Nations or in treaties and conventions in force.

The Court consists of 15 judges known as "members" of the Court. They are elected for 9-year terms by the General Assembly and the Security Council, voting independently; they may be reelected.

Secretariat The Secretariat consists of a Secretary-General and "such staff as the Organization may require." The Secretary-General, who is appointed by the General Assembly on the recommendation of the Security Council, is the chief administrative officer of the United Nations. He acts in that capacity for the General Assembly, the Security Council, the Economic and Social Council, and the Trusteeship Council. Under the Charter, the Secretary-General "may bring to the attention of the Security Council any matter that in his opinion may threaten the maintenance of international peace and security."

SELECTED BILATERAL ORGANIZATIONS

International Boundary Commission, United States and Canada

Room 150, 425 I Street NW., Washington, DC 20001. Phone, 202-632-8058.

International Boundary and Water Commission, United States and Mexico

United States Section: Suite C-310, 4171 N. Mesa Street, El Paso, TX 79902-1422. Phone, 915-534-6700.

Mexican Section: Avenida Universidad, No. 2180, Ciudad Juárez, Chihuahua, Mexico 32320.

International Joint Commission—United States and Canada

United States Section: 2001 S Street NW., Washington, DC 20440. Phone, 202-673-6222.

Canadian Section: 100 Metcalfe Street, Ottawa, ON K1P 5M1. Phone, 613-995-2984.

Regional Office: 100 Ouellette Avenue, Windsor, ON N9A 6T3. Phone, 519-256-7821 or 313-226-2170.

Joint Mexican-United States Defense Commission

United States Section: Suite 509, 1111 Jefferson Davis Highway, Arlington, VA 22202. Phone, 202-746-6342 or 202-746-6343.

Mexican Section: Mexican Embassy, Sixth Floor, 1911 Pennsylvania Avenue NW., Washington, DC 20006. Phone, 202-234-5492.

Permanent Joint Board on Defense—United States and Canada

Suite 511, 1111 Jefferson Davis Highway, Arlington, VA 22202. Phone, 202-746-6348.

Appendices

APPENDIX A: Standard Federal Regions and Federal Executive Boards

Standard Federal Regions

Standard Federal administrative regions were established to achieve more uniformity in the location and geographic jurisdiction of Federal field offices. Standard regions are a basis for promoting more systematic coordination among agencies and Federal, State, and local governments and for securing management improvements and economies through greater interagency and intergovernmental cooperation. OMB Circular A–105, *Standard Federal Regions,* provides further guidance on the policies and requirements governing standard administrative regions. Boundaries were drawn and regional office locations designated for 10 regions, and agencies are required to adopt the uniform system when changes are made or new offices established. A map showing the standard boundaries is printed on the following page.

The regional structures of agencies not conforming to the uniform regional system can be found in the tables accompanying their descriptions, when provided by the agency.

For further information, contact the General Management Division, Office of Management and Budget, New Executive Office Building, Washington, DC 20503. Phone, 202–395–5090.

Federal Executive Boards

Federal Executive Boards (FEB's) were established by Presidential directive (a memorandum for heads of Federal departments and agencies dated November 13, 1961) to improve internal Federal management practices and to provide a central focus for Federal participation in civic affairs in major metropolitan centers of Federal activity. They carry out their functions under the supervision and control of the Office of Personnel Management (OPM).

Federal Executive Boards are composed of heads of Federal field offices in the metropolitan area. A Chairman is elected annually from among the membership to provide overall leadership to the Board's operations. Committees and task forces carry out interagency projects consistent with the Board's missions.

Federal Executive Boards serve as a means for disseminating information within the Federal Government and for promoting discussion of Federal policies and activities of importance to all Federal executives in the field.

Currently, Federal Executive Boards are located in 27 metropolitan areas that are important centers of Federal activity. These areas are: Albuquerque-Santa Fe, Atlanta, Baltimore, Boston, Buffalo, Chicago, Cincinnati, Cleveland, Dallas-Fort Worth, Denver, Detroit, Honolulu-Pacific, Houston, Kansas City, Los Angeles, Miami, New Orleans, New York, Newark, Philadelphia, Pittsburgh, Portland, St. Louis, San Antonio, San Francisco, Seattle, and the Twin Cities (Minneapolis-St. Paul).

Federal Executive Associations, Councils, or Committees have been locally organized in over 100 other metropolitan areas to perform functions similar to the Federal Executive Boards but on a lesser scale of organization and activity.

For further information, contact the Assistant for Regional Operations, Office of Personnel Management, Room 5H36G, 1900 E Street NW., Washington, DC 20415–0001. Phone, 202–606–1001.

STANDARD FEDERAL REGIONS

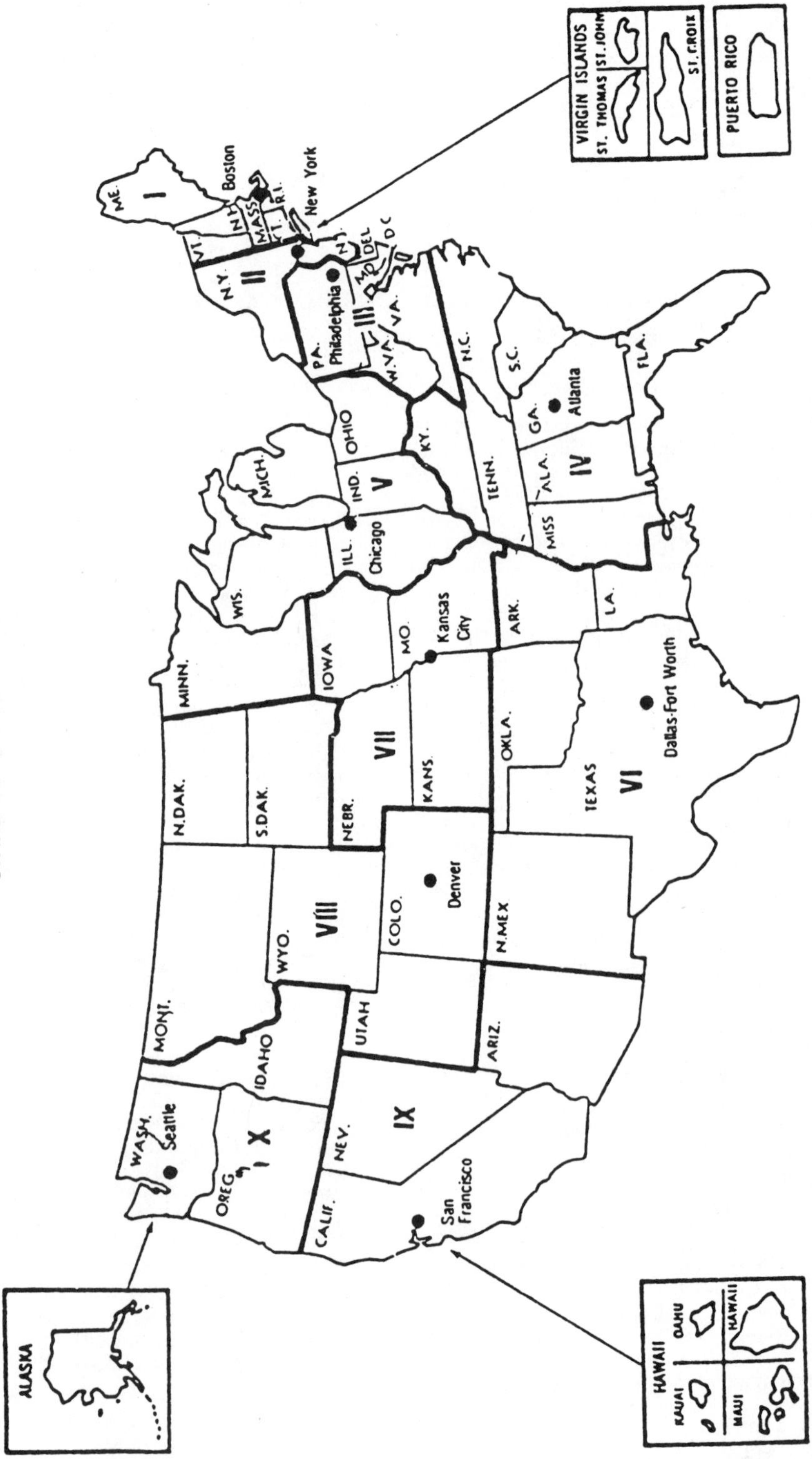

APPENDIX B: Commonly Used Abbreviations and Acronyms

ABMC	American Battle Monuments Commission
ACDA	United States Arms Control and Disarmament Agency
ACUS	Administrative Conference of the United States
ACYF	Administration for Children, Youth, and Families
ADA	Americans with Disabilities Act of 1990
ADAMHA	Alcohol, Drug Abuse, and Mental Health Administration
ADB	Asian Development Bank
ADD	Administration on Developmental Disabilities
AEDS	Atomic Energy Detection System
AFAA	Air Force Audit Agency
AFBCMR	Air Force Review Board for Correction of Military Records
AFCARA	Air Force Civilian Appellate Review Agency
AFPEO	Air Force Program Executive Offices
AFDB	African Development Bank
AFDC	Aid to Families with Dependent Children
AFDF	African Development Fund
AFIS	American Forces Information Service
AFPC	Armed Forces Policy Council
AFPPS	American Forces Press and Publications Service
AFRRI	Armed Forces Radiobiology Research Institute
AFRTS	Armed Forces Radio and Television Service
AFSC	Armed Forces Staff College
AGRICOLA	Agricultural OnLine Access
AID	Agency for International Development
AIDS	Acquired Immune Deficiency Syndrome
AMS	Agricultural Marketing Service
Amtrak	National Railroad Passenger Corporation
ANA	Administration for Native Americans
AOA	Administration on Aging
APHIS	Animal and Plant Health Inspection Service
ARC	Appalachian Regional Commission
ARS	Agricultural Research Service
ASCS	Agricultural Stabilization and Conservation Service
ATSDR	Agency for Toxic Substances and Disease Registry
BEA	Bureau of Economic Analysis
BIA	Bureau of Indian Affairs
BIB	Board for International Broadcasting
BJA	Bureau of Justice Assistance
BJS	Bureau of Justice Statistics
BLM	Bureau of Land Management
BLMRCP	Bureau of Labor-Management Relations and Cooperative Programs
BLS	Bureau of Labor Statistics
BPA	Bonneville Power Administration
BSC's	Business Service Centers
BVA	Board of Veterans Appeals

CBO	Congressional Budget Office
CCC	Commodity Credit Corporation; Customs Cooperation Council
CCEA	Cabinet Council on Economic Affairs
CCR	Commission on Civil Rights
CDBG	Community Development Block Grants
CDC	Centers for Disease Control
CEA	Council of Economic Advisers
CEQ	Council on Environmental Quality
CFA	Commission of Fine Arts
CFR	*Code of Federal Regulations*
CFTC	Commodity Futures Trading Commission
CG	Commanding General
CHAMPVA	Civilian Health and Medical Program of the Veterans Administration
C^3I	Command, Control, Communications, and Intelligence
C^4I	Communication, Command, Control, Computer, and Intelligence
CIA	Central Intelligence Agency
CIC	Consumer Information Center
CNO	Chief of Naval Operations
Conrail	Consolidated Rail Corporation
CPSC	Consumer Product Safety Commission
CRS	Congressional Research Service; Community Relations Service
CSA	Community Services Administration
CSRS	Cooperative State Research Service
CUFT	Center for the Utilization of Federal Technology
DA	Department of the Army
DARPA	Defense Advanced Research Projects Agency
DCAA	Defense Contract Audit Agency
DCASR's	Defense Contract Administration Services Regions
DCS	Defense Communications System
DEA	Drug Enforcement Administration
DIA	Defense Intelligence Agency
DINFOS	Defense Information School
DIPEC	Defense Industrial Plant Equipment Center
DIS	Defense Investigative Service
DISA	Defense Information Services Activity; Defense Information Systems Agency
DISAM	Defense Institute of Security Assistance Management
DLA	Defense Logistics Agency
DLSA	Defense Legal Services Agency
DMA	Defense Mapping Agency
DMFO	Defense Medical Facilities Office
DMS	Defense Mapping School
DMSA	Defense Medical Support Activity
DMSSC	Defense Medical Systems Support Center
DNA	Defense Nuclear Agency
DOC	Department of Commerce
DOD	Department of Defense
DODDS	Department of Defense Dependents Schools
DOE	Department of Energy
DOL	Department of Labor
DOT	Department of Transportation
DSAA	Defense Security Assistance Agency
DTSA	Defense Technology Security Administration
EDA	Economic Development Administration
EEOC	Equal Employment Opportunity Commission
EIA	Energy Information Administration
EO	Executive order
EOUSA	Executive Office for United States Attorneys

EPA	Environmental Protection Agency
ERA	Economic Regulatory Administration
ERS	Economic Research Service
ES	Extension Service
ESA	Employment Standards Administration
ETA	Employment and Training Administration
Eximbank	Export-Import Bank of the United States
FAA	Federal Aviation Administration
FAS	Foreign Agricultural Service
FBI	Federal Bureau of Investigation
FCA	Farm Credit Administration
FCC	Federal Communications Commission
FCIA	Foreign Credit Insurance Association
FCIC	Federal Crop Insurance Corporation
FDA	Food and Drug Administration
FDIC	Federal Deposit Insurance Corporation
FEB's	Federal Executive Boards
FEC	Federal Election Commission
FEMA	Federal Emergency Management Agency
FERC	Federal Energy Regulatory Commission
FFB	Federal Financing Bank
FGIS	Federal Grain Inspection Service
FHA	Federal Housing Administration
FHFB	Federal Housing Finance Board
FHWA	Federal Highway Administration
FIA	Federal Insurance Administration
FIC	Federal Information Centers
FIRS	Federal Information Relay Service
	Financing Corporation
FLETC	Federal Law Enforcement Training Center
FLRA	Federal Labor Relations Authority
FMC	Federal Maritime Commission
FMCS	Federal Mediation and Conciliation Service
FmHA	Farmers Home Administration
FMS	Financial Management Service
FNMA	Federal National Mortgage Association
FNS	Food and Nutrition Service
FOIA	Freedom of Information Act
FOMC	Federal Open Market Committee
FPRS	Federal Property Resources Service
FR	*Federal Register*
FRA	Federal Railroad Administration
FRS	Federal Reserve System
FSIS	Food Safety and Inspection Service
FSS	Federal Supply Service
FSTS	Federal Secure Telephone Service
FTC	Federal Trade Commission
FTS	Federal Telecommunications System
FWS	Fish and Wildlife Service
GAO	General Accounting Office
GATT	General Agreement on Tariffs and Trade
GNMA	Government National Mortgage Association
GPO	Government Printing Office
GSA	General Services Administration
HCFA	Health Care Financing Administration
HDS	Office of Human Development Services
HHS	Department of Health and Human Services
HIV	Human Immunodeficiency Virus
HNIS	Human Nutrition Information Service
HRA	Health Resources Administration

HUD	Department of Housing and Urban Development
IAEA	International Atomic Energy Agency
IAF	Inter-American Foundation
IBRD	International Bank for Reconstruction and Development
ICAF	Industrial College of the Armed Forces
ICAO	International Civil Aviation Organization
ICC	Interstate Commerce Commission
ICO	International Coffee Organization
IDA	International Development Association; Institute for Defense Analyses
IDB	Inter-American Development Bank
IDCA	United States International Development Cooperation Agency
IEVS	Income Eligibility Verification Systems
IFAD	International Fund for Agricultural Development
IFC	International Finance Corporation
IGDOD	Inspector General, Department of Defense
IHA's	Indian Housing Authorities
IHS	Indian Health Service
ILO	International Labor Organization
IMF	International Monetary Fund
IMS	Institute of Museum Services
INF	Intermediate-range nuclear forces
INS	Immigration and Naturalization Service
INTERPOL	International Criminal Police Organization
IOM	International Organization for Migration
IRMS	Information Resources Management Service
IRS	Internal Revenue Service
ITA	International Trade Administration
ITU	International Telecommunication Union
IVHS	Intelligent Vehicle-Highway System
JAG	Judge Advocate General
JCEWS	Joint Command, Control, and Electronic Warfare School
JCS	Joint Chiefs of Staff
JCSOS	Joint and Combined Staff Officer School
JTC^3A	Joint Tactical Command, Control, and Communications Agency
MA	Maritime Administration
MBDA	Minority Business Development Agency
MBFR	Mutual and balanced force reduction
MED	Office of Medical Services (State)
MMS	Minerals Management Service
MSHA	Mine Safety and Health Administration
MSPB	Merit Systems Protection Board
MSSD	Model Secondary School for the Deaf
MTB	Materials Transportation Bureau
NARA	National Archives and Records Administration
NASA	National Aeronautics and Space Administration
NASS	National Agricultural Statistics Service
NATO	North Atlantic Treaty Organization
NBS	National Bureau of Standards
NCC	National Coordinating Committee
NCI	National Cancer Institute
NCIC	National Cartographic Information Center
NCJRS	National Criminal Justice Reference Service
NCPC	National Capital Planning Commission
NCS	National Cemetery System
NCUA	National Credit Union Administration
NDU	National Defense University

NEH	National Endowment for the Humanities
NEL	National Engineering Laboratory
NHPRC	National Historical Publications and Records Commission
NHTSA	National Highway Traffic Safety Administration
NIC	National Institute of Corrections
NIE	National Institute of Education
NIH	National Institutes of Health
NIJ	National Institute of Justice
NIS	Naval Investigative Service
NIST	National Institute of Standards and Technology
NLM	National Library of Medicine
NLRB	National Labor Relations Board
NMCS	National Military Command System
NML	National Measurement Laboratory
NOAA	National Oceanic and Atmospheric Administration
NOS	National Ocean Survey
NRC	Nuclear Regulatory Commission
NSA	National Security Agency
NSC	National Security Council
NSF	National Science Foundation
NSTL	National Space Technology Laboratories
NTIA	National Telecommunications and Information Administration
NTID	National Technical Institute for the Deaf
NTIS	National Technical Information Service (Commerce)
NTSB	National Transportation Safety Board
NWC	National War College
OA	Office of Administration
OAS	Organization of American States
OASTP	Office of the Assistant Secretary for Technology Policy
OCHAMPUS	Office of Civilian Health and Medical Program of the Uniformed Services
OCS	Office of Community Services; Officer Candidate School; Outer Continental Shelf
OCSE	Office of Child Support Enforcement
OECD	Organization for Economic Cooperation and Development
OES	Office of Employment Security
OFCC	Office of Federal Contract Compliance
OFM	Office of Financial Management
OFPP	Office of Federal Procurement Policy
OFR	Office of the Federal Register
OGE	Office of Government Ethics
OGPS	Office of Grants and Program Systems
OICD	Office of International Cooperation and Development
OJJDP	Office of Juvenile Justice and Delinquency Prevention
OJP	Office of Justice Programs
OLMS	Office of Labor-Management Standards
OMB	Office of Management and Budget
OMIS	Office of Management and Information Systems
OPD	Offfice of Policy Development
OPFI	Office of Program and Fiscal Integrity
OPIC	Overseas Private Investment Corporation
OPM	Office of Personnel Management
ORM	Office of Regional Management
ORR	Office of Refugee Relief
OSC	Office of Special Counsel
OSCE	Office of Child Support Enforcement

OSDBU	Office of Small and Disadvantaged Business Utilization
OSF	Office of Space Flight
OSHA	Occupational Safety and Health Administration
OSHRC	Occupational Safety and Health Review Commission
OSM	Office of Surface Mining Reclamation and Enforcement
OSTP	Office of Science and Technology Policy
OT	Office of Transportation
OTA	Office of Technology Assessment
OTAA	Office of Trade Adjustment Assistance
OTS	Office of Thrift Supervision
OVC	Office for Victims of Crime
OVI	Office of Voluntarism Initiatives
OWBO	Office of Women's Business Ownership
PADC	Pennsylvania Avenue Development Corporation
PAHO	Pan American Health Organization
PBGC	Pension Benefit Guaranty Corporation
PBS	Public Buildings Service
PCC	Panama Canal Commission
PHA's	Public Housing Agencies
PHS	Public Health Service
PRC	Postal Rate Commission
PTO	Patent and Trademark Office
PWBA	Pension and Welfare Benefits Administration
REA	Rural Electrification Administration
REFCORP	Resolution Funding Corporation
RETRF	Rural Electrification and Telephone Revolving Fund
RFE	Radio Free Europe
RICO	Racketeer Influenced and Corrupt Organizations
RIT	Rochester Institute of Technology
RL	Radio Liberty
ROTC	Reserve Officer Training Corps
RRB	Railroad Retirement Board
RSA	Rehabilitation Services Administration
RSPA	Research and Special Programs Administration
RTB	Rural Telephone Bank
RTC	Resolution Trust Corporation
SAIF	Savings Association Insurance Fund
SAO	Smithsonian Astrophysical Observatory
SAVE	Systematic Alien Verification for Entitlement
SBA	Small Business Administration
SCS	Soil Conservation Service
SDIO	Strategic Defense Initiative Organization
SEC	Securities and Exchange Commission
SERC	Smithsonian Environmental Research Center
SGLI	Servicemen's Group Life Insurance
SIDS	Sudden Infant Death Syndrome
SITES	Smithsonian Institution Traveling Exhibition Service
SLS	Saint Lawrence Seaway Development Corporation
SPC	South Pacific Commission
SSA	Social Security Administration
SSI	Supplemental Security Income Program
SSS	Selective Service System
START	Strategic arms reduction talks
Stat.	United States Statutes at Large
TDP	Trade and Development Program
TFCS	Treasury Financial Communication System
TSC	Transportation Systems Center

TVA Tennessee Valley Authority
UDAG Urban Development Action Grants
UIS Unemployment Insurance Service
UMTA Urban Mass Transportation Administration
U.N. United Nations [1]
UNESCO United Nations Educational, Scientific and Cultural Organization
UNICEF United Nations Children's Fund (formerly United Nations International Children's Emergency Fund)
UNICOR Federal Prison Industries, Inc.
UPU Universal Postal Union
USA United States Army
USAF United States Air Force
U.S.C. United States Code
USCG United States Coast Guard
USDA United States Department of Agriculture
USES United States Employment Service
USIA United States Information Agency
USITC United States International Trade Commission
USMC United States Marine Corps
USN United States Navy
USNCB United States National Central Bureau
USRA United States Railway Association
USTTA United States Travel and Tourism Administration
VA Department of Veterans Affairs
VETS Veterans' Employment and Training Service
VGLI Veterans Group Life Insurance
VISTA Volunteers in Service to America
VOA Voice of America
WAPA Western Area Power Administration
WHO World Health Organization
WHS Washington Headquarters Services
WIC Special supplemental food program for Women, Infants, and Children
WIN Work Incentive program
WMO World Meteorological Organization
WTO World Tourism Organization
WWMCCS Worldwide Military Command and Control System
YCC Youth Conservation Corps

[1] Acronyms for other U.N. agencies can be found under Selected Multilateral Organizations, beginning on page 793.

APPENDIX C: Federal Executive Agencies Terminated, Transferred, or Changed in Name Subsequent to March 4, 1933

NOTE: Italicized terms indicate obsolete agencies, organizations, and entities. In most instances, explanatory remarks are written at those terms elsewhere in this appendix. Dates prior to March 4, 1933, are included to provide additional information about the agencies.

This appendix is indexed in a format considered to be useful to the reader. Entries are carried at the most significant term in their titles, or when there is more than one significant term, the entry is carried at the first significant term. Thus, **Bureau of the Budget** is found at **Budget, Bureau of the,** and **Bureau of Agricultural Engineering** is found at **Agricultural Engineering, Bureau of.** Reader comments on the format are encouraged and should be sent to the address shown on page iv of the *Manual.*

Accounts, Bureau of Functions transferred to Bureau of Government Financial Operations by Treasury Order 229 of Jan. 14, 1974.

Acts of Congress *See* **State Department**

Advisory Board, Commission, Committee. *See other part of title*

Aeronautical Board Organized in 1916 by agreement of *War* and Navy Secretaries. Placed under supervision of President by military order of July 5, 1939. Dissolved by Defense Secretary's letter of July 27, 1948, and functions transferred to *Munitions Board* and *Research and Development Board.* Military order of July 5, 1939, revoked by military order of Oct. 18, 1948.

Aeronautics, Bureau of Established in Navy Department by act of July 12, 1921 (42 Stat. 140). Abolished by act of Aug. 18, 1959 (73 Stat. 395) and functions transferred to *Bureau of Naval Weapons.*

Aeronautics, National Advisory Committee for Established by act of Mar. 3, 1915 (38 Stat. 930). Terminated by act of July 29, 1958 (72 Stat. 432), and functions transferred to National Aeronautics and Space Administration, established by same act.

Aeronautics Administration, Civil *See* **Aeronautics Authority, Civil**

Aeronautics Authority, Civil Established under act of June 23, 1938 (52 Stat. 973). Renamed *Civil Aeronautics Board* and Administrator transferred to Commerce Department by Reorg. Plan Nos. III and IV of 1940, effective June 30, 1940. Office of Administrator designated *Civil Aeronautics Administration* by Department Order 52 of Aug. 29, 1940. *Administration* transferred to *Federal Aviation Agency* by act of Aug. 23, 1958 (72 Stat. 810). Functions of *Board* under act of Aug. 23, 1958 (72 Stat. 775), transferred to National Transportation Safety Board by act of Oct. 15, 1966 (80 Stat. 931). Functions of *Board* terminated or transferred—effective in part Dec. 31, 1981; in part Jan. 1, 1983; and in part Jan. 1, 1985—by act of Aug. 23, 1958 (92 Stat. 1744). Most remaining functions transferred to Transportation Secretary, remainder to U.S. Postal Service. Termination of *Board* finalized by act of Oct. 4, 1984 (98 Stat. 1703).

Aeronautics Board, Civil *See* **Aeronautics Authority, Civil**

Aeronautics Branch Established in Commerce Department to carry out provisions of act of May 20, 1926 (44 Stat. 568). Renamed *Bureau of Air Commerce* by Secretary's administrative order of July 1, 1934. Personnel and property transferred to *Civil Aeronautics Authority* by EO 7959 of Aug. 22, 1938.

Aeronautics and Space Council, National Established by act of July 29, 1958 (72 Stat. 427). Abolished by Reorg. Plan No. 1 of 1973, effective June 30, 1973.

Aging, Administration on Established by *Health, Education, and Welfare Secretary* (*see reference*) on Oct. 1, 1965, to carry out provisions of act of July 14, 1965 (79 Stat. 218). Reassigned to *Social and Rehabilitation Service* by Department reorganization of Aug. 15, 1967. Transferred to Office of Assistant Secretary for Human Development by Secretary's order of June 15, 1973. Transferred to the Office of the Secretary of Health and Human Services by Secretary's reorganization notice dated Apr. 15, 1991.

Aging, Federal Council on Established by Presidential memorandum of Apr. 2, 1956.

Reconstituted at Federal level by Presidential letter of Mar. 7, 1959, to *Health, Education, and Welfare Secretary.* Abolished by EO 11022 of May 15, 1962, which established *President's Council on Aging.*

Aging, Office of Established by *Health, Education, and Welfare Secretary* June 2, 1955, as *Special Staff on Aging.* Terminated Sept. 30, 1965, and functions assumed by Administration on Aging.

Aging, President's Council on Established by EO 11022 of May 14, 1962. EO 11022 revoked by EO 12379 of Aug. 17, 1982.

Agricultural Adjustment Administration Established by act of May 12, 1933 (48 Stat. 31). Consolidated into *Agricultural Conservation and Adjustment Administration* as *Agricultural Adjustment Agency,* Agriculture Department, by EO 9069 of Feb. 23, 1942. Grouped with other agencies to form *Food Production Administration* by EO 9280 of Dec. 5, 1942. Transferred to *War Food Administration* by EO 9322 of Mar. 26, 1943. Administration terminated by EO 9577 of June 29, 1945, and functions transferred to Agriculture Secretary. Transfer made permanent by Reorg. Plan No. 3 of 1946, effective July 16, 1946. Functions of *Agricultural Adjustment Agency* consolidated with *Production and Marketing Administration* by Secretary's Memorandum 1118 of Aug. 18, 1945.

Agricultural Adjustment Agency *See* **Agricultural Adjustment Administration**

Agricultural Advisory Commission, National Established by EO 10472 of July 20, 1953. Terminated Feb. 4, 1965, on resignation of members.

Agricultural Chemistry and Engineering, Bureau of *See* **Agricultural Engineering, Bureau of**

Agricultural Conservation and Adjustment Administration Established by EO 9069 of Feb. 23, 1942, consolidating *Agricultural Adjustment Agency, Sugar Agency, Federal Crop Insurance Corporation,* and *Soil Conservation Service.* Consolidated into *Food Production Administration* by EO 9280 of Dec. 5, 1942.

Agricultural Conservation Program Service Established by Agriculture Secretary Jan. 21, 1953, from part of *Production and Marketing Administration.* Merged with *Commodity Stabilization Service* by Secretary's Memorandum 1446, supp. 2, of Apr. 19, 1961.

Agricultural Developmental Service, International Established by Agriculture Secretary's memorandum of July 12, 1963. Functions and delegations of authority transferred to *Foreign Agricultural Service* by Secretary's memorandum of Mar. 28, 1969. Functions transferred by Secretary to *Foreign Economic Development Service* Nov. 8, 1969.

Agricultural Economics, Bureau of Established by act of May 11, 1931 (42 Stat. 532). Functions transferred to other units of Agriculture Department, including *Consumer and Marketing Service* and *Agricultural Research Service,* under Secretary's Memorandum 1320, supp. 4, of Nov. 2, 1953.

Agricultural Engineering, Bureau of Established by act of Feb. 23, 1931 (46 Stat. 1266). Merged with *Bureau of Chemistry and Soils* by Secretarial order of Oct. 16, 1938, to form *Bureau of Agricultural Chemistry and Engineering.*

Agricultural and Industrial Chemistry, Bureau of *Bureau of Chemistry* and *Bureau of Soils,* created in 1901, combined into *Bureau of Chemistry and Soils* by act of Jan. 18, 1927 (44 Stat. 976). Soils units transferred to other agencies of Agriculture Department and remaining units of *Bureau of Chemistry and Soils* and *Bureau of Agricultural Engineering* consolidated with *Bureau of Agricultural Chemistry and Engineering* by Secretary's order of Oct. 16, 1938. In February 1943 agricultural engineering research made part of *Bureau of Plant Industry, Soils, and Agricultural Engineering,* and organization for continuing agricultural chemistry research relating to crop utilization named *Bureau of Agricultural and Industrial Chemistry,* in accordance with Research Administration Memorandum 5 issued pursuant to EO 9069 of Feb. 23, 1942, and in conformity with Secretary's Memorandums 960 and 986. Functions transferred to *Agricultural Research Service* under Secretary's Memorandum 1320, supp. 4, of Nov. 2, 1953.

Agricultural Library, National Established by Agriculture Secretary's Memorandum 1496 of Mar. 23, 1962. Consolidated into Science and Education Administration by Secretary's order of Jan. 24, 1978. Reestablished as National Agricultural Library by Secretary's order of June 16, 1981.

Agricultural Marketing Administration Established by EO 9069 of Feb. 23, 1942, consolidating *Surplus Marketing Administration, Agricultural Marketing Service,* and *Commodity Exchange Administration. Division of Consumers' Counsel* transferred to *Administration* by Secretary's memorandum of Feb. 28, 1942. Consolidated into *Food Distribution Administration* in Agriculture Department by EO 9280 of Dec. 5, 1942.

Agricultural Marketing Service Established by Agriculture Secretary pursuant to act of June 30, 1939 (53 Stat. 939). Merged into *Agricultural Marketing Administration* by EO 9069 of Feb. 23, 1942. Renamed *Consumer and Marketing Service* by Secretary's Memorandum 1567, supp. 1, of Feb. 8, 1965.

Agricultural Relations, Office of Foreign *See* **Agricultural Service, Foreign**

Agricultural Research Administration Established by EO 9069 of Feb. 23, 1942. Superseded by *Agricultural Research Service.*

Agricultural Research Service Established by Agriculture Secretary's Memorandum 1320, supp. 4, of Nov. 2, 1953. Consolidated into *Science and Education Administration* by Secretary's Order of Jan. 24, 1978. Reestablished as Agricultural Research Service by Secretarial order of June 16, 1981.

Agricultural Service, Foreign Established by act of June 5, 1930 (46 Stat. 497). Economic research and agricultural attaché activities administered by *Foreign*

Agricultural Service Division, Bureau of Agricultural Economics, until June 29, 1939. Transferred by Reorg. Plan No. II of 1939, effective July 1, 1939, from Agriculture Department to State Department. Economic research functions of *Division* transferred to *Office of Foreign Agricultural Relations* June 30, 1939. Functions of *Office* transferred to *Foreign Agricultural Service* Mar. 10, 1953. Agricultural attachés placed in Agriculture Department by act of Aug. 28, 1954 (68 Stat. 908).

Agricultural Statistics Division Transferred to *Bureau of Agricultural Economics* by EO 9069 of Feb. 23, 1942.

Agriculture, Division of *See* **Farm Products, Division of**

Aid, Advisory Committee on Voluntary Foreign Established by President May 14, 1946. Transferred from State Department to Director, *Mutual Security Agency,* and later to Director, *Foreign Operations Administration,* by Presidential letter of June 1, 1953.

Air Commerce, Bureau of *See* **Aeronautics Branch**

Air Coordinating Committee Established Mar. 27, 1945, by interdepartmental memorandum; formally established by EO 9781 of Sept. 19, 1946. Terminated by EO 10883 of Aug. 11, 1960, and functions transferred for liquidation to *Federal Aviation Agency.*

Air Force Management Engineering Agency Established in 1975 in Air Force as separate operating unit. Made subordinate unit of *Air Force Military Personnel Center* (later Air Force Manpower and Personnel Center) in 1978. Reestablished as separate operating unit of Air Force, effective Mar. 1, 1985, by Secretarial order.

Air Force Manpower and Personnel Center Certain functions transferred on activation of *Air Force Management Engineering Agency,* which was made separate operating unit from Air Force Manpower and Personnel Center in April 1985 by general order of Chief of Staff.

Air Force Medical Service Center Renamed Air Force Office of Medical Support by Program Action Directive 85-1 of Mar. 6, 1985, approved by Air Force Vice Chief of Staff.

Air Mail, Bureau of Established in Interstate Commerce Commission to carry out provisions of act of June 12, 1934 (48 Stat. 933). Personnel and property transferred to *Civil Aeronautics Authority* by EO 7959 of Aug. 22, 1938.

Air Patrol, Civil Established in *Civilian Defense Office* by Administrative Order 9 of Dec. 8, 1941. Transferred to *War Department* as auxiliary of Army Air Forces by EO 9339 of Apr. 29, 1943. Transferred to Air Force Department by Defense Secretary's order of May 21, 1948. Established as civilian auxiliary of U.S. Air Force by act of May 26, 1948 (62 Stat. 274).

Air Safety Board Established by act of June 23, 1938 (52 Stat. 973). Functions transferred to *Civil Aeronautics Board* by Reorg. Plan No. IV of 1940, effective June 30, 1940.

Airways Modernization Board Established by act of Aug. 14, 1957 (71 Stat. 349). Transferred to *Federal Aviation Agency* by EO 10786 of Nov. 1, 1958.

Alaska, Board of Road Commissioners for Established in *War Department* by act of Jan. 27, 1905 (33 Stat. 616). Functions transferred to Interior Department by act of June 30, 1932 (47 Stat. 446), and delegated to *Alaska Road Commission.* Functions transferred to Commerce Department by act of June 29, 1956 (70 Stat. 377), and terminated by act of June 25, 1959 (73 Stat. 145).

Alaska, Federal Field Committee for Development Planning in Established by EO 11182 of Oct. 2, 1964. Abolished by EO 11608 of July 19, 1971.

Alaska, Federal Reconstruction and Development Planning Commission for Established by EO 11150 of Apr. 2, 1964. Abolished by EO 11182 of Oct. 2, 1964, which established *President's Review Committee for Development Planning in Alaska* and *Federal Field Committee for Development Planning in Alaska.*

Alaska, President's Review Committee for Development Planning in Established by EO 11182 of Oct. 2, 1964. Superseded by Federal Advisory Council on Regional Economic Development established by EO 11386 of Dec. 28, 1967. EO 11386 revoked by EO 12553 of Feb. 25, 1986.

Alaska Communication System Operational responsibility vested in Army Secretary by act of May 26, 1900 (31 Stat. 206). Transferred to Air Force Secretary by Defense Secretary's reorganization order of May 24, 1962.

Alaska Engineering Commission *See* **Alaska Railroad**

Alaska Game Commission Established by act of Jan. 13, 1925 (43 Stat. 740). Expired Dec. 31, 1959, pursuant to act of July 7, 1958 (72 Stat. 339).

Alaska International Rail and Highway Commission Established by act of Aug. 1, 1956 (70 Stat. 888). Terminated June 30, 1961, under terms of act.

Alaska Power Administration Established by Interior Secretary in 1967. Transferred to Energy Department by act of Aug. 4, 1977 (91 Stat. 578).

Alaska Railroad Built pursuant to act of Mar. 12, 1914 (38 Stat. 305), which created *Alaska Engineering Commission.* Placed under Interior Secretary by EO 2129 of Jan. 26, 1915, and renamed Alaska Railroad by EO 3861 of June 8, 1923. Authority to regulate tariffs granted to Interstate Commerce Commission by EO 11107 of Apr. 25, 1963. Authority to operate Railroad transferred to Transportation Secretary by act of Oct. 15, 1966 (80 Stat. 941), effective Apr. 1, 1967.

Railroad purchased by State of Alaska, effective Jan. 5, 1985.

Alaska Road Commission *See* **Alaska, Board of Road Commissioners for**

Alcohol, Bureau of Industrial Established by act of May 27, 1930 (46 Stat. 427). Consolidated into *Bureau of Internal Revenue* by EO 6166 of June 10, 1933. Consolidation deferred until May 11, 1934, by EO 6639 of Mar. 10, 1934. Order also transferred to Internal Revenue Commissioner certain functions imposed on Attorney General by act of May 27, 1930, with relation to enforcement of criminal laws concerning intoxicating liquors remaining in effect after repeal of 18th amendment; personnel of, and appropriations for, *Bureau of Industrial Alcohol;* and necessary personnel and appropriations of *Bureau of Prohibition,* Justice Department.

Alcohol, Commissioner of Industrial Office created in Treasury Department by act of May 27, 1930 (46 Stat. 427). Abolished by EO 6639 of Mar. 10, 1934.

Alcohol Administration, Federal *See* **Alcohol Control Administration, Federal**

Alcohol Control Administration, Federal Established by EO 6474 of Dec. 4, 1933. Abolished Sept. 24, 1935, on induction into office of Administrator, *Federal Alcohol Administration,* as provided in act of Aug. 29, 1935 (49 Stat. 977). Abolished by Reorg. Plan No. III of 1940, effective June 30, 1940, and functions consolidated with activities of Internal Revenue Service.

Alien Property, Office of Transferred to Civil Division, Justice Department, by Attorney General Order 249–61 of Sept. 1, 1961. Abolished by EO 11281 of May 13, 1966, and foreign funds control functions transferred to *Office of Foreign Assets Control, Treasury Department.* Remaining functions continued by *Civil Division, Justice Department.* Remaining functions abolished by act of Aug. 23, 1988 (102 Stat. 1370).

Alien Property Custodian Appointed by President Oct. 22, 1917, under authority of act of Oct. 6, 1917 (40 Stat. 415). Office transferred to *Alien Property Division,* Justice Department, by EO 6694 of May 1, 1934. Powers vested in President by act delegated to Attorney General by EO 8136 of May 15, 1939. Authority vested in Attorney General by EOs 6694 and 8136 transferred by EO 9142 of Apr. 21, 1942, to *Office of Alien Property Custodian, Office for Emergency Management,* as provided for by EO 9095 of Mar. 11, 1942.

Alien Property Custodian, Office of Established in *Office for Emergency Management* by EO 9095 of Mar. 11, 1942. Terminated by EO 9788 of Oct. 14, 1946, and functions transferred to Justice Department. Transfer made permanent by Reorg. Plan No. 1 of 1947, effective July 1, 1947.

Alien Property Division *See* **Alien Property Custodian**

American. *See also other part of title*

American Republics, Office for Coordination of Commercial and Cultural Relations between the Established by *Council of National Defense* order approved by President Aug. 16, 1940. Succeeded by *Office of the Coordinator of Inter-American Affairs, Office for Emergency Management,* established by EO 8840 of July 30, 1941. Renamed *Office of Inter-American Affairs* by EO 9532 of Mar. 23, 1945. Information functions transferred to State Department by EO 9608 of Aug. 31, 1945. Terminated by EO 9710 of Apr. 10, 1946, and functions transferred to State Department, functioning as *Institute of Inter-American Affairs.* Transferred to *Foreign Operations Administration* by Reorg. Plan No. 7, effective Aug. 1, 1953.

American Revolution Bicentennial Administration *See* **American Revolution Bicentennial Commission**

American Revolution Bicentennial Commission Established by act of July 4, 1966 (80 Stat. 259). *American Revolution Bicentennial Administration* established by act of Dec. 11, 1973 (87 Stat. 697), to replace *Commission. Administration* terminated June 30, 1977, pursuant to terms of act. Certain continuing functions transferred to Interior Secretary by EO 12001 of June 29, 1977.

American Studies, Office of Renamed American Studies Program by Smithsonian Institution administrative order in 1990.

Anacostia Neighborhood Museum Renamed Anacostia Museum by Smithsonian Institution announcement of Apr. 3, 1987.

Animal Industry, Bureau of Established in Agriculture Department by act of May 29, 1884 (23 Stat. 31). Functions transferred to *Agricultural Research Service* by Secretary's Memorandum 1320, supp. 4, of Nov. 2, 1953.

Apprenticeship, Federal Committee on Previously known as *Federal Committee on Apprentice Training,* established by EO 6750–C of June 27, 1934. Functioned as part of *Division of Labor Standards,* Labor Department, pursuant to act of Aug. 16, 1937 (50 Stat. 664). Transferred to *Office of Administrator, Federal Security Agency,* by EO 9139 of Apr. 18, 1942. Transferred to *Bureau of Training, War Manpower Commission,* by EO 9247 of Sept. 17, 1942. Returned to Labor Department by EO 9617 of Sept. 19, 1945.

Architect, Office of the Supervising *See* **Construction Branch**

Archive of Folksong Renamed Archive of Folk Culture by administrative order of Deputy Librarian of Congress, effective Sept. 21, 1981.

Archives Council, National Established by act of June 19, 1934 (48 Stat. 1122). Transferred to General Services Administration by act of June 30, 1949 (63 Stat. 378). Terminated on establishment of Federal Records Council by act of Sept. 5, 1950 (64 Stat. 583).

Archives Establishment, National *Office of Archivist of the U.S.* and *National Archives* created by act of June 19, 1934 (48 Stat. 1122). Transferred to General Services Administration by act of June 30, 1949 (63 Stat. 381), and incorporated as *National Archives and Records Service* by order of General Services Administrator, together with functions of *Division of the Federal Register, National Archives Council, National Historical Publications Commission, National Archives Trust Fund Board, Trustees of the Franklin D. Roosevelt Library,* and *Administrative Committee of the Federal Register.* Transferred from General Services Administration to National Archives and Records Administration by act of Oct. 19, 1984 (98 Stat. 2283), along with certain functions of Administrator of General Services transferred to Archivist of the United States, effective Apr. 1, 1985.

Archives and Records Service, National *See* **Archives Establishment, National**

Archives Trust Fund Board, National *See* **Archives Establishment, National**

Area Redevelopment Administration Established May 8, 1961, by Commerce Secretary pursuant to act of May 1, 1961 (75 Stat. 47) and Reorg. Plan No. 5 of 1950, effective May 24, 1950. Terminated Aug. 31, 1965, by act of June 30, 1965 (79 Stat. 195). Functions transferred to Economic Development Administration in Commerce Department by Department Order 4-A, effective Sept. 1, 1965.

Arlington Memorial Amphitheater Commission Established by act of Mar. 4, 1921 (41 Stat. 1440). Abolished by act of Sept. 2, 1960 (74 Stat. 739), and functions transferred to Defense Secretary.

Arlington Memorial Bridge Commission Established by act of Mar. 4, 1913 (37 Stat. 885; D.C. Code (1951 ed.) 8-158). Abolished by EO 6166 of June 10, 1933, and functions transferred to *Office of National Parks, Buildings, and Reservations.*

Armed Forces Medical Library Founded in 1836 as *Library of the Surgeon General's Office,* U.S. Army. Later known as *Army Medical Library,* then *Armed Forces Medical Library* in 1952. Personnel and property transferred to National Library of Medicine established in Public Health Service by act of Aug. 3, 1956 (70 Stat. 960).

Armed Forces Museum Advisory Board, National Established by act of Aug. 30, 1961 (75 Stat. 414). Functions discontinued through lack of funding

Armed Services Renegotiation Board Established by Defense Secretary's directive of July 19, 1948. Abolished by Defense Secretary's letter of Jan. 18, 1952, and functions transferred to *Renegotiation Board.*

Army, Communications Command, U.S. Renamed U.S. Army Information Systems Command by Department General Orders No. 26 of July 25, 1984.

Army Materiel Development and Readiness Command, U.S. Renamed U.S. Army Materiel Command by Department General Order No. 28 of Aug. 15, 1984.

Army and Navy, Joint Board— Placed under direction of President by military order of July 5, 1939. Abolished Sept. 1, 1947, by joint letter of Aug. 20, 1947, to President from Secretaries of *War* and Navy.

Army and Navy Staff College Established Apr. 23, 1943, and operated under Joint Chiefs of Staff. Redesignated National War College, effective July 1, 1946.

Army Specialist Corps Established in *War Department* by EO 9078 of Feb. 26, 1942. Abolished by *War Secretary* Oct. 31, 1942, and functions merged into central Officer Procurement Service.

Arthritis, Diabetes, and Digestive and Kidney Diseases, National Institute of Renamed National Institute of Diabetes and Digestive and Kidney Diseases by act of Nov. 20, 1985 (99 Stat. 820).

Arthritis, Metabolism, and Digestive Diseases, National Institute of Renamed National Institute of Arthritis, Diabetes, and Digestive and Kidney Diseases by Secretary's order of June 15, 1981, pursuant to act of Dec. 19, 1980 (94 Stat. 3184).

Arts, Advisory Committee on the Established under authority of act of Sept. 20, 1961 (75 Stat. 527). Terminated July 1973 by act of Oct. 6, 1972. Formally abolished by Reorg. Plan No. 2 of 1977, effective Apr. 1, 1978.

Arts, National Council on the Established in Executive Office of the President by act of Sept. 3, 1964 (78 Stat. 905). Transferred to National Foundation on the Arts and the Humanities by act of Sept. 29, 1965 (79 Stat. 845).

Assay Commission, Annual Established initially by act of Apr. 2, 1792 (1 Stat. 250) and by act of Feb. 12, 1873 (Revised Statute sec. 3647; 17 Stat. 432). Terminated and functions transferred to Treasury Secretary by act of Mar. 14, 1980 (94 Stat. 98).

Assistance, Bureau of Public Renamed *Bureau of Family Services* by order of *Health, Education, and Welfare Secretary,* effective Jan. 1, 1962. Functions redelegated to *Social and Rehabilitation Service* by Secretary's reorganization of Aug. 15, 1967.

Assistance Coordinating Committee, Adjustment Established by act of Jan. 3, 1975 (88 Stat. 2040). Inactive since 1981.

Assistance Payments Administration Established by *Health, Education, and Welfare Secretary's* reorganization of Aug. 15, 1967. Transferred by Secretary's reorganization of Mar. 8, 1977 (42 FR 13262), from *Social and Rehabilitation Service* to Social Security Administration.

Athletics, Interagency Committee on International Established by EO 11117 of Aug. 13, 1963. Terminated by EO 11515 of Mar. 13, 1970.

Atlantic-Pacific Interoceanic Canal Study Commission Established by act of Sept. 22, 1964 (78 Stat. 990). Terminated Dec. 1, 1970, pursuant to terms of act.

Atomic Energy Commission Established by act of Aug. 1, 1946 (60 Stat. 755). Abolished by act of Oct. 11, 1974 (88 Stat. 1237) and functions transferred to *Energy Research and Development Administration* and Nuclear Regulatory Commission.

Aviation, Interdepartmental Committee on Civil International Established by Presidential letter of June 20, 1935. Terminated on organization of *Civil Aeronautics Authority.*

Aviation Agency, Federal Established by act of Aug. 23, 1958 (72 Stat. 731). Transferred to Transportation Secretary by act of Oct. 15, 1966 (80 Stat. 931).

Aviation Commission, Federal Established by act of June 12, 1934 (48 Stat. 938). Terminated Feb. 1, 1935, under provisions of act.

Beltsville Research Center Established to operate with other agencies of Agriculture Department under *Agricultural Research Administration.* Consolidated into *Agricultural Research Administration,* Agriculture Department, by EO 9069 of Feb. 23, 1942.

Biological Survey, Bureau of Established by Secretary's order July 1, 1885, as part of *Division of Entomology,* Agriculture Department. Made separate bureau by act of Apr. 23, 1904 (33 Stat. 276). Transferred to Interior Department by Reorg. Plan No. II of 1939, effective July 1, 1939. Consolidated with *Bureau of Fisheries* into Fish and Wildlife Service by Reorg. Plan No. III of 1940, effective June 30, 1940.

Blind, Inc., American Printing House for the Established in 1858 as privately owned institution in Louisville, KY. Functions of Treasury Secretary, except that relating to perpetual trust funds, transferred to *Federal Security Agency* by Reorg. Plan No. II of 1939, effective July 1, 1939. Functions performed by *Health, Education, and Welfare Department* transferred to Education Department.

Blind-Made Products, Committee on Purchases of Established by act of June 25, 1938 (52 Stat. 1196). Renamed *Committee for Purchase of Products and Services of the Blind and Other Severely Handicapped* by act of June 23, 1971 (85 Stat. 77). Renamed Committee for Purchase from the Blind and Other Severely Handicapped by act of July 25, 1974 (88 Stat. 392).

Blind and Other Severely Handicapped, Committee for Purchase of Products and Services of the *See* **Blind-Made Products, Committee on Purchases of**

Blockade and Supply Division Established by State departmental order of Aug. 27, 1943, in *Office of Foreign Economic Coordination.* Office abolished by departmental order of Nov. 6, 1943, pursuant to EO 9380 of Sept. 25, 1943, which established *Foreign Economic Administration.*

Board. *See other part of title*

Bond and Spirits Division Established as *Taxes and Penalties Unit,* as announced by Assistant to Attorney General in departmental circular of May 25, 1934, pursuant to EO 6639 of May 10, 1934. Abolished by administrative order of October 1942, and functions transferred to Tax, Claims, and Criminal Divisions, Justice Department.

Bonneville Power Administration Established by Interior Secretary pursuant to act of Aug. 20, 1937 (50 Stat. 731). Transferred to Energy Department by act of Aug. 4, 1977 (91 Stat. 578).

Boston National Historic Sites Commission Established by joint resolution of June 16, 1955 (69 Stat. 137). Terminated June 16, 1960, by act of Feb. 19, 1957 (71 Stat. 4).

Brazil-U.S. Defense Commission, Joint Established in May 1942 by agreement between the U.S. and Brazil. Terminated in September 1977 at direction of Brazilian Government.

Broadcast Bureau Merged with *Cable Television Bureau* to form Mass Media Bureau by Federal Communications Commission order, effective Nov. 30, 1982.

Broadcast Intelligence Service, Foreign *See* **Broadcast Monitoring Service, Foreign**

Broadcast Monitoring Service, Foreign Established in Federal Communications Commission by Presidential directive of Feb. 26, 1941. Renamed *Foreign Broadcast Intelligence Service* by FCC order of July 28, 1942. Transferred to *War Department* by *War* Secretarial order of Dec. 30, 1945. Act of May 3, 1945 (59 Stat. 110), provided for liquidation 60 days after Japanese armistice. Transferred to *Central Intelligence Group* Aug. 5, 1946, and renamed Foreign Broadcast Information Service.

Budget, Bureau of the Established by act of June 10, 1921 (42 Stat. 20), in Treasury Department under immediate direction of President. Transferred to Executive Office of the President by Reorg. Plan No. I, effective July 1, 1939. Reorganized by Reorg. Plan No. 2 of 1970, effective July 1, 1970, and renamed Office of Management and Budget.

Buildings Administration, Public Established as part of *Federal Works Agency* by Reorg. Plan No. I of 1939, effective July 1, 1939. Abolished by act of June 30, 1949 (63 Stat. 380), and functions transferred to General Services Administration.

Buildings Branch, Public Organized in *Procurement Division,* established in Treasury Department by EO 6166 of June 10, 1933. Consolidated with *Branch of Buildings Management,* National Park Service, to form *Public Buildings Administration, Federal Works Agency,* under Reorg. Plan No. I of 1939, effective July 1, 1939.

Buildings Commission, Public Established by act of July 1, 1916 (39 Stat. 328). Abolished by EO 6166 of June 10, 1933, and functions transferred to *Office of National Parks, Buildings, and Reservations,* Interior Department. Functions transferred to *Public Buildings Administration, Federal Works Agency,* under Reorg. Plan No. I of 1939, effective July 1, 1939.

Buildings Management, Branch of Functions of National Park Service (except those relating to monuments and memorials) consolidated with *Public Buildings Branch, Procurement Division,* Treasury Department, to form *Public Buildings Administration, Federal Works Agency,* in accordance with Reorg. Plan No. I of 1939, effective July 1, 1939.

Buildings and Public Parks of the National Capital, Office of Public Established by act of Feb. 26, 1925 (43 Stat. 983), by consolidation of *Office of Public Buildings and Grounds* under Chief of Engineers, U.S. Army, and *Office of Superintendent of State, War, and Navy Department Buildings.* Abolished by EO 6166 of June 10, 1933, and functions transferred to *Office of National Parks, Buildings, and Reservations,* Interior Department.

Bureau. *See other part of title*

Business, Cabinet Committee on Small Established by Presidential letter of May 31, 1956. Dissolved January 1961.

Business Administration, Domestic and International *See* **Business and Defense Services Administration**

Business Cooperation, Division of Established in *National Recovery Administration* by EO 7075 of June 15, 1935. Transferred to Commerce Department by EO 7252 of Dec. 21, 1935. By same order, functions of *Division* ordered terminated by Apr. 1, 1936. *Committee of Industrial Analysis* created by EO 7323 of Mar. 21, 1936, to complete work of *Division.*

Business and Defense Services Administration Established by Commerce Secretary Oct. 1, 1953, and operated under Department Organization Order 40-1. Abolished by Department Organization Order 40-1A of Sept. 15, 1970, and functions transferred to *Bureau of Domestic Commerce.* Functions transferred to *Domestic and International Business Administration,* effective Nov. 17, 1972. *Administration* terminated by Secretary's order of Dec. 4, 1977, and functions assumed by *Industry and Trade Administration.*

Business Economics, Office of Established by Commerce Secretary Jan. 17, 1946. Renamed Office of Economic Analysis Jan. 1, 1972. Transferred to *Social and Economic Statistics Administration.*

Business Operations, Bureau of International Established by Commerce Secretary Aug. 8, 1961, by Departmental Orders 173 and 174. Abolished by Departmental Order 182 of Feb. 1, 1963, which established *Bureau of International Commerce.* Functions transferred to *Domestic and International Business Administration,* effective Nov. 17, 1972.

Cabinet Committee. *See other part of title*

Cable Television Bureau Merged with *Broadcast Bureau* by Federal Communications Commission order to form Mass Media Bureau, effective Nov. 30, 1982.

California Debris Commission Established by act of Mar. 1, 1893 (27 Stat. 507). Abolished by act of Nov. 17, 1986 (100 Stat. 4229), and functions transferred to Interior Secretary.

Canal Zone Government Established by act of Aug. 24, 1912 (37 Stat. 561). Abolished by act of Sept. 27, 1979 (93 Stat. 454).

Capital Housing Authority, National Established by act of June 12, 1934 (48 Stat. 930). Made agency of District of Columbia government by act of Dec. 24, 1973 (87 Stat. 779), effective July 1, 1974.

Capital Park Commission, National Established by act of June 6, 1924 (43 Stat. 463). *National Capital Park and Planning Commission* named successor by act of Apr. 30, 1926 (44 Stat. 374). Functions transferred to *National Capital Planning Commission* by act of July 19, 1952 (66 Stat. 781).

Capital Park and Planning Commission, National *See* **Capital Park Commission, National**

Capital Regional Planning Council, National Established by act of July 19, 1952 (66 Stat. 785). Terminated by Reorg. Plan No. 5 of 1966, effective Sept. 8, 1966.

Capital Transportation Agency, National Established by act of July 14, 1960 (74 Stat 537). Authorized to establish rapid rail transit system by act of Sept. 8, 1965 (79 Stat. 663). Functions transferred to Washington Metropolitan Area Transit Authority by EO 11373 of Sept. 20, 1967.

Career Executive Board Established by EO 10758 of Mar. 4, 1958. Terminated July 1, 1959, and EO 10758 revoked by EO 10859 of Feb. 5, 1960.

Caribbean Organization Act of June 30, 1961 (75 Stat. 194), provided for acceptance by President of Agreement for the Establishment of the Caribbean Organization, signed at Washington, June 21, 1960. Article III of Agreement provided for termination of *Caribbean Commission,* authorized by Agreement signed Oct. 30, 1946, on first meeting of Caribbean Council, governing body of *Organization.* Terminated, effective Dec. 31, 1965, by resolution adopted by Council.

Cemeteries and Memorials in Europe, National Supervision transferred from *War Department* to American Battle Monuments Commission by EO 6614 of Feb. 26, 1934, which transfer was deferred to May 21, 1934, by EO 6690 of Apr. 25, 1934.

Cemeteries and Parks, National *War Department* functions regarding National Cemeteries and Parks located in continental U.S. transferred to *Office of National Parks, Buildings, and Reservations,* Interior Department, by EO 6166 of June 10, 1933.

Censorship, Office of Established by EO 8985 of Dec. 19, 1941. Terminated by EO 9631 of Sept. 28, 1945.

Censorship Policy Board Established by EO 8985 of Dec. 19, 1941. Terminated by EO 9631 of Sept. 28, 1945.

Census, Bureau of the Vital statistics functions transferred to *Federal Security Administration* by Reorg. Plan No. 2 of 1946, effective July 16, 1946, to be performed through *Public Health Service* or other facilities of *Federal Security Agency.*

Center. *See other part of title*

Central. *See other part of title*

Chemistry and Soils, Bureau of *See* **Agricultural and Industrial Chemistry, Bureau of**

Chesapeake Bay Center for Environmental Studies Established in 1965 in Annapolis, MD, as part of Smithsonian Institution by Secretarial order. Merged with *Radiation Biology Laboratory* by Secretarial Order July 1, 1983, to form Smithsonian Environmental Research Center.

Child Development, Office of *See* **Children's Bureau**

Child Support Enforcement, Office of Established in Health and Human Services Department by act of Jan. 4, 1975 (88 Stat. 2351). Replaced by Family Support Administration.

Children's Bureau Established by act of Apr. 9, 1912 (37 Stat. 79). Placed in Labor Department by act of Mar. 4, 1913 (37 Stat. 737). Transferred, with exception of child labor functions, to *Social Security Administration, Federal Security Agency,* by Reorg. Plan No. 2 of 1946, effective July 16, 1946. Continued under *Administration* when *Agency* functions assumed by *Health, Education, and Welfare Department.* Reassigned to *Welfare Administration* by Department reorganization Jan. 28, 1963. Reassigned to *Social and Rehabilitation Service* by Department reorganization Aug. 15, 1967. Reassigned to *Office of Child Development* by Department reorganization order of Sept. 17, 1969.

China, U.S. Court for Established by act of June 30, 1906 (34 Stat. 814). Transferred to Justice Department by EO 6166 of June 10, 1933, effective Mar. 2, 1934. Act of June 30, 1906, repealed effective Sept. 1, 1948 (62 Stat. 992).

Civil defense. *See* **Defense**

Civil Service Commission, U.S. Established by act of Jan. 16, 1883 (22 Stat. 403). Redesignated as Merit Systems Protection Board and functions transferred to Board and Office of Personnel Management by Reorg. Plan No. 2 of 1978, effective Jan. 1, 1979.

Civil War Centennial Commission Established by act of Sept. 7, 1957 (71 Stat. 626). Terminated May 1, 1966, pursuant to terms of act.

Civilian Conservation Corps Established by act of June 28, 1937 (50 Stat. 319). Made part of *Federal Security Agency* by Reorg. Plan No. I of 1939, effective July 1, 1939. Liquidation provided for by act of July 2, 1942 (56 Stat. 569), not later than June 30, 1943.

Civilian Production Administration Established by EO 9638 of Oct. 4, 1945. Consolidated with other agencies to form *Office of Temporary Controls, Office for Emergency Management,* by EO 9809 of Dec. 12, 1946.

Civilian Service Awards Board, Distinguished Established by EO 10717 of June 27, 1957. Terminated by EO 12014 of Oct. 19, 1977, and functions transferred to *U.S. Civil Service Commission.*

Claims, U.S. Court of Established Feb. 25, 1855 (10 Stat. 612). Abolished by act of Apr. 2, 1982 (96 Stat. 26) and trial jurisdiction transferred to *U.S. Claims Court* and appellate functions merged with those of *U.S. Court of Customs and Patent Appeals* to form U.S. Court of Appeals for the Federal Circuit.

Claims Commission of the United States, International Established in State Department by act of Mar. 10, 1950 (64 Stat. 12). Abolished by Reorg. Plan No. 1 of 1954, effective July 1, 1954, and functions transferred to Foreign Claims Settlement Commission of the United States.

Claims Settlement Commission of the United States, Foreign Established by Reorg. Plan No. 1 of 1954, effective July 1, 1954. Transferred to Justice Department by act of Mar. 14, 1980 (94 Stat. 96).

Clark Sesquicentennial Commission, George Rogers Established by Public Resolution 51 (45 Stat. 723). Expenditures ordered administered by Interior Department by EO 6166 of June 10, 1933.

Classification Review Committee, Interagency Established by EO 11652 of Mar. 8, 1972. Abolished by EO 12065 of June 28, 1978.

Clemency Board, Presidential Established in Executive Office of the President by EO 11803 of Sept. 16, 1974. Final recommendations submitted to President Sept. 15, 1975, and *Board* terminated by EO 11878 of Sept. 10, 1975.

Coal Commission, National Bituminous Established under authority of act of Aug. 30, 1935 (49 Stat. 992). Abolished by Reorg. Plan No. II of 1939, effective July 1, 1939, and functions transferred to *Bituminous Coal Division.*

Coal Consumers' Counsel, Office of the Bituminous Established by act of Apr. 11, 1941 (55 Stat. 134), renewing provisions of act of Apr. 23, 1937 (50 Stat. 72) for 2 years to continue functions of *Consumers' Counsel Division,* Interior Department. Functions continued by acts of Apr. 24, 1943 (57 Stat. 68), and May 21, 1943 (57 Stat. 82). Terminated Aug. 24, 1943.

Coal Division, Bituminous Established July 1, 1939, by Interior Secretary's Order 1394 of June 16, 1939, as amended by Order 1399, of July 5, 1939, pursuant to act of Apr. 3, 1939 (53 Stat. 562) and Reorg. Plan No. II of 1939, effective July 1, 1939. Administered functions vested in *National Bituminous Coal Commission* by act of Apr. 23, 1937 (50 Stat. 72). Act extended to Aug. 24, 1943, on which date it expired.

Coal Labor Board, Bituminous Established by act of July 12, 1921 (42 Stat. 140). Abolished as result of

U.S. Supreme Court decision, May 18, 1936, in case of *Carter* v. *Carter Coal Company et al.*

Coal Leasing Planning and Coordination, Office of Established Mar. 22, 1978, by Interior Department manual release 2075. Abolished Aug. 4, 1981, by departmental manual release 2342.

Coal Mine Safety Board of Review, Federal Established by act of July 16, 1952 (66 Stat. 697). Inactive after Mar. 30, 1970, pursuant to act of Dec. 30, 1969 (83 Stat. 803).

Coal Mines Administration Established by Interior Secretary July 1, 1943. Abolished by Secretary's Order 1977 of Aug. 16, 1944, as amended by Order 1982 of Aug. 31, 1944, and functions assumed by *Solid Fuels Administration for War. Administration* reestablished in Interior Department by EO 9728 of May 21, 1946. Terminated June 30, 1947, by act of March 27, 1942 (56 Stat. 176).

Coal Research, Office of Established in Interior Department by act of July 7, 1960 (74 Stat. 336). Functions transferred to *Energy Research and Development Administration* by act of Oct. 11, 1974 (88 Stat. 1237).

Coast and Geodetic Survey *See* **Coast Survey**

Coast Guard, U.S. Transferred from Treasury Department to Navy Department by EO 8929 of Nov. 1, 1941. Returned to Treasury Department by EO 9666 of Dec. 28, 1945. Transferred to Transportation Department by act of Oct. 15, 1966 (80 Stat. 931).

Coast Survey Established by act of Feb. 10, 1807 (2 Stat. 413). Redesignated as *Coast and Geodetic Survey* by act of June 20, 1878 (20 Stat. 206). Transferred to *Environmental Science Services Administration* by Reorg. Plan No. 2 of 1965, effective July 13, 1965.

Codification Board Established by act of June 19, 1937 (50 Stat. 304). Abolished by Reorg. Plan No. II of 1939, effective July 1, 1939, and functions transferred to *Division of the Federal Register.*

Coinage, Joint Commission on the Established by act of July 23, 1965 (79 Stat. 258). Expired Jan. 4, 1975, pursuant to act of Oct. 6, 1972 (88 Stat. 776).

Collection of Fine Arts, National Renamed National Museum of American Art in Smithsonian Institution by act of Oct. 13, 1980 (94 Stat. 1884).

Columbia Institution for the Instruction of the Deaf and Dumb, and the Blind Established by act of Feb. 16, 1857 (11 Stat. 161). Renamed *Columbia Institution for the Instruction of the Deaf and Dumb* by act of Feb. 23, 1865 (13 Stat. 436). Renamed *Columbia Institution for the Deaf* by act of Mar. 4, 1911 (36 Stat. 1422). Renamed *Gallaudet College* by act of June 18, 1954 (68 Stat. 265). Functions of *Health, Education, and Welfare Department* transferred to Education Department by act of Oct. 17, 1979 (93 Stat. 695). Renamed Gallaudet University by act of Aug. 4, 1986 (100 Stat. 781).

Commander in Chief, U.S. Fleet, and Chief of Naval Operations Duties of two positions prescribed by EO 8984 of Dec. 18, 1941. Combined under one officer by EO 9096 of Mar. 12, 1942.

Commerce, Bureau of Domestic *See* **Business and Defense Services Administration**

Commerce, Bureau of Foreign Established by Commerce Secretary Oct. 12, 1953, by Reorg. Plan No. 5 of 1950. Abolished by department order of Aug. 7, 1961, and functions vested in *Bureau of International Programs* and *Bureau of International Business Operations.*

Commerce, Bureau of Foreign and Domestic Established by act of Aug. 23, 1912 (37 Stat. 407). Functions reassigned to other offices of Commerce Department through internal reorganizations.

Commerce, Bureau of International *See* **Business Operations, Bureau of International**

Commerce Commission, Interstate Certain functions as cited in act of Oct. 15, 1966 (80 Stat. 931) transferred to Commerce Secretary. Functions relating to railroad and pipeline safety transferred to Federal Railroad Administrator and motor carrier safety to Federal Highway Administrator by act.

Commerce Department, Solicitor for Transferred from Justice Department to Commerce Department by EO 6166 of June 10, 1933.

Commerce Service, Foreign Established in *Bureau of Foreign and Domestic Commerce,* Commerce Department, by act of Mar. 3, 1927 (44 Stat. 1394). Transferred to State Department as part of Foreign Service by Reorg. Plan No. II of 1939, effective July 1, 1939.

Commercial Company, U.S. Established Mar. 27, 1942, as subsidiary of *Reconstruction Finance Corporation.* Transferred to *Office of Economic Warfare* by EO 9361 of July 15, 1943. *Office* consolidated into *Foreign Economic Administration* by EO 9380 of Sept. 25, 1943. Functions returned to *Corporation* by EO 9630 of Sept. 27, 1945, until June 30, 1948.

Commercial Policy, Executive Committee on Established by Presidential letter of Nov. 11, 1933, to Secretary of State. Abolished by EO 9461 of Aug. 7, 1944.

Commercial Services, Office of Foreign Established by Commerce Secretary Feb. 1, 1963, and operated under Department Organization Order 40-4. Abolished Sept. 15, 1970, by Department Organization Order 40-2A and functions transferred to Bureau of International Commerce.

Commercial Standards, Division of Transferred with *Division of Simplified Trade Practice* from National Bureau of Standards to Commerce Secretary by Reorg. Plan No. 3 of 1946, effective July 16, 1946, to permit reassignment to Office of Domestic Commerce. Functions transferred to National Bureau of Standards by Commerce Department Order 90, June 7, 1963.

Commercial Standards Division Transferred with *Division of Simplified Trade Practice* from National Bureau of Standards to Commerce Secretary by Reorg. Plan No. 3 of 1946, effective July 16, 1946, to permit reassignment to Office of Domestic Commerce. Functions transferred to National Bureau of Standards by Commerce Department Order 90, June 7, 1963, pursuant to Reorg. Plan No. 5 of 1950.

Commission. *See other part of title*

Committee. *See also other part of title*

Committee Management Secretariat Established in Office of Management and Budget Jan. 5, 1973, by act of Oct. 6, 1972 (86 Stat. 772). Functions transferred to General Services Administrator by Reorg. Plan No. 1 of 1977, effective Apr. 1, 1978. Reassigned to *National Archives and Records Service* by GSA order of Feb. 22, 1979. Transferred in Archives to Office of the Federal Register by GSA order of Oct. 14, 1980. Transferred to Office of the Archivist of the United States by GSA order of Sept. 24, 1982. Reassigned to Office of Program Initiatives, GSA, by GSA order of May 18, 1984. Transferred to Office of Management Services, GSA, by GSA order of April 7, 1986.

Commodities Corporation, Federal Surplus *See* **Relief Corporation, Federal Surplus**

Commodity Credit Corporation Organized by EO 6340 of Oct. 16, 1933, and managed in close affiliation with *Reconstruction Finance Corporation.* Transferred to Agriculture Department by Reorg. Plan No. I of 1939, effective July 1, 1939.

Commodity Exchange Administration *See* **Grain Futures Administration**

Commodity Exchange Authority *See* **Grain Futures Administration**

Commodity Exchange Commission Established by act of Sept. 21, 1922 (42 Stat. 998). Functions transferred to Commodity Futures Trading Commission by act of Oct. 23, 1974 (88 Stat. 1414).

Commodity Stabilization Service Established Nov. 2, 1953, by Secretary's Memorandum 1320, supp. 4. Renamed Agricultural Stabilization and Conservation Service by Secretary's Memorandum 1458 of June 14, 1961, effective June 5, 1961.

Communication Agency, International *See* **Information Agency, U.S.**

Communications Program, Joint Tactical Combined with *Joint Interoperability of the Tactical Command and Control Systems Programs* to form Joint Tactical Command, Control, and Communications Agency in July 1984, pursuant to Defense Department Directive 5154.28.

Community Development Corporation Established in Housing and Urban Development Department by act of Dec. 31, 1970 (84 Stat. 1791). Renamed *New Community Development Corporation* by act of Aug. 22, 1974 (88 Stat. 725). Abolished Nov. 30, 1983, by act of Nov. 30, 1983 (97 Stat. 1238), and functions transferred to Assistant Secretary for Community Planning and Development, Housing and Urban Development Department.

Community Development Corporation, New *See* **Community Development Corporation**

Community Facilities, Bureau of Established in 1945 by *Federal Works Administrator.* Transferred by act of June 30, 1949 (63 Stat. 380), to General Services Administration, functioning as *Community Facilities Service.* Certain functions transferred to various agencies, including Interior Department, *Housing and Home Finance Agency,* and *Federal Security Agency* by Reorg. Plans Nos. 15, 16, and 17 of 1950, effective May 24, 1950.

Community Facilities Administration Established in *Housing and Home Finance Agency* by Administrator's Organizational Order 1 of Dec. 23, 1954. Terminated by act of Sept. 9, 1965 (79 Stat. 667), and functions transferred to Housing and Urban Development Department.

Community Organization, Committee on Established in *Office of Defense Health and Welfare Services* Sept. 10, 1941. Functions transferred to *Federal Security Agency* by EO 9338 of Apr. 29, 1943.

Community Relations Service Established July 2, 1964, in Commerce Department by act of July 2, 1964 (78 Stat. 241). Transferred to Justice Department by Reorg. Plan No. 1 of 1966, effective Apr. 22, 1966.

Community Services, Office of Established in Health and Human Services Department by act of Aug. 13, 1981 (95 Stat. 516). Replaced by Family Support Administration.

Community Services Administration Established by act of Jan. 4, 1975 (88 Stat. 2291) as successor to *Office of Economic Opportunity.* Abolished as independent agency through repeal of act of Aug. 20, 1964 (except titles VIII and X of such act) by act of Aug. 13, 1981 (95 Stat. 519).

Community Services Administration Functions concerning Legal Services Program transferred to Legal Services Corporation by act of July 25, 1974 (88 Stat. 389). Renamed Public Services Administration by Health, Education, and Welfare departmental notice of Nov. 3, 1976. Transferred to *Office of Human Development* by Secretary's reorganization of Mar. 8, 1977 (42 FR 13262).

Community War Services Established in Office of the Administrator under EO 9338 of Apr. 29, 1943, and Federal Security Agency order. Terminated Dec. 31, 1946, by act of July 26, 1946 (60 Stat. 695).

Conciliation Service, U.S. Established by act of Mar. 4, 1913 (37 Stat. 738). Functions transferred to Federal Mediation and Conciliation Service, established by act of June 23, 1947 (61 Stat. 153).

Constitution, transfer of functions *See* **Statutes at Large and other matters**

Construction, Collective Bargaining Committee in Established by EO 11849 of Apr. 1, 1975. Inactive since Jan. 7, 1976. Formally abolished by EO 12110 of Dec. 28, 1978.

Construction, Equipment and Repairs, Bureau of Established in Navy Department by act of Aug. 31, 1842 (5 Stat. 579). Abolished by act of July 5, 1862 (12 Stat. 510), and functions distributed among *Bureau of Equipment and Recruiting, Bureau of Construction and Repair,* and *Bureau of Steam Engineering.*

Construction Branch Established in Treasury Department in 1853 and designated *Bureau of Construction* under control of *Office of Supervising Architect* by Sept. 30, 1855. *Office* incorporated into *Public Buildings Branch, Procurement Division,* by EO 6166 of June 10, 1933. Transferred to *Federal Works Agency* by Reorg. Plan No. I of 1939, effective July 1, 1939, when *Public Buildings Branch* of *Procurement Division, Bureau of Buildings Management,* National Park Service, Interior Department—so far as latter concerned with operation of public buildings for other departments or agencies—and *U.S. Housing Corporation* consolidated with *Public Buildings Administration, Federal Works Agency.*

Construction Industry Stabilization Committee Established by EO 11588 of Mar. 29, 1971. Abolished by EO 11788 of June 18, 1974.

Construction and Repair, Bureau of Established by act of July 5, 1862 (12 Stat. 510), replacing *Bureau of Construction, Equipment and Repairs.* Abolished by act of June 20, 1940 (54 Stat. 492), and functions transferred to *Bureau of Ships.*

Consumer Advisory Council Established by EO 11136 of Jan. 3, 1964. *Office of Consumer Affairs* established in Executive Office of the President by EO 11583 of Feb. 24, 1971, and Council reestablished in *Office.*

Consumer Affairs, Office of Established by EO 11583 of Feb. 24, 1971. Transferred to *Health, Education, and Welfare Department* by EO 11702 of Jan. 25, 1973.

Consumer Affairs Staff, National Business Council for Established in Commerce Department by departmental organization order of Dec. 16, 1971. Terminated by departmental order of Dec. 6, 1973, through lack of funds.

Consumer agencies Consumer agencies of *National Emergency Council* and *National Recovery Administration* reorganized and functions transferred, together with those of *Consumers' Advisory Board, NRA,* and *Cabinet Committee on Price Policy,* to *Consumers' Division, NRA,* by EO 7120 of July 30, 1935. *Division* transferred to Labor Department by EO 7252 of Dec. 21, 1935. Transferred to *Division of Consumers' Counsel, Agricultural Adjustment Administration,* Agriculture Department, by Labor Secretary's letter of Aug. 30, 1938, to Agriculture Secretary. Continued as *Consumer Standards Project* until June 30, 1941. Research on consumer standards continued by *Consumer Standards Section, Consumers' Counsel Division,* transferred to *Agricultural Marketing Administration* by administrative order of Feb. 28, 1942. Other project activities discontinued.

Consumer Cooperative Bank, National Established by act of Aug. 20, 1978 (92 Stat. 499). Removed from mixed-ownership, Government corporation status by acts of Sept. 13, 1982 (96 Stat. 1062) and Jan. 12, 1983 (96 Stat. 2478).

Consumer Interests, President's Committee on Established by EO 11136 of Jan. 3, 1964. Abolished by EO 11583 of Feb. 24, 1971.

Consumer and Marketing Service Established by Agriculture Secretary Feb. 2, 1965. Renamed Agricultural Marketing Service Apr. 2, 1972, by Secretary's order and certain functions transferred to Animal and Plant Health Inspection Service.

Consumers' Counsel Established in *National Bituminous Coal Commission* by act of Aug. 30, 1935 (49 Stat. 993). Office abolished by Reorg. Plan No. II of 1939, effective July 1, 1939, and functions transferred to Office of Solicitor, Interior Department, to function as *Consumers' Counsel Division* under direction of Interior Secretary. Functions transferred to *Office of the Bituminous Coal Consumers' Counsel* June 1941 by act of Apr. 11, 1941 (55 Stat. 134).

Consumers' Counsel Division *See* **Consumers' Counsel**

Consumers' Counsel, Division of Established by act of May 12, 1933 (48 Stat. 31). Transferred by order of Agriculture Secretary from *Agricultural Adjustment Administration* to supervision of Director of Marketing, effective Feb. 1, 1940. Transferred to *Agricultural Marketing Administration* by administrative order of Feb. 28, 1942.

Consumers' Problems, Adviser on *See* **Consumer agencies**

Contract Committee Government *See* **Contract Compliance, Committee on Government**

Contract Compliance, Committee on Government Established by EO 10308 of Dec. 3, 1951. Abolished by EO 10479 of Aug. 13, 1953, which established successor *Government Contract Committee.* Abolished by EO 10925 of Mar. 6, 1961, and records and property transferred to *President's Committee on Equal Employment Opportunity.*

Contract Settlement, Office of Established by act of July 1, 1944 (58 Stat. 651). Transferred to *Office of War Mobilization and Reconversion* by act of Oct. 3, 1944 (58 Stat. 785). Terminated by EO 9809 of Dec. 12, 1946, and Reorg. Plan No. 1 of 1947, effective July 1, 1947, and functions transferred to Treasury Department. Functions transferred to General Services Administration by act of June 30, 1949 (63 Stat. 380).

Contract Settlement Advisory Board Established by act of July 1, 1944 (58 Stat. 651). Transferred to Treasury Department by EO 9809 of Dec. 12, 1946, and by Reorg. Plan No. 1 of 1947, effective July 1, 1947. Transferred to General Services Administration by act of June 30, 1949 (63 Stat. 380) and

290-950 O 91 - 27

established as *Contract Review Board.* Renamed Board of Contract Appeals in 1961 by Administrator's order. Board established as independent entity within General Services Administration Feb. 27, 1979, pursuant to act of Nov. 1, 1978 (92 Stat. 2383).

Contract Settlement Appeal Board, Office of Established by act of July 1, 1944 (58 Stat. 651). Transferred to Treasury Department by EO 9809 of Dec. 12, 1946, and by Reorg. Plan No. 1 of 1947, effective July 1, 1947. Functions transferred to General Services Administration by act of June 30, 1949 (63 Stat. 380). Abolished by act of July 14, 1952 (66 Stat. 627).

Contract Termination Board, Joint Established Nov. 12, 1943, by *Director of War Mobilization.* Functions assumed by *Office of Contract Settlement.*

Contracts Division, Public Established in Labor Department to administer act of June 30, 1936 (49 Stat. 2036). Consolidated with Wage and Hour Division by order of Secretary Aug. 21, 1942. Absorbed by Wage and Hour Division by order of Secretary May 1971.

Cooperation Administration, International Established by State Department Delegation of Authority 85 of June 30, 1955, pursuant to EO 10610 of May 9, 1955. Abolished by act of Sept. 4, 1961 (75 Stat. 446), and functions redelegated to Agency for International Development pursuant to Presidential letter of Sept. 30, 1961, and EO 10973 of Nov. 3, 1961.

Coordinating Service, Federal *Office of Chief Coordinator* created by Executive order promulgated in *Bureau of the Budget* Circular 15, July 27, 1921, and duties enlarged by other *Bureau* circulars. Abolished by EO 6166 of June 10, 1933. Contract form, Federal traffic, and surplus property functions transferred to *Procurement Division* by order of Treasury Secretary, approved by President Oct. 9, 1933, issued pursuant to EOs 6166 of June 10, 1933, and 6224 of July 27, 1933.

Copyrighted Works, National Commission on New Technological Uses of Established by act of Dec. 31, 1974 (88 Stat. 1873). Terminated Sept. 29, 1978, pursuant to terms of act.

Corporate Payments Abroad, Task Force on Questionable Established by Presidential memorandum of Mar. 31, 1976. Terminated Dec. 31, 1976, pursuant to terms of memorandum.

Corporation, Federal Facilities Established in Treasury Department by EO 10539 of June 22, 1954. Placed under supervision of Director appointed by General Services Administrator by EO 10720 of July 11, 1957. Dissolved by act of Aug. 30, 1961 (75 Stat. 418), and functions transferred to Administrator of General Services.

Corregidor-Bataan Memorial Commission Established by act of Aug. 5, 1953 (67 Stat. 366). Terminated May 6, 1967, by act of Dec. 23, 1963 (77 Stat. 477).

Cost Accounting Standards Board Established by act of Aug. 15, 1970 (84 Stat. 796). Terminated Sept. 30, 1980, through lack of funding.

Cost of Living Council Established by EO 11615 of Aug. 15, 1971. Abolished by EO 11788 of June 18, 1974.

Cotton Stabilization Corporation Organized June 1930 under laws of Delaware by *Federal Farm Board* pursuant to act of June 15, 1929 (46 Stat. 11). Certificate of dissolution filed with Corporation Commission of Delaware Dec. 27, 1934.

Council. *See other part of title*

Courts Under act of Aug. 7, 1939 (53 Stat. 1223), and revised June 25, 1948 (62 Stat. 913), to provide for administration of U.S. courts, administrative jurisdiction over all continental and territorial courts transferred to Administrative Office of the U.S. Courts, including U.S. courts of appeals and district courts, District Court for the Territory of Alaska, U.S. District Court for the District of the Canal Zone, District Court of Guam, District Court of the Virgin Islands, Court of Claims, Court of Customs and Patent Appeals, and Customs Courts.

Credit Unions, Bureau of Federal *See* **Credit Union System, Federal**

Credit Union System, Federal Established by act of June 26, 1934 (48 Stat. 1216), to be administered by *Farm Credit Administration.* Transferred to Federal Deposit Insurance Corporation by EO 9148 of Apr. 27, 1942, and Reorg. Plan No. 1 of 1947, effective July 1, 1947. Functions transferred to *Bureau of Federal Credit Unions, Federal Security Agency,* established by act of June 29, 1948 (62 Stat. 1091). Functions transferred to *Health, Education, and Welfare Department* by Reorg. Plan No. 1 of 1953, effective Apr. 11, 1953. Functions transferred to National Credit Union Administration by act of Mar. 10, 1970 (84 Stat. 49).

Crime, National Council on Organized Established by EO 11534 of June 4, 1970. Terminated by EO 12110 of Dec. 28, 1978.

Crop Production Loan Office Authorized by Presidential letters of July 26, 1918, and July 26, 1919, to Agriculture Secretary. Further authorized by act of Mar. 3, 1921 (41 Stat. 1347). Transferred to Farm Credit Administration by EO 6084 of Mar. 27, 1933.

Cultural Center, National Established in Smithsonian Institution by act of Sept. 2, 1958 (72 Stat. 1698). Renamed John F. Kennedy Center for the Performing Arts by act of Jan. 23, 1964 (78 Stat. 4).

Customs, Bureau of Functions relating to award of numbers to undocumented vessels, vested in Collectors of Customs, transferred to Commandant of Coast Guard by EO 9083 of Feb. 27, 1942. Transfer made permanent by Reorg. Plan No. 3 of 1946, effective July 16, 1946. Redesignated U.S. Customs Service by Treasury Department Order 165-23 of Apr. 4, 1973.

Customs Court, U.S. Renamed U.S. Court of International Trade by act of Oct. 10, 1980 (94 Stat. 1727).

Customs and Patent Appeals, U.S. Court of Established by act of Mar. 2, 1929 (45 Stat. 1475). Abolished by act of Apr. 2, 1982 (96 Stat. 28) and functions merged with appellate functions of *U.S. Court of Claims* to form U.S. Court of Appeals for the Federal Circuit.

Dairy Industry, Bureau of *Bureau of Dairying* established in Agriculture Department by act of May 29, 1924 (43 Stat. 243). *Bureau of Dairy Industry* designation first appeared in act of May 11, 1926 (44 Stat. 499). Functions transferred to *Agricultural Research Service* by Secretary's Memorandum 1320, supp. 4, of Nov. 2, 1953.

Defense, Advisory Commission to the Council of National *See* **Defense, Council of National**

Defense, Council of National Established by act of Aug. 29, 1916 (39 Stat. 649). *Advisory Commission*—composed of Advisers on Industrial Production, Industrial Materials, Employment, Farm Products, Price Stabilization, Transportation, and Consumer Protection—established by *Council* pursuant to act and approved by President May 29, 1940. *Commission* decentralized by merging divisions with newly created national defense units. Agencies evolved from *Commission,* except *Office of Agricultural War Relations* and *Office of Price Administration,* made units of *Office for Emergency Management. Council* inactive.

Defense, Office of Civilian Established in *Office for Emergency Management* by EO 8757 of May 20, 1941. Terminated by EO 9562 of June 4, 1945.

Defense Administration, Federal Civil Established in *Office for Emergency Management* by EO 10186 of Dec. 1, 1950; subsequently established as independent agency by act of Jan. 12, 1951 (64 Stat. 1245). Functions transferred to *Office of Defense and Civilian Mobilization* by Reorg. Plan No. 1 of 1958, effective July 1, 1958.

Defense Advisory Council, Civil Established by act of Jan. 12, 1951 (64 Stat. 1245). Transferred to *Office of Defense and Civilian Mobilization* by Reorg. Plan No. 1 of 1958, effective July 1, 1958.

Defense Aid Reports, Division of Established in *Office for Emergency Management* by EO 8751 of May 2, 1941. Abolished by EO 8926 of Oct. 28, 1941, which created *Office of Lend-Lease Administration.*

Defense Air Transportation Administration Established Nov. 12, 1951, by Commerce Department Order 137. Abolished by Amendment 3 of Sept. 13, 1962, to Department Order 128 (revised) and functions transferred to Office of the Under Secretary of Commerce for Transportation.

Defense Atomic Support Agency Renamed Defense Nuclear Agency by General Order No. 1 of July 1, 1971.

Defense Audiovisual Agency Established by Defense Department Directive 5040.1 of June 12, 1979. Abolished by Secretary's memorandum of Apr. 19, 1985, and functions assigned to the military departments.

Defense Audit Service Established by Defense Department directive of Oct. 14, 1976. Abolished by Deputy Secretary's memorandum of Nov. 2, 1982, and functions transferred to Office of the Inspector General.

Defense Civil Preparedness Agency Functions transferred from Defense Department to Federal Emergency Management Agency by EO 12148 of July 20, 1979.

Defense and Civilian Mobilization Board Established by EO 10773 of July 1, 1938. Redesignated *Civil and Defense Mobilization Board* by act of Aug. 26, 1958 (72 Stat. 861). Abolished by *Office of Emergency Preparedness* Circular 1200.1 of Oct. 31, 1962.

Defense Communications Agency Established by direction of the Secretary of Defense on May 12, 1960. Renamed Defense Intelligence Systems Agency by DOD Directive 5105.19 dated June 25, 1991.

Defense Communications Board Established by EO 8546 of Sept. 24, 1940. Renamed *Board of War Communications* by EO 9183 of June 15, 1942. Abolished by EO 9831 of Feb. 24, 1947, and property transferred to Federal Communications Commission.

Defense Coordinating Board, Civil Established by EO 10611 of May 11, 1955. EO 10611 revoked by EO 10773 of July 1, 1958.

Defense Electric Power Administration Established by Interior Secretary's Order 2605 of Dec. 4, 1950. Abolished June 30, 1953, by Secretary's Order 2721 of May 7, 1953. Reestablished by Departmental Manual Release No. 253 of Aug. 6, 1959. Terminated by Departmental Manual Release No. 1050 of Jan. 10, 1977.

Defense Fisheries Administration Established by Interior Secretary's Order 2605 of Dec. 4, 1950. Abolished June 30, 1953, by Secretary's Order 2722 of May 13, 1953.

Defense Health and Welfare Services, Office of Established by EO 8890 of Sept. 3, 1941. Terminated by EO 9338 of Apr. 29, 1943, and functions transferred to *Federal Security Agency.*

Defense Homes Corporation Incorporated pursuant to President's letter to Treasury Secretary of Oct. 18, 1940. Transferred to *Federal Public Housing Authority* by EO 9070 of Feb. 24, 1942.

Defense Housing Coordination, Division of Established in *Office for Emergency Management* by EO 8632 of Jan. 11, 1941. Functions transferred to *National Housing Agency* by EO 9070 of Feb. 24, 1942.

Defense Housing Coordinator Office established July 21, 1940, by *Advisory Commission to Council of National Defense.* Functions transferred to *Division of Defense Housing Coordination, Office* *for Emergency Management,* by EO 8632 of Jan. 11, 1941.

Defense Housing Division, Mutual Ownership Established by Administrator of *Federal Works Agency* under provisions of act of June 28, 1941 (55 Stat. 361). Functions transferred to *Federal Public Housing Authority, National Housing Agency,* by EO 9070 of Feb. 24, 1942.

Defense Manpower Administration Established by Labor Secretary by General Order 48, pursuant to EO 10161 of Sept. 9, 1950, and Reorg. Plan No. 6 of 1950, effective May 24, 1950. General Order 48 revoked by General Order 63 of Aug. 25, 1953, which established *Office of Manpower Administration* in Department.

Defense Materials Procurement Agency Established by EO 10281 of Aug. 28, 1951. Abolished by EO 10480 of Aug. 14, 1953, and functions transferred to General Services Administration.

Defense Materials Service *See* **Emergency Procurement Service**

Defense Mediation Board, National Established by EO 8716 of Mar. 19, 1941. Terminated on creation of *National War Labor Board, Office for Emergency Management* by EO 9017 of Jan. 12, 1942. Transferred to Labor Department by EO 9617 of Sept. 19, 1945. *Board* terminated by EO 9672 of Dec. 31, 1945, which established *National Wage Stabilization Board* in Labor Department. Terminated by EO 9809 of Dec. 12, 1946, and functions transferred to Labor Secretary and Treasury Department, effective Feb. 24, 1947.

Defense Minerals Administration Established by Interior Secretary's Order 2605 of Dec. 4, 1950. Functions assigned to *Defense Materials Procurement Agency.* Functions of exploration for critical and strategic minerals redelegated to Interior Secretary and administered by *Defense Minerals Exploration Administration* by Secretary's Order 2726 of June 30, 1953. Termination of program announced by Secretary June 6, 1958. Certain activities continued in *Office of Minerals Exploration,* Interior Department.

Defense Minerals Exploration Administration *See* **Defense Minerals Administration**

Defense Mobilization, Office of Established in Executive Office of the President by EO 10193 of Dec. 16, 1950. Superseded by *Office of Defense Mobilization* established by Reorg. Plan No. 3 of 1953, effective June 12, 1953, which assumed functions of former *Office, National Security Resources Board,* and critical materials stockpiling functions of Army, Navy, Air Force, and Interior Secretaries and of *Army and Navy Munitions Board.* Consolidated with *Federal Civil Defense Administration* into *Office of Defense and Civilian Mobilization* by Reorg. Plan No. 1 of 1958, effective July 1, 1958, and offices of Director and Deputy Director terminated.

Defense Mobilization Board Established by EO 10200 of Jan. 3, 1951, and restated in EO 10480 of Aug. 14, 1953. Terminated by EO 10773 of July 1, 1958.

Defense Plant Corporation Established by act of June 25, 1940 (54 Stat. 572). Transferred from *Federal Loan Agency* to Commerce Department by EO 9071 of Feb. 24, 1942. Returned to *Federal Loan Agency* pursuant to act of Feb. 24, 1945 (59 Stat. 5). Dissolved by act of June 30, 1945 (59 Stat. 310), and functions transferred to *Reconstruction Finance Corporation.*

Defense Plants Administration, Small Established by act of July 31, 1951 (65 Stat. 131). Terminated July 31, 1953, by act of June 30, 1953 (67 Stat. 131). Functions relating to liquidation transferred to Small Business Administration by EO 10504 of Dec. 1, 1953.

Defense Production Administration Established by EO 10200 of Jan. 3, 1951. Terminated by EO 10433 of Feb. 4, 1953, and functions transferred to *Office of Defense Mobilization.*

Defense Property Disposal Service Renamed Defense Reutilization and Marketing Service by Defense Logistics Agency General Order 10–85, effective July 1, 1985.

Defense Public Works Division Established in *Public Works Administration.* Transferred to *Office of Federal Works Administrator* by administrative order of July 16, 1941. Abolished by administrative order of Mar. 6, 1942, and functions transferred to *Office of Chief Engineer, Federal Works Agency.*

Defense Purchases, Office for the Coordination of National Established by order of *Council of National Defense,* approved June 27, 1940. Order revoked Jan. 7, 1941, and records transferred to Executive Office of the President.

Defense Research Committee, National Established June 27, 1940, by order of *Council of National Defense.* Abolished by order of *Council* June 28, 1941, and reestablished in *Office of Scientific Research and Development* by EO 8807 of June 28, 1941. *Office* terminated by EO 9913 of Dec. 26, 1947, and property and records transferred to *National Military Establishment.*

Defense Resources Committee Established by Administrative Order 1496 of June 15, 1940. Replaced by *War Resources Council* by Administrative Order 1636 of Jan. 14, 1942. Inactive.

Defense Solid Fuels Administration Established by Interior Secretary's Order 2605 of Dec. 4, 1950. Abolished June 29, 1954, by Secretary's Order 2764.

Defense Stockpile Manager, National Established by act of Nov. 14, 1986 (100 Stat. 4067). Functions transferred from General Services Administrator to Defense Secretary by EO 12626 of Feb. 25, 1988.

Defense Supplies Corporation Established under act of June 25, 1940 (54 Stat. 572). Transferred from *Federal Loan Agency* to Commerce Department by EO 9071 of Feb. 24, 1942. Returned to *Federal Loan Agency* by act of Feb. 24, 1945 (59 Stat. 5).

Dissolved by act of June 30, 1945 (59 Stat. 310), and functions transferred to *Reconstruction Finance Corporation.*

Defense Supply Agency Renamed Defense Logistics Agency by DOD Directive 5105.22 of Jan. 22, 1977.

Defense Supply Management Agency Established in Defense Department by act of July 1, 1952 (66 Stat. 318). Abolished by Reorg. Plan No. 6 of 1953, effective June 30, 1953, and functions transferred to Defense Secretary.

Defense Transport Administration Established Oct. 4, 1950, by order of Commissioner of Interstate Commerce Commission in charge of Bureau of Service, pursuant to EO 10161 of Sept. 9, 1950. Terminated by DTA Commissioner's order, effective July 1, 1955, and functions transferred to Bureau of Safety and Service, Interstate Commerce Commission.

Defense Transportation, Office of Established in *Office for Emergency Management* by EO 8989 of Dec. 18, 1941. Terminated by EO 10065 of July 6, 1949.

Director. *See other part of title*

Disarmament Administration, U.S. Established in State Department. Functions transferred to U.S. Arms Control and Disarmament Agency by act of Sept. 26, 1961 (75 Stat. 638).

Disarmament Problems, President's Special Committee on Established by President Aug. 5, 1955. Dissolved in February 1958.

Disaster Assistance Administration, Federal Functions transferred from Housing and Urban Development Department to Federal Emergency Management Agency by EO 12148 of July 20, 1979.

Disaster Loan Corporation Grouped with other agencies to form *Federal Loan Agency* by Reorg. Plan No. I of 1939, effective July 1, 1939. Transferred to Commerce Department by EO 9071 of Feb. 24, 1942. Returned to *Federal Loan Agency* by act of Feb. 24, 1945 (59 Stat. 5). Dissolved by act of June 30, 1945 (59 Stat. 310), and functions transferred to *Reconstruction Finance Corporation.*

Disease Control, Center for Renamed Centers for Disease Control by Health and Human Services Secretary's notice of Oct. 1, 1980 (45 FR 67772).

Displaced Persons Commission Established by act of June 25, 1948 (62 Stat. 1009). Terminated Aug. 31, 1952, pursuant to terms of act.

District of Columbia Established by acts of July 16, 1790 (1 Stat. 130), and Mar. 3, 1791. Corporations of Washington and Georgetown and levy court of Washington County abolished in favor of territorial form of government in 1871. Permanent commission government established July 1, 1878. District Government created as municipal corporation by act of June 11, 1878 (20 Stat. 102). Treated as branch of U.S. Government by various statutory enactments of Congress. District Government altered by Reorg. Plan No. 3 of 1967, effective Nov. 3, 1967. Charter for local government in District of Columbia provided by act of Dec. 24, 1973 (87 Stat. 774).

District of Columbia, Highway Commission of the Established by act of Mar. 2, 1893 (27 Stat 532). *National Capital Park and Planning Commission* named successor by act of Apr. 30, 1926 (44 Stat. 374). Functions transferred to *National Capital Planning Commission* by act of July 19, 1952 (66 Stat. 781).

District of Columbia, Reform-School of the Established by act of May 3, 1876 (19 Stat. 49). Renamed *National Training School for Boys* by act of May 27, 1908 (35 Stat. 380). Transferred to Justice Department by Reorg. Plan No. II of 1939, effective July 1, 1939, to be administered by Director of Bureau of Prisons.

District of Columbia Auditorium Commission Established by act of July 1, 1955 (69 Stat. 243). Final report submitted to Congress Jan. 31, 1957, pursuant to act of Apr. 27, 1956 (70 Stat. 115).

District of Columbia Redevelopment Land Agency Established by act of Aug. 2, 1946 (60 Stat. 790). Agency established as instrumentality of District Government by act of Dec. 24, 1973 (87 Stat. 774), effective July 1, 1974.

District of Columbia-Virginia Boundary Commission Established by act of Mar. 21, 1934 (48 Stat. 453). Terminated Dec. 1, 1935, to which date it had been extended by Public Resolution 9 (49 Stat. 67).

Division. *See other part of title.*

Domestic Council Established in *Executive Office of the President* by Reorg. Plan No. 2 of 1970, effective July 1, 1970. Abolished by Reorg. Plan No. 1 of 1977, effective Mar. 26, 1978, and functions transferred to President and staff designated as *Domestic Policy Staff.* Pursuant to EO 12045 of Mar. 27, 1978, *Staff* assisted President in performance of transferred functions. Renamed Office of Policy Development.

Domestic Policy Staff *See* **Domestic Council**

Dominican Customs Receivership Transferred from *Division of Territories and Island Possessions,* Interior Department, to State Department by Reorg. Plan No. IV of 1940, effective June 30, 1940.

Drug Abuse, President's Advisory Commission on Narcotic and Established by EO 11076 of Jan. 15, 1963. Terminated November 1963 under terms of order.

Drug Abuse Control, Bureau of Established in *Food and Drug Administration, Health and Human Services Department,* to carry out functions of act of July 15, 1965 (79 Stat. 226). Functions transferred to *Bureau of Narcotics and Dangerous Drugs,* Justice Department, by Reorg. Plan No. 1 of 1968, effective Apr. 8, 1968. Abolished by Reorg. Plan No. 2 of 1973, effective July 1, 1973, and functions transferred to Drug Enforcement Administration.

Drug Abuse Law Enforcement, Office of Established by EO 11641 of Jan. 28, 1972. Terminated by EO 11727 of July 6, 1973, and functions transferred to Drug Enforcement Administration.

Drug Abuse Policy, Office of Established in Executive Office of the President by act of Mar. 19, 1976 (90 Stat. 242). Abolished by Reorg. Plan No. 1 of 1977, effective Mar. 26, 1978, and functions transferred to President.

Drug Abuse Prevention, Special Action Office for Established by EO 11599 of June 17, 1971, and act of Mar. 21, 1972 (86 Stat. 65). Terminated June 30, 1975, pursuant to terms of act.

Drug Abuse Prevention, Treatment, and Rehabilitation, Cabinet Committee on Established Apr. 27, 1976, by Presidential announcement. Terminated by Presidential memorandum of Mar. 14, 1977.

Drug Law Enforcement, Cabinet Committee for Established Apr. 27, 1976, pursuant to Presidential message to Congress of Apr. 27, 1976. Abolished by Presidential memorandum of Mar. 14, 1977.

Drugs, Bureau of Narcotics and Dangerous *See* **Drug Abuse Control, Bureau of**

Drugs and Biologics, National Center for Renamed Center for Drugs and Biologics by Food and Drug Administration notice of Mar. 9, 1984 (49 FR 10166). Reestablished as Center for Drug Evaluation and Research and Center for Biologics Evaluation and Research by Secretary's notice of Oct. 6, 1987 (52 FR 38275).

Drunk Driving, Presidential Commission on Established by EO 12358 of Apr. 14, 1982. Terminated Dec. 31, 1983, by EO 12415 of Apr. 5, 1983.

Dryden Research Center, Hugh L. Formerly separate field installation of National Aeronautics and Space Administration. Made component of Ames Research Center by NASA Management Instruction 1107.5A of Sept. 3, 1981.

Economic Administration, Foreign Established in *Office for Emergency Management* by EO 9380 of Sept. 25, 1943. Functions of *Office of Lend-Lease Administration, Office of Foreign Relief and Rehabilitation Operations, Office of Economic Warfare* (together with *U.S. Commercial Company, Rubber Development Corporation, Petroleum Reserves Corporation,* and *Export-Import Bank of Washington* and functions transferred thereto by EO 9361 of July 15, 1943), and foreign economic operations of *Office of Foreign Economic Coordination* transferred to *Administration.* Foreign procurement activities of *War Food Administration* and *Commodity Credit Corporation* transferred by EO 9385 of Oct. 6, 1943. Terminated by EO 9630 of Sept. 27, 1945, and functions redistributed to State, Commerce, and Agriculture Departments and *Reconstruction Finance Corporation.*

Economic Cooperation Administration Established by act of Apr. 3, 1948 (62 Stat. 138). Abolished by act of Oct. 10, 1951 (65 Stat. 373), and functions transferred to *Mutual Security Agency* pursuant to EO 10300 of Nov. 1, 1951.

Economic Coordination, Office of Foreign *See* **Board of Economic Operations**

Economic Defense Board Established by EO 8839 of July 30, 1941. Name changed to *Board of Economic Warfare* by EO 8982 of Dec. 17, 1941. *Board* terminated by EO 9361 of July 15, 1943, and *Office of Economic Warfare* established in *Office for Emergency Management. Office of Economic Warfare* consolidated with *Foreign Economic Administration* by EO 9380 of Sept. 25, 1943.

Economic Development, Office of Regional Established by Commerce Secretary Jan. 6, 1966, pursuant to act of Aug. 26, 1965 (79 Stat. 552). Abolished by Department Order 5A, Dec. 22, 1966, and functions vested in Economic Development Administration.

Economic Development Service, Foreign Established by order of Agriculture Secretary Nov. 8, 1969. Abolished by order of Secretary Feb. 6, 1972, and functions transferred to *Economic Research Service.*

Economic Growth and Stability, Advisory Board on Established by Presidential letter of June 1, 1953, to Congress. Superseded by *National Advisory Board on Economic Policy* by Presidential direction Mar. 12, 1961. *Cabinet Committee on Economic Growth* established by President Aug. 21, 1962, to succeed *Board.*

Economic Management Support Center Established by Agriculture Secretary's Memorandum 1836 of Jan. 9, 1974. Consolidated with other Department units into *Economics, Statistics, and Cooperatives Service* by Secretary's Memorandum 1927, effective Dec. 23, 1977.

Economic Operations, Board of Established by State departmental order of Oct. 7, 1941. Abolished by departmental order of June 24, 1943, and functions transferred to *Office of Foreign Economic Coordination* established by same order. *Office* abolished by Departmental order of Nov. 6, 1943, pursuant to EO 9380 of Sept. 25, 1943.

Economic Opportunity, Office of Established in Executive Office of the President by act of Aug. 20, 1964 (78 Stat. 508). All OEO programs except three transferred by administrative action to *Health, Education, and Welfare,* Labor, and Housing and Urban Development Departments July 6, 1973. Community Action, Economic Development, and Legal Services Programs transferred to *Community Services Administration* by act of Jan. 4, 1975 (88 Stat. 2310).

Economic Policy, Council on Established by Presidential memorandum of Feb. 2, 1973. Functions absorbed by *Economic Policy Board* Sept. 30, 1974.

Economic Policy, Council on Foreign Established Dec. 22, 1954, by Presidential letter of Dec. 11, 1954. Abolished by President Mar. 12, 1961, and functions transferred to Secretary of State.

Economic Policy, Council on International Established in Executive Office of the President by Presidential memorandum January 1971. Reestablished by act of Aug. 29, 1972 (86 Stat. 646). Terminated Sept. 30, 1977, on expiration of statutory authority.

Economic Policy, National Advisory Board on *See* **Economic Growth and Stability, Advisory Board on**

Economic Policy Board, President's Established by EO 11808 of Sept. 30, 1974. Terminated by EO 11975 of Mar. 7, 1977.

Economic Research Service Established by Agriculture Secretary's Memorandum 1446, supp. 1, of Apr. 3, 1961. Consolidated with other Agriculture Department units into *Economics, Statistics, and Cooperatives Service* by Secretary's Memorandum 1927, effective Dec. 23, 1977. Redesignated as Economic Research Service by Secretarial order of Oct. 1, 1981.

Economic Security, Advisory Council on Established by EO 6757 of June 29, 1934. Terminated on approval of act of Aug. 14, 1935 (49 Stat. 620) Aug. 14, 1935.

Economic Security, Committee on Established by EO 6757 of June 29, 1934. Terminated as formal agency in April 1936, as provided in act, but continued informally for some time thereafter.

Economic Stabilization, Office of Established in *Office for Emergency Management* by EO 9250 of Oct. 3, 1942. Terminated by EO 9620 of Sept. 20, 1945, and functions transferred to *Office of War Mobilization and Reconversion.* Reestablished in *Office for Emergency Management* by EO 9699 of Feb. 21, 1946. Transferred by EO 9762 of July 25, 1946, to *Office of War Mobilization and Reconversion.* Consolidated with other agencies to form *Office of Temporary Controls* by EO 9809 of Dec. 12, 1946.

Economic Stabilization Agency Established by EO 10161 of Sept. 9, 1950, and EO 10276 of July 31, 1951. Terminated, except for liquidation purposes, by EO 10434 of Feb. 6, 1953. Liquidation completed Oct. 31, 1953, pursuant to EO 10480 of Aug. 14, 1953.

Economic Stabilization Board Established by EO 9250 of Oct. 3, 1942. Transferred to *Office of War Mobilization and Reconversion* by EO 9620 of Sept. 20, 1945. Returned to *Office of Economic Stabilization* on reestablishment by EO 9699 of Feb. 21, 1946. *Board* returned to *Office of War Mobilization and Reconversion* by EO 9762 of July 25, 1946. Functions terminated by EO 9809 of Dec. 12, 1946.

Economic Warfare, Board of *See* **Economic Defense Board**

Economic Warfare, Office of *See* **Economic Defense Board**

Economics, Bureau of Industrial Established by Commerce Secretary Jan. 2, 1980, in conjunction with Reorg. Plan No. 3 of 1979 and operated under Department Organization Order 35-5B. Abolished at bureau level by Secretarial order (49 FR 4538), effective Jan. 22, 1984. Industry-related functions realigned and transferred from Under Secretary for Economic Affairs to Under Secretary for International Trade. Under Secretary for Economic Affairs retained units to support domestic macroeconomic policy functions.

Economics, Statistics, and Cooperatives Service Renamed *Economics and Statistics Service* by Agriculture Secretary's Memorandum 2025 of Sept. 17, 1980. Redesignated as Economic Research Service and Statistical Reporting Service by Secretarial order of Oct. 1, 1981.

Economy Board, Joint Placed under direction of President by military order of July 5, 1939. Abolished Sept. 1, 1947, by joint letter of Aug. 20, 1947, from Secretaries of *War* and Navy to President.

Education, Federal Board for Vocational Established by act of Feb. 23, 1917 (39 Stat. 929). Functions transferred to Interior Department by EO 6166 of June 10, 1933. Functions assigned to *Commissioner of Education* Oct. 10, 1933. *Office of Education* transferred from Interior Department to *Federal Security Agency* by Reorg. Plan No. I of 1939, effective July 1, 1939. *Board* abolished by Reorg. Plan No. 2 of 1946, effective July 16, 1946.

Education, National Institute of Established by act of June 23, 1972 (86 Stat. 327). Transferred to Office of Educational Research and Improvement, Education Department, by act of Oct. 17, 1979 (93 Stat. 678), effective May 4, 1980.

Education, Office of Established as independent agency by act of Mar. 2, 1867 (14 Stat. 434). Transferred to Interior Department by act of July 20, 1868 (15 Stat. 106). Transferred to *Federal Security Agency* by Reorg. Plan No. I of 1939, effective July 1, 1939. Functions of *Federal Security Administrator* administered by *Office of Education* relating to student loans and defense-related education transferred to *War Manpower Commission* by EO 9247 of Sept. 17, 1942.

Education, Office of Bilingual Abolished by act of Oct. 17, 1979 (93 Stat. 675), and functions transferred to Office of Bilingual Education and Minority Languages Affairs, Education Department.

Education Beyond the High School, President's Committee on Established by act of July 26, 1956 (70 Stat. 676). Terminated Dec. 31, 1957. Certain activities continued by *Bureau of Higher Education, Office of Education.*

Education Division Established in *Health, Education, and Welfare Department* by act of June 23, 1972 (86 Stat. 327). Functions transferred to Education Department by act of Oct. 17, 1979 (93 Stat. 677).

Education Statistics, National Center for Established within the *Department of Health and Human Services, Office of the Assistant Secretary,* by act of Aug. 21, 1974 (88 Stat. 556). Transferred to the *Office of Educational Research and Improvement,* by act of Oct. 17, 1979 (93 Stat.

678), effective May 4, 1980. Renamed *Center for Education Statistics* by act of Oct. 17, 1986 (100 Stat. 1579). Renamed *National Center for Education Statistics* by act of Apr. 28, 1988 (102 Stat. 331).

Educational and Cultural Affairs, Bureau of Established by Secretary of State in 1960. Terminated by Reorg. Plan No. 2 of 1977 and functions transferred to *International Communication Agency*, effective Apr. 1, 1978.

Educational and Cultural Affairs, Interagency Council on International Established Jan. 20, 1964, by Foreign Affairs Manual Circular, under authority of act of Sept. 21, 1961 (75 Stat. 527). Terminated Oct. 1973 following creation of Subcommittee on International Exchanges by National Security Council directive.

Educational Exchange, U.S. Advisory Commission on Established by act of Jan. 27, 1948 (62 Stat. 10). Abolished by act of Sept. 21, 1961 (75 Stat. 538), and superseded by U.S. Advisory Commission on International Educational and Cultural Affairs.

Efficiency, Bureau of Organized under act of Feb. 28, 1916 (39 Stat. 15). Abolished by act of Mar. 3, 1933 (47 Stat. 1519), and records transferred to *Bureau of the Budget*.

Elderly, Committee on Mental Health and Illness of the Established by act of July 29, 1975 (89 Stat. 347). Terminated Sept. 30, 1977.

Electoral votes for President and Vice President, transfer of functions *See* **State Department**

Electric Home and Farm Authority Incorporated Aug. 1, 1935, under laws of District of Columbia. Designated as U.S. agency by EO 7139 of Aug. 12, 1935. Continued by act of June 10, 1941 (55 Stat. 248). Grouped with other agencies in *Federal Loan Agency* by Reorg. Plan. No. I of 1939, effective July 1, 1939. Functions transferred to Commerce Department by EO 9071 of Feb. 24, 1942. Terminated by EO 9256 of Oct. 13, 1942.

Electric Home and Farm Authority, Inc. Organized Jan. 17, 1934, under laws of State of Delaware by EO 6514 of Dec. 19, 1933. Dissolved Aug. 1, 1935, and succeeded by *Electric Home and Farm Authority*.

Emergency Administration of Public Works, Federal Established by act of June 16, 1933 (48 Stat. 200). Operation continued by subsequent legislation, including act of June 21, 1938 (52 Stat. 816). Consolidated with *Federal Works Agency* as *Public Works Administration* by Reorg. Plan No. I of 1939, effective July 1, 1939. Functions transferred to *Office of Federal Works Administrator* by EO 9357 of June 30, 1943.

Emergency Conservation Work Established by EO 6101 of Apr. 5, 1933. Succeeded by *Civilian Conservation Corps*.

Emergency Council, National Established by EO 6433-A of Nov. 17, 1933. Consolidated with *Executive Council* by EO 6889-A of Oct. 29, 1934. Abolished by Reorg. Plan No. II of 1939, effective July 1, 1939, and functions (except those relating to *Radio Division* and *Film Service*) transferred to Executive Office of the President.

Emergency Council, Office of Economic Adviser to National Established by EO 6240 of Aug. 3, 1933, in connection with *Executive Council*, which later consolidated with *National Emergency Council*. Records and property used in preparation of statistical and economic summaries transferred to *Central Statistical Board* by EO 7003 of Apr. 8, 1935.

Emergency Management, Liaison Officer for Resignation of Liaison Officer for Emergency Management accepted by Presidential letter of Nov. 3, 1943, and no successor appointed. Liaison facilities terminated pursuant to optional provisions of administrative order of Jan. 7, 1941.

Emergency Management, Office for Established in Executive Office of the President by administrative order of May 25, 1940, in accordance with EO 8248 of Sept. 8, 1939. Inactive.

Emergency Mobilization Preparedness Board Established Dec. 17, 1981, by the President. Abolished by Presidential directive of September 16, 1985.

Emergency Planning, Office of Established as successor to *Office of Civil and Defense Mobilization* by act of Sept. 22, 1961 (75 Stat. 630). Renamed *Office of Emergency Preparedness* by act of Oct. 21, 1968 (82 Stat. 1194).

Emergency Preparedness, Office of Designated by act of Oct. 21, 1968 (82 Stat. 1194). Terminated by Reorg. Plan No. 2 of 1973, effective July 1, 1973, and functions transferred to Treasury and Housing and Urban Development Departments and General Services Administration.

Emergency Procurement Service Established Sept. 1, 1950, by Administrator of General Services. Renamed *Defense Materials Service* Sept. 7, 1956. Functions transferred to *Property Management and Disposal Service* July 29, 1966. *Service* abolished July 1, 1973, and functions transferred to Office of Federal Supply and Services, Public Buildings Service, Federal Property Resources Service.

Emergency Relief Administration, Federal Established by act of May 12, 1933 (48 Stat. 55). Expired June 30, 1938, having been liquidated by *Works Progress Administrator* pursuant to act of May 28, 1937 (50 Stat. 352).

Employee-Management Relations Program, President's Committee on the Implementation of the Federal Established by EO 10988 of Jan. 17, 1962. Terminated on submission of report to President June 21, 1963.

Employees' Compensation, Bureau of Transferred from *Federal Security Agency* to Labor Department by Reorg. Plan No. 19 of 1950, effective May 24, 1950. Functions absorbed by Employment Standards Administration Mar. 13, 1972.

Employees' Compensation Appeals Board Transferred from *Federal Security Agency* to Labor

Department by Reorg. Plan No. 19 of 1950, effective May 24, 1950.

Employees' Compensation Commission, U.S. Established by act of Sept. 7, 1916 (39 Stat. 742). Abolished by Reorg. Plan No. 2 of 1946, effective July 16, 1946, and functions transferred to *Federal Security Administrator.*

Employment Board, Fair Established by *U.S. Civil Service Commission* pursuant to EO 9980 of July 26, 1948. Abolished by EO 10590 of Jan. 18, 1955.

Employment of the Physically Handicapped, President's Committee on Established by EO 10640 of Oct. 10, 1955, continuing *Committee* established by act of July 11, 1949 (63 Stat. 409). Superseded by President's Committee on Employment of the Handicapped established by EO 10994 of Feb. 14, 1962.

Employment Policy, President's Committee on Government Established by EO 10590 of Jan. 18, 1955. Abolished by EO 10925 of Mar. 6, 1961, and functions transferred to *President's Committee on Equal Employment Opportunity.*

Employment Practice, Committee on Fair Established in *Office of Production Management* by EO 8802 of June 25, 1941. Transferred to *War Manpower Commission* by Presidential letter effective July 30, 1942. Committee terminated on establishment of *Committee on Fair Employment Practice, Office for Emergency Management,* by EO 9346 of May 27, 1943. Terminated June 30, 1946, by act of July 17, 1945 (59 Stat. 743).

Employment Security, Bureau of Transferred from *Federal Security Agency* to Labor Department by Reorg. Plan No. 2 of 1949, effective Aug. 20, 1949. Abolished by Labor Secretary's order of Mar. 14, 1969, and functions transferred to *Manpower Administration.*

Employment Service, U.S. Established in Labor Department in 1918 by departmental order. Abolished by act of June 6, 1933 (48 Stat. 113), and created as bureau with same name. Functions consolidated with unemployment compensation functions of *Social Security Board, Bureau of Employment Security,* and transferred to *Federal Security Agency* by Reorg. Plan No. I of 1939, effective July 1, 1939. *Service* transferred to *Bureau of Placement, War Manpower Commission,* by EO 9247 of Sept. 17, 1942. Returned to Labor Department by EO 9617 of Sept. 19, 1945. Transferred to *Federal Security Agency* by act of June 16, 1948 (62 Stat. 443), to function as part of *Bureau of Employment Security,* Social Security Administration. *Bureau,* including *U.S. Employment Service,* transferred to Labor Department by Reorg. Plan No. 2 of 1949, effective Aug. 20, 1949. Abolished by reorganization of *Manpower Administration,* effective Mar. 17, 1969, and functions assigned to *U.S. Training and Employment Service.*

Employment Stabilization Board, Federal Established by Feb. 10, 1931 (46 Stat. 1085). Abolished by EO 6166 of June 10, 1933. Abolition deferred by EO 6623 of Mar. 1, 1934, until functions of *Board* transferred to *Federal Employment Stabilization Office,* established in Commerce Department by same order. *Office* abolished by Reorg. Plan No. I of 1939, effective July 1, 1939, and functions transferred from Commerce Department to *National Resources Planning Board,* Executive Office of the President.

Employment Stabilization Office, Federal. *See* **Employment Stabilization Board, Federal**

Employment and Training, Office of Comprehensive Established in Labor Department. Terminated through expiration of authority for appropriations after fiscal year 1982. Replaced by *Office of Employment and Training Programs.*

Employment and Training Programs, Office of Renamed Office of Job Training Programs by Employment and Training Administration reorganization in Labor Department, effective June 1984.

Endangered Species Scientific Authority Established by EO 11911 of Apr. 13, 1976. Terminated by act of Dec. 28, 1979 (93 Stat. 1228), and functions transferred to Interior Secretary.

Energy Administration, Federal Established by act of May 7, 1974 (88 Stat. 96). Assigned additional responsibilities by acts of June 22, 1974 (88 Stat. 246), Dec. 22, 1975 (89 Stat. 871), and Aug. 14, 1976 (90 Stat. 1125). Terminated by act of Aug. 4, 1977 (91 Stat. 577), and functions transferred to Energy Department.

Energy Conservation, Office of Established by Interior Secretarial Order 2953 May 7, 1973. Functions transferred to *Federal Energy Administration* by act of May 7, 1974 (88 Stat. 100).

Energy Data and Analysis, Office of Established by Interior Secretarial Order 2953 of May 7, 1973. Functions transferred to *Federal Energy Administration* by act of May 7, 1974 (88 Stat. 100).

Energy Policy Office Established in Executive Office of the President by EO 11726 of June 29, 1973. Abolished by EO 11775 of Mar. 26, 1974.

Energy Programs, Office of Established by Commerce Department Organization Order 25–7A, effective Sept. 24, 1975. Terminated by act of Aug. 4, 1977 (91 Stat. 581), and functions transferred to Energy Department.

Energy Research and Development Administration Established by act of Oct. 11, 1974 (88 Stat. 1234). Assigned responsibilities by acts of Sept. 3, 1974 (88 Stat. 1069, 1079), Oct. 26, 1974 (88 Stat. 1431), and Dec. 31, 1974 (88 Stat. 1887). Terminated by act of Aug. 4, 1977 (91 Stat. 577), and functions transferred to Energy Department.

Energy Resources Council Established in Executive Office of the President by act of Oct. 11, 1974 (88 Stat. 1233). Establishing authority repealed by act of Aug. 4, 1977 (91 Stat. 608), and *Council* terminated.

Energy Supplies and Resources Policy, Presidential Advisory Committee on Established July 30, 1954, by President. Abolished Mar. 12, 1961, by President and functions transferred to Interior Secretary.

Enforcement Commission, National Established by General Order 18 of *Economic Stabilization Administrator,* effective July 30, 1952. Functions transferred to Director, *Office of Defense Mobilization,* and Attorney General by EO 10494 of Oct. 14, 1953.

Engineering, Bureau of *See* **Steam Engineering, Bureau of**

Entomology, Bureau of *See* **Entomology and Plant Quarantine, Bureau of**

Entomology and Plant Quarantine, Bureau of *Bureau of Entomology* and *Bureau of Plant Quarantine* created by acts of Apr. 23, 1904 (33 Stat. 276), and July 7, 1932 (47 Stat. 640), respectively. Consolidated with disease control and eradication functions of *Bureau of Plant Industry* into *Bureau of Entomology and Plant Quarantine* by act of Mar. 23, 1934 (48 Stat. 467). Functions transferred to *Agricultural Research Service* by Secretary's Memorandum 1320, supp. 4, of Nov. 2, 1953.

Environment, Cabinet Committee on the *See* **Environmental Quality Council**

Environmental Financing Authority Established by act of Oct. 18, 1972 (86 Stat. 899). Expired June 30, 1975, pursuant to terms of act.

Environmental Quality Council Established by EO 11472 of May 29, 1969. Renamed *Cabinet Committee on the Environment* by EO 11514 of Mar. 5, 1970. EO 11514 terminated by EO 11541 of July 1, 1970.

Environmental Science Services Administration Established in Commerce Department by Reorg. Plan No. 2 of 1965, effective July 13, 1965, by consolidating *Weather Bureau* and *Coast and Geodetic Survey.* Abolished by Reorg. Plan No. 4 of 1970, effective Oct. 3, 1970, and functions transferred to National Oceanic and Atmospheric Administration.

Equal Employment Opportunity, President's Committee on Established by EO 10925 of Mar. 6, 1961. Abolished by EO 11246 of Sept. 24, 1965, and functions transferred to Labor Department and *U.S. Civil Service Commission.*

Equal Opportunity, President's Council on Established by EO 11197 of Feb. 5, 1965. Abolished by EO 11247 of Sept. 24, 1965, and functions transferred to Justice Department.

Equipment, Bureau of Established as *Bureau of Equipment and Recruiting* by act of July 5, 1862 (12 Stat. 510), replacing *Bureau of Construction, Equipment and Repairs.* Designated as *Bureau of Equipment* in annual appropriation acts commencing with fiscal year 1892 (26 Stat. 192) after cognizance over enlisted personnel matters transferred, effective July 1, 1889, to *Bureau of Navigation.* Functions distributed among bureaus and offices in Navy Department by act of June 24, 1910 (61 Stat. 613). Abolished by act of June 30, 1914 (38 Stat. 408).

Ethics, Office of Government Established in the *Office of Personnel Management* by act of Oct. 26, 1978 (92 Stat. 1862). Changed to independent executive agency status by act of Nov. 3, 1988 (102 Stat. 3031).

European Migration, Intergovernmental Committee for Renamed Intergovernmental Committee for Migration by Resolution 624, passed by Intergovernmental Committee for European Migration Council, effective Nov. 11, 1980.

Evacuation, Joint Committee on *See* **Health and Welfare Aspects of Evacuation of Civilians, Joint Committee on**

Exchange Service, International Established in 1849 in Smithsonian Institution. Renamed Office of Publications Exchange by Secretary's internal directive of Jan. 11, 1985.

Executive Branch of the Government, Commission on Organization of the Established by act of July 7, 1947 (61 Stat. 246). Terminated June 12, 1949, pursuant to terms of act. Second *Commission on Organization of the Executive Branch of the Government* established by act of July 10, 1953 (67 Stat. 142). Terminated June 30, 1955, pursuant to terms of act.

Executive Council Established by EO 6202-A of July 11, 1933. Consolidated with *National Emergency Council* by EO 6889-A of Oct. 29, 1934.

Executive Exchange, President's Commission on *See* **Personnel Interchange, President's Commission on**

Executive orders *See* **State Department**

Executive Organization, President's Advisory Council on Established by President Apr. 5, 1969. Terminated May 7, 1971.

Executives, Active Corps of Established in ACTION by act of Oct. 1, 1973 (87 Stat. 404). Transferred to Small Business Administration by EO 11871 of July 18, 1975.

Exhibits, Supervisor of Established by Interior Department. Abolished in 1941 through lack of funding.

Export Control, Administrator of Functions delegated to Administrator by Proc. 2413 of July 2, 1940, transferred to *Office of Export Control, Economic Defense Board,* by EO 8900 of Sept. 15, 1941. Renamed *Board of Economic Warfare* by EO 8982 of Dec. 17, 1941.

Export Control, Office of *See* **Administrator of Export Control**

Export-Import Bank of Washington Organization of District of Columbia banking corporation directed by EO 6581 of Feb. 2, 1934. Certificate of incorporation filed Feb. 12, 1934. Grouped with other agencies to form *Federal Loan Agency* by Reorg. Plan No. I of 1939, effective July 1, 1939. Transferred to Commerce Department by EO 9071 of Feb. 24, 1942. Functions transferred to *Office of Economic Warfare* by EO 9361 of July 15, 1943. Established as permanent independent agency by act of July 31, 1945 (59 Stat. 526). Renamed Export-Import Bank of the U.S. by act of Mar. 13, 1968 (82 Stat. 47).

Export-Import Bank of Washington, D.C., Second Authorized by EO 6638 of Mar. 9, 1934. Abolished by EO 7365 of May 7, 1936, and records transferred to *Export-Import Bank of Washington,* effective June 30, 1936.

Export Marketing Service Established by Agriculture Secretary Mar. 28, 1969. Merged with Foreign Agricultural Service by Secretary's memorandum of Dec. 7, 1973, effective Feb. 3, 1974.

Exports and Requirements, Division of Established in *Office of Foreign Economic Coordination* by State Departmental order of Feb. 1, 1943. Abolished by departmental order of Nov. 6, 1943, pursuant to EO 9380 of Sept. 25, 1943.

Extension Service Established by act of May 14, 1914 (38 Stat. 372). Consolidated into *Science and Education Administration* by Secretary's order of Jan. 24, 1978. Reestablished as Extension Service by Secretarial order of June 16, 1981.

Facts and Figures, Office of Established in *Office for Emergency Management* by EO 8922 of Oct. 24, 1941. Consolidated with *Office of War Information* in *Office for Emergency Management* by EO 9182 of June 13, 1942.

Family Security Committee Established in *Office of Defense Health and Welfare Services* Feb. 12, 1941, by administrative order. Terminated Dec. 17, 1942.

Family Services, Bureau of *See* **Assistance, Bureau of Public**

Family Support Administration Established on Apr. 4, 1986, in the Department of Health and Human Services under authority of section 6 of Reorganization Plan No. 1 of 1953 (*see also* 51 FR 11641). Merged into Administration for Children and Families by Secretary's reorganization notice dated Apr. 15, 1991.

Farm Board, Federal Established by act of June 15, 1929 (46 Stat. 11). Renamed *Farm Credit Administration* and certain functions abolished by EO 6084 of Mar. 27, 1933. *Administration* placed under Agriculture Department by Reorg. Plan No. I of 1939, effective July 1, 1939. Made independent of Agriculture Department by act of Aug. 6, 1953 (67 Stat. 390).

Farm Credit Administration *See* **Federal Farm Board**

Farm Loan Board, Federal Established in *Treasury Department* to administer act of July 17, 1916 (39 Stat. 360). Offices of appointed members of *Board,* except member designated as *Farm Loan Commissioner,* abolished by EO 6084 of Mar. 27, 1933, and *Board* functions transferred to *Farm Loan Commissioner,* subject to jurisdiction and control of *Farm Credit Administration.* Title changed to *Land Bank Commissioner* by act of June 16, 1933. Abolished by act of Aug. 6, 1953 (67 Stat. 393).

Farm Loan Bureau, Federal Established in Treasury Department under supervision of *Federal Farm Loan Board* and charged with execution of act of July 17, 1916 (39 Stat. 360). Transferred to *Farm Credit Administration* by EO 6084 of Mar. 27, 1933.

Farm Loan Commissioner *See* **Federal Farm Loan Board**

Farm Mortgage Corporation, Federal Established by act of Jan. 31, 1934 (48 Stat. 344). Transferred to Agriculture Department by Reorg. Plan No. I of 1939, effective July 1, 1939, to operate under supervision of *Farm Credit Administration.* Abolished by act of Oct. 4, 1961 (75 Stat. 773).

Farm Products, Division of (Also known as *Division of Agriculture*) Established by Advisory Commission to Council of National Defense pursuant to act of Aug. 29, 1916 (39 Stat. 649). *Office of Agricultural Defense Relations* (later known as *Office for Agricultural War Relations*) established in Agriculture Department by Presidential letter of May 5, 1941, which transferred to Agriculture Secretary functions previously assigned to *Division of Agriculture.* Functions concerned with food production transferred to *Food Production Administration* and functions concerned with food distribution transferred to *Food Distribution Administration* by EO 9280 of Dec. 5, 1942.

Farm Security Administration *See* **Resettlement Administration**

Farmer Cooperative Service Established by Agriculture Secretary's Memorandum 1320, supp. 4, of Dec. 4, 1953. Consolidated with other Agriculture Department units into *Economics, Statistics, and Cooperatives Service* by Secretary's Memorandum 1927, effective Dec. 23, 1977.

Federal. *See also other part of title*

Federal Advisory Council Established in *Federal Security Agency* by act of June 6, 1933 (48 Stat. 116). Transferred to Labor Department by Reorg. Plan No. 2 of 1949, effective Aug. 20, 1949.

Federal Register, Administrative Committee of the *See* **Archives Establishment, National**

Federal Register, Division of the Established by act of July 26, 1935 (49 Stat. 500). Transferred to General Services Administration as part of *National Archives and Records Service* by act of June 30, 1949 (63 Stat. 381). Renamed Office of the Federal Register by order of General Services Administrator, Feb. 6, 1959. National Archives and Records Administration established by act of Oct. 19, 1984 (98 Stat. 2283).

Federal Reserve Board Renamed Board of Governors of the Federal Reserve System, and Governor and Vice Governor designated as

Chairman and Vice Chairman, respectively, of Board by act of Aug. 23, 1935 (49 Stat. 704).

Field Services, Office of Established by Commerce Secretary Feb. 1, 1963, by Department Organization Order 40-3. Terminated by Department Organization Order 40-1A of Sept. 15, 1970, and functions transferred to *Bureau of Domestic Commerce.*

Filipino Rehabilitation Commission Established by act of June 29, 1944 (58 Stat. 626). Inactive pursuant to terms of act.

Film Service, U.S. Established by *National Emergency Council* in September 1938. Transferred to *Office of Education, Federal Security Agency,* by Reorg. Plan No. II of 1939, effective July 1, 1939. Terminated June 30, 1940.

Films, Coordinator of Government Director of *Office of Government Reports* designated *Coordinator of Government Films* by Presidential letter of Dec. 18, 1941. Functions transferred to *Office of War Information* by EO 9182 of June 13, 1942.

Financial Operations, Bureau of Government Renamed Financial Management Service by Treasury Secretary's Order 145-21, effective Oct. 10, 1984.

Fire Administration, U.S. *See* **Fire Prevention and Control Administration, National**

Fire Council, Federal Established by EO 7397 of June 20, 1936. Transferred July 1, 1939, to *Federal Works Agency* by EO 8194 of July 6, 1939, with functions under direction of *Federal Works Administrator.* Transferred with *Federal Works Agency* to General Services Administration by act of June 30, 1949 (63 Stat. 380). Transferred to Commerce Department by EO 11654 of Mar. 13, 1972.

Fire Prevention and Control, National Academy for Established in Commerce Department by act of Oct. 29, 1974 (88 Stat. 1537). Transferred to Federal Emergency Management Agency by Reorg. Plan No. 3 of 1978, effective Apr. 1, 1979.

Fire Prevention and Control Administration, National Renamed *U.S. Fire Administration* by act of Oct. 5, 1978 (92 Stat. 932). Transferred to Federal Emergency Management Agency by Reorg. Plan No. 3 of 1978, effective Apr. 1, 1979.

Fish Commission, U.S. *Commissioner of Fish and Fisheries* established as head of *U.S. Fish Commission* by joint resolution of Feb. 9, 1871 (16 Stat. 594). *Commission* established as *Bureau of Fisheries* in *Department of Commerce and Labor* by act of Feb. 14, 1903 (32 Stat. 827). Labor Department created by act of Mar. 4, 1913 (37 Stat. 736), and *Bureau* remained in Commerce Department. Transferred to Interior Department by Reorg. Plan No. II of 1939, effective July 1, 1939. Consolidated with *Bureau of Biological Survey* into Fish and Wildlife Service by Reorg. Plan No. III of 1940, effective June 30, 1940.

Fish and Wildlife Service Established by Reorg. Plan No. III of 1940, effective June 30, 1940, consolidating *Bureau of Fisheries* and *Bureau of Biological Survey.* Succeeded by U.S. Fish and Wildlife Service.

Fisheries, Bureau of *See* **Fish Commission, U.S.**

Fisheries, Bureau of Commercial Organized in 1959 under U.S. Fish and Wildlife Service, Interior Department. Abolished by Reorg. Plan No. 4 of 1970, effective Oct. 3, 1970, and functions transferred to National Oceanic and Atmospheric Administration.

Fishery Coordination, Office of Established in Interior Department by EO 9204 of July 21, 1942. Terminated by EO 9649 of Oct. 29, 1945.

Flood Indemnity Administration, Federal Established in *Housing and Home Finance Agency* by Administrator's Organizational Order 1, effective Sept. 28, 1956, redesignated as Administrator's Organizational Order 2 Dec. 7, 1956, pursuant to act of Aug. 7, 1956 (70 Stat. 1078). Abolished by Administrator's Organizational Order 3, effective July 1, 1957, because of lack of appropriations.

Food, Cost of Living Council Committee on Established by EO 11695 of Jan. 11, 1973. Abolished by EO 11788 of June 18, 1974.

Food, Drug, and Insecticide Administration Established by act of Jan. 18, 1927 (44 Stat. 1002). Renamed *Food and Drug Administration* by act of May 27, 1930 (46 Stat. 422). Transferred from *Agriculture Department* to *Federal Security Agency* by Reorg. Plan No. IV of 1940, effective June 30, 1940. Transferred to *Health, Education, and Welfare Department* by Reorg. Plan No. 1 of 1953, effective Apr. 11, 1953.

Food Distribution Administration Established in Agriculture Department by EO 9280 of Dec. 5, 1942, consolidating *Agricultural Marketing Administration, Sugar Agency,* distribution functions of *Office for Agricultural War Relations,* regulatory work of *Bureau of Animal Industry,* and food units of *War Production Board.* Consolidated with other agencies by EO 9322 of Mar. 26, 1943, to form *Administration of Food Production and Distribution.*

Food and Drug Administration. *See* **Food, Drug, and Insecticide Administration**

Food Industry Advisory Committee Established by EO 11627 of Oct. 15, 1971. Abolished by EO 11781 of May 1, 1974.

Food Production Administration Established in Agriculture Department by EO 9280 of Dec. 5, 1942, which consolidated *Agricultural Adjustment Agency, Farm Credit Administration, Farm Security Administration, Federal Crop Insurance Corporation, Soil Conservation Service,* and food production activities of *War Production Board, Office of Agricultural War Relations,* and *Division of Farm Management and Costs, Bureau of Agricultural Economics.* Consolidated with other agencies by EO 9322 of Mar. 26, 1943, to form *Administration of Food Production and Distribution.*

Food Production and Distribution, Administration of Established by consolidation of *Food Production Administration, Food Distribution Administration, Commodity Credit Corporation,* and *Extension Service,* Agriculture Department, by EO 9322 of Mar. 26, 1943, under direction of Administrator, directly responsible to President. Renamed *War Food Administration* by EO 9334 of Apr. 19, 1943. Terminated by EO 9577 of June 29, 1945, and functions transferred to Agriculture Secretary. Transfer made permanent by Reorg. Plan No. 3 of 1946, effective July 16, 1946.

Food Safety and Quality Service Renamed Food Safety and Inspection Service by Agriculture Secretary's memorandum of June 19, 1981.

Foods, Bureau of Renamed Center for Food Safety and Applied Nutrition by Food and Drug Administration notice of Mar. 9, 1984 (49 FR 10166).

Foreign. *See also other part of title*

Foreign Operations Administration Established by Reorg. Plan No. 7 of 1953, effective Aug. 1, 1953, and functions transferred from *Office of Director of Mutual Security, Mutual Security Agency, Technical Cooperation Administration, Institute of Inter-American Affairs.* Abolished by EO 10610 of May 9, 1955, and functions and offices transferred to State and Defense Departments.

Foreign Scholarships, Board of. Renamed J. William Fulbright Foreign Scholarship Board by the act of Feb. 16, 1990 (104 Stat. 49).

Forest Reservation Commission, National Established by act of Mar. 1, 1911 (36 Stat. 962). Terminated by act of Oct. 22, 1976 (90 Stat. 2961), and functions transferred to Agriculture Secretary.

Forests, Director of Established by Administrative Order 1283 of May 18, 1938. Made part of *Office of Land Utilization,* Interior Department, by Administrative Order 1466 of Apr. 15, 1940.

Freedmen's Hospital Established by act of Mar. 3, 1871 (16 Stat. 506; T. 32 of D.C. Code). Transferred from Interior Department to *Federal Security Agency* by Reorg. Plan No. IV of 1940, effective June 30, 1940.

Fuel Yards Established by act of July 1, 1918 (40 Stat. 672). Transferred from *Bureau of Mines,* Commerce Department, to *Procurement Division,* Treasury Department, by EO 6166 of June 10, 1933, effective Mar. 2, 1934.

Fuels Coordinator for War, Office of Solid *See* **Fuels Administration for War, Solid**

Fuels Corporation, U.S. Synthetic Established by act of June 30, 1980 (94 Stat. 636). Terminated Apr. 18, 1986, by act of Dec. 19, 1985 (99 Stat. 1249), and functions transferred to Treasury Secretary.

Fund-Raising Within the Federal Service, President's Committee on Established by EO 10728 of Sept. 6, 1957. Abolished by EO 10927 of Mar. 18, 1961, and functions transferred to *U.S. Civil Service Commission.*

Gallaudet College *See* **Columbia Institution for the Instruction of the Deaf and Dumb, and the Blind**

General Programs, Office of Renamed Office of Public Programs by the Chairman, National Endowment for the Humanities, in Jan. 1991.

Geographic Board, U.S. Established by EO 27-A of Sept. 4, 1890. Abolished by EO 6680 of Apr. 17, 1935, and duties transferred to *U.S. Board on Geographical Names,* Interior Department, effective June 17, 1934. *Board* abolished by act of July 25, 1947 (61 Stat. 457), and duties assumed by *Board on Geographic Names.*

Geographical Names, U.S. Board on *See* **Geographic Board, U.S.**

Geography, Office of Function of standardizing foreign place names placed in Interior Department conjointly with *Board on Geographic Names* by act of July 25, 1947 (61 Stat. 456). Functions transferred to Defense Department by memorandum of understanding by Interior and Defense Departments and *Bureau of the Budget* Mar. 9, 1968.

Germany, Mixed Claims Commission, U.S. and Established by agreement of Aug. 10, 1922, between U.S. and Germany. Duties extended by agreement of Dec. 31, 1928. Time limit for filing claims expired June 30, 1928. All claims disposed of by Oct. 30, 1939. Terminated June 30, 1941.

Goethals Memorial Commission Established by act of Aug. 4, 1935 (49 Stat. 743). Placed under jurisdiction of *War Department* by EO 8191 of July 5, 1939.

Government. *See other part of title*

Grain Futures Administration Established in Agriculture Department under provisions of act of Sept. 21, 1922 (42 Stat. 998). Superseded by *Commodity Exchange Administration* by order of Secretary, effective July 1, 1936. Consolidated with other agencies into *Commodity Exchange Branch, Agricultural Marketing Administration,* by EO 9069 of Feb. 23, 1942. Functions transferred to Agriculture Secretary by EO 9577 of June 29, 1945. Transfer made permanent by Reorg. Plan No. 3 of 1946, effective July 16, 1946. Functions transferred to *Commodity Exchange Authority* by Secretary's Memorandum 1185 of Jan. 21, 1947. Functions transferred to Commodity Futures Trading Commission by act of Oct. 23, 1974 (88 Stat. 1414).

Grain Stabilization Corporation Organized as Delaware corporation to operate in connection with *Federal Farm Board* pursuant to act of June 15, 1929 (46 Stat. 11). Terminated by filing of certificate of dissolution with Corporation Commission of State of Delaware Dec. 14, 1935.

Grants and Program Systems, Office of Abolished and functions transferred to Cooperative State Research Service, Agriculture Department, by Secretarial Memorandum 1020-26 of July 1, 1986.

Grazing Service Consolidated with *General Land Office* into Bureau of Land Management, Interior

Department, by Reorg. Plan No. 3 of 1946, effective July 16, 1946.

Great Lakes Basin Commission Established by EO 11345 of Apr. 20, 1967. Terminated by EO 12319 of Sept. 9, 1981.

Great Lakes Pilotage Administration Established in Commerce Department to administer act of June 30, 1960 (74 Stat. 259). Administration of act transferred to Transportation Secretary by act of Oct. 15, 1966 (80 Stat. 931).

Hamilton, Bicentennial Commission, Alexander Established by act of Aug. 20, 1954 (68 Stat. 746). Terminated Apr. 30, 1958.

Handicapped, National Center on Education Media and Materials for the Established by agreement between *Health, Education, and Welfare Secretary* and Ohio State University, pursuant to acts of Aug. 20, 1969 (83 Stat. 102) and Apr. 13, 1970 (84 Stat. 187). Authorization deleted by act of Nov. 29, 1975 (89 Stat. 795), and Secretary authorized to enter into agreements with non-Federal organizations to establish and operate centers for handicapped.

Handicapped, National Council on the Established in *Health, Education, and Welfare Department* by act of Nov. 6, 1978 (92 Stat. 2977). Transferred to Education Department by act of Oct. 17, 1979 (93 Stat. 677). Reorganized as independent agency by act of Feb. 22, 1984 (98 Stat. 26).

Handicapped Employees, Interagency Committee on Alternately renamed Interagency Committee on Employment of People with Disabilities by EO 12704.

Handicapped Individuals, White House Conference on Established by act of Dec. 7, 1974 (88 Stat. 1617). Terminated Dec. 30, 1977, pursuant to terms of act.

Handicapped Research, National Institute of Renamed National Institute on Disability and Rehabilitation Research by act of Oct. 21, 1986 (100 Stat. 1820).

Health, Cost of Living Council Committee on Established by EO 11695 of Jan. 11, 1973. Abolished by EO 11788 of June 18, 1974.

Health, Education, and Welfare, Department of Established by Reorganization Plan No. 1 of 1953 (5 U.S.C. app.), effective Apr. 11, 1953. Renamed Health and Human Services Department by act of Oct. 17, 1979 (93 Stat. 695).

Health, Welfare, and Related Defense Activities, Office of the Coordinator of *Federal Security Administrator* designated as Coordinator of health, welfare, and related fields of activity affecting national defense, including aspects of education under *Federal Security Agency,* by *Council of National Defense,* with approval of President, Nov. 28, 1940. Office of Coordinator superseded by *Office of Defense Health and Welfare Services,* established in *Office for Emergency Services* by EO 8890 of Sept. 3, 1941.

Health Care Technology, National Council on Established by act of July 1, 1944, as amended (92 Stat. 3447). Name changed to *Council on Health Care Technology* by act of Oct. 30, 1984 (98 Stat. 2820). Name lowercased by act of Oct. 7, 1985 (99 Stat. 493). Terminated by act of Dec. 19, 1989 (103 Stat. 2205).

Health Facilities, Financing, Compliance, and Conversion, Bureau of Renamed Bureau of Health Facilities by Health and Human Services Secretary's order of Mar. 12, 1980 (45 FR 17207).

Health Industry Advisory Committee Established by EO 11695 of Jan. 11, 1973. Abolished by EO 11781 of May 1, 1974.

Health Manpower, Bureau of Renamed Bureau of Health Professions by Health and Human Services Secretary's order of Mar. 12, 1980 (45 FR 17207).

Health and Medical Committee Established by *Council of National Defense* order of Sept. 19, 1940. Transferred to *Federal Security Agency* by *Council* order approved by President Nov. 28, 1940. Reestablished in *Office of Defense Health and Welfare Services, Office for Emergency Management,* by EO 8890 of Sept. 3, 1941. *Committee* transferred to *Federal Security Agency* by EO 9338 of Apr. 29, 1943.

Health Resources Administration Established in Public Health Service. Abolished by Health and Human Services Secretarial reorganization of Aug. 20, 1982 (47 FR 38409), and functions transferred to Health Resources and Services Administration.

Health Service, Public Originated by act of July 16, 1798 (1 Stat. 605). Transferred from Treasury Department to *Federal Security Agency* by Reorg. Plan No. I of 1939, effective July 1, 1939.

Health Services Administration. Established in Public Health Service. Abolished by Health and Human Services Secretarial reorganization of Aug. 20, 1982 (47 FR 38409), and functions transferred to Health Resources and Services Administration.

Health Services Industry, Committee on the Established by EO 11627 of Oct. 15, 1971. Abolished by EO 11695 of Jan. 11, 1973.

Health Services and Mental Health Administration Established in Public Health Service Apr. 1, 1968. Abolished by *Health, Education, and Welfare Department* reorganization order and functions transferred to Centers for Disease Control, Health Resources Administration, and Health Services Administration, effective July 1, 1973.

Health Services Research, National Center for Established by act of July 23, 1974 (88 Stat. 363). Transferred from *Health Resources Administration* to Office of the Assistant Secretary for Health by departmental reorganization, effective Dec. 2, 1977. Renamed *National Center for Health Services Research and Health Care Technology Assessment* by Secretary's order, pursuant to act of Oct. 30, 1984 (98 Stat. 2817). Terminated by act of Dec. 19, 1989 (103 Stat. 2205).

Health Statistics, National Center for Established by act of July 23, 1974 (88 Stat. 363). Transferred from *Health Resources Administration* to Office of the Assistant Secretary for Health by departmental reorganization, effective Dec. 2, 1977. Transferred to Centers for Disease Control by Secretary's notice of Apr. 2, 1987 (52 FR 13318).

Health and Welfare Activities, Interdepartmental Committee to Coordinate Appointed by President Aug. 15, 1935, and reestablished by EO 7481 of Oct. 27, 1936. Terminated in 1939.

Health and Welfare Aspects of Evacuation of Civilians, Joint Committee on Established August 1941 as joint committee of *Office of Defense Health and Welfare Services* and *Office of Civilian Defense*. Reorganized in June 1942 and renamed *Joint Committee on Evacuation. Office of Defense Health and Welfare Services* abolished by EO 9388 of Apr. 29, 1943, and functions transferred to *Federal Security Agency. Committee* terminated.

Heart and Lung Institute, National Renamed National Heart, Lung, and Blood Institute by act of Apr. 22, 1976 (90 Stat. 402).

Heritage Conservation and Recreation Service Established by Interior Secretary Jan. 25, 1978. Abolished by Secretarial Order 3060 of Feb. 19, 1981, 1981, and functions transferred to National Park Service.

Highway Safety Agency, National Established in Commerce Department by act of Sept. 9, 1966 (80 Stat. 731). Functions transferred to Transportation Department by act of Oct. 15, 1966 (80 Stat. 931). Functions transferred to *National Highway Safety Bureau* by EO 11357 of June 6, 1967. *Bureau* renamed National Highway Traffic Safety Administration by act of Dec. 31, 1970 (84 Stat. 1739).

Highway Safety Bureau, National *See* **Highway Safety Agency, National**

Home Economics, Bureau of Human Nutrition and *See* **Home Economics, Office of**

Home Economics, Office of Renamed *Bureau of Home Economics* by Secretary's Memorandum 436, effective July 1, 1923, pursuant to act of Feb. 26, 1923 (42 Stat. 1289). Redesignated *Bureau of Human Nutrition and Home Economics* February 1943 in accordance with *Research Administration* Memorandum 5 issued pursuant to EO 9069 of Feb. 23, 1942, and in conformity with Secretary's Memorandums 960 and 986. Functions transferred to *Agricultural Research Service* by Secretary's Memorandum 1320, supp. 4, of Nov. 2, 1953.

Home Loan Bank Administration, Federal *See* **Home Loan Bank Board, Federal**

Home Loan Bank Board *See* **Home Loan Bank Board, Federal**

Home Loan Bank Board, Federal Established by acts of July 22, 1932 (47 Stat. 725), June 13, 1933 (48 Stat. 128), and June 27, 1934 (48 Stat. 1246). Grouped with other agencies to form *Federal Loan Agency* by Reorg. Plan No. I of 1939, effective July 1, 1939. Functions transferred to *Federal Home Loan Bank Administration, National Housing Agency,* by EO 9070 of Feb. 24, 1942. Abolished by Reorg. Plan No. 3, effective July 27, 1947, and functions transferred to *Home Loan Bank Board, Housing and Home Finance Agency.* Renamed *Federal Home Loan Bank Board* and made independent agency by act of Aug. 11, 1955 (69 Stat. 640). Abolished by act of Aug. 9, 1989 (103 Stat. 354, 415) and functions transferred to *Office of Thrift Supervision, Resolution Trust Corporation, Federal Deposit Insurance Corporation,* and *Federal Housing Finance Board.*

Home Loan Bank System, Federal Grouped with other agencies to form *Federal Loan Agency* by Reorg. Plan No. I of 1939, effective July 1, 1939. Functions transferred to *Federal Home Loan Bank Administration, National Housing Agency,* by EO 9070 of Feb. 24, 1942. Transferred to *Housing and Home Finance Agency* by Reorg. Plan No. 3 of 1947, effective July 27, 1947.

Home Mortgage Credit Extension Committee, National Voluntary Established by act of Aug. 2, 1954 (68 Stat 638). Terminated Oct. 1, 1965, pursuant to terms of act.

Home Owners' Loan Corporation Established by act of June 13, 1933 (48 Stat. 128), under supervision of *Federal Home Loan Bank Board.* Grouped with other agencies to form *Federal Loan Agency* by Reorg. Plan No. I of 1939, effective July 1, 1939. Transferred to *Federal Home Loan Bank Administration, National Housing Agency,* by EO 9070 of Feb. 24, 1942. Board of Directors abolished by Reorg. Plan No. 3 of 1947, effective July 27, 1947, and functions transferred, for liquidation of assets, to *Home Loan Bank Board, Housing and Home Finance Agency.* Terminated by order of *Home Loan Bank Board Secretary,* effective Feb. 3, 1954, pursuant to act of June 30, 1953 (67 Stat. 121).

Homesteads, Division of Subsistence Established by act of June 16, 1933 (48 Stat. 205). Interior Secretary authorized to administer section 208 of act by EO 6209 of July 21, 1933. *Federal Subsistence Homesteads Corporation* created by Secretary's order of Dec. 2, 1933, and organization incorporated under laws of Delaware. Transferred to *Resettlement Administration* by EO 7041 of May 15, 1935.

Homesteads Corporation, Federal Subsistence *See* **Homesteads, Division of Subsistence**

Hospitalization, Board of Federal Organized Nov. 1, 1921. Designated as advisory agency to *Bureau of the Budget* May 7, 1943. Terminated June 30, 1948, by Director's letter of May 28, 1948.

Housing, President's Committee on Equal Opportunity in Established by EO 11063 of Nov. 20, 1962. Inactive as of June 30, 1968.

Housing Administration, Federal Established by act of June 27, 1934 (48 Stat. 1246). Grouped with other agencies to form *Federal Loan Agency* by Reorg. Plan No. I of 1939, effective July 1, 1939.

Functions transferred to *Federal Housing Administration, National Housing Agency,* by EO 9070 of Feb. 24, 1942. Transferred to *Housing and Home Finance Agency* by Reorg. Plan No. 3, effective July 27, 1947. Functions transferred to Housing and Urban Development Department by act of Sept. 9, 1965 (79 Stat. 667).

Housing Administration, Public Established as constituent agency of *Housing and Home Finance Agency* by Reorg. Plan No. 3 of 1947, effective July 27, 1947. Functions transferred to Housing and Urban Development Department by act of Sept. 9, 1965 (79 Stat. 667).

Housing Agency, National Established by EO 9070 of Feb. 24, 1942, to consolidate housing functions relating to *Federal Home Loan Bank Board, Federal Home Loan Bank System, Federal Savings and Loan Insurance Corporation, Home Owners' Loan Corporation, U.S. Housing Corporation, Federal Housing Administration, U.S. Housing Authority, Defense Homes Corporation, Division of Defense Housing Coordination, Central Housing Committee, Farm Security Administration* with respect to nonfarm housing, *Public Buildings Administration, Division of Defense Housing, Mutual Ownership Defense Housing Division, Office of Administrator of Federal Works Agency,* and *War* and Navy Departments with respect to housing located off military installations. Agency dissolved on creation of *Housing and Home Finance Agency* by Reorg. Plan No. 3 of 1947, effective July 27, 1947.

Housing Authority, Federal Public Established by EO 9070 of Feb. 24, 1942. Public housing functions of *Federal Works Agency, War* and Navy Departments (except housing located on military installations), and *Farm Security Administration* (nonfarm housing) transferred to *Authority,* and *Defense Homes Corporation* administered by *Authority's* Commissioner. Functions transferred to *Public Housing Administration, Housing and Home Finance Agency,* by Reorg. Plan No. 3 of 1947, effective July 27, 1947.

Housing Authority, U.S. Established in Interior Department by act of Sept. 1, 1937 (50 Stat. 888). Transferred to *Federal Works Agency* by Reorg. Plan No. I of 1939, effective July 1, 1939. Transferred to *Federal Public Housing Authority, National Housing Agency,* by EO 9070 of Feb. 24, 1942. Office of Administrator abolished by Reorg. Plan No. 3 of 1947, effective July 27, 1947, and functions transferred to *Public Housing Administration, Housing and Home Finance Agency.*

Housing Corporation, U.S. Incorporated July 10, 1918, under laws of New York. Transferred from Labor Department to Treasury Department by EO 7641 of June 22, 1937. Transferred from Treasury Department to *Public Buildings Administration, Federal Works Agency,* by EO 8186 of June 29, 1939. Functions transferred for liquidation to *Federal Home Loan Bank Administration, National Housing Agency,* by EO 9070 of Feb. 24, 1942. Terminated Sept. 8, 1952, by Secretary, *Home Loan Bank Board.*

Housing Council, National Established in *Housing and Home Finance Agency* by Reorg. Plan No. 3 of 1947, effective July 27, 1947. Terminated by Reorg. Plan No. 4 of 1965, effective July 27, 1965, and functions transferred to President.

Housing Division Established July 1933 in *Public Works Administration* by act of June 16, 1933 (48 Stat. 195). Functions transferred to *U.S. Housing Authority* by EO 7732 of Oct. 27, 1937.

Housing Expediter, Office of the Established in *Office of War Mobilization and Reconversion* by Presidential letter of Dec. 12, 1945, to *Housing Expediter.* Functions of *Housing Expediter* defined by EO 9686 of Jan. 26, 1946. *Housing Expediter* confirmed in position of *National Housing Administrator* Feb. 6, 1946. *Office of the Housing Expediter* established by act of May 22, 1946 (60 Stat. 208). Functions of *Office* and *National Housing Administrator* segregated by EO 9820 of Jan. 11, 1947. Housing functions of *Civilian Production Administration* transferred to *Office* by EO 9836 of Mar. 22, 1947, effective Apr. 1, 1947. Rent control functions of *Office of Temporary Controls* transferred to *Office* by EO 9841 of Apr. 23, 1947. *Office* terminated by EO 10276 of July 31, 1951, and functions transferred to *Economic Stabilization Agency.*

Housing and Home Finance Agency Established by Reorg. Plan No. 3 of 1947, effective July 27, 1947. Terminated by act of Sept. 9, 1965 (79 Stat. 667), and functions transferred to Housing and Urban Development Department.

Howard University Established by act of Mar. 2, 1867 (14 Stat. 438). Functions of Interior Department transferred to *Federal Security Agency* by Reorg. Plan No. IV of 1940, effective June 30, 1940. Functions of *Health, Education, and Welfare Department* transferred to Education Department by act of Oct. 17, 1979 (93 Stat. 678).

Human Development, Office of Established in the Department of Health, Education, and Welfare (*see reference*). Renamed Office of Human Development Services and component units transferred to or reorganized under new administrations in Office by *Health, Education, and Welfare Secretary's* reorganization order of July 26, 1977. Merged into the Administration for Children and Families by Secretary's reorganization notice dated Apr. 15, 1991.

Human Development Services, Office of *See* **Human Development, Office of**

Hydrographic Office Jurisdiction transferred from *Bureau of Navigation* to Chief of Naval Operations by EO 9126 of Apr. 8, 1942, and by Reorg. Plan No. 3 of 1946, effective July 16, 1946. Renamed U.S. Naval Oceanographic Office by act of July 10, 1962 (76 Stat. 154).

Immigration, Bureau of Established as branch of Treasury Department by act of Mar. 3, 1891 (26 Stat. 1085). Transferred to *Department of Commerce and Labor* by act of Feb. 14, 1903 (34 Stat. 596). Made *Bureau of Immigration and*

Naturalization by act of June 29, 1906 (37 Stat. 736). Made separate division after Labor Department created by act of Mar. 4, 1913 (37 Stat. 736). Consolidated into *Immigration and Naturalization Service,* Labor Department, by EO 6166 of June 10, 1933. Transferred to Justice Department by Reorg. Plan No. V of 1940, effective June 14, 1940.

Immigration, Commissioners of Offices of commissioners of immigration of the several ports created by act of Aug. 18, 1894 (28 Stat. 391). Abolished by Reorg. Plan No. III of 1940, effective June 30, 1940, and functions transferred to *Bureau of Immigration and Naturalization,* Labor Department.

Immigration and Naturalization, Bureau of *See* **Immigration, Bureau of**

Immigration and Naturalization, District Commissioner of Created by act of Aug. 18, 1894 (28 Stat. 391), and abolished by Reorg. Plan No. III of 1940, effective June 30, 1940. Functions administered by Immigration and Naturalization Commissioner, Justice Department, through district immigration and naturalization directors.

Immigration and Naturalization Service *See* **Immigration, Bureau of**

Import Programs, Office of Established by Commerce Secretary Feb. 14, 1971. Functions transferred to *Domestic and International Business Administration,* effective Nov. 17, 1972.

Indian Claims Commission Established by act of Aug. 13, 1946 (60 Stat. 1049). Terminated by act of Oct. 8, 1976 (90 Stat. 1990), and pending cases transferred to *U.S. Court of Claims* Sept. 30, 1978.

Indian Commissioners, Board of Established by section 2039, Revised Statutes. Abolished by EO 6145 of May 25, 1933.

Indian Medical Facilities Functions transferred from Interior Department to *Health, Education, and Welfare Department,* to be administered by Surgeon General of Public Health Service, by act of Aug. 5, 1954 (68 Stat. 674).

Indian Opportunity, National Council on Established by EO 11399 of Mar. 6, 1968. Terminated Nov. 26, 1974, by act of Nov. 26, 1969 (83 Stat. 220).

Indian Policy Review Commission, American Established by act of Jan. 2, 1975 (88 Stat. 1910). Terminated June 30, 1977, pursuant to terms of act.

Industrial Analysis, Committee of Established by EO 7323 of Mar. 21, 1936. Terminated Feb. 17, 1937.

Industrial Cooperation, Coordinator for Established by EO 7193 of Sept. 26, 1935. Continued by EO 7324 of Mar. 30, 1936. Terminated June 30, 1937.

Industrial Emergency Committee Established by EO 6770 of June 30, 1934. Consolidated with *National Emergency Council* by EO 6889-A of Oct. 29, 1934.

Industrial Pollution Control Council Staff, National Established by Commerce Departmental Organization Order 35-3 of June 17, 1970. *Staff* abolished by Departmental Organization Order of Sept. 10, 1973. Council inactive.

Industrial Recovery Board, National Established by EO 6859 of Sept. 27, 1934. Terminated by EO 7075 of June 15, 1935.

Industrial Recovery Board, Special Established by EO 6173 of June 16, 1933. Functions absorbed by *National Emergency Council* under terms of EO 6513 of Dec. 18, 1933.

Industrial Relations, Office of Activated in Navy Department Sept. 14, 1945. Superseded June 22, 1966, by creation of *Office of Civilian Manpower Management.*

Industry and Trade Administration *See* **Business and Defense Services Administration**

Information, Committee for Reciprocity Established by EO 6750 of June 27, 1934; reestablished by EO 10004 of Oct. 5, 1948, which revoked EO 6750. Superseded by EO 10082 of Oct. 5, 1949; abolished by EO 11075 of Jan. 15, 1963, which revoked EO 10082.

Information, Coordinator of Established by Presidential order of July 11, 1941. Functions exclusive of foreign information activities transferred by military order of June 13, 1942, to jurisdiction of Joint Chiefs of Staff, *War Department,* as *Office of Strategic Services.* Foreign information functions transferred to *Office of War Information* by EO 9182 of June 13, 1942.

Information, Division of Established pursuant to Presidential letter of Feb. 28, 1941, to Liaison Officer, *Office of Emergency Management.* Abolished by EO 9182 of June 13, 1942. Functions relating to public information on war effort transferred and consolidated with *Office of War Information,* and publication services relating to specific agencies of OEM transferred to those agencies.

Information, Office of Coordinator of Transferred, exclusive of foreign information activities, to *Office of War Information* by EO 9182 of June 13, 1942. Designated *Office of Strategic Services* and transferred to jurisdiction of Joint Chiefs of Staff by Military Order of June 13, 1942. Terminated by EO 9621 of Sept. 20, 1945, and functions distributed to State and *War* Departments.

Information Administration, International Transferred from State Department to U.S. Information Agency by Reorg. Plan No. 8 of 1953, effective Aug. 1, 1953.

Information Agency, U.S. Established by Reorg. Plan No. 8 of 1953, effective Aug. 1, 1953. Abolished by Reorg. Plan No. 2 of 1977, effective Apr. 1, 1978, and functions transferred to *International Communication Agency.* Renamed U.S. Information Agency by act of Aug. 24, 1982 (96 Stat. 291).

Information and Public Affairs, Office of Merged with *Office of Intergovernmental Affairs* to form Office of Public and Intergovernmental Affairs by Labor Secretary's Order 1–85 of June 5, 1985.

Information Security Committee, Interagency Established by EO 12065 of June 28, 1978. Abolished by EO 12356 of Apr. 2, 1982.

Information Security Oversight Office Established in General Services Administration by EO 12065 of June 28, 1978. EO 12065 revoked by EO 12356 of Apr. 2, 1982, which provided for continuation of Office.

Information Service, Government *See* **U.S. Information Service**

Information Service, Interim International Established in State Department by EO 9608 of Aug. 31, 1945. Abolished Dec. 31, 1945, pursuant to terms of order.

Information Service, U.S. Established in March 1934 as division of *National Emergency Council.* Transferred to *Office of Government Reports* by Reorg. Plan No. II of 1939, effective July 1, 1939. Consolidated, along with other functions of *Office,* into *Division of Public Inquiries, Bureau of Special Services, Office of War Information,* by EO 9182 of June 13, 1942. *Bureau of Special Services* renamed *Government Information Service* and transferred to *Bureau of the Budget* by EO 9608 of Aug. 31, 1945. *Service* transferred to *Office of Government Reports* by EO 9809 of Dec. 12, 1946.

Insane, Government Hospital for the Established by act of Mar. 3, 1855 (10 Stat. 682). Renamed Saint Elizabeths Hospital by act of July 1, 1916 (39 Stat. 309). Transferred from Interior Department to *Federal Security Agency* by Reorg. Plan No. IV of 1940, effective June 30, 1940. Transferred to *Health, Education, and Welfare Department* by Reorg. Plan No. 1 of 1953, effective Apr. 11, 1953. Functions redelegated to National Institute of Mental Health by Secretary's reorganization order of Aug. 9, 1967. Property and administration transferred to District of Columbia Government by act of Nov. 8, 1984 (98 Stat. 3369).

Installations, Director of Established in Defense Department by act of July 14, 1952 (66 Stat. 625). Abolished by Reorg. Plan No. 6 of 1953, effective June 30, 1953, and functions transferred to Defense Secretary.

Insular Affairs, Bureau of Transferred from *War Department* to *Division of Territories and Island Possessions,* Interior Department, by Reorg. Plan No. II of 1939, effective July 1, 1939.

Insurance Administrator, Federal Established by act of Aug. 1, 1968 (82 Stat. 567). Functions transferred to Federal Emergency Management Agency by Reorg. Plan No. 3 of 1978, effective Apr. 1, 1979.

Intelligence Activities, President's Board of Consultants on Foreign Established by EO 10656 of Feb. 6, 1956. EO 10656 revoked by EO 10938 of May 4, 1961, and *Board* terminated. Functions transferred to *President's Foreign Intelligence Advisory Board.*

Intelligence Advisory Board, President's Foreign Established by EO 11460 of Mar. 20, 1969. Abolished by EO 11984 of May 4, 1977. Reestablished by EO 12331 of Oct. 20, 1981.

Intelligence Authority, National Established by Presidential directive of Jan. 22, 1946. Terminated on creation of Central Intelligence Agency under National Security Council by act of July 26, 1947 (61 Stat. 497).

Intelligence Group, Central Terminated on creation of Central Intelligence Agency by act of July 26, 1947 (61 Stat. 497).

Inter-American Affairs, Institute of *See* **American Republics, Office for Coordination of Commercial and Cultural Relations between the**

Inter-American Affairs, Office of *See* **American Republics, Office for Coordination of Commercial and Cultural Relations between the**

Inter-American Affairs, Office of the Coordinator of *See* **American Republics, Office for Coordination of Commercial and Cultural Relations between the**

Interagency. *See other part of title*

Interdepartmental. *See also other part of title*

Interdepartmental Advisory Council Established January 1941 to advise *Coordinator of Health, Welfare, and Related Defense Activities.* Terminated on creation of *Office of Defense Health and Welfare Service* Sept. 3, 1941.

Interest and Dividends, Committee on Established by EO 11695 of Jan. 11, 1973. Abolished by EO 11781 of May 1, 1974.

Intergovernmental Affairs, Office of Merged with *Office of Information and Public Affairs* to form Office of Public and Intergovernmental Affairs by Labor Secretary's Order 1–85 of June 5, 1985.

Intergovernmental Relations, Commission on Established by act of July 10, 1953 (67 Stat. 145). Final report submitted to Congress by June 30, 1955, pursuant to act of Feb. 7, 1955 (69 Stat. 7).

Intergovernmental Relations, Office of Established by EO 11455 of Feb. 14, 1969. Functions transferred to Domestic Council by EO 11690 of Dec. 14, 1972.

Interim Compliance Panel Established by Dec. 30, 1969 (83 Stat. 774). Terminated June 30, 1976, pursuant to terms of act.

Internal Revenue Service Functions relating to alcohol, tobacco, firearms, and explosives transferred to Bureau of Alcohol, Tobacco and Firearms by Treasury Departmental order July 1, 1972.

Internal Security Division Established July 9, 1945, by transfer of functions from Criminal

Division. Abolished Mar. 22, 1973, and functions transferred to Criminal Division, Justice Department.

International. *See also other part of title*

International Activities, Office of Renamed Office of Service and Protocol by Smithsonian Institution Secretary's internal directive of Jan. 11, 1985.

International Development, Agency for Transferred from State Department to U.S. International Development Cooperation Agency by Reorg. Plan No. 2 of 1979, effective Oct. 1, 1979. Continued as agency in IDCA by IDCA Delegation of Authority No. 1 of Oct. 1, 1979.

Investigation, Bureau of Established by act of May 22, 1908 (35 Stat. 235). Functions consolidated with investigative functions of *Bureau of Prohibition, Division of Investigation,* Justice Department, by EO 6166 of June 10, 1933, effective Mar. 2, 1934.

Investigation, Division of Designated as Federal Bureau of Investigation in Justice Department by act of Mar. 22, 1935 (49 Stat. 77).

Investigation and Research, Board of Established by act of Sept. 18, 1940 (54 Stat. 952). Extended to Sept. 18, 1944, by Proc. 2559 of June 26, 1942.

Investigations, Division of Established by administrative order of Apr. 27, 1933. Abolished Jan. 17, 1942, by administrative order and functions transferred to *Branch of Field Examination, General Land Office,* Interior Department.

Investments, Office of Foreign Direct Established in Commerce Department Jan. 2, 1968, by Departmental Organization Order 25-3 to carry out provisions of EO 11387 of Jan. 1, 1968. Controls on foreign investments terminated Jan. 29, 1974.

Jamestown-Williamsburg-Yorktown National Celebration Commission Established by act of Aug. 13, 1953 (67 Stat. 576). Terminated on submission of final report to Congress Mar. 1, 1958.

Joint. *See also other part of title.*

Joint Resolutions of Congress *See* **State Department**

Judicial Procedure, Commission on International Rules of Established by act of Sept. 2, 1958 (72 Stat. 1743). Terminated Dec. 31, 1966, by act of Aug. 30, 1964 (78 Stat. 700).

Justice Assistance, Research, and Statistics, Office of Established in Justice Department by act of Dec. 27, 1979 (93 Stat. 1201). Abolished by act of Oct. 12, 1984 (98 Stat. 2091).

Kennedy, Commission To Report Upon the Assassination of President John F. Established by EO 11130 of Nov. 29, 1963. Report submitted Sept. 24, 1964, and *Commission* discharged by Presidential letter of same date.

Labor, President's Committee on Migratory Appointed by Presidential letter of Aug. 26, 1954. Formally established by EO 10894 of Nov. 15, 1960. Terminated Jan. 6, 1964, by Labor Secretary in letter to members, with approval of President.

Labor and Commerce, Department of Established by act of Feb. 14, 1903 (32 Stat. 825). Reorganized into separate Departments of Labor and Commerce by act of Mar. 4, 1913 (37 Stat. 736).

Labor Department, Solicitor for Transferred from Justice Department to Labor Department by EO 6166 of June 10, 1933.

Labor-Management Advisory Committee Established by EO 11695 of Jan. 11, 1973. Abolished by EO 11788 of June 18, 1974.

Labor-Management Policy, President's Advisory Committee on Established by EO 10918 of Feb. 16, 1961. Abolished by EO 11710 of Apr. 4, 1973.

Labor-Management Relations Services, Office of Established by Labor Secretary's Order 3-84 of May 3, 1984. Renamed Bureau of Labor-Management Relations and Cooperative Programs by Secretarial Order 7-84 of Sept. 20, 1984 (49 FR 38374).

Labor-Management Services Administration *Office of Pension and Welfare Benefit Programs* transferred from *Administration* and constituted as separate unit by Labor Secretary's Order 1-84 of Jan. 20, 1984 (49 FR 4269). Remaining labor-management relations functions reassigned by Labor Secretary's Order 3-84 of May 3, 1984.

Labor Organization, International Established in 1919 by Treaty of Versailles with U.S. joining in 1934. U.S. membership terminated Nov. 1, 1977, at President's direction.

Labor Relations Council, Federal Established by EO 11491 of Oct. 29, 1969. Abolished by Reorg. Plan No. 2 of 1978, effective Jan. 1, 1979, and functions transferred to Federal Labor Relations Authority.

Labor Standards, Apprenticeship Section, Division of Transferred to *Federal Security Agency* by EO 9139 of Apr. 18, 1942, functioning as *Apprentice Training Service.* Transferred to *War Manpower Commission* by EO 9247 of Sept. 17, 1942, functioning in *Bureau of Training.* Returned to Labor Department by EO 9617 of Sept. 19, 1945.

Labor Standards, Bureau of Established by Labor departmental order in 1934. Functions absorbed by Occupational Safety and Health Administration in May 1971.

Land Bank Commissioner *See* **Farm Loan Board, Federal**

Land Law Review Commission, Public Established by act of Sept. 19, 1964 (78 Stat. 982). Terminated Dec. 31, 1970, pursuant to terms of act.

Land Office, General Consolidated with *Grazing Service* into Bureau of Land Management, Interior Department, by Reorg. Plan No. 3 of 1946, effective July 16, 1946.

Land Office, Office of Recorder of the General Created in Interior Department by act of July 4, 1836

(5 Stat. 111). Abolished by Reorg. Plan No. III of 1940, effective June 30, 1940, and functions transferred to *General Land Office.*

Land Policy Section Established in 1934 as part of *Program Planning Division, Agricultural Adjustment Administration.* Personnel taken over by *Resettlement Administration* in 1935.

Land Problems, Committee on National Established by EO 6693 of Apr. 28, 1934. Abolished by EO 6777 of June 30, 1934.

Land Program, Director of Basis of program found in act of June 16, 1933 (48 Stat. 200). *Special Board of Public Works* established by EO 6174 of June 16, 1933. Land Program established by *Board* by resolution passed Dec. 28, 1933, and amended July 18, 1934. *Federal Emergency Relief Administration* designated to administer program Feb. 28, 1934. Land Program transferred to *Resettlement Administration* by EO 7028 of Apr. 30, 1935. Functions of *Administration* transferred to Agriculture Secretary by EO 7530 of Dec. 31, 1936. Land conservation and land-utilization programs administered by *Administration* transferred to *Bureau of Agricultural Economics* by Secretary's Memorandum 733. Administration of land programs placed under *Soil Conservation Service* by Secretary's Memorandum 785 of Oct. 6, 1938.

Land Use Coordination, Office of Established by Agriculture Secretary's Memorandum 725 of July 12, 1937. Abolished Jan. 1, 1944, by General Departmental Circular 21 and functions administered by *Land Use Coordinator.*

Land Use and Water Planning, Office of Established in Interior Department by Secretarial Order No. 2953 of May 7, 1973. Abolished by Secretarial Order No. 2988 of Mar. 11, 1976.

Law Enforcement Assistance Administration Established by act of June 19, 1968 (82 Stat. 197). Operations closed out by Justice Department through lack of appropriations and remaining functions transferred to Office of Justice Assistance, Research, and Statistics.

Law Enforcement Training Center, Consolidated Federal Renamed Federal Law Enforcement Training Center by Amendment No. 1 of Aug. 14, 1975, to Treasury Department Order 217 (Revision 1).

Legislative Affairs, Office of Renamed Office of Intergovernmental and Legislative Affairs Feb. 24, 1984, by Attorney General's Order 1054–84 (49 FR 10177).

Lend-Lease Administration, Office of Established by EO 8926 of Oct. 28, 1941, to replace *Division of Defense Aid Reports.* Consolidated with *Foreign Economic Administration* by EO 9380 of Sept. 25, 1943.

Lewis and Clark Trail Commission Established by act of Oct. 6, 1964 (78 Stat. 1005). Terminated October 1969 by terms of act.

Lighthouses, Bureau of Established in Commerce Department by act of Aug. 7, 1789 (1 Stat. 53). Consolidated with U.S. Coast Guard by Reorg. Plan No. II of 1939, effective July 1, 1939.

Lincoln Sesquicentennial Commission Established by joint resolution of Sept. 2, 1957 (71 Stat. 587). Terminated Mar. 1, 1960, pursuant to terms of joint resolution.

Liquidation, Director of Established in *Office for Emergency Management* by EO 9674 of Jan. 4, 1946. Terminated by EO 9744 of June 27, 1946.

Liquidation Advisory Committee Established by EO 9674 of Jan. 4, 1946. Terminated by EO 9744 of June 27, 1946.

Loan Agency, Federal Established by Reorg. Plan No. I of 1939, effective July 1, 1939, by consolidating *Reconstruction Finance Corporation*—including subordinate units *RFC Mortgage Company, Disaster Loan Corporation, Federal National Mortgage Association, Defense Plant Corporation, Defense Homes Corporation, Defense Supplies Corporation, Rubber Reserve Company, Metals Reserve Company,* and *War Insurance Corporation* (later known as *War Damage Corporation*)—with *Federal Home Loan Bank Board, Home Owners' Loan Corporation, Federal Savings and Loan Insurance Corporation, Federal Housing Administration, Electric Home and Farm Authority,* and *Export-Import Bank of Washington. Federal Home Loan Bank Board, Federal Savings and Loan Insurance Corporation, Home Owners' Loan Corporation, Federal Housing Administration,* and *Defense Homes Corporation* transferred to *National Housing Agency* by EO 9070 of Feb. 24, 1942. *Reconstruction Finance Corporation* and its units (except *Defense Homes Corporation*), *Electric Home and Farm Authority,* and *Export-Import Bank of Washington* transferred to Commerce Department by EO 9071 of Feb. 24, 1942. *RFC* and units returned to *Federal Loan Agency* by act of Feb. 24, 1945 (59 Stat. 5). *Agency* abolished by act of June 30, 1947 (61 Stat. 202), and all property and records transferred to *Reconstruction Finance Corporation.*

Loan Fund, Development Established in *International Cooperation Administration* by act of Aug. 14, 1957 (71 Stat. 355). Created as independent corporate agency by act of June 30, 1958 (72 Stat. 261). Abolished by act of Sept. 4, 1961 (75 Stat. 445), and functions redelegated to Agency for International Development.

Loan Policy Board Established by act of July 18, 1958 (72 Stat. 385). Abolished by Reorg. Plan No. 4 of 1965, effective July 27, 1965, and functions transferred to Small Business Administration.

Longshoremen's Labor Board, National Established in Labor Department by EO 6748 of June 26, 1934. Terminated by Proc. 2120 of Mar. 11, 1935.

Low-Emission Vehicle Certification Board Established by act of Dec. 31, 1970 (84 Stat. 1701). Terminated by act of Mar. 14, 1980 (94 Stat. 98).

Lowell Historic Canal District Commission Established by act of Jan. 4, 1975 (88 Stat. 2330). Expired January 1977 pursuant to terms of act.

Loyalty Review Board Established Nov. 10, 1947, by *U.S. Civil Service Commission,* pursuant to EO 9835 of Mar. 21, 1947. Abolished by EO 10450 of Apr. 27, 1953.

Management Improvement, Advisory Committee on Established by EO 10072 of July 29, 1949. Abolished by EO 10917 of Feb. 10, 1961, and functions transferred to *Bureau of the Budget.*

Management Improvement, President's Advisory Council on Established by EO 11509 of Feb. 11, 1970. Inactive as of June 30, 1973.

Manpower, President's Committee on Established by EO 11152 of Apr. 15, 1964. Terminated by EO 11515 of Mar. 13, 1970.

Manpower Administration Renamed Employment and Training Administration by Labor Secretary's Order 14-75 of Nov. 12, 1975.

Manpower Management, Office of Civilian Renamed Office of Civilian Personnel by Navy Secretary Notice 5430 of Oct. 1, 1976.

Marine Affairs, Office of Established by Interior Secretary Apr. 30, 1970, to replace *Office of Marine Resources,* created by Secretary Oct. 22, 1968. Abolished by Secretary Dec. 4, 1970.

Marine Corps Memorial Commission, U.S. Established by act of Aug. 24, 1947 (61 Stat. 724). Terminated by act of Mar. 14, 1980 (94 Stat. 98).

Marine Inspection and Navigation, Bureau of *See* **Navigation and Steamboat Inspection, Bureau of**

Marine Resources and Engineering Development, National Council on Established in Executive Office of the President by act of June 17, 1966 (80 Stat. 203). Terminated Apr. 30, 1971, through lack of funds.

Maritime Administration Established in Commerce Department by Reorg. Plan No. 21 of 1950, effective May 24, 1950. Transferred to Transportation Department by act of Aug. 6, 1981 (95 Stat. 151).

Maritime Advisory Committee Established by EO 11156 of June 17, 1964. Terminated by EO 11427 of Sept. 4, 1968.

Maritime Board, Federal *See* **Maritime Commission, U.S.**

Maritime Commission, U.S. Established by act of June 29, 1936 (49 Stat. 1985), as successor agency to *U.S. Shipping Board* and *U.S. Shipping Board Merchant Fleet Corporation.* Training functions transferred to Commandant of Coast Guard by EO 9083 of Feb. 27, 1942. Functions further transferred to *War Shipping Administration* by EO 9198 of July 11, 1942. Abolished by Reorg. Plan No. 21 of 1950, effective May 24, 1950, which established *Federal Maritime Board* and *Maritime Administration* as successor agencies. *Board* abolished, regulatory functions transferred to Federal Maritime Commission, and functions relating to subsidization of merchant marine transferred to Commerce Secretary by Reorg. Plan No. 7 of 1961, effective Aug. 12, 1961.

Maritime Labor Board Authorized by act of June 23, 1938 (52 Stat. 968). Mediatory duties abolished by act of June 23, 1941 (55 Stat. 259); title expired June 22, 1942.

Marketing Administration, Surplus Established by Reorg. Plan No. III of 1940, effective June 30, 1940, consolidating functions vested in *Federal Surplus Commodities Corporation* and *Division of Marketing and Marketing Agreements, Agricultural Adjustment Administration.* Consolidated with other agencies into *Agricultural Marketing Administration* by EO 9069 of Feb. 23, 1942.

Marketing and Marketing Agreements, Division of Established in Agriculture Department by act of June 3, 1937 (50 Stat. 246). Consolidated with *Federal Surplus Commodities Corporation* into *Surplus Marketing Administration* by Reorg. Plan No. III of 1940, effective June 30, 1940.

Mediation, U.S. Board of Established by act of May 20, 1926 (44 Stat. 577). Abolished by act of June 21, 1934 (48 Stat. 1193), and superseded by National Mediation Board, July 21, 1934.

Medical Information Systems Program Office, Tri-Service Renamed Defense Medical Systems Support Center by memorandum of Assistant Defense Secretary (Health Affairs) May 3, 1985.

Medical Services Administration Established by *Health, Education, and Welfare Secretary's* reorganization of Aug. 15, 1967. Transferred from *Social and Rehabilitation Service* to Health Care Financing Administration by Secretary's reorganization of Mar. 8, 1977 (42 FR 13262).

Medicine and Surgery, Department of Established in the Veterans Administration by act of Sept. 2, 1958 (72 Stat. 1243). Renamed *Veterans Health Services and Research Administration* in the Department of Veterans Affairs by act of Oct. 25, 1988 (102 Stat. 2640). Renamed Veterans Health Administration, by act of May 7, 1991 (105 Stat. 187).

Memorial Commission, National Established by Public Resolution 107 of Mar. 4, 1929 (45 Stat. 1699). Terminated by EO 6166 of June 10, 1933, and functions transferred to *Office of National Parks, Buildings, and Reservations,* Interior Department.

Metals Reserve Company Established June 28, 1940, by act of Jan. 22, 1932 (47 Stat. 5). Transferred from *Federal Loan Agency* to Commerce Department by EO 9071 of Feb. 24, 1942. Returned to *Federal Loan Agency* by act of Feb. 24, 1945 (59 Stat. 5). Dissolved by act of June 30, 1945 (59 Stat. 310), and functions transferred to *Reconstruction Finance Corporation.*

Metric Board, U.S. Established by act of Dec. 23, 1975 (89 Stat. 1007). Terminated Oct. 1, 1982, through lack of funding.

Mexican-American Affairs, Interagency Committee on Established by Presidential memorandum of June 9, 1967. Renamed *Cabinet Committee on Opportunities for Spanish-Speaking People* by act of Dec. 30, 1969 (83 Stat. 838). Terminated Dec. 30, 1974, pursuant to terms of act.

Mexican Claims Commission, American Established by act of Dec. 18, 1942 (56 Stat. 1058). Terminated Apr. 4, 1947, by act of Apr. 3, 1945 (59 Stat. 59).

Mexican Claims Commission, Special Established by act of Apr. 10, 1935 (49 Stat. 149). Terminated by EO 7909 of June 15, 1938.

Mexico Commission for Border Development and Friendship, U.S.- Established through exchange of notes of Nov. 30 and Dec. 3, 1966, between U.S. and Mexico. Terminated Nov. 5, 1969.

Micronesian Claims Commission Established by act of July 1, 1971 (85 Stat. 92). Terminated Aug. 3, 1976, pursuant to terms of act.

Migration, Intergovernmental Committee for European Renamed Intergovernmental Committee for Migration by Resolution 624, passed by Intergovernmental Committee for European Migration Council, effective Nov. 11, 1980.

Migration, International Committee for Created in 1951. Renamed International Organization for Migration pursuant to article 29, paragraph 2, of the ICM constitution, effective Nov. 14, 1989.

Migratory Bird Conservation Commission Chairmanship transferred from Agriculture Secretary to Interior Secretary by Reorg. Plan No. II of 1939, effective July 1, 1939.

Military Air Transport Service Renamed Military Airlift Command in U.S. Air Force by HQ MATS/ MAC Special Order G-164 of Jan. 1, 1966.

Military Establishment, National Established as executive department of the Government by act of July 26, 1947 (61 Stat. 495). Designated Department of Defense by act of Aug. 10, 1949 (63 Stat. 579).

Military Purchases, Interdepartmental Committee for Coordination of Foreign and Domestic Informal liaison committee created on Presidential notification of Dec. 6, 1939, to Treasury and *War* Secretaries and Acting Navy Secretary. Committee dissolved in accordance with Presidential letter to Treasury Secretary Apr. 14, 1941, following approval of act of Mar. 11, 1941 (55 Stat. 31).

Military Renegotiation Policy and Review Board Established by directive of Defense Secretary July 19, 1948. Abolished by Defense Secretary's letter of Jan. 18, 1952, which transferred functions to Renegotiation Board.

Military Sea Transportation Service Renamed Military Sealift Command in U.S. Navy by COMSC notice of Aug. 1, 1970.

Militia Bureau Established in 1908 as *Division of Militia Affairs, Office of War Secretary.* Superseded in 1933 by National Guard Bureau.

Mine Health and Safety Academy, National Transferred from Interior Department to Labor Department by act of July 25, 1979 (93 Stat. 111).

Minerals Exploration, Office of Established by act of Aug. 21, 1958 (72 Stat. 700). Functions transferred to Geological Survey by Interior Secretary's Order 2886 of Feb. 26, 1965.

Minerals Mobilization, Office of Established by Interior Secretary pursuant to act of Sept. 8, 1950 (64 Stat. 798) and EO 10574 of Nov. 5, 1954, and by order of *Office of Defense Mobilization.* Succeeded by *Office of Minerals and Solid Fuels* Nov. 2, 1962. *Office of Minerals Policy Development* combined with *Office of Research and Development* in Interior Department May 21, 1976, under authority of Reorg. Plan No. 3 of 1950, to form *Office of Minerals Policy and Research Analysis.* Abolished Sept. 30, 1981, by Secretarial Order 3070 and functions transferred to Bureau of Mines.

Minerals Policy and Research Analysis, Office of *See* **Minerals Mobilization, Office of**

Minerals and Solid Fuels, Office of Established by Interior Secretary Oct. 26, 1962. Abolished and functions assigned to Deputy Assistant Secretary—Minerals and Energy Policy, Office of the Assistant Secretary—Mineral Resources, effective Oct. 22, 1971.

Mines, Bureau of Established in Interior Department by act of May 16, 1910 (36 Stat. 369). Transferred to Commerce Department by EO 4239 of June 4, 1925. Transferred to Interior Department by EO 6611 of Feb. 22, 1934.

Mining Enforcement and Safety Administration Established by Interior Secretary's Order 2953 of May 7, 1973. Terminated by departmental directive Mar. 9, 1978, and functions transferred to Mine Safety and Health Administration, Labor Department, established by act of Nov. 9, 1977 (91 Stat. 1319).

Minority Business Enterprise, Office of Renamed Minority Business Development Agency by Commerce Secretarial Order DOO-254A of Nov. 1, 1979.

Mint, Bureau of the Renamed U.S. Mint by Secretarial order of Jan. 9, 1984 (49 FR 5020).

Missile Sites Labor Commission Established by EO 10946 of May 26, 1961. Abolished by EO 11374 of Oct. 11, 1967, and functions transferred to Federal Mediation and Conciliation Service.

Missouri Basin Survey Commission Established by EO 10318 of Jan. 3, 1952. Report of Commission submitted to President Jan. 12, 1953, pursuant to EO 10329 of Feb. 25, 1952.

Missouri River Basin Commission Established by EO 11658 of Mar. 22, 1972. Terminated by EO 12319 of Sept. 9, 1981.

Mobilization, Office of Civil and Defense *See* **Mobilization, Office of Defense and Civilian**

Mobilization, Office of Defense and Civilian Established by Reorg. Plan No. 1 of 1958, effective July 1, 1958. Redesignated as *Office of Civil and Defense Mobilization* by act of Aug. 26, 1958 (72 Stat. 861), consolidating functions of *Office of Defense Mobilization* and *Federal Civil Defense Administration.* Civil defense functions transferred to Defense Secretary by EO 10952 of July 20, 1961, and remaining organization redesignated *Office of Emergency Planning* by act of Sept. 22, 1961 (75 Stat. 630).

Mobilization Policy, National Advisory Board on Established by EO 10224 of Mar. 15, 1951. EO 10224 revoked by EO 10773 of July 1, 1958.

Monetary and Financial Problems, National Advisory Council on International Established by act of July 31, 1945 (59 Stat. 512). Abolished by Reorg. Plan No. 4 of 1965, effective July 27, 1965, and functions transferred to President. Functions assumed by National Advisory Council on International Monetary and Financial Policies, established by EO 11269 of Feb. 14, 1966.

Monument Commission, National Established by act of Aug. 31, 1954 (68 Stat. 1029). Final report submitted in 1957, and audit of business completed September 1964.

Monuments in War Areas, American Commission for the Protection and Salvage of Artistic and Historic Established by President June 23, 1943; announced by Secretary of State Aug. 20, 1943. Activities assumed by State Department Aug. 16, 1946.

Mortgage Association, Federal National Chartered Feb. 10, 1938, by act of June 27, 1934 (48 Stat. 1246). Grouped with other agencies to form *Federal Loan Agency* by Reorg. Plan No. I of 1939, effective July 1, 1939. Transferred to Commerce Department by EO 9071 of Feb. 24, 1942. Returned to *Federal Loan Agency* by act of Feb. 24, 1945 (59 Stat. 5). Transferred to *Housing and Home Finance Agency* by Reorg. Plan No. 22 of 1950, effective July 10, 1950. Rechartered by act of Aug. 2, 1954 (68 Stat. 590) and made constituent agency of *Housing and Home Finance Agency.* Transferred with functions of *Housing and Home Finance Agency* to Housing and Urban Development Department by act of Sept. 9, 1965 (79 Stat. 667). Made Government-sponsored, private corporation by act of Aug. 1, 1968 (82 Stat. 536).

Motor Carrier Claims Commission Established by act of July 2, 1948 (62 Stat. 1222). Terminated Dec. 31, 1952, by acts of July 11, 1951 (65 Stat. 116), and Mar. 14, 1952 (66 Stat. 25).

Mount Rushmore National Memorial Commission Established by act of Feb. 25, 1929 (45 Stat. 1300). Expenditures ordered administered by Interior Department by EO 6166 of June 10, 1933. Transferred to National Park Service, Interior Department, by Reorg. Plan No. II of 1939, effective July 1, 1939.

Munitions Board Established in Defense Department by act of July 26, 1947 (61 Stat. 499). Abolished by Reorg. Plan No. 6 of 1953, effective June 30, 1953, and functions vested in Defense Secretary.

Munitions Board, Joint Army and Navy Organized in 1922. Placed under direction of President by military order of July 5, 1939. Reconstituted Aug. 18, 1945, by order approved by President. Terminated on establishment of *Munitions Board* by act of July 26, 1947 (61 Stat. 505).

Museum of History and Technology, National Renamed National Museum of American History in Smithsonian Institution by act of Oct. 13, 1980 (94 Stat. 1884).

Museum Services, Institute of Established by act of June 23, 1972 (86 Stat. 327). Transferred to Office of Educational Research and Improvement, Education Department, by act of Oct. 17, 1979 (93 Stat. 678), effective May 4, 1980. Transferred to National Foundation of the Arts and the Humanities by act of Dec. 23, 1981 (95 Stat. 1414).

Narcotics, Bureau of Established in Treasury Department by act of June 14, 1930 (46 Stat. 585). Abolished by Reorg. Plan No. 1 of 1968, effective Apr. 8, 1968, and functions transferred to *Bureau of Narcotics and Dangerous Drugs,* Justice Department.

Narcotics Control, Cabinet Committee on International Established by Presidential memorandum of Aug. 17, 1971. Terminated by Presidential memorandum of Mar. 14, 1977.

National. *See other part of title*

Naval Material, Office of Established by act of Mar. 5, 1948 (62 Stat. 68). Abolished by Defense Department Reorg. Order of Mar. 9, 1966, and functions transferred to Navy Secretary (31 FR 7188).

Naval Material Command *See* **Naval Material Support Establishment**

Naval Material Support Establishment Established by Navy Department General Order 5 of July 1, 1963 (28 FR 7037). Replaced by *Naval Material Command* pursuant to General Order 5 of Apr. 29, 1966 (31 FR 7188). Functions realigned to form Office of Naval Acquisition Support, and termination of *Command* effective May 6, 1985.

Naval Observatory Jurisdiction transferred from *Bureau of Navigation* to Chief of Naval Operations by EO 9126 of Apr. 8, 1942, and by Reorg. Plan No. 3 of 1946, effective July 16, 1946.

Naval Petroleum and Oil Shale Reserves, Office of Established by Navy Secretary, as required by law (70A Stat. 457). Jurisdiction transferred to Energy Department by act of Aug. 4, 1977 (91 Stat. 581).

Naval Weapons, Bureau of Established by act of Aug. 18, 1959 (73 Stat. 395), to replace *Bureau of Ordnance and Aeronautics.* Abolished by Defense Department reorg. order of Mar. 9, 1966, and functions transferred to Navy Secretary (31 FR 7188), effective May 1, 1966.

Navigation, Bureau of Created by act of July 5, 1884 (23 Stat. 118), as special service under

Treasury Department. Transferred to *Department of Commerce and Labor* by act of Feb. 4, 1903 (32 Stat. 825). Consolidated with *Bureau of Navigation and Steamboat Inspection* by act of June 30, 1932 (47 Stat. 415).

Navigation, Bureau of Renamed Bureau of Naval Personnel by act of May 13, 1942 (56 Stat. 276).

Navigation and Steamboat Inspection, Bureau of Renamed *Bureau of Marine Inspection and Navigation* by act of May 27, 1936 (49 Stat. 1380). Functions transferred to Bureau of Customs, Treasury Department, and U.S. Coast Guard by EO 9083 of Feb. 28, 1942. Transfer made permanent and *Bureau* abolished by Reorg. Plan. No. 3 of 1946, effective July 16, 1946.

Navy Commissioners, Board of Established by act of Feb. 7, 1815 (3 Stat. 202). Abolished by act of Aug. 31, 1842 (5 Stat. 579).

Navy Department Defense housing functions transferred to *Federal Public Housing Authority, National Housing Agency,* by EO 9070 of Feb. 24, 1942.

Neighborhoods, National Commission on Established by act of Apr. 30, 1977 (91 Stat. 56). Terminated May 4, 1979, pursuant to terms of act.

Neighborhoods, Voluntary Associations and Consumer Protection, Office of Abolished and certain functions transferred to Office of the Assistant Secretary for Housing—Federal Housing Commissioner and Office of the Assistant Secretary for Community Planning and Development. Primary enabling legislation, act of Oct. 31, 1978 (92 Stat. 2119), repealed by act of Aug. 13, 1981 (95 Stat. 398). Abolishment of office and transfer of functions carried out by Housing and Urban Development Secretarial order.

New England River Basins Commission Established by EO 11371 of Sept. 6, 1967. Terminated by EO 12319 of Sept. 9, 1981.

Nicaro Project Responsibility for management of Nicaro nickel producing facilities in Oriente Province, Cuba, transferred from *Office of Special Assistant to the Administrator (Nicaro Project)* to *Defense Materials Service* by General Services Administrator, effective July 7, 1959. Facilities expropriated by Cuban Government and nationalized Oct. 26, 1960.

Northern Mariana Islands Commission on Federal Laws Created by joint resolution of Mar. 24, 1976 (90 Stat. 263). Terminated with submission of final report in August 1985.

Nutrition Division Functions transferred from *Health, Education, and Welfare Department* to Agriculture Department by EO 9310 of Mar. 3, 1943.

Ocean Mining Administration Established by Interior Secretarial Order 2971 of Feb. 24, 1975. Abolished by Department Manual Release 2273 of June 13, 1980.

Oceanography, Interagency Committee on Established by *Federal Council for Science and Technology* pursuant to EO 10807 of Mar. 13, 1959. Absorbed by *National Council on Marine Resources and Engineering Development* pursuant to Vice Presidential letter of July 21, 1967.

Office. *See also other part of title*

Office Space, President's Advisory Commission on Presidential Established by act of Aug. 3, 1956 (70 Stat. 979). Terminated June 30, 1957, by act of Jan. 25, 1957 (71 Stat. 4).

Official Register Function of preparing *Official Register* vested in Director of the Census by act of Mar. 3, 1925 (43 Stat. 1105). Function transferred to *U.S. Civil Service Commission* by EO 6166 of June 10, 1933. Yearly compilation and publication required by act of Aug. 28, 1935 (49 Stat. 956). Act repealed by act of July 12, 1960 (74 Stat. 427), and last *Register* published in 1959.

Ohio River Basin Commission Established by EO 11578 of Jan. 13, 1971. Terminated by EO 12319 of Sept. 9, 1981.

Oil and Gas, Office of Established by Interior Secretary May 6, 1946, in response to Presidential letter of May 3, 1946. Transferred to *Federal Energy Administration* by act of May 7, 1974 (88 Stat. 100).

Oil Import Administration Established in Interior Department by Proc. 3279 of Mar. 10, 1959. Merged into *Office of Oil and Gas* Oct. 22, 1971.

Oil Import Appeals Board Established by Commerce Secretary Mar. 13, 1959, and made part of Office of Hearings and Appeals Dec. 23, 1971.

Operations Advisory Group Established by EO 11905 of Feb. 18, 1976. Abolished by Presidential Directive No. 2 of Jan. 20, 1977.

Operations Coordinating Board Established by EO 10483 of Sept. 2, 1953, which was superseded by EO 10700 of Feb. 25, 1957. EO 10700 revoked by EO 10920 of Feb. 18, 1961, and *Board* terminated.

Ordnance, Bureau of Established in Navy Department by act of July 5, 1862 (12 Stat. 510), replacing *Bureau of Ordnance and Hydrography.* Abolished by act of Aug. 18, 1959 (73 Stat. 395), and functions transferred to *Bureau of Naval Weapons.*

Ordnance and Hydrography, Bureau of Established in Navy Department by act of Aug. 31, 1842 (5 Stat. 579). Replaced under act of July 5, 1862 (12 Stat. 510), by *Bureau of Ordnance* and *Bureau of Navigation.*

Organization, President's Advisory Committee on Government Established by EO 10432 of Jan. 24, 1953. Abolished by EO 10917 of Feb. 10, 1961, and functions transferred to *Bureau of the Budget* for termination.

Organizations Staff, International Functions merged with *Foreign Agricultural Service* by Agriculture Secretary's memorandum of Dec. 7, 1973, effective Feb. 3, 1974.

Overseas Private Investment Corporation Transferred as separate agency to U.S. International Development Cooperation Agency by Reorg. Plan No. 2 of 1979, effective Oct. 1, 1979.

Pacific Northwest River Basins Commission Established by EO 11331 of Mar. 6, 1967. Terminated by EO 12319 of Sept. 9, 1981.

Packers and Stockyards Administration Established by Agriculture Secretary's Memorandum 1613, Supplement 1, of May 8, 1967. Consolidated into Agricultural Marketing Service by Secretary's Memorandum 1927 of Jan. 15, 1978.

Panama Canal Operation of piers at Atlantic and Pacific terminals transferred to Panama Railroad by EO 7021 of Apr. 19, 1935. Panama Canal reestablished as *Canal Zone Government* by act of Sept. 26, 1950 (64 Stat. 1038).

Panama Canal Company Established by act of June 29, 1948 (62 Stat. 1076). Abolished and superseded by Panama Canal Commission (93 Stat. 454).

Panama Railroad Company Incorporated Apr. 7, 1849, by New York State Legislature. Operated under private control until 1881, when original *French Canal Company* acquired most of its stock. *Company* and its successor, *New Panama Canal Company,* operated railroad as common carrier and also as adjunct in attempts to construct canal. In 1904 their shares of stock in *Panama Railroad Company* passed to ownership of U.S. as part of assets of *New Panama Canal Company* purchased under act of June 28, 1902 (34 Stat. 481). Remaining shares purchased from private owners in 1905. *Panama Railroad Company* reincorporated by act of June 29, 1948 (62 Stat. 1075) pursuant to requirements of act of Dec. 6, 1945 (59 Stat. 597). Reestablished as *Panama Canal Company* by act of Sept. 26, 1950 (64 Stat. 1038). Army Secretary directed to discontinue commercial operations of *Company* by Presidential letter of Mar. 29, 1961.

Paperwork, Commission on Federal Established by act of Dec. 27, 1974 (88 Stat. 1789). Terminated January 1978 pursuant to terms of act.

Park Service, National Functions in District of Columbia relating to space assignment, site selection for public buildings, and determination of priority in construction transferred to *Public Buildings Administration, Federal Works Agency,* under Reorg. Plan No. I of 1939, effective July 1, 1939.

Park Trust Fund Board, National Established by act of July 10, 1935 (49 Stat. 477). Terminated by act of Dec. 18, 1967 (81 Stat. 656), and functions transferred to National Park Foundation.

Parks, Buildings, and Reservations, Office of National Established in Interior Department by EO 6166 of June 10, 1933. Renamed National Park Service by act of Mar. 2, 1934 (48 Stat. 362).

Parole, Board of Established by act of June 25, 1948 (62 Stat. 854). Abolished by act of Mar. 15, 1976 (90 Stat. 219), and functions transferred to U.S. Parole Commission.

Patent Office Provisions of first patent act administered by State Department, with authority for granting patents vested in board comprising Secretaries of State and *War* and Attorney General. Board abolished, authority transferred to Secretary of State, and registration system established by act of Feb. 21, 1793 (1 Stat. 318). *Office* made bureau in State Department in October 1802, headed by *Superintendent of Patents. Office* reorganized in 1836 by act of June 4, 1836 (5 Stat. 117) under *Commissioner of Patents. Office* transferred to Interior Department in 1849. *Office* transferred to Commerce Department by EO 4175 of Mar. 17, 1925.

Patents Board, Government Established by EO 10096 of Jan. 23, 1950. Abolished by EO 10930 of Mar. 24, 1961, and functions transferred to Commerce Secretary.

Pay Board Established by EO 11627 of Oct. 15, 1971. Abolished by EO 11695 of Jan. 11, 1973.

Peace Corps Established in State Department by EO 10924 of Mar. 1, 1961, and continued by act of Sept. 22, 1961 (75 Stat. 612), and EO 11041 of Aug. 6, 1962. Functions transferred to ACTION by Reorg. Plan No. 1 of 1971, effective July 1, 1971. Made independent agency in executive branch by act of Dec. 29, 1981 (95 Stat. 1540).

Pennsylvania Avenue, Temporary Commission on Established by EO 11210 of Mar. 25, 1956. Inactive as of Nov. 15, 1969, through lack of funding.

Pension and Welfare Benefit Programs, Office of *See* **Labor-Management Services Administration**

Pensions, Commissioner of Provided for by act of Mar. 2, 1833 (4 Stat. 668). Continued by act of Mar. 3, 1835 (4 Stat. 779), and other acts as *Office of the Commissioner of Pensions.* Transferred to Interior Department as bureau by act of Mar. 3, 1849 (9 Stat. 395). *Bureau* consolidated with other bureaus and agencies into Veterans Administration by EO 5398 of July 21, 1930.

Pensions, Office of the Commissioner of *See* **Commissioner of Pensions**

Perry's Victory Memorial Commission Created by act of Mar. 3, 1919 (40 Stat. 1322). Administration of Memorial transferred to National Park Service by act of June 2, 1936 (49 Stat. 1393). Commission terminated by terms of act and membership reconstituted as advisory board to Interior Secretary.

Personal Property, Office of Renamed Office of Federal Supply and Services by General Services Administration order of Jan. 22, 1983.

Personnel, National Roster of Scientific and Specialized Established by *National Resources Planning Board* pursuant to Presidential letter of June 18, 1940, to Treasury Secretary. After Aug. 15, 1940, administered jointly by *Board* and *U.S. Civil Service Commission.* Transferred to *War Manpower Commission* by EO 9139 of Apr. 18, 1942. Transferred to Labor Department by EO 9617 of Sept. 19, 1945. Transferred with *Bureau of*

Employment Security to *Federal Security Agency* by act of June 16, 1948 (62 Stat. 443). Transferred to Labor Department by Reorg. Plan No. 2 of 1949, effective Aug. 20, 1949, and became inactive. Roster functions transferred to National Science Foundation by act of May 10, 1950 (64 Stat. 154). Reactivated in 1950 as *National Scientific Register* by *Office of Education, Federal Security Agency*, through *National Security Resources Board* grant of funds, and continued by National Science Foundation funds until December 1952, when *Register* integrated into Foundation's National Register of Scientific and Technical Personnel project in Division of Scientific Personnel and Education.

Personnel Administration, Council of Established by EO 7916 of June 24, 1938, effective Feb. 1, 1939. Made unit in *U.S. Civil Service Commission* by EO 8467 of July 1, 1940. Renamed *Federal Personnel Council* by EO 9830 of Feb. 24, 1947. Abolished by act of July 31, 1953 (67 Stat. 300), and personnel and records transferred to *Office of Executive Director, U.S. Civil Service Commission.*

Personnel Council, Federal *See* **Personnel Administration, Council of**

Personnel Interchange, President's Commission on Established by EO 11451 of Jan. 19, 1969. Continued by EO 12136 of May 15, 1979, and renamed *President's Commission on Executive Exchange.* Continued by EO 12493 of Dec. 5, 1984. Abolished by EO 12760 of May 2, 1991.

Personnel Management, Liaison Office for Established by EO 8248 of Sept. 8, 1939. Abolished by EO 10452 of May 1, 1953, and functions transferred to *U.S. Civil Service Commission.*

Petroleum Administration for Defense Established under act of Sept. 8, 1950 (64 Stat. 798) by Interior Secretary's Order 2591 of Oct. 3, 1950, pursuant to EO 10161 of Sept. 9, 1950. Continued by Order 2614 of Jan. 25, 1951, pursuant to EO 10200 of Jan. 3, 1951, and DPA Delegation 1 of Jan. 24, 1951. Abolished by Secretary's Order 2755 of Apr. 23, 1954.

Petroleum Administration for War *See* **Petroleum Coordinator for War, Office of**

Petroleum Administrative Board Established Sept. 11, 1933, by Interior Secretary. Terminated Mar. 31, 1936, by EO 7076 of June 15, 1935. Interior Secretary authorized to execute functions vested in President by act of Feb. 22, 1935 (49 Stat. 30) by EO 7756 of Dec. 1, 1937. Secretary also authorized to establish *Petroleum Conservation Division* to assist in administering act. Records of *Petroleum Administrative Board* and *Petroleum Labor Policy Board* housed with *Petroleum Conservation Division, Office of Oil and Gas,* acting as custodian for Interior Secretary.

Petroleum Coordinator for War, Office of Interior Secretary designated *Petroleum Coordinator for National Defense* by Presidential letter of May 28, 1941, and approved *Petroleum Coordinator for War* by Presidential letter of Apr. 20, 1942. *Office* abolished by EO 9276 of Dec. 2, 1942, and functions transferred to *Petroleum Administration for War,* established by same EO. *Administration* terminated by EO 9718 of May 3, 1946.

Petroleum Labor Policy Board Established by Interior Secretary, as Administrator of Code of Fair Competition for Petroleum Industry, on recommendation of Planning and Coordination Committee Oct. 10, 1933. Reorganized by Secretary Dec. 19, 1933, and reorganization confirmed by order of Mar. 8, 1935. Terminated Mar. 31, 1936, when *Petroleum Administrative Board* abolished by EO 7076 of June 15, 1935.

Petroleum Reserves Corporation Established June 30, 1943, by *Reconstruction Finance Corporation.* Transferred to *Office of Economic Warfare* by EO 9360 of July 15, 1943. *Office* consolidated into *Foreign Economic Administration* by EO 9380 of Sept. 25, 1943. Functions transferred to *Reconstruction Finance Corporation* by EO 9630 of Sept. 27, 1945. *RFC's* charter amended Nov. 9, 1945, to change name to *War Assets Corporation. Corporation* designated by *Surplus Property Administrator* as disposal agency for all types of property for which *Reconstruction Finance Corporation* formerly disposal agency. Domestic surplus property functions of *Corporation* transferred to *War Assets Administration* by EO 9689 of Jan. 31, 1946. *Reconstruction Finance Corporation* Board of Directors ordered by President to dissolve *War Assets Corporation* as soon after Mar. 25, 1946, as practicable.

Philippine Alien Property Administration Established in *Office for Emergency Management* by EO 9789 of Oct. 14, 1946. Abolished by EO 10254 of June 15, 1951, and functions transferred to Justice Department.

Philippine War Damage Commission Established by act of Apr. 30, 1946 (60 Stat. 128). Terminated Mar. 31, 1951, by act of Sept. 6, 1950 (64 Stat. 712).

Physical Fitness, Committee on Established in *Office of Federal Security Administrator* by EO 9338 of Apr. 29, 1943. Terminated June 30, 1945.

Physical Fitness, President's Council on Established by EO 11074 of Jan. 8, 1963. Renamed President's Council on Physical Fitness and Sports by EO 11398 of Mar. 4, 1968.

Planning Board, National Established by *Administrator of Public Works* July 30, 1933. Terminated by EO 6777 of June 30, 1934.

Plant Industry, Bureau of Established by act of Mar. 2, 1902 (31 Stat. 922). Soil fertility and soil microbiology work of *Bureau of Chemistry and Soils* transferred to *Bureau* by act of May 17, 1935. Soil chemistry and physics and soil survey work of *Bureau of Chemistry and Soils* transferred to *Bureau* by Secretary's Memorandum 784 of Oct. 6, 1938. In February 1943 engineering research of *Bureau of Agricultural Chemistry and Engineering* transferred to *Bureau of Plant Industry, Soils, and Agricultural Engineering* by Research Administration Memorandum 5 issued pursuant to EO 9069 of Feb. 23, 1942, and in conformity with Secretary's

Memorandums 960 and 986. Functions transferred to *Agricultural Research Service* by Secretary's Memorandum 1320, supp. 4, of Nov. 2, 1953.

Plant Industry, Soils, and Agricultural Engineering, Bureau of *See* **Plant Industry, Bureau of**

Plant Quarantine, Bureau of *See* **Entomology and Plant Quarantine, Bureau of**

Post Office Department *See* **Postal Service**

Postal Savings System Established by act of June 25, 1910 (36 Stat. 814). System closed by act of Mar. 28, 1966 (80 Stat. 92).

Postal Service Created July 26, 1775, by Continental Congress. Temporarily established by Congress by act of Sept. 22, 1789 (1 Stat. 70), and continued by subsequent acts. *Post Office Department* made executive department under act of June 8, 1872 (17 Stat. 283). Offices of First, Second, Third, and Fourth Assistant Postmasters General abolished and Deputy Postmaster General and four Assistant Postmasters General established by Reorg. Plan No. 3 of 1949, effective Aug. 20, 1949. Reorganized as U.S. Postal Service in executive branch by act of Aug. 12, 1970 (84 Stat. 719), effective July 1, 1971.

Power Administration, Southeastern Established by Interior Secretary in 1943 to carry out functions under act of Dec. 22, 1944 (58 Stat. 890). Transferred to Energy Department by act of Aug. 4, 1977 (91 Stat. 578).

Power Administration, Southwestern Established by Interior Secretary in 1943 to carry out functions under act of Dec. 22, 1944 (58 Stat. 890). Transferred to Energy Department by act of Aug. 4, 1977 (91 Stat. 578).

Power Commission, Federal Established by act of June 10, 1920 (41 Stat. 1063). Terminated by act of Aug. 4, 1977 (91 Stat. 578), and functions transferred to Energy Department.

Preparedness, Office of Renamed *Federal Preparedness Agency* by General Services Administrator's order of June 26, 1975.

Preparedness Agency, Federal Functions transferred from General Services Administration to Federal Emergency Management Agency by EO 12148 of July 20, 1979.

Presidential. *See other part of title.*

President's. *See other part of title*

Press Intelligence, Division of Established in August 1933. Made division of *National Emergency Council* July 10, 1935. Continued in *Office of Government Reports* by Reorg. Plan No. II of 1939, effective July 1, 1939. Transferred to *Office of War Information* by EO 9182 of June 13, 1942, functioning in *Bureau of Special Services. Office* abolished by EO 9608 of Aug. 31, 1945, and *Bureau* transferred to *Bureau of the Budget.* Upon reestablishment of *Office of Government Reports,* by EO 9809 of Dec. 12, 1946, *Division of Press Intelligence* made unit of *Office.*

Price Administration, Office of Established by EO 8734 of Apr. 11, 1941, combining *Price Division* and *Consumer Division* of *National Defense Advisory Commission.* Renamed *Office of Price Administration* by EO 8875 of Aug. 28, 1941, which transferred *Civilian Allocation Division* to *Office of Production Management.* Consolidated with other agencies into *Office of Temporary Controls* by EO 9809 of Dec. 12, 1946, except *Financial Reporting Division,* transferred to Federal Trade Commission.

Price Commission Established by EO 11627 of Oct. 15, 1971. Abolished by EO 11695 of Jan. 11, 1973.

Price Decontrol Board Established by act of July 25, 1946 (60 Stat. 669). Effective period of act of Jan. 30, 1942 (56 Stat. 23), extended to June 30, 1947, by joint resolution of June 25, 1946 (60 Stat. 664).

Price Stability for Economic Growth, Cabinet Committee on Established by Presidential letter of Jan. 28, 1959. Abolished by Presidential direction Mar. 12, 1961.

Price Stabilization, Office of Established by General Order 2 of *Economic Stabilization Administrator* Jan. 24, 1951. *Director of Price Stabilization* provided for in EO 10161 of Sept. 9, 1950. Terminated Apr. 30, 1953, by EO 10434 of Feb. 6, 1953, and provisions of acts of June 30, 1952 (66 Stat. 296) and June 30, 1953 (67 Stat. 131).

Prices and Costs, Committee on Government Activities Affecting Established by EO 10802 of Jan. 23, 1959. Abolished by EO 10928 of Mar. 23, 1961.

Priorities Board Established by order of *Council of National Defense,* approved Oct. 18, 1940, and by EO 8572 of Oct. 21, 1940. EO 8572 revoked by EO 8629 of Jan. 7, 1941.

Prison Industries, Inc., Federal Established by EO 6917 of Dec. 11, 1934. Transferred to Justice Department by Reorg. Plan No. II of 1939, effective July 1, 1939.

Prison Industries Reorganization Administration Functioned from Sept. 26, 1935, to Sept. 30, 1940, under authority of act of Apr. 8, 1935 (49 Stat. 115), and of EOs 7194 of Sept. 26, 1935, 7202 of Sept. 28, 1935, and 7649 of June 29, 1937. Terminated through lack of funding.

Private Sector Programs, Office of Functions transferred to the Office of Citizen Exchanges within the Bureau of Educational and Cultural Affairs, USIA, by the act of Feb. 16, 1990 (104 Stat. 56).

Processing tax *Agricultural Adjustment Administration's* function of collecting taxes declared unconstitutional by U.S. Supreme Court Jan. 6, 1936. Functions under acts of June 28, 1934 (48 Stat. 1275), Apr. 21, 1934 (48 Stat. 598), and Aug. 24, 1935 (49 Stat. 750) discontinued by repeal of these laws by act of Feb. 10, 1936 (49 Stat. 1106).

Processing Tax Board of Review Established in Treasury Department by act of June 22, (49 Stat. 1652). Abolished by act of Oct. 21, 1942 (56 Stat. 967).

Proclamations *See* **State Department**

Procurement, Commission on Government Established by act of Nov. 26, 1969 (83 Stat. 269). Terminated Apr. 30, 1973, through expiration of statutory authority.

Procurement and Assignment Service Established by President Oct. 30, 1941. Transferred from *Office of Defense Health and Welfare Services* to *War Manpower Commission* by EO 9139 of Apr. 18, 1942. Transferred to *Federal Security Agency* by EO 9617 of Sept. 19, 1945, which terminated *Commission.*

Procurement Division Established in Treasury Department by EO 6166 of June 10, 1933. Renamed *Bureau of Federal Supply* by Treasury Department order 73 of Nov. 19, 1946, effective Jan. 1, 1947. Transferred to General Services Administration as *Federal Supply Service* by act of June 30, 1949 (63 Stat. 380).

Product Standards Policy, Office of Formerly separate operating unit under Assistant Secretary for Productivity, Technology and Innovation, Commerce Department. Transferred to National Bureau of Standards by departmental reorganization order, effective Apr. 27, 1982.

Production Areas, Committee for Congested Established in Executive Office of the President by EO 9327 of Apr. 7, 1943. Terminated Dec. 31, 1944, by act of June 28, 1944 (58 Stat. 535).

Production Authority, National Established in Commerce Department Sept. 11, 1950, by EOs 10161 of Sept. 9, 1950, 10193 of Dec. 16, 1950, and 10200 of Jan. 3, 1951. Abolished by Commerce Secretary order of Oct. 1, 1953, and functions merged into *Business and Defense Services Administration.*

Production Management, Office of Established in *Office for Emergency Management* by EO 8629 of Jan. 7, 1941. Abolished by EO 9040 of Jan. 24, 1942, and personnel and property transferred to *War Production Board.*

Production and Marketing Administration Established by Agriculture Secretary's Memorandum 1118 of Aug. 18, 1945. Functions transferred under Department reorganization by Secretary's Memorandum 1320, supp. 4 of Nov. 2, 1953.

Productivity Council, National Established by EO 12089 of Oct. 23, 1978. EO 12089 revoked by EO 12379 of Aug. 17, 1982.

Programs, Bureau of International Established by Commerce Secretary Aug. 8, 1961, by Departmental Orders 173 and 174. Abolished by Departmental Order 182 of Feb. 1, 1963, which established *Bureau of International Commerce.* Functions transferred to *Domestic and International Business Administration,* effective Nov. 17, 1972.

Prohibition, Bureau of Established by act of May 27, 1930 (46 Stat. 427). Investigative functions consolidated with functions of *Bureau of Investigation* into *Division of Investigation,* Justice Department, by EO 6166 of June 10, 1933, which set as effective date Mar. 2, 1934, or such later date as fixed by President. All other functions performed by *Bureau of Prohibition* ordered transferred to such division in Justice Department as deemed desirable by Attorney General.

Property, Office of Surplus Established in *Procurement Division,* Treasury Department, by EO 9425 of Feb. 19, 1944, and act of Oct. 3, 1944 (58 Stat. 765), under general direction of *Surplus Property Board* established by same legislation. Transferred to Commerce Department by EO 9541 of Apr. 19, 1945. Terminated by EO 9643 of Oct. 19, 1945, and activities and personnel transferred to *Reconstruction Finance Corporation.*

Property Administration, Surplus *See* **War Property Administration, Surplus**

Property Board, Surplus *See* **War Property Administration, Surplus**

Property Council, Federal Established by EO 11724 of June 25, 1973, and reconstituted by EO 11954 of Jan. 7, 1977. Terminated by EO 12030 of Dec. 15, 1977.

Property Management and Disposal Service *See* **Emergency Procurement Service**

Property Office, Surplus Established in *Division of Territories and Island Possessions,* Interior Department, under Regulation 1 of *Surplus Property Board,* Apr. 2, 1945. Transferred to *War Assets Administration* by EO 9828 of Feb. 21, 1947.

Property Review Board Established by EO 12348 of Feb. 25, 1982. EO 12348 revoked by EO 12512 of Apr. 29, 1985.

Provisions and Clothing, Bureau of Established by acts of Aug. 31, 1842 (5 Stat. 579), and July 5, 1862 (12 Stat. 510). Designated *Bureau of Supplies and Accounts* by act of July 19, 1892 (27 Stat. 243). Abolished by Defense Department reorg. order of Mar. 9, 1966, and functions transferred to Navy Secretary (31 FR 7188).

Public. *See other part of title*

Publications Commission, National Historical Renamed National Historical Publications and Records Commission by act of Dec. 22, 1974 (88 Stat. 1734).

Puerto Rican Hurricane Relief Commission Established by act of Dec. 21, 1928 (45 Stat. 1067). No loans made after June 30, 1934, and *Commission* abolished June 3, 1935, by Public Resolution 22 (49 Stat. 320). Functions transferred to *Division of Territories and Island Possessions,* Interior Department. After June 30, 1946, collection work performed in *Puerto Rico Reconstruction Administration.* Following termination of *Administration,* remaining collection functions transferred to Agriculture Secretary by act of July 11, 1956 (70 Stat. 525).

Puerto Rico, U.S.-Puerto Rico Commission on the Status of Established by act of Feb. 20, 1964 (78 Stat. 17). Terminated by terms of act.

Puerto Rico Reconstruction Administration Established in Interior Department by EO 7057 of May 28, 1935. Terminated Feb. 15, 1955, by act of Aug. 15, 1953 (67 Stat. 584).

Radiation Biology Laboratory *See* **Radiation and Organisms, Division of**

Radiation Council, Federal Established by EO 10831 of Aug. 14, 1959, and act of Sept. 23, 1959 (73 Stat. 688). Abolished by Reorg. Plan No. 3 of 1970, effective Dec. 2, 1970, and functions transferred to Environmental Protection Agency.

Radiation and Organisms, Division of Established by Secretarial order of May 1, 1929, as part of Smithsonian Astrophysical Observatory. Renamed *Radiation Biology Laboratory* by Secretarial order of Feb. 16, 1965. Merged with *Chesapeake Center for Environmental Studies* by Secretarial order of July 1, 1983, to form Smithsonian Environmental Research Center.

Radio Commission, Federal Established by act of Feb. 23, 1927 (44 Stat. 1162). Abolished by act of June 19, 1934 (48 Stat. 1102), and functions transferred to Federal Communications Commission.

Radio Division Established by *National Emergency Council* July 1, 1938. Transferred to *Office of Education, Federal Security Agency,* by Reorg. Plan No. II of 1939, effective July 1, 1939. Terminated June 30, 1940.

Radio Propagation Laboratory, Central Transferred from National Bureau of Standards to *Environmental Science Services Administration* by Commerce Department Order 2-A, effective July 13, 1965.

Radiological Health, National Center for Devices and Renamed Center for Devices and Radiological Health by Food and Drug Administration notice of Mar. 9, 1984 (49 FR 10166).

Rail Public Counsel, Office of Established by act of Feb. 5, 1976 (90 Stat. 51). Terminated Dec. 1, 1979, through lack of funding.

Railroad Administration, U.S. *See* **Railroads, Director General of**

Railroad and Airline Wage Board Established by *Economic Stabilization Administrator's* General Order 7 of Sept. 27, 1951, pursuant to act of Sept. 8, 1950 (64 Stat. 816). Terminated Apr. 30, 1953, by EO 10434 of Feb. 6, 1953, and acts of June 30, 1952 (66 Stat. 296), and June 30, 1953 (67 Stat. 131).

Railroads, Director General of Established under authority of act of Aug. 29, 1916 (39 Stat. 645). Organization of *U.S. Railroad Administration* announced Feb. 9, 1918. Office abolished by Reorg. Plan No. II of 1939, effective July 1, 1939, and functions transferred to Treasury Secretary.

Railway Association, U.S. Established by act of Jan. 2, 1974 (87 Stat. 985). Terminated Apr. 1, 1987, by act of Oct. 21, 1986 (100 Stat. 1906).

Railway Labor Panel, National Established by EO 9172 of May 22, 1942. EO 9172 revoked by EO 9883 of Aug. 11, 1947.

Real Estate Board, Federal Established by EO 8034 of Jan. 14, 1939. Abolished by EO 10287 of Sept. 6, 1951.

Reclamation, Bureau of *See* **Reclamation Service**

Reclamation Service Established July 1902 in Geological Survey by Interior Secretary, pursuant to act of June 17, 1902 (32 Stat. 388). Separated from Survey in 1907 and renamed *Bureau of Reclamation* June 1923. Power marketing functions transferred to Energy Department by act of Aug. 4, 1977 (91 Stat. 578). *Bureau* renamed *Water and Power Resources Service* by Secretarial Order 3042 of Nov. 6, 1979. Renamed Bureau of Reclamation by Secretarial Order 3064 of May 18, 1981.

Reconciliation Service Established by Director of Selective Service pursuant to EO 11804 of Sept. 16, 1974. Program terminated Apr. 2, 1980.

Reconstruction Finance Corporation Established Feb. 2, 1932, by act of Jan. 22, 1932 (47 Stat. 5). Grouped with other agencies to form *Federal Loan Agency* by Reorg. Plan No. I of 1939, effective July 1, 1939. Transferred to Commerce Department by EO 9071 of Feb. 24, 1942. Returned to *Federal Loan Agency* by act of Feb. 24, 1945 (59 Stat. 5). *Agency* abolished by act of June 30, 1947 (61 Stat. 202), and functions assumed by *Corporation.* Functions relating to financing houses or site improvements, authorized by act of Aug. 10, 1948 (61 Stat. 1275), transferred to *Housing and Home Finance Agency* by Reorg. Plan No. 23 of 1950, effective July 10, 1950. *Corporation* Board of Directors, established by act of Jan. 22, 1932 (47 Stat. 5), abolished by Reorg. Plan No. 1 of 1951, effective May 1, 1951, and functions transferred to Administrator and *Loan Policy Board* established by same plan, effective Apr. 30, 1951. Act of July 30, 1953 (67 Stat. 230), provided for *RFC* succession until June 30, 1954, and for termination of its lending powers Sept. 28, 1953. Certain functions assigned to appropriate agencies for liquidation by Reorg. Plan No. 2 of 1954, effective July 1, 1954. *Corporation* abolished by Reorg. Plan No. 1 of 1957, effective June 30, 1957, and functions transferred to *Housing and Home Finance Agency,* General Services Administration, Small Business Administration, and Treasury Department.

Records and Information Management, Office of Functions transferred from *National Archives and Records Service* to *Automated Data and Telecommunications Service* by General Services Administrator's decision, effective Jan. 10, 1982, regionally and Apr. 1, 1982, in Washington, DC.

Recovery Administration, Advisory Council, National Established by EO 7075 of June 15, 1935. Transferred to Commerce Department by EO 7252 of Dec. 21, 1935, and functions ordered terminated not later than Apr. 1, 1936, by same order. *Committee of Industrial Analysis* created by EO 7323 of Mar. 21, 1936, to complete work of *Council.*

Recovery Administration, National Established by President pursuant to act of June 16, 1933 (48 Stat. 194). Provisions of title I of act repealed by Public Resolution 26 of June 14, 1935 (49 Stat. 375), and extension of *Administration* in skeletonized form authorized until Apr. 1, 1936. *Office of Administrator, National Recovery Administration,* created by EO 7075 of June 15, 1935. *Administration* terminated by EO 7252 of Dec. 21, 1935, which transferred *Division of Review, Division of Business Corporation,* and *Advisory Council* to Commerce Department for termination of functions by Apr. 1, 1936. *Consumers' Division* transferred to Labor Department by same order.

Recovery Review Board, National Established by EO 6632 of Mar. 7, 1934. Abolished by EO 6771 of June 30, 1934.

Recreation, Bureau of Outdoor Established in Interior Department by act of May 28, 1963 (77 Stat. 49). Terminated by Secretary's order of Jan. 25, 1978, and functions assumed by *Heritage Conservation and Recreation Service.*

Recreation and Natural Beauty, Citizens' Advisory Committee on Established by EO 11278 of May 4, 1966. Terminated by EO 11472 of May 29, 1969.

Recreation and Natural Beauty, President's Council on Established by EO 11278 of May 4, 1966. Terminated by EO 11472 of May 29, 1969.

Recreation Resources Review Commission, Outdoor Established by act of June 28, 1958 (72 Stat. 238). Final report submitted to President January 1962 and terminated Sept. 1, 1962.

Regional Action Planning Commissions Authorized by act of Aug. 26, 1965 (79 Stat. 552). Federal role abolished through repeal by act of Aug. 13, 1981 (95 Stat. 766). At time of repeal, eight commissions—Coastal Plains, Four Corners, New England, Old West Ozarks, Pacific Northwest, Southwest Border, Southwest Border Region, and Upper Great Lakes—affected.

Regional Councils, Federal Established by EO 12314 of July 22, 1981. Abolished by EO 12407 of Feb. 22, 1983.

Regional Operations, Executive Director of Established in Food and Drug Administration by *Health, Education, and Welfare Secretary's* order of May 20, 1971. Merged into Office of Regulatory Affairs by Health and Human Services Secretary's order of Nov. 5, 1984.

Regulatory Council, U.S. Disbanded by Vice Presidential memorandum of Mar. 25, 1981. Certain functions continued in Regulatory Information Service Center.

Regulatory Relief, Presidential Task Force on Establishment announced in President's remarks Jan. 22, 1981. Disbanded and functions transferred to Office of Management and Budget in August 1983.

Rehabilitation Services Administration Functions transferred from *Health, Education, and Welfare Department* to Office of Special Education and Rehabilitative Services, Education Department, by act of Oct. 17, 1979 (93 Stat. 678), effective May 4, 1980.

Relief Corporation, Federal Surplus Organized under powers granted to President by act of June 16, 1933 (48 Stat. 195). Charter granted by State of Delaware Oct. 4, 1933, and amended Nov. 18, 1935, changing name to *Federal Surplus Commodities Corporation* and naming Agriculture Secretary, *Administrator of Agricultural Adjustment Administration,* and *Governor of Farm Credit Administration* as Board of Directors. Continued as agency under Agriculture Secretary by acts of June 28, 1937 (50 Stat. 323) and Feb. 16, 1938 (52 Stat. 38). Consolidated with *Division of Marketing and Marketing Agreements* into *Surplus Marketing Administration* by Reorg. Plan No. III of 1940, effective June 30, 1940. Merged into *Agricultural Marketing Administration* by EO 9069 of Feb. 23, 1942.

Relief and Rehabilitation Operations, Office of Foreign Established in State Department as announced by White House Nov. 21, 1942. Consolidated with *Foreign Economic Administration* by EO 9380 of Sept. 25, 1943.

Renegotiation Board Established by act of Mar. 23, 1951 (65 Stat. 7). Terminated Mar. 31, 1979, by act of Oct. 10, 1978 (92 Stat. 1043).

Rent Advisory Board Established by EO 11632 of Nov. 22, 1971. Abolished by EO 11695 of Jan. 11, 1973.

Rent Stabilization, Office of Established by General Order 9 of *Economic Stabilization Administrator* July 31, 1951, pursuant to act of June 30, 1947 (61 Stat. 193), and EOs 10161 of Sept. 9, 1950, and 10276 of July 31, 1951. Abolished by EO 10475 of July 31, 1953, and functions transferred to *Office of Defense Mobilization. Office of Research and Development* combined with *Office of Minerals Policy Development* in Interior Department May 21, 1976, under authority of Reorg. Plan No. 3 of 1950, to form *Office of Minerals Policy and Research Analysis.* Abolished Sept. 30, 1981, by Secretarial Order 3070 and functions transferred to Bureau of Mines.

Reports, Office of Government Established July 1, 1939, to perform functions of *National Emergency Council* abolished by Reorg. Plan No. II of 1939, effective July 1, 1939. Established as administrative unit of Executive Office of the President by EO 8248 of Sept. 8, 1939. Consolidated with *Office of War Information, Office for Emergency Management,* by EO 9182 of June 13, 1942. Reestablished in Executive Office of the President by EO 9809 of Dec. 12, 1946, which transferred to it functions of *Media Programming Division* and *Motion Picture Division, Office of War Mobilization and Reconversion,* and functions transferred from *Bureau* *of Special Services, Office of War Information,* to *Bureau of the Budget* by EO 9608 of Aug. 31, 1945. Subsequent to enactment of act of July 30, 1947 (61 Stat. 588), functions of *Office* restricted to advertising and motion picture liaison and operation of library. Terminated June 30, 1948.

Research, Office of University Transferred from *Office of Program Management and Administration,* Research and Special Programs Administration, to Office of Economics, Office of the Assistant Secretary for Policy and International Affairs, under authority of Transportation Department appropriation request for FY 1985, effective Oct. 1, 1984.

Research and Development Board Established in Defense Department by act of July 26, 1947 (61 Stat. 499). Abolished by Reorg. Plan No. 6 of 1953, effective June 30, 1953, and functions vested in Defense Secretary.

Research and Development Board, Joint Established June 6, 1946, by charter of Secretaries of *War* and Navy. Terminated on creation of *Research and Development Board* by act of July 26, 1947 (61 Stat. 506).

Research and Intelligence Service, Interim Established in State Department by EO 9621 of Sept. 20, 1945. Abolished Dec. 31, 1945, pursuant to terms of order.

Research Resources, Division of Established in National Institutes of Health, Health and Human Services Department, Renamed National Center for Research Resources by secretarial notice of Feb. 23, 1990 (55 FR 6455).

Research Service, Cooperative State Established by Agriculture Secretary's Memorandum 1462, supp. 1, of Aug. 31, 1961. Consolidated into *Science and Education Administration* by Secretary's order of Jan. 24, 1978. Reestablished as Cooperative State Research Service by Secretarial order of June 16, 1981.

Research and Service Division, Cooperative Functions transferred to Agriculture Secretary in *Farmer Cooperative Service* by act of Aug. 6, 1953 (67 Stat. 390).

Resettlement Administration Established by EO 7027 of Apr. 30, 1935. Functions transferred to Agriculture Department by EO 7530 of Dec. 31, 1936. Renamed *Farm Security Administration* by Secretary's Memorandum 732 of Sept. 1, 1937. Abolished by act of Aug. 14, 1946 (60 Stat. 1062).

Resources Board and Advisory Committee, National Established by EO 6777 of June 30, 1934. Abolished by EO 7065 of June 7, 1935, and functions transferred to *National Resources Committee.*

Resources Committee, National Established by EO 7065 of June 7, 1935. Abolished by Reorg. Plan No. I of 1939, effective July 1, 1939, and functions transferred to *National Resources Planning Board* in Executive Office of the President. *Board* terminated by act of June 26, 1943 (57 Stat. 169).

Resources Planning Board, National *See* **Resources Committee, National**

Retired Executives, Service Corps of Established in ACTION by act of Oct. 1, 1973 (87 Stat. 404). Transferred to Small Business Administration by EO 11871 of July 18, 1975.

Retraining and Reemployment Administration Established by EO 9427 of Feb. 24, 1944, and act of Oct. 3, 1944 (58 Stat. 788). Transferred from *Office of War Mobilization and Reconversion* to Labor Department by EO 9617 of Sept. 19, 1945. Terminated pursuant to terms of act.

Revenue Sharing, Office of Established by Treasury Secretary to administer programs authorized by acts of Oct. 20, 1972 (86 Stat. 919), and July 22, 1976 (90 Stat. 999). Transferred from Office of the Secretary to Assistant Secretary (Domestic Finance) by Treasury Department Order 242, Revision 1, of May 17, 1976.

Review, Division of Established in *National Recovery Administration* by EO 7075 of June 15, 1935. Transferred to Commerce Department by EO 7252 of Dec. 21, 1935, and functions terminated by Apr. 1, 1936. *Committee of Industrial Analysis* created by EO 7323 of Mar. 21, 1936, to complete work of *Division.*

RFC Mortgage Company Organized under laws of Maryland Mar. 14, 1935, pursuant to act of Jan. 22, 1932 (47 Stat. 5). Grouped with other agencies to form *Federal Loan Agency* by Reorg. Plan No. I of 1939, effective July 1, 1939. Transferred to Commerce Department by EO 9071 of Feb. 24, 1942. Returned to *Federal Loan Agency* by act of Feb. 24, 1945 (59 Stat. 5). Assets and liabilities transferred to *Reconstruction Finance Corporation* by act of June 30, 1947 (61 Stat. 207).

River Basins, Neches, Trinity, Brazos, Colorado, Guadalupe, San Antonio, Nueces, and San Jacinto, and Intervening Areas, U.S. Study Commission on Established by act of Aug. 28, 1958 (72 Stat. 1058). Terminated June 30, 1962.

River Basins, Savannah, Altamaha, Saint Marys, Apalachicola-Chattahoochee, and Perdido-Escambia, and Intervening Areas, U.S. Study Commission on Established by act of Aug. 28, 1958 (72 Stat. 1090). Terminated Dec. 23, 1962.

Road Inquiry, Office of Established by Agriculture Secretary under authority of act of Aug. 8, 1894 (28 Stat. 264). Federal aid for highways to be administered by Agriculture Secretary through *Office of Public Roads and Rural Engineering* authorized by act of July 11, 1916 (39 Stat. 355), known as *Bureau of Public Roads* after July 1918. Transferred to *Federal Works Agency* by Reorg. Plan No. I of 1939, effective July 1, 1939, and renamed *Public Roads Administration.* Transferred to General Services Administration as *Bureau of Public Roads* by act of June 30, 1949 (63 Stat. 380). Transferred to Commerce Department by Reorg. Plan No. 7 of 1949, effective Aug. 20, 1949. Transferred to Transportation Secretary by act of Oct. 15, 1966 (80

Stat. 931), and functions assigned to Federal Highway Administration.

Roads, Bureau of Public *See* **Road Inquiry, Office of**

Roads Administration, Public *See* **Road Inquiry, Office of**

Roads and Rural Engineering, Office of Public *See* **Road Inquiry, Office of**

Rock Creek and Potomac Parkway Commission Established by act of Mar. 14, 1913 (37 Stat. 885). Abolished by EO 6166 of June 10, 1933, and functions transferred to *Office of National Parks, Buildings, and Reservations,* Interior Department.

Roosevelt Centennial Commission, Theodore Established by joint resolution of July 28, 1955 (69 Stat. 383). Terminated Oct. 27, 1959, pursuant to terms of act.

Roosevelt Library, Franklin D. Functions assigned to National Park Service by Reorg. Plan No. 3 of 1946, effective July 16, 1946, transferred to General Services Administration by Reorg. Plan No. 1 of 1963, effective July 27, 1963.

Roosevelt Library, Trustees of the Franklin D. Established by joint resolution of July 18, 1939 (53 Stat. 1063). Transferred to General Services Administration by act of June 30, 1949 (63 Stat. 381). Abolished by act of Mar. 5, 1958 (72 Stat. 34), and Library operated by *National Archives and Records Service,* General Services Administration.

Rubber Development Corporation Establishment announced Feb. 20, 1943, by Commerce Secretary. Organized under laws of Delaware as subsidiary of *Reconstruction Finance Corporation.* Assumed all activities of *Rubber Reserve Company* relating to development of foreign rubber sources and procurement of rubber therefrom. Functions transferred to *Office of Economic Warfare* by EO 9361 of July 15, 1943. *Office* consolidated into *Foreign Economic Administration* by EO 9380 of Sept. 25, 1943. *Office* returned to *Reconstruction Finance Corporation* by EO 9630 of Sept. 27, 1945. Certificate of incorporation expired June 30, 1947.

Rubber Producing Facilities Disposal Commission Established by act of Aug. 7, 1953 (67 Stat. 408). Functions transferred to *Federal Facilities Corporation* by EO 10678 of Sept. 20, 1956.

Rubber Reserve Company Established June 28, 1940, under act of Jan. 22, 1932 (47 Stat. 5). Transferred from *Federal Loan Agency* to Commerce Department by EO 9071 of Feb. 24, 1942. Returned to *Federal Loan Agency* by act of Feb. 24, 1945 (59 Stat. 5). Dissolved by act of June 30, 1945 (59 Stat. 310), and functions transferred to *Reconstruction Finance Corporation.*

Rural Areas Development, Office of Established by Agriculture Secretary's memorandum in 1961 (revised Sept. 21, 1962). Renamed *Rural Community Development Service* by Secretary's Memorandum 1570 of Feb. 24, 1965.

Rural Community Development Service Established by Agriculture Secretary's Memorandum 1570 of Feb. 25, 1965, to supersede *Office of Rural Areas Development.* Abolished Feb. 2, 1970, by Secretary's Memorandum 1670 of Jan. 30, 1970, and functions transferred to other agencies in department.

Rural Development Committee *See* **Rural Development Program, Committee for**

Rural Development Policy, Office of Established initially as *Office of Rural Development Policy Management and Coordination,* Farmers Home Administration, by Agricultural Secretary's Memorandum 1020-3 of Oct. 26, 1981. Abolished 1986 through lack of funding.

Rural Development Program, Committee for Established by EO 10847 of Oct. 12, 1959. Abolished by EO 11122 of Oct. 16, 1963, which established *Rural Development Committee. Committee* superseded by EO 11307 of Sept. 30, 1966, and functions assumed by Agriculture Secretary.

Rural Development Service Established by Agriculture Secretarial order in 1973. Functions transferred to Office of Rural Development Coordination and Planning, Farmers Home Administration, by Secretarial order in 1978.

Rural Electrification Administration Established by EO 7037 of May 11, 1935. Functions transferred by EO 7458 of Sept. 26, 1936, to *Rural Electrification Administration* established by act of May 20, 1936 (49 Stat. 1363). Transferred to Agriculture Department by Reorg. Plan No. II of 1939, effective July 1, 1939.

Rural Rehabilitation Division Established April 1934 by act of May 12, 1933 (48 Stat. 55). Functions transferred to *Resettlement Administration* by *Federal Emergency Relief Administrator's* order of June 19, 1935.

Saint Elizabeths Hospital *See* **Government Hospital for the Insane**

Saint Lawrence Seaway Development Corporation Established by act of May 13, 1954 (68 Stat. 92). Commerce Secretary given direction of general policies of *Corporation* by EO 10771 of June 20, 1958. Transferred to Transportation Department by act of Oct. 15, 1966 (80 Stat. 931).

Salary Stabilization, Office of *See* **Salary Stabilization Board**

Salary Stabilization Board Established May 10, 1951, by *Economic Stabilization Administrator's* General Order 8. Stabilization program administered by *Office of Salary Stabilization.* Terminated Apr. 30, 1953, by EO 10434 of Feb. 6, 1953, and acts of June 30, 1952 (66 Stat. 296), and June 30, 1953 (67 Stat. 131).

Sales Manager, Office of the General Established by Agriculture Secretary Feb. 29, 1976. Consolidated with Foreign Agricultural Service by Secretary's Memorandum 2001 of Nov. 29, 1979.

Saving Bonds, Interdepartmental Committee for the Voluntary Payroll Savings Plan for the Purchase of U.S. Established by EO 11532 of June 2, 1970. Superseded by EO 11981 of Mar. 29, 1977, which established Interagency Committee for the Purchase of U.S. Savings Bonds.

Savings and Loan Advisory Council, Federal Established by act of Oct. 6, 1972 (86 Stat. 770). Continued by act of Dec. 26, 1974 (88 Stat. 1739). Terminated by act of Aug. 9, 1989 (103 Stat. 422).

Savings and Loan Insurance Corporation, Federal Established by act of June 27, 1934 (48 Stat. 1246). Grouped with other agencies to form *Federal Loan Agency* by Reorg. Plan No. I of 1939, effective July 1, 1939. Transferred to *Federal Home Loan Bank Administration, National Housing Agency,* by EO 9070 of Feb. 24, 1942. Board of Trustees abolished by Reorg. Plan No. 3 of 1947, effective July 27, 1947, and functions transferred to *Home Loan Bank Board.* Abolished by act of Aug. 9, 1989 (103 Stat. 354).

Science, Engineering, and Technology, Federal Coordinating Council for Established by act of May 11, 1976 (90 Stat. 471). Abolished by Reorg. Plan No. 1 of 1977, effective Feb. 26, 1978, and functions transferred to President. Functions redelegated to Director of the Office of Science and Technology Policy and Federal Coordinating Council for Science, Engineering, and Technology, established by EO 12039 of Feb. 24, 1978.

Science, Engineering, and Technology Panel, Intergovernmental Established by act of May 11, 1976 (90 Stat. 465). Abolished by Reorg. Plan No. 1 of 1977, effective Feb. 26, 1978, and functions transferred to President. Functions redelegated to Director of Office of Science and Technology Policy by EO 12039 of Feb. 24, 1978, which established Intergovernmental Science, Engineering, and Technology Advisory Panel.

Science Advisory Committee, President's Established by President Apr. 20, 1951, and reconstituted Nov. 22, 1957. Terminated with *Office of Science and Technology,* effective July 1, 1973.

Science Exhibit-Century 21 Exposition, U.S. Established Jan. 20, 1960, by Commerce Department Order 167. Abolished by revocation of order June 5, 1963.

Science and Technology, Federal Council for *See* **Scientific Research and Development, Interdepartmental Committee on**

Science and Technology, Office of Established by Reorg. Plan No. 2 of 1962, effective June 8, 1962. *Office* abolished by Reorg. Plan No. 1 of 1973, effective June 30, 1973, and functions transferred to National Science Foundation.

Science and Technology, President's Committee on Established by act of May 11, 1976 (90 Stat. 468). Abolished by Reorg. Plan No. 1 of 1977, effective Feb. 26, 1978, and functions transferred to President.

Scientific Research and Development, Interdepartmental Committee on Established by EO 9912 of Dec. 24, 1947. EO 9912 revoked by EO 10807 of Mar. 13, 1959, which established *Federal Council for Science and Technology.* Abolished by act of May 11, 1976 (90 Stat. 472).

Scientific Research and Development, Office of Established in *Office for Emergency Management* by EO 8807 of June 28, 1941. Terminated by EO 9913 of Dec. 26, 1947, and property transferred to *National Military Establishment* for liquidation.

Scientists and Engineers, National Committee for the Development of Established by President Apr. 3, 1956. Renamed *President's Committee on Scientists and Engineers* May 7, 1957. Final report submitted Dec. 17, 1958, and expired Dec. 31, 1958.

Scientists and Engineers, President's Committee on *See* **Scientists and Engineers, National Committee for the Development of**

Screw Thread Commission, National Established by act of July 18, 1918 (40 Stat. 912). Terminated by EO 6166 of June 10, 1933, and records transferred to Commerce Department, effective Mar. 2, 1934. Informal Interdepartmental Screw Thread Committee established on Sept. 14, 1939, consisting of *War,* Navy, and Commerce Department representatives.

Security, Commission on Government Established by act of Aug. 9, 1955 (69 Stat. 595). Terminated Sept. 22, 1957, pursuant to terms of act.

Security, Office of the Director for Mutual *See* **Security Agency, Mutual**

Security Agency, Federal Established by Reorg. Plan No. 1 of 1939, effective July 1, 1939, grouping under one administration *Office of Education, Public Health Service, Social Security Board, U.S. Employment Service, Civilian Conservation Corps,* and *National Youth Administration.* Abolished by Reorg. Plan No. 1 of 1953, effective Apr. 11, 1953, and functions and units transferred to *Health, Education, and Welfare Department.*

Security Agency, Mutual Established and continued by acts of Oct. 10, 1951 (65 Stat. 373) and June 20, 1952 (66 Stat. 141). *Agency* and *Office of Director for Mutual Security* abolished by Reorg. Plan No. 7 of 1953, effective Aug. 1, 1953, and functions transferred to *Foreign Operations Administration,* established by same plan.

Security and Individual Rights, President's Commission on Internal Established by EO 10207 of Jan. 23, 1951. Terminated by EO 10305 of Nov. 14, 1951.

Security Resources Board, National Established by act of July 26, 1947 (61 Stat. 499). Transferred to Executive Office of the President by Reorg. Plan No. 4 of 1949, effective Aug. 20, 1949. Functions of *Board* transferred to Chairman and *Board* made advisory to him by Reorg. Plan No. 25 of 1950, effective July 10, 1950. Functions delegated by Executive order transferred to *Office of Defense Mobilization* by EO 10438 of Mar. 13, 1953. *Board* abolished by Reorg. Plan No. 3 of 1953, effective

290-950 O 91 - 28

June 12, 1953, and remaining functions transferred to *Office of Defense Mobilization.*

Security Training Commission, National Established by act of June 19, 1951 (65 Stat. 75). Expired June 30, 1957, pursuant to Presidential letter of Mar. 25, 1957.

Seed Loan Office Authorized by Presidential letters of July 26, 1918, and July 26, 1919, to Agriculture Secretary. Further authorized by act of Mar. 3, 1921 (41 Stat. 1347). *Office* transferred to Farm Credit Administration by EO 6084 of Mar. 27, 1933.

Selective Service Appeal Board, National Established by EO 9988 of Aug. 20, 1948. Inactive as of Apr. 11, 1975.

Selective Service Records, Office of *See* **Selective Service System**

Selective Service System Established by act of Sept. 16, 1940 (54 Stat. 885). Placed under jurisdiction of *War Manpower Commission* by EO 9279 of Dec. 5, 1942, as *Bureau of Selective Service.* Designated Selective Service System, separate agency, by EO 9410 of Dec. 23, 1943. Transferred for liquidation to *Office of Selective Service Records* established by act of Mar. 31, 1947 (61 Stat. 31). Transferred to Selective Service System by act of June 24, 1948 (62 Stat. 604).

Self-Help Development and Technical Development, Office of Established in *National Consumer Cooperative Bank* by act of Aug. 20, 1978 (92 Stat. 499). Abolished by act of Aug. 13, 1981 (95 Stat. 437), and assets transferred to Consumer Cooperative Development Corporation, Commerce Department, Dec. 30, 1982.

Services, Bureau of Special *See* **Office of War Information**

Services, Division of Central Administrative Established by *Liaison Officer for Emergency Management* pursuant to Presidential letter of Feb. 28, 1941. Terminated by EO 9471 of Aug. 25, 1944, and functions discontinued or transferred to constituent agencies of *Office for Emergency Management* and other agencies.

Shipbuilding Stabilization Committee Originally organized by *National Defense Advisory Commission* in 1940. Established August 1942 by *War Production Board.* Transferred to Labor Department from *Civilian Production Administration,* successor agency to *Board,* by EO 9656 of Nov. 15, 1945. Terminated June 30, 1947.

Shipping Board, U.S. Established by act of Sept. 7, 1916 (39 Stat. 729). Abolished by EO 6166 of June 10, 1933, and functions, including those in respect to *U.S. Shipping Board Merchant Fleet Corporation,* transferred to *U.S. Shipping Board Bureau,* Commerce Department, effective Mar. 2, 1934. Separation of employees deferred until Sept. 30, 1933, by EO 6245 of Aug. 9, 1933. Functions assumed by *U.S. Maritime Commission* Oct. 26, 1936, pursuant to act of June 29, 1936 (49 Stat. 1985).

Shipping Board Bureau, U.S. *See* **Shipping Board, U.S.**

Shipping Board Emergency Fleet Corporation, U.S. Established Apr. 16, 1917, under authority of act of Sept. 7, 1916 (39 Stat. 729). Renamed *U.S. Shipping Board Merchant Fleet Corporation* by act of Feb. 11, 1927 (44 Stat. 1083). Terminated Oct. 26, 1936, under provisions of act of June 29, 1936 (49 Stat. 1985), and functions transferred to *U.S. Maritime Commission.*

Shipping Board Merchant Fleet Corporation, U.S. *See* **Shipping Board Emergency Fleet Corporation, U.S.**

Ships, Bureau of Established by act of June 20, 1940 (54 Stat. 493), to replace *Bureau of Engineering* and *Bureau of Construction and Repair.* Abolished by Defense Department reorg. order of Mar. 9, 1966, and functions transferred to Navy Secretary (31 FR 7188).

Simpson Historical Research Center, Albert F. Renamed Headquarters USAF Historical Research Center by Defense Secretary's special order of Dec. 16, 1983.

Smithsonian Symposia and Seminars, Office of Renamed Office of Interdisciplinary Studies by Smithsonian Institution announcement of Mar. 16, 1987.

Social Development Institute, Inter-American Established by act of Dec. 30, 1969 (83 Stat. 821). Renamed Inter-American Foundation by act of Feb. 7, 1972 (86 Stat. 34).

Social Protection, Committee on Established in *Office of Defense Health and Welfare Services* by administrative order June 14, 1941. Functions transferred to *Federal Security Agency* by EO 9338 of Apr. 29, 1943.

Social and Rehabilitation Service Established by *Health, Education, and Welfare Secretary's* reorganization of Aug. 15, 1967. Abolished by Secretary's reorganization of Mar. 8, 1977 (42 FR 13262), and constituent units—*Medical Services Administration, Assistance Payments Administration, Office of Child Support Enforcement, and Public Services Administration*—transferred.

Social Security Board Established by act of Aug. 14, 1935 (49 Stat. 620). Incorporated into *Federal Security Agency* by Reorg. Plan No. I of 1939, effective July 1, 1939. Abolished by Reorg. Plan No. 2 of 1946, effective July 16, 1946, and functions transferred to *Federal Security Administration.*

Soil Conservation Service *See* **Soil Erosion Service**

Soil Erosion Service Established in Interior Department following allotment made Aug. 25, 1933. Transferred to Agriculture Department by Interior Secretary's administrative order of Mar. 25, 1935. Made *Soil Conservation Service* by order of Agriculture Secretary, Apr. 27, 1935, pursuant to provisions of act of Apr. 27, 1935 (49 Stat. 163). Certain functions of *Soil Conservation Service* under jurisdiction of Interior Department transferred from Agriculture Department to Interior Department by Reorg. Plan No. IV of 1940, effective June 30, 1940.

Soils, Bureau of *See* **Agricultural and Industrial Chemistry, Bureau of** and **Plant Industry, Bureau of**

Solicitor General, Office of Assistant Established in Justice Department by act of June 16, 1933 (48 Stat. 307). Terminated by Reorg. Plan No. 2 of 1950, effective May 24, 1950.

Space Science Board Renamed Space Studies Board by authority of the National Research Council, National Academy of Sciences, effective May 8, 1989.

Space Station, Office of Established in the *National Aeronautics and Space Administration.* Abolished in 1990 and remaining functions transferred to the *Office of Space Flight.*

Space Technology Laboratories, National Renamed John C. Stennis Space Center by EO 12641 of May 20, 1988.

Space and Terrestrial Applications, Office of *and* **Office of Space Science** Combined to form Office of Space Science and Applications by National Aeronautics and Space Administrator's announcement of Sept. 29, 1981.

Space Tracking and Data Systems, Office of Name changed to Office of Space Operations by National Aeronautics and Space Administrator's announcement of Jan. 9, 1987.

Space Transportation Operations, Office of *and* **Office of Space Transportation Systems** Combined to form Office of Space Transportation Systems, National Aeronautics and Space Administration, effective July 1982.

Spanish-Speaking People, Cabinet Committee on Opportunities for *See* **Mexican-American Affairs, Interagency Committee on**

Special. *See other part of title*

Specifications Board, Federal Established by *Bureau of the Budget* Circular 42 of Oct. 10, 1921. Transferred from *Federal Coordinating Service* to *Procurement Division* by Treasury Secretary's order of Oct. 9, 1933. *Board* superseded by *Federal Specifications Executive Committee,* set up by *Director of Procurement* under Circular Letter 106 of July 16, 1935.

Sport Fisheries and Wildlife, Bureau of Established in Interior Department by act of Aug. 8, 1956 (70 Stat. 1119). *Bureau* replaced by U.S. Fish and Wildlife Service pursuant to act of Apr. 22, 1974 (88 Stat. 92).

State Department Duty of Secretary of State of procuring copies of all statutes of the States, as provided for in act of Sept. 28, 1789 (R.S. 206), abolished by Reorg. Plan No. 20 of 1950, effective May 24, 1950. Functions of numbering, editing, and distributing proclamations and Executive orders transferred from State Department to *Division of the Federal Register, National Archives,* by EO 7298 of Feb. 18, 1936. Duty of Secretary of State of publishing Executive proclamations and treaties in newspapers in District of Columbia, provided for in act of July 31, 1876 (19 Stat. 105), abolished by Reorg. Plan No. 20 of 1950, effective May 24, 1950. Functions concerning publication of U.S. Statutes at Large, acts and joint resolutions in pamphlet form known as slip laws, and amendments to the Constitution; electoral votes for President and Vice President; and Territorial papers transferred from State Department to General Services Administrator by Reorg. Plan No. 20 of 1950. (*See also* **Archives Establishment, National**)

State and Local Cooperation, Division of Established by *Advisory Commission to Council of National Defense* Aug. 5, 1940. Transferred to *Office of Civilian Defense.*

State and Local Government Cooperation, Committee on Established by EO 11627 of Oct 15, 1971. Abolished by EO 11695 of Jan. 11, 1973.

State Technical Services, Office of Established by Commerce Secretary Nov. 19, 1965, pursuant to act of Sept. 14, 1965 (79 Stat. 697). Abolished by Secretary, effective June 30, 1970.

Statistical Board, Central Organized Aug. 9, 1933, by EO 6225 of July 27, 1933. Transferred to *Bureau of the Budget* by Reorg. Plan No. I of 1939, effective July 1, 1939. Expired July 25, 1940, and functions taken over by *Division of Statistical Standards, Bureau of the Budget.*

Statistical Committee, Central Established by act of July 25, 1935 (49 Stat. 498). Abolished by Reorg. Plan No. I of 1939, effective July 1, 1939, and functions transferred to *Bureau of the Budget.*

Statistical Policy Coordination Committee Established by EO 12013 of Oct. 7, 1977. Abolished by EO 12318 of Aug. 21, 1981.

Statistical Reporting Service Established by Agriculture Secretary's Memorandum 1446, Supplement 1, of pr. 3, 1961. Consolidated with other departmental units into *Economics, Statistics, and Cooperatives Service* by Secretary's Memorandum 1927, effective Dec. 23, 1977. Redesignated as Statistical Reporting Service by Secretary's order of Oct. 1, 1981.

Statistics Administration, Social and Economic Established Jan. 1, 1972, by Commerce Secretary. Terminated by Commerce Department Organization Order 10–2, effective Aug. 4, 1975 (40 FR 42765). Bureau of Economic Analysis and Bureau of the Census restored as primary operating units of Commerce Department by Organization Orders 35–1A and 2A, effective Aug. 4, 1975.

Statutes at Large *See* **State Department**

Statutes of the States *See* **State Department**

Steam Engineering, Bureau of Established in Navy Department by act of July 5, 1862 (12 Stat. 510). Redesignated as *Bureau of Engineering* by act of June 4, 1920 (41 Stat. 828). Abolished by act of June

20, 1940 (54 Stat. 492), and functions transferred to *Bureau of Ships.*

Steamboat Inspection Service President authorized to appoint *Service* by act of June 28, 1838 (5 Stat. 252). Treasury Secretary authorized to establish boards of local inspectors at enumerated ports throughout the U.S. by act of Feb. 28, 1871 (16 Stat. 440). Authority to appoint boards of local inspectors delegated to *Secretary of Commerce and Labor* by act of Mar. 4, 1905 (33 Stat. 1026). Consolidated with *Bureau of Navigation and Steamboat Inspection* by act of June 30, 1932 (47 Stat. 415).

Stock Catalog Board, Federal Standard Originated by act of Mar. 2, 1929 (45 Stat. 1461). Transferred from *Federal Coordinating Service* to *Procurement Division* by Treasury Secretary's order of Oct. 9, 1933.

Strategic Services, Office of *See* **Information, Office of Coordinator of**

Subversive Activities Control Board Established by act of Sept. 23, 1950 (64 Stat. 987). Terminated June 30, 1973, through lack of funding.

Sugar Division Created by act of May 12, 1933 (48 Stat. 31), authorized by act of Sept. 1, 1937 (50 Stat. 903). Taken from *Agricultural Adjustment Administration* and made independent division of Agriculture Department by Secretary's Memorandum 783, effective Oct. 16, 1938. Placed under *Agricultural Conservation and Adjustment Administration* by EO 9069 of Feb. 23, 1942, functioning as *Sugar Agency.* Functions transferred to *Food Distribution Administration* by EO 9280 of Dec. 5, 1942.

Sugar Rationing Administration Established by Agriculture Secretary's Memorandum 1190 of Mar. 31, 1947, under authority of act of Mar. 31, 1947 (61 Stat. 35). Terminated Mar. 31, 1948, on expiration of authority.

Supplies and Accounts, Bureau of *See* **Provisions and Clothing, Bureau of**

Supplies and Shortages, National Commission on Established by act of Sept. 30, 1974 (88 Stat. 1168). Terminated Mar. 31, 1977, pursuant to terms of act.

Supply, Bureau of Federal *See* **Procurement Division**

Supply, Office of Renamed Procurement and Property, Office of by Smithsonian Institution announcement of Nov. 4, 1986.

Supply Committee, General Established by act of June 17, 1910 (36 Stat. 531). Abolished by EO 6166 of June 10, 1933, effective Mar. 2, 1934, and functions transferred to *Procurement Division,* Treasury Department.

Supply Priorities and Allocations Board Established in *Office for Emergency Management* by EO 8875 of Aug. 28, 1941. Abolished by EO 9024 of Jan. 16, 1942, and functions transferred to *War Production Board.*

Supply Service, Federal Renamed *Office of Personal Property* by General Services Administration order, effective Sept. 28, 1982; later renamed Office of Federal Supply and Services by GSA order of Jan. 22, 1983.

Surveys and Maps, Federal Board of *See* **Surveys and Maps of the Federal Government, Board of**

Surveys and Maps of the Federal Government, Board of Established by EO 3206 of Dec. 30, 1919. Renamed *Federal Board of Surveys and Maps* by EO 7262 of Jan. 4, 1936. Abolished by EO 9094 of Mar. 10, 1942, and functions transferred to Director, *Bureau of the Budget.*

Tariff Commission, U.S. Renamed U.S. International Trade Commission by act of Jan. 3, 1975 (88 Stat. 2009).

Tax Court of the United States Renamed U.S. Tax Court by act of Dec. 30, 1969 (83 Stat. 730).

Technical Cooperation Administration Transferred from State Department to *Mutual Security Agency* by EO 10458 of June 1, 1953. Transferred to *Foreign Operations Administration* by Reorg. Plan No. 7 of 1953, effective Aug. 1, 1953.

Technical Services, Office of Designated unit of Office of the Commerce Secretary by Department Order 179, July 23, 1962. Functions transferred to National Bureau of Standards by Order 90 of Jan. 30, 1964.

Technology, Automation, and Economic Progress, National Commission on Established by act of Aug. 19, 1964 (78 Stat. 463). Terminated January 1966 pursuant to terms of act.

Telecommunications Advisor to the President Established in *Executive Office of the President* by EO 10297 of Oct. 9, 1951. EO 10297 revoked by EO 10460 of June 16, 1953, and functions transferred to Director of *Office of Defense Mobilization.*

Telecommunications Management, Director of Established in *Office of Emergency Planning* by EO 10995 of Feb. 16, 1962. Assignment of radio frequencies delegated to Government agencies and foreign diplomatic establishments by EO 11084 of Feb. 16, 1963. Abolished by Reorg. Plan No. 1 of 1970, effective Apr. 20, 1970.

Telecommunications Policy, Office of Established in *Executive Office of the President* by Reorg. Plan No. 1 of 1970, effective Apr. 20, 1970. Abolished by Reorg. Plan No. 1 of 1977, effective Mar. 26, 1978, and certain functions transferred to President with all other functions transferred to Commerce Department.

Telecommunications Service, Automated Data Renamed Office of Information Resources Management by General Services Administration order of Aug. 17, 1982.

Temporary Controls, Office of Established in *Office for Emergency Management* by EO 9809 of Dec. 12, 1946, consolidating *Office of War*

Mobilization and Reconversion, Office of Economic Stabilization, Office of Price Administration, and *Civilian Production Administration.* Functions with respect to Veterans' Emergency Housing Program transferred to *Housing Expediter* by EO 9836 of Mar. 22, 1947. Functions with respect to distribution and price of sugar products transferred to Agriculture Secretary by act of Mar. 31, 1947 (61 Stat. 36). Office terminated by EO 9841 of Apr. 23, 1947, and remaining functions redistributed.

Territorial Affairs, Office of Established by Interior Secretarial Order 2951 of Feb. 6, 1973. Abolished by Departmental Manual Release 2270 of June 6, 1980, and functions transferred to Office of Assistant Secretary for Territorial and International Affairs.

Territorial papers *See* **State Department**

Territories, Office of Established by Interior Secretary July 28, 1950. Functions reassigned to Deputy Assistant Secretary for Territorial Affairs in Office of the Assistant Secretary—Public Land Management, Interior Department by Secretarial Order 2942, effective July 1, 1971.

Terrorism, Cabinet Committee To Combat Established by Presidential memorandum of Sept. 25, 1972. Terminated by National Security Council memorandum of Sept. 16, 1977.

Textile Industry, Board of Inquiry for the Cotton Established by EO 6840 of Sept. 5, 1934. Abolished by EO 6858 of Sept. 26, 1934.

Textile National Industrial Relations Board Established by administrative order of June 28, 1934. Abolished by EO 6858 of Sept. 26, 1934, which created *Textile Labor Relations Board* in connection with Labor Department. *Board* terminated July 1, 1937, and functions absorbed by *U.S. Conciliation Service,* Labor Department.

Textile National Industrial Relations Board, Cotton Established by original Code of Fair Competition for the Cotton Textile Industry, as amended July 10, 1934. Abolished by EO 6858 of Sept. 26, 1934.

Textile Work Assignment Board, Cotton Amendments to Code of Fair Competition for Cotton Textile Industry approved by EO 6876 of Oct. 16, 1934, and *Cotton Textile Work Assignment Board* appointed by *Textile Labor Relations Board. Board* expired June 15, 1935.

Textile Work Assignment Board, Silk Appointed by *Textile Labor Relations Board* following President's approval of amendments to Code of Fair Competition for Silk Textile Industry by EO 6875 of Oct. 16, 1934. Terminated June 15, 1935.

Textile Work Assignment Board, Wool Established by EO 6877 of Oct. 16, 1934. Terminated June 15, 1935.

Textiles, Office of Established by Commerce Secretary Feb. 14, 1971. Functions transferred to *Domestic and International Business Administration,* effective Nov. 17, 1972.

Trade, Special Adviser to the President on Foreign Established by EO 6651 of Mar. 23, 1934. Terminated on expiration of *National Recovery Administration.*

Trade Administration, International *See* **Business and Defense Services Administration**

Trade Agreements, Interdepartmental Committee on Established by Secretary of State in 1934 and reestablished by EO 9832 of Feb. 25, 1947. Abolished by EO 11075 of Jan. 15, 1963.

Trade Expansion Act Advisory Committee Established by EO 11075 of Jan. 15, 1963. Abolished by EO 11846 of Mar. 27, 1975, and records transferred to Trade Policy Committee established by same EO.

Trade Negotiations, Office of the Special Representative for Renamed Office of the U.S. Trade Representative by EO 12188 of Jan. 4, 1980.

Trade Policy Committee Established by EO 10741 of Nov. 25, 1957. Abolished by EO 11075 of Jan. 15, 1963.

Traffic Safety, President's Committee for Established by Presidential letter of Apr. 14, 1954. Continued by EO 10858 of Jan. 13, 1960. Abolished by EO 11382 of Nov. 28, 1967.

Traffic Safety Agency, National Established in *Commerce Department* by act of Sept. 9, 1966 (80 Stat. 718). Activity transferred to Transportation Department by act of Oct. 15, 1966 (80 Stat. 931). Responsibility placed in *National Highway Safety Bureau* by EO 11357 of June 6, 1967.

Training and Employment Service, U.S. Established in *Manpower Administration, Labor Department,* Mar. 17, 1969. Abolished by Secretary's letter of Dec. 6, 1971, and functions assigned to Office of Employment Development Programs and *U.S. Employment Service.*

Training School for Boys, National *See* **District of Columbia, Reform-School of the**

Transportation, Federal Coordinator of Established by act of June 16, 1933 (48 Stat. 211). Expired June 16, 1936, under provisions of Public Resolution 27 (49 Stat. 376).

Transportation, Office of Established in the Agriculture Department by Secretary's Memorandum 1966 dated Dec. 12, 1978. Abolished by Secretary's Memorandum 1030-25 dated Dec. 28, 1990.

Transportation Administration, Urban Mass Established by act of July 9, 1964 (78 Stat. 302). Most functions transferred to Transportation Department by Reorg. Plan No. 2 of 1968, effective June 30, 1968, and joint responsibility assigned to Transportation and Housing and Urban Development Departments for functions relating to research, technical studies, and training. Transportation and Housing and Urban Development Under Secretaries agreed in November 1969 that Transportation Department should be focal point for urban mass transportation grant administration.

Transportation and Communications Service Established by General Services Administrator Oct. 19, 1961. Abolished by Administrator's order, effective July 15, 1972. Motor equipment, transportation, and public utilities responsibilities assigned to Federal Supply Service; telecommunications function assigned to Automated Data and Telecommunications Service.

Transportation and Public Utilities Service Abolished by General Services Administration order of Aug. 17, 1982. Functions transferred to various GSA organizations.

Transportation Research and Technology, Director of Renamed Science and Technology Adviser to Secretary by Transportation Secretary's order of Feb. 12, 1985.

Transportation Safety Board, National Established in Transportation Department by act of Oct. 15, 1966 (80 Stat. 935). Abolished by act of Jan. 3, 1975 (88 Stat. 2156), which established independent National Transportation Safety Board.

Travel Service, U.S. Replaced by U.S. Travel and Tourism Administration, Commerce Department, pursuant to act of Oct. 16, 1981 (95 Stat. 1014).

Treasury, Office of the Assistant Secretary of the—Electronics and Information Technology Established by Secretary's Order 114-1 of Mar. 14, 1983. Abolished by Secretary's Order 114-3 of May 17, 1985, and functions transferred to Office of the Assistant Secretary for Management. Certain provisions effective Aug. 31, 1985 (50 FR 23573).

Treasury, Solicitor of the Position established when certain functions of *Solicitor of the Treasury* transferred to Justice Department by EO 6166 of June 10, 1933. *Solicitor of the Treasury* transferred from Justice Department to Treasury Department by same order. *Office of Solicitor of the Treasury* abolished by act of May 10, 1934 (48 Stat. 758), and functions transferred to General Counsel, Treasury Department.

Treasury Secretary, Assistant Office abolished by Reorg. Plan No. III of 1940, effective June 30, 1940, and functions transferred to Fiscal Assistant Secretary, Treasury Department.

Treaties *See* **State Department**

Typhus Commission, U.S. of America Established in *War Department* by EO 9285 of Dec. 24, 1942. Abolished June 30, 1946, by EO 9680 of Jan. 17, 1946.

U.S. *See other part of title*

Uniformed Services University of the Health Sciences, School of Medicine of the Renamed F. Edward Hébert School of Medicine by act of Sept. 24, 1983 (97 Stat. 704).

United Nations Educational, Scientific and Cultural Organization U.S. membership in UNESCO authorized by act of July 30, 1946 (60 Stat. 712). Announcement of U.S. intention to withdraw made Dec. 28, 1983, in accordance with UNESCO constitution. Official U.S. withdrawal effective Dec. 31, 1984, by Secretary of State's letter of Dec. 19, 1984. U.S. maintains status as observer mission in UNESCO.

Upper Mississippi River Basin Commission Established by EO 11659 of Mar. 22, 1972. Terminated by EO 12319 of Sept. 9, 1981.

Urban Affairs, Council for Established in Executive Office of the President by EO 11452 of Jan. 23, 1969. Terminated by EO 11541 of July 1, 1970.

Urban Renewal Administration Established in *Housing and Home Finance Agency* by Administrator's Organizational Order 1 of Dec. 23, 1954. Functions transferred to Housing and Urban Development Department by act of Sept. 9, 1965 (78 Stat. 667), and *Administration* terminated.

Utilization and Disposal Service Established July 1, 1961, by Administrator of General Services and assigned functions of *Federal Supply Service* and *Public Buildings Service*. Functions transferred to *Property Management and Disposal Service* July 29, 1966.

Veterans Administration Legal work in defense of suits against the U.S. arising under act of June 7, 1924 (43 Stat. 607), transferred to Justice Department by EO 6166 of June 10, 1933. Transfer deferred to Sept. 10, 1933, by EO 6222 of July 27, 1933. *Administration* renamed Veterans Affairs Department by act of Oct. 25, 1988 (102 Stat. 2635).

Veterans Education Appeals Board *See* **Veterans Tuition Appeals Board**

Veterans Employment Service Renamed Veterans Employment and Training Service by Labor Secretary's Order 4-83 of Mar. 24, 1983 (48 FR 14092).

Veterans Health Administration *See* **Medicine and Surgery, Department of**

Veterans Health Services and Research Administration *See* **Medicine and Surgery, Department of**

Veterans Placement Service Board Established by act of June 22, 1944 (58 Stat. 293). Abolished by Reorg. Plan No. 2 of 1949, effective Aug. 20, 1949, and functions transferred to Labor Secretary.

Veterans Tuition Appeals Board Established by act of Aug. 24, 1949 (63 Stat. 654). Functions assumed by *Veterans Education Appeals Board* established by act of July 13, 1950 (64 Stat. 336). *Board* terminated by act of Aug. 28, 1957 (71 Stat. 474).

Veterinary Medicine, Bureau of Renamed Center for Veterinary Medicine by FDA notice of Mar. 9, 1984 (49 FR 10166).

Virgin Islands Public works programs under act of Dec. 20, 1944 (58 Stat. 827), transferred from General Services Administrator to Interior Secretary by Reorg. Plan No. 15 of 1950, effective May 24, 1950.

Virgin Islands Company Established in 1934. Reincorporated as Government corporation by act of June 30, 1949 (63 Stat. 350). Program terminated June 30, 1965, and *Corporation* dissolved July 1, 1966.

Virgin Islands Corporation *See* **Virgin Islands Company**

Visitor Facilities Advisory Commission, National Established by act of Mar. 12, 1968 (82 Stat. 45). Expired Jan. 5, 1975, pursuant to act of Oct. 6, 1972 (86 Stat. 776).

Vocational Rehabilitation, Office of Established to administer provisions of act of July 6, 1943 (57 Stat. 374). Other duties delegated by acts of Aug. 3, 1954 (68 Stat. 652), Nov. 8, 1965 (79 Stat. 1282), July 12, 1960 (74 Stat. 364), and July 10, 1954 (68 Stat. 454). Redesignated *Vocational Rehabilitation Administration* Jan. 28, 1963.

Vocational Rehabilitation Administration Made component of newly created *Social and Rehabilitation Service* as *Rehabilitation Services Administration* by *Health, Education, and Welfare Department* reorganization Aug. 15, 1967.

Voluntary Citizen Participation, State Office of Renamed State Office of Voluntarism in ACTION by notice of Apr. 18, 1986 (51 FR 13265), effective May 18, 1986.

Volunteer Service, International, Secretariat for Established in 1962 by International Conference on Middle Level Manpower called by President. Terminated Mar. 31, 1976, through insufficient funding.

Volunteers in Service to America Established by act of Nov. 8, 1966 (80 Stat. 1472). *Service* administered by *Office of Economic Opportunity* and functions transferred to ACTION by Reorg. Plan No. 1 of 1971, effective July 1, 1971.

Wage Adjustment Board Established May 29, 1942, by Labor Secretary at Presidential direction of May 14, 1942, to accomplish purpose of act of Mar. 3, 1931 (46 Stat. 1494), as amended by acts of Aug. 30, 1935 (49 Stat. 1011), and Jan. 30, 1942 (56 Stat. 23). Disbanded on termination of *National Wage Stabilization Board*.

Wage and Price Stability, Council on Established in Executive Office of the President by act of Aug. 24, 1974 (88 Stat. 750). Abolished by EO 12288 of Jan. 29, 1981. Funding ceased beyond June 5, 1981, by act of June 5, 1981 (95 Stat. 74), and authorization for appropriations repealed by act of Aug. 13, 1981 (95 Stat. 432).

Wage and Price Stability Program *See* **Wage and Price Stability, Council on**

Wage Stabilization Board Established by EO 10161 of Sept. 9, 1950. Reconstituted by EO 10377 of July 25, 1952. Terminated Apr. 30, 1953, by EO 10434 of Feb. 6, 1953, and acts of June 30, 1952 (66 Stat. 296), and June 30, 1953 (67 Stat. 131).

Wage Stabilization Board, National *See* **Defense Mediation Board, National**

Wallops Flight Center, Wallops Island, VA Formerly separate field installation of National Aeronautics and Space Administration. Made component of Goddard Space Flight Center by NASA Management Instruction 1107.10A of Sept. 3, 1981.

War, Solid Fuels Administration for Established in *Interior Department* by EO 9332 of Apr. 19, 1943. Absorbed *Office of Solid Fuels Coordinator for War* (originally established as *Office of Solid Fuels Coordinator for National Defense*) pursuant to Presidential letter of Nov. 5, 1941, later changed by Presidential letter of May 25, 1942. Terminated by EO 9847 of May 6, 1947.

War Assets Administration Established in *Office for Emergency Management* by EO 9689 of Jan. 31, 1946. Functions transferred to *Surplus Property Administration* by Reorg. Plan No. 1 of 1947, effective July 1, 1947, and agency renamed *War Assets Administration.* Abolished by act of June 30, 1949 (63 Stat. 738), and functions transferred for liquidation to General Services Administration.

War Assets Corporation *See* **Petroleum Reserves Corporation**

War Claims Commission Established by act of July 3, 1948 (62 Stat. 1240). Abolished by Reorg. Plan No. 1 of 1954, effective July 1, 1954, and functions transferred to Foreign Claims Settlement Commission of the U.S.

War Commodities Division Established in *Office of Foreign Economic Coordination* by State Departmental Order of Aug. 27, 1943. *Office* abolished by Departmental Order of Nov. 6, 1943, pursuant to EO 9380 of Sept. 25, 1943, which established *Foreign Economic Administration* in *Office for Emergency Management.*

War Communications, Board of *See* **Defense Communications Board**

War Contracts Price Adjustment Board Established by act of Feb. 25, 1944 (58 Stat. 85). Abolished by act of Mar. 23, 1951 (65 Stat. 7), and functions transferred to *Renegotiation Board,* established by same act, and General Services Administrator.

War Damage Corporation *See* **War Insurance Corporation**

War Department Established by act of Aug. 7, 1789 (1 Stat. 49), succeeding similar department established prior to adoption of the Constitution. Three military departments—Army; Navy, including naval aviation and U.S. Marine Corps; and Air Force—reorganized under *National Military Establishment* by act of July 26, 1947 (61 Stat. 495).

War Finance Corporation Established by act of Apr. 5, 1918 (40 Stat. 506). Functions and obligations transferred by Reorg. Plan No. II of 1939, effective July 1, 1939, to Treasury Secretary for liquidation not later than Dec. 31, 1939.

War Food Administration *See* **Food Production and Distribution, Administration of**

War Information, Office of Established in *Office of Emergency Management* by EO 9182 of June 13, 1942, consolidating *Office of Facts and Figures; Office of Government Reports; Division of Information, Office for Emergency Management;* and *Foreign Information Service—Outpost, Publications, and Pictorial Branches, Coordinator of Information.* Abolished by EO 9608 of Aug. 31, 1945. *Bureau of Special Services* and functions with respect to review of publications of Federal agencies transferred to *Bureau of the Budget.* Foreign information activities transferred to State Department.

War Insurance Corporation Established Dec. 13, 1941, by act of June 10, 1941 (55 Stat. 249). Charter filed Mar. 31, 1942. Renamed *War Damage Corporation* by act of Mar. 27, 1942 (56 Stat. 175). Transferred from *Federal Loan Agency* to Commerce Department by EO 9071 of Feb. 24, 1942. Returned to *Federal Loan Agency* by act of Feb. 24, 1945 (59 Stat. 5). *Agency* abolished by act of June 30, 1947 (61 Stat. 202), and functions assumed by *Reconstruction Finance Corporation.* Powers of *War Damage Corporation,* except for purposes of liquidation, terminated as of Jan. 22, 1947.

War Labor Board, National *See* **Defense Mediation Board, National**

War Manpower Commission Established in *Office for Emergency Management* by EO 9139 of Apr. 18, 1942. Terminated by EO 9617 of Sept. 19, 1945, and functions, except *Procurement and Assignment Service,* transferred to Labor Department.

War Mobilization, Office of Established by EO 9347 of May 27, 1943. Transferred to *Office of War Mobilization and Reconversion* by EO 9488 of Oct. 3, 1944.

War Mobilization and Reconversion, Office of Established by act of Oct. 3, 1944 (58 Stat. 785). Consolidated with other agencies by EO 9809 of Dec. 12, 1946, to form *Office of Temporary Controls. Media Programming Division* and *Motion Picture Division* transferred to *Office of Government Reports,* reestablished by same order. Certain other functions transferred to President and Commerce Secretary.

War Mobilization and Reconversion Advisory Board, Office of Established by act of Oct. 3, 1944 (58 Stat. 788). Transferred to *Office of Temporary Controls* by EO 9809 of Dec. 12, 1946.

War Plants Corporation, Smaller Established by act of June 11, 1942 (56 Stat. 351). Functions transferred by EO 9665 of Dec. 27, 1945, to *Reconstruction Finance Corporation* and Commerce Department. Abolished by act of June 30, 1947 (61 Stat. 202), and functions transferred for liquidation to General Services Administration by Reorg. Plan No. 1 of 1957, effective July 1, 1957.

War and Post War Adjustment Policies, Advisory Unit on Established in *Office of War Mobilization* by Presidential direction Nov. 6, 1943. Report submitted Feb. 15, 1944, and Unit Director and Assistant Director submitted letter to Director of *War Mobilization* ending their work May 12, 1944.

War Production Board Established in *Office for Emergency Management* by EO 9024 of Jan. 16, 1942. *Board* terminated and successor agency, *Civilian Production Administration,* established by EO 9638 of Oct. 4, 1945.

War Property Administration, Surplus Established in *Office of War Mobilization* by EO 9425 of Feb. 19, 1944. Terminated on establishment of *Surplus Property Board* by act of Oct. 3, 1944 (58 Stat. 768). *Surplus Property Administration* established in *Office of War Mobilization and Reconversion* by act of Sept. 18, 1945 (59 Stat. 533), and *Board* abolished. Domestic functions of *Administration* merged into *War Assets Corporation, Reconstruction Finance Corporation,* by EO 9689 of Jan. 31, 1946. Foreign functions transferred to State Department by same order. Transfers made permanent by Reorg. Plan No. 1 of 1947, effective July 1, 1947.

War Refugee Board Established in Executive Office of the President by EO 9417 of Jan. 22, 1944. Terminated by EO 9614 of Sept. 14, 1945.

War Relations, Agricultural, Office for *See* **Farm Products, Division of**

War Relief Agencies, President's Committee on Established by Presidential letter of Mar. 13, 1941. *President's War Relief Control Board* established by EO 9205 of July 25, 1942, to succeed *Committee. Board* terminated by EO 9723 of May 14, 1946, and functions transferred to State Department.

War Relief Control Board, President's *See* **President's Committee on War Relief Agencies**

War Relocation Authority Established in *Office for Emergency Management* by EO 9102 of Mar. 18, 1942. Transferred to Interior Department by EO 9423 of Feb. 16, 1944. Terminated by EO 9742 of June 25, 1946.

War Resources Board Established in August 1939 as advisory committee to work with *Joint Army and Navy Munitions Board.* Terminated by President Nov. 24, 1939.

War Resources Council *See* **Defense Resources Committee**

War Shipping Administration Established in *Office for Emergency Management* by EO 9054 Feb. 7, 1942. Terminated by act of July 8, 1946 (60 Stat. 501), and functions transferred to *U.S. Maritime Commission,* effective Sept. 1, 1946.

Water, Office of Saline Established to perform functions vested in Interior Secretary by act of July 29, 1971 (85 Stat. 159). Merged with *Office of Water Resources Research* to form *Office of Water Research and Technology* by Secretary's Order 2966 of July 26, 1974.

Water Commission, National Established by act of Sept. 26, 1968 (82 Stat. 868). Terminated Sept. 25, 1973, pursuant to terms of act.

Water Policy, Office of Established by Interior Department Manual Release 2374 of Dec. 29, 1981, under authority of Assistant Secretary. Abolished by Secretarial Order No. 3096 of Oct. 19, 1983, and functions transferred to Geological Survey and Office of Policy Analysis.

Water Pollution Control Administration, Federal Established under *Health, Education, and Welfare Secretary* by act of Oct. 2, 1965 (79 Stat. 903). Transferred to Interior Department by Reorg. Plan No. 2 of 1966, effective May 10, 1966. Renamed *Federal Water Quality Administration* by act of Apr. 3, 1970. Abolished by Reorg. Plan No. 3 of 1970, effective Dec. 2, 1970, and functions transferred to Environmental Protection Agency.

Water and Power Resources Service Renamed Bureau of Reclamation May 18, 1981, by Interior Secretarial Order 3064.

Water Quality Administration, Federal *See* **Water Pollution Control Administration, Federal**

Water Research and Technology, Office of Established by Interior Secretarial Order 2966 of July 26, 1974. Abolished by Secretarial order of Aug. 25, 1982, and functions transferred to Bureau of Reclamation, Geological Survey, and *Office of Water Policy.*

Water Resources Council Established by act of July 22, 1965 (89 Stat 575). Inactive as of Oct. 1, 1982.

Water Resources Research, Office of Established to perform functions vested in Interior Secretary by act of July 17, 1964 (78 Stat. 329). Merged with *Office of Saline Water* to form *Office of Water Research and Technology* by Secretary's Order 2966 of July 26, 1974.

Watergate Special Prosecution Force Established by Attorney General order, effective May 25, 1973. Terminated by Attorney General order, effective June 20, 1977.

Waterways Corporation, Inland Incorporated under act of June 3, 1924 (43 Stat. 360). Transferred from *War Department* to Commerce Department by Reorg. Plan No. II of 1939, effective July 1, 1939. *Corporation* sold to *Federal Waterways Corporation* under contract of July 24, 1953. Renamed *Federal Barge Lines, Inc.* Liquidated by act of July 19, 1963 (77 Stat. 81).

Weather Bureau Established in Agriculture Department by act of Oct. 1, 1890 (26 Stat. 653). Transferred to Commerce Department by Reorg. Plan No. IV of 1940, effective June 30, 1940. Functions transferred to *Environmental Science Services Administration* by Reorg. Plan No. 2 of 1965, effective July 13, 1965.

Weather Control, Advisory Committee on Established by act of Aug. 13, 1953 (67 Stat. 559). Act of Aug. 28, 1957 (71 Stat. 426), provided for termination by Dec. 31, 1957.

Welfare Administration Established by *Health, Education, and Welfare Secretary's* reorganization of Jan. 28, 1963. Components consisted of *Bureau of Family Services, Children's Bureau, Office of Juvenile Delinquency and Youth Development,* and *Cuban Refugee Staff.* These functions reassigned to *Social and Rehabilitation Service* by Department reorganization Aug. 15, 1967.

Wilson Memorial Commission, Woodrow Established by act of Oct. 4, 1961 (75 Stat. 783). Terminated on submittal of final report to President and Congress Sept. 29, 1966.

Women, Interdepartmental Committee on the Status of Established by EO 11126 of Nov. 1, 1963. Terminated by EO 12050 of Apr. 4, 1978.

Women, President's Commission on the Status of Established by EO 10980 of Dec. 14, 1961. Submitted final report to President Oct. 11, 1963.

Women's Army Auxiliary Corps Established by act of May 14, 1942 (56 Stat. 278), repealed in part and superseded by act of July 1, 1943 (57 Stat. 371), which established *Women's Army Corps. Corps* abolished by Defense Secretary Apr. 24, 1978, pursuant to provisions of 10 U.S.C. 125A.

Women's Business Enterprise Division Renamed *Office of Women's Business Enterprise* by Small Business Administrator's reorganization, effective Aug. 19, 1981. Renamed Office of Women's Business Ownership Aug. 19, 1982.

Women's Reserve Established in U.S. Coast Guard by act of Nov. 23, 1942 (56 Stat. 1020).

Women's Year, 1975, National Commission on the Observance of International Established by EO 11832 of Jan. 9, 1975. Continued by act of Dec. 23, 1975 (89 Stat. 1003). Terminated Mar. 31, 1978, pursuant to terms of act.

Wood Utilization, National Committee on Established by Presidential direction in 1925. Abolished by EO 6179–B of June 16, 1933.

Work Projects Administration *See* **Works Progress Administration**

Work-Training Programs, Bureau of Abolished by reorganization of *Manpower Administration* and functions assigned to *U.S. Training and Employment Service,* effective Mar. 17, 1969.

Working Life, Productivity and Quality of, National Center for Established by act of Nov. 28, 1975 (89 Stat. 935). Authorized appropriations expired Sept. 30, 1978, and functions assumed by *National Productivity Council.*

Works, Advisory Committee on Federal Public Established by President Oct. 5, 1955. Abolished by President Mar. 12, 1961, and functions assigned to *Bureau of the Budget.*

Works Administration, Federal Civil Established by EO 6420–B of Nov. 9, 1933. Function of employment expired March 1934. Function of settling claims continued under *Works Progress Administration.*

Works Administration, Public *See* **Emergency Administration of Public Works, Federal**

Works Agency, Federal Established by Reorg. Plan No. I of 1939, effective July 1, 1939. Functions relating to defense housing transferred to *Federal Public Housing Authority, National Housing Agency,* by EO 9070 of Feb. 24, 1942. Abolished by act of June 30, 1949 (63 Stat. 380), and functions transferred to General Services Administration.

Works Emergency Housing Corporation, Public Established by EO 6470 of Nov. 29, 1933. Incorporated under laws of State of Delaware. Abolished and liquidated as of Aug. 14, 1935, by filing of certificate of surrender of corporate rights.

Works Emergency Leasing Corporation, Public Incorporated Jan. 3, 1934, under laws of Delaware by direction of Administrator of Public Works. Terminated with filed certificate of dissolution with secretary of state of Delaware Jan. 2, 1935.

Works Progress Administration Established by EO 7034 of May 6, 1935, and continued by subsequent yearly emergency relief appropriation acts. Renamed *Work Projects Administration* by Reorg. Plan No. I of 1939, effective July 1, 1939, which provided for consolidation of *Works Progress Administration* into *Federal Works Agency.* Transferred by President to *Federal Works Administrator* Dec. 4, 1942.

Works, Special Board of Public *See* **Land Program, Director of**

Yards and Docks, Bureau of Established by acts of Aug. 31, 1842 (5 Stat. 579), and July 5, 1862 (12 Stat. 510). Abolished by Defense Department reorg. order of Mar. 9, 1966, and functions transferred to Navy Secretary (31 FR 7188).

Youth Administration, National Established in *Works Progress Administration* by EO 7086 of June 26, 1935. Transferred to *Federal Security Agency* by Reorg. Plan No. I of 1939, effective July 1, 1939. Transferred to *Bureau of Training, War Manpower Commission,* by EO 9247 of Sept. 17, 1942. Terminated by act of July 12, 1943 (57 Stat. 539).

Youth Crime, President's Committee on Juvenile Delinquency and Established by EO 10940 of May 11, 1961. Terminated by EO 11529 of Apr. 24, 1970.

Youth Fitness, President's Council on Established by EO 10673 of July 16, 1956. Renamed *President's Council on Physical Fitness* by EO 11074 of Jan. 8, 1963.

Youth Opportunity, President's Council on Established by EO 11330 of Mar. 5, 1967. Inactive as of June 30, 1971; EO 11330 revoked by EO 12379 of Aug. 17, 1982.

Youth Programs, Office of Established in Interior Department by Secretarial Order No. 2985 of Jan. 7, 1965. Functions moved to Office of Historically Black Colleges and Universities and Job Corps, Office of the Secretary, by Departmental Manual Release 2788 of Mar. 22, 1988.

APPENDIX D: Agencies Appearing in the Code of Federal Regulations

(This section contains an alphabetical listing of agencies appearing in the *Code of Federal Regulations* (CFR). The listing was revised as of June 21, 1991.)

Agency	CFR Title, Subtitle or Chapter
ACTION	45, XII
Administrative Committee of the Federal Register	1, I
Administrative Conference of the United States	1, III
Advisory Commission on Intergovernmental Relations	5, VII
Advisory Committee on Federal Pay	5, IV
Advisory Council on Historic Preservation	36, VIII
African Development Foundation	22, XV; 48, 57
Agency for International Development	22, II; 48, 7
Agricultural Marketing Service	7, I, IX, X, XI
Agricultural Research Service	7, V
Agricultural Stabilization and Conservation Service	7, VII
Agriculture Department	
Agricultural Marketing Service	7, I, IX, X, XI
Agricultural Research Service	7, V
Agricultural Stabilization and Conservation Service	7, VII
Animal and Plant Health Inspection Service	7, III; 9, I
Commodity Credit Corporation	7, XIV
Contract Appeals, Board of	7, XXIV
Cooperative State Research Service	7, XXXIV
Economic Analysis Staff	7, XXXIX
Economic Research Service	7, XXXVII
Economics Management Staff	7, XL
Energy, Office of	7, XXIX
Environmental Quality, Office of	7, XXXI
Farmers Home Administration	7, XVIII
Federal Acquisition Regulation	48, 4
Federal Crop Insurance Corporation	7, IV
Federal Grain Inspection Service	7, VIII
Finance and Management, Office of	7, XXX
Food and Nutrition Service	7, II
Food Safety and Inspection Service	9, III
Foreign Agricultural Service	7, XV
Foreign Economic Development Service	7, XXI
Forest Service	36, II
General Sales Manager, Office of	7, XXV
Grants and Program Systems, Office of	7, XXXII
Information Resources Management, Office of	7, XXVII
Inspector General, Office of	7, XXVI
International Cooperation and Development Office	7, XXII
National Agricultural Library	7, XLI
National Agricultural Statistics Service	7, XXXVI
Operations Office	7, XXVIII
Packers and Stockyards Administration	9, II
Rural Electrification Administration	7, XVII
Rural Telephone Bank	7, XVI
Secretary of Agriculture, Office of	7, Subtitle A
Soil Conservation Service	7, VI
Transportation, Office of	7, XXXIII

Agency	CFR Title, Subtitle or Chapter
World Agriculture Outlook Board	7, XXXVIII
Air Force Department	32, VII; Subtitle C, Ch. 132
Federal Acquisition Regulation Supplement	48, 53
Alaska Natural Gas Transportation System, Office of the Federal Inspector	10, XV
Alcohol, Tobacco and Firearms, Bureau of	27, I
AMTRAK	49, VII
American Battle Monuments Commission	36, IV
Animal and Plant Health Inspection Service	7, III; 9, I
Appalachian Regional Commission	5, IX
Architectural and Transportation Barriers Compliance Board	36, XI
Arms Control and Disarmament Agency, U.S.	22, VI
Army Department	32, V
Engineers, Corps of	33, II; 36, III
Federal Acquisition Regulation	48, 51
Assistant Secretary for Technology Policy (Commerce Department)	37, IV
Benefits Review Board	20, VII
Bicentennial of the United States Constitution, Commission on the	45, XX
Bilingual Education and Minority Languages Affairs, Office of	34, V
Blind and Other Severely Handicapped, Committee for Purchase from	41, 51
Board for International Broadcasting	22, XIII
Budget, Office of Management and	5, III
Census Bureau	15, I
Central Intelligence Agency	32, XIX
Child Support Enforcement, Office of	45, III
Christopher Columbus Quincentenary Jubilee Commission	45, XXII
Civil Rights Commission	45, VII
Civil Rights, Office for (Education Department)	34, I
Claims Collection Standards, Federal	4, II
Coast Guard	33, I; 46, I, III; 49, IV
Commerce Department	44, IV
Assistant Secretary for Technology Policy	37, IV
Census Bureau	15, I
Economic Affairs, Under Secretary	37, V
Economic Analysis, Bureau of	15, VIII
Economic Development Administration	13, III
Endangered Species Committee	50, IV
Export Administration Bureau	15, VII
Federal Acquisition Regulation	48, 13
Fishery Conservation and Management	50, VI
International Trade Administration	15, III; 19, III
National Institute of Standards and Technology	15, II
National Marine Fisheries Service	50, II, IV
National Oceanic and Atmospheric Administration	15, IX; 50, II, III, IV, VI
National Telecommunications and Information Administration	15, XXIII; 47, III
Patent and Trademark Office	37, I
Productivity, Technology and Innovation, Assistant Secretary for	37, IV
Secretary of Commerce, Office of	15, Subtitle A
Technology Administration	15, XI
Under Secretary for Technology	37, V
United States Travel and Tourism Administration	15, XII
Commercial Space Transportation, Office of (Transportation Department)	14, III
Commission on the Bicentennial of the United States Constitution	45, XX
Committee for Purchase from the Blind and Other Severely Handicapped	41, 51
Commodity Credit Corporation	7, XIV

Agency	CFR Title, Subtitle or Chapter
Commodity Futures Trading Commission	17, I
Community Planning and Development, Office of Assistant Secretary for	24, V, VI
Community Services, Office of	45, X
Comptroller of the Currency	12, I
Construction Industry Collective Bargaining Commission	29, IX
Consumer Product Safety Commission	16, II
Contract Appeals, Board of	7, XXIV
Cooperative State Research Service	7, XXXIV
Copyright Office	37, II
Copyright Royalty Tribunal	37, III
Cost Accounting Standards Board, Office of Federal Procurement Policy	48, 99
Council on Environmental Quality	40, V
Customs Service, United States	19, I
Defense Department	32, Subtitle A
Air Force Department	32, VII
Army Department	32, V; 33, II; 36, III, 48, 51
Engineers, Corps of	33, II; 36, III
Federal Acquisition Regulation	48, 2
Navy Department	32, VI; 48, 52
Secretary of Defense, Office of	32, I
Defense Logistics Agency	32, XII; 41, Subtitle C, Ch. 132
Defense Nuclear Facilities Safety Board	10, XVII
Delaware River Basin Commission	18, III
Drug Enforcement Administration	21, II
East-West Foreign Trade Board	15, XIII
Economic Affairs, Under Secretary (Commerce Department)	37, V
Economic Analysis, Bureau of	15, VIII
Economic Analysis Staff (Agriculture Department)	7, XXXIX
Economic Development Administration	13, III
Economic Research Service	7, XXXVII
Economics Management Staff	7, XL
Education, Department of	
Bilingual Education and Minority Languages Affairs, Office of	34, V
Civil Rights, Office for	34, I
Educational Research and Improvement, Office of	34, VII
Elementary and Secondary Education, Office of	34, II
Federal Acquisition Regulation	48, 34
Postsecondary Education, Office of	34, VI
Secretary of Education, Office of	34, Subtitle A
Special Education and Rehabilitative Services, Office of	34, III
Vocational and Adult Education, Office of	34, IV
Educational Research and Improvement, Office of	34, VII
Elementary and Secondary Education, Office of	34, II
Employees' Compensation Appeals Board	20, IV
Employees Loyalty Board, International Organizations	5, V
Employment and Training Administration	20, V
Employment Standards Administration	20, VI
Endangered Species Committee	50, IV
Energy, Department of	10, II, III, X; 41, 109
Federal Acquisition Regulation	48, 9
Federal Energy Regulatory Commission	18, I
Energy, Office of (Agriculture Department)	7, XXIX
Engineers, Corps of	33, II; 36, III
Engraving and Printing, Bureau of	31, VI
Environmental Protection Agency	40, I; 41, 115; 48, 15
Environmental Quality, Office of (Agriculture Department)	7, XXXI
Equal Employment Opportunity Commission	29, XIV
Equal Opportunity, Office of Assistant Secretary for	24, I
Executive Office of the President	3, I
Administration, Office of	5, XV
Export Administration Bureau	15, VII
Export-Import Bank of the United States	12, IV

Agency	CFR Title, Subtitle or Chapter
Family Assistance, Office of	45, II
Family Support Administration	45, II, III, IV, X
Farm Credit Administration	12, VI
Farm Credit System Assistance Board	12, XIII
Farm Credit System Insurance Corporation	12, XIV
Farmers Home Administration	7, XVIII
Federal Acquisition Regulation	48, 1
Federal Aviation Administration	14, I
Federal Claims Collection Standards	4, II
Federal Communications Commission	47, I
Federal Contract Compliance Programs, Office of	41, 60
Federal Crop Insurance Corporation	7, IV
Federal Deposit Insurance Corporation	12, III
Federal Election Commission	11, I
Federal Emergency Management Agency	44, I; 48, 44
Federal Energy Regulatory Commission	18, I
Federal Financial Institutions Examination Council	12, XI
Federal Financing Bank	12, VIII
Federal Grain Inspection Service	7, VIII
Federal Highway Administration	23, I, II; 49, III
Federal Home Loan Mortgage Corporation	1, IV
Federal Housing Finance Board	12, IX
Federal Information Resources Management Regulations	41, Subtitle E, Ch. 201
Federal Inspector for the Alaska Natural Gas Transportation System, Office of	10, XV
Federal Labor Relations Authority, and General Counsel of the Federal Labor Relations Authority	5, XIV; 22, XIV
Federal Law Enforcement Training Center	31, VII
Federal Maritime Commission	46, IV
Federal Mediation and Conciliation Service	29, XII
Federal Mine Safety and Health Review Commission	29, XXVII
Federal Pay, Advisory Committee on	5, IV
Federal Prison Industries, Inc.	28, III
Federal Procurement Policy Office	48, 99
Federal Property Management Regulations	41, 101
Federal Property Management Regulations System	41, Subtitle C
Federal Railroad Administration	49, II
Federal Register, Administrative Committee of	1, I
Federal Register, Office of	1, II
Federal Reserve System	12, II
Federal Retirement Thrift Investment Board	5, VI
Federal Service Impasses Panel	5, XIV
Federal Trade Commission	16, I
Federal Travel Regulation System	41, Subtitle F
Finance and Management (Agriculture Department)	7, XXX
Fine Arts Commission	45, XXI
Fiscal Service	31, II
Fish and Wildlife Service, United States	50, I, IV
Fishery Conservation and Management	50, VI
Fishing and Whaling, International Regulatory Agencies	50, III
Food and Drug Administration	21, I
Food and Nutrition Service	7, II
Food Safety and Inspection Service	9, III
Foreign Agricultural Service	7, XV
Foreign Assets Control, Office of	31, V
Foreign Claims Settlement Commission of United States	45, V
Foreign Economic Development Service	7, XXI
Foreign Service Grievance Board	22, IX
Foreign Service Impasse Disputes Panel	22, XIV
Foreign Service Labor Relations Board	22, XIV
Foreign-Trade Zones Board	15, IV
Forest Service	36, II
General Accounting Office	4, I, II, III
General Sales Manager, Office of	7, XXV
General Services Administration	
Contract Appeals Board	48, 61

Agency	CFR Title, Subtitle or Chapter
Federal Acquisition Regulation	48, 5
Federal Information Resources Management Regulations	41, Subtitle E, Ch. 201
Federal Property Management Regulations System	41, 101, 105
Federal Travel Regulation System	41, Subtitle F
Payment of Expenses Connected With the Death of Certain Employees	41, 303
Reduction in Meeting and Training Allowance Payments	41, 304
Relocation Allowances	41, 302
Travel Allowances	41, 301
Geological Survey	30, IV
Government Ethics, Office of	5, XVI
Government National Mortgage Association	24, III
Grants and Program Systems, Office of	7, XXXII
Great Lakes Pilotage	46, III
Harry S Truman Scholarship Foundation	45, XVIII
Health and Human Services, Department of	45, Subtitle A
Child Support Enforcement, Office of	45, III
Community Services, Office of	45, X
Family Assistance, Office of	45, II
Family Support Administration	45, II, III, IV, X
Federal Acquisition Regulation	48, 3
Food and Drug Administration	21, I
Health Care Financing Administration	42, IV
Human Development Services Office	45, XIII
Inspector General, Office of	42, V
Public Health Service	42, I
Refugee Resettlement, Office of	45, IV
Social Security Administration	20, III; 45, IV
Health Care Financing Administration	42, IV
Housing and Urban Development, Department of	
Community Planning and Development, Office of Assistant Secretary for	24, V, VI
Equal Opportunity, Office of Assistant Secretary for	24, I
Federal Acquisition Regulation	48, 24
Government National Mortgage Association	24, III
Housing—Federal Housing Commissioner, Office of Assistant Secretary for	24, II, VIII, X, XX
Inspector General, Office of	24, XII
Mortgage Insurance and Loan Programs Under Emergency Homeowners' Relief Act	24, XV
Public and Indian Housing, Office of Assistant Secretary for	24, IX
Secretary of Housing and Urban Development, Office of	24, Subtitle B, VII
Solar Energy and Energy Conservation Bank	24, XI
Housing—Federal Housing Commissioner, Office of Assistant Secretary for	24, II, VIII, X, XX
Human Development Services Office	45, XIII
Immigration and Naturalization Service	8, I
Indian Affairs, Bureau of	25, I
Indian Arts and Crafts Board	25, II
Information Agency, United States	22, V; 48, 19
Information Resources Management, Office of (Agriculture Department)	7, XXVII
Information Security Oversight Office	32, XX
Inspector General, Office of (Agriculture Department)	7, XXVI
Inspector General, Office of (Health and Human Services Department)	42, V
Inspector General, Office of (Housing and Urban Development Department)	24, XII
Inter-American Foundation	22, X
Intergovernmental Relations, Advisory Commission on	5, VII
Interior Department	
Endangered Species Committee	50, IV
Federal Acquisition Regulation	48, 14
Federal Property Management Regulations System	41, 114
Fish and Wildlife Service, United States	50, I, IV

Agency	CFR Title, Subtitle or Chapter
Geological Survey	30, IV
Indian Affairs, Bureau of	25, I
Indian Arts and Crafts Board	25, II
Land Management Bureau	43, II
Minerals Management Service	30, II
Mines, Bureau of	30, VI
National Park Service	36, I
Reclamation Bureau	43, I
Secretary of the Interior, Office of	43, Subtitle A
Surface Mining and Reclamation Appeals, Board of	30, III
Surface Mining Reclamation and Enforcement, Office of	30, VII
United States Fish and Wildlife Service	50, I, IV
Internal Revenue Service	26, I
International Boundary and Water Commission, United States and Mexico	22, XI
International Cooperation and Development Office (Agriculture Department)	7, XXII
International Development, Agency for	22, II
International Development Cooperation Agency	22, XII
International Development, Agency for	22, II
Overseas Private Investment Corporation	22, VII
International Joint Commission, United States and Canada	22, IV
International Organizations Employees Loyalty Board	5, V
International Regulatory Agencies (Fishing and Whaling)	50, III
International Trade Administration	15, III; 19, III
International Trade Commission, United States	19, II
Interstate Commerce Commission	49, X
Japan-United States Friendship Commission	22, XVI
Joint Board for the Enrollment of Actuaries	20, VIII
Justice Department	28, I; 41, 128
Drug Enforcement Administration	21, II
Federal Acquisition Regulation	48, 28
Federal Claims Collection Standards	4, II
Federal Prison Industries, Inc.	28, III
Foreign Claims Settlement Commission of the United States	45, V
Immigration and Naturalization Service	8, I
Offices of Independent Counsel	28, VI
Prisons, Bureau of	28, V
Labor Department	
Benefits Review Board	20, VII
Employees' Compensation Appeals Board	20, IV
Employment and Training Administration	20, V
Employment Standards Administration	20, VI
Federal Acquisition Regulation	48, 29
Federal Contract Compliance Programs, Office of	41, 60
Federal Procurement Regulations System	41, 50
Labor-Management Relations and Cooperative Programs, Bureau of	29, II
Labor-Management Standards, Office of	29, IV
Mine Safety and Health Administration	30, I
Occupational Safety and Health Administration	29, XVII
Pension and Welfare Benefits Administration	29, XXV
Public Contracts	41, 50
Secretary of Labor, Office of	29, Subtitle A
Veterans' Employment and Training, Office of the Assistant Secretary for	41, 61; 20, IX
Wage and Hour Division	29, V
Workers' Compensation Programs, Office of	20, I
Labor-Management Relations and Cooperative Programs, Bureau of	29, II
Labor-Management Standards, Office of	29, IV
Land Management, Bureau of	43, II
Legal Services Corporation	45, XVI
Library of Congress	36, VII
Copyright Office	37, II

Agency	CFR Title, Subtitle or Chapter
Management and Budget, Office of	5, III; 48, 99
Marine Mammal Commission	50, V
Maritime Administration	46, II
Merit Systems Protection Board	5, II
Micronesian Status Negotiations, Office for	32, XXVII
Mine Safety and Health Administration	30, I
Minerals Management Service	30, II
Mines, Bureau of	30, VI
Minority Business Development Agency	15, XIV
Miscellaneous Agencies	1, IV
Monetary Offices	31, I
Mortgage Insurance and Loan Programs Under the Emergency Homeowners' Relief Act (Housing and Urban Development Department)	24, XV
National Aeronautics and Space Administration	14, V; 48, 18
National Agricultural Library	7, XLI
National Agricultural Statistics Service	7, XXXVI
National Archives and Records Administration	36, XII
National Bureau of Standards	15, II
National Capital Planning Commission	1, IV
National Commission for Employment Policy	1, IV
National Commission on Libraries and Information Science	45, XVII
National Credit Union Administration	12, VII
National Foundation on the Arts and the Humanities	45, XI
National Highway Traffic Safety Administration	23, II, III; 49, V
National Institute of Standards and Technology	15, II
National Labor Relations Board	29, I
National Marine Fisheries Service	50, II, IV
National Mediation Board	29, X
National Oceanic and Atmospheric Administration	15, IX; 50, II, III, IV, VI
National Park Service	36, I
National Railroad Adjustment Board	29, III
National Railroad Passenger Corporation (AMTRAK)	49, VII
National Science Foundation	45, VI; 48, 25
National Security Council	32, XXI
National Security Council and Office of Science and Technology Policy	47, II
National Telecommunications and Information Administration	15, XXIII; 47, III
National Transportation Safety Board	49, VIII
Navajo and Hopi Indian Relocation Commission	25, IV
Navy Department	32, VI; 48, 52
Neighborhood Reinvestment Corporation	24, XXV
Nuclear Regulatory Commission	10, I
Occupational Safety and Health Administration	29, XVII
Occupational Safety and Health Review Commission	29, XX
Office of Independent Counsel	28, VII
Offices of Independent Counsel (Justice Department)	28, VI
Operations Office, Department of Agriculture	7, XXVIII
Overseas Private Investment Corporation	22, VII
Oversight Board	12, XV
Packers and Stockyards Administration	9, II
Panama Canal Commission	48, 35
Panama Canal Regulations	35, I
Patent and Trademark Office	37, I
Payment of Expenses Connected With the Death of Certain Employees	41, 303
Peace Corps	22, III
Pennsylvania Avenue Development Corporation	36, IX
Pension and Welfare Benefits Administration (Labor Department)	29, XXV
Pension Benefit Guaranty Corporation	29, XXVI
Personnel Management, Office of	5, I; 45, VIII; 48, 17
Federal Employees Health Benefits Acquisition Regulation	48, 16
Postal Rate Commission	39, III

Agency	CFR Title, Subtitle or Chapter
Postal Service, United States	39, I
Postsecondary Education, Office of	34, VI
Presidential Documents	3
President's Commission on White House Fellowships	1, IV
Prisons, Bureau of	28, V
Productivity, Technology and Innovation, Assistant Secretary (Commerce Department)	37, IV
Property Management Regulations System, Federal	41, Subtitle C
Public Contracts (Labor Department)	41, 50
Public Health Service	42, I
Railroad Retirement Board	20, II
Reclamation Bureau	43, I
Reduction in Meeting and Training Allowance Payments	41, 304
Refugee Resettlement, Office of	45, IV
Regional Action Planning Commissions	13, V
Relocation Allowances	41, 302
Research and Special Programs Administration	49, I
Resolution Trust Corporation	12, XVI
Rural Electrification Administration	7, XVII
Rural Telephone Bank	7, XVI
Saint Lawrence Seaway Development Corporation	33, IV
Science and Technology Policy, Office of	32, XXIV
Science and Technology Policy, Office of, and National Security Council	47, II
Secret Service	31, IV
Securities and Exchange Commission	17, II
Selective Service System	32, XVI
Small Business Administration	13, I; 48, 22
Smithsonian Institution	36, V
Social Security Administration	20, III; 45, IV
Soil Conservation Service	7, VI
Solar Energy and Energy Conservation Bank (Housing and Urban Development Department)	24, XI
Soldiers' and Airmen's Home, United States	5, XI
Special Counsel, Office of	5, VIII
Special Education and Rehabilitative Services, Office of	34, III
State Department	22, I
Federal Acquisition Regulation	48, 6
Surface Mining and Reclamation Appeals, Board of	30, III
Susquehanna River Basin Commission	18, VIII
Technology Administration	15, XI
Tennessee Valley Authority	18, XIII
Thrift Supervision Office (Treasury Department)	12, V
Trade Representative, United States, Office of	15, XX
Transportation, Department of	44, IV
Coast Guard	33, I; 46, I, III; 49, IV
Commercial Space Transportation, Office of	14, III
Contract Appeals Board	48, 63
Federal Acquisition Regulation	48, 12
Federal Aviation Administration	14, I
Federal Highway Administration	23, I, II; 49, III
Federal Railroad Administration	49, II
Maritime Administration	46, II
National Highway Traffic Safety Administration	23, II, III; 49, V
Research and Special Programs Administration	49, I
Saint Lawrence Seaway Development Corporation	33, IV
Secretary of Transportation, Office of	14, II; 49, Subtitle A
Urban Mass Transportation Administration	49, VI
Transportation, Office of (Agriculture Department)	7, XXXIII
Travel Allowance	41, 301
Travel and Tourism Administration, United States	15, XII
Treasury Department	17, IV
Alcohol, Tobacco and Firearms, Bureau of	27, I
Comptroller of the Currency	12, I
Customs Service, United States	19, I
Engraving and Printing, Bureau of	31, VI

Agency	CFR Title, Subtitle or Chapter
Federal Acquisition Regulation	48, 10
Federal Law Enforcement Training Center	31, VII
Fiscal Service	31, II
Foreign Assets Control, Office of	31, V
Internal Revenue Service	26, I
Monetary Offices	31, I
Secret Service	31, IV
Secretary of the Treasury, Office of	31, Subtitle A
Thrift Supervision Office	12, V
United States Customs Service	19, I
Truman, Harry S, Scholarship Foundation	45, XVIII
Under Secretary for Technology (Commerce Department)	37, V
United States and Canada, International Joint Commission	22, IV
United States Arms Control and Disarmament Agency	22, VI
United States Customs Service	19, I
United States Fish and Wildlife Service	50, I, IV
United States Information Agency	22, V; 48, 19
United States International Development Cooperation Agency	22, XII
United States International Trade Commission	19, II
United States Postal Service	39, I
United States Soldiers' and Airmen's Home	5, XI
United States Trade Representative, Office of	15, XX
United States Travel and Tourism Adminstration	15, XII
Urban Mass Transportation Administration	49, VI
Veterans Affairs Department	38, I; 48, 8
Veterans' Employment and Training, Office of the Assistant Secretary for	41, 61; 20, IX
Vice President of the United States, Office of	32, XXVIII
Vocational and Adult Education, Office of	34, IV
Wage and Hour Division	29, V
Water Resources Council	18, VI
Workers' Compensation Programs, Office of	20, I
World Agriculture Outlook Board	7, XXXVIII

Name Index

NOTE: Separate listings of Senators and Representatives can be found beginning on pages 32 and 34, respectively. Any other references to said persons can be found in this index.

B

C

D

E

G

I

J

K

L

M

N

O

P

Q

R

S

T

U

V

Y

Z

Agency/Subject Index

NOTE: This index does not include material appearing in the appendices.

A

B

C

D

K

L

M

N

O

P

R

S

T

U

V

W

Y

Z

RECENT CHANGES

Personnel actions brought to the attention of *Manual* editors July 2–Aug. 8, 1991

Page	Position	Action

U.S. Courts of Appeals

72	U.S. Circuit Judge for the Fourth Circuit	Clyde H. Hamilton confirmed July 18 (new position).
72	U.S. Circuit Judge for the Fourth Circuit	J. Michael Luttig confirmed July 29 (new position).

Defense Department

202	Assistant Secretary of the Army (Civil Works)	Nancy Patricia Dorn confirmed July 16, vice Robert W. Page.

Education Department

264	General Counsel	Jeffrey C. Martin confirmed July 18, vice Edward C. Stringer.
265	Assistant Secretary for Educational Research and Improvement	Diane S. Ravitch confirmed July 18, vice Christopher T. Cross.

Energy Department

273	Director of Energy Research	William Happer confirmed Aug. 2, vice Robert O. Hunter, Jr.

Housing and Urban Development Department

329	President, Government National Mortgage Association	Raoul Lord Carroll confirmed July 11, vice Arthur J. Hill.

Interior Department

339	Assistant Secretary (Policy, Management and Budget)	John Schrote confirmed Aug. 2, vice Lou Gallegos.

Justice Department

369	U.S. Attorney for the Northern District of Mississippi	Robert Q. Whitwell confirmed July 26 (reappointment).

Labor Department

399	Assistant Secretary for Public Affairs	Steven I. Hoffman confirmed July 18, vice Dale T. Tate.

State Department

432	U.S. Ambassador to Bolivia	Charles R. Bowers confirmed July 30, vice Robert S. Gelbard.
433	U.S. Ambassador to Colombia	Morris D. Busby confirmed July 30, vice Thomas Edmund McNamara.
433	U.S. Ambassador to Costa Rica	Luis Guinot, Jr., confirmed July 30, vice Deane Roesch Hinton.
433	U.S. Ambassador to Germany	Robert Michael Kimmitt confirmed July 30, vice Vernon A. Walters.
433	U.S. Ambassador to the Philippines	Frank G. Wisner confirmed July 30, vice Nicholas Platt.
433	U.S. Ambassador to Syria	Christopher W.S. Ross confirmed July 30, vice Edward P. Djerejian.
433	U.S. Ambassador to Thailand	David Floyd Lambertson confirmed July 18, vice Daniel A. O'Donohue.
434	U.S. Ambassador to Trinidad and Tobago	Sally G. Cowal confirmed July 30, vice Charles A. Gargano.
434	U.S. Ambassador to the Union of Soviet Socialist Republics	Robert S. Strauss confirmed July 30, vice Jack F. Matlock.

RECENT CHANGES—Continued

Personnel actions brought to the attention of *Manual* editors July 2–Aug. 8, 1991

Page	Position	Action
434	U.S. Ambassador to Yemen	Arthur Hayden Hughes confirmed July 30, vice Charles F. Dunbar, Jr.

Treasury Department

Page	Position	Action
477	Assistant Secretary (International Affairs)	Olin L. Wethington confirmed July 26, vice Charles H. Dallara.

Export-Import Bank of the United States

Page	Position	Action
559	Member, Board of Directors	Constance Bastine Harriman confirmed July 11, vice Richard C. Houseworth.

Federal Reserve System

Page	Position	Action
590	Member, designation as Vice Chairman	David W. Mullins, Jr., confirmed July 11, vice Manuel H. Johnson.

United States Information Agency

Page	Position	Action
734	Associate Director for Broadcasting and Director, Voice of America	Charles Graves Untermeyer confirmed July 30, vice Richard W. Carlson.

GPO : 1991 0 - 290-950